W9-AAS-932

# UNDERSTANDING CRIMINAL PROCEDURE

## Third Edition

**By**
**Joshua Dressler**

*Frank R. Strong Chair in Law*
*Michael E. Moritz College of Law*
*Ohio State University*

LexisNexis™

**Library of Congress Cataloging-in-Publication Data**

Dressler, Joshua.
  Understanding criminal procedure / Joshua Dressler.--3rd ed.
    p. cm. --(Understanding series)
  Includes index.
  ISBNUM NO = 0-8205-5405-7 (softbound)
  1. Criminal procedure--United States. I. Title. II. Understanding series (New York, N.Y.)


KF9619 .D74 2002
345.73'05--dc21

2001050834

This publication is designed to provide accurate and authoritative information in regard to the subject matter covered. It is sold with the understanding that the publisher is not engaged in rendering legal, accounting, or other professional services. If legal advice or other expert assistance is required, the services of a competent professional should be sought.

LexisNexis, the knowledge burst logo, and Michie are trademarks of Reed Elsevier Properties Inc, used under license. Matthew Bender is a registered trademark of Matthew Bender Properties Inc.

Copyright © 2002 Matthew Bender & Company, Inc., a member of the LexisNexis Group. All Rights Reserved. Published .

No copyright is claimed in the text of statutes, regulations, and excerpts from court opinions quoted within this work. Permission to copy material exceeding fair use, 17 U.S.C. § 107, may be licensed for a fee of 10¢ per page per copy from the Copyright Clearance Center, 222 Rosewood Drive, Danvers, Mass. 01923, telephone (978) 750-8400.

Editorial Offices
744 Broad Street, Newark, NJ 07102 (973) 820-2000
201 Mission Street, San Francisco, CA 94105-1831 (415) 908-3200
www.lexis.com

(Matthew Bender & Co., Inc.)                                          (Pub.791)

**To David: My Son, the Rabbi–to–be**

**&**

**To Debra and Casey: Who Have Joined the Dressler Family**

# PREFACE TO THE THIRD EDITION

*Purpose of the text.* This book is primarily designed for students enrolled in a class in Criminal Procedure. It parallels the curriculum in virtually all three-unit and four-unit versions of the law school course. In schools that offer two Criminal Procedure classes, one on police investigatory practices and the other focusing on the adjudicatory phase, this text will assist students taking either course, although primary emphasis in this edition of the book is on police practices. Based on previous editions, I expect that scholars, courts, and practicing attorneys will also find the text of considerable use. Nonetheless, I have written the text with the special needs of law students in mind. Put another way, my intention was to prepare a text that students can use with confidence that it will help them in their course preparation, and that professors can recommend or assign to their students with confidence that it will enhance the classroom dialogue.

Most teachers want students to think at least as much about the forest as they do about the individual trees. They want students to come away from class with an understanding of the law that has developed, but also with an appreciation of the values that have shaped it. They want their students to be sensitive to some of the broader issues in the field, relating to the use of judicial power to effectuate legal reform, to judicial craftsmanship, to the roles of race and poverty (just to name a few factors) in the enforcement of the law, and, of course, to the proper role of the government *vis a vis* the individual in the investigation and prosecution of crime. This book assists students in understanding these topics and, thus, improving class discussion.

The text covers the most important United States Supreme Court cases in the field. Where pertinent, the Federal Rules of Criminal Procedure, federal statutes, and lower federal and state court cases are discussed or cited. The broad overarching policy issues of criminal procedure are laid out; and some of the hottest debates— *e.g.*, the Fourth Amendment exclusionary rule, the *Miranda* decision, to name a couple—are considered in depth and (I believe) objectively.

Readers should find the book user-friendly. Students who want a thorough grasp of a topic may read the relevant chapter in its entirety. However, each chapter is divided into subsections, so that readers with more refined research needs can answer their questions efficiently. I also include citations to important scholarship, both classic and recent, that readers may wish to consider if they want to delve more deeply into specific topics. And, because so many of the topics interrelate, cross-referencing footnotes are included, so that readers can deftly move from one part of the book to another, if necessary.

*Changes in the third edition.* This edition of the text is approximately ten percent longer than the second edition. To a limited extent, this is the result of the ever-increasing number of important judicial decisions that must be surveyed. But, also, I concluded that various subjects, *e.g.*, racial profiling, deserved enhanced coverage. The chapters on police interrogation (Chapters 22–25) include increased discussion of the relationship between the Due Process Clause and the Fifth Amendment Self-Incrimination Clause. Previous users of the text will also find Chapter 2 (Overarching Policy Issues in Criminal Procedure) reorganized and significantly expanded. Chapter 19, dealing with non-criminal-investigatory searches, has been retitled, reorganized, and expanded as a result of the Supreme Court's recent activity in this area.

*Gender policy of the text.* In today's system of criminal justice, women are not simply crime victims: they are also lawyers, judges, police officers, legislators and criminal suspects. To deal with this modern reality, I have tried to balance the accounts in the text: in even-numbered chapters, I use the male pronoun to describe hypothetical and generic parties in the criminal justice system; in odd-numbered chapters, women get equal time. Based on comments I have received about the policy, most readers like the approach or, at worst, find it only temporarily distracting.

*Acknowledgments.* Many people helped me in many ways to write this book. I can name only a few of them here. With the first edition, Lee Lamborn and Joe Grano, my former colleagues at Wayne State University Law School, read and commented on every page of every chapter I wrote. George Thomas (Rutgers-Newark) did the same with the second edition. Many people, too many to mention here, commented on drafts of chapters of the third edition. The text is much better because of their generous assistance. I also thank Stanley Fisher (Boston University) and Rory Little (University of California, Hastings College of Law) for their careful written comments and suggestions based on the last edition. Mistakes and omissions are the result of my stubborn refusal to listen to advice.

Gerald Caplan, who was Dean of McGeorge School of Law (University of the Pacific) during my eight years there, also deserves special acknowledgment. He came to McGeorge in 1992 with the intention of improving the Law School's scholarly reputation. He provided faculty members with considerable financial assistance in their research and, in my case, a teaching load that allowed me to work on this and my other writing projects in a more productive manner. I greatly appreciate his support.

I am grateful to Jennifer McGeorge and Darin Marx (McGeorge Class of '02), for their excellent research assistance on this edition. The footnotes would not be the same (or as accurate) without them. I also thank David Lamb (now a successful and reasonably happy Public Defender in San Diego, California) for his earlier, unacknowledged assistance on the second edition.

My wife, Dottie, deserves the greatest thanks for everything she has done over the years to make my life so satisfying. I appreciate and love her beyond words.

*Looking to the future.* My new Ohio State colleague, friend, and first-rate scholar, Alan Michaels, is joining this book. He will co-author the annual Supplements to Understanding Criminal Procedure, beginning immediately. (He will also co-author the Fourth Edition, which will be significantly expanded in coverage from this and prior editions.) I greatly welcome his addition to the project.

*Plea.* I received many letters from users (professors and students alike) of the second edition. They wrote not only with kind words about the book, but with constructive suggestions for improvement. I hope that readers of this edition will be as generous with their comments. I may be contacted by electronic mail <dressler.11@osu.edu>. Alan Michaels, my future partner, may be reached at <michaels.23@osu.edu>.

Joshua Dressler
March, 2002

# TABLE OF CONTENTS

## CHAPTER 1

## INTRODUCTION TO CRIMINAL PROCEDURE

## CHAPTER 2

## OVERARCHING POLICY ISSUES IN CRIMINAL PROCEDURE

## CHAPTER 3

## INCORPORATION OF THE BILL OF RIGHTS

# CHAPTER 4

## GENERAL CONSTITUTIONAL LAW DOCTRINES

# CHAPTER 5

## FOURTH AMENDMENT: OVERVIEW

## CHAPTER 6

## FOURTH AMENDMENT:
## "PERSONS, HOUSES, PAPERS, AND EFFECTS"

## CHAPTER 7

## FOURTH AMENDMENT TERMINOLOGY:
## "SEARCH"

## CHAPTER 8

## FOURTH AMENDMENT TERMINOLOGY: "SEIZURE"

## CHAPTER 9

## FOURTH AMENDMENT: "PROBABLE CAUSE"

# CHAPTER 10

## ARRESTS

# CHAPTER 11

## SEARCH WARRANTS: IN GENERAL

## CHAPTER 12

## WARRANTLESS SEARCHES: EXIGENT CIRCUMSTANCES

## CHAPTER 13

## SEARCHES INCIDENT TO LAWFUL ARRESTS

## CHAPTER 14

## SEARCHES OF CARS AND CONTAINERS THEREIN

## CHAPTER 15

## "PLAIN VIEW" AND RELATED DOCTRINES

## CHAPTER 16

## INVENTORY SEARCHES

## CHAPTER 17

## CONSENT SEARCHES

## CHAPTER 18

## *TERRY v. OHIO*: THE "REASONABLENESS" BALANCING STANDARD IN CRIMINAL INVESTIGATIONS

## CHAPTER 19

## MORE "REASONABLENESS" BALANCING: SEARCHES AND SEIZURES PRIMARILY CONDUCTED FOR NON-CRIMINAL LAW PURPOSES

## CHAPTER 20

## FOURTH AMENDMENT: STANDING

# CHAPTER 21

# FOURTH AMENDMENT: EXCLUSIONARY RULE

## CHAPTER 22

## INTERROGATION LAW: OVERVIEW

## CHAPTER 23

## COERCED ("INVOLUNTARY") CONFESSIONS

## CHAPTER 24

## *MIRANDA v. ARIZONA*

          

## CHAPTER 25

## INTERROGATION LAW: SIXTH AMENDMENT RIGHT TO COUNSEL

# CHAPTER 26

# PRIVILEGE AGAINST SELF-INCRIMINATION: GENERAL PRINCIPLES

# CHAPTER 27

# EYEWITNESS IDENTIFICATION PROCEDURES

# CHAPTER 28

# ENTRAPMENT

## CHAPTER 29

## THE RIGHT TO COUNSEL: AT TRIAL
## AND ON APPEAL

# CHAPTER 30

## PRETRIAL RELEASE OF THE DEFENDANT

# CHAPTER 31

## PLEA BARGAINING AND GUILTY PLEAS

# CHAPTER 32

# DOUBLE JEOPARDY

## CHAPTER 1

# INTRODUCTION TO CRIMINAL PROCEDURE

## § 1.01 The Relationship of "Criminal Law" to "Criminal Procedure"

At one level, the relationship of criminal procedure to criminal law is straightforward. Criminal procedural law ("criminal procedure," for short) is composed of the rules that regulate the inquiry into whether a violation of a criminal law ("substantive" criminal law, to distinguish it from "procedural" criminal law) has occurred, and whether the person accused of the crime committed it.

Logically, substance is anterior to procedure.[1] The substantive criminal code defines the conduct that society wishes to deter and to punish. Procedural law functions as the means by which society implements its substantive goals. For example, assume the criminal law makes it a crime to possess cocaine. Criminal procedure sets the rules for discovering violations of this criminal statute—*e.g.*, police may not entrap suspects, subject them to unreasonable searches and seizures, or coerce confessions. If the police violate these or other procedural rules, various procedural consequences may arise, such as exclusion of evidence at trial or dismissal of the charge.

Unfortunately, the relationship of procedure to substance is more complicated than the simple description in the preceding paragraph suggests. First, procedural rules can frustrate the implementation of a community's substantive goals. For example, if the rules unduly hinder the police and prosecutors in their pursuit of law violators, some persons who deserve to be punished are apt to avoid criminal sanction, and the deterrent value of the criminal law is likely to be undermined. On the other hand, if the rules are lax, the police may mistreat suspects, and prosecutors may be able to introduce unreliable evidence against the accused, enhancing the likelihood of unjust convictions and punishment.

Second, the existence of some procedural rules may motivate lawmakers not to enact proposed criminal statutes. For example, suppose that a

---

[1] Herbert L. Packer, *Two Models of the Criminal Process*, 113 U. Pa. L. Rev. 1, 3 (1964).

legislature is debating whether to prohibit consensual homosexual conduct by adults in private places, *i.e.*, their homes. Further assume that the lawmakers determine that the only realistic way to seriously combat such conduct is for police officers to entrap suspects in the investigation of this offense. If procedural rules provide that entrapment (however defined) is illegal, lawmakers might hesitate to prohibit the conduct in the first place, even though they wish to deter or condemn it.[2]

Third, some legal doctrines involve a mixture of procedure and substance. Consider the constitutional rule that the government must prove beyond a reasonable doubt "every fact necessary to constitute the crime . . . charged."[3] This is a procedural rule, but it cannot properly be enforced unless the term "crime," a substantive criminal law concept, is defined. For example, does the "crime" of murder include as an ingredient the "absence of a legitimate claim of self-defense"—that is, is "murder" a killing that occurs in the absence of self-defense—or is self-defense an affirmative defense to the "crime" of murder? In short, the answer to the procedural question—who has the burden of proof regarding the matter of self-defense?—depends on the definition of murder, a substantive criminal law concept.

## § 1.02 Sources of Procedural Law

### [A] Formal Sources

Various layers of laws and regulations govern the conduct of the participants in the criminal justice system. First, starting at the highest level, various provisions of the United States Constitution, in particular those found in amendments 4, 5, 6, 8, and 14 thereto, restrict the power of law enforcement officers in their relations to persons suspected of criminal activity, and also govern the way in which pre-trial and criminal trials and appeals are conducted. The United States Supreme Court and lower federal and state courts frequently are called upon to interpret the federal constitutional provisions. As a result of substantial constitutional litigation, the study of some aspects of criminal procedure—in particular, police practices—is principally a study of constitutional law.

Second, at the state level, state constitutions are an increasingly important source of procedural law. In the past few decades, as the United States Supreme Court and lower federal courts have become less sympathetic to the *federal* constitutional claims of individual petitioners, a body of *state* constitutional jurisprudence has developed, in which some state courts,

---

[2] *See id.* at 4.

[3] In re Winship, 397 U.S. 358, 364 (1970).

interpreting their own constitutions, have granted relief to their residents that would be unavailable under the federal Constitution.[4] This trend is significant because a state supreme court is the final arbiter of the meaning of its own constitution.[5]

Third, legislatures have enacted statutes and courts have adopted written rules of criminal procedure governing many aspects of the state and federal criminal justice systems. For example, at the federal level, Congress has

---

[4] *See* Barry Latzer, *The Hidden Conservatism of the State Court "Revolution,"* 74 Judicature 190 (1991) (providing a list, by state, of the number of cases in which each state's highest court has rejected or adopted United States Supreme Court's criminal procedure decisions, from the late 1960s through 1989); Ronald K.L. Collins & David M. Skover, *The Future of Liberal Legal Scholarship*, 87 Mich. L. Rev. 189, 217 (1988) (reporting that, in their research, state courts in at least 450 cases recognized rights not available under the federal constitution). This treatise provides non-exhaustive citations to state constitutional law decisions.

Not all state courts have the authority to interpret their constitution differently than the United States Constitution. *E.g.,* Calif. Const. art. I, § 24 (in which the state constitution was amended by the initiative process to provide that in criminal cases various enumerated constitutional rights of the defendant "shall be construed by the courts of this state in a manner consistent with the Constitution of the United States"); Fla. Const. art. I, § 12 (in which the state charter was amended by initiative to provide that it "shall be construed in conformity with the 4th amendment to the United States Constitution, as interpreted by the United States Supreme Court").

It should be noted that a state court may interpret its own constitutional charter *less* protectively than its federal constitutional counterpoint, but if it does so, then the state court "must go on to decide the claim under federal law, assuming it has been raised." Hans A. Linde, *E Pluribus—Constitutional Theory and State Courts*, 18 Ga. L. Rev. 165, 179 (1984). If a state court interprets the state law *more* protectively to the individual, however, it need not turn to federal law—the state petitioner wins her claim.

[5] The importance of state constitutional law cannot easily be overstated, in terms of its potential impact on litigation in the early decades of the twenty-first century. For thoughtful discussion of so-called "judicial federalism" generally, or of its application in criminal cases, *see generally* Barry Latzer, State Constitutional Criminal Law (1995); Barry Latzer, State Constitutions and Criminal Justice (1991); Shirley S. Abrahamson, *Criminal Law and State Constitutions: The Emergence of State Constitutional Law*, 63 Tex. L. Rev. 1141 (1985); Catherine Greene Burnett & Neil Colman McCabe, *A Compass in the Swamp: A Guide to Tactics in State Constitutional Law Challenges*, 25 Tex. Tech. L. Rev. 75 (1993); William J. Brennan, Jr., *State Constitutions and the Protection of Individual Rights*, 90 Harv. L. Rev. 489 (1977); Paul G. Cassell, *The Mysterious Creation of Search and Seizure Exclusionary Rules Under State Constitutions: The Utah Example*, 1993 Utah L. Rev. 751 (1993); George E. Dix, *Judicial Independence in Defining Criminal Defendants' Texas Constitutional Rights*, 68 Tex. L. Rev. 1369 (1990); James A. Gardner, *The Failed Discourse of State Constitutionalism*, 90 Mich. L. Rev. 761 (1992); Paul Marcus, *State Constitutional Protection for Defendants in Criminal Prosecutions*, 20 Ariz. St. L.J. 151 (1988); Stanley Mosk, *State Constitutionalism: Both Liberal and Conservative*, 63 Tex. L. Rev. 1081 (1985); Special Project, *State Constitutions and Criminal Procedure: A Primer for the 21st Century*, 67 Ore. L. Rev. 689 (1988).

enacted laws governing such matters as electronic surveillance of private conversations, [6] pretrial detention of dangerous persons, [7] and the qualifications for jury service. [8] Also, Congress has granted authority to the Supreme Court to promulgate written rules to govern proceedings in the federal courts, which the Court has done in the form of the Federal Rules of Criminal Procedure. In turn, Federal Rule 57 authorizes District Courts (trial courts) to make rules governing local practice.

Fourth, some law enforcement agencies promulgate written regulations that their employees are required to follow. For example, police departments frequently have rules governing, among other matters, the use of deadly force to effectuate arrests, the techniques to be followed in conducting lineups, and the procedures to be used in inspecting the contents of automobiles taken into police custody. Although these regulations do not have the force of law, their violation may result in internal sanctions.

Fifth, on occasion the Supreme Court invokes its so-called "supervisory authority" over the administration of criminal justice in the federal courts to announce rules that apply throughout the federal judicial system. Similarly, some federal circuit courts have developed rules that apply to the district courts within their jurisdiction. Federal supervisory authority rules do not apply in the state courts and are subject to revision by Congress. [9]

### [B]  Informal Sources: A Taste of Reality

Although criminal procedural rules are primarily promulgated "from on high"—by the United States Supreme Court, state supreme courts, and federal and state legislatures—the law that is enforced daily on the streets often looks considerably different. As Professor Anthony Amsterdam once observed about United States Supreme Court case law: "[o]nce uttered, these pronouncements will be interpreted by arrays of lower appellate courts, trial judges, magistrates, commissioners and police officials. *Their* interpretation . . ., for all practical purposes, will become the word of god." [10] Put more bluntly, the law at the end of a billy club or police firearm may look very different than the law handed down by nine Justices of the United States Supreme Court or by a legislative body. [11]

---

[6] 18 U.S.C. §§ 2510–2521 (1997).

[7] 18 U.S.C. §§ 3141–3150 (1997).

[8] 28 U.S.C. § 1865 (1997).

[9] The concept of "supervisory authority" is discussed more fully at § 4.04, *infra.*

[10] Anthony G. Amsterdam, *The Supreme Court and the Rights of Suspects in Criminal Cases*, 45 N.Y.U. L. Rev. 785, 786 (1970).

[11] Gregory Howard Williams, *Police Discretion: The Institutional Dilemma—Who Is In Charge?*, 68 Iowa L. Rev. 431, 437 (1983) ("There is little assurance that policy established by the Supreme Court will be implemented by patrol officers").

This dichotomy between formal and informal law is inevitable. The United States Supreme Court, and each state's highest court, lack daily supervisory control over the actions of the police. Judicial authority is limited to litigated cases, and most of what occurs on the street between police officers and the citizenry is legally invisible. Even if a police officer breaches a constitutional or statutory rule, the victim of the breach may not bring the matter to the attention of a judicial body. Even if she does, state supreme courts and the United States Supreme Court can only hear a tiny fraction of the cases affecting criminal suspects.

## § 1.03  Stages of a Criminal Prosecution

### [A]  In General

Analytically and in law school curricula, "criminal procedure" is often divided into two parts, the investigatory and the adjudicatory stages. In the investigatory phase, the primary actors in the "drama" are police officers and those whom they suspect of criminal activity. This is the "cops and (alleged) robbers" stage of the process.

The adjudicatory phase begins when the government commits itself to bringing a suspect to trial for her alleged criminal conduct. In this stage, the focus of attention turns to the legal profession—the prosecutors, defense lawyers, and judges—who participate in the adversarial judicial system. This is the "bail-to-maybe-jail" phase of the process.

In studying criminal procedure, it is important to understand the procedural context in which the legal rules apply. What follows, therefore, is a brief overview of the stages of a typical criminal prosecution. Because adjudicatory procedures differ by state and depend on whether the defendant is charged with a felony or a misdemeanor, primary emphasis is on *felony* prosecutions in the *federal* system.

### [B]  Investigatory Stage

A criminal investigation commonly begins when a police officer, on the basis of her own observations and/or those of an informant, comes to believe that criminal activity may be afoot or has already occurred. Because there are no formal stages of a criminal investigation, most Criminal Procedure courses survey the constitutional law pertaining to the most common police investigative practices.

Police officers usually search and seize persons and property during the investigatory stage. Searches and seizures occur in an almost infinite variety of ways: for example, by stopping ("seizing") a suspect on the street and frisking her ("searching") for weapons or evidence; by entering a house in order to look for a suspect or evidence of a crime; by opening containers found in an automobile stopped on the highway; and by wiretapping in order to monitor the conversations of suspects.

The Fourth Amendment to the United States Constitution prohibits unreasonable searches and seizures. At one time, most especially in the late 1950s through the early-to-mid 1970s, this proscription was interpreted to mean that, except in limited circumstances, police officers were not allowed to search or seize property without a search warrant, supported by probable cause, issued by a judge (or "magistrate"). This warrant requirement (or, at least, warrant presumption) came to be honored primarily in the breach, and is of limited value today in determining the lawfulness of police conduct. Not only do police officers today rarely seek a warrant, but many searches and seizures can be conducted on less than probable cause.[12]

The police also interrogate suspects and witnesses during criminal investigations. Some interrogations occur in a police-dominated atmosphere, such as in a police station. In other circumstances, questioning occurs in a less coercive environment, such as in a person's home, automobile, or on the street, sometimes in the presence of family or friends. An interrogation may trigger various constitutional questions, including: (1) is the suspect entitled to be represented by counsel during the questioning?; and (2) was any ensuing confession obtained voluntarily? In particular, the Fifth Amendment privilege against compulsory self-incrimination, the due process clauses of the Fifth and Fourteenth Amendments, and the Sixth Amendment guarantee of assistance of counsel during criminal prosecutions, are potentially implicated during police interrogations.[13]

The police also conduct lineups, show witnesses photographs of potential suspects, take handwriting and voice exemplars, and conduct other identification procedures. The police may conduct many of these activities without prior judicial approval, and without intervention by defense counsel. Nonetheless, in some cases the Sixth Amendment right-to-counsel provision applies and, in all cases, the procedures must be conducted in a constitutionally reliable manner.[14]

Assuming that a criminal investigation results in a police determination that there is probable cause to believe that the suspect committed a crime, she may be arrested. When a routine arrest occurs in a private home, the police must ordinarily be armed with a warrant to take the suspect into custody. Arrests in public places usually can be made without an arrest warrant.[15]

---

[12] *See generally* chapters 18–19, *infra*.

[13] *See generally* chapters 22–25, *infra*.

[14] *See generally* chapter 27, *infra*.

[15] *See generally* chapter 10, *infra*.

Upon arrest, the suspect is usually searched and taken to the police station or to a jail, where she is "booked" (*i.e.,* her name is logged in an arrest book or on a computer), photographed, fingerprinted, and more fully searched. Typically, any personal belongings found in her possession at the station or jail are inventoried and placed in custody for safekeeping.

## [C] Adjudicatory Stage

### [1] Issuance of a Complaint

After a suspect is arrested and booked, a complaint is prepared by the police or a prosecutor and is filed with the court. A "complaint" is "a written statement of the essential facts constituting the offense charged."[16] It serves as the official charging document until either an "information" or an "indictment," each of which is discussed below,[17] is issued.

### [2] Probable Cause (*Gerstein*) Hearing

The police may not constitutionally arrest a person unless they have probable cause to believe that a crime has occurred and that the suspect committed it. In order to implement the Fourth Amendment bar on unreasonable seizures of persons, the Supreme Court has held that, whenever practicable, a probable cause determination should be made by a neutral and detached magistrate, rather than by a police officer.[18]

If the police apply for an arrest warrant, the requisite judicial oversight occurs. However, when the police arrest a suspect without an arrest warrant—the vast majority of cases—a prior judicial determination of probable cause is lacking. Therefore, the Supreme Court ruled in *Gerstein v. Pugh*[19] that, following a *warrantless* arrest, the Fourth Amendment requires that a prompt judicial determination of probable cause be made as a precondition to any extended restraint of the arrestee's liberty.

Because a so-called "*Gerstein* hearing" serves as a post-arrest equivalent of a pre-arrest warrant-application hearing,[20] the proceeding may be conducted in the same manner as a warrant hearing—in the defendant's absence, and the probable cause determination may be based on hearsay testimony. If the arrestee is permitted to be present during the hearing, she is not constitutionally entitled to representation by counsel or to the full panoply of adversarial safeguards available at trial. In many jurisdictions, the probable cause hearing is conducted in the suspect's presence at her

---

[16] Fed. R. Crim. P. 3.

[17] *See* §§ 1.03[C][4]–[5], *infra.*

[18] *See* Johnson v. United States, 333 U.S. 10 (1948).

[19] 420 U.S. 103 (1975).

[20] *See* § 11.02, *infra.*

first appearance before a judicial officer, a proceeding which is discussed immediately below.[21]

### [3]  First Appearance Before the Magistrate

An arrested person must be taken "without unnecessary delay,"[22] usually within 24 hours except on weekends, before a judicial officer, for a hearing variously called the "initial arraignment," "arraignment on a warrant," "arraignment on a complaint," or, simply the "first" or "initial" "appearance."

At the hearing, the arrestee receives formal notice of the charges against her, her constitutional rights in the impending prosecution are explained to her, and a date is set for a preliminary hearing. If the suspect is indigent and not presently represented by counsel, a lawyer is appointed for her at this time. If the suspect was arrested without a warrant, a probable cause determination (a *Gerstein* hearing) is usually made at the first appearance. Finally, and perhaps most significantly, the magistrate determines at this time whether the arrestee should be set free on her own recognizance, released on bail, or detained pending further proceedings.[23]

### [4]  Preliminary Hearing

In most jurisdictions, a preliminary hearing (or "preliminary examination") is held within two weeks after the arrestee's initial appearance before the magistrate, unless the defendant waives the hearing.[24] The primary purpose of a preliminary hearing is to determine whether there is probable cause to believe that a criminal offense has occurred and that the arrestee committed it.[25]

---

[21] How promptly must the *Gerstein* hearing be held? In County of Riverside v. McLaughlin, 500 U.S. 44 (1991), the Supreme Court stated that the Constitution "permits a reasonable postponement of a probable cause determination while the police cope with the everyday problems of processing suspects through an overly burdened criminal justice system." Therefore, if a state wishes to combine the probable cause hearing with other pretrial proceedings, such as the first appearance before the magistrate, it may do so as long as the hearing occurs, as a general matter, within 48 hours from the time of arrest. However, a delay "for delay's sake," out of ill-will toward the suspect, or in order to secure evidence that will justify the arrest, is constitutionally unreasonable, even if it falls within the presumptive 48-hour period.

[22] Fed. R. Crim. P. 5(a).

[23] *See generally* chapter 30, *infra.*

[24] In the federal system, the hearing must be held no later than 10 days following the initial appearance, if the arrestee is in custody, or within 20 days if she is not. Fed. R. Crim. P. 5(c).

[25] Fed. R. Crim. P. 5.1(a).

A preliminary hearing is adversarial in nature, and runs somewhat like a trial. Because it is considered a critical stage of the prosecution, the defendant is constitutionally entitled to representation by counsel.[26] At the hearing, the prosecutor and the defendant may call witnesses on their behalf and cross-examine adverse witnesses. However, many jurisdictions permit the introduction of hearsay and of evidence obtained in an unconstitutional manner, although such evidence usually is inadmissible at trial.[27]

The significance of the preliminary hearing in the criminal process depends on whether the state is an "indictment jurisdiction" (*i.e.*, a state in which the defendant ordinarily cannot be brought to trial unless she is indicted by a grand jury) or an "information jurisdiction" (*i.e.*, a state in which an indictment by a grand jury is not required). In *information* jurisdictions, once the magistrate determines that there is sufficient evidence to "bind over" the defendant for trial, the prosecutor files an "information" with the trial court. The "information" is a document stating the charges against the defendant and the essential facts relating to them. The information replaces the complaint as the formal charging document.

In the alternative, if the magistrate in an information jurisdiction does *not* find sufficient evidence to bind over the defendant, the complaint is dismissed and the defendant is discharged. If the prosecutor wishes to proceed with the dismissed case, various options are available: (1) she may file a new complaint, in which case the prosecution begins anew;[28] (2) in some states, she may appeal the magistrate's dismissal to the trial court; and/or (3) in some circumstances, she is permitted to seek an indictment from a grand jury.

In indictment jurisdictions, by contrast, the preliminary hearing functions as little more than an adversarial *Gerstein*-type hearing.[29] Indeed, the magistrate's probable cause determination may be superseded by the actions of the grand jury, *i.e.*, if the grand jury does not indict the defendant, she must be released, even if the preliminary hearing magistrate previously determined that there was probable cause to believe that the arrestee committed an offense. In the federal system, which is an indictment jurisdiction, the preliminary examination is not held if the defendant is indicted before the date set for the preliminary hearing.[30]

---

[26] Coleman v. Alabama, 399 U.S. 1 (1970).

[27] Fed. R. Crim. P. 5.1(a).

[28] This is not a violation of the double jeopardy clause of the United States Constitution. *See* § 32.01[A][2], *infra*.

[29] *See* § 1.03[C][2], *supra*.

[30] Fed. R. Crim. P. 5(c).

### [5] Grand Jury Proceeding

In indictment jurisdictions, a person may not be brought to trial for a serious offense unless she is indicted by a grand jury or waives her right to a grand jury hearing. The purpose of a grand jury is to stand "between the accuser and the accused . . . [in order] to determine whether a charge is founded upon reason or was dictated by an intimidating power or by malice and personal ill will." [31] Because of the grand jury's historical role as the guardian of the rights of the innocent, the Fifth Amendment to the United States Constitution provides that in federal prosecutions, "[n]o person shall be held to answer for a capital, or otherwise infamous crime, unless on a[n] . . . indictment of a Grand Jury . . . ." The constitutional term "infamous crime" encompasses all felony prosecutions.

Today, for various reasons, a grand jury proceeding may not in fact shield an innocent person as well as a preliminary hearing. First, the putative defendant, *i.e.,* the person targeted for indictment, is not permitted to be present during the grand jury proceedings, except if and when she is called as a witness. Only the grand jurors, the prosecutor, the witness, and a transcriber of the proceedings, is present in the jury room during the hearing.

Second, witnesses, including the putative defendant, do not have a constitutional right to have counsel present while they testify before the grand jury. [32] Third, because no judge is present during the proceedings, rules of evidence do not apply. An indictment is not invalid even if it is based solely on inadmissible hearsay evidence [33] or unconstitutionally obtained information. [34] Fourth, the prosecutor is not required to disclose to the grand jurors evidence in her custody that might exculpate the putative defendant. [35]

Upon conclusion of the prosecutor's presentation of her case, the grand jurors deliberate privately. If a majority of them determine that sufficient evidence was introduced by the prosecutor, [36] the jury (through the prosecutor) issues an "indictment," a document that states the charges and the relevant facts relating to them. If the jury does not vote to indict the

---

[31] Wood v. Georgia, 370 U.S. 375, 390 (1962).

[32] In re Groban, 352 U.S. 330 (1957) (dictum); United States v. Mandujano, 425 U.S. 564 (1976) (dictum) (plurality opinion).

[33] Costello v. United States, 350 U.S. 359 (1956).

[34] *See* United States v. Calandra, 414 U.S. 338 (1974).

[35] United States v. Williams, 504 U.S. 36 (1992).

[36] Most jurisdictions, including the federal courts (*see* United States v. Calandra, 414 U.S. at 343), apply a probable cause standard, similar to that employed in preliminary hearings. Some states use a higher, "directed verdict," standard, *i.e.,* whether there is evidence which, if unexplained, would warrant a conviction at trial.

defendant (a "no-bill"), the complaint issued against the defendant is dismissed and she is discharged.

### [6] Arraignment

If an indictment or information is filed, the defendant is arraigned in open court. At the arraignment, at which time defense counsel is permitted to be present, the accused is provided with a copy of the indictment or information, after which she enters a plea to the offenses charged in it. She may plead "not guilty," "guilty," "*nolo contendere*,"[37] or (in some states) "not guilty by reason of insanity."

### [7] Pretrial Motions

After arraignment, the defendant may make various pretrial motions. Among the defenses, objections, and requests that often are raised prior to trial are: (1) that the indictment or information is defective, in that it fails to allege an essential element of the crime charged, or that it fails to give the defendant sufficient notice of the facts relating to the charge against her;[38] (2) that the venue of the prosecution is improper or inconvenient;[39] (3) that the indictment or information joins offenses or parties in an improper or prejudicial manner;[40] (4) that evidence in the possession of one of the parties should be disclosed to the opposing party;[41] (5) that evidence should be suppressed because it was obtained in an unconstitutional manner; and (6) that the prosecution is constitutionally barred, such as by the double jeopardy and/or speedy trial clauses of the Constitution.[42]

In some circumstances, if a defendant's pretrial motions are successful, the judge will dismiss the charges on her own or on the prosecutor's motion.[43] For example, if the prosecution is barred by the double jeopardy clause, dismissal is obligatory. Or, if the judge grants the defendant's motion to suppress key evidence, the prosecutor might determine that continuation of the proceedings would be futile and, therefore, request dismissal of the charges.

---

[37] Literally, the plea means "I will not contest it [the charge]." For most purposes in a criminal proceeding, the plea is treated the same as a guilty plea.

[38] *See, e.g.,* Fed. R. Crim. P. 12(b)(2).

[39] *See, e.g.,* Fed. R. Crim. P. 18, 21(a).

[40] *See, e.g.,* Fed. R. Crim. P. 8, 14.

[41] *See, e.g.,* Fed. R. Crim. P. 16.

[42] U.S. Const. amend. V (". . .nor shall any person be subject for the same offence to be twice put in jeopardy of life or limb . . ."); U.S. Const. amend. VI ("In all criminal prosecutions, the accused shall enjoy the right to a speedy . . .trial. . . .").

[43] *See, e.g.,* Fed. R. Crim. P. 48.

## [8]  Trial

### [a]  Right to Trial by Jury

If a defendant does not plead guilty and the charges are not dismissed, a trial is held. The Sixth Amendment entitles a defendant to trial by jury in the prosecution of any serious, *i.e.,* non-petty, offense. Although the boundaries of the term "non-petty" have not been fully laid out, the right to a jury trial applies, at a minimum, to any offense for which the maximum potential punishment is incarceration in excess of six months.[44]

Trial juries usually consist of twelve persons.[45] However, a jury as small as six in number is constitutionally permitted.[46] In most jurisdictions, the jury verdict to acquit or to convict must be unanimous.[47] However, state laws permitting non-unanimous verdicts have been upheld as constitutional.[48]

### [b]  Composition of the Jury

The Sixth Amendment guarantees a defendant trial "by an impartial jury." An individual juror is not impartial if her state of mind as to any individual involved in the trial, or as to the issues involved in the case, would substantially impair her performance as a juror in accordance with the law and the court's instructions.[49]

Moreover, although the accused is not entitled to a jury that mirrors the community as a whole, she is entitled to one drawn from a pool of persons constituting a fair cross-section of the community. This right is violated if large, distinctive groups of persons, such as women or members of a racial group, are systematically excluded from the jury pool.[50]

### [c]  Selection of Jurors

In order to discover possible bias, the trial judge and (in some jurisdictions) the attorneys examine the prospective jurors ("venirepersons")

---

[44] Blanton v. City of North Las Vegas, 489 U.S. 538 (1989). A defendant who is prosecuted in a single proceeding for multiple petty offenses does not have a Sixth Amendment right to a jury trial, even if the aggregate prison terms authorized for the offenses exceeds six months. Lewis v. United States, 518 U.S. 322 (1996).

[45] *See, e.g.,* Fed. R. Crim. P. 23(b).

[46] Williams v. Florida, 399 U.S. 78 (1970) (jury of six is allowed); Ballew v. Georgia, 435 U.S. 223 (1978) (jury of five is not allowed).

[47] *See, e.g.,* Fed. R. Crim. P. 31(a).

[48] Johnson v. Louisiana, 406 U.S. 356 (1972) (upholding a 9-3 guilty verdict because the vote constituted a "substantial majority" of the jurors); *but see* Burch v. Louisiana, 441 U.S. 130 (1979) (striking down a statute permitting 5-1 guilty verdicts by six-person juries).

[49] *See* Adams v. Texas, 448 U.S. 38 (1980).

[50] Taylor v. Louisiana, 419 U.S. 522 (1975).

regarding their attitudes and beliefs relating to the case (*i.e.,* conduct a *"voir dire"*). If either side believes that a venireperson is partial, that side may challenge the juror "for cause." If the judge grants the challenge, the prospective juror is excused.

The law also recognizes "peremptory" challenges, *i.e.,* challenges not based on cause. The primary purpose of a peremptory challenge is to allow a party to exclude a person from the jury if it believes, as a matter of intuition or as the result of the *voir dire,* that the individual is biased, but whose partiality has not been proved to the satisfaction of the judge. Both the defense and prosecution are entitled to exercise a specified number of peremptories.[51]

Peremptory challenges may not be exercised in an unfettered manner. Under the equal protection clause of the Fourteenth Amendment, neither the prosecution,[52] nor the defense,[53] may exercise challenges to remove persons from the venire *solely* on the basis of the prospective juror's race or gender,[54] *i.e.,* on the assumption or intuitive judgment that the person will be biased in the case solely because of the defendant's and juror's shared (or different) race or sex.

### [d]  Other Constitutional Trial Rights

The defendant is constitutionally entitled to employ counsel at trial. An indigent is entitled to the appointment of counsel in all felony prosecutions, as well as at any misdemeanor trial in which she will be incarcerated if convicted.[55] The defendant may also call witnesses on her own behalf, and confront and cross-examine the witnesses who testify against her.[56] The defendant is not required to testify in her own behalf, and she "must pay no court-imposed price for the exercise of [her Fifth Amendment] constitutional privilege not to testify."[57]

---

[51] *E.g.,* Fed. R. Crim. P. 24(b) (in non-capital felony trials, the government is entitled to 6, and the defense to 10, peremptory challenges; in capital trials, each side is entitled to 20 peremptories).

[52] Batson v. Kentucky, 476 U.S. 79 (1986).

[53] Georgia v. McCollum, 505 U.S. 42 (1992).

[54] Batson v. Kentucky, 476 U.S. 79 (1986) (race); J.E.B. v. Alabama ex rel. T.B., 511 U.S. 127 (1994) (gender).

[55] Gideon v. Wainwright, 372 U.S. 335 (1963) (felony cases); Argersinger v. Hamlin, 407 U.S. 25 (1972) (misdemeanor cases). *See generally* chapter 29, *infra.*

[56] U.S. Const. amend. VI ("In all criminal prosecutions, the accused shall the enjoy the right . . .to be confronted with the witnesses against him; [and] to have compulsory process for obtaining witnesses in his favor. . . .").

[57] Carter v. Kentucky, 450 U.S. 288, 301 (1981); *see also* Griffin v. California, 380 U.S. 609 (1965).

### [9] Appeal

If the defendant is acquitted by the jury or by the judge in a bench trial, the government is barred by the double jeopardy clause to appeal the acquittal.[58]

If the defendant is convicted, she has no constitutional right to appeal her conviction.[59] However, all jurisdictions statutorily permit a convicted defendant (now the "appellant") to appeal. In state court systems, she may appeal to an appellate court below the state supreme court or, if there is none, directly to the state supreme court. In the federal courts, a defendant may appeal her conviction to the United States Court of Appeals for the circuit with jurisdiction over the case.

If the appellant is unsuccessful in her statutory appeal of right, she may be entitled to discretionary appeals to a higher court. For example, in a state in which an appeal of right is brought to an intermediate appellate court, the state supreme court is permitted, but usually is not required except in capital cases, to hear the appellant's second appeal. She may also petition the United States Supreme Court to consider her case. If her appeal is ultimately successful, she ordinarily may be reprosecuted.[60]

### [10] Collateral Attack of a Conviction: Habeas Corpus[61]

After a defendant's appeals are exhausted—*i.e.*, once her conviction is final—she may file a petition for a writ of habeas corpus in a federal district court, if she believes that her continued incarceration is in violation of the United States Constitution or of a federal law.[62] A post-conviction habeas corpus proceeding is not part of the criminal appeal process itself. It is a

---

[58] *See* § 32.03[A][1], *infra.*

[59] *See* McKane v. Durston, 153 U.S. 684 (1894) (dictum); Jones v. Barnes, 463 U.S. 745 (1983) (dictum).

[60] *See* § 32.05[A], *infra.*

[61] *See generally* Graham Hughes, The Decline of Habeas Corpus (Occasional Papers from the Center for Research in Crime and Justice, N.Y.U. School of Law, No. VIII, 1990); Joseph L. Hoffmann, *The Supreme Court's New Vision of Federal Habeas Corpus for State Prisoners,* 1989 Sup. Ct. Rev.165; Kathleen Patchel, *The New Habeas,* 42 Hastings L.J. 939 (1991); Yale L. Rosenberg, *Kaddish for Federal Habeas Corpus,* 59 Geo. Wash. L. Rev. 362 (1991); Robert Weisberg, *A Great Writ While It Lasted,* 81 J. Crim. L. & Criminology 9 (1990); Larry W. Yackle, *A Primer on the New Habeas Corpus Statute,* 44 Buffalo L. Rev. 381 (1996); Note, *The Avoidance of Constitutional Questions and the Preservation of Judicial Review: Federal Court Treatment of the New Habeas Provisions,* 111 Harv. L. Rev. 1578 (1998).

[62] 28 U.S.C. §§ 2241–2244, 2253–2255, 2261–2266 (1997). Some states have their own habeas corpus procedures, which must be exhausted before a convicted person seeks *federal* habeas relief.

civil action designed to overturn a presumptively valid criminal judgment. As such, it is considered a collateral attack on a criminal conviction, as distinguished from a direct criminal appeal. The purpose of a habeas petition is to convince the district (trial) court that it should compel the warden of the jail or prison holding the petitioner to bring her before the court so that it can determine whether she is being held in custody against the law.

Federal habeas corpus jurisprudence involves exceedingly intricate rules, and recent legislation has made it more difficult than in the past for petitioners to obtain a hearing on the merits of their federal claims. However, if the proper allegations are made, the district court may grant the petition and conduct an evidentiary hearing into the federal claim.

Because a habeas corpus petition constitutes a collateral attack on a judgment that is already final, and because federal courts are hesitant to intrude on state proceedings, the standards that a petitioner must satisfy to obtain ultimate relief in habeas are often stricter than those that apply on direct appeals. However, if the district court determines that the petitioner is being held in custody in violation of federal law or the Constitution, it may vacate the conviction. The ruling of the district court—whether to grant or deny the petition—is subject to appeal by the losing party.

## § 1.04   Studying Constitutional Law Cases

The study of many aspects of criminal procedure, particularly the law relating to police practices, is largely the study of constitutional law, especially the decisions of the United States Supreme Court. Consequently, the following suggestions are offered to students inexperienced in analysis of constitutional cases.

### [A]   Read Concurring and Dissenting Opinions

To the extent that your casebook permits, pay attention to concurring and dissenting opinions, if any, in the assigned cases. Various reasons support this recommendation. First, the ideas expressed in the concurring or dissenting opinions of today sometimes become the majority views of tomorrow.

Second, sometimes a concurring or dissenting opinion explains the views of the majority better than the latter's own opinion, calls attention to unresolved issues, or suggests where the logic of the majority opinion may lead. Indeed, on occasion a concurring opinion takes on a life of its own, and is cited or applied in subsequent opinions in preference to the majority opinion.[63]

---

[63] *E.g.*, Justice Harlan's concurring opinion in Katz v. United States, 389 U.S. 487 (1967). *See generally* § 7.03[C], *infra*.

Third, as discussed in subsection [C], it is often necessary to analyze these opinions in order to determine the long-term significance of a constitutional holding.

## [B]  Learn Case Names

Pay attention to the names of Supreme Court cases. Unlike cases applying common law doctrine, which often are fungible, a United States Supreme Court constitutional decision represents the final official[64] word on the issue in question.[65] These opinions have the "power to shake the assembled faithful with awful tremors of exultation and loathing."[66] Consequently, lawyers tend to talk about constitutional issues in a shorthand (*e.g.*, "Was the suspect Mirandized[67] ?"). It is helpful to understand and speak this language.

## [C]  Count Votes

If the casebook permits, take note of the vote breakdown in important cases. For various reasons, vote counting can prove insightful, and sometimes is essential. First, the long-term importance of a decision may depend on the size of the majority. A 5-4 decision is not equivalent to a 9-0 ruling. A unanimous opinion often carries greater moral suasion with the public and within the legal community than one decided by the slimmest of margins. Moreover, a 5-4 precedent is a prime target for overruling (or, at least, narrowing) when a Justice in the majority leaves the Court.

Second, vote counting is essential in ascertaining the precedential value of some cases. For example, suppose that *D* appeals her conviction on two independent grounds: (1) that police officers conducted an unconstitutional search of her house (issue A); and (2) that the officers coerced a confession from her (issue B). Assume that if either of these claims is successful *D*'s conviction must be overturned.

Assume the following scenario: four judges agree with *D* on issue A, but express no opinion regarding issue B. One judge concurs in the judgment; she rules against *D* on issue A, but in *D*'s favor on issue B. Four dissenters reject both of *D*'s claims. Thus, *D* gets what she wants: she wins her appeal, as five judges believe that she is entitled to a new trial, albeit for different reasons.

However, a good lawyer with a client who wishes to raise issue A on similar facts would observe that her chances of success with the same court

---

**64** *But see* § 1.02[B], *supra*, for a "taste of reality."

**65** Of course, the Supreme Court can overrule itself, or the Constitution can be amended to override an unpopular decision.

**66** Amsterdam, Note 10, *supra*, at 786.

**67** Miranda v. Arizona, 384 U.S. 436 (1966).

are not good: four members of the court are likely to favor her client's claim regarding issue A, while five (the dissenters and the concurring judge) will probably oppose her. Likewise, another attorney, but one who seeks to raise issue B, can expect that at least four judges will oppose, and only one will favor, her client. The case would depend on the views of the four court members who expressed no opinion on issue B.

## [D]    Learn the Views of Individual Justices[68]

Suppose that a lawyer is considering the wisdom of appealing a criminal conviction in a case in which the law is fuzzy, *i.e.,* there is no rule or precedent on point. In order to determine whether to recommend an appeal and, if so, what arguments are most apt to be persuasive, the attorney needs to "get into the head" of the judges on the court that will hear the case. One aspect of this is to identify each judge's judicial and legal philosophy, as well as her overall belief-system.[69]

It is usually too simplistic (although not always[70] ) to treat a judge as a "liberal" or a "conservative" (or as an "activist" or a "non-activist"), whatever these terms may mean to the user. Some judges are "liberal," for example, in matters relating to freedom of speech but are "conservative" on question of criminal justice. Even in the latter area, a particular judge

---

[68] For discussion of the jurisprudence of various currently sitting Justices, *see generally* Richard A. Cordray & James T. Vradelis, Comment, *The Emerging Jurisprudence of Justice O'Connor,* 52 U. Chi. L. Rev. 389 (1985); M. David Gelfand & Keith Werham, *Federalism and Separation of Powers on a "Conservative" Court: Currents and Cross-Currents from Justices O'Connor and Scalia,* 64 Tul. L. Rev. 1443 (1990); George Kannar, *The Constitutional Catechism of Antonin Scalia,* 99 Yale L.J. 1297 (1990); Christopher E. Smith, *Justice Antonin Scalia and Criminal Justice Cases,* 81 Ky. L.J. 187 (1992); Christopher E. Smith, *Supreme Court Surprise: Justice Anthony Kennedy's Move Toward Moderation,* 45 Okla. L. Rev. 459 (1992). For one analysis of a recently retired Justice, see Kit Kinports, *Justice Blackmun's Mark on Criminal Law and Procedure,* 26 Hastings Const. L.Q. 219 (1998).

[69] The focus here is on the appellate court level, but lawyers must especially be sensitive to the belief-system of *trial* judges, where the vast majority of cases are ultimately resolved. In regard to the backgrounds and voting patterns of President Bill Clinton's appointments to the federal court of appeals, *see* Rorie L. Spill & Kathleen A. Bratton, *Clinton and Diversification of the Federal Judiciary,* 84 Judicature 256 (2001) and Susan B. Haire, Martha Anne Humphries, & Donald R. Songer, *The Voting Behavior of Clinton's Court of Appeals Appointees,* 84 Judicature 274 (2001).

[70] As an example, Justice William Douglas took the "civil libertarian" position in 90 percent of the cases in which he cast a vote between 1953 and 1975. In contrast, Justice William Rehnquist took a civil libertarian position in only 19.6% of the cases decided between 1972, when he joined the Court, and 1985. Jeffrey A Segal & Harold J. Spaeth, *Decisional Trends on the Warren and Burger Courts: Results from the Supreme Court Data Base Project,* 73 Judicature 103, 105–06 (1989).

might believe that the police should not generally be required to obtain warrants before they conduct searches (a pro-police position), but that they should usually be required to have probable cause before they conduct the searches (a pro-defense position).

In the field of Criminal Procedure, where the focus is primarily on the Supreme Court, lawyers and law students need to pay attention to the voting patterns of individual members of the Supreme Court. Over time, an observer can develop a sense of a Justice's philosophy and can more accurately predict her vote on specific issues.

## [E]  Be Sensitive to Supreme Court History[71]

Just as individual Justices have specific philosophical perspectives, the Supreme Court as a body—or, more correctly, a majority of it—possesses, at any given time, an institutional philosophy or attitude regarding constitutional adjudication or, in the case of criminal procedure, criminal law

---

[71] For discussion of the so-called Warren Court, *see generally* Francis A. Allen, *The Judicial Quest for Penal Justice: The Warren Court and the Criminal Cases*, 1975 U. Ill. L.F. 518; A. Kenneth Pye, *The Warren Court and Criminal Procedure*, 67 Mich. L. Rev. 249 (1968); Yale Kamisar, *The Warren Court and Criminal Justice: A Quarter-Century Retrospective*, 31 Tulsa L.J. 1 (1995).

Regarding the Burger Court and a comparison of it to the Warren Court, *see generally* The Burger Years (H. Schwartz ed. 1987); Albert W. Alschuler, *Failed Pragmatism: Reflections on the Burger Court*, 100 Harv. L. Rev. 1436 (1987); Peter Arenella, *Rethinking the Functions of Criminal Procedure: The Warren and Burger Courts' Competing Ideologies*, 72 Geo. L.J. 185 (1983); Jerold H. Israel, *Criminal Procedure, the Burger Court, and the Legacy of the Warren Court*, 75 Mich. L. Rev. 1319 (1977); Stephen A. Saltzburg, *The Flow and Ebb of Constitutional Criminal Procedure in the Warren and Burger Courts*, 69 Geo. L.J. 151 (1980); Stephen J. Schulhofer, *The Constitution and the Police: Individual Rights and Law Enforcement*, 66 Wash. U. L.Q. 11 (1988); Louis Michael Seidman, *Factual Guilt and the Burger Court: An Examination of Continuity and Change in Criminal Procedure*, 80 Colum. L. Rev. 436 (1980); Robert Weisberg, *Criminal Procedure Doctrine: Some Versions of the Skeptical*, 76 J. Crim. L. & Criminology 832 (1985).

Regarding the Rehnquist Court, *see generally* Tinsley E. Yarbrough, The Rehnquist Court and the Constitution (2000); Craig M. Bradley, *Criminal Procedure in the Rehnquist Court: Has the Rehnquisition Begun?*, 62 Ind. L.J. 273 (1987); Brian K. Landsberg, *Race and the Rehnquist Court*, 66 Tul. L. Rev. 1267 (1992); Robert H. Smith, *Uncoupling the "Centrist Bloc"—An Empirical Analysis of the Thesis of a Dominant, Moderate Bloc on the United States Supreme Court*, 62 Tenn. L. Rev. 1 (1994); Carol S. Steiker, *Counter-Revolution in Constitutional Criminal Procedure? Two Audiences, Two Answers*, 94 Mich. L. Rev. 2466 (1996).

For a political history of the appointments to the Supreme Court, see Henry J. Abraham, Justices and Presidents (1974). For a perspective on various twentieth century Justices, see The Supreme Court and Its Justices (Jesse Choper, ed. 1987). For a valuable statistical analysis of each Supreme Court term, including figures on voting alignments, see the annual study of the Supreme Court term, published in the first issue of each volume of the Harvard Law Review.

jurisprudence. Moreover, certain small-group dynamics develop among the sitting Justices, which affect interpersonal relations, and ultimately, shape the work product. It is worthwhile, therefore, to be sensitive to the place of a Supreme Court opinion in the larger historical constitutional and institutional picture.

Lawyers tend to talk in general terms about the philosophical views of the "Warren Court," the "Burger Court," and the "Rehnquist Court," the shorthand titles for the Supreme Court, and the opinions decided by it, under the three most recent Chief Justices, Earl Warren (1953-1969), Warren Burger (1969-1986), and William Rehnquist (1986-Present).

As the footnote at the beginning of this subsection may suggest, countless book and articles have been written about the philosophies of the Warren, Burger, and Rehnquist Courts. As a generalization, the Warren Court was an activist Court that used its judicial power to develop rules favorable to individuals *vis a vis* the government. In the context of criminal procedure, the Warren Court was responsible for most of the constitutional decisions that expanded the rights of persons accused of crime. Indeed, the "criminal justice revolution"—as it has often been called—was largely led by the Warren Court (or, more accurately, a majority of its members).[72]

In contrast, the current-day Rehnquist Court (and, somewhat less so, the Burger Court) has favored the "crime control" model of criminal procedure,[73] in that it has granted legislatures and prosecutorial agencies considerable discretion in defining, investigating, and prosecuting crime. The Rehnquist Court has usually placed greater emphasis than did the Warren Court on the matter of obtaining (or, at least, its critics would claim, more rhetoric of obtaining) a factually reliable outcome at trial, and less emphasis than the earlier Court on the methods employed by the government to obtain the evidence used to convict defendants.

Some criminal procedure casebooks include a chart showing the dates on which individual Justices joined the Court. If your book has such a chart, look at it often to see where specific cases fit in. If your book does not have such a chart, the following brief review may be helpful.

In theory, the Warren Court began in 1953 when President Dwight Eisenhower appointed Earl Warren as Chief Justice. However, the civil libertarian thrust of the Court did not develop immediately, but rather took effect gradually as new appointments were made. Already on the Court in 1953, and sympathetic to the Chief Justice's views as they developed, was

---

[72] For a summary of the "revolution" (or, failed revolution, according to the author) see Craig M. Bradley, The Failure of the Criminal Procedure Revolution 6–36 (1993).

[73] *See* § 2.02[B], *infra*.

William Douglas, who was appointed in 1939 by President Franklin D. Roosevelt. After the Chief Justice was appointed, William Brennan (1956) and Potter Stewart (1958) joined the Court. Brennan was a major participant in the Warren Court decisions, and Stewart sometimes provided a crucial fifth vote.

The Warren Court reached its civil libertarian peak in the mid-1960s, after Presidents John F. Kennedy and Lyndon B. Johnson replaced outgoing members of the Court with: Arthur Goldberg (1962, by J.F.K.), who was himself replaced by Abe Fortas (1965, by L.B.J.); Byron White (1962, by J.F.K.); and Thurgood Marshall (1967, by L.B.J.). Of the replacements, only Justice White was often critical of Warren Court values.

The shift away from the Warren Court philosophy was as gradual as its ascendancy. It began in 1969 with the election of Richard Nixon, who campaigned for office in part on the promise to nominate "law and order" justices.[74] President Nixon almost immediately filled two Court vacancies: Warren Burger (1969) and Harry Blackmun (1970), who replaced Chief Justice Warren and Justice Fortas respectively. He subsequently appointed two more Justices: William Rehnquist (1972) and Lewis Powell (1972), who replaced centrist Justices John Harlan and Hugo Black, respectively. President Gerald Ford appointed John Stevens (1975) to replace Justice Douglas. In the context of criminal procedure, each of these changes in personnel resulted in a high court somewhat more disposed to crime control outcomes. (However, over time, Stevens has become the Court's most consistent advocate of the displaced Warren Court values.)

It was not until the 1980s that the shift away from Warren Court values became clearly evident. During this decade, Sandra Day O'Connor (1981), Antonin Scalia (1985), and Anthony Kennedy (1988) were appointed by President Ronald Reagan, replacing Justice Stewart, Chief Justice Burger,[75] and Justice Powell, respectively. With the appointment of Justice Kennedy, the balance of power definitively tipped in favor of the crime control model of criminal justice, and the Court increasingly cut back on the holdings of the Warren Court era.

The 1990s saw the departure of the remaining members of the Warren Court. Justices Brennan (1990) and Marshall (1991), strong believers in Warren Court values, retired. President George Bush replaced them with David Souter and Clarence Thomas, respectively. In 1993, the last member of the Warren Court, Byron White, retired. President William Clinton

---

[74] Liva Baker, Miranda: Crime, Law and Politics 221–324 (1983).

[75] Technically, Chief Justice Burger was replaced by Justice Rehnquist, who was elevated to Chief Justice. Justice Scalia filled Justice Rehnquist's old spot.

appointed Ruth Bader Ginsburg as his replacement. The year 1994 saw the first departure of a Burger Court Justice, Harry Blackmun, with Stephen Breyer taking his place on the Court. The criminal justice opinions of Justices Souter, Ginsburg, and Breyer have frequently run counter to the now prevailing pro-government position of the Rehnquist Court;[76] in contrast, Justice Thomas is a consistent advocate for crime control values.

---

[76] *See generally* Karen O'Connor & Barbara Palmer, *The Clinton Clones: Ginsburg, Breyer, and the Clinton Legacy*, 84 Judicature 262 (2001).

CHAPTER 2

# OVERARCHING POLICY ISSUES IN CRIMINAL PROCEDURE

The law thankfully does not develop in a philosophical or policy vacuum. Lawyers, students, and scholars must be sensitive to various overarching controversies affecting the field if they are to appreciate—and be able sensibly to critique—the law of criminal procedure. At times, lawmakers expressly consider the issues discussed in this chapter in formulating criminal procedure doctrine; more often, however, these subjects silently animate lawmaking.

## § 2.01 Norms of the Criminal Process[1]

The legitimacy of the United States system of criminal procedure seems to depend on four not altogether consistent norms: (1) the accuracy of verdicts; (2) the fairness of the process itself; (3) the degree to which the justice system limits the power of government in relation to citizens ensnared in the criminal process; and (4) the efficiency of the process. These norms are considered in greater detail in this chapter, particularly in Sections 2.02 through 2.04.

Regarding accuracy, a perfectly accurate criminal process would result in no arrests of innocent persons or, somewhat less perfectly, innocent persons would be released prior to trial or (still less perfectly) as the result of acquittal at trial. Similarly, in an entirely reliable system, all guilty persons would be arrested or, at least, all those guilty who are arrested would be convicted. All systems that process and evaluate information, of course, make errors in evaluation, but in light of what is at stake in the criminal law if errors are made—loss of liberty or life as the result of punishment of the innocent, and the acquittal and release of culpable and potentially dangerous guilty persons—a process that does not value accuracy cannot easily be characterized as legitimate.

---

[1] For a more thorough version of the material considered in this chapter section, *see* Joshua Dressler & George C. Thomas III, Criminal Procedure: Principles, Policies and Perspectives 47–53 (1999).

A second way to measure the legitimacy of the American criminal justice system is by how fairly it treats persons suspected of, or prosecuted for, alleged criminal activity. Although the "fairness" and "accuracy" norms will sometimes overlap, they represent different and sometimes conflicting concerns, because the concept of fairness suggests that even guilty persons should be treated in a manner consistent with human dignity. Of course, "fairness" and "human dignity" are imprecise concepts, so controversies abound in this realm. For example, does fairness require that, prior to questioning, the police inform a suspect of his constitutional privilege not to be witness against himself? Is it unfair to prevent defense lawyers from being present to assist their clients during police questioning? Is it unfair to deny a defendant the opportunity personally to confront and cross-examine his accuser when the accuser is a young child who claims he sexually abused her?

A third concern of the American criminal process is to limit governmental overreaching. Sometimes this norm overlaps accuracy: use of police torture to secure a confession can result in inaccuracy (a false confession) and represents obvious overreaching. Moreover, torture of a suspect is, rather uncontroversially, a violation of the fairness norm. But, the desire to promote limited government is sometimes an independent value. For example, a rule requiring the exclusion of evidence secured by the police, without a search warrant, from a suspect's bedroom may result in a *less* accurate outcome (because the excluded evidence is reliable). One can also plausibly argue that exclusion of such evidence is the "fair thing to do," but it is plausible as well to reason that it is unfair that "the criminal is to go free because the constable has blundered."[2] However one decides the fairness issue, something more is involved in a rule prohibiting the police from entering the bedroom without a warrant: it is the principle that explains the ratification of most of the provisions of the Bill of Rights, namely, that we are a political system that values individual rights and favors limited governmental power in the lives of its citizens. Therefore, we prefer that, emergencies aside, the police obtain judicial approval (a search warrant) before they enter the private confines of a home.

A fourth norm is that of efficiency. An inefficient system is wasteful of human and institutional resources. A system that is slow to reach an outcome can also undermine social protection by delaying the confinement and punishment of the guilty; it can also render more agonizing the experience of the innocent accused. On the other hand, the same grease that permits the wheels of justice to turn smoothly can sometimes undermine accuracy (*e.g.,* if the system encourages the innocent to plead guilty) or occur at the

---

[2] People v. Defore, 150 N.E. 585, 587 (N.Y. 1926) (opinion of Cardozo, J.)

arguable cost of fairness to the accused (*e.g.*, by denying defendants the assistance of delay-producing legal representation).

## § 2.02   Alternative Models of Criminal Justice[3]

### [A]   Overview

As is evident from the preceding chapter section, criminal procedural law is shaped by various overlapping but also sometimes conflicting norms. Although society desires a reliable criminal justice system—one that accurately sorts out the innocent from the guilty—the criminal process is intended to vindicate other goals, as well, such as fair treatment of criminal suspects and racial, sexual, and economic equality in the justice system.[4] Vindication of the latter goals, however, may impair the efficiency of the criminal system, still another norm, so the matter of criminal justice goals comes down to setting priorities.

How have we—and should we—set priorities? For more than a generation, various scholars have sought to answer these questions by constructing models of an adversarial system of criminal justice that can account for the procedural rules that have developed and/or suggest how a sensible system might be formulated.

Professor Herbert Packer once identified two models of criminal procedure, each possessing identifiable value systems, "that compete for priority in the operation of the criminal process."[5] He termed them the "Crime Control" (hereafter, CC) and "Due Process" (DP) models of criminal justice.[6] Packer's analysis has been criticized,[7] and alternative models of criminal justice have been suggested by other commentators.[8] Nonetheless, his articulation of the models has greatly influenced thought in the field.

---

[3] *See generally* Herbert L. Packer, The Limits of the Criminal Sanction 149–246 (1968); Peter Arenella, *Rethinking the Functions of Criminal Procedure: The Warren and Burger Courts' Competing Ideologies*, 72 Geo. L.J. 185 (1983); Douglas Evan Beloof, *The Third Model of Criminal Process: The Victim Participation Model*, 1999 Utah L. Rev. 289; John Griffiths, *Ideology in Criminal Procedure or A Third "Model" of the Criminal Process*, 79 Yale L. J. 359 (1970); Kent Roach, *Four Models of the Criminal Process*, 89 J. Crim. L. & Criminology 671 (1999).

[4] Susan R. Klein, *Enduring Principles and Current Crises in Constitutional Criminal Procedure*, 24 Law & Social Inquiry 533, 536 (1999).

[5] Packer, Note 3, *supra*, at 153.

[6] Packer first set out the models in Herbert L. Packer, *Two Models of the Criminal Process*, 113 U. Pa. L. Rev. 1 (1964).

[7] *E.g.*, Arenella, Note 3, *supra*, at 209–228; John Griffiths, *The Limits of Criminal Law Scholarship*, 79 Yale L.J. 1388 (1970).

[8] *E.g.*, Arenella, Note 3, *supra*, at 213–228 (re-conceptualizing Packer's models); Beloof,

The models are summarized below. Although they are usually discussed as if they represent mutually exclusive visions, some commentators believe that with slight modifications of the goals, many disputes disappear.[9] Nonetheless, the reader may find it useful to evaluate procedural law, as set out in this text, in light of these models.

## [B] Crime Control Model of Criminal Justice

The CC Model is founded on the principle that repression of crime is the most important domestic goal of government. The criminal sanction is "a positive guarantor of social freedom" and essential to the maintenance of "public order."[10] In light of the paramount significance of crime prevention, CC advocates place a premium on efficiency in the investigation and prosecution of alleged law violators.

How do we make the process efficient? First, speed and informality are desirable. This means that, to the extent feasible, nonjudicial processes are preferable to formal, judicial ones. Great faith is placed in the expertise of police and prosecutors. "Most fact-finding in the crime control model is conducted by the police in the streets and station-houses, not by lawyers and judges in the courts."[11] Police officers are permitted substantial opportunity to function free of legal impediments ("ceremonious rituals"),[12] including lawyers,[13] as they investigate criminal activity, screen out the innocent, and "as expeditiously as possible, [secure] the conviction of the rest, with a minimum of occasions for challenge . . . ."[14] Trials, with their

---

Note 3, *supra* (advocating a "victim participation model"); Griffiths, Note 3, *supra* (advocating a "family" model of criminal justice premised on the view that rehabilitation and reintegration of an offender into society is desirable); Roach, Note 3, *supra* (describing punitive and non-punitive victims' rights models). For consideration of procedural systems in other countries, and discussion of what the United States might learn from these systems, *see* Mirjan Damaska, *Evidentiary Barriers to Conviction and Two Models of Criminal Procedure: A Comparative Study*, 121 U. Pa. L. Rev. 506 (1973); Daniel H. Foote, *The Benevolent Paternalism of Japanese Criminal Justice*, 80 Cal. L. Rev. 317 (1992); Richard S. Frase, *Comparative Criminal Justice as a Guide to American Law Reform: How Do the French Do It, How Can We Find Out, and Why Should We Care?*, 78 Cal. L. Rev. 542 (1990).

[9] *See generally* Donald A. Dripps, *Beyond the Warren Court and Its Conservative Critics: Toward a Unified Theory of Constitutional Criminal Procedure*, 23 U. Mich. J.L. Ref. 591 (1990).

[10] Packer, Note 3, *supra*, at 158.

[11] Roach, Note 3, *supra*, at 678.

[12] Packer, Note 3, *supra*, at 159.

[13] "A lawyer's place is in court. He should not enter a criminal case until it is in court." *Id.* at 203.

[14] *Id.* at 160.

formality, rigid rules of evidence, and adversarial conditions, are delayed as long as possible, or avoided entirely through guilty pleas.[15]

Besides efficiency, the CC Model favors uniformity. That is, if large numbers of cases are to be handled efficiently, the criminal process must be "routine" and "stereotyped." According to Packer, the CC Model should look like "an assembly-line conveyor belt down which moves an endless stream of cases, never stopping."[16] Cases should not be taken off the belt unless informal procedures indicate that the suspect did not commit the offense.

Third, the CC Model functions on the premise that most suspects are factually guilty of the offense for which they are being prosecuted.[17] By assuming the factual guilt of a suspect, the CC advocate expresses confidence in the criminal justice system; and the presumption helps reinforce society's desire to promote an efficient system. The CC Model is less enamored of—and certainly less concerned with—the *legal* guilt requirement, applicable at trials, that presumes the innocence of the accused.

### [C]  Due Process Model of Criminal Justice

The values of the DP Model may be understood by contrasting them to the CC Model. First, DP advocates, while not discounting the desirability of preventing crime, believe in the liberal view of "the primacy of the individual and the complementary concept of limitation on official power."[18] Therefore, in its efforts to guard the rights of individuals, including persons suspected of crime, the DP model imposes many restraints on government, especially on the police.

Second, advocates of the DP Model question the reliability of informal systems of criminal justice. Whereas the CC system pictures police officers as skilled investigators likely to ascertain the truth if obstacles are not placed in their way, the DP Model emphasizes the risks of human error and bias in informal investigative processes. For the DP advocate, reliability is enhanced by a process involving early intervention of judges and lawyers— and, thus, of formality—in the justice system.

Third, while the CC Model is predicated on the assumed *factual* guilt of suspects, the DP system focuses on the doctrine of *legal* guilt. That is,

---

[15] The "center of gravity [in the CC Model] . . .lies in the early, administrative fact-finding stages." *Id.* at 162.

[16] *Id.* at 160.

[17] Alan M. Dershowitz, The Best Defense xxi (1982) (stating that two rules of "the justice game" are: (1) "[a]lmost all criminal defendants are in fact guilty"; and (2) "[a]ll defense lawyers, prosecutors and judges understand and believe" the first rule).

[18] Packer, Note 3, *supra*, at 165.

a criminal suspect is not legally guilty of a crime unless and until (guilty pleas aside) the prosecutor proves the defendant's guilt beyond a reasonable doubt in the courtroom, through the adversarial process, on the basis of legally admissible evidence.[19] The legal presumption of innocence, like the CC Model's belief in the factual guilt of the suspect, represents a mood, a way of thinking about criminal cases: by thinking of suspects as innocent persons, DP Model advocates believe that we are more apt to appreciate the value of setting limits on governmental power. Moreover, the presumption of innocence decreases the likelihood of conviction of innocent persons, although it increases the possibility that factually guilty persons will escape conviction.

Fourth, the models differ in their evaluation of the importance of redressing economic inequality in the criminal justice system. Adherents of the DP Model agree with the principle that "[t]here can be no equal justice where the kind of trial a man gets depends on the amount of money he has."[20] Therefore, to the extent possible, they seek to place indigent individuals in the same position as more wealthy suspects. In contrast, in the efficiency-driven CC system, an indigent is entitled to a fair, but not necessarily equal, opportunity to demonstrate his factual innocence. Likewise, the DP model would devise rules to reduce the likelihood and effects of other forms of inequality, such as racial discrimination. This is not a priority of the CC Model.

Finally, the judiciary as an institution has a more active role to play in the DP Model than in the CC system, which favors legislative supremacy. Judicial activism is appropriate in the DP Model because its advocates believe that the "central purpose of our written Constitution, and more specifically of its unique creation of a life-tenured federal judiciary, [is] to ensure that certain rights [*i.e.,* those included in the Bill of Rights] are firmly secured *against* possible oppression by the Federal or State Governments."[21]

---

[19] Packer's factual/legal guilt distinction, as set out in the text, is too simplistic. Packer assumes that factual guilt is merely an empirical question: did the suspect (and not some unidentified person) commit the acts that constitute the offense, *e.g.,* did the accused (kill) (rob) (rape) the victim? This is a matter that may, indeed, be provable through informal investigatory processes. The trial process, then, appears accordingly to consist, simply, of rules for proving factual guilt to a high degree of certainty. But factual guilt is more than an empirical judgment: to be *guilty* of a *crime*—and not simply to have done a harmful act—a person must commit the *actus reus* of an offense with the requisite degree of moral culpability and accountability. In short, a *normative* judgment must always be made before it may be said that a person is factually guilty of a crime. Quite simply, even factual guilt *cannot* be determined informally. *See* Arenella, Note 3, *supra,* at 214.

[20] Griffin v. Illinois, 351 U.S. 12, 19 (1956).

[21] Florida v. Meyers, 466 U.S. 380, 385 (1984) (Stevens, J., dissenting).

(Matthew Bender & Co., Inc.)                                                    (Pub.791)

Thus, all else being equal, a system modeled on DP values will be less efficient, more inclined to favor an active judiciary *vis a vis* the legislature, more apt to protect individual liberties, more interested in bringing about equality in the justice system, less likely to convict innocent persons, and more likely to allow the guilty to go free, than one based on CC values.

## § 2.03    The Role of "Truth" In the Criminal Justice System[22]

Everyone agrees that truth—reliable trial outcomes, in which the guilty are convicted and the innocent are acquitted—is a critical goal of the criminal justice system. All else being equal, the criminal process should advance, rather than retard, the truth-seeking process.

Nonetheless, controversies abound in this field. First, there is disagreement regarding the best methods for enhancing reliability. For example, as noted in § 2.02, some people believe that the adjudicatory process, with its formality, diminishes reliability, whereas others believe that it promotes truth-finding better than the more informal fact-finding processes of the police.

A second vital question of policy—indeed, one of fundamental moral values—is whether erroneous convictions and erroneous acquittals are equally undesirable. That is, once we accept that no system of fact adjudication by humans is error-free, one must determine whether the system should be indifferent to the direction of the error.

Whereas the civil law uses a "guilt-innocent neutral"[23] approach to error allocation, the traditional view of American criminal justice, reflected by the constitutional presumption of innocence and by other doctrines such as the constitutional privilege against compulsory self-incrimination, is that

---

[22] *See generally* William T. Pizzi, Trials Without Truth (1999); Thomas Weigend, *Criminal Procedure: Comparative Aspects* in 2 Encyclopedia of Crime and Justice (Joshua Dressler, Editor-in-Chief 2001); Albert W. Alschuler, *The Search for Truth Continued, The Privilege Retained: A Response to Judge Frankel,* 54 U. Colo. L. Rev. 67 (1982); William J. Brennan, Jr., *The Criminal Prosecution: Sporting Event or Quest for Truth?,* 1963 Wash. U. L.Q. 279; Marvin E. Frankel, *The Search for Truth: An Umpireal View,* 123 U. Pa. L. Rev. 1031 (1975); Monroe H. Freedman, *Judge Frankel's Search for Truth,* 123 U. Pa. L. Rev. 1060 (1975); Henry J. Friendly, *Is Innocence Irrelevant? Collateral Attack on Criminal Judgments,* 38 U. Chi. L. Rev. 142 (1970); Gary Goodpaster, *On the Theory of American Adversary Criminal Trial,* 78 J. Crim. L. & Criminology 118 (1987); Klein, Note 4, *supra*; William S. Laufer, *The Rhetoric of Innocence,* 70 Wash. L. Rev. 329 (1995); Charles Pulaski, Jr., *Criminal Trials: A "Search for Truth" or Something Else?,* 16 Crim. L. Bull. 41 (1980); A. Kenneth Pye, *The Role of Counsel in the Suppression of Truth,* 1978 Duke L.J. 921; Irene Merker Rosenberg & Yale L. Rosenberg, *Guilt: Henry Friendly Meets the MaHaRaL of Prague,* 90 Mich. L. Rev. 604 (1991); Tom Stacy, *The Search for the Truth in Constitutional Criminal Procedure,* 91 Colum. L. Rev. 1369 (1991).

[23] Stacy, Note 22, *supra,* at 1407.

an "innocence-weighted" approach is preferable: "it is far worse to convict an innocent man than to let a guilty man go free."[24] Blackstone went so far as to claim that "the law holds than it is better that ten guilty persons escape, than that one innocent suffer."[25] In short, there is particular evil in infliction of undeserved pain; and there may also be utilitarian reasons for the rule, in that "the moral force of the criminal law [is] diluted by a [legal process] that leaves people in doubt whether innocent men are being condemned."[26] Under this view, a process that devises an even playing field is, in fact, improperly balanced; rather, the law should place a heavy thumb "on the defendant's side of the scales of justice."[27]

This position is not universally accepted, and may be less in vogue today than in centuries past.[28] From a purely retributive perspective, it may be claimed that the two forms of error are equally wrong: it is wrong to punish an innocent person, but it is equally unjust for a guilty person to avoid paying his debt to society. From a utilitarian viewpoint, a system of rules that makes it easier for guilty people to go free may send a dangerous message to would-be offenders; and the wrongful release of particularly dangerous individuals may result in more societal pain than is imposed by the infliction of punishment of an equal number of innocent persons.[29]

Professor and Judge Richard Posner contends that "unless the resources devoted to determining guilt and innocence are increased, the only way to reduce the probability of convicting the innocent is to reduce the probability of convicting the guilty as well."[30] That is, with finite resources, every dollar spent to protect the innocent is money not spent to convict the guilty. If we assume that most people charged with crime are factually guilty, the reasoning continues, concern for protecting innocence will result in a less reliable outcome than a process evenly balanced. Indeed, if one accepts Posner's view, a guilt-weighted system is preferable: the principle that we should give the fox—under this view, most persons suspected of crime—a

---

[24] In re Winship, 397 U.S. 358, 372 (1970) (Harlan, J., concurring).

[25] 4 William Blackstone, Commentaries on the Laws of England 358 (1765).

[26] In re Winship, 397 U.S. at 364.

[27] Barbara D. Underwood, *The Thumb on the Scales of Justice: Burdens of Persuasion in Criminal Cases,* 86 Yale L.J. 1299 (1977).

[28] *See especially* Stacy, Note 23, *supra* (contending that the Supreme Court's emerging view is that wrongful acquittals are as bad as wrongful convictions).

[29] For debate on this subject, *see* Jeffrey Reiman & Ernest van den Haag, *On the Common Saying that it is Better that Ten Guilty Persons Escape than that One Innocent Suffer: Pro and Con,* 7 Soc. Phil. & Policy (Spring, 1990) at 226.

[30] Richard A. Posner, The Problems of Jurisprudence 216 (1990).

chance of surviving the hunt "makes for good sports, but in a criminal investigation we should be seeking truth rather than entertainment."[31]

This debate brings us close to a third serious controversy: *is* the truth of a defendant's guilt or innocence the only value that should be considered in the criminal justice system? Some commentators suggest as much: subordination of the truth to *any* other value is indefensible; when the truth is not discovered, or its implications ignored, the system necessarily fails in its mission. One scholar has argued that, properly interpreted, the constitutional provisions relating to criminal procedure exist only "to protect the innocent. The guilty, in general, receive . . . protection only as an incidental and unavoidable by-product of protecting the innocent *because* of their innocence."[32] It follows from this view, for example, that a rule of law that requires the exclusion at trial of trustworthy evidence because it was illegally secured by the police is an unwise rule.

The contrary position, held by most legal commentators, is that the criminal justice system should not focus exclusively on the truth-finding process. As one English court put it, "[t]ruth, like all other good things, may be loved unwisely—may be pursued too keenly—may cost too much."[33] From this perspective, "truth must find its place in the context of a larger concern to do justice."[34] That is, "justice" means more than, simply, a reliable result in a particular prosecution. Many observers would claim that the truth is too expensive if it is obtained by government use of torture or violation of other important human rights. In such circumstances, society may consider it preferable to allow a potentially guilty party to go free—either out of respect for the accused's human rights, concern about the moral integrity of the justice system, or as a means of deterring future official abuses—than to use the tainted evidence to obtain a conviction.[35] In particular in regard to constitutional law, many would agree with the observation that "the pursuit of truth . . . is not the only, or even, perhaps, the most important, principle at work . . . ."[36]

---

[31] Joseph D. Grano, *Selling the Idea to Tell the Truth: The Professional Interrogator and Modern Confessions Law*, 84 Mich. L. Rev. 662, 677 (1986).

[32] Akhil Reed Amar, The Constitution and Criminal Procedure: First Principles 154 (1997).

[33] Pearse v. Pearse, 63 Eng. Rep. 957, 970 (1846).

[34] Law Reform Commission of Canada, Our Criminal Procedure (Report 32) 10 (1988).

[35] *See* Sawyer v. Whitley, 505 U.S. 333, 356 (1992) (Blackmun, J., concurring in the judgment) (criticizing the Court's "single-minded focus" on truth-finding, and stating that "[t]he accusatorial system of justice adopted by the Founders affords a defendant certain process-based protections that do not have accuracy of truth-finding as their primary goal").

[36] Klein, Note 4, *supra*, at 534.

## § 2.04 Accusatorial versus Inquisitorial Systems of Justice [37]

Judges often state that "ours is an accusatorial and not an inquisitorial system" [38] of criminal justice. But, is it? And, more significantly for present purposes, *should* it be accusatorial?

Generally speaking, in its pure form, an accusatorial system of criminal justice is one founded on the belief that "to respect the inviolability of the human personality, . . . the government seeking to punish an individual [must] produce the evidence against him by its own independent labors." [39] The government must "shoulder the entire load." [40] It may not convict a person by obtaining evidence of guilt involuntarily from the accused. As one scholar has explained, "an accusatorial system . . . assigns great social value in keeping the state out of disputes, especially when stigma and sanction may follow"; therefore, the defendant in the accusatorial system is treated "*as if* he is innocent and need lend no aid to those who would convict him." [41]

At trial, the accusatorial system is founded on the adversarial theory of trial practice. The adversary system is "a regulated storytelling contest between champions of competing, interpretive stories." [42] That is, the parties in dispute, normally represented by attorneys, present their conflicting versions of the events to a passive and impartial decisionmaker.

In contrast, an inquisitorial system in its most extreme form permits the government to obtain evidence of a defendant's guilt through the "simple expedient of compelling it" [43] from the accused party. During the trial, the

---

[37] *See generally* Joseph Grano, Police Interrogation and Confessions: A Rebuttal to Misconceived Objections (Occasional Papers from the Center for Research in Crime and Justice, N.Y.U. School of Law, 1987); Damaska, Note 8, *supra*; Abraham S. Goldstein, *Reflections on Two Models: Inquisitorial Themes in American Criminal Procedure*, 26 Stan. L. Rev. 1009 (1974); Abraham S. Goldstein & Martin Marcus, *The Myth of Judicial Supervision in Three 'Inquisitorial' Systems: France, Italy, and Germany*, 87 Yale L.J. 240 (1977); Goodpaster, Note 22, *supra*; John H. Langbein & Lloyd L. Weinreb, *Continental Criminal Procedure: "Myth" and Reality*, 87 Yale L.J. 1549 (1978); Myron Moskovitz, *The O.J. Inquisition: A United States Encounter With Continental Criminal Justice*, 28 Vand. J. Transnat'l L. 1121 (1995); Gregory W. O'Reilly, *England Limits the Right to Silence and Moves Towards an Inquisitorial System of Justice*, 85 J. Crim. L. & Criminology 402 (1994); Weigend, Note 22, *supra*;.

[38] Rogers v. Richmond, 365 U.S. 534, 541 (1961).

[39] Miranda v. Arizona, 384 U.S. 436, 460 (1966).

[40] *Id.* (quoting 8 Wigmore, Evidence 317 (McNaughton rev. 1961)).

[41] Goldstein, Note 37, *supra*, at 1017.

[42] Goodpaster, Note 22, *supra*, at 120.

[43] Miranda v. Arizona, 384 U.S. at 460.

judge (as inquisitor), conducts the factual and legal investigation himself, rather than leaving the matter to attorneys to present the facts in a pro and con manner. In this system, as well, the judge may compel the defendant to be a witness against himself.

Sloganeering aside, it is not true that the American system of criminal justice is purely accusatorial in character (just as few, if any, countries on the European continent today perfectly fit the inquisitorial mold). Indeed, the Supreme Court has recently stated that "[o]ur system of justice is, and has always been, an inquisitorial one at the investigatory stage . . . ."[44] Even if this is an over-statement, as is developed in this text the government is *not* required to "shoulder the entire load" to convict a suspect. For example, a suspect may be compelled to participate in a lineup, to be fingerprinted, and to have his blood extracted from his veins against his will,[45] all of which events often assist in his conviction and punishment. On the other hand, the Supreme Court has sometimes taken steps to "even the playing field" in the police station, such as by allowing defense lawyers to be present during post-indictment lineups, and to permit suspects to request the assistance of counsel before and during police interrogations.[46]

If the investigatory phase is often inquisitorial in nature, the adjudicatory phase of the criminal justice system—with the adversarial process fully in play, and the recognized Fifth Amendment right of a defendant not to be "compelled in any criminal case to be a witness against himself"—is mostly accusatorial in nature. But, even here, some non-accusatorial features may be found, such as the rule that the government may require a defendant to notify the prosecutor regarding his intended trial defenses,[47] a rule that makes it easier for the government to prepare and win its case.

The critical question is whether the justice system should be more (or less) accusatorial/adversarial than it presently is. To the extent that truth-production is the goal of the criminal process, some have argued that the adversarial trial system is appropriate because "truth is best discovered by powerful statements on both sides of the question."[48] Only this way, it is asserted, will an arbiter avoid the tendency to judge a controversy too swiftly.

---

[44] McNeil v. Wisconsin, 501 U.S. 171, 181 n.2 (1991).

[45] *See* § 26.05[D][1], *infra.*

[46] *See* §§ 27.02[A] (at lineups), 24.04[B][1][b], *infra.*

[47] *See* Williams v. Florida, 399 U.S. 78 (1970).

[48] United States v. Cronic, 466 U.S. 648, 655 (1984) (quoting Lord Eldon in Kaufman, *Does the Judge Have a Right to Qualified Counsel?*, 61 A.B.A. J. 569, 569 (1975) (internal quotation marks omitted)).

Other commentators claim that the adversarial process is not conducive to a reliable verdict.[49] They would agree with the view of one jurist who complained that the adversary process achieves truth "only as a convenience, a byproduct, or an accidental approximation."[50] If what we want is the truth, they assert, the judge should take a more active role at trial, and there should be no bar to the production of reliable evidence, including the defendant's own trial testimony, simply because it was obtained involuntarily from the accused.

An alternative defense of the adversary system, one that is particularly aimed at the pre-trial investigatory phase, is that such a system places a needed protective barrier between the accused, a potentially innocent person, and the far more powerful State. In this context, an observation by the Supreme Court may be relevant:

> We have learned the lesson of history, ancient and modern, that a system of criminal law enforcement which comes to depend on the "confession" [and other evidence secured from the accused] will, in the long run, be less reliable and more subject to abuses than a system which depends on extrinsic evidence independently secured through skillful investigation.[51]

However, even if the accusatorial system can be justified on this ground, the question remains whether more truth-enhancing techniques can safely be permitted in the adversarial system.

## § 2.05  Race, Gender, Economic Class (and Other Characteristics) in the Law[52]

Issues related to race, gender, and economic class are very often at the center of attention in criminal procedure. For example, a rich person can hire an attorney and, if convicted, pay to file an appeal. An indigent cannot

---

[49] *See* Goodpaster, Note 22, *supra*, at 121–22.

[50] Frankel, Note 22, *supra*, at 1037.

[51] Escobedo v. Illinois, 378 U.S. 478, 488–89 (1964) (footnotes omitted).

[52] *See generally* Randall Kennedy, Race, Crime and the Law (1997); Feminist Legal Theory: Readings in Law & Gender (Katherine T. Bartlett & Rosanne Kennedy, eds. 1991); Gary Minda, Postmodern Legal Movements 106-48, 167-85 (1995); Richard Delgado & Jean Stefancic, *Critical Race Theory: An Annotated Bibliography*, 79 Va. L. Rev. 461 (1993); Duncan Kennedy & Karl E. Klare, *A Bibliography of Critical Legal Studies*, 94 Yale L.J. 461 (1984); Andrew D. Leipold, *Objective Tests and Subjective Bias: Some Problems of Discriminatory Intent in the Criminal Law*, 73 Chi.-Kent. L. Rev. 559 (1998); Christopher Stone, *Race, Crime and the Administration of Justice*, National Institute of Justice Journal 26 (April 1999). In addition, scholarship specifically relating to the effects of race, gender, and economic class on the law of criminal procedure are cited throughout the text, where appropriate.

afford a private attorney or pay court filing costs. Therefore, courts and legislatures must determine *whether* (and, if so, *how*) to ensure that indigent defendants obtain access to the criminal process on the same basis as non-indigent persons, and obtain representation of similar quality and energy as that which can be secured by a wealthy individual.[53]

In regard to issues of gender, many issues arise, such as whether legislatures should be permitted to permit women to seek release from jury duty on more lenient grounds than are available to males,[54] and whether lawyers should be permitted to exclude persons from a criminal jury based solely on the person's sex.[55]

And, perhaps most tragically of all, racism has permeated the criminal justice system on many levels. Studies show, for example, that minority youths are treated more harshly than non-minority youths in the juvenile justice system,[56] jurors are influenced by the race of defendants in criminal cases;[57] and there is growing and conceded evidence of "racial profiling,"[58]

---

[53] *See, e.g.*, §§ 29.02[B] (appointment of trial counsel for indigents), 29.03 (*id.*, on some appeals), and 31.06[B][2][e] (risk that innocent indigents, represented by overharried lawyers, may be compelled to plead guilty), *infra*.

[54] Taylor v. Louisiana, 419 U.S. 522 (1975) (holding that a statute permitting women, but not men, to file a written declaration of their desire not to be subject to jury service violated the Sixth Amendment right of a defendant to a jury pool that is a representative cross-section of the community).

[55] J.E.B. v. Alabama ex rel. T.B. 511 U.S. 127 (1994) (holding that exercise of peremptory challenges based solely on gender violates the equal protection clause of the Fourteenth Amendment; therefore, a party's efforts to remove male jurors in a child custody and paternity action cannot properly be based on the assumption that men (or women) will decide such cases solely on the basis of their sex).

[56] Fox Butterfield, *Racial Disparities Seen as Pervasive in Juvenile Justice*, New York Times, April 26, 2000, at A1 (reporting on findings compiled by the Department of Justice and six national foundations).

[57] Samuel R. Sommers & Phoebe C. Ellsworth, *Race in the Courtroom: Perceptions of Guilt amd Dispositional Attributions*, 26 Personality & Soc. Psych. Bulletin 1367 (2000) (among the findings is that in cases in which race was not a salient factor, white jurors rated African-American defendants more guilty, aggressive, and violent than they did white defendants).

[58] David A. Harris, *"Driving While Black" and All Other Traffic Offenses: The Supreme Court and Pretextual Traffic Stops*, 87 J. Crim. L. & Criminology 544 (1997); Tracey Maclin, *Race and the Fourth Amendment*, 51 Vand. L. Rev. 333 (1998); David A. Sklansky, *Traffic Stops, Minority Motorists, and the Future of the Fourth Amendment*, 1997 Sup. Ct. Rev. 271. At least on occasion, police departments have known of the existence of racial profiling by their officers but have withheld information on the problem. David Barstow and David Kocieniewski, *Records Show New Jersey Police Knew of Racial Profiling in '96*, New York Times, October 12, 2000, at A1. In some cases, racial profiling has been "routine." David Kocieniewski and Robert Hanley, *Racial Profiling Was the Routine, New Jersey Finds*, New York Times, Nov. 28, 2000, at A1.

in which police officers stop, question, and often search African-Americans (and other minorities) and their automobiles based on racial stereotyping.[59] Lawmakers must determine how best to combat such discrimination, and courts frequently are called upon to determine what weapons against racism are provided by the United States and/or state constitutions.

But, even as courts, lawyers, and commentators seek to find ways to develop a more race-and gender-blind criminal justice system, other commentators believe that, in some regards, the law should take race and gender *more* into account. For example, in determining what conduct may be expected of a "reasonable person" in a confrontation with a police officer, Professor Tracey Maclin has argued that "the dynamics surrounding an encounter between a police officer and a black male are quite different from those that surround an encounter between an officer and the so-called average, reasonable person"?[60] If this is correct, the issue arises whether the "reasonable person" standard should be race-specific, rather than race-neutral.[61]

Issues of race, gender, economic status call on society—and lawyers—to ask difficult and painful questions. As these matters affect the contours of the law—and the way it is enforced—they should be kept in mind throughout.

## § 2.06 Who Should Devise the Rules of Criminal Procedure?[62]

The United States Supreme Court took the leading role in formulating rules of criminal justice during the 1950s, continuing through the early 1970s. In more recent years, the Court has accepted a more passive role, leaving many matters of procedure to legislative bodies or, at least, to state courts.

---

[59] *E.g.,* State v. Soto, 734 A.2d 350 (N.J. Super. 1996) (citing statistical evidence that New Jersey State Police engaged in racial discrimination in its enforcement of traffic laws); Iver Peterson, *Whitman Concedes Troopers Used Race in Stopping Drivers,* New York Times, April 21, 1999, at A1 (the Governor of New Jersey conceded that state troopers singled out African American and Hispanic motorists on the highway for stops, and then searched their vehicles three times more often than in the case of white motorists). *See also* §§ 2.07[B], 9.02[F], and 18.03[B][5], *infra.*

[60] Tracey Maclin, *"Black and Blue Encounters"—Some Preliminary Thoughts About Fourth Amendment Seizures: Should Race Matter?,* 26 Val. U. L. Rev. 243, 250 (1991); *see also* Tracey Maclin, *Terry v. Ohio's Fourth Amendment Legacy: Black Men and Police Discretion,* 72 St. John's L. Rev. 1271 (1998).

[61] *See* § 8.03[C][3], *infra.*

[62] *See generally* Craig M. Bradley, The Failure of the Criminal Procedure Revolution 38–94 (1993); Anthony G. Amsterdam, *The Supreme Court and the Rights of Suspects in Criminal Cases,* 45 N.Y.U. L. Rev. 785 (1970); Dripps, Note 9, *supra*; Henry J. Friendly, *The Bill of Rights as a Code of Criminal Procedure,* 53 Cal. L. Rev. 929 (1965).

Which approach is better? That is, should the judiciary, or should some other institution, formulate procedural rules? And, whichever body takes the lead, should the rules be uniform throughout the country, or should local bodies have substantial discretion to determine what limits are placed on police power, how state and local prosecutors enforce the criminal laws, and how state courts adjudicate charges of criminal conduct?

As noted elsewhere in this chapter,[63] advocates of the due process model of criminal justice generally favor an active judiciary, particularly that of the United States Supreme Court. Crime control advocates favor fewer rules and, where rules are required, prefer that they be devised by the police and local legislative bodies, which (they believe) can better evaluate local needs.

Beyond this philosophical disagreement about criminal justice, some scholars advocate a limited federal judicial role on the ground that, in the words of Justice Louis Brandeis, "[i]t is one of the happy incidents of the federal system that a single courageous State may, if its citizens choose, serve as a laboratory"[64] that experiments on ways to improve the justice system. In contrast, a Supreme Court decision based on the Constitution announces a national rule of criminal procedure, which (according to advocates of federalism) stifles local ingenuity.[65]

Even among advocates of national rules of criminal procedure, there is dispute whether the judiciary is the proper body for formulating legal doctrine. Professor Craig Bradley contends, for example, that "any [Supreme Court] attempt to resolve an issue of constitutional law will tend to create more uncertainty than it resolves."[66] He suggests that, because the Court is composed of lawyers, every opinion is backed up with multiple explanations, which can only confuse the parties that must interpret and apply the Court's rulings on a daily basis. Moreover, courts necessarily act on a case-by-case basis, announcing rules to resolve specific controversies, thereby leaving gaps in the law. Bradley's solution is for Congress to legislate a comprehensive code of criminal procedure, binding on the states.

Among advocates of a strong federal judicial role, there is recognition of the fact that few conflicts between the police and private individuals reach the courts, much less that they can be decided by the Supreme Court.[67] Thus, although Supreme Court pronouncements may be valuable because "they have vast mystical significance" and "state our aspirations,"[68] society

---

[63] See generally § 2.02, supra.

[64] New State Ice Co. v. Liebmann, 285 U.S. 262, 311 (1932) (dissenting opinion).

[65] Friendly, Note 62, supra, at 954–55.

[66] Bradley, Note 62, supra, at 62.

[67] See § 1.02[B], supra.

[68] Amsterdam, Note 62, supra, at 793.

ultimately must look beyond the judiciary for meaningful protection of the rights of persons accused of crime. But, Congress does not presently desire to adopt rules of criminal procedure binding on local authorities, and there is considerable question whether such rules would violate constitutional principles of federalism.

Where does that leave those who want to limit police power, but who do not look to the Supreme Court as primary guardian? According to Professor Anthony Amsterdam, reform "must be done . . . by local legislators, executives, the police command structure and citizens in their communities. In light of past performance—or, rather, nonperformance—by all of these persons, this may seem a vain hope."[69] Thus, many supporters of the due process model return to the judiciary as the principal, if not exclusive, source for rule-making.

Users of this text will see how this controversy plays out between those who want the judiciary to take a less active role in criminal procedure (either for philosophical or practical reasons) and those who believe that the Supreme Court must be the main architect of a just and efficient criminal process.

## § 2.07 Formulating the Rules of Criminal Procedure: Some Overarching Controversies

### [A] Bright-Line Rules versus Case-by-Case Adjudication[70]

An ongoing and critically important issue in criminal procedure is this: Should courts (and other lawmaking institutions) develop bright-line rules of criminal procedure, or should they formulate "blurry line" rules, the implementation of which requires case-by-case adjudication?

Both types of rules abound in the criminal law. For example, in police interrogation law, the Supreme Court has held that, pursuant to the due process clause, a statement obtained from a suspect by means of police coercion, *i.e.*, obtained involuntarily, is inadmissible at the suspect's criminal trial.[71] However, the voluntariness of a confession is assessed from

---

[69] *Id.* at 810.

[70] *See generally* Albert W. Alschuler, *Bright Line Fever and the Fourth Amendment*, 45 U. Pitt. L. Rev. 227 (1984); Craig M. Bradley, *Two Models of the Fourth Amendment*, 83 Mich. L. Rev. 1468 (1985); Joseph D. Grano, *Miranda v. Arizona and the Legal Mind: Formalism's Triumph Over Substance and Reason*, 24 Am. Crim. L. Rev. 243 (1986); Wayne R. LaFave, *Being Frank About the Fourth: On Allen's "Process of 'Factualization' in the Search and Seizure Cases"*, 85 Mich. L. Rev. 427 (1986); Wayne R. LaFave, *The Fourth Amendment in an Imperfect World: On Drawing "Bright Lines" and "Good Faith"*, 43 U. Pitt. L. Rev. 307 (1982); Wayne R. LaFave, *"Case-by-Case Adjudication" Versus "Standardized Procedures": The Robinson Dilemma*, 1974 Sup. Ct. Rev. 127.

[71] *See generally* chapter 23, *infra*.

a totality of the circumstances. There is "no talismanic definition of 'voluntariness' "[72] : the court looks at all of the circumstances surrounding the confession (*e.g.*, the length of detention, the physical conditions in the interrogation room, the interrogation techniques used, the age and mental state of the suspect) in order to determine whether the statement was freely given. Under a totality-of-the-circumstances standard, "everything [is] relevant but nothing [is] determinative."[73]

On the other hand, the Supreme Court has also announced bright-line interrogation rules. The so-called "*Miranda*[74] rule" is bright-line in nature, in that any statement obtained during custodial interrogation in inadmissible against the speaker during the government's case-in-chief, unless the police initially informed the suspect of certain specified constitutional rights. Subject to certain exceptions and the inevitable fuzziness at the definitional edges of "custody" and "interrogation," this rule is absolute: in the absence of the warnings, *any and all* statements are inadmissible, *regardless* of whether the suspect was aware of his rights, and *regardless* of how the statement was secured.

Fourth Amendment jurisprudence, as well, contains both types of rules. For example, when the police arrest an occupant of a home, they may search the "area within the arrestee's immediate control"—the so-called "grabbing area"—without a search warrant.[75] The quoted language states a blurry-line rule, because the size of the grabbing area depends on the particular circumstances of the case, including the nature and contents of the room in which the arrest occurs, and the dexterity of the arrestee, thereby requiring case-by-case adjudication. In contrast, when the police arrest an occupant of an automobile, the police are permitted to search the entire passenger compartment of the vehicle and all containers found therein, without regard for the size of the car, whether the containers are closed or open, and whether the arrestee is standing near or far away from the vehicle.[76] This rule is bright-line.

Which approach to rule-making is preferable? Advocates of case-by-case adjudication argue that their approach is more apt to lead to the "correct" result, *i.e.*, to the result that is consistent with the underlying justification for the rule. They contend that bright-line rule-making can do no more than be right much of the time, whereas the goal of case-by-case adjudication

---

[72] Schneckloth v. Bustamonte, 412 U.S. 218, 224 (1973).

[73] Grano, Note 70, *supra*, at 243.

[74] Miranda v. Arizona, 384 U.S. 436 (1966). *See generally* chapter 24, *infra*.

[75] Chimel v. California, 395 U.S. 752 (1969). *See* § 13.03, *infra*.

[76] New York v. Belton, 453 U.S. 454 (1981). *See* § 13.05, *infra*.

is to be correct all of the time. For example, the Supreme Court has expressed a strong preference for police officers to secure warrants before they conduct searches, in order to protect citizens' privacy concerns.[77] The justification for *warrantless* searches incident to arrests, notwithstanding this preference, is to protect an arresting officer's safety by letting him look for weapons that an arrestee might secure, and to prevent the destruction of evidence in the arrestee's proximity. The "grabbing area" rule, therefore, fits this justification by allowing the police to search the area within the suspect's physical control, but to go no further. When that principle is converted to a bright-line rule, however, as with automobiles, the police are permitted to conduct warrantless searches in some, perhaps many, cases in which the need to act in the absence of a search warrant is lacking.

Advocates of bright lines contend that law enforcement officers must make split-second constitutional determinations. To do their job properly, "[a] single, familiar standard is essential to guide police officers, who have only limited time and expertise to reflect on and balance the social and individual interests involved in the specific circumstances they confront."[78] Put another way, those who enforce the law need clear guidance, rather than rules that are "qualified by all sorts of ifs, ands, and buts [that] . . . requir[e] the drawing of subtle nuances and hairline distinctions."[79] In contrast to bright-line rules, case-by-case, totality-of-the-circumstances, adjudication adds up to little more than "I know it when I see it" jurisprudence,[80] "in which the courts provide a lengthy factual description followed by a conclusion . . ., without anything to connect the two."[81] Such a rule fails to assist the police in their daily affairs.

Professor Anthony Amsterdam has reasoned that although a blurry-line rule may be "splendid in its flexibility," it is apt to be "awful in its unintelligibility, unadministrability, and . . . general ooziness."[82]

---

[77] *See* § 11.01, *infra.*

[78] Dunaway v. New York, 442 U.S. 200, 213–14 (1979); *see also* Atwater v. Lago Vista, 121 S. Ct. 1536, 1553–54 (2001) ("Often enough, the Fourth Amendment has to be applied on the spur (and in the heat) of the moment, and the object in implementing its command of reasonableness is to draw standards sufficiently clear and simple to be applied with a fair prospect of surviving judicial second-guessing months and years after the arrest or search is made.").

[79] LaFave, *"Case-by-Case Adjudication"* . . ., Note 70, *supra,* at 141.

[80] Ronald J. Bacigal, *Putting the People Back Into the Fourth Amendment,* 62 Geo. Wash. U. L. Rev. 359, 363 n. 19 (1994).

[81] Lloyd L. Weinreb, *Generalities of the Fourth Amendment,* 42 U. Chi. L. Rev. 47, 57 (1974).

[82] Anthony G. Amsterdam, *Perspectives on the Fourth Amendment,* 58 Minn. L. Rev. 349, 415 (1974).

Therefore, the argument proceeds, it is preferable to have a clear rule that can be obeyed nearly all of the time, even if it will lead to a correct result in, perhaps, only ninety percent of the cases, than it is to implement *unclear* rules that should lead to the correct result all of the time, but which well-intentioned officers are able to apply correctly in only seventy-five percent of the cases.[83]

It is not necessarily the case, however, that police officers understand bright-line rules better than they do non-bright-line ones.[84] Moreover, even assuming their virtue, do bright-line rules remain bright? Justice William Rehnquist has observed that lawyers are "trained to attack 'bright lines' the way hounds attack foxes."[85] Lawyers want rules to be "responsive to every relevant shading of every relevant variation of every relevant complexity" that might arise in a criminal case.[86] The tendency of courts—forced to confront real-world gray issues with black-and-white rules—is to develop hairline distinctions that inevitably muddy the water.[87]

Some commentators take a middle position in the debate.[88] They favor bright lines, but only if certain conditions are met. First, a bright-line rule should be implemented only when there is evidence of a genuine need for it, *i.e.*, when case-by-case adjudication provides inadequate guidance. Second, a bright-line rule should parallel the result that would be reached in a high percentage of cases if case-by-case adjudication were involved. Third, the bright-line rule should not readily be susceptible to abuse by those enforcing it.

----

[83] LaFave, *The Fourth Amendment in an Imperfect World . . .*, Note 70, *supra*, at 321.

[84] William C. Heffernan & Richard W. Lovely, *Evaluating the Fourth Amendment Exclusionary Rule: The Problem of Police Compliance with the Law*, 24 U. Mich. J.L. Ref. 311, 356 (1991) (in a study of four mid-sized police departments, the authors found that officers were no more likely to understand bright-line search-and-seizure rules than non-bright-line rules).

[85] Robbins v. California, 453 U.S. 420, 443 (1981).

[86] Amsterdam, Note 82, *supra*, at 375.

[87] *See* Bradley, Note 62, *supra*, at 77–81.

[88] *E.g.*, LaFave, *The Fourth Amendment in an Imperfect World . . .*, Note 70, *supra*, at 325–33.

## [B] Subjectivity versus Objectivity: Rule-Making to Avoid Pretextual Police Conduct[89]

Should the legitimacy of police conduct depend on the subjective state of mind of a law enforcement officer, *i.e.*, whether he is acting for a constitutionally appropriate or inappropriate reason? Or, should courts disregard an officer's hidden motivations, even if they are malicious, and measure police performance solely on objective grounds?

The Supreme Court has formulated both subjective and objective rules of criminal procedure. For example, in the interrogation field, the Court has held that a police officer violates the Sixth Amendment right to counsel if the officer "deliberately and designedly"—a subjective standard—sets out to elicit information in the absence of the accused's counsel.[90] On the other hand, the Court has crafted an objective standard to determine whether police conduct, short of actual questioning, constitutes the functional equivalent of "interrogation" for purposes of requiring *Miranda* warnings ("words or actions on the part of the police . . . that the police *should know are reasonably likely* to elicit an incriminating response from the suspect").[91]

Fourth Amendment jurisprudence, too, includes both subjective and objective standards, although the clear emphasis is on the latter. The Court has stated that "evenhanded law enforcement is best achieved by the application of objective standards of conduct, rather than standards that depend upon the subjective state of mind of the officer."[92] As a consequence, for example, the Justices have held that the police may search a home based on consent given by one who has no authority to let them enter (*e.g.,* someone who once lived at the residence, but has since moved out), as long "as the facts available to the officer at the moment . . . warrant a man of reasonable caution in the belief that the consenting party had authority."[93]

---

[89] *See generally* John M. Burkoff, *The Pretext Search Doctrine Returns After Never Leaving,* 66 U. Det. L. Rev. 363 (1989); Edwin J. Butterfoss, *Solving the Pretext Puzzle: The Importance of Ulterior Motives and Fabrications in the Supreme Court's Fourth Amendment Pretext Doctrine,* 79 Ky. L.J. 1 (1990); James B. Haddad, *Pretextual Fourth Amendment Activity: Another Viewpoint,* 18 U. Mich. J.L. Ref. 639 (1985); Harris, *Note 58,* supra; Leipold, Note 52, *supra;* Maclin, Note 58, *supra;* Sklansky, Note 58, *supra.*

[90] Brewer v. Williams, 430 U.S. 387, 389 (1977). *See* § 25.05, *infra.*

[91] Rhode Island v. Innis, 446 U.S. 291, 301 (1980) (emphasis added) (footnotes omitted). *See* § 24.08, *infra.*

[92] Horton v. California, 496 U.S. 128, 138 (1990).

[93] Illinois v. Rodriguez, 497 U.S. 177, 188 (1990) (internal quotations omitted). *See* § 17.06, *infra.*

On the other hand, sometimes an officer's state of mind will affect the legitimacy of the conduct. For example, although the police may inventory an automobile that they have impounded, as long as they apply standardized procedures, the police may *not* use such procedures as a ruse for investigating suspected criminal activity.[94]

Which approach—standards based on objective factors, or ones that take into consideration the motives of the police—is preferable? Frequently, the question is characterized in terms of how to deal with "pretextual" police conduct, *i.e.*, a situation in which "the officer does not have the state of mind which is hypothecated by the reasons which provide the legal justification for the officer's action."[95] For example, an officer who issues a traffic ticket to a speeder solely so that he can look inside the automobile on the hunch that the driver might be in possession of illegal narcotics is acting "pretextually." Similarly, an officer might delay a valid arrest until the suspect is at a friend's home. The delay might be motivated by the officer's desire to search the third person's residence, in the absence of probable cause, in the hope of linking the resident to the crime.

The most obvious way to deal with a claim of pretext is to take into consideration subjective motivations, and to consider each claim of pretext on a case-by-case basis, in order to determine whether the officer acted for proper or improper reasons. The primary difficulty with this approach is that "the catch is not worth the trouble of the hunt when courts set out to bag the secret motivations of policemen."[96] People rarely act of a single mind: conflicting motivations, some proper and others not, often incite action. Even the most truthful officer may be unable to testify with certainty regarding his thought processes on an earlier occasion; and a dishonest officer has a strong incentive to lie if his subjective beliefs will control the admissibility of the evidence. Realistically, a judge, forced to divine a police officer's motivations, is likely to give the officer the benefit of the doubt.

Alternatively, the Supreme Court might devise constitutional rules that limit police power in those classes of cases in which the risk of pretext is especially high. Occasionally, the Court has done this. In the house-search example above, for example, the Supreme Court ruled that a police officer may not ordinarily enter a person's home to arrest a guest, even if the officer has an arrest warrant, unless he is also armed with a warrant to search the third person's premises.[97] The Court observed that if a search warrant were

---

[94] *See* Colorado v. Bertine, 479 U.S. 367, 375–76 (1987); South Dakota v. Opperman, 428 U.S. 364, 376 (1976). *See* § 16.02[B][1], *infra*.

[95] Scott v. United States, 436 U.S. 128, 138 (1978).

[96] Amsterdam, Note 82, *supra*, at 436 (footnote omitted).

[97] Steagald v. United States, 451 U.S. 204 (1981). *See* § 10.06, *infra*.

not required, an arrest warrant might "serve as the pretext for entering a home in which the police have a suspicion, but not probable cause to believe, that illegal activity is taking place."[98]

Far more often, however, the Court has refused to draft rules to limit the risk of pretext. For example, the Supreme Court has held that if an officer has probable cause to stop a motorist in order to issue a traffic citation, the detention is valid under the Fourth Amendment, even if the stop was a pretext to conduct an investigation of the driver for drug activities.[99] Put simply, the Court has said, "[s]ubjective intentions play no role in ordinary, probable-cause Fourth Amendment analysis."[100]

In the study of criminal procedure, readers should consider whether the risk of pretextual conduct is sufficiently great to justify greater judicial focus on the subject.

---

[98] *Id.* at 215; *see also* Maine v. Moulton, 474 U.S. 159, 180 (1985) (the police obtained incriminating statements from *M* about Crime X, in violation of *M*'s right to counsel, while they were *legitimately* asking *M* questions about Crime Y; held: the statements about Crime X were inadmissible, despite the officers' possible good faith; "[t]o allow the admission of evidence obtained from the accused in violation of his Sixth Amendment rights whenever the police assert an alternative, legitimate reason for their surveillance invites abuse . . .in the form of fabricated investigations . . . .").

[99] Whren v. United States, 517 U.S. 806 (1996). *See* § 9.02[F], *infra.*

[100] *Id.* at 813.

CHAPTER 3

# INCORPORATION OF THE BILL OF RIGHTS

## § 3.01 Incorporation: The Nature of the Issue[1]

The first ten amendments to the United States Constitution—the Bill of Rights—were adopted contemporaneously with the ratification of the Constitution. These provisions were designed to limit the power of the federal government; they were not intended as restrictions on the actions of state government.[2] Most criminal prosecutions, however, originate in state courts, as the result of criminal investigations conducted by state or local police officers. Consequently, the provisions of the Bill of Rights that pertain to criminal procedure—primarily, the fourth, fifth, sixth, and eighth amendments—have no direct effect on the majority of criminal cases that arise in this country.

The Fourteenth Amendment, adopted in 1868, imposes limits on state action. Section 1 of that amendment limits the states in three ways:

No State shall [1] make or enforce any law which shall abridge the privileges or immunities of citizens of the United States; [2] nor shall

---

[1] *See generally* Akhil Reed Amar, *The Bill of Rights and the Fourteenth Amendment*, 101 Yale L.J. 1193 (1992); Richard L. Aynes, *Charles Fairman, Felix Frankfurter, and the Fourteenth Amendment*, 70 Chi.-Kent L. Rev. 1197 (1995); Robert L. Cord, *The Incorporation Doctrine and Procedural Due Process Under the Fourteenth Amendment: An Overview*, 1987 B.Y.U. L. Rev. 867; William Winslow Crosskey, *Charles Fairman, "Legislative History," and the Constitutional Limitations on State Authority*, 22 U. Chi. L. Rev. 1 (1954); William O. Douglas, *The Bill of Rights Is Not Enough*, 38 N.Y.U. L. Rev. 207 (1963); Charles Fairman, *Does the Fourteenth Amendment Incorporate the Bill of Rights? The Original Understanding*, 2 Stan. L. Rev. 5 (1949); Jerold H. Israel, *Free-Standing Due Process and Criminal Procedure: The Supreme Court's Search for Interpretive Guidelines*, 45 St. Lous U.L.J. 303 (2001); Barry Latzer, *Toward the Decentralization of Criminal Procedure: State Constitutional Law and Selective Disincorporation*, 87 J. Crim. L. & Criminology 63 (1996); Gary L. McDowell & Judith A. Baer, *The Fourteenth Amendment: Should the Bill of Rights Apply to the States? The Disincorporation Debate*, 1987 Utah L. Rev. 951; Bryan H. Wildenthal, *The Lost Compromise: Reassessing the Early Understanding in Court and Congress on Incorporation of the Bill of Rights in the Fourteenth Amendment*, 61 Ohio St. L.J. 1051 (2000); Bryan H. Wildenthal, *The Road to Twining: Reassessing the Disincorporation of the Bill of Rights*, 61 Ohio St. L.J. 1457 (2000).

[2] Barron v. Baltimore, 32 U.S. (7 Pet.) 243 (1833).

any State deprive any person of life, liberty, or property, without due process of law; [3] nor deny to any person within its jurisdiction the equal protection of the laws.[3]

A matter of considerable dispute is what the relationship is between the Fourteenth Amendment and the Bill of Rights. At the center of the debate, commonly called the "incorporation" debate, is the second clause of section 1, namely, the due process clause.[4] The essential question is this: To what extent, if at all, does the Fourteenth Amendment due process clause "incorporate" (or "absorb") the Bill of Rights, so as to make the Bill's restrictions on *federal* power applicable to the *states*? A related question is whether the due process clause guarantees any rights not enumerated in the Constitution. According to one scholar, "despite the importance of the topic and all the attention devoted to it, we still lack a fully satisfying account of the relationship between the first ten amendments and the Fourteenth."[5]

The incorporation debate is important for various reasons. First, the extent to which people are protected from overreaching by agents of the state depends in large measure on the extent to which the Fourteenth Amendment incorporates the Bill of Rights.[6] At one extreme, if none of the provisions of the Bill of Rights apply to the states, citizens may be subjected to (just to note a few examples) warrantless entries of the home by local police, coercive interrogation techniques, and felony trials without the assistance of counsel.[7] On the other hand, if the due process clause incorporates the Bill of Rights in its entirety, the latter charter becomes a national code of criminal procedure; federal and state action would be restricted in identical manner.

---

[3] U.S. Const. amend. XIV, § 1 (numbers in brackets added).

[4] Early on, the Supreme Court rejected the plausible claim that the Fourteenth Amendment "privileges and immunities" clause prohibits states from abridging the rights set out in the Bill of Rights. The Court ruled that this clause only bars states from abridging privileges and immunities *inherent in national citizenship*, which the Court determined did not include the provisions of the Bill of Rights. *See* Slaughter-House Cases, 83 U.S. (16 Wall.) 36 (1873). For a very different interpretation of the *Slaughter-House Cases*—one that "proposes to overturn more than a century of conventional wisdom regarding" the 1873 opinion—*see* Wildenthal, *The Lost Compromise*, Note 1, *supra*.

[5] Amar, Note 1, *supra*, at 1196.

[6] Usually unstated in the incorporation debate is the belief of many advocates of incorporationism that states are "chronically . . . backward" in their protection of individual rights. Without incorporationism, the argument goes, states would trample on citizens' rights. There is some historical support for this view. According to some modern commentators, however, "the state courts are no longer rights-antediluvians, and that therefore an entire set of assumptions underlying incorporation has eroded." Latzer, Note 1, *supra*, at 65–66.

[7] However, a state constitution may prohibit such conduct.

Second, as the latter observation suggests, the values of federalism are at stake in the incorporation debate. The broader the scope of the Fourteenth Amendment due process clause, the less free are the states to develop their own rules of criminal procedure. Yet, uniformity among the states is said to be "inimical to traditional notions of federalism."[8]

Third, incorporationism raises questions regarding the proper role of the judiciary in the enforcement of constitutional rights. As discussed below, some critics claim that certain incorporation theories exacerbate the risk that judges will apply their personal views of proper governmental action, rather than enforce the terms of the Constitution.

## § 3.02  Incorporation Theories: An Overview

### [A]  Total Incorporation

Justice Hugo Black was the judicial architect of an incorporation approach described as "total" or "full" incorporation.[9] According to Black, "one of the chief objects that the provisions of the [Fourteenth] Amendment's first section, separately, and as a whole, were intended to accomplish was to make the Bill of Rights, applicable to the states."[10] In other words, the Fourteenth Amendment in general, and the due process clause in particular, incorporates all of the rights included in the Bill of Rights, nothing more or less. This principle has never received the support of a majority of the members of the Supreme Court.

### [B]  Fundamental Rights

In contrast to total incorporation is the "fundamental rights" or "ordered liberty" doctrine. Originally asserted in 1884,[11] this approach gained ascendancy in the 1930s with the influential support of Justices Benjamin Cardozo[12] and Felix Frankfurter.[13] The essence of this doctrine is that the Fourteenth Amendment "neither comprehends the specific provisions by which the founders deemed it appropriate to restrict the federal government nor is it confined to them. The Due Process Clause . . . has an independent potency . . . ."[14]

---

[8] Rummel v. Estelle, 445 U.S. 263, 282 (1980).

[9] *See* Adamson v. California, 332 U.S. 46, 68–123 (1947) (Black, J. dissenting); Rochin v. California. 342 U.S. 165, 174–77 (1952) (Black, J., concurring).

[10] *Adamson*, 332 U.S. at 71–72.

[11] Hurtado v. California, 110 U.S. 516, 546 (1884) (Harlan, J., dissenting).

[12] *See* Palko v. Connecticut, 302 U.S. 319 (1937), *overruled* in Benton v. Maryland, 395 U.S. 784 (1969).

[13] *E.g.*, *Adamson*, 332 U.S. at 59-68 (concurring opinion); *Rochin*, 342 U.S. at 166–74 (majority opinion).

[14] *Adamson*, 332 U.S. at 66 (Frankfurter, J., concurring).

According to Justice Frankfurter, the due process clause did not incorporate, as such, any of the provisions of the Bill of Rights. Instead, the Fourteenth Amendment due process clause requires that states honor " 'principle[s] of justice so rooted in the traditions and consciences of our people as to be ranked as fundamental'." [15] These fundamental rights "might indeed happen to overlap wholly or in part with some of the rules of the Bill of Rights, but [they] bear no logical relationship to those rules." [16]

Notice that according to this doctrine a right may be included in the Bill of Rights (and thus be protected against encroachment by the federal government) and yet not be deemed fundamental (and, therefore, not be protected against state overreaching). On the other hand, a right may be fundamental, and yet not be an express provision of the Bill of Rights. Thus, under this view, the Fourteenth Amendment, potentially, is both more and less than the Bill of Rights.

Over the years, the Supreme Court has variously articulated the test by which "fundamentalness" is determined. [17] For example, a right is fundamental if: it is "of the very essence of a scheme of ordered liberty"; a "fair and enlightened system of justice would be impossible without [it]"; it is "at the base of all our civil and political institutions"; its denial would "offend those canons of decency and fairness which express the notions of justice of English-speaking people"; or it is "fundamental to the American scheme of justice"; [18] or conduct in derogation of the right "shocks the conscience."

### [C] Total-Incorporation-Plus

Justices Frank Murphy, Wiley Rutledge, and William Douglas posited the broadest interpretation of the Fourteenth Amendment. According to these Justices, the due process clause incorporates the Bill of Rights in its entirety (total incorporation), as well as all fundamental rights that fall outside the express language of the Constitution (a component of fundamental-rights doctrine). [19]

### [D] Selective Incorporation (or Pseudo-Fundamental-Rights)

Selective incorporation includes features of both fundamental-rights theory and total incorporation, without following the logic of either doctrine.

---

[15] *Palko,* 302 U.S. at 325 (*quoting* Snyder v. Massachusetts, 291 U.S. 97, 105 (1934)).

[16] Amar, Note 1, *supra,* at 1196.

[17] *See generally* the cases cited at notes 12–13, *supra.*

[18] Duncan v. Louisiana, 391 U.S. 145, 149 (1968).

[19] *See Adamson,* 332 U.S. at 123–25 (Murphy and Rutledge, JJ., dissenting); Poe v. Ullman 367 U.S. 497, 516 (1961) (Douglas, J., dissenting).

It represents, as one judicial critic put it, "an uneasy and illogical compromise"[20] between the two doctrines.

Selective incorporationists go along with fundamental-rights theorists in stating that not all rights included in the Bill of Rights are inevitably absorbed by the Fourteenth Amendment. On the other hand, contrary to fundamental-rights theory, and more in keeping with incorporationism, selective incorporationists believe that once a right is deemed to be fundamental, it is "applicable to the States with all the subtleties and refinements born of history and embodied in case experience developed in the context of federal adjudication."[21]

The latter quotation is critical to understanding why this theory conflicts with the doctrines from which it is derived. The point of fundamental-rights theory is that a right is protected by the due process clause because it is crucial to the maintenance of justice; its inclusion in the Bill of Rights is logically irrelevant. Consequently, under the latter theory, the constitutional law that has developed regarding the *federal* right is not determinative of the scope of the *state* version of the analogous right emanating from the Fourteenth Amendment.

For example, the Fourth Amendment prohibits unreasonable searches and seizures by federal officers. Pursuant to fundamental right theory, the Fourteenth Amendment also prohibits such conduct by state officers.[22] However, it does not follow from the latter theory that the entirety of federal Fourth Amendment jurisprudence regarding what constitutes an "unreasonable search or seizure" is carried over to the states via the Fourteenth Amendment.

Selective incorporation, however, absorbs "all of the bag and baggage"[23] of the Bill of Rights. Once a right is determined to be fundamental, *every* feature of the federal right applies to the states. That is why selective-incorporationism is a *pseudo*-fundamental-rights theory: although inclusion of the right in the Fourteenth Amendment is selective (only fundamental rights are protected by the due process clause), once it is identified as fundamental, the right perfectly mirrors the federal provision (*i.e.*, it is incorporated).

---

[20] Duncan v. Louisiana, 391 U.S. at 172 (Harlan, J., dissenting).

[21] Williams v. Florida, 399 U.S. 78, 130–31 (1970) (Harlan, J., concurring) (explaining the theory).

[22] Wolf v. Colorado, 338 U.S. 25 (1949), *overruled on other grounds* in Mapp v. Ohio, 367 U.S. 643 (1961).

[23] Duncan v. Louisiana, 391 U.S. at 213 (Fortas, J., concurring).

## § 3.03  The Incorporation Debate

### [A]  Overview of the Debate

Debate regarding the relationship of the Fourteenth Amendment to the Bill of Rights has focused primarily on the total-incorporation and fundamental-rights doctrines. Some of the debate is "interpretivist" in nature.[24] That is, the discourse turns on concerns of textualism (*i.e.*, which approach is more consistent with the language of the Fourteenth Amendment?) and originalism (*i.e.*, which doctrine more closely approximates the intent of the framers of the provision?).

Two other important considerations arise in the debate: libertarianism (*i.e.*, which due process approach is more protective of individual liberty?); and structuralism (*i.e.*, which theory is more consistent with concepts of federalism and separation-of-powers?). A brief review of the debate follows.

### [B]  What Did the Framers Intend?

Justice Black and some scholars have accumulated evidence to support their assertion that the framers of the Fourteenth Amendment intended to incorporate the entirety of the Bill of Rights.[25]

Other scholars[26] and Justices of the Supreme Court have disputed this claim. Justice Frankfurter obliquely questioned the total-incorporationist

---

[24] "Interpretivism" describes the view of constitutional interpretation that judges should confine themselves to enforcing those rights that are stated or are clearly implicit in a constitution. Others apply a somewhat broader, but still relatively constrained approach, that seeks "inspiration and discipline in the amended Constitution's specific words and word patterns, the historical experiences that birthed and rebirthed the text, and the conceptual schemas and structures organizing the document." Akhil Reed Amar, *The Document and the Doctrine*, 114 Harv. L. Rev. 26, 26 (2000) (using the term "documentarians" to describe those who follow this constitutional interpretive approach).

A competing approach to interpretivism asserts that judges should not interpret constitutions as they would examine contracts or statutes: they should look beyond the text, structure, and history to discover the meaning of a constitutional provision. *See generally* John Hart Ely, Democracy and Distrust: A Theory of Judicial Review (1980); Michael Perry, The Constitution, the Courts and Human Rights (1982); Robert H. Bork, *Neutral Principles and Some First Amendment Problems*, 47 Ind. L.J. 1 (1971); John Hart Ely, *Constitutional Interpretivism: Its Allure and Impossibility*, 53 Ind. L.J. 399 (1978); John Hart Ely, *On Discovering Fundamental Values*, 92 Harv. L. Rev. 5 (1978); Thomas C. Grey, *Do We Have an Unwritten Constitution?*, 27 Stan. L. Rev. 703 (1975); Michael J. Perry, *Interpreting the Constitution*, 1987 B.Y.U. L. Rev. 1157; Herbert Wechsler, *Toward Neutral Principles of Constitutional Law*, 73 Harv. L. Rev. 1 (1959).

[25] Justice Black provided a 31-page appendix to his dissent in *Adamson*, *supra*, in support of his claim; *see also* Crosskey, Note 1, *supra*; Wildenthal, Note 1, *supra* (both articles).

[26] *E.g.*, Fairman, Note 1, *supra*. While not accepting "Black's band of mechanical incorporation," Professor Amar is critical of Professor Charles Fairman's "130 pages of Black-

claim by observing that all but one ("an eccentric exception"[27] ) of the Supreme Court Justices who had previously considered the question had rejected incorporationism. Frankfurter doubted that the state legislators, by ratifying the Fourteenth Amendment, thought that they were agreeing to dismantle their own systems of justice and replace them with the federal system.

A recent commentator has concluded that the framers' intent is "to a considerable degree . . . shrouded in the mists of history. There is simply no clear answer [to the historical question]."[28]

### [C]    Textual Claims: What Does "Due Process" Mean?

Opponents of incorporationism frequently point out that if the words "due process of law" are meant to incorporate the Bill of Rights, as Justice Black asserts, "it is a strange way of saying it."[29] If incorporationism was the framers' purpose, why did they not say so directly? Why would they have used this oblique shorthand? Indeed, since the phrase "due process of law" also rests in the Fifth Amendment, why would the phrase mean one thing in the Fourteenth Amendment and another in the Fifth?[30]

Fundamental-rights adherents are not out of the textual woods, either. "Due process of law" is also an odd way of saying "fundamental rights" or "rights implicit in the concept of ordered liberty." Moreover, in light of the fact that the due process clause has been interpreted to protect fundamental substantive rights not found in the Constitution, such as a right of privacy,[31] it is hard to see how a *substantive* right can be textually defended by language that speaks merely of providing due *process*.[32]

### [D]    Which Doctrine is More Libertarian?

On its face, total-incorporationism is more libertarian because, with one sweep of the wand, the entire Bill of Rights is nationalized. In contrast,

---

bashing." Amar observes that "Fairman spent so much energy attacking Justice Black that he failed to offer any sustained narrative in support of an alternative reading of the Fourteenth Amendment." Amar, Note 1, *supra*, at 1238.

[27] *Adamson*, 332 U.S. at 62.

[28] McDowell & Baer, Note 1, *supra*, at 956–57 (statement of McDowell in debate with Baer).

[29] *Adamson*, 332 U.S. at 63 (Frankfurter, J., concurring).

[30] In other words, under total incorporation, "due process of law" is a shorthand for freedom of speech, freedom of religion, the right to bear arms, and so on; yet, in the Fifth Amendment, the words "due process of law" could not logically have this meaning since these other rights are enumerated elsewhere in the Bill of Rights.

[31] *See* Griswold v. Connecticut, 381 U.S. 479 (1965).

[32] Ely, *Constitutional Interpretivism*. . ., Note 24, *supra*, at 419–20 ("[T]here is simply no blinking the fact that the word that follows 'due' is 'process.' ").

the fundamental-rights doctrine is like an accordion: it can "periodically . . . expand and contract . . . to conform to the Court's conception of what at a particular time constitutes 'civilized decency' and 'fundamental liberty and justice.' "[33]

But this perspective is somewhat misleading. Fundamental-rights doctrine allows for the recognition of rights not found within the four corners of the Constitution. Thus, whereas incorporationists do not recognize a constitutionally-based right of privacy because it is not expressly found in the document, fundamental-rights theory permits such possibilities.

### [E] Which Theory Is Structurally Preferable?

Incorporationism runs afoul of traditional views of federalism because it compels states to uproot their established methods for prosecuting crimes and fastens upon them the federal version of due process. Under concepts of fundamental rights, states can run their criminal justice systems more freely, as they must ensure only those rights that are essential to fundamental justice.

The fundamental-rights doctrine, however, is subject to criticism on separation-of-powers grounds. Incorporationists argue that one need only look at the various tests of "fundamental rights" to conclude that the latter doctrine invites judges "to roam at large in the broad expanses of policy and morals and to trespass, all too freely, on the legislative domain of the States as well as the Federal Government."[34] The doctrine allows federal judges, unelected and serving life appointments, to behave like "dictators or philosopher kings,"[35] as they determine (for example) whether a "fair and enlightened system of justice" would be possible in the absence of a particular protection.

### [F] Which Theory Has "Won" the Debate?

Precedent can be overruled, so no Fourteenth Amendment theory can gain a permanent victory in the Supreme Court. Nonetheless, various observations are possible. First, fundamental-rights doctrine has won the rhetorical war with total-incorporationism. No majority opinion of the Court has ever accepted the latter principle, nor does it have any support on the Court at this time.

Second, as a practical matter, and notwithstanding the first point, Justice Black's goal of incorporating the Bill of Rights has nearly been realized. In the realm of criminal procedure, all but two provisions of the Bill of

---

[33] *Adamson*, 332 U.S. at 69 (Black, J., dissenting).

[34] *Id.* at 90 (Black, J., dissenting).

[35] Ely, *Constitutional Interpretivism.* . ., Note 24, *supra*, at 445.

Rights apply to the states, albeit via fundamental-rights analysis.[36] Also, in light of the advent of selective-incorporationism, these rights apparently include all of the "baggage" from the federal system.

Finally, consistent with fundamental-rights doctrine, the Supreme Court has recognized rights not enumerated in the Constitution, such as the right of privacy. Thus, ironically, if "winners" are to be declared, they may be those few Justices who favored total-incorporation-plus.

---

[36] The exceptions are the Fifth Amendment provision that no person shall be held to answer for a serious crime except by indictment or presentment of a grand jury, Hurtado v. California, 110 U.S. 516 (1884), and the Eighth Amendment "no excessive bail" provision. The Supreme Court has not ruled on the fundamental-rights status of the latter provision.

CHAPTER 4

# GENERAL CONSTITUTIONAL LAW DOCTRINES

This chapter considers five constitutional (or quasi-constitutional) law doctrines that are frequently asserted in criminal procedure litigation.

## § 4.01 Retroactivity[1]

### [A] Explanation of the Issue

When the Supreme Court announces a new criminal procedural rule or right, it ultimately must determine whether the rule applies retroactively and, if so, to what extent. This is a problem of far-reaching consequences.

Assume that the Supreme Court announces a new rule restricting police investigations on March 15, 2000. Obviously, this new rule will apply *prospectively* to all police investigations that occur after that date. But, should the rule also be applied *retroactively* and, if so, *how far back*? There are various possibilities. First, the new rule might only apply to cases that go to trial after March 15, although the police investigation may have occurred before that date (the police were acting within the then-existing rules when they conducted the investigation).

---

[1] *See generally* Richard H. Fallon, Jr. & Daniel J. Meltzer, *New Law, Non-Retroactivity, and Constitutional Remedies*, 104 Harv. L. Rev. 1731 (1991); Jill E. Fisch, *Retroactivity and Legal Change: An Equilibrium Approach*, 110 Harv. L. Rev. 1055 (1997); Patrick E. Higginbotham, *Notes on Teague*, 66 S. Cal. L. Rev. 2433 (1993); Joseph L. Hoffmann, *Retroactivity and the Great Writ: How Congress Should Respond to Teague v. Lane*, 1990 B.Y.U. L. Rev. 183; Joseph L. Hoffmann, *The Supreme Court's New Vision of Federal Habeas Corpus for State Prisoners*, 1989 Sup. Ct. Rev. 165; Linda Meyer, *"Nothing We Say Matters": Teague and New Rules*, 61 U. Chi. L. Rev. 423 (1994); Paul J. Mishkin, *The Supreme Court, 1964 Term — Foreword: The High Court, The Great Writ, and the Due Process of Time and Law*, 79 Harv. L. Rev. 56 (1965); Yale L. Rosenberg, *Kaddish for Federal Habeas Corpus*, 59 Geo. Wash. L. Rev. 362 (1991); Herman Schwartz, *Retroactivity, Reliability, and Due Process: A Reply to Professor Mishkin*, 33 U. Chi. L. Rev. 719 (1966); Pamela J. Stephens, *The New Retroactivity Doctrine: Equality, Reliance and Stare Decisis*, 48 Syracuse L. Rev. 1515 (1998); Ann Woolhandler, *Demodeling Habeas*, 45 Stan. L. Rev. 575 (1993); Larry W. Yackle, *The Habeas Hagioscope*, 66 S. Cal. L. Rev. 2331 (1993).

Second, the new rule might apply retroactively to all criminal cases not yet final[2] on March 15, 2000. Thus, even a defendant who was tried and convicted *before* that date could take advantage of the new decision if it were handed down while he was appealing his conviction.

Finally, the new rule might be fully retroactive. That is, an inmate who has exhausted all of his appeals by March 15, 2000 and is now simply serving his criminal sentence, would be permitted to attack his conviction collaterally in a habeas corpus proceeding on the basis of the newly announced rule.[3]

Competing policies animate retroactivity debate. Opponents of retroactivity argue that a person only has a right to be treated in conformity with the rules in existence at the time of the disputed action. It is not unfair, therefore, to apply new rules prospectively only. Furthermore, full retroactive application of new constitutional rules undermines the desired finality of criminal judgments. With full retroactivity, prisoners whose trials may have been held many years earlier could return to the courts seeking relief, thereby clogging the courts and potentially emptying the prisons.

Proponents of full retroactivity argue that fundamentally like cases should be treated alike. They believe that it is unfair to deny the benefits of a new rule to people "languishing in prison who have suffered precisely the same deprivations at the hands of government that now invalidate the convictions of those fortunate enough to have run afoul of the law after, not before, the new constitutional rule was made effective."[4] Should a person be executed, for example, because his conviction was final on March 14, 2000, whereas another inmate can have his conviction and sentence overturned by asserting the new rule, because his appeal extended for an additional day or two?

The Supreme Court has struggled with these and other policy concerns in an effort to develop a sensible jurisprudence of retroactivity. Current law is the result of a tortuous and inconsistent legal history.[5]

---

[2] For purposes of retroactivity law, a conviction is "final" when all direct appeals have been exhausted, and the time to petition for certiorari to the United States Supreme Court has elapsed or the petition to the Court has been finally denied. Linkletter v. Walker, 381 U.S. 618, 622 n.5 (1965).

[3] A full understanding of retroactivity law requires an understanding of the nature of habeas corpus proceedings. For an explanation, *see* § 1.03[C][10], *supra*.

[4] Francis A. Allen, *The Judicial Quest for Penal Justice: The Warren Court and the Criminal Cases*, 1975 U. Ill. L.F. 518, 529.

[5] Note, *Retroactivity and the Exclusionary Rule: A Unifying Approach*, 97 Harv. L. Rev. 961, 961 (1984).

## [B]  Common Law of Retroactivity

At common law, newly announced judicial rules applied retroactively to *all* cases brought to the judiciary's attention. This retroactivity rule followed logically from the then-existing view, expressed by Blackstone, that judges do not make law, but instead "discover" or "declare" pre-existing law.[6] In other words, common law courts "believed they were finding rather than making law."[7]

It follows from this so-called "declaratory theory" of judicial decision-making that when a court announced a legal principle in conflict with prior judicial pronouncements on the same subject, the court was merely recognizing the pre-existing law that earlier judges failed to discover. Consequently, as the "true law" had *not* changed, there was no "retroactivity" problem to resolve.

## [C]  The *Linkletter* Doctrine

In general, the common law full-retroactivity principle applied to constitutional law until the Supreme Court's seminal decision in *Linkletter v. Walker*.[8] It is not coincidental that the same Supreme Court—the Warren Court—that announced many far-reaching new constitutional rules became skittish with the potential impact of its decisions, and backed away from the common law retroactivity rule.

In *Linkletter*, the Court considered the question of whether *Mapp v. Ohio*,[9] which held for the first time that evidence obtained as the result of an unreasonable police search or seizure must be excluded from the defendant's criminal trial, should be applied retroactively to grant relief to a habeas corpus petitioner whose conviction became final before *Mapp* was decided. The Supreme Court rejected the common law full-retroactivity rule, and replaced it with a three-factor standard for determining whether, and to what extent, new constitutional rules would be applied retroactively. The three factors were: "(a) the purpose to be served by the new standards, (b) the extent of the reliance by law enforcement authorities on the old standards, and (c) the effect on the administration of justice of a retroactive application of the new standards."[10]

*Linkletter* predictably resulted in "incompatible rules and inconsistent principles."[11] Some new rules were applied prospectively only, other new

---

[6] 1 W. Blackstone, Commentaries on the Laws of England *69–70 (1769).

[7] Rogers v. Tennessee, 121 S. Ct. 1693, 1700 (2001).

[8] 381 U.S. 618 (1965).

[9] 367 U.S. 643 (1961). *See* §§ 5.04[B], 21.01[E], *infra*.

[10] Stovall v. Denno, 388 U.S. 293, 297 (1967).

[11] Desist v. United States, 394 U.S. 244, 258 (1969) (Harlan, J., dissenting).

rules (as in *Linkletter*) were applied retroactively to cases not yet final when the new law was announced, whereas still other rules received full retroactive application.

### [D] Abandonment of *Linkletter*

#### [1] In General

Legal scholars had a "field day"[12] with the post-*Linkletter* decisions, criticizing them for their inconsistency. However, the most influential critic of the Court's retroactivity jurisprudence was one of its own members, Justice John Harlan, who called on his colleagues to rethink retroactivity law.[13]

The linchpin of Harlan's analysis was that constitutionally similar cases ordinarily should be treated alike. As he put it, it is wrong for the Court to "fish[] one case from the stream of appellate review, using it as a vehicle for pronouncing new constitutional standards, and then permit[] a stream of similar cases subsequently to flow by unaffected by that new rule."[14] He contended that new rules should be enforced in all criminal cases that have not resulted in a final judgment of conviction.

Justice Harlan also advocated abandonment of the *Linkletter* formula in cases subject to collateral habeas corpus review. However, in light of society's interest in leaving litigation in a state of final repose, he reasoned that in adjudicating habeas corpus petitions, courts should, subject to two exceptions, apply the law prevailing at the time the petitioner's conviction became final, *i.e.*, new rules should not apply retroactively to convictions already final.

In 1982, the Supreme Court began to shift course,[15] agreeing with Justice Harlan that its retroactivity law needed to be rethought, and embracing to a significant degree his criticisms of its prior retroactivity jurisprudence. The new law of retroactivity, which closely resembles Justice Harlan's suggestions, is described below.

#### [2] Current Retroactivity Law

##### [a] Cases Not Yet Final: Direct Review

In 1987, in *Griffith v. Kentucky*,[16] the Court clearly broke with the past and formally abandoned *Linkletter*'s three-factor test. In its place, per Justice

---

[12] Francis X. Beytagh, *Ten Years of Non-Retroactivity: A Critique and a Proposal*, 61 Va. L. Rev. 1557, 1558 (1975).

[13] *See* Desist v. United States, 394 U.S. at 256–69 (dissenting opinion); Mackey v. United States, 401 U.S. 667, 675–702 (1971) (separate opinion).

[14] *Mackey*, 401 U.S. at 679.

[15] United States v. Johnson, 457 U.S. 537 (1982).

[16] 479 U.S. 314 (1987).

Harlan's suggestion, the court adopted the retroactivity principle that "a new rule . . . is to be applied retroactively to all cases, state or federal, pending on direct review or not yet final. . . ."[17]

## [b]  Cases Already Final: Collateral Review

### [i]  General Rule

Until 1989, the Supreme Court resisted Justice Harlan's approach to habeas corpus review. However, beginning with its plurality opinion in *Teague v. Lane*,[18] which became a majority position in *Penry v. Lynaugh*,[19] the Supreme Court adopted the basic features of Harlan's no-retroactivity rule in the context of habeas proceedings. Under *Teague*, the Court no longer announces or applies new constitutional procedural rules in cases on collateral review, unless they fall within one of two very limited exceptions.

Essentially, the *Teague* inquiry is conducted in three steps.[20] First, the date on which the petitioner's conviction became final is determined. Second, as more fully described in subsection [ii] below, the habeas court must determine whether "a state court considering [the defendant's] claim at the time his conviction became final would have felt compelled by existing precedent to conclude that the rule [he] seeks was required by the Constitution."[21] If existing precedent would *not* have compelled the result requested by the petitioner, then the rule sought is new, and the general no-retroactivity presumption comes into play.[22] The final step in the *Teague* analysis is to determine whether the new rule falls within one of the two narrow exceptions to *Teague*.[23]

---

[17] For the definition of "new rule"—a critical term of art in retroactivity jurisprudence—*see* § 4.01[D][2][b][ii], *infra*.

[18] 489 U.S. 288 (1989).

[19] 492 U.S. 302 (1989).

[20] O'Dell v. Netherland, 521 U.S. 151, 156 (1997).

[21] *Id.* at 156 (*quoting* Saffle v. Parks, 494 U.S. 484, 488 (1990)).

[22] This means, for example, that under *Teague*, exceptions aside, a person sentenced to death by a state court cannot take advantage of a new rule announced by the Supreme Court *after* his conviction and sentence becomes final, even though the new rule, if applied to him, would require reversal of his death sentence. *E.g.*, O'Dell v. Netherland, 521 U.S. 151 (1997).

[23] As this three-step process suggests, the issue of retroactivity is now considered a "threshold question." *Teague*, 489 U.S. at 305. That is, the Supreme Court will not consider a habeas petition on its merits unless and until it determines that any new rule it might announce would apply to the immediate case. The practical effect of the threshold requirement is that the Court today reviews on the merits many fewer habeas petitions than in the past. Most habeas petitions either raise uninteresting legal issues (*e.g.*, a lower court misapplied an old

The first exception is that new rules apply retroactively to cases on collateral review if they "place an entire category of primary conduct beyond the reach of the criminal law, . . . [or] prohibit imposition of a certain type of punishment for a class of defendants because of their status or offense."[24] For example, a new rule that decriminalizes possession of obscene literature in the home[25] would be applied retroactively to cases on collateral review, as would a new rule that the death penalty may not be imposed on adults convicted of rape.[26]

The second, "even more circumscribed,"[27] exception is that a new rule applies on collateral review if it involves a "watershed rule[] of criminal procedure"[28] that is necessary to guarantee the fundamental fairness of the criminal proceeding, *i.e.*, a rule "without which the likelihood of an accurate conviction is seriously diminished."[29] This exception has been explained as follows:

> It is . . . not enough . . . to say that a new rule is aimed at improving the accuracy of [a] trial. More is required. A rule that qualifies under this exception must not only improve accuracy, but also " 'alter our understanding of the *bedrock procedural elements*' " essential to the fairness of a proceeding.[30]

For example, the rule that an indigent defendant is entitled to representation by counsel at trial[31] is entitled to full retroactive application.

### [ii]  Meaning of "New Rule"

A constitutional rule is "new" for purposes of retroactivity jurisprudence if: (1) it "breaks new ground or imposes a new obligation on the States or the Federal Government," such as when the Supreme Court overrules

---

rule, which ordinarily is considered to be an uncertworthy matter), or they raise interesting new issues that cannot be decided in the petitioner's favor because, to do so, would require the retroactive implementation of a new rule. The effect of *Teague*, therefore, is largely to shift constitutional decisionmaking to state courts. Hoffmann, *Supreme Court's New Vision . . .*, Note 1, *supra*, at 187.

[24] Sawyer v. Smith, 497 U.S. 227, 241 (1990).

[25] Stanley v. Georgia, 394 U.S. 557 (1969).

[26] Coker v. Georgia, 433 U.S. 584 (1977).

[27] O'Dell v. Netherland, 521 U.S. at 157.

[28] *Teague*, 489 U.S. at 311.

[29] *Id.* at 313.

[30] Sawyer v. Smith, 497 U.S. at 242 (quoting *Teague*, which in turn quoted Justice Harlan in Mackey v. United States, 401 U.S. 667, 693 (1971)) (emphasis added).

[31] Gideon v. Wainwright, 372 U.S. 335 (1963).

a prior decision; or (2) "the result was not *dictated* by precedent existing at the time the defendant's conviction became final."[32]

The Supreme Court rarely overrules itself, so the second type of "new rule" is more significant and less easy to identify. However, the key word in the standard set out above is "dictated": the Court has warned that a case announces a "new rule"—even if its holding is within the "logical compass" of a previous holding, or even if it can be said to be "controlled" by an earlier case—unless a state court, applying "reasonable, good-faith interpretations"[33] of case law existing "at the time [a petitioner's] conviction became final would have felt compelled by existing precedent"[34] to rule in his favor. Put differently, the Court "will not disturb a final state conviction or sentence unless it can be said that, at the time the conviction or sentence became final, a state court would have acted objectively unreasonably by not extending the relief later sought in federal court."[35]

The line between a rule that is "controlled," but not "dictated," by prior case law, is exceedingly difficult to draw. For example, in *Butler v. McKellar*,[36] the Supreme Court concluded that a prior holding favorable to the petitioner (call it *Case 2*), decided after the petitioner's conviction became final, constituted a new rule (and, thus, did not inure to the petitioner), although it admittedly was "controlled" by an earlier decision (*Case 1*), which was decided *before* the petitioner's conviction became final. The *Butler* Court held that the rule announced in *Case 2* was not "dictated" (only, perhaps, "controlled") by *Case 1*, as evidenced in part by the fact that, prior to *Case 2*, a "significant difference of opinion [existed] on the part of several lower courts" regarding the import of *Case 1* as it related to the issues decided in *Case 2*.

*Butler* should not be read, however, as suggesting that a rule is new simply because a few stray lower court opinions, decided after *Case 1*, but prior to *Case 2*, reached a result contrary to the Supreme Court's later holding in *Case 2*. According to *Stringer v. Black*:[37]

> The purpose of the new rule doctrine is to validate reasonable interpretations of existing precedents. Reasonableness . . . is an objective standard, and the ultimate decision whether [*Case 2*] was dictated by precedent [*Case 1*] is based on an objective reading of the relevant cases. The short

---

[32] *Teague*, 489 U.S. at 301.

[33] Butler v. McKellar, 494 U.S. 407, 414 (1990).

[34] Saffle v. Parks, 494 U.S. 484, 488 (1990).

[35] O'Dell v. Netherland, 521 U.S. 151, 156 (1997).

[36] 494 U.S. 407 (1990).

[37] 503 U.S. 222, 237 (1992).

answer to the State's argument [that *Case 2* announced a new rule, as evidenced by the fact that one lower federal court read *Case 1* differently than the Supreme Court did in *Case 2*] is that the [lower court] made a serious mistake.

Essentially, the purpose of the broad definition of "new rule" is to "ensure that gradual developments in the law over which *reasonable* jurists may disagree are not later used to upset the finality of state convictions valid when entered."[38] But, *Teague* does *not* stand for the proposition that all state court opinions are reasonable; federal courts are duty bound to scrutinize the existing law in order to determine, for themselves, whether a particular outcome is dictated by precedent.[39]

## § 4.02 Waiver of Constitutional Rights[40]

### [A] Definition of "Waiver": The *Zerbst* Test

Virtually any constitutional right may be waived by a criminal suspect or defendant during a criminal investigation or prosecution. Consequently, issues of waiver permeate criminal procedure litigation and are discussed throughout this text.

A traditional starting point for understanding waiver law is *Johnson v. Zerbst*.[41] *Zerbst* provides that a constitutional right may not be waived unless there is "an intentional relinquishment or abandonment of a known right or privilege." This standard is divisible into three parts. First, the person must in fact have relinquished or abandoned the constitutional right in question.[42] Second, the relinquishment must be "voluntary in the sense that it was the product of a free and deliberate choice rather than intimidation, coercion, or deception."[43] Third, the holder of the right must be aware of the nature of the right and of the primary consequences of its relinquishment.[44]

---

[38] Sawyer v. Smith, 497 U.S. 227, 234 (1990) (emphasis added).

[39] Williams v. Taylor, 529 U.S. 362, 383–84 (2000).

[40] *See generally* George E. Dix, *Waiver in Criminal Procedure: A Brief for More Careful Analysis*, 55 Tex. L. Rev. 193 (1977); Edward L. Rubin, *Toward a General Theory of Waiver*, 28 UCLA L. Rev. 478 (1981); William J. Stuntz, *Waiving Rights in Criminal Procedure*, 75 Va. L. Rev. 761 (1989); Michael E. Tigar, *The Supreme Court, 1969 Term—Foreword: Waiver of Constitutional Rights: Disquiet in the Citadel*, 84 Harv. L. Rev. 1 (1970); Peter Westen, *Away From Waiver: A Rationale for the Forfeiture of Constitutional Rights in Criminal Procedure*, 75 Mich. L. Rev. 1214 (1977).

[41] 304 U.S. 458 (1938).

[42] *See* Brewer v. Williams, 430 U.S. 387, 404 (1977).

[43] Moran v. Burbine, 475 U.S. 412, 421 (1986).

[44] *Id.*

Under *Zerbst*, the validity of a waiver is based on the totality of the circumstances of the case. However, a court is required to "indulge every reasonable presumption against waiver"[45] of constitutional rights.

## [B]  When the *Zerbst* Test Does Not Apply

The *Zerbst* rule does not always apply. As the Supreme Court observed in *New York v. Hill*,[46] "[w]hat suffices for waiver depends on the nature of the right at issue." A less strict rule, therefore, applies in some circumstances. And, at times, a waiver is not really a waiver. That is, the Supreme Court will treat what seems to constitute a waiver of a constitutional right as something else.

According to the Supreme Court, "[w]e have been unyielding in our insistence that a defendant's waiver of his *trial rights* cannot be given effect unless it is 'knowing' and 'intelligent.' "[47] By "trial rights," the Court has in mind those rights that enhance the reliability of the truth-determining process, such as the right to trial counsel. A right that protects some other constitutional value is not always treated with the same solicitude.

For example, suppose that *D*, unaware that he has a right to refuse, permits the police to conduct a warrantless search of his home. Is the subsequent search permissible? Under *Zerbst* waiver principles, the answer would seem to be no: *D* has not relinquished or abandoned a *known* right or privilege, *i.e.*, the right to demand that the police secure a warrant before searching. Nonetheless, assuming that coercion was not involved in the case, the search will likely be upheld, on the ground that what has taken place is not a "waiver" of a constitutional right, but simply is voluntary "consent" to conduct the warrantless search, a recognized exception to the requirement of a search warrant.[48] This ruling may be explained on the alternative ground that a less strict waiver standard applies to the Fourth Amendment, because the bar on unreasonable searches and seizures is not a trial right, but instead protects the different constitutional value of "the right of each individual to be let alone."[49]

Similarly, a defendant who requests a mistrial due to prosecutorial misconduct ordinarily may be prosecuted again for the same offense, notwithstanding the Fifth Amendment double jeopardy prohibition. Yet, it would be plausible to argue in such a case that the defendant was coerced by the governmental misconduct into making the mistrial motion; therefore,

---

[45] *Zerbst*, 304 U.S. at 464 (internal quotation marks omitted).

[46] 528 U.S. 110 (2000).

[47] Illinois v. Rodriguez, 497 U.S. 177, 183 (1990) (emphasis added).

[48] *See* Schneckloth v. Bustamonte, 412 U.S. 218 (1973). *See* § 17.03[D], *infra*.

[49] Tehan v. United States ex rel. Shott, 382 U.S. 406, 416 (1966).

the "waiver" should be deemed invalid. According to the Supreme Court, however, "traditional" waiver principles do not apply in this context; instead, the issue is whether the defendant "retain[ed] primary control over the course to be followed" in the case of governmental misconduct.[50]

Sometimes a right is lost as a matter of law, without *any* regard to the right-holder's wishes. For example, a defendant may lose his constitutional right to be present at his own trial if he is disruptive in the courtroom.[51] He is also precluded from raising constitutional defenses if he does not bring them to the court's attention in timely fashion.[52] Although courts do not always make the point clear, the loss of a right in such circumstances involves a "forfeiture"[53] of the right, or a "preclusionary penalty,"[54] rather than a waiver.[55]

## § 4.03 Harmless Error[56]

### [A] Overview of the Issue

Given human fallibility, there is virtually no such thing as an error-free trial.[57] It is unfair to the public and wasteful of finite resources, therefore, to overturn convictions and conduct new trials whenever any error, no matter how trivial, occurs. Nonetheless, until the twentieth century, state and federal appellate courts usually reversed convictions automatically if they discovered errors in the trial process. Today the rule of thumb is that a defendant is entitled to a fair trial, but not a perfect one.[58]

---

[50] United States v. Dinitz, 424 U.S. 600, 609 (1976). *See* § 32.02[C][1], *infra*.

[51] Illinois v. Allen, 397 U.S. 337, 343 (1970).

[52] *E.g.*, Fed R. Crim. P. 12(f).

[53] Westen, Note 40, *supra*, at 1214–19.

[54] Dix, Note 40, *supra*, at 209.

[55] United States v. Olano, 507 U.S. 725, 733 (1993) ("Waiver is different from forfeiture"; whereas waiver is the "intentional relinquishment or abandonment of a known right," "forfeiture is the failure to make the timely assertion of a right.").

[56] *See generally* John H. Blume & Stephen P. Garvey, Harmless Error in Federal Habeas Corpus After Brecht v. Abrahamson, 35 Wm. & Mary L. Rev. 163 (1993); Steven H. Goldberg, *Harmless Error: Constitutional Sneak Thief*, 71 J. Crim. L. & Criminology 421 (1980); Craig Goldblatt, *Harmless Error as Constitutional Common Law: Congress's Power to Reverse Arizona v Fulminante*, 60 U. Chi. L. Rev. 985 (1993); Stuart P. Green, *The Challenge of Harmless Error*, 59 La. L. Rev. 1101 (1999); William Landes & Richard Posner, *Harmless Error*, 30 J. Legal Studies 161 (2001); Daniel J. Meltzer, *Harmless Error and Constitutional Remedies*, 61 U. Chi. L. Rev. 1 (1994); Gregory Mitchell, *Against "Overwhelming" Appellate Activism: Constraining Harmless Error Review*, 82 Cal. L. Rev. 1335 (1994); Stephen A. Saltzburg, *The Harm of Harmless Error*, 59 Va. L. Rev. 988 (1973); Tom Stacy & Kim Dayton, *Rethinking Harmless Constitutional Error*, 88 Colum. L. Rev. 79 (1988).

[57] United States v. Hasting, 461 U.S. 499, 508–09 (1983).

[58] Delaware v. Van Arsdall, 475 U.S. 673, 681.

When an appellate court determines that an error was made at the trial below, it must determine if the error was prejudicial or harmless. In making *that* determination, a court must distinguish between non-constitutional and constitutional errors. The latter type of error, because it is more serious than the former type, is more likely to be deemed prejudicial. But, even among constitutional errors, it is necessary for an appellate court to distinguish between two types of mistakes, "trial errors" and the more serious "structural errors." And, finally, the harmless-error rules differ depending on what type of appellate review is involved, a direct appeal or, instead, a collateral attack on a conviction in a habeas corpus proceeding. All of these distinctions are considered below.

Contrary to common myth, convictions of criminal defendants are rarely reversed. In one study of the appeals process in California,[59] for example, convictions were reversed in so few cases—only about five percent of the appeals—that one scholar observed that "despite the more-rigorous restrictions on public authority that ostensibly surround the determination of criminal guilt, the procedural standards actually enforced by many appellate courts are higher in civil than in criminal cases."[60]

## [B]　Non-Constitutional Trial Errors

Most trial errors do not implicate the Constitution. A trial judge may, for example, violate a state evidentiary rule by excluding evidence that should have been admitted, or vice-versa. There is no uniform test for determining whether such a non-constitutional trial error was harmless or, instead, prejudicial. However, the federal rule, originally adopted by statute, and now incorporated in the Federal Rules of Criminal Procedure,[61] is that an error is harmless if "it does not affect substantial rights."

In *Kotteakos v. United States*,[62] the Supreme Court interpreted the "substantial rights" rule to mean that a conviction cannot stand "if one cannot say, with fair assurance, after pondering all that happened," that the error did *not* have a "substantial and injurious effect or influence in determining the jury's verdict." Stripped of the multiple negatives, this means that a conviction must be reversed if (again in the language of *Kotteakos*) "the error itself had a substantial influence" on the verdict. "If

---

[59] Thomas Y. Davies, *Affirmed: A Study of Criminal Appeals and Decision-Making Norms in a California Court of Appeal*, 1982 Am. B. Found. Res. J. 543.

[60] Francis A. Allen, The Habits of Legality 32 (1996). In another study of federal appellate criminal cases, convictions were overturned in 13 percent of the cases. Landes & Posner, Note 56, *supra*, at 183–84.

[61] Fed. R. Crim. P. 52(a).

[62] 328 U.S. 750, 765, 776 (1946).

so, or if one is left in grave doubt [that it had a substantial influence], the conviction cannot stand."

### [C]   Constitutional Errors

#### [1]   Direct Appeals

##### [a]   Classification of Errors

Constitutional errors, *e.g.*, admission at trial of a coerced confession, are matters of graver concern to appellate courts than non-constitutional mistakes. As a result, the Supreme Court has devised relatively stringent standards for determining whether a conviction must be reversed due to constitutional error.

Constitutional errors are divided into two categories for purposes of harmless-error analysis. First, is a constitutional "trial error," *i.e.*, an "error which occurred during the presentation of the case to the jury, and which may therefore be quantitatively assessed in the context of other evidence presented in order to determine whether its admission was harmless."[63] Second, are "structural defects in the constitution of the trial mechanism," which are errors that "defy analysis by 'harmless-error' standards."[64] The harmless-error rules differ, depending on the type of error involved, as discussed immediately below.

##### [b]   Trial Errors: The *Chapman* Doctrine

Most constitutional-law harmless-error issues involve trial errors. Examples of constitutional trial error include the wrongful admission at trial of: evidence obtained in violation of Fourth Amendment search-and-seizure rules;[65] statements secured by the police through coercion[66] or in violation of the accused's Sixth Amendment right to counsel;[67] and evidence of a pretrial identification procedure conducted in violation of the accused's constitutional rights.[68] Sometimes the error involves a trial judge's constitutionally wrongful *restriction* on the presentation of the defendant's case.[69]

Constitutional trial errors are subject to the so-called "*Chapman* rule." In *Chapman v. California*,[70] the Supreme Court held that if a constitutional

---

[63] Arizona v. Fulminante, 499 U.S. 279, 307–08 (1991).

[64] *Id.* at 309.

[65] Chambers v. Maroney, 399 U.S. 42 (1970).

[66] Arizona v. Fulminante, 499 U.S. 279 (1991).

[67] Milton v. Wainwright, 407 U.S. 371 (1972).

[68] *E.g.*, Moore v. Illinois, 434 U.S. 220 (1977).

[69] *E.g.*, Delaware v. Van Arsdall, 475 U.S. 673 (1986) (wrongful restriction on *D*'s right to impeach a prosecution witness, in violation of the Sixth Amendment Confrontation Clause).

[70] 386 U.S. 18 (1967).

error occurs, the government must prove *beyond a reasonable doubt* that the error was harmless, *i.e.*, "that the error complained of did not contribute to the verdict obtained." Put somewhat differently, a conviction *will* be upheld, notwithstanding constitutional trial error, if the Government convinces the appellate court beyond a reasonable doubt that, but for the error(s), the same verdict would have resulted. However, in applying this standard, the inquiry for the reviewing court "is not whether, in a trial that occurred without the error, a guilty verdict would surely have been rendered, but whether the guilty verdict actually rendered in *this* trial was surely unattributable to the error."[71]

The *Chapman* rule is grounded on the view "that the central purpose of a criminal trial is to decide the factual question of the defendant's guilt or innocence."[72] If overwhelming error-free evidence of a defendant's guilt was introduced at the trial, the proceeding has fulfilled its mission and, therefore, the conviction should not be reversed.

The principle that a conviction will not inevitably be overturned, notwithstanding constitutional violations, is controversial. Among the criticisms leveled at it are the following. First, *Chapman* assumes that appellate courts can "reconstruct the world of the criminal trial"[73] by subtracting the constitutionally inadmissible evidence that the violation produced and/or by adding to the trial testimony the evidence that the constitutional violation kept from the factfinder, so as to determine whether the violation(s) contributed to the verdict. But, such reconstruction requires a court to speculate regarding a counter-factual reality. How can a court say with confidence what a jury would have done in that entirely different and non-existent world?[74]

Second, as the latter criticism suggests, the *Chapman* rule requires appellate courts to function as an appellate jury, a role for which it is particularly ill-suited, and which arguably violates the spirit of the defendant's Sixth Amendment right to trial by jury. Critics argue that appellate

---

[71] Sullivan v. Louisiana, 508 U.S. 275, 279 (1993) (emphasis added).

[72] Delaware v. Van Arsdall, 475 U.S. at 681.

[73] Robert Weisberg, *Foreword: Criminal Procedure Doctrine: Some Versions of the Skeptical*, 76 J. Crim. L. & Criminology 832, 846 (1985).

[74] Chief Justice Rehnquist concedes this point. He has written: "[A]ny time an appellate court conducts harmless-error review it necessarily engages in some speculation as to the jury's decisionmaking process; for in the end no judge can know for certain what factors led to the jury's verdict." Sullivan v. Louisiana, 508 U.S. at 284 (concurring opinion). But, "harmless-error review has become an integral component of our criminal justice system." *Id.*

courts should only focus "on the *process* used at trial rather than on the *evidence* that process produced."[75]

Third, the *Chapman* rule arguably acts like a "constitutional sneak thief."[76] The gist of this criticism is that, by focusing on the reliability of the verdict, the harmless-error rule de-emphasizes the values underlying the constitutional rights that were violated and, by allowing some convictions to stand, undermines the deterrent value of excluding the evidence.[77] In effect, the argument is made, the harmless-error doctrine, which is not a constitutionally-based rule, trumps express constitutional rights.

### [c]  Structural Defects: *Per Se* Rule

For many years, the Supreme Court recognized a small number of errors that it deemed so fundamental that it would not conduct harmless error analysis. Proof of the constitutional violation constituted *per se* prejudice and required automatic reversal of the conviction. For example, the wrongful admission of a coerced confession was deemed prejudicial *per se*.

Today, the Supreme Court treats the wrongful admission of a coerced confession as "trial error," subject to harmless error analysis.[78] The Court now reserves the "prejudice *per se*" approach to so-called structural defects in the trial mechanism, *i.e.*, defects that "affect the framework within which the trial proceeds."[79] Structural defects include: failure to provide a trial attorney to an indigent defendant;[80] representation of a defendant by a lawyer with an active conflict of interest;[81] adjudication by a biased judge;[82] selection of a jury by a judge without jurisdiction to preside over

---

[75] *The Supreme Court, 1985 Term—Leading Cases*, 100 Harv. L. Rev. 100, 116 (1986).

[76] Goldberg, Note 56, *supra*, at 421.

[77] But, maybe not. There is considerable public and political pressure on judges to affirm criminal convictions. If there were no harmless-error rule, judges might be inclined to find no constitutional violation and, therefore, weaken constitutional rights. With a harmless error doctrine, however, judges can reach the constitutional issues with candor—find a violation, which may be of value as precedent in a later case—while affirming the instant conviction. Green, Note 56, *supra*, at 1102–03.

[78] Arizona v. Fulminante, 499 U.S. 279 (1991).

[79] *Id.* at 310.

[80] Gideon v. Wainwright, 372 U.S. 335 (1963); *see also* Geders v. United States, 425 U.S. 80 (1976) (direct interference with the defendant's counsel, such as by ordering the defendant not to consult with his attorney during an overnight recess).

[81] Holloway v. Arkansas, 435 U.S. 475 (1978).

[82] Tumey v. Ohio, 273 U.S. 510 (1927).

the procedure,[83] and a constitutionally deficient reasonable-doubt instruction to the jury.[84]

The structural-defect *per se* rule may be justified on two grounds. First, structural defects are not susceptible to harmless-error analysis. How does an appellate court objectively determine, for example, how a trial would have proceeded if an uncounseled defendant had been furnished an attorney? There is no realistic way to quantify the harm caused or its effect on a jury.[85] Second, it is hard to conceive of a prejudice-free structurally defective trial. The likelihood of prejudice is so great—for example, if the case is heard before a biased judge—that it would be wasteful of judicial resources to invoke harmless-error analysis, even if it were possible.

### [2]  Collateral Appeals (Habeas Corpus Proceedings)[86]

Until 1993, the United States Supreme Court applied the *Chapman* standard in federal habeas corpus proceedings. That is, for purposes of harmless-error analysis in cases involving constitutional trial errors, federal courts did not distinguish between a direct appeal of a criminal conviction and a collateral attack on a state conviction in a habeas corpus proceeding. The Court changed directions, however, in *Brecht v. Abrahamson*.[87]

In *Brecht*, the Supreme Court held that the less stringent harmless-error standard used by federal courts in cases of *non*-constitutional trial error—the *Kotteakos* standard of whether an error "had substantial and injurious effect or influence in determining the jury's verdict"[88] —applies, as well, in determining whether habeas relief should be granted in cases of constitutional trial error.[89] Although it avoids the term "burden of proof" in harmless-error analysis, the Supreme Court has stated that when a federal habeas court finds constitutional trial error, and "the record is so evenly balanced that a conscientious judge is in grave doubt as to the harmlessness of an error" under the *Kotteakos* standard, the error is prejudicial.[90]

---

[83] Gomez v. United States, 490 U.S. 858 (1989).

[84] Sullivan v. Louisiana, 508 U.S. 275 (1993).

[85] For a questionable variation on this rationale, *see id.* at 280 ("There being no jury verdict of guilty-beyond-a-reasonable-doubt, the question whether the *same* verdict of guilty-beyond a reasonable doubt would have been rendered absent the constitutional error [of a defective instruction on reasonable doubt] is utterly meaningless. There is no *object*, so to speak, upon which harmless-error scrutiny can operate.") (emphasis added).

[86] For an explanation of habeas corpus proceedings, *see* § 1.03[C][10], *supra*.

[87] 507 U.S. 619 (1993).

[88] *See* § 4.03[B, *supra*.

[89] The *Kotteakos* standard does not apply to structural defects. California v. Roy, 519 U.S. 2, 4 (1996).

[90] O'Neal v. McAninch, 513 U.S. 432, 437 (1995).

The Court reasoned that the *Kotteakos* standard is better suited than the *Chapman* doctrine in habeas proceedings for dealing with constitutional trial errors made in state courts. Chief Justice Rehnquist reasoned that it was illogical to require a federal court to engage in the same *Chapman* harmless-error analysis that is already required of the state courts on direct review, prior to the matter reaching the federal courts. Furthermore, concerns for finality in criminal proceedings, and comity with the states, justified enforcement of the "less onerous" *Kotteakos* standard.

## § 4.04 Supervisory Power[91]

When a federal court renders a decision in the field of criminal procedure, its source of authority usually is the Constitution, a federal statute, or a provision of the Federal Rules of Criminal Procedure.[92] Occasionally, however, the Supreme Court and lower federal courts exercise their so-called "supervisory power" or "supervisory authority" over the federal courts.

The Supreme Court first invoked this power in 1943, in *McNabb v. United States*.[93] In *McNabb*, the Justices were troubled that federal law enforcement agents were regularly violating a statute that required them to take arrested persons before the nearest available federal magistrate "without unnecessary delay."[94] Although the statute provided no remedy for its violation, the Court exercised its supervisory authority to rule that any confession obtained by the police during an unlawful detention was inadmissible at trial even if it was obtained voluntarily.

Since *McNabb*, the supervisory power has been exerted by the Supreme Court "to improve the truth-finding process of the trial, . . . [and] also to prevent parties from reaping benefit or incurring harm from violations of substantive or procedural rules (imposed by the Constitution or laws) governing matters apart from the trial itself. . . ."[95] Lower federal courts, as well, have exercised supervisory power in compelling circumstances. For example, federal circuit courts and district judges have suppressed evidence obtained by prosecutors in violation of ethical canons,[96] have barred

---

[91] *See generally* Sara Sun Beale, *Reconsidering Supervisory Power in Criminal Cases: Constitutional and Statutory Limits on the Authority of the Federal Courts*, 84 Colum. L. Rev. 1433 (1984); George E. Dix, *Nonconstitutional Exclusionary Rules in Criminal Procedure*, 27 Am. Crim. L. Rev. 53 (1989); Alfred Hill, *The Bill of Rights and the Supervisory Power*, 69 Colum. L. Rev. 181 (1969).

[92] *See* § 1.02[A], *supra.*

[93] 318 U.S. 332 (1943).

[94] *See* § 23.01[C], *infra.*

[95] United States v. Williams, 504 U.S. 36, 46 (1992).

[96] *See* United States v. Hammad, 858 F.2d 834 (2d Cir. 1988) (holding that a district

deceptive use of hearsay evidence in grand jury proceedings,[97] have recognized new evidentiary privileges at trial,[98] and have developed procedures for taking guilty pleas.[99]

Constitutional decisionmaking should be distinguished from supervisory rulings. The Supreme Court's constitutional jurisprudence has national scope; federal supervisory authority extends only within the federal system.[100] Similarly, a circuit court's supervisory power cannot extend beyond the district courts in its circuit. It is also easier to repeal a supervisory rule: not only may the court that promulgated it change its mind (or a higher federal court overrule it), but because it is not based on constitutional principles, a supervisory ruling may be revised or negated by Congress.[101]

Courts and commentators have questioned the source of the federal courts' supervisory authority. The Supreme Court once suggested that the power emanates from a federal statute,[102] but this view is no longer generally accepted. Instead, the power apparently arises from article III of the Constitution, which confers general judicial power on the federal courts. Although article III does not expressly grant federal courts supervisory authority, advocates of its use contend that it is implied or inherent in the judicial role.[103]

---

court may, in its discretion, suppress evidence for violation of ethical canons); United States v. Howard, 426 F. Supp. 1067 (W.D.N.Y. 1977) (suppressing evidence, alternatively, on constitutional and supervisory grounds).

[97] United States v. Estepa, 471 F.2d 1132 (2d Cir. 1972) (per Friendly, C.J.).

[98] Mullen v. United States, 263 F.2d 275 (D.C. Cir. 1958).

[99] Moody v. United States, 497 F.2d 359 (7th Cir. 1974).

[100] Dickerson v. United States, 530 U.S. 428, 438 (2000).

[101] *Id.* at 437 ("This Court has supervisory authority over the federal courts, and we may use that authority to prescribe rules of evidence and procedure that are binding in those tribunals. . . . [However,] Congress retains the ultimate authority to modify or set aside any judicially created rules of evidence and procedure that are not required by the Constitution.").

[102] La Buy v. Howes Leather Co., 352 U.S. 249, 260 (1957) (invoking the All Writs Act, 28 U.S.C. § 1651).

[103] Professor Sara Beale claims that "[s]upervisory power as such does not exist," Beale, Note 91, *supra*, at 1520, although she believes that some judicial exercises of authority under the "supervisory power" label are legitimate on other grounds. Beale doubts that circuit courts have authority to establish procedural rules for the district courts, and she contends that, in the absence of statutory authority, the Supreme Court has inherent power only to develop rules that relate to the efficiency and reliability of the judicial process (*e.g.*, rules that reduce the risk of perjured testimony). Supervisory rulings intended to influence the police and other extrajudicial parties are improper, according to Beale. As noted in the text, however, the Supreme Court has taken a more expansive view of its authority.

(Matthew Bender & Co., Inc.)      (Pub.791)

Although the Supreme Court continues to exercise its supervisory authority on occasion, it has sent a clear message to lower courts that they may not use the power to undercut the high court's constitutional jurisprudence. Two cases demonstrate the Court's modern view.

In *United States v. Payner*,[104] the Internal Revenue Service launched an investigation ("Operation Trade Winds") of the financial activities of American citizens living in the Bahamas. In this regard, I.R.S. agents employed a private investigator to obtain and photograph the contents of a bank official's briefcase, which resulted in incriminating evidence against a third person, *D*. Under Fourth Amendment "standing" law,[105] *D* could not object to the search, although it was illegal, because it was the bank official's, and not *D*'s, briefcase that was searched.

According to the district court, the I.R.S. not only "knowingly and willfully participated in the unlawful seizure," but it affirmatively counseled its agents that Fourth Amendment standing law permitted them to conduct unconstitutional seizures of the kind involved in the present case. Troubled by the government's conduct here, the trial court ignored the standing rules and exercised supervisory power to exclude the evidence obtained from the briefcase.

The Supreme Court reversed. Although stating that it understood the district court's "commendable desire" to deter deliberate lawless activities by government agents, the Court warned that lower courts are not permitted to use non-constitutional supervisory law to upset the "careful balance of interests" embodied in previous constitutional decisions.

In a second case, *United States v. Hasting*,[106] a federal circuit court, concerned that prosecutors were repeatedly violating a constitutional rule announced by the Supreme Court, used its supervisory power to reverse a conviction, without consideration of whether the violation in the instant case was prejudicial under the harmless-error rule.[107] As in *Payner*, the Supreme Court reversed the lower court. It ruled that lower courts may not invoke their supervisory authority "in a vacuum." In particular, a reviewing court may not ignore constitutional harmless-error doctrine in its exercise of its supervisory power.

The Supreme Court has also warned federal courts that whatever the proper scope of supervisory authority, "it does not include the power to develop rules that circumvent or conflict with the Federal Rules of Criminal

---

[104] 447 U.S. 727 (1980).

[105] *See* § 20.07, *infra*.

[106] 461 U.S. 499 (1983).

[107] *See generally* § 4.03, *supra*.

Procedure."[108] For example, in *Carlisle v. United States*,[109] the Court held that a trial judge had no authority to grant a defendant's postconviction motion for judgment of acquittal that, due to attorney error, was filed one day outside the 7-day time limit established by Federal Rule 29(c). The Court stated that federal courts do not have " 'inherent power' to act in contravention of applicable Rules" and federal statutes.[110]

## § 4.05 Prophylactic Rules[111]

On occasion, the Supreme Court identifies a rule that it has promulgated as "prophylactic" in nature. The term has various meanings, in various contexts. Generally speaking, a "prophylactic rule" is one devised by a court for the purpose of preventing a violation of a constitutional right. Thus, for example, the Supreme Court has on various occasions described the rule requiring the police to give suspects certain warnings before conducting custodial interrogation—the so-called *Miranda*[112] warnings—as prophylactic in nature. The warnings must be given, in other words, to make sure that any resulting incriminating statement made by the suspect is not coerced, in violation of the Constitution.

What is the significance of characterizing a rule as "prophylactic"? Based on language in various post-*Miranda* decisions, some[113] commentators concluded that prophylactic rules are non-constitutional in nature, *i.e.*, it is possible to violate a prophylactic rule without actually violating the Constitution itself.[114] Therefore, the reasoning follows, a non-constitutional prophylactic rule, like a rule promulgated by a federal court through its supervisory authority,[115] does not apply to the states and may be modified

---

[108] Carlisle v. United States, 517 U.S. 416, 426 (1996).

[109] *Id.*

[110] *See also* Bank of Nova Scotia v. United States, 487 U.S. 250 (1988) (a federal court may not invoke its supervisory power to circumvent harmless-error inquiry prescribed by Fed. R. Crim. P. 52(a)).

[111] *See generally* Joseph D. Grano, *Prophylactic Rules in Criminal Procedure: A Question of Article III Legitimacy*, 80 Nw. U. L. Rev. 100 (1985); Brian K. Landsberg, *Safeguarding Constitutional Rights: The Uses and Limits of Prophylactic Rules*, 66 Tenn. L. Rev. 925 (1999); Daryl J. Levinson, *Rights Essentialism and Remedial Equilibration*, 99 Colum. L. Rev. 857 (1999); Henry P. Monaghan, *The Supreme Court, 1974 Term—Foreword: Constitutional Common Law*, 89 Harv. L. Rev. 1 (1975); David A. Strauss, *The Ubiquity of Prophylactic Rules*, 55 U. Chi. L. Rev. 190 (1988). *See also* the cites in Note 118, *infra*.

[112] Miranda v. Arizona 384 U.S. 436 (1966).

[113] *E.g.*, Grano, Note 111, *supra*.

[114] *E.g.*, Oregon v. Elstad, 470 U.S. 298, 306 (1985) ("The *Miranda* exclusionary rule . . .serves the Fifth Amendment and sweeps more broadly than the Fifth Amendment itself. *It may be triggered even in the absence of a Fifth Amendment violation*.") (emphasis added).

[115] *See* § 4.04, *supra*.

in the federal system by Congressional legislation. In contrast, other commentators have characterized prophylactic rules as a species of constitutional common law,[116] or as "a central and necessary feature of constitutional law"[117] created out of necessity to protect express constitutional rights. Understood this way, prophylactic rules must be followed by the states and are not subject to Congressional repeal.

The Supreme Court's recent efforts to explain *Miranda* and, one had hoped, to clarify the role of prophylactic rules in constitutional jurisprudence, have resulted in considerable dispute and much scholarly analysis.[118] In *Dickerson v. United States*,[119] the Court stated that, despite its prior characterization of *Miranda* warnings as prophylactic, *Miranda v. Arizona* announced a constitutional rule applicable to the states and not subject to being overruled by legislation. Whatever *Dickerson* may mean to *Miranda* jurisprudence—a matter considered elsewhere[120]—what the case seems to be saying about prophylactic rules generally is that they *are* of constitutional pedigree, in the sense that unless and until the Supreme Court or a legislative body can devise a different prophylaxis that is at least as effective as the original one in protecting an express constitutional right, the original prophylactic rule (*e.g.*, the *Miranda* warnings) must be followed by all parties in the criminal justice system.

---

[116] *E.g.,* Monaghan, Note 111, *supra.*

[117] Strauss, Note 111, *supra* at 190.

[118] For recent analysis of prophylactic rules in light of the *Dickerson* case (cited in the text immediately *infra*), *see generally* Michael C. Dorf & Barry Friedman, *Shared Constitutional Interpretation*, 2000 Sup. Ct. Rev. 1; Susan R. Klein, *Identifying and (Re)Formulating Prophylactic Rules, Safe Harbors and Incidental Rights in Constitutional Criminal Procedure*, 99 Mich. L. Rev. 1030 (2001); David A Strauss, *Miranda, The Constitution, and Congress*, 99 Mich. L. Rev. 958 (2001).

[119] 530 U.S. 428 (2000).

[120] *See* § 24.06[C], *infra.*

CHAPTER 5

# FOURTH AMENDMENT: OVERVIEW

## § 5.01 A Warning Before Beginning the Fourth Amendment Journey[1]

According to one commentator, the Fourth Amendment contains "both the virtue of brevity and the vice of ambiguity."[2] Another scholar has stated that the amendment is "brief, vague, general, [and] unilluminating."[3] For almost a century the text remained "largely unexplored territory."[4] It did

---

[1] There is a voluminous literature relating to the Fourth Amendment. Citations to some excellent sources will be provided throughout this text. By far the most cited Fourth Amendment source is Professor Wayne LaFave's five-volume treatise, Search and Seizure (3d ed. 1996).

For general discussion of Fourth Amendment jurisprudence, *see generally* Akhil Reed Amar, *Fourth Amendment First Principles*, 107 Harv. L. Rev. 757 (1994); Anthony G. Amsterdam, *Perspectives On The Fourth Amendment*, 58 Minn. L. Rev. 349 (1974); Ronald J. Bacigal, *Choosing Perspectives in Criminal Procedure*, 6 Wm. & Mary Bill of Rts J. 677 (1998); Susan Bandes, *"We the People" and our Enduring Values*, 96 Mich. L. Rev. 1376 (1998); Gerard V. Bradley, The Constitutional Theory of the Fourth Amendment, 38 DePaul L. Rev. 817 (1989); Morgan Cloud, *Pragmatism, Positivism, and Principles in Fourth Amendment Theory*, 41 UCLA L. Rev. 199 (1993); Sherry F. Colb, *Innocence, Privacy, and Targeting in Fourth Amendment Jurisprudence*, 96 Colum. L. Rev. 1456 (1996); Tracey Maclin, *When the Cure for the Fourth Amendment Is Worse than the Disease*, 68 S. Cal. L. Rev. 1 (1994); Louis Michael Seidman, *The Problems With Privacy's Problem*, 93 Mich. L. Rev. 1079 (1995); David A. Sklansky, *The Fourth Amendment and Common Law*, 100 Colum. L. Rev. 1739 (2000); Carol S. Steiker, *Second Thoughts About First Principles*, 107 Harv. L. Rev. 820 (1994); William J. Stuntz, *Privacy's Problem and the Law of Criminal Procedure*, 93 Mich. L. Rev. 1016 (1995); Scott E. Sundby, *"Everyman"'s Fourth Amendment: Privacy or Mutual Trust Between Government and Citizen?*, 94 Colum. L. Rev. 1751 (1994); Silas J. Wasserstrom & Louis Michael Seidman, *The Fourth Amendment as Constitutional Theory*, 77 Geo. L.J. 19 (1988); Lloyd L. Weinreb, *Generalities of the Fourth Amendment*, 42 U. Chi. L. Rev. 47 (1974).

[2] Jacob W. Landynski, Search and Seizure and the Supreme Court: A Study in Constitutional Interpretation 42 (1966).

[3] Amsterdam, Note 1, *supra*, at 353–54.

[4] Landynski, Note 2, *supra*, at 49.

not take "full flower"[5] until 1961, when the Supreme Court extended the provision's judicially-implied exclusionary rule to the states.[6]

Many years ago, Justice Felix Frankfurter observed that "[t]he course of true law pertaining to [the Fourth Amendment] . . . has not . . . run smooth."[7] This is an understatement. "Almost no one has a kind word to say about fourth amendment jurisprudence."[8] According to one critic, "[t]he Fourth Amendment today is an embarrassment."[9] And, whether one agrees with the observation that "Fourth Amendment case law is a sinking ocean liner—rudderless and badly off course,"[10] it is true that criticism of Fourth Amendment law comes from widely divergent, and even opposite, political and philosophical poles.

Put simply, the single sentence that constitutes the Fourth Amendment (as set out in subsection [B]) has resulted in billions of words of interpretive text by the Supreme Court, state and lower federal courts, and commentators. The Fourth Amendment today looks to some like a Rorschach blot,[11] its jurisprudence described by one observer as "a mass of contradictions and obscurities."[12] The goal of anyone studying Fourth Amendment law, therefore, is to make as much sense of it as possible, as well as to consider ways to improve upon what has been constructed (or, to continue one metaphor, to save the ocean liner before it sinks).

## § 5.02 The Text[13]

The Fourth Amendment to the United States Constitution is a mere 54 words long. It reads:

The right of the people to be secure in their persons, houses, papers, and effects, against unreasonable searches and seizures, shall not be violated,

---

[5] Wayne R. LaFave, *The Fourth Amendment Today: A Bicentennial Appraisal*, 32 Vill. L. Rev. 1061, 1064 (1987).

[6] Mapp v. Ohio, 367 U.S. 643 (1961). For discussion of the exclusionary rule, *see* § 5.04[B] and chapter 21, *infra*.

[7] Chapman v. United States, 365 U.S. 610, 618 (1961) (concurring opinion).

[8] Wasserstrom & Seidman, Note 1, *supra*, at 19.

[9] Amar, Note 1, *supra*, at 757.

[10] *Id.* at 759.

[11] Amsterdam, Note 1, *supra*, at 375.

[12] Craig M. Bradley, *Two Models of the Fourth Amendment*, 83 Mich. L. Rev. 1468, 1468 (1985).

[13] For shorthand purposes, this treatise speaks of the provisions of the Fourth Amendment as if they applied directly to the states, although it is the Fourteenth Amendment due process clause that recognizes the fundamental right to be secure from unreasonable searches and seizures by state agents. Wolf v. Colorado, 338 U.S. 25 (1949), *overruled on other grounds*, Mapp v. Ohio, 367 U.S. 643 (1961). *See generally* chapter 3, *supra*.

and no Warrants shall issue, but upon probable cause, supported by Oath or affirmation, and particularly describing the place to be searched, and the persons or things to be seized.

In reading the text, one can divide the Fourth Amendment into two general parts. The first portion of the Fourth Amendment tells us what the amendment seek to prohibit (or, if you will, what right we hold against the government). In this portion, the text states *who* is covered ("the people"); *what* is covered ("persons, houses, papers, and effects"); and the nature of the protection ("to be secure . . . against unreasonable searches and seizures"). This portion of the Fourth Amendment, in particular the latter language, is sometimes described as the "Reasonableness Clause" (or "reasonableness requirement") of the Fourth Amendment.

The second portion of the Fourth Amendment relates to warrants. It tells us what is required for a warrant to be issued ("probable cause [for the search or seizure], supported by oath or affirmation"), and tells us something about the form of the warrant itself ("particularly describing the place to be searched, and the persons or things to be seized"). This portion of the text is often described as the "Warrant Clause," with its "particularity requirement."

One of the great debates in Fourth Amendment jurisprudence relates to the connection, if any, between the Reasonableness Clause and the Warrant Clause. How does one clause inform the other, if at all? More particularly, does the Fourth Amendment stand for the proposition that any search or seizure conducted without a valid warrant is unreasonable (or, at least, presumptively unreasonable) and, thus, impermissible in view of the reasonableness requirement of the Fourth Amendment?

On the hand, is the Warrant Clause independent of the Reasonableness Clause? That is, does the Warrant Clause tell us simply *how* warrants should be issued (with probable cause, etc.), but tell us nothing whatsoever about *whether* or *when* warrants need to be issued?[14] The debate on this critical matter is summarized elsewhere in this text,[15] and is at the center of most of the controversy in Fourth Amendment jurisprudence.

## § 5.03　What Does the Fourth Amendment Seek to Protect?

The ultimate question that lawyers, and specifically the Supreme Court, have sought to answer over the past century or more is: What is the purpose of the Fourth Amendment? Sometimes the answer to the question focuses

---

[14] Under this view, "[t]he Warrant Clause says only when warrants may not issue [in the absence of probable cause], not when they may, or must." Amar, Note 1, *supra*, at 774.

[15] *See* § 11.01, *infra*.

on the text of the Fourth Amendment. As noted above, there is considerable—even raging—debate regarding the relationship of the Warrant Clause to the Reasonableness Clause of the Fourth Amendment. But, the text does not definitively answer the question, so scholars have looked to history to divine the intent of the framers of the Constitution.

In that regard, the Supreme Court has observed that "the Fourth Amendment's commands grew in large measure out of the colonists' experience with the writs of assistance and their memories of the general warrants formerly in use in England."[16] Specifically, writs of assistance authorized the use of "assistants"—local officials, such as the sheriff—to aid the Crown's agents to forcibly enter and search a colonist's home (or any other place), virtually at will, for smuggled goods. Similarly, general warrants were used in England to ferret out supposed seditious publications. Search warrants empowered agents of the Crown, on very little basis, to forcibly enter and search (indeed, ransack) homes for books and papers for use in seditious libel prosecutions.[17]

Although abusive general warrants and writs constituted the immediate evils that the framers sought to prohibit (the "aboriginal subject of the fourth amendment"[18] ), the Supreme Court has since asserted "that the evil the Amendment was designed to prevent was broader than the[se] abuse[s]."[19] What other evils may the framers have had in mind? Although the Court has never said so expressly, some members of the Court (a majority, in some eras), have viewed "the fourth amendment as quintessentially a regulation of the police—that, in enforcing the fourth amendment, courts *must* police the police."[20] Or, put more generally, "the larger purpose for which the Framers adopted the text . . . [was] to curb the exercise of discretionary authority by officers."[21]

For some scholars and Justices, the drafters' intent is the predominant, if not sole, basis for interpreting the Fourth Amendment. Other members of the Court and various commentators have expressed doubt that the original meaning of the amendment, whatever it is, can or should be directly enforced in the twenty-first century.[22] For those who do not feel constrained

---

[16] United States v. Chadwick, 433 U.S. 1, 7–8 (1977).

[17] *See* Osmond K. Fraenkel, *Concerning Searches and Seizures*, 34 Harv. L. Rev. 361, 362–63 (1920).

[18] Amsterdam, Note 1, *supra*, at 363.

[19] Payton v. New York, 445 U.S. 573, 585 (1980).

[20] Amsterdam, Note 1, *supra*, at 371.

[21] Thomas Y. Davies, *Recovering the Original Fourth Amendment*, 98 Mich. L. Rev. 547, 556 (1999).

[22] *Id.*; *see also* Susan R. Klein, *Enduring Principles and Current Crises in Constitutional Criminal Procedure*, 24 Law & Social Inquiry 533, 542–43 (1999).

by the original meaning of the Fourth Amendment, the goal is to determine how to ensure the viability of the amendment in modern times while remaining reasonably faithful to the amendment's text and history.

One way to strive for both historical faithfulness and modern relevance is to ask and answer the following question: Beyond the specific *means* of intrusion historically barred by the Fourth Amendment (intrusion of homes by means of general warrants or writs), what broad overriding *values* inspired the framers of the Fourth Amendment? Originally, the Supreme Court claimed that the Fourth Amendment primarily was intended to prevent violations of the "sacred and incommunicable" right to private property, which was described as "[t]he great end for which men entered into society."[23] The more recent interpretation of the amendment is that the framers intended to protect people's legitimate expectations of privacy in their "persons, houses, papers, and effects."[24]

Under both historical interpretations, the Court has suggested that "physical entry of the home [without a valid warrant] is the chief evil against which the . . . Fourth Amendment is directed."[25] The unwarranted "breach of the entrance to an individual's home"[26] is the clearest violation of Fourth Amendment values, whether those values are primarily property or privacy based. As will be seen, even as the Court's devotion to search warrants has ebbed and flowed, the Justices have remained comparatively firm in their commitment to the protection of the home and other "privately owned building[s]."[27]

Some contemporary scholars believe that the Court's modern privacy analysis is wrong-footed. In reading subsequent chapters of this text, students of the Fourth Amendment may wish to consider various suggestions for change. Professor William Stuntz, for example, believes that the law of criminal procedure, in particular the Fourth Amendment, has focused too much on informational privacy—on the right to keep information hidden from the government—rather than on dignitary interests. According to Stuntz,

> criminal procedure would be better off with less attention to privacy, at least as privacy is defined in the doctrine today. Were the law of criminal

---

[23] Boyd v. United States, 116 U.S. 616, 627 (1886) (quoting Lord Camden).

[24] However, the Fourth Amendment "cannot be translated into a general constitutional 'right to privacy.' " Katz v. United States, 389 U.S. 347, 350 (1967). For fuller discussion of the property rights and privacy interpretations, *see* §§ 7.02–7.03, *infra*.

[25] United States v. United States District Court, 407 U.S. 297, 313 (1972).

[26] Payton v. New York, 445 U.S. 573, 589 (1980).

[27] California v. Acevedo, 500 U.S. 565, 585 (1991) (Scalia, J., concurring).

procedure to focus more on force and coercion [used by the government] and less on information gathering . . ., it would square better with other constitutional law and better protect the interests most people value most highly.[28]

In reply, Professor Michael Seidman contends that the focus of Fourth Amendment law is precisely where Stuntz would want it, on the matters of "violence, disruption, and humiliation."[29] For example, Seidman suggests, the harm of a forcible entry and search of a home is less "the revelation of information [inside] but [more] the invasion of broader, more amorphous, but no less real, dignity interests."[30] The distinction between informational privacy and freedom from "violence, disruption, and humiliation" is one that lawyers and scholars may focus on more carefully in coming years.

Another approach to the Fourth Amendment has been suggested by Professor Scott Sundby. He would choose a new "constitutional metaphor" by which to think about the amendment: "Justice Brandeis's famous image of 'the right to let alone,' no longer fully captures the values that are at stake. . . . [T]he animating principle . . . is the idea of reciprocal government-citizen trust."[31]

According to Sundby, government action draws its legitimacy from the trust that the people place in their representatives by choosing them to govern. This mandate is not valid, however, unless there is voluntary consent of the governed, which only occurs if the government acts in a manner manifesting its trust in the people to exercise liberty responsibly. That trust, however, "is jeopardized when the government is allowed to intrude into the citizenry's lives without a finding that the citizenry has forfeited society's trust to exercise its freedoms responsibly."[32]

Sundby believes that the value of the metaphor of trust is not that it offers a simple rule for evaluating police conduct in specified circumstances, but rather that it directs attention beyond the privacy expectations of the individual, and beyond the short-term justifications for the government intrusion, to the broader normative issue of what relationship should exist between citizens and their government in a democratic, rather than totalitarian, society. In essence, Professor Sundby would have us (and the courts)

---

[28] Stuntz, Note 1, *supra*, at 1020.

[29] Seidman, Note 1, *supra*, at 1087.

[30] *Id.* at 1088.

[31] Sundby, Note 1, *supra*, at 1754.

[32] *Id.* at 1777.

think more about "the long-term dangers attendant to not protecting the citizen's independence from the government."[33]

## § 5.04  Some Things To Know at the Outset

### [A]  Standing to Raise Fourth Amendment Claims

A defendant in a criminal prosecution may not raise a claim of a Fourth Amendment violation unless she is the alleged victim of the unreasonable search or seizure. In other words, Fourth Amendment rights are personal; they may not be vicariously asserted. This is sometimes called the "standing" requirement. This subject is discussed in detail in chapter 20.

Conceptually, standing to raise a Fourth Amendment claim is a threshold issue. A defense lawyer who believes evidence seized by the police should be suppressed at trial pursuant to the Fourth Amendment "exclusionary rule" (see [B] below) must first demonstrate that her client was the alleged victim of the unreasonable search or seizure.

The Supreme Court no longer treats the issue of standing separately from the substantive merits of the defendant's Fourth Amendment claim.[34] Nonetheless, it is often preferable to treat "standing" as a distinct inquiry, because it is possible to have authority to raise a claim that will ultimately be lost on the merits, just as there are cases in which Fourth Amendment interests *have* been violated, but the particular person who wishes to raise the claim is not the proper one to do so.

### [B]  Exclusionary Rule

The issue of the scope of the Fourth Amendment—*i.e.*, what constitutes an unreasonable search or seizure—must be distinguished from the matter of the *remedy* for a Fourth Amendment violation. Since 1914 in federal criminal proceedings,[35] and since 1961 in state criminal trials,[36] the primary Fourth Amendment remedy has been the so-called "exclusionary rule." In very general terms, this rule provides that evidence seized by the police in violation of the Fourth Amendment may not be introduced by the prosecution in a criminal trial of the victim of the unreasonable search or seizure.

The Fourth Amendment exclusionary rule is exceedingly controversial, and is under both judicial and legislative attack, because its prevents the government from introducing reliable evidence of a defendant's guilt. As

---

[33] *Id.* at 1809.

[34] Rakas v. Illinois, 439 U.S. 128 (1978).

[35] Weeks v. United States, 232 U.S. 383 (1914).

[36] Mapp v. Ohio, 367 U.S. 643 (1961).

a result, significant limits have been placed on the rule in recent years, and there are continuing efforts to abolish the doctrine. Those limits, and the arguments for and against the rule, are surveyed in chapter 21.

### [C] Pretrial Nature of Fourth Amendment Issues

In light of the exclusionary rule, the ultimate Fourth Amendment issue in criminal proceedings is whether particular items of evidence, seized by the police, are admissible at defendant's trial. Under present law, the admissibility issue is raised by defense motion, and resolved prior to trial by a judge, whose responsibility it is to determine whether the search and seizure was reasonable. Typically, the *petit* jury is not involved in this determination.

There is historical irony in this process. As Professor Akhil Amar has noted, in the eyes of the framers of the Constitution, judges were "the heavies, not the heroes, of our [Fourth Amendment] story,"[37] because it was they who authorized the abusive general warrants and writs of assistance that the amendment sought to abolish.[38] Traditionally, as well, reasonableness is "a classic question of fact for the jury."[39] According to some, the current approach of "having judges decide what police conduct violates the Fourth Amendment reflects a distrust of society's ability or willingness to apply the Fourth Amendment properly."[40] Some scholars, therefore, have argued for jury participation in the process.[41]

As matters presently are handled, the trial judge makes all findings of fact and rulings of law on Fourth Amendment matters. She decides whose version of the facts—the police version or the defendant's description of the events—should be believed and, based on her findings of fact, renders a legal ruling on the reasonableness of the police conduct under applicable constitutional law. In any subsequent appeal of her determination, an appellate court must accept the lower court's factual findings, absent an abuse of discretion.

### [D] "Private" Searches and Seizures[42]

The Fourth Amendment limits *government* action. The amendment does *not* restrict the actions of private parties, *i.e.*, persons who are not directly

---

[37] Akhil R. Amar, *The Bill of Rights as a Constitution*, 100 Yale L.J. 1131, 1179 (1991).

[38] *See* § 5.03, *supra*.

[39] Amar, Note 37, *supra*, at 1179.

[40] George C. Thomas III & Barry S. Pollack, *Saving Rights from a Remedy: A Societal View of the Fourth Amendment*, 73 B.U. L. Rev. 147, 149 (1993).

[41] *E.g.*, Amar, Note 1, *supra*, at 817–19; Bacigal, Note 1, *supra*; and Thomas & Pollack, Note 40, *supra*.

[42] *See generally* 1 LaFave, Note 1, *supra*, at § 1.8.

or indirectly acting for the government. Put starkly, the Fourth Amendment has nothing to say regarding private searches and seizures. Therefore, evidence secured by a private party—no matter how unreasonable or illegal the methods used to obtain it—is constitutionally admissible in a criminal proceeding against the victim of the improper conduct.[43] For example, if a private security guard searches an office without cause, or if one neighbor breaks into the house of another, these actions do not violate the Fourth Amendment, even if they violate federal or state criminal laws.

The Fourth Amendment applies if a private person acts "as an instrument or agent of the Government."[44] For example, a Fourth Amendment violation may be found if, at the request of law enforcement officer, a private individual conducts surveillance of a citizen or opens a package belonging to another. Whether a private person should be deemed an agent of the government for Fourth Amendment purposes depends on the degree of government involvement in the situation, and is determined by the totality of the circumstances.[45]

Although most Fourth Amendment litigation involves searches and seizures by police officers, the amendment applies to other public employees, such as firefighters,[46] public school teachers,[47] and housing inspectors.[48]

### [E]　Extraterritorial Searches and Seizures[49]

The Fourth Amendment does not restrict the conduct of *foreign* law enforcement officers acting *outside* the United States. Therefore, United States citizens cannot assert constitutional protection in such circumstances, and evidence secured by a foreign officer, if turned over to an American court, may be admitted against the victim of the search. On the other hand, if there is sufficient American involvement in the extraterritorial search of the American citizen, the Fourth Amendment applies.

A different question arises when the victim of the extraterritorial search is, herself, a foreigner. In *United States v. Verdugo-Urquidez,*[50] D, a

---

[43] *See* Burdeau v. McDowell, 256 U.S. 465 (1921).

[44] Skinner v. Railway Labor Executives' Ass'n, 489 U.S. 602, 614 (1989); *see* United States v. Jacobsen, 466 U.S. 109, 113–14 (1984).

[45] *Skinner*, 489 U.S. at 614.

[46] *E.g.*, Michigan v. Tyler, 436 U.S. 499 (1978).

[47] *E.g.*, New Jersey v. T. L. O., 469 U.S. 325 (1985).

[48] *E.g.*, Camara v. Municipal Court, 387 U.S. 523 (1967).

[49] *See generally* 1 LaFave, Note 1, *supra*, at § 1.8(h); Eric Bentley, Jr., *Toward an International Fourth Amendment: Rethinking Searches and Seizures Abroad After Verdugo-Urquidez*, 27 Vand. J. Trans. L. 329 (1991); Note, *The Extraterritorial Applicability of the Fourth Amendment*, 102 Harv. L. Rev. 1672 (1989).

[50] 494 U.S. 259 (1990).

Mexican citizen and resident, temporarily in custody in an American correctional facility, was subjected to a warrantless search of his Mexican property by agents of the United States Drug Enforcement Agency working along with Mexican police. The Supreme Court held that *D* could not claim the protection of the Fourth Amendment, despite U.S. involvement, and despite *D*'s presence in the United States when the extraterritorial search occurred.

According to Chief Justice Rehnquist, the words "the people" in the Fourth Amendment text "refer[] to a class of persons who are part of a national community or who have otherwise developed sufficient connection with this country to be considered part of that community." He suggested that nonresident aliens located outside the United States or its territories, as well as those who are temporarily and involuntarily in the country (such as *D*), are not protected against foreign searches, even if those searches are conducted by United States government officers.

Various issues remain after *Verdugo-Urquidez*. First, concurring Justices Stevens and Kennedy and three dissenters rejected Chief Justice Rehnquist's reasoning that *D* was not among "the people" protected by the Fourth Amendment. The concurring Justices concluded, instead, that the Warrant Clause does not apply to extraterritorial searches, and that the search here was otherwise reasonable. Based on the split opinion, Professor LaFave has observed that "the *most* that can be definitely concluded . . . is that the Fourth Amendment's warrant clause is inapplicable to a search conducted under the circumstances present" in the case.[51]

Second, the Court expressly left for another day the question of whether a nonresident alien, whose *involuntary* presence in the country is prolonged (such as an alien serving a terms of years in a state or federal prison) has sufficient connection with the country to be entitled to raise Fourth Amendment claims as the result of an extraterritorial search.

Third, and perhaps more significantly, the Court merely assumed, but did not decide, that undocumented immigrants living *voluntarily* in the United States, but who "presumably have accepted some societal obligations," possess Fourth Amendment rights.

## § 5.05 Fourth Amendment Checklist

In criminal prosecutions, Fourth Amendment issues arise in an evidentiary context. That is, the question that normally must be considered is this:

*Should a particular tangible object or oral communication, secured by government agents, and which the prosecutor intends to introduce at trial*

---

[51] 1 LaFave, Note 1, *supra*, at 282.

*against the defendant (D) in the government's case-in-chief, be excluded because it was obtained in violation of the Fourth Amendment?*

Answering this question is rarely simple. Nor is there a fool-proof way to go about determining the answer. Nonetheless, the following checklist of questions may help to clarify matters. Although the list may seem overwhelming at the outset, the reader should find it helpful to return to it frequently, to see how the materials explained in later chapters fit into the larger picture.

In answering the evidentiary question stated above, one should focus on the police activity that resulted in discovery of the particular evidence at issue, and consider as many of the following questions as are relevant. *Assuming that there are multiple items of evidence to consider, it is preferable to consider them in chronological order, i.e., in the order in which the evidence was secured by the police.*

1. *Does D have standing to raise a Fourth Amendment challenge to the specific item of evidence in question?* As will be seen in chapter 20, if your answer is "no," the evidence is admissible, in so far as the Fourth Amendment is concerned. If the answer is "yes," the analysis continues. In a multi-defendant criminal prosecution, this question must be asked separately as to each defendant. One person may have standing to raise the claim, while another does not.

2. *Did the police activity in question implicate a "person, house, paper, or effect"?* As discussed in chapter 6, if the answer to this question is "no"—which is rare—the Fourth Amendment does not apply.

3. *Did the police activity constitute a "search" and/or "seizure"?* These words have specialized meanings in Fourth Amendment jurisprudence, as explained in chapters 7–8. If the police activity in question does not constitute either a search or seizure, the Fourth Amendment does not apply.

4. *Was the search and/or seizure reasonable or unreasonable?* This is the ultimate substantive issue, because it tells us whether the Fourth Amendment was violated. Nonetheless, one cannot answer this question without considering sub-issues, including the following:

A. *Did the police have adequate grounds to conduct the search and/or seizure?* For searches and seizures, the police traditionally must have "probable cause," a constitutional term of art considered in chapter 9. Many searches and seizures, however, are permitted on a lesser ground, called "reasonable suspicion," a concept discussed in chapter 18. And, the Supreme Court has approved random, no-suspicion-required searches and/or seizures in a few cases. Those exceptional circumstances are considered in chapters 18–19.

In light of the different rules here, one must look at the particular search and/or seizure in question, and determine whether it is the type for which probable cause is required (many cases), or whether it is the type for which reasonable suspicion is sufficient (many cases), or whether this is one of the few cases in which the police may act at random. Then, assuming some level of cause is required, you must determine whether the police possessed probable cause or reasonable suspicion, as the case may be.

B. *Did the police act on the basis of a search warrant and/or arrest warrant?* If the answer is "no," the sub-question is: *Did the police have a valid reason for failing to obtain a warrant?* As will be seen in chapter 10, *arrest* warrants are required only in very limited circumstances. *Search* warrants are required more often. However, their constitutional role has undergone considerable change—and dilution—over time (see chapters 11–18). When the issue is the absence of a search warrant, one must often consider various "exceptions" to the "warrant requirement."

If the answer to question 4B is "yes"—a warrant *was* issued—a number of sub-issues may arise: (i) *did the police obtain the warrant in a proper manner?*; (ii) *was the party issuing the warrant a neutral and detached magistrate?*; (iii) *was the warrant in proper form, e.g., does it satisfy the constitutional particularity requirement?*; and (iv) *did the police execute the warrant properly?* These matters are considered in chapter 11. Of course, there will also be the issue of whether the magistrate who issued the warrant was correct in her determination that there was probable cause for the police conduct. That issue, however, was considered above.

5. Assuming that the preceding questions justify the conclusion that the police conducted an unreasonable search or seizure in violation of *D*'s rights, the evidence in question *probably* is inadmissible. And, the violation may taint evidence obtained later in the criminal investigation. However, in order to determine admissibility, the following questions should be asked and answered. These matters are considered fully in chapter 21.

A. *Did the police conduct the search and/or seizure on the basis of a warrant later declared to be invalid?* If the answer is "yes," this implicates the so-called "good-faith" exception to the exclusionary rule, which requires determination of whether the officers executing the warrant acted on the basis of an objective good faith belief that the warrant was valid. If they did, the evidence is admissible, notwithstanding the invalidity of the warrant. If they did *not* act in objective good faith, the exclusionary rule applies.

B. Assuming the exclusionary rule applies, ask: *Is there evidence that is a fruit of the poisonous tree, i.e. was other evidence obtained due to the initial illegality?* If the answer is "yes," the "fruits of the poisonous tree" are also inadmissible, subject to two limiting doctrines: (i) the inevitable-discovery doctrine; and (ii) the attenuated-connection doctrine.

(Matthew Bender & Co., Inc.)                                                    (Pub.791)

CHAPTER **6**

# FOURTH AMENDMENT: "PERSONS, HOUSES, PAPERS, AND EFFECTS"

## § 6.01  Significance of the Constitutional Phrase

The Fourth Amendment provides that the "right of the people to be secure in their *persons, houses, papers, and effects*, against unreasonable searches and seizures, shall not be violated . . . ."[1]

There are two plausible ways to interpret the relationship between the italicized words and the prohibitory phrase, "unreasonable searches and seizures." First, the text could be (and has on occasion been[2]) interpreted to mean that government activity that does not impinge upon a "person, house, paper, or effect" is not a "search" or "seizure" within the meaning of the Fourth Amendment. Alternatively, and more plausibly as a textual matter, the language may inform us that the Fourth Amendment only prohibits "unreasonable searches and seizures" *of* "persons, houses, papers, and effects." That is, the latter phrase tells us *what* is protected by the Fourth Amendment, while the former phrase describes the nature of the protection provided.

Either interpretation leads to the same conclusion: police activity that does *not* involve a person, house, paper, or effect—whether the police activity is reasonable or unreasonable, conducted with or without a warrant, and whether supported by probable cause, reasonable suspicion, or no credible evidence at all—is lawful under the Fourth Amendment.

Very few cases turn on the meaning of this constitutional phrase. Occasionally, however, the Supreme Court defines a component of the phrase narrowly and, thus, rules that the contested government action falls outside the scope of the Fourth Amendment.

---

[1] Emphasis supplied.

[2] *E.g.*, Olmstead v. United States, 277 U.S. 438 (1928), *overruled by* Katz v. United States, 389 U.S. 347 (1967) (oral communication is not a "person, house, paper, or effect"; therefore, the tapping of telephone wires outside of a speaker's house or office is not a "search" or "seizure" of the conversation).

## § 6.02 "Persons"

The word "person" in the Fourth Amendment phrase "persons, houses, papers, and effects" includes: (1) *D*'s body, as a whole, such as when he is arrested;[3] (2) the exterior of *D*'s body (including his clothing), as when he is patted down for weapons or the contents of his clothing are searched;[4] and (3) the interior of *D*'s body, such as when blood is extracted to test for alcohol content.[5]

Early in the twentieth century, the Supreme Court held that the Fourth Amendment applied only to searches and seizures of material things. Based on that interpretation, oral communication was not a "person, house, paper, or effect"; therefore, warrantless electronic surveillance of conversations did not violate the Fourth Amendment.[6] The Court subsequently reversed itself[7] and construed the amendment's protection of "persons" to encompass electronic eavesdropping of their conversations.[8]

## § 6.03 "Houses"

"Houses" is broadly construed. It includes virtually all structures that people commonly use as a residence, whether on a temporary basis, such as a hotel room,[9] or on a long-term basis, such as an apartment.[10] It also encompasses buildings attached to the residence, such as a garage,[11] and even buildings that are not physically connected to the house if they are used for intimate activities of the home.

For constitutional purposes, the word "house" also includes the *curtilage* of the home, that is, "the area to which extends the intimate activity associated with the 'sanctity of a man's home and the privacies of life.' "[12] However, so-called "open fields," or unoccupied and undeveloped real property outside the curtilage of a home, are excluded.[13]

---

[3] *See, e.g.*, Chimel v. California, 395 U.S. 752 (1969).

[4] *See, e.g.*, Terry v. Ohio, 392 U.S. 1 (1968).

[5] *See, e.g.*, Schmerber v. California. 384 U.S. 757 (1966).

[6] Olmstead v. United States, 277 U.S. 438 (1928).

[7] Katz v. United States, 389 U.S. 347 (1967).

[8] Oliver v. United States, 466 U.S. at 176 n.6 (interpreting *Katz*).

[9] *See, e.g.*, Stoner v. California, 376 U.S. 483 (1964).

[10] *See, e.g.*, Clinton v. Virginia, 377 U.S. 158 (1964) (per curiam).

[11] *See, e.g.*, Taylor v. United States, 286 U.S. 1 (1932).

[12] Oliver v. United States, 466 U.S. at 180 (quoting Boyd v. United States, 116 U.S. 616, 630 (1886)).

[13] Hester v. United States, 265 U.S. 57 (1924); Oliver v. United States, 466 U.S. 170 (1984); see generally 1 Wayne R. LaFave, Search and Seizure § 2.4(a) (3d ed. 1996). The factors that distinguish a curtilage from an open field are considered at § 7.06[B], *infra*.

Offices, stores, and other commercial buildings are included within the term "houses,"[14] a conclusion that the Supreme Court has stated has "deep roots in the history of the Amendment."[15] However, this does not mean that the *scope* of Fourth Amendment coverage is the same: commercial structures are treated differently than residential property, primarily because one's expectations of privacy in the former are less than with homes.[16] The point is, simply, that commercial structures are encompassed within the Fourth Amendment and receive *some* constitutional protection.

## § 6.04   "Papers and Effects"

The term "papers" encompasses personal items, such as letters and diaries, as well as impersonal business records.[17]

The word "effects" represents the residual component of the constitutional phrase. For example, "effects" include automobiles, luggage and other containers, clothing, weapons, and even the fruits of a crime.[18] The term is less inclusive, however, than the word "property." In that light, the Supreme Court has determined that an "open field," which is not a "house," is also not an "effect."[19]

---

[14] *See, e.g.*, See v. City of Seattle, 387 U.S. 541 (1967); see generally 1 LaFave, Note 13, *supra*, at § 2.4(b).

[15] Oliver v. United States, 466 U.S. at 178 n.8.

[16] Minnesota v. Carter, 525 U.S. 83, 90 (1998); New York v. Burger, 482 U.S. 691, 700 (1987).

[17] *See, e.g.*, Andresen v. Maryland, 427 U.S. 463 (1976) (business records).

[18] *See, e.g.*, Chambers v. Maroney, 399 U.S. 42 (1970) (automobile); United States v. Chadwick, 433 U.S. 1 (1977) (luggage); United States v. Edwards, 415 U.S. 800 (1974) (clothing); Warden v. Hayden, 387 U.S. 294 (1967) (weapons, money from a robbery).

[19] Oliver v. United States, 466 U.S. at 177.

CHAPTER 7

# FOURTH AMENDMENT TERMINOLOGY: "SEARCH"

## § 7.01 Constitutional Significance of the Term "Search"

The Fourth Amendment prohibits unreasonable searches and seizures. This chapter considers the meaning of the word "search," and answers the question: when is a search not a "search"?[1]

"Search" is a technical term of art in Fourth Amendment jurisprudence. The word is not employed by lawyers in its ordinary and popular sense. At times, the difference between the lay and legal meaning of the word is so great that lawyers, including those sitting on the Supreme Court, find it difficult to avoid describing police activity as a "search," even as it is judged to be a "non-search" in the Fourth Amendment context.[2]

The importance of the question at hand cannot be overstated. A search may be reasonable or unreasonable—the Fourth Amendment may be satisfied or not satisfied—but if the police activity is not a "search" (or a "seizure," as that term is explained in the next chapter), *the Fourth Amendment simply does not apply to the case.* Put more starkly, if a court determines that no search or seizure occurred in a specific situation, Fourth Amendment analysis ceases at that point. As Judge Charles Moylan of the Maryland Court of Special Appeals bluntly put it, "the law does not give a constitutional damn" about non-search and non-seizure police activity.[3]

Consequently, in considering the law discussed in this chapter the reader should not lose sight of the fact that the question, "Was the Fourth Amendment satisfied?" is preceded by the threshold question, "Does the Fourth Amendment apply?" A court may answer the basic question

---

[1] *See* John M. Burkoff, *When Is a Search Not a "Search?": Fourth Amendment Doublethink*, 15 U. Tol. L. Rev 515 (1984).

[2] *See, e.g.*, Oliver v. United States, 466 U.S. 170, 173 (1984) (in which the Court framed the issue to be whether the "open fields" doctrine "permits police officers to . . .search a field," although the Court went on to hold, in part, that inspection of an open field is not a Fourth Amendment "search").

[3] Charles E. Moylan, *The Fourth Amendment Inapplicable vs. The Fourth Amendment Satisfied: The Neglected Threshold of "So What?"*, 1 So. Ill. U.L.J. 75, 76 (1977).

affirmatively—the conduct *is* a search, and, therefore, *is* governed by the Fourth Amendment—and yet still determine that the search was reasonable and, thus, constitutionally permissible. But, if a court answers the is-it-a-search question in the negative, any claim that the police acted without a warrant or without probable cause may be answered with the remark, "So what?" As Judge Moylan explained, "[w]hen the fourth amendment is inapplicable, good and evil have no relevance."[4]

## § 7.02 "Search": Original Pre-*Katz* Analysis

Fourth Amendment "search" analysis is divisible into two historical periods. In the first period, which ended in 1967 when the Supreme Court announced its landmark decision in *Katz v. United States*,[5] the Justices generally treated Fourth Amendment issues as a property-focused inquiry.

*Boyd v. United States*,[6] the first Supreme Court case seriously to consider the nature of the Fourth Amendment, laid the seeds of the property-rights interpretation of the amendment.[7] According to *Boyd*, the odious English practice of issuing general warrants, which authorized officials of the Crown to search and, often, ransack houses was "fresh in the memories" of the drafters of the Fourth Amendment.[8] The Court quoted extensively from the "memorable discussion" and condemnation of general warrants set out in *Entick v. Carrington*,[9] in which Lord Camden stated that "every invasion of private property, be it ever so minute, is a trespass."

According to Lord Camden, as quoted in *Boyd*, "[t]he great end for which men entered into society was to secure their property. That right is preserved sacred and incommunicable in all instances where it has not been taken away . . . by some public law for the good of the whole." The *Boyd* Court concluded from these remarks that "[i]t is not the breaking of his doors, and the rummaging of his drawers, that constitutes the essence of the [Fourth Amendment] offence; but it is the invasion of his indefeasible right of personal security, personal liberty, and private property. . . ."

Based on *Boyd*, the pre-*Katz* Fourth Amendment did not apply in the absence of a physical intrusion—a trespass—into a "constitutionally

---

[4] *Id.* at 75.

[5] 389 U.S. 347 (1967).

[6] 116 U.S. 616 (1886).

[7] *Boyd* also provided support for the privacy-oriented view of the Fourth Amendment that ultimately developed. *See* Tom Bush, Comment, *A Privacy-Based Analysis for Warrantless Aerial Surveillance Cases*, 75 Cal. L. Rev. 1767, 1789-91 (1987).

[8] *See also* § 5.03, *supra.*

[9] 19 Howell St. Tr. 1029, 1066 (1765) (Eng.).

protected area,"[10] most especially a "house," as that term was defined in the constitutional phrase, "persons, houses, papers, and effects."[11]

*Olmstead v. United States*[12] provides perhaps the most famous example of the Court's pre-*Katz* property rights/trespass approach to the Fourth Amendment. In *Olmstead*, federal officers, without obtaining a search warrant, used wiretaps to intercept the conversations of *D* and others, conducted by telephone from their homes and offices. The Court, per Chief Justice Taft, ruled that this conduct fell outside the reach of the Fourth Amendment.

The explanatory portion of the opinion was brief and unrevealing. The reasoning, however, came down to this: conversations are not "persons, house, papers, or effects," so they are unprotected;[13] the houses and offices from which the conversations arose *are* protected by the Fourth Amendment, but only from physical intrusions or trespasses; eyes and ears cannot "search" or "seize," as neither can trespass; and, the wiretaps used to listen to the conversations, which *can* trespass, did not do so here because they were installed on telephone lines *outside D*'s property.

In other pre-*Katz* decisions applying the trespass doctrine, the Supreme Court concluded that the use of a searchlight was not a "search," in essence because light cannot trespass.[14] It also held that no "search" occurs when an undercover agent consensually enters a criminal suspect's premises with a hidden transmitter[15] or tape recorder[16] on her body, and there engages the suspect in incriminating conversations, since the invited agent is not a trespasser.

On the other hand, in *Silverman v. United States*,[17] a "search" occurred when a spike-microphone inserted into a party wall intruded minutely into the speakers' side of the wall. The Justices observed, however, that the decision was not based on the fact that there was a "technical trespass under . . . local property law." The property-rights/trespass conception of Fourth Amendment "search" law was eroding.

---

[10] Lanza v. New York, 370 U.S. 139, 142 (1962).

[11] *See* § 6.03, *supra.*

[12] 277 U.S. 438 (1928), *overruled by* Katz v. United States, 389 U.S. 347 (1967).

[13] *See* § 6.02, *supra.*

[14] United States v. Lee, 274 U.S. 559 (1927).

[15] On Lee v. United States, 343 U.S. 747 (1952).

[16] Lopez v. United States, 373 U.S. 427 (1963).

[17] 365 U.S. 505 (1961).

## § 7.03 "Search": The Modern *Katz v. United States* Analysis[18]

### [A] The Fall of the Trespass Doctrine

*Katz v. United States*[19] is the seminal case in modern "search" law, indeed in Fourth Amendment jurisprudence generally. Although many critics of recent Supreme Court cases, including some members of the Court,[20] have accused the Justices of abandoning *Katz*'s underlying principles—and still other members of the Court are themselves critical of the *Katz* opinion itself[21] —contemporary Fourth Amendment analysis begins (if it does not ultimately end) with *Katz*, rather than with the property-rights/trespass approach discussed in the preceding section of this chapter.

In *Katz*, D was the subject of warrantless surveillance of his conversations by federal officers, who attached an electronic listening device to the outside of a telephone booth from which he conducted conversations. In light of the Court's original jurisprudence, the parties pressed their Fourth Amendment claims in terms of whether the telephone booth, like a house, was a "constitutionally protected area," and whether a physical intrusion of it was necessary to raise a Fourth Amendment "search" claim.

The Court rejected this line of analysis. With the advent of modern technology as it existed in the 1960s—and, thus, with the government's capacity electronically to intercept conversations without physical intrusion into any enclosure—the Court arrived at the view that the trespass doctrine constituted "bad physics as well as bad law."[22] Consequently, the Court announced "that the 'trespass' doctrine . . . can no longer be regarded as controlling."

### [B] Majority Opinion: In Search of a New Test

Justice Potter Stewart wrote the Court's opinion in *Katz*. One scholar has described the majority opinion as an "efficient dismantler, but neglectful

---

[18] *See generally* Anthony G. Amsterdam, *Perspectives On The Fourth Amendment*, 58 Minn. L. Rev. 349 (1974); Burkoff, Note 1, *supra*; Lewis R. Katz, *In Search of a Fourth Amendment for the Twenty-first Century*, 65 Ind. L.J. 549 (1990); Edmund W. Kitch, *Katz v. United States: The Limits of the Fourth Amendment*, 1968 Sup. Ct. Rev. 133; James J. Tomkovicz, *Beyond Secrecy for Secrecy's Sake: Toward an Expanded Vision of the Fourth Amendment Privacy Province*, 36 Hastings L.J. 645 (1985); Note, *A Reconsideration of the Katz Expectation of Privacy Test*, 76 Mich. L. Rev. 154 (1977).

[19] 389 U.S. 347 (1967).

[20] *E.g.*, Florida v. Riley, 488 U.S. 445, 456 (1989) (Brennan, J., dissenting, with whom Marshall and Stevens, JJ. joined, observing that the plurality opinion "reads almost as if *Katz* . . . had never been decided.").

[21] *See* Note 33, infra.

[22] *Katz*, 389 U.S. at 362 (Harlan, J., concurring).

reconstructor."[23] That is, *Katz* buried the trespass doctrine, but the majority opinion offered no evident test in its place. Although *Katz* "bestowed a controlling role upon privacy,"[24] Justice Stewart rejected "privacy" as a new talisman. In fact, he warned that "the Fourth Amendment cannot be translated into a general constitutional 'right to privacy.' That Amendment protects individual privacy against certain kinds of governmental intrusion, but its protections go further, and often have nothing to do with privacy at all."

Justice Stewart stated that "the Fourth Amendment protects people, not places." Although this statement is surely true—the Amendment begins with the phrase "[t]he right of the people"—it is less helpful than it might seem because, as Justice Harlan wisely observed in his concurring opinion, the ultimate "question . . . is what protection [the Fourth Amendment] affords to those people. Generally, . . . the answer to that question requires reference to a 'place.' "

Although Justice Stewart offered no bright-line definition of a "search," he did state in language that has proven quite important in post-*Katz* cases—if there is anything like a "test" in the majority opinion, it is this— that "[w]hat a person knowingly exposes to the public, even in his own home or office, is not a subject of Fourth Amendment protection," whereas "what he seeks to preserve as private, even in an area accessible to the public, may be constitutionally protected."

In this "knowing public exposure"/"seek to preserve as private" context, Justice Stewart distinguished in *D*'s situation in the telephone booth between the uninvited ear (the electronic bug) and intruding eyes. Because the telephone booth was made of glass, *D*'s physical actions were knowingly exposed to the public, but what he sought to exclude when he entered the booth was the uninvited ear. Therefore, by shutting the door on the booth and paying the toll, *D* was "surely entitled to assume that the words he utter[ed] . . . [would] not be broadcast to the world." As a result, "the Government's activities . . . violated the privacy upon which he justifiably relied. . . ."

### [C]  Concurring Opinion: A New "Search" Test

If Justice Stewart's opinion was devoid of a definition of a Fourth Amendment "search," Justice John Marshall Harlan's concurring opinion filled the void. He interpreted the case "to hold only" that a telephone booth, like a home, and unlike an open field, is an area in which "a person has a constitutionally protected 'reasonable expectation of privacy'. . . ."

---

[23] Tomkovicz, Note 18, *supra*, at 650–51.

[24] *Id.* at 651.

Although Justice Harlan asserted that this holding "emerged from prior decisions," it is this language from *Katz* that has survived as the operative definition—the new talisman—of a Fourth Amendment "search."

As Justice Harlan explained, the "reasonable expectation of privacy" standard has a subjective and an objective component. First, the individual must have "exhibited an actual (subjective) expectation of privacy." Second, she must prove[25] that the expectation she exhibited is one that "society is prepared to recognize as 'reasonable' " or—to use the Court's variants— "legitimate"[26] or "justifiable."[27]

Police conduct does not constitute a "search" if either prong of the test is lacking. For example, as Justice Harlan observed, if *D* in *Katz* had spoken "in the open" where he could have been overheard, rather than in the closed telephone booth that shut out the uninvited ears of others,[28] *D*'s subjective expectation of privacy would not have been reasonable under the circumstances. Therefore, *D* could not have claimed successfully that he was searched.

Similarly, *D* would not have had a valid "search" claim if he had realized that the telephone booth was bugged. Thus, although people *in general* may have a reasonable expectation of privacy in their telephone conversations, *D*'s subjective realization that his conversations were not private would have undermined his Fourth Amendment claim.

---

[25] *Katz* did not consider the question of who has the burden of proof in search cases. However, in Florida v. Riley, 488 U.S. 445 (1989), four Justices inferentially, at 451, and a fifth justice (Justice O'Connor) expressly, at 455, suggested that the defendant must provide facts that would support the claim that her expectation of privacy was reasonable. Four Justices dissented on this issue, at 465. In issues of standing—which the Court has equated to the was-there-a-search question, *see* § 20.01[B], *infra*—the Court has expressly held that the defendant "bears the burden of proving . . . that he had a legitimate expectation of privacy" in the item allegedly searched. Rawlings v. Kentucky, 448 U.S. 98, 104 (1980).

[26] *E.g.*, Illinois v. Andreas, 463 U.S. 765, 771 (1983).

[27] Smith v. Maryland, 442 U.S. 735, 740 (1979); *see also Katz*, 389 U.S. 347, 353 (1967) ("The Government's activities . . .violated the privacy upon which [*D*] justifiably relied . . . .").

[28] Suppose that *X*, a lip reader, had stood outside the booth and "listened" to *D*'s conversation? If *D* had observed *X* watching his lips, would he have had a reasonable expectation of privacy regarding *this* mode of interception of his conversation? Perhaps not, if *D* had understood that *X* was reading his lips. Under such circumstances, *D* "knowingly exposed" (to use Justice Stewart's language) his words to *X*; his conversations were "in the open" (to use Justice Harlan's words) insofar as *X* was concerned. As well, Stewart explicitly distinguished between "intruding eyes" and "uninvited ears." One could reason, therefore, that *Katz* stands for the proposition that a person may have a reasonable expectation of privacy regarding one mode of intrusion, and yet have none if the same information is intercepted in another manner. *See* § 7.04[B], *infra*.

## [D]  Analysis and Critique of the New Test

### [1]  Did We Need a New Test and Is This the Right One?

Should Justice Harlan have provided a new "search" definition? Professor Anthony Amsterdam has observed that Justice Stewart's opinion "was written to resist captivation in any formula."[29] The Court dismantled the prior law because it had become too rigid: thoughtful analysis had given way to formulas and talismans, such as "trespass." Therefore, according to this criticism, Harlan's "search" test violated the essence of *Katz* because it substituted one talisman for another.

Justice Harlan came to agree, at least in part, with this criticism. He later acknowledged that his expectations formula, although "an advance over the unsophisticated trespass analysis of the common law," also had its "limitations and can, ultimately, lead to the substitution of words for analysis."[30] Based on a survey of post-*Katz* Supreme Court decisions, especially the Court's treatment of the objective prong of the "search" standard, some critics would maintain that Justice Harlan's warning about his own test has proved prescient.[31]

Potential problems with the "reasonable expectation of privacy" test are set out below. But, there is a more basic question that may be asked at the outset: if the Court was going to provide a definition of the term "search," why did it not define it in an ordinary, common sense manner—perhaps it should have used an ordinary dictionary meaning[32] —and then focus on the Fourth Amendment prohibition on "unreasonable *searches* and seizures"?[33] According to this approach, courts would no longer be

---

[29] Amsterdam, Note 18, *supra*, at 385.

[30] United States v. White, 401 U.S. 745, 786 (1971) (dissenting opinion).

[31] See § 7.04, *infra*, for an overview of post-*Katz* search jurisprudence.

[32] Indeed, in an opinion authored by Justice Scalia, a *Katz* critic (*see* Note 33, *infra*), the Supreme Court recently stated that "[w]hen the Fourth Amendment was adopted, as now, to 'search' meant '[t]o look over or through for the purpose of finding something; to explore; to examine by inspection; as, to *search* the house for a book; to *search* the woods for a thief.' N. Webster, An American Dictionary of the English Language 66 (1828) (reprint 6th ed. 1989)." Kyllo v. United States, 121 S. Ct. 2038, 2043 n.1 (2001). It remains to be seen whether the Court will at some future time abandon the Harlan standard and define "search" in this manner.

[33] This seems to be what Justices Scalia and Thomas would like to do. Scalia has observed that "[w]hen that self-indulgent [*Katz*] test is employed . . . to determine whether a 'search or seizure' within the meaning of the Constitution has *occurred* (as opposed to whether that 'search or seizure' is an 'unreasonable' one), it has no plausible foundation in the text of the Fourth Amendment." Minnesota v. Carter, 525 U.S. 83, 97 (1998) (Scalia and Thomas, JJ., concurring).

concerned with the question, "[w]as the police action a search?"—almost all police investigations involve searches in the Webster's Dictionary sense of the term. Instead, the question would be the far more straightforward one, "[w]as the specific warrantless search conducted by the police a reasonable one?"

### [2] Should We Have the Subjective Prong?

Many commentators fault Justice Harlan for including a subjective prong in the expectations formula.[34] Their thesis is that if the subjective component is taken seriously, the government can eliminate privacy expectations—and, thus, render the Fourth Amendment inapplicable—by the simple act of announcing its intention to conduct Orwellian surveillance. Once people know that the government is reading their mail, listening to their conversations, and generally intruding on their privacy, they will possess no subjective expectation of privacy.[35]

Beyond this, *non*-government intrusions can undermine our right to be free of government intrusions. For example, technology makes it possible for private parties to track our movements electronically, as well as for corporations to discover private information about us by computer. Furthermore, increased crime and urbanization accustom us to a less private way of life. With these lesser expectations of privacy, the scope of our Fourth Amendment protections potentially narrows, which further increases the government's legal ability to invade individuals' privacy.[36]

Justice Harlan ultimately agreed with this criticism of his test. He concluded that the critical focus should be on *objective* expectations. Privacy analysis, he concluded, should "transcend the search for subjective expectations" because "[o]ur expectations . . . are in large part reflections of laws

---

[34] *E.g.*, Amsterdam, Note 18, *supra*, at 384; Burkoff, Note 1, *supra*, at 537–39; Wayne R. LaFave, *The Fourth Amendment Today: A Bicentennial Appraisal*, 32 Vill. L. Rev. 1061, 1080–81 (1987); Note, Note 18, *supra*, at 157–58.

[35] In this regard, *see* Joel Brinkley, *Israel in Uproar Over TV Report Confirming Existence of Secret Army Unit*, New York Times, June 24, 1991, at A3 (a military security film showing two Israeli soldiers disguised as Arabs catching a "Palestinian suspect" was shown on Israeli television; the stated purpose was "simply to scare the Arabs"; according to an Army spokesman, "Now they will be aware of the fact that nothing is secured. No one they see can be immediately identified as a friend or an enemy; they don't know; that's exactly [the atmosphere] we are trying to create").

[36] The same observation applies to Justice Stewart's "*knowing* exposure to the public" test. In view of modern technological and other incursions into citizens' private lives, virtually everyone *knowingly* exposes intimate and private details of their lives to others. Had Justice Stewart substituted the word "purposely" for "knowingly," the result would have been different, because "purposeful" exposure only occurs when it is the conscious motive of the individual to expose the information to others.

that translate into rules the customs and values of the past and present."[37] The task of the law, he noted, is "to form and project, as well as mirror and reflect."

The Court as a whole has acknowledged the potential danger inhering in the subjective prong. It has stated that if the situation should ever occur that a person's subjective expectations were " 'conditioned' by influences alien to well-recognized Fourth Amendment freedoms," the subjective element "obviously could play no meaningful role."[38] The Court has not elaborated on this remark.

### [3]    The Objective Prong: What *Precisely* Is The Standard?[39]

Justice Harlan stated in *Katz* that, in order for the Fourth Amendment to apply, the expectation exhibited by an individual must be one that "society is prepared to recognize as 'reasonable'." In the majority opinion, Justice Stewart stated that the electronic surveillance in that case violated the privacy upon which *D* "justifiably" relied in the telephone booth.[40] In stating or applying the objective prong, some post-*Katz* cases have also used the word "justifiable," and still others have employed the word "legitimate." The Court treats these words interchangeably, and yet a distinction arguably could be drawn between, on the one hand, "reasonable" expectations and, on the other hand, "legitimate" or "justifiable" ones. The potential distinction merits notice.

Typically, to say that a person's belief or expectation is "reasonable" means that her belief or expectation is one that an ordinary person would possess. In the privacy context, this would mean that an expectation of privacy is "reasonable" when a reasonable person would not expect that her privacy is at serious risk. So understood, "reasonableness" contains a significant empirical component, a "matter[] of statistical probability,"[41] *e.g.*, how likely is it that there will be a privacy incursion.

In contrast, to say that a person has a "legitimate" or "justifiable" expectation of privacy is to draw a normative conclusion—a value

---

[37] United States v. White, 401 U.S. 745, 786 (1971) (dissenting opinion).

[38] Smith v. Maryland, 442 U.S. 735, 740 n.5 (1979).

[39] *See generally* Christopher Slobogin & Joseph E. Schumacher, *Reasonable Expectations of Privacy and Autonomy in Fourth Amendment Cases: An Empirical Look at "Understandings Recognized and Permitted by Society"*, 42 Duke L.J. 727 (1993); Scott E. Sundby, *"Everyman" 's Fourth Amendment: Privacy or Mutual Trust Between Government and Citizen?*, 94 Colum. L. Rev. 1751 (1994); Note, Note 18, *supra*; Note, *From Private Places to Personal Privacy: A Post-Katz Study of Fourth Amendment Protection*, 43 N.Y.U. L. Rev. 968, 983 (1968).

[40] *See* Note 27, *supra*.

[41] LaFave, Note 34, *supra*, at 1081.

judgment—that she has a right to that expectation.[42] As one court has put it, the privacy protected by the Fourth Amendment under this view "is not the privacy that one reasonably *expects* but the privacy to which one has a *right*."[43] Professor Amsterdam has asked the normative question this way:

> [W]hether, if the particular form of surveillance practiced by the police is permitted to go unregulated by constitutional restraints, the amount of privacy and freedom remaining to citizens would be diminished to a compass inconsistent with the aims of a free and open society.[44]

Based on this distinction, a privacy expectation could be empirically "reasonable" and yet normatively "illegitimate" or "unjustifiable"; on the other hand, an "unreasonable" expectation of privacy could be "justifiable" or "legitimate." For example, suppose that D commits a crime in a secluded spot in a park during the middle of the night after carefully ascertaining that the area is frequented at that hour only once every 672 days. Based on this information, D expects that her actions will not be observed. That expectation might be "reasonable" in the sense that most persons would expect, as a matter of statistical probability, to be free from observation. Nonetheless, if a police officer happened by and observed the criminal conduct, commentators would likely agree with the Supreme Court that D's subjective privacy expectation should not be protected.[45] This is because D's expectations, although perhaps "reasonable," were "unjustifiable" or "illegitimate." That is, as a normative matter, people have no right to expect privacy if they conduct activities in the open, no matter how unlikely it is that they will be discovered on any given occasion.

On the other hand, suppose that D lives in a high-crime area in which police helicopters routinely hover at a very low altitude over the backyards of homes scanning the area. On a particular occasion, suppose that the helicopter comes down sufficiently low that the pilot observes a marijuana plant growing in D's backyard. As a matter of foreseeability, it would have been unreasonable for D to expect privacy in the heavily surveyed curtilage of her home. As a value judgment, however, it is an open issue as to whether this type of government conduct should be approved.[46]

---

[42] Note, Note 18, *supra*, at 155–56.

[43] State v. Campbell, 759 P.2d 1040, 1044 (Or. 1988).

[44] Amsterdam, Note 18, *supra*, at 403.

[45] This conclusion follows from Justice Harlan's remark in *Katz* that "conversations in the open would not be protected against being overheard, for the expectation of privacy under the circumstances would be unreasonable." As the words are being used in the text, Harlan should have said that the expectation would be "unjustifiable" or "illegitimate."

[46] For the Court's judgment in this regard, *see* § 7.08, *infra*.

Which form of analysis—empirical or normative—did Justice Harlan intend by his test? His concurring opinion in *Katz* provides no definitive answer. However, he described the objective component in terms of an expectation "that *society is prepared to recognize* as 'reasonable'." The italicized words may connote a normative inquiry.

Harlan's view became clearer after *Katz*. In a reflective post-*Katz* opinion, he placed himself definitively on the side of a normative interpretation of the objective prong. He stated that judges must determine "the desirability of saddling" people with particular risks to their privacy. He wrote that "[t]he critical question . . . is whether under our system of government, as reflected in the Constitution, we should impose on our citizens . . . [particular privacy] risks . . . without at least the protection of a warrant requirement."[47]

Justice Harlan's views notwithstanding, the Court's approach to the issue has been mixed. At times, it has stated that a normative inquiry is proper.[48] Other times, however, the Court has treated the empirical fact of privacy incursions—*e.g.*, that people trespass,[49] conduct aerial surveillance of residential backyards,[50] or look through other people's trash[51] —as justification for concluding that subjective expectations of privacy were unreasonable and, therefore, unprotected by the Fourth Amendment.

It is submitted here that Justice Harlan was correct in treating the issue normatively. If he is right, the critical question that remains is whether courts should attempt to determine *society's* normative judgment in regard to particular forms of surveillance, or whether it is the responsibility of the judges themselves (in the words of Justice Harlan) "to form and project, as well as mirror and reflect" privacy expectations. The benefit of researching public attitudes is that the normative judgment will not consist solely of the views of nine (or even five) justices on the United States Supreme Court.[52] The detriment in this approach is that the law may end up mirroring current attitudes, which have themselves been conditioned by prior

---

[47] United States v. White, 401 U.S. 745, 786 (1971) (dissenting opinion).

[48] *E.g.*, Smith v. Maryland, 442 U.S. 735, 740 n.5 (1979).

[49] *See* § 7.06, *infra*.

[50] *See* § 7.08, *infra*.

[51] *See* § 7.10, *infra*.

[52] *See* Minnesota v. Carter, 525 U.S. 83, 97 (1998) (Scalia and Thomas, JJ, concurring) ("In my view, the only thing the past three decades have established about the *Katz* test . . . is that, unsurprisingly, those 'actual (subjective) expectation[s] of privacy' 'that society is prepared to recognize as "reasonable"' bear an uncanny resemblance to those expectations of privacy that this Court considers reasonable.").

incursions authorized by the courts, rather than projecting a twenty-first century view of the proper relationship between the government and citizenry.[53]

## § 7.04 Post-*Katz* "Search" Jurisprudence: An Overview[54]

### [A] What Has *Katz* Wrought?

### [1] Subjective Prong

In Supreme Court Fourth Amendment "search" jurisprudence, the Court has generally found that the Fourth Amendment claimant possessed an expectation of privacy, was willing to assume that she did, or simply moved on without discussion to the objective prong.[55]

However, on at least two occasions the Court has suggested that the claimant's subjective expectation was not, or may not have been, present. In one case,[56] the Court did not seek to determine the defendant's subjective expectations, but rather expressed doubt that people "in general" would

---

[53] The Supreme Court has never sought to use reliable social science literature to determine public expectations of privacy. One study in this regard suggests that "the Supreme Court's conclusions about the scope of the Fourth Amendment are often not in tune with commonly held attitudes about police investigative techniques." Slobogin & Schumacher, Note 39, *supra*, at 774.

[54] *See generally* Burkoff, Note 1, *supra*; Melvin Gutterman, *A Formulation of the Value and Means Models of the Fourth Amendment in the Age of Technologically Enhanced Surveillance*, 39 Syracuse L. Rev. 647 (1988); John M. Junker, *The Structure of the Fourth Amendment: The Scope of the Protection*, 79 J. Crim. L. & Criminology 1105 (1989); Katz, Note 18, *supra*; Tracey Maclin, *Constructing Fourth Amendment Principles from the Government Perspective: Whose Amendment Is It, Anyway?*, 25 Am. Crim. L. Rev. 669 (1988); Brian J. Serr, *Great Expectations of Privacy: A New Model for Fourth Amendment Protection*, 73 Minn. L. Rev. 583 (1989); Christopher Slobogin, *Technologically-Assisted Physical Surveillance: The American Bar Association's Tentative Draft Standards*, 10 Harv. J. L. & Techn. 383 (1997); Slobogin & Schumacher, Note 39, *supra*; David E. Steinberg, *Making Sense of Sense-Enhanced Searches*, 74 Minn. L. Rev. 563 (1990); Sundby, Note 39, *supra*; Tomkovicz, Note 18, *supra*; Richard G. Wilkins, *Defining the "Reasonable Expectation of Privacy": An Emerging Tripartite Analysis*, 40 Vand. L. Rev. 1077 (1987); Daniel B. Yeager, *Search, Seizure and the Positive Law: Expectations of Privacy Outside the Fourth Amendment*, 84 J. Crim. L. & Criminology 249 (1993).

[55] *E.g.*, California v. Greenwood, 486 U.S. 35, 39 (1988) ("It may well be that respondents did not expect that the contents of their garbage bags would become known to the police or other members of the public."); Oliver v. United States, 466 U.S. 170, 177 (1984) (not discussing the subjective prong, and simply stating that "[t]he Amendment does not protect the merely subjective expectation of privacy . . . ."); United States v. White, 401 U.S. 745, 751 (1971) ("Very probably, individual defendants neither know nor suspect that their colleagues have gone or will go to the police or are carrying recorders or transmitters. Otherwise, conversation would cease . . . .").

[56] Smith v. Maryland, 442 U.S. 735 (1979). *See* § 7.07[A], *infra*.

possess a subjective expectation of the sort claimed by the defendant. In the other case,[57] the Court distinguished between a subjective "intent" or "hope" for privacy (which the defendant "clearly" possessed) and a subjective "expectation" (which the Court said was "not entirely clear" from the circumstances).

### [2]  Objective Prong

Most "search" litigation has focused on the objective component of Justice Harlan's *Katz* test. Although most legal observers immediately following *Katz* expected the Supreme Court to interpret the Fourth Amendment more broadly—and, thus, provide more protection of citizens—than it did during the pre-*Katz* trespass era, the reality has been the opposite. With a few notable exceptions, the Court has applied the objective prong strictly, often reaching a no-search conclusion.

At least three often interrelated factors have proved particularly important in "objective prong" analysis. First, the nature of the property inspected. Although Justice Stewart observed in *Katz* that the Fourth Amendment "protects people, not places," the reality is that (as the Court sees it) the extent to which a person has a reasonable expectation of privacy is significantly tied to the place where the police activity occurred. For example, as discussed in this chapter, "open fields" fall outside the protection of the Fourth Amendment, the "curtilage" of a person's home is entitled to somewhat greater protection, and activities within the home are rather strictly protected.[58]

Second, the extent to which a person has taken measures to keep information, her property, or an activity private is vital. In this context, two rules are frequently asserted: (1) a rule drawn from Justice Stewart's majority opinion in *Katz* is that person cannot possess a reasonable expectation of privacy in that which she knowingly exposes to the public or is in open view;[59] and (2) one who voluntarily conveys information or property to another person assumes the risk that the latter individual is a

---

[57] California v. Ciraolo, 476 U.S. 207 (1986). *See* § 7.08[B], *infra*.

[58] *See* Payton v. New York, 445 U.S. 573, 590 (1980) (the Fourth Amendment draws "a firm line at the entrance to the house"); Kyllo v. United States, 121 S. Ct. 2038, 2043 (2001) (noting in "search" analysis that it is "difficult" to determine the proper line of protection when dealing with "telephone booths, automobiles, or even the curtilage and uncovered portions of residences," but stating that the interior of a home "is a ready criterion, with roots deep in the common law, of the minimal expectation of privacy that *exists* and that is acknowledged to be *reasonable*").

[59] To a considerable extent, this factor simply restates the previous factor: one has a more reasonable expectation of privacy if she keeps property hidden in the interior of one's residence than if she leaves it outside the home.

government agent or will transmit the information or property to the government. The effect of the latter "limited exposure" doctrine is that "the fourth amendment is eliminated from a great many aspects of modern life. The Court requires the individual who seeks full . . . protection to live an isolated life within his house with the shades drawn."[60]

Third, the degree of intrusion experienced by the police activity is relevant. For example, whether very low-altitude aerial surveillance of the backyard of a person's home by helicopter constitutes a "search" may depend on whether the helicopter causes noise and dust, thereby disrupting legitimate activities therein.[61]

Similarly, police surveillance that provides only very limited information to the government, such as whether a locked suitcase contains illegal drugs, but which provides no further information as to its contents, is more likely to be considered a "non-search" than surveillance techniques that provides intimate information about the individual. However, in light of the special protections accorded to persons in their homes, the Supreme Court recently declared that "the Fourth Amendment's protection of the home has never been tied to measurement of the quality or quantity of information obtained [by the government]. . . In the home, . . . *all* details are intimate details . . . ."[62]

### [B] Lurking Issues Worth Keeping In Mind

Various interrelated "search" questions are worthy of consideration in evaluating the Supreme Court's post-*Katz* jurisprudence discussed in the remainder of this chapter. First, how should the Court resolve the issue raised earlier[63] regarding the difference between an empirically "reasonable" expectation of privacy and a normatively "legitimate" or "justifiable" one?

Second, to what extent should the *mode* of government intrusion matter to search analysis? Should the Court conclude that a citizen may have a reasonable expectation of privacy regarding one form of intrusion or mode of surveillance, even if she does not have such an expectation as to another? For example, suppose that two persons are performing a sexual act in an open stall in a public restroom. Should we conclude that they have no reasonable expectation of privacy if an officer enters the bathroom and observes them, but that they maintain a legitimate expectation that the government will not observe them from a more clandestine vantage point,

---

[60] Katz, Note 18, *supra*, at 568.

[61] *See* § 7.08[C], *infra*.

[62] Kyllo v. United States, 121 S. Ct. at 2045

[63] *See* § 7.03[D][3], *supra*.

such as through a peephole in the back wall or by use of a hidden overhead camera?[64] The Court's consideration of this issue has not been consistent. For example, in one case,[65] the Supreme Court suggested, in part, that a person does not have an objectively reasonable expectation of privacy from visual observations made by trespassing into an open field because the same observations are possible by lawful aerial surveillance. And yet the Court recently stated that "[t]he fact that equivalent information could sometimes be obtained by other means does *not* make lawful the use of means that violate the Fourth Amendment."[66] Indeed, in *Katz*, it will be remembered, Justice Stewart distinguished between the metaphorically uninvited ear in the telephone booth and intruding eyes.

Third, should it matter *who* intrudes on our privacy? Should we say that a person may have a legitimate expectation of privacy from government intrusion, even though she may not have a similar expectation of freedom from private invasions? For example, should we be permitted to assume that government agents will not inspect our garbage without a warrant, even if we know that our neighbors or the homeless might sift through our trash?[67] Or, should a property owner who knows that her land is often the subject of unlawful trespass by private individuals be allowed to maintain a legitimate expectation of privacy from similar trespasses by police officers?[68]

As you consider these questions, students of search law might also ask themselves whether the reasonable-expectation-of-privacy test should be discarded. Does it meet the needs of the technologically enhanced twenty-first century? If the rule should be abandoned, what should replace it? Should Fourth Amendment jurisprudence be concerned less with privacy *per se*, and more interested in some other value?[69] Should the Court simply

---

[64] *E.g.*, People v. Triggs, 506 P.2d 232 (Cal. 1973) (police observation from a hidden "plumbing access area" of activities in a doorless public toilet stall constitutes a "search"), *overruled on other grounds*, People v. Lilienthal 587 P.2d 706 (Cal. 1978); *see* State v. Bonnell, 856 P.2d 1265 (Haw. 1993) (in which the court applying the state constitution, but defining "search" in *Katz*-ian terms, stated that the mode of governmental intrusion is a relevant factor in determining whether a person maintains a reasonable expectation of privacy; therefore, the police conducted a "search" when they secretly videotaped activities in a room used by public employees during their work breaks, although the room was not private and could be entered freely by anyone). *See also* Note 28, *supra*.

[65] Oliver v. United States, 466 U.S. 170 (1984); *see* § 7.06, *infra*.

[66] Kyllo v. United States, 121 S. Ct. 2038, 2043 n.2 (2001) (emphasis added).

[67] For the Court's answer to this question, *see* § 7.10, *infra*.

[68] For the Court's answer to this question, *see* § 7.06, *infra*.

[69] *See* § 5.03, *supra*, for suggestions of two alternative visions of the Fourth Amendment.

use a dictionary definition of "search" and, thereby, shift the issue in most cases from "Was it a search?" to "Was the search reasonable?"?[70]

## § 7.05 Surveillance of Conversations By "False Friends"[71]

### [A] "False Friends" versus *Katz*

*Katz v. United States*[72] involved electronic monitoring by the government of private conversations to which neither of the speakers consented. That is, while D and X spoke on the telephone, unbeknownst to either, government agents listened to their conversations. *Katz* concluded that the speakers had a reasonable expectation of privacy in their telephone conversations. Therefore, the government was required to conduct the search in a constitutionally reasonable manner by obtaining a search warrant to conduct electronic eavesdropping.

*Katz* must be distinguished from cases in which the police acquire a suspect's statements without electronically monitoring her conversations, or by monitoring them with the consent of the other party. Two categories of cases of this sort are the subject of this section. Both involve situations in which X, a police informant or covert ("undercover") police agent, insinuates herself into D's confidence in order to elicit incriminating information from D. In such circumstances, X might be termed a "false friend" of D, essentially a visible "bug" with an invisible purpose.

In the first category of false-friend cases—the plain version—D makes statements to X, or makes statements to another person in X's known presence. X gathers the information from D by listening, and then reports the statements to other police officers.

The second category might be termed the "wired false friend" cases, which differ from the first scenario in that the "friend," X, also has in her possession a hidden transmitter that permits the police simultaneously to monitor their conversations, or has with her a hidden tape recorder that registers D's words.

### [B] False Friends

No "search" occurs if X, a police informant or undercover agent who is visibly present but is masquerading as D's friend, business associate, or

---

[70] *See also* § 7.03[D][1], *supra*.

[71] *See generally* Tracey Maclin, *Informants and the Fourth Amendment: A Reconsideration*, 74 Wash. U.L.Q. 573 (1996); Slobigin, Note 54, *supra*; Geoffrey R. Stone, *The Scope of the Fourth Amendment: Privacy and the Police Use of Spies, Secret Agents, and Informers*, 1976 Am. B. Found. Res. J. 1193; H. Richard Uviller, *Evidence from the Mind of the Criminal Suspect: A Reconsideration of the Current Rules of Access and Restraint*, 87 Colum. L. Rev. 1137 (1987).

[72] 389 U.S. 347 (1967).

colleague in crime, listens to and reports to the government $D$'s statements to $X$ or to another person in $X$'s presence. Prior to *Katz*, the Supreme Court invoked an "assumption of the risk" doctrine to reach this conclusion; after *Katz*, it reaffirmed this rule but framed its reasoning in expectation-of-privacy terms.

In the leading pre-*Katz* false-friend case, *Hoffa v. United States*,[73] $D$ conversed with $X$ in $D$'s hotel suite. $X$ was an acquaintance of $D$, but at the time of their conversations the Supreme Court assumed that $X$ was serving as a paid government informant. The government sought to introduce $D$'s statements at his later trial.

The Court rejected $D$'s claim that his statements were obtained in violation of the Fourth Amendment. The Justices held that although the hotel room in which the conversations arose was a constitutionally protected area, "no interest legitimately protected by the Fourth Amendment [was] involved" because $D$ "was not relying on the security of the hotel room; he was relying upon his misplaced confidence that [$X$] would not reveal his wrongdoing."

The lesson of *Hoffa* is that when a person voluntarily speaks to another, *i.e.*, deliberately reveals her mental impressions to a second person, she assumes the risk that the listener is not whom she claims to be—a friend—or is a friend who will ultimately betray her. According to the Court, such a possibility is "inherent in the conditions of human society. It is the kind of risk we necessarily assume whenever we speak."

*Hoffa* was reaffirmed after *Katz* in *United States v. White*.[74] According to *White*, *Katz* left the holding of *Hoffa* "undisturbed," but the Court restated *Hoffa* in "*Katz*ian" terms, stating that a person does not have "a justifiable and constitutionally protected expectation that a person with whom he is conversing will not then or later reveal the conversation to the police."

*Hoffa* and *White* may be defended on this ground: whereas a person can control the extent to which she gives up her privacy in her home, she cannot similarly control her privacy regarding her thoughts once she has disclosed them to another. That is, $D$ can admit $X$ into her home, and yet remain fully protected from unreasonable entry by others. When $D$ discloses her thoughts to $X$, however, she cannot selectively surrender them. She "necessarily entrust[s] the recipient with complete control over their dissemination, relying wholly on [the] listener's discretion."[75]

---

[73] 385 U.S. 293 (1967).

[74] 401 U.S. 745 (1971).

[75] Uviller, Note 71, at 1198.

Despite this justification, the Court's holdings in *Hoffa* and *White* are controversial for various reasons. First, people doubtlessly must assume the risk that their friends will later betray them, as this possibility always exists in interpersonal relations. It does not necessarily follow, however, that people should be expected to assume the risk in a free society that their "friends" are government agents at the moment they speak.

Second, one critic has argued that the false-friend rule jeopardizes the conversational confidentiality "necessary for the maintenance of personal autonomy and the development of creative individuality."[76] He contends that if a person must assume the risk of disclosure of her private comments, she cannot "discard [her] social mask, blow off steam, and disregard minor social conventions." Intimacy is lost, for its essence is the sharing of feelings and ideas not revealed to the public as a whole. Arguably, therefore, government-initiated seizure of conversations should ordinarily be forbidden unless a search warrant is obtained.[77]

Notwithstanding these criticisms, as well as the not inconsiderable risk—and reality—that some police informants will fabricate conversations,[78] the Supreme Court has consistently upheld the use of covert government agents to conduct conversational surveillance. The Justices' tolerance of this investigative technique is likely founded on their pragmatic recognition of the fact that the use of "false friends" is essential to the detection of otherwise inaccessible information about crime.[79]

---

[76] Stone, Note 71, *supra*, at 1233.

[77] But, these criticisms have a largely *First* Amendment texture to them.

[78] The risk is not small because, as one prosecutor observed about informants, "[t]hey are scum, the underbelly of the system. Informants will not testify because they are nice guys. . . . [W]e are trading something for something." Robert Reinhold, *California Shaken Over an Informer*, New York Times, Feb. 17, 1989, at 1; *e.g., A Snitch's Story: In L.A., an Informer Blows the Whistle—On Himself*, Time Magazine, Dec. 12, 1988, at 32 (informant admitted to concocting false confessions in as many as 120 criminal cases resulting in convictions).

[79] Uviller, Note 71, *supra*, at 1199. In a companion case to *Hoffa*, the Supreme Court ruled that the Fourth Amendment was not violated when *X*, a federal agent, misrepresented his identity and purpose and thereby obtained an invitation to *D*'s home, where an illegal narcotics sale occurred in his presence. Lewis v. United States, 385 U.S. 206 (1966). The Court held that *X*'s testimony regarding the sale was admissible because his activities inside *D*'s premises remained within the scope of *D*'s invitation. Chief Justice Warren observed that "[w]ere we to hold the deceptions of the agent in this case constitutionally prohibited, we would come near to a rule that the use of undercover agents in any manner is virtually unconstitutional *per se*."

### [C]  "Wired" False Friends

Prior to *Katz*, the fact that a false friend was "wired" with a transmitter or tape recorder was irrelevant to "search" analysis. As long as the agent did not trespass, no search occurred.[80]

*Katz* left this rule undisturbed. In *United States v. White*,[81] the Court held that there is no constitutional difference between the plain false-friend case, in which *X* converses with *D* and then testifies at trial as to her recollection of the conversation, and the situation in which *X* uses the more reliable technique of recording the conversation, or where she carries a microphone that transmits the conversation to other agents who can then corroborate *X*'s testimony. To the Court, the "wired" false-friend doctrine follows simply, almost inevitably, from the pure false-friend doctrine: "[i]f the law gives no protection to the wrongdoer whose trusted accomplice is or becomes a police agent [as in *Hoffa*], neither should it protect him when the same agent has recorded or transmitted the conversations which are later offered in evidence to prove the State's case."

Justice Harlan dissented in *White*. He accepted the *Hoffa* false-friend doctrine, but he believed that the practice of monitoring conversations undermined "that confidence and sense of security with one another that is characteristic of individual relationships between citizens in a free society." He reasoned that people will measure their words more carefully if they fear that their conversations are being transmitted to third persons than they will in an ordinary false-friend situation. The fear of bugging, he predicted, will "smother that spontaneity—reflected in frivolous, impetuous, sacrilegious, and defiant discourse—that liberates daily life."

## § 7.06   Open Fields[82]

### [A]  Rule

Entry into and exploration of so-called "open fields" does not amount to a "search" within the meaning of the Fourth Amendment. This "open-fields doctrine," first announced by the Supreme Court prior to *Katz*,[83] was reaffirmed by it in *Oliver v. United States*.[84]

---

[80] *See* Notes 15–16, and accompanying text, *supra*.

[81] 401 U.S. 745 (1971) (plurality opinion); *but see* State v. Blow, 602 A.2d 552 (Vt. 1991) (rejecting in part the rule in *White*, holding that electronic participant monitoring conducted in a person's home offends the core values of the state constitution and, therefore, ordinarily require a search warrant).

[82] 1 Wayne R. LaFave, Search and Seizure § 2.4(a) (3d ed. 1996).

[83] Hester v. United States, 265 U.S. 57 (1924).

[84] 466 U.S. 170 (1984); *contra under the state constitution,* Barnard v. State, 124 So. 479 (Miss. 1929) (an open field is subject to protection); People v. Scott, 593 N.E.2d 1328

*Oliver* involved two cases in which officers without search warrants entered private property, ignored "No Trespassing" signs, walked around either a locked gate or a stone wall, and there they observed marijuana plants that were not visible from outside the property.

The Supreme Court, per Justice Lewis Powell, held that people do not have a legitimate expectation of privacy in activities occurring in open fields, even if the activity could not be observed from the ground except by trespassing in violation of civil or criminal law.[85] According to *Oliver*, the Fourth Amendment reflects the constitutional framers' belief that certain "enclaves," such as a house, should be free from governmental interference. In contrast, "open fields do not provide the setting for those intimate activities that the Amendment is intended to shelter from government interference or surveillance." The Court stated that "[t]here is no societal interest in protecting the privacy of those activities, such as cultivation of crops, that occur in open fields."

Furthermore, as a practical matter, open fields usually are accessible to the public and the police in ways that homes and offices are not. The Court observed that "No Trespassing" signs do not effectively bar intruders. Moreover, the same activities that police officers observe by trespassing can be observed lawfully by air. Therefore, any expectation that a home-owner may have in her open fields is not one that society is prepared to recognize as reasonable.

### [B] "Open Field" versus "Curtilage"

*Oliver* did not define the term "open field," but it did state that it "may include any unoccupied or undeveloped area outside the curtilage." It also stated that it "need be neither 'open' nor a 'field' as those terms are used in common speech."

---

(N.Y. 1992) (*id.*); Welch v. State, 289 S.W. 510 (Tenn. 1926); State v. Kirchoff, 587 A.2d 988 (Vt. 1991) (*id.*); State v. Myrick, 688 P.2d 151 (Wash. 1984) (*id.*); *see also* State v. Bullock, 901 P.2d 61 (Mont. 1995) (holding that a person may have an expectation of privacy in an open field, and that where that expectation is evidenced by fencing, a "no trespassing" sign, or by some other means that unmistakably indicates that entry is not permitted, entry by law enforcement requires consent or a warrant); State v. Dixson, 766 P.2d 1015 (Or. 1988) (*id.*).

[85] The Court also held that an open field falls outside the scope of the "persons, houses, papers, and effects" language of the Fourth Amendment. *See* §§ 6.03-.04, *supra*.

An issue not decided by the Court in *Oliver* or since is whether a person may retain a reasonable expectation of privacy regarding the interior of a structure, such as a barn, found in an open field. The Court has only assumed *arguendo* that a search occurs if an officer, while in an open field, enters a structure, where she then observes activities not visible from outside. United States v. Dunn, 480 U.S. 294, 303 (1987).

Distinguished from an open field is the "curtilage," which is entitled to Fourth Amendment protection, although not as much as is accorded to the interior of a home.[86] The curtilage is "the land immediately surrounding and associated with the home." At common law it is the "area to which extends the intimate activity associated with the 'sanctity of a man's home and the privacies of life.' "[87]

As set out in *United States v. Dunn*,[88] four factors are relevant in determining whether land falls within the curtilage: (1) the proximity of the land to the home; (2) whether the area is included within enclosures surrounding the house; (3) the nature of the use to which the area is put; and (4) the steps taken by the resident to protect the land in question from observation.

For example, in *Dunn*, *D* owned a ranch enclosed by a fence. Another fence surrounded *D*'s ranch house. Approximately 50 yards beyond the latter fence were two barns, each enclosed by its own fence. A federal officer, who had received information that *D* was producing illegal drugs on his property, climbed over *D*'s perimeter fence and an interior fence. The officer smelled an acidic odor commonly associated with drug production emanating from the barns. He climbed over the barn fences and, without entering the structures, peered in. He observed incriminating evidence in one barn.

The Court determined that the barns were not within the curtilage of the ranch house: they were 60 yards from it, and 50 yards outside the fence surrounding the house; the officer had objective evidence that the barns were not being used for intimate, home-related, activities; and the Court did not believe that *D* took sufficient steps to prevent observation into the barn from the open-field vantage point.

### [C]   Criticism of the Doctrine

*Oliver* is a controversial decision. Various criticisms of the opinion merit note, especially because they raise broader questions about Fourth Amendment "search" jurisprudence. First, the Court resolved the issue by providing a bright-line rule—*i.e.*, an expectation of privacy in an open field is never legitimate. It might have chosen to resolve the question on a case-by-case basis, by holding that a person may have a legitimate expectation of privacy in an open field in some cases, depending on such circumstances as the use to which the land is being put, and the methods taken to protect privacy.

---

[86] *See* the text to Note 58, *supra; see also* § 7.08, *infra.*

[87] *Oliver*, 466 U.S. at 180 (quoting Boyd v. United States, 116 U.S. 616, 630 (1886)).

[88] 480 U.S. 294 (1987).

The Justices rejected this approach because they believed it would provide police officers insufficient guidance.

However, even if a bright-line rule is preferable to case-by-case adjudication, a matter of considerable importance and controversy,[89] the Court could have drawn an alternative bright line. The dissenters suggested that a better rule would have been: "Private land marked in a fashion sufficient to render entry thereon a criminal trespass under the law of the state in which the land lies is protected by the Fourth Amendment. . . ." It should be remembered that such a rule would not bar police entry onto open fields; it would simply render the Fourth Amendment applicable to the case: the police could still enter with a search warrant or if they had good reason not to secure one.

Second, the Court justified its conclusion that an expectation of privacy in an open field is unreasonable, in part on the ground that people frequently trespass on open fields. But, this raises a basic question: Should the foreseeability or actuality of criminal wrongdoing undercut the privacy rights of citizens? At a minimum, perhaps the appropriate question the Court ought to have asked is whether people have a right to expect that law enforcement officers, as distinguished from private persons, will obey criminal laws and respect property rights.

Third, *Oliver* is based in part on the ground that, since the police may observe an open field lawfully from the air, the Fourth Amendment is not violated by entry on foot. In short, the Court does not distinguish here between the *means* of governmental intrusion. Yet, such a distinction might have been intended in *Katz* when Justice Stewart distinguished between "the intruding eye . . . [and] the uninvited ear."[90]

## § 7.07 Technological Information Gathering[91]

### [A] In General

The Supreme Court shifted away from the trespass doctrine in *Katz v. United States* in considerable part because, as Justice Harlan put it then, the trespass doctrine constituted "bad physics as well as bad law."[92] Technology had reached the point that the trespass doctrine no longer served

---

[89] *See* § 2.07[A], *supra.*

[90] *See* § 7.04[B], *supra.*

[91] *See generally* Clifford S. Fishman, *Technologically Enhanced Visual Surveillance and the Fourth Amendment: Sophistication, Availability, and the Expectation of Privacy,* 26 Am. Crim. L. Rev. 315 (1988); Gutterman, Note 54, *supra;* Slobogin, Note 54, *supra;* Steinberg, Note 54, *supra.*

[92] 389 U.S. 347, 362 (1967) (Harlan, J., concurring).

as a meaningful limitation on governmental intrusion, since by 1967 it was possible for the police to intercept conversations without ever trespassing on private property. But, of course, the technology of 1967 pales in comparison to that which has developed in the past few decades, thus placing increasing pressure on the reasonable-expectation-of-privacy doctrine.

The Supreme Court long ago ruled in *United States v. Lee*[93] that the use of a flashlight or searchlight to observe in the dark what would be visible to the naked eye in the light does not constitute a search. Although *Katz* adopted a new Fourth Amendment "search" standard, Justice Stewart cited *Lee* in support of his "knowingly exposes to the public" standard.[94]

*Lee* equated searchlights to binoculars (what *Lee* called "a field glass"), which suggests that the Court also saw no constitutional obstacle to the police using devices that *magnify* a distant object that is otherwise in plain view. Indeed, the Court later (but pre-*Katz*) remarked in dicta in *On Lee v. United States*[95] that "[t]he use of bifocals, field glasses or the telescope to magnify the object of a witness' vision is not a forbidden search or seizure, even if they focus without his knowledge or consent upon what one supposes to be private indiscretions." In short, *One Lee* teaches that the sighting of an object in plain view from a lawful vantage point—even if this sighting occurs through the use of binoculars or other magnifying devices—does not constitute a search.

In the post-*Katz* era, the Supreme Court has been willing to stand by this pre-*Katz* law. For example, in *Dow Chemical Co. v. United States*,[96] agents of the Environmental Protection Agency seeking evidence against Dow photographed its 2000-acre industrial complex from altitudes of 1,200 to 12,000 feet with the use of what the Court described as a "standard, floor-mounted, precision aerial mapping camera." The Court did not treat this surveillance as a search because "[h]ere, EPA was not employing some unique sensory device that, for example, could penetrate the walls of buildings and record conversations in Dow's plants, offices, or laboratories, but rather was using a conventional, albeit precise, commercial camera commonly used in mapmaking." The Court stated in dicta, however, that "surveillance of private property by using highly sophisticated surveillance equipment not generally available to the public . . . might be constitutionally proscribed absent a [search] warrant."

---

[93] 274 U.S. 559 (1927).

[94] *See* § 7.03[B], *supra*.

[95] 343 U.S. 747, 754 (1952).

[96] 476 U.S. 227 (1986).

When the police use modern technology to gather information, the *Katz* doctrine seemingly requires a court to consider the nature of the technology used (does it permit the government to "see" what would otherwise be invisible to the naked eye, even in daylight, from a lawful vantage point) and the nature of the place being observed (is it an open field, the curtilage of a home, commercial property as in *Dow Chemical*, or the interior of a home).

The subsections below consider the Court's treatment of various forms of modern technology, some used to provide information to the police about activities going on in private residences, and other times to survey less private areas. As will be seen in subsection [D], the Court recently determined in *Kyllo v. United States* [97] that it needed to devise rules to take into account that sophisticated technology, now or in the future, may allow the government to "see" through walls and other opaque barriers. *Kyllo* promises to be an exceedingly important case in the Court's effort to avoid having to conclude that the *Katz* standard, like the predecessor trespass doctrine, constitutes bad physics as well as bad law. As will be noted below, *Kyllo* calls into question the Court's treatment of pen registers, the subject of the next subsection. [98]

### [B]  Pen Registers [99]

The Supreme Court held in *Smith v. Maryland* [100] that the installation and use of a pen register by the telephone company, at the behest of the government, to record the telephone numbers dialed from a private residence is not a "search" within the meaning of the Fourth Amendment.

The Court distinguished pen registers from the electronic surveillance that occurred in *Katz*. In *Katz*, a telephone booth was bugged in order to permit the police to acquire the *contents* of private communications. Pen registers, however, have a far more limited capacity, in that they only disclose the telephone numbers dialed. The device does not inform its user what was said, or even if a conversation occurred; nor are the identities of the persons called disclosed. Thus, the narrow issue, as the *Smith* Court put it, was whether the defendant "had a 'legitimate expectation of privacy' regarding the numbers he dialed on his phone."

---

[97] 533 U.S. 27 (2001).

[98] *See* Note 115, *infra.*

[99] 1 LaFave, Note 82, *supra,* at § 2.7(b).

[100] 442 U.S. 735 (1979); *contra under the state constitution,* People v. Sporleder, 666 P.2d 135 (Colo. 1983); State v. Rothman, 779 P.2d 1 (Haw. 1989); State v. Thompson, 760 P.2d 1162 (Idaho 1988); State v. Hunt, 450 A.2d 952 (N.J. 1982); Commonwealth v. Melilli, 555 A.2d 1254 (Pa. 1989); Richardson v. State, 865 S.W.2d 944 (Tex. Crim. App. 1993); State v. Gunwall, 720 P.2d 808 (Wash. 1986).

*Smith* discussed both elements of the "search" test. First, it expressed doubt "that people in general entertain any actual expectation of privacy in the numbers they dial." The Justices reasoned that telephone users know that they convey the numbers they are dialing to the telephone company, and they know that the phone company has the capacity to record this information, because customers see a list of toll calls on their monthly bills.[101] Also, the Court observed, "[a]lthough most people may be oblivious to a pen register's esoteric functions, they presumably have some awareness"—from notices in phone books—"of one common use: to aid in the identification of persons making annoying or obscene calls." Therefore, the Court inferred that, "[a]lthough subjective expectations cannot be scientifically gauged, it is too much to believe" that telephone users harbor subjective privacy expectations regarding the numbers they call. Consequently, the Court concluded, "in all probability" the defendant entertained no actual expectation of privacy in the numbers he dialed.

The Court did not rest there, and chose to move to the objective prong of the *Katz* test. It concluded that even if the defendant *did* harbor a subjective expectation of privacy regarding the phone numbers he dialed, this expectation was unreasonable. Citing the false-friend conversational surveillance cases[102] and *United States v. Miller*,[103] it concluded that a person has no legitimate expectation of privacy in any information that she voluntarily turns over to third parties. By knowingly exposing information (the numbers dialed) to a third party (here, the telephone company), the telephone user assumes the risk that it will be transmitted to law enforcement agents.

The dissenters distinguished the false-friend cases from pen registers. They argued that a person can "exercise some discretion in deciding who should enjoy his confidential communications." In contrast, people have no choice in modern society but to use telephones. Moreover, the dissent reasoned that "[p]rivacy is not a discrete commodity, possessed absolutely

---

[101] Even if the Court was right in this global assumption, it seems doubtful that most people at the time of *Smith* knew that the telephone company registered *uncompleted* phone calls (*i.e.*, numbers dialed in which the customer received a busy signal, nobody answered the telephone, or the caller prematurely hung up), as such calls—toll or otherwise—were not listed on monthly phone bills.

[102] *See* § 7.05, *supra.*

[103] 425 U.S. 435 (1976). In *Miller*, the Court held that a bank customer has no legitimate expectation of privacy in financial information that she "voluntarily conveys" to bank employees in the ordinary course of business. No search occurs, therefore, if the bank hands over the customer's financial records to the government. *Contra under the state constitution*, People v. Jackson, 452 N.E.2d 85 (Ill. 1983); Commonwealth v. De John, 403 A.2d 1283 (Pa. 1979); State v. Thompson, 810 P.2d 415 (Utah 1991).

or not at all." The rule should not be that if one discloses information to a telephone company, that individual assumes the risk that the facts will be disclosed to the rest of the world for other purposes.

Although the majority considered the information disclosed by pen registers relatively non-intrusive—mere phone numbers called (but from a private home!), and not the conversations themselves—the dissenters found the "prospect of unregulated governmental monitoring . . . disturbing even to those with nothing illicit to hide. Many individuals, including members of unpopular political organizations or journalists with confidential sources, may legitimately wish to avoid disclosure of their personal contacts."

### [C]  Electronic Tracking Devices[104]

Police officers increasingly use "beepers" to track the movement of suspects. A "beeper" is a small battery-operated device that can be installed in a suspect's vehicle or in some object that the suspect will have in her possession, which emits periodic radio signals that can be picked up by officers in police cars, airplanes, or helicopters. *Installation* of such a device in or on the suspect's property raises a "seizure" issue.[105] *Use* of the device to monitor the suspect's movements raises a "search" question. The Court's "beeper cases" have focused less on the nature of the device used and more on the site of the information disclosed by the beeper.

In *United States v. Knotts*,[106] federal officers suspected *D* of manufacturing drugs. Without obtaining a warrant, they installed a beeper in a chemical drum that they knew would be sold to *D*. With the assistance of the beeper, the officers followed *D*'s automobile as he drove from one state to another. At one point, due to *D*'s evasive maneuvers, the police ended visual surveillance of the vehicle. They also temporarily lost the signal from the beeper, but they later regained contact with it by helicopter. The signal indicated that the chemical drum was located outside a certain cabin. Based on this information, the police secured a warrant to search the cabin. *D* reasoned that the warrant was invalid because critical information used to obtain the warrant was secured unconstitutionally, *i.e.*, as the result of electronic surveillance conducted without a warrant.

The Supreme Court held the use of the beeper did not constitute a search and, therefore, no warrant was required to monitor *D*'s movements. The Court focused on two interrelated factors. First, the beeper did not provide

---

[104] 1 LaFave, Note 82, *supra*, at § 2.7(e).

[105] *See* § 8.02[B], *infra*.

[106] 460 U.S. 276 (1983); *contra under the state constitution*, State v. Campbell, 759 P.2d 1040 (Or. 1988).

the police with any information that they could not have secured by visual surveillance from public places along the route. In essence, *D* knowingly exposed to others the information of his movements by driving on public roads. The fact that a beeper was used instead of visual surveillance did not alter the analysis—the mode of surveillance was irrelevant. [107] Second, the beeper had "limited use" in this case: it did not reveal information as to *D*'s movements within any private place, such as within the cabin.

The latter distinction proved significant in *United States v. Karo*. [108] In *Karo*, the beeper allowed the police to monitor the movement of a container of chemicals inside various homes as well as in public places. The information secured in this manner was used to obtain a warrant to search a house for drug-related evidence. The Court held that the Fourth Amendment protected against use of the beeper located inside the house. It observed that "[i]ndiscriminate monitoring of property that has been withdrawn from public view would present far too serious a threat to privacy interests in the home to escape entirely some sort of Fourth Amendment oversight."

*Knotts* and *Karo* suggest a few intriguing points about Fourth Amendment "search" analysis. First, the implication of *Knotts* is that as long as monitoring is limited to movements of persons in non-private areas, the government is free to conduct constant surveillance of citizens. The *Knotts* Court, aware of this troubling implication, observed that "if such dragnet-style . . . practices . . . should eventually occur, there will be time enough then to determine whether different constitutional principles may be applicable."

Second, the suggestion in *Knotts* that *D* did not have a legitimate expectation of privacy because the officers could have obtained the same information by visual surveillance, obscures the fact that "to learn what the beeper revealed . . . would have taken an army of bystanders in ready and willing communication with one other" along the route traveled. [109] The implication of *Knotts* is that as long as it is hypothetically conceivable (although, in some cases, nearly impossible practically) to obtain information in a non-technologically-enhanced manner from a lawful vantage point, it is irrelevant that, instead, the government uses an electronic tracking device to obtain the same information.

---

[107] On the mode-of-intrusion issue, *see* § 7.04[B], *supra*.

[108] 468 U.S. 705 (1984).

[109] LaFave, Note 34, *supra*, at 1082.

## [D]  Thermal Imagers

As the Supreme Court explained in *Kyllo v. United States*,[110] a thermal imager is a device that can "detect infrared radiation, which virtually all objects emit but which is not visible to the naked eye. The imager converts radiation into images based on relative warmth. . . . [I]n that respect, it operates somewhat like a video camera showing heat images."

In *Kyllo*, a federal agent, suspicious that *K* was using high-intensity lamps in his home to grow marijuana, used a thermal imager to scan the triplex in which *K* lived. The agent conducted the imaging from his vehicle across the street from *K*'s residence. The scanning showed that the roof of the garage and a side wall of *K*'s home were substantially warmer than the rest of the building. Based on this information and other evidence, the agent obtained a warrant to search the residence. The issue in *Kyllo*, as Justice Scalia put it for the Court, was "whether the use of a thermal-imaging device aimed at a private home from a public street to detect relative amounts of heat within the home constitutes a 'search' within the meaning of the Fourth Amendment."

By a vote of 5-4, the Court answered the question in the affirmative and, in the process, announced a new rule to deal with technological advances in existence or in development[111] —that may impinge on the privacy of home dwellers. The majority, quoting language from the pre-*Katz* era *Silverman*[112] case, stated that

> [w]e think that obtaining by sense-enhancing technology any information regarding the interior of the home that could not otherwise have been obtained without physical "intrusion into a constitutionally protected area," *Silverman* . . ., constitutes a search—at least where (as here) the technology in question is not in general public use.

In such circumstances, the police presumptively need a warrant to use the technology. Moreover, the Court hinted in a footnote that it might in some later case reexamine the not-in-general-use limitation on the rule.

Justice Scalia used the opportunity of *Kyllo* again[113] to criticize the *Katz* test as "circular, and hence subjective and unpredictable," and one that may

---

[110] 533 U.S. 27 (2001).

[111] Justice Scalia conceded that the technology used in the present case was "relatively crude." But, citing a Department of Justice website, he noted that the "ability to 'see' through walls and other opaque barriers is a clear, and scientifically feasible, goal of law enforcement research and development."

[112] Silverman v. United States, 365 U.S. 505 (1961).

[113] *See* Note 33, *supra.*

answer the wrong question.[114] He stated that it is "difficult" to refine the *Katz* test in the context of telephone booths, curtilages of homes, and automobiles, but "in the case of the search of the interior of homes . . . there is a ready criterion, with roots deep in the common law." Again quoting the *Silverman* case, the majority stated that " '[a]t the very core' of the Fourth Amendment 'stands the right of a man to retreat into his own home and there be free from unreasonable governmental intrusion.' "

But, what about the fact that thermal imagers only detect relative heat emanations from the home and not intimate details about life inside the dwelling? The Court's answer, in language likely to be quoted often in the future, was: "[i]n the home . . . all details are intimate details, because the entire area is held safe from prying government eyes."[115] According to Scalia, "[t]he Fourth Amendment's protection of the home has never been tied to measurement of the quality or quantity of information." A "search" occurs if there is "any physical invasion of the structure of the home, 'by even a fraction of an inch',"[116] or if a police officer "barely cracks open the front door and sees nothing but the nonintimate rug on the vestibule floor," or, as seen in *United States v. Karo*,[117] the beeper-in-a-cabin case, if "the only thing detected is a can of ether in the home."

The dissenters would have distinguished between "through-the-wall" surveillance—the type Justice Scalia fears in the future—and "off-the-wall" surveillance. Justice Stevens, author of the dissent, explained:

> [T]his case involves nothing more than off-the-wall surveillance . . . to gather information exposed to the general public from the outside of petitioner's home. All that the infrared camera did . . . was passively measure heat emitted from the exterior surfaces of [*K*'s] home. . . . [N]o

---

[114] "One might think that . . . examining the portion of a house that is in plain public view, while it is a 'search' despite the absence of trespass, is not an 'unreasonable' one under the Fourth Amendment. . . . But in fact we have held that the visual observation is no 'search' at all . . . ."

[115] This language seemingly undercuts the holding of the Court in Smith v. Maryland, 442 U.S. 735 (1979), the pen register case discussed in subsection [A]. There, it will be remembered, the Court distinguished between the *contents* of private conversations—which *Katz* protects—and the supposedly more limited information (the phone numbers called from within a home) provided by a pen register. If the police can use a pen register to obtain phone numbers—perhaps, as the dissent in *Smith* hypothesized, the phone numbers of unpopular political organizations or the confidential sources of journalists—being called by a home-dweller, it should surely be permissible to use a thermal imaging device to determine relative heat emanations from a home. Or, put another way, assuming the Court intends to stand by *Kyllo*, the Court should reconsider *Smith*.

[116] The Court again cited the pre-*Katz Silverman* case for this proposition.

[117] 468 U.S. 705 (1984). *See* § 7.07[C], *supra*.

details regarding the interior of [*K*'s] home were revealed. Unlike an x-ray scan, or other possible "through-the-wall" techniques, the detection of infrared radiation emanating from the home did not accomplish "an unauthorized physical penetration into the premises," nor did it "obtain information that it could not have obtained by observation from outside the curtilage of the house."

In reasoning not dissimilar to that found in *United States v. Knotts*,[118] the beeper-on-the-highway case, Justice Stevens explained that with "ordinary use of the senses" a neighbor could observe the heat emanating from the building, if (as here) it was vented; furthermore, "any member of the public might notice that one part of a house is warmer than another part . . . if, for example, rainwater evaporates or snow melts at different rates across its surfaces."[119] Thus, to the dissent, the imager provided information to the police that came "off the wall" and not through it; all the police did is use that information (and tips they had received elsewhere) to *infer* what was taking place inside.

## § 7.08 Aerial Surveillance[120]

### [A] Rule

As explained more fully below, non-sense-enhanced aerial surveillance by the government of activities occurring within the curtilage of a house does not constitute a search if the surveillance: (1) occurs from public navigable airspace; (2) is conducted in a physically nonintrusive manner; and (3) does not reveal intimate activities traditionally connected with the use of a home or curtilage.[121]

### [B] Surveillance by Airplanes

In *California v. Ciraolo*,[122] *O*, a police officer, received an anonymous tip that *D* was growing marijuana in his backyard. *O* attempted to observe

---

[118] 460 U.S. 276 (1983). *See* § 7.07[C], *supra.*

[119] Justice Scalia responded in *Kyllo* that "[t]he fact that equivalent information could sometimes be obtained by other means does not make lawful use of means that violate the Fourth Amendment. The police might, for example, learn how many people are in a particular house by setting up year-round surveillance; but that does not make breaking and entering to find out the same information lawful." Thus, Scalia is drawing a mode-of-intrusion distinction. *See* § 7.04[B], *supra.* In contrast, the Supreme Court in *Oliver v. United States*, *see* § 7.06, *supra*, *justified* trespassing in open fields, in part on the ground that the police could have obtained the same information lawfully by aerial surveillance, *i.e.*, by a different mode of intrusion.

[120] *See generally* 1 LaFave, Note 82, *supra*, at § 2.3(g); Bush, Note 7, *supra*; Fishman, Note 91, *supra*; Steinberg, Note 54, *supra*.

[121] California v. Ciraolo 476 U.S. 207 (1986); Florida v. Riley, 488 U.S. 445 (1989).

[122] 476 U.S. 207 (1986).

*D*'s yard from ground-level but was thwarted by a six-foot-high outer fence and a ten-foot-high inner fence. Therefore, *O* obtained a private plane to fly over the backyard at an altitude of approximately 1,000 feet, which was within public navigable airspace according to Federal Aviation Administration (F.A.A.) regulations. From that vantage point, *O* observed marijuana plants in *D*'s backyard.

The Supreme Court held that the aerial surveillance of *D*'s backyard, an area that the Court agreed was within the curtilage of the house, did not constitute a search. Regarding the subjective prong of the *Katz* test, Chief Justice Warren Burger stated that "[c]learly . . . [*D*] has met the test of manifesting his own subjective intent and desire to maintain privacy as to his unlawful agriculture." Remarkably, however, this did not necessarily satisfy the subjective prong, for all that the ten-foot-high fence demonstrated is *D*'s "intent and desire" to maintain privacy; it did not necessarily demonstrate his *expectation* of such privacy.

The Court pointed out that the fence "might not shield these plants from the eyes of a citizen or a policeman perched on the top of a truck or a 2-level bus."[123] Therefore, the Court stated that it was "not entirely clear" whether *D* maintained a "subjective expectation of privacy from *all* observations of his backyard," or only from ground-level observations. The implication from this comment may be that one cannot satisfy the first prong of *Katz* unless the person has an expectation of privacy regarding all modes of surveillance possible under the circumstances.

The Court also held that the second prong of the expectation-of-privacy standard was not satisfied. Chief Justice Burger observed that police officers need not shield their eyes from information or activities knowingly exposed to them, even in the curtilage of a house. And, the fact that a person has taken measures to restrict some views of her activities within the curtilage does not preclude the police from observing them from a public vantage point where they have a right to be.

According to *Ciraolo*, a person is not entitled to assume that what she grows in the backyard will not be observed in a nonintrusive manner by passing aircraft in public airspace or, for that matter, "by a power company repair mechanic on a pole overlooking the yard." The Court stated that "[i]n an age where private and commercial flights in the public airways is routine," it was unreasonable for *D* to expect privacy from the air.

*Ciraolo* has been criticized on various grounds. First, this case points up the problem of determining privacy expectations in an empirical, rather

---

[123] There were no such buses in the community in which the surveillance occurred. Wayne R. LaFave, *The Forgotten Motto of Obsta Principiis in Fourth Amendment Jurisprudence*, 28 Ariz. L. Rev. 291, 298 (1986).

than normative, manner.[124] The Court essentially holds that the Fourth Amendment does not protect citizens from aerial snooping in public airspace because airplane flights over private property are common. This fact of modern life, however, does not answer the question of whether a person should have a *right* to expect privacy in this regard, *at least from government surveillance.*

Second, the Court equates the unfocused, momentary observations of a private party sitting in the window seat of a commercial airplane with the focused, less-brief observations—indeed, surveillance—of a trained police officer involved in a criminal investigation. There seems little doubt that the two cases are not similar to the average person; the degree of privacy intrusion is much greater in the latter case than in the former.

Third, the practical message of the case is that one who wishes to retain Fourth Amendment privacy rights in her backyard must cover or enclose it. Yet, this destroys the value and purpose of the curtilage, which is to maintain the privacies of the home, but in an outside venue.

### [C] Surveillance by Helicopters

In *Florida v. Riley*,[125] the Supreme Court applied the reasoning of *Ciraolo* to inspections by helicopter, which allow for much lower-altitude surveillance. In *Riley*, *O*, an officer in a police helicopter, observed marijuana plants growing in *D*'s within-the-curtilage greenhouse, which was missing two roof panels. In order to observe the inside of the structure, *O* descended to an altitude of 400 feet, which would have been impermissible under F.A.A. regulations if the flight had occurred in a fixed-wing aircraft, but which was lawful for helicopter flights.

The Supreme Court held, 5-4, that the police action was not a search. Justice White's four-Justice plurality opinion stated that *D* knowingly exposed his greenhouse to the surveillance because "any member of the public could legally have been flying over [*D*'s] property in a helicopter at the altitude of 400 feet and could have observed [his] greenhouse." He observed that private and commercial helicopter flights in public airways are routine, and *D* offered no evidence—the burden was on *D* to prove— "that such flights [were] unheard of" in the vicinity of his house.

But, the plurality opinion contained considerable limiting language. Justice White indicated that it "would have [been] a different case if flying at that altitude had been contrary to law or regulation." The implication of this remark is that the surveillance would have constituted a search if

---

[124] *See* § 7.03[D][3], *supra.*

[125] 488 U.S. 445 (1989).

an airplane rather than a helicopter had surveyed *D*'s greenhouse from precisely the same vantage point. In short, the mode of intrusion—the type of flying machine used—would have mattered in this case.

Justice White also warned that "an inspection of the curtilage of a house from an aircraft will [not] always pass muster under the Fourth Amendment simply because the place is within navigable airspace specified by law." He suggested that the result might have been different if there had been "any intimation that the helicopter interfered with [*D*'s] normal use of the greenhouse or of other parts of the curtilage." The plurality considered it significant that the record did not reveal that "intimate details connected with the use of the home or curtilage were observed, and there was no undue noise, no wind, dust, or threat of injury."

This language is intriguing. Why should it matter whether the officer spots marijuana crops or, instead, observes "intimate" activities in the curtilage of the home?[126] Can the Court possibly mean that if the same helicopter had observed the contents of the greenhouse as well as consensual but illegal sexual acts in the backyard, the surveillance would have been a "search" of one but not of the other activity? Yet, as the Court frequently observes, the police need not shield their eyes to activities visible to them from vantage points where they have a right to be. Nor is it clear why helicopter-caused dust, as an example, triggers a privacy right that is not otherwise implicated. This harkens back, as the dissenters pointed out, to the pre-*Katz* "intrusion" and "trespass" concepts of the Fourth Amendment.[127]

Justice O'Connor, who concurred in the judgment, and the four dissenters in *Riley*, minimized the significance of the lawfulness of the helicopter flight. The issue to them was not whether the flight was lawful, or even whether *police* helicopter flights at 400 feet were common, but rather whether, as Justice O'Connor phrased the issue, "members of the public travel with sufficient regularity [at such low altitudes] that [*D*'s] expectation of privacy from aerial observation" was unreasonable. In other words, five Justices in *Riley* apparently believed that a person may have a reasonable expectation of privacy regarding *police* aerial surveillance, regardless of frequency, if *non-police* helicopter flights (in general, as distinguished from flights over the specific individual's curtilage) are rare.

---

[126] Kyllo v. United States, 533 U.S. 27 (2001), discussed in § 7.07[D], *supra*, teaches that *in the home* "all details are intimate details." In the curtilage, however, the Court may draw distinctions.

[127] *See also id.*, in which the Court frequently cited pre-*Katz* language to support its holding that use of a thermal imager to detect heat escaping from a home constitutes a search.

## § 7.09 Dog Sniffs and Other Tests for Contraband[128]

In *United States v. Place*,[129] Drug Enforcement Agency (D.E.A.) agents seized luggage belonging to *D*, a deplaning airline passenger whom they suspected of drug possession, and subjected it to a "sniff test" by a dog trained to discover narcotics. The dog "reacted positively" to one piece of luggage.

The Supreme Court was anxious to resolve the validity of this type of investigatory procedure. Although resolution of the issue was unnecessary to the decision, and the matter had not been briefed or argued in the Court, the Justices declared that the dog sniff in this case—critically limited to "exposure of [*D*'s] luggage, which was located in a public place, to a trained canine"[130] —did not constitute a search.

The Court focused on two facts. First, the information was secured in a comparatively nonintrusive manner: the luggage, observed in a public

---

[128] *See generally* 1 LaFave, Note 82, *supra*, at § 2.2(f); Hope Walker Hall, Comment, *Sniffing Out the Fourth Amendment: United States v. Place—Dog Sniffs—Ten Years Later*, 46 Me. L. Rev. 151 (1994); Steinberg, Note 54, *supra*.

[129] 462 U.S. 696 (1983); *contra under the state constitution*, Pooley v. State, 705 P.2d 1293 (Alaska Ct. App. 1985) (dog sniff of luggage constitutes a search, requiring reasonable suspicion); People v. Boylan, 854 P.2d 807 (Colo. 1993) (*id.*, dog sniff of a private express courier package); People v. Cox, 739 N.E.2d 1066 (Ill. App. 2000), *appeal granted*, 747 N.E.2d 354 (Ill. 2001) (dog sniff of a vehicle is a search, requiring reasonable suspicion); State v. Pellicci, 580 A.2d 710 (1990) (*id.*); Commonwealth v. Martin, 626 A.2d 556 (Pa. 1993) (dog sniff of a person is a search, requiring probable cause); *see also* Note 130, *infra*.

[130] This limitation is significant. The holding of *Place* only reaches the use of a dog to smell for contraband in a public area. It is an open issue whether the Fourth Amendment applies to the use of a dog to sniff the exterior of private enclaves, such as a house. Various courts, applying their respective state constitutions, have rejected *Place* in such circumstances. *See* McGahan v. State, 807 P.2d 506 (Alaska Ct. App. 1991) (dog sniff of the exterior of a commercial building is a search, requiring reasonable suspicion); State v. Ortiz, 600 N.W.2d 805 (Neb. 1999) (*id.*, dog sniff of an apartment residence from the hallway); People v. Dunn, 564 N.E.2d 1054 (N.Y. 1990) (*id.*); Commonwealth v. Johnston, 530 A.2d 74 (Pa. 1987) (*id.*, dog sniff of a storage place); State v. Dearman, 962 P.2d 850 (Wash. 1998) (use of a trained narcotics dog to detect marijuana growing in the defendant's garage constitutes a "search").

The Supreme Court might reach a similar conclusion. In Kyllo v. United States, 533 U. S. 27 (2001), *see* § 7.07[D], *supra*, the Court ruled that police use of sense-enhancing "technology" to secure information regarding activities in the interior of a home that could not have been obtained without physical intrusion into the dwelling constitutes a search (at least where the technology in question is not in general public use). "Dog sniffing," of course, is not "technology," but it *is* sense-enhancing, in that specially trained dogs can smell contraband in circumstances in which human beings cannot. The *Kyllo* Court's exceedingly strong language about the sanctity of the home may prove important in any post-*Place* case dealing with the use of a dog outside a home, to sniff for contraband *inside* a residence.

area, was not opened and, thus, noncontraband items were never exposed to the public eye. Second, the information revealed by the test was extremely limited, as "the sniff discloses only the presence or absence of narcotics, a contraband item." The Court observed that "the canine sniff is *sui generis*. We are aware of no other investigative procedure that is so limited both in the manner in which the information is obtained and in the content of the information revealed by the procedure."

Dog sniffs soon proved not to be *sui generis*. In *United States v. Jacobsen*,[131] a D.E.A. agent conducting a drug investigation came upon white powder in a plastic bag belonging to *D*. Because the agent suspected that it was cocaine, he conducted an on-the-scene test: he placed a small amount of the powder in three test tubes containing liquids; the liquids took on a certain sequence of colors, which confirmed that the powder was cocaine.

The Supreme Court, in a conclusion "dictated" by *Place*, ruled that any chemical test that "merely discloses whether or not a particular substance is cocaine does not compromise any legitimate interest in privacy," and is, therefore, not a search. As Congress has determined that private possession of certain items is illegitimate, "government conduct that can reveal whether a substance is [contraband], and no other arguably 'private' fact, compromises no legitimate privacy interest." In contrast, if a substance is not tested to determine if it is contraband, but rather to find out whether it contains evidence of a person's use of contraband, the test is a search.[132]

## § 7.10   Inspection of Garbage[133]

The Supreme Court held in *California v. Greenwood*[134] that a person has no reasonable expectation of privacy in garbage enclosed in a bag and left for collection outside the curtilage of her home. No search occurs, therefore, when an officer opens a trash bag left at the curb and sifts through its contents.

In *Greenwood*, the Court conceded that *D*, the homeowner whose garbage was inspected by the police, might have had a subjective expectation that the trash bag would not be opened by the police or the public. However, it concluded that *D*'s Fourth Amendment claim failed on objective grounds,

---

[131] 466 U.S. 109 (1984).

[132] Skinner v. Railway Labor Executives' Ass'n, 489 U.S. 602 (1989) (tests of blood and urine for evidence of drug usage is a "search").

[133] *See generally* 1 LaFave, Note 82, *supra*, at § 2.6(c).

[134] 486 U.S. 35 (1988); *contra under the state constitution*, State v. Hempele, 576 A.2d 793 (N.J. 1990) (police may *seize* a garbage bag left for collection without a warrant or probable cause, but a warrant is required to *search* its contents).

because "it is common knowledge" that plastic garbage bags left on the curb for pickup "are readily accessible to animals, children, scavengers, snoops, and other members of the public."

In light of this common knowledge, the Court invoked two related "search" rules. First, applying *Katz* and the aerial surveillance decisions,[135] it stated that the Fourth Amendment does not protect information knowingly exposed to the public. Second, citing *Smith v. Maryland*,[136] the pen register case, it noted that one cannot have a reasonable expectation of privacy in information voluntarily turned over to others.

However, *Greenwood* goes further than the cases the Court cited. In those cases, the individuals exposed *information* to others (by conducting activities in an area visible to aircraft, and by making telephone calls, the numbers of which were being recorded by the telephone company). In *Greenwood*, D only knowingly exposed the *container* that enclosed the information. As the dissent pointed out, D did not "flaunt[] his intimate activity" by exposing the contents of his trash.

Essentially, under *Greenwood*, D's expectation of privacy was illegitimate because of, as the dissent put it, the "mere *possibility* that unwelcome meddlers [might] open and rummage through the containers." That is, because private persons *might* snoop, individuals have no constitutionally recognized reasonable expectation of privacy when and if the police—not private persons—*in fact* snoop. But, if that is enough to render the Fourth Amendment inapplicable, the dissenters asked rhetorically, would the Court suggest that "the possibility of a burglary negates an expectation of privacy in the home[?]"

---

[135] *See* § 7.08, *supra.*

[136] 442 U.S. 735 (1979), discussed at § 7.07[A], *supra.*

## CHAPTER 8

# FOURTH AMENDMENT TERMINOLOGY: "SEIZURE"

## § 8.01  Constitutional Significance of the Term "Seizure"

This chapter defines the term "seizure." Unlike the word "search," which has a single constitutional definition, the word "seizure" has two definitions, one relating to property, and the other to seizures of persons. As is the case with searches, the issue of whether police conduct constitutes a seizure is a matter of threshold significance: unless the police action is a "seizure" (or a "search"), the restrictions of the Fourth Amendment do not apply.

Assuming that police conduct constitutes a seizure, the remaining constitutional issue is whether it was reasonable. With property, this means that the police must often have a search warrant, based on probable cause, or a justification for not securing the warrant.[1] In the case of seizure of persons, the police must have adequate cause to seize the individual and, in the case of an arrest in a home, must usually have an arrest warrant.[2] In the case of arrests or other seizures tantamount to an arrest, probable cause is required.[3] With less intrusive seizures, a lesser standard— reasonable suspicion—is satisfactory, and in relatively few circumstances, the police may lawfully briefly seize a person without any suspicion at all.[4]

## § 8.02  Seizure of Property

### [A]  General Rule

In contrast to a search, which affects a person's privacy interest, a seizure of property invades a person's possessory interest in that property.[5] Tangible[6] property is "seized" in Fourth Amendment terms "when there

---

[1] *See especially* chapter 11, *infra.*

[2] *See* § 10.05, *infra.*

[3] *See* §§ 9.01 (arrests), 10.03[A] (*id.*), and 18.04 (seizures tantamount to arrests), *infra.*

[4] *See, e.g.,* §§ 18.01–.03 (*Terry* detentions, explained), 19.03 (border seizures), 19.04 (vehicle-use searches and seizures), and 19.05 ("special needs" searches and seizures), *infra.*

[5] Texas v. Brown, 460 U.S. 730, 747 (1983) (Stevens J., concurring).

[6] The Supreme Court originally ruled that the Fourth Amendment applied only to searches

is some meaningful interference with an individual's possessory interests in that property."[7]

A "seizure" occurs when a police officer exercises control over $D$'s property by destroying it,[8] or by removing it from $D$'s actual or constructive possession.[9] A house or office and its contents are "seized" when an officer secures the premises, *i.e.*, prevents persons from entering and taking away or destroying personal property.[10] On the other hand, no "seizure" occurs when an officer merely picks up an object to look at it or moves it a small distance, because any interference with $D$'s possessory interest in such circumstances is not "meaningful."[11]

## [B]  Installation of Electronic Devices On or In Personal Property

The installation of an electronic device on or in personal property, in order to monitor a person's movements or to intercept conversations, can raise difficult "seizure" issues. At least in some contexts, installation of an electronic device is not a seizure. For example, in *United States v. Karo*,[12] federal agents learned that $D$ intended to obtain ether from $X$, a merchant, for use in the production of illegal drugs. With $X$'s consent, the agents installed an electronic "beeper" inside an ether can that $X$ agreed to transfer to $D$, so that the agents could monitor $D$'s movements as he transported the can in an automobile.[13]

The Court held that the placement of the device in the can was not a seizure, since the container at the time of installation did not belong to $D$,

---

and seizures of material things, which excluded conversations; but the word "person" in the phrase "persons, houses, papers and effects" is now interpreted to encompass an individual's conversations. *See* § 6.02, *supra*. Current constitutional law treats the act of monitoring a conversation as both a search and seizure of the words. *See* Berger v. New York, 388 U.S. 41 (1967).

[7] United States v. Jacobsen, 466 U.S. 109, 113 (1984).

[8] *Id.* at 124–25.

[9] *E.g.*, United States v. Place, 462 U.S. 696 (1983) (detention of $D$'s luggage for 90 minutes in order to take it from La Guardia Airport to JFK Airport to permit a trained narcotics dog to smell it).

[10] Illinois v. McArthur, 531 U.S. 326 (2001).

[11] *See, e.g.*, Arizona v. Hicks, 480 U.S. 321 (1987) (officer slightly moved stereo equipment in order to read a serial number on the back: no "seizure" issue raised); New York v. Class, 475 U.S. 106 (1986) (officer slightly moved a piece of paper in $D$'s car to see underneath: no "seizure" issue raised); Texas v. Brown, 460 U.S. 730 (1983) (officer moved a balloon a few feet in order to better view its contents: no "seizure" issue raised).

[12] 468 U.S. 705 (1984).

[13] Regarding the *monitoring* of $D$'s movements by means of the electronic device, as distinguished from its *installation*, see § 7.07[C], *supra*.

and thus did not invade *his* possessory interests in it.[14] More controversially, the Court also held that no seizure occurred when the "beeper"-infested can was transferred to *D* by *X*. According to the Court, "[a]lthough the can may have contained an unknown and unwanted foreign object, it cannot be said that anyone's possessory interest was interfered with in a meaningful way."

Justice Stevens, joined by Justices Brennan and Marshall, dissented from this conclusion. They contended that a possessory interest in property includes the right to exclude others from it, which was meaningfully interfered with the moment the can was transferred to *D* with the monitoring device secreted inside. As the dissent put it, "the character of the property is profoundly different when infected with an electronic bug than when it is entirely germ free."

## § 8.03   Seizure of Persons[15]

### [A]   Overview

The arrest of a suspect uncontroversially constitutes a "seizure" of that person.[16] In 1968, however, the Supreme Court held for the first time that a person may be "seized" under circumstances short of an arrest.[17] As a consequence, the high court had to provide a working definition of a "seizure" of a person. The Court's definition, the *"Terry-Mendenhall"* rule, is explained in subsections [B] and [C] below. However, students must also be aware of the *Hodari D.* embellishment on that definition, described in subsection [D], which applies in police-pursuit cases.

### [B]   The *Terry* Definition

The Supreme Court first defined "seizure" (of persons) in *Terry v. Ohio*,[18] when it stated:

---

[14] Of course, there was no meaningful interference of the *merchant's* possessory interest in the property, as he consented to the installation.

[15] *See generally* 4 Wayne R. LaFave, Search and Seizure § 9.3 (3d ed. 1996); Ronald J. Bacigal, *In Pursuit of the Elusive Fourth Amendment: The Police Chase Cases*, 58 Tenn. L. Rev. 73 (1990); Thomas K. Clancy, *The Future of Fourth Amendment Seizure Analysis after Hodari D. and Bostick*, 28 Am. Crim. L. Rev. 799 (1991); Wayne R. LaFave, *Pinguitudinous Police, Pachydermatous Prey: Whence Fourth Amendment "Seizures"?*, 1991 U. Ill. L. Rev. 729 (1991); Wayne R. LaFave, *"Seizures" Typology: Classifying Detentions of the Person to Resolve Warrant, Grounds, and Search Issues*, 17 U. Mich. J.L. Ref. 417, 420–26 (1984); Tracey Maclin, *"Black and Blue Encounters"—Some Preliminary Thoughts About Fourth Amendment Seizures: Should Race Matter?*, 26 Val. U. L. Rev. 243 (1991).

[16] *E.g.*, Henry v. United States, 361 U.S. 98 (1959).

[17] Terry v. Ohio, 392 U.S. 1, 16–19 (1968).

[18] 392 U.S. 1 (1968).

Obviously, not all personal intercourse between policemen and citizens involves "seizures" of persons. Only when the officer, by means of physical force or show of authority, has in some way restrained the liberty of a citizen may we conclude that a "seizure" has occurred.

According to this definition, *D* is "seized" by an officer when he is: physically restrained or ordered to stop so that he can be frisked or questioned on the street;[19] intentionally shot by the officer;[20] taken into custody and brought to a police station for questioning[21] or fingerprinting;[22] ordered to pull his automobile off the highway for questioning or to receive a traffic citation;[23] or intentionally forced to stop his car by means of a roadblock.[24]

### [C] The *Mendenhall* "Reasonable Person" Test

### [1] In General

Some police-citizen encounters are not as clear-cut as the examples set out in subsection [B]. For example, in *United States v. Mendenhall*,[25] two male federal drug agents approached *D*, an African-American woman, in an airport concourse. They identified themselves as federal agents, and asked to see her identification and airline ticket, which she handed to them. Did this brief encounter constitute a seizure of *D*? If so, the agents needed to have cause for approaching her and requesting her identification and ticket; if not, they could stop her—or anyone else at the airport—at random to make such a request.

Justice Stewart announced the judgment of the Court, and in a portion of the opinion in which only Justice Rehnquist joined, but which now commands the support of the full Court,[26] he added an objective component to the "seizure" definition: "We conclude that a person has been 'seized' within the meaning of the Fourth Amendment only if, in view of all of the circumstances surrounding the incident, a reasonable person would have believed that he was not free to leave."

The implication of *Mendenhall* is that in determining whether a seizure has occurred, the subjective intention of a police officer to forcibly detain

---

[19] *Id.*

[20] *E.g.,* Tennessee v. Garner, 471 U.S. 1 (1985).

[21] *E.g.,* Dunaway v. New York, 442 U.S. 200 (1979).

[22] *E.g.,* Hayes v. Florida, 470 U.S. 811 (1985).

[23] *E.g.,* United States v. Hensley, 469 U.S. 221 (1985).

[24] *E.g.,* Brower v. Inyo County, 489 U.S. 593 (1989).

[25] 446 U.S. 544 (1980).

[26] The test was adopted as the majority rule in INS v. Delgado, 466 U.S. 210 (1984).

a suspect if he attempts to leave is irrelevant, except insofar as that intention is conveyed to the suspect and, thus, might affect the impressions of a reasonable person in the suspect's shoes. It follows that the subjective impressions of the person accosted is also irrelevant, except to the extent that a reasonable person in that individual's situation would possess the same beliefs.

### [2]   Application of the Test [27]

### [a]   Seizure by Questioning?

The Court stated in *Terry v. Ohio* that "[o]bviously, not all personal intercourse between policemen and citizens involves 'seizures' of persons." In the simplest case, if an officer asks a person on the street for the time of day, no reasonable person would believe that his freedom of movement is restricted because of the question. Under *Terry-Mendenhall*, no seizure has occurred.

However, even when police question an individual about suspected criminal activity, brief questioning *by itself* is unlikely ever to amount to a "seizure." The Court's reasoning is frankly pragmatic: "[C]haracterizing every street encounter between a citizen and the police as a 'seizure,' while not enhancing any interest secured by the Fourth Amendment, would impose wholly unrealistic restrictions upon a wide variety of legitimate law enforcement practices." [28]

Specifically, the Supreme Court has held that "interrogation relating to one's identity or a request for identification by the police does not, by itself, constitute a Fourth Amendment seizure." [29] In this context, consider the Court's treatment of the facts in *Mendenhall*. Justices Stewart and Rehnquist concluded that, based on the totality of the circumstances in that case, no seizure occurred when the agents first accosted *D* and requested her identification and airline ticket. It was irrelevant to the analysis whether the officers would have physically restrained *D* or ordered her to remain in their custody had she refused to cooperate. In the view of the two Justices—a view that seems unrealistic to many people and may best be explained on the pragmatic ground noted in the last paragraph—a reasonable person in *D*'s situation would have believed that she was free to leave. [30] Justice Stewart explained:

---

[27] For application of the test in the context of police pursuit of a fleeing suspect, *see* § 18.03[D][4], *infra*.

[28] United States v. Mendenhall, 446 U.S. at 554.

[29] *Delgado*, 466 U.S. at 216.

[30] Three Justices did not determine whether she was seized, stating only that the question

The events took place in the public concourse. The agents wore no uniforms and displayed no weapons. They did not summon [*D*] to their presence, but instead approached her . . . . They requested, but did not demand to see [her] identification and ticket. . . .

What *would* have converted the encounter into a seizure? Justice Stewart stated:

Examples of circumstances that might indicate a seizure, even where the person did not attempt to leave, would be the threatening presence of several officers, the display of a weapon by an officer, some physical touching of the person of the citizen, or the use of language or tone of voice indicating that compliance with the officer's request might be compelled.

The line between a finding of "no seizure" and "seizure" is exceedingly thin. Contrast *Mendenhall* to the facts in *Florida v. Royer.* [31] In *Royer*, two detectives accosted *D*, an embarking airline passenger, identified themselves, and asked to see his ticket and driver's license, which he provided them. When the officers spotted a discrepancy in the documents, they informed him that he was suspected of transporting narcotics. Without returning his ticket and license, they requested that he accompany them to a nearby small room, which *D* did.

As in *Mendenhall*, the Supreme Court held that the initial encounter— when the officers asked *D* for identification—was not a seizure, but the plurality opinion stated that *D* was seized when the agents asked him to accompany them to the room. The Court reasoned that because the officers retained *D*'s ticket and driver's license without indicating that he was free to depart, a reasonable person in *D*'s situation—one who needed the ticket to embark—would have believed that he was not free to leave, *i.e.*, that he had to accompany them to the room.

### [b] Factory Sweeps

The Supreme Court applied the *Terry-Mendenhall* rule strictly and, arguably, unrealistically, in *Immigration and Naturalization Service v. Delgado.* [32] *Delgado* involved a so-called "factory sweep" or "factory survey," in which I.N.S. agents, without warning, enter a factory or other employment cite where the agents believe they might find illegal aliens, and question the workers. In this case, the agents entered *en masse*. While

---

was "extremely close." The four dissenters pointed out that the "seizure" question had not been raised below; therefore they would have remanded to the district court for an evidentiary hearing on the question.

[31] 460 U.S. 491 (1983).

[32] 466 U.S. 210 (1984).

several agents stood at the building exits, other agents dispersed throughout the factory to question many workers. The agents were armed, displayed badges, and carried walkie-talkies. When they confronted an employee, they asked one to three questions relating to citizenship. During the sweep, which lasted between one and two hours, employees continued their work and were free to walk about the factory.

The Supreme Court, per Justice Rehnquist, held that such factory sweeps did not constitute seizure of all of the workers inside the factory. The Court reasoned that when people are at work, "their freedom to move about has been meaningfully restricted, not by the actions of law enforcement officials, but by the workers' voluntary obligations to their employers." Second, the workers could move about the factory freely. Third, the employees were subjected to "nothing more than a brief encounter."

The reasoning in *Delgado* is questionable. First, although a worker's freedom of action *is* restricted by the employment relation, as the Court itself noted this restriction is the result of the *voluntary* obligations of the employees. Ordinarily, if a worker wants to leave his job during the day, he may do so; he might lose his job or, more likely, be docked some salary, but he *can* leave. During the factory sweep, however, armed agents blocked the way.

Second, in view of the near-military method of entrance, it is unrealistic to think that a factory worker, even a United States citizen or legal alien, would feel, as a reasonable person, that he could discontinue his contact with the I.N.S. agents. Yet, as manifested in *Mendenhall*, the Court assumes that a reasonable person has considerable fortitude, and that such a person not only could, but would, discontinue an encounter with government agents if that were his wish.

### [c]  Bus Sweeps

In *Florida v. Bostick*,[33] two sheriff's deputies boarded an interstate bus while it was temporarily stopped to pick up passengers, in order to intercept drug traffickers who might be aboard. Dressed in "raid" jackets bearing the department's insignia, the deputies approached *D*, who was sitting in the back of the bus, identified themselves as narcotics agents, and questioned him. The deputies requested and received permission to search *D*'s luggage. The search turned up illegal drugs. The trial court ruled that *D* was not seized by the deputies' actions.

The state supreme court reversed. It ruled that a reasonable person in *D*'s position would not have felt free to leave the bus, *i.e.*, that *D* was

---

[33] 501 U.S. 429 (1991).

"seized." Because the deputies concededly lacked any basis for suspecting *D* of wrongdoing when they approached him—indeed, the purpose of bus sweeps is to question as many passengers as possible and seek consent to search their belongings, based on hunches or acting at random—the state court held that *D*'s subsequent consent to search his luggage was invalid.

The United States Supreme Court, per Justice Sandra O'Connor, did not determine whether *D* was seized; it remanded the case to the state court to evaluate the matter "under the correct legal standard."[34] Nonetheless, the Court's reasoning left no doubt as to its view that, on the facts developed, *D* was not seized.

Justice O'Connor stated that "[o]ur cases [citing *Mendenhall, Delgado*, and *Royer*, discussed in subsections [a] and [b] above] make it clear that a seizure does not occur simply because a police officer approaches an individual and asks a few questions." She stated as well that there was "no doubt that if the same encounter had taken place before [*D*] boarded the bus or in the lobby of the terminal, it would not rise to the level of a seizure."

The fact that the encounter occurred on a cramped bus, about to depart, did not appreciably affect the Court's analysis. Although O'Connor conceded that "[w]here the encounter takes place is one factor, . . . it is not the only one." The majority found the *Delgado* factory-sweep case dispositive, and analytically indistinguishable. As with the workers in that case, the bus passengers' freedom of movement "was restricted by a factor independent of police conduct"—their status as passengers. In such a case, "the degree to which a reasonable person [in *D*'s position] would feel that he or she could leave is not an accurate measure of the coercive effect of the encounter." *D*'s feeling of confinement, the Court suggested, was "the natural result of his decision to take the bus." The proper test in such circumstances is whether "a reasonable person would feel free to decline the officers' requests or otherwise terminate the encounter." Absent coercion in that process, no seizure occurs.

### [3] An Issue of Importance: The Nature of the "Reasonable Person"

In view of the fact that the *Terry-Mendenhall* "seizure" test is evaluated on the basis of the perceptions of a "reasonable person," it is critical to determine the nature of this fictional character. The Supreme Court has made clear that the "reasonable person" standard "presupposes an innocent person."[35] Thus, in determining whether a person accosted by the police

---

[34] On remand, the state supreme court affirmed the finding of the trial court that no seizure occurred. Bostick v. State, 593 So.2d 494 (Fla. 1992).

[35] Florida v. Bostick, 501 U.S. at 438.

on the street, in a bus, an airline terminal, or anywhere else, is seized, a court will evaluate the situation on the assumption that the individual has nothing to hide, rather than to ask whether a reasonable *law violator* would believe that he is free to terminate the encounter.

Beyond this, to what extent does—or *should*—the "reasonable person" possess the subjective characteristics of the individual accosted by the police?[36] For example, was it relevant in *Mendenhall* that *D* was a woman, and that the agents were males? Should the test be whether a reasonable *woman* accosted by two *male* federal agents would feel free to leave? Is it relevant that *D* was 22 years old, rather than, for example, 50 years old or, on the other hand, a youth?

The Supreme Court has rarely confronted this issue. In *Mendenhall*, however, Justices Stewart and Rehnquist stated that "these factors"—her age and gender, and the agents' gender—"were not irrelevant" in determining whether a reasonable person, in view of all of the circumstances surrounding the incident, would have believed that (s)he was not free to leave.

A touchier issue, but one of even greater practical significance, is whether the racial characteristics of the parties should be considered in determining how a reasonable person would behave. In *Mendenhall*, the federal agents were white and *D* was African-American. Professor Tracey Maclin has forcefully argued that "the dynamics surrounding an encounter between a police officer and a black male are quite different from those that surround an encounter between an officer and the so-called average, reasonable person."[37]

Maclin contends that the ordinary encounter between a black male suspect and the police, even when the suspect is middle-class or professional, involves a degree of coercion ordinarily absent in other encounters. Therefore, he reasons, courts should "abandon a naive theory of the Fourth Amendment, and consider the real world that exists on the street,"[38] including the fact that racial minorities, especially black males, are not treated the same as white people in day-to-day encounters with the police.

As an empirical matter, it is hard to deny the accuracy of Maclin's observations. Many African-Americans, especially black males, are the

---

[36] This question extends well beyond the subject at hand and, indeed, beyond criminal procedural law. The nature of the "reasonable person" is a matter of considerable controversy in tort and criminal law generally. In regard to criminal law, *see generally* Joshua Dressler, Understanding Criminal Law §§ 10.04[D][2][d], 18.05[A], and 31.07[B][2][b][ii] (3d ed. 2001).

[37] Maclin, Note 15, *supra*, at 250.

[38] *Id.* at 279.

victims of racial profiling by police officers.[39] And, at least some Justices of the United States Supreme Court have observed that in the minority community, even an innocent person may often "believe[] that contact with the police can itself be dangerous."[40] Therefore, the ordinary African-American, compared to a non-minority person, is likely to treat almost any encounter with the police as a more coercive event and is more likely to believe that his freedom of movement is significantly curtailed. Again, the two-Justice *Mendenhall* opinion indicated that the racial characteristics of the parties in the case "were not irrelevant" to the "seizure" issue, although it concluded that the racial aspects of the case were not determinative.

### [D] The *Hodari D.* Embellishment on the *Terry-Mendenhall* Test: The Submission-by-Authority Problem

There is more to the *Terry-Mendenhall* test than was explained in subsection [B] and [C] above, and it is most clearly seen in the police-pursuit cases. The question in such cases is this: When does pursuit of a suspect constitute a seizure of the person? For example, suppose that *O*, a police officer, observes *D* standing on the sidewalk. *D* notices *O*'s attention and flees. If *O* pursues *D* by car or on foot, is *D* "seized" the moment the pursuit begins, or only if and when he is captured? Or, might a "seizure" occur at some intermediate stage, on a case-by-case basis?

The issue is significant. If a pursuit is not a seizure, the police may chase someone without any basis for believing that he is involved in wrongdoing. Furthermore, if the pursued party discards an object during such a chase, and assuming that the pursuit does not implicate the Fourth Amendment, the police may retrieve the object without the latter action constituting a fruit of an unlawful seizure.

The Supreme Court provided a controversial answer to the pursuit problem in *California v. Hodari D.*[41] And, in doing so, it explained (or, some would say, changed) the *Terry-Mendenhall* standard. Speaking for the majority, Justice Antonin Scalia stated that the latter definition "says

---

[39] *See* § 2.05, *supra*, and §§ 9.02[F] and 18.03[B][5], *infra*.

[40] Illinois v. Wardlow, 528 U.S. 119, 132 (2000) (Stevens J., with whom Souter, Ginsburg, and Breyer, JJ, joined, dissenting).

[41] 499 U.S. 621 (1991); *contra, interpreting state constitutional law*, State v. Oquendo, 613 A.2d 1300 (Conn. 1992) (defining "seizure" exclusively by means of the *Mendenhall* test); State v. Quino, 840 P.2d 358 (Haw. 1992) (*id*); Commonwealth v. Stoute, 665 N.E.2d 93 (Mass. 1996) (*Id.*); In re Welfare of E.D.J., 502 N.W.2d 779 (Minn. 1993) (*id.*); State v. Tucker, 642 A.2d 401 (N.J. 1994) (*Id.*); People v. Madera, 580 N.Y.S.2d 984 (Sup. Ct. 1992), *aff'd*, 596 N.Y.S.2d 766 (App. Div. 1993), *aff'd*, 624 N.E.2d 675 (N.Y. 1993) (*id.*); Commonwealth v. Matos, 672 A.2d 769 (Pa. 1996) (*id.*); Commonwealth v. Young, 957 P.2d 681 (Wash 1998) (*id.*).

that a person has been seized 'only if,' not that he has been seized 'whenever' " a reasonable person would have believed that he was not free to leave. That is, the *Terry-Mendenhall* test "states a *necessary*, but not a *sufficient*, condition for seizure—or, more precisely, for seizure effected through a 'show of authority.' "

In order words, in determining whether and when a seizure has occurred, it is necessary after *Hodari D.* to distinguish between a show-of-authority case and one in which the officer uses physical force to detain an individual. In the former case, a seizure is not proven simply by showing that a reasonable person in the suspect's situation would have believed that he was not free to end the encounter. More must be shown. Speaking for the Court, Justice Scalia explained:

> The word "seizure" readily bears the meaning of a laying on of hands or application of physical force to restrain movement, even when it is ultimately unsuccessful. ("She seized the purse-snatcher, but he broke out of her grasp.") It does not remotely apply, however, to the prospect of a policeman yelling "Stop, in the name of the law!" at a fleeing form that continues to flee. That is no seizure. . . . [A seizure] requires *either* physical force . . . *or*, where that is absent, *submission* to the assertion of authority.

For example, if *O*, a police officer, chases *D*, a suspect, and grabs him, a seizure has occurred at that instant, even if *D* pulls away from *O*'s grasp and flees. However, if *O* does not touch *D*, but instead orders him to stop or fires a warning shot in the air, *D* is not seized (although a reasonable person in *D*'s situation would very likely believe that he is not free to end the encounter as he wishes) *unless and until D submits to O's authority.*

Justices Stevens and Marshall dissented in *Hodari D.* They accused the majority of "adopt[ing] a definition of 'seizure' that is unfaithful to a long line of Fourth Amendment cases," including *Mendenhall.*[42]

---

[42] The dissenters also believed that *Hodari D.* was inconsistent with the Court's reasoning in Michigan v. Chesternut, 486 U.S. 567 (1988). In that case, *D*, standing on a corner, fled by foot when he observed a marked police vehicle. Suspicious of *D*'s flight, the officers caught up to him in their vehicle and followed alongside him a short distance. Although *D* was later arrested, at no time during the initial pursuit was he stopped by the police.

The *Chesternut* Court concluded that the pursuit was not so intimidating that it communicated to a reasonable person in *D*'s situation "an attempt to capture or otherwise intrude upon [*D*'s] freedom of movement." In dictum, the Court suggested that the result might have been different if the officers had used their siren, drawn their guns, or "operated the car in an aggressive manner to block [*D*'s] course or otherwise control the direction or speed of his movement." In other words, upon the right facts, an "attempt to capture" could constitute a "seizure." *Hodari D.* rejects such an implication.

They also attacked the ruling as "profoundly unwise." The dissenters' worry relates to the potentially "significant time interval between the initiation of the officer's show of [authority] and the complete submission by the citizen," which is when the "seizure" occurs according to *Hodari D.* Following the majority's approach, the police may now lawfully chase a person—even if the pursuit includes a command to "freeze," the use of sirens, or other coercive actions—without reasonable suspicion of wrongdoing, in the hope that during the pursuit the citizen's response, *e.g.*, a furtive motion, will justify a subsequent seizure. Indeed, the flight itself may often provide the police with the requisite justification for seizing the individual.[43] Yet, anomalously, if an officer barely touches the suspect in an effort to detain him, and the citizen immediately escapes, such "laying on of hands" is a seizure, and the subsequent furtive behavior by the citizen cannot justify the prior seizure.[44]

*Hodari D.* does not indicate how one decides when the requisite submission of authority occurs. Does a fleeing suspect, for example, submit to authority (and, thus, is seized) as soon as he stops running, or only when he indicates by words or action (*e.g.,* raising his hands above his head) that he has submitted? Or, when does the driver of an automobile submit to authority when the police seek to have him pull over on the highway: is it as soon as the driver sees the officer's red lights flashing in the rear view mirror, slows down, and begins to change lanes to pull over, or only when the vehicle comes to a complete stop? The bright-line rule of *Hodari D.*, therefore, will need further judicial clarification.

---

[43] *See* § 18.03[B][4], *infra.*

[44] Only somewhat tongue-in-cheek, Professor Wayne LaFave suggests that the message of *Hodari D.* to police departments is that when they chase a person on a wild and unsupported hunch, a "fat cop" is preferable to one of "slim, trim, and of athletic build," because the latter officer is too likely to catch up to the suspect and grab him "by the scruff of the neck *before* the [contraband is] ditched." LaFave, *Pinguitudinous Police . . .,* Note 15, *supra*, at 730, 731.

## CHAPTER 9

# FOURTH AMENDMENT: "PROBABLE CAUSE"

## § 9.01   The Constitutional Role of "Probable Cause"[1]

One clause of the Fourth Amendment prohibits "unreasonable searches and seizures." Another clause provides that "no Warrants shall issue, but upon probable cause." The interrelationship of these two clauses is a matter of considerable dispute,[2] but what is not in dispute is that "probable cause" is a critical feature of Fourth Amendment jurisprudence. Indeed, one may fairly say that "the concept of probable cause lies at the heart" of the amendment.[3] As the Supreme Court has suggested,[4] the "rule of probable cause is a practical, nontechnical conception affording the best compromise that has been found" for balancing competing needs—"safeguard[ing] citizens from rash and unreasonable interferences with privacy and from unfounded charges of crime" while, at the same time, "giv[ing] fair leeway for enforcing the law in the community's protection."

The importance of probable cause in Fourth Amendment jurisprudence is evident from three general constitutional principles that should be kept in mind at the outset. First, the text of the Fourth Amendment itself provides that arrest and search warrants may *only* be issued if supported by probable cause. Second, *all* arrests (even those that do *not* require a warrant) require probable cause. That is, an arrest—a seizure of that person—on less than

---

[1] *See generally* Akhil Reed Amar, *Fourth Amendment First Principles*, 107 Harv. L. Rev. 757, 782–85 (1994); Tracey Maclin, *When the Cure for the Fourth Amendment Is Worse Than the Disease*, 68 S. Cal. L. Rev. 1, 25–32 (1994).

[2] *See* § 5.02, *supra*, and § 11.01 *infra*.

[3] Albert W. Alschuler, *Bright Line Fever and the Fourth Amendment*, 45 U. Pitt. L. Rev. 227, 243 (1984). Not everyone agrees with this appraisal. Professor Akhil Amar, see Note 1, *supra*, at 785, points out that the "probable cause" standard is found only in the Warrant Clause of the Fourth Amendment; therefore, he argues, "probable cause" is central only to cases in which the police apply for a warrant. As for warrant*less* searches and seizures, he reasons from the text and history of the amendment that police conduct need only be "reasonable," a much more flexible standard than "probable cause." For a vigorous response to Professor Amar's views, *see* Maclin, Note 1, *supra*.

[4] Brinegar v. United States, 338 U.S. 160, 176 (1949).

probable cause is *always* constitutionally unreasonable.[5] Third, in computer terms we might say that "probable cause" is the default position for searches and seizures of property: with rare exceptions, searches and seizures are reasonable if they are conducted with probable cause;[6] absent special justification, however, searches and seizures conducted on less than probable cause are constitutionally *un*reasonable.

## § 9.02 Probable Cause: General Principles[7]

### [A] "Probable Cause": Definition

"Probable cause" exists when the facts and circumstances within an officer's personal knowledge, and of which she has reasonably trustworthy information, are sufficient in themselves to warrant a person of reasonable caution in the belief that: (1) in the case of an arrest, an offense has been committed and the person to be arrested committed it; and (2) in the case of a search, a specifically described item subject to seizure will be found in the place to be searched.[8]

### [B] "Probable Cause": Objective versus Subjective

As the definition in subsection [A] suggests, "probable cause" is an objective concept. An officer's subjective belief, no matter how sincere, that she has sufficient cause to arrest a person or to conduct a search does not in itself constitute probable cause.[9] Moreover, an officer's *lack* of belief that she has probable cause does not foreclose a finding to the contrary.[10] If there is objective probable cause, the officer's subjective motivations for making the arrest or search are irrelevant.[11]

On the other hand, in determining what a "person of reasonable caution" would believe, a court will take into account the specific experiences and expertise of the officer whose actions are under scrutiny. For example, an officer's specialized knowledge of the appearance or odor of a narcotic is relevant in determining whether an arrest based on that knowledge was valid.[12]

---

[5] *See* Henry v. United States, 361 U.S. 98, 100–101 (1959).

[6] Whren v. United States, 517 U.S. 806, 817 (1996).

[7] *See generally* 2 Wayne R. LaFave, Search and Seizure § 3.2 (3d ed. 1996); Akhil Reed Amar, *Terry and Fourth Amendment First Principles*, 72 St. John's L. Rev. 1097 (1998).

[8] *Brinegar*, 338 U.S. at 175–76.

[9] Beck v. Ohio, 379 U.S. 89, 97 (1964).

[10] Florida v. Royer, 460 U.S. 491, 507 (1983).

[11] Whren v. United States, 517 U.S. 806 (1996). *See* § 9.02[F], *infra*.

[12] *E.g.*, Johnson v. United States, 333 U.S. 10 (1948).

(Matthew Bender & Co., Inc.)

## [C]  "Probable Cause": Arrests versus Searches

The methodology for making a probable cause determination is the same for arrests as it is for searches. However, the result need not be the same in a specific case: that is, an officer might have probable cause to arrest a person but not to conduct a search, or vice-versa. For example, *O*, an officer, might have probable cause to believe that she will find contraband in *D*'s automobile, and yet lack probable cause to arrest *D*, because she may lack sufficient evidence that *D* is aware of the contraband. Conversely, *O* might have probable cause to arrest *D* for manufacturing drugs, but if *D*'s arrest occurs at *X*'s house, about which *O* has no evidence of drug activity, she might lack probable cause to search *X*'s residence for drugs.

Furthermore, evidence that would justify a search is apt to become "stale" sooner than information that is used to justify an arrest.[13] For example, information obtained on January 1 that a small quantity of drugs will be found in *D*'s bedroom might be insufficient to warrant a search one month later because the drugs might have been moved or consumed by then.

In contrast, if an officer has probable cause to arrest *D* for possession of drugs on January 1, the arrest will be valid a month later—the "probable cause" is still fresh—unless intervening information casts doubt on the trustworthiness of the earlier information. For example, "probable cause" might no longer exist if the officer subsequently learned that the informant who implicated *D* had a motive to lie.

## [D]  "Probable Cause": With or Without Warrants

A central feature of traditional Fourth Amendment jurisprudence is that the constitutionally preferable arbiter of probable cause is a "neutral and detached magistrate" rather than a police officer "engaged in the often competitive enterprise of ferreting out crime."[14]

Even when the police are justified in acting without prior judicial authorization—that is, without a warrant—probable cause usually is required. If an officer acts without a warrant, a court subsequently called on to determine whether her actions were reasonable must determine whether the officer had probable cause at the time of the Fourth Amendment activity—*i.e.*, whether a magistrate *would* have issued a warrant if one had been sought.

In view of "the Fourth Amendment's strong preferences for searches conducted pursuant to a warrant,"[15] the Supreme Court has indicated that

---

[13] *See generally* Comment, *A Fresh Look at Stale Probable Cause: Examining the Timeliness Requirement of the Fourth Amendment*, 59 Iowa L. Rev. 1308 (1974).

[14] Johnson v. United States, 333 U.S. at 13–14. *See generally* §§ 11.01 and 11.03, *infra*.

[15] Illinois v. Gates, 462 U.S. 213, 236 (1983).

"the resolution of doubtful or marginal cases [of probable cause] . . . should be largely determined by the preference to be accorded to warrants."[16] That is, in close probable-cause cases, a search conducted with a warrant may be upheld where a warrantless search would be rejected for lack of probable cause.

### [E] "Probable Cause": Search For and Seize What?

### [1] "Mere Evidence" Rule

Originally, a search was unjustifiable unless there was probable cause to believe that it would result in the seizure of one of three categories of evidence: (1) a "fruit" of a crime (*e.g.*, money obtained in a robbery); (b) an instrumentality of a crime (*e.g.*, the gun used to commit a robbery, or the car used in the get-away); or (c) contraband (*e.g.*, illegal narcotics). So-called "mere evidence," that is, items that have only evidentiary value in the apprehension or conviction of a person for an offense, could not be seized.[17]

The so-called "mere evidence rule" was founded on property-based concepts consistent with the original understanding of the Fourth Amendment. The justification for the rule was that the government could search for and seize property only if it asserted an interest in the property superior to that of the person from whom it would be seized. Such a superior right was said to exist in relation to fruits, instrumentalities, and contraband, but not as to "mere evidence."

The superior-interest theory was largely a fiction, but it was based on the following assumptions. In the case of fruits, the government, representing a private complainant, had a greater interest in the stolen items than did the alleged criminal. Regarding contraband, the government had a superior property right because a private person has no right whatsoever to possess such property. In the case of a criminal instrumentality, the property was considered forfeited to the government because of its use in criminal activities (and to prevent its use in later crimes). Regarding "mere evidence" of crime, however, no justification existed for subordinating the individual's property rights to the government.

### [2] Abolition of the "Mere Evidence" Rule

The Supreme Court abolished the mere evidence rule in *Warden v. Hayden*.[18] Police officers may now seize not only fruits, instrumentalities,

---

[16] United States v. Ventresca, 380 U.S. 102, 109 (1965).

[17] *See* Gouled v. United States, 255 U.S. 298 (1921).

[18] 387 U.S. 294 (1967).

and contraband, but also "mere evidence," *i.e.*, an article for which there is a nexus between it and criminal activity. According to *Hayden*, this nexus exists if there is probable cause "to believe that the evidence sought will aid in a particular apprehension or conviction."[19]

The Court abolished the mere evidence rule because it believed that the doctrine was indefensible in light of modern Fourth Amendment privacy principles. It concluded that a search for evidence disturbs privacy no more than one directed at fruits, instrumentalities, or contraband because, in all of these cases, a magistrate can intervene, "and the requirements of probable cause and specificity [in the warrant] can be preserved intact."

The Court also concluded that nothing in the nature of property seized as "mere evidence" is more private than other types of property. Indeed, the same item that constitutes evidence in one case might be a fruit or instrumentality in another. For example, a diary might be seized in one case because it includes evidence that ties the defendant to the crime, but a diary might also be a fruit of a crime.[20]

In general, the reasoning of *Hayden* is unexceptionable. Nonetheless, abolition of the mere evidence rule is not without some significant privacy repercussions. First, persons who possess the fruits of a crime, criminal instrumentalities, or contraband are usually guilty of wrongdoing. Innocent persons, however, may unwittingly come into possession of evidence that relates to a criminal investigation. As a practical matter, therefore, *Hayden* enlarges the class of persons who may be subjected to searches.[21]

Second, although *Hayden* involved seizure of clothing rather than of papers that might provide evidence of a crime, the implication of the case is that private papers are no longer immune from search and seizure as "mere evidence." Yet, as the Supreme Court has acknowledged, "there are grave dangers inherent in executing a warrant authorizing a search and seizure of a person's papers that are not necessarily present in executing a warrant to search for physical objects whose relevance is more easily ascertainable."[22] The "grave danger" is that in searching for evidentiary papers, the police must often examine innocent-but-private documents in order to find the incriminating items.

---

[19] Some jurisdictions also provide for warrants to be issued to search for and seize any "person . . . who is unlawfully restrained." *E.g.*, Fed. R. Crim. P 41(b). This provision is justified on the ground that the person seized, *e.g.*, a kidnap victim, is evidence of a crime.

[20] *E.g.*, Matthews v. Correa, 135 F.2d 534 (2nd Cir. 1943).

[21] *E.g.*, Zurcher v. Stanford Daily, 436 U.S. 547 (1978) (police obtained a warrant to search the files of a student newspaper for photographs revealing the identity of persons who attacked police officers during a demonstration).

[22] Andresen v. Maryland, 427 U.S. 463, 482 n.11 (1976).

Despite the special privacy concerns relating to searches of papers, the Supreme Court has approved the seizure of business records as long as the police seek to minimize unwarranted intrusions on privacy.[23] There is no reason to believe that it will devise any greater protections for personal papers, such as diaries and letters.[24]

### [F] Special Problem: "Probable Cause" and Pretextual Police Conduct[25]

According to the Court in one of its most controversial[26] and potentially far-reaching Fourth Amendment pronouncements, "[s]ubjective intentions play no role in ordinary, probable-cause Fourth Amendment analysis."[27] That is, generally speaking, if probable cause objectively exists to conduct an arrest or search, the Court will look no further: it is of no Fourth Amendment consequence that the officer may subjectively have an ulterior motive—even, for example, a racially biased reason—for her conduct.[28]

For example, in *Whren v. United States*,[29] *O*, an officer, had probable cause to stop *D*, a motorist, in order to issue traffic citations for turning

---

[23] *Id.*

[24] Arguably, a heightened level of probable cause for searches and seizures of personal papers should be demanded. *See* Joseph D. Grano, *Perplexing Questions About Three Basic Fourth Amendment Issues: Fourth Amendment Activity, Probable Cause, and the Warrant Requirement*, 69 J. Crim. L. & Criminology 425, 452 (1978). The concept of a sliding scale of probable cause is considered at § 9.07[C], *infra*.

[25] *See generally* David A. Harris, *"Driving While Black" and All Other Traffic Offenses: The Supreme Court and Pretextual Traffic Stops*, 87 J. Crim. L. & Criminology 544 (1997); Andrew D. Leipold, *Objective Tests and Subjective Bias: Some Problems of Discriminatory Intent in the Criminal Law*, 73 Chi.-Kent. L. Rev. 559 (1998); Tracey Maclin, *Race and the Fourth Amendment*, 51 Vand. L. Rev. 333 (1998); David A. Sklansky, *Traffic Stops, Minority Motorists, and the Future of the Fourth Amendment*, 1997 Sup. Ct. Rev. 271; Christopher Slobogin, *Deceit, Pretext, and Trickery: Investigative Lies By the Police*, 76 Or. L. Rev.775 (1997); Anthony C. Thompson, *Stopping the Usual Suspects: Race and the Fourth Amendment*, 74 N.Y.U. L. Rev. 956 (1999). *See also* §§ 2.05, 2.07[B], *supra* and § 18.03[B][5], *infra*, for further consideration of racial profiling, in particular.

[26] *See* Note 29, *infra*.

[27] Whren v. United States, 517 U.S. 806, 813 (1996).

[28] If there is evidence of intentional discrimination, the victim of racial bias may assert a claim on the basis of the Equal Protection Clause, but the Fourth Amendment does not apply. *Id.*

[29] 517 U.S. 806 (1996); *contra, under state constitution*, State v. Ladson, 979 P.2d 833 (Wash. 1999) (pretextual traffic stops are made without "authority of law" and, therefore, prohibited). *Whren* has been subjected to extensive scholarly criticism. Tracey Maclin, *What Can Fourth Amendment Doctrine Learn from Vagueness Doctrine?*, 3 U. Pa. J. Const. L. 398, 402 n.17 (2001) (and also providing citations therein to widespread literature criticizing *Whren*).

without signaling and for speeding. In view of the relatively trivial nature of the offenses, *O* might not have stopped *D* but for the fact that he had a hunch—perhaps grounded on racial grounds—that the occupants of the vehicle were involved in drug activities. When *O* approached the stopped vehicle, he observed plastic bags of crack cocaine in plain view in the car.

The Court stated that (warrant issues aside) a search or seizure supported by probable cause is constitutionally reasonable under the Fourth Amendment without regard to the officer's motives for the action.[30] Even if an officer stops an automobile driver for malicious reasons, for example, to harass the car occupant on racial grounds or, as in *Whren*, if he has a hunch *un*supported by probable cause that he might observe contraband in the vehicle if he can find a basis for stopping the car, the officer's conduct—based on objective probable cause that the driver has violated traffic laws—does not run afoul of the Fourth Amendment.[31] Likewise, an officer may make a full custodial arrest based on probable cause, as a pretext to conducting a search of evidence unrelated to the arrest.[32]

*Whren* is exceptionally controversial. Pretextual police conduct, especially but not limited to traffic stops, is not a rare occurrence.[33] And,

---

[30] However, although the Court will *not* inquire into an officer's motives in a probable-cause context, the Supreme Court *will* look beyond the claim of objective probable cause and conduct individualized "reasonableness" review—that is, probable cause is sometimes insufficient to render a search or seizure reasonable—when the Fourth Amendment activity was "conducted in an extraordinary manner, unusually harmful to an individual's privacy or even physical interests—such as, for example, seizure by means of deadly force, unannounced entry into a home, entry into a home without a warrant, or physical penetration of the body." *Whren*, 517 U.S. at 818; *see also* Atwater v. Lago Vista, 121 S. Ct. 1536, 1557 (2001).

[31] The *Whren* Court did not deny that it has on occasion suggested that an officer's pretextual motivations may be relevant in Fourth Amendment analysis, for example, in inventory search cases. *See* § 16.02[B], *infra*. But, *Whren* said, "we were addressing [there] the validity of a search conducted in the absence of probable cause." *See also* City of Indianapolis v. Edmond, 531 U.S. 32 (2000) (in which the Court considered the purpose of a drug interdiction checkpoint program, in which the police conducted suspicionless vehicle stops; the Court distinguished *Whren* on the ground that in the latter case the Justices "expressly distinguished cases where we had addressed the validity of searches conducted in the absence of probable cause").

[32] Arkansas v. Sullivan, 532 U.S. 769 (2001) (per curiam) (officer arrested *D* for various driving violations as a pretext to search the vehicle for narcotics).

[33] In one exceptional case, a single state trooper claimed to have arrested 250 persons on drug charges after "routine" traffic stops. In these cases he either observed drugs in plain view after the stop or subsequently obtained permission to search the vehicle. In one case, the drug arrest occurred after he stopped a van containing four African-Americans; the stated reason for the stop was that the driver changed lanes without signaling and drove 58 miles per hour in a 55 mile-per-hour zone. United States v. Roberson, 6 F. 3d 1088 (5th Cir. 1993).

according to one court, "[b]y all indications, pretextual traffic stops have increased markedly all over the country since the *Whren* decision."[34] Whether or not this assertion is accurate, there is increasing evidence that, even before *Whren*, police officers frequently used racial profiling to determine which vehicles to stop on the road for supposed traffic violations, in order to investigate more serious crimes.[35] At a minimum, *Whren* invites such profiling by denying victims of the process a Fourth Amendment basis for objecting.

## § 9.03 Determining "Probable Cause": Overview

### [A] Types of Information: In General

When a magistrate is asked to determine whether probable cause exists to arrest a person or to conduct a search, she must ask herself two questions: (1) is the information being offered sufficiently trustworthy to be considered?; and (2) if it is, is the quantum of evidence sufficient to constitute probable cause? The first question is the subject of this section and Sections 9.04 and 9.05. The second question in considered in Section 9.07.

In general, a police officer might furnish a magistrate with two types of information when she applies for a warrant: (1) "direct information," *i.e.*, information the officer secured by personal observation; and (2) "hearsay information," *i.e.*, information she received from another person who is not present for questioning by the magistrate. Because the officer provides her information under oath by affidavit, she is commonly described in probable cause nomenclature as the "affiant," whereas one whose hearsay information is tendered in the affidavit is the "informant."

Regarding hearsay, which is often inadmissible at trial, a magistrate may consider it for purposes of determining probable cause, as long as the

---

[34] Whitehead v. United States, 698 A.2d 1115, 1117 (Md. App. 1997).

[35] New Jersey has been at the center of the profiling controversy, where the statistics are the most developed at this time. David Barstow and David Kocieniewski, *Records Show New Jersey Police Knew of Racial Profiling in '96*, New York Times, October 12, 2000, at A1; David Kocieniewski and Robert Hanley, *Racial Profiling Was the Routine, New Jersey Finds*, New York Times, Nov. 28, 2000, at A1; *see also* State v. Soto, 734 A.2d 350 (N.J. Super. 1996) (granting a suppression motion of 17 black defendants who provided statistical evidence demonstrating that the New Jersey State Police engaged in racial discrimination in the enforcement of traffic laws on the New Jersey Turnpike). A California statute that would have required police agencies in that state to compile traffic stop data, including the race of persons stopped, was vetoed by the Governor. Dan Smith, *"Profiling" Measure Vetoed by Governor*, Sacramento Bee, Sept. 29, 1999, at A1. In 1999, President Bill Clinton directed the Departments of Justice, Treasury and Interior to collect data on the race, ethnicity, and gender of persons stopped and searched by agents in those departments, to determine whether racial profiling is occurring. Bureau of National Affairs, Criminal Law Reporter, Vol. 65, No. 11, June 16, 1999, at 292.

information is reasonably trustworthy.[36] Moreover, the informant's identity need not be disclosed to the magistrate unless the court doubts the affiant's credibility regarding the hearsay.[37] For example, disclosure may be compelled if the magistrate has reason to believe that the affiant lied regarding the informant's existence or misstated the nature of the information received.

### [B] "Bald and Unilluminating" Assertions

A "bald and unilluminating assertion of suspicion" is entitled to no weight in the probable cause determination.[38] For example, a magistrate should not consider an affiant's assertion that she "has cause to suspect and does believe" that seizable articles will be found in a particular place, unless the affiant provides the reasons for her belief.[39] Similarly, the magistrate should give no weight to an unsupported claim by the affiant that she has information that *D* "is known [to others] as a gambler."[40]

In view of the fact that a neutral and detached magistrate, rather than the police officer, is the preferred arbiter of probable cause, the preceding rule make sense. If a magistrate were to consider wholly conclusory statements made in an affidavit, she "would be serving simply as the rubber stamp of the source's conclusion."[41]

### [C] Direct Information

Unless a magistrate has reason to believe that the affiant has committed perjury or recklessly misstated the truth,[42] she may consider all direct information (as distinguished from "bald and unilluminating" assertions) provided by the affiant. The affiant's information is considered reasonably trustworthy because the oath she takes affirms her honesty,[43] and the fact

---

[36] Brinegar v. United States, 338 U.S. 160, 173–74 (1949).

[37] *See* McCray v. Illinois, 386 U.S. 300 (1967).

[38] Spinelli v. United States, 393 U.S. 410, 414 (1969); *see* Nathanson v. United States, 290 U.S. 41, 47 (1933); *see* Illinois v. Gates, 462 U.S. 213, 239 (1983).

[39] *Nathanson*, 290 U.S. 41 (1933).

[40] *Spinelli*, 393 U.S. 410 (1969).

[41] Charles E. Moylan, Jr., Illinois v. Gates: What It Did and What It Did Not Do, 20 Crim. L. Bull. 93, 101 (1984).

[42] In such circumstances, see § 11.04, *infra*.

[43] However, Ninth Circuit federal judge Alex Kozinski has been quoted as saying that "[i]t is an open secret long shared by prosecutors, defense lawyers and judges that perjury is widespread among law enforcement officers." Stuart Taylor, Jr., *For the Record*, Am. Law., Oct. 1995, at 72. This problem prevails throughout the criminal justice process, and not simply at probable-cause hearings. Generally speaking, however, despite the open secret, judges usually accept police testimony they suspect is perjurious. The reasons for this vary, including the wish to help law enforcement officers convict persons whom the judge believes

that the information was personally observed by her attests to the basis of her knowledge.[44]

Of course, the fact that the magistrate may consider direct information provided by the affiant does not mean that there is probable cause to issue a warrant based on it. The magistrate must still determine whether the information, alone or in conjunction with any trustworthy hearsay information provided,[45] satisfies the probable cause standard.

### [D] Hearsay ("Informant") Information

An informant's assertions are not always trustworthy. The difficulty with hearsay is not just that it is second-hand in nature, but that it often comes from untrustworthy sources. As one commentator has observed, the ordinary police informant is not a former Boy Scout and present-day prince of the church.[46] Typically, an informant is a person involved in criminal activities, perhaps as a small-time drug pusher, or as a middle-or even high-level member of an organized crime syndicate, and, therefore, not from a trustworthy milieu. Frequently, as well, the tipster provides the information in consideration for some benefit from the police or the prosecutor (*e.g.*,

---

are guilty. Other reasons include a desire not to be portrayed in the media as "soft on crime," thus jeopardizing their re-election. Andrew J. McClurg, *Good Cop, Bad Cop: Using Cognitive Dissonance Theory to Reduce Police Lying*, 32 U.C. Davis L. Rev. 389, 405 (1999).

For general discussion of the problem of policy perjury (or what has come to be called "testilying"), as well as consideration of the moral issues relating to police deceit, *see generally* Gabriel J. Chin & Scott C. Wells, *The "Blue Wall of Silence" as Evidence of Bias and Motive to Lie: A New Approach to Police Perjury*, 59 U. Pitt. L. Rev. 233 (1998); McClurg, *supra*; Robert P. Mosteller, *Moderating Investigative Lies by Disclosure and Documentation*, 76 Or. L. Rev. 833 (1997); Margaret L. Paris, *Lying to Ourselves*, 76 Or. L. Rev. 817 (1997); Slobogin, Note 25, *supra*; Christopher Slobogin, *Testilying: Police Perjury and What to Do About It*, 67 U. Colo. L. Rev. 1037 (1996).

[44] *Spinelli*, 393 U.S. at 423 (White, J., concurring).

[45] If the direct evidence alone constitutes probable cause, hearsay information is "redundant and can simply be factored out." Moylan, Note 41, *supra*, at 101.

[46] Charles E. Moylan, Jr., *Hearsay and Probable Cause: An Aguilar and Spinelli Primer*, 25 Mercer L. Rev. 741, 758 (1974). Stephen Trott, a former prosecutor, now United States Circuit Court of Appeals judge, has warned that informants' "willingness to do anything [to help themselves] includes not only truthfully spilling the beans on friends and relatives, but also lying, committing perjury, manufacturing evidence, soliciting others to corroborate their lies with more lies, and double-crossing anyone with whom they come into contact, including . . . the prosecutor." Mark Curriden, *Secret Threat to Justice*, National Law Journal, Feb. 20, 1995, at 1A.

money that may be used to feed a drug habit, or immunity from criminal prosecution) which calls into question her motives.[47]

Not only are some informants untrustworthy by nature, but the source of *their* information varies. In some cases, the informant's "knowledge" of the facts that she relates to the officer arises from first-hand participation in the criminal activities reported, but in other cases she may be relating no more than a vague rumor that she has heard on the streets.

The difficult question that must be answered in probable cause determinations, then, is this: Under what circumstances is information obtained from an informant sufficiently trustworthy to justify its consideration? The Supreme Court has wrestled mightily with this question. At one time it applied the so-called "*Aguilar*" or "*Aguilar-Spinelli*" two-pronged test. In 1983, it abandoned that test in favor of the *Gates* "totality-of-the-circumstances test." However, the full import of the prevailing *Gates* test cannot be appreciated without an understanding of the *Aguilar* test. The old and new tests are discussed in the two sections that follow.

## § 9.04   The *Aguilar* Two-Pronged Test[48]

### [A]   In General

The two-pronged test for determining the trustworthiness of hearsay ("informant") information was stated in *Aguilar v. Texas*,[49] a case in which the validity of a warrant to search for drugs was at issue:

Although an affidavit may be based on hearsay information and need not reflect the direct personal observations of the affiant, . . . the magistrate must be informed of some of the underlying circumstances from which the informant concluded that the narcotics were where he claimed they were, and some of the underlying circumstances from which the officer concluded that the informant . . . was "credible" or his information "reliable."

This statement, more fully explained in *Spinelli v. United States*,[50] suggests two inquiries regarding hearsay evidence: (1) "[h]ow did the informant get the information?"; and (2) "[w]hy should I [the magistrate]

---

[47] E.g., Carey Goldberg, *At Stake in a Messy Boston Trial: How to Handle Informers' Crimes*, New York Times, March 13, 1999, at A1 (describing the problems confronting prosecutors who protected two men who committed assorted crimes in exchange for information they provided about activities in the Mafia).

[48] See generally Wayne R. LaFave, *Probable Cause From Informants: The Effects of Murphy's Law on Fourth Amendment Adjudication*, 1977 U. Ill. L.F. 1; Moylan, Note 46, *supra*.

[49] 378 U.S. 108 (1964).

[50] 393 U.S. 410 (1969).

believe this person?" These two questions represent the two prongs of *Aguilar*: (1) the *basis-of-knowledge* prong; and (2) the *veracity* prong, of which there are two alternative spurs, the "credibility-of-the-informant spur" and the "reliability-of-the-information spur."[51]

Under *Aguilar*, if both prongs of the test are satisfied, the informant's assertions are sufficiently trustworthy to be considered by the magistrate in her probable cause determination. If either of the prongs is not satisfied, however, the hearsay evidence standing alone is insufficiently trustworthy to be considered. Its trustworthiness, however, may be resuscitated by at least partial corroboration of the informant's tip, as discussed in subsection [D].

### [B]  Basis-of-Knowledge Prong

#### [1]  In General

The point of the basis-of-knowledge prong—"[h]ow did the informant get the information?"—is that the tipster might be passing along information based on her personal knowledge, which is good, but it is also possible that she is reporting nothing more reliable than "an offhand remark heard at a neighborhood bar."[52]

This prong is satisfied if the informant explicitly states that she personally observed the reported facts. For example, the basis-of-knowledge is proved if *I*, the informant, tells *O*, the officer-affiant, that "*D* is using her house to sell drugs. *I know this because I bought drugs from her at her house yesterday.*" The italicized words demonstrate *I*'s first-hand knowledge.[53]

On the other hand, suppose that *I* tells *O*, "A friend of mine told me that *D* is selling drugs at her home." Here, *I* has her own informant. In that case, under *Aguilar*, the two-pronged test must be applied one step further down the hearsay chain, and the magistrate must ascertain how *I*'s informant got *her* information, and how reliable *that* informant is.

#### [2]  "Self-Verifying Detail"

If an informant does not indicate how she obtained her information, and the officer fails to question her regarding this omission, the officer might be unable to satisfy the magistrate's need for sufficient underlying information to ascertain the basis of the informant's knowledge. For example, if *I* tells *O* only that "*D* is using her house to sell drugs," neither *O* nor the magistrate can ascertain the basis of *I*'s knowledge. Without clarification, the basis-of-knowledge prong is not met.

---

[51] Moylan, Note 46, *supra*, at 755.

[52] *Spinelli*, 393 U.S. at 417.

[53] Of course, the informant could be lying, but this goes to the veracity prong.

In some circumstances, however, the Court has allowed indirect proof of this prong, on the basis of what has been described as "self-verifying detail,"[54] of which the facts in *Draper v. United States*,[55] a pre-*Aguilar* case, are said to "provide a suitable benchmark."[56] In *Draper*, *I*, without stating how he obtained his information, told the police that *D* had gone to Chicago on a specified date by train, that he would return by train with three ounces of heroin on one of two particular dates, that he would be wearing specifically described clothing, that he would carry a tan zipper bag, and that he walked "habitually fast."

The Court in *Draper* considered *I*'s information trustworthy. *Spinelli* explained *Draper* this way: "the tip describe[d] the accused's criminal activity in sufficient detail that the magistrate may know that he is relying on something more substantial than a casual rumor . . . or an accusation based merely on an individual's general reputation." In other words, *I*'s information was so rich in detail that it was reasonable to conclude that he obtained the information first hand.

The reasoning of *Spinelli* on this point is not persuasive. Even if *I* did not make up the story (a veracity issue), the detail demonstrates at most that *someone* apparently had first-hand knowledge of *D*'s plans. *I* might have been passing along the detailed information of *X*, a third person, whose own veracity would then be at issue. In light of the importance of the warrant procedure, a magistrate should not assume on an ambiguous record that *I* was reporting first-hand information.

### [C]  Veracity Prong

Even if an informant states that her information was obtained first hand, she may be lying or her information-gathering skills might be poor. For these reasons, evidence is required under *Aguilar* to demonstrate either that *I* is a credible person (the credibility spur of the veracity prong) or, if that cannot be shown, that her information in the present case is reliable (the reliability spur).[57]

The Supreme Court has provided relatively little guidance regarding how an affiant should demonstrate an informant's veracity. Lower federal and

---

[54] Moylan, Note 46, *supra*, at 749.

[55] 358 U.S. 307 (1959).

[56] *Spinelli*, 393 U.S. at 416.

[57] Courts do not carefully attend to the veracity prong if the informant was the victim of the offense or an ordinary citizen who witnessed the crime. Although such persons are "informants" (they are sometimes called "citizen-informers" in an effort to distinguish them from the unsavory characters who ordinarily provide tips), courts assume their reliability absent special circumstances. *See generally* 2 LaFave, Note 7, *supra*, at § 3.4.

state courts have exercised primary responsibility to fashion an answer.[58] *Aguilar* itself states only that reliability cannot be proved on the ground of a mere assertion by the affiant that the informant is reliable.

Typically, an affiant proves the informant's veracity by providing the magistrate with the informant's "track record" or "batting average." For example, an assertion that the informant's prior tips have led to arrests culminating in convictions is an especially suitable way to prove *I*'s credibility.[59] Of course, if the affiant informs the magistrate regarding the tipster's successes, she should also report any failures. That is the only way to measure the informant's batting average.

The veracity prong may also be satisfied through the reliability-of-the-information spur. This approach is apt to be fruitful in circumstances in which the informant has a questionable (or no) track record. A statement by *I* that constitutes a declaration against her penal interest may be adequate under this spur. For example, when an affiant reports that the informant "has personal knowledge of and has purchased illicit whiskey from within the residence described, for a period of more than 2 years, and most recently within the past 2 weeks,"[60] this statement might be sufficient to satisfy both prongs, as it states the basis of the informant's knowledge, and the claim constitutes an admission of a crime by the tipster, which may tend to make the other assertions more believable.[61]

## [D] Corroboration

A tipster's information that would not otherwise satisfy the two-pronged *Aguilar* test may be considered by a magistrate if the police verify aspects of the informant's facts, as long as it can "fairly be said that the [corroborated] tip . . . is as trustworthy as a tip which would pass *Aguilar*'s tests without independent corroboration."[62]

*Draper v. United States*[63] again provides a benchmark. In that case, after *I* provided detailed information regarding *D*'s activities, the police corroborated some of *I*'s assertions, including *D*'s presence at the train station on one of the dates predicted, his clothing, and his fast gait. The verification

---

[58] *Id.* at § 3.3.

[59] *See* McCray v. Illinois, 386 U.S. 300 (1967).

[60] United States v. Harris, 403 U.S. 573, 575 (1971).

[61] But, is an incriminating statement *really* a declaration against penal interest in light of the fact the police often reward informants by not prosecuting them for their admitted offenses. *See* the text to Note 47, *supra*.

[62] *Spinelli*, 393 U.S. at 415.

[63] 358 U.S. 307 (1959). *See* the text following Note 56, *supra*.

in this case "is simply the present-tense equivalent of a good past track record."[64]

In contrast, in *Spinelli* the police "corroborated" an informant's claim that *D* was a gambler using a particular residence for bookmaking by learning independently that the residence had two telephone numbers. Corroboration of this "one small detail" was deemed insufficient.

## § 9.05   The *Gates* "Totality of the Circumstances" Test[65]

### [A]   The Test Explained

In *Illinois v. Gates*,[66] Bloomingdale, Illinois police officers received an anonymous letter that accused a married couple of selling drugs at a specified address. The letter described in detail the couple's alleged *modus operandi*, including the fact that they usually bought drugs in Florida and brought them to Illinois by car. The letter also stated that on a specific date the wife would drive to Florida, drop off the car and fly home, and the husband would fly down a few days later and drive back alone with a large quantity of drugs in the trunk.

The police and federal agents verified facts alleged in the letter, including the Florida trip. The letter was wrong, however, in predicting that the wife would fly home immediately after dropping off the car; instead, she remained and accompanied her husband on the trip north. As they began driving north "on an interstate frequently used by travelers to the Chicago area," the police sought and secured a warrant to search the suspects' automobile and home.

The anonymous tip standing alone did not meet either prong of the *Aguilar v. Texas*[67] standard,[68] although possibly the police department's

---

[64] Moylan, Note 41, *supra*, at 101.

[65] *See generally* Joseph D. Grano, *Probable Cause and Common Sense: A Reply to the Critics of Illinois v. Gates*, 17 U. Mich. J.L. Ref. 465 (1984); Roger S. Hanson, *The Aftermath of Illinois v. Gates and United States v. Leon: A Comprehensive Evaluation of Their Impact Upon the Litigation of Search Warrant Validity*, 15 West. St. U.L.Rev. 393 (1988); Yale Kamisar, *Gates, "Probable Cause," "Good Faith," and Beyond*, 69 Iowa L. Rev. 551 (1984); and Moylan, Note 41, *supra*.

[66] 462 U.S. 213 (1983); *contra, continuing to apply the Aguilar test under the state constitution*: State v. Jones, 706 P.2d 317 (Alaska 1985); Commonwealth v. Upton, 476 N.E.2d 548 (Mass. 1985); State v. Cordova, 784 P.2d 30 (N.M. 1989); People v. Griminger, 524 N.E.2d 409 (N.Y. 1988); and State v. Jackson, 688 P.2d 136 (Wash. 1984).

[67] 378 U.S. 108 (1964); *see* § 9.04, *supra*.

[68] The letter writer was unknown to the police, so there was no way to judge his or her veracity. The Court also stated that the letter gave "absolutely no indication of the basis for the writer's predictions regarding the criminal activities."

corroboration was sufficient to permit a finding of probable cause under *Aguilar*.[69] Nonetheless, Justice Rehnquist, writing for five Justices, abandoned *Aguilar* and what he described as "the elaborate set of legal rules" that developed from it, and in its place substituted "the totality-of-the-circumstances analysis that traditionally has informed probable cause determinations." On the basis of that standard, the Court held that the warrant was supported by probable cause.[70]

According to *Gates*, a magistrate must conduct a "balanced assessment of the relative weights of all the various indicia of reliability (and unreliability) attending an informant's tip." The factors enunciated in *Aguilar*—basis-of-knowledge and veracity—remain "highly relevant" in determining the value of an informant's tip. However, the prongs are no longer treated as separate, independent requirements. Now, the strength of one prong or some other indicia of reliability may compensate for weakness in the other prong.

The Court justified abandonment of *Aguilar* on the ground that probable cause is a "fluid," nontechnical, common sense conception, based on "the factual and practical considerations of everyday life on which reasonable and prudent men, not legal technicians, act." According to *Gates*, "probable cause" is not "reduc[ible] to a neat set of legal rules," as supposedly were developed under *Aguilar*.

Justice Rehnquist also defended the change on the ground that the earlier test's alleged rigidity seriously impeded effective law enforcement. He also contended that this inflexibility tempted police officers to avoid the warrant process entirely, thereby reducing the desired influence of magistrates in the search-and-seizure process.

### [B]  Criticism of *Gates*

*Gates* has been criticized by many,[71] but not all,[72] commentators and rejected by some courts.[73] Critics most especially question the essence of

---

[69] This was the position taken by Justice White, who concurred in the judgment.

[70] Justices Stevens and Brennan, in dissent, contended that probable cause was lacking for the search of the house at the time the police sought the warrant. They were troubled by the incorrect prediction by the informant that the wife would fly home immediately, which she did not do. Her actual conduct—waiting for her husband to arrive, and driving north with him—was much less suspicious than the predicted event.

The dissent also pointed out that, prior to seeking the warrant, the police did not confirm that the Gates's were returning home after a suspiciously short stay in Florida. The highway on which they were spotted was one "commonly used by travelers to Disney World, Sea World," the circus, Cocoa Beach, Cape Canaveral, and other tourist spots.

[71] *E.g.*, Wayne R. LaFave, *The Fourth Amendment Today: A Bicentennial Appraisal*, 32 Vill. L. Rev. 1061, 1065–70 (1987); Kamisar, Note 65, *supra*.

[72] *E.g.*, Grano, Note 65, *supra*.

[73] *See* Note 66, *supra*.

the opinion, which is that the two-pronged *Aguilar* "test relied too much on logic and not enough on experience to decide what the reasonably cautious police officer would and should do under the circumstances."[74]

Specifically, many critics disagree with *Gates* that the strength of one prong can compensate for the weakness of the other. First, Justice Rehnquist asserts in *Gates* that if an informant, is "known for the unusual reliability of his predictions . . . his failure, in a particular case, to thoroughly set forth the basis of his knowledge surely should not serve as an absolute bar to a finding of probable cause based on his tip." Great strength in the veracity prong, in other words, may make up for lack of evidence regarding the informant's basis of knowledge.

This conclusion is not self-evident. Suppose that *A*, a person of great trustworthiness—say, a rabbi or nun—claims that *D* is a murderer. As a matter of logic, critics maintain, there is no more reason to believe *A*'s claim than that of an unproven stranger, unless and until we know how *A* came to her conclusion. If she obtained incriminating information about *D* from an unreliable source, *e.g.*, from a pathological liar, then the assertion of *D*'s guilt is no more trustworthy than the liar whose claims were filtered through the nun or rabbi.

Moreover, as Justice White argued in his concurring opinion in *Gates*, if Justice Rehnquist is correct in the view that the veracity of an informant may compensate for the lack of information regarding the tipster's basis of knowledge, then it follows that a similar conclusory assertion by an honest and experienced police officer should also be acceptable. Yet, the Supreme Court has repeatedly held that the wholly unsupported ("bald and unilluminating") assertions of an officer do not satisfy the probable cause requirement.[75]

Defenders of *Gates* respond that if an informant has provided, for example, ten reliable reports in the past, but in the present case does not indicate how he obtained his information, "it may be reasonable to infer that [he] . . . does not report information unless it has been reliably obtained."[76] Likewise, our common experiences tell us that we *are* apt to believe the nun or rabbi, even without knowing how she obtained her information, because we trust her not to accept and repeat the claims of unreliable persons.

Perhaps the defenders of *Gates* are correct in this regard, but in light of the constitutional interests at stake, it is preferable for courts to require

---

[74] Grano, Note 65, *supra*, at 469.

[75] *See* § 9.03[B], *supra*.

[76] Grano, Note 65, *supra*, at 513.

magistrates to question affiants carefully to determine the source of their information and, likewise, for officers to question their informants, so that magistrates later are not tempted to infer a reliable basis of knowledge that might not exist.

Whether one agrees with Justice Rehnquist or his critics on this matter, the *Gates* majority is probably wrong in its other assertion, namely, that strength in the basis-of-knowledge prong logically can make up for weakness in the informant's veracity. On this matter, Justice Rehnquist states: "[E]ven if we entertain some doubt as to an informant's motives, his explicit and detailed description of alleged wrongdoing, along with a statement that the event was observed firsthand, entitles the tip to greater weight than might otherwise be the case."

Even taking into consideration the soft language used—"entitles the tip to *greater* weight than *might* otherwise be the case"—Justice Rehnquist provides no case support whatsoever for a notion that Professor Wayne LaFave has described as "bizarre."[77] In computer lingo, the answer to the Justice is "garbage in, garbage out." That is, a liar can just as easily provide specific non-existent "details" as she can give a more general statement. Indeed, it is probably reasonable to assume that a liar, to appear more credible, will be as specific as her creativity allows. It is submitted here that an informant's claims should not be considered by a magistrate unless the veracity prong is independently satisfied.

## § 9.06 Probable Cause and the Reasonableness Standard: The *Camara* Principle[78]

The Fourth Amendment was once considered a "monolith."[79] That is, a search was an all-or-nothing matter: there were no degrees of searches. It was assumed as well that all searches required probable cause, and that "probable cause" had the same meaning in every context.

Such a monolith no longer exists, if it ever did. Not all searches require probable cause.[80] And, it is fair to say that, today, "probable cause" is a

---

[77] 2 LaFave, Note 7, *supra*, at 99.

[78] *See generally* Ronald J. Bacigal, *The Fourth Amendment in Flux: The Rise and Fall of Probable Cause*, 1979 U. Ill. L.F. 763; Wayne R. LaFave, *Administrative Searches and the Fourth Amendment: The Camara and See Cases*, 1967 Sup. Ct. Rev. 1; Barry Jeffrey Stern, *Warrants Without Probable Cause*, 59 Brook. L. Rev. 1385 (1994); Scott E. Sundby, *A Return to Fourth Amendment Basics: Undoing the Mischief of Camara and Terry*, 72 Minn. L. Rev. 383 (1988).

[79] Anthony G. Amsterdam, *Perspectives On the Fourth Amendment*, 58 Minn. L. Rev. 349, 388 (1974).

[80] *See especially* chapters 18–19, *infra*.

"somewhat variable concept."[81] Some of this variability is considered in § 9.07, but an important starting point for understanding the issue is *Camara v. Municipal Court.*[82]

In *Camara*, housing inspectors wanted to conduct a routine annual administrative inspection of *D*'s apartment in order to ascertain whether the municipal housing code was being honored. The inspectors lacked suspicion of any criminal law or administrative code violation on *D*'s premises. Application of traditional "probable cause" standards, therefore, would have prevented their entry onto *D*'s premises without his consent, which he refused to grant.

The Supreme Court's response to this situation was to retain the Fourth Amendment warrant requirement in this case,[83] but to recognize a different kind of "probable cause" for issuance of a search warrant in what has come to be known as an "administrative search" case. The Court, per Justice White, started by pointing out that " 'probable cause' is the standard by which a particular decision to search is tested against the constitutional mandate of reasonableness." In turn, "there can be no ready test for determining reasonableness other than by balancing the need to search against the invasion which the search entails."

The Court proceeded to balance the competing interests. On the side of permitting housing-code inspections was the public's long acceptance of such programs, and the Court's realization that their effectiveness would be seriously threatened if inspectors could not readily enter premises in order to check for violations not visible from public vantage points. Weighed against this was "a relatively limited invasion of the urban citizen's privacy," because such inspections "are neither personal in nature nor aimed at the discovery of evidence of crime."

Based on this balancing approach, the Court developed a special "probable cause" standard to apply in such circumstances: probable cause exists to issue a warrant to inspect premises for administrative code violations as long as there are "reasonable legislative or administrative standards for conducting an area inspection [that] are satisfied with respect to a particular dwelling." In other words, unlike traditional "probable cause," which requires *individualized* suspicion that *criminal* evidence will be found in the area to be searched, administrative "probable cause" may be founded on the basis of somewhat more generalized factors, such as the passage of time since the last inspection, the nature of the building in question, and

---

[81] LaFave, Note 71, *supra*, at 1070.

[82] 387 U.S. 523 (1967).

[83] Warrants are not required for all administrative searches. *See* § 19.02, *infra*.

the condition of the entire area to be searched, and there is no requirement of suspicion of criminal wrongdoing as distinguished from the possibility of finding administrative code violations based on the factors just noted.

*Camara*'s new version of probable cause is critical, of course, in the specialized but increasingly important area of administrative law. But *Camara*'s significance in Fourth Amendment jurisprudence far exceeds this role. By defining "probable cause" in terms of "reasonableness," *Camara* brought a balancing approach to the Fourth Amendment "through the portal of probable cause."[84] As discussed elsewhere,[85] this balancing approach is now at the core of Fourth Amendment analysis in criminal investigations, even outside the realm of "probable cause."

### § 9.07 How Probable Is "Probable Cause"?[86]

#### [A] Governing Law

Suppose that *O*, a police officer, observes *A* and *B* standing over *V*'s body. Assume further that *O* has reason to believe, nearing one hundred percent certainty, that *A* or *B*, but not both, murdered *V*. The odds, however, are equal as to which one is guilty.[87] May *O* constitutionally arrest both suspects? Is the answer different if three, rather than two, suspects are at the scene, and only one is guilty? Or, what if *O* is virtually certain that a murder suspect is hiding in one of two (or three) houses. May she search both (or all three) houses, if needed, to find the suspect? The essential question raised by these scenarios is this: how certain must the "person of reasonable caution" be before she arrests a suspect or conducts a search and seizure, or before a magistrate authorizes such activity?

The Supreme Court has never quantified "probable cause." To the contrary, the Court in *Illinois v. Gates*[88] described probable cause as a "fluid concept" that turns on "assessment of probabilities in particular factual contexts" and, therefore, is "not readily, or even usefully, reduced" to a mathematical formula. Instead, the Court used phrases such as "fair probability" and "substantial basis" to articulate the quantum of evidence necessary to prove "probable cause."

---

[84] Sundby, Note 78, *supra*, at 399.

[85] *See* chapters 18–19, *infra*.

[86] *See generally* Alschuler, Note 3, *supra*, at 243–56; Amar, Note 1, *supra*, at 782–85; Grano, Note 65, *supra*; Maclin, Note 1, *supra*, at 25–32; Christopher Slobogin, *The World Without a Fourth Amendment*, 39 UCLA L. Rev. 1, 38–78 (1991).

[87] If *O* had reason to believe that *A* and *B* acted jointly, the problem raised in the text would disappear.

[88] 462 U.S. 213 (1983).

While the Court eschews a precise quantification of the concept, this much is known: less evidence is required to justify an arrest or search than to convict a person at trial, but more is required than "bare" or "mere" or even "reasonable suspicion."[89] More specifically, the "probable cause" standard "does *not* demand any showing that such a belief be correct or more likely true than false."[90] In other words, "probable cause" involves less than a "50% + " likelihood of accuracy.

Consequently, in the arrest hypothetical described above, it would seem to follow—although it is counter-intuitive—that *O* has probable cause to arrest *A and B* for murder, although she knows that one of the suspects is innocent, or she could flip a coin and arrest one based on her knowledge that there is a fifty percent chance that she picked the right person. On the other hand, Supreme Court dictum implies that the arrest of three persons, only one of whom is guilty, is unconstitutional for want of probable cause.[91]

### [B]   Reflections on the Issue

Precedent and dictum aside, is the Court justified in permitting arrests and searches on less than a preponderance of the evidence? One quite plausible answer is, "[i]t depends." That is, "probable cause" might be determined on a sliding scale, in which the degree of suspicion required would depend on the individual and societal interests implicated in the specific case. This possibility is discussed in subsection [C]. However, even if the degree of "probable cause" were to vary depending on the circumstances, the question would remain: How probable *should* "probable cause" be in the ordinary arrest or search case, before one looks at the exceptional cases that justify a heightened or reduced level of probability?

In an ideal world, problems such as those hypothesized in part [A] would not occur. For example, *O* might be able to avoid the dilemma of arresting *A* and *B* by very briefly detaining both suspects rather than arresting them, and questioning them long enough to determine which person is (even slightly) more likely guilty. But, even if she did so, *A* and *B* might refuse to answer her questions, or their answers might not assist her in focusing suspicion on one of them, in which case *O* would be back where she started.

The question that ultimately must be answered is in what type of society do we wish to live. Do we think it is better that both persons, one of whom

---

[89] Brinegar v. United States, 338 U.S. 160, 175 (1949) ("bare suspicion"); Mallory v. United States 354 U.S. 449, 454 (1957) ("mere suspicion"). "Reasonable suspicion" is a term of art that justifies some relatively less intrusive searches and seizures. *See* chapter 18, *infra*.

[90] Texas v. Brown, 460 U.S. 730, 742 (1983) (emphasis added).

[91] Mallory v. United States, 354 U.S. at 456 (condemning "arrests at large," in which one of three suspects was arrested in order to interrogate him).

is nearly certainly a murderer, remain free at least temporarily while the police seek more evidence, than that *O* arrest them both, knowing that one of them is innocent, and seek post-arrest evidence that incriminates one and/or exculpates the other?

The conclusion that *O* may arrest *A and B* for a crime that she knows only one committed is troubling, but arguably is correct. To permit *O* to arrest both suspects provides her and society needed leeway without "leav[ing] law-abiding citizens at the mercy of the officers' whim or caprice."[92] An officer who acts on a fifty percent likelihood that the person arrested is a guilty party has arguably conducted a reasonable seizure of the person—which, after all, is the constitutional standard—at least if the alternative is to arrest neither suspect and, thus, knowingly allow a murderer to be free. As the Court has observed in a different context, "what is generally demanded of the many factual determinations that must regularly be made by agents of the government . . . is not that they always be correct, but that they always be reasonable."[93]

Even if an arrest or search based on a fifty percent chance of accuracy satisfies us,[94] this only shifts the debate to the more difficult question: how improbable are we willing to let "probable cause" be? That is, how much lower are we prepared to reduce the odds of accuracy before we conclude that the interest in protecting the community from crime must give way to the Fourth Amendment interest in safeguarding citizens from rash and unreasonable interferences with privacy?

Professor Joseph Grano has gone so far as to say that an officer who suspects ten persons of a crime, but who has no way of distinguishing among them, should be permitted in some circumstances to arrest all ten, and then seek evidence to clear the nine innocent parties.[95] Grano believes that focusing on the ten percent accuracy figure "distorts our perspective." He would concentrate on the fact that the police have successfully narrowed their investigation "from the universe of all possible suspects, which may include much of the population, to ten individuals."

---

[92] *Brinegar*, 338 U.S. at 176.

[93] Illinois v. Rodriguez, 497 U.S. 177, 185 (1990).

[94] The reasonableness of the arrest seems stronger in the more ordinary case in which the police focus attention on just one person, and the evidence against that person suggests to a person of reasonable caution that the odds are 50-50 that the suspect is guilty.

[95] Grano, Note 65, *supra*, at 496–97. Apparently, he would allow the police to hold the suspects until their first appearance before a magistrate, which usually occurs within a day or two of arrest, *see* § 1.03[C][3], *supra*, or until a preliminary hearing is conducted, usually within two weeks after the first appearance, *see* § 1.03[C][4], *supra*, at which time the prosecutor would be required to meet a somewhat higher standard of proof.

But, what about the nine innocent persons? Why are they not justified in demanding that the police narrow their investigation further before they are arrested? Grano's answer is that we should construct a "community model" of criminal justice that is premised on the view that individuals cannot act "oblivious to the community's needs." According to this model, even in a society "traditionally and properly dedicated to individual rights," the community may legitimately demand that the nine innocent individuals sacrifice "some liberty or privacy in order to unmask the offender."

All models of criminal justice are controversial in their value judgments. However, Grano's view of the proper balance between the individual and society is one that many people—and certainly this author—would reject on the ground that it unduly minimizes the interests of the nine innocent persons arrested. An arrest—even one that lasts just a few days or weeks—entails more than trivial liberty and privacy loss: an arrest (here, multiplied times nine innocent persons) results in loss of liberty, stigmatization, personal humiliation (such as when the arrestee is compelled to undergo a strip search prior to incarceration), any physical or mental trauma that occurs in the jail system (hardly a rarity), as well as collateral harm, such as legal fees, possible loss of employment, and a permanent arrest record.

How far might Grano's reasoning take us? Suppose there is statistical proof that during a specified range of hours at night, in a particular urban area, ten percent of all males on the street between the ages of sixteen and twenty-five are in possession of illegal narcotics.[96] During the specified hours in that geographical region, may a police officer arrest *every* male in the appropriate age bracket, because the chance of finding a guilty person is ten percent?

Grano would not permit such arrests, distinguishing them from the first case. In the original hypothetical the police developed cause to suspect ten *specific* individuals of a crime; in the new case, no individualized suspicion is involved. The society may require personal sacrifice in the former case, Grano argues, but not "when no cause whatsoever exists to believe that the individual, as opposed to anyone else, is involved with crime."[97]

But, if it is fair to demand sacrifice by innocent people in the first example, why is it not fair in the second? Once we are prepared to say that the community has a right to demand nine of us to sacrifice our liberty for awhile in order to permit the police to discover the guilty tenth person, it is a small step to demand that nine innocent urban youths give up some liberty and privacy in order to attack the scourge of narcotics in their own community.

---

[96] *See* Alschuler, Note 3, *supra*, at 246.

[97] Grano, Note 65, *supra*, at 498.

The demand that police meet relatively high standards of probable cause may result in them catching fewer criminals or, at least, having to work harder to make arrests and conduct searches, than if one follows Grano's model. But, this may be "the price the framers anticipated and were willing to pay to ensure the sanctity of the person, the home, and property against unrestrained governmental power."[98]

None of this discussion ultimately tells us where the probable cause line ideally should be drawn once we agree (or accept, as we must, the precedent) that the doctrine falls below the civil preponderance-of-evidence standard, and that "probable cause" is, at least to some extent, a fluid concept. But, if it *is* fluid, why not say so expressly and develop a sliding-scale version of probable cause. That idea is considered next.

## [C] "Probable Cause" as a Sliding Scale?[99]

### [1] *Is* There a Sliding Scale?

*Camara v. Municipal Court*[100] demonstrated that there are different *kinds* of "probable cause": one that applies to criminal investigations and another that is used in administrative search cases. But, are there also different *degrees* of "probable cause"? Is there, in other words, a sliding scale of "probable cause"?

The Supreme Court has rejected such a concept, preferring instead to retain the "single, familiar standard"[101] of probable cause. However, although the Court is unwilling to acknowledge different degrees of probable cause, it has developed an alternative sliding-scale approach to searches and seizures: it has said that some searches and seizures may be conducted on a lesser level of suspicion than probable cause.

In the watershed case of *Terry v. Ohio*,[102] the Supreme Court held that searches and seizures that are less-than-ordinarily intrusive may be conducted on the basis of a lesser quantum of evidence than "probable cause." That lesser amount is termed "reasonable suspicion." Furthermore, in a few circumstances, where the intrusion on a person's privacy is especially slight,

---

[98] Potter Stewart, *The Road to Mapp v. Ohio and Beyond: The Origins, Development and Future of the Exclusionary Rule in Search-and-Seizure Cases*, 83 Colum. L. Rev. 1365, 1393 (1983).

[99] *See generally* Amar, Note 7, *supra*; Christopher Slobogin, *Let's Not Bury Terry: A Call for Rejuvenation of the Proportionality Principle*, 72 St. John's L. Rev. 1053 (1998); Scott E. Sundby, *An Ode to Probable Cause: A Brief Response to Professors Amar and Slobogin*, 72 St. John's L. Rev. 1133 (1998).

[100] 387 U.S. 523 (1967). See § 9.06, *supra*.

[101] Dunaway v. New York, 442 U.S. 200, 213 (1979).

[102] 392 U.S. 1 (1968). *See generally* chapter 18, *infra*.

and society's interest in conducting the search or seizure is considered unusually great, government officers may act without any individualized suspicion whatsoever.[103]

Does the sliding-scale slide in the other direction? Do *more*-than-ordinarily intrusive searches and seizures require a quantum of evidence greater than probable cause? Logic, if not the laws of gravity, would suggest that they should, but the Supreme Court has never acknowledged the existence of a requirement of "probable cause-plus," despite various opportunities to do so.

For example, in *Zurcher v. Stanford Daily*,[104] the Court justified the search of a newspaper office for photographic evidence of a crime on the basis of ordinary probable cause, although heightened probable cause might have been justified on either of two grounds: that the police searched the premises of individuals not personally suspected of crime;[105] or that the police conduct threatened First Amendment values.[106]

Similarly, the Supreme Court does not require the police to have heightened probable cause in order to obtain permission to have surgery conducted on a person believed to be in possession of criminal evidence. For example, in *Schmerber v. California*,[107] a physician, at the direction of a police officer, extracted blood from a suspect to test for alcohol content. This intrusion "implicated . . . [the] most personal and deep-rooted expectations of privacy."[108] Yet, the Court held that the intrusion only required "a clear indication," rather than "mere chance," that the evidence would be found. The precise meaning of the phrase "clear indication" is in doubt, but subsequent cases suggest that bodily intrusions do not require more than probable cause, and might even require less in some circumstances.[109]

---

[103] *E.g.*, Mich. Dept. of State Police v. Sitz, 496 U.S. 444 (1990) (permitting brief random seizures of drivers at sobriety checkpoints).

[104] 436 U.S. 547 (1978).

[105] *Id.* at 577 (Stevens, J., dissenting).

[106] Grano, Note 24, *supra*, at 450–52; *see also* New York v. P.J. Video, Inc., 475 U.S. 868 (1986) (providing that a warrant application authorizing the seizure of materials presumptively protected by the First Amendment is evaluated by traditional standards of "probable cause").

[107] 384 U.S. 757 (1966).

[108] Winston v. Lee, 470 U.S. 753, 760 (1985).

[109] *Compare* Winston v. Lee, 470 U.S. 753, 760 (1985) (in which the Court stated that *Schmerber* "noted the importance of probable cause") *with* United States v. Montoya de Hernandez, 473 U.S. 531, 540 (1985) (in which the Court observed that the words "clear indication" in *Schmerber* "were used to indicate the necessity for particularized suspicion that the evidence sought might be found within the body of the individual."). However, the

### [2] *Should* There Be a Sliding Scale?

The summary of the law in subsection [1] demonstrates that, although the Supreme Court has not implemented a sliding-scale of "probable cause," it has developed a downward-directed sliding-scale of "reasonable" searches and seizures, *i.e.*, those that require probable cause, and those that require less than probable cause ("reasonable suspicion" or no individualized suspicion). Although it may be too late to change directions now, would it have been preferable for the Court to have expressly recognized a sliding-scale of "probable cause" (but, presumably, one that slides in *both* directions), than to have devised the concept of "reasonable suspicion" (words not even found in the Fourth Amendment) and have allowed some searches and seizures on the basis of no cause at all?

Justice Robert Jackson once advocated what essentially was a sliding-scale version of probable cause.[110] He conceded that he would "strive hard" to justify a roadblock around a neighborhood in which all outgoing automobiles were searched if its purpose was to prevent a kidnapper from leaving with his victim, but that he would not justify the same conduct, based on the same information, in order "to salvage a few bottles of bourbon and catch a bootlegger."

Or, consider this example: the police have reason to believe that a bomb is set to explode in a locker in a busy airport.[111] Although the odds might be small that the bomb will be found in any particular locker, it is intuitively appealing to permit the police to conduct warrantless searches of each locker until the bomb is found, even as we would prohibit searches of the same lockers, based on the same degree of likelihood of success, in order to find a small quantity of marijuana.

Professor Akhil Amar contends that the Supreme Court went wrong when it decided that the concept of "probable cause" was at the heart of the Fourth Amendment. He reasons that the probable cause requirement is found only in the Warrant Clause of the amendment. In *that* context—when the police seek to obtain a warrant—he would require "a standard akin to more than fifty percent." However, with *warrantless* searches and seizures—which are *not* textually linked to the probable cause requirement—all that would be

---

Court did state in *Winston, supra,* that a "more substantial [than ordinary] justification" is required to "intrude upon an area in which our society recognizes a significantly heightened privacy interest." *See* § 12.02, *infra.*

[110] *Brinegar,* 338 U.S. at 182–83 (Jackson, J., dissenting); *see also* United States v. Chaidez, 919 F.2d 1193, 1197 (7th Cir. 1990) (favoring a sliding-scale approach, the court observed that "circumstances defy . . .simple categorization, and if a [probable-cause] line must nonetheless be drawn it will be arbitrary, with nearly identical cases on opposite sides.").

[111] Alschuler, Note 3, *supra,* at 246–47.

required is that the search or seizure be "reasonable," a concept that "obviously does require different levels of cause in different contexts, and not always a high probability of success."

But, there are dangers inherent in sliding-scales, which have been articulated well by Professor Anthony Amsterdam. Once a sliding-scale approach is recognized, the Fourth Amendment becomes "one immense Rorschach blot."[112] One potential effect of the sliding-scale, troubling to persons interested in an efficient criminal justice system, is a "graduated fourth amendment . . . splendid in its flexibility, [but] awful in its unintelligibility, unadministrability, unenforcibility and general ooziness."[113] Given its "ooziness," a second effect of a sliding-scale, disturbing to civil libertarians, is that it is likely to "produce more slide than scale," because "courts are seldom going to say that what [the police] did was unreasonable."[114]

---

[112] Amsterdam, Note 79, *supra,* at 393.

[113] *Id.* at 415.

[114] *Id.* at 394.

CHAPTER **10**

# ARRESTS

## § 10.01  Nature of an "Arrest"[1]

The term "arrest" is often used in court opinions and statutes, but is rarely defined. Indeed, the word "arrest" is sometimes modified by adjectives such as "formal,"[2] "custodial,"[3] and "traditional,"[4] from which one may infer that some arrests are "informal," "noncustodial," and "nontraditional."

Operationally (and in the traditional sense of the term), a person is "arrested" when he is taken into custody by lawful authority, for the purpose of holding him in order to answer for a criminal charge. In constitutional terms, an arrest constitutes a "seizure" of the person, as that term is used in Fourth Amendment jurisprudence.

Although all arrests are Fourth Amendment seizures, not all seizures constitute arrests in the taken-into-custody sense of the term. Use of the word "arrest" ordinarily implies that the individual's freedom of movement has been curtailed for an indefinite period of time—at least long enough so that he can be taken to police headquarters for booking—whereas a person can be detained against his will for a brief time—and, thus, be "seized"[5] —without being arrested in the latter sense.

Nonetheless, some states by statute or judicial opinion characterize the temporary detention of a person for the purpose of issuing a summons or to write a traffic citation as an arrest.[6] This use of the term is uncommon. Unless otherwise specified in this chapter, the term "arrest" is used in the operational taken-into-custody sense of the term.

---

[1] *See generally* David A. Moran, *Traffic Stops, Littering Tickets, and Police Warnings: The Case for a Fourth Amendment Non-Custodial Arrest Doctrine*, 37 Am. Crim. L. Rev. 1143 (2000).

[2] *E.g.*, Berkemer v. McCarty, 468 U.S. 420, 425 (1984).

[3] *E.g.*, United States v. Robinson, 414 U.S. 218, 235 (1973).

[4] *E.g.*, Dunaway v. New York, 442 U.S. 200, 212 (1979).

[5] *See* § 8.03, *supra*.

[6] *E.g.*, People v. Bland, 884 P.2d. 312, 315–16 (Colo. 1994) (interpreting a state statute as authorizing "noncustodial" arrests); Thomas v. State, 614 So.2d 468, 470–71 (Fla. 1993).

## § 10.02 Making An Arrest: Common Law and Statutory Arrest Rules

At common law, a police officer could not arrest a person for an offense unless he had reasonable grounds to believe that a crime had been committed and that the person to be arrested committed it.[7] The common law term "reasonable grounds" is equivalent to the constitutional term "probable cause."[8]

Today, most statutes[9] provide that the police may make a felony arrest without a warrant. However, a warrant is required for a misdemeanor arrest unless the offense occurs in the officer's presence.[10] As discussed below, however, warrantless arrests in some circumstances are unconstitutional, notwithstanding common law and statutory precedent.

The Fourth Amendment does not prohibit the police from taking a person into custody (as distinguished from simply issuing a citation) without a warrant merely because the arrest offense is an exceedingly minor one (for example, failure of a motorist to fasten his seatbelt), punishable only by a fine.[11]

## § 10.03 Arrest Warrants: Constitutional Law Overview

### [A] General Rules

Here is a categorical rule: all custodial arrests must be founded on probable cause.[12] An arrest not founded on probable cause constitutes an unreasonable seizure of the person, in violation of the Fourth Amendment.

---

[7] *See generally* Joshua Dressler, Understanding Criminal Law § 21.02[A][1] (3d ed. 2001); Akhil Reed Amar, *Fourth Amendment First Principles,* 107 Harv. L. Rev. 757, 782 (1994).

[8] Draper v. United States, 358 U.S. 307, 310 n.3 (1959).

[9] *See, e.g.,* Cal. Penal Code § 836 (West 1985 & Supp. 2001).

[10] For the common law meaning of the phrase "in the presence," *see* 3 Wayne R. LaFave, Search and Seizure § 5.1(c) (3d ed. 1996).

[11] Atwater v. Lago Vista, 532 U.S. 318 (2001); *contra under state constitution,* State v. Jones, 727 N.E.2d 886 (Ohio 2000) (decided before *Atwater*). The holding in *Atwater* was based in considerable part on the Court's survey of pre-Constitutional English common law, statutes enacted by the Parliament before the founding of the United States, and its examination of American history during the constitutional framing era. The Court concluded from this historical analysis that the Fourth Amendment did not intend to bar custodial arrests for minor "fine-only" offenses. The Court also concluded that it was impractical to devise a constitutional line between jailable and "fine-only" offenses, because "we cannot expect every police officer to know the details of frequently complex penalty schemes," and because "penalties for ostensibly identical conduct can vary on account of facts difficult (if not impossible) to know at the scene of an arrest."

[12] *See* Henry v. United States, 361 U.S. 98 (1959); Dunaway v. New York, 442 U.S. 200 (1979).

The law regarding arrest warrants is less categorical. As a constitutional matter, a police officer: (1) may arrest a person in a public place without a warrant, even if it is practicable to secure one; (2) may *not* arrest a person in his home without an arrest warrant, absent exigent circumstances or valid consent; and (3) absent exigent circumstances or valid consent, may not arrest a person in another person's home without a search, and perhaps an arrest, warrant. These rules are discussed in detail in Sections 10.04 through 10.06.

### [B]  How Arrest Warrant Issues Arise

An arrest that is invalid because it was executed without a warrant does not render unlawful the continued custody of the suspect and, therefore, does not in itself void a conviction.[13] Instead, the constitutionality of a warrantless arrest arises as an issue in a criminal prosecution in an evidentiary context, that is, *when the arrest results in the seizure of evidence that the government wishes to use against the arrestee at his criminal trial.*

For example, if the police seek to justify a warrantless *search* of *D*'s home for evidence on the basis that it was an incident to *D*'s lawful arrest in the residence, or if the police claim that the evidence was in lawful "plain view" at the time of *D*'s arrest, then the lawfulness of *D*'s arrest that gave rise to the search and/or seizure is brought into question. In such circumstances, the absence of an arrest warrant will sometimes serve as a basis for excluding the seized evidence. Similarly, a post-arrest confession is often inadmissible if produced by an unconstitutional arrest.

### § 10.04  Arrest in a Public Place: the *Watson* No-Warrant Rule[14]

In *United States v. Watson*,[15] federal postal inspectors arrested *D* in a restaurant for possession of stolen credit cards. Although based on probable cause, the arrest was conducted without a warrant, under authority of a federal statute similar to those in nearly all states that permits warrantless arrests on the basis of probable cause (or "reasonable grounds" for believing) that the suspect "has committed or is committing a felony."

The Court upheld the constitutionality of the statute in the context of arrests in public places. The Court largely grounded its ruling on history. The majority observed that warrantless felony arrests were permitted at

---

13 *See* United States v. Crews, 445 U.S. 463 (1980); Gerstein v. Pugh, 420 U.S. 103 (1975); Frisbie v. Collins, 342 U.S. 519 (1952).

14 *See generally* 3 LaFave, Note 10, *supra*, at § 5.1(b).

15 423 U.S. 411 (1976); *contra*, Campos v. State, 870 P.2d 117 (N.M. 1994) (under the state constitution, the validity of a warrantless arrest in a public place depends on exigent circumstances).

common law, and that this rule "survived substantially intact" in nearly all states, as well as in the federal system. The Court particularly noted the 1792 Congressional passage of a law providing federal marshals with, in the words of the original statute, "the same powers in executing the laws of the United States, as sheriffs and their deputies in the several states have by law." Since sheriffs at that time had authority to arrest felons *without* a warrant, this legislation demonstrated that contemporaries of the drafters of the Constitution saw no inconsistency between the Fourth Amendment and legislation authorizing warrantless felony arrests.

Justice Powell concurred in the opinion, but with reservations. He conceded that the holding of the Court "created a certain anomaly." The anomaly is that seizures of persons in public places are subject to less judicial scrutiny than searches and seizures of property. As he observed:

> There is no more basic constitutional rule in the Fourth Amendment area than that which makes a warrantless search unreasonable except in a few "jealously and carefully drawn" exceptional circumstances. . . . [¶ ] Since the Fourth Amendment speaks equally to both searches and seizures, and since an arrest, the taking hold of one's person, is quintessentially a seizure, it would seem that the constitutional provision should impose the same limitations upon arrests that it does upon searches. Indeed, as an abstract matter an argument can be made that the restrictions upon arrest should be greater. A search may cause only annoyance and temporary inconvenience to the law-abiding citizen . . . . An arrest, however, is a serious personal intrusion regardless of whether the person seized is guilty or innocent . . . . [¶ ] But logic sometimes must defer to history and experience.

The dissenters questioned the Court's reliance on common law authority. They pointed out that only the most serious crimes were identified as felonies at common law. Many modern-day felonies, such as assault with the intent to commit murder, were common law misdemeanors and, therefore, required an arrest warrant. The holding in *Watson*, therefore, "result[ed] in contravention of the common law."

### § 10.05 Arrest in the Home: the *Payton* Warrant-Requirement Rule[16]

#### [A] In General

The Supreme Court ruled in *Payton v. New York*[17] that the Fourth Amendment prohibits the warrantless, nonconsensual entry into a suspect's

---

[16] *See generally* 3 LaFave, Note 10, *supra*, at § 6.1.

[17] 445 U.S. 573 (1980).

home in order to make a "routine" (non-exigent) felony [18] arrest.

In *Payton*, police officers had probable cause to arrest *D1* for a felony. They went to *D1*'s home to arrest him without a warrant. They heard music playing inside the home, and knocked, but received no reply. After a brief wait, they broke in with the assistance of a crow bar. Nobody was inside, but they seized evidence in plain view. In a companion case, the police knocked at *D2*'s door, his three-year-old son opened it, and the officers, observing *D2* inside, entered and arrested him without a warrant.

The Supreme Court, per Justice Stevens, held that the Fourth Amendment prohibited the police conduct in these two cases. The Court stated that, absent exigent circumstances, which it did not define, nonconsensual entry into a suspect's home in order to make an arrest requires an arrest warrant and "reason to believe the suspect is within." If the officer is armed with a warrant, however, she has implicit authority to search anywhere in the home that the person named in the warrant might be found until she is taken into custody. [19]

The *Payton* Court justified the warrant requirement primarily on the ground that "physical entry of a home is the chief evil against which the wording of the Fourth Amendment is directed." The purpose of the arrest warrant, in other words, is not to protect the suspect from unreasonable seizure, but rather is to safeguard the integrity of the home from entry—and the occupants' privacy therein—in the absence of a prior determination of probable cause by a magistrate. [20]

Justice Stevens pointed out that general warrants and writs of assistance were the immediate evils that motivated the adoption of the Fourth Amendment. [21] However, he said, "[i]t is . . . perfectly clear that the evil the Amendment was designed to prevent was broader than the abuse of the general warrant." A broader purpose of the amendment is to protect against government intrusion into "the sanctity of a man's home and the privacies of life." According to the Court, absent an emergency or consent, the Fourth Amendment bars (in crucial language) the warrantless "breach of the entrance to an individual's home." Although the amendment protects privacy in various settings, "[i]n none is the zone of privacy more clearly

---

[18] Although *Payton* concerned felony arrests and, consequently, the rule was stated in those terms, the doctrine applies to misdemeanor arrests in the home as well. See Welsh v. Wisconsin, 466 U.S. 740 (1984).

[19] Maryland v. Buie, 494 U.S. 325, 330 (1990). Under limited circumstances, arresting officers may also conduct a "protective sweep" of the home for other persons who might pose a danger to the officers or others. See § 18.08, *infra*.

[20] Minnesota v. Olson, 495 U.S. 91, 95 (1990) (explaining *Payton*).

[21] See § 5.03, *supra*.

defined than when bounded by the unambiguous physical dimensions of an individual's home."

The dissenters found the majority's historical argument faulty. They argued that at the time of the adoption of the Fourth Amendment, law enforcement officers had broad inherent power to arrest without a warrant. The evil of general warrants and writs of assistance was that they gave magistrates the power to expand upon this inherent authority, and it was *this* judicial expansion that the Fourth Amendment sought to prohibit. As one scholar has put it, in the Framers' minds, "judges and warrants are the heavies, not the heroes, of our story."[22] On this view, the Framers would have considered it perverse to require a warrant to make *any* kind of arrest.

## [B]  Scope of the Rule

### [1]  *Payton* versus *Watson*: "Home" versus "Public Place"

An arrest warrant is required (absent consent) for a routine arrest of the defendant in his home (*Payton*), including his temporary residence (*e.g.* a motel room). However, warrantless arrests in public places are constitutional (*Watson*). It is critical, therefore, to distinguish between a "home" and a "public place" for Fourth Amendment purposes.

Clearly, an arrest on the street, in a public park, or on or in any other public site, falls within the *Watson* no-warrant-requirement rule. It is also clear that "public place" includes the inside of a privately owned commercial building open to the public, since the arrest in *Watson* occurred in a restaurant during working hours. There is a split of lower court authority, however, on whether *Watson* or *Payton* applies to the entry of a commercial facility not open to the general public.[23]

The *Watson-Payton* distinction is sometimes difficult to draw, even when an arrest occurs in the context of an arrestee's home. For example, in *United States v. Santana*,[24] the arresting officer testified that he found *D* standing directly in the open doorway of her house when he arrived without a warrant to arrest her. The Court stated that "one step forward would have put her outside [the house], one step backward would have put her in the vestibule of her residence." The *Santana* Court stated that although the threshold of her dwelling is "private" in the same way that her yard is, for purposes of the arrest-warrant rule *D* was standing in a "public place." According

---

[22] Akhil R. Amar, *The Bill of Rights as a Constitution*, 100 Yale L.J. 1131, 1179 (1991). *See generally* § 11.01, *infra*.

[23] *Compare* United States v. Ponce, 488 F. Supp. 226 (S.D.N.Y. 1980) (permitting entry of a warehouse through an ajar door) *with* United States v. Driver, 776 F.2d 807 (9th Cir. 1985) (requiring a warrant to enter a closed office inside a warehouse).

[24] 427 U.S. 38 (1976).

to the Court, she was standing in open view; as such, she was "as exposed to view, speech, hearing, and touch as if she had been standing completely outside her house."

In *Santana*, *D* retreated into her house after she spotted the officers, who followed her inside. The Court justified the police entry on the ground of hot pursuit, an exception to *Payton* discussed in the next subsection. However, if *D* had stood motionless in the doorway, her warrantless arrest would have been constitutional, as much so as if she had been on a public street.

A more difficult and controversial question relates to the following common scenario: in a non-emergent situation, *O*, a police officer, comes to *D*'s home without an arrest warrant; *O* knocks at the door; *D* opens the door; *O* arrests *D*. Here, unlike *Santana*, the arrestee is in his home, with the door shut, when the officer arrives. Under these circumstances, is a warrantless arrest valid? Does it matter whether *D* happens to be standing partially outside the home when the arrest occurs? Does it matter whether *O* enters the home to make the arrest? Suppose, instead, that *O* asks *D* to come outside, at which moment the arrest occurs?

Lower courts are divided on how to deal with these and related scenarios.[25] A court will sometimes uphold a warrantless arrest without being precise regarding where the arresting officer and home dweller were standing at the moment of seizure. Some courts take the view that if the arrestee is fully within the house, a warrantless arrest is invalid, even if the officer accomplishes the arrest without entering the home, on the ground that the critical issue is "not the location of the arresting officer," but rather is "the location of the arrestee."[26] But, it should be remembered that *Payton* made much of the fact that there should not be a "breach of the entrance to an individual's home." As a consequence, some courts allow warrantless arrests if, but only if, the arrest can be effectuated without such a breach.[27] The latter approach allows police officers to avoid the strictures of *Payton* by careful planning,[28] but can also result in violations of a very technical

---

[25] See 3 LaFave, Note 10, *supra*, at 256–63 (and cases cited therein).

[26] State v. Holeman, 693 P.2d 89, 91 (Wash. 1985).

[27] *E.g.*, State v. Santiago, 619 A.2d 1132 (Conn. 1993); *see* United States v. Berkowitz, 927 F.2d 1376, 1386 (7th Cir. 1991) ("*Payton* prohibits only a warrantless *entry* into the home, not a policeman's use of his voice to convey a message of arrest from outside the home.").

[28] *E.g.*, State v. White, 838 P.2d 605, 608 (Or. App. 1992) (*Watson*, rather than *Payton*, applies if the police surround a house, order the suspect by telephone to come out, and arrest him when he complies, as long as there "was no entry into an enclave of [the defendant's] privacy").

nature.[29]

## [2] Exigencies Justifying Warrantless Entry

### [a] Hot Pursuit

Warrantless entry of a home is permitted in hot pursuit of a fleeing felon. As the Court explained in *United States v. Santana*,[30] "hot pursuit" involves "some sort of chase [of the suspect], but it need not be an extended hue and cry 'in and about [the] public streets.' "

In *Santana*, police officers had probable cause, but no warrant, to arrest D for a felony. They drove to D's house, where they observed her standing in the doorway. Constitutionally speaking, this placed her in a "public place." When she observed the officers, she retreated into the house, although she left the door open. The officers entered to arrest her.

The police entry of the home took the case outside of the *Watson* "public place" rule. Nonetheless, the Court justified the entry and warrantless arrest according to the hot pursuit doctrine: that is, the pursuit to arrest began in a public place and ended, albeit quickly, in the home.[31]

### [b] Other Exigencies

The Supreme Court has rarely indicated what exigencies, beyond hot pursuit, justify a warrantless entry of a home to make an arrest. However, in *Minnesota v. Olson*,[32] the Court said that the Minnesota Supreme Court "applied essentially the correct standard" for determining what circumstances justify a warrantless entry of a home to make an arrest.

---

[29] *E.g.*, State v. Johnson, 501 N.W.2d 876 (Wis. Ct. App. 1993) (citing *Payton*, the Fourth Amendment is violated if an officer, without a warrant, positions himself in the suspect's doorway, with his "toenails" to the "balls of [the] feet" inside the home).

[30] 427 U.S. 38 (1976).

[31] Sometimes the hot pursuit doctrine is invoked in questionable circumstances. For example, in Warden v. Hayden, 387 U.S. 294 (1967), the police had probable cause to believe that D had committed an armed robbery moments earlier and had entered a particular house. The Court upheld the officers' warrantless entry of the house to search for and arrest D on the basis of the "exigencies of the situation." Because the officers did not chase D from the scene of the crime to the house, *Hayden* did not "involve a 'hot pursuit' in the sense that that term would normally be understood." *Santana*, 427 U.S. at 43 n.3. Nonetheless, the Court often treats *Hayden* as if it were a "hot pursuit" case. *E.g.*, Welsh v. Wisconsin, 466 U.S. 740, 750 (1984) (citing *Hayden* as a hot pursuit case); *see also* State v. Dow, 844 P.2d 780 (Mont. 1992) (in which the court upheld D's warrantless arrest in a motel room for a rape that occurred outdoors two hours earlier, supposedly pursuant to the hot pursuit doctrine—although the court also described the doctrine in terms of "fresh pursuit" and "warm pursuit"—after the police discovered D's footprints in the snow leading from the scene of the crime to the motel room).

[32] 495 U.S. 91 (1990).

Based on *Olson*, apparently the police may nonconsensually enter a home without a warrant in hot pursuit of a felon, or if they have probable cause to believe that if they do not enter immediately: (1) evidence will be destroyed; (2) the suspect will escape; or (3) harm will result to the police or others, either inside or outside the dwelling. In assessing the exigency, the gravity of the crime and the likelihood that the suspect is armed must be considered.

The gravity of the crime is sometimes a critical factor. *Olson* involved a felony arrest. The Supreme Court indicated in *Welsh v. Wisconsin*,[33] however, that "application of the exigent-circumstances exception in the context of a home entry should rarely be sanctioned when there is probable cause to believe that only a minor offense . . . has been committed." In *Welsh*, the Court declared unconstitutional the warrantless entry of *D*'s home in order to arrest *D* for driving his car under the influence of alcohol, an offense which constituted a noncriminal violation for which *D* could have been fined $200. The Court rejected the government claim that the entry was necessary because the evidence of the crime—the alcohol in *D*'s bloodstream—would have been imminently "destroyed" by bodily processes if the police could not enter quickly in order to test *D*'s blood-alcohol content.

The Court stopped short of deciding whether the Constitution "impose[s] an absolute ban on warrantless home arrests for certain minor offenses." However, it observed that "it is difficult to conceive of a warrantless home arrest that would not be unreasonable . . . when the underlying offense is extremely minor."

## § 10.06   Arrest in a Third Person's Home: The *Steagald* Warrant Principle

*Payton v. New York*[34] teaches that when the police seek to enter a person's home in order to arrest him, they must have an *arrest* warrant, although the primary reason for the warrant is to safeguard the sanctity of the home, which would ordinarily be protected by a *search* warrant. Suppose, however, that the police have reason to believe that *D*, the person to be arrested, is not at home, but is a guest in *X*'s house. Does the arrest warrant provide the police with the limited authority to enter *X*'s residence and search for *D*, or is a search warrant required? *Payton* left the question open. *Steagald v. United States*[35] answered it.

---

[33] 466 U.S. 740 (1984).

[34] 445 U.S. 573 (1980). See § 10.05, *supra*.

[35] 451 U.S. 204 (1981).

In *Steagald*, the police had information that *D*, for whom they had an arrest warrant, could be "reached during the next 24 hours" at *X*'s home. The officers did not go to *X*'s premises for a few days. When they did, they entered without consent, did not find *D*, but observed illegal drugs that resulted in *X*'s arrest.

The Supreme Court held that the arrest warrant for *D* was an inadequate safeguard of *X*'s independent Fourth Amendment right to privacy in his own home. The arrest warrant primarily served to prevent *D*'s arrest on less than probable cause; it did not protect *X*'s right to reasonable security in his home.

The Court ruled that a person whose home is searched for the presence of a guest is entitled, absent an emergency or consent, to a prior judicial determination of probable cause to search the premises for the person to be arrested. Without this protection, the Court observed, there would be a "significant potential for abuse," in that the police, armed only with an arrest warrant, "could search all the homes of that individual's friends and acquaintances" in the speculative hope of finding evidence against the latter parties.

*Steagald* does not indicate whether an arrest warrant, obtained in this case, is also required. Although the Court pointed out that the police can easily obtain a search warrant "when they obtain an arrest warrant," Professor Wayne LaFave reasons that a search warrant alone ought to be adequate if the magistrate also determines that there is probable cause to arrest the suspect who is the object of the search.[36]

*Steagald* creates line-drawing problems. When the residence that is entered is, as *Payton* put it, the "dwelling in which the suspect lives," an arrest warrant is required, but a search warrant need not be obtained. When *D* is a "guest" in another person's home, a search warrant (and possibly an arrest warrant) is required. The line between a householder (*Payton*) and a guest (*Steagald*) can be thin.

Some cases are easy to decide. After all, in *Payton* itself, other people— *D*'s family—lived with *D*. *Their* privacy rights were threatened by the police entry, but the arrest warrant was sufficient. It follows, therefore, that where *D* and *X* are co-residents of a home, *Payton* applies. At the other extreme, *Steagald* applies if *D* is merely a short-term daytime guest in *X*'s home.

What about an overnight guest? In *Steagald*, *D* was expected to be at *X*'s house "during the next 24 hours," which would suggest he was staying overnight. Furthermore, the police did not enter for a few more days, which

---

[36] 3 LaFave, Note 10, *supra*, at 238–39.

suggests that they may have assumed that he was still living there. Yet, on these facts, the majority required a search warrant. Thus, a brief stay, even if this includes sleeping on the premises, apparently does not convert a guest into a householder for *Payton-Steagald* purposes.

Perhaps the proper line between a guest and a householder should depend on whether the person's stay, either on the basis of duration or shared understanding of the parties, entitles him to consent to police entry of the premises over the householder's objection.[37] In such circumstances, the individual has such control over the premises that it may be appropriate to treat him as a householder (in which case *Payner*, not *Steagald*, applies), and no longer simply as a guest. The Court has not yet clarified the matter.

## § 10.07  Beyond Warrants: Executing an Arrest[38]

### [A]  Arrests in the Home: When and How Entry of the Residence Is Permitted

The Fourth Amendment "require[s] that police actions in execution of a warrant be related to the objectives of the authorized intrusion."[39] This means that a valid arrest warrant "carries with it the limited authority to enter a dwelling in which the suspect lives *when there is reason to believe the suspect is within*."[40] In the absence of a reasonable basis for believing that the suspect is inside the residence, the police may not justify entry of a home on the basis of an arrest warrant.

Even if a police officer has reason to know that the suspect is inside a residence, the common law rule provides that the officer is not ordinarily permitted to forcibly enter the home to execute a search warrant unless he knocked, announced his purpose for entering, requested admittance, and was refused entry. As discussed more fully elsewhere in the text,[41] the Supreme Court ruled in *Wilson v. Arkansas*[42] that this common law "principle forms a part of the reasonableness inquiry under the Fourth Amendment." Specifically, a police officer—even one armed with a warrant—may not ordinarily enter a residence without satisfying the knock-and-announce requirement. This rule seemingly applies to arrests, as well as to searches.

---

[37] In cases of joint access or control of premises, each co-inhabitant ordinarily has a right to consent to a search; the other person assumes the risk of such consent. See § 17.05, *infra.*

[38] *See also* § 10.02, *supra* (the Fourth Amendment permits police officers to execute warrantless *custodial* arrests for violations of minor non-jailable offenses).

[39] Wilson v. Layne, 526 U.S. 603, 611 (1999).

[40] 445 U.S. 573, 603 (1980) (emphasis added).

[41] See § 11.06[C], *infra.*

[42] 514 U.S. 927 (1995).

## [B] Force in Making an Arrest

## [1] Deadly Force[43]

Until the fourteenth century, agents of the Crown were permitted to use deadly force to kill fleeing felons, regardless of the felony, and regardless of whether such force was necessary in order to prevent the escape. Eventually a necessity component was added to the rule, but it remained the case that deadly force was permissible to prevent any felon, even a non-violent one, from avoiding arrest.[44]

In *Tennessee v. Garner*,[45] the Supreme Court held that this common law rule, codified in many states, is unconstitutionally broad.[46] In *Garner*, *O*, an officer, was dispatched to a home on a "prowler inside call." He observed *D* fleeing in the direction of a six-foot-high chain-link fence. By use of his flashlight, *O* could tell that *D* was young, 5'5" to 5'7" tall, and apparently unarmed. He ordered *D* to halt; when the youth began to scale the fence, *O* shot and killed him.

The Supreme Court, per Justice White, held that *O*'s use of deadly force—force intended or likely to cause death or serious bodily harm—to prevent the escape of *D*, an apparently unarmed felon, violated the Fourth Amendment. It stated that "[t]he use of deadly force to prevent the escape of all felony suspects, whatever the circumstances, is constitutionally unreasonable. It is not better that all felony suspects die than that they escape."

*Garner* provides that use of deadly force to make an arrest is unreasonable unless two conditions are met. First, the officer must have "probable cause

---

[43] *See generally* Kevin P. Jenkins, *Police Use of Deadly Force Against Minorities: Ways to Stop the Killing,* 9 Harv. BlackLetter J. 1 (1992); Edward J. Littlejohn, *Deadly Force and its Effects on Police-Community Relations,* 27 How. L.J. 1131 (1984); Lawrence W. Sherman, *Execution Without Trial: Police Homicide and the Constitution,* 33 Vand. L. Rev. 71 (1980); Jerry R. Sparger & David J. Giacopassi, *Memphis Revisited: A Reexamination of Police Shootings After the Garner Decision,* 9 Just. Q. 211 (1992); Abraham N. Tennebaum, *The Influence of the Garner Decision on Police Use of Deadly Force,* 85 J. Crim. L. & Criminology 241 (1994); H. Richard Uviller, *Seizure by Gunshot: The Riddle of the Fleeing Felon,* 14 N.Y.U. Rev. L. & Soc. Change, 705 (1986).

[44] See Dressler, Note 7, *supra,* at § 21.03[B].

[45] 471 U.S. 1 (1985).

[46] In most cases, as in *Garner*, the issue of the alleged use of unnecessary force arises in the context of a civil suit against the officer for the wrongful death of the suspect or, less often, for the violation of the deceased's constitutional rights under 42 U.S.C. § 1983 (1994 & Supp. 2000), or in a prosecution of the officer for criminal homicide. The rule announced in *Garner* only raises potential Fourth Amendment exclusionary rule issues if a non-violent suspect survives the "deadly force," and the prosecutor seeks to introduce evidence obtained from the arrestee as the result of the unreasonable police conduct.

to believe that the suspect poses a significant threat of death or serious physical injury to the officer or others." Justice White suggested that deadly force would be reasonable if the suspect threatened him with a deadly weapon, or if the officer had probable cause to believe that the suspect had committed a felony involving the actual or threatened use of deadly force.

Second, deadly force may only be used if the officer reasonably believes that such force is necessary to make the arrest or prevent escape. If the officer could reasonably effectuate the arrest with non-deadly force, he must do so. Moreover, when feasible, the officer must warn the suspect before deadly force is employed.

### [2]   Non-Deadly Force[47]

As explained above, the Supreme Court ruled in *Garner* that deadly force, used to prevent the escape of a non-deadly felony suspect, constitutes an unreasonable seizure of that person. But *Garner*'s reasoning is not confined to deadly-force cases. The issue, after all, is one of reasonableness: if use of deadly force is unreasonable in the case of some fleeing felons, the use of non-deadly force to arrest a petty criminal might also be excessive in some circumstances.

The Supreme Court has acknowledged *Garner*'s relevance beyond the deadly-force realm. In *Graham v. Connor*,[48] the Court—stating that it was making "explicit what was implicit in *Garner*'s analysis"—held "that *all* claims that law enforcement officers have used excessive force—deadly or not—in the course of an arrest, investigatory stop, or other 'seizure' of a free citizen should be analyzed under the Fourth Amendment . . . 'reasonableness' standard." The issue is "whether the officers' actions are objectively reasonable in light of the facts and circumstances confronting them, without regard to their underlying intent or motivation." Among the relevant factors to be considered are the seriousness of the crime, the extent to which the suspect poses an immediate threat to the safety of others, and the extent to which the suspect is resisting arrest or attempting to escape.

---

[47] *See generally* Uviller, Note 43, *supra*; Gregory Howard Williams, *Controlling the Use of Non-Deadly Force: Policy and Practice*, 10 Harv. BlackLetter J. 79 (1993).

[48] 490 U.S. 386 (1989).

CHAPTER **11**

# SEARCH WARRANTS: IN GENERAL

## § 11.01 The Debate Regarding the Constitutional Role of Search Warrants[1]

### [A] Nature and Significance of the Debate

The first clause of the Fourth Amendment (the Reasonableness Clause) provides that "the right of the people to be secure . . . against unreasonable searches and seizures shall not be violated." The Amendment's second clause (the Warrant Clause) states that "no Warrants shall issue, but upon probable cause, supported by Oath or affirmation, and particularly describing the place to be searched, and the persons or things to be seized." The relationship, if any, of these two clauses is a "syntactical mystery,"[2] and is—as the long and far from complete list of articles cited in footnote one attests—a matter of considerable controversy.

---

[1] *See generally* Akhil Reed Amar, *Fourth Amendment First Principles*, 107 Harv. L. Rev. 757 (1994); Craig M. Bradley, *The Court's "Two Model" Approach to the Fourth Amendment: Carpe Diem!*, 84 J. Crim. L. & Criminology 429 (1993); Craig M. Bradley, *Two Models of the Fourth Amendment*, 83 Mich. L. Rev. 1468 (1985) (hereafter, Bradley, *Two Models . . .*); Sherry F. Colb, *The Qualitative Dimension of Fourth Amendment "Reasonableness,"* 98 Colum. L. Rev. 1642 (1998); Thomas Y. Davies, *Recovering the Original Fourth Amendment*, 98 Mich. L. Rev. 547 (1999); Joseph D. Grano, *Rethinking the Fourth Amendment Warrant Requirement*, 19 Am. Crim. L. Rev. 603 (1982); William W. Greenhalgh & Mark J. Yost, *In Defense of the "Per Se" Rule: Justice Stewart's Struggle to Preserve the Fourth Amendment's Warrant Clause*, 31 Am. Crim. L. Rev. 1013 (1994); Tracey Maclin, *The Complexity of the Fourth Amendment: A Historical Review*, 77 B.U. L. Rev. 925 (1997); Tracey Maclin, *When the Cure For the Fourth Amendment Is Worse Than the Disease*, 68 S. Cal. L. Rev. 1 (1994); Carol S. Steiker, *Second Thoughts About First Principles*, 107 Harv. L. Rev. 820 (1994); William J. Stuntz, *Warrants and Fourth Amendment Remedies*, 77 Va. L. Rev. 881 (1991); James J. Tomkovicz, *California v. Acevedo: The Walls Close In On The Warrant Requirement*, 29 Am. Crim. L. Rev. 1103 (1992); H. Richard Uviller, *Reasonability and the Fourth Amendment: A (Belated) Farewell to Justice Potter Stewart*, 25 Crim. L. Bull. 29 (1989); Silas J. Wasserstrom, *The Court's Turn Toward a General Reasonableness Interpretation of the Fourth Amendment*, 27 Am. Crim. L. Rev. 119 (1989).

[2] Uviller, Note 1, *supra*, at 33.

There are two schools of thought regarding the relationship of the two clauses. One view is that the clauses are vitally linked; specifically, "the Warrant Clause defines and interprets the Reasonableness Clause."[3] According to this view, "[t]he command of the Fourth Amendment to the American police officer and the American prosecutor is simple: 'You always have to get a warrant—UNLESS YOU CAN'T.' "[4] Or, as one scholar put it, "a warrant is *always* required for *every* search and seizure when it is practicable to obtain one."[5] The Supreme Court has expressed this "warrant requirement" (or "warrant preference") rule in *Katz v. United States*,[6] when it provided that "searches conducted outside the judicial process, without prior approval by judge or magistrate, are *per se* unreasonable under the Fourth Amendment—subject only to a few specifically established and well-delineated exceptions." Advocates of this rule believe that exceptions to the warrant requirement should be "jealously and carefully drawn,"[7] and permitted only on "a showing . . . that the exigencies of the situation made that course imperative."[8]

The competing position is that the preference for search warrants was "judicially created"[9] and is not constitutionally required. According to this view, the Warrant Clause does not inform the Reasonableness Clause; the clauses are independent of each other. Advocates of this model believe that the first clause of the Fourth Amendment "speaks globally to all searches and seizures,"[10] and provides simply that they must be reasonable, taking into consideration all relevant factors.[11] As the Supreme Court stated in *United States v. Rabinowitz*,[12] the appropriate test of police conduct "is not whether it is reasonable to procure a search warrant, but whether the search is reasonable." According to this view, then, what *is* the purpose

---

[3] Maclin, *When the Cure. . .*, Note 1, *supra*, at 20.

[4] Dyson v. State, 712 A.2d 573, 577 (Md. App. 1997), *reversed*, Maryland v. Dyson, 527 U.S. 465 (1999).

[5] Bradley, *Two Models . . .*, Note 1, *supra*, at 1471.

[6] 389 U.S. 347 (1967).

[7] Jones v. United States, 357 U.S. 493, 499 (1958).

[8] McDonald v. United States, 335 U.S. 451, 456 (1948).

[9] Robbins v. California, 453 U.S. 420, 438 (1981) (Rehnquist, J., dissenting).

[10] Amar, Note 1, *supra*, at 762.

[11] *See* Terry v. Ohio, 392 U.S. 1, 21 (1968) (*quoting* Camara v. Municipal Court, 387 U.S. 523, 536–37 (1967)) ("there is 'no ready test for determining reasonableness other than by balancing the need to search [or seize] against the invasion which the search [or seizure] entails' "); Bradley, *Two Models . . .*, Note 1, *supra*, at 1471 ("[a] search or seizure must be reasonable, considering all relevant factors on a case-by-case basis").

[12] 339 U.S. 56 (1950), *overruled on other grounds*, Chimel v. California, 395 U.S. 752 (1969).

of the Warrant Clause? It tells us "when warrants may not issue, not when they may, or must."[13] The Warrant Clause informs us that "any warrant that *does* issue is per se unreasonable if not supported by probable cause, particular description, and the rest."[14]

The practical significance of the debate is enormous. Strict enforcement of a warrant requirement would compel police officers to apply for warrants in the vast majority of cases. In such a system, judges, rather than police, would make nearly all probable cause determinations. On the other hand, warrants would be a rarity under the alternative model. The police would determine whether to intrude on a citizen's privacy, and the judiciary would have the more limited role of determining, after the incursion, whether the police conduct was reasonable.

## [B] The Substance of the Debate

### [1] Historical Debate

Professor Telford Taylor contends that those "who have viewed the fourth amendment primarily as a requirement that searches be covered by warrants, have stood the amendment on its head."[15] Opponents of a warrant requirement reason that the framers of the Fourth Amendment were not concerned about the executive branch of government, including the police; instead, they feared the judiciary, which in the colonial era authorized abusive warrants, in the form of general warrants and writs of assistance.[16] In short, in the framers' eyes, judges were "the heavies, not the heroes, of our story."[17] It makes no sense, therefore, to think that the Amendment is intended to compel the police to seek judicial approval before they conduct searches.

In further support of this reading of history, opponents of a warrant requirement point out that, at common law, arrests without warrants were permissible in many circumstances, and warrantless searches incident to arrests were also allowed. Moreover, the First Congress, which proposed the Fourth Amendment, also passed legislation authorizing federal naval inspectors to enter and conduct warrantless searches of ships. According to Professor Akhil Amar, "[i]f any members of the early Congresses objected to or even questioned these warrantless searches and seizures on

---

[13] Amar, Note 1, *supra*, at 774.

[14] *Id.* at 762 (emphasis added).

[15] Telford Taylor, Two Studies in Constitutional Interpretation 46–47 (1969).

[16] *See* § 5.03, *supra*.

[17] Akhil Reed Amar, *The Bill of Rights as a Constitution*, 100 Yale L.J. 1131, 1179 (1991).

Fourth Amendment grounds, supporters of the so-called warrant requirement have yet to identify them."[18]

Proponents of the warrant-requirement rule contend that the preceding arguments go too far. They agree that the drafters of the Fourth Amendment intended for the Warrant Clause to prevent abusive warrants. But, they do not believe that this was the sole purpose of the clause. They make a textual claim: "[o]n any fair reading, this language appears to assume that searches and seizures will be conducted, at least sometimes, pursuant to warrants."[19] Were it otherwise, a legislature could evade the probable cause and particularity requirements of the Warrant Clause by the simple expedient of abolishing all warrants. Thus, unless there is at least *some* warrant requirement, a legislature could render the constitutional text useless.

Moreover, the history of the Fourth Amendment is not quite as clear as the opponents of the warrant requirement suggest. As Professor Joseph Grano observed, "[w]hile the colonists did not object to warrantless searches, the reason for the absence of such objection was that such searches, except perhaps in the context of lawful arrests, simply did not exist."[20] Indeed, Telford Taylor concluded from his historical survey that the correct principle of law at that time was that "searches incident to arrests are permissible, and in exceptional cases, *if authorized by warrant*, searches independent of arrest may be carried out."[21]

According to some advocates of a warrant requirement, the "history of the Fourth Amendment *is* about controlling executive power."[22] Professor Anthony Amsterdam suggests that "the fourth amendment is quintessentially a regulation of the police—that, in enforcing the fourth amendment, courts *must* police the police."[23]

So, who is right? The historical debate will doubtlessly continue for years to come. However, Professor Thomas Davies's recent scholarly research may come the closest to date to providing insights into the Framers' collective minds. His research finds that, indeed, the "Framers' complaints were not about warrantless intrusions but were almost exclusively about . . . searches of houses under general warrants."[24] Nonetheless, Professor

---

[18] Amar, Note 1, *supra*, at 766–67.

[19] Grano, Note 1, *supra*, at 617.

[20] *Id.*

[21] Taylor, Note 15, *supra*, at 49.

[22] Maclin, Note 1, *supra*, at 5 (emphasis added).

[23] Anthony G. Amsterdam, *Perspectives On the Fourth Amendment*, 58 Minn. L. Rev. 349, 371 (1974).

[24] Davies, Note 1, *supra*, at 553.

Davies contends that the "warrant-preference construction [of the Fourth Amendment] is more faithful to the Framers' concerns than the generalized-reasonableness construction. *In fact, the latter is nearly the antithesis of the Framers' understanding.*"[25]

Davies believes that the Framers' lack of attention to warrantless police action was a function of historical factors not relevant in modern time:

> [I]t made sense for the Framers to focus only on clarifying warrant standards because the *ex officio* authority of the framing-era officer was still rather meager. For example, the framing-era constable's arrest authority was much narrower than is generally supposed, and nowhere near that of a modern police officer. Likewise, the justifications available for a warrantless entry of a house were especially limited. At common law, controlling the warrant *did* control the officer for all practical purposes.[26]

As Davies reads the historical evidence, although the immediate purpose of the Fourth Amendment was to prohibit general warrants and their like, "the larger purpose for which the Framers adopted the text . . . [was] to curb the exercise of discretionary authority by officers."[27]

### [2] Policy Debate

Proponents of a warrant-requirement rule respond that even if history conclusively supported the claims of opponents, this would not resolve the debate. They favor a principle of "constitutional dynamism—the principle that interpretations of the Constitution will and should change over time to accommodate the needs of different historical ages."[28] Warrant advocates contend that there are compelling reasons to demand that a police officer—an agent of the government[29] —ordinarily obtain a warrant before

---

[25] *Id.* at 556 (emphasis added).

[26] *Id.* at 554. Davies explains, as well, that there was a second reason for the Framers' lack of attention to warrantless intrusions: "they did not antiticipate that a wrongful act by an officer might constitute a form of government illegality—rather, they viewed such misconduct as only a *personal* trespass by the person who held the office." *Id.* The notion that police misconduct constitutes *government* misconduct appears to have been a nineteenth century development.

[27] *Id.* at 556.

[28] Steiker, Note 1, *supra*, at 825–26; *see* Maclin, *When the Cure. . .*, Note 1, *supra*, at 11 (the Amendment "states an ideal; it is not a constitutional wrench that 'locks-in' search and seizure practices of a vanished era"); *see also* Davies, Note 1, *supra*, at 556 ("I . . . doubt[] that the original meaning [of the Amendment] can be directly applied to address modern issues. . . . [I]t would be inappropriate to employ framing-era doctrines selectively to answer specific modern issues because historic doctrines often do not accomplish the same ends in the modern context as they did during the framing era.").

[29] *See* Note 26, *supra*.

conducting a search. In *Johnson v. United States*,[30] the Supreme Court explained the policy in favor of warrants this way:

> The point of the Fourth Amendment, which often is not grasped by zealous officers, is not that it denies law enforcement the support of the usual inferences which reasonable men draw from evidence. Its protection consists in requiring that those inferences be drawn by a neutral and detached magistrate instead of being judged by the officer engaged in the often competitive enterprise of ferreting out crime. Any assumption that evidence sufficient to support a magistrate's disinterested determination to issue a search warrant will justify the officers in making a search without a warrant would reduce the Amendment to nullity and leave the people's homes secure only in the discretion of police officers.

Essentially, the argument is this: the Fourth Amendment "is designed to prevent, not simply to redress, unlawful police action."[31] Therefore, if people are going to be secure in their persons, houses, papers and effects from unreasonable searches and seizures, as the Fourth Amendment guarantees, a neutral party—the judge, and not the police officer or the person whose privacy or security is at risk—should make the initial determination whether there is sufficient basis to intrude on an individual's security. Warrant advocates also suggest that a magistrate's intervention between the police and a citizen is even more important today than in the eighteenth century, in light of the enhanced authority claimed by government over the lives of individuals, the more intrusive crime-prevention methods available to law enforcement, and racial divisions.[32]

In response, opponents of the warrant requirement contend that "if taken seriously, a warrant requirement makes no sense."[33] Professor Akhil Amar defends this position by noting that nobody truly believes that warrants are *always* required. There must be an exception for exigent circumstances. It also makes no sense to him that the police should be barred from conducting a warrantless search if they receive consent to do so. Moreover, nobody would seriously claim that a warrant is required before an officer seizes an object in plain view, or before guards x-ray luggage in an airport. He contends that, in view of the "vast number of real-life, unintrusive, nondiscriminatory searches and seizures to which modern day Americans are routinely subjected,"[34] the warrant requirement cannot withstand scrutiny.

---

[30] 333 U.S. 10 (1948).

[31] Chimel v. California, 395 U.S. 752, 766 n.12 (1969).

[32] *See* Steiker, Note 1, *supra*, at 830–44.

[33] Amar, Note 1, *supra*, at 767–68.

[34] *Id.* at 769.

The fall-back position of advocates of a warrant requirement is that there are exceptions to the warrant requirement. In essence, there is not a constitutional warrant *requirement*, but rather a constitutional *preference* for warrants. Professor Amar contends, however, that since there are no exceptions to the supposed warrant requirement in the Fourth Amendment— the courts just make them up as they go along—this "modification seems to concede that the ultimate touchstone of the amendment is not warrants, but reasonableness." [35] Our common sense tells us that "reasonableness" is the proper rule; if the Supreme Court accepted this proposition, Amar argues, it and lower courts would not have to play "word games" to avoid the Warrant Clause, such as by suggesting that some searches are not really searches at all, [36] and that "probable cause" does not really mean "probable." [37]

But, if reasonableness is the touchstone, what then? Amar concedes that this standard involves a "complex equation" that demands of police officers and the courts that they balance a myriad of factors, including the probability of finding the evidence in question, "the intrusiveness of the search, the identity of the search target, the availability of other means of achieving the purpose of the search, and so on." [38] As noted in the context of "probable cause," [39] "reasonableness" converts the Fourth Amendment into "one immense Rorschach blot," [40] which would be "splendid in its flexibility, [but] awful in its unintelligibility, unadministrability, unenforcibility and general ooziness." [41] And, in view of the vagueness—ooziness—of the standard, proponents of the warrant requirement fear that "courts are seldom going to say that what [the police] did was unreasonable." [42]

### [C]  Who Has "Won" the Debate?

Justice Antonin Scalia has observed that the Supreme Court's Fourth Amendment "jurisprudence [has] lurched back and forth between imposing a categorical warrant requirement and looking to reasonableness alone." [43] In the early years of Fourth Amendment law, a long line of cases suggested that searches had to be conducted "pursuant to a warrant or . . . fall within

---

[35] *Id.* at 771.

[36] *See* § 7.01, *supra.*

[37] *See* § 9.07[A], *supra.*

[38] Amar, Note 1, *supra,* at 801.

[39] *See* § 9.07[C][2], *supra.*

[40] Amsterdam, Note 23, *supra,* at 393.

[41] *Id.* at 415.

[42] *Id.* at 394.

[43] California v. Acevedo, 500 U.S. 565, 582 (1991) (concurring opinion).

one of the exceptions to the warrant requirement."[44] The Court's position became muddy in the late 1940's and 1950s, however, and remained so until the Supreme Court's *Katz*[45] decision in 1967.

The warrant-requirement rule re-emerged forcefully with *Katz*. During the next fifteen years or so, the Court fairly consistently reaffirmed the supremacy of the Warrant Clause. Yet, even as it did so, it approved new and broader exceptions to the "warrant requirement." As a consequence, "the Supreme Court . . . created a jurisprudential mare's nest,"[46] in which the exceptions to the "requirement" seemingly gobbled up the rule. A leading judicial advocate of the warrant requirement during this era was Justice Potter Stewart, who retired in 1981. Justice Byron White was the leading advocate of the competing "reasonableness" interpretation of the Fourth Amendment.

With Justice Stewart's departure, the Supreme Court increasingly moved away from the principle of a warrant requirement. "Warrant requirement" language is now predominantly found in dissenting opinions.[47] The clear and unmistakable trend of Fourth Amendment law is toward the primacy of the Reasonableness Clause. Majority opinions now state that "[t]he touchstone of the Fourth Amendment is reasonableness."[48] Indeed, it now appears that a majority of the Justices on the Supreme Court believe not only that the reasonableness rule should predominate, but that courts should look initially to the common law for an understanding of what constitutes a reasonable search or seizure. In *Wyoming v Houghton*,[49] the Court stated:

> [I]n determining whether a particular governmental action violates [the Fourth Amendment], we inquire first whether the action was regarded as an unlawful search or seizure under the common law when the Amendment was framed. Where that inquiry yields no answer, we must evaluate the search or seizure under traditional standards of reasonableness by assessing, on the one hand, the degree to which it intrudes upon an individual's privacy and, on the other hand, the degree to which it is needed for the promotion of legitimate governmental interests.

---

[44] Greenhalgh & Yost, Note 1, *supra*, at 1041.

[45] Katz v. United States, 389 U.S. 347 (1967).

[46] Hulit v. State, 982 S.W.2d 431, 436 (Tex. Crim. App. 1998).

[47] *E.g.*, California v. Acevedo, 500 U.S. at 586 (Stevens and Marshall, JJ., dissenting) ("The [warrant] requirement . . . reflects the sound policy judgment that, absent exceptional circumstances, the decision to invade the privacy of an individual's personal effects should be made by a neutral magistrate rather than an agent of the Executive").

[48] *E.g.*, Florida v. Jimeno, 500 U.S. 248, 250 (1991).

[49] 526 U.S. 295, 299–300 (1999); *see generally* David A. Sklansky, *The Fourth Amendment and Common Law*, 100 Colum. L. Rev. 1739 (2000).

This sea-change in the Court's attitude may also be seen in the following justification for dispensing with a warrant requirement for the search of containers found in automobiles:[50]

To the extent that the [warrant-requirement] rule protects privacy, its protection is minimal. Law enforcement officers may seize a container and hold it until they obtain a search warrant. . . . "Since the police, by hypothesis, have probable cause to seize the property, we can assume that a warrant will be routinely forthcoming in the overwhelming majority of cases."[51]

The hypothesis that the police have probable cause to conduct their searches and, therefore, that warrants will be "routinely forthcoming," demonstrates that the Court no longer believes that there is a need to impose a neutral arbiter between the police and the citizenry. In light of this reasoning, one scholar has predicted that "the Court is 'substantively,' if not 'formally,' headed toward" the conclusion that "the warrant rule is unsound or [at least] that it has no application outside the home."[52]

The latter proposition—that the Court might retain a warrant requirement, subject to various exceptions, in the limited context of a home[53] —seems more likely than that the Court will abandon warrants entirely. Indeed, Justice Scalia, an ardent advocate of the "reasonableness" rule, has indicated that he believes that warrants are required in limited circumstances—"where the common law required a warrant [presumably, in searches of homes]; and it may even be that changes in the surrounding legal rules . . . may make a warrant indispensable to reasonableness where it once was not."[54]

Moreover, even today, it is often necessary for lawyers and courts to talk about the "warrant requirement" or, more accurately, about "exceptions" to the "warrant requirement." This is because the Supreme Court has not

---

[50] See generally § 14.07, infra.

[51] California v. Acevedo, 500 U.S. at 575 (quoting the dissenting opinion in Arkansas v. Sanders, 442 U.S. 753, 770 (1979)).

[52] Tomkovicz, Note 1, supra, at 1176–77.

[53] Where would such a rule leave the homeless? Indeed, do the homeless have a reasonable expectation of privacy in their belongings, or are they shut out of Fourth Amendment protection entirely? This issue has rarely been considered by the courts. But see State v. Mooney, 588 A.2d 145 (Conn. 1991) (involving a search of a homeless person's belongings left unattended under a bridge). Mooney inspired considerable scholarly attention. E.g., Mark A. Godsey, Comment, Privacy and the Growing Plight of the Homeless: Reconsidering the Values Underlying the Fourth Amendment, 53 Ohio St. L.J. 869 (1992); Peter Mancini, Mooney and Privacy: Some Tough Questions, 72 B.U. L. Rev. 425 (1992); Kevin Royer, The Mooney Blues: Homelessness and Constitutional Security from Unreasonable Searches, 72 B.U. L. Rev. 443 (1992).

[54] Acevedo, 500 U.S. at 583 (concurring opinion).

cleared the deck of many of its rulings from the earlier era. Thus, there are many "exceptions" to the "warrant requirement" that were formulated in the middle of the twentieth century that remain good law today. The rules from those cases still apply, even if the underlying reasoning may increasingly seem dated.

## § 11.02  The Warrant Application Process[55]

An investigating officer who seeks a warrant prepares an application for a search (or arrest) warrant; an affidavit, sworn under oath or by affirmation, setting out the facts supporting the warrant; and the warrant itself. The officer then seeks approval of the documents from a supervisor or, in some jurisdictions, an assistant prosecutor.

Once approval is obtained, the officer goes to the courthouse or, if necessary, to the home of a judge.[56] When choices are available, such as in large urban areas, judge-shopping is common: the officer seeks a judge known to issue warrants liberally. During the daytime, the officer ordinarily presents the application to the judge while she is on the bench, during a court recess.

In theory, the judge carefully reads the officer's documents and questions her regarding any ambiguities in the materials. When the application includes hearsay information, which is common, the judge will question the officer to ensure that the informant's basis of knowledge was good and her veracity high. Although it is exceedingly rare, the judge may require the informant to be identified or produced, if necessary to the probable cause determination.[57]

In practice, warrant proceedings are brief. According to one study, the average time taken by a reviewing magistrate to consider an application was two minutes, 48 seconds; the median time was two minutes, 12 seconds. Ten percent of all applications were reviewed in less than one minute. Fewer than ten percent of all applications were rejected.[58]

After a warrant is approved and signed by the judge, she gives the original warrant and a copy to the officer, and retains a copy and the supporting documentation. Frequently, a clerk will establish a file for the case. After

---

[55] *See generally* Richard Van Duizend, L. Paul Sutton, & Charlotte Carter, The Search Warrant Process: Preconceptions, Perceptions, and Practices (National Center for State Courts 1984); Abraham S. Goldstein, *The Search Warrant, the Magistrate, and Judicial Review*, 62 N.Y.U. L. Rev. 1173 (1987).

[56] In some jurisdictions, a warrant may be issued on sworn oral testimony via telephone. *E.g.*, Fed. R. Crim. P 41(c)(2)(A).

[57] McCray v. Illinois, 386 U.S. 300 (1967).

[58] R. Van Duizend, *et al.*, Note 55, *supra*, at 25–32.

execution of the warrant, the officer files a "return" with the court, indicating when the search occurred and what, if anything, was seized.

## § 11.03 "Neutral and Detached Magistrate" Requirement

Although the Fourth Amendment does not expressly so require, warrants must be issued by "neutral and detached magistrate[s]."[59] This requirement is not met if the person issuing the warrant is a member of the executive branch, such as the state attorney general, rather than a member of the judiciary.[60]

Even if a warrant is issued by a member of the judiciary, she must be neutral and detached, rather than a "rubber stamp for the police."[61] Thus, an unsalaried magistrate who receives a fee for each warrant issued, but no compensation for applications denied, lacks the requisite detachment.[62]

A warrant is also invalid if the issuing magistrate, by her behavior in a particular case, manifests a lack of neutrality. For example, a judge who accompanies officers to a bookstore suspected of selling obscene material, and who there inspects the materials to determine which ones are obscene, is "not acting as a judicial officer but as an adjunct law enforcement officer."[63]

On the other hand, the magistrate or judge need not be a lawyer. In *Shadwick v. City of Tampa*,[64] the Supreme Court approved the issuance of misdemeanor arrest warrants by non-lawyer court clerks. Although the case dealt only with misdemeanor arrests, the Court's language was broad and cited felony search warrant cases in support. Indeed, the Supreme Court observed uncritically in *Illinois v. Gates*[65] that "search and arrest warrants long have been issued by persons who are neither lawyers nor judges, and who certainly do not remain abreast of each judicial refinement of the nature of 'probable cause.' "

---

[59] Johnson v. United States, 333 U.S. 10, 14 (1948).

[60] Coolidge v. New Hampshire, 403 U.S. 443, 453 (1971).

[61] United States v. Leon, 468 U.S. 897, 914 (1984) (*quoting* Aguilar v. Texas, 378 U.S. 108, 111 (1964)). Unfortunately, a perception among many persons involved in the criminal justice system is that many magistrates "knowingly accept police perjury as truthful," in part because they wish to assist the police in their investigations, and in order to improve their own re-election chances. Myron W. Orfield, Jr., *Deterrence, Perjury, and the Heater Factor: An Exclusionary Rule in the Chicago Criminal Courts*, 63 U. Colo. L. Rev. 75, 83 (1992) (study of Cook County criminal justice system).

[62] Connally v. Georgia, 429 U.S. 245 (1977).

[63] Lo-Ji Sales, Inc. v. New York, 442 U.S. 319, 327 (1979).

[64] 407 U.S. 345 (1972).

[65] 462 U.S. 213, 235 (1983).

## § 11.04 "Oath or Affirmation"

The Fourth Amendment provides that warrants may not be issued unless they are "supported by Oath or affirmation." Therefore, a warrant defective for want of probable cause cannot be saved by post-warrant proof that the police had additional information that they failed to disclose to the judge.[66]

A more complex situation arises when an officer provides false information to the magistrate.[67] Under limited circumstances outlined in *Franks v. Delaware*,[68] a defendant may mount a post-search attack on a facially valid warrant on the ground that, but for the falsity in the affidavit, a warrant would not have been issued.

According to *Franks*, an affidavit supporting a search warrant is presumed valid. A defendant is not entitled to a hearing to attack the affidavit (and, thus, the warrant) unless she makes a "substantial preliminary showing"[69] that: (1) a false statement was included in the affidavit, *e.g.*, the affiant did not observe the events that she swore that she saw, did not have the conversations she claimed to have had, or fabricated the existence of a confidential informant and the details supposedly received from her[70] ; (2) the affiant made the false statement "knowingly and intentionally" or with

---

[66] Whiteley v. Warden, 401 U.S. 560 (1971), *questioned on other grounds*, Arizona v. Evans, 514 U.S. 1 (1995).

[67] For general discussion of the problem of policy perjury (or what has come to be called "testilying"), *see* Gabriel J. Chin & Scott C. Wells, *The "Blue Wall of Silence" as Evidence of Bias and Motive to Lie: A New Approach to Police Perjury*, 59 U. Pitt. L. Rev. 233 (1998); Andrew J. McClurg, *Good Cop, Bad Cop: Using Cognitive Dissonance Theory to Reduce Police Lying*, 32 U.C. Davis L. Rev. 389 (1999); Christopher Slobogin, *Testilying: Police Perjury and What to Do About It*, 67 U. Colo. L. Rev. 1037 (1996).

[68] 438 U.S. 154 (1978).

[69] Such a showing is made in the form of specific allegations and an offer of proof, including the use of affidavits or other reliable statements of witnesses.

[70] *E.g.* Allan R. Gold, *Dead Officer, Dropped Charges: a Scandal in Boston*, New York Times, March 20, 1989, at A12 (charges were dropped in a homicide case due to "egregious misconduct" by the prosecutor and the police, including the fact that a police officer applied for several warrants based on hearsay information of "John," who did not exist).

Professor Donald Dripps has suggested that at suppression hearings where the outcome of the proceeding depends on the credibility of witnesses, "the court should inquire whether either party is willing to supplement the record with a polygraph examination of the party's witness or witnesses." Although the judge would not be bound by the results of the polygraph examinations, she could consider them along with all of the other evidence, and the results would become part of the record to be considered, as appropriate, by an appellate court. Donald A. Dripps, *Police, Plus Perjury, Equals Polygraphy*, 86 J. Crim. L. & Criminology 693, 694 (1996).

reckless disregard for the truth;[71] and (3) the false statement was necessary to the magistrate's finding of probable cause.

If these allegations are proved at a hearing by a preponderance of the evidence, the warrant is void, and the fruits of the search must be excluded from evidence at the criminal trial. As stated in *Franks*, "it would be an unthinkable imposition upon the [the magistrate's] authority if a warrant affidavit, revealed after the fact to contain a deliberately or recklessly false statement, were to stand beyond impeachment."

*Franks* does not permit impeachment of a "nongovernmental informant."[72] Therefore, a warrant is not voidable if an informant lies to the affiant, who then innocently or negligently (but not recklessly or deliberately) passes along this false information to the magistrate. The rationale for drawing this distinction is that the general credibility of the *informant* must be shown as part of the probable cause requirement, while the veracity of the *affiant* is assumed at the probable cause stage. Thus, a *Franks* challenge is the only opportunity to demonstrate the unworthiness of the affiant's information, but would arguably be redundant as a check on the informant.

## § 11.05  Search Warrant "Particularity" Requirement

### [A]  In General

The Fourth Amendment provides that warrants must "particularly describ[e] the place to be searched, and the persons or things to be seized." Particularity is required in order to avoid the abuses, exemplified by general warrants and writs of assistance, that occurred under the English and colonial common law.[73] A warrant that lacks particularity permits police officers too much discretion in its execution and undercuts the probable cause requirement.

### [B]  "Place to be Searched"

A place to be searched must be described in the warrant in a manner sufficiently precise that the officer executing the warrant can identify it with reasonable effort.[74] For example, it is sufficient if the search warrant

---

[71] In other contexts the Court has defined "reckless disregard for the truth" to mean that the person "in fact entertained serious doubts as to the truth" of the statement made. St. Amant v. Thompson, 390 U.S. 727, 731 (1968).

[72] The Court did not explain the meaning of the adjectival limitation. Seemingly, it would be permissible to impeach another police officer who, although not the affiant, provided information that went into the affidavit.

[73] *See* § 5.03, *supra*.

[74] Steele v. United States, 267 U.S. 498, 503 (1925).

provides the street address of a single-unit house to be searched. If the structure is a multiple-unit building, additional information, such as an apartment number, is required.

If the officer who applies for a warrant has reason to believe that the building to be searched is a single-unit structure, so that a street address is sufficient, but the officer executing the warrant learns that the structure contains multiple units, the warrant itself is not invalid for want of particularity, because its validity "must be assessed on the basis of the information that the officers disclosed, or had a duty to discover and to disclose, to the issuing Magistrate."[75] The more difficult problem in such a case relates to the *execution* of the facially valid warrant. If the warrant directs the police to search "the home belonging to *D*, who lives at 123 Main Street," and upon arriving there they learn (or should have learned) that the building at that address is a duplex, the officers are obligated to limit their search to *D*'s unit, which they can ascertain by reasonable effort, such as by checking names on the mailbox or by asking neighbors.[76]

A warrant to search an automobile is sufficient if it describes the vehicle in a manner that will make it easy for the officer to determine what car may be searched. For example, the license or vehicle identification number of the vehicle is adequate. So, too, it could be sufficient simply to identify it by its location, if the location is a one-car garage, but not if it is a two-car garage or public parking lot.

### [C] "Persons or Things to be Seized"

The phrase "persons . . . to be seized" primarily relates to arrest warrants, because an arrest is a seizure of a person.[77]

The "things to be seized" should be described in search warrants with sufficient particularity that, in the words of the Supreme Court in *Marron v. United States*,[78] "seizure of one thing under a warrant describing another

---

[75] Maryland v. Garrison, 480 U.S. 79, 85 (1987).

[76] However, a search of the wrong premises may be reasonable. In *Garrison, id.*, the officers executed a warrant of a "third floor apartment" at a particular address. The officers did not learn (and had no reason to know) until after they had entered the "third floor apartment" and had seized evidence that the premises actually were a two-apartment unit, and that they were in the wrong apartment. The Court approved the search and seizure, observing that it must "allow some latitude for honest mistakes that are made by officers in the dangerous and difficult process of making arrests and executing search warrants." Once they became aware of their error, however, the officers were required to desist from searching the apartment further.

[77] Some jurisdictions permit the seizure of a person "who is unlawfully restrained," such as a kidnap victim, as "evidence" of the crime. *E.g.*, Fed. R. Crim. P. 41(b).

[78] 275 U.S. 192, 196 (1927).

[cannot occur]. As to what is to be taken, nothing is left to the discretion of the officer executing the warrant."

In practice, neither the Supreme Court nor lower courts have applied the *Marron* test strictly. In his treatise, Professor Wayne LaFave has helpfully summarized the general principles that he has distilled from the numerous cases in the field.[79] Among the principles he identified are: (1) vagueness in the warrant description is tolerated to a greater degree when the police have described the item with as much particularity as can reasonably be expected;[80] and (2) less specificity is required regarding contraband[81] than is required regarding stolen goods[82] or items, such as books and papers, that retain special First Amendment protection.[83]

## § 11.06　Execution of Search Warrants[84]

### [A]　In Anticipation of Execution

In the ordinary course of events, the police will obtain a search warrant and then proceed to the site of the search and execute it according to the principles laid out in this chapter section beginning in subsection [B]. On occasion, however, the police may find themselves in a situation in which an exigency justifying an immediate warrantless search does not exist,[85] but they have reason to fear that such an exigency will develop during the period in which they apply for the warrant. In such circumstances, the police may wish to cordon off the area in anticipation of the warrant. Yet, such an action may itself constitute a warrantless seizure of the property in question.

For example, in *Illinois v. McArthur*,[86] police officers had probable cause to believe that *D* had hidden illegal drugs in his trailer home. They went

---

[79] 2 Wayne R. LaFave, Search and Seizure § 4.6 (3d ed. 1996).

[80] *E.g.*, Andresen v. Maryland, 427 U.S. 463, 479 (1976) (a warrant authorizing the seizure of items pertaining to a real estate fraud, but which included a residual clause authorizing the seizure of "fruits, instrumentalities, and evidence of crime at this [time] unknown," was upheld by the Court in part because of the complexity of the real estate scheme and the inability of the police to be more specific).

[81] *E.g.*, it is satisfactory for the warrant to direct the officers to seize "gambling paraphernalia," "controlled substances," or "drugs unlawfully possessed."

[82] *E.g.*, it is insufficient to describe the item to be seized as "the stolen automobile" or "the jewelry," if a more specific description is possible.

[83] Stanford v. Texas, 379 U.S. 476, 485 (1965) ("The constitutional requirement [of particularity] . . . is to be accorded the most scrupulous exactitude when the 'things' are books, and the basis for their seizure is the ideas which they contain.").

[84] *See generally* 2 LaFave, Note 79, *supra*, at §§ 4.7–4.12.

[85] *See generally* § 12.04, *infra* (when a warrantless entry of a home is justified on exigent grounds).

[86] 531 U.S. 326 (2001).

to *D*'s home and asked for permission to search it, but *D* refused. One officer immediately sent a second officer to apply for a search warrant. In the meantime, *D* had left his trailer and was standing on his porch. The officer informed *D* that, until a warrant was obtained, he could not reenter his trailer unless an officer accompanied him inside. During the wait, *D* reentered his home a few times (to get cigarettes and make telephone calls), and each time the officer stood guard just inside the door. Two hours later, warrant in hand, the police searched the trailer and discovered the contraband.

The Court upheld the police action here. Although the Court said that in "the ordinary case" a warrantless *seizure* of personal property, just like a warrantless *search*, is unreasonable, the Court believed that the warrantless temporary seizure of the premises here was reasonable. [87] The Court pointed to the following circumstances, which it noted existed in combination: (1) the police had probable cause to conduct the search for contraband; (2) the police "had good reason to fear that, unless restrained, [*D*] would destroy the drugs"; (3) "the police made reasonable efforts to reconcile their law enforcement needs with the demands of personal privacy," for example, they avoided significant intrusions into the house until the warrant was obtained; and (4) the length of time of the restraint was limited.

*McArthur* is a narrow opinion and does not justify all anticipatory warrantless seizures of personal premises. But a temporary seizure, supported by probable cause, "designed to prevent the loss of evidence while the police diligently obtain[] a warrant in a reasonable period of time" is permissible.

### [B] Time of Execution

Some jurisdictions, by statute or rule of procedure, require that search warrants be executed within a specified period of time from the date that the warrant was signed by the magistrate, often within ten days. [88] This rule reduces the risk that the justification for the search—the basis for the finding of probable cause—will become stale.

Some jurisdictions bar nighttime execution of warrants, "unless the issuing authority, by appropriate provision in the warrant, and for reasonable cause shown" authorizes it. [89] The Supreme Court has not determined

---

[87] The police action constituted a seizure because it resulted in a meaningful interference with *D*'s possessory interest in his trailer. *See* § 8.02[A], *supra*.

[88] *E.g.,* Fed. R. Crim. P 41(c)(1).

[89] *Id.*

whether non-exigent nighttime warrant executions are constitutionally reasonable.[90]

### [C]  Means of Entry

At common law, absent special circumstances, an officer was not permitted to enter a home forcibly to execute a warrant, unless he knocked at the door (or otherwise indicated his presence), identified himself as an officer, stated his purpose for entering, requested admittance, and was refused admission.[91]

In *Wilson v. Arkansas*,[92] the Supreme Court, per Justice Clarence Thomas, unanimously held that the common law knock-and-announce "principle forms a part of the reasonableness inquiry under the Fourth Amendment." Justice Thomas stated that the common law rule "was woven quickly into the fabric of early American law," because most states that ratified the Fourth Amendment also enacted statutes or constitutional provisions incorporating English common law. History, therefore, "leaves no doubt that the reasonableness of a search of a dwelling may depend in part on whether law enforcement officers announced their presence and authority prior to entering."

The knock-and-announce rule, however, is qualified. First, there are exceptions to the requirement. Justice Thomas did not provide a comprehensive list of circumstances in which no-knock entries are permitted, choosing instead to leave the matter initially to lower courts for determination. Nonetheless, he cited cases that have acknowledged the authority of the police to enter without notice "under circumstances presenting a threat of physical violence," in hot-pursuit cases ("in cases where a prisoner escapes . . . and retreats to his dwelling"), and "where police officers have reason to believe that evidence would likely be destroyed if advance notice were given."

Application of these exceptions must be determined on a case-by-case basis. That is, the police cannot justify their failure to satisfy the knock-and-announce principles by simply categorizing the case as, for example, a drug investigation. As the Court explained in *Richards v. Wisconsin*, "[i]f a *per*

---

[90] *But see* Gooding v. United States, 416 U.S. 430 (1974) (involving the interpretation of a statute, the Court approved the execution of a nighttime search authorized in a warrant without a showing of need; the constitutionality of the statute was not addressed in the case).

[91] Federal law provides that an officer may break open any outer or inner door or window of a house in order to execute a search warrant "if, after notice of his authority and purpose, he is refused admittance or when necessary to liberate himself or a person aiding him in the execution of the warrant." 18 U.S.C. § 3109 (1985).

[92] 514 U.S. 927 (1995).

*se* exception were allowed for each category of criminal investigation that included a considerable—albeit hypothetical—risk of danger to officers or destruction of evidence, the knock-and-announce element of the Fourth Amendment's reasonableness requirement would be meaningless."[93]

But, *Richards* also created a substantial loophole in the knock-and-announce rule. In order to satisfy one of the exceptions to the requirement, the police need only possess reasonable suspicion, rather than probable cause, "that knocking and announcing their presence, under the particular circumstances, would be dangerous or futile, or that it would inhibit the effective investigation of the crime by, for example, allowing the destruction of evidence." The Court stated that the reasonable suspicion standard "strikes the appropriate balance between the legitimate law enforcement concerns . . . and the individual privacy interests."[94] Because "reasonable suspicion" requires little more than a hunch,[95] the effect of *Richards* is apt to be that the exceptions will gobble up the knock-and-announce requirement.[96]

### [D]  Search of Persons While Executing a Warrant[97]

### [1]  In Premises Open to the Public

A warrant may properly authorize the search of a named individual who is expected to be found on the premises to be searched. On the other hand, a warrant authorizing the search of "all persons found on the premises," without identifying the individuals, is unconstitutionally broad except in the unlikely event that there is probable cause to believe that anyone who might be present at the time of the search will be in possession of criminal evidence.

The more difficult issue is under what circumstances, if any, an officer executing a valid search warrant of premises may search persons found at the scene who are *not* named in the warrant. *Ybarra v. Illinois*[98] provides

---

[93] 520 U.S. 385, 394 (1997).

[94] Moreover, the "reasonable suspicion" standard applies, even if the police know that they will need to destroy property, *e.g.*, break a window, in order to enter a residence. United States v. Ramirez, 523 U.S. 65, 70 (1998).

[95] *See* § 18.03[A], *infra*.

[96] As a result, *contra under the state constitution*, Commonwealth v. Macias, 711 N.E.2d 130 (Mass. 1999) (unannounced entry into a residence, founded on police officers' belief that evidence will be destroyed if they comply with the knock-and-announce rule, is not justified unless the belief satisfies the probable cause standard).

[97] *See generally* Daniel L. Rotenberg, *An Essay on the Unexpected Person Factor in Searches and Seizures*, 39 St. Louis U.L.J. 505 (1995).

[98] 444 U.S. 85 (1979).

guidelines for determining the scope of an officer's authority to search persons while executing a search warrant of premises open to the public.

In *Ybarra*, police officers had a warrant to search a tavern, and a specifically named bartender, for heroin. Eight officers executing the warrant entered the bar while it was open to the public and frisked each of the customers for weapons. One of the customers, *D*, who had not acted suspiciously, was frisked while he was standing at a pinball machine. The officer felt something in *D*'s pocket, which seemed to be "a cigarette pack with objects in it." Although the officer did nothing immediately, he returned a few minutes later, pulled out the object, which was a cigarette pack as predicted, and opened it to find tin foil packets of heroin.

The Supreme Court concluded that "a person's mere propinquity to others independently suspected of criminal activity does not, without more, give rise to probable cause to search that person." That is, every customer on the premises had personal Fourth Amendment protection. The officers' authority to search the bartender and the premises, therefore, did not justify a full search of the customers.

This does not mean that officers executing a warrant on public premises must necessarily bypass people present at the scene. Based on the principles of *Terry v. Ohio*,[99] an officer executing a warrant may pat down (frisk) an occupant for weapons if she has reasonable suspicion, based on specific articulable facts, that the person to be frisked is armed and dangerous. If the officer conducting the pat-down feels what appears to be a weapon, she may then conduct a full search in order to seize the weapon. In this case, however, the officer lacked reasonable suspicion to believe that *D* was armed and dangerous; therefore, even the initial pat-down was unconstitutional.

### [2]　In Private Homes

*Ybarra* involved the execution of a search warrant on premises open to the general public, in which there was no evidence that any customer was linked to the criminal activities that brought the officers to the tavern. What should the rule be when the police execute a warrant to search a private residence?

The Supreme Court has not answered this question directly. A few lower courts permit the police, while executing a search warrant of a home for narcotics, automatically to frisk occupants for weapons. Other courts require particularized suspicion that the person frisked is armed and dangerous.[100]

---

[99] 392 U.S. 1 (1968). *See* § 18.02, *infra*.

[100] 2 LaFave, Note 79, *supra*, at 640–42.

Even if reasonable suspicion is required, it will often be much easier to justify a pat-down in a residence than in a building open to the public. As the Supreme Court has observed in the context of arrests, "an in-home arrest puts the officer at the disadvantage of being on his adversary's 'turf.'"[101] Moreover, a private home, unlike the *Ybarra* bar, "does not attract casual visitors off the street."[102] Therefore, police officers in a residence will frequently have reason to fear that the occupants are connected to the suspected criminal activity going on there or, at least, that they have an incentive to protect the criminal interests of the residents of the home by using force against the arresting officers.

### [E] Detention of Persons During Searches[103]

In *Michigan v. Summers,*[104] police officers encountered *D* as he descended the front steps of a house that the officers had a warrant to search for narcotics. They requested and obtained *D*'s assistance in entering the premises, after which they forcibly detained (seized) him while they searched the house.

The search proved fruitful. After the officers learned that *D* was the owner of the house, they arrested and searched him incident to the arrest. More drugs were found on his person, and it was this evidence that *D* sought to exclude at his trial on the ground that it was a fruit of an unlawful detention in the home.

The Court held that *D*'s temporary seizure was reasonable. It noted various justifications for the detention of persons during the execution of search warrants: (1) to avoid the risk that an occupant might leave with the evidence sought; (2) to reduce the risk of bodily harm to the officers or others; and (3) to facilitate the search, by inducing the detained occupants to open locked containers or doors.

Although the police did not prove that any of the above-stated reasons applied in *Summers*, the Court chose to provide a bright-line rule. The bright-line rule is: a warrant to search for contraband includes the limited authority to detain all occupants of the premises to be searched while the warrant is executed.

---

[101] Maryland v. Buie, 494 U.S. 325, 333 (1990). In *Buie*, the Court ruled that the police may conduct a protective visual sweep of a home while they are completing an in-home arrest, but only if they possess reasonable suspicion that the area to be swept harbors a dangerous person. *See* § 13.02[C][3], *infra*. The Court did not state in *Buie* what the police may do if they find a person during a sweep.

[102] People v. Thurman, 257 Cal. Rptr. 517, 520 (Cal. App. 1989).

[103] *See generally* Rotenberg, Note 97, *supra*.

[104] 452 U.S. 692 (1981).

The potential limits of *Summers* should be noted. First, the Court did not determine whether the rule also applies to warrantless residential searches. The Court stated in a footnote, however, that its holding does not "preclude the possibility that comparable police conduct may be justified by exigent circumstances in the absence of a warrant."

Second, the *Summers* rule, as stated, was limited to searches for contraband. In a footnote, the Court left open the issue of whether the police may detain persons during searches for evidence of a crime. Apparently, therefore, the term "contraband" is used broadly to include the fruits and instrumentalities of criminal activity, but might not pertain to "mere evidence."[105]

Third, the Court used the word "occupants" in the holding and elsewhere in the opinion. But, the Court also used the word "residents," and observed in that context that "we may safely assume that most citizens . . . would elect to remain in order to observe the search of their possessions." Therefore, did the Court mean to limit the scope of its holding to persons who have a possessory connection to the premises searched, or may the police detain anyone who happens to be present when the warrant is executed? The Court has not answered this question, although one expert believes that "it would seem that the word 'occupants' is not to be loosely construed as covering anyone present . . . ."[106]

### [F]  Scope of the Search

A search warrant must satisfy the particularity requirement of the Fourth Amendment. However, assuming that a warrant describes the place to be searched with adequate precision, the authority to search that place includes the entire area in question, including containers found within it, as long as they are large enough to contain the object of the search.[107] For example, in a search of a house for stolen jewelry, the police may open dresser drawers and jewelry boxes that could hold the fruits of the crime. If they were searching the home for a stolen large-screen television set, however, they would not be justified in opening those containers for such a large object.

Police may constitutionally *seize* any item (even if it is not described in the warrant) if: (1) they see the item while searching a place which they have the authority to search; (2) the item is located in such an area; and (3) police have probable cause to believe the item is subject to seizure.

---

[105] Regarding the nature of "mere evidence," *see* § 9.02[E], *supra.*

[106] 2 LaFave, Note 79, *supra*, at 650.

[107] United States v. Ross, 456 U.S. 798, 820–21 (1982).

Once the articles particularly described in the warrant are discovered and seized, the search must cease.[108]

---

[108] Horton v. California, 496 U.S. 128, 141 (1990).

CHAPTER 12

# WARRANTLESS SEARCHES: EXIGENT
# CIRCUMSTANCES

## § 12.01   Nature of the Warrant Exception

Many exceptions to the so-called "warrant requirement" of the Fourth Amendment are based on exigent circumstances, that is, on the ground that time constraints make it impracticable for the officer to secure a warrant. Because an exigency is a situation that requires immediate action, it is reasonable for an officer in emergent circumstances to search without a warrant.

Certain types of exigent circumstances commonly recur. For example, an arrest triggers a threat to the police officer that the arrestee might use a concealed weapon or destroy evidence hidden on his person or in the area of his control before the officer can obtain a search warrant. Thus, there is a "search incident to lawful arrest" exception to the warrant requirement. Similarly, the mobility of an automobile makes it difficult to secure a warrant to search a car on the highway. Therefore, there is an "automobile" exception to justify warrantless car searches.

Other exigencies occur less frequently or arise in such disparate factual circumstances that courts have not classified them under a specific warrant exception. Therefore, these cases tend to be grouped together under the general umbrella of an "exigency" exception to the search warrant requirement.

Although the circumstances that fall within this exception vary, certain generalizations are possible. First, all of the cases that fall within this exception involve emergent situations in which the police act without a warrant due to a reasonable belief that criminal evidence will be destroyed or a suspect will avoid capture if the officers take the time to attempt to secure a search warrant. Second, the emergency that justifies the police action should limit the appropriate scope of the search. For example, if the exigency is that a box containing criminal evidence in a particular house may be destroyed, the right to search will extend only to those places in the house that could reasonably conceal the box. Third, although an exigency justifies the absence of a search warrant, it does not dispense with any underlying probable cause requirement that exists. Finally, it is important to keep in mind that the search warrant exception now under discussion relates to criminal investigations. In contrast, the Court has indicated that when the police or other law enforcement officers are engaged in "community caretaking functions, totally divorced from the detection, investigation or acquisition of evidence relating to the violation of a criminal statute,"[1] different principles apply, e.g., even probable cause may not be required.[2]

Some examples of warrantless searches that may be justified on the grounds of exigent circumstances are discussed in this chapter.

## § 12.02 Intrusions Into the Human Body[3]

The Supreme Court has wrestled various times with the question of whether, and under what circumstances, the government may conduct a search of a person that involves intrusion into the body of the suspect. In some cases, the police methods may "offend 'a sense of justice,' "[4] and consequently violate due process.[5] In the Fourth Amendment context, however, the fact that a search will involve an intrusion into the body does not in itself bar the government, in appropriate circumstances, from acting without a warrant. However, *with or without a warrant*, certain special protections must be taken.

In *Schmerber v. California*,[6] *D* was arrested at a hospital for driving under the influence of alcohol. On the order of the arresting officer, a physician took a blood sample from *D* to test for alcohol content. Although the Court stated that there was "plainly probable cause" for the arrest, the search and seizure were without a warrant. The Court held that the warrantless police conduct was justifiable on the ground that the evidence—the alcohol in the bloodstream—would have been lost if the police had been required to obtain a warrant, because the evidence was in the process of being "destroyed" as *D*'s body eliminated it from its system.

Although the warrantless search was permissible, the Court ruled that the police may not intrude into a person's body unless: (1) they are justified

---

[1] Cady v. Dombrowski, 413 U.S. 433, 441 (1973).

[2] In regard to non-criminal investigations, *see* chapters 16 (inventory searches) and 19 (various "special needs" circumstances), *infra. See also* § 12.04, *infra.*

[3] *See generally* Michael G. Rogers, Note, *Bodily Intrusion in Search of Evidence: A Study in Fourth Amendment Decisionmaking*, 62 Ind. L.J. 1181 (1987).

[4] Rochin v. California, 342 U.S. 165, 173 (1952).

[5] *See* § 21.01[D], *infra.*

[6] 384 U.S. 757 (1966).

in requiring the individual to submit to the test; and (2) the means and procedures employed are reasonable. The first requirement was met in this case: the officer had "plainly probable cause" to arrest $D$ for driving under the influence of alcohol; the test was not conducted "on the mere chance" that alcohol would be found in the bloodstream, but rather on the basis of a "clear indication" that such evidence would be discovered.[7]

The second requirement was also met here. The procedure involved— extraction of blood—is highly effective, commonplace, and rarely painful or traumatic. Also, the test was performed in a reasonable manner: by a physician, in a hospital environment, under accepted medical practices. Therefore, the search was reasonable.[8]

## § 12.03    External Searches of the Body

In *Cupp v. Murphy*,[9] the police had probable cause to arrest $D$ for the strangulation murder of his wife. $D$ voluntarily appeared at the police station for questioning, after which he was released. During the questioning, the officers observed a "dark spot" on $D$'s finger, which they suspected was dried blood from the murder. When they asked for permission to take a small scraping for testing, $D$ refused and rubbed his fingers together. He then put his hands in his pocket. The police heard a "metallic sound, such as keys or change rattling," which further suggested that $D$ was attempting to destroy the evidence on his hands that connected him to the crime. Therefore, an officer forcibly took scrapings from underneath $D$'s fingernails.

The Supreme Court, per Justice Potter Stewart, approved the warrantless police action. Stewart stated that the principles underlying "search incident to lawful arrest" law applied to the present case. That is, the Court has ruled that an arrestee taken into custody may be searched without a warrant because of the risk that he will use any weapon on him to escape, or that

---

[7] In light of this language as well as the underlying reasoning of *Schmerber*, some courts and commentators interpret the case to require probable cause for *any* nonconsensual intrusion into a person's body. However, the Court has cast some doubt on this proposition. *Compare* Winston v. Lee, 470 U.S. 753, 760 (1985) (*Schmerber* "noted the importance of probable cause") *with* United States v. Montoya de Hernandez, 473 U.S. 531, 540 (1985) (*Schmerber* "indicate[d] the necessity for particularized suspicion").

[8] Sometimes, this second requirement can prove fatal to the government's case, even with probable cause. *E.g.,* Winston v. Lee, 470 U.S. 753 (1985) (in which the Court held that surgical intrusion into a robbery suspect's chest, under general anaesthesia, to recover a bullet fired by the victim was unreasonable because the medical risks, though not extremely severe, were in dispute, and there was no compelling need to obtain the bullet, as there was other available evidence linking the suspect to the robbery).

[9] 412 U.S. 291 (1973).

he will destroy any evidence on his person.[10] In the present case, *D* was not under arrest and knew that he was going to be released. Consequently, the Court reasoned that, compared to a person under formal arrest, he was likely to "be less hostile to the police and less likely to take conspicuous, immediate steps to destroy incriminating evidence on his person." Based on this difference, the Court indicated that it would have been inappropriate for the police to conduct a full search of *D*. On the other hand, in view of "the existence of probable cause, the very limited intrusion undertaken. . ., and the ready destructibility of the evidence," the limited police action here was reasonable.

Because *D* was not arrested at the time of the search, this case is easier to justify on straightforward exigency principles than by analogy on search-incident-to-lawful-arrest grounds. Indeed, analyzed as an exigency case, the Court might have been too stringent in its analysis. After all, in light of the nature of the questioning that occurred, the police had good reason to fear—as much so as in an arrest context—that *D*, once released, would destroy *any* evidence on his person, and not simply the substance under his finger nails, that tied him to the crime. A full search of *D*'s person, therefore, might have been reasonable under the circumstances.

### § 12.04  Entry and Search of a Home

The Supreme Court has stated in ringing terms that "physical entry of the home is the chief evil against which the wording of the Fourth Amendment is directed."[11] Indeed, in no other circumstance is the requirement of a search warrant as jealously guarded. Nonetheless, exigent circumstances can justify a warrantless entry of a dwelling to make a felony arrest[12] or to conduct a search related to a serious offense.

In *Minnesota v. Olson*,[13] the Supreme Court concluded that a state court "applied essentially the correct standard" when it identified the following exigencies as circumstances justifying warrantless entry of a home: (1) hot pursuit of a fleeing felon; (2) imminent destruction of evidence; (3) the need to prevent a suspect's escape; or (4) risk of harm to the police or to others, inside or outside the dwelling. The police must apparently have probable cause to believe that one or more of the factors justifying the entry are present.

*Warden v. Hayden*[14] provides a good example of how entry into a home and a full-scale search of the premises may be justified on grounds of

[10] *See* § 13.01, *infra*.
[11] United States v. United States District Court, 407 U.S. 297, 313 (1972).
[12] *See* § 10.05[B][2], *supra*.
[13] 495 U.S. 91 (1990). *Olson* is discussed in greater detail at § 10.05[B][2][b], *supra*.
[14] 387 U.S. 294 (1967).

exigency. In *Hayden*, police officers had probable cause to believe that *D*, a man involved in an armed robbery, had moments earlier entered a particular house. An unspecified number of officers hurried to the address, knocked at the door, and were allowed to enter "without objection" by a woman living in the house. The officers spread out on both floors of the house and the basement looking for the suspect, in order to arrest him. *D* was discovered feigning sleep in his bedroom, where he was arrested. At the same time, other officers came upon and seized items related to the crime in other parts of the house.

The police officers' warrantless conduct was justified by the Supreme Court because "the exigencies of the situation made the course imperative." The officers were in pursuit of an armed robber and speed was essential. This justified their warrantless entry into *D*'s house in order to make an arrest. Once they entered and began their search for him, "only a thorough search of the house for persons and weapons could have insured that [*D*] was the only man present and that the police had control of all weapons which could be used against them or to effect escape."

In short, the exigency justified the warrantless conduct—the entry and search—and the nature of the exigency defined the legitimate scope of the search. In this case, at a minimum, the police had the right to search any place in the home where the armed robber, anyone else who might interfere with the arrest, and/or weapons, might be found.[15] But, the right to conduct the exigency search ended as soon as the robber was discovered and the threat to the officers' safety ended.[16]

It should be reiterated[17] that this chapter considers searches conducted in criminal investigations. Warrantless entry of a home may also be permitted in the police department's community caretaking function, but it is critical to distinguish between the two roles of the police—investigating crime and caretaking. For example, in *Mincey v. Arizona*,[18] undercover police officers went to an apartment as part of a drug investigation. While inside, a resident shot and killed one of the officers, after which the other officers arrested *M* and searched for other victims (two were discovered).

---

[15] The Court did not decide in *Hayden* whether the police would have been justified in searching for evidence of the crime, other than weapons, that might be destroyed before they discovered *D*. Although *Olson, supra*, concerns the exigencies that justify a warrantless *entry* of a home, the reasoning of that case would also justify the search and seizure of criminal evidence, while the police are in hot pursuit of a felon.

[16] Of course, as soon as the robber was arrested, a *different* warrant exception (search incident to a lawful arrest) came into play.

[17] *See* § 12.01, *supra*.

[18] 437 U.S. 385 (1978).

The officers then secured the premises. Ten minutes later homicide investigators arrived and, without a warrant, proceeded to search the entire apartment, during which time incriminating evidence was seized.

The Supreme Court drew an important line. It stated:

> We do not question the right of the police to respond to emergency situations. Numerous state and federal cases have recognized that the Fourth Amendment does not bar police officers from making warrantless entries and searches when they reasonably believe that a person within is in need of immediate aid. Similarly, when the police come upon the scene of a homicide they may make a prompt warrantless search of the area to see if there are other victims or if a killer is still on the premises.

For example, the police may enter a home without a warrant when they have good reason to believe that a person inside is in dire need of medical treatment. This is part of the caretaking function. The Warrant Clause has no role to play in such circumstances. And, even during a homicide, which has obvious criminal overtones, the caretaking function extends to the process of searching for victims.[19]

But, *Mincey* went on to make another point. Although the officers in the house at the time of the homicide were entitled, without a warrant, to search for victims, and if they had found criminal evidence during that search they could properly have seized it pursuant to the plain-view doctrine,[20] the homicide investigators who arrived ten minutes later—when the emergency caretaking process was over and the criminal investigation had commenced—were *not* entitled to enter without a search warrant. The Justices rejected Arizona's claim that there is a "murder scene exception" to the search warrant requirement.[21] Caretaking issues aside, a home may not be entered without a warrant in the absence of an exigency (or consent, an independent basis discussed elsewhere[22] ).

---

[19] *See generally* John F. Decker, *Emergency Circumstances, Police Responses, and Fourth Amendment Restrictions*, 89 J. Crim. L. & Criminology 433 (1999).

[20] *See* chapter 15, *infra.*

[21] *See also* Flippo v. West Virginia, 528 U.S. 11 (1999) (reaffirming *Mincey*).

[22] *See generally* Chapter 17, *infra.*

CHAPTER 13

# SEARCHES INCIDENT TO LAWFUL ARRESTS

## § 13.01  Search Warrant Exception: General Principles[1]

### [A]  Rule

Subject to substantial clarification in § 13.02, a police officer who makes a lawful *full custodial arrest*[2] may conduct a contemporaneous[3] warrantless search of: (1) the arrestee's person; (2) the area within the arrestee's immediate control (sometimes called the "grabbing" or "lunging" area); and (3) if the arrest occurs in a home, "closets and other spaces immediately adjoining the place of arrest from which an attack could be immediately launched."[4] This constitutes the "search incident to lawful arrest" (or, for short, "search incident") exception to the so-called warrant requirement.

### [B]  Rationale of the Warrant Exception

The leading cases in the "search incident to lawful arrest" area were handed down during a period in which the United States Supreme Court typically declared that there was a "warrant requirement" (or, at least, warrant presumption), *i.e.*, that warrantless searches are unreasonable in the absence of a compelling justification for permitting the police to act without prior judicial authorization.[5] Therefore, the Court explained the rule relating to searches incident to lawful arrests in this manner: a custodial arrest provides the suspect with the incentive to use any available weapon to resist the officer or to flee, and to destroy or conceal evidence of the crime. Further, an in-home arrest "puts the officer at the disadvantage of being

---

[1] *See generally* 3 Wayne R. LaFave, Search and Seizure §§ 5.2, 6.3, 7.1 (3d ed. 1996).

[2] Regarding the meaning and significance of the italicized words, *see* § 13.02[A][1], *infra*.

[3] The arrest must *precede* the search. If the *search* precedes the arrest, the police may not justify the warrantless search on the basis of "search incident" law. Sibron v. New York, 392 U.S. 40, 63 (1968) ("It is axiomatic that an incident search may not precede an arrest and serve as part of its justification.").

[4] Chimel v. California, 395 U.S. 752 (1969) (for principles (1) and (2)); Maryland v. Buie, 494 U.S. 325 (1990) (for principle (3)).

[5] For a review of the history of the Court's treatment of the Warrant Clause of the Fourth Amendment, *see* § 11.01, *supra*.

on his adversary's 'turf,' "[6] in that the arrest creates the risk that an accomplice, relative, or friend of the suspect will attack the officer.

In view of the risks just set out, the Court declared that it is reasonable for arresting officers immediately—without a warrant—to search a suspect and her "grabbing area" (the areas to which she could lunge) for weapons or destructible evidence, as well as to search immediately adjoining area for dangerous persons. Searches outside this area, however, cannot be justified on such exigent grounds. Therefore, as to these latter searches, the ordinary rule—searches should be conducted *with* warrants—comes back into play unless another warrant exception applies.

The Court's current mode of analysis is, simply, to determine whether a search is reasonable, rather than to start from a presumption against warrantless police conduct. Clearly, the types of warrantless searches authorized in this area remain reasonable, for the reasons previously given. What remains to be seen is whether the Supreme Court might, in the future, expand the range of legitimate warrantless searches incident to lawful arrests. To do so, however, the Court will need to overrule current case law.

### [C]   The Probable Cause Requirement

The existence of an exception to a search warrant "requirement" does not automatically dispose of the ordinary rule that a full search may not be conducted in the absence of probable cause.[7] However, in the context of searches incident to lawful arrests, the right of an officer to search the person of the arrestee for weapons and evidence, and to search the closets and other spaces adjoining the place of arrest for persons who might launch an attack, flows immediately and automatically from the arrest itself.[8] That is, the police may conduct a search of the person and of the adjoining closets and spaces, *even if there is no reason to believe that weapons, evidence, or dangerous persons will be discovered.*

The Supreme Court has never expressly held that the right to search the area within the arrestee's immediate control (as distinguished from the two areas described above) is also automatic. However, lower courts assume that the same rule applies,[9] and there is no reason to believe that the high court, if required to reach the issue, will treat this matter any differently.

---

[6] Maryland v. Buie, 494 U.S. at 333.

[7] *See* § 9.01, *supra.*

[8] United States v. Robinson, 414 U.S. 218 (1973) (search of the arrestee); Maryland v. Buie, 494 U.S. 325 (1990) (search of the adjoining area for dangerous persons).

[9] 3 LaFave, Note 1, *supra,* at 440.

## [D]   What May Be Seized During the Search

As explained above, the purpose of a warrantless search incident to a lawful arrest is to find weapons or evidence related to the crime, or to discover a person who represents a danger to the officer. However, a police officer may *seize* without a warrant *any* article found during the search, if she has probable cause to believe that it is criminal evidence related to this or another crime.[10] Thus, the officer need not have probable cause to conduct the *search*, but she must have probable cause to *seize* the evidence found in the search.

## § 13.02   Search Warrant Exception: In Greater Detail

### [A]   The Arrest

#### [1]   "Full Custodial"

The search-incident-to-lawful-arrest rule applies to arrests in which the officer takes the suspect into "full custody," which includes transporting her to the police station for booking.[11]

Do the search-incident rules discussed in this chapter apply, however, when an officer temporarily detains a suspect to issue a traffic citation or other summons? The first point to be made as to this question is that, typically, such an encounter between a police officer and a citizen is not characterized as an arrest, so that any warrant exception here would have to be classified as a warrantless "search incident to a lawful citation or summons." However, a few jurisdictions describe the citation process as an "arrest,"[12] albeit not a *custodial* arrest.

The Supreme Court has answered the traffic citation issue. In *Knowles v. Iowa*,[13] *O*, an Iowa police officer, stopped *D* for speeding. Under state law, *O* had authority to arrest *D*, take him into custody, and immediately transport him to a magistrate. Instead, *O* issued *D* a traffic citation and, also pursuant to statute, conducted a full search of the car, during which he discovered marijuana under the driver's seat.

The Court unanimously held that the warrantless search could not be justified on "search incident" grounds. The Court stated that neither of the

---

[10] *See* Warden v. Hayden, 387 U.S. 294, 307 (1967) (stating that there must be "a nexus . . . between the item to be seized and criminal behavior"); Arizona v. Hicks, 480 U.S. 321, 326 (1987) (the police must have probable cause to seize items found in plain view); United States v. Robinson, 414 U.S. 218 (1973) (the arresting officer properly seized heroin discovered during the search of a traffic violator).

[11] *E.g.*, United States v. Robinson, 414 U.S. 218 (1973) (dealing expressly with a "full custody arrest").

[12] *See* § 10.01, *supra*.

[13] 525 U.S. 113 (1998).

reasons for permitting warrantless searches at the time of an arrest—to disarm a suspect and to discover and preserve evidence—justifies a search of a car when an officer merely issues a speeding ticket, *i.e.*, does not take the individual into custody. The Court stated that although officer safety is a "legitimate and weighty" interest, the physical threat to an officer when issuing a citation "is a good deal less" than when she takes the individual into custody.[14] In the latter circumstance, she will be in close proximity to the arrestee for an extended period of time.

As for discovering evidence, the *Knowles* Court stated that "[a]s for the destruction of evidence relating to [the driver's] identity, if a police officer is not satisfied with the identification furnished by the driver, this may be a basis for arresting him rather than merely issuing a citation." And, regarding the possibility that the driver might destroy evidence of an *unrelated* offense, the Court said that such possibility "seems remote."

On its face, *Knowles* is a victory for advocates of restrictions on police encounters with citizens in "minor offense" contexts. But, it must be kept in mind that the Iowa statute in question gave the police the authority to issue a traffic citation to a speeder, as occurred in *Knowles, or* to take the driver into custody and then conduct a warrantless search incident to the lawful arrest. What if *O*, in *Knowles*, had chosen the option to take *D* into custody?

That is precisely what happened in *Atwater v. Lago Vista.*[15] In *Atwater*, an officer stopped *D* because she and her son were driving without their seatbelts, a misdemeanor punishable only by a small fine. The officer could have issued a traffic citation, but instead he took *D* into custody, which was also authorized by statute. The Court ruled, 5-4, that the Fourth Amendment does not prohibit the custodial arrest of a person for a minor, "fine-only" offense.[16] And, once such a custodial arrest is made, the arresting officer is automatically authorized to search the driver and the area within the driver's immediate control.[17] Thus, at least where officers have the option of taking misdemeanants into custody, the conjunction of *Knowles* and *Atwater* creates an incentive for officers, should they have a hunch that a traffic violator has criminal evidence in her possession or in the passenger compartment of her vehicle, to make a full custodial arrest in order to have authority to permit a search incident to the custodial arrest.

---

[14] The Court noted that an officer may be justified in non-custodial circumstances to take *some* precautions against the possible use of a weapon by a traffic violator, but a full car search is not required. As to those other precautions, *see* §§ 18.04[C][2] and 18.07, *infra*.

[15] 532 U.S. 318 (2001).

[16] *See* § 10.02, Note 11, *supra*, for further details on *Atwater*.

[17] In this regard, *see especially* § 13.04, *infra*.

### [2]   Lawfulness of the Arrest

The search-incident rule applies to a search conducted after a *lawful* arrest. Therefore, if an arrest is unlawful, the incidental warrantless search cannot be justified on the basis of this warrant exception. As discussed elsewhere,[18] to be lawful the police must have probable cause and, in certain circumstances, a warrant to make an arrest.

## [B]   Contemporaneousness of the Search

### [1]   Area Within Arrestee's Immediate Control

A police officer's right to conduct a search of the area within the immediate control of an arrestee is limited to searches substantially contemporaneous to the arrest. For example, if an officer arrests the driver of an automobile, but does not search the car until after she tows it to the police garage, the later search cannot be justified by the search-incident-to-lawful-arrest exception.[19] Quite simply, the search is no longer an "incident" of the arrest.

This limitation on the warrant exception is reasonable in light of the rule's purpose: once the arrestee is taken into custody, there is no risk that she can grab any weapons or destroy any articles of evidence that previously were in the lunging area.

### [2]   Closets and Other Spaces Adjoining the Place of Arrest

Once a person arrested in her home is removed from it, the justification vanishes for a search of closets and other spaces immediately adjoining the place of arrest. Therefore, although the Supreme Court has not yet dealt with a non-immediate search of such areas incident to an arrest, the contemporaneousness limitation should apply.

### [3]   Of the Person

The contemporaneousness limitation might not apply to searches of the person or, perhaps more to the point, the search-incident exception merges nearly imperceptibly into another warrant exception in most non-contemporaneous searches of arrestees.

For example, consider *United States v. Edwards*:[20] *D* was arrested at night and jailed for an attempted burglary of a Post Office. Soon after the arrest the police learned that the burglar had attempted to enter the building by prying open a window. Therefore, the police suspected that paint chips might be found on *D*'s clothing. The next morning, approximately ten hours

---

[18] *See* § 10.03, *supra.*

[19] Preston v. United States, 376 U.S. 364 (1964).

[20] 415 U.S. 800 (1974).

after the arrest, the police purchased new clothing for *D* and seized what he was wearing, which they inspected and held as evidence of the crime.

The Supreme Court upheld the warrantless search. Although its holding appears to be based on various warrant-exception rules,[21] the Court apparently had the search-incident rule in mind when it stated that a search of a person "that could be made on the spot at the time of arrest may legally be conducted later when the accused arrives at the place of detention."

*Edwards* is controversial. In support of the holding is the fact that, as the Court said, *D* "was no more imposed upon than he could have been at the time and place of arrest or immediately upon arrival at the place of detention." If the police could have inspected his clothing, even vacuumed it, at the scene of the crime, *D*'s privacy was not invaded any more because the search occurred ten hours later. Furthermore, any paint chips that were on *D*'s clothing remained in his grabbing area, and the incentive to conceal or destroy the evidence existed throughout the night. Finally, the delay in the search was reasonable, as the police needed time to obtain replacement clothing. On the other hand, the police had ten hours to secure a warrant, which distinguishes *Edwards* from the ordinary search-incident-to-lawful-arrest case. Moreover, to the extent that *D* had the inclination to destroy evidence on his clothing, he already had ample time to do so.

Cases like *Edwards* are rare. As a practical matter, when an arrestee is incarcerated the right to search her person incident to the arrest is followed quickly by the right of the police to conduct an arrest inventory that is likely to be at least as thorough as the search incident to the arrest.

### [C]   Scope of the Search

### [1]   Search of the Person

The right to search a person incident to a lawful arrest includes the right to search the pockets of the arrestee's clothing, and to open containers found therein,[22] as well as to search containers "immediately associated"[23] with the person, such as a purse or shoulder bag, as long as the containers are large enough to conceal a weapon or evidence of crime.

---

[21] Some language in *Edwards* supports the proposition that the search could be justified on principles analogous to the "arrest inventory" exception to the warrant requirement. *See* § 16.03, *infra.* The Court also said that another "closely related consideration" that justified the examination of the clothing was the "plain view" principle that "the police . . . are normally permitted to seize evidence of crime when it is lawfully encountered."

[22] *E.g.,* United States v. Robinson, 414 U.S. 218 (1973) (cigarette package in pocket of arrestee).

[23] United States v. Chadwick, 433 U.S. 1, 15 (1977).

The right to search the arrestee is not unlimited in scope. For example, because it implicates the "most personal and deep-rooted expectations of privacy,"[24] a warrantless search that involves penetration of the surface of the body, such as testing a person's blood for evidence of alcohol, may not be justified under ordinary search-incident doctrine, although it may be justifiable on other grounds.[25]

The Supreme Court has not determined under what Fourth Amendment circumstances, if any, a strip search or body-cavity search can be conducted as an incident to an arrest.[26] However, searches incident to an arrest or incarceration must not "violate the dictates of reason . . . because of . . . their manner of perpetration."[27]

### [2]   Area Within the Immediate Control

### [a]   In General

The area within the "immediate control" of an arrestee is the area into which the person might lunge for a weapon or for evidence to destroy. Accordingly, the arrest of a person in her three-bedroom home does not justify a search of the entire premises,[28] but it might justify the search of much of the room in which the arrest occurs, including all containers found in it that could contain a weapon or evidence.

In principle, the scope of the grabbing area depends on the circumstances of the individual case. There is no bright-line rule. Among the factors that may properly affect the scope of the arrestee's grabbing area are: whether she is handcuffed (and, if so, whether she is cuffed in front or behind her back); the size and dexterity of the arrestee; the size of the room; whether the containers in the room are open or shut, and if shut, whether they are locked or unlocked;[29] and the number of officers relative to suspects.

---

[24] Winston v. Lee, 470 U.S. 753, 760 (1985).

[25] See Schmerber v. California, 384 U.S. 757 (1966) (upholding a blood test of a person arrested for driving under the influence of alcohol, on search-incident-to-lawful-arrest grounds, but requiring that there be a "clear indication" that the test will discover alcohol, and that the search be performed in a reasonable manner). Schmerber may be justified as an "exigency exception" case. See § 12.02, supra.

[26] Strip searches of pretrial detainees who have had contact with visitors from outside the jail are reasonable under the Fourth Amendment if they are conducted in a reasonable manner. Bell v. Wolfish, 441 U.S. 520 (1979).

[27] United States v. Edwards, 415 U.S. 800, 808 n.9 (1974) (quoting Charles v. United States, 278 F.2d 386, 389 (9th Cir. 1960)).

[28] Chimel v. California 395 U.S. 752 (1969).

[29] Unfortunately, courts sometimes fail to distinguish between the container itself, which might be in the arrestee's grabbing area, and the *interior* of the container—where a weapon or evidence might be held—which might not be in the grabbing area if the container is locked.

As a practical matter, some courts apply a bright-line "one-room rule" to a search that is incident to a lawful arrest in a home, in that they permit a search of the entire room in which the arrest occurred, regardless of the room size or other circumstances. [30] Improperly, but commonly, as well, some courts treat the arrestee as "a combination acrobat and Houdini who might well free himself from his restraints and suddenly gain access to some distant place." [31]

In should be kept in mind that the grabbing area of a suspect changes if the arrestee moves. The Supreme Court has held that it is not unreasonable for an officer, "as a matter of routine, to monitor the movements of an arrested person, as his judgment dictates, following the arrest." [32] For example, if *D* is arrested in her bathrobe in the living room of her house, it is not unreasonable for the officer to allow her to enter the bedroom to get dressed before being taken to the police station. In such circumstances, the officer has "a right to remain literally at [*D*'s] elbow," [33] and to search the new grabbing area, which includes the clothes she intends to wear.

### [b]  Automobiles

In order to assist the police in determining the legally recognized grabbing area of a person arrested in her automobile, the Supreme Court, in *New York v. Belton*, [34] devised a bright-line rule for cars. [35] The *Belton* rule states that a police officer may, contemporaneous to the arrest of an occupant of an automobile, search the passenger compartment and all containers found therein, whether the containers are open or closed. For purposes of the rule, a "container" is "any object capable of holding another object." Under this rule, the glove compartment, consoles "or other receptacles," as well as luggage, clothing, boxes, "and the like" found in the passenger compartment are subject to warrantless search. The trunk and engine compartment fall outside the bright-line *Belton* rule.

Various observations regarding the scope of this rule are possible. First, it applies only if the arrestee was an "occupant" of the vehicle—the driver or a passenger—at the time of her contact with the police. [36] Thus, if a

---

[30] 3 LaFave, Note 1, *supra*, at 303.

[31] *Id.* at 304; *but see* United States v. Vasey, 834 F.2d 782, 787 (9th Cir. 1987) (the search-incident rule "does not allow the officers to presume that an arrestee is superhuman.").

[32] Washington v. Chrisman, 455 U.S. 1, 7 (1982).

[33] *Id.* at 6.

[34] 453 U.S. 454 (1981).

[35] For more on *Belton*, including the Court's rationale, *see* § 13.05, *infra*.

[36] *E.g.*, State v. Foster, 905 P.2d 1032 (Idaho Ct. App. 1995) (the *Belton* rule is limited to searches of cars occupied by the defendant when the police signal the driver to stop or when contact between police and defendant was otherwise initiated).

person is near her unoccupied automobile when the police arrive, and she never enters the car, ordinary search-incident doctrine, and not the *Belton* bright-line rule, should apply.

Second, "contemporaneous" means "substantially contemporaneous." The search need not take place when the arrestee is in the automobile. Indeed, the physical proximity of the arrestee to the automobile at the time of the search is immaterial, as long as she and the vehicle are still at the scene. The right to search does not depend on whether the automobile doors are open or shut, and the warrantless search may occur even if the occupants are handcuffed and in custody in the police car.[37]

Third, although *Belton* involved four arrestees and a single police officer to guard them, the bright-line nature of the rule suggests that it applies even if there is just one person in custody and multiple officers.

Less clear is whether the rule, which permits the police to open *closed* containers applies as well to *locked* containers. It strains credulity to believe that an arrestee, perhaps handcuffed in the police vehicle, would be able to grab a weapon or evidence in a locked glove compartment or a locked suitcase on the backseat of the car. Moreover, if the Court merely wishes to retain the bright-line nature of the *Belton* rule, it could do so by declaring locked containers off-limits. At the present time, the Supreme Court has not resolved this question, and lower court case law is divided.[38]

### [3]  Protective Searches for Dangerous Persons[39]

The traditional purpose of a search incident to a lawful arrest is to look for weapons or evidence that the arrestee might grab. However, in *Maryland v. Buie*,[40] the Supreme Court stated that as an incident to an arrest in a home, police officers may "as a precautionary matter and without probable cause or reasonable suspicion, look in closets and other spaces immediately

---

[37] 3 LaFave, Note 1, *supra*, at 448–49.

[38] *Belton* involved an ordinary automobile. The Supreme Court has not indicated whether a different rule might apply to a search of a motor home incident to a lawful arrest. Generally speaking, however, a motor home that is also used for transportation purposes is provided no greater Fourth Amendment protection than an ordinary motor vehicle. *See* California v. Carney, 471 U.S. 386 (1985), discussed at § 14.06, *infra*. One state court, applying it own constitution, has adopted a potentially restricted version of the bright-line *Belton* rule, providing that the police may search the interior quarters of a motor home, if such quarters are "readily accessible from the passenger compartment," as an incident to an arrest. However, the police may *not* open a locked container or locked glove compartment. State v. Vrieling, 983 P.2d 1150, 1154 (Wash. 1999).

[39] *See generally* Daniel L. Rotenberg, *An Essay on the Unexpected Person Factor in Searches and Seizures*, 39 St. Louis U. L.J. 505 (1995).

[40] 494 U.S. 325, 334 (1990).

adjoining the place of arrest from which an attack could be immediately launched" before the police have time to depart.[41]

The *Buie* opinion provides no clues as to the meaning of the phrase "immediately adjoining the place of arrest." Presumably, this language authorizes the police to look in places outside the arrestee's grabbing area. After all, the purpose of this search is not to prevent the person in custody from lunging for a weapon or evidence, but rather is to look for people who might threaten the officers' safety. On the other hand, because a *Buie* search is one for people, and not for weapons or evidence, the spaces in which the police may look must be large enough to hold a human being.

*Buie* does not state what an officer may do if she finds a person during such a search. However, especially if the arrest is for a crime of violence, it should certainly be the case that the police may conduct a limited pat-down for weapons of any person discovered in a closet or other space adjoining the place of the arrest.[42]

## § 13.03 *Chimel v. California*: Setting the Rule's Contours

*Chimel v. California*,[43] is the benchmark search-incident-to-lawful-arrest case. In *Chimel*, the police, armed with an arrest warrant but without a search warrant, arrested *D* in his three-bedroom home for burglary. After the arrest, the officers searched the entire premises, including the attic, garage, and a small workshop, for evidence connected to the crime. Various items were seized. The police contended that the warrantless search should be permitted on the ground that it was an incident to the lawful arrest.

Justice Potter Stewart delivered the opinion of the Court. He conceded that the prior law bearing on the issue was "far from consistent." Stewart detailed the Court's four decades of twists and turns in search-incident law, including twists in which it authorized searches as broad in scope as that which occurred in *Chimel*.[44]

In *Chimel*, the Court took another turn. It ruled, 7-2, that, as an incident to an arrest, the police may conduct a warrantless search of the arrestee and the area in her immediate control, but that they may not search the entire house without a warrant.

---

[41] Under more limited circumstances, they may also do a protective sweep of other parts of the home, but this action is not based on the search-incident exception to the warrant requirement. *See* § 18.08, *infra*.

[42] *See* Terry v. Ohio, 392 U.S. 1 (1968).

[43] 395 U.S. 752 (1969).

[44] *E.g.*, Harris v. United States, 331 U.S. 145 (1947); United States v. Rabinowitz, 339 U.S. 56 (1950). Both cases were overruled by *Chimel*.

The majority's treatment of the issue is illustrative of the Supreme Court's approach to search warrant cases generally in the 1960s and early 1970s.[45] The analysis centered on the Fourth Amendment Warrant Clause and the majority's belief that, in general, warrantless searches are *per se* unreasonable ("the Constitution requires a magistrate to pass on the desires of the police before they violate the privacy of the home"[46]). Accordingly, a warrantless search is prohibited unless the government demonstrates that an exigency made the warrantless conduct imperative. As the Court stated, "the burden is on those seeking [an] exemption [from the requirement] to show the need for it . . . ."[47]

Justice Stewart also stated that when a warrant exception *is* recognized, it "must be 'strictly tied to and justified by' the circumstances which rendered its initiation permissible."[48] Put somewhat differently, an exception to the warrant requirement should be defined as narrowly as possible, and the exception should not apply to situations in which the justification for the exception is absent.

In the case of a search incident to an arrest, the Court concluded that a warrantless search of an arrestee is justified in order to remove any weapons that she might seek to use in order to resist arrest or to effect an escape, as well as to seize any evidence that might be destroyed or concealed. For the same reasons, the scope of the search must include the "area within the immediate control" of the arrestee, which the Court defined as "the area into which an arrestee might reach in order to grab a weapon or evidentiary items."

On the other hand, the Court concluded that it is unreasonable to expand the scope of the search to the remainder of the premises on which a suspect is arrested. Such a rule would expand the exception beyond its stated justification of protecting the arresting officer from harm, and of preventing the destruction of evidence by the person arrested. Justice Stewart also expressed concern that if a full search of the premises of an arrestee were allowed, the police could pretextually avoid the warrant requirement "by the simple expedient of arranging to arrest suspects at home rather than elsewhere."[49]

---

[45] *See* § 11.01[B], *supra.*

[46] Chimel v. California, 395 U.S. at 761 (quoting McDonald v. United States, 335 U.S. 451, 455–56 (1948)).

[47] *Id.* at 762 (alteration in original) (quoting United States v. Jeffers, 342 U.S. 48, 51 (1951)).

[48] *Id.* (quoting Terry v. Ohio, 392 U.S. 1, 19 (1968)).

[49] Regarding the general issue of pretextual police conduct, *see* § 2.07[B], *supra.*

Justice Byron White, with whom Justice Hugo Black joined, dissented. The dissent started from a different Fourth Amendment jurisprudential perspective: according to Justice White, there is no Fourth Amendment "warrant requirement"; instead, the Reasonableness Clause of the amendment ("the right of the people to be secure . . . against unreasonable searches and seizures") governs search-and-seizure law. In his view, the issue in *Chimel* was not whether an exigency made it impracticable to secure a warrant, but rather was whether a search beyond the area of the arrestee's immediate control, if founded on probable cause, was reasonable.

The dissent reasoned that a search of an arrestee's home incident to an arrest, if supported by probable cause, is reasonable. An arrest in a home often creates exigent circumstances, including the risk that a family member (for example, *D*'s wife, who was present at the time of his arrest) or an accomplice will seek to destroy evidence after the police depart. "This must so often be the case," Justice White concluded, that it is "unreasonable to require a warrant for the search of the premises" of a person taken into custody in the home. That is, because many or most in-home arrests create an exigency, a bright-line rule should be announced permitting a search of the *entire* premises in *every* case (even one not involving an emergency), as long as the police have probable cause for the warrantless search beyond the grabbing area.

## § 13.04 *United States v. Robinson*: The Traffic Arrest Case [50]

### [A] The Holding

Only four years after the high court handed down its opinion in *Chimel v. California*,[51] but also after four changes in personnel on the Supreme Court, the Justices decided *United States v. Robinson*.[52] *Robinson* focused on the issue of whether the police, as an incident to a lawful custodial arrest for a routine traffic violation, may search an arrestee although they have no reason to believe that weapons or criminal evidence will be found on her.

---

[50] *See generally* Albert W. Alschuler, *Bright Line Fever and the Fourth Amendment*, 45 U. Pitt. L. Rev. 227, 256–60 (1984); Craig M. Bradley, *The Court's "Two Model" Approach to the Fourth Amendment: Carpe Diem!*, 84 J. Crim. L. & Criminology 429 (1993); Wayne R. LaFave, *"Case-by-Case Adjudication" Versus "Standardized Procedures": The Robinson Dilemma*, 1974 Sup. Ct. Rev. 127; Barbara C. Salken, *The General Warrant of the Twentieth Century? A Fourth Amendment Solution to Unchecked Discretion to Arrest for Traffic Offenses*, 62 Temp. L.Q. 221 (1989); James B. White, *The Fourth Amendment as a Way of Talking About People: A Study of Robinson and Matlock*, 1974 Sup. Ct. Rev. 165.

[51] 395 U.S. 752 (1969).

[52] 414 U.S. 218 (1973).

In *Robinson*, *O*, a District of Columbia police officer, observed *D* driving his automobile on a public road. Based on prior information, *O* had probable cause to believe that *D* was driving with a revoked operator's permit. *O* ordered *D* to pull over, after which he informed *D* that he was under arrest for "operating after revocation," an offense that required *D*'s custodial arrest, pursuant to police department regulations.

Because D.C. police procedures required him to do so, *O* searched *D*. First, *O* patted down the outside of *D*'s clothing. *O* felt an object in *D*'s breast pocket that he could not identify, but which he pulled out. It was a crumpled up cigarette package inside of which were objects that did not feel like cigarettes. *O* opened the package and found fourteen gelatin capsules that contained heroin, which *O* seized and which served as the basis for *D*'s prosecution on drug possession charges.

The Court of Appeals ruled that the officer acted unconstitutionally by conducting the full search. It focused on the fact that the arrest was for a minor traffic offense, rather than for a serious crime. The court reasoned that *O* had no basis for believing that *D* was in possession of destructible evidence relating to the offense of driving with a revoked license. As for a concern for weapons, the Court of Appeals concluded that with a traffic offense, a limited frisk was sufficient. As the frisk here did not disclose any object that felt like a weapon, the subsequent full searches (pulling out the cigarette package, and then opening it) were impermissible.

The Supreme Court, per Justice Rehnquist, rejected this analysis. It treated as speculative any assumption that people who violate traffic laws are less likely to possess dangerous weapons than those arrested for more serious crimes. However, its "more fundamental disagreement" with the lower court was with the latter's view that, as the Supreme Court put it, "there must be litigated in each case the issue of whether or not there was present one of the reasons supporting the authority for a search of the person incident to a lawful arrest."

According to *Robinson*, the authority to search a person incident to a lawful custodial arrest does not depend on "what a court may later determine was the probability in a particular arrest situation that weapons or evidence would in fact be found upon the person of the suspect." That is, "[a] custodial arrest of a suspect based on probable cause is a reasonable intrusion under the Fourth Amendment; *that intrusion being lawful, a search incident to the arrest requires no additional justification.*"[53] According to *Robinson*, "in the case of a lawful custodial arrest a full search of the person is not only an exception to the warrant requirement . . ., but is also a 'reasonable' search under the Amendment."

---

[53] 414 U.S. at 235 (emphasis added).

### [B]   *Robinson* versus *Chimel*

The holding of *Robinson* is not inconsistent with that of *Chimel*. *Chimel* was concerned with the scope of the search-incident-to-lawful-arrest warrant exception; the Court was not called upon in that case to determine whether probable cause (or any other level of suspicion) was required for searches that occurred within the scope of the exception. Nonetheless, the *Robinson* Court's Fourth Amendment analysis differs appreciably from the *Chimel* Court's reasoning and, therefore, is worthy of attention.

In *Chimel*, the Court focused on the Warrant Clause of the Fourth Amendment, placed the burden of proof on the government to justify *any* exception to the warrant requirement, and, in light of the presumption against warrantless searches, refused to announce an exception broader than was absolutely necessary to meet the circumstances of the situation. In contrast, the *Robinson* Court, while noting the warrant requirement of the Fourth Amendment, primarily focused on its view that a full search of a person arrested for an offense—any offense—is a reasonable search. Unlike *Chimel*, the *Robinson* Court did not require the government to show that a full warrantless search in the present case (as distinguished from a more limited pat-down) was needed; it did not demand (as *Chimel* did) proof of facts that justified dispensing with the warrant requirement.

In this vein, notice how the *Robinson* Court gave short shrift to the search of *D*'s cigarette package after it was removed from his pocket. That is, even granting the right of officers to search all arrestees for possible weapons and evidence, a remaining question is whether police should have the automatic right to open containers found on the person of the arrestee. If warrant exceptions are tied to the exigencies that justify them (as *Chimel* said), an officer should *seize* such a container without a warrant, place it in a safe place outside the arrestee's grabbing area, and thereby avoid the additional privacy intrusion of a warrantless *search* of the container. Justice Rehnquist's analysis of this issue in *Robinson* consisted simply of the statement that "the Fourth Amendment does not require [the officer's judgment] to be broken down in each instance into an analysis of each step in the search." Yet, the reasoning of *Chimel* would seem to suggest, if not require, such a step-by-step process.

Finally, notice the Court's treatment of the problem of pretextual conduct. In *Chimel*, the Court worried that a rule allowing a full search of the premises of an arrestee would invite police officers pretextually to make arrests in private residences.[54] But, in a case such as *Robinson* there is a risk that a D.C. police officer will use a minor violation of a vehicle

---

[54] *See* the text immediately preceding Note 49, *supra.*

ordinance—an ordinance that requires her to take the driver into custody—as a pretext to conduct a full search of someone whom the officer suspects, but has less than probable cause to believe, is in possession of criminal evidence.

Indeed, in *Gustafson v. Florida*,[55] a companion case of *Robinson*, the Supreme Court upheld a search factually similar to that in *Robinson*, except that in *Gustafson* there were no police departmental policies requiring that traffic violators be taken into custody or that full-body searches be conducted. In other words, the officer in *Gustafson* had the opportunity to choose whether to issue a traffic ticket and permit the driver to leave or, instead, take the violator into custody and conduct a search incident to the custodial arrest. The *Gustafson* Court was not troubled by the possibility that an officer, exercising her discretion, might choose to take the driver into custody simply so she could conduct a search that would not otherwise constitutionally be permitted. In essence, the Court did not consider the problem of pretextual conduct sufficiently serious to justify developing a rule that limited potential police overreaching.[56]

Whichever approach to the Fourth Amendment—that of *Chimel* or *Robinson*—is better, there is considerable basis for asserting that the two opinions do not fit comfortably with each other in terms of general Fourth Amendment jurisprudence.

## § 13.05 *New York v. Belton*: Bright Lines for Automobiles[57]

In *New York v. Belton*,[58] *O*, a police officer, arrested four occupants of an automobile that he had stopped for speeding, after he smelled burnt

---

[55] 414 U.S. 260 (1973).

[56] *See also* Whren v. United States, 517 U.S. 806, 812 (1996) (observing that the Court's cases, including *Robinson* and *Gustafson*, foreclose the argument "that an officer's [improper] motive invalidates objectively justifiable behavior under the Fourth Amendment").

[57] *See generally* Alschuler, Note 50, *supra*; Bradley, Note 50, *supra*; David M. Silk, *When Bright Lines Break Down: Limiting New York v. Belton*, 136 U. Pa. L. Rev. 281 (1987).

[58] 453 U.S. 454 (1981); *contra, under the state constitution*, State v. Hernandez, 410 So.2d 1381, 1385 (La. 1982) (in dictum, rejecting the bright-line *Belton* rule and requiring case-by-case adjudication of the proper scope of a car search incident to an arrest); State v. Pierce, 642 A.2d 947 (N.J. 1994) (*Belton* rule does not apply to a warrantless custodial arrest for a motor vehicle offense); People v. Belton, 432 N.E.2d 745 (N.Y. 1982) (warrantless search of car only allowed when the police have reason to believe that the car contains a weapon or evidence of a crime); State v. Brown, 588 N.E.2d 113 (Ohio 1992) (as an incident to an arrest, the police may not open a closed container found in a glove compartment after the suspect is in custody in the police car); State v. Kirsch, 686 P.2d 446 (Or. Ct. App. 1984) (stating that *Belton* is not the law in Oregon; requiring case-by-case adjudication of the grabbing area); Commonwealth v. White, 669 A.2d 896 (Pa. 1995) (absent exigent circumstances, the police may not conduct a warrantless search of a car after the occupants

marijuana in the vehicle and observed an envelope on the floor of the car marked "Supergold," a term that he associated with marijuana. *O* removed the occupants from the car and separated them from each other "so they would not be in physical touching area of each other." He returned to the vehicle, opened the envelope, and discovered marijuana. He then searched the remainder of the passenger compartment. In the backseat he found a jacket. He unzipped a pocket of it, in which he found cocaine.

In an opinion written by Justice Stewart, the author of *Chimel*, the Supreme Court approved the warrantless search, including that of the jacket, as an incident to the lawful arrest of the occupants. The Court lamented the lack of a "straightforward rule" respecting the question of what constitutes the grabbing area of persons arrested in automobiles. Therefore, the Court generated a bright-line rule: in all cases, an officer may conduct a contemporaneous warrantless search of the passenger compartment of a vehicle incident to a lawful custodial[59] arrest of the occupants.[60]

It is almost impossible to rationalize *Belton* in light of *Chimel*, and particularly perplexing is the fact that Justice Stewart wrote both opinions. As discussed earlier, *Chimel* was based on the principle that, in view of the constitutional importance of warrants, the scope of a search should be "strictly tied" to the circumstances that render the warrantless action permissible. In *Belton*, however, the bright-line rule clearly permits the police to dispense with the warrant requirement in cases in which no genuine exigency exists.

If the passenger compartment of a car, whose doors are closed, is within the grabbing area of an arrestee sitting handcuffed in a police car—as the *Belton* bright-line rule suggests—then it is not difficult to argue that the search condemned in *Chimel*—a search of the remainder of the house, while the arrestee and his wife were on the premises—should have been upheld. At the least, a bright-line "one room" or "one floor" rule, rather than the vague "area of immediate control" rule, could easily be defended after *Belton*. In short, if *Belton* is right in devising a bright-line rule to assist the police and courts in car cases, the case-by-case adjudication called for by *Chimel* in home-arrests is hard to justify. If *Chimel* is right, *Belton* is hard to fathom.

---

are arrested, outside the car, and in police custody); State v. Stroud, 720 P.2d 436 (Wash. 1986) (as an incident to an arrest of an occupant of a car, a warrant is needed to search a locked glove compartment or locked container); Vasquez v. State, 990 P.2d 476 (Wyo. 1999) (accepting the scope of a *Belton* search, but only if it is reasonable under the circumstances of the individual case).

**59** The *Belton* rule does not apply to a car search incident to the issuance of a traffic citation. Knowles v. Iowa, 525 U.S. 113 (1998). *See* § 13.02[A][1], *supra*.

**60** *See* § 13.02[C][2][b], *supra*.

Even if bright-line rules are desirable, a matter of considerable dispute,[61] a strong case can be made that *Belton* is not the proper bright-line rule. Bright-line rules ought to produce results similar to those that would occur by case-by-case adjudication.[62] It is implausible to believe that in the majority of cases in which a car occupant is arrested, the entire passenger compartment of the vehicle is in the arrestee's grabbing area after she is removed from the vehicle.

Assuming that the facts described in lower court cases are typical, the usual scenario after an occupant of a car is arrested is that she is removed from the vehicle, handcuffed, and placed in the police car. In light of this, it makes more sense, if a bright-line rule is desired, to declare that the interior of a vehicle is never in the arrestee's immediate control once she is removed from it or, at least, once she is placed in the police car.

---

[61] *See* § 2.07[A], *supra.*

[62] Wayne R. LaFave, *The Fourth Amendment in an Imperfect World: On Drawing "Bright Lines" and "Good Faith"*, 43 U. Pitt. L. Rev. 307, 325–26 (1982).

## CHAPTER 14

# SEARCHES OF CARS AND CONTAINERS THEREIN

## § 14.01 Automobile Search Warrant Exception: General Rules[1]

### [A] Important Overview

A warrantless nonconsensual search of an automobile can be justified on various grounds: as an incident to a lawful arrest; in the police department's community caretaking function of inventorying a vehicle after it has been lawfully seized and towed from a public road; and, in limited circumstances, when a driver is stopped on the highway for violating a traffic offense.[2] But, there is also a specific "automobile[3] exception" to the Fourth Amendment search warrant "requirement."[4]

The automobile exception has broadened dramatically over time. The Supreme Court once stated that "[t]he word 'automobile' is not a talisman in whose presence the Fourth Amendment fades away and disappears."[5]

---

[1] *See generally* 3 Wayne R. LaFave, Search and Seizure § 7.2(a)–(b) (3d ed. 1996); Martin R. Gardner, *Searches and Seizures of Automobiles and Their Contents: Fourth Amendment Considerations in a Post-Ross World*, 62 Neb. L. Rev. 1 (1983); Joseph D. Grano, *Rethinking the Fourth Amendment Warrant Requirement*, 19 Am. Crim. L. Rev. 603 (1982); Lewis R. Katz, *The Automobile Exception Transformed: The Rise of a Public Place Exemption to the Warrant Requirement*, 36 Case W. Res. L. Rev. 375 (1986); Lewis R. Katz, *United States v. Ross: Evolving Standards for Warrantless Searches*, 74 J. Crim. L. & Criminology 172 (1983); David E. Steinberg, *The Drive Toward Warrantless Auto Searches: Suggestions from a Back Seat Driver*, 80 B.U. L. Rev. 545 (2000); Note, *Warrantless Searches and Seizures of Automobiles*, 87 Harv. L. Rev. 835 (1974).

[2] *See* § 13.05, *supra* (search incident to a lawful arrest), § 16.01, *infra* (inventory search); and § 18.07, *infra* (during traffic stop).

[3] As used in this chapter, the word "automobile" applies to all motorized vehicles, including trucks, airplanes, motor homes, and motor boats. *See* California v. Carney, 471 U.S. 386, 393 n.2 (1985); *see also* United States v. Albers, 136 F.3d 670 (9th Cir. 1998) (applying the exception to houseboats that are readily mobile). It has even been applied to a bicycle being operated on a public street. People v. Allen, 92 Cal. Rptr.2d 869 (Cal. App. 2000).

[4] Some states refuse to recognize an independent "automobile exception" under their state constitutions. *See* Note 9, *infra*.

[5] Coolidge v. New Hampshire, 403 U.S. 443, 461–62 (1971) (plurality opinion).

Today, however, in nearly all circumstances, a citizen who enters an automobile surrenders the right to have the initial probable cause determination of a car search[6] made by a magistrate. Indeed, in many circumstances, the police may search or seize an *unoccupied* automobile without a warrant, as long as it is later determined that they possessed probable cause for the conduct.

The general rules are set out in the subsections that follow. But, the rules that have developed are controversial with many scholars and some state courts. Therefore, to appreciate the controversies—and to fully understand the road that the Supreme Court has taken to its current destination—some of the most critical automobile cases are discussed in §§ 14.02 through 14.06.

A separate issue must also be considered in relation to automobiles. Often, a search of an automobile includes a search of a container, *e.g.,* an occupant's purse or jacket, a paper bag, or a briefcase, found within the vehicle. The Court has wrestled specially with this specific issue. The container-in-car issue is considered in §14.07.

### [B] Searches "At the Scene"

A police officer may conduct an immediate ("at the scene") warrantless search of an automobile that he has probable cause to believe contains contraband, or fruits, instrumentalities, or evidence of a crime, if: (1) he stops the car on the highway;[7] or (2) the vehicle is readily capable of use on the highway, is found "in a setting that objectively indicates that [the vehicle] is being used for transportation," and is discovered "stationary in a place not regularly used for residential purposes."[8]

Although early automobile cases seemed to be based on a requirement of exigency—that the vehicle could immediately be moved and, therefore, lost to the police—the current law provides that "the 'automobile exception' has no separate exigency requirement."[9] It is now enough that "[i]f a car

---

[6] The warrantless search of an occupant of a vehicle, as distinguished from the automobile itself, does not fall within the scope of the automobile search warrant exception. The justification for *that* search must be found elsewhere, *e.g.*, as an incident to an arrest.

[7] Carroll v. United States, 267 U.S. 132, 153–54 (1925).

[8] California v. Carney, 471 U.S. at 392, 394.

[9] Maryland v. Dyson, 527 U.S. 465, 467 (1999); *contra*, State v. Miller, 630 A.2d 1315 (Conn. 1993); State v. Elison, 14 P.3d 456 (Mont. 2000); State v. Sterndale, 656 A.2d 409 (N.H. 1995); State v. Cooke, 751 A.2d 92 (N.J. 2000); State v. Kock, 725 P.2d 1285 (Or. 1986); State v. Larocco, 794 P.2d 460 (Utah 1990) (plurality opinion); State v. Patterson, 774 P.2d 10 (Wash. 1989) (all holding under their own state constitutions that absent an exigency beyond the inherent mobility of a car or some other independent warrant exception, a warrant supported by probable cause is required to conduct a search of an unoccupied vehicle).

is readily mobile and probable cause exists to believe it contains contraband [or, presumably, other seizable evidence], the Fourth Amendment . . . permits police to search the vehicle without more."[10]

It follows from this that, assuming probable cause to search, the police may conduct an immediate search of a vehicle—or, more accurately, of those portions of the vehicle for which the police have probable cause to search[11] —when they stop the car on a public road,[12] or which they discover off the highway, at a gas station,[13] or parked in a public place, such as in a parking lot.[14] In contrast, there is weak support for the proposition that a warrantless search of an unoccupied car parked in the user's driveway or garage is not permitted if the police have time to secure a warrant prior to the search.[15]

As a corollary of the preceding rules, the Fourth Amendment does not require the police to secure a warrant to *seize* an automobile parked in a public place—even if they have time to obtain a warrant—when they have probable cause to believe that the vehicle itself constitutes forfeitable contraband under state law (*e.g.*, because there is probable cause to believe that the car was used on some prior occasion in the commission of a criminal offense).[16] The police may seize the vehicle although they have no reason to believe that it contains objects subject to seizure.[17]

## [C]  Searches "Away From the Scene"

A warrantless search of an automobile that would be valid if it were conducted at the scene, *i.e.*, at the place where it was stopped or discovered, is also permitted if it takes place shortly thereafter away from the scene.[18]

---

[10] Pennsylvania v. Labron, 518 U.S. 938, 940 (1996).

[11] *See* § 10.01[D], *infra*.

[12] *E.g.*, Carroll v. United States, 267 U.S. 132 (1925).

[13] *See* Colorado v. Bannister, 449 U.S. 1 (1980) (per curiam) (the police observed the car on the road, but did not reach it until it had left the highway and entered a service station).

[14] *E.g.*, California v. Carney, 471 U.S. 386 (1985) (vehicle was occupied). Many courts have justified warrantless searches of *unoccupied* cars parked on the street, often on the ground that the suspect linked to the car is at large, that accomplices might arrive and drive away the car, or even that a stranger might tamper with it. 3 LaFave, Note 1, *supra*, at 466, 479–80 (and cases cited therein).

[15] *E.g.*, Coolidge v. New Hampshire, 403 U.S. 443 (1971) (plurality opinion). *Coolidge* is consider in Section 14.04, *infra*. Its current vitality is considered in Section 14.06, *infra*.

[16] Florida v. White, 526 U.S. 559 (1999).

[17] However, after the seizure, the police may be authorized to conduct a warrantless inventory *search* of the automobile. *See* § 16.01, *infra*. If so, evidence found during such a lawful inventory would be admissible at the car owner's trial.

[18] Chambers v. Maroney, 399 U.S. 42 (1970).

That is, if the police wish to do so—regardless of the reason for their decision[19] —they may seize a car without searching it, move it to another site (such as a police impoundment lot), and search it there without a warrant, on the day of the seizure,[20] or even a day[21] or a few days[22] later. On the other hand, a delay of a year to search an impounded vehicle without a warrant is unreasonable.[23]

## [D]  Probable Cause Requirement

As the preceding comments suggest, the police may conduct a search of an automobile without a warrant in most circumstances. But, the "automobile exception" to the Fourth Amendment is an exception only to the requirement of a search warrant; the probable cause requirement remains firm.

The Supreme Court has explained that "[t]he scope of a warrantless search of an automobile . . . is defined by the object of the search and places in which there is probable cause to believe that it may be found."[24] Thus, it does not follow that "probable cause to search" *always* applies to an entire automobile. In most circumstances, the police will receive reliable information that criminal evidence is somewhere in (or, perhaps, throughout) the vehicle, in which case the right to search *will* extend to the entire car. On the other hand, the police may possess more limited probable cause. For example, in *California v. Acevedo*,[25] the police observed *D* place a small paper bag in the trunk of a vehicle and drive away. The officers had probable cause to believe that the bag contained drugs; they had no other reason to believe that the car (beyond the bag) contained contraband. On these facts, the police had probable cause to search only the trunk to look for the paper bag.

A second point to understand is that once the police discover the criminal evidence for which they are searching, the search must cease, absent new

---

[19] Texas v. White, 423 U.S. 67 (1975) (per curiam).

[20] *E.g.*, Chambers v. Maroney, 399 U.S. 42 (1970).

[21] *E.g.*, Cardwell v. Lewis, 417 U.S. 583 (1974) (plurality opinion).

[22] *E.g.*, United States v. Johns, 469 U.S. 478, 487 (1985) (three-day delay was reasonable; however, the Court did not "foreclose the possibility" that a delay of that length could be deemed unreasonable if the owner proved that the delay "adversely affected [his] privacy or possessory interest" in the car or its contents).

[23] *E.g.*, Coolidge v. New Hampshire, 403 U.S. 443 (1971) (after a timely search, the car was re-searched more than a year after its seizure); United States v. Johns, 469 U.S. at 487 (citing *Coolidge*, the Court observed that "police officers may [not] indefinitely retain possession of a vehicle and its contents before they complete a vehicle search.").

[24] United States v. Ross, 456 U.S. 798, 824 (1982).

[25] 500 U.S. 565 (1991).

information that would justify a new search. Thus, in *Acevedo*, once the paper bag was found in the trunk, the police could not lawfully continue to search the car (as distinguished from the paper bag).

Third, as with searches executed by warrant,[26] the police may not search any portion of a vehicle that could not contain the object of the search. For example, if the police have probable cause to search a car for a stolen 25-inch television set, the police may not open the glove compartment. However, if they are looking for stolen jewelry, the glove compartment may be searched.

## § 14.02   *Carroll v. United States*: The "Mobility" Rationale

In *Carroll v. United States*,[27] a Prohibition era case, the Supreme Court first enunciated an automobile exception to the Fourth Amendment warrant requirement. In *Carroll*, federal officers stopped *D* and *X* in *D*'s automobile on the highway and searched it without a warrant for "bootleg" liquor. At the time *D*'s car was stopped, the officers had probable cause to search it for the contraband, but they lacked authority to arrest the occupants of the car unless and until they found the goods.[28]

The Court upheld the warrantless search for contraband.[29] In an opinion written by Chief Justice Taft, the Court stated that "[i]n cases where the securing of a warrant is reasonably practicable, it must be used." However, it also observed that "a necessary difference [exists] between a search of a . . . dwelling house or other structure in respect of which a proper official warrant readily may be obtained" and an automobile, because a "vehicle can be quickly moved out of the locality or jurisdiction in which the warrant must be sought."

The result in *Carroll* is unsurprising. Apparently, the police did not have probable cause to search the vehicle before they spotted it on the highway. Moreover, the police "were not looking for defendants at the particular time when they appeared." Therefore, the police could not be faulted for not possessing a warrant when they sighted the car. At that point, the car was

---

[26] See § 11.06[F], *supra*.

[27] 267 U.S. 132 (1925).

[28] Possession of the liquor was a misdemeanor, and the police could only arrest for a misdemeanor if the offense was committed in their presence, which required that they observe the liquor in the car.

[29] *Carroll* only authorized a warrantless search of the automobile for contraband and property "subject to seizure and destruction." However, as Professor LaFave has observed, "the specific reference to contraband appears to be no more than recognition of the then extant 'mere evidence' rule, ultimately abolished . . . ." 3 LaFave, Note 1, *supra*, at 460. For discussion of the "mere evidence" rule, see § 9.02[E], *supra*.

clearly mobile: it was in transit on the highway. And, significantly, the occupants could not be arrested prior to the search, so the police could not prevent the suspects from driving out of the jurisdiction. Therefore, a genuine exigency existed. The only practical solution was to conduct a warrantless search.

## § 14.03 *Chambers v. Maroney*: A Controversial View of "Mobility"

In *Chambers v. Maroney*,[30] police officers had probable cause to stop *D*'s car because it fit the description of one involved in a robbery in the vicinity. When the officers approached the car and saw that the occupants fit the robbers' descriptions, they lawfully arrested them. The police did not search the car at that time. Instead, they drove it and the suspects to the police station. Shortly thereafter, while the arrestees were in jail, the police searched the car without a warrant and found weapons and evidence of the crime concealed under the dashboard.

The Court, per Justice Byron White, upheld the warrantless search, ostensibly on the basis of the principles enunciated in *Carroll v. United States*.[31] Essentially, *Chambers* stands for the proposition that, as the Court later explained the case, "police officers with probable cause to search an automobile at the scene where it was stopped [may] constitutionally do so later at the station house without first obtaining a warrant."[32]

Justice White stated that "[n]either *Carroll*, . . . nor other cases in this Court require or suggest that in every conceivable circumstance the search of an auto even with probable cause may be made without the extra protection for privacy that a warrant affords." Nonetheless, as in *Carroll* and the present case, "the circumstances that furnish probable cause to search . . . are most often unforeseeable; moreover, the opportunity to search is fleeting since a car is readily movable."

The Court reasoned that when an automobile is stopped on the highway, an effective search is possible only if the police search the car at the scene, or seize it without a warrant and hold it until one is obtained. Justice White conceded that "arguably," in view of the preference for a magistrate's determination of probable cause, the latter option should have been followed here, on the ground that "the 'lesser' intrusion [of the seizure] is permissible until the magistrate authorizes the 'greater' [intrusion of the search]."

The Court rejected this "arguable" claim. It stated that the question of which is the greater intrusion "is itself a debatable question . . . the answer

---

[30] 399 U.S. 42 (1970).

[31] 267 U.S. 132 (1925). See § 14.02, *supra*.

[32] Texas v. White, 423 U.S. 67, 68 (1975).

[to which] may depend on a variety of circumstances." Consequently, the Court concluded, there is no constitutional difference between the options: "[g]iven probable cause to search, either course is reasonable under the Fourth Amendment."

But, the police in *Chambers* followed neither of these paths: they did not search the car at the scene without a warrant; and they did not seize it without a warrant and then submit the issue of probable cause to a neutral and detached magistrate. Instead, they seized the car without a warrant and searched it—again without a warrant—at the station. The Court justified the latter action on the ground that, "unless the Fourth Amendment permits a warrantless seizure of the car and the denial of its use to anyone until a warrant is secured," a car retains its mobility at the police station. Therefore, the officers' practical options at the stationhouse were the same as they were on the highway: search it immediately; or deny its use to others until a warrant could be obtained. Again, the Court ruled that there was no constitutional difference between these choices.

Two critical observations of *Chambers* are in order. First, "mobility," at least as existed in *Carroll*, plainly was absent in *Chambers*. In *Carroll*, the police were unable to arrest the occupants until they searched the vehicle on the highway. In *Chambers*, the occupants were in custody prior to the search, and the search occurred at the police station; therefore, there was no risk that the car would be quickly moved out of the jurisdiction or hidden. Nor did the government present any evidence that anyone who had a right to the car sought to take it while it was at the station.

Second, the Court was almost certainly wrong when it concluded that there was no constitutional difference between the warrantless search of *D*'s car in *Chambers*, on the one hand, and its warrantless seizure until a magistrate could make the probable cause determination, on the other hand. The latter option surely constituted a lesser intrusion, as Justice Harlan argued in his dissent.

Why is this? When a car is stopped by police on the highway, various constitutionally recognized interests of its occupants are at stake.[33] First, the occupants have an interest in being permitted to continue their travel unimpeded. Second, the car owner has a possessory interest in his vehicle. Third, the occupants have a privacy interest in the contents of the car. In *Chambers*, however, neither *D* nor the others were in position to assert either of the first two interests. The occupants were in custody, so their right of uninterrupted travel had lapsed. Nor could they realistically expect the police to leave the car on the highway; the officers' caretaking function

---

[33] Note, Note 1, *supra*, at 840–45.

required them to move it to a safer site, so the car owner's interest in control over his car could not be enforced. Thus, *D*'s only substantial Fourth Amendment concern was his privacy interest in the contents of the car, which could only be protected by the requirement that the police apply for a search warrant.

Can *Chambers* be justified? The only way it can make sense on the basis of the mobility rationale is to define "mobility" differently than in *Carroll*. In the latter case, the car was deemed "mobile" because it was occupied and in transit. Presumably, as well, a car is mobile if it is occupied and imminently will be on the road. In contrast, in *Chambers,* Justice White attached a much broader meaning to the concept: when he stated that an impounded automobile at a police station is "readily movable," he seemed to be focusing on the *inherent* nature of a motor vehicle. It follows from this that, after *Chambers,* the "exigency" that justifies a warrantless car search does not terminate simply because the car is unoccupied and the people to whom it belongs are in custody or otherwise unable to take the car.

This meaning of "mobility," however, applies nearly all of the time to any motorized vehicle. The logic of this approach is that there is no real exigency requirement at all.[34] Cars virtually fall outside the Fourth Amendment's warrant protection.

## § 14.04 *Coolidge v. New Hampshire*: **Departing From** *Chambers*

In *Coolidge v. New Hampshire,*[35] the police investigated *D*'s possible involvement in a recent murder. *D* and his wife fully cooperated with the police in the investigation. After three weeks, the authorities concluded that they had probable cause to arrest *D*, as well as probable cause to search his car for evidence related to the crime. The police arrested *D* at his home. His car was parked in the driveway. The police towed it to the police station, and thereafter searched it three times without a valid warrant two days after it was seized, nearly a year later, and a third time fourteen months after the original search.

Justice Potter Stewart delivered the opinion of the Court, but the portion of the opinion relating to the automobile exception to the warrant requirement mustered only four votes. The plurality held that the warrantless search of *D*'s car was unconstitutional. In an effort to distinguish the facts from *Carroll v. United States*[36] and *Chambers v. Maroney,*[37] where warrants

---

[34] *See* § 14.01[B], *supra.*

[35] 403 U.S. 443 (1971).

[36] 267 U.S. 132 (1925). *See* § 14.02, *supra*

[37] 399 U.S. 42 (1970). *See* § 14.03, *supra.*

were not required, Justice Stewart noted that "the police had known for some time of the probable role of the . . . car in the crime." Moreover, *D* "already had ample opportunity to destroy any evidence he thought incriminating." The Court also set out other facts it considered important, including that the vehicle was not stopped on the highway, as in the prior cases, but rather was "an unoccupied vehicle parked on the owner's private property."

These facts adequately distinguish *Coolidge* from *Carroll*. The car in the earlier case, but not here, was in transit, and the police had to act quickly. But, how can this case be distinguished from *Chambers*? Although the car in that case started on the highway, and this one did not, in both cases the searches occurred after the vehicle was impounded, and after the suspect was in custody.

The difference between the cases really comes down to the meaning of "mobility." Justice White, the author of *Chambers*, stated in *Coolidge* that "the difference between a moving and movable vehicle is tenuous at best. It is a metaphysical distinction without roots in the commonsense standard of reasonableness governing search and seizure cases." In contrast, consider Justice Stewart's view of mobility in *Coolidge*:

> It is frequently said that occupied automobiles stopped on the open highway may be searched without a warrant because they are "mobile," or "movable." . . . In this case, it is, of course, true that even though [D] was in jail, his wife was miles away in the company of two plainclothesmen, and the Coolidge property was under the guard of two other officers, the automobile was in a literal sense "mobile." . . . We attach no constitutional significance to this sort of mobility. . . . [A] good number of the containers that the police might discover on a person's property and want to search are equally movable, *e.g.*, trunks, suitcases, boxes, briefcases, and bags. How are such objects to be distinguished from an unoccupied automobile . . . sitting on the owner's property?

Justice White's view of mobility leaves automobiles nearly unprotected from warrantless searches.[38] In contrast, Justice Stewart stated that "[t]he word 'automobile' is not a talisman in whose presence the Fourth Amendment fades away and disappears." However, *Coolidge* was a plurality opinion and, as seen below, Justice Stewart's conception of mobility has not gained majority approval.

---

[38] However, Justice White did not approve the second and third searches of the Coolidge car: he believed that *Chambers* only justified a relatively short detention of a vehicle in order to conduct a warrantless search.

## § 14.05 From *Cady* to *Cardwell*: A New (and Disputable) Rationale is Discovered

Although *Coolidge v. New Hampshire*[39] quite arguably made good sense from a mobility perspective, it did not muster a majority vote. At least as to vehicles on the highway, it was difficult for the Court after *Chambers v. Maroney*[40] to justify the automobile exception on the mobility principle as that concept was first invoked in *Carroll v. United States*.[41] In 1982, the Justices conceded in *Michigan v. Thomas*[42] that the right to search a car without a warrant does not "depend upon a reviewing court's assessment of the likelihood in each particular case that the car would have been driven away, or that its contents would have been tampered with, during the period required for the police to obtain a warrant."

In view of this concession, the Court needed a new theory to explain its willingness to permit warrantless car searches. The seeds of the new theory were sown in *Cady v. Dombrowski*.[43] In *Cady*, a car driven by *D*, an off-duty police officer, was involved in a traffic accident. *D* was arrested for drunk driving, and the car was towed to a private garage. Shortly thereafter, an officer investigating the accident learned that *D*'s service revolver was probably still in the car. Because the gun was vulnerable to theft in the parking lot, the officer searched the car for the weapon. Inadvertently, he discovered evidence that tied *D* to a homicide.

In a 5-4 opinion, the Court held that the warrantless search—"standard police procedure" in the department under such community caretaking circumstances—was reasonable. However, *Cady*'s long-term significance is found in the Court's discussion of the automobile exception to the warrant requirement. It conceded that although the original justification for the exception "was the [car's] vagrant and mobile nature," subsequent warrant-less searches were upheld in cases in which mobility was "remote, if not non-existent." *Cady* provided an explanation of why, mobility aside, automobiles are different from houses:

> Because of the extensive regulation of motor vehicles and traffic, and also because of the frequency with which a vehicle can become disabled or involved in an accident on public highways, the extent of police-citizen contact involving automobiles will be substantially greater than police-citizen contact in a home or office.

---

[39] 403 U.S. 443 (1971). See § 14.04, *supra*.

[40] 399 U.S. 42 (1970). See § 14.03, *supra*.

[41] 267 U.S. 132 (1925). See § 14.02, *supra*.

[42] 458 U.S. 259 (1982) (per curiam).

[43] 413 U.S. 433 (1973).

(Matthew Bender & Co., Inc.)

A year later, in *Cardwell v. Lewis*,[44] a four-justice plurality developed this argument further. After noting the mobility of cars, the Court stated that "there is still another distinguishing factor," which was that:

[o]ne has a lesser expectation of privacy in a motor vehicle because its function is transportation and it seldom serves as one's residence or as the repository of personal effects. A car has little capacity for escaping public scrutiny. It travels public thoroughfares where both its occupants and its contents are in plain view.

A majority of Justices later accepted the lesser-expectation-of-privacy rationale in *South Dakota v. Opperman*,[45] a car inventory case.[46] The rationale was adopted as part of the automobile exception to the warrant requirement in *California v. Carney*,[47] a case involving the search of a motor home. *Carney* is considered in Section 14.06.

Is the lesser-expectation-of-privacy rationale persuasive? First, the fact that a car is visible to the public on the road does not distinguish it from any object that a person might carry in open view, for example, a suitcase or valise. Additionally, although a car on the road is visible, its *contents* often are not, as they may be placed under the seat, in the glove compartment, or the trunk.

Nor was the *Cardwell* Court accurate in stating that an automobile "seldom serves as one's residence or the repository of personal effects." People commonly use their cars, especially the trunk and glove compartment, to transport articles of considerable importance and of a personal nature. Although the car serves in such cases only as a temporary repository of these items, a car is no less important a source of privacy than a hotel room, which receives full Fourth Amendment protection. Indeed, the Court appears to have accepted this point in recent cases. It has conceded that "[c]ertainly the privacy interests in a car's trunk or glove compartment may be no less than those in a movable container."[48] Also, for homeless persons lucky enough to still have an automobile, and for people who live and travel in luxurious motor homes, the automobile may be their *only* repository for their treasured belongings.

Third, the fact that cars are the object of extensive governmental regulation, although true, does not wholly distinguish them from "fully" protected houses and offices, which are the subject of building, safety, and

---

[44] 417 U.S. 583 (1974).

[45] 428 U.S. 364 (1976).

[46] *See* § 16.01[B], *infra*.

[47] 471 U.S. 386 (1985).

[48] United States v. Ross, 456 U.S. 798, 823 (1982).

health code regulations and nonconsensual inspections.[49] Perhaps in view of the fact that the government regulates so many aspects of our lives—and, therefore, reduces our "reasonable expectations"—the issue regarding cars ought to be whether we have a *right* to an undiluted expectation of privacy in our cars, regardless of the heavily regulated nature of automobile usage.

### § 14.06 *California v. Carney*: The Mobility and Lesser-Expectation-of-Privacy Rationales at Work

*California v. Carney*[50] involved a warrantless search of a "fully mobile 'motor home' located in a public place." The police received uncorroborated information that *D* was using his motor home as a site for exchanging drugs for sex. At the time, *D* was parked in a city lot, near a courthouse where a warrant could have been secured. The police put the motor home under surveillance for one and one-quarter hours, during which time they saw a youth enter the vehicle, and later leave with marijuana. The youth confirmed that he received the drugs in exchange for sexual contacts by *D*. Although there was no indication that the vehicle was about to depart, or even that *D* knew that he under surveillance, the police entered the motor home without a warrant or consent, and seized drugs inside.

The Supreme Court, per Chief Justice Warren Burger, discussed both rationales for the automobile exception. Regarding mobility, it stated that the motor home was "obviously readily mobile by the turn of a switch key." This statement is true, of course, in the sense that the motor home had the capacity for movement; however, if that capacity had been utilized while an officer was seeking a warrant, the vehicle could and would have been immediately stopped. This sense of "mobility" approximates Justice White's understanding of the term in *Chambers v. Maroney*,[51] and is contrary to the plurality analysis in *Coolidge v. New Hampshire*.[52] Except, perhaps, for a motor vehicle without wheels or a battery—which is not really a motorized vehicle—nearly any car is "mobile" in the sense explained here.

As for the lesser-expectation-of-privacy rationale, the Court stated that even when an automobile is not "immediately mobile, the lesser expectation of privacy resulting from its use . . . justifie[s] application of the vehicular exception." Chief Justice Burger conceded that *D*'s vehicle "possessed some, if not many of the attributes of a home." Nonetheless, "it is equally clear that the vehicle falls within the scope of the exception laid down [in the automobile] cases." And, critically perhaps, "the vehicle was so situated

---

[49] *See* § 19.02, *infra.*

[50] 471 U.S. 386 (1985).

[51] 399 U.S. 42 (1970). *See* § 14.03, *supra.*

[52] 403 U.S. 443 (1971). *See* § 14.04, *supra.*

that an objective observer would conclude that it was being used not as a residence, but as a vehicle."

Of course, *D* might have been using his vehicle as *both* a residence and a mode of transportation. If this is the case, the automobile exception presumably applies. The Court did not decide whether the exception applies "to a motor home that is situated in a way or place that objectively indicates that it is being used as a residence." According to Chief Justice Burger:

> Among the factors that might be relevant in determining whether a warrant would be required in such a circumstance is its location, whether the vehicle is readily mobile or instead, for instance, elevated on blocks, whether the vehicle is licensed, whether it is connected to utilities, and whether it has convenient access to a public road.

Ultimately and critically, the Court described the automobile exception this way: "[w]hen a vehicle is being used on the highways, or if it is readily capable of such use and is found stationary in a place *not regularly used for residential purposes* . . . the two justifications for the vehicle exception come into play." The italicized language seems to allow the Court to reaffirm the plurality holding in *Coolidge*, if it chooses to do so. Except in this limited situation, however, any vehicle "readily capable" of use for transportation purposes, which is not objectively being used solely as a residence, may apparently be searched without a warrant (assuming probable cause for the search).

## § 14.07  Special Problem: Search of Containers Found in Cars[53]

### [A]  Clarification of the Issue

#### [1]  In General

The "car cases" generally involve the issue of whether the police may search an automobile without a warrant, assuming they have probable cause for the inspection. But, suppose that the officers come upon a container, *e.g.*, a suitcase, briefcase, or paper bag, during the car search. May they open it without a warrant? Or, suppose that the police are validly searching the car (without a warrant) looking for a particular container that they have reason to believe contains contraband. If they find it, may they open that container without a warrant? These questions are considered here.

---

[53] *See generally* 3 LaFave, Note 1, *supra*, at § 7.2(d); Craig M. Bradley, *The Court's "Two Model" Approach to the Fourth Amendment: Carpe Diem!*, 84 J. Crim. L. & Criminology 429 (1993); Katz, *The Automobile Exception Transformed*, Note 1, *supra*; James J. Tomkovicz, *California v. Acevedo: The Walls Close In On The Warrant Requirement*, 29 Am. Crim. L. Rev. 1103 (1992).

### [2]   What is a "Container"?

For current purposes, a "container" is "any object capable of holding another object."[54]

Containers are not all alike. Some containers are inexpensive, such as a simple paper bag, whereas others are expensive, such as an executive's attache case. Furthermore, people protect the contents of containers in different ways. One person with a paper bag might leave it open, another might fold it closed, and still another could staple it shut; luggage might be unlocked, locked, or even double-locked.

The Supreme Court has stated that "[w]hat one person may put into a suitcase, another may put into a paper bag."[55] Therefore, with one significant exception, the Court does not draw distinctions among containers in determining whether the police must obtain a warrant to open it. That is, whatever rules apply—they are discussed below—the Court will not treat some containers as more deserving of protection than others.

The exception is that the Fourth Amendment does not provide full protection for containers which "by their very nature cannot support any reasonable expectation of privacy because their contents can be inferred from their outward appearance."[56] The Court's examples of such containers are a kit of burglar's tools and a gun case. In essence, if the contents of a container are in literal plain view because the container is open or transparent, a person cannot possess a reasonable expectation of privacy as to the observation of its contents. Likewise, contents are in figurative plain view if the container's "distinctive configuration . . . proclaims its contents."[57] Perhaps, as well—the Court has left the issue open[58] —one may not possess a reasonable expectation of privacy in a container the contents of which can be determined by its distinctive odor.

### [B]   General Rule

The rule, which did not come easily to the Court, is that containers—even one belonging to a passenger of the automobile, who is not suspected of criminal activity[59] —may be searched without a warrant during an

---

[54] New York v. Belton, 453 U.S. 454, 460 n.4 (1981).

[55] Robbins v. California 453 U.S. 420, 426 (1981), *overruled on other grounds*, United States v. Ross, 456 U.S. 798 (1982).

[56] Arkansas v. Sanders, 442 U.S. 753, 764–65 n.13 (1979), *overruled on other grounds*, California v. Acevedo, 500 U.S. 565 (1991).

[57] Robbins v. California, 453 U.S. at 427.

[58] United States v. Johns, 469 U.S. 478 (1985).

[59] Wyoming v. Houghton, 526 U.S. 295 (1999). *See* Note 72, *infra*.

otherwise lawful "automobile exception" search.[60] And, if the container may be searched at the scene, it may also be seized and searched without a warrant shortly thereafter, at the police station.[61]

This rule applies in either of two general circumstances. First, as part of a valid warrantless car search, the police may come across a container. If so, they may open it without a warrant, assuming (as always[62] ) that the container is large enough to hold the criminal evidence for which the police are searching. In these circumstances, the existence of probable cause to search the car serves to justify the warrantless container search, even though the officer conducting the search lacks any specific probable cause as to that particular container.

Second, the police may have probable cause to believe that a particular container holding criminal evidence will be found in a car. In such circumstances, the police may conduct a warrantless search of the car for the container (per the automobile exception), and then open the container, also without a warrant.

On the other hand, absent exigent circumstances, consent, or as an incident to an arrest, the police may not open a container found outside a motor vehicle without obtaining a search warrant.

### [C]   How the Container Rules Developed

#### [1]   *United States v. Chadwick*

In *United States v. Chadwick*,[63] Amtrak officials observed two persons load an unusually heavy footlocker onto a train. One of the suspects fit a profile used to spot drug traffickers, and the footlocker was leaking talcum powder, a substance often used to mask the odor of illegal narcotics. The railroad employees transmitted this information to federal narcotics agents.

The agents put the suspects under surveillance when they got off the train two days later. Although the agents did not have a warrant, they came with a dog trained to detect marijuana. While the footlocker was sitting on the floor in the train station, the dog signaled the presence of an illegal narcotic inside. The agents then watched as *D* and two other persons lifted the double-locked footlocker into the trunk of a car. While the trunk was still open, and before the engine was started, the officers arrested the three persons, seized the footlocker, transported it to their headquarters, and there searched it 90 minutes later, still without a warrant.

---

[60] California v. Acevedo, 500 U.S. 565 (1991).

[61] United States v. Johns, 469 U.S. 478 (1985).

[62] *See* § 14.01[D], *supra.*

[63] 433 U.S. 1 (1977).

At the trial court level, the government sought to justify the warrantless conduct on various grounds, including the automobile exception.[64] The trial court rejected this claim, because it "saw the relationship between the footlocker and [D's] automobile as merely coincidental." Presumably, the court meant by this that the police had probable cause to search the container before it was placed in the vehicle; moreover, the footlocker was seized only seconds after its placement in the car, before the engine was started. On appeal to the Supreme Court, the government abandoned this argument.

Instead, the government made two other claims. First, in an argument that the dissent characterized as "extreme," the government asserted that the Fourth Amendment Warrant Clause "protects only interests traditionally identified with the home." Drawing on the history of the Fourth Amendment, and the framers' concern about writs of assistance and general warrants,[65] the government argued that "only homes, offices, and private communications implicate interests which lie at the core of the Fourth Amendment." Therefore, since the footlocker was seized outside a home or office, it could be opened without a warrant, if the search was supported by probable cause.

The Court, per Chief Justice Burger, rejected this argument. Although general warrants and writs of assistance "deeply concerned the colonists" and were "foremost in the minds of the Framers, . . . it would be a mistake to conclude . . . that the Warrant Clause was therefore intended to guard only against intrusions into the home." The Chief Justice observed that the Warrant Clause does not distinguish between searches in private homes and elsewhere, and that the initial clause of the Fourth Amendment draws no distinctions between "persons, houses, papers, and effects" in barring unreasonable search and seizures. In essence, the container and its contents are "effects"; they are textually entitled to as much Fourth Amendment protection as persons, houses, and papers.

---

[64] The government also argued that the search was an incident to the lawful arrest. However, the Supreme Court stated that once police reduce "property not immediately associated with the person of the arrestee to their exclusive control"—as here, by taking the container to headquarters—and, therefore, there is no danger of the arrestee grabbing it, "a search of that property is no longer an incident of that arrest."

A more difficult question is whether the search would have been justified if the officers had opened the double-locked footlocker at the scene. Justices Blackmun and Rehnquist, who dissented, believed that the police could have lawfully opened the footlocker at the scene because it was in the grabbing area of the arrestees. Justice Brennan, who concurred, believed it was "not at all obvious" that this was so, because he doubted that the *contents* of the "securely locked" container were in the grabbing area.

[65] *See* § 5.03, *supra*.

Beyond the textual and historical arguments, the Court noted that "we do not write from a clean slate." Quoting *Katz v. United States*,[66] it stated that the Fourth Amendment "protects people, not places." Therefore, it is wrong to assume that people are protected only in their homes. "Accordingly," the Chief Justice stated, "we have held warrantless searches unreasonable, and therefore unconstitutional, in a variety of settings." He also reasserted the traditional policy argument for warrants, stating that it "far more likely that [a search] will not exceed proper bounds when it is done pursuant to a judicial authorization."

The government had a second, less broad, explanation for the warrantless search of the footlocker. Although it did not reassert the automobile exception, it used the "car search" cases to argue that "luggage is . . . analogous to motor vehicles for Fourth Amendment purposes." The apparent reasoning is that a footlocker or other container is as mobile as an automobile. Therefore, as with a motor vehicle, assuming probable cause for the search, a container should be subject to a warrantless search at the scene or, as in *Chambers v. Maroney*,[67] at police headquarters shortly thereafter.

The Supreme Court rejected this argument, as well. It held that the warrantless *seizure* of *D*'s footlocker was permissible, but that the warrantless *search* of it ninety minutes later was unconstitutional, as no exigency existed at the time of the search. According to the Chief Justice:

> Once the federal agents had seized [the container] at the railroad station and had safely transferred it to the Boston Federal Building under their exclusive control, there was not the slightest danger that the footlocker or its contents could have been removed before a valid search warrant could be obtained. . . . With the footlocker safely immobilized, it was unreasonable to undertake the additional and greater intrusion of a search without a warrant.

Of course, in terms of mobility, the same might have been said about the automobile in *Chambers*. If the car in that case remained "mobile" at the police station, why is a footlocker any different? The Court distinguished the cases on the ground that the seizure of a car does not necessarily guarantee that the vehicle will not be wrongfully moved, since "[a]bsolutely secure storage facilities may not be available, . . . and the size and inherent mobility of a vehicle make it susceptible to theft or intrusion by vandals."

The Court drew another distinction between cars and containers: "[t]he answer lies in the diminished expectation of privacy which surrounds the automobile . . . ." According to *Chadwick*:

---

[66] 389 U.S. 347 (1967).

[67] Chambers v. Maroney, 399 U.S. 42 (1970). *See* § 14.03, *supra*.

The factors which diminish the privacy aspects of an automobile do not apply to [*D*'s] footlocker. Luggage[68] contents are not [ordinarily] open to public view . . .; nor is luggage subject to regular inspections and official scrutiny on a continuing basis. Unlike an automobile, whose primary function is transportation, luggage is intended as a repository of personal effects. In sum, a person's expectations of privacy in personal luggage are substantially greater than in an automobile.

According to the Court, the privacy distinction also explains the difference between the *Chambers* car and the *Chadwick* footlocker. The Court disingenuously stated that "[i]t was the greatly reduced expectation of privacy in the automobile, coupled with the transportation function of the vehicle, which made the Court in *Chambers* unwilling to decide whether an immediate search of an automobile, or its seizure and indefinite immobilization, constituted a greater interference with the rights of the owner." However, *Chambers* never made this point: the lesser-expectation-of-privacy rationale of the "car search" cases had not yet been developed.

The lesson of *Chadwick* is this: people have a greater expectation of privacy in containers than in their automobiles. Therefore, when the police unexpectedly encounter a container that they believe holds criminal evidence, and assuming that no other warrant exception applies, the police may *seize* the container without a warrant. However, they may not open it until they convince a magistrate that they have probable cause to search it.

The extent to which this lesson of *Chadwick* remains good law is considered below.

### [2]  *Arkansas v. Sanders*

In significant respects, the facts in *Arkansas v. Sanders*[69] were similar to those in *Chadwick*. As in *Chadwick*, the police possessed probable cause to search a particular container (here, a green suitcase). As in *Chadwick*, the police did not seize the container until it was placed in a vehicle, in this case a taxicab at an airport. However, unlike the facts in *Chadwick*, the police here allowed the taxi to drive away, whereupon the officers gave pursuit, stopped the cab a few blocks away, seized the suitcase, and opened it immediately.

Because the search involved a container found in a car stopped on the public road, the government defended the warrantless police activity on the ground that it was permissible under the automobile exception. Thus, the issue was whether the principles of *Chadwick* or the car cases controlled.

---

[68] Despite the Court's use of the term "luggage," the principles enunciated in *Chadwick* apply to other types of containers. *See* § 14.07[A][2], *supra*.

[69] 442 U.S. 753 (1979), *overruled by* California v. Acevedo, 500 U.S. 565 (1991).

Justice Lewis Powell delivered the opinion of the Court. He reasserted the primacy of the warrant requirement. He observed that "[t]he mere reasonableness of a search, assessed in the light of the surrounding circumstances, is not a substitute for the judicial warrant required under the Fourth Amendment." Although there are "some exceptions" to the warrant requirement, including one for automobiles, the Court concluded that the reasons justifying warrantless car searches—lesser expectation of privacy and mobility—do not apply to containers found in automobiles.

As to privacy, Justice Powell reasoned that "[o]ne is not less inclined to place private, personal possessions in a suitcase merely because the suitcase is to be carried in an automobile rather than transported by other means . . . ." Second, although the Court agreed that a suitcase in the trunk of an automobile is as mobile as the vehicle itself, "the exigency of mobility must be assessed at the point immediately before the search—after the police had seized the object to be searched and have it securely within their control." As the suitcase was in the officers' control when it was searched, it was not mobile. Therefore, Justice Powell stated, "as a general rule there is no greater need for warrantless searches of luggage taken from automobiles than of luggage taken from other places."

Notice the immediately preceding language, which was broader than was required to decide the case. *Sanders*, like *Chadwick*, involved a search of a container that the police had probable cause to seize and search *before* it was placed in a vehicle. In that sense, the container in *Sanders* was only (to use the language of *Chadwick*) "coincidentally" in a vehicle. Nonetheless, the general rule announced here seemed to be that containers found in cars *never* fall within the scope of the automobile exception. That is, *Chadwick*—and not *Carroll* and *Chambers*, the car cases[70]—applies to all containers taken from automobiles. This expansive reading of the Warrant Clause of the Fourth Amendment, however, was short-lived.

### [3]   *United States v. Ross*

In *United States v. Ross*,[71] the police had probable cause to search an entire car for contraband. During the search, they discovered a closed paper bag in the trunk, which they opened without a warrant. Thus, *Ross* differed from *Chadwick* and *Sanders* in the following way: in *Ross* the probable cause focused on an automobile, in which a container coincidentally was discovered; in *Chadwick* and *Sanders*, the probable cause was directed at a container, later coincidentally placed in a car.

---

[70] Carroll v. United States, 267 U.S. 132 (1925); Chambers v. Maroney, 399 U.S. 42 (1970). *See* §§ 14.02–14.03, *supra.*

[71] 456 U.S. 798 (1982).

As it turned out, this distinction mattered. Justice John Stevens, speaking for the Court, held that the warrantless search—including opening the paper bag—was constitutional. According to *Ross*, the permissible scope of a warrantless search "is defined by the object of the search and the places in which there is probable cause to believe that it may be found." In short, in *this* situation, the automobile exception took precedence: "[i]f probable cause justifies the search of a lawfully stopped vehicle [under the 'automobile exception'], it justifies the search of every part of the vehicle and its contents that may conceal the object of the search." The Court has since clarified that the *Ross* rule applies to *all* containers found in a car, even if the container belongs to a person not linked to the vehicle, such as a passenger of the suspect-driver or a person not in the vehicle at all.[72]

Although the Court adhered to the holding in *Sanders*, it undermined some of its reasoning. The Court compared the scope of a search of an automobile to that of a home. In the latter case, a warrant, supported by probable cause and which meets the particularity requirements of the Fourth Amendment, ordinarily is required. However, once the warrant is authorized, the police may search "the entire area in which the object of the search may be found and is not limited by the possibility that separate acts of entry or opening may be required to complete the search."

The same reasoning applies to a car search, according to *Ross*. Although a warrant is not required for the search of a car because of its mobility, the scope of the search should include all areas in the car that a magistrate, if it had been practicable to request a warrant, could have authorized.

---

[72] Wyoming v. Houghton, 526 U.S. 295 (1999). In *Houghton*, the police had probable cause to search the car for drugs based on their contact with the driver after they lawfully stopped the vehicle for traffic violations. In the car search, the police found and opened a purse belonging to a female passenger, in which drug paraphernalia was found, resulting in her arrest.

Justice Scalia, for the Court, pointed out that the critical issue in a search is not the owner of the property in question, but whether (quoting Zurcher v. Stanford Daily, 436 U.S. 547 (1978)) "there is reasonable cause to believe that the specific 'things' to be searched for and seized are located on the property to which entry is sought." Therefore, the *Houghton* Court declared, when there is probable cause to search a car for drugs, as here, the police may open any and all containers, "without a showing of individualized probable cause for each one."

In further support of this interpretation of the Fourth Amendment, the Court stated that "[p]assengers, no less than drivers, possess a reduced expectation of privacy with regard to the property they transport in cars . . . ." Moreover, a different rule would impair effective law enforcement as it might prevent the police from finding criminal evidence. Justice Scalia pointed out that a car passenger "will often be engaged in a common enterprise with the driver" and, therefore, will have the same interest in concealing contraband and other criminal evidence.

Therefore, immediately after *Ross*, there were two lines of container cases. If the police had probable cause to search a container, which was then placed in an automobile, *Chadwick-Sanders* applied, and the police needed a warrant to search the container. In contrast, if the police had probable cause to search a car, and a container happened to be found during the lawful search, the automobile exception applied, and the container could be opened as part of the car search (assuming its size allowed for concealment of the criminal evidence). Then, along came *Acevedo*.

### [4]  *California v. Acevedo*

In *California v. Acevedo*,[73] the Supreme Court erased what it described as the "curious line between the search of an automobile that coincidentally turns up a container [*Ross*] and the search of a container that coincidentally turns up in an automobile [*Chadwick-Sanders*]."

Justice Blackmun, who dissented in both *Chadwick* and *Sanders*, delivered the Court's opinion. Stating that "[t]he protections of the Fourth Amendment must not turn on such coincidences," the Court expressly overruled *Sanders*. It announced the following rule: "[t]he interpretation of the *Carroll* doctrine set forth in *Ross* now applies to all searches of containers found in an automobile. In other words, the police may search without a warrant if their search is supported by probable cause."

In *Acevedo*, as police looked on, *D* left a residence holding a closed paper bag that the officers had probable cause to believe contained illegal narcotics. *D* placed the bag in the trunk of a car, and drove away. The police stopped the car on the road, opened the trunk, and inspected the contents of the bag, which contained marijuana.

Thus, the case was factually similar to *Chadwick* and *Sanders* in a key respect: the police had probable cause to search a specific container before it was placed in the car. Moreover, as in *Sanders*, the container was not searched until the car was on the highway. The present case was unlike *Ross* in one important respect: in *Ross*, the police had probable cause to search a car trunk for contraband, during which search they unexpectedly discovered a closed paper bag; in *Acevedo*, probable cause to search did not extend beyond the closed paper bag, *i.e.*, the police had probable cause to search the trunk, *but only so that they could find the paper bag.*[74]

---

[73] 500 U.S. 565 (1991); *contra under the state constitution*, State v. Savva, 616 A.2d 774 (Vt. 1991).

[74] The italicized language is important. The police in *Acevedo* had the right to open *D*'s car trunk to search for the paper bag, and not to conduct a search of the trunk for contraband beyond that. Notice the significance of this distinction.

*Scenario 1*. The police in *Acevedo* open the trunk and immediately spot the paper bag.

Why did the Court overrule *Sanders*? Justice Blackmun stated that "[t]he discrepancy between the two rules has led to confusion for law enforcement officers," thus failing to provide "clear and unequivocal" guidelines. But, Fourth Amendment jurisprudence rarely provides clear and unequivocal rules. Nor is it evident that the law in this area was especially difficult: the officers in *Chadwick* and *Sanders* knew full well that they wanted to search a container and not the car *per se*, and the rule announced there sent a fairly clear message: if the police believe there is criminal evidence in a particular container, they should seize it, but seek a warrant.

Second, the Court said that the separate rules "may enable the police to broaden their power to make warrantless searches and disserve privacy interests." Justice Blackmun worried that "[i]f the police know that they may open a bag only if they are actually searching the entire car, they may search more extensively than they otherwise would in order to establish the general probable cause required by *Ross*."

The apparent point of this statement is that, in the pre-*Acevedo* world in which the police only have probable cause to search a particular container, Blackmun feared that the police might search the rest of the vehicle in the hope of discovering contraband, so as to convert the situation into a *Ross*-like car search, justifying a warrantless search of the container. Yet, as Professor LaFave has observed, this argument is "unmitigated poppycock," because "if any point is solidly grounded in Fourth Amendment jurisprudence, it is that the police cannot 'bootstrap' themselves into probable cause; a search may not be justified by what turns up in that search."[75]

Third, the majority maintained that, "[t]o the extent that the *Chadwick-Sanders* rule protects privacy, its protection is minimal." Why is this? Justice Blackmun observed:

[Under *Chadwick-Sanders*] [l]aw enforcement officers may seize a container and hold it until they obtain a search warrant. *"Since the police,*

---

According to this case, they may seize and search it without a warrant. The right to search the trunk further ceases.

*Scenario 2.* The same as 1, except that when they open the trunk they observe other criminal evidence in open view. They may seize *this* evidence under the plain view doctrine, see § 15.01, *infra*, as well as seize and search the paper bag. Moreover, the newly found criminal evidence in the trunk *might* give the police independent probable cause to conduct a greater search of the trunk or, perhaps, the rest of the car.

*Scenario 3.* The police in *Acevedo* open the trunk, and do not see the paper bag. They may now search the trunk until they find it. To do this, they may open *other* containers large enough to hold the paper bag. The police may seize any criminal evidence they find in plain view during the process.

[75] 3 LaFave, Note 1, *supra*, at 502.

*by hypothesis, have probable cause to seize the property, we can assume that a warrant will be routinely forthcoming in the overwhelming majority of cases.*" [Emphasis added.]

The italicized language—which originated in Blackmun's own *dissent* in *Sanders*—is interesting and especially disturbing to advocates of the warrant requirement. In essence, Justice Blackmun is rejecting the statement in *Sanders*, which expresses the essence of the warrant requirement, that "[t]he mere reasonableness of a search . . . is not a substitute for the judicial warrant . . . ." The warrant requirement is based on the premise that, in the words of Justice Stevens's dissent in *Acevedo*, "the decision to invade the privacy of an individual's personal effects should be made by a neutral magistrate rather than an agent of the Executive."

Fourth, Justice Blackmun believed that the prior container rules resulted in an anomaly: the more likely the police are to discover drugs in a container, the less authority they have to search it. That is, under *Ross*, if the police are conducting a warrantless car search, and they stumble upon a container, they may open it, although they have no particularized reason to believe they will find evidence inside; yet, if they have solid probable cause to search a particular container, but no basis for searching the rest of the car, *Chadwick-Sanders* required a warrant to open the container. But, this argument is flawed, at least if there is still a Fourth Amendment warrant requirement: it confuses the issue of probable cause with the requirement of a warrant. As the dissenters observed, "even proof beyond a reasonable doubt will not justify a warrantless search that is not supported by one of the exceptions to the warrant requirement."

### [5]   What Is Left of *Chadwick*?

*Acevedo* overruled *Sanders*, but it did not expressly overrule *Chadwick*. What remains, then, of *Chadwick*? The majority opinion in *Acevedo* does not openly question that opinion's basic premise that a person possesses a legitimate expectation of privacy in closed containers, outside the context of a vehicle.[76]

However, what if (exactly as in *Chadwick*) the police conduct a warrantless search of a container the moment it is placed in a car, but before the vehicle is taken onto the highway? The reasoning of *Acevedo* strongly suggests that such a search now falls within the automobile exception to the warrant requirement. Language in *Acevedo* supports this conclusion: according to Justice Blackmun, "*Ross* now applies to all searches of

---

[76] *See* United States v. $639,558 in United States Currency, 955 F.2d 712 (D.C. Cir. 1992) (ruling that the holding of *Chadwick* survives *Acevedo*; therefore, a warrantless search of a closed container, seized from *D*'s "sleeper" compartment on a train, is unconstitutional).

containers found in an automobile." *Chadwick*, it will be remembered, was not argued to the Supreme Court in terms of the automobile exception. Therefore, if a case factually on all fours with *Chadwick* arises, and if the government invokes the automobile exception, the Court seems poised to overrule the holding of *Chadwick*.[77]

Assuming *Chadwick* remains good law as to containers found and searched *outside* an automobile, *Acevedo* creates its own anomaly. If a person walks along a street holding a briefcase that the police have probable cause to believe contains evidence of a crime, the police may seize, but not search, it without a warrant. However, once the person puts the container, previously in open view, in an automobile, for example, in a locked car trunk, the police may search the trunk for the container, and open it without a warrant. There is little to commend this distinction in terms of reasonable privacy expectations or mobility concerns.

It should be noted, however, that much of the reasoning of *Acevedo* undermines the "warrant requirement" of the Fourth Amendment. If it is true that warrants provide only minimal privacy protection, as the Court stated there, there is little reason to require a warrant in the case of a container search outside an automobile. Therefore, the Court might be prepared to rethink the "extreme" government argument made and rejected in *Chadwick*, namely, that warrants are only needed to conduct searches inside a home or office. Perhaps outside a private building, the Court will declare that searches need only satisfy the reasonableness requirement of the Fourth Amendment.[78]

---

[77] Tomkovicz, Note 53, *supra*, at 1115.

[78] *See* Florida v. White, 526 U.S. 559, 565 (1999) (in part justifying the warrantless seizure of a car, parked in a public place, although its owner was already in custody, on the ground that "our Fourth Amendment jurisprudence has consistently accorded law enforcement officials greater latitude in exercising their duties in public places").

CHAPTER 15

# "PLAIN VIEW" AND RELATED DOCTRINES

## § 15.01 Plain View: General Principles[1]

### [A] Elements of the Doctrine

An object of an incriminating nature may be seized without a warrant if it is in "plain view" of a police officer lawfully present at the scene.

"Plain view" is a constitutional term of art. As explained more fully below, an article is in "plain view," and subject to warrantless seizure by a police officer, if: (1) she observes it from a lawful vantage point; (2) she has a right of physical access to it; and (3) its nature as an object subject to seizure (*i.e.*, that it is contraband or a fruit, instrumentality, or evidence of a crime) is immediately apparent when she observes it (*i.e.*, she has probable cause to seize it).[2]

For example, suppose that *O*, a police officer, has a valid warrant to search *D*'s garage for drug paraphernalia and illegal narcotics. As she is searching the garage pursuant to the warrant, she notices, to her surprise, that the automobile fits the description of one recently used in an unrelated murder. *O* seizes the car as evidence of the murder, although the warrant does not authorize her to do so.

Under the plain-view doctrine, the warrantless seizure of the car would be permissible because: (1) her entry into the garage (and, therefore, her sighting of the car) was proper, as it was authorized by the warrant; (2) her physical access to the car was lawful, as it was situated in the area she had a right to search pursuant to the warrant; and (3) when she observed the car it was immediately apparent to her that it was evidence of a crime.

### [B] Rationale of the Doctrine

The plain view doctrine, as set out above, does *not* serve as an exception to the supposed rule that a warrant ordinarily is required to conduct a *search*

---

[1] *See generally* 1 Wayne R. LaFave, Search and Seizure § 2.2(a) (3d ed. 1996).

[2] Horton v. California, 496 U.S. 128 (1990); *see* Coolidge v. New Hampshire, 403 U.S. 443 (1971); Arizona v. Hicks, 480 U.S. 321 (1987); Texas v. Brown, 460 U.S. 730 (1983).

of a person, house, paper, or effect. Instead, it functions as a justification for the police conducting a warrantless *seizure* of the evidence in plain view.[3]

A warrantless seizure of an object in plain view is not inconsistent with the purposes of the Fourth Amendment Warrant Clause. According to Justice Potter Stewart in *Coolidge v. New Hampshire*,[4] the Warrant Clause ensures that police officers, whenever practicable, seek a prior judicial determination of probable cause in order "to eliminate altogether searches not based on probable cause," as well as to prevent exploratory or general searches. Thus, in the example in subsection [A], *O* obtained a prior judicial determination of probable cause to search the garage. Furthermore, the search did not become exploratory in nature by seizing the car: her presence in the garage was authorized by the warrant; and the seizure did not expand on the lawful scope of the search.

Under such circumstances, a warrantless seizure of an object discovered in plain view is (in the words of *Coolidge*) only a "minor peril to Fourth Amendment protections, [but] . . . a major gain in effective law enforcement." To require an officer to obtain a warrant to seize what she discovers in plain view would be a "needless inconvenience, and sometimes [might be] dangerous—to the evidence or to the police themselves."

## § 15.02 "Plain View": Examining the Elements in Detail

### [A] Element 1: Lawful Vantage Point

The first requirement of the plain view doctrine is that the officer must observe the object from a lawful vantage point. The Supreme Court has observed that "it is important to keep in mind that, in the vast majority of cases, *any* evidence seized by the police will be in plain view, at least at the moment of seizure."[5] Therefore, "an essential predicate to any valid warrantless seizure of incriminating evidence [is] that the officer did not violate the Fourth Amendment in arriving at the place from which the evidence could be plainly viewed."[6]

Generally speaking, there are four ways in which an officer may observe evidence from a lawful vantage point. First, she may discover the article during the execution of a valid search warrant, such as in the example of the garage search discussed above.

---

[3] Horton v. California, 496 U.S. at 133–34.

[4] 403 U.S. 443 (1971).

[5] *Id.* at 465.

[6] Horton v. California, 496 U.S. at 136.

Second, the object may come into view during an in-home arrest pursuant to an arrest warrant. For example, an officer who enters $D$'s house armed with an arrest warrant may observe an incriminating object while looking for $D$ inside the residence.

Third, criminal evidence might be discovered by an officer during a search justified under an exception to the warrant requirement. For example, an officer may come across an article of evidence while she is in a house in hot pursuit of a felon,[7] or while she is conducting a warrantless consent search. In such circumstances, the *search* that turned up the evidence is justified by an independent warrant exception; the plain view doctrine justifies the warrantless *seizure* of the evidence found.

Fourth, an officer's view of an object may arise from an activity that does not constitute a search and, therefore, falls outside the scope of the Fourth Amendment. For example, $O$, a police officer, walking down a public sidewalk might glance toward a residence and, from that vantage point, observe marijuana plants sitting in open view on a table near the window in $D$'s living room. In this example, as no search has occurred—$D$ could hardly have a reasonable expectation of privacy in regard to the sighting— the first element of plain view is satisfied, but the second element presents a difficulty, as discussed below.

### [B]   Element 2: Right of Access to the Object

A police officer may observe an incriminating article from a lawful vantage point, but "she must also have a lawful right of access to the object itself."[8] Thus, in the example immediately above, the plain view doctrine does not allow $O$ to enter $D$'s home without a warrant to seize the marijuana visible from the street. Access to the living room requires a warrant or some independent search warrant exception.[9]

If an officer has a Fourth Amendment justification—not simply the fact that the article is visible to her—to enter a house, she may do so. For example, in *Washington v. Chrisman*,[10] $O$ arrested $D$, a college student, in a public place for underage possession of alcohol. $D$ claimed that he was over the minimum age for possession of the liquor. He sought permission to retrieve his identification from his dormitory room. $O$ agreed and followed him to the room. While $D$ was inside, $O$ remained just outside

---

[7] *E.g.*, Warden v. Hayden, 387 U.S. 194 (1967).

[8] Horton v. California, 496 U.S. at 137.

[9] Coolidge v. New Hampshire, 403 U.S. at 468 ("even where the object [in plain view] is contraband, this Court has repeatedly stated and enforced the basic rule that the police may not enter [private premises] and make a warrantless seizure").

[10] 455 U.S. 1 (1982).

the door, but from that spot he observed marijuana and drug paraphernalia inside the room. He entered and seized the items.

Because an arresting officer has the right to remain at an arrestee's elbow,[11] *O* had authority from the outset to follow *D* into the dormitory room. Consequently, the Court held that the warrantless entry after the objects came into his view was permissible. If the result were otherwise, the "perverse effect" would be to "penaliz[e] the officer for exercising more restraint than was required under the circumstances."

### [C] Element 3: Right to Seize is "Immediately Apparent"

A police officer may not seize an article without a search warrant merely because she has a right of access to it from a proper vantage point. For example, the fact that *O* is lawfully in *D*'s living room in order to make an arrest does not justify the seizure of every article that *O* observes in the room, regardless of its character. The Supreme Court stated in *Coolidge v. New Hampshire*[12] that seizure of an article in plain view is "legitimate only where it is immediately apparent to the police that they have evidence before them." As explained in *Arizona v. Hicks*,[13] "immediately apparent" means that the officer must have probable cause to seize the article in plain view.

The "immediately apparent"—or probable cause—requirement is consistent with the rationale of the doctrine of plain view. As explained above,[14] the doctrine is meant only to free the police from the inconvenience of securing a warrant to seize that which is found in plain view during an otherwise lawful search or non-search activity. It does not purport to dispense with the probable cause requirement for the seizure. Justice Antonin Scalia reminds us, "[d]ispensing with the need for a warrant [in plain view circumstances] is worlds apart from permitting a lesser standard of *cause* for the seizure than a warrant would require, *i.e.*, the standard of probable cause."[15]

## § 15.03 The Plain View Doctrine At Work: *Arizona v. Hicks*[16]

*Arizona v. Hicks*[17] provides an instructional, albeit controversial,[18]

---

[11] See § 13.02[C][2][a], *supra*.

[12] 403 U.S. 443 (1971).

[13] 480 U.S. 321 (1987).

[14] See § 15.01[B], *supra*.

[15] Arizona v. Hicks, 480 U.S. 321, 327 (1987).

[16] *See generally* 2 LaFave, Note 1, *supra*, at § 4.11(d); Denise Marie Cloutier, *Arizona v. Hicks: The Failure to Recognize Limited Inspections as Reasonable in Fourth Amendment Jurisprudence*, 24 Colum. J.L. & Soc. Probs. 351 (1991).

[17] 480 U.S. 321 (1987).

example of the interrelationship of the elements of the plain view doctrine. In *Hicks*, the police entered *D*'s apartment without a search warrant because a bullet had been fired through *D*'s floor into the apartment below it, wounding a man. The officers entered "to search for the shooter, for other victims, and for weapons."

While inside, *O*, one of the officers, observed two sets of expensive stereo components that seemed out of place in *D*'s "squalid" apartment. *O* reasonably suspected, but lacked probable cause to believe, that the components were stolen. Therefore, he either turned around or upside down one piece of the equipment—a turntable—in order to read and record its serial number. *O* reported the number to police headquarters, which confirmed that it had been taken in a robbery. *O* seized the turntable. Later, he secured a warrant to seize the remaining components.

The government sought to justify the warrantless seizure of the turntable on the basis of the plain view doctrine. Uncontroversially, the officers' warrantless entry into *D*'s apartment was proper due to the exigencies of the situation. Therefore, *O* had a right to be in a position in which the stereo components were visible and accessible to him as he looked for persons and weapons. Nonetheless, the Supreme Court, per Justice Scalia, held that the warrantless seizure of the turntable was unconstitutional.

The route that the Court took in reaching its conclusion merits careful attention. The difficulty in this case in the application of the plain view doctrine was with the third element of the rule, namely, the requirement that the incriminating nature of the article be immediately apparent to the police. To properly analyze this issue, and to see how this element relates to the other components of the plain view doctrine, it is useful to consider not only what occurred in *D*'s house but also what could have happened.

For example, if it had been immediately apparent to *O* as he looked at (without touching) the stereo components that they were stolen, it would have been proper for him to seize them under the plain view doctrine. But, as the situation actually materialized, *O* did not have probable cause to believe that the equipment was stolen when he first spotted the turntable. More was needed to bring his suspicion to the level of probable cause—he needed the serial number.

If *O* could have read the serial number without moving the equipment, there would have been no constitutional problem. His action—merely observing that which was in view from a place where he had a right to be—would not have constituted a search or seizure. Therefore, if this non-Fourth-Amendment activity—the non-search and non-seizure inspection of

---

[18] *E.g.* Cloutier, Note 16, *supra* (contending that *Hicks* should be overruled).

the serial number—had provided $O$ with probable cause to believe that the turntable was the fruit of a crime, $O$ would have been acting lawfully if he had seized it without a warrant.

But, in *Hicks* the facts were not as hypothesized. The turntable had to be moved to observe its serial number. Therefore, the question that the Court had to answer was whether *this* action—physically trivial as it was—constituted a new "search" or "seizure" that required an additional justification.

The slight movement of the turntable did not constitute a "seizure," as this action did not constitute a meaningful interference with $D$'s possessory interest in it.[19] But, the act of moving it was another "search" because it exposed to $O$ matters not previously visible to him; on these facts, $D$ had a reasonable expectation of privacy in the bottom of the turntable. As Justice Scalia explained, "a search is a search, even if it happens to disclose nothing but the bottom of a turntable."

The issue, therefore, was whether this new (warrantless) search was justified. To resolve this question the Court needed to reconsider the first element of the plain view doctrine. That is, in light of the original justification for the intrusion into the room (to look for the shooter, additional victims, and the weapon), was this additional search justified? If the answer had been yes—*e.g.*, if a weapon could realistically have been underneath the turntable—the new search would have been permissible and, as it incidentally resulted in the information that gave $O$ probable cause to believe that the turntable was stolen, he could lawfully have seized it. However, the search was conducted for reasons unrelated to the initial intrusion. Therefore, *Hicks* held, $O$ was unable to justify his actions on the basis of plain view.

Justice Scalia's analysis is controversial. The dissent argued that the act of moving the turntable was a "cursory inspection" rather than a "full-blown search." As such, it claimed, $O$ should have been allowed to inspect it on the basis of "reasonable suspicion" (which he possessed) rather than "probable cause." Scalia rejected this argument, however, because he was "unwilling to send police and judges into a new thicket of Fourth Amendment law, to seek a creature of uncertain description."

However, the "cursory inspection" concept would not have sent the police and courts into a new Fourth Amendment "thicket." Long before this case, the Court recognized the general principle that searches that are less than ordinarily intrusive may be conducted on less than probable cause.[20] Nor

---

[19] See § 8.02[A], *supra*.

[20] See chapter 18, *infra*.

is a "cursory inspection" inevitably a "creature of uncertain description": it might be defined, as Professor LaFave has suggested,[21] as the "picking up of an article to ascertain a serial number or other identifying characteristic on its exterior."

Justice Scalia defended his position by focusing on the importance of probable cause in Fourth Amendment jurisprudence. As he put it,

> there is nothing new in the realization that the Constitution sometimes insulates the criminality of a few in order to protect the privacy of us all. Our disagreement with the dissenters pertains to where the proper balance should be struck; we choose to adhere to the textual and traditional standard of probable cause.

In recent years, this attitude regarding the importance of probable cause has frequently been ignored by the Supreme Court. In *Hicks*, it was not.

## § 15.04  "Inadvertent Discovery": The Plain View Debate[22]

In the typical "plain view" case, *O*, an officer, conducting a valid search, will discover incriminating evidence in open view that she did not anticipate finding. In such circumstances, *O* may seize this inadvertently discovered evidence. However, suppose that *O* *anticipated* finding the evidence in plain view. For example, suppose that *O* has probable cause to search *D*'s premises for articles A and B. She obtains a warrant to seize article A, but she does not request authorization to seize article B, although she expects that she will find it during the search, and she intends to seize it if she discovers it. If *O* discovers article B during the execution of the warrant, may she seize it under the plain view doctrine?

In *Coolidge v. New Hampshire*,[23] Justice Stewart, author of the Court's four-Justice plurality opinion, answered the question in the negative. He stated that if an officer anticipates discovery of a particular object, but she fails to request a warrant to seize it, or if she fails to mention it in her application for a warrant to search for other articles, the subsequent search is analogous to an exploratory search, and the seizure of the anticipated articles "fl[ies] in the face of the basic rule that no amount of probable cause can justify a warrantless seizure." Thus, as the concept of plain view was explained in *Coolidge*, there was an inadvertency element to the doctrine.

The inadvertency element was never accepted by a majority of the members of the Supreme Court. Nonetheless, after *Coolidge* was decided,

---

[21] 2 LaFave, Note 1, *supra*, at 703.

[22] *See generally* 3 LaFave, Note 1, *supra*, at § 6.7(c).

[23] 403 U.S. 443 (1971).

virtually all of the states and lower federal courts endorsed the inadvertency rule.[24]

In *Horton v. California*,[25] the Supreme Court "revisited" the issue. In *Horton*, *O*, a police officer, obtained a warrant to search *D*'s home for the proceeds (jewelry) from a robbery. *O* anticipated finding the weapons used in the crime (including a machine gun and stun gun) during the search, and he intended to seize them, which he did, when they were discovered in plain view in the home. *D* argued that the latter seizure was impermissible: the warrant did not provide for the seizure of the weapons and, because their discovery was not inadvertent, their seizure could not be justified under the plain view doctrine, as set out in *Coolidge*.

The Supreme Court ruled, 7-2, per Justice John Stevens, that inadvertency, although "a characteristic of most legitimate 'plain view' seizures, . . . is not a necessary condition" of the doctrine. It concluded that "the absence of inadvertence was not essential to the Court's rejection of the State's 'plain view' argument in *Coolidge*." In short, although the holding in *Coolidge* was binding precedent, its plurality ruling regarding inadvertency was flawed.

As *Horton* pointed out, the inadvertency requirement is not necessary "to prevent the police from conducting general searches, or from converting specific warrants into general warrants." These Fourth Amendment evils are prevented by scrupulous adherence to the Fourth Amendment requirement that no warrant be issued unless it particularly describes "the place to be searched and the persons or things to be seized," and by the judicial rule that warrantless searches must "be circumscribed by the exigencies which justify its initiation." In other words, the area and duration of a search is limited by the latter requirements; the inadvertency element adds no additional privacy protection.

For example, in *Horton*, the inadvertency element would not have offered *D* any privacy protection that was not already guaranteed: the warrant entitled the officer to be in *D*'s home, in order to search for the fruits of a robbery; and the weapons were found in those areas of the home to which the officer had a constitutional right of access under the warrant. Furthermore, if the proceeds of the crime had been found before the weapons had been discovered, the search would have had to terminate at that time, so

---

[24] Forty-six states, the District of Columbia, and twelve United States Courts of Appeals subscribed to the requirement. Horton v. California, 496 U.S. 128, 149–53 (1990) (appendices A and B to the dissenting opinion of Brennan, J.).

[25] 496 U.S. 128 (1990); *contra*, State v. Meyer, 893 P.2d 159 (Haw. 1995) (under the state constitution, holding that inadvertency is a requirement of the plain view doctrine).

the omission of the weapons from the warrant did not lengthen the time the officers could legitimately stay on the premises.

The Court additionally expressed its disinclination to apply a doctrine that requires courts to divine an officer's subjective state of mind, *i.e.* to determine whether the officer expected to find the evidence in question. According to Justice Stevens, "evenhanded law enforcement is best achieved by the application of objective standards of conduct. . . ." He pointed out that if an officer has knowledge approaching certainty that certain evidence will be found during a search, there is no reason to believe that "she would deliberately omit a particular description of the item to be seized from the application for a search warrant."

On the other hand, if the officer has a warrant to search for one article, and merely suspects that she will find another item, whether or not the suspicion amounts to probable cause, the *Horton* Court did not believe that such a "suspicion should immunize the second item from seizure if it is found during a lawful search for the first." Borrowing from Justice White's dissent in *Coolidge*, the Court reasoned that there is no reason to draw a distinction between an article discovered inadvertently and one that is anticipated; the interference with the individual's possessory interest is the same in both cases, as is the inconvenience and danger of requiring the officer to depart and secure a warrant.

Justice Brennan, with whom Justice Marshall joined, dissented in *Horton*. The dissent agreed with the majority that the inadvertency requirement furthers no privacy interests. But, it argued, it does protect possessory interests: the message sent by the inadvertency requirement is that "we will not excuse officers from the general requirement of a warrant to seize if the officers know the location of the evidence, have probable cause to seize it, intend to seize it, and yet do not bother to obtain a warrant particularly describing that evidence." Exclusion of "evidence so seized will encourage officers to be more precise and complete in future warrant applications."

## § 15.05   Expanding on Plain View: Use of Other Senses[26]

### [A]   "Plain Hearing" and "Plain Smell" Doctrines

Courts have expanded on the "plain view" doctrine to recognize "plain hearing" and "plain smell" principles. These expansions make sense. What an officer observes from a lawful vantage point is not a search, because a person cannot maintain a reasonable expectation of privacy regarding anything visible to the naked eye from that position. For the same reason, a person cannot have a reasonable expectation of privacy regarding her oral

---

[26] *See generally* 1 LaFave, Note 1, *supra*, at 402–04.

communications, if they can he heard by someone, lawfully positioned, within ear shot ("plain hearing"); nor can she legitimately expect that an officer will not use her sense of smell to detect incriminating evidence from a lawful position.[27]

### [B] "Plain Touch" (or "Plain Feel") Doctrine[28]

In *Minnesota v. Dickerson*,[29] a unanimous Supreme Court recognized a "plain touch" or "plain feel" corollary to the plain view doctrine. Under this doctrine, the police may seize contraband detected solely through an officer's sense of touch if, comparable to plain view, the officer had a right to touch the object in question and, upon tactile observation, its identity as contraband was immediately apparent.

In *Dickerson*, *O*, a police officer, observed *D* acting suspiciously near a notorious "crack house." *O* frisked *D* for weapons, pursuant to the so-called "*Terry* doctrine,"[30] which permits an officer investigating possible criminal activity to pat down a suspect if she is justified in believing that the person may be armed and presently dangerous. The *Dickerson* Court stated that if it had been immediately apparent to *O* during the lawful frisk that the object he was touching was contraband, *O* could properly have reached into the pocket and seized it without a warrant pursuant to the plain *touch* doctrine.

In this case, however, when *O* frisked *D*, he felt a "small lump," which he realized was not a weapon, but which he could not otherwise immediately identify. Under *Terry*, the weapons-search should have ended at that instant. Instead, *O* continued to examine the object with his fingers and determined that it was probably crack cocaine. *O* reached into *D*'s pocket and retrieved a small plastic bag containing cocaine.

The Court held here that the warrantless seizure of the cocaine was unlawful. It reasoned that the second search—the act of examining the lump after the weapons-search was completed—fell outside the scope of the original lawful intrusion. Therefore, *O* acted improperly under the plain

---

[27] Complications arise if the government uses sensory-enhancements to see, hear, or smell evidence of a crime. *See generally id.* at § 2.2(a)–(d).

[28] *See generally* John A. Cecere, Note, *Searches Woven From Terry Cloth: How the Plain Feel Doctrine Plus Terry Equals Pretextual Search*, 36 B. C. L. Rev. 125 (1994); David L. Haselkorn, Comment, *The Case Against a Plain Feel Exception to the Warrant Requirement*, 54 U. Chi. L. Rev. 683 (1987); Susanne N. MacIntosh, Comment, *Fourth Amendment—The Plain Touch Exception to the Warrant Requirement*, 84 J. Crim. L. & Criminology 743 (1994); Anne Bowen Poulin, *The Plain Feel Doctrine and the Evolution of the Fourth Amendment*, 42 Vill. L. Rev. 741 (1997).

[29] 508 U.S. 366 (1993).

[30] Terry v. Ohio, 392 U.S. 1 (1968). See chapter 18, *infra*.

touch doctrine when he seized the object. In essence, once $O$ decided that $D$ was unarmed, $O$'s right to physical access to $D$ ended; the second search should not have occurred. [31]

Although the officer's conduct in *Dickerson* violated the Fourth Amendment, the line between a lawful and an unlawful search in such circumstances is extremely thin, even nearly non-existent. Even putting aside the possibility of police perjury, [32] an officer may be unable to reconstruct the fast moving events days or weeks later, when called upon to testify. Had $O$ testified in *Dickerson*, for example, that he determined *simultaneously* that the object was not a weapon, but was crack cocaine, the evidence would have been admissible under the plain touch doctrine.

---

[31] *See also* Bond v. United States, 529 U.S. 334 (2000), in which federal agents walked through a Greyhound bus and randomly squeezed the soft luggage passengers had placed in the overhead storage spaces. In $B$'s case, the officer squeezed a green canvas bag and felt a "brick-like" object. The government argued that this touching did not constitute a search, on the ground that passengers know that bus employees and other passengers may have reason to touch luggage placed in the overhead storage area; therefore, a passenger does not have a reasonable expectation of privacy in having her soft luggage physically manipulated.. However, the Supreme Court, 7-2, held in an opinion written by Chief Justice Rehnquist that although a passenger *does* expect that luggage may be moved and, therefore, handled, "[h]e does not expect that other[s] . . .will, as a matter of course, feel the bag in an exploratory manner." In essence, therefore, the officer had a right to physical access to the luggage, but the touching that occurred here exceeded the casual touching that could be expected in a bus. Had the brick been felt in casual touching, the plain-touch doctrine would have come into play.

[32] Unfortunately, some magistrates "knowingly accept police perjury as truthful," in part because they wish to assist the police in their investigations, and in order to improve their own re-election chances. Myron W. Orfield, Jr., *Deterrence, Perjury, and the Heater Factor: An Exclusionary Rule in the Chicago Criminal Courts*, 63 U. Colo. L. Rev. 75, 83 (1992) (study of Cook County criminal justice system).

CHAPTER **16**

# INVENTORY SEARCHES

## § 16.01 Automobile Inventories: General Principles[1]

### [A] Rule

In *South Dakota v. Opperman*,[2] the police towed *D*'s unoccupied car to an impoundment lot after it had been ticketed twice on the same morning for being illegally parked in a tow-away zone. At the lot, a police officer observed a watch on the dashboard and other valuables sitting on the back seat and back floorboard. Pursuant to standard procedures in the jurisdiction, the police unlocked the car door, inventoried the contents of the passenger compartment, and removed them for safekeeping. During the inventory, the police discovered marijuana in the unlocked glove compartment. *D* was prosecuted for possession of this contraband.

The Court, 5–4 (with Justice Lewis Powell, part of the slim majority, also writing a narrow concurring opinion), upheld the inventory of *D*'s car. Although there are features of *Opperman* that hint at potential limiting principles, subsequent inventory cases suggest that, generally speaking, a routine inventory search ("inventory," for short) of a lawfully impounded car is reasonable under the Fourth Amendment even though it is conducted without a warrant and in the absence of probable cause to believe—indeed, in the absence of *any* basis for believing—that evidence of a crime will be discovered.[3] Consequently, if police discover criminal evidence during

---

[1] See generally 3 Wayne R. LaFave, Search and Seizure §§ 7.4(a), 7.5(e) (3d ed. 1996); Wayne R. LaFave, *Controlling Discretion by Administrative Regulations: The Use, Misuse, and Nonuse of Police Rules and Policies in Fourth Amendment Adjudication*, 89 Mich. L. Rev. 442 (1990) (especially pp. 447–63).

[2] 428 U.S. 364 (1976); *contra, under the state constitution,* State v. Sawyer, 571 P.2d 1131 (Mont. 1977), *overruled in part on other grounds,* State v. Long, 700 P.2d 153 (Mont. 1985) (permitting only warrantless inventories to secure objects in plain view from outside the vehicle); State v. Opperman, 247 N.W.2d 673 (S.D. 1976) (*id.*).

[3] *Opperman* dealt primarily with the "search" aspect of the inventory. The Court perfunctorily approved the impoundment, which constituted a *seizure* of *D*'s car. It observed that the police must often remove and impound vehicles disabled on the road or in violation of parking ordinances. It described as "beyond challenge" the right "of police to seize and remove vehicles impeding traffic or threatening public safety and convenience."

an inventory, they may seize it pursuant to the plain view doctrine, and introduce it in a criminal prosecution.

### [B]  Rationale (and Critique) of the Rule

The rationale of the inventory cases could plausibly place them under the "administrative search" or "special needs" exceptions to the warrant and probable cause features of the Fourth Amendment, which exceptions are discussed elsewhere.[4] However, largely for historical reasons—the early "administrative search" cases focused on activities of non-police officials, and the "special needs" exception had not yet been devised—an independent "inventory exception" to the Fourth Amendment has developed.

Why is neither probable cause nor a warrant required to inventory a lawfully impounded automobile? The Court drew on the fact that an inventory is not part of a criminal investigation, but rather is an administrative act, *i.e.,* a part of a police department's community caretaking function. According to *Opperman*, the "probable cause" concept is a standard for use in *criminal investigations* and, therefore, is "unhelpful when analysis centers upon the reasonableness of routine administrative caretaking functions, particularly when no claim is made that the protective procedures are a subterfuge for criminal investigations."[5]

With the probable cause component of the Fourth Amendment deemed irrelevant, the Court disposed of the need for search warrants in inventory cases by noting that the warrant requirement is "linked . . . textually . . . to the probable-cause concept." That is, because the Warrant Clause provides that "no Warrants shall issue, but upon probable cause," there is no need for a warrant if there is no reason for determining probable cause. In view of the resulting inapplicability of the Warrant Clause to inventories, the Court looked exclusively at the Fourth Amendment reasonableness standard.

The *Opperman* opinion was drafted in unusually broad terms. The Court might have sought simply to explain why, based on the totality of the circumstances, the inventory of *D*'s car was reasonable. Instead, much of its reasoning focused on the reasonableness of car inventories *in general*. The Court stated that automobile inventories are a "response to three distinct needs": (1) to protect the police and the public from dangerous instrumentalities that might be hidden in the car; (2) to protect the police against claims of lost or stolen property; and (3) to protect the owner's property while

---

[4] *See generally* chapter 19, *infra.*

[5] This conclusion was not inevitable. It might have formulated a different type of "probable cause" standard, relevant to administrative inventory searches. The Court has done this with other administrative inspections. See § 9.06, *supra.*

it is in police custody. The Court concluded that these interests outweigh an owner's expectation of privacy in his automobile, which it described as "significantly less than that relating to one's home or office."[6]

Critics question the Court's analysis. First, they contend that the assertion that inventories are needed in order to protect the safety of the police and the public "borders on the ridiculous."[7] Cars rarely contain dangerous instrumentalities, and there is no reason to believe that an unsearched car sitting in an impoundment lot constitutes a greater danger than one parked on the street or in a public parking lot. Yet, a non-impounded car may not be searched without probable cause or consent. Justice Powell, concurring, conceded that "[e]xcept in rare cases, there is little danger associated with impounding unsearched automobiles." However, he was unwilling to discount this factor entirely because, he reasoned, in the rare case in which the danger materializes, the consequences are apt to be severe, and there is no way to identify a high-risk automobile without searching it.

Second, protection of the police against claims of theft, although a weightier concern, may not justify warrantless inventories. Police departments, as involuntary bailees, usually have only limited liability for losses in such circumstances; and as Justice Powell conceded, inventories might not discourage false claims, because a car owner could fraudulently assert that an object was stolen prior to the inventory, or was purposely or negligently left off the inventory list.

Third, automobile inventories supposedly protect the owner's property from theft. In fact, of course, it is the act of securing the belongings, not the inventory itself, that reduces the risk of loss. It is unclear, however, that this process provides much greater protection than the simpler and less intrusive procedure of rolling up the windows of an impounded car, locking its doors, and placing it in a secure place. Moreover, if the police are going to invade a car owner's privacy in order to protect his property, critics maintain that it is not unreasonable to suggest, as the dissenters did in *Opperman*, that an inventory should only be conducted after "the exhaustion and failure of reasonable efforts . . . to identify and reach the owner of the property in order to facilitate alternative means of security or to obtain his consent to the search."

Since *Opperman* was decided, the Court has discounted the potential relevance of alternative means of protecting a car owner's property from theft. It has stated that "[t]he reasonableness of any particular governmental activity does not necessarily or invariably turn on the existence of alternative

---

[6] The lesser-expectation-of-privacy principle regarding cars is discussed at § 14.05, *supra*.

[7] 3 LaFave, Note 1, *supra*, at 543.

'less intrusive' means. . . . [The Court is] hardly in a position to second-guess police departments as to what practical administrative method will best deter theft . . . ."[8]

## § 16.02   Automobile Inventories: In Detail

### [A]   Administrative Nature of the Search

In upholding specific inventories, the Supreme Court has noted more than once that the inventories were not subterfuges for criminal investigations. The implication from this is that evidence found during an inventory is inadmissible in a criminal trial if the search was a pretext for a criminal investigation. This interpretation is plausible in view of the Court's reasoning in *South Dakota v. Opperman*[9] that the Warrant Clause is "unhelpful" in analyzing the reasonableness of "routine, administrative caretaking" activities by the police: pretextual inventory searches are not routine administrative police activities.

On the other hand, this "no pretext" limitation on inventories conflicts with the frequently expressed view of the Court in other contexts,[10] especially in recent years, that the validity of an officer's actions should be based on objective criteria, without regard to his motivations. Indeed, in *Arkansas v. Sullivan*[11] —a case in which none of the inventory cases were considered—the Supreme Court ruled that the Fourth Amendment is *not* violated when a police officer lawfully, *i.e.*, with objective probable cause, arrests an individual for traffic violations in order to have the opportunity to conduct an automobile inventory search for drugs.

The no-criminal-investigation limitation, assuming there still is one, apparently applies only if the officer's "sole purpose"[12] in conducting the inventory is to investigate crime. An officer who hopes or even suspects that he will find criminal evidence during an inventory may nonetheless conduct one if he acts, at least in part, for legitimate administrative reasons.[13] Assuming that the inventory is required by departmental regulations, the defendant will be hard put to argue convincingly that the officer's sole purpose was to investigate a crime.

---

[8] Illinois v. Lafayette, 462 U.S. 640, 647–48 (1983) (arrest inventory); *see also* Colorado v. Bertine, 479 U.S. 367, 374 (1987) ("[R]easonable police regulations . . . administered in good faith satisfy the Fourth Amendment, even though courts might as a matter of hindsight be able to devise equally reasonable rules requiring a different procedure.").

[9] 428 U.S. 364 (1976). See § 16.01[B], *supra*.

[10] *See, e.g.,* §§ 2.07[B], 9.02[B], 9.02[F], and 15.04, *supra*.

[11] 532 U.S. 769 (2001) (per curiam).

[12] Colorado v. Bertine, 479 U.S. at 372.

[13] United States v. Frank, 864 F.2d 992, 1001 (3d Cir. 1988).

## [B] "Routine" Nature of the Inventory

### [1]  In General

A warrantless, suspicionless search of a car lawfully in police custody is not justifiable merely because it was conducted for administrative purposes. The inventory must be a "routine" or "standard" procedure of the department conducting it.[14] (Of course, the mere fact that an inventory is conducted pursuant to standard departmental regulations is insufficient basis for upholding the police action. As one court has observed, "[u]nconstitutional searches cannot be constitutionalized by standardizing them as a part of normal police practice."[15] ) The purpose of this requirement is to reduce the risk that inventories will be conducted arbitrarily, discriminatorily, or as "a ruse for a general rummaging in order to discover incriminating evidence."[16]

Although there is language in *Opperman*[17] that might suggest that a warrantless inventory is unreasonable unless it is triggered by police observation of valuables in plain view in the impounded car, subsequent cases do not support such an across-the-board limitation. Apparently, if a departmental regulation authorizes that all impounded cars be inventoried, whether or not valuables are in plain view, the inventory may proceed.

### [2]  Nondiscretionary Inventories

Ideally, the regulations authorizing an inventory should be similar to those involved in *Opperman*, namely, they should give no significant discretion to the individual officer. The procedures should require officers to "act more or less mechanically, according to a set routine."[18]

Nondiscretionary inventories are desirable. They "promote[] a certain equality of treatment. . . . [T]he minister's picnic basket and grandma's knitting bag [found in an automobile] are opened and inventoried right along with the biker's tool box and the gypsy's satchel."[19] Also, nondiscretionary inventories are less likely to function as a ruse for a criminal investigation.

---

[14] Colorado v. Bertine, 479 U.S. at 374 n.6 ("Our decisions have always adhered to the *requirement* that inventories be conducted according to standardized criteria.") (emphasis added).

[15] State v. Jewell, 338 So.2d 633, 640 (La. 1976).

[16] Florida v. Wells, 495 U.S. 1, 4 (1990).

[17] 428 U.S. at 376 & n.10 (in which the Court noted that the "inventory itself was prompted by the presence in plain view of a number of valuables inside the car" and that "once the policeman was lawfully inside the car to secure the personal property in plain view, it was not unreasonable to open the unlocked glove compartment . . . .").

[18] Commonwealth v. Sullo, 532 N.E.2d 1219, 1222 (Mass. App. Ct. 1989).

[19] State v. Shamblin, 763 P.2d 425, 428 (Utah Ct. App. 1988).

### [3] Discretionary Inventories

Inventories are problematic when they are conducted pursuant to regulations that allow individual officers discretion in determining whether to conduct the inventory and/or in deciding the scope of the search. With increased discretion comes the enhanced risk of arbitrariness, discrimination, and the use of the inventory as a disguise for a criminal investigation.

Nonetheless, the Supreme Court has upheld inventories that permit some police discretion. In *Colorado v. Bertine*,[20] the Court approved an inventory in which the regulations allowed officers in certain circumstances to choose whether to impound the car and conduct an inventory of it, on the one hand, or to park it in a public parking lot and lock it, on the other hand. Discretion regarding whether to conduct an inventory is allowed "as long as [it] . . . is exercised according to standard criteria and on the basis of something other than suspicion of evidence of criminal activity." The standardized criteria in *Bertine* included provisions that prohibited the police from parking vehicles in lots vulnerable to theft or vandalism.

### [C] Automobile Owner's Wishes

The right of the police to inventory an automobile does not depend on a finding that the car owner is unavailable to give his consent to the search, to take his belongings out of the car, or to waive any rights that he might have against the police for the theft of his property.

Originally, it was not implausible to interpret *Opperman* narrowly to permit warrantless inventories only when it was unreasonable for the police to contact the car owner. The majority in *Opperman* observed that the car owner in that case "was not present to make other arrangements for the safekeeping of his belongings."

Notwithstanding this language, the Supreme Court in *Bertine* upheld an inventory although the vehicle owner was in police custody and, therefore, could have been given the opportunity to make other arrangements to protect his property. Quoting from *Illinois v. Lafayette*,[21] an arrest inventory case, the *Bertine* Court stated that although such an alternative was possible, "the real question is not what 'could have been achieved,' but whether the Fourth Amendment *requires* such steps." The Court stated that the Fourth Amendment does not require the police to act in the least intrusive fashion possible.

---

[20] 479 U.S. 367 (1987).

[21] 462 U.S. 640 (1983). See § 15.03, *infra*.

## [D]  Scope of an Inventory

### [1]  Containers

The Supreme Court ruled in *Bertine* that as part of a valid automobile inventory, the police may open containers found in the car, without a warrant or probable cause. However, five Justices in *Bertine* appeared to accept the principle that the police may open and search containers without a warrant only "if they are following standard police procedures that *mandate* the opening of such containers in *every* impounded vehicle."[22]

*Florida v. Wells*[23] clouds the picture. Chief Justice Rehnquist stated in dictum for five Justices, over the strenuous objection of four dissenters, that "in forbidding uncanalized discretion to police officers conducting inventory searches, there is no reason to insist that they be conducted in a mechanical 'all-or-nothing' fashion." The Chief Justice further wrote that a "police officer may be allowed sufficient latitude to determine whether a particular container should or should not be opened in light of the nature of the search and characteristics of the container itself." As this is dictum, and members of both the majority and dissent have left the Court, it is uncertain whether this language will become law.

### [2]  Locked Portions of the Automobile

*Opperman* approved an inventory search of an unlocked glove compartment because it was a customary place for persons to store valuables. The Court did not consider, nor has it since considered, the justifiability of an inventory of a *locked* glove compartment or of an automobile trunk. However, many courts have authorized such searches when they are a required part of a routine inventory.[24]

The lower court trend is likely to receive the Court's approval when and if it considers the issue. The *Opperman* car was locked (although the glove compartment was not), yet the inventory was permitted; it is reasonable, therefore, to conclude that the fact that a glove compartment or the trunk is locked is not constitutionally significant, as long as the standard procedure in the jurisdiction requires the officer to open the locked portions of the car where valuables may reasonably be stored.

---

[22] Colorado v. Bertine, 479 U.S. at 377 (Blackmun, Powell, and O'Connor JJ., concurring) (emphasis added). Dissenting Justices Marshall and Brennan would have limited inventories of containers even further, so they would have accepted the limiting language in the concurring opinion.

[23] 495 U.S. 1 (1990).

[24] 3 LaFave, Note 1, *supra*, at 554.

### [3]  Inspection of Papers

The Supreme Court has not determined whether or to what extent the police may read papers and documents found during an otherwise valid inventory. However, five Justices in *Opperman* suggested that the reading of papers that touch upon intimate areas of a person's private life should not be routinely allowed.

Concurring, Justice Powell observed in *Opperman* that "[u]pholding [inventory] searches . . . provides no general license for the police to examine all the contents of such automobiles." In particular, he noted that there was no evidence in the case that the police, who found "miscellaneous papers," a checkbook, and a social security card, read these personal papers. The four dissenters, as well, stated that the police "would not be justified in sifting through papers secured under the procedures employed here." This conclusion seems correct, as none of the reasons for an inventory justifies reading personal papers.

Lower courts have frequently barred the introduction of evidence secured as the result of the inspection of private papers found during an inventory.[25] Line-drawing, however, is necessary. The police inevitably must handle papers found during an inventory, and they will often need to peruse them in order to identify them on an inventory sheet. Therefore, although the police should not read the documents beyond what is absolutely necessary to complete the inventory, they cannot be expected to blind themselves to what they see in plain view in the process.

## § 16.03  Arrest Inventories[26]

In *Illinois v. Lafayette*,[27] the Supreme Court held that the police may search an arrested person, as well as his personal effects, including containers, as part of a routine[28] inventory at a police station, incident to

---

[25] *E.g.*, Commonwealth v. Sullo, 532 N.E.2d 1219 (Mass. App. Ct. 1989).

[26] *See generally* 3 LaFave, Note 1, *supra*, at § 5.3(a).

[27] 462 U.S. 640 (1983); *contra, under the state constitution*, Reeves v. State, 599 P.2d 727 (Alaska 1979) (a warrantless arrest inventory may not be more intrusive than is absolutely necessary to prevent entry of weapons, drugs, or contraband inside the jail; therefore, any object taken from the arrestee's possession may not be further searched or opened, except pursuant to a warrant or valid warrant exception); State v. Perham, 814 P.2d 914 (Haw. 1991) (the police may not search the contents of an arrestee's wallet as part of an arrest inventory, in absence of evidence that such an exploratory search was the least intrusive means of accomplishing the purposes of safeguarding the property and of protecting the police against fraudulent claims).

[28] Regarding the requirement that inventories be routine, *see* § 16.02[B], *supra*.

his booking and jailing.[29] Neither a search warrant nor probable cause is required for an arrest inventory.

The Court's reasoning in *Lafayette* in support of arrest inventories parallels that pertaining to automobile inventories. The Court stated that an inventory is reasonable to prevent theft of the arrestee's property by inmates and jail employees, to protect the police from theft claims, and to prevent the arrestee from carrying dangerous instrumentalities or contraband into the jail.

In practice, the scope of an arrest inventory is broader than a search incident to an arrest. A search that would be impractical or embarrassing at the scene of the arrest can be conducted at the stationhouse. For example, as part of an arrest inventory, authorities are entitled not only to search the arrestee's clothing, but also to take the clothing and keep it in official custody.[30] The Court in *Lafayette* also left open the question of "the circumstances in which a strip search may or may not be appropriate" as part of the inventory process.

---

[29] Prior to *Lafayette*, the Court held in United States v. Edwards, 415 U.S. 800 (1974), that the police were entitled in that case, "with or without probable cause," to seize, search, and keep in official custody the clothing worn by *D*, a jail inmate, when he was arrested and jailed. Although the clothing was not taken from *D* until ten hours after his arrest, the Court stated that the police "did no more . . . than they were entitled to do incident to the usual custodial arrest and incarceration." Strictly speaking, *Edwards* did not involve an inventory search because of the 10-hour delay. *See* § 13.02[B][3], *supra*.

[30] *See id.*

## CHAPTER 17

# CONSENT SEARCHES

## § 17.01 Preliminary Observations: Pragmatism, the Police, and the Supreme Court

If warrantless searches are *per se* unreasonable, as the Supreme Court has often maintained (although far less often recently),[1] one of the most significant exceptions to the warrant "requirement" must be the so-called "consent search" exception. As one police officer explained:

[T]here are a lot of warrants that are not sought because of the hassle. You just figure it's not worth the hassle. . . . I don't think you can forego a case because of the hassle of a search warrant, but you can . . . work some other method. If I can get consent, I'm gonna do it.[2]

Another police officer, frustrated at delays in getting a warrant, expressed the situation this way: "[y]ou say to yourself, '[m]y God, you know, if I'm putting you [the magistrate] out, you know, I'll run back to the house and *try bargaining for consent, you know, 'cause I can get that done.'* "[3] Indeed, although there are no reliable figures on the number of warrantless searches justified on consent grounds, one police detective has estimated the figure as high as 98 percent.[4]

Put simply, there are few areas of Fourth Amendment jurisprudence of greater practical significance than consent searches. One of the more interesting and, for some, potentially troubling aspects of consent law, is how far the Supreme Court seemingly has bent to permit this form of warrantless activity. Justice Potter Stewart candidly explained the Court's attitude regarding consent searches in *Schneckloth v. Bustamonte*:

In situations where the police have some evidence of illicit activity, but lack probable cause to arrest or search, a search authorized by a valid

---

[1] *See* § 11.01, *supra.*

[2] Richard Van Duizend, L Paul Sutton, & Charlotte A. Carter, The Search Warrant Process: Preconceptions, Perceptions, and Practices 21 (National Center for State Courts 1984).

[3] *Id.* at 95 (emphasis added).

[4] *Id.* at 21.

consent may be the only means of obtaining important and reliable evidence. . . . And in those cases where there is probable cause to arrest or search, but where the police lack a warrant, a consent search may still be valuable. If the search is conducted and proves fruitless, that in itself may convince the police that an arrest with its possible stigma and embarrassment is unnecessary, or that a far more extensive search pursuant to a warrant is not justified. In short, a search pursuant to consent . . . is a constitutionally permissible and wholly legitimate aspect of effective police activity.[5]

Do these arguments hold up? In the situation in which the police believe they have probable cause, the primary justification for allowing them to act without a warrant—and, thus, to act without the preferred input of a neutral and detached magistrate—may be no more weighty than a claim of police efficiency or, less substantial still, police convenience. After all, the reasoning may be, why should an officer have to go to the trouble of requesting a warrant when the person whose rights the Constitution is seeking to protect consents to the police action? If this *is* the justification, however, one would hope that courts would be very careful to assure themselves that consent was properly granted.

The greater challenge in justifying warrantless consent searches occurs when the police know or suspect that they do not have probable cause— when they could *not* obtain a warrant even if they sought one—and so they "bargain" for consent. Justice Stewart's concern is that, in such circumstances, "a search authorized by a valid consent may be the only means of obtaining important and reliable evidence." But, surely this pragmatic explanation is weak *if* there *really* is a constitutional warrant requirement. As Justice Antonin Scalia has observed, "there is nothing new in the realization that the Constitution sometimes insulates the criminality of a few in order to protect the privacy of us all."[6]

Readers of this chapter should ask themselves whether the Court has acquitted itself adequately in explaining why and when warrantless consent searches are permitted. As will be seen, the consent warrant "exception" is far more comfortably explained in the current constitutional era in which the Supreme Court speaks, simply, about the reasonableness of searches rather than about warrant requirements.

---

[5] 412 U.S. 218, 227–28 (1973).

[6] Arizona v. Hicks, 480 U.S. 321, 329 (1987).

## § 17.02  Consent Searches: General Principles[7]

### [A]  General Rule

As explained in the chapter sections that follow, validly obtained consent justifies an officer in conducting a warrantless search, with or without probable cause. If the officer discovers evidence during a valid consent search, she may seize it without a warrant pursuant to the plain view doctrine.

### [B]  Rationale for the Warrant Exception

The Supreme Court has struggled to explain the "consent search" warrant exception. In comparatively early opinions, the Court sometimes justified consent searches on waiver principles, that is, on the ground that, by consenting, a person waives her right to be free from unreasonable searches and seizures.[8] Looked at this way, a consent search is not really an exception to the Fourth Amendment warrant requirement—consent does not make the warrantless action proper. Instead, by waiving her rights, the citizen gives up any claim she might otherwise have that her rights were violated.

The Supreme Court no longer justifies consent searches on waiver principles. Indeed, if waiver were the basis for consent searches, a number of important rulings of the Court would need to be reconsidered. First, a waiver of a constitutional right is "an intentional relinquishment or abandonment of a *known* right or privilege."[9] The Supreme Court has held, however, that a warrantless search may be upheld even if the consenting party did not know that she could refuse.[10]

Second, waiver principles may conflict with the Court's "third party" consent jurisprudence. For example, suppose that A and B jointly own and use certain premises, and A consents to a police search. Such consent is valid against B.[11] Yet, this outcome is of doubtful validity on waiver principles, because A, absent some agency relationship, cannot waive B's Fourth Amendment rights.

For the same reason, waiver principles fail to explain the "apparent authority" doctrine, which provides that the police may conduct a search

---

[7] *See generally* 3 Wayne R. LaFave, Search and Seizure § 8.1(a)–(b) (3d ed. 1996).

[8] *E.g.*, Johnson v. United States, 333 U.S. 10, 13 (1948) (consent is invalid if it is "granted in submission to authority rather than as an understanding and intentional waiver of a constitutional right"); Stoner v. California, 376 U.S. 483, 489 (1964) (the right to be free of a warrantless search "was a right . . .which only the petitioner could waive by word or deed . . . .").

[9] Johnson v. Zerbst, 304 U.S. 458, 464 (1938) (emphasis added). *See* § 4.02, *supra*.

[10] Schneckloth v. Bustamonte, 412 U.S. 218 (1973). *See* § 17.03[D], *infra*.

[11] United States v. Matlock, 415 U.S. 164 (1974). *See* § 17.05, *infra*.

without a warrant on the basis of consent granted by $X$, a stranger to the property, if the police reasonably believe that $X$ has authority to give consent.[12] Quite obviously, $X$ cannot waive the constitutional rights of a stranger, so the waiver principle fails to explain current consent law.

A second rationale of warrantless consent searches is that one who voluntarily consents to a search no longer has a reasonable expectation of privacy in the property in question. Under this view, a consent search is not really a "search" at all.

There is some support for this thesis in third-party consent cases. The Supreme Court has stated—in reasoning reminiscent of the "false friend" surveillance-of-conversation cases[13] —that one who shares authority over property with others "assume[s] the risk that one of their number might permit the common area to be searched."[14] As three members of the Court in *Illinois v. Rodriguez* explained, "a person may voluntarily limit his expectation of privacy by allowing others to exercise authority over his possessions."[15] However, this reading of consent law was rejected by the majority in *Rodriguez*. According to Justice Scalia, "[t]o describe a consented search as a non-invasion of privacy and thus a non-search is strange in the extreme."

So, ultimately, what justifies a warrantless consent search? The Court's current answer is that a consent search—simply because of the valid consent given—is a reasonable search. That is, "consent" is not really an exception to a warrant requirement: the current Court majority is hostile to the concept of such a requirement. Instead, "[t]here are various elements . . . that can make a search . . . 'reasonable'—one of which is the consent of the person" whose premises or effects will be searched.[16]

But, what makes a consent search reasonable? Perhaps the answer, simply, is that no cognizable harm of a privacy or dignitary nature occurs from a search that a person freely authorizes the government to conduct; if so, it is *not unreasonable* to search in such circumstances. But, perhaps the explanation lies in Justice Stewart's pragmatic observations in *Schneckloth v. Bustamonte*,[17] considered in Section 17.01,[18] including his admission that, in some circumstances, "a search authorized by a valid consent

---

[12] Illinois v. Rodriguez, 497 U.S. 177 (1990). *See* § 17.06, *infra.*

[13] *See* § 7.05, *supra.*

[14] United States v. Matlock, 415 U.S. at 171 n.7.

[15] 497 U.S. at 190 (Marshall, J., with whom Brennan and Stevens, JJ., joined, dissenting).

[16] *Rodriguez, id.* at 183–84.

[17] 412 U.S. 218 (1973).

[18] *See* the text at and following Note 5, *supra.*

may be the only means of obtaining important and reliable evidence." This argument may be unpersuasive to those who favor a warrant requirement (or, at least, strong presumption), but it can be justified as part of a reasonableness inquiry.

## § 17.03　Validity of Consent[19]

### [A]　Voluntariness: In General

Consent is legally ineffective unless the person granting consent does so voluntarily, rather than as "the result of duress or coercion, express or implied."[20] The burden of proof is on the prosecutor to demonstrate by the preponderance of the evidence that consent was freely given.[21]

There is "no talismanic definition of 'voluntariness.' "[22] It is an "amphibian"[23] notion, "reflect[ing] an accommodation of the complex of values implicated"[24] in the police conduct. In the case of consent searches, the competing values are "the legitimate need for such searches [as a means of obtaining "important and reliable evidence"] and the equally important requirement of assuring the absence of coercion."[25]

The "voluntariness" of consent is determined from the totality of the circumstances of the individual case. As with other applications of the totality-of-the-circumstances test,[26] it is impossible to predict with certainty what factors will render consent involuntary in a specific case. Among the factors that may support a finding of coercion are: (1) a show of force by the police, such as a display of guns, that would suggest to the person that she is not free to refuse consent; (2) the presence of a large number of officers, which may suggest to the person "that the police are contemplating an undertaking which does not depend upon the cooperation of the individual"[27] ; (3) repetitive requests for consent after an initial refusal; and (4) evidence relating to the consenting person's age, race,[28] sex, level

---

[19] 3 LaFave, Note 7, *supra*, at § 8.2.

[20] Schneckloth v. Bustamonte, 412 U.S. 218, 248 (1973).

[21] *See* Bumper v. North Carolina, 391 U.S. 543 (1968).

[22] Schneckloth v. Bustamonte, 412 U.S. at 224.

[23] Culombe v. Connecticut, 367 U.S. 568, 605 (1961).

[24] Schneckloth v. Bustamonte, 412 U.S. at 224.

[25] *Id.* at 227.

[26] *See* § 23.03, *infra*. Regarding the debate between bright-line rules and case-by-case adjudication, *see* § 2.07[A], *supra*.

[27] 3 LaFave, Note 7, *supra*, at 644.

[28] Will an African-American person, or a person of another racial minority, feel coerced to consent to a search under circumstances in which a non-minority person would not feel compelled? The Supreme Court has not spoken to this issue. However, many commentators

of education, emotional state, or mental condition, that suggests that her will was overborne by the officers' conduct. Other pertinent factors are discussed immediately below.

### [B] Claim of Authority by the Police

In *Bumper v. North Carolina*,[29] police officers told *X*, who was standing at the front door of her house, that they had a warrant to search her premises. *X* opened the door and said "go ahead." Although a warrant may have existed in the case, none was ever disclosed, and the prosecutor defended the search on the ground of consent.

The Supreme Court held that a state may not meet its burden of proof that consent was voluntarily granted "by showing no more than acquiescence to a claim of lawful authority." Specifically, consent is invalid when it "has been given only after the official conducting the search has asserted that he possesses a warrant." Such a situation "is instinct with coercion— albeit colorably lawful coercion. Where there is coercion there cannot be consent."

On its face, *Bumper* provides a bright-line rule: if an officer asserts authority to conduct a search on the basis of a warrant, whether that warrant is valid, invalid, or does not exist, any consent granted thereafter is invalid.[30] For example, if *D* indicates to the officer asserting authority, "You needn't have brought a search warrant. You are welcome to search,"[31] the consent may be legally effective, on the ground that *D*'s statement indicates that her consent was not linked to the officer's claim of authority.

### [C] Police Deception

Police officers sometimes use deception to obtain consent to search. Often the deception relates to the identity of the person seeking consent. That is, an undercover officer will actively misrepresent or fail to disclose her true identity in order to gain admission onto premises where she can observe

---

believe that people living in minority neighborhoods experience more coercive police conduct than occurs in other neighborhoods; in light of this, a minority person is likely to interpret a police request for consent very differently—perhaps, as a demand, rather than a request— than one living in the majority neighborhood. *See generally* Robert V. Ward, *Consenting to a Search and Seizure in Poor and Minority Neighborhoods: No Place for a "Reasonable Person"*, 36 How. L.J. 239 (1993). For discussion of the role of race in other Fourth Amendment contexts, *see* §§ 8.03[C][3], and 9.03, *supra*. *See also* §§ 18.01 and 18.03[B][5], *infra*.

[29] 391 U.S. 543 (1968).

[30] 3 LaFave, Note 7, *supra*, at 639–41.

[31] *E.g.*, Earls v. State, 496 S.W.2d 464 (Tenn. 1973) (upholding the consent as voluntary).

activities or conduct a search. As discussed elsewhere,[32] the Supreme Court in a long line of cases, beginning in the pre-*Katz*[33] "trespass" era and continuing into modern times, has held that when *A* talks to *B* or invites her into an otherwise constitutionally protected area, *A* assumes the risk that *B* is not whom she purports to be. Put differently, consent is not vitiated by the fact that, but for the misrepresentation or nondisclosure of a police officer's identity, the person would not have granted consent to the undercover officer to enter the individual's premises.

A different form of deception occurs when an officer deceives an individual regarding the purpose of a requested search. Sometimes, lower courts will invalidate a consent given in deceptive circumstances, but the deception itself might not actually explain the outcome. For example, in *United States v. Dichiarinte*,[34] the police obtained consent to search *D*'s premises by explaining that they wanted to search for narcotics; in fact, they intended to open and examine certain documents, which they did. The court invalidated the consent on the ground that police "may not obtain consent to search on the representation that they intend to look only for certain specified items and subsequently use the consent as a license to conduct a general exploratory search." However, as Professor LaFave has pointed out,[35] the search would have been invalid in any case—even if the police had been looking for narcotics as they claimed—on the ground that they exceeded the scope of the search to which consent had been granted.[36]

What if the police use deception, but do not exceed the legitimate scope of the search? For example, *O*, a police officer, might request consent to search *D*'s bedroom for evidence relating to a jewelry theft, when in fact she is looking for a bloody shirt that is evidence of a recent murder. *D* might consent, knowing that she has no jewelry, and assuming that *O* will not understand the significance of the bloody shirt if it is discovered. Does *O*'s deception vitiate *D*'s consent, although the search does not exceed the scope of consent?

The Supreme Court has said little on the matter, and state and lower federal courts have reached mixed results in such cases. The law is sufficiently muddled that LaFave has stated that "as unsettling as it may be to say," the test appears to be, simply, whether the police "deception [was] 'fair.' "[37] Even if "fair deception" is not an oxymoron, the concept

---

[32] *See* §§ 7.02 and 7.05[B], and most particularly Note 79 therein, *supra*.

[33] Katz v. United States, 389 U.S. 347 (1967).

[34] 445 F.2d 126 (7th Cir. 1971).

[35] 3 LaFave, Note 7, *supra*, at 707.

[36] Regarding scope-of-consent issues, *see* § 17.04, *infra*.

[37] 3 LaFave, Note 7, *supra*, at 711.

is obviously value-laden and, therefore, requires courts to determine whether, and to what extent, agents of the government should "play fair" in trying to investigate the activities of persons whom they suspect of not "playing fair."

### [D]  Awareness of Fourth Amendment Rights

In *Schneckloth v. Bustamonte*,[38] the police stopped a car in which *X* and *D* were passengers, because a headlight was burned out. After the driver failed to produce his driver's license and only *X* could provide identification, an officer asked for permission to search the car. *X*, the brother of the absent vehicle owner, consented. During the search, the police discovered evidence that connected *D* to a crime.

In the ensuing prosecution, *D* asserted that *X*'s consent to the car search was invalid. Although the state courts found that *X*'s consent was voluntary, a federal court ruled that the consent was not valid unless the prosecution proved that *X* knew that he had the right to refuse consent to the search.

The Supreme Court, per Justice Stewart, disagreed with the federal court's analysis. It framed the issue as follows: "[W]hat must the state prove to demonstrate that a consent was 'voluntarily' given[?]" To answer this question, Justice Stewart sought guidance from the cases in which the Court had determined the voluntariness of a suspect's confession under the Fourteenth Amendment due process clause. As Stewart explained, "[t]hose cases yield no talismanic definition of 'voluntariness' "; to the question of "whether a defendant's will was overborne in a particular case, the Court has assessed the totality of all the surrounding circumstances." Therefore, in the Fourth Amendment context as well, the Court rejected the principle that " 'voluntariness' requires proof of knowledge of a right to refuse as the *sine qua non* of an effective consent to search." Instead, a person's awareness—or lack thereof—of a right to refuse consent is simply one factor, among all of the surrounding circumstances, to be taken into account in determining the voluntariness of the consent given.[39]

Many commentators are critical of the reasoning of *Schneckloth*, if not also of its ultimate holding. These critics maintain (as Justice Thurgood Marshall argued in dissent) that the majority misstated the issue in the case. They reason that the issue was not whether *X*'s consent was *voluntary*, but

---

[38] 412 U.S. 218 (1973).

[39] *See also* Ohio v. Robinette, 519 U.S. 33 (1996) (the Fourth Amendment does not require that a lawfully seized person be advised that she is free to go before her consent to a car search will be recognized as voluntary; eschewing this bright-line rule, the Court followed the *Schneckloth* approach of treating voluntariness as a matter to be determined from all of the circumstances).

rather whether *X waived* his constitutional right to be free from unreasonable searches and seizures.

The distinction is a significant one. The traditional waiver principle, enunciated in *Johnson v. Zerbst*,[40] is that the state must prove "an intentional relinquishment . . . of a known right or privilege." In *Schneckloth*, such knowledge was not proved; therefore, there seemingly was no "waiver" of Fourth Amendment rights under this test.

Justice Stewart discounted the relevance of the *Zerbst* rule to consent searches. First, he suggested that a waiver approach to consent searches is inconsistent with the Court's "third party" consent law. As explained in Section 17.05, any person who possesses common authority over premises or effects may consent to a search of the property. Yet, Justice Stewart observed, "it is inconceivable that the Constitution could countenance the waiver of a defendant's [constitutional] right . . . by a third party."

Second, according to Stewart, the Court's waiver decisions "do not reflect an uncritical demand for a knowing and intelligent waiver in every situation where a person has failed to invoke a constitutional protection." The Court distinguished between, on the one hand, rights that protect a fair criminal trial, such as the right to trial counsel, which was at issue in *Zerbst*, and the rights guaranteed under the Fourth Amendment. In the former case, a "strict standard of waiver" is required because the reliability of the trial is at stake. In contrast, "[t]he [privacy] protections of the Fourth Amendment are of a wholly different order, and have nothing whatsoever to do with promoting the fair ascertainment of truth at a criminal trial." Therefore, even if one were to resolve the issue of consent in "waiver" terms—which the Court ultimately was not prepared to do—*Schneckloth* teaches that constitutional rights that affect the reliability of the trial process are protected more scrupulously than other constitutional rights.[41]

## § 17.04  Scope of Search[42]

A warrantless consent search is invalid if an officer exceeds the scope of the consent granted. For example, if *A* consents to a search of her bedroom, the police may not search other parts of the house on the basis of the consent.[43] If she consents to a ten-minute search, the police may

---

[40] 304 U.S. 458 (1938). See § 4.02, *supra*.

[41] *Schneckloth* has been rejected, at least in part, by one state court applying its own constitution. State v. Ferrier, 960 P.2d 927 (Wash. 1998) (an officer seeking consent to search a suspect's home without a warrant must warn the resident of the right to refuse consent).

[42] *See generally* 3 LaFave, Note 7, *supra*, at § 8.1(c).

[43] However, if the officer observes criminal evidence in view on the way to the bedroom, she may seize it pursuant to the plain view doctrine.

not invoke consent to justify the search after the consent expires.[44] Consent searches, however, are virtually never negotiated with the precision of a contract, so it is often unclear how extensively the police may search based on the permission given.

In *Florida v. Jimeno*,[45] the Supreme Court provided its clearest guidance to date on the "scope of consent" issue. In *Jimeno, O* stopped *D*'s car on the highway in order to issue a traffic citation. Because he had reason to suspect that *D* was carrying narcotics in the car, *O* requested permission to search the car for narcotics. *D* consented. During the search, *O* opened a folded paper bag, in which he discovered a kilogram of cocaine. The trial court suppressed the evidence on the ground that *D* had not expressly consented to a search of the container.

The Supreme Court reversed. Chief Justice Rehnquist declared that "[t]he standard for measuring the scope of a suspect's consent . . . is that of 'objective' reasonableness—what would the typical reasonable person have understood by the exchange between the officer and the suspect?" On the facts here, the Court maintained that "it was objectively reasonable for the police to conclude that the general consent to search [*D*'s] car included consent to search containers within that car which might bear drugs." In other words, whether or not *D* subjectively thought about the container when he gave consent to search, *O* acted reasonably in interpreting *D*'s consent to include the right to open the folded paper bag.

*Jimeno* does *not* stand for the broad proposition that the police may, in the absence of an express limitation, open *every* container discovered during *any* consent search of a residence or automobile. According to the Court, "[t]he scope of a search is generally defined by its expressed object." Therefore, it would be improper for the police to open a container too small to hide the object of the search.

Potentially more significantly, the Court in dictum distinguished the present case from one in which the police, pursuant to consent to search a car trunk, break open a locked suitcase found in the trunk. In the latter situation, the Court opined, "[i]t is very likely unreasonable to think that a suspect, by consenting to the search of his trunk, has agreed to the breaking open of [the suitcase] . . . ." However, the distinction drawn here—between a locked suitcase and a folded up paper bag—seemingly conflicts with the Supreme Court's other container cases, which have treated closed containers alike for Fourth Amendment purposes, on the ground that "[w]hat one

---

[44] However, if criminal evidence is found during the ten minutes, the police may be justified in arresting *A*, and conducting a separate search as incident to the arrest.

[45] 500 U.S. 248 (1991).

person may put into a suitcase, another"—presumably, for example, a homeless individual—"may put into a paper bag."[46]

## § 17.05  Third Party Consent[47]

More than one person may have an interest in real or personal property that the police want to search. A search of a residence, for example, typically intrudes on the privacy of several persons who inhabit it; a search of a container intrudes on the privacy interests of anyone who uses it as a depository of private effects.

In a criminal proceeding, no significant consent issues arises if *X* voluntarily consents to a search of premises or personal effects that also belong to *D*, as long as the evidence found during the search is introduced at trial only against *X*. The issue of "third-party consent" arises, however, when the person against whom the evidence is introduced (*D*) is not the one who granted consent (*X*).

In *Stoner v. California*,[48] the police obtained consent from a hotel clerk to enter *D*'s hotel room. The Court ruled that the consent was invalid, "[e]ven if it be assumed that a state law . . . gave a hotel proprietor blanket authority to authorize the police to search." The Court stated that Fourth Amendment rights are "not to be eroded by strained applications of the law of agency" or by the "subtle distinctions" of property law. In language that suggested that third-party consent might never be valid, the Court indicated that "[i]t is important to bear in mind that it was [*D*'s] constitutional right which was at stake here . . . . It was a right, therefore, which only . . . [*D*] could waive by word or deed, either directly or through an agent."

In *United States v. Matlock*,[49] however, the Court announced that a warrantless search is constitutionally valid if the police obtain consent from one who possesses common authority over the property searched. The burden of proof is on the government to establish common authority.[50]

---

[46] Robbins v. California, 453 U.S. 420, 426 (1981), *overruled on other grounds*, United States v. Ross, 456 U.S. 798 (1982). *See generally* § 14.07, *supra*.

[47] *See generally* 3 LaFave, Note 7, *supra*, at §§ 8.3–8.4; Mary I. Coombs, *Shared Privacy and the Fourth Amendment, or the Rights of Relationships*, 75 Cal. L. Rev. 1593 (1987); Robert Deschene, Comment, *The Problem of Third-Party Consent in Fourth Amendment Searches: Toward a "Conservative" Reading of the Matlock Decision*, 42 Me. L. Rev. 159 (1990); Peter Goldberger, *Consent, Expectations of Privacy, and the Meaning of "Searches" in the Fourth Amendment*, 75 J. Crim. L. & Criminology 319 (1984); James B. White, *The Fourth Amendment as a Way of Talking About People: A Study of Robinson and Matlock*, 1974 Sup. Ct. Rev. 165.

[48] 376 U.S. 483 (1964).

[49] 415 U.S. 164 (1974).

[50] Illinois v. Rodriguez, 497 U.S. 177, 181 (1990).

In *Matlock*, D was arrested in the front yard of a home in which he shared a room with X. The officers received consent from X to search the room. D's consent was not requested. The Court declared the law to be "clear" that consent to a search "of one who possesses common authority over premises or effects is valid as against the absent nonconsenting person with whom the authority is shared." It stated that "common authority" rests on "mutual use of the property by persons generally having joint access or control for most purposes."[51]

*Matlock* justified third-party common-authority consent on the ground that "it is reasonable to recognize that any of the co-inhabitants has the right to permit the inspection in his own right and that the others have assumed the risk that one of their number might permit the common area to be searched." Thus, two related principles arise from *Matlock*: (1) each person with common authority over property maintains her own right to consent to a search; and (2), because of (1), any person who shares property with another assumes the risk that such consent will be granted. In *Matlock*, this meant that X had the right to consent, and her consent justified the search, even though the police knew where they could find D to ask his permission (after all, they had just arrested him), and even though they wanted to search the premises for evidence against D, and not against X.

Various issues are raised by *Matlock*. For example, suppose that A and B, persons with common authority over property, are in an antagonistic relationship when the police seek consent. Indeed, suppose that the police know of their dispute, and purposely seek out A for consent, explaining that they are looking for evidence against B? Although there is case law to the contrary, the general rule seems to be that A's consent is effective. The reasoning of *Matlock* supports the majority rule: A has her own right to consent; indeed, in such circumstances, the assumption-of-risk doctrine takes on particular significance.

Suppose, however, that when the police request consent from A, B is present and objects to the search of their common belongings? *Matlock* referred to "absent, nonconsenting persons" in its description of the third-party consent rule. Does this mean that consent by one joint occupant is legally ineffective against another occupant who is also present, and who objects to the search? Lower court case law is split in this regard.[52] Some

---

[51] One who shares premises with another person may retain exclusive control over a portion of the premises or over particular effects within them. For example, a particular room in an apartment shared by college roommates might be used exclusively by one person. Lower courts agree that as to such areas or personal effects, consent is ineffective unless it is granted by the person with exclusive control.

[52] 3 LaFave, Note 7, *supra*, at 726–33.

courts have concluded that the consent of both parties is required when they are both present, on the theory that one co-tenant's right to restrict access to the premises is not subordinated to the other person's right to grant consent, at least if the former contemporaneously asserts her objection.[53]

On the other hand, the logic of *Matlock* suggests a contrary outcome. It should follow from *Matlock* that by sharing her privacy with *A*, *B* assumes the risk that *A* will voluntarily consent to a search of their joint property, even over *B*'s objection. Indeed, sometimes courts go so far as to the say that *Matlock* applies although the *consenting* co-occupant is *absent*, and the police conduct the warrantless search without obtaining consent of the physically *present* joint occupant.[54]

*Matlock* is controversial. The Court minimizes or ignores entirely the idea of "shared privacy." As Professor Mary Coombs has argued, some relationships are sufficiently intimate "to permit a presumption that the parties would shelter one another's interests."[55] At a minimum, therefore, "the more intimate the relationship between the parties is shown to be, the more skeptical the court should be that the consent was truly voluntary,"[56] when one party to the relationship "consents" and the other does not.

## § 17.06 "Apparent Authority"[57]

Suppose that *X*, a guest at *D*'s house, answers the door when the police arrive. The officers, believing that *X* lives at the residence, seek and receive consent from *X* to search the premises. Is such consent—consent based on apparent, not real, authority—effective? The issue cuts to the core of the rationale of consent searches.[58]

In *Stoner v. California*,[59] the Supreme Court stated that "the rights protected by the Fourth Amendment are not to be eroded . . . by unrealistic

---

[53] *E.g.*, State v. Leach, 782 P.2d 1035 (Wash. 1989) (holding that the state must prove, at the very least, that the defendant did not object to the search to which the joint occupant consented).

[54] *E.g.* People v. Sanders, 904 P.2d 1311 (Colo. 1995); *contra*, In re Welfare of D.A.G., 484 N.W.2d 787 (Minn. 1992) (under the state constitution, a present joint occupant's right to be free from a warrantless search of premises prevails over an absent joint occupant's right to consent to that search).

[55] Coombs, Note 47, *supra*, at 1653; *see* Lloyd L. Weinreb, *Generalities of the Fourth Amendment*, 42 U. Chi. L. Rev. 47, 63 (1974) ("[O]rdinarily, persons with equal 'rights' in a place would accommodate each other by not admitting persons over another's objection while he was present.").

[56] Coombs, Note 47, *supra*, at 1661.

[57] *See generally* 3 LaFave, Note 7, *supra*, at § 8.3(g).

[58] *See* § 17.02[B], *supra*.

[59] 376 U.S. 483 (1964).

doctrines of 'apparent authority.' " Ten years later, however, in *United States v. Matlock*,[60] the Court expressly left open the issue of whether "apparent authority" constitutes effective consent.

In *Illinois v. Rodriguez*,[61] the Court resolved the issue left open in *Matlock*. It held, 6–3, that a warrantless entry of a residence is valid when it is based on the consent of a person whom the police, at the time of entry, reasonably (but incorrectly) believe has common authority over the premises.

In *Rodriguez*, X reported to the police that she had been severely beaten that day by D in a specified apartment. X stated that D was now asleep on the premises, and she offered to let the police in with her key so that they could arrest him. During her conversation with the police, X referred to D's apartment as "our" apartment, and she stated that she had clothing and furniture there. In fact, however, although she had once shared the apartment with D, she had vacated it weeks earlier and had taken the key without D's knowledge. With X's consent, the police entered D's apartment. Inside, they observed drug paraphernalia and cocaine in plain view. D was arrested and charged with possession of illegal drugs. The trial court granted D's motion to exclude the evidence found in the apartment because X lacked common authority over the premises.

The Supreme Court, per Justice Scalia, reversed. According to *Rodriguez*, "what is at issue when a claim of apparent consent is raised is not whether the right to be free of searches has been *waived*, but whether the right to be free of *unreasonable* searches has been *violated*." Justice Scalia wrote:

> It is apparent that in order to satisfy the "reasonableness" requirement of the Fourth Amendment, what is generally demanded of the many factual determinations that must regularly be made by agents of the government—whether the magistrate issuing a warrant, the police officer executing a warrant, or the police officer conducting a search or seizure under one of the exceptions to the warrant requirement—is not that they always be correct, but that they always be reasonable.[62]

---

[60] 415 U.S. 164 (1974).

[61] 497 U.S. 177 (1990); *contra, under state constitution*, State v. Lopez, 896 P.2d 889 (Haw. 1995) (consent may not be based on apparent authority); State v. McLees, 994 P.2d 683 (Mont. 2000) (*id.*); State v. Wright, 893 P.2d 455 (N.M. Ct. App. 1995) (*id.*).

[62] Notice the Court's inclusion of exceptions to the warrant requirement within the general rubric that the police need not be correct in their actions, only that they be reasonable. This language may have profound future impact on "warrant exception" case law. For example, suppose that a police officer conducts a search, ostensibly incident to a lawful arrest, but she seizes evidence that a court later determines was slightly outside the arrestee's grabbing area. Under current law, that evidence is inadmissible. In light of *Rodriguez*, however, could the government argument that the officer's mistake was a reasonable one, thereby rendering the search reasonable?

In effect, therefore, a search based on a reasonable mistake of fact regarding the authority of the third person to give consent is a "reasonable" search within the meaning of the Fourth Amendment.[63]

The consent determination, as with other factual matters that arise under the Fourth Amendment, must be judged against an objective standard. The Court warned that an invitation by a person to conduct a search, even if accompanied by an explicit claim of authority to grant consent (*e.g.*, "I live here"), is insufficient to justify a consent search if "the surrounding circumstances [are] . . . such that a reasonable person would doubt its truth."

Specifically, the objective test announced in *Rodriguez* is: "[W]ould the facts available to the officer at the moment . . . 'warrant a man of reasonable caution in the belief' that the consenting party had authority over the premises?" If the answer is "no," then "warrantless entry without further inquiry is unlawful unless actual authority exists." If the answer is "yes," the warrantless search is valid.

---

[63] In the criminal law, a reasonable mistake of fact ordinarily serves to acquit a wrongdoer of an offense, on the ground that the mistake negates the requisite *mens rea* of the crime. Joshua Dressler, Understanding Criminal Law § 12.03 (3d ed. 2001). However, the mistake does not render the conduct justifiable. For example, if *D*, a hunter, shoots and kills *V*, another hunter, in the dark, mistakenly believing that *V* is a bear, *D* will not be convicted of murder and, if the mistake was a reasonable one, she is not guilty of any form of criminal homicide. But, the outcome—*V*'s death— is no less socially harmful.

*Query*: Shouldn't the same analysis apply here? An officer's reasonable mistake regarding consent shows us that she is not *culpable* for her actions. But, does it make her conduct any less harmful or wrongful? May we not say that a citizen's rights have been violated by a warrantless search of her home based on ineffective consent, even if we also conclude that the officer is not morally culpable for the violation? Many violations of the Fourth Amendment are unintentional, and sometimes they are not even the result of negligence, but they constitute violations nonetheless.

## CHAPTER 18

# *TERRY v. OHIO*: THE "REASONABLENESS" BALANCING STANDARD IN CRIMINAL INVESTIGATIONS

### § 18.01  *Terry v. Ohio*: An Overview to a Landmark Case[1]

The Fourth Amendment was once considered a monolith.[2] "Probable cause" had a single meaning, and "searches" and "seizures" were all-or-nothing concepts. The monolith was cracked by the Supreme Court in *Camara v. Municipal Court.*[3] In *Camara*, the Justices recognized a different form of "probable cause," applicable in administrative-search cases,[4] that does not require individualized suspicion of criminal wrongdoing and which is based on the general Fourth Amendment standard of "reasonableness." To determine "reasonableness," the *Camara* Court invoked a balancing test, in which the individual's and society's interests in the given type of administrative search were weighed against each other.

If *Camara* cracked the Fourth Amendment monolith, *Terry v. Ohio*[5] broke it entirely. Although the issue in *Terry* was described by the Court as "quite narrow"—"whether it is always unreasonable for a policeman to seize a person and subject him to a limited search for weapons unless there is probable cause to arrest"—the significance of the case to Fourth Amendment jurisprudence is, quite simply, monumental. In terms of the

---

[1] *See generally* 4 Wayne R. LaFave, Search and Seizure § 9.1 (3d ed. 1996); David A. Harris, *Frisking Every Suspect: The Withering of Terry*, 28 U.C. Davis L. Rev. 1 (1994); Wayne R. LaFave, *"Street Encounters" and the Constitution: Terry, Sibron, Peters, and Beyond*, 67 Mich. L. Rev. 39 (1968); Tracey Maclin, *The Decline of the Right of Locomotion: The Fourth Amendment on the Streets*, 75 Cornell L. Rev. 1258 (1990); Scott E. Sundby, *A Return to Fourth Amendment Basics: Undoing the Mischief of Camara and Terry*, 72 Minn. L. Rev. 383 (1988); Gregory Howard Williams, *The Supreme Court and Broken Promises: The Gradual But Continual Erosion of* Terry v. Ohio, 34 How. L.J. 567 (1991). *See also* the citations found in Note 15, *infra*.

[2] Anthony G. Amsterdam, *Perspectives on the Fourth Amendment*, 58 Minn. L. Rev. 349, 388 (1974).

[3] 387 U.S. 523 (1967). *See* § 9.06, *supra*.

[4] *See generally* § 19.02, *infra*.

[5] 392 U.S. 1 (1968).

daily activities of the police, as well as the experiences of persons "on the street," there is no Supreme Court Fourth Amendment case—not even *Katz v. United States*[6] —of greater practical impact.

The significance of *Terry* will be seen in this chapter, but a brief overview is appropriate. First, *Terry* transported *Camara*'s "reasonableness" balancing test from the realm of administrative searches to traditional criminal investigations, and used it to determine the reasonableness of warrantless searches and seizures, rather than merely to define "probable cause." The result has been a significant diminution in the role of the Warrant Clause in Fourth Amendment jurisprudence. That is, *Terry* provided the impetus, as well as the framework, for a move by the Supreme Court away from the proposition that warrantless searches are *per se* unreasonable, to the competing view that the appropriate test of police conduct "is not whether it is reasonable to procure a search warrant, but whether the search was reasonable."[7] Warrantless police conduct became much easier to justify after *Terry*.

Second, *Terry* recognized that searches and seizures can vary in their intrusiveness. The Court no longer treats all searches (and all seizures) alike. As a result of this case, many police-citizen on-the-street encounters that do not involve arrests or full-blown searches come within the scope of the Fourth Amendment, but are considered lawful, notwithstanding the absence of a warrant or probable cause.

Third, as a corollary of the last point, because of *Terry* the police may now conduct a wide array of searches and seizures that are considered less-than-ordinarily intrusive, on the basis of a lesser standard of cause than "probable cause," so-called "reasonable suspicion."[8]

Finally, although *Terry* does not require such a holding, the Supreme Court has applied the "reasonableness" balancing test that stems from it to hold that some seizures and searches of persons or property may be conducted without individualized suspicion of any kind.[9]

---

[6] 389 U.S. 347 (1967).

[7] United States v. Rabinowitz, 339 U.S. 56, 66 (1950). According to one scholar, *Terry* "established such a spongy test, one that allowed the police so much room to maneuver and furnished the courts so little bases for meaningful review, that the opinion must have been the cause for celebration in a goodly number of police stations." Yale Kamisar, *The Warren Court and Criminal Justice: A Quarter-Century Retrospective*, 31 Tulsa L.J. 1, 5 (1995).

[8] *See, e.g.*, §§ 18.08 (protective sweeps of residences), 19.05[B][1] (searches of public school students), and 19.05[B][2] (searches of public employees), *infra*.

[9] *See* § 16.01, *supra* (car inventories), and §§ 19.03 (border searches), 19.04[D] (sobriety checkpoints), and 19.05[C][2] (drug and alcohol testing of public employees and public school children), *infra*.

At least one other aspect of *Terry* deserves note here. Professor Akhil Amar suggests that this case may provide "one of the most open Fourth Amendment discussions of race to date."[10] Whether or not this assertion is accurate,[11] there is no gainsaying that when the police forcibly stop (seize) persons on the street to question them or to conduct full or cursory searches, highly sensitive issues of racial profiling (and to a lesser extent, issues of ethnicity, class, or gender) come to the fore.[12]

Some scholars believe that the *Terry* opinion (or, at least, the *Terry* doctrine as it has come to be interpreted over the years), and its move away from the warrant requirement, has done much to exacerbate racial tensions between the police and members of minority communities.[13] Others believe that the Court's movement in this case to a reasonableness standard is good, in part because it will force courts to confront issues, such as race and class, "honestly and openly."[14] Whoever is right in this regard, Chief Justice Earl Warren was surely correct when he observed in *Terry* that "[w]e would be less than candid if we did not acknowledge that this [case] thrusts to the fore, difficult and troublesome issues regarding a sensitive area of police activity."

[10] Akhil Reed Amar, *Fourth Amendment First Principles*, 107 Harv. L. Rev. 757, 808 (1994).

[11] It is not a universally held view. *E.g.*, Anthony C. Thompson, *Stopping the Usual Suspects: Race and the Fourth Amendment*, 74 N.Y.U. L. Rev. 956 (1999) (contending that the Supreme Court intentionally disguised the race-based aspects of the search and seizure in *Terry*).

[12] According to a New York County District Attorney *amicus* brief filed in the *Terry* case, 1600 police reports of stop-and-frisks by the New York City Police Department "showed [a] disproportionate racial impact of those actions." Michael R. Juviler, *A Prosecutor's Perspective*, 72 St. John's L. Rev. 741, 743 (1998).

[13] *See generally* David A. Harris, *"Driving While Black" and All Other Traffic Offenses: The Supreme Court and Pretextual Traffic Stops*, 87 J. Crim. L. & Criminology 544 (1997); Adina Schwartz, *"Just Take Away Their Guns": The Hidden Racism of* Terry v. Ohio, 23 Fordham Urb. L.J. 317 (1996). Among those scholars who believe that the Court made a wrong turn when it moved away from the warrant requirement, and that such a move has harmed racial minorities is Professor Tracey Maclin. *See* Tracey Maclin, *"Black and Blue Encounters"—Some Preliminary Thoughts About Fourth Amendment Seizures: Should Race Matter?*, 26 Val. U. L. Rev. 243 (1991); *see also* Developments in the Law, *Race and Criminal Process: III. Racial Discrimination on the Beat: Extending the Racial Critique to Police Conduct*, 101 Harv. L. Rev. 1472, 1494 (1988); David A. Harris, *Factors for Reasonable Suspicion: When Black and Poor Means Stopped and Frisked*, 69 Ind. L.J. 659 (1994); Sheri Lynn Johnson, *Race and the Decision to Detain a Suspect*, 93 Yale L.J. 214 (1983); Maclin, Note 1, *supra*; Randall S. Susskind, Note, *Race, Reasonable Articulable Suspicion, and Seizure*, 31 Am. Crim. L. Rev. 327 (1994); Williams, Note 1, *supra*.

[14] Amar, Note 10, *supra*, at 808.

## § 18.02   *Terry v. Ohio*: The Opinion[15]

### [A]   Majority Opinion

*O*,[16] a 39-year police veteran, became "thoroughly suspicious" when he observed two men walking back and forth repeatedly in front of a store, peering in. *O* testified that he suspected that the men were "casing a job," *i.e.*, planning to commit an armed robbery. *O* also observed the two men talk to a third individual.[17]

*O* approached the three suspects, identified himself as a police officer, asked for their names, and when he received only a mumbled reply from one, he grabbed *D*, spun him around, and patted down ("frisked") the outside of his clothing. *O* felt a pistol in the breast pocket of *D*'s overcoat, pulled it out, and arrested him and for carrying a concealed weapon. At a hearing to determine the admissibility of the weapon, *O* testified that he frisked

---

[15] *See generally* Terry v. Ohio *30 Years Later: A Symposium on the Fourth Amendment, Law Enforcement and Police-Citizen Encounters*, 72 St. John's L. Rev. 721–1524 (1998). For a fascinating study of how the Court reached its outcome in *Terry*, see John Q. Barrett, *Deciding the Stop and Frisk Cases: A Look Inside the Supreme Court's Conference*, 72 St. John's L. Rev. 749 (1998).

[16] *O* was Cleveland Police Detective Martin McFadden. Louis Stokes (now an Ohio Congressman), who represented Terry (*D*) in the fateful case, has described McFadden as follows:

He was a real character—a tall, stately guy, and basically a good policeman. "Mac," as we called him, was really a guy that we really liked. He was straight. One thing about him—as a police officer, he came straight down the line. You did not have to worry about him misrepresenting what the facts were.

Louis Stokes, *Representing John W. Terry*, 72 St. John's L. Rev. 727, 729 (1998).

[17] Although the *Terry* opinion is silent on matter, *D* and the second suspect were African-American; the third individual was white. *D*'s defense counsel questioned *O* about his suspicions. According to the counsel's modern-day recollections:

[Officer McFadden] said to us that he had seen these two fellows standing across the street from him, and he described them as being two Negroes, and then he talked of the white fellow who came up to them and talked with them. Then he [the third man] went on down the street. Mac then admitted to us they weren't doing anything, except one of the black fellows would leave the other one, walk down the street a little bit, turn around, peer into the window . . ., then walk back up to where the other fellow was. Then the other fellow would take a walk in a similar manner.

[*O*] was asked specifically what attracted him to them. On one occasion he said, "Well, to tell the truth, I just didn't like 'em." He was asked how long he'd been a police officer. "39 years." How long had he been a detective? "35 years." What did he think they were doing? "Well," he said, "I suspected that they were casing a joint for the purpose of robbing it." "Well," he was asked, "have you ever in your 39 years as a police officer, 35 as a detective, had the opportunity to observe anybody casing a place for a stickup?" He said, "No, I haven't." "Then what attracted you to them?" He indicated he just didn't like them.

*Id.* at 729–30.

the suspects only to see whether they were armed, and that he put his hands in D's clothing only after he felt the weapon. At the time of the pat-downs, O lacked probable cause to arrest the suspects or to search them.[18]

The Supreme Court, per Chief Justice Earl Warren, upheld O's action. In doing so, however, it rejected the government's claim that the "stop and frisk" procedure fell outside the purview of the Fourth Amendment. This argument, the Court stated, "seeks to isolate from constitutional scrutiny the initial stages of the contact between the policeman and the citizen." The Chief Justice rejected this "rigid all-or-nothing" analysis. In considerable part, perhaps, the Court sought to bring the stop-and-frisk process within the scope of the Fourth Amendment because of "[t]he wholesale harassment by certain elements of the police community, of which minority groups, particularly Negroes, frequently complain."

For the first time, the Court stated that a person can be "seized"—and, thus, the Fourth Amendment is implicated—short of being arrested. The Chief Justice stated that a "seizure" occurs "whenever a police officer accosts an individual and restrains his freedom to walk away." In slightly different language, *Terry* also states that "[o]nly when the officer, by means of physical force or show of authority, has in some way restrained the liberty of a citizen may we conclude that a 'seizure' has occurred."[19] The Court stated that D was seized, although less intrusively than if he had been arrested, at least as soon as O initiated physical contact with D in order to search him.

Likewise, the Supreme Court held that the pat-down that O conducted was a "serious intrusion" on D's privacy and, therefore, a "search," albeit "something less than a 'full' " one. Chief Justice Warren stated that "it is nothing less than sheer torture of the English language to suggest that a careful exploration of the outer surfaces of a person's clothing all over his or her body in an attempt to find weapons is not a 'search.' "[20]

Although the stop-and-frisk conducted by O involved Fourth Amendment activity, the Court concluded that the Warrant Clause does not apply to

---

[18] Subsequently, D (Terry) was confined to an asylum for the criminally insane. By the time the *Terry* case reached the high court, the second African-American suspect, who was also arrested, was killed in a robbery in Columbus, Ohio. Reuben M. Payne, *The Prosecutor's Perspective on* Terry: *Detective McFadden Had a Right to Protect Himself*, 72 St. John's L. Rev. 733, 733 (1998). The third person in the incident, although taken into custody by O, was not ultimately charged with any offense.

[19] Since *Terry*, the Court has refined this definition of "seizure." *See* § 8.03, *supra.*

[20] As the Court observed, a pat-down requires the officer to do a "thorough search" of the suspect's body, including "the groin and area about the testicles, and entire surface of the legs down to the feet." Indeed, quite arguably, a pat-down is *more* intrusive than a "full" search of the pocket of a person's clothing.

this type of police practice. The Chief Justice stated that the Court would "not retreat" from the ordinary rule that the police must, whenever practicable, secure a search warrant, but, he said, "we deal here with an entire rubric of police conduct—necessarily swift action predicated upon the on-the-spot observations of a police officer on the beat—which historically has not been, and as a practical matter could not be, subjected to the warrant procedure."

Because the Warrant Clause was deemed inapplicable to this "entire rubric of police conduct," the Court held that the "probable cause" standard, which is textually tied to the warrant requirement in the Fourth Amendment, also does not apply.[21] Instead, the Court stated, the "central inquiry" is "the reasonableness in all the circumstances of the particular governmental invasion of a citizen's personal security."

How does the Court go about determining whether a particular search or seizure is "reasonable"? Quoting *Camara v. Municipal Court*,[22] the Chief Justice observed that "there is 'no ready test for determining reasonableness other than by balancing the need to search [or seize] against the invasion which the search [or seizure] entails.' " The Court also warned in oft-quoted language that "in justifying the particular intrusion, the police officer must be able to point to specific and articulable facts which, taken together with rational inferences from those facts, reasonably warrant the intrusion."

The Court balanced the competing interests in this case. It focused first on the "nature and extent of the governmental interests involved." The Court pointed to the general interest of "effective crime prevention and detection" that would be impaired if the police could not confront suspects for investigative purposes on less than probable cause. It was this interest, the Chief Justice stated, that *O* was discharging when he decided to approach *D* and the other suspects to inquire about their activities.

The second governmental interest—and what the Court deemed to be "[t]he crux of the case"—involved *O*'s frisk of *D* for weapons. The Court stated that *O* had a legitimate immediate interest in assuring himself that the suspect was "not armed with a weapon that could unexpectedly and fatally be used against him." As the Chief Justice put it, "[c]ertainly it would be unreasonable to require that police officers take unnecessary steps in the performance of their duties. American criminals have a long tradition of violence . . . ."

---

[21] This conclusion need not follow. When an exigency justifies an exception to the warrant requirement, the Court may retain the probable cause standard, as it has done, for example, in the case of searches of cars stopped on the highway.

[22] 387 U.S. 523 (1967).

Viewed against these interests, of course, there was $D$'s interest in free locomotion on the street, and freedom from police intrusion. The initial detention/seizure, however, was not as severe an intrusion as an arrest; and the pat-down "constitutes a brief, though far from inconsiderable, intrusion upon the sanctity of the person."

Based on this balancing approach, the Court announced certain principles. The Chief Justice concluded that when an officer has what has come to be known in later cases as "reasonable suspicion" that "the individual whose suspicious behavior he is investigating at close range is armed and presently dangerous to the officer or others," an officer has the constitutional authority to ascertain whether the person in fact is armed and, if he is, to disarm him. The Court warned that, in determining whether an officer acted reasonably, "due weight must be given, not to his inchoate and unparticularized suspicion or 'hunch,' but to the specific reasonable inferences which he is entitled to draw from the facts in light of his experience."

Moreover, the procedure used by the officer to protect himself must be "strictly circumscribed [in manner] by the exigencies which justify its initiation." Specifically, the purpose of the *Terry* search is limited: to determine whether the suspect is armed. Unlike a search incident to an arrest, a *Terry*-type search "is not justified by any need to prevent the disappearance or destruction of evidence of crime."

The appropriate manner of the protective search depends on the facts of the case, but the Court approved the technique used here: a pat-down of the outside of the suspect's clothing that is reasonably designed to discover "guns, knives, clubs, or other hidden instruments for the assault of the police officer"; and, when a hard object that feels like a weapon is discovered during the pat-down, a full search under the clothing to remove it.

The majority opinion concludes with what is intended as a carefully worded, narrow holding:

> We merely hold today that where a police officer observes unusual conduct which leads him reasonably to conclude in light of his experience that criminal activity may be afoot and that the persons with whom he is dealing may be armed and presently dangerous, where in the course of investigating this behavior he identifies himself as a policeman and makes reasonable inquiries, and where nothing in the initial stages of the encounter serves to dispel his reasonable fear for his own or others' safety, he is entitled for the protection of himself and others in the area to conduct a carefully limited search of the outer clothing of such persons in an attempt to discover weapons which might be used to assault him.

Such a search is a reasonable search under the Fourth Amendment, and any weapons seized may properly be introduced in evidence against the person from whom they were taken.[23]

As will be seen in this chapter, the Court has taken the reasoning of *Terry*, in particular the balancing approach, and expanded considerably on the circumstances in which the police may conduct searches and seizures on less than probable cause and without a warrant.

### [B] Justice Harlan's Concurring Opinion

Justice Harlan, while "unreservedly agree[ing]" with the Court's holding, sought "to fill in a few gaps" in the majority opinion. In doing so, he provided two important insights into the stop-and-frisk process.

First, the majority opinion focused on the protective search—the pat-down—of *D*. But, as Justice Harlan rightly observed, the right to frisk ought to depend on whether the officer had authority in the first place to insist on the encounter that placed his safety in jeopardy. In short, before the search, there is likely to be a seizure of the person, which logically must be justified first. This is because, just as an officer may ask a citizen a question, the "person addressed [ordinarily] has an equal right to ignore his interrogator and walk away." In this case, Justice Harlan believed that *O* had a right to seize *D* because he "observed circumstances that would reasonably lead an experienced, prudent policeman to suspect that [*D*] was about to engage in burglary or robbery."

Second, Justice Harlan concluded that when a forcible stop is justified, "the right to frisk must be immediate and automatic if the reason for the stop is, as here, an articulable suspicion of a crime of violence." This comment is significant because the holding quoted above suggests that an officer, after seizing a suspect, needs to investigate further before conducting a pat-down. As discussed in § 18.06[A], Justice Harlan has had the better side of this controversy, as the Supreme Court has implicitly acknowledged.

---

[23] *Terry*, 392 U.S. at 30–31.

## § 18.03  "Reasonable Suspicion"[24]

### [A]  Quantum of Evidence Required

The Supreme Court has never quantified the concept of "probable cause."[25] The Court in *Illinois v. Gates*[26] described it as a "fluid concept" that is "not readily, or even usefully, reduced" to a mathematical formula. Basically, "probable cause" involves a "substantial basis" for concluding—a "fair probability" but less than a preponderance of the evidence—that a search will turn up criminal evidence or that the person seized is guilty of an offense.

The Supreme Court in *Terry v. Ohio* did not indicate what quantum of evidence is required to justify a less-than-ordinarily-intrusive seizure of a person or to conduct a less-than-full search (pat-down) of a suspect, although Chief Justice Warren did make the rather obvious point in the context of a pat-down that the officer need not be "absolutely certain" that the suspect is armed.

Since *Terry*, the Court has stated that the "reasonable suspicion"[27] standard is "obviously less demanding than that for probable cause."[28] It requires "considerably less"[29] proof of wrongdoing than proof by a preponderance of the evidence. As the Court has recently put it, "*Terry* accepts the risk that officers may stop [and/or frisk] innocent people."[30] All that is required to justify a *Terry*-level search or seizure is "some minimal level of objective justification."[31] Essentially, the police may not act on the basis of an "inchoate and unparticularized suspicion or hunch,"

---

[24] *See generally* 4 LaFave, Note 1, *supra*, at § 9.4; David A. Harris, *Particularized Suspicion, Categorical Judgments: Supreme Court Rhetoric versus Lower Court Reality Under* Terry v. Ohio, 72 St. John's L. Rev. 975 (1998); Margaret Raymond, *Down on the Corner, Out in the Street: Considering the Character of the Neighborhood in Evaluating Reasonable Suspicion*, 60 Ohio St. L.J. 99 (1999).

[25] *See* § 9.07[A], *supra*.

[26] 462 U.S. 213 (1983).

[27] A piece of trivia: the Court did not use the term "reasonable suspicion" in *Terry*, although it was used by a lower court, as quoted by the Supreme Court, in Sibron v. New York, 392 U.S. 40 (1968), a companion case to *Terry*. The Supreme Court apparently used the term itself, although in quotation marks, for the first time in a *Terry* context in Almeida-Sanchez v. United States, 413 U.S. 266, 268 (1973). The quotation marks were dropped in Gustafson v. Florida, 414 U.S. 260, 265 n.4 (1973), a non-*Terry* case, and later in United States v. Brignoni-Ponce, 422 U.S. 873, 882 (1975), a case involving a *Terry*-level seizure.

[28] United States v. Sokolow, 490 U.S. 1, 7 (1989).

[29] *Id.*

[30] Illinois v. Wardlow, 528 U.S. 119, 126 (2000).

[31] INS v. Delgado, 466 U.S. 210, 217 (1984).

which was expressly condemned in *Terry*; suspicion is "reasonable," however, if the officer can point to some (perhaps just a few) specific and articulable facts that, along with reasonable inferences from those facts, justify the intrusion.[32] The subsections that follow delve more deeply into the question of what facts and inferences typically constitute "reasonable suspicion."

## [B] Types of Information

### [1] In General

As with probable cause, the Supreme Court has declared that the "reasonable suspicion" standard cannot be "readily, or even usefully, reduced to a neat set of legal rules."[33] Instead, the justifiability of a *Terry*-type seizure or search, like a seizure or search based on probable cause, is supposed to be evaluated on "the totality of the circumstances—the whole picture."[34]

Typically, as in *Terry*, a seizure of a person (and pat-down) will be based in whole or in considerable part on an officer's personal observations of the suspect and the surrounding circumstances. A police officer is entitled to make "common-sense conclusions about human behavior,"[35] including those founded on his personal law enforcement expertise. The more difficult problems arise when an officer claims that he acted on the basis of suspicions grounded at least in part on the observations or experiences of others.

---

[32] Critics of post-*Terry* case law have assumed that lower courts now routinely uphold police stop-and-frisks. However, according to one concededly incomplete sampling of federal district court and state appellate court opinions, defendants won *Terry* motions to suppress in a not-insignificant 26% to 28% of the cases. George C. Thomas III, *Terry v. Ohio in the Trenches: A Glimpse at How Courts Apply "Reasonable Suspicion"*, 72 St. John's L. Rev. 1025, 1029–1034 (1998). Professor Thomas states, however, "we need much more data about how magistrates and trial judges are deciding *Terry* issues before we know with any kind of confidence" whether these figures will hold up. *Id.* at 1041.

[33] United States v. Sokolow, 490 U.S. at 7 (quoting Illinois v. Gates, 462 U.S. 213, 232 (1983)).

[34] United States v. Cortez, 449 U.S. 411, 417 (1981); *see also* United States v. Arvizu, 122 S.Ct. 744 (2002). However, according to some scholars, "lower courts have slowly and steadily adopted whole categories of cases which allow police to [stop and] frisk . . ., whatever the specific facts [of the individual case] are." Harris, Note 24, *supra*, at 976. That is, certain observations (for example, furtive behavior or flight by a suspect) or surrounding circumstances (for example, that the suspect is in a "high-crime area") can result in a virtual bright-line rule at the lower-court level that "reasonable suspicion" exists. See also Raymond, Note 24, *supra* (arguing that, in particular, the character of a neighborhood as crime-or drug-prone tends to dominate judicial analysis and push aside particularized facts that might result in a contrary outcome).

[35] United States v. Cortez, 449 U.S. at 418.

## [2]   Hearsay: When It Is and Is Not Sufficient

In *Terry*, the officer acted on the basis of his own personal observations of the suspects. Three cases—*Adams v. Williams*,[36] *Alabama v. White*,[37] and *Florida v. J. L.*[38] —teach, however, that "reasonable suspicion," like "probable cause," may be based on hearsay. Furthermore, because "reasonable suspicion" is a less demanding standard than "probable cause," it may be satisfied not only on the basis of a lesser quantum of evidence, but also on the basis of "information that is less reliable than that required to show probable cause."[39] The same factors that apply to information supplied by an informant in the probable cause context—the informant's basis of knowledge and veracity—apply in the *Terry* context, "although allowance must be made in applying them for the lesser showing required to meet that standard."[40] These three cases, *Adams*, *White*, and *J. L.*, usefully suggest rough guidelines regarding how informants may properly be used in the *Terry* context and how courts should oversee the process.

In *Adams*, the Supreme Court sustained a *Terry* stop and frisk based in part on an informant's tip that would not have justified an arrest or a search based on probable cause. In the case, late at night, a known informant told *O* that *D* was seated in a nearby car with narcotics in his possession and a gun concealed at his waist. The informant did not indicate the basis of his knowledge. As a result of the tip, *O* proceeded to *D*'s car. He ordered *D* to open the door; instead, *D* opened his window, at which point *O* reached in and removed a revolver from *D*'s waist.

The Supreme Court, per Justice Rehnquist, conceded that the unverified tip might not have been sufficient to justify any action that required probable cause. Nonetheless, it held that the tip "carried enough indicia of reliability" to justify a *Terry*-level seizure.

The Court considered the tipster's information sufficiently reliable because he had provided the police with information about a crime on a prior occasion, and because he personally came to *O* with the present information, rather than making an anonymous report. As a result, the informant subjected himself to the (theoretical) risk of arrest for making a false complaint if the information he provided had proven to be false. The Court was not dissuaded by the fact, pointed out by the dissenters, that

---

[36] 407 U.S. 143 (1972).

[37] 496 U.S. 325 (1990); *see generally* David S. Rudstein, *White on White: Anonymous Tips, Reasonable Suspicion, and the Constitution*, 79 Ky. L.J. 661 (1990-91).

[38] 529 U.S. 266 (2000).

[39] Alabama v. White, 496 U.S. at 330.

[40] *Id.* at 328–29.

the informant's prior track record consisted of a single tip, pertaining to a different type of conduct (alleged homosexual behavior in a railroad station), that did not result in an arrest. For purposes of reasonable suspicion, there were sufficient indicia of the informant's reliability.

The Court in *Adams* warned that "[s]ome tips, completely lacking in indicia of reliability, would either warrant no police response or require further investigation before a forcible stop of a suspect would be authorized." *Alabama v. White*[41] provides a good example of such an unsatisfactory tip, but one that was saved—although just barely so—by police investigation. In *White*, the police received a telephone call from an anonymous informant who stated that *D* (a woman she named) would be leaving a specified apartment at a specified time in a "brown Plymouth station wagon with the right taillight broken," and that she would drive to a specified motel, in possession of an ounce of cocaine in a brown attaché case.

The officers proceeded to the apartment, where they observed an automobile fitting the informant's description, parked in front of the apartment building. They spotted a woman, empty handed, enter the car and drive in the direction of the motel. Before the car reached its destination, however, the officers stopped the vehicle and ordered the driver, *D*, out of the car. A search based on consent resulted in seizure of marijuana, found in an attaché case in the car.

The Court held, 6-3, that the anonymous tip in this case, by itself, was insufficient to justify a forcible stop of *D*. It pointed out that the caller provided "absolutely no indication of the basis for the . . . predictions regarding [*D*'s] criminal activities"; furthermore, the call "provide[d] virtually nothing from which one might conclude that [the informant] . . . [was] either honest or his information reliable." Nonetheless, in what the Supreme Court crucially admitted was "a close case," the majority concluded that "under the totality of the circumstances the anonymous tip, as corroborated, exhibited sufficient indicia of reliability to justify the investigatory stop of [*D*'s] car."

Notice here that the corroboration was incomplete and imperfect. First, it was not clear prior to the stop that the woman the police were following was the person named by the informant. Second, the police did not corroborate that the suspect left the specified apartment at the specified address. Third, the police did not wait to see if *D* would drive her car to

---

[41] 496 U.S. 325 (1990); *contra, under the state constitution,* Commonwealth v. Lyons, 564 N.E.2d 390 (Mass. 1990) (rejecting the *Gates/White* totality-of-the-circumstances test in the context of probable cause/reasonable suspicion).

the motel, as predicted. Moreover, one fact not only was not corroborated but was false: *D* did not have the attache' case in her possession, as predicted, when she entered her car.

The Supreme Court instead focused on the fact that the informant predicted future conduct—that a particular person would come out of a specified apartment and drive a particular automobile to a particular location—some of which was corroborated. According to Rehnquist, "[w]hen significant aspects of the caller's predictions were verified, there was reason to believe not only that the caller was honest but also that he was well informed, at least well enough to justify the stop." Of course, as the dissent noted, every fact the police corroborated in *White* involved innocent conduct that could fit the description of countless people each day. The majority was not dissuaded by the fact that, as Justice Stevens warned in his dissent, "[a]nybody with enough knowledge about a given person to make her the target of a prank, or to harbor a grudge against her, will certainly be able to formulate a tip about her like the one predicting" *D*'s actions. Again, to meet the lower standard of "reasonable suspicion"—to conduct a brief detention or frisk—the information, as corroborated, was adequate.

But, there is a point past which the Supreme Court will not go in justifying a *Terry* stop or frisk based on the "reasonable suspicion" standard. It must be kept in mind that the Court described *White* as a "close case" and relied heavily on the fact that the informant there accurately predicted some future behavior. Contrast this with *Florida v. J. L.*,[42] in which an anonymous telephone caller reported to police, simply, that a young black male wearing a plaid shirt and standing at a particular bus stop was carrying a gun. Two officers proceeded to the site where they observed three young black males "hanging out" at the bus stop. The officers saw no firearm, nor did J. L., dressed in a plaid shirt as stated, make any threatening or unusual movements. As the Court stated, "*[a]part from the tip*, the officers had no reason to suspect any of the three of illegal conduct." Nonetheless, the officers frisked J. L. (and the other two males) and seized a gun they discovered in J. L.'s pocket.

The Court unanimously held that the officers lacked reasonable suspicion to justify frisking J. L. It observed that "[i]f *White* was a close case on the reliability of anonymous tips, this one surely falls on the other side of the line." Writing for the Court, Justice Ginsburg rejected the government's claim that the police could act on the basis of the informant's tip because it provided an accurate description of a particular person at a particular

---

[42] 529 U.S. 266 (2000).

location. Ginsburg declared that "[a]n accurate description of a subject's readily observable location and appearance is of course reliable in this limited sense: It will help the police correctly identify the person whom the tipster means to accuse." What the tip lacked—and what Ginsburg said was "essential" to the Court's holding in *White*—was predictive information that the police could corroborate.[43]

The government advanced a second argument in *J. L.*, namely, "that the standard *Terry* analysis should be modified to license a 'firearm exception.' Under such an exception, a tip alleging an illegal gun would justify a stop and frisk even if the accusation would fail standard pre-search reliability testing." The Court, again unanimously, declined to recognize such an exception, stating that it "would rove too far," by permitting an individual to harass another and to cause an intrusive search simply "by placing an anonymous call falsely reporting the target's unlawful carriage of a gun."

### [3] Drug-Courier Profiles[44]

The Supreme Court has stated that an officer's observations may properly be supplemented by "consideration of the modes or patterns of operation of certain kinds of lawbreakers."[45] In the drug-trafficking field, an officer's suspicions will often be buttressed by his awareness that the suspect's conduct or appearance conforms to a so-called "drug-courier profile," which is a set of characteristics purportedly often associated with drug traffickers, compiled by law enforcement agencies, such as the Drug Enforcement Administration.

Many litigated cases involving drug-courier profiles occur in the following context: law enforcement agents observe a person about to embark on, or disembarking from, an airplane, train, or bus; the individual's conduct is lawful in all respects, but it and the suspect's appearance fit a drug-courier profile; therefore, the officers stop the suspect in order to question him. If the investigation constitutes a *Terry*-level seizure, the police must possess reasonable suspicion for the encounter.[46]

---

[43] *J. L.* is also distinguishable from *Adams v. Williams*. Although the informant there, as here, only described a particular person at a particular location—he did not predict future conduct—the informant's reliability in *Adams* was somewhat stronger: he came to the police non-anonymously; therefore, his reputation could be better assessed and he could be held criminally responsible if his allegations proved to be fabricated. *See* Florida v. J. L., 529 U.S. at 270.

[44] *See generally* Stephen E. Hall, *A Balancing Approach to the Constitutionality of Drug Courier Profiles*, 1993 U. Ill. L. Rev. 1007 (1993).

[45] United States v. Cortez, 449 U.S. 411, 418 (1981).

[46] Initial contact between an officer and a suspect will often fall short of a seizure of the person, *see* § 8.03, *supra*, and therefore may lawfully take place in the absence of reasonable suspicion.

The fact mere that a suspect's behavior and/or appearance conforms to a drug-courier profile does not, without more, constitute reasonable suspicion.[47] As one court has explained, "[m]ere mechanical matching of characteristics thought to be common to all drug couriers can never meet the rigorous requirements of the fourth amendment. To be reasonable, an officer's suspicion must be specific and, to some extent, individualized to the particular characteristics exhibited by a particular person."[48] On the other hand, the fact that the suspect's conduct conforms to a reliable drug-courier profile "does not . . . detract from [the] evidentiary significance [of the factors] as seen by a trained agent."[49]

Therefore, each drug-courier profile case must be decided on its own merits, and it is difficult to draw broad principles from the cases the Supreme Court has decided.[50] The Court took a comparatively strict view of the subject in *Reid v. Georgia*.[51] In *Reid*, it held that an officer lacked reasonable suspicion to justify detaining a suspect in an airport who fit a drug profile in that he: (1) arrived from a "drug source" city; (2) arrived early in the morning, a time when law enforcement activity is reduced; (3) apparently tried to conceal the fact that he was traveling with another person; and (4) had no luggage except for shoulder bags.

Notwithstanding the profile, the Court believed that, except for the third factor, the facts "describe[d] a very large category of presumably innocent travelers, who would be subject to virtually random seizures were the Court to conclude that as little foundation as there was in this case could justify a seizure." The Court disposed of the furtive conduct on the ground that the officer's suspicion that the suspect was concealing something was no more than an inchoate and unparticularized hunch. The Court did warn, however, that "there could . . . be circumstances in which wholly lawful conduct might justify the suspicion that criminal activity was afoot."

The Court was presented with a case of lawful, but reasonably suspicious, conduct in *Florida v. Royer*.[52] In *Royer*, D, about to embark on an airplane, fit a drug-courier profile in that he: (1) was traveling from a major drug source city; (2) paid for his ticket in cash with a large number of small bills; (3) traveled under an assumed name; and (4) appeared to be nervous.

---

[47] *See* Reid v. Georgia, 448 U.S. 438 (1980) (per curiam).

[48] United States v. Hanson, 801 F.2d 757, 762 (5th Cir. 1986).

[49] United States v. Sokolow, 490 U.S. 1, 10 (1989).

[50] "[I]t cannot be said with assurance what combination of factors from the 'drug courier profile' will suffice to justify a *Terry* stop of a particular traveler." 4 LaFave, Note 1, *supra*, at 169.

[51] 448 U.S. 438 (1980) (per curiam).

[52] 460 U.S. 491 (1983).

For a four-Justice plurality, Justice Byron White stated that when the police learned that *D* was traveling under an assumed name, "this fact, and the facts already known to the officers" justified a temporary detention.

In *United States v. Sokolow*,[53] the conduct of *D*, a passenger disembarking from an airplane, was consistent with a drug-courier profile in that: (1) he paid for airplane tickets totaling $2,100 with a roll of $20 bills; (2) he traveled under a name different than that listed for his telephone number; (3) his original destination was Miami, a major drug source city; (4) he stayed in the city, in July, for only two days, although his round-trip flight from Hawaii lasted 20 hours; (5) he appeared nervous; and (6) he did not check any of his luggage.

The Court conceded that each of these factors was "quite consistent with innocent travel." On the other hand, it found factors (1) and (4) "out of the ordinary"; and it thought that the existence of factor (2) gave the police reasonable grounds for believing that *D* was traveling under an alias. Taken together, these three factors amounted to reasonable suspicion of drug trafficking.

Most drug courier profile cases at the lower court level tend to be evaluated "in a common-sense fashion," based on the particular factors present in the case, "without accepting the profile itself as establishing that certain combinations of factors are inevitably sufficient to support a *Terry* stop."[54] Indeed, in the absence of statistical evidence presented to the trial court by the law enforcement agency demonstrating the existence of a reasonable correlation between a profile and drug activity, courts have no logical basis for considering the drug courier profile, as such.[55] As always, each case should be decided on its own merits.

Indeed, one risk with drug courier profiles, if accepted uncritically, is that they can serve as a subterfuge for racial profiling,[56] particularly if the profile includes a racial or ethnic factor—for example, that the suspect is Hispanic—and the other "suspicious" factors are largely correlated with, rather than independent of, the racial or ethnic factor.[57]

---

[53] 490 U.S. 1 (1989).

[54] 4 LaFave, Note 1, *supra*, at 174.

[55] Derricott v. State, 611 A.2d 592 (Md. 1992).

[56] *See* § 18.03[B][5], *infra*.

[57] United States v. Ornelas-Ledesma, 16 F.3d 714 (7th Cir. 1994) (in which the profile considered the facts that: *D* was Hispanic; came from the "source" state of California; drove a 2-door vehicle, which is supposedly preferred by drug traffickers; checked into a motel without a reservation at 4:00 a.m.; and was accompanied by another man; the court was critical of the fact that these factors were correlated with the lower-income status of many innocent Hispanics on long-distance trips).

### [4]　Flight in "High-Crime Areas"[58]

The existence of drug courier profiles raises a related issue: are there certain neighborhoods, by their nature, that are sufficiently riddled with crime that there is a statistically significant possibility (say, 10 percent chance) that *anyone* found in the area is involved in criminal activity? Even if the chances of criminal activity are not high enough to justify a search or arrest based on probable cause,[59] what about a *Terry* stop? The Supreme Court has ruled out such a conclusion, stating that "[t]he fact that [a person] was in a neighborhood frequented by drug users, standing alone, is not a basis for concluding that [he] himself was engaged in criminal conduct."[60] So what more is needed?

In this regard, is one common-sense conclusion about human behavior the following: one who turns and walks quickly the other direction—or, more dramatically, "flees"—when the individual spots a police officer is probably guilty of wrongdoing or, at least, planned criminal wrongdoing? Can flight, standing alone, constitute reasonable suspicion, regardless of the character of the neighborhood? In *California v. Hodari D.*,[61] Justice Scalia, writing for seven Justices, hinted in dictum that unprovoked flight constitutes reasonable suspicion to stop a fleeing party, quoting the Bible, "The wicked flee when no man pursueth," *Proverbs* 28:1.

The Supreme Court directly confronted the unprovoked flight issue—and the relationship of flight and the character of a neighborhood—in *Illinois v. Wardlow*.[62] In *Wardlow*, officers in a police caravan converging on a Chicago area known for heavy drug trafficking observed *W* standing next to a building, in possession of an opaque bag. As the caravan arrived in his vicinity, *W* fled. Two officers in the last caravan vehicle pursued and seized *W*. At the suppression hearing, one of the pursuing officers testified that he was in uniform on that day, but he was not asked whether the other officers were in uniform, nor was he asked whether the caravan vehicles were marked.

The Supreme Court unanimously agreed that unprovoked flight, when coupled with other factors, can constitute *Terry*-level suspicion justifying a seizure, but they split 5-4 on whether the facts here were sufficient. Although *Wardlow* provides no express *per se* rule regarding flight, the practical lesson of the case appears to be that the coupling of two

---

[58] *See* Raymond, Note 24, *supra*.

[59] The issue in the probable cause context is considered in detail at § 9.07[B], *supra*.

[60] Brown v. Texas, 443 U.S. 47, 52 (1979).

[61] 499 U.S. 621 (1991).

[62] 528 U.S. 119 (2000).

circumstances—unprovoked flight motivated by the presence of police, and a high crime area—is sufficiently suspicious to justify the seizure of a fleeing individual, at least in the absence of circumstances that render the flight innocent in appearance.

Chief Justice Rehnquist, writing for the majority, agreed that "there are innocent reasons for flight from police and that, therefore, flight is not necessarily indicative of ongoing criminal activity." But, under *Terry*, "the determination of reasonable suspicion must be based on commonsense judgments and inferences about human behavior." And, the majority said, "[h]eadlong flight—wherever it occurs—is the consummate act of evasion; it is not necessarily indicative of wrongdoing, but it is certainly suggestive of such." According to the Chief Justice, *Terry* demonstrates that ambiguous conduct, although susceptible of an innocent explanation, can justify a seizure to investigate the ambiguities: "*Terry* accepts the risk that officers may stop innocent people." Although an individual's presence in a high crime area, standing alone, is insufficient to support *Terry*-level suspicion of criminal activity, the location of the events is a relevant factor; coupled with *W*'s unprovoked flight from the police, the majority held that the police acted lawfully here.

Justice Stevens, writing for four Justices in a partial dissent, agreed that unprovoked flight is a relevant factor in determining reasonable suspicion, but warned that it "describes a category of activity too broad and varied to permit a *per se* reasonable inference regarding the motivation for the activity." Stevens pointed to many innocent motivations for rapid movement: "to catch up with a friend a block or two away, to seek shelter from an impending storm, to arrive at a bus stop before the bus leaves, . . . any of which might coincide with the arrival of an officer in the vicinity." He also suggested reasons why a person might innocently flee the police: to avoid being called as a witness to a crime; concern that the officers' presence indicates dangerous criminal activity nearby, which the citizen sensibly wishes to escape; and—in remarkable recognition of concerns in the minority community about relations with the police—in the case of "minorities and those residing in high crime areas, there is . . . the possibility that the fleeing person is entirely innocent, but, with or without justification, believes that contact with the police can itself be dangerous . . . ."

According to the dissenters, unprovoked flight is not so rare as to be "aberrant" or "abnormal." Just as "innocent explanations surely do not establish that the Fourth Amendment is always violated whenever someone is stopped solely on the basis of an unprovoked flight, neither do the suspicious motivations establish that the Fourth Amendment is never violated when a *Terry* stop is predicated on that fact alone."

The dissenters were not impressed with the government's case here: the events occurred in the daytime; it was not even clear from the evidence presented at the hearing that the address where *W* was spotted "was the intended [drug-infested] destination of the caravan" or simply a building along the way; and it was uncertain whether *W* recognized the occupants of the vehicles as police officers. The testifying officer only stated, "[h]e looked in our direction and began fleeing." The dissenters believed that the prosecution failed to satisfy its burden of proof to justify the seizure.

*Wardlow* leaves a lot of issues undecided and subject to later clarification. The Court spoke about "unprovoked flight," but what does this term mean? Is flight truly "unprovoked" if, for example, a citizen runs away when he spots a police car with its lights on and sirens blaring? It may be one thing if there is reason for the person to assume that the police vehicle is seeking to stop him—a driver observing the police car in the rear-view mirror, immediately behind him—but what if the person is walking on the sidewalk, observes the police car, and begins to run? Just as critically, what are the parameters of the term "flight"? *Wardlow* supposedly involved "headlong flight," but what if an individual simply turns and walks quickly—or even slowly—in the opposite direction the moment he observes an officer?

There is also a need for the Court to provide more insight into the "high crime area" concept. What facts about the character of a neighborhood are sufficiently suspicious that, coupled with flight or other suspicious conduct, justify a forcible stop? The facts in *Wardlow* regarding the neighborhood were strong (although *W*'s specific location in the drug area was ambiguous), but how much less will qualify?

### [5]  The Role of Race in Determining "Reasonable Suspicion"[63]

A current controversy receiving national attention is so-called racial profiling. The term has various potential meanings, but it generally involves the police use of race as the predominant or sole factor in determining whether to forcibly stop an individual. Most frequently racial profiling arises when a police officer stops an automobile driver on the basis of race, a procedure sufficiently common that it has come to be termed "driving while black." As one court has observed,

> we cannot help but be aware that the burden of aggressive and intrusive police action falls disproportionately on African-American, and

---

[63] This subject is considered in greater detail, and citations relating to the subject are found, at §§ 2.05, 2.07[B], and 9.02[F], *supra*.

sometimes Latino, males. . . . [A]s a practical matter neither society nor our enforcement of the laws is yet color-blind. Cases, newspaper reports, books, and scholarly writings all make clear that the experience of being stopped by the police is a much more common one for black men than it is for white men.[64]

The problem extends to African-Americans of all economic classes, including lawyers, physicians, businesspeople, and academics.[65]

Most racial profiling cases arise in the probable cause context: an officer grows suspicious of an automobile driver on racial or ethnic grounds, waits until he has probable cause to issue a traffic citation—which, given the plethora of driving regulations is only a matter of time—and then uses that opportunity as a pretext to question the driver, observe the contents of the car in plain view, or seek consent to conduct a car search. In light of *Whren v. United States*,[66] such stops do not violate the Fourth Amendment solely because the officer is acting pretextually. Although *Whren* deals with probable cause, it may be assumed that its lessons apply as well to *Terry* stops.

*Terry* stops based solely on the race of a suspect are impermissible.[67] However, race or ethnicity is not an impermissible factor, when coupled with other criteria, in determining whether the police have "reasonable suspicion" justifying a stop. Thus, for example, courts have sometimes treated "racial incongruity"—the presence of a person of a particular race or ethnic group in a place he is not ordinarily found—as one legitimate factor in evaluating the lawfulness of a stop.[68]

## § 18.04 Distinguishing a *"Terry* Stop" From an Arrest[69]

### [A] Overview to the Issue

An encounter between a police officer and a private citizen can be so non-intrusive—for example, if an officer asks for the time of day—that it does not constitute a "seizure" and, therefore, does not trigger Fourth Amendment scrutiny.[70] On the other hand, a detention can be so intrusive that it constitutes a *de facto* arrest and, therefore, requires probable cause, and not mere reasonable suspicion. The line between a *Terry*-level seizure

---

[64] Washington v. Lambert, 98 F.3d 1181, 1187 (9th Cir. 1996).

[65] *Id.* at 1188.

[66] 517 U.S. 806 (1996).

[67] 4 LaFave, Note 1, *supra*, at 183 (and n. 220 citing cases).

[68] *Id.*

[69] *See generally* 4 LaFave, Note 1, *supra*, at § 9.7.

[70] *See* § 8.03, *supra*.

and a *de facto* arrest, therefore, is an important one. Unfortunately, the line is not bright. As with other *Terry* issues, courts consider the totality of circumstances surrounding the encounter. Various factors, however, deserve special note and are considered immediately below.

## [B] Length of the Detention

*Terry* involved a very brief detention of persons suspected of criminal activity. The Court has more than once stated that the justifiability of a seizure on less than probable cause is predicated in part on the brevity of the detention.[71]

Nonetheless, there is no bright-line time limitation to a *Terry*-type seizure. A seizure based on reasonable suspicion may be permitted although it lasts longer than those that occurred in *Terry*. For example, in *United States v. Sharpe*[72] the Court upheld a twenty-minute detention of suspects, stopped in their vehicles on a public highway, in order to investigate criminal activity. Although the Court upheld the seizures, their legitimacy was based on the presence of three critical temporal factors: (1) the officer "pursued his investigation in a diligent and reasonable manner"; (2) the method of investigation "was likely to confirm or dispel [the officers'] suspicions quickly"; and (3) the detention lasted no longer than was necessary to effectuate the purpose of the stop. A significant fact in *Sharpe* was that the length of detention was aggravated by evasive actions taken by the suspects in what otherwise would have been a much briefer detention.

*Sharpe* should not be interpreted to mean that a seizure of any length may be justified on the basis of reasonable suspicion as long as the police pursue their investigation diligently. Indeed, *Sharpe* warned that even if the three conditions stated above are met, a detention that "continues indefinitely at some point . . . can no longer be justified" as a *Terry* stop.

Despite this warning, the Supreme Court in *United States v. Montoya de Hernandez*[73] upheld a seizure, based on the lower standard of reasonable suspicion, lasting well over 16 hours. In the case, *D*, a woman whom customs agents suspected of concealing narcotics-filled balloons in her alimentary canal in order to smuggle them into the country, refused to undergo an x-ray. Therefore, the agents detained her in a small room, and

---

[71] *See, e.g.,* Dunaway v. New York, 442 U.S. 200, 209 (1979) (*Terry* "involved a brief, on-the-spot stop on the street . . . , a situation that did not fit comfortably within the traditional concept of an 'arrest' "); United States v. Place, 462 U.S. 696, 76 (1983) ("the principles of *Terry* and its progeny would permit the officer to detain . . .briefly to investigate the circumstances that aroused his suspicion").

[72] 470 U.S. 675 (1985).

[73] 473 U.S. 531 (1985).

told her that "if she went to the toilet she would have to use a wastebasket in the women's restroom," so that her stool could be inspected for balloons. The Court held that the seizure here "was not unreasonably long," in view of the fact that it occurred at the international border, the method of suspected smuggling did not allow for a speedy determination, *D* refused the only alternative method of investigation (an x-ray), and *D* made "heroic" efforts to avoid having the bowel movement.

### [C]  Forcible Movement of the Suspect

#### [1]  In General

In *Terry*, the suspects were seized and searched on the street. However, if the police move a suspect to another site for further investigation, a court may treat the seizure as tantamount to an arrest, requiring probable cause. This is especially likely to occur if the criminal investigation could have taken place where the detention arose.

For example, in *Dunaway v. New York*,[74] the police took *D* into custody at his neighbor's home, and transported him to a police station for questioning. Although *D* was told he was not under arrest, the Supreme Court treated the police action as a *de facto* arrest, requiring probable cause. Likewise, in *Florida v. Royer*,[75] the police moved *D*, originally encountered in an airport concourse, to a small room 40 feet away, where the investigation continued. Among the reasons given by the Court for treating this act as tantamount to an arrest was that there was no finding of a legitimate law enforcement purpose for moving the suspect.

#### [2]  Removal from An Automobile After a Lawful Stop

The Supreme Court has held that whenever a police officer lawfully stops a vehicle on the road, even for a minor traffic violation, it is reasonable for the officer to order the driver out of the car, even if he does this as a matter of routine for purposes of safety. According to *Pennsylvania v. Mimms*,[76] once a driver is pulled over in his car, the incremental intrusion from the request that he alight from his vehicle is *de minimis*. Therefore, the right to order the driver out of the car—again, assuming the initial seizure was lawful—is automatic, *i.e.* it requires no special justification.[77]

---

[74] 442 U.S. 200 (1979).

[75] 460 U.S. 491 (1983).

[76] 434 U.S. 106 (1977).

[77] *Contra under the state constitution*, Commonwealth v. Gonsalves, 711 N.E.2d 108 (Mass.1999) (a police officer must have a reasonable belief that his or another's safety is in danger before ordering a driver or other occupant out of a motor vehicle following a lawful stop of the vehicle).

Furthermore, the Supreme Court held, 7-2, in *Maryland v. Wilson*[78] that an officer, making a valid traffic stop, may "as a matter of course" order *passengers*, and not simply the driver, out of the car pending completion of the detention.[79] The Court conceded that a passenger's interest in liberty is "in one sense stronger than that for the driver," because the police have grounds to stop the driver for a vehicular offense, whereas there is no such basis for stopping or detaining passengers. Nonetheless, "as a practical matter, the passengers are already stopped by virtue of the stop of the vehicle." Therefore, the additional intrusion of being ordered out of the car is *de minimis*, and is outweighed by an officer's purported weighty interest in protecting himself from possible violence by passengers. In dissent, Justices Stevens and Kennedy stated that:

> the number of stops in which an officer is actually at risk is dwarfed by the far greater number of routine stops. . . . In contrast, the potential daily burden on thousands of innocent citizens is obvious. . . . [C]ountless citizens who cherish individual liberty and are offended, embarrassed, and sometimes provoked by arbitrary official commands may well consider the burden [of being ordered out of the car] to be significant.

In the dissenters' view, "wholly innocent passengers . . . have a constitutionally protected right to decide whether to remain comfortably seated within the vehicle rather than exposing themselves to the elements and the observations of curious bystanders."

The Court left open the issue of whether an officer may detain a passenger for the duration of the stop. For example, may a passenger in a taxicab stopped because the driver was speeding hop into another taxi to get to the airport, or may the police require him to remain until the officer is through with the driver? In view of the *Terry* "reasonableness" balancing standard, it is submitted here that the passenger's interest in locomotion should take precedence. An officer will have little legitimate interest in keeping a passenger—about whom the officer has no suspicions of wrongdoing—at the scene. Indeed, the individual's departure removes a theoretical threat to the officer's safety.[80]

---

[78] 519 U.S. 408 (1997).

[79] *Contra under the state constitution*, Commonwealth v. Gonsalves, 711 N.E.2d 108 (Mass. 1999) (requiring reasonable suspicion to order a passenger out of vehicle); State v. Mendez, 970 P.2d 722 (Wash. 1999) (*id.*).

[80] *See* Walls v. State, 714 N.E.2d 1266 (Ind. Ct. App. 1999) (holding that an officer who has lawfully stopped a car for a traffic citation may not routinely order a passenger, who has left the vehicle and walked away, to return; the officer must have reasonable suspicion that the person is armed and presently dangerous or have other legitimate grounds to detain him).

## [D] Existence of "Less Intrusive Means"[81]

In *Florida v. Royer*,[82] Justice White, author of the four-Justice plurality opinion, but with the apparent support of Justice Brennan,[83] asserted that when a suspect is seized according to *Terry*, "the investigative methods employed should be the least intrusive means reasonably available to verify or dispel the officer's suspicions in a short period of time.

In *Royer*, this principle was violated when the police moved *D*, an embarking airplane passenger suspected of drug smuggling, from the public concourse to a small room nearby so that the police could retrieve his luggage and search it, a process that took 15 minutes. According to Justice White, the government did not "touch[] on the question whether it would have been feasible to investigate the contents of [*D*'s] bag in a more expeditious way." In particular, he noted that "[t]he courts are not strangers to the use of trained dogs to detect the presence of controlled substances in luggage." Because there was no indication in this case that the latter investigatory technique "was not feasible and available," the officers' conduct was considered more intrusive than necessary.

Similarly, in *United States v. Place*,[84] another airport concourse case, the Court ruled that a 90-minute detention of *D*'s luggage, and implicitly of *D*, in order to get a dog to sniff the luggage, was unreasonable because the government agents had prior warning of *D*'s intended arrival in New York and, therefore, "could have minimized the intrusion on [*D*'s] Fourth Amendment interests," by having the dog available when he arrived.

The least-intrusive-means doctrine applies, if at all, only in the *Royer/Place* context, namely, when the issue is whether the length of an investigatory seizure was excessive. In contrast, consider *United States v. Sokolow*,[85] in which *D* claimed that the police were constitutionally required, if they could, to verify their suspicions that he was smuggling narcotics *before* they seized him. The Court quickly disposed of this argument by stating that Justice White's "statement" in *Royer* "was directed at the length of the investigative stop, not at whether the police had a less intrusive means to verify their suspicions before stopping [*D*]." According to *Sokolow*, "[t]he

---

[81] *See generally* Nadine Strossen, *The Fourth Amendment in the Balance: Accurately Setting the Scales Through the Least Intrusive Alternative Analysis*, 63 N.Y.U. L. Rev. 1173 (1988).

[82] 460 U.S. 491 (1983).

[83] Justice Brennan concurred in the judgment. He stated that a *Terry* seizure must be so short in duration that it would be "difficult to conceive of a less intrusive means that would be effective to accomplish the purpose of the stop."

[84] 462 U.S. 696 (1983).

[85] 490 U.S. 1 (1989).

reasonableness of the officer's decision to stop a suspect does not turn on the availability of less intrusive investigatory techniques."[86]

Even in length-of-detention cases, the Court has limited its use of the least-intrusive-means doctrine. In *United States v. Sharpe*,[87] D was detained for twenty minutes while the police sought to determine whether he was involved in transporting drugs in his pickup truck. The Court stated that in assessing whether this detention was too long to constitute a *Terry* stop, "[t]he question is not simply whether some other alternative was available, *but whether the police acted unreasonably in failing to recognize it or to pursue it.*" And, in answering the latter question, the Court warned reviewing courts "not [to] indulge in unrealistic second-guessing."

## § 18.05   Grounds for *"Terry* Stops"[88]

### [A]   Crime Prevention versus Crime Detection

*Terry* involved the brief seizure and limited search of a person suspected of imminent criminal activity. The brief seizure was reasonable in view of the government's interest in crime prevention. The Supreme Court unanimously held in *United State v. Hensley*[89] that a *Terry*-level seizure may also be reasonable in order to investigate a crime that has already occurred. However, a seizure that is reasonable in the crime-prevention context will not necessarily be permissible in the crime-investigation setting.

As the Court explained in *Hensley*, the factors that go into the *Terry* "reasonableness" balancing inquiry are not identical in the two contexts. The exigent circumstances that justify a brief detention when an officer reasonably suspects that serious crime is afoot may be missing in the crime-detection framework. Furthermore, in crime-detection cases, officers often can choose a time and place for the stop that is more convenient to the suspect than is possible when crime is afoot.

### [B]   Nature of the Crime

Most *Terry*-type seizures involve the detention of persons suspected of involvement in violent crimes. The principles of *Terry* extend, however, to the investigation of drug trafficking "or of any other serious crime."[90]

---

[86] *See also* Michigan v. Long, 463 U.S. 1032, 1052 (1983) (a *Terry*-type search of a car for weapons is valid even if the police could have "adopt[ed] alternative means to ensure their safety in order to avoid the intrusion involved in a *Terry* encounter.").

[87] 470 U.S. 675 (1985).

[88] *See generally* 3 LaFave, Note 1, *supra*, at § 9.4.

[89] 469 U.S. 221 (1985).

[90] Florida v. Royer, 460 U.S. 491, 499 (1983).

The Supreme Court has not determined whether or under what circumstances a *Terry*-level seizure is permitted for purposes of either crime prevention or detection, if the person is suspected of involvement in a very minor offense.[91]

### [C]  Fingerprinting

The Supreme Court considers fingerprinting a less serious intrusion on a person's security than other police practices. First, fingerprinting (unlike interrogations and some searches) does not probe a person's private life and thoughts. Second, the process is more reliable than lineups and confessions, and "is not subject to such abuses as the improper [suggestive] line-up and the 'third degree' [interrogation]."[92] Third, fingerprinting can be conducted at a time convenient to the suspect and need not be repeated.

In light of these differences, the transportation of a suspect to the police station for fingerprinting, if he is detained there only briefly, is permissible on the basis of probable cause or, the Court has hinted in dictum, "on less than probable cause" if it is "under judicial supervision."[93] The implication—it is only that—is that legislatures or courts may develop procedures for special "fingerprint search warrants," grounded on reasonable suspicion. Some courts have approved such warrants, even without legislation.[94]

Also, the Court has indicated that there is support in its prior cases for the view that a brief detention of a suspect "in the field" for fingerprinting at the scene is permissible if: (1) the belief that the suspect has committed a crime meets the reasonable suspicion standard; (2) there is a reasonable basis for believing that fingerprinting will establish or negate the suspect's connection with that crime; and (3) the fingerprinting is conducted "with dispatch."[95]

## § 18.06  Weapons Searches: Of Persons[96]

### [A]  Permissibility

Chief Justice Warren stated in *Terry* that a police officer, upon lawful seizure of a person, may pat down the individual for weapons if certain conditions are met. First, the officer must reasonably suspect that the person is "armed and presently dangerous." Second, the Court seemed to suggest

---

[91] The issue, at least for investigatory purposes, was explicitly left open by the Court in United States v. Hensley, 469 U.S. 221, 229 (1985).

[92] Davis v. Mississippi, 394 U.S. 721, 727 (1969).

[93] Hayes v Florida, 470 U.S. 811, 816–17 (1985).

[94] *E.g.*, In re Fingerprinting of M.B., 309 A.2d 3 (N.J. Super. Ct. App. Div. 1973).

[95] Hayes v. Florida, 470 U.S. at 817.

[96] *See generally* 4 LaFave, Note 1, *supra*, at § 9.5.

in its holding that the officer must use the least intrusive means to protect himself: he must investigate first, and only frisk the suspect if "nothing in the initial stages of the encounter serves to dispel his reasonable fear for his own or others' safety."[97]

In contrast, Justice Harlan argued in his concurrence that the right to conduct a weapons search of a detained suspect is immediate and automatic if the basis for the seizure is that the officer believes that violent crime is afoot, as in *Terry*. In other words, assuming that the officer was justified in seizing the suspect for investigation of a violent crime, the officer should not be required to jeopardize his safety by questioning the suspect before he conducts a weapons search.

The Supreme Court's treatment of the facts in *Adams v. Williams*[98] suggests that Justice Harlan's view is now accepted. In *Adams*, an officer received information that *D* was sitting in a parked car, carrying narcotics, with a handgun concealed at his waist. The officer confronted *D*, after which he seized the gun without asking *D* any questions that might have dispelled his concern. The Court upheld the conviction.

## [B]  Method

### [1]  Pat-Down (Frisk)

*Terry* did not mandate a particular weapons search procedure, although it approved the one conducted in that case. In *Terry*, *O* patted down the exterior of *D*'s clothing. Upon feeling a weapon, *O* searched *D*'s pocket and pulled out the weapon. In contrast, in *Sibron v. New York*,[99] a companion case to *Terry*, the Court disapproved a search in which the officer thrust his hand into the suspect's pocket without first frisking him.

Notwithstanding *Sibron*, a pat-down is not always a prerequisite to a valid weapons search. Rather obviously, if a suspect whom the officer has reason to believe is armed and dangerous suddenly moves his hand into a pocket or under a piece of clothing that might contain a weapon, the officer need not jeopardize himself by conducting a pat-down.[100]

The facts in *Adams v. Williams*[101] provide another example of a valid weapons search that was not preceded by a pat-down. In *Adams*, an officer who had been informed that *D* was in his parked car with a weapon concealed at his waist, asked *D* to open his car door; when *D* opened his

---

[97] *See* the text to Note 23, *supra*.

[98] 407 U.S. 143 (1972).

[99] 392 U.S. 40 (1968).

[100] 4 LaFave, Note 1, *supra*, at 273.

[101] 407 U.S. 143 (1972).

window instead, the officer reached into the car and, without frisking *D*, seized the gun from the suspect's waistband. The Court, without discussion of the procedure, approved the officer's conduct. Although an explanation by the Court would have been helpful, the officer's no-frisk approach can be justified on the ground that a pat-down in these circumstances would have been difficult, even dangerous. Because the officer reached only to the spot where he had been told that the gun was concealed, his actions were reasonable.

### [2] After the Pat-Down

If an officer feels no object during a pat-down, or he feels an object that does not appear to be a weapon, no further search is justifiable under the *Terry* principle, which is based exclusively on the concern for the officer's safety. If the initial pat-down—with no further touching—provides the officer with probable cause for believing that an object felt is contraband or other criminal evidence subject to seizure, he may pull out the object without a warrant, as part of the plain-touch doctrine.[102]

If the officer feels a hard object that he reasonably believes is a weapon, the officer may reach for the object. If the object he pulls out is a container, he may feel the container to see if it might contain a weapon inside. If his fears regarding the container are not reasonably dispelled by its size, weight, and feel, the officer may, at a minimum, retain possession of the container so as to separate the suspect from any weapon that might be inside. Probably, he may open the container and look inside, on the ground "that this is simply a continuation, in a sense, of the frisk of the person and thus may be carried out on the same terms."[103]

If the container pulled out by the officer could not reasonably contain a weapon, it may not be kept or searched under *Terry*. Of course, if something else in the encounter gives rise to probable cause to arrest, the suspect may be searched incident to arrest.

### § 18.07 Weapons Searches: Of Automobiles

People may lawfully be frisked under certain circumstances, but what about cars? The Supreme Court ruled in *Michigan v. Long*[104] that, in some circumstances, the police may conduct a weapons search—a "frisk,"[105] if

---

[102] Minnesota v. Dickerson, 508 U.S. 366 (1993). *See* § 15.05[B], *supra*.

[103] 4 LaFave, Note 1, *supra*, at 282.

[104] 463 U.S. 1032 (1983).

[105] *See* Maryland v. Buie, 494 U.S. 325, 332 (1990) ("In a sense, *Long* authorized a 'frisk' of an automobile for weapons.").

you will—of the passenger compartment of a lawfully stopped automobile.[106]

In *Long*, police officers in a rural region of Michigan, at night, observed D drive his car erratically, at an excessive rate of speed, and swerve into a ditch. The officers stopped to investigate. As they did, D got out of his car and, leaving the door open, met the police at the rear of the automobile. D appeared to be intoxicated.

The officers requested to see D's vehicle registration. After repeated requests, and no response, D began to walk towards the open door of the car. The officers followed him, and observed a hunting knife on the floor of the driver's side of the car. At that point, the officers frisked D, but they felt no weapon.

The officers then shone a light inside the car to look for other weapons. They noticed something, although they could not identify it, protruding from under the armrest on the front seat. One officer entered the car, lifted the armrest, and found an open pouch containing marijuana. D was arrested for possession of the contraband.

The Court upheld the search. It observed that investigative detentions of persons in cars "are especially fraught with danger to police officers," and that the passenger compartment of a car is within the immediate control of a suspect. Therefore, it reasoned, if a weapon is inside a car, it represents a danger to the police. Although this reasoning might suggest that the police may conduct a weapons search of the passenger compartment of any automobile they lawfully stop, the holding of *Long* is narrower than this. The Court stated that "the search of the passenger compartment of an automobile, limited to those areas in which a weapon may be placed or hidden, is permissible if the police officer possesses a reasonable belief . . . that the suspect is dangerous and the suspect may gain immediate control of weapons."

In *Long*, the Court noted specific, articulable facts that, in its view, justified the officers to enter the car to search for weapons. These facts included: (1) it was late at night; (2) the area was rural; (3) D appeared to be intoxicated; (4) the officers observed a hunting knife in the vehicle; and (5) D intended to re-enter the vehicle.

Should these factors add up to reasonable suspicion? The Court did not explain why the hour of the night was relevant, nor why the rural nature of the area was an aggravating, rather than an ordinary or even mitigating feature. As for the third fact, D was suspected of drunk driving, not of an

---

[106] *Contra, under the state constitution,* People v. Torres, 543 N.E.2d 61 (N.Y. 1989).

armed crime; as Justice Brennan pointed out in dissent, "a drunk driver is indeed dangerous while driving, but not while stopped on the roadside by the police."

The fact that a knife was observed in the automobile, the strongest point in favor of the search, does not demonstrate that $D$ was "presently dangerous," especially in light of the fact that the area in which the investigation occurred was one commonly frequented by lawful hunters. Finally, as for the fact that $D$ appeared to be re-entering the vehicle (very possibly in belated response to the police request for the car registration), the police could have ordered him to move away from the car, a less intrusive procedure than to search the entire passenger compartment of the automobile. [107]

## § 18.08  Protective Sweeps of Residences [108]

As explained by the Supreme Court in *Maryland v. Buie*, [109] a "protective sweep" of a residence "is a quick and limited search of a premises, incident to an arrest and conducted to protect the safety of police officers or others. It is narrowly confined to a cursory visual inspection of those places in which a person might be hiding."

In *Buie*, per Justice White, the Supreme Court ruled, as discussed elsewhere, [110] that as an incident to an arrest of an individual, the police may automatically—*i.e.*, without probable cause or reasonable suspicion— conduct a protective sweep of "spaces immediately adjoining the place of arrest." Moreover, beyond this limited area, the arresting officers may conduct a warrantless protective sweep of other parts of the residence if there exists reasonable suspicion "that the area [to be] swept harbor[s] an individual posing a danger to the officer or others."

In *Buie*, six or seven officers entered $D$'s house with a warrant to arrest him for a crime allegedly committed by $D$ and $X$. When they entered, they observed a basement; standing on the first floor, an officer ordered anyone in the basement to come out. Eventually, $D$ emerged and was arrested and handcuffed on the main floor. Thereafter, an officer entered the basement to see if anyone else was present. Although he found no one, he discovered evidence related to the crime in plain view, which he seized. The Court

---

[107] The Court pointed out that if $D$ had not been arrested, he would have returned to the car to leave the scene, and thus could have reached the knife and any other weapon in the car. However, if he were not under arrest and no longer in temporary custody, $D$ had little incentive to use the knife against the officers.

[108] *See generally* 3 LaFave, Note 1, *supra*, at § 6.4(c).

[109] 494 U.S. 325 (1990).

[110] See § 13.02[C][3], *supra*.

stated that the officer acted properly in entering the basement if there were facts that warranted him in suspecting that a person posing a danger to him or others was downstairs.[111]

In announcing the rule, the Supreme Court focused on the lessons to be learned from *Terry* and *Michigan v. Long*.[112] Justice White applied the reasonableness balancing test set out in *Terry*. In regard to the governmental interest in permitting the warrantless search, he observed that both *Terry* and *Long* justified weapons searches out of concern for the safety of police officers. Here, too, there was a concern for police safety, perhaps even graver than confronted the officers in *Terry* and *Long*: "unlike an encounter on the street or along a highway, an in-home arrest puts the officer at the disadvantage of being on his adversary's 'turf.' An ambush in a confined setting of unknown configuration is more to be feared than it is in open, more familiar surroundings."

In regard to individuals' privacy interests, the Court analogized protective sweeps to the limited intrusions allowed in *Terry* and *Long*. Although the Court conceded that a sweep of a home is not a *de minimis* intrusion, it is nonetheless a limited one, in that the sweep "may extend only to a cursory inspection of those spaces where a person may be found," and may "last[] no longer than is necessary to dispel the reasonable suspicion of danger and in any event no longer than it takes to complete the arrest and depart the premises."[113] According to the Court, the interest in the arresting officers' safety outweighs the intrusion that protective sweeps may entail.

## § 18.09 Temporary Seizures of Property

In *United States v. Place*,[114] federal officers had advance information that D would disembark from an airplane with luggage containing narcotics. When D arrived, the officers seized his luggage and, 90 minutes later,

---

[111] The Court remanded the case to the state court to determine whether the requisite reasonable suspicion existed. In a concurrence, Justice Stevens expressed doubt that the police could justify the protective sweep. He reasoned that the police may only conduct a sweep if it will *reduce* the risk of harm to themselves or others: "in short, the search must be protective." He described the officer's decision to enter the basement after D's arrest as "a surprising choice for an officer, worried about safety." On remand, however, the court found that the officers were justified in conducting the sweep. Buie v. State, 580 A.2d 167 (Md. 1990).

[112] 463 U.S. 1032 (1983). *See* § 18.07, *supra*.

[113] Nonetheless, it should be observed that the search is far more extensive than the one approved in *Terry* in that every room and hallway closet in the residence may be entered. In that sense, the Court has approved a *full* search of a residence on the basis of reasonable suspicion, rather than probable cause.

[114] 462 U.S. 696 (1983).

subjected it to a "non-search"[115] sniff by a trained narcotics detection dog. The dog's response confirmed the officers' suspicions, after which they applied for and received a warrant to search the suitcase.

The Supreme Court, per Justice Sandra O'Connor, ruled that police officers may, without a warrant, temporarily detain (seize) luggage on the basis of reasonable suspicion that it contains narcotics, in order to investigate the circumstances that aroused their suspicion. In short, *Terry* principles apply to seizures of property, and not simply to seizures of persons. However, the Court concluded that the hour-and-a-half detention in this case was excessive, and therefore disapproved the seizure here.

In reaching its conclusion, the Court applied the *Terry* reasonableness balancing test. It determined that the government's interest in seizing *D*'s personal property was substantial. Quoting *United States v. Mendenhall*,[116] the Court stated that "[t]he public has a compelling interest in detecting those who would traffic in deadly drugs for personal profit."

On the countervailing side, Justice O'Connor observed that "intrusion on possessory interests . . . can vary both in its nature and extent." She distinguished between a seizure of property "after the owner has relinquished control of the property to a third party or, as here, from the immediate custody and control of the owner." In the latter situation, the seizure not only intrudes upon a person's possessory interest in his property, but also on his "liberty interest in proceeding with his itinerary," since a person will ordinarily not feel free to leave an airport without his personal belongings. Consequently, the Court treated the seizure of the property in *Place* as if it included a seizure of *D* himself.

Under these circumstances, the Court concluded that the 90-minute detention was excessive. Justice O'Connor noted the importance of brevity in *Terry* cases, and the fact that the police did not diligently pursue their investigation. With their prior knowledge that *D* would be arriving with suspicious luggage, the Court felt that the officers should have brought the trained dog to the scene in advance of *D*'s arrival.

---

[115] *See* § 7.09, *supra.*

[116] 446 U.S. 544 (1980).

## CHAPTER 19

# MORE "REASONABLENESS" BALANCING: SEARCHES AND SEIZURES PRIMARILY CONDUCTED FOR NON-CRIMINAL LAW PURPOSES

## § 19.01 An Important Overview[1]

With one significant exception,[2] previous chapters focused on searches and seizures conducted by police officers in criminal investigations, *i.e.*, in pursuit of criminal evidence or a person suspected of a crime already committed, or as part of a police effort, as in *Terry v. Ohio*,[3] to investigate possible ongoing crime. In contrast, this chapter centers on searches and seizures, sometimes performed by police officers but often conducted by other public officers, that are *not* conducted (at least, primarily) in the enforcement of criminal laws.

As will be seen in later chapter sections, the line between, on the one hand, a criminal investigation and, on the other hand, searches and seizures designed primarily to serve non-criminal law enforcement goals, is thin and, quite arguably, arbitrary. Yet, it is a line of considerable constitutional significance.

On the "criminal investigatory" side of the line, the Supreme Court once declared that search warrants, supported by probable cause, were presumptively required. Although warrants today are the exception rather than the rule and, after *Terry*, "probable cause" is no longer the exclusive standard for determining the reasonableness of criminal investigatory searches and seizures, it remains the case that warrants are required in some realms (especially in regard to the home) and, as the Supreme Court recently put it, "[a] search or seizure is ordinarily unreasonable in the absence of

---

[1] *See generally* Stephen J. Schulhofer, *On the Fourth Amendment Rights of the Law-Abiding Public*, 1989 Sup. Ct. Rev. 87; William J. Stuntz, *Implicit Bargains, Government Power, and the Fourth Amendment*, 44 Stan. L. Rev. 553 (1992); Scott E. Sundby, *"Everyman"'s Fourth Amendment: Privacy or Mutual Trust Between Government and Citizen?*, 94 Colum. L. Rev. 1751 (1994).

[2] *See* chapter 16, *supra.*

[3] 392 U.S. 1 (1968); *see* § 18.02, *supra.*

individualized suspicion of wrongdoing."[4] But, on the other side of the criminal investigatory line, the Court has determined that individualized suspicion (and, of course, warrants) are "not an 'irreducible' component of reasonableness."[5]

The cases that fall on the non-criminal law enforcement side of the line are quite varied in nature. Some are labeled "administrative search" cases. Here, employees of administrative agencies (although, on occasion, police officers) inspect buildings or businesses to determine whether administrative code regulations have been violated. As the Court has put it, "[w]e have . . . allowed searches for certain administrative purposes without particularized suspicion of misconduct, provided that those searches are appropriately limited."[6] Second, the Court has upheld brief, warrantless, suspicionless seizures of motorists in certain circumstances, primarily at international borders and at traffic-safety and sobriety checkpoints.

Third, the Court has "upheld certain regimes of suspicionless [and warrantless] searches where the program was designed to serve 'special needs, beyond the normal need for law enforcement.' "[7] This "special needs" exception—one that can plausibly subsume the preceding two categories of cases—applies when special governmental needs "make the warrant and[/or] probable-cause requirement[s] impracticable."[8]

A remarkable irony is evident when one compares the law on the two sides of the criminal-investigatory line. On the non-criminal law enforcement side of the line, the Supreme Court has had the opportunity "to hear face-to-face, as Fourth Amendment claimants, those law-abiding citizens for whose ultimate benefits the constitutional restraints on public power were primarily intended."[9] And yet the Justices have on occasion required such law-abiding persons to open up their homes, businesses, papers, effects, and bodies to *greater* scrutiny than is compelled of criminal suspects.[10] As Professor Scott Sundby has observed, this is a matter of

---

[4] City of Indianapolis v. Edmond, 531 U.S. 32, 37 (2000).

[5] *Id.*

[6] *Id.*

[7] *Id.*

[8] Griffin v. Wisconsin, 483 U.S. 868, 872 (1987) (quoting New Jersey v. T.L.O., 469 U.S. 325, 351 (1985) (Blackmun, J., concurring in judgment)).

[9] Schulhofer, Note 1, *supra,* at 88.

[10] *Id.* at 89. Early on, the Court noted that "[i]t is surely anomalous to say that the individual and his private property are fully protected by the Fourth Amendment only when the individual is suspected of criminal behavior." Camara v. Municipal Court, 387 U.S. 523, 530 (1967).

considerable concern, because of the lesson being taught by some of these Fourth Amendment cases:

> The lesson is that, despite responsible individual behavior, the government has the power to exercise its judgment and discard trust of the individual in the name of a perceived greater good. It is this discarding of trust, however, that in the long run jeopardizes the greater good by upsetting the reciprocal government-citizen trust that forms the foundation of a legitimate government.[11]

However, the Supreme Court has demonstrated recent concern that suspicionless searches and seizures—especially in the roadblock and "special needs" fields—not expand too far, lest we reach the point at which "the Fourth Amendment would do little to prevent such intrusions from becoming a routine part of American life."[12] Recent Court opinions[13] leave the law muddier than before, and call into question the viability of some earlier more permissive case law. Although no sure-fire rule exists, the Court now suggests that ordinary Fourth Amendment principles—most especially the requirement of individualized suspicion of wrongdoing—apply if "the immediate objective" of a contested search or seizure is "to generate evidence *for law enforcement purposes*," even if the "ultimate goal" for using the evidence is to further some non-criminal-investigatory goal.[14]

## § 19.02　Administrative Searches[15]

Modern "administrative search" law began in 1967 with companion cases *Camara v. Municipal Court*[16] and *See v. City of Seattle*.[17] *Camara* involved the attempt of an employee of the San Francisco Department of Public Health to enter *D*'s apartment without a warrant or consent in order to conduct a routine inspection of the residence for possible violations of the city's housing code. *See* involved a fire department employee's warrantless entry of a warehouse pursuant to a city ordinance that authorized entry into

---

[11] Sundby, Note 1, *supra*, at 1812.

[12] City of Indianapolis v. Edmond, 531 U.S. at 42.

[13] In particular, City of Indianapolis v. Edmond, 531 U.S. 32 (2000) (*see* § 19.04[C], *infra*) and Ferguson v. City of Charleston, 121 S. Ct. 1281 (2001) (*see* § 19.05[C][3], *infra*).

[14] Ferguson v. City of Charleston, 121 S. Ct. at 1291.

[15] *See generally* 4 Wayne R. LaFave, Search and Seizure § 10.1–.02 (3d ed. 1996); Wayne R. LaFave, *Administrative Searches and the Fourth Amendment: The Camara and See Cases*, 1967 Sup. Ct. Rev. 1; Scott E. Sundby, *A Return to Fourth Amendment Basics: Undoing the Mischief of Camara and Terry*, 72 Minn. L. Rev. 383 (1988).

[16] 387 U.S. 523 (1967).

[17] 387 U.S. 541 (1967).

non-dwellings in order to inspect for fire code violations. In neither *Camara* nor *See* did the public employee who entered the building without a warrant possess probable cause to believe that evidence of a crime—or even of code violations—would be found in the inspected area.

*Camara* and *See* are important cases for two reasons. First, as discussed elsewhere in this text,[18] the Court in *Camara* developed an administrative search version of "probable cause" that does not require individualized suspicion of wrongdoing, and which requires only that an administrative search be "reasonable." To determine "reasonableness," *Camara* implemented a balancing test, later used in criminal investigations,[19] in which "the need to search [is weighed] against the invasion which the search entails."

Second, *Camara* and *See* considered the question of whether the Fourth Amendment warrant requirement applies to health and safety code inspections of homes and commercial buildings. The Court held in both cases that, except in the case of emergency or consent, the right of entry to conduct an administrative inspection requires a warrant, albeit one based on administrative, not ordinary, probable cause. The Court stated that "[i]t nowhere has been urged that fire, health and housing code inspection programs could not achieve their goals within the confines of a reasonable search warrant requirement."

Post-*See* cases demonstrate that under some circumstances, warrantless, non-exigent, nonconsensual administrative inspections of commercial premises *are* constitutional. As explained by the Court in *New York v. Burger*,[20] a "closely regulated" business[21] may be inspected without a warrant if three conditions are met. First, the administrative regulatory scheme must advance a "substantial interest," such as to protect the health and safety of workers.[22]

Second, warrantless inspections must be necessary to further the regulatory scheme. This element is met if there is a serious possibility that a

---

[18] *See* § 9.06, *supra.*

[19] Terry v. Ohio, 392 U.S. 1 (1968). *See* chapter 18, *supra.*

[20] 482 U.S. 691 (1987).

[21] A business is "closely regulated" if there is "a long tradition of close government supervision" of the business, Marshall v. Barlow's, Inc., 436 U.S. 307 (1978) or, in the case of new and emerging industries, if there is a "pervasiveness and regularity" of regulation. Donovan v. Dewey, 452 U.S. 594 (1981). Examples of "closely regulated businesses" are: liquor dealers, Colonnade Catering Corp. v. United States, 397 U.S. 72 (1970); gun dealers, United States v. Biswell, 406 U.S. 311 (1972); mining companies, Donovan v. Dewey, *supra*; and automobile junkyards, New York v. Burger, 482 U.S. 691 (1987).

[22] Donovan v. Dewey, 452 U.S. 594 (1981) (mine workers).

routine warrant requirement would allow the subjects of the regulations to conceal their violations of the rules, and thereby frustrate the administrative system.

Third, the ordinance or statute that permits warrantless inspections must, by its terms, provide an adequate substitute for the warrant, such as rules that limit the discretion of the inspectors, regarding the time, place, and scope of the search.

The line between administrative inspections and traditional criminal searches can be thin, as is demonstrated by the facts and the Court's treatment of them, in *Burger*. In that case, police officers—not employees of an administrative agency—entered *D*'s automobile junkyard, a closely regulated business, without a warrant or probable cause of penal wrongdoing. Pursuant to a statute that authorized them to do so, they requested to see *D*'s business license and "police book," *i.e.*, a record of automobiles and parts on the premises. *D* conceded that he had neither document, whereupon the officers searched the junkyard, found evidence of stolen vehicle parts, and arrested him for possession of stolen property.

The Court upheld the search.[23] It did not consider it fatal to the scheme that police officers, rather than administrative inspectors, conducted the search. The Justices observed that many communities lack the resources to hire inspectors to enforce non-penal regulations.

More significantly, the Court considered it irrelevant to the Fourth Amendment aspects of the case that the regulations had the same ultimate purpose as criminal larceny laws, namely, to deter car thefts. The saving feature of the regulations was that they had "different subsidiary purposes and prescribe[d] different methods of addressing the problems." In this case, the Court concluded, the regulations established the conditions under which vehicle-dismantling businesses could be operated, including the institution of a requirement that the businesses be licensed and maintain certain records.

In regard to the line-drawing problem, notice that *Burger* is troubling because *D* admitted to the police officers when they arrived that he was in violation of the regulations. Therefore, as soon as he made that admission, the ensuing contested search took on the obvious cast of a police effort to uncover evidence of criminal activity. But, the Court did not focus on the motives of the specific officers in this case, but rather on the fact that the administrative regulations were not "designed to gather evidence to enable convictions under the penal laws." As the Court has more recently

---

**23** *Contra*, People v. Scott, 593 N.E.2d 1328 (N.Y. 1992) (holding that the regulatory scheme involved in *Burger* violated the state constitution).

explained *Burger*, the discovery of evidence of criminal wrongdoing there was "merely incidental to the purposes of the administrative search."[24]

## § 19.03 International Border Searches and Seizures[25]

### [A] At the Border

#### [1] Routine Searches and Seizures

The Supreme Court ruled in *United States v. Ramsey*[26] what lower courts had long ago assumed, namely, that people may be stopped (seized) at the international border or its "functional equivalent" (*e.g.*, at an airport where an international flight arrives), and they and their belongings may be searched, without a warrant and in the absence of individualized suspicion of wrongdoing, "pursuant to the long-standing right of the sovereign to protect itself" from the entry of persons or objects dangerous to the nation. In short, such warrantless, suspicionless searches and seizures are "reasonable simply by virtue of the fact that they occur at the border."

Although *Ramsey* was not written in such terms, the Court could easily have placed its ruling under the general "special needs" rubric discussed later in this chapter—a special need, beyond traditional criminal law enforcement, that makes brief seizures and searches necessary, and which interest cannot realistically be achieved if the warrant and probable-cause requirements are enforced. Therefore, brief suspicionless border seizures and searches are reasonable.

#### [2] Non-Routine Searches and Seizures

A person lawfully stopped at the border may be detained further, beyond the scope of a routine customs search, if the agents have reasonable suspicion of criminal activity. For example, in *United States v. Montoya de Hernandez*,[27] in an opinion described by one scholar as "at best, a most distressing one,"[28] the Court approved a 16-hour detention of *D*, a woman who officers reasonably suspected of having swallowed balloons containing heroin in order to avoid detection. After *D* refused to undergo an x-ray (she claimed she was pregnant, although in fact she was not), she was compelled to remain incommunicado in a small room furnished only with hard chairs and a table, while the authorities waited for her to defecate. The Court concluded that the seizure was reasonable, although it conceded that *D*

---

[24] Ferguson v. City of Charleston. 121 S. Ct. 1281, 1291 n. 21 (2001).

[25] *See generally* 4 LaFave, Note 15, *supra*, at § 10.05.

[26] 431 U.S. 606 (1977).

[27] 473 U.S. 531 (1985).

[28] 4 LaFave, Note 15, *supra*, at 540.

underwent a "long, uncomfortable, indeed humiliating" detention. It found that *D*'s interest in personal freedom was outweighed by the substantial national interest in preventing the importation of illegal drugs.

### [B] Near the Border

#### [1] In General

Border officers frequently stop cars near, but not at the functional equivalent of, the Canadian and (far more often) Mexican borders, in order to question occupants regarding their citizenship, and/or to search the vehicles for contraband or aliens being smuggled into the country. In such circumstances, the border agents do not know for a fact that occupants of the car came across the border. The reasonableness of these seizures and searches depends in part on whether they take place at a fixed checkpoint or as the result of a so-called "roving" border patrol.

#### [2] Roving Border Patrols

Roving border patrols present significant Fourth Amendment concerns. First, the patrols occur without notice, often at night on seldom-traveled roads, and their approach is apt to alarm motorists. Therefore, the subjective intrusion, measured by the surprise and alarm of lawful travelers, is significant. Second, roving border patrol agents have considerable discretion regarding whom to stop. Such unbridled discretion can result in discriminatory enforcement.

As a consequence of these concerns, the Supreme Court has applied fairly traditional Fourth Amendment standards to searches and seizures conducted by roving border patrol agents. In *Almeida-Sanchez v. United States*,[29] *D*'s car was stopped and searched approximately 25 air miles from the Mexican border. Marijuana was found inside the car. The patrol officers had no warrant and, concededly, no probable cause to conduct the search. In a 5-4 opinion written by Justice Potter Stewart, the Supreme Court held that the search violated the Fourth Amendment according to ordinary car search principles.[30] The majority rejected the argument that the search was reasonable as a routine administrative search,[31] because the search here occurred solely at the "discretion of the official in the field," and not as the result of specified regulations.

The Court also applied traditional Fourth Amendment principles in *United States v. Brignoni-Ponce*,[32] a case in which roving border patrol

---

[29] 413 U.S. 266 (1973).

[30] *See* chapter 14, *supra.*

[31] *See* § 19.02, *supra.*

[32] 422 U.S. 873 (1975).

agents briefly stopped a vehicle to question the occupants solely on the ground that they appeared to be of Mexican ancestry. The Court held that roving agents may not detain a person in a vehicle even briefly for questioning in the absence of reasonable suspicion of illegal presence in the country. The Court noted some factors that may justify a brief seizure: information about recent illegal border crossings in the area; furtive behavior by the occupants of the vehicle; and evidence that the car has an "extraordinary number" of passengers. Reasonable suspicion may not be based, however, exclusively on the fact that occupants of the vehicle appear to be of foreign ancestry.

### [3] Fixed Interior Checkpoints

Fixed interior checkpoints do not present the same Fourth Amendment concerns set out above. In this realm, therefore, the Supreme Court determined in *United States v. Martinez-Fuerte*[33] that vehicle occupants may be stopped at fixed checkpoints, and briefly detained for questioning, *without* individualized suspicion of wrongdoing.

The Court distinguished fixed checkpoints from roving border patrols on two grounds. First, the subjective intrusion on the security of lawful travelers "is appreciably less in the case of a [fixed] checkpoint stop." In the latter circumstance, "the motorist can see that other vehicles are being stopped, he can see visible signs of the officers' authority, and he is much less likely to be frightened or annoyed by the intrusion." Second, fixed checkpoints involve less discretionary enforcement activity than roving patrols. The location of the fixed checkpoint is not determined by the officers, and they may only stop cars that pass through it.

In these circumstances, the Court balanced the government's interest in stopping cars near the border against the car occupants' interests in privacy and free locomotion. It determined that the objective intrusion was minimal, in that travelers were stopped only momentarily, and the subjective intrusion was less than in the case of roving border patrols. Balanced against these minimal intrusions was the "substantiality of the public interest" in preventing the entry of illegal aliens. Furthermore, evidence was presented that a requirement that detentions be based on reasonable suspicion was impractical, and would "eliminate any deterrent to the conduct of well-disguised smuggling operations."

The holding in *Martinez-Fuerte* is expressly limited "to the type of stops described in [the] opinion." That is, any further detention beyond that which is necessary to conduct brief questioning regarding citizenship "must be based on consent or probable cause."[34]

---

[33] 428 U.S. 543 (1976).

[34] *See* United States v. Ortiz, 422 U.S. 891 (1975).

## § 19.04   Vehicle-Use Searches and Seizures [35]

### [A]   License and Vehicle Registration Inspections

Automobiles have long been treated differently—and, from a Fourth Amendment, less protectively—than homes and, for that matter, many other forms of personal property. The Supreme Court has stated that motorists have a lesser expectation of privacy in their automobiles, in part because motor vehicles are the subject of extensive regulation. [36] Every state, of course, requires vehicles to be registered and their operators to be licensed. Moreover, each state and most local communities have regulations regarding the use and maintenance of automobiles.

Police officers frequently stop motorists on the road to issue traffic citations, presumably based on probable cause. But the Court has had to confront more troubling Fourth Amendment issues when motorists are stopped without probable cause *or even reasonable suspicion* of criminal wrongdoing. Relatively early on, the Court considered the constitutionality of random driver's license and vehicle registration checks. Its first step was a tentative one: the Court ruled *against* random stops, but dictum invited their use under certain conditions.

In *Delaware v. Prouse*, [37] an officer conducting a random driver's license and registration check, stopped a vehicle driven by *D*. After the stop, the officer observed marijuana in plain view inside the vehicle. The Supreme Court held that the marijuana was discovered in violation of the Fourth Amendment, on the ground that the officer did not have a right to order the car to pull over as part of a license/registration inspection. It reached this conclusion by applying the reasonableness balancing standard: by balancing the intrusion on the driver's interests "against the promotion of legitimate governmental interests."

In the latter regard, the Court agreed "that the States have a vital interest in ensuring that only those qualified to do so are permitted to operate motor vehicles, that these vehicles are fit for safe operation, and hence that

---

[35] *See generally* 4 LaFave, Note 15, *supra*, at § 10.8; James C. English, Comment, *Sobriety Checkpoints Under State Constitutions: What Has Happened to Sitz?*, 59 U. Pitt. L. Rev. 453 (1998); James B. Jacobs & Nadine Strossen, *Mass Investigations Without Individualized Suspicion: A Constitutional and Policy Critique of Drunk Driving Roadblocks*, 18 U.C. Davis L. Rev. 595 (1985); Wayne R. LaFave, *Controlling Discretion by Administrative Regulations: The Use, Misuse, and Nonuse of Police Rules and Policies in Fourth Amendment Adjudication*, 89 Mich. L. Rev. 442 (1990); Nadine Strossen, *Michigan Department of State Police v. Sitz: A Roadblock to Meaningful Enforcement of Constitutional Rights*, 42 Hastings L.J. 285 (1991).

[36] *See* § 14.05, *supra*.

[37] 440 U.S. 648 (1979).

licensing, registration, and vehicle inspection requirements are being observed."[38] On the other side of the scale, one might have assumed that the Court would consider the intrusion on the driver's interest in free locomotion relatively minor in comparison to the "vital" state interest it set out. But, what troubled the Court was, first, that the officer "was not acting pursuant to any standards, guidelines, or procedures pertaining to document spot checks, promulgated by either his department or [the state]." Thus, the risk of arbitrary and discriminatory enforcement was great.

Second, the Court seemed to question the wisdom of random stops. "Absent some empirical data to the contrary," the Court stated, "it must be assumed that finding an unlicensed driver among those who commit traffic violations [for which there is, therefore, probable cause to make the stop] is a much more likely event than finding an unlicensed driver by choosing randomly from the entire universe of drivers." The Court assumed in the absence of such data, that the "contribution to highway safety made by discretionary stops selected from among drivers generally will . . . be marginal at best." In disapproving of the procedure in this case, the Court announced that:

> except in those situations in which there is at least articulable and reasonable suspicion that a motorist is unlicensed or that an automobile is not registered, or that either the vehicle or an occupant is otherwise subject to seizure for violation of law, stopping an automobile and detaining the driver in order to check his driver's license and the registration of the automobile are unreasonable under the Fourth Amendment.

But, the Court did not rule out the possibility that suspicionless license/registration inspections would be upheld under different circumstances. In critical dictum, it stated that "[t]his holding does not preclude [a state] . . . from developing methods for spot checks that involve less intrusion or that do not involve the unconstrained exercise of discretion." The implication of *Prouse* is that routine checks *are* permissible if safeguards are devised to assure that "persons in automobiles on public roadways [do] not for that reason alone have their travel and privacy interfered with at the unbridled discretion of police officers." According to *Prouse*, "[q]uestioning of all oncoming traffic at roadblock-type stops is one possible alternative."

---

[38] The State suggested two other interests in conducting the stops: apprehension of stolen cars and identification of drivers under the influence of alcohol or narcotics. The Court responded in footnote: "[t]he latter interest is subsumed by the interest in roadway safety, as may be the former interest to some extent. The remaining governmental interest in controlling automobile thefts is not distinguishable from the general interest in crime control."

## [B]  Sobriety Checkpoints

The Supreme Court's next venture in the vehicle-use realm involved the constitutionality of highway sobriety checkpoints, at which the police randomly (without individualized suspicion) stop motorists to check drivers for evidence of intoxication. Law enforcement officials were concerned at one time that the Court might disapprove of suspicionless sobriety checkpoints. This concern was enhanced by the Court's rulings in three Court cases—*United States v. Brignoni-Ponce*,[39] *Brown v. Texas*,[40] and *Delaware v. Prouse*[41] —in which the Justices invalidated seizures of persons in the absence of individualized suspicion of wrongdoing.

Nonetheless, the Supreme Court upheld a highway sobriety checkpoint in *Michigan Department of State Police v. Sitz*.[42] In *Sitz*, Michigan state police devised guidelines for conducting sobriety checkpoints. In the only implementation of the state's procedures, 126 vehicles were stopped, and the drivers were briefly examined for signs of intoxication. On average,

---

[39] 422 U.S. 873 (1975) (disapproving of roving border patrol stops of vehicles in the absence of reasonable suspicion). *See* § 19.03[B][2], *supra*.

[40] 443 U.S. 47 (1979). In *Brown*, police officers in a patrol car observed *D* and *X* in an alley, walking in opposite directions. The officers believed that the two had been together or were about to meet when their police vehicle appeared. The officers did not detain *X*, but they stopped *D* and requested identification because he "looked suspicious" and had not been seen in the area before. The question on appeal was "whether [*D*] was validly convicted for refusing to comply with a policeman's demand that he identify himself," pursuant to a state criminal law making it an offense to refuse to provide identification to the police on request.

The Court held that application of the statute in the instant case violated *D*'s Fourth Amendment rights. Summarizing prior case law, including Terry v. Ohio, 392 U.S. 1 (1968), Chief Justice Warren Burger described a three-pronged test for determining whether a brief seizure of a person is reasonable: "Consideration of the constitutionality of such seizures involves a weighing of [1] the gravity of the public concerns served by the seizure, [2] the degree to which the seizure advances the public interest, and [3] the severity of the interference with individual liberty."

The Chief Justice stated that a "central concern in balancing these competing considerations" is "to assure that an individual's reasonable expectation of privacy is not subject to arbitrary invasions solely at the unfettered discretion of officers in the field." In order to prevent abuses of discretion, the Court stated that a seizure of a person must be based on reasonable suspicion or "be carried out pursuant to a plan embodying explicit, neutral limitations on the conduct of individual officers."

[41] 440 U.S. 648 (1979). *See* § 19.04[A], *supra*.

[42] 496 U.S. 444 (1990); *contra, under the state constitution*, Sitz v. Department of State Police, 506 N.W.2d 209 (Mich. 1993); Ascher v. Commissioner of Public Safety, 519 N.W.2d 183 (Minn. 1994); State v. Sims, 808 P.2d 141 (Utah Ct. App. 1991) (the police may not conduct a suspicionless highway roadblock unless and until the state legislature authorizes the practice).

each detention took 25 seconds. Two drivers who appeared to be intoxicated were required to move out of the traffic flow, to another point where a second officer could check their licenses and conduct sobriety tests. One of these drivers was arrested. Another motorist, who attempted to break through the checkpoint, was also arrested.

The state courts ruled that the checkpoint was unconstitutional. Applying the three-pronged test set out in *Brown v. Texas*,[43] the lower court held that, although the state's interest in curbing drunken driving was "grave and legitimate" (the first *Brown* prong), the checkpoint program was ineffective and, therefore, did not significantly advance the public interest (the second prong). Also, the lower court determined that the overall intrusion on drivers' liberty (the third factor) was considerable: the objective intrusion (a 25-second delay) was minimal, but the subjective intrusion was substantial, because the checkpoints generated fear and surprise among motorists in much the same way that roving border patrols were condemned by the Supreme Court in *Brignoni-Ponce*.

The Supreme Court disagreed with this analysis. In an opinion written by Chief Justice Rehnquist, the Court held that the sobriety checkpoint did not violate the Fourth Amendment in so far as it pertained to the initial stop and associated preliminary questioning and observation of each motorist. The Court did not address the legitimacy of the detention of motorists for more extensive field sobriety tests, which it stated "may require satisfaction of an individualized suspicion standard."

The initial seizures, the Court determined, were reasonable. Applying a balancing test, the Chief Justice not surprisingly stated that "[n]o one can seriously dispute the magnitude of the drunken driving problem or the States' interest in eradicating it." On the other scale, the Court described the intrusion on motorists' security as "slight." Unlike the state courts that equated the checkpoints to roving border patrols, the majority analogized the sobriety roadblock to a fixed interior border checkpoint set up to detect illegal aliens, a procedure previously approved by the Supreme Court in *United States v. Martinez-Fuerte*.[44] The *Sitz* Court saw "virtually no difference between the levels of intrusion on law-abiding motorists from the brief stops necessary to the effectuation of these two types of checkpoints . . . ."

Perhaps the most significant aspect of *Sitz* is the fact that the majority discounted the state court's finding that the checkpoint was an ineffective

---

[43] *See* Note 40, *supra*.

[44] 428 U.S. 543 (1976) (holding that a brief detention of a driver at a permanent interior checkpoint is lawful, even in the absence of individualized suspicion of criminal activity, in order to combat the entry of illegal aliens into the country). *See* § 19.03[B][3], *supra*.

way to combat drunken driving and, therefore, did not satisfy the *Brown* prong that required courts to weigh "the degree to which the seizure advances the public interest." Isn't it more effective, for example, to patrol the roads for observable evidence of intoxicated driving than to set up checkpoints? The Chief Justice stated, in critical language, that the *Brown* test "was not meant to transfer from politically accountable officials to the courts the decision as to which among reasonable alternative law enforcement techniques should be employed to deal with a serious public danger."

But, didn't *Prouse* weigh the degree to which the seizure in that case advanced the public interest? It did, but *Sitz* distinguished *Prouse* on the ground that the latter case involved a "complete absence of empirical data," whereas the state here provided data and expert testimony[45] regarding the effect of the checkpoints. This evidence satisfied the Court that a sobriety roadblock is "among reasonable alternative law enforcement techniques" that may be employed to combat drunken driving. Having overcome that hurdle, courts are required by *Sitz* to leave the matter of *comparative* efficacy to "politically accountable officials."

In dissent, Justice Stevens, joined by Justices Brennan and Marshall, asserted that:

> [t]he Court overvalues the law enforcement interest in using sobriety checkpoints, undervalues the citizen's interest in freedom from random, unannounced investigatory seizures, and mistakenly assumes that there is "virtually no difference" between a routine stop at a permanent, fixed checkpoint and a surprise stop at a sobriety checkpoint.

Justice Stevens stated that the element of surprise, and thus the subjective intrusion on the security of motorists, is the "most obvious distinction" between a sobriety roadblock and the suspicionless interior-border stops approved in *Martinez-Fuerte*. In the latter case, the checkpoint site was known to all drivers because of its permanent nature, whereas the procedures implemented in Michigan called for roving checkpoints. Furthermore, in *Martinez-Fuerte*, many of the stops occurred during the daytime; in contrast, sobriety checkpoints are usually set up at nighttime, when fear is more easily generated.

The dissent also criticized the majority's treatment of the public interest factor. Justice Stevens—unwilling to transfer oversight of the comparative efficacy issue to "politically accountable officials"—accused the majority of "tampering with the scales of justice" by "plac[ing] a heavy thumb on the law enforcement interest by looking only at gross receipts instead of

---

[45] An expert testified that checkpoints in other states had resulted in approximately a 1% arrest rate among persons stopped.

net benefits." He stated that "there is absolutely no evidence" that the arrest rate for intoxication at the checkpoint "represents an increase over the number of arrests that would have been made by using the same law enforcement resources in conventional patrols."

### [C] Drug Interdiction Checkpoints

As discussed at the beginning of this chapter, the Supreme Court has sought to draw a Fourth Amendment distinction between searches and seizures conducted in criminal investigations and ones that are performed for non-criminal law purposes. But, this line is a hard one to draw, as the *Michigan Department of State Police v. Sitz*[46] sobriety-checkpoint case demonstrates: although the purpose of such checkpoints is to enhance roadway safety, police officers are the agents for promoting that safety, *and they do so by stopping and arresting intoxicated drivers*. So, sobriety checkpoints have a criminal law enforcement aspect to them.

The importance of this distinction (and the difficulty in drawing it) came to the forefront in *City of Indianapolis v. Edmond*,[47] in which the Court considered the constitutionality of a narcotics interdiction checkpoint. The City of Indianapolis conducted six roadblocks during a four-month period in order to discover illegal drugs. During this time, pursuant to a written plan, more than 1000 vehicles were stopped on the highway, mostly in the daytime, for two to three minutes each. Each driver was informed that she was being stopped at a drug checkpoint and was asked to produce a license and registration. A police officer also looked for signs of impairment. Meanwhile, a narcotics-detection dog walked around the outside of each vehicle and conducted a "non-search"[48] sniff for contraband. The "hit rate" of the program—arrests for drug and non-drug related offenses—was nine percent, of which more than half of the arrests were for drug-related crimes.

Despite the success of the checkpoint and the vital societal interest in combating drug use, the Supreme Court ruled, 6-3, that the drug interdiction checkpoint violated the Fourth Amendment. It drew a line between the border-stop[49] and sobriety-checkpoint cases—cases "designed primarily to serve purposes closely related to the problems of policing the border or the necessity of ensuring roadway safety"—and the case at hand, namely, a roadblock "whose primary purpose was to detect evidence of ordinary criminal wrongdoing."

---

[46] 496 U.S. 444 (1990). *See* § 19.04[B], *supra*.

[47] 531 U.S. 32 (2000).

[48] *See* § 7.09, *supra*.

[49] *See* § 19.03, *supra*.

The City sought to bring the checkpoint under the border-stop and sobriety-checkpoint umbrella by arguing that those "checkpoints . . . had the same ultimate purpose of arresting those suspected of committing crimes." The *Edmond* Court, per Justice O'Connor, would have none of this. In an effort to draw some firmer lines, O'Connor wrote:

> If we were to rest the case at this high level of generality, there would be little check on the ability of the authorities to construct roadblocks for almost any conceivable law enforcement purpose. Without drawing the line at roadblocks designed primarily to serve the general interest in crime control, the Fourth Amendment would do little to prevent such intrusions from becoming a routine part of American life.

Although the social harm resulting from drugs is "of the first magnitude," the Court explained that the "gravity of the threat alone cannot be dispositive of questions concerning what means law enforcement officers may employ to pursue a given purpose. . . . We are particularly reluctant to recognize exceptions to the general rule of individualized suspicion where governmental authorities primarily pursue their general crime control ends." Justice O'Connor stated: "[w]hen law enforcement authorities pursue primarily general crime control purposes at checkpoints . . ., stops can only be justified by some quantum of individualized suspicion."[50]

The impact of *Edmond* is this: when the police seek to defend a checkpoint program that authorizes suspicionless seizures of individuals, courts are required to determine the "primary purpose" of the police plan—is it, for example, to police the border, ensure roadway safety, or is "just" to conduct non-specific crime control?—because that test will determine whether individualized suspicion is required. But, didn't the Court suggest in *Whren v. United States*[51] that courts are not supposed to inquire into the motivations of police officers? *Edmond* explained that *Whren* stands for the principle that an inquiry into an officer's subjective motivations has no place in *probable cause* analysis; in contrast, "programmatic purposes"—but not the motivations of the individual officers acting at the scene—"may be relevant to the validity of Fourth Amendment

---

[50] The emphasis here is on "*general* crime control purposes": the Court stated in dictum that "[o]f course, there are circumstances that may justify a law enforcement checkpoint where the primary purpose would otherwise, but for some emergency, relate to ordinary criminal control." According to the Court, "the Fourth Amendment would almost certainly permit an appropriately tailored roadblock set up to thwart an imminent terrorist attack or to catch a dangerous criminal who is likely to flee by way of a particular route." For a pre-*Edmond* analysis of this issue, *see generally* John F. Decker, *Emergency Circumstances, Police Responses, and Fourth Amendment Restrictions*, 89 J. Crim. L. & Criminology 433 (1999).

[51] 517 U.S. 806 (1996). *See* § 9.02[F], *supra*.

intrusions undertaken pursuant to a general scheme without individualized suspicion."

Notice the difficulty *Edmond* presents: the officers here asked to see the licenses and registration materials of motorists, a procedure potentially permitted under *Delaware v. Prouse*, and they checked for intoxication, a procedure approved by the Court in *Sitz*. Therefore, what if the City had *not* identified the process as a "drug interdiction checkpoint," as it did, but had characterized it as a sobriety checkpoint during which the dog sniffed for drugs as well? Would *that* have been allowed?

The Court expressly left open the issue of "whether the State may establish a checkpoint program with the primary purpose of checking licenses or driver sobriety and a secondary purpose of interdicting narcotics." If the Court eventually answers this question in the affirmative, the potentially exceedingly thin line between "primary" and "secondary" purposes will become critical to Fourth Amendment analysis and the long-term significance of *Edmond*.[52] But, one may then ask, as the dissenters essentially did in *Edmond*, why this distinction should matter, as long as *one* of its purposes meets Fourth Amendment standards.

## § 19.05 "Special Needs" Searches and Seizures[53]

### [A] In General

An increasingly significant exception to the Fourth Amendment principle that searches and seizures are unreasonable if they are not authorized by a warrant and/or supported by probable cause is the so-called "special needs" (or "special governmental needs") doctrine. As explained in the next subsection, this exception began slowly—indeed, it was not initially characterized as a "special needs" rule—but now is said to apply when "special needs, beyond the normal need for law enforcement, make the warrant and[/or] probable-cause requirement[s] impracticable."[54] Although

---

[52] Since *Edmond* was decided, the Court has stated that "[i]n looking to the programmatic purpose, we consider all the available evidence in order to determine the relevant primary purpose." Ferguson v. City of Charleston, 121 S. Ct. 1281, 1290 (2001). Thus, the police cannot simply change the label on a checkpoint to escape the strictures of the Fourth Amendment.

[53] *See generally* Jennifer Y. Buffaloe, Note, *"Special Needs" and the Fourth Amendment: An Exception Poised to Swallow the Warrant Preference Rule*, 32 Harv. C.R.-C.L. L. Rev. 529 (1997); Robert D. Dodson, *Ten Years of Randomized Jurisprudence: Amending the Special Needs Doctrine*, 51 S.C. L. Rev. 258 (2000); Gerald S. Reamey, *When "Special Needs" Meet Probable Cause: Denying the Devil Benefit of Law*, 19 Hastings Const. L.Q. 295 (1992); Schulhofer, Note 1, *supra*; Stuntz, Note 1, *supra*; Sundby, Note 1, *supra*.

[54] Griffin v. Wisconsin, 483 U.S. 868, 872 (1987) (quoting New Jersey v. T.L.O., 469 U.S. 325, 351 (1985) (Blackmun, J., concurring in judgment)).

the early cases only dispensed with the warrant and/or probable-cause provisions of the Fourth Amendment, more recent cases have authorized *suspicionless* searches.

Professor William Stuntz has observed that "little or no effort has been made to explain what these 'special needs' are; the term turns out to be no more than a label that indicates when a lax standard will apply."[55] Essentially, when the Court determines that "special needs" exist, it evaluates the governmental activity—the special need—by the "reasonableness" balancing standard first invoked by Supreme Court in *Camara v. Municipal Court.*[56] Nearly always, the government interest "trumps" the requirements of a warrant and/or probable cause (or reasonable suspicion).[57]

Two initial points are worth making. First, although the Supreme Court has treated the administrative-search, border-search, and checkpoint cases (discussed in the immediately preceding sections of this chapter) separately from the "special need" cases,[58] there is little reason for this distinction. Those cases involved specific governmental interests—special needs, if you will—beyond ordinary criminal investigations. Moreover, the process of determining the legitimacy of the governmental action was the same: application of the "reasonableness" balancing standard.

Second, the "special needs" exception does not apply, the Court has recently explained, when "the immediate objective" of the search is "to generate evidence *for law enforcement purposes*," even if the "ultimate goal" is to promote some value other than general crime control.[59] Most "special needs" cases have involved searches conducted by persons others than police officers, which has made it easier for the Court to conclude that a special need, beyond ordinary law enforcement, justified the special rule. "Extensive entanglement of law enforcement" in the process jeopardizes a "special needs" claim.[60]

## [B]  Searches of Personal Property and Premises

### [1]  Searches Directed at Public School Students

The "special needs" doctrine was born in *New Jersey v. T.L.O,*[61] although explicit enunciation of the principle is found in a concurring opinion,[62]

---

[55] Stuntz, Note 1, *supra*, at 554.

[56] 387 U.S. 523 (1967). *See* §§ 9.06 and 19.02, *supra*.

[57] Reamey, Note 53, *supra*, at 314.

[58] *E.g.,* Michigan Department of State Police v. Sitz, 496 U.S. 444, 450 (1990); City of Indianapolis v. Edmond, 531 U.S. 32, 37 (2000).

[59] Ferguson v. City of Charleston, 121 S. Ct. 1281, 1291 (2001).

[60] *See* § 19.05[C][3], *infra*.

[61] 469 U.S. 325 (1985).

[62] *See* Note 54, *supra*.

rather than in Justice Byron White's opinion for the Court. In *T.L.O.*, two female students were caught smoking in a school lavatory, in violation of school rules. The students were brought to the vice-principal. When one of them, *D*, denied that she had been smoking, the administrator demanded her purse, opened it, and observed a package of cigarettes. He removed the cigarettes, and in doing so discovered cigarette paper, which is often used to make marijuana cigarettes. Based on that observation, he conducted a full search of *D*'s purse, during which he found other evidence that implicated her in the sale of marijuana. The evidence was handed over to the police and used in a juvenile court proceeding against her.

The Supreme Court rejected the state's initial claim that the Fourth Amendment does not apply to the conduct of school officials,[63] and agreed that public school students retain a legitimate expectation of privacy in the private property they bring to school. Nonetheless, the Court determined that neither the warrant requirement nor the traditional doctrine of probable cause applies to public school searches. The Court disposed of the warrant requirement summarily. It stated that it is "unsuited to the school environment," as it would "unduly interfere with the maintenance of the swift and informal disciplinary proceedings needed in the schools."

Regarding probable cause, Justice White observed that "[w]here a careful balancing of governmental and public interests suggests that the public interest is best served by a Fourth Amendment standard of reasonableness that stops short of probable cause, we have not hesitated to adopt such a standard." The Court found that this was such a case, and ruled that public school teachers and administrators may search students without a warrant if two conditions are met: (1) "there are reasonable grounds"—not necessarily "probable cause" in the criminal law context—"for suspecting that the search will turn up evidence that the student has violated or is violating either the law or the rules of the school"; and (2) once initiated, the search is "not excessively intrusive in light of the age and sex of the student and the nature of the infraction."

Justices Brennan and Marshall dissented. They agreed with the majority that school officials should not be required to obtain warrants to conduct searches. However, as the search in this case was full-scale in nature, they "emphatically" rejected the majority's decision to "cast aside" the probable cause standard. They criticized the majority for "jettison[ing]" the latter

---

[63] The government's argument was based on the premise that school officials act *in loco parentis*, as mere agents of the parents, and, thus, are private parties whose actions fall outside the scope of the Fourth Amendment. The Court stated that this argument was "in tension with contemporary reality" and inconsistent with its prior rulings that school officials are subject to the commands of the Constitution.

standard, "the only standard that finds support in the text of the Fourth Amendment," and replacing it with the "Rohrschach [*sic*]-like 'balancing test.' "

Justice Stevens also dissented. In an opinion that the other two dissenters joined, he contended that a search by a school official should not be permitted at all if it is intended to "reveal evidence of . . . the most trivial school regulation." He complained that under the majority rule, "a search for curlers and sunglasses in order to enforce the school dress code is . . . just as important as a search for evidence of heroin addiction or violent gang activity." He would have limited warrantless searches to "uncover evidence that the student is violating the law or engaging in conduct that is seriously disruptive of school order, or the educational process."

## [2]  Searches Directed at Public Employees

The second step in the development of the "special needs" doctrine came in *O'Connor v. Ortega*,[64] a case involving the reasonableness of a search conducted by a public employer of the office, including the desk and file cabinets, of an employee suspected of employment improprieties. In a sharply divided opinion, a four-justice plurality, adopting the "special needs" terminology from the concurring opinion in *T.L.O.*,[65] approved the use of the "reasonableness" balancing test to determine the scope of an employee's Fourth Amendment rights in regard to searches and seizures conducted by an employer.

Regarding search warrants, the plurality concluded that "the realities of the workplace . . . strongly suggest that a warrant requirement would be unworkable." In the view of the plurality, "requiring an employer to obtain a warrant whenever the employer wished to enter an employee's office, desk, or file cabinets for a work-related purpose would seriously disrupt the routine conduct of the business and would be unduly burdensome."

Regarding probable cause, the plurality was careful to note that it was only considering the issue in regard to "a noninvestigatory work-related intrusion" or "an investigatory search for evidence of suspected work-related employee misfeasance." In such circumstances, as with searches in the public school context, the employer's conduct is "judged by the standard of reasonableness," both at its inception and regarding the scope of the intrusion. For a search to be reasonable at its inception, there must exist "reasonable grounds for suspecting that the search will turn up evidence that the employee is guilty of work-related misconduct, or that the search is necessary for a noninvestigatory work-related purpose such as to retrieve

[64] 480 U.S. 709 (1987).

[65] *Id.* at 720.

a needed file." As for the scope of the search, the measures taken must be "reasonably related to the objectives of the search and not excessively intrusive in light of . . . the nature of the [misconduct]."

### [3] Searches Directed at Probationers

The "special needs" doctrine reached majority opinion status in *Griffin v. Wisconsin*.[66] In *Griffin*, the Court approved a warrantless, non-exigent search by a probation officer (accompanied by the police) of the home of a probationer. The search, based on information provided to the probation officer by the police, was conducted pursuant to a Wisconsin administrative regulation that authorized such searches if there were "reasonable grounds" to believe that contraband would be discovered on the premises. In a 5-4 opinion, Justice Scalia announced that the warrantless search of the residence in conformity with the regulation was a reasonable response to a special governmental need.

Justice Scalia stated that a warrant requirement "would interfere to an appreciable degree with the probation system, setting up a magistrate rather than the probation officer as the judge of how close a supervision the probationer requires." Similarly, the Court felt that the concept of "probable cause" could properly be replaced (as in the earlier "special needs" cases) by the "reasonable grounds" standard.

The Court characterized the probationer as the "client" of his probation officer. The Court noted that "[a]lthough a probation officer is not an impartial magistrate, neither is he the police officer who normally conducts searches against the ordinary citizen." As the Court explained it, application of traditional warrant procedures would impair the "individualized counseling designed to foster growth and development" by the probationer's "client."

### [C] Drug and Alcohol Testing[67]

### [1] Overview of Factors

The Supreme Court has, in limited circumstances, approved drug and alcohol testing (by taking blood, urine, or breath samples) of some public employees and public school students, in the absence of a search warrant and even in the absence of individualized suspicion. The Court's rulings

---

[66] 483 U.S. 868 (1987).

[67] *See generally* George M. Dery III, *Are Politicians More Deserving of Privacy than Schoolchildren? How Chandler v. Miller Exposed the Absurdities of Fourth Amendment "Special Needs" Balancing*, 40 Ariz. L. Rev. 73 (1998); Jennifer E. Smiley, Comment, *Rethinking the "Special Needs" Doctrine: Suspicionless Drug Testing of High School Students and the Narrowing of Fourth Amendment Protections*, 95 Nw. U.L. Rev. 811 (2001).

in these areas are considered in subsection [2]. Perhaps emboldened by the Court's decisions, legislatures and local officials have sought to expand the use of drug testing to other categories of persons, only to have the Court declare some of these efforts unconstitutional. The latter cases are considered in subsection [3].

Although the cases do not fit together perfectly, as clarified below, certain factors tend to support a finding that suspicionless alcohol or drug testing is constitutionally reasonable. First, regardless of the ultimate goal of the testing, the immediate objective of the testing must *not* be to generate evidence for criminal law enforcement purposes.

Second, consistent with the administrative-search cases,[68] testing is more likely to be treated favorably if those being tested are working in a job already pervasively regulated by the government or, in non-employment contexts, have a reduced expectation of privacy.

Third, in the employment context, there should be a significant relationship between the employee's job responsibilities and the employer's concern about drug or alcohol use. In other circumstances, there should be a significant societal reason for identifying drug users or alcohol abusers.

Fourth, the case for testing is strengthened by the introduction of empirical evidence of a substantial need for the random testing program in question. Specifically, random testing is much more likely to be approved if there is evidence that a system based on individualized suspicion is impracticable, and that the testing scheme devised will be reasonably effective in satisfying the governmental need motivating the testing.

Fifth, testing is more likely to be upheld if the regulations authorizing it remove most, if not all, of the discretion of the government agency in determining who will be tested and under what circumstances the testing will occur.

Finally, scrupulous care must be taken to ensure that the dignity of persons being tested is respected in the specimen-collection process. This is particularly a matter of concern with urine collection.

### [2]  Approved Testing

In the companion cases of *Skinner v. Railway Labor Executives' Association*[69] and *National Treasury Employees Union v. Von Raab*,[70] the Supreme Court upheld warrantless blood, breath, and urine testing of some public

---

[68] *See* § 19.02, *supra.*

[69] 489 U.S. 602 (1989).

[70] 489 U.S. 656 (1989).

employees, conducted pursuant to administrative regulations, in the absence of individualized suspicion, in order to detect drug or alcohol usage.

In *Skinner*, the Federal Railroad Administration (F.R.A.) adopted regulations requiring railroad companies to conduct blood and urine tests for alcohol and drugs, of certain employees, such as engineers, following major train accidents, and permitting them to administer breath or urine tests to employees who violate safety rules. The regulations were a response to detailed findings of the F.R.A., to the effect that drug or alcohol use by railroad employees was a causal factor in a significant number of accidents that had resulted in death or property damage, and that railroad companies were unable to detect on-the-job drug or alcohol use on the basis of visual observation.

In *Von Raab*, the United States Customs Service developed a drug-screening program to conduct urinalysis tests of employees seeking transfer or promotion to positions having a direct involvement in the Service's drug interdiction program or requiring the person to carry a firearm or handle classified materials.

As a beginning point, the Supreme Court concluded in *Skinner* that blood, breath, and urine tests intrude on Fourth Amendment interests. Blood tests, because they involve intrusions beneath the skin, constitute a search; the subsequent chemical testing of the blood to obtain "physiological data" invades an individual's privacy interests still further. In cursory fashion, the Court also held that a breath test "implicates . . . concerns about bodily integrity" similar to blood testing. Urine collection, "which may in some cases involve visual or aural monitoring of the act of urination," is a search. Moreover, a urine test "might also be characterized as a . . . seizure, since it may be viewed as a meaningful interference with the employee's possessory interest in his bodily fluids."

Although the testing constituted Fourth Amendment activity, the Supreme Court held that the tests in these cases fell within the "special needs" exception to the warrant and probable-cause requirements of the Fourth Amendment. The *Skinner* Court disposed of the warrant requirement on three grounds. First, it concluded that a warrant was not needed because the circumstances under which the testing was required or permitted, *i.e.*, after serious train incidents or violations of safety rules, were specifically set out in the regulations authorizing the tests: "[i]ndeed, in light of the standardized nature of the tests and the minimal discretion vested in those charged with administering the program, there [we]re virtually no facts for a neutral magistrate to evaluate."

Second, because evidence of the ingestion of alcohol and drugs is eliminated from the body quickly, imposing a warrant requirement would have "significantly hinder[ed], and in many cases frustrat[ed], the objectives of the Government testing program." Finally, the Court considered it unreasonable to impose "unwieldy warrant procedures" on the railroad companies, who are unfamiliar with the intricacies of the system.

The Court disposed of the probable-cause requirement on the ground that the privacy interests implicated by the testing were minimal. It characterized as "not significant" the bodily intrusion occasioned by blood testing; breath testing was treated as less intrusive still, because it does not involve physical penetration of the skin.

*Skinner* was more troubled by urine testing. The Court conceded that the excretory function "traditionally [is] shielded by great privacy." Nevertheless, the Court was satisfied that the employees' privacy needs were satisfied in this case, because the regulations did not require the employees to be observed while they urinated, and the urine was collected "in a medical environment" by non-employer personnel. Furthermore, and "more importantly" to the privacy issue, the Court found that the employees' expectations of privacy regarding the testing were "diminished by reason of their participation in an industry that is regulated pervasively to ensure safety."

Weighed against the employees' "minimal" privacy interests in this case was the government's "compelling" interest in random testing. In support of this proposition, the Court pointed to the conclusions of the F.R.A. that impaired employees generally were able to escape visual detection. Furthermore, the Court concluded that the suspicionless testing in this case was an effective way to deter violations of safety regulations, because the employees were aware that testing would take place "upon the occurrence of a triggering event, the timing of which no employee [could] predict with certainty," *e.g.*, a railroad accident.

The Court applied similar reasoning in *Von Raab* to justify the testing of Customs Service employees. It approved the regulations on various grounds, including the need to reduce the risk of bribe-taking, mishandling of weapons, use of drugs by employees with ready access to contraband, and "unsympathetic" enforcement of the narcotics laws by persons whose mission it would be to interdict narcotics.

Justice Antonin Scalia, who joined the majority in *Skinner*, and Justice Stevens, who concurred in *Skinner*, dissented in *Von Raab*. Justice Scalia stated their reason for dissenting: the majority in *Von Raab* failed to present "real evidence of a real problem that [would] be solved by urine testing of Customs Service employees." As he put it:

What is absent in the Government's justifications—notably absent, revealingly absent, and as far as I am concerned dispositively absent—is the recitation of *even a single instance* in which any of the speculated horribles [of bribe-taking, poor aim, or unsympathetic law enforcement as the result of drug-usage] actually occurred.

The dissenters warned that "the impairment of individual liberties cannot be the means of making a point; that symbolism, even symbolism for so worthy a cause as the abolition of unlawful drugs, cannot validate an otherwise unreasonable search."

These two cases, then, suggest that warrantless, suspicionless drug testing of public employees is reasonable when: (1) the employee is working in a job already pervasively regulated; (2) there is a close relationship between the employee's job responsibilities and the employer's concern about drug or alcohol use; (3) the regulations authorizing the testing remove most or all of the employer's discretion in determining which employees will be tested and under what circumstances it will occur; (4) there is evidence presented that a system based on an individualized system is impracticable or would frustrate the non-law-enforcement purpose of the testing; and (5) care is taken to protect the dignitary interest of employees in the specimen-collection process.

The Supreme Court has also authorized random drug testing of public school students in limited circumstances. In *Vernonia School District 47J v. Acton*,[71] the Supreme Court, 6-3, per Justice Scalia, upheld random urinalysis drug testing of students voluntarily participating in the petitioner school district's athletics programs. Pursuant to the policy of the Vernonia school district, all students wishing to play sports were required to sign a form consenting to urinalysis drug testing. Parental consent was also required.

Athletes were tested at the beginning of the season for their sport; and, once each week, ten percent of the athletes were selected blindly for follow-up testing. An athlete undergoing testing was accompanied by an adult of the same sex into a restroom. Each boy selected would produce a sample at a urinal, while fully clothed, with his back to the monitor, who would stand about 12 to 15 feet behind. The monitor was permitted to watch while the sample was produced, and to listen for "normal sounds of urination." Girls produced their samples in an enclosed bathroom stall, where they could be heard but not observed. If a sample tested positive, a second test was required; if it also proved positive, the student had the option of participating in a six-week assistance program including weekly urinalysis, or suspension from athletics for a specified period of time.

---

[71] 515 U.S. 646 (1995); *see generally* Wayne R. LaFave, *Computers, Urinals, and the Fourth Amendment: Confessions of a Patron Saint*, 94 Mich. L. Rev. 2553 (1996).

According to the trial court, Vernonia administered the testing after it observed a sharp increase in drug use by students, open discussion and glorification of the drug culture, and serious disciplinary problems. The trial court found that student athletes, "admired in their schools and in the community," were the leaders of the drug culture.

The Supreme Court approved the mass testings involved in this case, although they were conducted without warrants or individualized suspicion of wrongdoing. Citing *New Jersey v. T.L.O.*,[72] the majority stated that the warrant and probable-cause requirements were impracticable in the public school context. In *T.L.O.*, however, the Court approved a search based on individualized suspicion of wrongdoing, whereas the testing conducted by Vernonia lacked this element. Justice Scalia stated, however, that there is no "irreducible" Fourth Amendment requirement of reasonable suspicion. Ultimately, the Court stated, the "measure of the constitutionality of a governmental search is 'reasonableness.' "

The Court balanced the competing interests. First, Justice Scalia considered the nature of the privacy interest upon which the search intruded: "Central . . . to the present case is the fact that the subjects of the [p]olicy are (1) children, who (2) have been committed to the temporary custody of the State as schoolmaster." As a result, school children have a lesser expectation of privacy than adults possess. Moreover, school athletes have further reduced expectations of privacy, because they must suit up and shower in public locker rooms, and must "voluntarily subject themselves to a degree of regulation even higher than that imposed on students generally," including the requirement of a preseason physical examination and adequate insurance coverage.

Regarding the character of the intrusion, the Court reiterated its comment in *Skinner* that collecting samples for urinalysis intrudes upon "an excretory function traditionally shielded by great privacy." The manner in which the production of the sample is monitored, therefore, is of critical importance. Here, the male students were fully clothed, and observed only from behind; the females had even greater privacy. As such, the conditions were nearly identical to those encountered by students in the restrooms on a regular basis. The Court also considered it significant that the information disclosed by the urine samples was limited: Vernonia only tested for drugs, and not for other medical conditions, such as epilepsy, pregnancy, or diabetes.

Finally, the Court considered the "nature and immediacy of the governmental concern at issue here, and the efficacy of this means for meeting it." The Court described the governmental interest in deterring drug use

---

[72] 469 U.S. 325 (1985). *See* § 19.05[B][1], *supra*.

by schoolchildren as "important—indeed, perhaps compelling," and "at least as important" as the goals furthered by random drug testing in *Skinner* and *Von Raab*. Significantly, the Court was armed with the trial court finding that there was a serious drug problem in Vernonia, resulting in disruptions to the educational process, and requiring disciplinary actions of "epidemic proportions"; moreover, Justice Scalia wrote, "it must not be lost sight of that this program is directed more narrowly to drug use by school athletes, where the risk of immediate physical harm to the drug user or those with whom he is playing his sport is particularly high."

As to the efficacy of the means for addressing the drug problem, the Court stated that it is "self-evident that a drug problem largely fueled by the 'role model' effect of athletes' drug use, and of particular danger to athletes, is effectively addressed by making sure that athletes do not use drugs." The Court rejected the claim that a less intrusive means existed, namely, drug testing of students suspected of drug use. The Court noted, first, that it has "repeatedly refused to declare that only the 'least intrusive' search practicable can be reasonable under the Fourth Amendment." It also noted difficulties with the alternative approach: parents willing to accept random drug testing might be unwilling "to accept accusatory drug testing . . ., which transforms the process into a badge of shame." Such a system might also result in arbitrary enforcement, and subsequent expensive litigation.

*Vernonia School District* is an important expansion of the "special needs" doctrine. It authorizes random suspicionless drug-testing outside the public-employment sphere to which some commentators hoped the doctrine would be limited. But, the case may not have substantial influence outside the public school context. According to Justice Scalia:

> We caution against the assumption that suspicionless drug testing will readily pass constitutional muster in other contexts. The most significant element in this case is the first we discussed: that the [p]olicy was undertaken in furtherance of the government's responsibilities, under a public school system, as guardian and tutor of children entrusted to its care.

Indeed, Justice Ginsburg, while joining the majority, wrote in a concurrence that, in her view, an essential feature of the majority opinion is that the petitioner school district's drug-testing policy was limited to those voluntarily participating in athletics. According to Ginsburg, there remains a serious constitutional question whether drug testing may be compelled of *all* students attending school.

Indeed, as with *Skinner* and *Von Raab*, *Vernonia School District* is a limited decision: (1) testing was limited to persons voluntarily participating in extra-curricular activities; (2) there was considerable evidence presented at trial of a serious drug problem in Vernonia; (3) the drug problem was undermining the educational mission of the school district and, thus, there was an "important," "perhaps compelling" need to tackle the problem; (4) a regime based on individualized suspicion would have been impracticable, thus making random testing more reasonable; (5) the procedures mitigated the risk of arbitrary enforcement; and (6) the procedures for collecting the urine samples were respectful of the students' privacy interests.

### [3] Disapproved Testing

If observers—and lawmakers—interpreted the cases discussed in the preceding subsection as providing a green light from the Supreme Court to devise any form of suspicionless drug testing desired, this "understanding" has proved to be false. The *Skinner, Von Raab* and *Vernonia School District* cases offered only a cautionary yellow light to such testing programs.

Indeed, one caution light illuminated by the *dissenters* in *Von Raab* has proved significant. As quoted above, they warned that "symbolism, even symbolism for so worthy a cause as the abolition of unlawful drugs, cannot validate an otherwise unreasonable search." In *Chandler v. Miller*,[73] that warning proved prophetic. The Supreme Court in *Chandler* ruled, 8-1, that Georgia's requirement that various candidates for state office pass a drug test did "not fit within the closely guarded category of constitutionally permissible suspicionless searches."

The Georgia statute required candidates for state office to submit to urinalysis drug tests within 30 days prior to qualifying for nomination or election. A candidate could not be placed on the ballot if the tests were positive for specified illegal drugs. Writing for the Court, Justice Ginsburg stated that the Fourth Amendment "shields society" from a urinalysis drug test that "diminishes personal privacy [solely] for a symbol's sake."

The problem with the Georgia testing regime was not its invasiveness. Justice Ginsburg stated that the procedure was "relatively noninvasive"— indeed, it was less so than the process approved in *Vernonia School District*—as the intended candidate could provide the requisite urine specimen in the privacy of his or her private physician's office. Instead, what was missing was proof of a "substantial" special need "sufficiently vital" to override the privacy interest of the candidates. Unlike *Vernonia*, in which evidence of a serious drug problem was proven, "[n]otably lacking in [the State of Georgia's] presentation [was] any indication of a concrete danger demanding departure from the Fourth Amendment's main rule" that

---

[73] 520 U.S. 305 (1997).

individualized suspicion is required. The Court wrote that a "demonstrated problem of drug abuse, while not in all cases necessary to the validity of a testing regime, . . . would shore up an assertion of a special need for a suspicionless general search program." Here, the law was not passed in response to *any* fear or suspicion of drug use by state officials.

But, this was not the only failing of the testing program. The Court stated that, unlike the testing approved in *Skinner, Von Raab,* and *Vernonia,* the scheme here was "not well designed to identify candidates who violate antidrug laws. Nor [was] the scheme a credible means to deter illicit drug users from seeking election to state office." Because the test date was no secret and could be scheduled anytime within 30 days prior to the individual qualifying for a place on the ballot, a drug-taking candidate could "abstain for a pretest period sufficient to avoid detection."

Also, the State of Georgia failed to show why suspicionless testing was necessary. Unlike the circumstances in *Von Raab,* for example, in which it was not feasible to subject employees to day-to-day scrutiny for drugs, "[c]andidates for public office . . . are subject to relentless scrutiny—by their peers, the public, and the press." Consequently, all that was left to the Georgia testing regime was "the image the State seeks to protect." "However well-meant," the Court said, "[t]he Fourth Amendment shields society against that state action."

The Supreme Court also sent a very significant limiting message in *Ferguson v. City of Charleston.*[74] In *Ferguson,* the Supreme Court invalidated procedures to identify and nonconsensually test any maternity patient suspected of drug use—who, thereby, was jeopardizing the health of her unborn child—who came to the Charleston public hospital operated by the Medical University of South Carolina. The procedures were formulated by a task force composed of representatives of the hospital, police, and local officials. According to the policy, if the results of a urine test proved incriminating, they were handed over to the police for prosecution of the mother. As the Court explained, the procedures:

> provided that a patient should be tested for cocaine through a urine drug screen if she met one or more of nine criteria. It also stated that a chain of custody should be followed when obtaining and testing urine samples, presumably to make sure that the results could be used in subsequent criminal proceedings. The policy also provided for education and referral to a substance abuse clinic for patients who tested positive. Most important, it added the threat of law enforcement intervention that "provided the necessary 'leverage' to make the [p]olicy effective." . . .

---

[74] 121 S. Ct. 1281 (2001).

That threat was, as respondents candidly acknowledge, essential to the program's success in getting women into treatment and keeping them there.

Despite the importance of the ultimate goal—"protecting the health of both mother and child"—and despite the fact that the program was limited to mothers who fit a medical drug-user profile, six members of the Court[75] declared the warrantless testing program constitutionally unreasonable. "As an initial matter," the Court noted that "the invasion of privacy in this case [was] far more substantial" than in the earlier "special need" drug-testing cases, because the individuals being tested in the earlier cases—even in *Chandler*—knew precisely the purpose of the testing and "there were protections against the dissemination of the results to third parties." Here, the Court stated, the pregnant mothers had "[t]he reasonable expectation of privacy enjoyed by the typical patient undergoing diagnostic tests in a hospital . . . that the results of those tests will not be shared with nonmedical personnel"—such as the police—"without her consent."

But, this was not the most critical fault with the procedure in the Court's analysis. What distinguished this case from the earlier ones, "lies in the nature of the 'special need' asserted as justification for the warrantless searches." In the prior cases, the special need "advanced as a justification . . . was one divorced from the State's general interest in law enforcement." In such circumstances, the majority wrote, the Court "tolerated suspension of the Fourth Amendment's warrant and probable cause requirement in part because there was no law enforcement purpose behind the searches . . . and there was little, if any, entanglement with law enforcement."

In contrast, here the Court found that the policy's "central and indispensable feature . . . was the use of law enforcement from its inception to coerce patients into substance abuse treatment." Even though the policy's "ultimate purpose" was a beneficent one, "the immediate objective of the [testing] was to generate evidence *for law enforcement purposes* in order to reach that [beneficent] goal." In such circumstances, the Court announced, the "special needs" exception does not apply and, therefore, a valid search warrant is required.

How did the Court determine the "immediate objective" (or "relevant primary purpose") of the program? It stated that it would consider all the available evidence. Here, "an initial and continuing focus of the policy was on the arrest and prosecution of drug-abusing mothers." The Court was troubled by the fact that the document setting out the policies and procedures

---

[75] Justice Stevens delivered the opinion of the Court for himself and Justices O'Connor, Souter, Ginsburg, and Breyer. Justice Kennedy, the sixth vote, concurred in the judgment.

devoted attention to chain-of-custody matters, to the range of possible criminal charges that could be brought, and to the procedures for notifying the police. Indeed, "Charleston prosecutors and police were extensively involved in the day-to-day administration of the policy."[76] Meanwhile, "[n]owhere . . . [did] the document discuss different courses of medical treatment for either mother or infant, aside from the treatment for the mother's addiction."

The dissenters, with Justice Scalia writing, sharply criticized the majority's analysis. First, they disputed the implication they drew from the majority opinion, namely, that the "medical rationale [of the testing] was merely a pretext; there was no special need." Justice Scalia pointed to the fact that the testing began "neither at police suggestion nor with police involvement." A few months after the testing began, however, a Medical Center nurse learned that the local prosecutor was arresting cocaine-taking pregnant mothers for child abuse. She informed her superiors, and the hospital's counsel contacted the prosecutor, resulting in the disputed policy. To the dissent, this history demonstrated that the original purpose of the testing was to provide health benefits, and that it would be "incredible" to believe that this was no longer the goal after formulation of the policy. Thus, the dissent reasoned, there was no basis for distinguishing the policy from a case in which a physician, in the course of ordinary medical procedures, comes across incriminating information that the physician is required by law to report to the police.

To the dissent, "the *addition* of a law-enforcement-related purpose *to* a legitimate medical purpose [should not] destroy [the] applicability of the 'special-needs' doctrine." Moreover, the dissent argued, this limitation is inconsistent with *Griffin v. Wisconsin*,[77] in which the Court approved a "special needs" search by a probation officer who conducted the search *with the police present, and based on information provided by the police.*

There is, indeed, considerable tension between *Ferguson* and *Griffin*. Despite the Court's efforts to explain away *Griffin*,[78] *Ferguson*, like *City*

---

[76] It is this aspect of the case that convinced Justice Kennedy to concur in the judgment. He rejected the majority's distinction between "ultimate goals" and "immediate purposes." However, "[n]one of our special needs precedents has sanctioned the routine inclusion of law enforcement, both in the design of the policy and in using arrests, either threatened or real, to implement the system designed for the special needs objectives."

[77] 483 U.S. 868 (1987). *See* § 19.05[B][3], *supra.*

[78] The Court quoted language from *Griffin* that "[a]lthough a probation officer is not an impartial magistrate, neither is he a police officer who normally conducts searches against the ordinary citizen." *Griffin*, 483 U.S. at 876. The Court also indicated that "*Griffin* is properly read as limited by the fact that probationers have a lesser expectation of privacy than the public at large."

*of Indianapolis v. Edmond,*[79] are demonstrations of the Court's new-found concern that the reasonableness standard, and most particularly the "special needs" doctrine, not be extended to that point that "the Fourth Amendment would do little to prevent such intrusions from becoming a routine part of American life."[80]

---

[79] 531 U.S. 32 (2000). *See* § 19.04[C], *supra.*

[80] *Id.* at 42.

## CHAPTER 20

# FOURTH AMENDMENT: STANDING

## § 20.01 The Role of "Standing" in Fourth Amendment Law[1]

### [A]  In General

The Fourth Amendment guarantees "[t]he right of the people to be secure in their persons, houses, papers, and effects against unreasonable searches and seizures." Generally speaking, this right is enforced by application of the exclusionary rule, which provides that evidence secured in violation of the Fourth Amendment may not be used in a criminal trial.[2]

It has long been the case, however, that nearly all claims to enforce constitutional rights may be raised only by those who have "standing" to assert them. The Fourth Amendment is no exception to this principle. That is, a person who makes a motion to suppress evidence that the government intends to use against him at trial[3] must show that he was "a victim of a search or seizure . . . as distinguished from one who claims prejudice only through the use of evidence gathered as a consequence of a search or seizure directed at someone else."[4]

In short, Fourth Amendment rights are personal. They may not vicariously be asserted.[5] The fact that X was the victim of an unreasonable search

---

[1] *See generally* 5 Wayne R. LaFave, Search and Seizure § 11.3 (3d ed. 1996); Mary I. Coombs, *Shared Privacy and the Fourth Amendment, or the Rights of Relationships*, 75 Cal. L. Rev. 1593 (1987); Melvin Gutterman, *Fourth Amendment Privacy and Standing: "Wherever the Twain Shall Meet"*, 60 N.C. L. Rev. 1 (1981); Richard B. Kuhns, *The Concept of Personal Aggrievement in Fourth Amendment Standing Cases*, 65 Iowa L. Rev. 493 (1980); Lloyd L. Weinreb, *Your Place or Mine? Privacy of Presence under the Fourth Amendment*, 1999 Sup. Ct. Rev. 253.

[2] *See* chapter 21, *infra*.

[3] A person aggrieved by a Fourth Amendment violation may make a pretrial motion to have the seized property returned to him as well to exclude the evidence at his trial. *E.g.*, Fed. R. Crim. P. 41(e).

[4] Jones v. United States, 362 U.S. 257, 261 (1960), *overruled on other grounds*, United States v. Salvucci, 448 U.S. 83 (1980).

[5] Alderman v. United States, 394 U.S. 165, 174 (1969).

or seizure, during which time evidence was seized that incriminates *D*, does not give *D* a right to have such evidence excluded at *his* trial—even though the same evidence would be inadmissible against *X*—unless *D* can show that *his* Fourth Amendment rights were violated by the police action, *i.e.*, that he, too, was a victim of the unconstitutional activity. In some sense of the constitutional phrase, *D* must show that *his* person, house, papers, and/or effects were implicated by the police conduct.

### [B] Is "Standing" a Separate Concept?

Conceptually, "standing" is a threshold issue: a person seeking to have evidence excluded at his trial must first demonstrate that he has standing to contest the search and seizure. If he does not have standing, the court does not need to evaluate the police conduct—the defendant is, as it were, locked out of court in regard to the merits of the suppression issue. However, the Supreme Court stated in *Rakas v. Illinois*:[6]

> [T]he question necessarily arises whether it serves any useful analytical purpose to consider this principle [that Fourth Amendment rights may not be vicariously asserted] a matter of standing, distinct from the merits of a defendant's Fourth Amendment claim. . . . [T]he type of standing requirement discussed in [prior cases] . . . is more properly subsumed under substantive Fourth Amendment doctrine. . . . The inquiry under either approach is the same. But we think the better analysis forthrightly focuses on the extent of a particular defendant's rights under the Fourth Amendment, rather than on any theoretically separate, but invariably intertwined concept of standing.

In other words, following *Rakas*, "standing," as such, is no longer the issue that the Supreme Court wants lower courts to resolve.[7] Instead, the Court prefers now to ask the question: were *D*'s Fourth Amendment rights—as distinguished from someone else's—violated by the police action? This, as will be seen,[8] usually means that a court should ask, simply, whether the defendant had a legitimate expectation of privacy in the area searched by the police.

However, as Justice Blackmun,[9] Professor LaFave,[10] and some lower

---

[6] 439 U.S. 128, 138–39 (1978) (footnote omitted).

[7] Minnesota v. Carter, 525 U.S. 83, 87 (1998) (criticizing the state court for analyzing the facts of the case "under the rubric of 'standing' doctrine, an analysis which this Court expressly rejected 20 years ago in *Rakas*").

[8] *See* § 20.07, *infra*.

[9] Rawlings v. Kentucky, 448 U.S. 98, 112 (1980) (concurring opinion).

[10] 5 LaFave, Note 1, *supra*, at 121–22.

courts[11] have demonstrated, it is not *analytically* improper for a court, as before, to treat "standing" and the issue of whether a substantive Fourth Amendment violation has occurred, as distinct inquiries. The "standing" question is whether the police have intruded upon the *movant's* Fourth Amendment sphere of protection, whereas the substantive "non-standing" question (if relevant) is whether the police activity violated the Fourth Amendment. It is important to keep in mind that it is possible for a claimant to have standing to raise a Fourth Amendment challenge, but to lose on the merits. To lose sight of this analytical distinction can invite confusion.

Consider the facts in *Minnesota v. Carter*.[12] In *Carter*, the police observed *X* and his two guests, *D1* and *D2*, conducting illegal activities in *X*'s ground-level apartment. A police officer saw the parties' conduct through a gap in the window shades covering *X*'s window. *D1* and *D2* sought to have the evidence later seized by the police from their host's apartment (and other evidence) suppressed at their trial on the ground that the police surveillance was unconstitutional.

Notice that under traditional "standing" analysis, the first issue in *Carter* would be whether *D1* and *D2* had standing to contest the police "snooping" and then, if they did have standing, the second issue would be whether that surveillance constituted a "search." However, when these two questions are collapsed into one, as *Rakas* would have courts do, it is easy to confuse the issue of whether a "search" occurred (whether *someone's* reasonable expectation of privacy was violated) with the issue of whether *D1* and *D2*, in particular, were victimized.

Indeed, in *Carter*, three dissenting Justices (Ginsburg, Stevens and Souter) did not seem to notice the conceptual distinction. They defended the proposition that *D1* and *D2* had the right to challenge the police conduct, but they never reached the second question—one raised in the petition for certiorari—whether the police conduct violated their reasonable expectation of privacy. Justice Breyer saw this problem. Although he agreed with the dissenters on the first ("standing") issue, he found no Fourth Amendment violation because, in his view, no search occurred. In short, in the pre-*Rakas* world, Breyer's opinion suggests that the defendants had standing to contest the police conduct, but that they should lose on the merits.

So, the lesson is this: first, a defendant must have standing to raise a Fourth Amendment challenge. However, second, the previously distinct issues (does the movant have standing?; and if so, what should the result

---

[11] *E.g.*, State v. Alston, 440 A.2d 1311, 1314 n.2 (N.J. 1981) (describing the *Rakas* Court's suggestion as a "semantic difference without much significant analytic distinction").

[12] 525 U.S. 83 (1998).

be on the merits of the motion?) now have become just one question: were the *movant's* Fourth Amendment rights violated. Finally, unless lawyers are *very* careful, the *Rakas* Court's approach to "standing" can result in incomplete or incorrect analysis.

## § 20.02 Rationale of the Standing Requirement

Professor Anthony Amsterdam once noted that there are two competing perspectives on the Fourth Amendment. One view, the "atomistic" perspective, is that the Fourth Amendment is "a collection of protections of atomistic spheres of interest of individual citizens." That is, the Fourth Amendment protects isolated individuals ("atoms"), in the sense that the amendment "safeguard[s] *my* person and *your* house and *her* papers and *his* effects against unreasonable searches and seizures."[13] The second view, the "regulatory" perspective, is that the Fourth Amendment functions "as a regulation of governmental conduct." In other words, the amendment is intended to safeguard the collective "people"—as in "we, the people"—from governmental overreaching.

As Fourth Amendment jurisprudence has developed, standing—based as it is on the premise that a person may raise a Fourth Amendment challenge only if he *personally* was a victim of unreasonable police activity—is based on the atomistic philosophy. In contrast, the exclusionary rule is regulatory in nature, in that its purpose is to deter police misconduct, in order to safeguard society as a whole.

Understood this way, the standing requirement and the exclusionary rule act, at least in part, in opposition to each other. This is because evidence seized in violation of the Fourth Amendment is excluded at trial in order to deter police misconduct; but, the requirement of standing to raise a Fourth Amendment claim often undercuts this deterrence goal, as it limits the number of people ("atoms") who can bring the misconduct to the attention of the courts so that the exclusionary rule can be applied.

For example, consider *United States v. Payner*.[14] In *Payner*, Internal Revenue Service (I.R.S.) agents launched an investigation into the financial activities of United States citizens living in the Bahamas. As part of "Operation Trade Winds," the I.R.S. approved a plan in which a private investigator it hired illegally photographed the contents of a bank official's briefcase in order to uncover incriminating evidence against *D*, a target of the I.R.S. investigation. A district court found that the I.R.S. "affirmatively

---

[13] Anthony G. Amsterdam, *Perspectives on the Fourth Amendment*, 58 Minn. L. Rev. 349, 367 (1974).

[14] 447 U.S. 727 (1980).

counsel[ed] its agents that the Fourth Amendment standing limitation permits them to purposefully conduct an unconstitutional search and seizure of one individual in order to obtain evidence against third parties."

*Payner* points up this problem: government agents purposely flouted Fourth Amendment values by securing evidence against the suspects by invading the privacy of other people, knowing that the targets of their investigation would lack standing to object to the misconduct. From a regulatory perspective, this was a nearly perfect case for application of the exclusionary rule. But, the atomistic standing requirement frustrated that effort; indeed, it functioned as an incentive to the government to act unlawfully.[15]

As a policy matter, the Fourth Amendment standing requirement makes sense only if it is treated as a purposeful limitation on the goals of the exclusionary rule.[16] As examined in the next chapter, the exclusionary rule is a potentially expensive doctrine. That is, in the law's efforts to deter unreasonable searches and seizures, courts suppress relevant and reliable evidence—the fruits of the police misconduct—at criminal trials. The consequence of this is that guilty people may be convicted less often than they would be if society were willing to use the wrongfully gathered evidence.

Essentially, the standing requirement is the Supreme Court's declaration that the cost of the exclusionary rule can become too great to bear. Even understood this way, the question remains how narrowly or broadly should courts define the concept of a "victim" in the context of the standing requirement, because the term is not self-defining. The Court has explained in this context that, in determining where the standing line should be drawn, the Supreme Court must decide whether "the additional benefits of extending the exclusionary rule to other defendants would justify further encroachment upon the public interest in prosecuting those accused of crime and having them acquitted or convicted on the basis of all the evidence which exposes the truth."[17] In turn, analysis of this matter depends on the resolution of two empirical questions: how expensive *really* is the exclusionary rule?; and to what extent does the standing requirement actually undermine the purposes of the exclusionary rule?

---

[15] For an argument that standing should be conferred on defendants like Payner as a penalty for the government's bad-faith conduct, *see* George C. Thomas III & Barry S. Pollack, *Balancing the Fourth Amendment Scales: The Bad-Faith "Exception" to Exclusionary Rule Limitations*, 45 Hastings L.J. 21 (1993).

[16] Kuhns, Note 1, *supra*, at 509–13.

[17] Alderman v. United States, 394 U.S. 165, 175 (1969).

As discussed in the next chapter, the Supreme Court has become increasingly critical of the exclusionary rule. At the same time, it does not believe that a narrow interpretation of the standing requirement appreciably undermines any justifiable goals of the exclusionary rule. Therefore, it is more difficult now to raise a Fourth Amendment claim than it was decades ago.

## § 20.03 Target Standing[18]

Does a person have standing to raise a Fourth Amendment claim simply because he was the target of the search that resulted in the seizure of evidence against him? For example, suppose that the police enter X's house without a search warrant in order to seize evidence belonging to D. May D—the target of the search—contest the police action, although it was X's privacy that was invaded? Plausibly, D should have standing. Presumably, there would be a beneficial deterrent effect in a rule that informs the police that the target of their search will always have standing to challenge their conduct if they violate the Fourth Amendment, even if the direct victim of their activity is another person.

Notwithstanding this argument, as well as language in some cases that appeared to make a point of the fact that the defendant was the target of the contested search,[19] the Supreme Court rejected the doctrine of target standing in *Rakas v. Illinois*.[20] The Court concluded that target standing is not required to obtain the beneficial deterrent effect of the exclusionary rule. According to *Rakas*, an officer will be deterred from improperly intruding on X's (the non-target's) privacy, even without target standing by D, because X will have ample motivation to raise his own Fourth Amendment claim; and, where X is not charged with a crime, the officer will be deterred because X may recover damages in a civil action for violation of his privacy.

## § 20.04 Derivative Standing[21]

In 1948 in *McDonald v. United States*,[22] the Supreme Court reversed D's conviction because evidence used against him had been seized in

---

[18] 5 LaFave, Note 1, *supra*, at § 11.3(h).

[19] *E.g.*, United States v. Jeffers, 342 U.S. 48, 52 (1951) (the search and seizure were "bound together by one sole purpose—to locate and seize the narcotics of [defendant]"); Jones v. United States, 362 U.S. 257, 261 (1960) (describing a person with standing as one who is "a victim of a search or seizure, *one against whom the search was directed*") (emphasis added).

[20] 439 U.S. 128 (1978).

[21] 5 LaFave, Note 1, *supra*, at § 11.3(i).

[22] 335 U.S. 451 (1948).

violation of the Fourth Amendment rights of *X*, his co-defendant. The Court reasoned that *X* had the right to have his property returned to him prior to trial as the result of the Fourth Amendment violation;[23] therefore, the evidence would not have been in the government's custody to use against *D*.

Although *McDonald* did not speak in terms of "standing," many lower courts interpreted the case to mean that so-called "derivative standing" exists: a defendant has the right to raise a Fourth Amendment claim if the rights of any co-defendant or co-conspirator were violated.

The doctrine of derivative standing, if it ever existed at the Supreme Court level, was overruled *sub silentio* in *Wong Sun v. United States*,[24] when the Court held that evidence unconstitutionally seized from one defendant, James Toy, was admissible against another defendant, Wong Sun, because the unlawful police conduct relating to Toy invaded no Fourth Amendment right of Wong Sun.

The Court made the point explicit in *Alderman v. United States*,[25] when it stated that "[c]oconspirators and codefendants [are] . . . accorded no special standing."[26] The Court concluded that the potential deterrent benefit of applying the exclusionary rule to co-defendants who did not otherwise have standing was outweighed by the costs of such an approach.

## § 20.05  Automatic Standing[27]

For a little more than a decade, the Supreme Court recognized the doctrine of "automatic standing." First announced in a unanimous opinion by Justice Felix Frankfurter in *Jones v. United States*,[28] the rule was that a defendant did not have to prove standing to raise a Fourth Amendment claim if possession of the evidence seized was a necessary element of the crime for which he was prosecuted. For example, in *Jones*, federal agents seized narcotics belonging to *D* in a search of *X*'s apartment. *D* was prosecuted for possession of the narcotics. Under the automatic standing rule announced in the case, *D* was allowed to contest the legality of the search of *X*'s apartment. In practical terms, this meant that *D* did not have to prove that

---

[23] *See* Note 3, *supra*.

[24] 371 U.S. 471 (1963).

[25] 394 U.S. 165 (1969).

[26] *See also* United States v. Padilla, 508 U.S. 77, 82 (1993) (per curiam) ("Participants in a criminal conspiracy may have [standing to contest a search], but the conspiracy itself neither adds to nor detracts from [the claim].").

[27] 5 LaFave, Note 1, *supra*, at 11.3(g).

[28] 362 U.S. 257 (1960), *overruled in* United States v. Salvucci, 448 U.S. 83 (1980).

the narcotics belonged to him, which would have been the usual basis for securing standing in such circumstances.[29]

Automatic standing was permitted for two reasons. First, in what was subsequently described as the "cornerstone" rationale of the *Jones* opinion,[30] the Court expressed concern about the dilemma confronting a defendant charged with a crime of possession who wished to contest a search: to prove standing to raise a Fourth Amendment claim he might have to testify in a pretrial hearing that he owned or possessed the seized evidence, the very "facts the proof of which would tend, if indeed not be sufficient to convict him"; at the same time, lower courts had held that such incriminating testimony could be used against the defendant at his trial. The automatic standing rule freed the defendant from that dilemma.

Second, the *Jones* Court believed that a prosecutor should not "have the advantage of contradictory positions," *i.e.*, that *D* possessed the contraband in violation of the law, and yet that he lacked standing to contest the search because he did not have a possessory interest in the seized materials.

The Court abandoned the automatic standing rule in *United States v. Salvucci.*[31] In *Salvucci*, the Court observed that the self-incrimination dilemma described in *Jones* was eliminated by the Court in *Simmons v. United States.*[32] In *Simmons*, the Court held that the testimony of a defendant in support of a Fourth Amendment motion to suppress evidence may not be used against him at trial, over his objection, on the issue of guilt.[33]

*Salvucci* disposed of the remaining justification for the automatic standing rule—that prosecutors should not be permitted the advantage of contradictory claims—by stating that post-*Jones* "standing" decisions, in particular the Court's watershed opinion in *Rakas v. Illinois*,[34] demonstrated that there is nothing inherently self-contradictory about a prosecutor charging a defendant with possession of contraband and simultaneously maintaining that the defendant was not the victim of an unconstitutional search.

---

[29] *See* § 27.06, *infra.*

[30] Brown v. United States, 411 U.S. 223, 228 (1973).

[31] 448 U.S. 83 (1980); *contra, under the state constitution*, Commonwealth v. Amendola, 550 N.E.2d 121 (Mass. 1990); State v. Sidebotham, 474 A.2d 1377 (N.H. 1984); State v. Wright, 596 A.2d 925 (Vt. 1991); State v. Simpson, 622 P.2d 1199 (Wash. 1980)

[32] 390 U.S. 377 (1968).

[33] *Salvucci* expressly reserved the question of whether the *Simmons* rule prevents the prosecutor from using the defendant's testimony at the suppression hearing to impeach his trial testimony.

[34] 439 U.S. 128 (1978). *See* § 27.07, *infra.*

This conclusion stems from the fact that, as discussed below, according to *Rakas*, standing to contest a search requires that the person asserting the claim have had a reasonable expectation of privacy in the area searched at the time. Therefore, it is possible for a person to possess contraband and yet lack standing to object to the search that turned it up, if the contraband was seized from a place in which *D* lacked a legitimate privacy expectation, such as another person's residence or vehicle.

## § 20.06　General Principles of Standing: Pre-*Rakas*

The doctrine of standing took a significant turn in 1978, when the Court decided *Rakas v. Illinois*.[35] The implications of *Rakas* are discussed in Section 20.07. Prior to *Rakas*, the Supreme Court handed down only twelve opinions dealing with the scope of the doctrine of standing.[36] However, based on the Court's few opinions and lower court jurisprudence, the following summary of the pre-*Rakas* law is possible.

A defendant had standing to raise a Fourth Amendment claim if he: (1) owned or had a possessory interest in the premises searched;[37] (2) was legitimately on the premises at the time of the search;[38] (3) owned the property seized;[39] or (4) had lawful possession of the property seized, such as in the status of a bailee.[40] Automatic standing existed in limited circumstances.[41]

## § 20.07　Standing to Contest a Search: *Rakas v. Illinois*

### [A]　The New Approach

*Rakas v. Illinois*[42] is the leading Supreme Court case in modern "standing" jurisprudence. It brought a new language and a different approach to the doctrine.

In *Rakas*, police officers stopped an automobile that purportedly met the description of the car used in a robbery that had occurred moments earlier. The four occupants, including its owner who had been driving, were ordered

---

[35] 439 U.S. 128 (1978).

[36] Kuhns, Note 1, *supra*, at 514 & n.143 (listing the cases, some of which did not use the term "standing," and some of which dealt only peripherally with the question).

[37] *See* Brown v. United States, 411 U.S. 223, 229 (1973).

[38] Jones v. United States, 362 U.S. 257 (1960).

[39] *See* United States v. Jeffers, 342 U.S. 48 (1951).

[40] 5 LaFave, Note 1, *supra*, at 202.

[41] *See* § 20.05, *supra*.

[42] 439 U.S. 128 (1978); *contra, under the state constitution*, State v. Wood, 536 A.2d 902 (Vt. 1987) (to establish standing, a defendant need only assert a possessory, proprietary, or participatory interest in the item seized or the area to be searched).

out, after which the police searched the passenger compartment. Rifle shells were found in the locked glove compartment, and a sawed-off rifle was found under the front passenger seat.

*D*,[43] a passenger, moved to suppress the rifle and the shells found in the car, apparently on the ground that the police lacked adequate cause for the search. As the Court pointed out various times in the opinion, *D* did not base his claim for standing on the ground that he had an ownership interest in the vehicle or in the property seized, grounds for standing prior to *Rakas*.[44] Instead, his key[45] standing claim was that he was "legitimately on the premises" at the time of the search, a basis for standing authorized by the Court in *Jones v. United States*.[46]

By a 5-4 vote, the Court, per Justice Rehnquist, held that *D*'s motion to suppress the evidence on the basis of his status as a legitimate passenger in the car was properly denied by the trial court. In so holding, the Court announced a new way to look at the issue of standing: according to the majority, the question of standing should not be considered "distinct from the merits of a defendant's Fourth Amendment claim."[47] That is, beginning with this case, the issue of standing to contest a search collapses into the basic "*Katz*-ian"[48] matter of whether the defendant had a reasonable or legitimate expectation of privacy in the area searched.[49] According to *Rakas*, the new test for standing to contest a search—or what the Court described as the "capacity to claim the protection of the Fourth Amendment"—is "whether the person who claims the protection of the Amendment has a legitimate expectation of privacy in the invaded place." The Court minimized the significance of this restatement of standing law. It stated that "[w]e can think of no decided cases of this Court that would have come out differently had we concluded, as we do now, that the . . . standing requirement . . . is more properly subsumed under substantive Fourth Amendment doctrine."

Justice Rehnquist explained that the holding in *Jones* was proper,[50] but

---

[43] Actually, there were two petitioners in the *Rakas* appeal. For purposes of clarity, they are subsumed under "*D*."

[44] *See* § 20.06, *supra*.

[45] *D* also claimed standing on the ground that he was the target of the search, a theory rejected by the Court. *See* § 20.03, *supra*.

[46] 362 U.S. 257 (1960).

[47] For further discussion of this point, *see* § 20.01[B], *supra*.

[48] Katz v. United States, 389 U.S. 347 (1967).

[49] But, notice: The "standing" issue is whether *the defendant* has a legitimate expectation of privacy in the area searched, whereas the "search" issue is whether *anyone* has a legitimate expectation of privacy in the area searched.

[50] *Jones* is more fully discussed in subsection § 20.07[B][1][a], *infra*.

the phrase used in that case—"legitimately on premises"—"creates too broad a gauge for measurement of Fourth Amendment rights." According to the *Jones* standard, the *Rakas* Court reasoned, a casual visitor to another person's home would have standing to contest a search of the basement that the visitor had never seen or been permitted to enter. Similarly "a casual visitor who walks into a house one minute before a search of the house commences and leaves one minute after the search ends would be able to contest the legality of the search." Yet, to the *Rakas* Court neither outcome was sensible, as the first visitor had no legitimate expectation of privacy in the basement, and the second visitor had no expectation of privacy in the home at all.[51] Rehnquist pointed out, however, that "[t]his is not to say that such visitors could not contest the lawfulness of the seizure of evidence or the search if their own property were seized. . . ."[52]

On the facts of *Rakas*, the majority concluded that *D* failed to prove that he had any legitimate expectation of privacy in the areas searched, namely, in the locked glove compartment and the area under the front passenger seat. According to the Court, "[l]ike the trunk of an automobile, these are areas in which a passenger *qua* passenger simply would not normally have a legitimate expectation of privacy." Therefore, *D* could not successfully claim the protections of the Fourth Amendment.

Justice White, with whom Justices Brennan, Marshall, and Stevens joined, dissented. He warned that the Court had "declare[d] an 'open season' on automobiles." Specifically, he interpreted the case to stand for the proposition that "a legitimate occupant of an automobile may not invoke the exclusionary rule and challenge a search of that vehicle unless he happens to own or have a possessory interest in it."

---

[51] Rehnquist's first example seems correct to this extent: if I invite a guest into my home, and give her access only to one part of the home, she has no reason to object to a search of an entirely different part of the house. As a guest, she does not have a reasonable expectation of privacy in the area searched (the basement). But, what if the police have to enter, say, the kitchen, where my guest is sitting with me, in order to get to the basement to conduct the unlawful search? If the *entry of the house*—as distinguished from the specific basement search—is also at issue, I see no reason why my guest should not have standing to contest *that* aspect of the police conduct.

In regard to the second hypothetical, I have difficulty understanding why a casual visitor to my home, present there for just a few minutes, has no legitimate expectation of privacy if the police, for example, break into the house in violation of the Fourth Amendment during precisely those few minutes of her presence there. If she is there permissively, I would think that her expectations of privacy begin as soon as she enters the sanctuary of "my castle," and that her expectations that the police won't break in are no less legitimate because it is a short visit.

[52] *But see* § 20.07[B][4], *infra.*

The dissent argued that the holding in *Rakas* would undercut the purpose of the exclusionary rule, as it would serve as an invitation to the police to search any automobile containing more than one person, on the ground that any evidence unlawfully found in it would probably be admissible against at least some of the occupants.

The dissent objected to the Court's approach on two other grounds. First, it criticized the majority for rejecting *Jones*'s legitimately-on-the-premises rule, which was relatively easy to apply by police and courts, and substituting for it a non-bright-line test ("legitimate expectation of privacy in the invaded place"), which it predicted would present greater difficulties of application.[53]

Second, the dissent accused the Court of returning to pre-*Katz* property rights distinctions, even as it denied that it was doing so. As the dissent viewed the facts in *Rakas*, D was in a private place (an automobile) with the permission of the owner of that place, yet this did not entitle him under the Court's analysis to a legitimate expectation of privacy. "But," the dissent asked rhetorically, "if that is not sufficient, what would be?" Its answer was that "it is hard to imagine anything short of a property interest [in the car] that would satisfy the majority."

As a matter of privacy rights, Justice White believed that the holding was not only contrary to precedent, "but also to the everyday expectations of privacy that we all share." He suggested that if the owner of the car in *Rakas* had invited D to be a passenger and had said, "I give you a temporary possessory interest in my vehicle so that you will share the right of privacy that the Supreme Court says that I own," then the majority "apparently" would have reached a different conclusion. "But," he said, "people seldom say such things, though they may mean their invitation to encompass them if only they had thought of the problem."

In view of the dissent's claims regarding the meaning of *Rakas* and the majority's observation that "[i]t is not without significance that these statements of today's 'holding' come from the dissenting opinion, and not from the Court's opinion,"[54] a closer look at the impact of *Rakas* is in order.

---

[53] The majority replied that the *Jones* rule had only "superficial clarity" and concealed "underneath that thin veneer all of the problems of line drawing which must be faced in any conscientious effort to apply the Fourth Amendment."

[54] *Rakas*, 439 U.S. at 149 n.17.

### [B]   The Impact of *Rakas*: A Closer Look

### [1]   Search of Another Person's Residence

#### [a]   When the Owner or Lessor is Absent

Nothing in *Rakas* suggests any change in the previous rule that a person with a possessory interest in premises searched by the police has standing to contest the search of his own residence, even if he is temporarily not present at the time of the intrusion.[55] After *Rakas*, however, a person may not challenge a search of *another person*'s residence merely on the ground that he was "legitimately on the premises" at the time of the intrusion. Although such a basis was satisfactory in *Jones v. United States*,[56] it is now necessary to determine whether the guest had a reasonable expectation of privacy in the premises searched.

A non-resident defendant should have standing to contest a search if he was the sole occupant of the premises, with the permission of the resident. For example, the defendant in *Jones* was alone in his friend's apartment when the search occurred. He had a key to the premises, which he used to admit himself to the apartment, had clothing in the closet, had slept there "maybe a night," and had "complete dominion and control" (*Rakas*'s words) over the apartment, except *vis a vis* the absent host. As *Rakas* analyzed *Jones*, the latter case stood "for the unremarkable proposition that a person can have a legally sufficient interest in a place other than his own home so that the Fourth Amendment protects him from unreasonable governmental intrusion into that place."

#### [b]   When the Owner or Lessor is Present

A person may sometimes successfully challenge a search of another person's residence, *even when the resident is present*. This is evident from *Minnesota v. Olson*.[57] In *Olson*, the Supreme Court held, 7-2, that *D*, an overnight guest in his girl friend's home, could challenge the police entry of the premises, notwithstanding the fact that *D* was never alone in the home, did not have a key, and lacked dominion and control over the premises.

Speaking for the Court, Justice White (the author of the *Rakas* dissent) stated that "[w]e do not understand *Rakas* . . . to hold that an overnight guest can never have a legitimate expectation of privacy except when his host is away and he has a key . . . ." Instead, *Olson* holds, any overnight

---

[55] 5 LaFave, Note 1, *supra*, at 122.

[56] 362 U.S. 247 (1960).

[57] 495 U.S. 91 (1990).

guest, even one who lacks "untrammeled power to admit and exclude" others because the host is present, can challenge a search in his host's home.

According to White, the holding in *Olson* "merely recognizes the everyday expectations of privacy that we all share." If a guest were required to have complete dominion and control in order to have standing, Justice White pointed out, "an adult daughter living temporarily in the home of her parents would have no legitimate expectation of privacy because her right to admit or exclude would be subject to her parents' veto."

If an overnight guest may challenge a search, will a lesser connection to the premises suffice? The Supreme Court has provided insights into this question. In *Minnesota v. Carter*,[58] X, the lessee of a ground-level apartment, and *D1* and *D2*, his guests, sat bagging cocaine in *X*'s apartment. These activities were observed by a police officer who looked through a gap in a drawn window blind. *D1* and *D2* were from out-of-town and (as explained by the Court) "had come to the apartment for the sole purpose of packaging the cocaine. [They] had never been to the apartment before and were only in the apartment for approximately 2 ½ hours."

The Court held, 5-4, that the Fourth Amendment rights of *D1* and *D2* were not violated by the officer's surveillance of their activities. Whereas an overnight guest may claim the protections of the Fourth Amendment (*Olson*), "one who is merely present with the consent of the householder may not." Chief Justice Rehnquist, writing for the majority, explained:

> If we regard the overnight guest in *Minnesota v. Olson* as typifying those who may claim the protection of the Fourth Amendment in the home of another, and one merely "legitimately on the premises" as typifying those who may not do so, the present case is obviously somewhere in between.

The Court then focused on three factors that, in its view, placed this case on the no-right-to-challenge side of the line:

> [T]he purely commercial nature of the transaction engaged in here, the relatively short period of time on the premises, and the lack of any previous connections between [*D1* and *D2*] and [*X*], all lead us to conclude that [their] situation is closer to that of one simply permitted on the premises.

This language, however, does not mean that only an overnight guest may challenge a search in another person's home. Although this is the view of Justices Scalia and Thomas—they joined the Rehnquist opinion but also separately concurred[59] —the separate opinions of Justice Kennedy (who,

---

[58] 525 U.S. 83 (1998).

[59] According to Justices Scalia and Thomas, the text of the Fourth Amendment (which

like Scalia and Thomas, joined the majority opinion), Justice Breyer (who concurred only in the judgment), and the three dissenters (Justices Ginsburg, Stevens, and Souter) suggest a less narrow reading of the case.

It may be worthwhile, first, to look at the dissent. The three dissenters, per Justice Ginsburg, announced a much broader "standing" rule than the majority: "[W]hen a homeowner or lessor personally invites a guest into her home to share in a common endeavor, whether it be for conversation, to engage in leisure activities, or for business purposes licit or illicit, that guest should share his host's shelter against unreasonable searches and seizures."[60] Their position in this regard was joined by Justice Breyer, who concurred in the judgment against the defendants, but who stated that he agreed with the dissent that *D1* and *D2* "can claim the Fourth Amendment protection." Thus, there are four votes for the Ginsburg rule.

That brings us to Justice Kennedy, the swing vote. He explained that he joined the majority opinion because he believed that "its reasoning is consistent with my view that almost all social guests have a legitimate expectation of privacy, and hence protection against unreasonable searches, in their host's home." Why, then, did he join the opinion, since *D1* and *D2* were in *X*'s residence with the latter's consent? According to Kennedy:

> In this case, [*D1* and *D2*] have established nothing more than a fleeting and insubstantial connection with [*X*'s] home. For all that appears in the record, [they] used [*X*'s] house simply as a convenient processing station . . . . There is no suggestion that [*D1* and *D2*] engaged in confidential communications with [*X*] about their transaction. [They] had not been to [*X*'s] apartment before, and they left it even before their arrest.

Kennedy concluded that the defendants' Fourth Amendment rights were not violated because they had "established no meaningful tie or connection to the owner, the owner's home, or the owner's expectation of privacy."

Thus, it seems that Justice Kennedy would have ruled for the defendants if one, or certainly more, of the following factors were present: (1) they had been in the residence for non-commercial reasons; (2) they had spoken

---

protects people in "their" persons, houses, papers, and effects) and common law precedent support the view that the Fourth Amendment does not protect a person in *another*'s home. What about *Olson*? "We went to the absolute limit of what text and tradition permits . . ., when we protected a mere overnight guest against an unreasonable search of his hosts' apartment." In *Olson*, however, unlike in the present case, "it is plausible to regard a person's overnight lodging as at least his 'temporary' residence . . . ."

[60] Justice Ginsburg observed, "[o]ur decisions indicate that people have a reasonable expectation of privacy in their homes in part because they have the prerogative to exclude others. The power to exclude implies the power to include. Our Fourth Amendment decisions should reflect these complementary prerogatives."

confidentially to *X* regarding their commercial (and illegal) activities; and/or (3) they had had prior or more substantial connections to the premises (although 2 ½ hours on this occasion hardly seems fleeting). Thus, his ruling against the defendants was exceedingly narrow. When coupled with the dissenters' and Breyer's position, there is reason to believe that on occasion a social, or even business, guest will be permitted to challenge a search in the host's residence, even if the guest does not stay overnight.

### [2]  Search of One's Own Automobile When Absent

A person retains a legitimate expectation of privacy in his own home even when he is temporarily absent from it.[61] Does the same rule apply to the owner of an automobile who is not present when his vehicle is searched? Lower court case law is split. Most courts have held that when a car owner lends his vehicle to another, at least if the bailment is of short duration, the owner maintains a legitimate expectation of privacy in it and, therefore, can challenge a search of the car that takes place in his absence.[62]

A few courts have held that possession, and not ownership of the car is the key; therefore, a nonpresent owner of an automobile lacks standing to contest the search of his vehicle.[63] More often, however, a court may rule that the owner lacks standing if he gives another person complete control of the car and its contents for an extended period of time, especially if the vehicle will be driven a considerable distance away from the owner.[64]

### [3]  Search of Another Person's Automobile

### [a]  When the Owner Is Absent

The general rule after *Rakas* is easy to state, but difficult to apply: a person has standing to contest a search of an automobile in which he is an occupant, although he is not its owner, if he has a reasonable expectation of privacy in the area of the automobile searched. Despite the concerns of Justice White in the dissent in *Rakas* (that the majority "declare[d] 'open season' on automobiles"), a non-owner occupant may have standing in limited circumstances.

---

[61] *See* the text to Note 55, *supra*.

[62] United States v. Eldridge, 302 F.2d 463, 464–65 (4th Cir. 1962) (court noting that the "bailment was to be of short duration"); United States v. Dotson, 817 F.2d 1127, *modified*, 821 F.2d 1034 (5th Cir. 1987) (*D* had standing after he loaned his car to a friend for a brief time to get the car washed); State v. Bartlett, 999 P.2d 274 (Kan. 2000) (*D* loaned the car to another to take it to fill a water container).

[63] United States v. Dall, 608 F.2d 910, 915 (1st Cir. 1979)

[64] State v. Abramoff, 338 N.W.2d 502 (Wis. 1983) (*D* permitted others to drive his car for a trip between Florida and Wisconsin).

The most likely case for standing occurs when the owner of the car is absent, and the person challenging the search has a possessory interest in the vehicle comparable to that of the occupant of the premises in *Jones*. For example, if *X*-owner lends his car to *D* for a week, *D* should be able to challenge a search of the vehicle if it is stopped while he is driving it in *X*'s absence. At the time of the search, *D* has exclusive dominion and control over the car and, thus, would have a legitimate expectation of privacy in it.

Under some circumstances, a non-owner may only have a legitimate expectation of privacy in some portions of the automobile. Standing is not necessarily an all-or-nothing proposition. It should be remembered that *Rakas* found that *D* lacked a reasonable expectation of privacy *in the particular areas of the car searched*. Similarly, regarding the right of a guest in a house to contest a search, the Court distinguished between a search of the kitchen, where a hypothetical guest was invited to be, and the basement, to which the guest was not invited.[65] Suppose, therefore, car owner *X* has two keys to the vehicle: an ignition key that also unlocks the doors to the automobile; and a separate trunk key. If *X* loans the car to *D*, but does not furnish the trunk key, it is likely that *D*—if he has no other access to the trunk[66] —would not have standing to contest a trunk search, although he could challenge a search of the passenger compartment.

### [b]    When the Owner Is Present

May a "mere"[67] passenger in a vehicle containing the owner of the car have a reasonable expectation of privacy in the automobile, or at least in portions of it?

Before answering, it is important to clarify the issue at hand. The question is whether an occupant may challenge a *search* of the car in which the owner is present. A separate question arises if the occupant wishes to challenge the *forcible stop*—the initial *seizure* of the vehicle—preceding the search. This question is considered in Section 20.08. Nor are we concerned here with a case in which an occupant of a car is *himself* searched; although a person may not have an expectation of privacy in premises, he retains a legitimate expectation of privacy regarding his own person, even as he sits in another person's car.

---

[65] *See* the text following Note 50, *supra.*

[66] In many modern automobiles, however, the trunk can be opened from inside the car without a key by pulling a latch.

[67] Of course, a special relationship between the passenger and the car owner, such as by marriage, would differentiate it from the "mere" passenger situation. In such circumstances, the spouse-passenger should have standing to object, as lower courts have consistently held. 5 LaFave, Note 1, *supra*, at 191–92.

What, then, about a search of an automobile driven by the owner, in which *D* is a passenger? May *D* *ever* have standing to challenge such a search? Some courts have answered this question in the negative.[68] But, is this result inevitable? For example, suppose that, in a week-long cross-country drive, *X*, the owner of a vehicle, gives *D* a trunk key, with the explicit understanding that *D* may place his belongings in the trunk any time he wishes. Does *X*'s presence in the car preclude a finding that *D* has a protectible privacy interest in the trunk?

Although the matter is disputable, *D* should have standing. Indeed, in view of the Court's holding in *Minnesota v. Olson*,[69] namely, that an overnight guest in a home may have a reasonable expectation of privacy in that dwelling even if the host is present at all times, it should be possible for *D* to challenge a search of at least some portions of a car in which he is a week-long guest.[70] As the Court said in *Olson*, "hosts will more likely than not respect the privacy interests of their guests, who are entitled to a legitimate expectation of privacy despite the fact they have no legal interest in the premises and do not have the legal authority to determine who may or may not enter."

On the other hand, *Rakas* expressly left open the issue of "whether the same expectations of privacy are warranted in a car as would be justified in a dwelling house in analogous circumstances."[71] In view of the long lines of cases that provide that a person possesses a lesser expectation of privacy in an automobile than in a home, it is conceivable that the reasoning of *Olson* will not transfer to an automobile.

### [4] Contesting a Search Resulting in the Seizure of One's Own Property

The preceding discussion considered the question of whether a defendant may challenge a search of another's person's residence or car in which the defendant was an occupant. But, suppose that we add an additional factor: the property seized in the search belongs to the defendant. Assuming that the defendant does not otherwise have standing, may he now challenge the search because it resulted in the seizure of his own property?[72] Prior to

---

[68] *Id.* at 172.

[69] 495 U.S. 91 (1990). *See* § 20.07[B][1][b], *supra*.

[70] *See also* Minnesota v. Carter, 525 U.S. 83 (1998) (in which five Justices indicated support for the proposition that a *non*-overnight guest in a home will usually have standing to challenge a search that occurs in his presence). *Carter* is discussed at § 20.07[B][1][b], *supra*.

[71] *Rakas*, 439 U.S. at 148.

[72] Again, this must be distinguished from the question of whether the *seizure* of his property may be challenged, a matter considered in Section 20.08, *infra*.

*Rakas,* the answer was clear: a person had standing to contest a search if he claimed an ownership or possessory interest in the property seized during the search.[73]

*Rakas* did not expressly overrule this principle. In fact, a fair reading of the opinion is that the Court left the old law undisturbed in this regard. The Court various times stated that *D,* a passenger in the car, had not claimed that either the rifle or ammunition seized in the search were his, the implication of which was that had either been his property, *D* would have had standing to object to the search. The Court also implied in *Rakas* that a casual visitor to a house, even one who lacks a reasonable expectation of privacy in it, could contest a search that culminated in the seizure of his own property on the premises.[74]

Nonetheless, the holding of *Rawlings v. Kentucky*[75] belies the implications of *Rakas. Rawlings* holds that a person may *not* successfully challenge a search of an area in which he has no reasonable expectation of privacy even though he has a possessory or ownership interest in the property seized during the search.

In *Rawlings, D* placed a jar and vials containing controlled substances in *X*'s purse shortly before the police entered a home in which *D* and *X* were guests in order to arrest the owner of the house. When the police arrived, they smelled marijuana smoke and observed marijuana seeds, so two officers left to apply for a search warrant. The remaining officers informed the occupants that they could not leave pending the execution of the warrant, unless they submitted to a body search. Shortly thereafter, after the warrant was obtained, the police ordered *X* to empty her purse.[76] When she did, the officers discovered the controlled substances. *D,* who was sitting next to *X* on a couch, admitted ownership of them.

The Court held that, following *Rakas, D* could not contest the search of *X*'s purse simply on the basis that he had an ownership interest in the property seized. The Court, again per Justice Rehnquist, stated that *Rakas* rejected the view that "arcane" concepts of property law controlled the issue; therefore, the question that had to be considered was whether *D* had a reasonable expectation of privacy in *X*'s purse, of which *D*'s ownership of the drug vial was only one factor in that determination.

---

[73] *See* § 20.06, *supra.*

[74] *See* the text accompanying Note 52, *supra.*

[75] 448 U.S. 98 (1980).

[76] The police incorrectly believed that the warrant authorized them to search the persons in the house.

The Court held that $D$ did not have a reasonable expectation of privacy in $X$'s purse. Among the reasons given by the Court were: (1) at the time of the "sudden bailment" $D$ had known $X$ for only a few days; (2) $D$ had never before sought or received access to $X$'s purse; (3) $D$ did not have a right to exclude others from the purse; (4) $Y$, a "longtime acquaintance and frequent companion" of $X$, had "free access" to her purse and, in fact, had rummaged through it for a hairbrush that morning; (5) the "precipitous nature of the transaction hardly supports a reasonable inference that [$D$] took normal precautions to maintain his privacy"; and (6) the record of the suppression hearing "contains a frank admission by [$D$] that he had no subjective expectation that [$X$'s] purse would remain free from governmental intrusion."

Professor LaFave has written that "[n]o one of the several points made by Justice Rehnquist can withstand close scrutiny. . . ."[77] There is no reason why a bailor—here, $D$—should not expect privacy in the area in which his goods are kept by the bailee. Indeed, the selection of a bailee is made in large part on the basis of the bailor's belief that his goods will be protected and his privacy in them respected. In any case, any expectation of privacy that would otherwise exist is not diminished merely because the bailor recently met the bailee (point 1) or was using that person for the first time (point 2).

Nor should it be fatal to the bailor's claim that he cannot exclude others from the bailee's "premises" (here, the purse) (point 3). The *Rawlings* Court's conclusion is inconsistent with the Court's later reasoning in *Minnesota v. Olson*[78] that the mere fact that a homeowner has the right to admit persons into a house in which he has a guest does not deprive the guest of a legitimate expectation of privacy in the premises. It should follow from this that $X$'s right to allow others to look in her purse, even over $D$'s objection, should not render $D$'s expectation of privacy in the purse illegitimate.

As for $Y$'s access to the purse (point 4), this point should add very little. The right to privacy is not lost merely because it is shared, as long as it is not shared with the public at large.

The Court's fifth point, that $D$ did not take reasonable precautions to protect his privacy, is also unpersuasive. $D$ did not leave the jar and vials on a table; he put it in $X$'s purse. A person ordinarily has a reasonable expectation of privacy in a container as long as it is closed.[79] $X$'s purse was such a container.

---

[77] 5 LaFave, Note 1, *supra*, at 154.

[78] 495 U.S. 91 (1990). *See* § 20.07[B][1][b], *supra*.

[79] *See* United States v. Ross, 456 U.S. 798, 822 (1982).

Finally, as to the sixth point, the "frank admission" noted by the majority was a "[n]o, sir" answer to the question, "[d]id you feel that [X's] purse would be free from the intrusion of the officers as you sat there?" As the question demonstrates, D was being asked whether he thought X's purse would remain inviolate *after* the police had already entered the home and told the guests that they could not leave without submitting to a personal search. As Professor LaFave has cogently pointed out,[80] if D's admission precludes a challenge to the search of X's purse, it would also preclude D from challenging a search of his own person, a silly result.

## § 20.08   Standing to Contest a Seizure: Post-*Rakas*

Nearly everything the Supreme Court has said about standing, both before and after its benchmark ruling in *Rakas v. Illinois*,[81] has concerned challenges to police searches, rather than to seizures. For example, in *Rakas*, D challenged the search of X's car, in which property apparently not belonging to D was seized and used against him at his trial. In *Rawlings v. Kentucky*,[82] D challenged the search of X's purse, in which drugs belonging to D were discovered and seized.

Although the case law, even in the lower courts, is thin, there is apparently no doubt that a person may challenge a seizure of his own person, but lacks standing to challenge the seizure of someone else.[83] However, the former point is an important one. Suppose that the police stop a car on the highway in which D is an occupant, without probable cause or reasonable suspicion of any criminal activity. After the stop, they conduct a search of the car, during which they find illegal drugs belonging to D in the trunk. Based on *Rakas*, it is doubtful that D would have standing to challenge the trunk *search*, but he *would* have standing to challenge the forcible stop of the car, because *that* act constituted an unlawful *seizure* of his person (and, of course, of everyone else in the car). As various courts have recognized, if a defendant successfully challenges the seizure of his person, the evidence found in the car may be excluded as a fruit of that unlawful conduct.[84]

Under what circumstances may a person challenge the *seizure* of an *object*? For example, suppose that in *Rawlings* D had placed a sealed envelope containing drugs in X's purse. Suppose further that when the police ordered X to empty her purse, they found the sealed envelope and, although they had no idea what was inside, seized it. Four days later, after a dog

---

80 5 LaFave, Note 1, *supra*, at 158.

81 439 U.S. 128 (1978). *See* § 20.07[A], *supra*.

82 448 U.S. 98 (1980). *See* § 20.07[B][3], *supra*.

83 5 LaFave, Note 1, *supra*, at 120.

84 *Id.* at 173 & n.231 (and cases cited therein).

sniff of the envelope confirmed their hunch that it contained illegal drugs, assume they obtained a warrant to search the envelope. On these facts, *D* would not have standing to contest the *search* of *X*'s purse, but would he have standing to contest the four-day-long *seizure* of the envelope? If so, and assuming that this seizure was unlawful,[85] the subsequent search would be tainted.

If the Supreme Court is consistent, it should treat seizures as it does searches. That is, if the issue of standing to contest a *search* is subsumed under substantive Fourth Amendment doctrine, the same should occur here. If so, as a seizure of an object occurs "when there is some meaningful interference with an individual's possessory interest in that property,"[86] the issue of standing would be whether the seizure constituted a meaningful interference with the *defendant's* possessory interest in the property seized. In the hypothetical *Rawlings* scenario, *D* would have standing to contest the seizure of the envelope.

---

[85] *See* United States v. Place, 462 U.S. 696 (1983). *See* § 18.09, *supra.*

[86] United States v. Jacobsen, 466 U.S. 109, 113 (1984). *See* § 8.02[A], *supra.*

CHAPTER **21**

# FOURTH AMENDMENT: EXCLUSIONARY RULE

## § 21.01 Development of the Exclusionary Rule[1]

### [A] Overview

The Fourth Amendment text describes "[t]he right of the people": it is "to be secure in [our] persons, houses, papers, and effects, against unreasonable searches and seizures." And, we are told that "no Warrants shall issue, but upon probable cause, supported by Oath or affirmation, and particularly describing the place to be searched, and the persons or things to be seized."

Rights presumably come with remedies for their violation. What is the remedy for the violation of a Fourth Amendment right? The text is silent in this regard, as it is with many other provisions of the Bill of Rights. Over time, the Supreme Court has come to conclude that an exclusionary rule—generally speaking, evidence gathered in violation of the Fourth Amendment is inadmissible in a criminal trial—is the primary (although not exclusive) remedy available to victims of unreasonable searches and seizures. As will be seen in later sections of this chapter,[2] however, the exclusionary rule is exceptionally controversial, its scope has changed—largely, narrowed—over time, and there is reason to question its long-term vitality.

---

[1] *See generally* 1 Wayne R. LaFave, Search and Seizure § 1.1(a)–(e) (3d ed. 1996); Francis A. Allen, *Federalism and the Fourth Amendment: A Requiem for Wolf*, 1961 Sup. Ct. Rev. 1; Yale Kamisar, *Wolf and Lustig Ten Years Later: Illegal State Evidence in State and Federal Courts*, 43 Minn. L. Rev. 1083 (1959); Potter Stewart, *The Road to Mapp v. Ohio and Beyond: The Origins, Development and Future of the Exclusionary Rule in Search-and-Seizure Cases*, 83 Colum. L. Rev. 1365 (1983); Silas Wasserstrom & William J. Mertens, *The Exclusionary Rule on the Scaffold: But Was It a Fair Trial?*, 22 Am. Crim. L. Rev. 85 (1984). For an examination of the exclusionary rule under Canada's Charter of Rights, *see* David C. McDonald, *The Exclusion of Evidence Obtained by Constitutionally Impermissible Means in Canada*, 9 Crim. Just. Ethics (Summer/Fall 1990), at 43.

Other constitutional rights have exclusionary rules, which are discussed in this text in conjunction with the specific rights in question. Various non-constitutional rules have exclusionary rules. As to them, *see* George E. Dix, *Nonconstitutional Exclusionary Rules in Criminal Procedure*, 27 Am. Crim. L. Rev. 53 (1989).

[2] *See especially* §§ 21.05–25.07, *infra.*

## [B]  *Weeks v. United States*

The Supreme Court adopted the Fourth Amendment exclusionary rule for the first time in 1914 in *Weeks v. United States*.[3] In *Weeks*, the Court held that in *federal* trials the Fourth Amendment bars the use of evidence unconstitutionally seized by federal law enforcement officers. Without such a rule, the Court subsequently explained, the Fourth Amendment would be reduced to a mere "form of words."[4]

## [C]  *Wolf v. Colorado*

When *Weeks* was decided, the Supreme Court had not yet held that the guarantees of the Fourth Amendment applied to the states pursuant to the Fourteenth Amendment due process clause.[5] Therefore, the Court in *Weeks* did not have reason to consider whether the exclusionary rule applied in *state* criminal trials.

In 1949, however, in *Wolf v. Colorado*,[6] the Court, per Justice Felix Frankfurter, held that "security of one's privacy against arbitrary intrusion by the police—which is at the core of the Fourth Amendment—is basic to a free society." As a consequence of *Wolf*, therefore, states are now subject to the substantive provisions of the Fourth Amendment.

On the other hand, the *Wolf* Court indicated that "the ways of enforcing such a basic right raise questions of a different order." According to *Wolf*, the exclusionary rule adopted in *Weeks* "was not derived from the explicit requirements of the Fourth Amendment. . . . The decision was a matter of judicial implication." The Court seemed to be hinting by this remark that the federal exclusionary rule of *Weeks* might not be constitutionally required. It stated that "a different question [than was raised in *Weeks*] would be presented if Congress . . . were to pass a statute purporting to negate the *Weeks* doctrine." In "default of that judgment," the Court indicated, it would "stoutly adhere" to *Weeks*.

Although the Court was unwilling to back down from its holding in *Weeks*, it refused to extend the exclusionary rule to the states. The Court concluded that the states were not compelled to exclude "logically relevant evidence" from their trials, even if that evidence was obtained unconstitutionally as a result of an unreasonable search or seizure. Justice Frankfurter noted that none of the ten jurisdictions that had considered the issue within

---

[3] 232 U.S. 383 (1914).

[4] Silverthorne Lumber Co. v. United States, 251 U.S. 385, 392 (1920).

[5] *See* chapter 3, *supra*, for an explanation of the relationship of the Fourteenth Amendment to the Bill of Rights.

[6] 338 U.S. 25 (1949), *overruled on other grounds*, Mapp v. Ohio, 367 U.S. 643 (1961).

the United Kingdom and the British Commonwealth excluded evidence obtained by illegal search and seizure, and that a majority of the states in this country, left to their own devices, had rejected the *Weeks* doctrine.

### [D]  *Rochin v. California* and Its Progeny

Although *Wolf v. Colorado* held that evidence was not inadmissible in a state trial merely because it was gathered in violation of the principles underlying the Fourth Amendment, the Court demonstrated in *Rochin v. California*[7] that it was prepared to require the adoption of an exclusionary rule in state trials, albeit by a different route.

In *Rochin*, police officers, acting without a search warrant and perhaps without probable cause, entered *D*'s home at night, forcibly opened his second-floor bedroom door, and found *D* and his wife on the bed. When *D* swallowed capsules that had been on a night stand, three officers "jumped" on him and unsuccessfully tried to extract them from his mouth. They failed, so they took *D*, handcuffed, to a hospital where they directed physicians to force an emetic solution through a tube into his stomach in order to cause him to expel the capsules, which he did. The capsules contained morphine. *D* was prosecuted for the possession of the morphine.

The Court, per Justice Frankfurter (the author of *Wolf*), held that the police conduct in this case—specifically, "[i]llegally breaking into the privacy of the petitioner, the struggle to open his mouth and remove what was there, the forcible extraction of his stomach's contents"—"shock[ed] the conscience." It said that the police conduct was "bound to offend even hardened sensibilities," and was "too close to the rack and the screw to permit."

The Court concluded that the Fourteenth Amendment due process clause prohibits the use at trial of evidence, even of a reliable nature, secured in a manner that violates "certain decencies of civilized conduct." To hold otherwise, *Rochin* concluded, "would be to afford brutality the cloak of law. Nothing would be more calculated to discredit law and thereby to brutalize the temper of society."

In subsequent cases, the Court interpreted *Rochin* narrowly. In *Irvine v. California*,[8] the Court ruled, 5-4, over Justice Frankfurter's dissent, that the government was within its rights to introduce at trial statements that the police had obtained illegally by entering *D*'s home to install and then later move a hidden microphone. *Rochin* was distinguished on the ground that it, unlike the present case, involved "coercion, violence, or brutality to the person."

---

[7] 342 U.S. 165 (1952).

[8] 347 U.S. 128 (1954).

*Rochin* was again distinguished in *Breithaupt v. Abram.*[9] In *Breithaupt*, the police took a blood sample from *D* while he was unconscious. Because the blood was extracted nonviolently by a physician in a hospital, the Court concluded that the "sense of justice of which we spoke in *Rochin*" was not offended.

The shock-the-conscience test of *Rochin* remains good law. However, in light of its narrow scope, and the Supreme Court's post-*Rochin* Fourth Amendment exclusionary rule jurisprudence that brings that constitutional right into play, the doctrine is rarely invoked today to exclude real evidence secured from a person in a violent manner.[10]

### [E] *Mapp v. Ohio*

In *Mapp v. Ohio*,[11] officers who claimed they were conducting an investigation of a bombing sought to enter *D*'s house in order to find and question a suspect they believed was hiding there. When they demanded entrance, *D* telephoned her attorney and, on his advice, refused to admit them without a search warrant.

After keeping the house under surveillance for three hours, and apparently[12] still without a warrant, the officers returned to the house. When *D* did not come to the door immediately, they forcibly entered, damaging the door in the process. Once inside, the officers displayed a piece of paper that they claimed was a search warrant. *D* grabbed it and "placed it in her bosom." A struggle ensued, in which *D*'s hand was twisted, after which the police removed the "warrant" from her clothing.

*D* was forcibly taken upstairs to her bedroom, where the officers searched her belongings. Later, the rest of the house, including her child's bedroom, the living room, the kitchen, and the basement were thoroughly searched. Nobody, nor any evidence regarding the bombing, was found. However, "obscene materials"[13] were found and seized. *D* was convicted for their possession.

---

[9] 352 U.S. 432 (1957).

[10] The Supreme Court has acknowledged that *Rochin* "today would be treated under the Fourth Amendment, albeit with the same result." County of Sacramento v. Lewis, 523 U.S. 833, 849 n.9 (1998). The doctrine still "point[s] the way" to courts, however, when they must identify the point at which abusive use of executive power violates the Constitution. *Id.* at 847.

[11] 367 U.S. 643 (1961).

[12] No warrant was produced by the prosecutor, nor was this failure ever explained.

[13] The materials consisted of four books—*Affairs of a Troubadour, Little Darlings, London Stage Affairs,* and *Memories of a Hotel Man* — and a hand-drawn picture "of a very obscene nature." Stewart, Note 1, *supra*, at 1367.

Although the Fourth[14] Amendment aspects of the case were not briefed, argued, or discussed in the state courts, nor raised by *D*'s attorney,[15] the Supreme Court granted hearing in the case and used it as its vehicle to overrule *Wolf*.

*Mapp* holds that the Fourth Amendment exclusionary rule applies in state criminal trials, just as it does in the federal system via *Weeks*. Justice Tom Clark, for the Court, stated that "it was logically and constitutionally necessary that the exclusion doctrine . . . be also insisted upon as an essential ingredient of the right . . . recognized by the *Wolf* case." In short, the exclusionary rule is of constitutional origin. To hold otherwise, *Mapp* said, would be "to grant the right [to be free from unreasonable searches and seizures] but in reality to withhold its privilege and enjoyment."

## § 21.02    Rationale of the Exclusionary Rule[16]

*Mapp v. Ohio*[17] provided two justifications for the exclusionary rule. First, and primarily, the "purpose of the exclusionary rule 'is to deter—to compel respect for the constitutional guaranty in the only effectively available way—by removing the incentive to disregard it.' "[18] In essence, the reasoning follows,[19] if we assume that threat of punishment deters many would-be criminals from violating penal laws, we may assume that police officers, too, will be deterred from violating constitutional rights if they know that the government cannot take advantage of the fruits of their illegal conduct by use of the evidence at a criminal trial.

A second justification for the exclusionary rule is "the imperative of judicial integrity."[20] This rationale was first identified by the Court (although not in "integrity" terms) in *Weeks v. United States*.[21] In *Weeks*,

---

[14] Although the Fourteenth, and not the Fourth, Amendment applies in state prosecutions, *see* chapter 3, *supra*, the text uses "Fourth Amendment" as a shorthand for those fundamental rights in the Fourth Amendment that have been incorporated to the states through the Fourteenth Amendment.

[15] *D*'s counsel raised two constitutional claims: (1) that the police conduct shocked the conscience, in violation of *Rochin v. California* (*see* § 21.01[D], *supra*); and (2) that the conviction for possession of obscene materials violated First Amendment principles. An *amicus* brief included one paragraph calling on the Court to overrule *Wolf*. When *D*'s attorney was questioned about this in oral argument, he indicated that he had never heard of *Wolf*. Stewart, Note 1, *supra*, at 1367.

[16] 1 LaFave, Note 1, *supra*, at § 1.1(f); Jerry E. Norton, *The Exclusionary Rule Reconsidered: Restoring the Status Quo Ante*, 33 Wake Forest L. Rev. 261 (1998).

[17] 367 U.S. 643 (1961).

[18] *Id.* at 656 (quoting Elkins v. United States, 364 U.S. 206, 217 (1960)).

[19] On the question of whether the deterrence reasoning is valid, *see* § 21.04[C], *infra*.

[20] Mapp v. Ohio, 367 U.S. at 659 (quoting Elkins v. United States, 364 U.S. at 222).

[21] 232 U.S. 383 (1914).

the Court stated that the judiciary is "charged at all times with support of the Constitution" and that "people . . . have a right to appeal [to the courts] for the maintenance of . . . fundamental rights." To permit prosecutors to use unconstitutionally seized evidence, *Weeks* reasoned, "would be to affirm by judicial decision a manifest neglect if not an open defiance of the prohibitions of the Constitution." In such circumstances, judges would be acting as "accomplices in the willful disobedience of a Constitution they are sworn to uphold."[22] Judges "shouldn't soil their hands by allowing in unconstitutionally acquired evidence."[23]

Since *Mapp* was decided, however, the Supreme Court has de-emphasized the judicial integrity justification of the exclusionary rule to the point of practical extinction.[24] "[W]hile it is quite true," Justice Rehnquist has observed, "that courts are not to be participants in 'dirty business,' neither are they to be ethereal vestal virgins of another world."[25] The Court now states that the judicial integrity theory has only a "limited role [to play] . . . in the determination whether to apply the rule in a particular context."[26] Deterrence is the " 'prime purpose' of the rule, if not the sole one."[27]

The subordination of "judicial integrity" to "deterrence" in exclusionary rule jurisprudence has a pragmatic explanation. The concept of judicial integrity potentially functions as a moral imperative—"thou shalt not be an accessory to an illegal act"—and, as such, does not easily allow for cost-benefit analysis of the exclusionary rule. Indeed, as the Court has pointed out,[28] if judicial integrity is taken seriously, evidence obtained unlawfully would need to be suppressed in *all* judicial proceedings, not merely (as is now the case) in criminal trials, and it would seemingly require abandonment of the "standing" requirement. These are consequences that the Court, even during the Warren Court era, was unprepared to accept.

---

[22] Elkins v. United States, 364 U.S. at 223.

[23] McGuigan, *An Interview with Judge Robert H. Bork*, Judicial Notice, June, 1986, at 1, 6 (quoting Judge Bork, who rejects this theory).

[24] For arguments in favor of retention of the doctrine, *see* Fred Gilbert Bennett, Note, *Judicial Integrity and Judicial Review: An Argument for Expanding the Scope of the Exclusionary Rule*, 20 UCLA L. Rev. 1129 (1973).

[25] California v. Minjares, 443 U.S. 916, 924 (1979) (Rehnquist, J., dissenting); *see also* McGuigan, Note 23, *supra* (in which Judge Bork observed that "I have never been convinced by that [judicial integrity] argument because it seems the conscience of the court ought to be at least equally shaken by the idea of turning a criminal loose upon society.").

[26] Stone v. Powell, 428 U.S. 465, 485 (1976).

[27] United States v. Janis, 428 U.S. 433, 446 (1976).

[28] Stone v. Powell, 428 U.S. at 485.

## § 21.03  Is the Exclusionary Rule Constitutionally Required?[29]

*Weeks v. United States*[30] implicitly, and *Mapp v. Ohio*[31] explicitly, determined that the exclusionary rule is an essential component—"part and parcel" according to *Mapp*—of the Fourth (and Fourteenth) Amendment. That is, according to *Mapp*, the Fourth Amendment not only safeguards people against unreasonable searches and seizures, but it guarantees that evidence obtained in violation of their Fourth Amendment rights will not be used against them in criminal trials. Indeed, even Justice Harlan, who dissented in *Mapp* because he did *not* believe that the exclusionary rule was constitutionally required, had no doubt that this was the holding of the *Mapp* Court. As he observed:

> Essential to the majority's argument against *Wolf* [*v. Colorado*[32] ] is the proposition that the [exclusionary] rule . . . derives not from the "supervisory power" of this Court over the federal judiciary system, but from Constitutional requirement. This is so because no one, I suppose, would suggest that this Court possesses any general supervisory power over the state courts.

Despite Harlan's unassailable observations and the explicit reasoning of the *Mapp* majority, the Supreme Court implicitly overruled the constitutional reasoning, although not the holding, of *Mapp*—an exclusionary rule remains, but its constitutional pedigree has been lost—in *United States v. Calandra*.[33] In *Calandra*, Justice Lewis Powell, speaking for six members of the Court, described the exclusionary rule as "a judicially created remedy designed to safeguard Fourth Amendment rights generally through its deterrent effect, rather than a personal constitutional right of the party aggrieved." In other words, the exclusionary rule is no longer considered an essential component of the Fourth Amendment, but is merely a remedy devised by the Justices to deter unconstitutional governmental misconduct. As the Court has recently expressed, "the rule is prudential rather than constitutionally mandated . . . ."[34]

What is the significance of the de-constitutionalization of the Fourth Amendment exclusionary rule? Justice William Brennan, dissenting in

---

[29] *See generally* Lawrence Crocker, *Can the Exclusionary Rule Be Saved?*, 84 J. Crim. L. & Criminology 310 (1993); Thomas S. Schrock & Robert C. Welsh, *Up From Calandra: The Exclusionary Rule as a Constitutional Requirement*, 59 Minn. L. Rev. 251 (1974).

[30] 232 U.S. 383 (1914). *See* § 21.01[B], *supra.*

[31] 367 U.S. 643 (1961). *See* § 21.01[E], *supra.*

[32] *See* § 21.01[C], *supra.*

[33] 414 U.S. 338 (1974).

[34] Pennsylvania Bd. of Probation and Parole v. Scott, 524 U.S. 357 (1998).

*Calandra*, expressed his concern this way: "I am left with the uneasy feeling that today's decision may signal that a majority of my colleagues have positioned themselves to . . . abandon altogether the exclusionary rule in search-and-seizure cases." Indeed, if the exclusionary rule is *not* constitutionally commanded by the Constitution—if it is merely a "prudential" rule devised by the Supreme Court—then what the Court "giveth" it can "taketh" away or, at a very minimum, narrow dramatically.

In fact, since *Calandra* was decided, the Court *has* narrowed the exclusionary rule's scope.[35] And, if the only basis for the exclusionary rule is an empirical claim that it deters official misconduct, then the Justices have the authority, if it also has the will, to abolish the exclusionary rule because the Court determines it lacks sufficient deterrent bite to outweigh its costs (loss of reliable evidence).[36]

The de-constitutionalization the exclusionary rule also means that Congress should have authority to abolish the rule, if it replaces it with remedial protections sufficient to meet some yet unclear constitutional minimum standard.[37] And, perhaps, most significantly, since the Court does not have authority to require states to apply a rule not derived from the Constitution, the legitimacy of federal cases that enforce the judicially-created exclusionary rule against the states is called into question. State legislatures, like Congress, may have authority to replace the exclusionary rule with another,

---

[35] *See* §§ 21.05–21.07, *infra.*

[36] It remains to be seen if the Court has sufficient will (votes) to take that step. In an analogous area, the Supreme Court apparently de-constitutionalized the controversial holding of Miranda v. Arizona, 384 U.S. 436 (1966), but then seemingly turned 180 degrees and re-constitutionalized it when confronted with the question of whether to uphold a federal statute that purported to overrule *Miranda.* See Dickerson v. United States, 530 U.S. 428 (2000), discussed at § 24.06[C], *infra.*

[37] Congress has considered *narrowing* the exclusionary rule. *E.g.*, H.R. 666, 104th Cong., 1st Sess. (1995). The "Exclusionary Rule Reform Act of 1995" passed the House of Representatives, 289-142, on February 8, 1995. In the version sent to the Senate, it provided under 18 U.S.C. § 3510(a):

Evidence which is obtained as the result of a search or seizure shall not be excluded in a [federal criminal] proceeding . . . on the ground that the search or seizure was in violation of the fourth amendment to the Constitution . . ., if the search or seizure was carried out in circumstances justifying an objectively reasonable belief that it was in conformity with the fourth amendment. The fact that evidence was obtained pursuant to and within the scope of a warrant constitutes prima facie evidence of the existence of such circumstances.

The Exclusionary Rule Reform Act was not enacted.

perhaps civil or administrative, remedy of sufficient bite to safeguard Fourth Amendment rights.[38]

## § 21.04   Exclusionary Rule: Should It Be Abolished?[39]

### [A]   Political and Historical Overview

Justice William Douglas predicted that *Mapp v. Ohio*[40] would end the "storm of constitutional controversy" evoked by *Wolf*.[41] It did nothing of the sort. Debate regarding *Mapp* and the exclusionary rule commenced almost as soon as the decision was announced, and it has not ceased. Indeed, in light of *United States v. Calandra*,[42] discussed in Section 21.03, *Mapp* and the exclusionary rule are on thin constitutional ice that can crack at any time.

---

[38] *E.g.*, California Assembly Bill 988, as amended on January 4, 1996, would have abolished the exclusionary rule and created a new cause of action in equity "against any state or local public agency whose employees or agents have violated the constitutional rights of any citizen during the courses of a criminal investigation." Upon a finding of a constitutional violation, the law would have authorized a court to issue an injunction commanding that no further violations occur and/or impose "immediate civil penalties [of up to $100,000] payable by the agency employing or directing the offender." The penalties would not have been paid to the victim of the constitutional violation, but would have been payable to a state Restitution Fund. The bill did not become law.

[39] *See generally* Gary S. Goodpaster, *An Essay on Ending the Exclusionary Rule*, 33 Hastings L.J. 1065 (1982); William C. Heffernan & Richard W. Lovely, *Evaluating the Fourth Amendment Exclusionary Rule: The Problem of Police Compliance with the Law*, 24 U. Mich. J.L. Ref. 311 (1991); Yale Kamisar, *Does (Did) (Should) the Exclusionary Rule Rest on a "Principled Basis" Rather than an "Empirical Proposition"?*, 16 Creighton L. Rev. 565 (1983); John Kaplan, *The Limits of the Exclusionary Rule*, 26 Stan. L. Rev. 1027 (1974); William J. Mertens & Silas Wasserstrom, *The Good Faith Exception to the Exclusionary Rule: Deregulating the Police and Derailing the Law*, 70 Geo. L.J. 365 (1981); Arval A. Morris, *The Exclusionary Rule, Deterrence, and Posner's Economic Analysis of Law*, 57 Wash. L. Rev. 647 (1982); Norton, Note 16, *supra*; Dallin H. Oaks, *Studying the Exclusionary Rule in Search and Seizure*, 37 U. Chi. L. Rev. 665 (1970); Myron W. Orfield, Jr., *Deterrence, Perjury, and the Heater Factor: An Exclusionary Rule in the Chicago Criminal Courts*, 63 U. Colo. L. Rev. 75 (1992); Myron A. Orfield, Jr., Note, *The Exclusionary Rule and Deterrence: An Empirical Study of Chicago Narcotics Officers*, 54 U. Chi. L. Rev. 1016 (1987); Richard A. Posner, *Rethinking the Fourth Amendment*, 1981 Sup. Ct. Rev. 49; Christopher Slobogin, *Why Liberals Should Chuck the Exclusionary Rule*, 1999 U. Ill. L. Rev. 363; Stewart, Note 1, *supra*; William J. Stuntz, *The Virtues and Vices of the Exclusionary Rule*, 20 Harv. J.L. & Pub. Pol'y 443 (1997); William J. Stuntz, *Warrants and Fourth Amendment Remedies*, 77 Va. L. Rev. 881 (1991); Lane V. Sunderland, *Liberals, Conservatives, and the Exclusionary Rule*, 71 J. Crim. L. & Criminology 343 (1980); George C. Thomas III & Barry S. Pollack, *Saving Rights from a Remedy: A Societal View of the Fourth Amendment*, 73 B.U. L. Rev. 147 (1993).

[40] 367 U.S. 643 (1961). *See* § 21.01[E], *supra*.

[41] Wolf v. Colorado, 338 U.S. 25 (1949). *See* § 21.01[C], *supra*.

[42] 414 U.S. 338 (1974).

One scholar—and now liberal critic—of the exclusionary rule has observed that the rule "is one of the mainstays of liberal ideology. Among those who place themselves somewhere left of center, a stance against using unconstitutionally seized evidence is as *de rigueur* as being anti-death penalty or pro-choice."[43] In part, liberal support for the exclusionary rule is a response to the almost-immediate attack on the rule that arose from political conservatives, who rejected it even before its effects could be measured.

There is some irony in the development of this left/right dichotomy. One view of post-*Mapp* Fourth Amendment jurisprudence suggests that the controversial nature of the exclusionary rule induced the Supreme Court— even during the heyday of the Warren Court era, and certainly after— to narrow the scope of *substantive* Fourth Amendment doctrine. That is, to avoid the application of the exclusionary rule and consequent potential acquittal of faculty guilty defendants, the Court interpreted the text of the amendment narrowly, so it would be harder for a defendant to demonstrate that her rights were violated. There is also reason to believe that many trial judges have chosen to accept questionable testimony by police officers regarding searches and seizures, in order to prevent the exclusion of otherwise reliable evidence of a defendant's guilt.[44] Thus, it is possible that the "political right" has gained far more from the exclusionary rule than has the rule's defenders on the "political left."

Some of the controversies surrounding the exclusionary rule are considered below.

### [B] Is There Historical Foundation for the Exclusionary Rule?

*What the critics say*: Some critics attack the doctrine on historical grounds. Professor Akhil Amar argues, for example, that "[t]he modern Court has not only misunderstood the nature of Fourth Amendment rights, but has also distorted Fourth Amendment remedies."[45] He reasons that the amendment's text (the "right of the people to be secure in their persons, houses, papers, and effects, against unreasonable searches and seizures") "should remind us of background common law principles protecting these interests of personhood, property, and privacy—in a word, the law of tort."[46]

---

[43] Slobogin, Note 39, *supra*, at 364.

[44] *See* § 21.04[D][2][b], *infra*.

[45] Akhil Reed Amar, *Fourth Amendment First Principles*, 107 Harv. L. Rev. 757, 785 (1994).

[46] *Id.*

According to Amar, when a person, house, paper or effect was "unreasonably trespassed upon" in pre-Revolutionary England and America, the remedy was a civil action against the trespasser. In Amar's view, therefore, tort remedies against constitutional wrongdoers were "clearly the ones presupposed by the Framers of the Fourth Amendment and counterpart state constitutional provisions."[47]

*What defenders of the rule say*: Justice Potter Stewart, an advocate of the exclusionary rule, believes that "[t]he actual 'legislative history' of the fourth amendment reveals little about the . . . origin and development of the exclusionary rule."[48] According to Stewart, the history of the Fourth Amendment's "immediate ancestors" in state constitutions "provides little guidance," and the Congressional debates over the text of the Fourth Amendment "shed no light on whether it was intended to require the exclusion of illegally obtained evidence."[49]

In any case, defenders of the exclusionary rule contend that history should not be determinative. "[T]he framers meant the Constitution to mean more than it says, and more than they could conceive."[50] That is, for advocates of "constitutional dynamism—the principle that interpretations of the Constitution will and should change over time to accommodate the needs of different historical ages,"[51] the Framers' intentions, although important, are best formulated "at a level of abstraction that leaves room for changing particular applications."[52] We should ask ourselves what *values* the Framers held dear, and then determine what *means* of enforcing those values will best work in modern times. The "fact that colonial history [arguably] does not support the [exclusionary rule] . . . does not suggest that *nothing* supports it."[53] As there are strong non-historical reasons for an exclusionary rule in modern times, the rule should be supported.

---

[47] *Id.* at 786.

[48] Stewart, Note 1, *supra*, at 1371.

[49] *Id.*

[50] Telford Taylor, Two Studies in Constitutional Interpretation 43 (1969); *see* Tracey Maclin, *When the Cure for the Fourth Amendment is Worse than the Disease*, 68 S. Cal. L. Rev. 1, 46 (1994) ("If constitutional interpretation was simply a matter of identifying whether a particular historical practice was permitted in 1789 . . ., it would be better to appoint historians to the Court and leave the lawyers on the sidelines.").

[51] Carol S. Steiker, *Second Thoughts About First Principles*, 107 Harv. L. Rev. 820, 825–26 (1994).

[52] *Id.* at 826.

[53] *Id.* at 830.

## [C]   Does the Exclusionary Rule Deter Constitutional Violations?

The exclusionary rule applies after a victim's Fourth Amendment rights have been violated, *i.e.*, after an unreasonable search or seizure has already occurred. But, "[t]he rule is calculated to prevent, not to repair."[54] That is, privacy lost as the result of police wrongdoing "cannot be restored. Reparation comes too late."[55] Therefore, in determining whether the exclusionary rule represents good policy, a critical question to ask is: does the exclusionary rule serve the stated purpose of preventing unlawful searches and seizures in the first place?

*What the critics say*: Empirical studies[56] suggest, and common sense tells us, that the exclusionary rule does not and cannot function as a meaningful deterrent. Most violations of the Fourth Amendment occur at its edges: an officer in good faith misunderstands a complex Fourth Amendment rule[57] or interprets the facts regarding a search or seizure differently than a court does. These errors cannot be prevented; by definition, they are inadvertent. In any case, we would not want to deter good-faith police activity: all we can ask of the police is that they make reasonable, good-faith efforts to obey the Constitution.

In contrast, those who knowingly violate the Fourth Amendment *can* theoretically be deterred, but the exclusionary rule is too indirect and attenuated a form of punishment to do the job adequately.[58] For the exclusionary rule to be fully effective, the undesired conduct must always be detected, and the "punishing stimulus" of the exclusion of evidence must be given *immediately* after *every* incident of misconduct. But, experience teaches us that most constitutionally questionable searches and seizures on the street are not litigated because the police do not make an arrest (they may act solely in order to establish authority, to obtain information, or to harass) or, when they do arrest, many harried defense lawyers plea bargain rather than litigate. Furthermore, suppression motions are often unsuccessful even when litigated. Bad faith officers believe, perhaps with reason,[59] that

---

[54] Elkins v. United States, 364 U.S. 206, 217 (1960).

[55] Linkletter v. Walker, 381 U.S. 618, 637 (1965).

[56] *E.g.*, Ronald L. Akers & Lonn Lanza-Kaduce, *The Exclusionary Rule: Legal Doctrine and Social Research on Constitutional Norms*, 2 Sam Houston St. U. Crim. Just. Center Res. Bull. 1 (1986); Oaks, Note 39, *supra*; James E. Spiotto, *Search and Seizure: An Empirical Study of the Exclusionary Rule and its Alternatives*, 2 J. Legal Stud. 243 (1973).

[57] *See* Heffernan & Lovely, Note 39, *supra*, at 332–45 (finding that even well-trained officers are mistaken about Fourth Amendment jurisprudence approximately 25% of the time).

[58] Slobogin, Note 39, *supra*, at 374–77.

[59] Kaplan, Note 39, *supra*, at 1032 & n.40.

by committing perjury they can avoid suppression of evidence.[60] Finally, suppression of evidence, if it occurs at all, happens long after the wrongful conduct has occurred and may not even be communicated to the offending officer.

Beyond these deterrence problems, bad-faith officers may find the suppression of evidence, even if communicated to them, of marginal concern. Although officers doubtlessly want those whom they arrest to be convicted, the possibility that evidence may be excluded at trial does not diminish other powerful motivations to act unlawfully: malicious officers obtain considerable satisfaction from the knowledge that they have imposed other hardships on a suspect, such as invasion of privacy, the expense and ordeal of a criminal prosecution, family disruption, and loss of employment.

Studies also report that police institutional norms have more influence on the conduct of individual officers than court decisions.[61] Police officers "on the beat" are more interested in the views of their peers and supervisors than in the opinions of "elitist" or "bleeding-heart liberal" judges. A search that a court might later consider unreasonable is apt to be viewed with sympathy by other law enforcement agents, so that the loss of the evidence may not deter the ordinary officer.[62]

*What defenders of the rule say:* As with all arguments regarding deterrence, it is easier to prove that a penalty has *not* had a deterrent effect

---

[60] Police perjury "disturbingly [is] a well-documented aspect of criminal justice administration." Richard Van Duizend, L. Paul Sutton, & Charlotte Carter, The Search Warrant Process: Preconceptions, Perceptions, and Practices 108 (National Center for State Courts 1984); Orfield, Note 39, *supra*, at 82–83 (in a study of Cook County, Illinois criminal courts, the author discovered "pervasive police perjury," including "systematic fabrications in case reports and affidavits for search warrants, creating artificial probable cause"). *See also* § 21.04[D][2][b], *infra*.

For general discussion of the problem of policy perjury (or what has come to be called "testilying"), as well as consideration of the moral issues relating to police deceit, *see* Gabriel J. Chin & Scott C. Wells, *The "Blue Wall of Silence" as Evidence of Bias and Motive to Lie: A New Approach to Police Perjury*, 59 U. Pitt. L. Rev. 233 (1998); Robert P. Mosteller, *Moderating Investigative Lies by Disclosure and Documentation*, 76 Or. L. Rev. 833 (1997); Margaret L. Paris, *Lying to Ourselves*, 76 Or. L. Rev. 817 (1997); Christopher Slobogin, *Deceit, Pretext, and Trickery: Investigative Lies By the Police*, 76 Or. L. Rev. 775 (1997); Christopher Slobogin, *Testilying: Police Perjury and What to Do About It*, 67 U. Colo. L. Rev. 1037 (1996).

[61] *See* Jerome Skolnick, Justice Without Trial: Law Enforcement in Democratic Society 219–25 (1966).

[62] *See* Stephen L. Wasby, *Police Training About Criminal Procedure: Infrequent and Inadequate*, 7 Pol'y Stud. J. 461, 466 (1978) ("The spirit and tone of communication about the law [during police training], particularly when the law is favorable to defendants' rights, is often negative, with the need for compliance stressed only infrequently.").

than that it is to show that it has succeeded. One commentator has stated, "there is virtually no likelihood that the Court is going to receive any 'relevant statistics' which objectively measure the 'practical efficacy' of the exclusionary rule."[63] For this reason, all arguments—pro or con—based on deterrence are "partly a matter of logic and psychology, [but] largely a matter of faith."[64]

Fair-minded critics of the exclusionary rule admit that "[n]o one actually knows how effective the exclusionary rule is as a deterrent."[65] Indeed, Professor Dallin Oaks, the author of the classic study most commonly cited by the rule's critics, candidly warned that his study "obviously fall[s] short of an empirical substantiation or refutation of the deterrent effect of the exclusionary rule."[66] His harshest comments about the exclusionary rule are found in the postscript to the study, in which he presented his self-described "polemic on the rule," one which "brushes past the uncertainties identified in the discussion of the data."[67]

To a considerable extent, criticisms based on deterrence are misdirected. They seek to show that the exclusionary rule does not directly deter specific police officers. But, systemic (or general) deterrence, not specific deterrence, is the primary goal of the exclusionary rule.[68] According to Justice Brennan, "the chief deterrent function of the rule is its tendency to promote institutional compliance with Fourth Amendment requirements on the part of law enforcement agencies generally."[69]

The exclusionary rule is meant to deter unconstitutional police conduct by promoting professionalism within the ranks, specifically by creating an incentive for police departments to hire individuals sensitive to civil liberties, to better train officers in the proper use of force, to keep officers updated on constitutional law, and to develop internal guidelines that reduce the likelihood of unreasonable arrests and searches.

There is anecdotal evidence that *Mapp* has had these effects in many police departments. Justice Stewart said after he left the Court that "[t]he

---

[63] Critique, *On the Limitations of Empirical Evaluations of the Exclusionary Rule: A Critique of the Spiotto Research and United States v. Calandra*, 69 Nw. U. L. Rev. 740, 763–64 (1974).

[64] Roger B. Dworkin, *Fact Style Adjudication and the Fourth Amendment: The Limits of Lawyering*, 48 Ind. L.J. 329, 333 (1973).

[65] Posner, Note 39, *supra*, at 54 (footnote deleted).

[66] Oaks, Note 39, *supra*, at 709.

[67] *Id.* at 755.

[68] Mertens & Wasserstrom, Note 39, *supra*, at 394.

[69] United States v. Leon, 468 U.S. 897, 953 (1984) (dissenting opinion).

world has changed . . . since the *Mapp* decision was announced."[70]
Various observers of police practices have reported that *Mapp* promoted
professionalism. For example, Oaks found that police adherence to constitutional doctrine increased after *Mapp* was decided, and that the rule
"contributed to an increased awareness of constitutional requirements by
the police,"[71] and more recent studies support this conclusion.[72]

Furthermore, search warrants were sought more often after *Mapp* than
before. Police departments and prosecutors that once paid no attention to
the Fourth Amendment now "at least . . . consider the parameters of an
unconstitutional search and seizure."[73] And, flagrant cases of police
misconduct—such as occurred in *Mapp*—appear to have diminished.

Some defenders of the exclusionary rule attack the issue differently. They
reason that deterrence criticisms of the sort summarized earlier are disingen-
uous. According to Professors Wasserstrom and Seidman, "it is difficult
to believe that the exclusionary rule debate would have the same intensity
if the rule's opponents believed that it should be replaced by a more
effective deterrent."[74] They point out that most critics of the rule, besides
arguing that the rule does not deter, also claim that the rule results in too
many criminals being set free. Yet, "[t]his state of affairs would be made
worse, not better, if fourth amendment violations were more effectively
deterred." That is, if a remedy for Fourth Amendment violations does its
job exceptionally well, there will be more, not fewer, cases of important
evidence *not* coming to light, and guilty people avoiding conviction. Thus,
these scholars reason, "[i]t seems likely . . . that the real source of the
opponents' discontent is not with the rule's *ineffectiveness* but with its
*effectiveness*."[75]

### [D]   Is the Rule (Even If It Deters) Worth Its Cost?

### [1]   Should This Question Even Be Asked?[76]

Exclusionary rule critics provide a list of the alleged costs to society of
the doctrine, the sum of which, they argue, is greater than the rule's possible

---

[70] Stewart, Note 1, *supra*, at 1386.

[71] Oaks, Note 39, *supra*, at 708.

[72] *E.g.*, Orfield, Note 39, *supra*, at 80, 94 (in a study of Cook County, Illinois criminal
courts, the author found that the exclusionary rule had an "institutional deterrent effect,"
in that "police and prosecutorial institutions respond[ed] to the exclusionary rule by designing
programs and procedures to ensure compliance with the Fourth Amendment.").

[73] Kaplan, Note 39, *supra*, at 1034.

[74] Silas J. Wasserstrom & Louis Michael Seidman, *The Fourth Amendment as Constitutional Theory*, 77 Geo. L.J. 19, 36–37 (1988).

[75] *Id.* at 37.

[76] *See generally* Kamisar, Note 39, *supra*.

deterrent benefits. Advocates of the exclusionary rule believe that the costs have been exaggerated, just as its deterrent benefits have allegedly been undervalued. A brief discussion of some of the alleged costs of the rule follows.

However, at the outset it should be noted that cost-benefit calculations of the sort described here are not without its critics. According to Justice Brennan, "the language of deterrence and of cost/benefit analysis . . . can have a narcotic effect. It creates an illusion of technical precision and ineluctability."[77] These critics maintain that it is nearly impossible to analyze objectively the costs and benefits of the rule, because the process involves "measuring imponderables and comparing incommensurables."[78] For example, how much does privacy weigh in the balance? Is one unreasonable search that is deterred equal to one guilty person going free?

Some defenders of the exclusionary rule believe that courts ought to focus more on the principled, rather than pragmatic, grounds for the exclusionary rule. Court ought to focus on the need to preserve judicial integrity—to "avoid the taint of partnership in official lawlessness"—by barring unconstitutionally seized evidence. Others, too, warn that the government should "not profit from its lawless behavior."[79] The exclusionary rule, they argue, is defensible not because it deters the police (which it may or may not do) but because it is fair: it puts the citizen and the government back in the procedural position they would have found themselves if the Constitution had not been violated.[80]

At the current time, however, non-consequentialist arguments of this sort carry little sway with the Supreme Court.

### [2] The "Costs"

### [a] The Rule Protects the Wrong People

*What the critics say*: The purpose of a criminal trial is to learn the truth regarding a defendant's innocence or guilt, to "sort[] the innocent from the guilty."[81] When a murderer's bloody knife is introduced at her trial, the truth is learned, the guilty person is convicted, and people are more secure in their persons, houses, papers, and effects.[82] The Fourth Amendment

---

[77] United States v. Leon, 468 U.S. 897, 929 (1984) (dissenting opinion).

[78] Yale Kamisar, *Gates, "Probable Cause," "Good Faith," and Beyond*, 69 Iowa L. Rev. 551, 613 (1984).

[79] United States v. Calandra, 414 U.S. 338, 357 (1974) (Brennan, J., joined by Douglas and Marshal, JJ, dissenting).

[80] *See generally* Norton, Note 16, supra.

[81] Amar, Note 45, *supra*, at 759.

[82] *Id.* at 793.

exclusionary rule, however, "deflects the truthfinding process"[83] by excluding reliable evidence, such as the murderer's bloody knife.

As a result of the suppression of the truth, the exclusionary rule "often frees the guilty."[84] Without the bloody knife, the murderer goes free, and people are *less* secure in their persons, houses, papers, and effects. And, while the guilty go free, innocent people receive no benefit from the rule. This is because an innocent person has nothing to be seized. Therefore, she must turn to a civil remedy to obtain redress if her privacy is unconstitutionally invaded.

*What defenders of the rule say*: First, the preceding argument is misdirected. If the criminal justice system is an obstacle course, it is the Fourth Amendment itself—*e.g.*, the requirements of a warrant and probable cause—and not the exclusionary rule that constructs the barriers that make it harder to convict the guilty.[85]

Second, the cost of guilty people going free is vastly overstated by the critics.[86] A study by Professor Thomas Davies[87] —described by Professor Wayne LaFave as "the most careful and balanced assessment of all available empirical data"[88] —suggests that the "most striking feature of the data is the concentration of illegal searches in drug arrests . . . and the extremely small effects in arrests for other offenses, including violent crimes."[89] In short, if one considers the exclusionary rule critics' "favorite stalking horse"[90] —the murderer's bloody knife—there is little reason to worry about the exclusion doctrine. Although nonprosecutions or nonconvictions in the drug area due to illegal searches were not insignificant in the period of time studied—2.8 percent to 7.1 percent—Davies concluded that "available empirical evidence casts considerable doubt on both the alleged 'high costs' of the exclusionary rule and the purported prevalence of 'legal technicalities' as the cause of illegal searches."[91]

---

[83] Stone v. Powell, 428 U.S. 465, 490 (1976).

[84] *Id.*

[85] Stewart, Note 1, *supra*, at 1393.

[86] Maclin, Note 50, *supra*, at 43 (describing the criticisms as "[s]care tactics").

[87] Thomas Y. Davies, *A Hard Look at What We Know (and Still Need to Learn) About the "Costs" of the Exclusionary Rule: The NIJ Study and Other Studies of "Lost" Arrests*, 1983 Am. B. Found. Res. J. 611.

[88] Wayne R. LaFave, *"The Seductive Call of Expediency": United States v. Leon, Its Rationale and Ramifications*, 1984 U. Ill. L. Rev. 895, 904.

[89] Davies, Note 87, *supra*, at 680.

[90] Maclin, Note 50, *supra*, at 44.

[91] Davies, Note 87, *supra*, at 688.

Other studies support Davies' conclusions. A 1979 survey by the General Accounting Office—a study of a period when the Fourth Amendment was more vigorously enforced than today—showed that Fourth Amendment problems explained only 0.4 percent of the total number of cases declined for federal prosecution.[92] Another study of the impact of the exclusionary rule in seven communities found that in cases in which warrants had been issued, evidence was found in more than 90 percent of the resulting searches, yet motions to suppress evidence seized during those successful searches were filed in only 39 percent of the prosecutions, and were granted in just 12 percent of the cases, for an overall suppression rate of slightly less than 5 percent of the total number of warrant-related prosecutions.[93] Perhaps even more significantly, convictions were obtained in at least 70 percent of the cases in which suppression motions were granted. Overall, therefore, the exclusionary rule prevented the conviction of criminal defendants in no more than 1.4% of the cases studied.

Third, it is inaccurate to say that innocent people do not benefit from an exclusionary rule. If the rule serves its deterrent purpose, the police will not enter the homes, search the cars, or otherwise intrude upon the privacy of those about whom there is little or no objective evidence of guilt. There is no way to know, of course, how many innocent people have *not* been the victims of unreasonable searches and seizures because of *Mapp*. In any case, even if it were true that only the guilty derive benefit from the rule, this would not demonstrate "that the rule is not a necessary remedy, only that it is not a sufficient one."[94]

### [b] The Rule Promotes Cynicism

*What the critics say*: The exclusionary rule promotes cynicism among members of the public and parties in the criminal justice system, including trial judges and even criminal defendants.

The exclusionary rule treats a criminal defendant as a "surrogate for the larger public interest in restraining the government. The criminal defendant is a kind of private attorney general."[95] But, the defendant is "the worst kind" of surrogate, because he is "self-serving." As a person in possession of criminal evidence, he is "often unrepresentative of the larger class of law-abiding citizens, and his interests regularly conflict with theirs."[96] No

---

[92] Comptroller General, U.S. General Accounting Office, Impact of the Exclusionary Rule on Federal Criminal Prosecutions 14 (1979) (Rep. No. GGD-79-45).

[93] R. Van Duizend, *et al.*, Note 60, *supra*, at 48–56.

[94] Stewart, Note 1, *supra*, at 1396.

[95] Amar, Note 45, *supra*, at 796.

[96] *Id.*

wonder, then, that a "solid majority of Americans rejects the idea that '[t]he criminal is to go free because the constable has blundered.' "[97] "The public is *revulsed* [*sic*]"[98] by the sight of guilty people going free because reliable evidence that could convict them is suppressed by judges on the basis of a "technicality."

This cynicism runs even deeper. Police officers lie in order to avoid suppression of evidence, and some trial judges wink at the dishonesty in order to avoid allowing guilty defendants to go free. Professor William Pizzi writes:

> Rather than contributing to police professionalism, a draconian exclusionary rule feeds into . . . [an] "us versus them" mentality among police officers and encourages cynicism about the system and even the practice referred to by police as "testilying," meaning that officers "embellish" the actual facts in their suppression hearing testimony to avoid the possibility of suppression. When the crime is a serious one and the consequences of suppression would mean that the guilty person will go free, judges are tempted to credit testimony that they have good reason to believe has been embellished, to avoid suppression. . . .
>
> . . . [A] system with harsh rules becomes less honest all around as we struggle to avoid the harshness of the rules. . . . An attitude of cynicism starts to pervade courthouses as the criminal justice system comes to expect and tolerate dishonesty under oath."[99]

The dishonesty inspired by the exclusionary rule even affects guilty defendants who are likely to think to themselves, "if the police are allowed to lie, and the judges permit it, why am I expected to act honestly?" The legal system, in short, pays a high cost in lost respect when it violates natural feelings of justice.

*What defenders of the rule say:* If the public is outraged by the exclusionary rule, it should not be. First, as noted above, fewer guilty people go free than is believed. Second, although the rule obstructs the truth by suppressing reliable evidence, responsibility for this should be placed at the door of the government, whose officers violated the Fourth Amendment. As Justice Harlan has explained, judges "do not release a criminal from jail because

---

[97] Kaplan, Note 39, *supra,* at 1035 (quoting Justice Benjamin Cardozo in People v. Defore, 150 N.E. 585, 587 (N.Y. 1926)).

[98] Statement of the Co-Chairman of the Attorney-General's Task Force on Violent crime, *quoted in* New York Times, Aug. 18, 1981, at 10, *as reported in* Wayne R. LaFave, *The Fourth Amendment in an Imperfect World: On Drawing "Bright Lines" and "Good Faith",* 43 U. Pitt. L. Rev. 307, 336 (1982).

[99] William T. Pizzi, Trials Without Truth 38–39 (1999).

we like to do so, or because we think it is wise to do so, but only because the government has offended constitutional principles in the conduct of [the defendant's] case."[100] The public's outrage should be aimed, therefore, at those who fail to obey the Constitution's edicts and at those who lie under oath and countenance it at trial.

### [c] The Rule Results in Disproportionate Punishment[101]

*What the critics say*: Even if the exclusionary rule should not be abandoned entirely, the *Mapp* version of the doctrine goes too far because the "penalty" for violation of the Fourth Amendment is often disproportionate to the "crime" committed by the police.

First, *Mapp* applies as much to the inadvertent mistake of a good-faith police officer as it does to the malicious conduct of a bad-faith actor. Although "[f]reeing either a tiger or a mouse in a schoolroom is an illegal act, . . . no rational person would suggest that these two acts should be punished in the same way."[102] Second, the rule does not distinguish between a trial for a serious crime and one for a minor offense. Therefore, a potentially dangerous offender may escape incarceration, even if the wrong committed by the officer was trivial in nature. Evidence of a crime should be excluded, if at all, when "the reprehensibility of the officer's illegality is greater than the defendant's."[103]

*What defenders of the rule say*: The proportionality argument wrongly assumes that the exclusionary rule is intended as compensation of the victim for a Fourth Amendment violation. In fact, its purpose is to instill professionalism in police ranks, in order to prevent *future* violations. Just as punishment of a criminal is not calibrated to the facts of a particular case if we seek general deterrence, it is wrong to measure the effect of the exclusionary rule in an individual case.

### [E] Are There Better Remedies?

*What the critics say*: Even if the exclusionary rule deters, and even if its benefits slightly outweigh its costs, there are other remedies that would provide greater net benefits. Furthermore, as long as the exclusionary rule is in place, courts and legislatures have no incentive to implement alternative remedies.

---

[100] Desist v. United States, 394 U.S. 244, 258 (1969) (dissenting opinion).

[101] *See generally* Kaplan, Note 39, *supra*; Yale Kamisar, *"Comparative Reprehensibility" and the Fourth Amendment Exclusionary Rule*, 86 Mich. L. Rev. 1 (1987).

[102] Bivens v. Six Unknown Named Agents, 403 U.S. 388, 419 (1971) (Burger, C.J. dissenting).

[103] Kamisar, Note 101, *supra*, at 3 (articulating, but rejecting, the argument).

Some commentators believe that the primary remedy for a Fourth Amendment violation should be a civil action. Whether the suit is in the form of a common law tort (*e.g.*, battery or trespass), a federal civil rights action,[104] or a newly developed state "constitutional tort" proceeding, a jury would apply a tort concept of reasonableness, in order to determine whether the Fourth Amendment was violated. The defendants—the individual police officers and government agencies—would pay compensatory and punitive damages, when appropriate.[105] With the abolition of the exclusionary rule, a criminal trial could focus on determining the guilt or innocence of the defendant; at the same time, a plaintiff (whether guilty or innocent of a crime) could obtain redress for violation of her Fourth Amendment rights. And, substantial money judgments would send a direct, more powerful message than the exclusionary rule to police departments to train and supervise their officers.

Other remedies, potentially in conjunction with actions for money damages, have been mentioned, including: criminal prosecutions of officers who maliciously violate the Fourth Amendment;[106] injunctive relief; implementation of police review boards with authority to discipline or fire officers for constitutional wrongdoing; and statutory procedures to decertify wrongdoing police officers, so that they cannot be re-employed by another department in the same jurisdiction.[107]

*What defenders of the rule say*: In a perfect world, a complete spectrum of civil and criminal remedies, such as those suggested by abolitionists, would be "superior to evidentiary exclusion as a system for deterring

---

[104] *E.g.*, 42 U.S.C.A. § 1983 (2000) (it is actionable for any person "under color of any statute, ordinance, regulation, custom, or usage, of any State" to subject any person "to the deprivation of any rights, privileges, or immunities secured by the Constitution"); 28 U.S.C.A. § 2680(h) (2000) (permitting a civil suit against federal officers for constitutional violations).

[105] Contrary to the suggestions in the text, Professor Donald Dripps has proposed that the exclusionary rule be retained, but that judge should be authorized to enter a *contingent* suppression order when the police violate the Fourth Amendment; the suppression could be avoided if the state pays damages in an amount determined by the judge. Donald Dripps, *The Case for the Contingent Exclusionary Rule*, 38 Am. Crim. L. Rev. 1 (2001). This proposal is analyzed and critiqued in part in George C. Thomas III, *Judges Are Not Economists and Other Reasons to Be Skeptical of Contingent Suppression Orders: A Response to Professor Dripps*, 38 Am. Crim. L. Rev. 47 (2001) (ultimately proposing that juries, not judges, decide whether to fine the state or suppress the evidence).

[106] *E.g.*, 18 U.S.C.A. § 242 (2000) (making it a federal crime for anyone acting under color of law to deprive a person of her constitutional rights).

[107] Roger Goldman & Steven Puro, *Decertification of Police: An Alternative to Traditional Remedies for Police Misconduct*, 15 Hastings Const. L.Q. 45, 48 (1987).

governmental misconduct."[108] Nonetheless, "[d]espite its many flaws, the exclusionary rule is . . . the best we can realistically do."[109]

The key word is "realistically." Criminal prosecutions of the police for Fourth Amendment violations are virtually unheard of. The reason is obvious: prosecutors rarely want to proceed against their natural allies, the police. Civil suits, too, "are few and far between, and therefore relatively punchless as punishing mechanisms."[110] The difficulties with this remedy are considerable. First, individual officers and the government itself are immune from civil liability in many circumstances, so legislatures would have to fashion a system that allows for entity liability. It is unclear whether legislative bodies, buffeted by political forces, would be prepared to abolish a structure set up to protect public officials, particularly police officers, from monetary liability. As Professor Steiker recounts, "[t]he history of attempts to regulate police practices should make us extremely doubtful about reliance on legislatures to create effective remedial structures."[111]

Second, many defenders of the exclusionary rule doubt that "we [can] be confident that juries would award Fourth Amendment remedies sufficient to create litigation incentives and thus to promote adequate deterrence."[112] Jurors, fearful of crime, will hesitate, as they have in the past, to rule against the police, even in flagrant cases in which there is videotaped or other eyewitness evidence of the disputed police conduct. Jurors are apt to focus less on the police behavior, and more on their assessment of the plaintiff's character,[113] which in turn invites the jury to decide whether they "fear the robbers more than the cops."[114]

Policing the police is a good idea. However, according to Professor Tracey Maclin, "[c]ivilian review boards, commonly hailed as a panacea for police abuse and illegality, do not work in isolation and are often weak substitutes for effective control of police misconduct."[115]

---

[108] Steiker, Note 51, *supra*, at 848.

[109] *Id.*

[110] Slobogin, Note 39, *supra*, at 385.

[111] Steiker, Note 51, *supra*, at 849.

[112] *Id.*

[113] Maclin, Note 50, *supra*, at 64.

[114] Steiker, Note 51, *supra*, at 850. To mitigate these problems, some commentators advocate the use of judicial decisionmakers, rather than juries, in such proceedings. *E.g.*, Slobogin, Note 39, *supra*, at 388. *See also* Note 38, *supra* (a proposed state law creating an action in equity, with a judicial decisionmaker).

[115] Maclin, Note 50, *supra*, at 64–65.

## § 21.05  When the Exclusionary Rule Does Not Apply: In General

### [A]  Non-Criminal Proceedings

#### [1]  In General

The Supreme Court has stated that, "[a]s with any remedial device, the application of the [exclusionary] rule [should be] restricted to those areas where its remedial objectives are thought most efficaciously served."[116] In other words, in determining whether the rule should be applied to a particular proceeding, the issue is whether the cost of its use in the particular context is likely to outweigh the incremental deterrent benefit of extending the doctrine to the new situation.

The Court has held that the exclusionary rule applies in some quasi-criminal contexts, such as in proceedings in which property will be forfeited because of criminal wrongdoing.[117] On the other hand, the rule does not apply in ordinary civil suits, civil tax proceedings,[118] or deportation hearings.[119]

#### [2]  Habeas Corpus[120]

Although the exclusionary rule applies to state criminal trials, it has only limited applicability in federal habeas corpus proceedings brought to overturn state criminal convictions. In *Stone v. Powell*,[121] the Supreme Court balanced "the utility of the exclusionary rule against the costs of extending it to collateral review of Fourth Amendment claims." It characterized the costs of the rule "even at trial and on direct review" as "well known." As for the deterrent benefits of the rule, it stated that "[t]here is no reason to believe . . . that the overall educative effect of the exclusionary rule would be appreciably diminished if search-and-seizure claims could not be raised in federal habeas corpus review of state convictions." Therefore, the Court held that "where the State has provided an opportunity for full and fair litigation of a Fourth Amendment claim, the Constitution does not require that a state prisoner be granted federal habeas corpus relief on the ground that evidence obtained in an unconstitutional search or seizure was introduced at his trial."

---

[116] United States v. Calandra, 414 U.S. 338, 348 (1974) (alteration in original).

[117] One 1958 Plymouth Sedan v. Pennsylvania, 380 U.S. 693 (1965).

[118] United States v. Janis, 428 U.S. 433 (1976).

[119] I.N.S. v. Lopez-Mendoza, 468 U.S. 1032 (1984); *but see* Gonzalez-Rivera v. I.N.S., 22 F.3d 1441 (9th Cir. 1994) (suppressing evidence in a deportation hearing because of the government's bad-faith conduct in stopping a deportee based solely on his Hispanic appearance; finding an egregious-violation exception to the holding in *Lopez-Mendoza*).

[120] For an explanation of habeas corpus, *see* § 1.03[C][10], *supra*.

[121] 428 U.S. 465 (1976).

The Supreme Court did not explain in *Stone*, nor has it since clarified, what it meant by the phrase "an opportunity for a full and fair litigation of a Fourth Amendment claim." Applying *Powell*, it is evident that a habeas petitioner may not raise a claim if her basis for objection is simply that a state court misapplied search-and-seizure doctrine. Professor LaFave suggests, however, that "[i]t may be that a state decision could be so patently in error and so wide of the Fourth Amendment mark as to constitute a prima facie showing of the absence of 'full and fair consideration.' "[122] Nonetheless, according to LaFave, the effect of *Stone* is "there will be few occasions when a state prisoner will be able to obtain an adjudication of his Fourth Amendment claim in a federal habeas court."[123]

## [B] Criminal Proceedings

### [1] Non-Trial Proceedings

Evidence seized unconstitutionally may be introduced in grand jury proceedings without violation of the Fourth Amendment.[124] Apparently, such evidence may also be used in preliminary hearings,[125] at bail proceedings,[126] in sentencing,[127] and at proceedings to revoke parole.[128]

### [2] At a Criminal Trial

#### [a] "Good Faith" Exception

In specified circumstances, the Fourth Amendment does not bar the use at a criminal trial of evidence obtained by a police officer acting in reasonable reliance on a search warrant that subsequently is determined to be invalid.[129] Because of the complexity of this exception to the exclusionary rule, it is considered in Section 21.06.

---

[122] 5 LaFave, Note 1, supra, at 455.

[123] *Id.* at 448. For a survey of lower court interpretations of *Stone*, see *id.* at 448–58.

[124] United States v. Calandra, 414 U.S. 338 (1974).

[125] *See* Giordenello v. United States, 357 U.S. 480 (1958) (magistrates lack authority to adjudicate the admissibility of evidence); Fed. R. Crim. P. 5.1(a) ("[o]bjections to evidence based on the ground that it was acquired by unlawful means are not properly made at the preliminary examination.").

[126] *E.g.*, 18 U.S.C.A. § 3142(f) (2000) ("The rules concerning the admissibility of evidence in criminal trials do not apply to the presentation and consideration of information at the hearing").

[127] United States v. McCrory, 930 F.2d 63 (D.C. Cir. 1991) (evidence seized in violation of the Fourth Amendment may be considered by the judge in determining the defendant's appropriate sentence under the federal sentencing guidelines).

[128] Pennsylvania Bd. of Probation and Parole v. Scott, 524 U.S. 357 (1998).

[129] United States v. Leon, 468 U.S. 897 (1984).

## [b]   Impeachment Exception

As the result of a string of complicated and seemingly conflicting Supreme Court opinions, [130] a prosecutor may introduce evidence obtained from a defendant in violation of her Fourth Amendment rights for the limited purpose of impeaching her: (1) direct testimony; or (2) answers to legitimate questions put to her during cross-examination. However, the government may not use evidence obtained in violation of the defendant's Fourth Amendment rights to impeach *all* defense witnesses.

For example, if *D* testifies in a drug prosecution that she has never seen narcotics, [131] or denies in cross-examination that she previously possessed particular evidence of a crime, [132] the prosecutor may introduce testimony that contradicts these claims in order to impeach her credibility, even though the impeachment evidence was secured in violation of *D*'s Fourth Amendment rights. On the other hand, the prosecutor may not use a statement obtained from *D* in violation of the Fourth Amendment to impeach witnesses other than the defendant, who provide testimony in conflict with that statement. [133]

The Supreme Court has determined that use of Fourth Amendment tainted evidence to impeach a defendant's false testimony significantly furthers the truth-seeking process by deterring perjury; at the same time, the use of such evidence in this limited manner creates only a speculative possibility that the police will be encouraged to violate the Fourth Amendment.

In contrast, in *James v. Illinois*, [134] the Court refused, 5-4, to extend the impeachment exception to all defense witness' testimony. Speaking for the majority, Justice William Brennan stated that such a rule would not further the truth-seeking process to the same degree, because it might deter defendants from calling witnesses who would otherwise provide truthful and probative evidence, out of fear that the truthful witnesses might unexpectedly make a statement "in sufficient tension with the tainted evidence" to allow impeachment. The *James* Court also felt that expansion of the exception to all defense witnesses would significantly weaken the exclusionary rule's deterrent effect, as it would greatly increase the number of times such evidence could be used during a trial.

---

[130] *See generally* 5 LaFave, Note 1, *supra*, at § 11.6(a); James L. Kainen, *The Impeachment Exception to the Exclusionary Rules: Policies, Principles, and Politics*, 44 Stan. L. Rev. 1301 (1992).

[131] Walder v. United States, 347 U.S. 62 (1954).

[132] United States v. Havens, 446 U.S. 620 (1980).

[133] James v. Illinois, 493 U.S. 307 (1990).

[134] *Id.*

## § 21.06 When the Exclusionary Rule Does Not Apply: The "Good Faith" Exception[135]

### [A] Rule

#### [1] In General

In *United States v. Leon,*[136] police officers executed a facially valid search warrant. Later, a district court held that, "while recognizing that the case was a close one," the warrant was invalid because it was not supported by probable cause.

In *Massachusetts v. Sheppard,*[137] a companion case, the police seized evidence related to a homicide pursuant to a warrant later declared invalid because of a technical error committed by the issuing magistrate. The error was that the magistrate signed a warrant form normally used to conduct searches for illegal drugs, and he forgot to cross out the language in the form that authorized the police to search for controlled substances. The executing officer did not look at the warrant after the magistrate signed it because he was assured by the judge that the offending language had been excised. As a consequence of the judge's error, the warrant did not satisfy the particularity requirement of the Fourth Amendment.

Under ordinary exclusionary rule principles, the evidence obtained in these cases would have been inadmissible at the defendants' criminal trials, except for impeachment purposes, because the warrants supporting the

---

[135] *See generally* 1 LaFave, Note 1, *supra,* at § 1.3; Craig M. Bradley, *The "Good Faith Exception" Cases: Reasonable Exercises in Futility,* 60 Ind. L.J. 287 (1985); Donald Dripps, *Living With Leon,* 95 Yale L.J. 906 (1986); Steven Duke, *Making Leon Worse,* 95 Yale L.J. 1405 (1986); David Clark Esseks, Note, *Errors in Good Faith: The Leon Exception Six Years Later,* 89 Mich. L. Rev. 625 (1990); Abraham S. Goldstein, *The Search Warrant, the Magistrate, and Judicial Review,* 62 N.Y.U. L. Rev. 1173 (1987); Roger S. Hanson, *The Aftermath of Illinois v. Gates and United States v. Leon: A Comprehensive Evaluation of Their Impact Upon the Litigation of Search Warrant Validity,* 15 W. St. U. L. Rev. 393 (1988); Kamisar, Note 78, *supra;* Wayne R. LaFave, *The Fourth Amendment in an Imperfect World: On Drawing "Bright Lines" and "Good Faith",* 43 U. Pitt. L. Rev. 307 (1982).

[136] 468 U.S. 897 (1984). The good-faith exception to the exclusionary rule announced in this case has been rejected by various states. *E.g.,* Dorsey v. State, 761 A.2d 807 (Del. 2000); State v. Guzman, 842 P.2d 660 (Idaho 1992); State v. Cline, 617 N.W.2d 277 (Iowa 2000); People v. Jackson, 446 N.W.2d 891 (Mich. Ct. App. 1989) (*Leon* does not apply unless the state supreme court so holds); State v. Canelo, 653 A.2d 1097 (N.H. 1995); State v. Novembrino, 519 A.2d 820 (N.J. 1987); State v. Gutierrez, 863 P.2d 1052 (N.M. 1993); People v. Bigelow, 488 N.E.2d 451 (N.Y. 1985); Commonwealth v. Edmunds, 586 A.2d 887 (Pa. 1991); State v. Oakes, 598 A.2d 119 (Vt. 1991); *see also* Gary v. State, 422 S.E.2d 426 (Ga. 1992) (*Leon* does not apply in light of a legislatively-mandated exclusionary rule that does not recognize the good-faith exception).

[137] 468 U.S. 981 (1984).

searches were invalid. Nonetheless, the Supreme Court permitted the evidence to be introduced at the trials.

As a result of these two cases, there now exists a so-called "good faith" (or *Leon*) exception to the Fourth Amendment exclusionary rule. According to *Leon*, as clarified below, evidence obtained pursuant to a search warrant later declared to be invalid may be introduced at a defendant's criminal trial in the prosecutor's case-in-chief, if a reasonably well-trained officer would have believed that the warrant was valid. As explained more fully in subsection [B], the *Leon* rule is founded on the belief that there is insufficient justification for applying the exclusionary rule when the police obtain a warrant, reasonably rely on its validity, and later learn that the magistrate erred in authorizing the search.

### [2]  "Good Faith"

Notwithstanding the "good faith" label often attached to the *Leon* rule, evidence is not admissible merely on a finding that the officer involved in the search honestly believed that the warrant she was executing was valid. *Leon* states that the inquiry into "good faith" is limited "to the objectively ascertainable question whether a reasonably well trained officer would have known the search was illegal despite the magistrate's authorization." The test, in short, is an objective one.

Does this mean, as a literal reading of the *Leon* test would suggest, that evidence obtained by a "bad faith" officer—one who knew or suspected the warrant she was executing was invalid—is admissible, as long as a "reasonably well trained officer" *would have believed* that the warrant was good? Probably not, as Professor LaFave has shown by way of the following example: Officer takes her affidavit for a warrant to Prosecutor for a judgment as to its sufficiency. Prosecutor informs her in no uncertain terms that the affidavit is insufficient to show probable cause. Officer ignores this appraisal and goes to a magistrate who (mistakenly) issues a warrant on it.

According to Professor LaFave, the likely state of mind of the "reasonably well trained officer" would take into account Officer's awareness that Prosecutor, a trained lawyer, believed there was insufficient basis for a warrant. This conclusion follows from the language in *Leon* that, in determining whether an officer's reliance on a warrant was objectively reasonable, "all of the circumstances—including whether the warrant application had previously been rejected by a different magistrate—may be considered." It is unclear what other circumstances known to the officers involved in the search warrant process are relevant in measuring the beliefs of the "reasonable officer."

### [3] When *Leon* Does Not Apply

### [a] In General

*Leon* represents an exception to the exclusionary rule. The exception potentially comes into play when an officer obtains a search warrant and abides by its terms, but the warrant is later declared defective. *Leon*, however, has its own exceptions—or, more accurately, the *Leon* opinion notes four (there could be more[138]) situations in which, in the Court's opinion, a reasonably well trained officer would *not* rely on a warrant.

First, the non-suppression rule of *Leon* does not apply if the magistrate who issued the warrant relied on information supplied by an affiant who knew that the statements in the document were false or who recklessly disregarded the truth, in violation of the principles of *Franks v. Delaware*.[139]

Second, evidence is properly excluded if, in the language of *Leon*, the "issuing magistrate wholly abandoned his judicial role in the manner condemned in *Lo-Ji Sales, Inc. v. New York*."[140] In other words, *Leon* does not apply if the magistrate's behavior was so lacking in neutrality that a reasonable officer would have realized that the magistrate was not functioning in an impartial, judicial manner.[141] Despite *Leon*'s specification of *Lo-Ji Sales*, it is likely that the exclusionary rule applies to any situation in which the magistrate acts as a rubber stamp for the police, for example, if she signs the warrant without reading it, while in the presence of the officer who later claims reliance.[142]

Third, an officer may not rely "on a warrant based on an affidavit 'so lacking in indicia of probable cause as to render official belief in its existence entirely unreasonable.' "[143] But, what does this mean? A search based on a warrant not supported by probable cause is, by definition, an *unreasonable* search. How can an officer's execution of a warrant in such circumstances satisfy the reasonableness standard of *Leon*? Are we to believe, as dissenters Brennan and Marshall rhetorically suggested in *Leon*, that "we . . . have to entertain the mind boggling concept of objectively reasonable reliance upon an objectively unreasonable warrant"?

---

[138] Goldstein, Note 135, *supra*, at 1204–05.

[139] 438 U.S. 154 (1978). *See* § 11.04, *supra*.

[140] *Lo-Ji Sales, Inc.*, 442 U.S. 319 (1979) (magistrate accompanied police to an "adult bookstore" and selected the materials to be seized). *See generally* § 11.03, *supra*.

[141] O'Connor v. Madera County Superior Court, 76 Cal.Rptr.2d 138, 145 (Cal. App. 1998), *opinion withdrawn by court of court*, 1998 Cal. Lexis 6851 (Cal. Oct. 14, 1998).

[142] United States v. Decker, 956 F.2d 773 (8th Cir. 1992).

[143] United States v. Leon, 468 U.S. 897, 923 (quoting Brown v. Illinois, 422 U.S. 590, 610–11 (1975)).

Although the scope of this "exception" to *Leon* is not self-evident,[144] the Court seemingly means that an officer may not rely on a warrant issued by a magistrate based on a wholly conclusory—"bare bones"—affidavit, in *gross* violation of the totality-of-the-circumstances test of probable cause enunciated in *Illinois v. Gates*.[145]

To explain further, *Gates* concerned the propriety of a *magistrate's* probable cause determination. In contrast, *Leon* focuses on an *officer's* decision to seek and execute the warrant; the magistrate's thought processes regarding probable cause are not the key.[146] The lesson of *Leon* seems to be that, ordinarily, an officer may reasonably rely on the assumption that a magistrate knows what she is doing when she makes a probable cause finding. Even if it turns out later, based on a higher court ruling, that the magistrate's probable cause judgment was faulty, the officer's reliance on the magistrate will protect the evidence from exclusion. Only if the magistrate's finding of probable cause is grossly off the mark, such as when the affidavit consists of little or nothing more than conclusory statements, will this exception to *Leon* apply.

The fourth *Leon* exception to the exclusionary rule applies when an officer relies on a warrant "so facially deficient—*i.e.*, in failing to particularize the place to be searched or the things to be seized—that the executing officers cannot reasonable presume it is valid." For example, an officer may not reasonably rely on a warrant authorizing her to search "an apartment" of a multi-unit building, or to seize "all stolen goods" in a particularly described house. In these cases, unrelated to any question of probable cause, the warrant is facially deficient because it fails to meet the particularity clause of the Fourth Amendment.

How, then, do we explain *Sheppard*, in which the warrant was invalid on particularity grounds, but the Court allowed the evidence to be introduced? In that case, the magistrate forgot to cross out irrelevant portions of the form. But he assured the officer seeking the warrant, *who was also the one who executed it*, that the corrections had been made. On these facts, reliance on the magistrate's assurances was reasonable. *Sheppard* left open the question of "[w]hether an officer who is . . . [un]familiar with the warrant application or who has unalleviated concerns about the proper scope of the search would be justified in failing to notice a defect [in the warrant]."

---

[144] For more complete analysis, *see* 1 LaFave, Note 1, *supra*, at 83–92.

[145] 462 U.S. 213 (1983). *See* § 9.05, *supra*.

[146] 1 LaFave, Note 1, *supra*, at 87.

### [b] Improperly Executed Warrants

The Court in *Leon* warned in a footnote that the reasoning of the case "assumes, of course, that the officers properly executed the warrant and searched only those places and for those objects that it was reasonable to believe were covered by the warrant." In other words, the *Leon* "good faith" rule does not cover *improperly executed* warrants.

For example, suppose that *O*, an officer, executes a warrant authorizing her to search *D*'s bedroom for clothing related to a rape. If *O*, conducting the bedroom search, inspects files and seizes incriminating papers found in them, this latter search will not be protected by *Leon*, as it was not reasonable for *O* to believe that a warrant authorizing her to search for clothing would permit her to look through written materials. Likewise, if *O* seizes clothing from *D*'s garage, an area that clearly falls outside the coverage of the warrant, this clothing is excludable. The errors here were perpetrated by *O*, and not by the magistrate, and consequently fall outside the reasoning of *Leon*, discussed immediately below.

### [B] Why the Exception?: The Reasoning of *Leon*

Much of the Court's opinion in *Leon*, written by Justice Byron White, reads like a well-reasoned, but not out-of-the-ordinary, general criticism of the exclusionary rule. These aspects of *Leon* can be used to defend a broader exception to *Mapp*—such as a good-faith exception in non-warrant cases[147]—or the outright abolition of the rule. Other features of *Leon* are directed to the narrower question before it, namely, whether the deterrent benefits of the exclusionary rule outweigh its costs in the context of an officer's reasonable reliance on a warrant that has been authorized by a magistrate.

Drawing from language of earlier Supreme Court cases critical of the exclusionary rule, Justice White stated that the exclusionary rule exacts "substantial social costs." It "impedes" the "truth-finding functions of judge and jury." It results in the "objectionable collateral consequence" of the release of some guilty persons and reduced sentences for others. Furthermore, "[p]articularly when law enforcement officers have acted in objective good faith or their transgressions have been minor, the magnitude of the benefit conferred on such guilty defendants offends basic concepts of the criminal justice system." In short, the penalty inflicted for a violation of the Fourth Amendment often is grossly disproportional to the "crime" of the violation. As a result, the rule may "generat[e] disrespect for the law and the administration of justice."

The Court drew a distinction between bad-faith and good-faith police conduct. Quoting *Franks v. Delaware*,[148] Justice White observed that the

---

[147] *See* § 21.07, *infra.*
[148] 438 U.S. 154 (1978).

Court has "not seriously questioned, 'in the absence of a more efficacious sanction, the continued application of the rule . . . where a Fourth Amendment violation has been substantial and deliberate.' " However, *Leon* goes on, "the balancing approach that has evolved in various contexts . . . 'forcefully suggests that the exclusionary rule be . . . modified' " in the context of "reasonable good-faith" police conduct.

The fact that the police secured warrants—albeit defective ones—in *Leon* and *Sheppard* was important in the Court's analysis of the efficacy of the exclusionary rule in these cases. Justice White provided a three-fold justification for limiting the scope of the suppression rule in circumstances in which a warrant has been secured:

> First, the exclusionary rule is designed to deter police misconduct rather than to punish the errors of judges and magistrates. Second, there exists no evidence suggesting that judges and magistrates are inclined to ignore or subvert the Fourth Amendment or that lawlessness among these actors requires application of the extreme sanction of exclusion. [¶] Third, and most important, we discern no basis, and are offered none, for believing that exclusion of evidence seized pursuant to a warrant will have a significant deterrent effect on the issuing judge or magistrate.[149]

On the third—"and most important"—point, the Court reasoned that "[m]any of the factors that indicate that the exclusionary rule cannot provide an effective . . . deterrent for individual offending law enforcement officers applies as well to judges or magistrates." As for systemic deterrence, the rule "clearly" cannot have such an influence, since judges are not adjunct law enforcement officers and, therefore, "have no stake in the outcome of particular criminal prosecutions." Therefore, the threat of exclusion of evidence "cannot be expected significantly to deter them."

If the exclusionary rule will not deter judges and magistrates, the rule can only make sense if it will "alter the behavior of individual law enforcement officers or the policies of their department." The Court doubted that a change in the exclusionary rule such as that announced in *Leon* would have a counter-deterrent effect on police officers. First, it treated as "speculative" the fear that the rule would result in "magistrate shopping," *i.e.*, officers seeking out more lenient judges to issue warrants. In any case, "[i]f a magistrate serves merely as a 'rubber stamp' for the police or is unable to exercise mature judgment, closer supervision or removal provides a more effective remedy than the exclusionary rule."

Beyond this, Justice White stated, "even assuming that the rule effectively deters some police misconduct"—the Court said "[n]o empirical researcher,

---

[149] *Leon*, 468 U.S. at 916.

(Matthew Bender & Co., Inc.)

proponent or opponent . . . has yet been able to establish [this] with any assurance"—exclusion of evidence "cannot be expected, and should not be applied, to deter objectively reasonable law enforcement activity." In such circumstances, exclusion of the evidence "will not further the ends of the exclusionary rule in any appreciable way; for it is painfully apparent that . . . the officer is acting as a reasonable officer would and should act in similar circumstances."

Not surprisingly, *Leon* is controversial and, as a consequence, some states have rejected the "good faith" exception to the exclusionary rule.[150] Some critics believe that, even if a cost-benefit analysis is appropriate in determining whether to retain the exclusionary rule—itself a controversial issue[151]—the *Leon* majority's approach to the subject was skewed.[152] According to Justice Brennan in dissent, the Court created a "curious world where the 'costs' of excluding illegally obtained evidence loom to exaggerated heights and where the 'benefits' . . . are made to disappear with a mere wave of the hand."

In particular, the Court included on the scale *all* of the supposed costs of the exclusionary rule—not simply those that might be avoided by the good-faith principle—while it considered *only* those benefits of the exclusionary rule that arise in "objective good-faith" cases. For example, the Court cited existing data on prosecutions lost as a result of the exclusionary rule.[153] Those figures are not especially high in percentage terms, but in any case the only data that should have been considered are those costs that will be avoided by the *Leon* rule. Some lost prosecutions are the result of bad-faith police conduct or objectively unreasonable conduct by officers armed with search warrants, while some prosecutions are lost due to errors by police in non-warrant cases. These losses will continue after *Leon* and, therefore, should not have been placed on the scales.

Also, the Court arguably understated the value of the exclusionary rule in inducing magistrates to act more carefully. Current data suggest that many magistrates already provide little oversight of the warrant process.[154] Perhaps in some cases, judges *do* function as adjunct law officers, albeit

---

[150] *See* Note 136, *supra.*

[151] *See* § 21.04[D][1], *supra.*

[152] *See* Yale Kamisar, *The Warren Court and Criminal Justice: A Quarter-Century Retrospective,* 31 Tulsa L.J. 1, 32 (1995) (accusing the post-Warren Court of doing its balancing "in an empirical fog" and of conducting cost-benefit analysis by giving "back the values and assumptions the Court fed into it").

[153] Justice White cited data provided by Davies, Note 87, *supra.* For the data, *see* the text accompanying Note 91, *supra.*

[154] *See* § 11.02, *supra.*

while "disguised" in judicial robes; if so, the message of *Leon* is not a good one, as it allows these magistrates to protect the prosecution from the exclusion of evidence. Furthermore, one factor in the minds of some magistrates is that they do not want their decisions to be overturned by a higher court. If so, *Leon* might undercut their incentive to scrutinize warrant applications with care, because appellate courts have less reason after *Leon* to decide whether a warrant was invalid: they can skip directly to the good-faith issue and rule in favor of the government.

## § 21.07    The Exclusionary Rule, Good Faith, and Warrantless Police Conduct

### [A]    Should *Leon* Extend to Warrantless Police Action?

The *Leon*[155] "objective good-faith" rule applies to searches conducted with warrants. However, as a practical matter, the police do not usually seek prior judicial authorization for searches: Fourth Amendment jurisprudence provides the police ample leeway to act without a search warrant. Therefore, although *Leon* narrowed the scope of the amendment's exclusionary rule, it did so in a relatively small class of cases. The major question that remains is whether the Court will take another step—this time a very large one—and hold that the good-faith exception applies to *non*-warranted searches.[156]

### [1]    Arguments in Favor of Extending *Leon*

There is language or reasoning in *Leon* that gives comfort to those who want the good-faith exception extended to searches without warrants. Indeed, some of the reasoning could serve as a starting point for outright abolition of the exclusionary rule.

The argument for outright abolition assumes, as an initial premise, that the exclusionary rule is not constitutionally required, which appears to be the Court's current position on the subject.[157] If this is so, then the Court could abolish the rule if it does not believe it is satisfying its deterrent purpose, or if a less costly remedy would deter Fourth Amendment violations at least as well as the present-day rule. As summarized earlier,[158] Justice White's opinion in *Leon* is critical of the exclusionary rule. Even

---

[155] United States v. Leon, 468 U.S. 897 (1984). *See* § 21.06, *supra*.

[156] The Fifth Circuit of the United States Court of Appeals purports to recognize a *Leon*-like exception to the exclusionary rule in cases involving warrantless arrests and investigatory stops. United States v. Ramirez-Lujan, 976 F.2d 930 (5th Cir. 1992); United States v. De Leon-Reyna, 930 F.2d 396 (5th Cir. 1991).

[157] *See* § 21.03, *supra*.

[158] *See* § 21.06[B], *supra*.

with bad-faith police conduct, the Court only goes so far as to say that "in the absence of a more efficacious sanction," it will apply the rule to a "substantial and deliberate" violation. One might infer from this language that the Justices who signed the majority opinion in *Leon* would abolish the rule altogether if an appropriate alternative sanction could be found.

The less extreme option of extending the good-faith exception to non-warrant cases could be a step in the direction of outright abolition. Moreover, much of *Leon*'s reasoning would justify a good-faith exception for warrantless searches. The Court could argue that, just as with warranted searches, a police officer who acts in an objectively reasonable manner, albeit without a warrant, is not deterrable and, in any case, does not need to be deterred. To quote Justice Scalia in a different, but relevant, situation:

> It is apparent that in order to satisfy the "reasonableness" requirement of the Fourth Amendment, what is generally demanded of the many factual determinations that must regularly be made by agents of the government—whether the magistrate issuing a warrant, the police officer executing a warrant, or *the police officer conducting a search or seizure under one of the exceptions to the warrant requirement*—is not that they always be correct, but that they always be reasonable.[159]

### [2] Arguments Against Extending *Leon*

The Court set out a three-pronged defense of the good-faith exception in *Leon*.[160] Those three interrelated arguments focused on the fact that the blame for the Fourth Amendment violation in the case rested primarily with a member of the judiciary—the magistrate—and not with a member of the executive (the police officer).

The Court considered it significant that the exclusionary rule is meant to deter police, not judges. It saw no basis for believing that judges need to be deterred. And, beyond this, according to Justice White, exclusion of evidence would not have a deterrent effect on members of the judiciary. Even if these arguments are persuasive, they do not support the conclusion that the exclusionary rule cannot have a deterrent effect on police officers who do not seek prior judicial authorization for their actions. Moreover, to extend *Leon* to non-warrant cases runs counter to the Court's overall policy of providing incentives to the police to seek warrants rather than to act on their own.[161]

---

[159] Illinois v. Rodriguez, 497 U.S. 177, 185–86 (1990) (emphasis added).

[160] *See* the text to Note 149, *supra*.

[161] *E.g., see* § 9.02[D], *supra*.

## [B]   Answering the Question: Post-*Leon* Law

In *Arizona v. Evans*,[162] the Court extended the good-faith exception to a non-warrant search. However, the error in *Evans* was committed by a court employee, rather than by a police officer. Therefore, the Court found it relatively easy to apply *Leon* in this atypical situation.

In *Evans*, *D* was arrested during a routine traffic stop, after the patrol car's computer reported that there was an outstanding misdemeanor warrant for *D*'s arrest. A subsequent warrantless search incident to the arrest revealed marijuana. As it turned out, the arrest warrant had previously been quashed, but *D*'s name had not been removed from the computer, due to a clerical error by a court employee responsible for updating the records.

Seven Justices held that the exclusionary rule did not require suppression of the marijuana. According to Chief Justice Rehnquist, *Leon*'s reasoning justified the holding here. It made the same three-pronged argument set out in the latter case,[163] except that it focused on the fact that the error here was committed by a court employee, rather than a magistrate.

First, the Chief Justice stated, the "exclusionary rule was historically designed as a means of deterring police misconduct, not mistakes by court employees." Second, there was no evidence to suggest that "court employees are inclined to ignore or subvert the Fourth Amendment or that lawlessness among these actors requires application of the extreme sanction of exclusion." Third, "and most important, there is no basis for believing that application of the exclusionary rule in these circumstances will have a significant effect on court employees responsible for informing the police that a warrant has been quashed." Therefore, applying the objective good-faith rule of *Leon*, the Court observed that "[t]here is no indication that the arresting officer was not acting objectively reasonably when he relied upon the police computer record."

However, computer errors of the sort involved in *Evans* are common.[164] This concern apparently stirred Justices O'Connor, Souter and Breyer to write a concurring opinion. Although they joined the majority opinion, these Justices warned that it "would *not* be reasonable for the police to rely, say, on a recordkeeping system, their own or some other agency's, that has no

---

[162] 514 U.S. 1 (1995); *see generally* Wayne R. LaFave, *Computers, Urinals, and the Fourth Amendment: Confessions of a Patron Saint*, 94 Mich. L. Rev. 2553 (1996).

[163] *See* the text to Note 149, *supra*.

[164] According to projections of the Federal Bureau of Investigation, as many as 12,000 invalid or inaccurate reports on suspects wanted for arrest are transmitted *daily* to federal, state, and local police agencies. David Burnham, *F.B.I. Says 12,000 Faulty Reports on Suspects Are Issued Each Day*, New York Times, Aug. 25, 1985, at 1.

mechanism to ensure its accuracy over time and that routinely leads to false arrests." Although the police "are entitled to enjoy the substantial advantage" of computer technology, they may not "rely on it blindly."

In a separate concurrence, Justices Souter and Breyer observed that the Court did not answer "another question that may reach us in due course, that is, how far, in dealing with fruits of computerized error, our very concept of deterrence by exclusion of evidence should extend to the government as a whole, not merely the police, on the ground that there would otherwise be no reasonable expectation of keeping the number of resulting false arrests within an acceptable minimum limit."

Justice Stevens dissented. He objected to the extension of the good-faith rule to a non-warrant situation. According to Stevens, *Leon* "stands for the dubious but limited proposition that courts should not look behind the face of a warrant on which police have relied in good faith."

Justice Ginsburg also dissented. She believed that certiorari was improvidently granted. However, she also expressed considerable concern about computer recordkeeping of the sort involved in *Evans*, and she was skeptical of the ability to distinguish between errors caused by court employees and those working for other branches of government: "In this electronic age, particularly with respect to recordkeeping, court personnel and police officers are not neatly compartmentalized actors."[165] According to Ginsburg, few would disagree with the state supreme court's finding that it is "repugnant to the principles of a free society" to take an individual "into police custody because of a computer error precipitated by government carelessness."

Although *Evans* demonstrates that a majority of the Court is willing to apply *Leon* in a non-warrant circumstance, the case provides no direct clues regarding whether the good-faith exception will apply to Fourth Amendment violations that are the result of misjudgments by police officers, or even the result of faulty information in *police*-managed computers.[166]

---

[165] In this regard, *see* Shadler v. State, 761 So.2d 279 (Fla. 2000) (in which the court determined that a computer error by the driver's license division of the state's Department of Highway Safety and Motor Vehicles fell outside the scope of *Evans*, because the Department "essentially" was a law enforcement agency; the court reached this conclusion based in part on statements made by the Department on its Internet web page that stressed its role in highway safety; the court refused to focus solely on the role of the license subdivision of the Department ).

[166] *See* State v. White, 660 So. 2d 664, 667 (Fla. 1995) (refusing to apply the good-faith exception because the error in the instant case "boils down to one unmistakable fact—failure of the police to maintain up-to-date and accurate computer records").

## § 21.08   "Fruit of the Poisonous Tree" Doctrine[167]

### [A]   Overview

#### [1]   General Principles

In general, the Fourth Amendment exclusionary rule extends not only to the direct products of governmental illegality, but also to secondary evidence that is the "fruit of the poisonous tree."[168] For example, suppose that *P*, a police officer, on a sheer hunch, unconstitutionally searches *D*'s house for evidence of her suspected connection to a murder. During the search, the officer seizes a diary. The diary names a witness (*W*) to the murder, who agrees to testify against *D* at her trial.

The unconstitutional search of the house constitutes the initial illegality: it is the "poisonous tree." Under ordinary exclusionary rule principles, of course, the diary is inadmissible at *D*'s trial because it was the direct product of the unlawful search. However, is *W*'s testimony admissible? The government obtained the evidence from a diary that was searched as the result of the initial illegality; as such *W*'s testimony—"secondary" or "derivative" evidence—is a fruit of the poisonous tree.

Assuming that the exclusionary rule is otherwise applicable, evidence that is a fruit of the poisonous tree is ordinarily inadmissible. However, the fruit-of-the-poisonous-tree doctrine is subject to three qualifications: (1) the independent source doctrine; (2) the inevitable discovery rule; and (3) the attenuated connection principle. The first doctrine defines a circumstance in which the evidence is question is *not* a fruit of the poisonous tree and, therefore, is not subject to exclusion on this ground. The remaining two doctrines serve as exceptions to the rule that a fruit of a poisonous tree must be excluded at the criminal trial.

#### [2]   Identifying the Poisonous Tree

The fruit-of-the-poisonous-tree doctrine applies to constitutional provisions other than the Fourth Amendment, *i.e.*, there are Fifth Amendment and Sixth Amendment poisonous trees, as well.[169] On the other hand, *apparently* there is no *Miranda*[170] poisonous tree doctrine.[171] Therefore, it is important to identify the nature of the poisonous tree.

---

[167] *See generally* 5 LaFave, Note 1, *supra*, at § 11.4.

[168] Nardone v. United States, 308 U.S. 338, 341 (1939).

[169] *See* §§ 23.02[E][3] (Fifth Amendment, interrogations), 25.07[D] (Sixth Amendment right to counsel, interrogations), and 27.02[A] (*id.*, eyewitness identification procedures), *infra*.

[170] Miranda v. Arizona, 384 U.S. 436 (1966).

[171] *See* § 24.12[B], *infra*.

For example, suppose that *D* is arrested without probable cause, informed of her *Miranda* rights, voluntarily waives those rights, and confesses. The confession is not inadmissible under Fifth Amendment, Sixth Amendment, or *Miranda* principles. Nonetheless, the confession might be inadmissible as a fruit of a *Fourth Amendment* poisonous tree (the unlawful arrest).

On the other hand, suppose that *D* is *lawfully* arrested, *not* informed of her *Miranda* rights, and subjected to custodial interrogation, during which time she informs the police where she concealed a gun used in the crime. Here, as we will see, *D*'s confession is inadmissible under *Miranda* principles. The gun is a fruit of that *Miranda* violation. Therefore, its admissibility is a matter of *Miranda* jurisprudence, and not of Fourth Amendment law.

### [B]  Independent Source Doctrine[172]

The threshold issue in any fruit-of-the-poisonous-tree claim is whether "the challenged evidence is in some sense the product of illegal governmental activity."[173] Evidence that is not causally linked to governmental illegality is admissible pursuant to the "independent source doctrine."[174] Such evidence is a fruit of a *non*-poisonous tree. As the Supreme Court has explained:

> [T]he interest of society in deterring unlawful police conduct and the public interest in having juries receive all probative evidence of a crime are properly balanced by putting the police in the same, not a *worse* position that they would have been in if no police error or misconduct had occurred. . . . When the challenged evidence has an independent source, exclusion of such evidence would put the police in a worse position than they would have been in absent any error or violation.[175]

In its simplest application, the independent source doctrine applies if the challenged evidence is discovered for the first time during *lawful* police activity. For example, suppose that the police *lawfully* seize *D*'s diary in a criminal investigation. The diary identifies *W*, an eye-witness to *D*'s conduct. The police contact *W*, who agrees to testify against *D*. Later, the police search *D*'s premises again, but this time *unlawfully*. In the second search, the police discover *W*'s name in another document. Under the independent source doctrine, *D* may not successfully challenge *W*'s trial

---

[172] *See generally* Craig M. Bradley, *Murray v. United States: The Bell Tolls for the Search Warrant Requirement*, 64 Ind. L.J. 907 (1989).

[173] United States v. Crews, 445 U.S. 463, 471 (1980).

[174] *See* Silverthorne Lumber Co. v. United States, 251 U.S. 385 (1920).

[175] Nix v. Williams, 467 U.S. 431, 443 (1984).

testimony as a fruit of the poisonous tree, because the police originally obtained *W*'s name in the first—lawful—search.

The independent source doctrine also applies if evidence is initially discovered *unlawfully*, but is later obtained lawfully in a manner independent of the original discovery. This lesson is learned from the Court's controversial analysis in *Murray v. United States*.[176] In *Murray*, officers unconstitutionally, for lack of warrant, entered a warehouse and observed burlap-wrapped bales, which they suspected contained marijuana. The officers left without seizing the bales. While they kept the area under surveillance, other officers obtained a warrant to search the building based on an untainted affidavit, *i.e.*, an affidavit only containing information the police gathered lawfully before the entry. The officers then seized the bales, pursuant to the warrant.

Justice Scalia, speaking for a four-Justice plurality, remanded the case to a lower court "for determination whether the warrant-authorized search of the warehouse was an independent source of the challenged evidence in the sense we have described." As the Court analyzed the situation, the warrant may have been an independent source because it was supported by probable cause, which in turn was based on an affidavit that did not include anything learned by the police during the illegal entry. Under such circumstances, the evidence seized was a product of the second—lawful— warranted search, and not a product of the first—unlawful—warrantless search.

According to the plurality, there was one way that the second search could be a fruit of the original illegality, namely, "if the agents' decision to seek the warrant was prompted by what they had seen during the initial entry." Put differently, if the police would not have applied for the warrant (although they had enough lawfully obtained information to do so) *but for* the illegal search, then the second search *would* be a fruit of the illegality. On such hypothesized facts, the warrant would be a fruit of the unlawful entry because the latter search *motivated* the request for the warrant.

How does a court determine whether an officer's decision to apply for a warrant was prompted by an unlawful search? Does *Murray* invite an officer to testify that she would have sought a warrant even if she had not illegally entered the premises? Such an invitation is undesirable. As the Court has stated elsewhere, "evenhanded law enforcement is best achieved by the application of objective standards of conduct, rather than standards

---

[176] 487 U.S. 533 (1988); *contra under the state constitution,* Commonwealth v. Melendez, 676 A.2d 226 (Pa.1996) (application of the "independent source doctrine" is proper only if, unlike the facts in *Murray*, the "independent source" is independent of the police or investigative team that engaged in the initial unlawful conduct).

that depend upon the subjective state of mind of the officer."[177] Under *Murray*, a finding regarding the agents' state of mind *is* required. However, according to the plurality, an officer's assurance on the point—"I would have requested this warrant anyway"—is not dispositive: "[w]here the facts render those assurances implausible, the independent source doctrine will not apply."

A controversial feature of *Murray* is that it arguably provides an incentive to police to conduct unlawful confirmatory searches, *i.e.*, warrantless searches "to make sure that what they expect to be on the premises is in fact there."[178] The fear is that because the warrant application process is inconvenient, officers will want to confirm their suspicions before they apply for a warrant. If they unlawfully search and find nothing, they save the time of applying for a warrant. On the other hand, thanks to *Murray*, if the police find criminal evidence, they may request a warrant and, as long as they leave out their observations from the unlawful search, seize the evidence pursuant to the warrant.

Justice Scalia discounted this concern. He reasoned that if the police have probable cause before the confirmatory search, as in *Murray*, they would be "foolish" to conduct it, because they will later have to prove that all of the information in the warrant affidavit was obtained lawfully, and that they were not motivated to apply for the warrant by the fact of the confirmatory search, an "onerous" burden. On the other hand, if they lack probable cause before the confirmatory search, nothing learned during the search may be used to strengthen their case.

### [C] Inevitable Discovery Rule

The independent source doctrine provides that evidence is admissible, despite police illegality, if the evidence seized was not causally linked to the wrongdoing. Suppose, however, that the government concedes that the evidence in question *is* causally tied to earlier governmental illegality, but it asserts that the police would have discovered the evidence lawfully, even in the absence of the unconstitutional conduct. If the court accepts the prosecutor's claim, is the derivative evidence admissible?

The Supreme Court held in *Nix v. Williams*[179] that evidence linked to an earlier illegality *is* admissible in a criminal trial if the prosecutor proves

---

[177] Horton v. California, 496 U.S. 128, 138 (1990).

[178] Murray v. United States, 487 U.S. at 539.

[179] 467 U.S. 431 (1984); *contra under the state constitution*, Smith v. State, 948 P.2d 473 (Alaska 1997) (requiring proof by "clear and convincing" standard); State v. Garner, 417 S.E.2d 502 (N.C. 1992) (*id.*); Commonwealth v. O'Connor, 546 N.E.2d 336 (Mass. 1989) ("certain as a practical matter").

by a preponderance of the evidence that the challenged evidence "ultimately or inevitably would have been discovered by lawful means." This is the so-called "inevitable discovery" (or "hypothetical independent source") rule. Although the violation in *Nix* was of the Sixth Amendment right to counsel, the fruit-of-the-poisonous-tree analysis applies in the same manner in Fourth Amendment cases.

In *Nix*, police officers, in violation of *D*'s Sixth Amendment right to counsel, deliberately elicited incriminating information from him and induced him to lead them to the body of the murder victim. At the time that *D* agreed to show the police where the body would be found, a search team was within a few miles of the corpse; however, the search was temporarily called off, after *D* agreed to cooperate.

The Court ruled that the evidence relating to the victim's body was admissible, notwithstanding the Sixth Amendment illegality, on the basis of the inevitable discovery doctrine. The trial court found that the body would have been discovered "within a short time" in "essentially the same condition" even if the police had not violated *D*'s Sixth Amendment rights. Consequently, society should not be punished for the officer's illegality by placing the prosecution in a worse position than it would have been had the police acted lawfully.

Justices Brennan and Marshall dissented. They agreed that evidence that would ultimately be discovered lawfully should be admissible, but they would have required the prosecutor to prove such inevitability by the higher standard of "clear and convincing evidence." They reasoned that the inevitable discovery doctrine, although akin to the independent source doctrine, differs from it in the key respect that there is *not* an independent source, only a hypothetically independent one. The higher burden of proof is needed in order to confine the inevitable discovery rule to circumstances that closely resemble the independent source doctrine.

### [D]  Attenuated Connection Principle (The *Wong Sun* Rule)[180]

### [1]  General Rule

In *Nardone v. United States*[181] the Supreme Court held that evidence secured as the result of police illegality is admissible if the connection between the illegality and the challenged evidence has "become so attenuated as to dissipate the taint."

---

[180] *See generally* Brent D. Stratton, Comment, *The Attenuation Exception to the Exclusionary Rule: A Study in Attenuated Principle and Dissipated Logic*, 75 J. Crim. L. & Criminology 139 (1984).

[181] 308 U.S. 338 (1939).

The Court explained the attenuated connection principle a bit more in *Wong Sun v. United States*.[182] In *Wong Sun*, the Court stated that not all evidence "is 'fruit of the poisonous tree' simply because it would not have come to light but for the illegal actions of the police." Instead, the correct question is "whether, granting establishment of the primary illegality, the evidence to which instant objection is made has been come at by exploitation of that illegality or instead by means sufficiently distinguishable to be purged of the primary taint."

There is generally no bright-line test for determining whether derivative evidence is free of the original taint. Each case is determined on its own facts, and no single fact is dispositive. Ultimately, "the 'dissipation of the taint' concept . . . 'attempts to mark the point at which the detrimental consequences of illegal police action become so attenuated that the deterrent effect of the exclusionary rule no longer justifies its cost.'"[183]

### [2]  Attenuation Factors

### [a]  Temporal Proximity

The shorter the time lapse between the initial illegality and the acquisition of the challenged evidence, the more likely that a court will conclude that the evidence is tainted. For example, in *Wong Sun*, the police obtained a statement from *D* in his bedroom immediately after his unlawful arrest. The Court suppressed this evidence, "which derive[d] so immediately from the unlawful entry."

### [b]  Intervening Events

### [i]  In General

The more factors that intervene between the initial illegality and the seizure of the challenged evidence, the more likely that the evidence will be admitted. As the causal chain of events lengthens, the less likely it is that the police "foresaw the challenged evidence as a probable product of their illegality."[184] Consequently, the deterrent value of the exclusionary rule is reduced.

### [ii]  Intervening Act of Free Will

An intervening act of free will very often remove the taint of an earlier illegality. For example, in *Wong Sun, D* was released from jail after his

---

[182] 371 U.S. 471 (1963).

[183] United States v. Leon, 468 U.S. 897, 911 (1984) (quoting Brown v. Illinois, 422 U.S. 590, 609 (1975) (Powell, J., concurring)).

[184] Comment, *Fruit of the Poisonous Tree—A Plea for Relevant Criteria*, 115 U. Pa. L. Rev. 1136, 1148–49 (1967).

unlawful arrest. Subsequently, he voluntarily returned to the police station and provided a written statement. The Court found that the voluntary nature of *D*'s conduct—returning to police headquarters and answering questions propounded to him—rendered his statement sufficiently free of taint to be admissible.

On the other hand, the Court has consistently held that "*Miranda* warnings, *alone* and *per se*, cannot always make the act [of confessing] a product of free will to break, for Fourth Amendment purposes, the causal connection between the illegality and the confession." [185] Therefore, if the police arrest a suspect on less than probable cause, read her the *Miranda* warnings, obtain a waiver, and thereafter secure a confession, the question of whether the subsequent statement was the product of the suspect's free will—and, thus, whether the taint of the initial illegality has been sufficiently dissipated—must be determined on the totality of the circumstances.

### [iii]  Special Issue: Statement Obtained After an Unlawful Entry of a Home

As just noted, the taint of a statement obtained from a suspect after an unlawful arrest is not necessarily dissipated simply because *Miranda* warnings were given after the illegality occurred and prior to the taking of the confession. But, the Supreme Court ruled in *New York v. Harris* [186] that in one very specific circumstance there is a bright-line rule of admissibility: "[W]here the police have probable cause to arrest a suspect, the exclusionary rule does not bar the State's use of a statement made by the defendant outside of his home, even though the statement is taken after an arrest made in a home in violation of *Payton* [*v. New York*]."

It will be remembered that the Court held in *Payton v. New York* [187] that the Fourth Amendment prohibits the police from entering a suspect's home without a warrant or consent in order to make a routine felony arrest. In *Harris*, the police violated *Payton*'s strictures by arresting *D* in his home without an arrest warrant. The police then transported *D* to the police station where they informed *D* of his *Miranda* rights. *D* waived his constitutional rights, and made a statement that the police sought to introduce at his trial. Under ordinary principles, the Court would have weighed all of the circumstances surrounding the confession to determine whether the taint

---

[185] Brown v. Illinois, 422 U.S. 590, 603 (1975); *e.g.*, Dunaway v. New York, 442 U.S. 200 (1979).

[186] 495 U.S. 14 (1990); *contra*, State v. Geisler, 610 A.2d 1225 (Conn. 1992) (rejecting *Harris* under the state constitution, and applying ordinary attenuated connection principles); People v. Harris, 570 N.E.2d 1051 (N.Y. 1991) (*Id.*).

[187] 445 U.S. 573 (1980). *See* § 10.05, *supra*.

from the *Payton* violation was dissipated by the *Miranda* warnings. *Harris* held, however, that the statement was admissible on the basis of just one factor: *D*'s statement was not the product of that aspect of the police conduct that was illegal.

The Court reasoned that the purpose of the *Payton* rule is to protect the sanctity of the home from unwarranted entry. According to *Harris*, "[n]othing in the reasoning of that case suggests that an arrest in a home without a warrant but with probable cause somehow renders unlawful continued custody of the suspect once he is removed from the house." As the Court has consistently held, a person is not immune from prosecution merely because her person is the fruit of an illegal arrest.[188] Therefore, as the Court explained:

> [b]ecause the officers had probable cause to arrest [*D*] for a crime, [*D*] was not unlawfully in custody when he was removed to the station house . . . . For Fourth Amendment purposes, the legal issue is the same as it would be had the police arrested [*D*] on his doorstep, illegally entered his home to search for evidence, and later interrogated [*D*] at the station house.

In short, *D*'s "statement taken at the police station was not the product of being in unlawful custody. Neither was it the fruit of having been arrested in the home rather than someplace else. . . . [H]is subsequent statement was not an exploitation of the illegal entry into [*D*'s] home." Whether one reads this case as an application of the independent-source doctrine[189] or, instead, of the attenuated-connection (dissipation-of-taint) principle, a violation of *Payton* loses its Fourth Amendment significance (in regard to any statement made by the arrestee) the instant the individual, arrested on probable cause, is outside the confines of the home.

### [c]  Flagrancy of the Violation

Derivative evidence is less likely to be free of taint if the initial illegality was flagrant rather than accidental.[190] Metaphorically, a flagrant violation results in greater poison, and thus takes longer to dissipate. It is justifiable to apply the exclusionary rule more extensively if the secondary evidence is causally linked to egregious police misconduct and, thus, to police behavior in greater need of deterrence.[191]

---

[188] *See* § 10.03[B], *supra.*

[189] *See* § 21.08[B], *supra.*

[190] *See* Brown v. Illinois, 422 U.S. 590, 604 (1975).

[191] *See* George C. Thomas III & Barry S. Pollack, *Balancing the Fourth Amendment Scales: The Bad-Faith Exception to Exclusionary Rule Limitations,* 45 Hastings L.J. 21 (1993) (arguing that government bad-faith conduct in obtaining evidence not only requires a more

### [d]  Nature of the Derivative Evidence

According to the Supreme Court, some contested evidence, by its nature, is more susceptible to dissipation of the taint than other evidence. In particular, verbal evidence is more likely to be admissible than physical evidence.

In *United States v. Ceccolini*,[192] the police unlawfully obtained the name of *X*, a witness to a crime, through an unlawful search. When contacted by the police, *X* offered to provide important testimony against *D*. *D* sought to exclude *X*'s testimony as a fruit of the unlawful search.

The Court rejected the prosecutor's claim that the testimony of a witness should never "be excluded at trial no matter how close and proximate the connection between it and a violation of the Fourth Amendment." But, the Court also rejected language from *Wong Sun*, which stated that "the policies underlying the exclusionary rule [do not] invite any logical distinction between physical and verbal evidence."

Instead, the Court held that a witness' testimony is more likely than physical evidence to be free of taint. It offered two reasons in support of this proposition. First, witnesses often come forward of their own volition, whereas inanimate objects must be discovered by others. Therefore, there is a greater likelihood that the police will discover a witness by lawful means; consequently, the police have less incentive to violate the Constitution in order to obtain witness testimony.

But, this argument is debatable. Essentially, the majority's reasoning is that testimony will often be admissible under the independent source or inevitable discovery doctrine, because witnesses (unlike inanimate objects) can and often do come forward voluntarily. But, *Ceccolini* suggests that even if a witness does *not* come forward in a particular case, the mere possibility that she *might* do so renders the taint more attenuated. This reasoning, however, amounts to nothing more than, as the dissent put it, "judicial double counting" of the free-will factor.

The second reason for the Court's belief that the testimony of witnesses should more easily be purged of taint than physical evidence is that if this were not the case, relevant and material testimony of witnesses would be "permanently disabled." However, as the dissent in *Ceccolini* observed, physical evidence is also susceptible to permanent disability, and witness testimony is more apt to be unreliable than physical evidence. It is unclear,

---

extensive application of the exclusionary rule to secondary evidence, but also justifies use of the rule when it otherwise would not be available—*e.g.*, when victims of bad-faith conduct lack standing, and in civil actions brought by the government).

[192] 435 U.S. 268 (1978).

therefore, why a special rule should be devised to make it easier to introduce verbal testimony than physical evidence.

## CHAPTER 22

# INTERROGATION LAW: OVERVIEW

## § 22.01  Initial Observations About Interrogation Law

Police interrogation law has come a long way since the "stone age"[1] —or "the good old days," depending on one's view of the subject—of American criminal procedure. Although the Supreme Court in 1884 adopted the common law rule of evidence that a suspect's statement to the police is inadmissible at trial if it was made involuntarily,[2] this rule did not become a part of constitutional law until 1897 in the federal courts,[3] and 1936 in the state courts.[4]

The second half of the twentieth century was a volatile and controversial period in interrogation law, and there is little reason to believe that the new century will bring an end to the controversies. The law and the various controversies surrounding the confession process are considered in detail in the next three chapters of this text. As will be seen, some rulings, and broad language in various Supreme Court opinions particularly in the 1960s, suggested to many contemporary legal observers that "the doctrines converging upon the institution of police interrogation are threatening to push on to their logical conclusion—*to the point where no questioning of suspects will be permitted.*"[5]

This prediction proved wildly faulty. It is clear, however, that interrogation law experienced significant changes during the Warren Court era, as a majority of the Court sought to "even the playing field" in the interrogation room—or, at least, to make it less one-sided—by setting limits on interrogation techniques, requiring the police to inform suspects of their constitutional rights relating to interrogations, and implementing procedures making it possible for suspects to have counsel present during questioning.

---

[1] Yale Kamisar, *Kauper's "Judicial Examination of the Accused" Forty Years Later—Some Comments on a Remarkable Article*, 73 Mich. L. Rev. 15, 16 (1974).

[2] Hopt v. Utah, 110 U.S. 574 (1884).

[3] Bram v. United States, 168 U.S. 532 (1897).

[4] Brown v. Mississippi, 297 U.S. 278 (1936).

[5] Walter V. Schaefer, The Suspect and Society 9 (1967) (emphasis added).

In large part, the trend toward expansion of the rights of criminal suspects in the interrogation room ended when the balance of power on the Supreme Court shifted,[6] as Justices with "due process model" values were replaced by advocates of the "crime control model" of criminal justice.[7] Although the leading Warren Court interrogation cases have not been overruled, they are mostly "battered and bruised."[8] The "new" Court has applied existing law narrowly, sometimes reinterpreted precedent, and announced various exceptions to the old rules. The effect is an uneasy alliance of the old and the new: of old law founded on considerable suspicion of the interrogation process, and new law that views confessions not only as good for the soul but as necessary in a crime-fighting society.

## § 22.02 Police Interrogation Techniques: Historically and At Present

In order to appreciate the reasons why the United States Supreme Court and, to a lesser extent, state courts, became involved in setting limits on police interrogation procedures, it is necessary to put the police practices in historical context.

According to sociologist and lawyer Richard Leo, the typical American police department of the nineteenth century was "brutal and corrupt."[9] Indeed, through the first third of the twentieth century, police interrogations typically involved the use of the so-called "third degree": the police "routinely threatened, beat, and tortured suspects" in order to wring confessions from the guilty and, not rarely, the innocent.[10]

---

[6] See 1.04[E], supra.

[7] See § 2.02, supra.

[8] Yale Kamisar, *The Warren Court and Criminal Justice: A Quarter-Century Retrospective*, 31 Tulsa L.J. 1, 54 (1995).

[9] See generally Richard A. Leo, Police Interrogation in America: A Study in Violence, Civility and Social Change (1994) (unpublished doctoral dissertation) (on file with the Stanford Law Review) (see especially chapter 2).

[10] Richard J. Ofshe & Richard A. Leo, *The Social Psychology of Police Interrogation: The Theory and Classification of True and False Confessions*, 16 Studies in Law, Politics and Society 189, 189 (1997). Unfortunately, false confessions—confessions by innocent persons—remain a problem. Jan Hoffman, *Police Refine Methods So Potent, Even the Innocent Have Confessed*, New York Times, March 10, 1998, at A1 (although there is considerable dispute regarding the frequency of false confessions, their number "is shaking the confidence of both prosecutors and juries in the reliability of confessions"); Ofshe & Leo, *supra*, at 190 ("False confessions are caused by inappropriate, improper and inept use of the methods of psychological interrogation."); Welsh S. White, *What is an Involuntary Confessions Now?*, 50 Rutgers L. Rev. 2001, 2005 (1998) ("[o]ver the past few decades, standard interrogation techniques have apparently led to false confessions in a significant number of cases" (and citing sources in support of this proposition)); *see generally* Welsh S. White, *False Confessions and the Constitution: Safeguards Against Untrustworthy Confessions*, 32 Harv. C.R.-C.L. L. Rev. 105 (1997).

Police interrogations were conducted incommunicado, which insured not only that the suspect was isolated—and, thus, more susceptible to the tactics used—but that the violence occurring in the interrogation room would largely go undocumented. Although there is no way to know with certainty how often brutality was used, Leo and other scholars[11] believe that it was regularly practiced by the police to obtain confessions and as an extra-legal method of retribution against those whom the police believed were guilty of wrongdoing.

At its most extreme, the police used brutal physical force to secure confessions. Some suspects were beaten all over the body, but more often the assaults were limited to those regions of the body that would not be visible when the individual was taken before a judge. Sometimes, however, the police violence could not be disguised. For example, in one case reported by Leo,[12] police officers hung a handcuffed suspect over the top of an open door and used him as a "human punching bag."

The beginnings of change occurred in 1931, when the federal government published the findings of a blue-ribbon commission study, "Report on Lawlessness in Law Enforcement," headed by then United States Attorney General George Wickersham. The report exposed the third-degree interrogation techniques to a largely shocked public. As a result of public revulsion and increased judicial attention to the problem, police departments initiated reforms. Physical coercion declined as a consequence in the 1930s and 1940s, as departmental professionalization took place.

By the 1960s, police interrogation techniques had become relatively sophisticated. Sociologist Gary Marx has observed, however, that "[t]here is an interesting irony at work here: restrict police use of coercion, and the use of deception increases."[13] That is, with limitations placed on the use of violence to secure confessions, the police turned to psychological pressures and deceptions. Consistent with the social psychology literature of the time,[14] police manuals instructed officers on the proper arrangement of interrogation rooms,[15] on the characteristics of the ideal interrogator,[16] and on the most effective means to manipulate suspects to confess.

---

[11] *E.g.,* Lawrence Friedman, Crime and Punishment in American History 303 (1993).

[12] *See* Note 9, *supra.*

[13] Gary T. Marx, Undercover: Police Surveillance in America 47 (1988).

[14] *See* Edwin D. Driver, *Confessions and the Social Psychology of Coercion,* 82 Harv. L. Rev. 42 (1968).

[15] *E.g.,* they should give the suspect the "illusion that the environment . . .is withdrawing." Arthur S. Aubry & Rudolph R. Caputo, Criminal Interrogation 38 (1965).

[16] *E.g.,* the interrogator should be male, tall, deep voiced, and dressed in a business suit.

Contemporary police strategy has been described as possessing "many of the essential hallmarks of a confidence game."[17] According to one police officer, "interrogation [now] is *not* a matter of forcing suspects to confess but of 'conning' them. Really what we do is just bullshit them."[18] Less generously, an observer of police tactics has characterized contemporary interrogations as less violent than in the past, on occasion "ingenious," but still "uncivilized, at best."[19]

Since the 1960s and largely continuing today,[20] police officers try to foster anxiety in suspects, for example, by stating (often falsely) that they have sufficient evidence to convict, and then using this disclosure to convince a suspect that it is hopeless to resist the officers' entreaties. Or, the police may follow the very different tactic of displaying false sympathy for the suspect, blaming the victim, and minimizing the moral significance of the charges against the arrestee, in order to secure the individual's confidence and convince him that the court and jury will show leniency.

In summary, police procedures have evolved over the past century from use of violence to psychological manipulation of suspects. These changes have been brought about as a result of public demands for change following disclosures of police brutality and, more often, by pressure exerted by the judiciary.

---

[17] Richard A. Leo, *Miranda's Revenge: Police Interrogation as a Confidence Game*, 30 Law & Soc. Rev. 259, 260–61 (1996).

[18] Richard A. Leo, *From Coercion to Deception: The Changing Nature of Police Interrogation in America*, 18 Crime, Law & Soc. Change 35, 35 (1992) (quoting from William Hart, *The Subtle Art of Persuasion*, Police Magazine (January, 1981) at 15–16) (emphasis added).

[19] "Some of the techniques used by detectives could aptly be described as physically intimidating, teetering on the brink of violence. . . . [D]etectives [were] doing everything from slamming doors and kicking chairs, swearing, and interrogating late at night to lying about the evidence against the suspect and about the detective's ability and willingness to get the suspect a lower sentence. Several of the techniques are ingenious . . . . But most people would find them uncivilized, at best." Akhil Reed Amar & Reneé B. Lettow, *Fifth Amendment First Principles: The Self-Incrimination Clause*, 93 Mich. L. Rev. 857, 873-74 (1995) (footnote omitted) (summarizing the findings of David Simon, who observed a homicide police unit for a year, as reported in David Simon, Homicide: A Year on the Killing Streets (1991)).

[20] *See generally* Ofshe & Leo, Note 10, *supra*; Hoffman, Note 10, *supra*.

## § 22.03  Interrogation Law: Constitutional Issues

### [A]  Was the Confession Coerced (Obtained Involuntarily)?

#### [1]  Due Process Clause

The Fifth Amendment, which applies to the actions of the federal government, provides that "[n]o person shall . . . be deprived of life, liberty, or property, without due process of law." The Fourteenth Amendment, which applies to state and local governments, has a similar due process clause. As examined and clarified in the next chapter, a person is denied due process of law if an involuntary statement, *i.e.*, a statement obtained as the result of undue police pressure, is used against him at a criminal trial.

#### [2]  Fifth Amendment Compulsory Self-Incrimination Clause

The Fifth Amendment provides that "[n]o person . . . shall be compelled in any criminal case to be a witness against himself." This right has come to be known, in shorthand, as the "privilege against self-incrimination," but more accurately is the "privilege against *compelled* self-incrimination." The Fifth Amendment privilege applies most obviously at a federal criminal trial: a defendant may not be compelled to testify (to be a witness) against himself.[21] The role of the Fifth Amendment privilege in the pre-trial context, most particularly in the interrogation room, is more controversial.

In 1964, the Supreme Court held that the privilege against compelled self-incrimination is a fundamental right, applicable to the states pursuant to the Fourteenth Amendment due process clause.[22] Consequently, the admissibility of a confession in a state criminal prosecution can now be tested by either self-incrimination or due process principles.

Outside the police interrogation context, "compulsion" (the Fifth Amendment term) and "involuntariness" (the due process clause prohibition) are separate concepts and, therefore, are not properly equated.[23] However, in the interrogation context, the Supreme Court has conflated the concepts: there is little evident difference in the case law between a confession that

---

[21] The general principles of the Fifth Amendment privilege are discussed in chapter 26, *infra*.

[22] Malloy v. Hogan, 378 U.S. 1 (1964).

[23] For example, a threat to discharge a police officer if he refuses to testify at a hearing renders his statement *compelled* under the Fifth Amendment. Garrity v. New Jersey, 385 U.S. 493, 497 (1967). But such a statement is far from *involuntary* in the sense that the latter concept is used in the confession cases. Stephen J. Schulhofer, *Reconsidering Miranda*, 54 U. Chi. L. Rev. 435, 440–46 (1987); Stephen J. Schulhofer, *Miranda, Dickerson and the Puzzling Persistence of Fifth Amendment Exceptionalism*, 99 Mich. L. Rev. 941 (2001).

is barred at trial because it was "compelled" and one that was secured "involuntarily."[24]

### [B] Was the Confession Obtained in Violation of *Miranda v. Arizona*?

In *Miranda v. Arizona*,[25] the Supreme Court devised a set of warnings that the police must give a suspect in custody before they may interrogate him, in order to protect his privilege against compulsory self-incrimination. The Court stated that in the absence of the procedural safeguards set out in the case, "no statement obtained from the defendant [during custodial interrogation] can truly be the product of his free choice."

The original understanding of *Miranda* was that a violation of the rules set out in that opinion constituted a breach of the Fifth Amendment privilege against compulsory self-incrimination. Subsequently, however, the Supreme Court characterized the *Miranda* safeguards as "prophylactic" in nature.[26] The Court stated that the *Miranda* rules "serve" the Fifth Amendment, but "sweep more broadly than the Fifth Amendment itself."[27] That is, one can violate the *Miranda* rules *without* violating the Fifth Amendment, *i.e.*, not all statements obtained in violation of *Miranda* are involuntary or compelled.

In 2000, the Supreme Court re-characterized *Miranda* as "constitutional decision"[28] and "constitutional rule."[29] Nonetheless, the Court did not disavow any of its prior rulings that have distinguished *Miranda* violations from traditional "involuntariness" claims. Consequently, although *Miranda* must be seen as a branch of Fifth Amendment law, it is necessary for analytical purposes to treat *Miranda* jurisprudence separately from "pure" self-incrimination law.

### [C] Was the Defendant Entitled to Counsel?

#### [1] Sixth Amendment

Whether or not a statement was obtained by the police in a coercive manner, it is inadmissible at trial if it was obtained in violation of the accused's constitutional right to counsel. The Sixth Amendment provides that "[i]n all criminal prosecutions, the accused shall enjoy the right to . . .

---

[24] *See generally* § 23.01[B][3], *infra.*

[25] 384 U.S. 436 (1966).

[26] The concept of a "prophylactic rule" is discussed at § 4.05, *supra.*

[27] Oregon v. Elstad, 470 U.S. 298, 306 (1985).

[28] Dickerson v. United States, 530 U.S. 428, 432, 438 (2000)

[29] *Id.* at 437, 438, 441, 444.

the Assistance of Counsel for his defence." This right applies to the states through the Fourteenth Amendment due process clause.[30]

The Sixth Amendment right to counsel is violated if the government deliberately elicits statements from a suspect in the absence of his counsel or waiver of the right. However, the Sixth Amendment right does not attach until adversary judicial criminal proceedings commence, such as when a suspect is arraigned or indicted.

### [2] *"Miranda"* Right to Counsel

The Fifth Amendment does not expressly contain a right to counsel. However, as a result of the *Miranda* opinion, a suspect—even before adversary judicial criminal proceedings have commenced—is entitled to what may be best described as the *"Miranda* right to counsel." This right attaches when a suspect is subjected to custodial interrogation. The purpose of this right to counsel is very narrow: to protect the suspect's privilege against compulsory self-incrimination.

It is necessary to treat the *Miranda* and Sixth Amendment versions of the right to counsel separately. They attach at different times, under different circumstances, and for different reasons.[31]

## § 22.04   Interrogation Law: An Overview to The Policy Debate[32]

### [A]   Societal Ambivalence Regarding Confessions

Interrogation law is controversial. In large part this is because there is an "uneasy conflict of worthy interests [that] produces a curious ambivalence of attitudes toward the confession of crime by one taken into police custody."[33] This "uneasy conflict of worthy interests" is considered in detail in subsequent chapters, but readers should be sensitive to the debate at the outset.

### [1]   Why the Public Favors Confessions

On one level, the public likes the idea of wrongdoers confessing. People believe it is good for wrongdoers to admit their guilt. One who confesses and accepts responsibility for his actions has taken a significant step toward

---

[30] Gideon v. Wainwright, 372 U.S. 335 (1963).

[31] *See* § 25.08, *infra*.

[32] *See generally* Joseph P. Grano, Confessions, Truth, and the Law (1993); Yale Kamisar, Police Interrogation and Confessions (1980); Yale Kamisar, *Remembering the "Old World" of Criminal Procedure: A Reply to Professor Grano*, 23 U. Mich. J.L. Ref. 537 (1990).

[33] Arthur E. Sutherland, Jr., *Crime and Confession*, 79 Harv. L. Rev. 21, 22 (1965); *see also* Peter Brooks, Troubling Confessions 2 (2000) ("We want confessions, yet we are suspicious of them.").

paying his debt to society. The admission of responsibility may also be the first step in the criminal's rehabilitation.[34]

From a law enforcement perspective, confession is good because a statement of guilt is often the best evidence of a person's guilt. In some cases, a conviction may be impossible without it. Moreover, if a defendant confesses, this relieves the public of its fear that it may be prosecuting an innocent person. The public considers confessions reliable. As Justice Jackson observed, "[i]t probably is the normal instinct to deny and conceal any shameful or guilty act."[35] Therefore, when an accused person takes the "unnatural" step of admitting his guilt we assume that the admission is true. Why else would a person confess?

### [2] Why the Public Is Concerned About Confessions

As much as society values confessions, it also worries them. The answer to the question ending the last subsection—"Why would a person confess if he were not guilty?"—might be: "Because he was coerced to do so." That is, it is precisely because the act of confession runs contrary to ordinary behavior (at least in the criminal law context) we are suspicious that it might be the result of police overreaching.

The public fears police overreaching for at least two reasons. First, if a confession is coerced, its reliability is called into serious question; the truth-seeking process of the criminal trial is jeopardized rather than advanced by its admission.

Second, if the police are left to their own devices to obtain confessions from persons they suspect are guilty, there is an enhanced risk that they will turn to inquisitorial techniques that not only create an undue risk of false confessions but also violate "the law's ethical or moral responsibility to treat criminal suspects and defendants in a manner consistent with their dignity as autonomous human beings."[36] As Justice Arthur Goldberg once observed: "[w]e have learned the lesson of history . . . that a system of criminal law enforcement which comes to depend on the 'confession' will, in the long run, be less reliable and more subject to abuses than a system which depends on extrinsic evidence independently secured through skillful investigation."[37]

---

[34] Brooks, Note 33, *supra*, at 2 ("Confession of wrongdoing is considered fundamental to morality because it constitutes a verbal act of self-recognition as wrongdoer and hence provides the basis of rehabilitation.").

[35] Ashcraft v. Tennessee, 322 U.S. 143, 160 (1944) (dissenting opinion).

[36] George E. Dix, *Federal Constitutional Confession Law: The 1986 and 1987 Supreme Court Terms,* 67 Tex. L. Rev. 231, 261 (1988).

[37] Escobedo v. Illinois 378 U.S. 478, 488–89 (1964).

## [B]   Has the Law Gone Too Far to Disfavor Confessions?

In view of society's conflicting attitudes regarding confessions, an overarching question in the interrogation law field is whether the Supreme Court has placed adequate restrictions on the police.

People who are suspicious of police interrogations have argued that there should be as much justice "in the gatehouses" of American criminal procedure as in its "mansions."[38] That is, just as the defendant in the courtroom (the mansion) is provided many adversarial protections—rules intended to ensure that he can tell his side of the story effectively—the suspect in the police station (the gatehouse) needs comparable safeguards. Indeed, a criminal trial, with all of its adversarial protections, may prove meaningless if an accused person is left relatively helpless during the pre-trial, police investigatory, period. Therefore, some people favor providing broad constitutional protections to the suspect in the interrogation room: "If the exercise of constitutional rights will thwart the effectiveness of a system of law enforcement, then there is something very wrong with that system."[39]

In contrast, many persons believe that "a civilized, decent society need not be embarrassed by police interrogation and confessions."[40] They argue that courts have created an "equality in the police station [that] thwarts rather than serves the goal of truth."[41] In particular, they claim it is unwise—even downright silly—to allow defense lawyers into the interrogation room, for their only purpose can be to prevent their clients from talking and, far more often than not, this means that the truth-seeking process is retarded.[42]

Critics of "pro-defendant" interrogation law contend that the Supreme Court has devised a system of criminal justice intended to "even the playing field" between the criminal suspect and the police. But, they ask, why would we want to do this? This "sporting view of justice"[43] is irrational. As long

---

[38] Yale Kamisar, *Equal Justice in the Gatehouses and Mansions of American Criminal Procedure, reprinted in* Yale Kamisar, Police Interrogation and Confessions 27 (1980).

[39] Escobedo v. Illinois 378 U.S. at 490.

[40] Joseph D. Grano, Police Interrogation and Confessions: A Rebuttal to Misconceived Objections 1 (Occasional Papers from the Center for Research in Crime and Justice, New York University School of Law, No. 1, 1987).

[41] *Id.* at 4.

[42] William J. Stuntz, *Lawyers, Deception, and Evidence Gathering*, 79 Va. L. Rev. 1903, 1906, 1955 (1993) (contending that "the earlier lawyers become part of the process, the greater the likelihood that their participation will be a relative benefit to the least deserving parties"; lawyers "retard evidence gathering by their opponents," yet "evidence gathering facilitates the separation of good claims or defenses from bad ones.").

[43] Roscoe Pound, *The Causes of Popular Dissatisfaction With the Administration of Justice*, 40 Am. Law Rev. 729, 738 (1906).

as police procedures do not create an undue risk of false confessions, the system *should* be unequal, because it is desirable to give the police—more accurately, society—the upper hand in the battle to convict the guilty. Put simply, we should want confessions. Justice Antonin Scalia has expressed this perspective as follows:

> [E]ven if I were to concede that an honest confession is a foolish mistake [by the suspect], I would welcome rather than reject it; a rule that foolish mistakes do not count would leave most offenders not only unconvicted but undetected. More fundamentally, however, it is wrong, and subtly corrosive of our criminal justice system, to regard an honest confession as a "mistake." . . . We should . . . rejoice at an honest confession, rather than pity the "poor fool" who has made it; and we should regret the attempted retraction of that good act, rather than seek to facilitate and encourage it.[44]

### [C]   Questions to Think About

In studying interrogation law, the key policy question to consider is the one raised in the last subsection: has the law gone far enough—or too far?—in protecting suspects in the interrogation process? But, there are a number of sub-issues and independent questions, some empirical in nature and others normative, that should be considered.

1. *To what extent were confessions unreliable before the Supreme Court became involved?* The answer to this question may be the easiest one to answer: third-degree abuse was common (although we cannot tell with certainty *how* commonplace it was) before the Supreme Court sought to fix the system.

2. *Why do we want to avoid coerced confessions: is it solely a function of seeking the truth or are there other concerns as well?* Just because a confession is coerced does not mean that it is false. Coerced confessions, standing alone, are inherently unreliable; but coerced confessions coupled with independent corroborating evidence of guilt are not unreliable. Sometimes people are coerced to tell the truth. To what extent, if at all, should our concern with police overreaching extend beyond the risk of false confessions?

3. *To what extent are current police techniques, which generally eschew violence, but which involve psychological pressures and manipulations, acceptable?* This question ties in directly to the last question: are confessions obtained in this more subtle manner reliable? And, if our concerns go beyond this factor, are we troubled by the police use of these techniques to secure incriminating statements?

---

[44] Minnick v. Mississippi, 498 U.S. 146, 166–67 (1990) (dissenting opinion).

4. *How important are confessions in the prosecution of crime?* Is police interrogation "an indispensable instrumentality of justice."[45] To what extent, are there other reliable (or even more reliable) methods to prove a person's guilt, such that a reduction in the number of confessions would not be a matter of legitimate societal concern?

5. *To what extent, in fact, has the Supreme Court made it more difficult for the police to obtain reliable confessions?* The empirical questions here are various. First, have the constitutional rules significantly reduced the number of confessions obtained by the police? If the answer is "no," is police efficiency undermined in other ways? On the other hand, if there has been a reduction in confessions attributable to the Court's decisions, does this mean that the truth-seeking process has been hurt, or are the police primarily "losing" the unreliable confessions that they used to obtain by third-degree methods? Is it also possible that the stringent rules have provided an incentive for the police to seek more reliable methods to prove guilt?

6. *Have the constitutional rules created equality in the interrogation room? If they have, is that a good or bad outcome?* The empirical question is whether suspects are now on an equal footing with the police in the interrogation room. The normative question is: is equality in this context irrational, or does it further valid concerns for human dignity and fair play?

7. *Regardless of the answers to the preceding questions, is the Supreme Court the proper institution to develop interrogation rules?* This question has two components. First, has the Supreme Court gone beyond its legitimate constitutional authority to develop the confession rules? Second, even if the Court has not exceeded its authority, is the federal judiciary the best institution to develop the law, or should it defer more often to others, such as to state courts and legislatures?

---

[45] Ashcraft v. Tennessee, 322 U.S. 143, 160 (1944) (dissenting opinion).

## CHAPTER 23

# COERCED ("INVOLUNTARY") CONFESSIONS

## § 23.01 Coerced Confession Law: Historical Development[1]

### [A] Common Law

In early English common law, all statements of a suspect, even those obtained by torture, were admissible at trial. By the end of the eighteenth century, however, the rule had changed, and it was determined that "no credit" was to be given to "a confession forced from the mind by the flattery of hope, or by the torture of fear."[2] This rule was applied strictly. Over the years, as interpreted by English courts, confessions gathered by brutality or threat of force were inadmissible at a defendant's criminal trial, but so also were statements induced by promises not to prosecute or to seek leniency in sentencing.

A crucial purpose of the English common law exclusionary rule was to remove from consideration by the factfinder statements obtained in a manner likely to produce a false confession, which thus might result in the conviction of an innocent person.[3] With that goal in mind, English courts phrased the issue to be whether the defendant's statement was made voluntarily or involuntarily. Over time, the involuntariness of the confession itself became the basis for its exclusion, "irrespective of any attempt to measure its influence to cause a false confession."[4]

---

[1] *See generally* Laurence A. Benner, *Requiem for Miranda: The Rehnquist Court's Voluntariness Doctrine in Historical Perspective*, 67 Wash. U. L.Q. 59 (1989); Lawrence Herman, *The Unexplored Relationship Between the Privilege Against Compulsory Self-Incrimination and the Involuntary Confession Rule (pts 1 & 2)*, 53 Ohio St. L.J. 101, 497 (1992); Yale Kamisar, *What is an "Involuntary" Confession? Some Comments on Inbau and Reid's Criminal Interrogation and Confessions*, 17 Rutgers L. Rev. 728 (1963); Welsh S. White, *What is an Involuntary Confession Now?*, 50 Rutgers L. Rev. 2001 (1998).

[2] Rex v. Warickshall, 1 Leach C.L. 263, 264, 168 Eng. Rep. 234, 235 (K.B. 1783).

[3] *Cf.* George C. Thomas III & Marshall D. Bilder, *Aristotle's Paradox and the Self-Incrimination Puzzle*, 82 J. Crim. L. & Criminology 243, 249–53 (1991) (noting the concern with trustworthiness, but arguing that the rationale of protecting free choice is an equally good explanation of the early English cases).

[4] 3 Wigmore on Evidence § 825, at 346 (Chadbourne Rev. 1970).

American state and federal courts, including the Supreme Court, generally followed the English lead. In *Hopt v. Utah*,[5] for example, the Supreme Court adopted for the federal courts the common law rule of evidence regarding confessions. The Court stated that a "confession, if freely and voluntarily made, is evidence of the most satisfactory character." However, it warned that a confession is inadmissible if it is obtained "because of a threat or promise by or in the presence of [one in authority], which, operating upon the fears or hopes of the accused . . . deprives him of that freedom of will or self-control essential to make his confession voluntary within the meaning of the law."

### [B]  Constitutional Law

### [1]  Privilege Against Compelled Self-Incrimination

In 1897, the Supreme Court announced in *Bram v. United States*[6] that the Fifth Amendment privilege against compelled self-incrimination "was but a crystallization of the [common law] doctrine relative to confessions." As one judge has put it, *Bram* "produced a seismic shift of the tectonic plates, though it did so without rattling in any way the surface test."[7] That is, *Bram* brought the common law rule under the umbrella of the Fifth Amendment: thereafter, compelled statements were inadmissible in *federal* criminal trials as a matter of constitutional law.

*Bram* announced a strict, virtual bright-line, rule:

[A] confession, in order to be admissible, must be free and voluntary: that is, must not be extracted by *any* sort of threats or violence, nor obtained by *any* direct or implied promises, *however slight*, nor by the exertion of *any* improper influence. . . . A confession can *never* be received in evidence where the prisoner has been *influenced* by *any* threat or promise.[8]

Because the constitutional privilege against compelled self-incrimination was not then considered a fundamental right, *Bram* did not apply to the states. In 1964, however, the Court ruled in *Malloy v. Hogan*[9] that the Fifth Amendment privilege against self-incrimination is a fundamental right applicable to the states through the Fourteenth Amendment. Consequently, a defendant in a *state* trial may now assert the privilege against compulsory self-incrimination as a basis for excluding a coerced confession.

---

[5] 110 U.S. 574 (1884).

[6] 168 U.S. 532 (1897).

[7] Hof v. State, 629 A.2d 1251, 1265 (Md. Ct. Spec. App. 1993) (per Moylan, J. ).

[8] *Bram*, 168 U.S. at 542–43 (emphasis added) (omission in original).

[9] 378 U.S. 1 (1964).

## [2] Due Process

There was no constitutional basis for excluding a coerced confession in a *state* criminal trial until 1936. In that year, the Supreme Court, in *Brown v. Mississippi*,[10] invoked the Fourteenth Amendment due process clause for the first time to invalidate a murder conviction obtained solely on the basis of confessions "shown to have been extorted by officers of the State by brutality and violence."

In *Brown*, three defendants, "all ignorant negroes" who denied involvement in a murder, were brutalized by sheriff's deputies, and in one case by a mob of white vigilantes with a deputy's participation. One suspect was hung by a rope to the limb of a tree twice and tied to a tree and whipped; two others were stripped, laid over chairs in the jail, and whipped with a leather strap so severely that their backs were "cut to pieces."

The Court stated that "[i]t would be difficult to conceive of methods more revolting to the sense of justice than those taken to procure the confessions of these [defendants]." It compared the actions of the state officials— "[c]ompulsion by torture to extort a confession"—to use of "[t]he rack and torture chamber," and concluded that a conviction secured in this manner "was a clear denial of due process."

The facts in *Brown* were so shocking that the Supreme Court did not need to examine in any useful way what constitutes an involuntary confession. Later cases, at least prior to the Court's watershed decision in *Miranda v. Arizona*,[11] suggest that a confession may be considered involuntary if the police interrogation methods were "repellant to civilized standards of decency or which, under the circumstances, [were] thought to apply a degree of pressure to an individual which unfairly impair[ed] his capacity to make a rational choice."[12]

## [3] Two Constitutional Provisions (and Standards?) Become One[13]

The Fifth Amendment privilege against self-incrimination prohibits the admission of *compelled* confessions. The due process clause, as interpreted by the Supreme Court, prohibits the admissibility of *involuntary* confessions. Are these two standards—one based on compulsion and the other on involuntariness—the same?

---

[10] 297 U.S. 278 (1936).

[11] 384 U.S. 436 (1966).

[12] *Id.* at 507 n.4 (Harlan, J., dissenting) (quoting Paul M. Bator & James Vorenberg, *Arrest, Detention, Interrogation and the Right to Counsel*, 66 Colum. L. Rev. 62, 73 (1966)).

[13] *See generally* Herman, Note 1, *supra*, at 502–511; Stephen J. Schulhofer, *Reconsidering Miranda*, 54 U. Chi. L. Rev. 435, 440–46 (1987).

Initially, the two lines of cases—federal self-incrimination cases and state due process decisions—may have been traveling down different paths. The leading Fifth Amendment self-incrimination case, *Bram v. United States*, seemingly applied a strict, nearly bright-line rule to determine what constitutes compulsion in the interrogation process.[14] In contrast, the early due process cases seemingly required proof either that the suspect's will was broken by the police—a factor not required under *Bram*—or that the police methods used were the sort likely to result in a false confession—again, not necessarily a Fifth Amendment self-incrimination requirement.

Moreover, in contrast to the bright-line aspects of *Bram*, the due process cases are generally decided on a case-by-case totality-of-the-circumstances basis. Moreover, if one looks at how the Fifth Amendment privilege has been applied in non-interrogation contexts,[15] the Supreme Court "ordinarily does not balance the government's interest in obtaining information against the individual's interest in avoiding compulsion"—the latter interest prevails. In contrast, "the due process rule frankly acknowledges balancing as a norm . . . ."[16]

So, it would seem that the standards are different. Therefore, once *Malloy v. Hogan*[17] incorporated the privilege against self-incrimination to the states, one might have expected that state defendants contesting interrogation practices would have asserted the privilege against self-incrimination, rather than due process, on the ground that the tough *Bram* test is preferable to the more flexible due process standard. One might have predicted that the due process clause standard would essentially fall by the side due to non-use.

But, there is a historical quirk that cannot be ignored in the interrogation field. During the nearly seven-decade period in which the Fifth Amendment privilege applied exclusively in the federal courts—from the time of *Bram* to *Malloy*—the Supreme Court decided fewer than a dozen cases dealing with coerced confessions in federal trials. Meanwhile, during the less than thirty years in which state confessions had to be resolved according to due process principles—from *Brown v. Mississippi*[18] to *Malloy*—the high court decided no fewer than 35 coerced-confession cases.[19] As a result of this disparity, the Court had many opportunities to focus on the due process

---

[14] *See* the text to Note 8, *supra*.

[15] *See generally* chapter 26, *infra*.

[16] Herman, Note 1, *supra*, at 503, 509.

[17] 378 U.S. 1 (1964). *See generally* § 23.01[B][2], *supra*.

[18] 297 U.S. 278 (1936).

[19] Hof v. State, 629 A.2d at 1269.

clause voluntariness standard. In contrast, the Fifth Amendment self-incrimination privilege cases were "low-visibility events."[20] Consequently, as one legal historian reported, "*Bram* had little impact [on interrogation law] . . . and, as late as 1951, it was not clear whether the exclusion of involuntary confessions in *federal* cases was based on the Fifth Amendment's self-incrimination provision, the Fifth Amendment's due process provision, or the common law confession rule."[21]

So, ironically perhaps, the incorporation process tended to work in an opposite direction than one would have expected: rather than move the case law in state cases to the more vigorous federal standard, courts seemingly moved toward the due process standard in all cases, state and federal. In *Arizona v. Fulminante*,[22] the Supreme Court observed that the Fifth Amendment self-incrimination bright-line rule of *Bram* "does not state the standard for determining the voluntariness of a confession."[23] And, in *Dickerson v. United States*,[24] in the Court's historical account of state and federal confession law, it stated that "we evaluate[] the admissibility of a suspect's confession under a voluntariness test"—the totality-of-circumstances test—indicating that "[o]ver time, our cases [have] recognized two constitutional bases for the requirement that a confession be voluntary to be admitted into evidence," namely, the Fifth Amendment privilege against self-incrimination and the due process clause.

In short, at the present time, there is no apparent legal difference between the meaning of a "compelled" confession in the Fifth Amendment self-incrimination context and an "involuntary" one in the due process framework. *Bram*'s bright line has given way to the totality-of-circumstances approach, an approach that is described in greater detail in Sections 23.02 and, especially, 23.03.

### [C]  A Non-Constitutional Bright-Line Rule for the Federal Courts?: The *McNabb-Mallory* Rule

There is no litmus test for determining the voluntariness of a confession.[25] Each case must be decided on its own facts, a judicially inefficient way to filter out coerced confessions. Consequently, beginning in the 1940s,

---

[20] *Id.*

[21] Herman, Note 1, *supra*, at 500.

[22] 499 U.S. 279 (1991).

[23] *See also* Colorado v. Connelly, 479 U.S. 157, 163 (1986) (noting that the "Court has retained [the] due process focus, even after holding, in [*Malloy*], that the Fifth Amendment privilege against compulsory self-incrimination applies to the States").

[24] 530 U.S. 428 (2000).

[25] See § 23.03, *infra*.

the Supreme Court developed a bright-line rule, applicable only in federal courts, that excludes a category of confessions that might have been coerced, but which the Supreme Court did not want lower courts to have to evaluate on a case-by-case basis. The rule has come to be known as the *McNabb-Mallory*[26] rule.

By federal statute then, and by federal rule now, an arrestee must be brought before a magistrate "without unnecessary delay" following her arrest.[27] In *McNabb* and *Mallory* (and some intervening cases), the Supreme Court used its supervisory power over the federal courts to define the phrase "unnecessary delay" and to provide a remedy for violations of the "prompt-arraignment rule."

The essence of the *McNabb-Mallory* rule was that although the police could properly delay a suspect's first appearance before a magistrate for booking purposes, they could not delay the appearance in order to interrogate her. The Court's remedy for a violation of the prompt-arraignment rule was to exclude from federal trials any statement obtained during the unnecessary delay, whether or not the confession was involuntary under traditional principles.

The *McNabb-Mallory* rule was not applied enthusiastically by federal courts and was criticized in Congress. In 1968, Congress purported to overrule the doctrine when it enacted the Omnibus Crime Control and Safe Streets Act, which provides in part that any confession obtained in the first six hours after arrest for a federal offense is admissible notwithstanding any delay, and that a confession obtained thereafter may also be admissible, depending on the totality of the circumstances.[28]

Because the *McNabb-Mallory* rule is not of constitutional origin, it does not apply to the states (which generally do not have a similar rule of automatic exclusion[29] ), and Congress likely had authority to override it by the 1968 legislation.[30] In any case, the rule is of little practical significance in view of the Supreme Court's later *Miranda* ruling.

---

[26] McNabb v. United States, 318 U.S. 332 (1943); Mallory v. United States, 354 U.S. 449 (1957).

[27] Fed. R. Crim. P. 5(a). A similar requirement exists in virtually every state.

[28] 18 U.S.C.A. § 3501(c) (2000). The provisions of this section do not apply to statements made by a person being held solely on state charges, even if the interrogators are federal officers. United States v. Alvarez-Sanchez, 511 U.S. 350 (1994).

[29] Commonwealth v. Rosario, 661 N.E.2d 71, 76 n.4 (Mass. 1996).

[30] The federal circuit courts are divided on the effect of Section 3501(c) on confessions obtained in violation of the *McNabb-Mallory* rule. *See* United States v. Alvarez-Sanchez, 511 U.S. at 361 & n.* (1994) (cases cited therein).

## § 23.02    Coerced Confession Law: General Principles

### [A]    Voluntariness Rule

A statement obtained from a suspect as a result of police coercion is inadmissible in her state or federal criminal trial under the due process clauses of the Constitution and the Fifth Amendment privilege against compulsory self-incrimination.[31] As explained in Section 23.03, the voluntariness of a confession is determined based on the totality of the circumstances.

The Supreme Court ruled in *Arizona v. Fulminante*[32] that if a defendant's coerced confession is introduced into evidence at trial over her objection,[33] and she is convicted, the judgment must be reversed unless the government proves beyond a reasonable doubt that the erroneous admission of the confession did not affect the trial outcome. Until *Fulminante*, the consistent rule had been that the wrongful admission of a coerced confession required automatic reversal of the conviction, even if there was overwhelming independent evidence of the defendant's guilt.[34]

---

[31] *E.g.*, Spano v. New York, 360 U.S. 315 (1959) (due process); Ziang Sung Wan v. United States, 266 U.S. 1 (1924) (Fifth Amendment).

[32] 499 U.S. 279 (1991).

[33] A defendant must make a timely pretrial motion to suppress a confession. *E.g.*, Fed. R. Crim. P. 12(b)(3). Failure to do so results in forfeiture of the claim. Fed. R. Crim. P. 12(f). If the motion is made, the judge must suppress the evidence unless she finds by a preponderance of the evidence that the confession was not coerced by the police. Lego v. Twomey, 404 U.S. 477 (1972). In most jurisdictions, the judge's determination of the matter is final pending appeal. In contrast, some states follow the "Massachusetts procedure": the judge makes the initial voluntariness determination, which is final if she rules that the confession was coerced; if she finds that it was not, the jury is allowed to hear the confession and the circumstances surrounding its acquisition, and is instructed that it may consider the confession only if it determines that it was voluntarily given.

[34] *E.g.*, Payne v. Arkansas, 356 U.S. 560 (1958). Confessions are the "queen of proofs." Peter Brooks, Troubling Confessions 4 (2000). Therefore, the change in the law brought about by *Fulminante* is disturbing, most especially if appellate courts are not exceptionally vigilant in measuring the possible impact of coerced confessions on juries. *See generally* Saul M. Kassin & Holly Sukel, *Coerced Confessions and the Jury: An Experimental Test of the "Harmless Error" Rule*, 21 Law & Hum. Behav. 27 (1997) (in two mock-juror studies, the authors found that a confession increases the conviction rate, even when jurors treated it as coerced and later claimed that the confession had no influence on their deliberations). Regarding *Fulminante*, *see* Charles J. Ogletree, Jr., *Arizona v. Fulminante: The Harm of Applying Harmless Error to Coerced Confessions*, 105 Harv. L. Rev. 152 (1991). "Harmless error" law is considered at § 4.03, *supra*.

## [B]  Rationale of the Voluntariness Requirement[35]

According to the Supreme Court, a "complex of values"[36] underlie the voluntariness requirement in coerced confession jurisprudence.[37] First, and most obviously, there is a heightened risk of false confessions—and, thus, of convicting innocent persons—if the police are permitted to obtain statements from suspects through coercive means.[38]

But, the Supreme Court and scholars have noted other reasons, as well, for excluding coerced confessions. Even if there is independent evidence corroborating a coerced confession, such a statement should be excluded because the police should "obey the law while enforcing the law."[39] A third reason coerced confessions are inadmissible is because their use is "so offensive to a civilized system of justice that they must be condemned."[40]

Fourth, "ours is an accusatorial and not an inquisitorial system."[41] One principle of an accusatorial system is that "the mind, as the center of the self, may not be pressed by the government into an instrument of its own destruction."[42] Indeed, the use of coercion to obtain a confession "was the chief inequity, the crowning infamy of . . . the Inquisition . . . ."[43]

---

[35] *See generally* George E. Dix, *Federal Constitutional Confession Law: The 1986 and 1987 Supreme Court Terms*, 67 Tex. L. Rev. 231 (1988); Kamisar, Note 1, *supra*; Welsh S. White, *False Confessions and the Constitution: Safeguards Against Untrustworthy Confessions*, 32 Harv. C.R-C.L. L. Rev. 105 (1997); White, Note 1, *supra*; Comment, *The Coerced Confession Cases in Search of a Rationale*, 31 U. Chi. L. Rev. 313 (1964).

[36] Blackburn v. Alabama, 361 U.S. 199, 207 (1960).

[37] In light of the Supreme Court's merger of Fifth Amendment self-incrimination jurisprudence with the due process cases in the interrogation context, *see* § 23.01[B][3], *supra*, the values that support the self-incrimination clause are commingled here with the justifications for the more general due process standard.

[38] Spano v. New York, 360 U.S. 315, 320 (1959) (expressing concern regarding the "inherent untrustworthiness" of coerced confessions). How great a risk is there today that police interrogation techniques will result in false confessions and miscarriages of justice? For discussion of this issue, *see* Richard A. Leo & Richard J. Ofshe, *The Consequences of False Confessions: Deprivations of Liberty and Miscarriages of Justice in the Age of Psychological Interrogation*, 88 J. Crim. L. & Criminology 429 (1998); Paul G. Cassell, *Protecting the Innocent From False Confessions and Lost Confessions—And From Miranda*, 88 J. Crim. L. & Criminology 497 (1998) (reply to the Leo & Ofshe article). *See also* § 22.02, especially Note 10, *supra*.

[39] *Spano*, 360 U.S. at 320.

[40] Miller v. Fenton, 474 U.S. 104, 109 (1985).

[41] Rogers v. Richmond, 365 U.S. 534, 541 (1961).

[42] H. Richard Uviller, *Evidence from the Mind of the Criminal Suspect: A Reconsideration of the Current Rules of Access and Restraint*, 87 Colum. L. Rev. 1137, 1146 (1987).

[43] Brown v. Mississippi, 297 U.S. 278, 287 (1936) (quoting Fisher v. State, 110 So. 361, 365 (Miss. 1926)).

Fifth, values of human dignity, personal autonomy and mental freedom support the premise that a person should not be convicted on the basis of a confession unless it is the "untrammeled exercise of personal determination."[44] Finally, of course, the exclusion of a coerced confession should deter police overreaching and, thus, prevent the wrongs described above.[45]

Although all of these concerns retain some force in current litigation, the unreliability of a coerced confession is neither a necessary nor sufficient basis for its exclusion. That is, a coerced confession is inadmissible, although perhaps trustworthy in a particular case, if the police interrogation techniques are fundamentally unfair.[46] Seemingly, this occurs if the interrogation method is likely, in the ordinary run of cases, to induce a false confession, even if in the present case the confession has been corroborated by independent evidence.[47] At the same time, as explained immediately below, a confession that is both involuntary *and* unreliable is *not* constitutionally inadmissible if the coercing party is not a government agent.[48]

### [C]  Official Overreaching: Requirement of State Action

*Colorado v. Connelly*[49] provides that "[t]he most outrageous behavior by a private party seeking to secure evidence against a defendant does not make that evidence inadmissible under the Due Process Clause." In order to exclude a confession on due process grounds, there must be a "link between coercive activity of the State, on the one hand, and a resulting confession by a defendant, on the other."

In *Connelly, D*, a person suffering from chronic schizophrenia, in a psychotic state and responding to "command hallucinations" (he heard "the

---

[44] Uviller, Note 42, *supra*, at 1146; *see also* Bram v. United States, 168 U.S. 532, 544 (1897) (the Fifth Amendment privilege embodies "principles of humanity and civil liberty, which had been secured in the mother country only after years of struggle"); Miranda v. Arizona, 384 U.S. 436, 460 (1966) ("[T]he constitutional foundation underlying the privilege [against compulsory self-incrimination] is the respect a government . . . must accord to the dignity and integrity of its citizens. . . . [It must] respect the inviolability of the human personality . . . .").

[45] Colorado v. Connelly, 479 U.S. 157, 165–66 (1986).

[46] Lisenba v. California, 314 U.S. 219, 236 (1941) ("The aim of the [voluntariness] requirement . . . is not to exclude presumptively false evidence, but to prevent fundamental unfairness in the use of evidence, whether true or false.").

[47] White, Note 1, *supra*, at 2019–2020.

[48] Colorado v. Connelly, 479 U.S. 157 (1986).

[49] *Id.*; *contra, under the state constitution*, State v. Bowe, 881 P.2d 538 (Haw. 1994) (coercive conduct of a private person is sufficient to render a confession inadmissible); State v. Rees, 748 A.2d 976 (Me. 2000) (police coercion is not the *sine qua non* for exclusion; therefore, a statement made by a suspect suffering from dementia must be excluded as involuntary).

voice of God" order him to confess or commit suicide), approached a police officer on the street and confessed to a murder. The perplexed officer ascertained that $D$ was not drunk or on drugs, but was told by $D$ that he had been a patient in several mental hospitals. After the officer informed $D$ of his constitutional rights, $D$ answered questions about the crime.

According to expert testimony, $D$'s mental condition "interfered with [his] 'volitional abilities; that is, his ability to make free and rational choices'," including the decision whether to confess. $D$'s confession, motivated as it was by perceived orders from God, was as involuntary—and, potentially as untrustworthy—as a confession wrung from him by the police. Nonetheless, the Court concluded that the " 'involuntary confession' jurisprudence is entirely consistent with the settled law requiring some sort of 'state action' to support a [due process clause] violation."

The Court stated that the potential unreliability of a confession is a matter that "the Constitution rightly leaves . . . to be resolved by state laws governing the admission of evidence." As Justice Stevens observed in his partial concurrence, "[t]he fact that the statements [made by $D$] were involuntary—just as the product of Lady Macbeth's nightmare was involuntary—does not mean that their use for whatever evidentiary value they may have is fundamentally unfair or a denial of due process."

The dissenters contended that "due process derives much of its meaning from a conception of fundamental fairness that emphasizes the right to make vital choices voluntarily." Although they conceded that police overreaching had been an element of every previous confession case, "it is also true that in every case [until now] the Court has made clear that ensuring that a confession is a product of free will is an independent concern."

### [D] Standing to Raise a Coerced Confession Claim

Suppose that the police coerce $X$ to make a statement in which she incriminates $D$. Is $X$'s statement (or other evidence incriminating $D$ gathered as a fruit of $X$'s coerced confession[50]) inadmissible at $D$'s criminal trial, or is the direct victim of the coercion the only person with standing to seek suppression of the evidence?

The Supreme Court has not ruled directly on the standing question in the context of a coerced confession claim, but there is virtually no doubt that standing is a requirement.[51] The Court has stated that the Fifth

---

[50] This is a more likely scenario, because a common evidentiary rule is that a confession may only be admitted as substantive evidence against the confessor.

[51] The issue of "standing" most commonly arises in the Fourth Amendment context. See chapter 20, *supra*.

Amendment privilege against compulsory self-incrimination is "intimate and personal,"[52] and that "it adheres basically to the person, not to information that may incriminate him."[53] Moreover, the abandonment of a standing requirement in coerced confession cases, whether litigated on self-incrimination or due process grounds, would expand the applicability of the exclusionary rule, an unlikely outcome in view of the Court's expressed concern "that the exclusionary rule imposes a substantial cost on the societal interest in law enforcement."[54]

## [E]  Exclusionary Rule

### [1]  Constitutional Basis of the Exclusionary Rule[55]

The Fifth Amendment provides that a person shall not be "compelled to be a witness against himself." As this language suggests, *use* at trial of a compelled statement is unconstitutional, for its admission effectively makes the defendant a "witness against himself." In short, exclusion of a coerced confession—unlike exclusion of evidence obtained as a result of an unreasonable search or seizure—is not simply a remedy for violation of a constitutional right; *it is an element of the right itself.*

From a due process perspective, two constitutional wrongs apparently exist: obtaining a confession by coercive police conduct, and using that confession at trial. As Professor Arnold Loewy has observed, using *Brown v. Mississippi*[56] as an example, the beating Brown suffered was "clearly wrong in itself, regardless of whether any confession [was] used or even obtained."[57] Thus, if that torture had occurred today, Brown could have sued the police for violation of his constitutional rights. But, beyond this, the *Brown* opinion provided that "use of the confessions thus obtained as the basis for conviction and sentence was a clear denial of due process." In short, exclusion of a coerced confession is constitutionally required by the due process clause. It is not simply a remedy for a constitutional violation.

---

[52] Couch v. United States, 409 U.S. 322, 327 (1973) (a summons served on *X*, *D*'s accountant, requiring *X* to hand over *D*'s personal business records, does not violate *D*'s Fifth Amendment privilege; the compulsion by subpoena was directed at *X*).

[53] *Id.* at 328.

[54] Colorado v. Connelly, 479 U.S. 157, 166 (1986) (quoting United States v. Janis, 428 U.S. 433, 448–49 (1976)).

[55] *See generally* Arnold H. Loewy, *Police-Obtained Evidence and the Constitution: Distinguishing Unconstitutionally Obtained Evidence from Unconstitutionally Used Evidence*, 87 Mich. L. Rev. 907 (1989).

[56] 297 U.S. 278 (1936). *See* § 23.01[B][2], *supra*.

[57] Loewy, Note 55, *supra*, at 934.

### [2]  Scope of the Exclusionary Rule: Impeachment

A coerced confession is inadmissible at the defendant's criminal trial for *all* purposes. That is, a coerced confession may not be introduced in the prosecutor's case-in-chief to prove the defendant's guilt, *and* it is also inadmissible for impeachment purposes.[58] As such, this exclusionary rule is broader than the exclusionary rules related to the Fourth Amendment, *Miranda*, and to at least certain aspects of the Sixth Amendment right to counsel.[59]

### [3]  Fruit-of-the-Poisonous-Tree Doctrine

If *D*'s confession is coerced, the incriminating statement is inadmissible, but may the government introduce at trial other evidence, *e.g.*, an instrumentality used in the offense, that would not have been obtained but for the information provided in the coerced statement? In short, is there a fruit-of-the-poisonous-tree doctrine[60] applicable to coerced confessions? The Supreme Court has not expressly answered the question, but it is generally assumed that the doctrine applies.[61]

The Court has applied the poisonous-tree principle in a related context. In *Harrison v. United States*,[62] a prosecutor improperly introduced at trial three confessions that the police obtained from *D* in violation the *McNabb-Mallory* rule.[63] As a result, *D* changed his trial strategy, and testified in his own behalf. Ultimately, *D*'s conviction was overturned because of the *McNabb-Mallory* violations. At *D*'s second trial, at which the confessions were properly excluded, the prosecutor sought to introduce *D*'s testimony from the first trial. However, the Court held that this testimony was

---

[58] Mincey v. Arizona, 437 U.S. 385 (1978) (due process); *see also* New Jersey v. Portash, 440 U.S. 450 (1979) (Fifth Amendment privilege, involving the attempted use at trial, for impeachment purposes, of *D*'s testimony, obtained by compulsion before a grand jury).

[59] *See* § 21.05[B][2][b], *supra* (Fourth Amendment); §§ 24.12[A] (*Miranda*) and 25.07[C] (Sixth Amendment), *infra*.

[60] *See generally* § 21.08, *supra*.

[61] In the context of the Fifth Amendment privilege against self-incrimination, not all scholars agree that the fruit-of-the-poisonous-tree doctrine should apply to tangible evidence. Amar and Lettow make the following textual argument: the Fifth Amendment prohibits a defendant from being a "witness" against herself; tangible evidence is not a "witness," as it does not testify. Therefore, they conclude, "[p]hysical evidence . . . can be introduced at trial whatever its source—even if that source is a compelled pretrial utterance." Akhil Reed Amar & Reneé B. Lettow, *Fifth Amendment First Principles: The Self-Incrimination Clause*, 93 Mich. L. Rev. 857, 900 (1995). For the contrary (and more accepted) view, *see* Yale Kamisar, *On the "Fruits" of Miranda Violations, Coerced Confessions, and Compelled Testimony*, 93 Mich. L. Rev. 929 (1995).

[62] 392 U.S. 219 (1968).

[63] The *McNabb-Mallory* rule is discussed at § 23.01[C], *supra*.

inadmissible because the prosecutor had not adequately proved that it "was obtained 'by means sufficiently distinguishable' from the underlying illegality 'to be purged of the primary taint.' " Since the "poisonous tree" in *Harrison* was a *non*-constitutional supervisory-authority rule, it follows that a violation of the Constitution itself (the Fifth Amendment or the due process clause) requires implementation of the poisonous-tree doctrine.

## § 23.03   The Voluntariness Requirement: In Greater Detail[64]

### [A]   Critical Overview

In *Bram v. United States*,[65] the Supreme Court's first effort to define "compulsion" in a constitutional context, the Court stated that a confession "must not be extracted by any sort of threat or violence, nor obtained by any direct or implied promises, however slight, nor by the exertion of any improper influence." The Court warned that because "the law cannot measure the force of the influence used, or decide upon its effect upon the mind of the prisoner," it would hold a confession inadmissible "if any degree of influence" was exerted.

This bright-line rule has not prevailed. The voluntariness of a confession is now assessed—whether a court applies the due process clause or the Fifth Amendment privilege against compulsory self-incrimination—from "the totality of all the circumstances—[considering] both the characteristics of the accused and the details of the interrogation."[66]

There are at least two problems with this standard. First, as with any rule that must be determined from the totality of the circumstances, the police receive less guidance than if they were required to obey a bright-line rule, and courts can become overwhelmed adjudicating highly fact-sensitive claims of coercion. Second, the Supreme Court has wavered in regard to

---

[64] *See generally* Joseph D. Grano, Confessions, Truth, and the Law (1993); Yale Kamisar, Police Interrogation and Confessions (1980); George E. Dix, *Mistake, Ignorance, Expectation of Benefit, and the Modern Law of Confessions*, 1975 Wash. U. L.Q. 275; Joseph D. Grano, *Voluntariness, Free Will, and the Law of Confessions*, 65 Va. L. Rev. 859 (1979); Catherine Hancock, *Due Process Before Miranda*, 70 Tul. L. Rev. 2195 (1996); Richard J. Ofshe & Richard A. Leo, *The Social Psychology of Police Interrogation: The Theory and Classification of True and False Confessions*, 16 Law, Politics, & Society 189 (1997); Margaret L. Paris, *Trust, Lies, and Interrogation*, 3 Va. J. Soc. Pol'y & L. 3 (1995); Daniel W. Sasaki, Note, *Guarding the Guardians: Police Trickery and Confessions*, 40 Stan. L. Rev. 1593 (1988); Welsh S. White, *Confessions Induced by Broken Government Promises*, 43 Duke L.J. 947 (1994); Welsh S. White, *Police Trickery in Inducing Confessions*, 127 U. Pa. L. Rev. 581 (1979); White, Note 1, *supra*; and White, Note 35, *supra*.

[65] 168 U.S. 532 (1897).

[66] Dickerson v. United States, 530 U.S. 428, 434 (2000) (quoting Schneckloth v. Busta-monte, 412 U.S. 218, 226 (1973)).

a critical question: to what extent is (and should) the test focus on the *specific* confession—and whether *this* defendant's will was overborne by the police methods—or, instead, on whether the interrogation methods were of the sort that should be condemned—regardless of whether *this* defendant's will was overborne—because the means used to extract the confession created too great a risk of inducing a false confession in the ordinary situation.[67]

The Supreme Court often applies—or, at least, purports to apply—the "overborne will" standard. Thus, it has described the issue of voluntariness this way:

> Is the confession the product of an essentially free and unconstrained choice by its maker? If it is, *if he has willed to confess*, it may be used against him. If it is not, *if his will has been overborne* and his capacity for self-determination critically impaired, the . . . confession [is inadmissible].[68]

The implication of this language is that voluntariness is an empirical issue. It is as if a court can look within the accused person's psyche or soul and determine whether she "freely chose" to confess or, instead, had her will overborne by the police. As the Court in *Bram* acknowledged, however, there is no practical way to measure the influence of a particular police practice on a particular suspect. Ultimately, the issue of coerced confessions, like the defense of duress in the substantive criminal law,[69] presents a normative question: how much, and what kind of, pressure placed on a person is morally permissible?

Ultimately, a normative analysis is inevitable. All confessions, even those obtained by torture, are "free" in the sense that the speaker preferred confessing to the continuation of the pressures. Professor George Thomas has observed that "[i]f . . . 'voluntary' means only that one exercises choice between alternatives, then . . . '[a]ll conscious verbal utterances are and must be voluntary.' "[70] On the other hand, nearly all confessions are

---

[67] For discussion of how the pre-*Miranda* Supreme Court wavered between these two standards, *see* Kamisar, Note 1, *supra*; for a more recent analysis, *see* White, Note 1, *supra*.

[68] Culombe v. Connecticut, 367 U.S. 568, 602 (1961) (opinion of Frankfurter, J.) (emphasis added); *see also* Dickerson v. United States, 530 U.S. at 434 (the due process cases "refined the test into an inquiry that examines 'whether a defendant's will was overborne' by the circumstances surrounding the giving of a confession") (quoting Schneckloth v. Bustamonte, 412 U.S. 218, 226 (1973).

[69] *See* Joshua Dressler, *Exegesis of the Law of Duress: Justifying the Excuse and Searching for Its Proper Limits*, 62 S. Cal. L. Rev. 1331 (1989).

[70] George C. Thomas III, *Justice O'Connor's Pragmatic View of Coerced Self-Incrimination*, 13 Women's Rts. L. Rep. 117, 121 (1991) (quoting 2 John Henry Wigmore on Evidence § 824 n.1 (2d ed. 1923)).

"unfree" in the sense that they are the result of pressures on the individual's will, and surely few would disagree with the view that any police interrogation, no matter how benign, exerts significant pressures on the person undergoing questioning. Under this latter interpretation, however, "voluntary" means the absence of any influence—an impossibility—or, at least, the absence of any *external* influence to confess (thus, allowing for the possibility of "the conscience-stricken urge to 'rid one's soul of a sense of guilt' ").[71] So, the issue must come down to this: how "free" is "free enough"?

The Supreme Court has conceded that voluntariness is "an amphibian"[72] notion. Although the determination of voluntariness requires a finding of the "crude historical facts"[73] regarding the acquisition of the suspect's confession, the ultimate issue is a legal one.[74] In resolving the legal issue, the Court's decisions inevitably "reflect a . . . recognition that the Constitution requires the sacrifice of neither security nor liberty."[75] That is, the Court has balanced society's perceived need for confessions against the importance of ensuring that the interrogation process does not undermine the "complex of values" supporting the privilege against self-incrimination.[76]

The result of this balancing process, not surprisingly, has been a collection of Supreme Court cases expressing conflicting value judgments, and results that are not always easily explained (or explained away). As a practical matter, the totality-of-the-circumstances test makes "everything relevant but nothing determinative."[77] The typical coerced confession case is one "in which the court[] provide[s] a lengthy factual description followed by a conclusion . . ., without anything to connect the two."[78]

A very brief review of some of the cases and relevant interrelated factors are considered immediately below.

---

[71] *Id.* at 120 (quoting Ashcraft v. Tennessee, 322 U.S. 143, 161 (1944) (Jackson J., dissenting).

[72] Culombe v. Connecticut, 367 U.S. at 605.

[73] *Id.* at 603.

[74] Miller v. Fenton, 474 U.S. 104, 110 (1985).

[75] Schneckloth v. Bustamonte, 412 U.S. 218, 225 (1973).

[76] And yet, outside the interrogation context, the Supreme Court has ordinarily avoided such a balancing process in the Fifth Amendment context. *See* § 23.02[B][3], *supra*.

[77] Joseph D. Grano, *Miranda v. Arizona and the Legal Mind: Formalism's Triumph Over Substance and Reason*, 24 Am. Crim. L. Rev. 243, 243 (1986).

[78] Lloyd L. Weinreb, *Generalities of the Fourth Amendment*, 42 U. Chi. L. Rev. 47, 57 (1974).

## [B] "Voluntariness": Factors

### [1] Actual or Threatened Physical Force or Deprivation

A confession obtained by threatened or actual use of violence is inadmissible. The Court has consistently condemned such police practices as whipping[79] or slapping[80] a suspect in order to obtain a confession. "[O]ne truncheon blow on the head"[81] will render a statement inadmissible, as will express or credible implied threats of violence, such as holding a gun to a suspect's head.[82]

Confessions have also been invalidated when the police have "warned" a suspect that, unless he confesses, he may be the victim of mob violence[83] or deadly attacks from fellow prisoners.[84] Confessions have also been suppressed in cases in which the police deprived a suspect of food, water, or sleep, for an extended period of time.[85]

It should be noted that in most (if not all) of the preceding examples, whether or not a particular suspect's will was overborne by the police conduct, a court could be expected to suppress the incriminating statement on the ground that the police used unlawful inquisitorial techniques to gather the evidence—methods that might also induce an incriminating statement from an innocent person of ordinary firmness.

Arguably, however, even a *lawful* threat to inflict pain may render a confession inadmissible in unusual circumstances. For example, in one Nebraska case, a court invalidated an incriminating statement—an admission by a rape suspect, after initial denial, that he had had intercourse with the victim—secured after the interrogating officer warned the suspect that if he did not admit to the intercourse, he would have to submit to a penile swab for a semen sample. After the suspect asked for details, the officer described the procedure (which includes placing a Q-tip inside the penis)

---

[79] Brown v. Mississippi, 297 U.S. 278 (1936).

[80] Haynes v. Washington, 373 U.S. 503 (1963).

[81] Fikes v. Alabama, 352 U.S. 191, 198 (1957) (Frankfurter and Brennan, JJ., concurring) (assuming that it is "common ground" that a confession obtained in this manner violates due process).

[82] Beecher v. Alabama, 389 U.S. 35 (1967).

[83] Payne v. Arkansas, 356 U.S. 560 (1958) (*D* was told that there would be "30 or 40 people" arriving at the police station to do violence to him, but that if *D* told the truth, the police would prevent them from hurting him).

[84] Arizona v. Fulminante, 499 U.S. 279 (1991) (*D*, a prison inmate, was physically threatened by fellow prisoners because of a rumor that he was suspected of an unsolved child murder; *X*, a paid government informant, offered to protect *D* from violence in exchange for an admission about the crime).

[85] Brooks v. Florida, 389 U.S. 413 (1967); Reck v. Pate, 367 U.S. 433 (1961).

and, when asked by the suspect if the procedure was painful, confirmed that it would be.[86] The court observed that "to render a defendant's statement involuntary, [the procedure] need not be of such nature or degree that would have resulted in recoil by Tomas de Torquemada of the Spanish Inquisition."

Why did making a lawful threat—to have medical personnel perform a legitimate medical procedure as part of a legitimate criminal investigation—render the statement coerced? The court was not specific. It would seem here that the confession was suppressed either because the trial court believed that this particular suspect's will was overborne by the description of the procedure or, perhaps, even if this were not the case, because the officer admitted in court that he raised the specter of the procedure in order to secure the confession ("it was an interrogation technique"). The former argument is based on an empirical claim (presumably founded on the fact that the suspect asserted his innocence until shortly after he learned about the medical procedure, which may suggest that the information broke his will), and the latter is founded on a normative claim that police officers should not tell suspects that the only way they can avoid a painful medical procedure is by making an inculpatory statement. As with any such normative claim, however, a court ought to explain why, precisely, such a police tactic deserves condemnation—is it because the court believes that there is too great a risk that it will compel an innocent person to confess, or is there another reason?

### [2] Psychological Pressures

"[C]oercion can be mental as well as physical, and . . . the blood of the accused is not the only hallmark of an unconstitutional inquisition."[87] Among the relevant factors in determining whether the psychological pressures are too great are: length of custodial detention; whether the interrogation was prolonged in nature; whether the questioning occurred in the daytime or at night; whether the interrogation is conducted incommunicado; and the personal characteristics of the suspect (*e.g.*, age,[88]

---

[86] State v. Phelps, 456 N.W.2d 290 (Neb. 1990).

[87] Blackburn v. Alabama, 361 U.S. 199, 206 (1960).

[88] A factor especially weighing against voluntariness of an interrogation of a juvenile is the failure of the police to permit the youth's parents to be present during the interrogation. *E.g.*, In re G.O., 727 N.E.2d 1003 (Ill. 2000) (police refusal to permit a 13-year-old suspect to confer with his parents was a factor favoring involuntariness; nonetheless, finding the confession voluntary); State v. Presha, 748 A.2d 1108 (N.J. 2000) (despite the "highly significant" factor that a 17-year-old youth was interrogated in the parents' absence, confession was voluntary; but announcing the rule that any interrogation of a juvenile under the age of fourteen that is conducted in the absence of a parent or other adult representative is inadmissible as a matter of law).

intelligence, level of education, psychological makeup, and prior experience with the police). Of course, if non-psychological factors are included—for example, food deprivation—a finding of involuntariness is enhanced. As before, a court may find a confession involuntary either because it believes that the individual's will was overborne—seemingly, the usual basis here—or because it considers the interrogation techniques morally unacceptable.

In relatively early, pre-*Miranda* cases, the Supreme Court took a fairly firm stand in this realm. It described nearly thirty-six hours of nonstop incommunicado interrogation "inherently coercive."[89] And, it suppressed a confession of a foreign-born suspect—who had limited education, no criminal record, and a history of emotional instability—obtained as the result of an eight-hour, middle-of-the-night, interrogation capped off by police use of a long-time friend of the suspect to manipulate the suspect's emotions.[90] The Court expressly stated that, "considering all the facts," the suspect's "will was overborne by official pressure, fatigue and sympathy falsely aroused."

### [3] Promises of Leniency and Threats of Harsh Legal Treatment

*Bram v. United States*[91] declared any confession involuntary if it was "obtained by any direct or implied promises, however slight." The Supreme Court has since repudiated this statement.[92] Today, some—but far from all—promises of leniency are considered coercive.

Supreme Court cases in this area are relatively rare. In *Lynumn v. Illinois*,[93] a Warren Court era case, *D* confessed to selling marijuana after the police told her that she could lose welfare payments, lose custody of her children, and get a ten-year prison sentence, but that if she cooperated, they would recommend leniency and help her keep her children.

The Supreme Court unanimously declared the confession coerced. Although the *Lynumn* Court did not refer to the promise of leniency as a justification for its ruling, many lawyers in the pre-repudiated *Bram* era interpreted the case as condemning police promises of leniency as a means of securing confessions. More recently, however, the Court has explained that the confession in *Lynumn* was involuntary because the police misrepresented the consequences of failing to confess.[94]

---

[89] Ashcraft v. Tennessee, 322 U.S. 143 (1944).

[90] Spano v. New York, 360 U.S. 315 (1959).

[91] 168 U.S. 532 (1897).

[92] Arizona v. Fulminante, 499 U.S. 279, 285 (1991).

[93] 372 U.S. 528 (1963).

[94] Colorado v. Spring, 479 U.S. 564, 576 n.8 (1987).

Lower courts have determined that some types of promises of leniency will render a confession involuntary. According to one survey, "lower courts have often held that a confession is involuntary if made in response to a promise that the result will be nonprosecution, the dropping of some charges, medical treatment, or a certain reduction in the punishment the defendant may receive."[95] Even here, however, courts are less inclined today to invalidate leniency-based confessions in light of *Bram*'s undercutting.[96] And, standing alone, courts rarely find involuntariness if the police merely promise to bring the defendant's cooperation to the prosecutor's attention, or promise that a prosecutor will *discuss* leniency in exchange for a confession.[97]

What if the police, rather than promising a benefit in exchange for a confession, threaten especially harsh legal treatment if the suspect refuses to confess? Such threats sometimes invalidate a confession. For example, in *Rogers v. Richmond*,[98] the Supreme Court suppressed a confession as involuntary because it was secured in response to a wrongful police threat to take the suspect's wife into custody. Some lower courts, as well, have ruled that a confession is involuntary if the police threaten to inform the prosecutor of a suspect's refusal to cooperate, since this is a threat to penalize the accused for asserting her privilege against compulsory self-incrimination.[99] Likewise, a confession may be involuntary if an officer tells a suspect that "if you try and hide [the truth] from me you're really going to get hammered [by the prosecutor]."[100]

### [4]    Deception[101]

When the Supreme Court began to suppress confessions obtained by violence and torture, the police turned to more sophisticated interrogation techniques, often including deception.[102] Among other strategies, a police officer may display false sympathy for the accused, falsely claim to have incriminating evidence proving the accused's guilt, or falsely assert that

---

[95] 2 Wayne R. LaFave, Jerold H. Israel & Nancy J. King, Criminal Procedure 453–54 (2d. ed. 1999).

[96] *Id.* at 454.

[97] *See, e.g.*, Commonwealth v. Mandile, 492 N.E.2d 74 (1986); United States v. Coleman 208 F.3d 786 (9th Cir. 2000).

[98] 365 U.S. 534 (1961).

[99] United States v. Harrison, 34 F3d 886 (9th Cir. 1994).

[100] Beavers v. State, 998 P.2d 1040, 1042 (Alaska 2000).

[101] *See generally* Paris, Note 64, *supra*; Christopher Slobogin, *Deceit, Pretext, and Trickery: Investigative Lies By the Police*, 76 Or. L. Rev. 775 (1997).

[102] *See* § 22.02, *supra*.

a co-defendant has implicated the accused in the crime. Sometimes, police officers concoct highly creative ways to "con" suspects into confessing.[103]

In *Miranda v. Arizona*,[104] the Court sharply criticized deceptive police practices.[105] Nonetheless, the high court's decisions in this area, especially in recent years, demonstrate that considerable police deception is permissible. Indeed, although the case law in this area is hardly consistent, one safe generalization is that deception *alone*—lying to the suspect—will almost never invalidate a confession. Thus, if the police falsely inform a suspect that the case against her is strong because a co-conspirator has already confessed, this lie, although relevant as is every factor in the voluntariness analysis, will not by itself render the confession involuntary.[106]

In the early years of the Warren Court era, the Court took a stricter approach to deception than in recent time. It suppressed a confession because the interrogating officers falsely claimed that the suspect's right to retain custody of her children was dependent on her cooperation with them.[107] It also held that the police violated due process when they masqueraded a police psychiatrist as a physician called in to treat the suspect's very painful sinus condition, during which "treatment" the "physician" interrogated him.[108] But, both of these cases, besides being early decisions of the Court, included aggravating features: in the first case, the police also promised leniency;[109] and the second ruse was especially extreme in light of the accused's physical pain at the time. In contrast, the Court has more recently approved the technique of placing an undercover officer, masquerading as a burglar, in a jail cell where the "fellow inmate" could purposely elicit incriminating statements from the suspect.[110]

---

[103] *E.g.*, consider the following ruse by *O*, a New York homicide investigator. In an effort to obtain a confession from *D*, a suspect in a murder investigation, *O* told *D* that "when a person is murdered the last thing a person sees is the person who killed them. And this image remains on the lens of their eyes after they die." *O* went on to say that modern technology made it possible to remove the eyes during autopsy and have them "developed" like film in a photo lab, and thereby identify the killer. Based on this deception, *D* confessed. Ron Rosenbaum, *Crack Murder: A Detective Story*, New York Times Magazine, Feb. 15, 1987, at 24.

[104] 384 U.S. 436 (1966).

[105] See § 24.04[C][1], *infra*.

[106] Frazier v. Cupp, 394 U.S. 731, 739 (1969) ("The fact that the police misrepresented the statements that [the other party] had made is, while relevant, insufficient . . . to make this otherwise voluntary confession inadmissible.").

[107] Lynumn v. Illinois, 372 U.S. 528 (1963).

[108] Leyra v. Denno, 347 U.S. 556 (1954).

[109] *See* § 23.03[B][3], *supra*.

[110] Illinois v. Perkins, 496 U.S. 292 (1990).

CHAPTER 24

# MIRANDA V. ARIZONA

## § 24.01 *Miranda*: A Brief Overview and Some Reflections

*Miranda v. Arizona*[1] is one of the most famous Supreme Court decisions in American history. Perhaps thanks to the media and "cop shows" on television, nearly every American and many citizens of other countries have heard of *Miranda*. According to one study of lawyers, it is the most memorable criminal case in Supreme Court jurisprudence, and the third most notable overall.[2]

Fame and acceptance, however, are two different concepts. The *Miranda* opinion itself mustered only five votes, and proved to be immediately controversial in many circles. According to one observer, the opinion "must rank as the most bitterly criticized, most contentious, and most diversely analyzed criminal procedure decision by the Warren Court."[3] The decision "evoked much anger and spread much sorrow"[4] among many police officers and legislators, who believed that the decision would impede law enforcement efforts to obtain confessions of guilt; yet, others in more recent years have criticized *Miranda* for not going far enough in protecting suspects from improper police interrogation procedures.[5] As a result of criticisms of *Miranda* from law enforcement agencies, Congress in 1968—just two years after the decision was handed down—sought to "overrule" the holding by legislation.[6]

*Miranda*'s influence has stretched well beyond the police interrogation room. The decision, the values underlying it, and the public's perception

---

[1] 384 U.S. 436 (1966).

[2] Jethro K. Lieberman, Milestones! 200 Years of American Law: Milestones in Our Legal History vi–vii (1976).

[3] Henry J. Abraham, Freedom and the Court 125 (4th ed. 1982).

[4] Yale Kamisar, *A Dissent From the Miranda Dissents: Some Comments on the "New" Fifth Amendment and the Old "Voluntariness" Test*, 65 Mich. L. Rev. 59, 59 (1966).

[5] Irene Merker Rosenberg & Yale L. Rosenberg, *A Modest Proposal for the Abolition of Custodial Confessions*, 68 N.C. L. Rev. 69, 73 (1989); Paul Marcus, *A Return to the "Bright Line Rule" of Miranda*, 35 Wm. & Mary L. Rev. 93, 109–10 (1993).

[6] 18 U.S.C.A. § 3501 (2000).

of it were factors in the refusal of the United States Senate to confirm Abe Fortas, a member of the *Miranda* majority, as Chief Justice of the Supreme Court, and *Miranda* may have helped elect Richard Nixon to the presidency.[7]

*Miranda*—the legal doctrine—is alive,[8] but not in the best of conditions.[9] One former member of the Court described the case as "twisting slowly in the wind."[10] As demonstrated in this chapter, the *Miranda* of 1966 is not the *Miranda* of the twenty-first century. Professor Yale Kamisar has observed that, with the departure of Earl Warren and other members of his Court, "almost all Court watchers expected the [Supreme] Court to treat *Miranda* unkindly. They did not have to wait very long."[11] In most regards, *Miranda* has been narrowly interpreted, and exceptions to the doctrine have been created, so that much of the case's potential impact for good or ill has been diminished.

## § 24.02  *Miranda*: **Placing the Case in Historical Context**[12]

Before *Miranda*, the police typically interrogated suspects in private. Defense lawyers were excluded from the interrogation room. The incommunicado nature of the process facilitated police brutality, which was common well into the twentieth century. By mid-century, as the result of public opposition to violent police practices and a judicial crackdown on the use of torture to obtain confessions, police departments shifted their interrogation strategy from the use of physical force to psychological ploys to secure confessions from unwilling suspects.

The new procedures troubled some observers who believed that they differed only in degree from those used in totalitarian societies.[13] The

---

[7] A major campaign position of Nixon, the candidate, was that he would fill Court vacancies with judges opposed to *Miranda*. *See generally* Liva Baker, Miranda: Crime, Law and Politics (1983).

[8] The Supreme Court had a very recent opportunity to overrule it, but refused to do so. Dickerson v. United States, 530 U.S. 428 (2000). *See* § 24.06, *infra.*

[9] That is more than can be said for Ernesto Miranda. He was killed in a barroom brawl ten years after the case bearing his name was decided. His suspected killer was given *Miranda* warnings. Baker, Note 7, *supra*, at 408–09.

[10] Arthur J. Goldberg, *Escobedo and Miranda Revisited*, 18 Akron L. Rev. 177, 182 (1984).

[11] Yale Kamisar, *The Warren Court and Criminal Justice: A Quarter-Century Retrospective*, 31 Tulsa L.J. 1, 13 (1995).

[12] *See* § 22.02, *supra*, for greater detail on pre-*Miranda* police procedures.

[13] David L. Sterling, *Police Interrogation and the Psychology of Confession*, 14 J. Pub. L. 25, 37 (1965) ("[I]f the American police manuals are examined, there is a striking similarity between their recommendations and Russian and Chinese interrogation techniques.").

authors of the police manuals, however, defended the new tactics on the ground that "[o]f necessity, criminal interrogators must deal with criminal offenders on a somewhat lower moral plane than that upon which ethical law-abiding citizens are expected to conduct their every day affairs."[14]

The move from force to psychological pressures did not satisfy a majority of the Supreme Court, which viewed confessions "darkly as the product of police coercion."[15] The Court came to believe that encounters in the interrogation room should be more evenly balanced between suspects and the police. The Justices' ultimate goal was to "protect those suspects who were the most vulnerable in police interrogations—minorities and the poor—by informing them of their rights and empowering them against coercive tactics."[16]

Moreover, by the early 1960s the Court had become thoroughly dissatisfied with the imprecise "voluntariness" test[17] as a mechanism for dealing with the interrogation techniques suggested in the police manuals. Based upon thirty years of struggle with the doctrine—with a test in which "[a]lmost everything was relevant, but almost nothing was decisive"[18]—the Court concluded that the test resulted in "intolerable uncertainty,"[19] and that a bright-line rule was needed.

Interrogation law took a dramatic turn in 1964. First, the Court held that the Fifth Amendment privilege against compulsory self-incrimination is a fundamental right applicable to the states through the Fourteenth Amendment.[20] Second, in *Massiah v. United States*,[21] the Court turned its sights toward the Sixth Amendment, and held that the government may not deliberately elicit statements from a person under indictment in the absence of counsel. Shortly thereafter, in *Escobedo v. Illinois*,[22] it extended the right to counsel to a pre-indictment interrogation.

*Massiah*, and especially *Escobedo*, generated confusion and controversy among observers.[23] The next year, the Court held a conference to consider

---

[14] Fred E. Inbau & John E. Reid, Criminal Interrogation and Confessions 208 (1962).

[15] Gerald M. Caplan, *Questioning Miranda*, 38 Vand. L. Rev. 1417, 1425 (1985).

[16] Charles D. Weisselberg, *Saving Miranda*, 84 Cornell L. Rev. 109, 125 (1998).

[17] *See* § 23.03, *supra.*

[18] Yale Kamisar, *Gates, "Probable Cause," "Good Faith," and Beyond*, 69 Iowa L. Rev. 551, 570 (1984).

[19] Joseph D. Grano, *Voluntariness, Free Will, and the Law of Confessions*, 65 Va. L. Rev. 859, 863 (1979).

[20] Malloy v. Hogan, 378 U.S. 1 (1964).

[21] 377 U.S. 201 (1964). *See* § 25.02, *infra.*

[22] 378 U.S. 478 (1964). *See* § 24.03, *infra.*

[23] Geoffrey R. Stone, *The Miranda Doctrine in the Burger Court*, 1977 Sup. Ct. Rev. 99, 103.

which of 101"*Escobedo* cases" it would use to clarify the latter Sixth Amendment right-to-counsel decision.[24] It chose four appeals now treated collectively as *Miranda v. Arizona*, but instead of clarifying *Escobedo*, the Justices used those cases to shift its focus from the Sixth Amendment right to counsel to the Fifth Amendment privilege against compulsory self-incrimination.

## § 24.03  The Road to *Miranda*: *Escobedo v. Illinois*

The road to *Miranda* runs through *Escobedo v. Illinois*.[25] In *Escobedo*, D, who was under arrest for murder, was taken into custody late in the evening and interrogated at the police station. During the questioning, he was handcuffed and kept standing.

At various times during the interrogation, D asked to consult with his privately-retained lawyer, but his requests were refused on the false ground that his lawyer "didn't want to see" him. The truth was that shortly after the questioning began, D's counsel arrived at the station, but he was not permitted to talk to his client because, as one officer candidly put it, "they hadn't completed questioning."

Later in the night, the police suggested to D that he confront X, an accomplice who (according to the police) had implicated D as the trigger-man. D agreed to talk to X in their presence. During the encounter, D made statements to X that, for the first time, indicated his familiarity with the crime. Later, D made additional statements to the police implicating himself as an accomplice. At no time was D informed by the police of his privilege against self-incrimination.

D sought to exclude his statements on the basis that they were coerced in violation of the due process clause, but the trial court found that they were voluntarily given. D was convicted. On appeal, the Supreme Court held that the confession was inadmissible because it was obtained in violation of D's Sixth Amendment right to counsel.

*Escobedo* was path-breaking. Never before had the Court held that the Sixth Amendment right to counsel applied to one against whom criminal proceedings had not yet formally commenced, such as by indictment. Speaking for the Court, Justice Arthur Goldberg stated that the fact that D had not been indicted when the statements were obtained was irrelevant because, "[w]hen [D] requested, and was denied, an opportunity to consult with his lawyer, the investigation had ceased to be a general investigation

---

[24] Weisselberg, Note 16, *supra*, at 117–118.

[25] 378 U.S. 478 (1964).

. . . ." By that time, the investigation had "focused" on *D*; for all practical purposes he had become the accused.

The Court observed that *D*, who had no prior criminal record, undoubtedly was unaware that his admissions of complicity were legally as damaging as an admission that he had fired the fatal shot. Therefore, he needed the "guiding hand of counsel" to advise him "in this delicate situation." According to *Escobedo*, it "would exalt form over substance to make the right to counsel . . . depend on whether at the time of the interrogation, the authorities had secured a formal indictment."

Despite broad language in the opinion, the Court's holding was narrow. It held only that a suspect's Sixth Amendment right to counsel is violated when, "as here": (1) the investigation focuses on him; (2) he is in custody; (3) the police interrogate him; (4) he requests and is denied an opportunity to consult with his lawyer; and (5) the police have not informed him of his privilege against self-incrimination.

*Escobedo* was controversial. Some criticized it for "opening the door" of the interrogation room to defense attorneys, while others criticized it for not going far enough in that direction. Critics of the latter variety pointed out that under *Escobedo* a person who did not ask to see his attorney was not protected. Effectively, this excluded indigents who lacked knowledge of the *Escobedo* ruling or who were too timid to ask for counsel during interrogation. However, criticisms of *Escobedo* were soon over-shadowed by *Miranda*.

*Escobedo*'s long-term impact as a Sixth Amendment case was soon undercut. The Court "in retrospect" concluded that the underlying rationale of the case was "not to vindicate the constitutional right to counsel as such, but, like *Miranda*, 'to guarantee full effectuation of the privilege against self-incrimination . . . .' "[26] In short, *Escobedo*, although nominally a right-to-counsel case, became a self-incrimination opinion.

The Supreme Court has limited the holding of *Escobedo* to its own facts.[27] Consequently, it is the only opinion of the Court to hold that the Sixth Amendment right to counsel attaches in advance of formal adversary criminal proceedings begin.

*Escobedo*'s long-term significance is not in its holding, but rather in the majority's expressed attitudes regarding interrogations and confessions, which formed the basis for *Miranda*.[28] *Escobedo* provides a classic defense

---

[26] Kirby v. Illinois, 406 U.S. 682, 689 (1972) (quoting Johnson v. New Jersey, 384 U.S. 719, 729 (1966)).

[27] Johnson v. New Jersey, 384 U.S. 719 (1966).

[28] *See* Joseph D. Grano, *Selling the Idea to Tell the Truth: The Professional Interrogator and Modern Confessions Law*, 84 Mich. L. Rev. 662, 666 (1986).

of the accusatorial system of criminal justice, which is founded on the view that the government must shoulder the entire load of proving a defendant's guilt, and that confessions—at least, uncounseled ones—are disfavored, if not disallowed. As one scholar recognized, "*Escobedo* launched such a broad attack on the government's reliance on confessions that it threatened (or promised) to eliminate virtually all police interrogation of suspects."[29]

The essence of the Court's reasoning was that *D*, as a suspect in custody on whom the police investigation had focused, needed the guiding hand of a lawyer in his encounter with the police. But, of course, had he been given that right, his lawyer almost certainly would have advised him not to talk. The Court's reaction to this was to state that this demonstrated why custodial interrogation is a critical stage in the criminal justice process. "The right to counsel would indeed be hollow," *Escobedo* intoned, "if it began at a period when few confessions were obtained." Quoting Wigmore, Justice Goldberg observed that "any system of administration which permits the prosecution to trust habitually to compulsory self-disclosure as a source of proof must itself suffer morally thereby." It was with this attitude toward confessions that the Warren Court turned to *Miranda*.

## § 24.04 *Miranda*: The Case

### [A] The Facts

*Miranda v. Arizona* involved four cases consolidated for appeal. In view of the *per se* holding of *Miranda*, the facts relating to the police investigations received little attention by the Court. Although the prosecutions involved police practices in four jurisdictions, there were significant common facts: (1) each of the suspects had been taken into custody (in three, by arrest; in one, before formal arrest); (2) they were questioned in an interrogation room; (3) the questioning occurred in a police-dominated environment in which each suspect was alone with the questioners; and (4) the suspects were never informed of their privilege against compulsory self-incrimination.

### [B] The Holding

#### [1] What Rights Does a Suspect Have In the Interrogation Room?

##### [a] Self-Incrimination

A suspect has a constitutional right not to be compelled to make incriminating statements in the interrogation process. To enforce this right,

---

[29] Kamisar, Note 11, *supra*, at 9; *see* Grano, Note 28, *supra*, at 666 ("if one takes *Escobedo*'s reasoning seriously, all police interrogation should be prohibited until the defendant has had an opportunity to consult with a lawyer").

*Miranda* holds that any statement, whether exculpatory or inculpatory, obtained as the result of custodial interrogation may not be used against the suspect in a criminal trial unless the prosecutor proves that the police provided procedural safeguards effective to secure the suspect's privilege against compulsory self-incrimination. [30]

"Custodial interrogation"—the triggering mechanism of *Miranda*—is defined as "questioning initiated by law enforcement officers after a person has been taken into custody or otherwise deprived of his freedom of action in any significant way." The Court said that "[t]his is what we meant in *Escobedo* [*v. Illinois* [31] ] when we spoke of an investigation which had focused on an accused." [32]

### [b]　Right to Counsel

*Miranda* observes that "[t]he circumstances surrounding in-custody interrogation can operate very quickly to overbear the will of one merely made aware of his privilege" against compulsory self-incrimination. Therefore, the Court held that an in-custody suspect also has a right to consult counsel prior to questioning and to have counsel present during interrogation. [33]

Under *Miranda*, the primary purpose of defense counsel during custodial interrogation is to assure that the suspect's ability to choose whether to speak or to remain silent is unfettered. The lawyer presence in the interrogation room also serves "significant subsidiary functions": his presence reduces the likelihood that the police will act coercively; he can more effectively reconstruct events and, thus, make a case of coercion, if necessary, at a subsequent hearing or trial; and he can ensure that any

---

[30] Exceptions to this rule now exist. *See* § 24.11, *infra.*

[31] 378 U.S. 478 (1964). *See* § 24.03, *supra.*

[32] According to one scholar, this "was surely one of the least honest sentences in the opinion." Marcus, Note 5, *supra,* at 114. The *Miranda*'s Court's definition of "custody" is *not* what was meant by "focus" in *Escobedo.* In *Escobedo, both* focus and custody were required. *Miranda* rejected the focus requirement. *See* § 24.07[B][1], *infra.*

[33] In an intriguing footnote in Berkemer v. McCarty, 468 U.S. 420, 434 n.21 (1984), the Court declined to answer the question "whether an indigent suspect has a right, under the Fifth Amendment, to have an attorney appointed to advise him regarding his responses to custodial interrogation when the alleged offense about which he is being questioned is sufficiently minor that he would not have a right, under the Sixth Amendment, to the assistance of appointed counsel at trial." (As discussed in § 29.02[B][4], *infra,* an indigent does not have a constitutional right to appointed counsel at trial of a misdemeanor offense for which he will not be incarcerated if convicted.)

statement given by his client is accurate and that it is reported correctly at trial.[34]

The right to counsel discussed in *Miranda* may be described as the Fifth Amendment, or *Miranda*, right to counsel. It should not be confused with the Sixth Amendment right to counsel, discussed in the next chapter, which differs in various respects.

### [2] Procedural Safeguards: The *"Miranda* Warnings"

According to *Miranda*, Congress and the states are free to develop procedural safeguards for protecting a suspect's Fifth Amendment rights during custodial interrogation. However, unless they are "fully as effective" as those described in the opinion, the following warnings must be provided by the police prior to custodial questioning.

First, the police must "in clear and unequivocal terms" indicate that the suspect has a right to remain silent.

Second, the consequence of foregoing the preceding right must be explained to the suspect. Specifically, the first statement "must be accompanied by the explanation that anything said can and will be used against the individual in court."

Third, a suspect held for interrogation must "clearly" be informed that "he has the right to consult with a lawyer and to have the lawyer with him during interrogation."

Fourth, because the financial ability of the suspect has no relation to the scope of the right to counsel or its importance, the police must inform him that "if he is indigent a lawyer will be appointed to represent him."

### [3] Waiver of a Suspect's *"Miranda* Rights"

#### [a] In General

A suspect may waive his privilege against self-incrimination and his *Miranda* right to counsel before or during interrogation. A "heavy burden" rests on the prosecutor, however, to demonstrate that the defendant "voluntarily, knowingly, and intelligently"[35] waived his rights.

---

[34] A twenty-first century debate is whether these subsidiary functions can adequately be satisfied by videotaping all custodial police interrogations. *E.g.* Paul G. Cassell, *The Paths Not Taken: The Supreme Court's Failures in Dickerson*, 99 Mich. L. Rev. 898 (2001) (arguing for videotaping as a substitute for the right to counsel); Stephen J. Schulhofer, *Miranda, Dickerson and the Puzzling Persistence of Fifth Amendment Exceptionalism*, 99 Mich. L. Rev. 941 (2001) (arguing that unless videotaping supplements *Miranda*, rather than serving as a substitute, it will make matters worse); *see also* William A. Geller, *Videotaping Interrogations and Confessions* in Miranda: Law, Justice, and Policing 303 (Richard A. Leo & George C. Thomas III eds. 1998).

[35] *See* Johnson v. Zerbst, 304 U.S. 458 (1938).

### [b]    Voluntariness of the Waiver

The Court stated that the mere "fact of lengthy interrogation or incommunicado incarceration before a statement is made is strong evidence" of involuntary relinquishment of the Fifth Amendment privilege. Furthermore, evidence that the suspect was "threatened, tricked, or cajoled into a waiver will . . . show that [he] did not voluntarily waive his privilege."

### [c]    Intelligence of the Waiver

A waiver is not "knowing and intelligent" unless the *Miranda* warnings are given. The Court stated that because the rights are fundamental, it "will not pause to inquire in individual cases whether the defendant was aware of his rights without a warning being given"; and "[n]o amount of circumstantial evidence that the person may have been aware of [his] right[s] will suffice to stand in its stead."

### [4]    Enforcing the Rights

### [a]    Privilege Against Self-Incrimination

After the warnings are given, an "express statement" by a suspect that he is willing to make a statement, and that he does not want an attorney present, "followed closely by a statement could constitute a waiver." A waiver of the privilege against self-incrimination "will not be presumed simply from the silence of the accused after warnings are given."

If the suspect "indicates in any manner, at any time prior to or during questioning, that he wishes to remain silent, the interrogation must cease." The Court stated that any statement obtained after the suspect invokes his privilege "cannot be other than the product of compulsion, subtle or otherwise." However, if a person asserts his privilege in his attorney's presence, the Court stated that "there may be some circumstances in which further questioning would be permissible," particularly "[i]n the absence of evidence of overbearing."

### [b]    Right to Counsel

As with a suspect's right to remain silent, once warnings are given, an express statement by a suspect that he is willing to be interrogated without counsel, "followed closely by a statement could constitute a waiver."

If a suspect at any time prior to or during the questioning states that he wants to consult with an attorney, "the interrogation must cease until an attorney is present." When the lawyer is furnished, "the individual must have an opportunity to confer with the attorney and to have him present during any subsequent questioning."

## [C]  Reasoning of the Court

### [1]  Custodial Interrogation As "Compulsion"

The Court was critical of police interrogation techniques, as evidenced by the police manuals available at the time and quoted extensively in the opinion. According to police procedures, the "guilt of the subject is to be posited as a fact." The manuals train officers to give a suspect the psychological impression that a confession would be nothing more than an "elaboration" of the obvious, the subject's guilt. When "appeals and tricks" fail, the officers "must rely on an oppressive atmosphere of dogged persistence."

Other ploys recommended in the manuals, and described by the Court, include the technique of the police interrogator offering excuses for the suspect's conduct in order to gain his confidence and elicit an admission of guilt, use of a "Mutt and Jeff" act in which a friendly police officer fends off a hostile officer to protect the subject, and outright trickery. In the latter category, the manuals at the time of *Miranda* advised police to use lineups in which fictitious witnesses identify the suspect, in order to convince him that there is no value in remaining silent.

Based on such police practices, the Court concluded that custodial interrogation "exacts a heavy toll on individual liberty and trades on the weakness of individuals." Suspects are "thrust into an unfamiliar atmosphere and run through menacing police interrogation procedures." They are "surrounded by antagonistic forces," kept "incommunicado" in a "police-dominated atmosphere," and "deprived of every psychological advantage."

As the preceding language would suggest, the most common reading of *Miranda* in 1966 was that the case stands for the proposition that "compulsion *inheres* in custodial interrogation to such an extent that *any* confession, in *any* case of custodial interrogation, is compelled."[36] That is, in the absence of procedural safeguards (*i.e.*, the *"Miranda* warnings" or their equivalent) custodial interrogation necessarily *will*—not simply *can*—result in unconstitutional compulsion.[37] In short, the Court appeared to replace the totality-of-the-circumstances "voluntariness" test with a bright-line, *per se* definition of "compulsion" in the custodial interrogation context.

Further support for this reading of *Miranda* is evident from the Court's observations that custodial interrogation "carries its own badge of intimidation," and that persons "subjected to the techniques of persuasion described

---

[36] Lawrence Herman, *The Supreme Court, the Attorney General, and the Good Old Days of Police Interrogation*, 48 Ohio. St. L.J. 733, 735 (1987).

[37] Stephen J. Schulhofer, *Reconsidering Miranda*, 54 U. Chi. L. Rev. 435, 447 (1987).

above cannot be otherwise than under compulsion to speak." The Court also stated that in the absence of warnings or their equivalent, which are "employed to dispel the compulsion inherent in custodial surroundings, no statements obtained from the defendant can truly be the product of his free choice."[38]

### [2] The Limited Importance of Confessions in Law Enforcement

As one scholar has observed, "*Miranda* . . . represents a preference for Fifth Amendment values over the interest of law enforcement officers in obtaining incriminating statements."[39] The *Miranda* Court stated that it was "not unmindful of the burdens which law enforcement officials must bear, often under trying circumstances," to obtain evidence to convict the guilty. But it was not persuaded by the "recurrent argument . . . that society's need for interrogation outweighs the privilege."

Although the Justices conceded that "confessions may play an important role in some convictions," it considered the cases at hand "graphic examples of the overstatement of the 'need' for confessions." The Court pointed out that in each case before it, the police had considerable incriminating evidence against the suspects that was obtained through standard non-interrogation investigatory practices.

### [3] Fifth Amendment Values and the Importance of the Adversarial System

In perhaps the most important explanatory language of the opinion—and certainly the most stirring—the Supreme Court described the Fifth Amendment privilege against compulsory self-incrimination as a "noble principle," based on the "individual's substantive right, a 'right to a private enclave where he may lead a private life. That right is the hallmark of our democracy.' " Chief Justice Earl Warren characterized the privilege as "the essential mainstay of our adversary system." According to *Miranda*, the principles underlying it add up "to one overriding thought":

> the respect a government . . . must accord to the dignity and integrity of its citizens. To maintain a "fair state-individual balance," to require the government "to shoulder the entire load," . . . to respect the inviolability of the human personality, our accusatory system of criminal

---

[38] Not all of the language in *Miranda* supports the thesis that custodial interrogation is inherently coercive. For example, the opinion states that "we might not find the defendants' statements [in these cases] to have been involuntary in traditional terms. . . . [However,] [t]he *potentiality* for compulsion is forcefully apparent . . . ." 384 U.S. at 457 (emphasis added).

[39] Weisselberg, Note 16, *supra*, at 121.

justice demands that the government seeking to punish an individual produce the evidence against him by its own independent labors, rather than by the cruel, simple expedient of compelling it from his own mouth.[40]

Consequently, *Miranda* suggested, it "is not for the authorities to decide" when a suspect should speak; rather, it is the right of the individual, with such assistance as he may wish to obtain from an attorney, to decide whether and when to talk to the police. When an attorney recommends to his client that he remain silent, he "is merely carrying out what he is sworn to do under his oath—to protect to the extent of his ability the rights of his client." As such, the defense attorney in the interrogation room "plays a vital role in the administration of criminal justice under our Constitution."

## § 24.05 Criticisms of *Miranda*[41]

Although it did not seem so to critics at the time, *Miranda* constituted a compromise, of sorts.[42] Although it apparently created a bright-line, *per se* rule of "involuntariness" to supplant the more flexible totality-of-circumstances standard, it did not eliminate altogether uncounseled custodial interrogations, as some observers wanted. What follows is a brief survey of some of the criticisms of *Miranda* from "both directions," as well as arguments in its favor.

---

[40] *Miranda*, 384 U.S. at 460. For fuller discussion of the history of, the policies supporting, and the general contours of, the privilege against compulsory self-incrimination, *see* chapter 26, *infra*.

[41] For criticisms of *Miranda* from a law enforcement perspective, *see generally* Caplan, Note 15, *supra*; Joseph D. Grano, *Miranda's Constitutional Difficulties: A Reply to Professor Schulhofer*, 55 U. Chi. L. Rev. 174 (1988); Joseph D. Grano, *Miranda v. Arizona and the Legal Mind: Formalism's Triumph over Substance and Reason*, 24 Am. Crim. L. Rev. 243 (1986); Grano, Note 28, *supra*; Office of Legal Policy, U.S. Dept. of Justice, Report to the Attorney General on the Law of Pre-Trial Interrogation (1986).

For a defense of *Miranda* or criticisms of it on the ground that it did not go far enough in limiting confessions, *see generally* Kamisar, Notes 4 and 11, *supra*; Charles J. Ogletree, *Are Confessions Really Good for the Soul?: A Proposal to Mirandize Miranda*, 100 Harv. L. Rev. 1826 (1987); Rosenberg & Rosenberg, Note 5, *supra*; Stephen J. Schulhofer, *Bashing Miranda Is Unjustified—And Harmful*, 20 Harv. J. Law & Pub. Pol'y 347 (1997); Schulhofer, Note 37, *supra*; Welsh S. White, *Miranda's Failure to Restrain Pernicious Interrogation Practices*, 99 Mich. L. Rev. 1211 (2001); Welsh S. White, *Defending Miranda: A Reply to Professor Caplan*, 39 Vand. L. Rev. 1 (1986).

For articles relating to the claim that *Miranda* applies a historically incorrect interpretation of the Fifth Amendment, *see* Note 48, *infra*; for empirical claims that *Miranda* has (or has not) resulted in fewer confessions, *see* Note 77, *infra*.

[42] Kamisar, Note 11, *supra*, at 11.

## [A]  "*Miranda* Did Not Go Far Enough"

*What the critics say:* The Court did not take the logic of *Escobedo*[43] and *Miranda* to its logical conclusion, which is to prohibit custodial confessions altogether,[44] permit questioning but only in the presence of a lawyer,[45] or, at a very minimum, prohibit interrogation until the suspect has consulted with counsel.[46]

If one takes seriously the principle stated in *Miranda* that the government must "shoulder the entire load" in an accusatorial system of justice, and that it must "respect the inviolability of the human personality," then it follows from this that the government should not be permitted to establish guilt by use of admissions obtained in the "inherently coercive" environment described by the Supreme Court. Even if this is too extreme a position, the Court acted inconsistently in stating that custodial interrogations are inherent coercive, yet allowing for suspects to "voluntarily" waive their rights in the same coercive environment. At a minimum, therefore, a lawyer needs to be present or consulted before a waiver can truly be effective.

*What the defenders say:* Defenders of *Miranda* do not necessarily disagree with the preceding criticisms, but they suggest that "these [critics] do not seem to appreciate the fact that in 1966 the Court was barely able to go as far as it did—that at the time it was probably not possible to persuade a majority of the Court to go one inch further . . . ."[47]

## [B]  "*Miranda* Went Too Far"

### [1]  "*Miranda* Lacks Historical and Textual Support"[48]

*What the critics say:* The holding of *Miranda* has "no significant support in the history of the privilege or in the language of the Fifth Amendment."[49] Professor Albert Alschuler has stated that "neither the English nor the American version of the privilege afforded suspects and defendants a right to refuse to respond to incriminating questions."[50] In England, the privilege

---

[43] Escobedo v. Illinois, 378 U.S. 478 (1964). *See* § 24.03, *supra*.

[44] Rosenberg & Rosenberg, Note 5, *supra*.

[45] Otis H. Stephens, Jr., The Supreme Court and Confessions of Guilt 205 (1973).

[46] Ogletree, Note 41, *supra*, at 1830.

[47] Kamisar, Note 11, *supra*, at 12.

[48] *See generally* Albert W. Alschuler, *A Peculiar Privilege in Historical Perspective: The Right to Remain Silent*, 94 Mich. L. Rev. 2625 (1996); John H. Langbein, *The Historical Origins of the Privilege Against Self-Incrimination at Common Law*, 92 Mich. L. Rev. 1047 (1994); Eben Moglen, *Taking the Fifth: Reconsidering the Origins of the Constitutional Privilege Against Self-Incrimination*, 92 Mich. L. Rev. 1086 (1994).

[49] *Miranda*, 384 U.S. at 526 (White, J., dissenting).

[50] Alschuler, Note 48, *supra*, at 2631.

against compulsory self-incrimination applied only to *judicial* interrogations. Wigmore, too, concludes that the American privilege against compulsory self-incrimination does not apply to police interrogations.[51] Moreover, the most sensible reading of the text of the Fifth Amendment—"No person . . . shall be compelled to be a *witness* against himself"—is that the privilege was intended only to prevent the compulsion of oral testimony by the defendant in his criminal trial.

*What the defenders say:* The preceding criticism is not really directed at *Miranda*, but at the general (and pre-*Miranda*) proposition that the Fifth Amendment privilege requires the exclusion of statements obtained by police coercion. Wigmore's historical review of the Fifth Amendment has been questioned by some legal historians.[52] Beyond this, it is wrong to tie the Fifth Amendment privilege to an historical period in which investigatory and trial procedures differed so markedly from present-day processes. Divining the Framers' intent is always a murky enterprise, but it is odd to think that they would have intended to allow modern-day police coercion while they barred judicial compulsion.[53] Even the Office of Legal Policy in the Department of Justice, which called in 1986 for the Court to overrule *Miranda*, conceded that the applicability of the Fifth Amendment to custodial police interrogations is consistent with a historical understanding of the privilege.[54]

### [2] "The Rule Is Unnecessary and Irrational"

*What the critics say:* The *per se* rule of *Miranda* is unnecessary. The "Due Process Clauses [of the Fifth and Fourteenth Amendments] provide an adequate tool for coping with confessions."[55] The totality-of-the-circumstances voluntariness test is workable, effective, sophisticated, and sensitive. The claim that it provides inadequate guidance to the police is a "great exaggeration."[56] Supreme Court case law makes clear that if the police engage in certain types of conduct (*e.g.*, physical abuse of any kind, prolonged detention, food or sleep deprivation), they do so at their risk.

---

[51] 3 John H. Wigmore, Evidence 401 (Chadbourn rev. 1970).

[52] *E.g.*, Lawrence Herman, *The Unexplored Relationship Between the Privilege Against Compulsory Self-Incrimination and the Involuntary Confession Rule (Part I)*, 53 Ohio St. L.J. 101 (1992); *contra, see* the sources in Note 48, *supra.*

[53] "[I]f the police are permitted to interrogate an accused under the pressure of compulsory detention to secure a confession . . . they are doing the very same acts which historically the judiciary was doing in the seventeenth century but which the privilege against self-incrimination abolished." Beisel, Control Over Illegal Enforcement of the Criminal Law: Role of the Supreme Court 104 (1955) (*quoted in* Kamisar, Note 4, *supra*, at 73–74).

[54] Office of Legal Policy, Note 41, *supra*, at 42.

[55] *Miranda*, 384 U.S. at 505 (Harlan, J., dissenting).

[56] Caplan, Note 15, *supra*, at 1432.

In contrast, the *Miranda* rule is formalistic.[57] The premise that *every* custodial interrogation is coercive is counter-intuitive and empirically false. If a suspect in custody blurts out a confession, it is admissible despite the compulsion inherent in custody. But, a single question—"Did you commit the crime?"—asked of the suspect in the absence of warnings and waiver supposedly renders the process coercive. But, "[c]ommon sense informs us to the contrary."[58] It cannot be the case that *any* question of *any* person— regardless of the subject's internal fortitude, and regardless of the nature of the custodial interrogation—overbears the will.

*What the defenders say:* Only a person with "an extravagant faith" in the voluntariness test "could fail to see that the safeguards provided by [it] . . . were largely 'illusory.' "[59] Even a critic of *Miranda* has conceded that the old test resulted in "intolerable uncertainty."[60] As with other bright-line rules, *Miranda* sends a clearer message to the police than the totality-of-the-circumstances test could ever send.

Moreover, criticism of the *per se* nature of the rule is historically misguided: *Miranda* merely returned the law to the point at which it began.[61] In *Bram v. United States*,[62] the Supreme Court applied a similar definition of Fifth Amendment "compulsion." Although the *Bram* Court used the term "involuntary" in its analysis, it did not mean by this that the suspect's will had to be overborne in the due process sense for there to be a constitutional violation. Quite the contrary. Only later did the Court begin to use the term "involuntariness" interchangeably with "compulsion."[63]

In self-incrimination analysis, the amount of pressure required to invalidate a confession should be less than is required in the due process context, and should not be balanced against law enforcement interests,[64] because the Fifth Amendment is linked to the anti-inquisitorial values of the Fifth Amendment's framers. The critical question should be, as in *Miranda*, whether the pressure was "imposed for the *purpose* of discouraging the silence of a criminal suspect."[65]

---

[57] *See* Grano, *Legal Mind*, Note 41, *supra*, at 246.

[58] *Miranda*, 384 U.S. at 534 (White, J., dissenting).

[59] Kamisar, Note 4, *supra*, at 62.

[60] Grano, Note 19, *supra*, at 863.

[61] *See* Schulhofer, Note 37, *supra*, at 440–46.

[62] 168 U.S. 532 (1897). *See* § 23.01[B][1], *supra*.

[63] *See* § 23.01[B][3], *supra*.

[64] *Id.*

[65] Schulhofer, Note 37, *supra*, at 445.

### [3] *"Miranda* is Anti-Confessions and Pro-Fox Hunts"

*What the critics say:* The "obvious underpinning of [*Miranda*] . . . is a deep-seated distrust of all confessions." The "not so subtle overtone of the opinion [is] . . . that it is inherently wrong for the police to gather evidence from the accused himself."[66] Whatever else the Court may say, "the thrust of the new rules is to negate all pressures, to reinforce the nervous or ignorant suspect, and ultimately to discourage any confession at all."[67]

The *Miranda* majority opinion seeks a pure adversary system, but the American system of justice is and should be one mixed with non-adversarial procedures. *Miranda* ignores the fact that "[t]he most basic function of any government is to provide for the security of the individual and of his property." Respect for the inviolability of the suspect is not all that is valued by the Constitution: "the human personality of others in the society must also be preserved."[68]

*Miranda* treats criminal suspects as if they were underdogs in need of lawyers to match wits with the police, and to protect them against the pressures generated by custodial interrogation.[69] *Miranda* places the suspect on an even playing field with the police.[70] It gives an underdog suspect a sporting chance to be acquitted, even when he is factually guilty.

But, this "sporting theory of justice"[71] is senseless. Bentham contemptuously labeled this impulse to give the guilty a chance to avoid punishment as the "fox hunter's reason," that is, "[t]he fox is to have a fair chance for his life: he must have . . . leave to run a certain length of way, for the express purpose of giving him a chance for escape."[72] Nobody who believes in the basic legitimacy of a society, however, should "endorse the view that a guilty suspect, like a fox during a hunt, must be given a sporting chance to escape conviction and punishment."[73] We should want guilty people to confess, and not make it easier for them to remain silent.[74]

---

[66] *Miranda*, 384 U.S. at 537, 538 (White J., dissenting).

[67] *Id.* at 505 (Harlan, J., dissenting).

[68] *Id.* at 537 (White, J., dissenting).

[69] *See* Caplan, Note 15, *supra*, at 1441.

[70] It may do more: "it gives the suspect too great an advantage. If the police are too formidable for the average offender, a lawyer will be too formidable for the average investigator." *Id.* at 1443.

[71] Roscoe Pound, *The Causes of Popular Dissatisfaction with the Administration of Justice*, 29 A.B.A. Re. 395 (1906) (*reprinted in* 35 F.R.D. 273, 281 (1964)).

[72] 5 Jeremy Bentham, Rationale of Judicial Evidence 238–39 (1827).

[73] Grano, Note 28, *supra*, at 677.

[74] *See* Rosenberg & Rosenberg, Note 5, *supra*, at 70–71 (reproducing portions of the comic strip "Amazing Spider-Man," in which Peter Parker, the web-slinger alter ego, expresses

*What the defenders say:* The critics' real objection is not to *Miranda*, but to the Fifth Amendment privilege against self-incrimination, and the accusatorial system of justice that underlies it. It is the Constitution, not the Supreme Court, that prohibits compulsory self-incrimination. It is the Fifth Amendment, not *Miranda*, that values a system of justice in which the government must prove guilt by its independent labors.

*Miranda* is not based on a "fox hunt" or "sporting" approach to justice. It is based on the premise that it is "unseemly" for the police "systematically to . . . take advantage of the psychological vulnerabilities of a citizen."[75] The weak—which is what a suspect is when dealing alone with the police while in custody—should not be exploited by agents of the government. Values of human autonomy and dignity require no less than what *Miranda* safeguards.[76]

### [4] "*Miranda* Is Injurious to Law Enforcement"[77]

*What the critics say:* Police questioning of suspects "is an indispensable instrumentality of justice."[78] "[W]e cannot read an undiscriminating hostility to mere interrogation into the Constitution without unduly fettering the States in protecting society from the criminal."[79] The logical implication of *Miranda* is that once a suspect is informed of his privilege against compulsory self-incrimination and of his right to talk to a lawyer before any interrogation occurs, he *will* talk to his lawyer, and any lawyer worth his salt will tell his client to remain silent. *Miranda*'s effect, therefore, is

dismay at the release of the evil bad-guy "just because of a technicality"—the absence of *Miranda* warnings; Parker says "[w]e're treating justice like a game! The crook is "safe at first" because the cop dropped the ball! That's insanity.").

[75] Stephen J. Schulhofer, *Confessions and the Court*, 79 Mich. L. Rev. 865, 872 (1981).

[76] *See* R. Kent Greenawalt, *Silence as a Moral and Constitutional Right*, 23 Wm. & Mary L. Rev. 15, 40–41 (1981).

[77] *See generally* Paul G. Cassell, *Miranda's Social Costs: An Empirical Reassessment*, 90 Nw. U. L. Rev. 387 (1996); Paul G. Cassell, *All Benefits, No Costs: The Grand Illusion of Miranda's Defenders*, 90 Nw. U. L. Rev. 1084 (1996); Paul G. Cassell & Bret S. Hayman, *Police Interrogation in the 1990s: An Empirical Study of the Effects of Miranda*, 43 UCLA L. Rev. 839 (1996); Richard L. Leo, *The Impact of Miranda Revisited*, 86 J. Crim. L. & Criminology 621 (1996); Richard L. Leo, *Inside the Interrogation Room*, 86 J. Crim. L. & Criminology 266 (1996); Stephen J. Schulhofer, *Miranda's Practical Effect: Substantial Benefits and Vanishingly Small Social Costs*, 90 Nw. U. L. Rev. 500 (1996); George C. Thomas III, *Is Miranda a Real-World Failure? A Plea for More (and Better) Empirical Evidence*, 43 UCLA L. Rev. 821 (1996); George C. Thomas III, *Plain Talk About the Miranda Empirical Debate: A "Steady-State" Theory of Confessions*, 43 UCLA L. Rev. 933 (1996).

[78] Ashcraft v. Tennessee, 322 U.S. 143, 160 (1944) (Jackson, J., dissenting).

[79] *Id.*

to make it more difficult for the police to obtain critical confessions. As a consequence, more guilty people will escape justice.

*Miranda* has taken its toll. Researchers in Pittsburgh found that, before *Miranda*, 48.5% of suspects confessed their offenses; immediately after, the rate dropped to 32.3%, and a somewhat later sample produced an even lower figure of 27.1 percent.[80] Before-and-shortly-after figures obtained in other communities (New York County, Philadelphia, New Haven, Washington D.C., Kansas City, Chicago, and Los Angeles) suggest that *Miranda* results in a lost *confession* in about one out of every six criminal cases in this country, and in a lost *conviction* in 3.8% of all serious criminal cases.[81]

*Miranda* continues to hamper the police. Figures from a recent study in Salt Lake City suggest that the police were successful in obtaining confessions in only one-third of the cases surveyed, compared to a 55% to 60% rate before *Miranda*.[82] According to Professor Paul Cassell, the various *Miranda* studies conducted at various times in various jurisdictions demonstrate that *Miranda* has resulted in dismissal of charges in approximately 28,000 violent felony cases yearly.[83]

*What the defenders say:* The practical effect of *Miranda* has been "substantial benefits and vanishingly small social costs."[84] Indeed, many early critics of *Miranda* now concede that the decision has not handcuffed the police.[85]

The studies reported above are flawed on various complicated empirical grounds.[86] Nonetheless, critics of *Miranda* "devote[] considerable effort to milking them for empirical conclusions."[87] Even if we had rigorous empirical calculations of lost confessions, which we do not, there would be reasons "to be skeptical of evidence of a *Miranda* effect: (1) the

---

[80] Richard H. Seeburger & R. Stanton Wettick, Jr., *Miranda in Pittsburgh—A Statistical Study*, 29 U. Pitt. L. Rev. 1 (1967).

[81] Cassell, *Empirical Reassessment*, Note 77, *supra*, at 417, 438.

[82] Cassell & Hayman, Note 77, *supra*, at 871.

[83] Cassell, *Empirical Reassessment*, Note 77, *supra*, at 440.

[84] Schulhofer, Note 77, *supra*.

[85] *See* Schulhofer, Note 37, *supra*, at 456.

[86] Obviously, empirical criticisms of *Miranda* can be no more reliable than the studies themselves that seek to show *Miranda*'s deleterious effects on the interrogation process. For a thorough critique of the methodologies in the *Miranda* studies, *see especially* Schulhofer, Note 77, *supra*; and Thomas, *Plain Talk*, Note 74, *supra*.

[87] Schulhofer, Note 77, *supra*, at 505.

possibility of independent long-term trends; (2) the likelihood of competing causal events; and (3) the instability in the confession rates."[88]

Probably "[t]he only reliable evidence of a statistically significant reduction in confessions is the . . . study in Pittsburgh."[89] Yet, even in that city the Chief of Police told the researchers that *Miranda* had been good for his department, as it "provided an opportunity to professionalize the police."[90] As for the Salt Lake City 3.8% lost-conviction figure, closer scrutiny by Professor Schulhofer suggests that the figure is based on "inconsistent and highly partisan procedures," which when removed, results in a finding of, *at most*, a lost-conviction figure of "a mere seventy-eight one-hundredths of one percent [0.78%] for the immediate post-*Miranda* period, and most likely even less today. For all practical purposes, *Miranda*'s empirically detectable harm to law enforcement shrinks virtually to zero."[91] It follows, therefore, that the Cassell calculation of dismissed cases is grossly over-inflated.[92]

One reason why *Miranda* has had so little impact on the confession rate is that, as one critic of *Miranda* has conceded, "[a]ll the studies suggest that suspects frequently waive their [*Miranda*] rights."[93] Police almost always read suspects the warnings, the suspects predictably[94] and commonly[95] waive their rights, and the interrogations proceed. As a result, *Miranda* "liberate[s] the police,"[96] because the warnings reduce the likelihood that a court will find that the interrogation process was coercive under traditional voluntariness principles.[97]

---

[88] Thomas, *Plain Talk*, Note 77, *supra*, at 937 (crediting Schulhofer, Note 77, *supra*, for identifying these reasons).

[89] Thomas, *Real-World Failure*, Note 77, *supra*, at 830; *see* White, *Defending Miranda*, Note 41, *supra*, at 18–19.

[90] Yale Kamisar, *Landmark Ruling's Had No Detrimental Effect*, Boston Globe, Feb. 1, 1987, at A27, *as quoted in* Schulhofer, Note 37, *supra*, at 458 n.59.

[91] Schulhofer, Note 77, *supra*, at 502.

[92] Schulhofer, *id.* at 546, warns, as well, against citing absolute numbers of dismissed cases that are mere extrapolations based on inherently soft figures and assumptions. Thus, the specific figure Cassell quoted of lost felony cases—or, indeed, *any* specific figure—necessarily tells a misleading story, because it gives a false impression of precision.

[93] Caplan, Note 15, *supra*, at 1466.

[94] As previously noted, *Miranda* is a compromise. The Court did not take its own reasoning to its logical conclusion, namely, to prohibit waivers in the coercive environment of the interrogation room until suspects consult with counsel.

[95] In the Salt Lake City study, *Miranda* waivers were obtained in 83.7% of the cases. Cassell & Hayman, Note 77, *supra*, at 860.

[96] Schulhofer, Note 37, *supra*, at 454.

[97] Berkemer v. McCarty, 468 U.S. 420, 433 n.20 (1984) ("cases in which a defendant can make a colorable argument that a self-incriminating statement was 'compelled' despite the fact that the law enforcement authorities adhered to the dictates of *Miranda* are rare").

## § 24.06 Is *Miranda* a Constitutionally Based Decision?

### [A] Congress and *Miranda*[98]

In 1968, Congress passed the Omnibus Crime Control and Safe Streets Act. It provides in pertinent part:

### [18 U.S.C.] § 3501 Admissibility of confessions

(a) In any criminal prosecution brought by the United States or by the District of Columbia, a confession . . . shall be admissible in evidence if it is voluntarily given. Before such confession is received in evidence, the trial judge shall, out of the presence of the jury, determine any issue as to voluntariness. If the trial judge determines that the confession was voluntarily made it shall be admitted in evidence . . . .

(b) The trial judge in determining the issue of voluntariness shall take into consideration all the circumstances surrounding the giving of the confession, including (1) the time elapsing between arrest and arraignment of the defendant making the confession, if it was made after arrest and before arraignment, (2) whether such defendant knew the nature of the offense for which he was charged or of which he was suspected at the time of making the confession, (3) whether or not such defendant was advised or knew that he was not required to make any statement and that any such statement could be used against him, (4) whether or not such defendant had been advised prior to questioning of his right to the assistance of counsel; and (5) whether or not such defendant was without the assistance of counsel when questioned and when giving such confession.

The presence or absence of any of the above-mentioned factors to be taken into consideration by the judge need not be conclusive on the issue of voluntariness of the confession.

As the Supreme Court observed in *Dickerson v. United States*,[99] "[g]iven § 3501's express designation of voluntariness as the touchstone of admissibility, its omission of any warning requirement, and the instruction for trial

---

[98] For scholarly literature relating to Congress's efforts to overrule *Miranda*, all written before the Supreme Court's opinion in *Dickerson v. United States* (discussed below), *see generally* Paul G. Cassell, *The Statute That Time Forgot: 18 U.S.C. § 3501 and the Overhauling of Miranda*, 85 Iowa L. Rev. 175 (1999); Donald Dripps, *Is the Miranda Caselaw Really Inconsistent? A Proposed Fifth Amendment Synthesis*, 17 Const. Commentary 19 (2000); Yale Kamisar, *Can (Did) Congress "Overrule" Miranda?*, 85 Cornell L. Rev. 883 (2000); Michael Edmund O'Neill, *Undoing Miranda*, 2000 B.Y.U. L. Rev. 185; George C. Thomas III, *The End of the Road for Miranda v. Arizona? On the History and Future of Rules for Police Interrogation*, 37 Am. Crim. L. Rev. 1 (2000).

[99] 530 U.S. 428, 436 (2000).

courts to consider a nonexclusive list of factors relevant to the circumstances of a confession, . . . Congress intended by its enactment to overrule *Miranda*."

Since Congress cannot overrule a constitutional rule, the legitimacy of Section 3501—and *Miranda*'s continued vitality—was placed in issue with enactment of this legislation. For approximately three decades, however, Section 3501 remained dormant: federal law enforcement officers continued to give *Miranda* warnings as a matter of course, and federal prosecutors did not seek admission of confessions when *Miranda* warnings were not properly given.

## [B]  The Early Decisions on *Miranda*'s Constitutionality

The constitutional underpinnings of *Miranda* were seemingly cut out from under it by the Supreme Court in *Michigan v. Tucker*.[100] In *Tucker*, D was not fully informed of his constitutional rights as mandated by *Miranda*. Consequently, the statement obtained by the police was excluded at D's trial. At issue, however, was whether the fruits of the confession—the testimony of a witness whose name was mentioned in the *Miranda*-less statement—was also inadmissible, as a "fruit of the poisonous tree."[101]

In order to resolve the fruit issue, the Court, per Justice William Rehnquist, asked a foundational question: "[W]hether the police conduct complained of directly infringed upon [D's] right against compulsory self-incrimination or whether it instead violated only the prophylactic rules developed to protect that right." The Court's answer was that "[c]ertainly no one could contend that the interrogation faced by [D] bore any resemblance to the historical practices at which the right against compulsory self-incrimination was aimed," namely, the "ecclesiastical inquisitions and Star Chamber proceedings occurring several centuries ago." Therefore, "the police conduct here did not deprive [D] of his privilege against compulsory self-incrimination as such, but rather failed to make available to him the full measure of procedural safeguards associated with that right since *Miranda*."

What did Justice Rehnquist and the Court mean by speaking of *Miranda* as "only" a "prophylactic" rule?[102] Essentially, what most lawyers took from *Tucker* was this: the failure of police to provide proper warnings to a suspect prior to custodial interrogation does not by itself render a confession involuntary in violation of the Fifth Amendment; rather, the omission of full warnings only violates procedural safeguards devised by

---

[100] 417 U.S. 433 (1974).

[101] The *Miranda* fruit issue is considered in § 24.12[B], *infra*.

[102] Regarding prophylactic rules generally, *see* § 4.05, *supra*.

the Court in *Miranda in order to prevent an actual violation of the Constitution.* As the Court subsequently put it, "[t]he *Miranda* exclusionary rule . . . serves the Fifth Amendment and *sweeps more broadly than the Fifth Amendment itself. It may be triggered even in the absence of a Fifth Amendment violation.*"[103]

The *Tucker* Court's interpretation of *Miranda* was criticized as "an outright rejection of [its] core premises,"[104] and inconsistent with language in *Miranda*[105] and various pre-*Tucker* Court explanations of the case.[106] Although the Court in *Miranda* stated that Congress could devise alternative means to prevent involuntary confessions, it also indicated that in the absence of the warnings or remedies at least as effective, *any* custodial interrogation was *inherently coercive.*

*Tucker* seemingly deconstitutionalized *Miranda*. It provided support for the argument that Congress possessed the authority to reject *Miranda* and either return the law to its pre-*Miranda* position or (at a minimum) develop alternatives to the *Miranda* warnings. Moreover, since the Supreme Court lacks general supervisory authority over state judicial proceedings,[107] *Tucker* called into question whether the federal judiciary could require states to enforce the *Miranda* warnings.

### [C] The Answer: *Dickerson v. United States*[108]

In *Dickerson, D* moved to suppress statements he made to F.B.I. agents during custodial interrogation on the ground that he had not received his *Miranda* warnings. The trial court granted his motion, but the United States Court of Appeals for the Fourth Circuit reversed on the ground that Section 3501 superseded *Miranda*; and, applying that statute, the Fourth Circuit concluded that *D*'s statements were voluntarily made. The Supreme Court granted a hearing in *Dickerson* to decide, at last, whether Section 3501 was constitutional.

Writing for a seven-member majority, Chief Justice Rehnquist—the author of the *Tucker* opinion that seemed to deconstitutionalize

---

[103] Oregon v. Elstad, 470 U.S. 298, 306 (1985) (emphasis added).

[104] Stone, Note 23, *supra*, at 118.

[105] *See* § 24.04[C][1], *supra*.

[106] *E.g.*, Orozco v. Texas, 394 U.S. 324, 326 (1969) ("[T]he use of these admissions obtained in the absence of the required warnings was a *flat violation of the Self-Incrimination Clause of the Fifth Amendment* . . . .") (emphasis added).

[107] Smith v. Phillips, 455 U.S. 209, 221 (1982); *see generally* § 4.04, *supra*.

[108] 530 U.S. 428 (2000); *see generally* Donald A. Drips, *Constitutional Theory for Criminal Procedure:* Dickerson, Miranda *and the Continuing Quest for Broad-but-Shallow*, 43 Wm. and Mary 1 (2001); Yale Kamisar, *Miranda Thirty-Five Years Later: A Close Look at the Majority and Dissenting Opinions in* Dickerson, 33 Ariz St. L.J. 387 (2001).

*Miranda*—stated that *Miranda* was "a constitutional decision" and, as he also put it, *Miranda* has "constitutional origin," "constitutional underpinnings," and a "constitutional basis." Therefore, the majority held, *Miranda* could not be overruled by an Act of Congress. Moreover, the Court declined to overrule *Miranda* itself.[109] Although defenders of *Miranda* were obviously pleased by this outcome, early scholarly analysis of *Dickerson* suggests that virtually nobody has found the Court's opinion intellectually satisfying.[110]

The Supreme Court found support for the constitutional basis of *Miranda* in the language of *Miranda* itself, and in various post-*Miranda* cases.[111] The Chief Justice conceded "that there is language in some of our opinions that supports the view" that *Miranda* is not constitutionally based. But, Rehnquist parsed the language of the *Miranda* opinion to show that it was "replete with statements indicating that the majority thought it was announcing a constitutional rule." Of course, this observation is correct: that is why the Chief Justice's opinion in *Tucker*, the first case to characterize *Miranda* as a prophylactic rule, was criticized for rejecting *Miranda*'s core premises.

The Chief Justice also found support for the proposition that *Miranda* is based on the Constitution from the Court's "invitation for legislative action to protect the constitutional right against coerced self-incrimination." Rehnquist stated that the *Miranda* decision, by inviting Congressional action, intended to avoid creating a "constitutional straightjacket," but that "a review of our opinion . . . clarifies that this disclaimer was intended to indicate that the Constitution does not require police to administer the particular *Miranda* warnings, not that the Constitution does not require a procedure that is effective in securing Fifth Amendment rights."

These arguments, founded largely on language in *Miranda*, were of secondary importance compared to another basis: "first and foremost of the factors on the other side—that *Miranda* is a constitutional decision—is that both *Miranda* and two of its companion cases applied the rule to proceedings in state courts . . . ." That is, since the Supreme Court lacks supervisory authority over state proceedings, and since the high court enforced the

---

[109] Although the Court's ruling meant that Dickerson's confession had to be excluded, as frequently occurs in such circumstances the suppression did not result in a lost conviction for the government. Dickerson was convicted of robbery in a retrial, even without use of the statement. He was sentenced to ten years' imprisonment. *Man Sentenced in Case That Upheld Miranda*, New York Times, Jan. 6, 2001, at A9.

[110] Scholarship relating to *Dickerson* is burgeoning. *See especially* Symposium, *Miranda After Dickerson: The Future of Confession Law*,, 99 Mich. L.Rev. 879-1247 (2001); *see also* Note 103, *supra*.

[111] *Dickerson*, 530 U.S. at 440 n.5 (citing and quoting post-*Miranda* cases that "referred to *Miranda*'s constitutional underpinnings").

rule it announced in *Miranda* in state cases, this means that *Miranda must* be a constitutional decision.

Justice Scalia (writing also for Justice Thomas) described the latter argument as "a classic example of begging the question." To him, the issue is not whether the Court once (or even now) considered *Miranda* a constitutional decision, but rather whether the dictates of *Miranda*, in fact, are constitutionally based. If not, Scalia wrote, "our continued application of the *Miranda* code to the States despite our consistent statements that running afoul of its dictates does not necessarily—or even usually—result in an actual constitutional violation, represents not the source of *Miranda*'s salvation but rather evidence of its ultimate illegitimacy."

The majority in *Dickerson* also refused to overrule *Miranda,* but it provided no ringing endorsement of the case. The Chief Justice stated that "[w]hether or not we would agree with *Miranda*'s reasoning and its resulting rule, were we addressing the issue in the first instance, the principles of *stare decisis* weigh heavily against overruling it now." The majority stated that while " '*stare decisis* is not an inexorable command,' " the doctrine should be followed absent some special justification. Here, there "is [no] such justification for overruling *Miranda. Miranda* has become embedded in routine police practice to the point where the warnings have become part of our national culture."

The outcome in *Dickerson* presumably pleases those who wanted *Miranda* retained. And, there is no longer significant opposition to *Miranda* in police ranks, perhaps because, as Rehnquist stated, the Court's "subsequent cases have reduced the impact of the *Miranda* rule on legitimate"— and, some would say, even illegitimate—"law enforcement" techniques. But, *Dickerson* leaves important questions unanswered, not the least of which is whether prior Supreme Court opinions limiting the scope of *Miranda* have been undercut by *Dickerson.* As is developed below,[112] the Court has created exceptions to the it;Miranda rules on the ground that *Miranda* announced a mere prophylactic rule. With that distinction seemingly lost, Justice Scalia has suggested that "the Court must [now] come up with some other explanation" for the *Miranda* exceptions. And, he observes, "[t]hat will take quite a bit of doing."

Another aspect of *Dickerson*, which goes beyond the significance of *Miranda*, deserves attention. To the extent that *Dickerson* stands for the proposition that *Miranda* announced a prophylactic rule (the requirement of *Miranda* warnings) to protect a constitutional right—*and that this makes the case a constitutional decision*—this seems to mean that prophylactic

---

[112] *See especially* § 24.12, *infra.*

rules have nearly as much power as constitutional rights. *Dickerson* may teach—although it never speaks to the question explicitly—that states and Congress cannot tamper with prophylactic rules except to devise alternative rules that are as or more effective in guarding against constitutional violations.

Justice Scalia declared in *Dickerson* that this means that the Court "has the power not merely to apply the Constitution but to expand it, imposing what it regards as useful 'prophylactic' restrictions upon Congress and the States"? According to Scalia this is "frightening antidemocratic power." But, many scholars believe that there is nothing inconsistent about the Court saying that the legislature can do as a good a job as the judiciary in designing rules to protect constitutional rights, but also saying that in the absence of acceptable legislatively-devised safeguards, the judiciary has the right—and even obligation—to set out and require the enforcement of prophylactic rules.[113]

## § 24.07   Meaning of *Miranda*: "Custody"[114]

### [A]   General Principles

*Miranda* warnings prior to questioning are required "only where there has been such a restriction on a person's freedom as to render him 'in custody.' "[115] According to *Miranda*, "custody" arises when a person is "taken into custody or otherwise deprived of his freedom of action in any significant way." As the Court has subsequently explained that phrase, a person is "in custody" for purposes of receiving *Miranda* warnings if "there is a 'formal arrest or restraint on freedom of movement' of the degree associated with a formal arrest."[116]

In determining whether a person is in custody, "a court must examine all of the circumstances surrounding the interrogation."[117] Ironically, therefore, although *Miranda* was intended to serve as a bright-line alternative to the totality-of-the-circumstances voluntariness standard, there is often no bright line (formal arrests aside) for determining whether "custody" exists and, therefore, whether *Miranda* applies.

---

[113] *See* David A. Strauss, *Miranda, The Constitution, and Congress*, 99 Mich. L. Rev. 958 (2001).

[114] *See generally* Daniel Yeager, *Rethinking Custodial Interrogation*, 28 Am. Crim. L. Rev. 1 (1990).

[115] Oregon v. Mathiason, 429 U.S. 492, 495 (1977).

[116] California v. Beheler, 463 U.S. 1121, 1125 (1983) (quoting Oregon v. Mathiason, 429 U.S. at 495)).

[117] Stansbury v. California, 511 U.S. 318, 322 (1994).

One matter that is *not* a factor, however, in determining whether a subject is in custody is an "officer's subjective and undisclosed view concerning whether the person being interrogated is a suspect."[118] Instead, "the only relevant inquiry is how a reasonable man in the suspect's position would have understood his situation."[119]

For example, in *Berkemer v. McCarty*,[120] *O*, a police officer, observed *D* driving erratically on a highway. *O* forced *D* to pull over and get out of the car. When *D* complied, *O* noticed that *D* had difficulty standing. At that moment, *O* *subjectively* determined that *D* would be charged with a driving offense and taken to jail. Without informing *D* of his *Miranda* rights, *O* asked *D* whether he had been using intoxicants.

The Supreme Court held that *D*'s answer to the question was admissible, because *D* was not in custody. *O*'s unarticulated plan to arrest *D* had no bearing on the issue. The Court concluded that at the moment of the brief questioning, a reasonable driver in *D*'s situation would *not* have believed that he was in a situation that could "fairly be characterized as the functional equivalent of formal arrest." In contrast, if an officer's conduct in relation to a suspect would cause a reasonable person in the suspect's position to believe that he is functionally under arrest, although he is not, *Miranda* warnings are required prior to interrogation. The relevant inquiry in all cases is, simply, "how a reasonable person in the position of the individual being questioned would gauge the breadth of his or her 'freedom of action.' "[121]

## [B]  General Principles: In Greater Detail

### [1]  Does "Focus" Equal "Custody"?

The *Miranda* opinion suggested that "custody" and "focus" (as the latter term was used in *Escobedo v. Illinois*[122] ) were synonyms.[123] In fact, however, as the Court has since conceded, "focus" can exist in the absence of "custody," in which case *Miranda* warnings are not required.

For example, in *Beckwith v. United States*,[124] *D* was questioned by Internal Revenue Service agents at his home. At the time of the questioning, *D* was the focus of a criminal tax investigation. Nonetheless, because *D*

---

[118] *Id.* at 319.

[119] Berkemer v. McCarty, 468 U.S. 420, 442 (1984).

[120] 468 U.S. 420 (1984).

[121] Stansbury v. California, 511 U.S. at 324 (quoting Berkemer v. McCarty, 468 U.S. at 440).

[122] 378 U.S. 478 (1964). *See* § 24.03, *supra.*

[123] *See* the text accompanying Note 32, *supra.*

[124] 425 U.S. 341 (1976).

was not in custody at the time of the questioning — a reasonable person in *D*'s situation would have believed that he was free to leave or to ask the agents to go — *Miranda* warnings were not required.

### [2]   Does *Miranda* Apply Outside the Police Station?

*Miranda* warnings are required prior to custodial interrogation, regardless of the site of the interrogation.

A person may be in custody in his own home. In *Orozco v. Texas*,[125] the Court held that *D* was in custody when four police officers entered his bedroom and questioned him there at 4:00 a.m. One of the officers testified that *D* was under arrest at the time of the questioning, although *D* had not been informed of this fact. Presumably, however, in light of the timing of the interrogation, the pointed nature of the questions, and the fact that four armed officers were present, a reasonable person in *D*'s situation would have believed that he was in custody. Therefore, *Miranda* warnings were required.

On the other hand, a person is not necessarily in custody in an interrogation room. In *California v. Beheler*,[126] *D* voluntarily agreed to accompany police to the station house, in order to be questioned about a homicide that he had reported to them. At the police station, he answered questions that the police did not preface with *Miranda* warnings. The questioning took 30 minutes, after which he was permitted to leave. Five days later, *D* was arrested in connection with the homicide. The Court held that the *Miranda*-less statements *D* made were admissible: although the interrogation occurred in a police station, *D* was not in custody.

### [3]   Does *Miranda* Apply to Minor Offenses?

In *Berkemer v. McCarty*,[127] *D* was arrested for driving his car under the influence of alcohol, a misdemeanor offense. He was transported by patrol car to the jail, where he was questioned without *Miranda* warnings. The government argued that *Miranda* warnings should not be required prior to questioning for minor traffic offenses. With such offenses, it argued, "the police have no reason to subject . . . . a suspect to the sort of interrogation that most troubled the Court in *Miranda*." Also, enforcement of minor traffic offenses "would be more expeditious and effective" without the warnings.

The Court refused to carve out the suggested exception. *Miranda* warnings are required prior to custodial interrogation for *any* criminal

---

[125] 394 U.S. 324 (1969).

[126] 463 U.S. 1121 (1983).

[127] 468 U.S. 420 (1984).

offense.[128] According to Justice Thurgood Marshall, "[o]ne of the principal advantages of the [*Miranda*] doctrine . . . is the clarity of that rule," which would be undermined by the proposed exception. Justice Marshall pointed out that the police are often unaware whether the person they have arrested has committed a felony or a misdemeanor; therefore, they would not know whether *Miranda* warnings were required. There is also the possibility that questioning about one offense, a misdemeanor, might move imperceptibly into questioning about another, more serious, crime. The Court also discounted the assumption that police abuses never occur during interrogations for offenses denominated by the state as minor.

### [4] Does *Miranda* Apply to a *"Terry* Stop"?

*Miranda* warnings are required if a person is deprived of his freedom of action "in any significant way." The key word is "significant." A person is not in custody for purposes of *Miranda* merely because his freedom of movement has been curtailed by the police, *i.e.*, that he has been "seized" in a Fourth Amendment *Terry v. Ohio*[129] sense of that term.

The Supreme Court held in *Berkemer v. McCarty*[130] that a motorist is not "in custody" if he is subjected to roadside questioning during a routine traffic stop. Traffic stops are brief, occur in public, and usually involve only one or two officers. Consequently, the motorist does not feel "completely at the mercy of the police." "Custody" does not take place in the absence of coercive conditions at the scene that would cause a reasonable person to believe that he is in a situation that may "fairly be characterized as the functional equivalent of formal arrest."

### [5] Are *Miranda* Warnings Required In All "Coercive Environments"?

As the preceding analysis of *Miranda* "custody" law might suggest, there is no necessary correlation between "custody" and a "coercive environment." In a significant sense, therefore, the law of "custody" has been cut off from the conceptual underpinnings of *Miranda*.

For example, in *Oregon v. Mathiason*,[131] *D* was a parolee suspected of a burglary. At the request of the police, *D* agreed to come to the police station, where he was questioned in the absence of *Miranda* warnings, in an office with the door closed. A reviewing court found that the questioning took place in a coercive environment. Moreover, the police used a technique

---

[128] *But see* Note 33, *supra*.

[129] 392 U.S. 1 (1968). *See* chapter 18, *supra*.

[130] 468 U.S. 420 (1984).

[131] 429 U.S. 492 (1977).

noted and criticized in *Miranda*: they falsely told *D* that they had evidence implicating him in the crime.

The Supreme Court held that, on these facts, *Miranda* warnings were not required because *D* was not in custody during the interview: prior to questioning he was told he was not under arrest, and he left the station after the questioning. According to *Mathiason*, "[s]uch a non-custodial situation is not converted to one in which *Miranda* applies simply because a reviewing court concludes that . . . the questioning took place in a 'coercive environment.' " In dissent, Justice Marshall complained that "surely formalities alone cannot control." Justice John Stevens, also in dissent, called the majority's reasoning "formalistic." But, in this case, form trumped substance.

The converse may also be the case. For example, suppose that the police arrest Donald in his home for a very minor offense. Without giving *Miranda* warnings, the police ask a single question, "Did you do it?" Because Donald is in custody, his incriminating answer would be inadmissible under *Miranda*, yet the environment in which the one question was asked—in Donald's home, perhaps in the presence of family members; a minor offense; and no threats or tricks—is far less coercive than the conditions that confronted the suspect in *Mathiason*.

The reasons that animated the *Miranda* Court to require warnings were far more in place in the interrogation room in which parolee Mathiason found himself than in Donald's home. Bright-line rules, by their nature, will result in anomalous outcomes in some cases, but the *Miranda* Court intended for the bright-line rule to redound to the benefit of the suspect.

## § 24.08  Meaning of *Miranda*: "Interrogation"[132]

### [A]  In General

#### [1]  Rule

In *Rhode Island v. Innis*,[133] *D* was arrested for a murder in which the weapon used in the crime had not yet been discovered. *D* was placed in a police car with three officers. En route to the station, one of the officers said to a colleague that a school for handicapped children was in the vicinity, and that "God forbid one of [the children] might find a weapon with shells and they might hurt themselves." After the officer added that "it would be too bad if a little girl would pick up the gun, maybe kill herself," *D*

---

[132] *See generally* Welsh S. White, *Interrogation Without Questions: Rhode Island v. Innis and United States v. Henry*, 78 Mich. L. Rev. 1209 (1980); Yeager, Note 105, *supra*.

[133] 446 U.S. 291 (1980).

interrupted and offered to show the police where he had abandoned the weapon.

These events occurred after *Miranda* warnings had been given. However, because *D* had previously requested to see a lawyer, the police were required to cease interrogation until *D* talked to his attorney.[134] The precise issue in the case, therefore, was whether the handicapped-children statement by the officer constituted "interrogation," so as to violate the "cease interrogation" rule.

According to *Innis*, for purposes of *Miranda*, "interrogation" refers not only to "express questioning," but also to its "functional equivalent." The "functional equivalent" of express questioning is "any words or actions on the part of the police (other than those normally attendant to arrest and custody) that the police should know are reasonably likely to elicit an incriminating response from the suspect."

### [2] A Closer Look at the Rule

According to *Innis*, the "functional equivalent" form of interrogation "focuses primarily upon the perceptions of the suspect, rather than the intent of the police." In other words, the officer's subjective intent to elicit an incriminating response by his words or actions is not the key. Instead, the *Innis* test is primarily objective: *should* the officer have realized that his acts or words were *reasonably likely* to result in an incriminating response from the suspect? In criminal *mens rea* terms, an "interrogation" occurs if an officer was negligent in failing to foresee that his words or actions were likely to result in a statement from the suspect.

Although the mental state of the police officer is not the focus of the *Innis* test, it may be relevant in determining whether an interrogation has occurred. The Court warned that "any knowledge the police may have had concerning the susceptibility of a defendant to a particular form of persuasion might be an important factor in determining whether the police should have known that their words or actions were reasonably likely to elicit an incriminating response."

*Brewer v. Williams*,[135] a Sixth Amendment case,[136] provides an example of what the Court probably had in mind in *Innis*. In *Williams*, the police

---

[134] *See* § 24.10[B][3][a], *infra*.

[135] 430 U.S. 387 (1977).

[136] *Innis* states that the definition of "interrogation" for *Miranda* purposes is *not* informed by the Court's Sixth Amendment right-to-counsel jurisprudence. Under the latter provision, the government may not "deliberately elicit" an incriminating response from a person formally charged with a crime in the absence of the accused's lawyer. Thus, the latter test is subjective, not objective. *See* §§ 25.02 and 25.05[A], *infra*.

subjected *D*, a person whom they knew to be a highly religious man and a recent escapee from a mental hospital, to a "Christian burial speech." The speech was designed to convince *D* to tell the officers where the body of a young rape-homicide victim had been hidden, so that her parents could give her a "Christian burial." Although *D* did not respond immediately, he eventually made incriminating remarks and led them to the body.

The Court in *Williams* did not consider the implications of the police conduct in light of *Miranda*. However, under the definition of "interrogation" developed in *Innis*, and in light of the officers' knowledge of *D*'s mental instability and his susceptibility to religious pleas, the "Christian burial speech" very likely would have satisfied the *Innis* "interrogation" test.

In *Innis*, however, the majority concluded that the handicapped-children statement did not amount to the functional equivalent of "interrogation." The Court implicitly distinguished *Williams*: it noted that the police conversation here was brief (it was not "a lengthy harangue in the presence of the suspect"); the comments were not especially "evocative"; and there was no evidence that the officers knew that *D* was "peculiarly susceptible to an appeal to conscience,"[137] or that he was disoriented or upset when the remarks were made.[138]

The state of mind of a police officer may be relevant for a second reason, notwithstanding the objective nature of the *Innis* test. In a footnote, the Court stated that the officer's intent "may well have a bearing on whether the police should have known that their words or actions were reasonably likely to evoke an incriminating response."

How can this be, in light of the objective nature of the *Innis* test? One scholar has suggested that "the best reading of the *Innis* test is that it turns upon the *objective* purpose *manifested* by the police."[139] That is, an officer

---

[137] This conclusion is dubious. As Justice Marshall pointed out in dissent, an appeal to a suspect's conscience is a classic interrogation technique recommended in the police manuals criticized in *Miranda*. An officer's call-to-conscience will often succeed where a direct, accusatorial question will not.

[138] Many lower courts not favorably inclined to *Miranda* have interpreted the Supreme Court's analysis in *Innis* as giving them permission to apply the test announced in the case in an exceptionally narrow—some would say, unrealistic—way. *E.g.,* Gates v. Commonwealth, 516 S.E.2d 731 (Va. App. 1999) (the police did not engage in "interrogation" by bringing *D* from his jail cell, where he was incarcerated on other charges, to a police interrogation room, where officers executed an arrest warrant by informing *D* that he was under arrest for murder and proceeding to read the warrant to the defendant; *D*, angry, interrupted the reading and made a statement).

[139] White, Note 127, *supra,* at 1231.

should know that his words or actions are reasonably likely to result in an incriminating response when he "should realize that the . . . conduct will probably be viewed by the suspect as designed to achieve this purpose." Under this reading, not yet confirmed by the Supreme Court, the following standard would apply: "if an objective observer (with the same knowledge of the suspect as the police officer) would, on the sole basis of hearing the officer's remarks, infer that the remarks were designed to elicit an incriminating response, then the remarks should constitute 'interrogation.' "[140]

### [B]   When Is an Interrogation Not a *Miranda* "Interrogation"?

The "interrogation" standard examined above is subject to two limitations. First, *Miranda* warnings are not required, even in response to direct questioning or its functional equivalent, if the person interrogated does not know that the questioner is a law enforcement officer. In short, custodial interrogation by an undercover officer is not the type of "interrogation" that triggers a requirement of *Miranda* warnings.[141]

Second, *Miranda* warnings are intended to protect a custodial suspect's Fifth Amendment privilege against compulsory self-incrimination. However, the Fifth Amendment does *not* protect a person from being compelled to produce "real or physical evidence," as distinguished from evidence of a "testimonial or communicative" nature.[142] Therefore, the Fifth Amendment is not violated if a person is ordered, for example, to produce a blood sample or voice exemplar, even though the results may incriminate him.

It follows from this that *Miranda* only applies if the "testimonial or communicative" component of the Fifth Amendment privilege is implicated by the police interrogation. For example, suppose that *O* arrests *D* for drunk driving. Without providing *Miranda* warnings, *O* conducts a sobriety test in which *D*'s responses to direct questions (*e.g.*, "what is your name?"; "how old are you?"; "who is the President of the United States?") are videotaped. *D*'s answers to these direct questions—interrogation—are not rendered inadmissible by *Miranda* merely because the slurred nature of his answers will incriminate him. As the Court has explained, "[r]equiring a suspect to reveal the physical manner in which he articulates words, like requiring him to reveal the physical properties of the sound produced by his voice . . . does not, without more, compel him to provide a 'testimonial' response for purposes of the privilege."[143]

---

[140] *Id.* at 1232.

[141] Illinois v. Perkins, 496 U.S. 292 (1990). *See* § 24.11[B], *infra.*

[142] Schmerber v. California, 384 U.S. 757 (1966). This important distinction is explained in detail at § 26.05[D][1], *infra.*

[143] Pennsylvania v. Muniz, 496 U.S. 582, 592 (1990).

In contrast, the Fifth Amendment (and, therefore, *Miranda*) is implicated if the *content* of *D*'s answers—*e.g.*, if *D*'s answers the questions incorrectly—suggests that his mental state is confused. In this situation, the inference of *D*'s intoxication is drawn from a testimonial act (his answers) and not from physical evidence (slurred speech).[144]

## § 24.09 Adequacy of *Miranda* Warnings

The Supreme Court announced in *California v. Prysock*[145] that no "talismanic incantation" of the *Miranda* warnings is required, as long as the officer's explanation of the suspect's constitutional rights is a "fully effective equivalent" of the *Miranda* warnings. Thus, although a benefit of *Miranda* is its supposed bright-line nature, and the *Miranda* warnings themselves are easily stated, the Court has approved a case-by-case factual inquiry when officers "ad lib" or a police department develops a different version of the warnings.

Although this rule is not in direct conflict with *Miranda*, the Court's application of it in *Duckworth v. Eagan*[146] arguably "dealt *Miranda* a heavy blow."[147] In *Duckworth*, the police read *D* a set of warnings that included the following remarks:

> Anything you say can be used against you in court. *You have a right to talk to a lawyer for advice before we ask you any questions, and to have him with you during questioning.* You have this right to the advice and presence of a lawyer even if you cannot afford to hire one. *We have no way of giving you a lawyer, but one will be appointed for you, if you wish, if and when you go to court. . . .*

In view of the second italicized remark, a federal court concluded that the warnings were defective because *D*, an indigent, could reasonably have interpreted the words to mean that a lawyer would not be available to him until formal charges were brought, even if the questioning proceeded immediately.

The Supreme Court declared the warnings adequate. According to Chief Justice Rehnquist, "[t]he inquiry is simply whether the warnings reasonably 'conve[y] to [a suspect] his rights as required by *Miranda*.' "[148] He stated

---

[144] *Id.* at 593.

[145] 453 U.S. 355 (1981).

[146] 492 U.S. 195 (1989).

[147] Yale Kamisar, *Duckworth v. Eagan: A Little-Noticed Miranda Case That May Cause Much Mischief*, 25 Crim. L. Bull. 550, 552 (1989).

[148] *Duckworth*, 492 U.S. at 203 (alteration in original) (quoting California v. Prysock, 453 U.S. at 361).

that, in view of the first italicized sentence above, the warnings made sufficiently clear that questioning would not occur until *D* had a lawyer or waived the right. The warnings "touched all of the bases required by *Miranda*," and the officer's additional comment was accurate in terms of state law and under *Miranda*.[149] Professor Yale Kamisar has observed, however, that "if [*D*] were a smart, sophisticated fellow, he might have dissected the . . . police warning the way [the Court] did . . . . But the *Miranda* warnings weren't designed for smart, sophisticated people."[150]

## § 24.10 Waiver of *Miranda* Rights

### [A] In General

#### [1] Overview

Most suspects in custody waive their constitutional rights after receiving *Miranda* warnings.[151] Therefore, *Miranda* waiver jurisprudence is of great significance. If the prosecution wishes to introduce a statement at trial obtained by the police as the result of custodial interrogation, a court must determine whether the suspect validly waived his rights. The general principles relating to waiver are considered in this subsection. Special issues arise if, before or during interrogation, a custodial suspect asserts his Fifth Amendment privilege against self-incrimination, or if he requests assistance of counsel. The law in *this* regard in considered in subsection [B].

#### [2] Types of Waiver: Express versus Implied

*Miranda* states that "a valid waiver will not be presumed simply from the silence of the accused after warnings are given or simply from the fact that a confession was in fact actually obtained." It states that an express waiver, followed "closely" by a statement, "could" constitute a valid waiver. The implication seems to be that the *Miranda* Court envisioned that waivers would be expressed, rather than implied.

Nonetheless, the Court held in *North Carolina v. Butler*[152] that "an explicit statement of waiver is not invariably necessary to support a finding that the defendant waived the right to remain silent or the right to counsel

---

[149] That is, *Miranda* does not require the presence of a "stationhouse lawyer." Waiver issues aside, *Miranda* only requires that the police not interrogate a suspect who cannot be furnished immediate legal assistance until counsel can be obtained.

[150] Kamisar, Note 142, *supra*, at 554.

[151] *See* Notes 92–97 and the text thereto, *supra*; for discussion of the techniques used by police to secure waivers, *see* Richard A. Leo & Welsh S. White, *Adapting to Miranda: Modern Interrogators' Strategies for Dealing with the Obstacles Posed by Miranda*, 84 Minn. L. Rev. 397, 431–450 (1999).

[152] 441 U.S. 369, 375–76 (1979).

guaranteed by the *Miranda* case." According to *Butler*, although the burden of proof is on the government to prove that the suspect validly waived his *Miranda* rights, "in at least some cases waiver can be clearly inferred from the actions and words of the person interrogated," after *Miranda* warnings are given.

The Court has had little more to say on the matter, leaving to lower courts the task of determining when a waiver may be inferred from a suspect's actions or words.

### [3]   Elements of a Valid Waiver

### [a]   Generally

*Miranda* provides that a "defendant may waive effectuation of [his] rights, provided that the waiver is made voluntarily, knowingly and intelligently." As such, the Court effectively applied the strict waiver standard first announced in *Johnson v. Zerbst*,[153] which declared that a constitutional right may not be waived unless there is "an intentional relinquishment or abandonment of a known right or privilege."

According to *Miranda*, a suspect's waiver is not valid unless the prosecutor overcomes an undefined "heavy burden" of proof that the waiver was voluntary, knowing, and intelligent. In *Colorado v. Connelly*,[154] however, the Court held that this "heavy burden" is met if the prosecutor proves the validity of the waiver by a preponderance of the evidence. The matter of waiver "depends in each case 'upon the particular facts and circumstances surrounding that case, including the background, experience, and conduct of the accused.' "[155]

### [b]   Voluntariness of the Waiver

A waiver must be voluntary, *i.e.*, "the product of a free and deliberate choice rather than intimidation, coercion, or deception."[156] In determining voluntariness, the Court has stated that "[t]here is obviously no reason to require more in the way of a 'voluntariness' inquiry in the *Miranda* waiver context than in the Fourteenth Amendment confession context."[157]

As with rights located in the due process clause, a waiver of *Miranda* rights is not involuntary if the "moral and psychological pressures to confess

---

[153] 304 U.S. 458 (1938); *see* Edwards v. Arizona, 451 U.S. 477, 482 (1981) (acknowledging that *Zerbst* is the applicable test).

[154] 479 U.S. 157 (1986).

[155] Edwards v. Arizona, 451 U.S. at 482 (quoting Johnson v. Zerbst, 304 U.S. at 464).

[156] Moran v. Burbine, 475 U.S. 412, 421 (1986).

[157] Colorado v. Connelly, 479 U.S. 153, 169–70 (1986).

emanat[e] from sources other than official coercion."[158] For example, a suspect's waiver of his *Miranda* rights is valid if he was "coerced" to do so by his belief that God commanded him to confess or commit suicide.[159] Furthermore, the Court has held that the internal psychological pressures that arise from having a "guilty secret" do not invalidate a subsequent decision to confess.[160] Beyond this, due process jurisprudence applies to the voluntariness prong of *Miranda* waiver law, and may be incorporated by reference here.[161]

Thus, there is a historical irony. *Miranda* was intended as a bright-line alternative to the much-criticized, totality-of-the-circumstances "voluntariness" standard that preceded it. Nonetheless, "voluntariness" jurisprudence has returned, although this time in the disguise of *Miranda* waiver law.

### [c] Knowing and Intelligent Waiver

To be valid, a "waiver must have been made with a full awareness of both the nature of the right being abandoned and the consequences of the decision to abandon it."[162]

The Court has not enforced this rule strictly. For example, in *Oregon v. Elstad*,[163] D confessed to a crime before *Miranda* warnings were given. Thereafter, the police read D the *Miranda* warnings, after which D waived his rights and provided more incriminating statements. D argued that his post-*Miranda* statements should be excluded, in part on the ground that he wrongly believed that "the cat was out of the bag." That is, he did not know when he made the second statement that his earlier confession was inadmissible; therefore, he wrongly believed that he had nothing to lose in confessing a second time, and his waiver was thus not knowingly and intelligently made.

The Court disagreed. It explained that "[t]his Court has never embraced the theory that a defendant's ignorance of the full consequences of his decisions vitiates their voluntariness." It is not true that "the *sine qua non* for a knowing and voluntary waiver of the right to remain silent is a full and complete appreciation of all of the consequences flowing from the nature and quality of the evidence in the case." Thus, a defendant must have a "full awareness" of the consequences of abandoning the *Miranda* rights, but need not have awareness of the *full* consequences.

---

[158] Oregon v. Elstad, 470 U.S. 298, 305 (1985).

[159] Colorado v. Connelly, 479 U.S. 157 (1986).

[160] Oregon v. Elstad, 470 U.S. 298 (1985).

[161] *See* § 23.03, *supra.*

[162] Moran v. Burbine, 475 U.S. 412, 421 (1986).

[163] 470 U.S. 298 (1985).

For example, a waiver is valid even if the suspect is not aware of the possible topics of the interrogation. In *Colorado v. Spring*, [164] *D* was arrested for interstate transportation of stolen firearms. Based on prior information that linked him to a murder, the after-waiver interrogation turned quickly from the firearms charge to the uncharged murder. *D* ultimately confessed to the latter crime. The Court held that *D*'s waiver was knowing and intelligent, although he did not know he was going to be questioned about the murder when he gave up his rights: he knew what his rights were, including the right to cut off questioning at any time; and he knew that *any* statement he made could be used against him.

### [4]  *Moran v. Burbine*: Waiver in the Post-*Miranda* Era

*Moran v. Burbine* [165] is a case that deserves special attention. It is important not only for what it says about *Miranda* waiver law, but also for what it demonstrates, namely, the distance the Court has traveled since the days of *Escobedo v. Illinois* [166] and *Miranda*.

In *Burbine*, *D* was arrested for a murder. As a result of *D*'s sister's efforts, an attorney called the police station in the evening and informed a detective that she would act as *D*'s counsel in the event that the police intended to interrogate him. The officer assured the lawyer that *D* would not be interrogated that night, In fact, however, less than an hour later, the police conducted the first of a series of interviews with *D* regarding the homicide. Prior to each session, *D* was informed of his *Miranda* rights, and he signed written forms waiving his right to counsel. At no time, however, was *D* informed that his sister had retained counsel for him, nor was he aware of his counsel's telephone conversation with the police.

In an opinion written by Justice Sandra O'Connor, the Court held, 6-3, that the police followed acceptable *Miranda* procedures, and that the record

---

[164] 479 U.S. 564 (1987).

[165] 475 U.S. 412 (1986); *contra, under state constitution*, Bryan v. State, 571 A.2d 170 (Del. 1990) (waiver is invalid if police intentionally or negligently fail to inform a suspect during custodial interrogation that his lawyer wants to confer); People v. McCauley, 645 N.E.2d 923 (Ill. 1994) (due process is violated if police interfere with an attorney-client relationship by preventing a custodial suspect, under interrogation, from receiving the immediately available assistance of his own attorney); People v. Bender, 551 N.W.2d 71 (Mich. 1996) (plurality opinion) (suspect has a right to know that his lawyer wishes to seem him, whether the request comes in person, over telephone, or by way of messenger); Commonwealth v. Mavredakis, 725 N.E.2d 169 (Mass. 2000) (information regarding the immediate availability of an identified attorney who is actually able to provide assistance has a bearing on the suspect's ability to knowingly and intelligently waive his constitutional rights); State v. Reed, 627 A.2d 630 (N.J. 1993) (waiver is invalid if the police refuse to inform the suspect before or during interrogation that an attorney wishes to confer with him).

[166] 378 U.S. 478 (1964). *See* § 24.03, *supra*.

supported the state court finding that *D*'s waiver of his *Miranda* rights, his right to counsel in particular, was voluntary, knowing, and intelligent.

The Court granted that the police conduct was "objectionable as a matter of ethics." It "share[d] [*D*'s] distaste for the deliberate misleading of an officer of the court." However, "even deliberate deception of an attorney could not possibly affect a suspect's decision to waive his *Miranda* rights." That is, unlike in *Escobedo*, in which the police falsely told the *suspect* that his attorney did not want to see him, the deception here was directed at the *attorney*. Therefore, the police misconduct, unknown to *D*, could not have affected the voluntariness of his waiver.

The Court concluded, as well, that the undisclosed information did not deprive *D* of the "knowledge essential to his ability to understand the nature of his rights and the consequences of abandoning them." Once the prosecutor shows that a suspect was fully informed of his *Miranda* rights and that he was not coerced to waive them, "the analysis is complete and the waiver is valid as a matter of law."

In essence, *Burbine* teaches that, although a suspect must be informed of his right to assistance of counsel, he is not constitutionally entitled to know that his counsel wishes to see him. As Justice O'Connor wrote, the information withheld by the police "would have been useful to [*D*]; perhaps even it might have affected his decision to confess." "But," she wrote, "we have never read the Constitution to require that the police supply a suspect with a flow of information to help him calibrate his self-interest in deciding whether to speak or stand by his rights." The Court lacked "the authority to mandate a code of behavior for state officials wholly unconnected to any federal right or privilege."

The Court that decided *Escobedo* and *Miranda* would probably have disallowed the confession here. The Warren Court distrusted confessions, was critical of police deception, and inclined to set up an even "playing field" in the interrogation room. To the *Escobedo-Miranda* Court, defense lawyers play a critical and positive role in the adversary system, by neutralizing some of the coercive influences in the interrogation process and by assisting the suspect in deciding whether to invoke his constitutional rights.

The Supreme Court that decided *Burbine* was a Court of a different philosophical cast. Whereas the Warren Court viewed suspects as underdogs in need of assistance, most members of the current Court are critical of the "fox hunt" theory of justice,[167] and are disinclined to apply *Miranda*

---

[167] *See* § 24.05[B][3], *supra.*

more broadly than necessary. Consequently, the officers' efforts to keep defense counsel away from her client was permitted on the ground that any rule to the contrary would be "wholly unconnected to any federal right or privilege."

### [B]  Waiver Law: If a Suspect Asserts His Rights

#### [1]  Overview

Subsection [A] described what the government must show in order to convince a court that a suspect validly waived his constitutional rights, after receiving *Miranda* warnings.

The present subsection considers a related question: What procedures must the police follow if a defendant asserts his Fifth Amendment privilege against self-incrimination, *i.e.*, if he asserts his right to remain silent and/or if he requests assistance of counsel? Under what circumstances may the police obtain a valid waiver once the custodial suspect asserts one or both of these rights? As will be seen, the rules differ considerably depending on which right is asserted: the police must follow stricter rules when a suspect asks to consult with a lawyer.

#### [2]  Right to Remain Silent

The *Miranda* opinion states that, once warnings are given, if the suspect "indicates in any manner, at any time prior to or during questioning, that he wishes to remain silent, the interrogation must cease." Is the required cessation permanent?

In *Michigan v. Mosley*,[168] the Court held that the preceding language did not mean that the police may never resume interrogation after a suspect asserts his right to silence, but neither does it mean that they need only cease questioning momentarily. Instead, the Court ruled, the suspect's right to cut off questioning is satisfied if the police "scrupulously honor" his right to silence after he asserts the privilege. Again, this means that a bright-line rule gives way to case-by-case adjudication.

In *Mosley*, *D* was arrested and read his *Miranda* rights. *D* invoked his Fifth Amendment privilege. The police ceased interrogation and placed *D* in a jail cell. Two hours later, a different officer, who wanted to interrogate *D* about a different crime (one for which *D* was not in custody), went to the cell and re-read the *Miranda* warnings. *D* signed a waiver form and answered questions. The Court held that on these facts—interrogation ceased immediately upon request; two hours elapsed; the subsequent questioning was by a different officer, in a different location, for a different

---

[168] 423 U.S. 96 (1975).

crime; and *Miranda* warnings were restated—the police scrupulously honored the suspect's Fifth Amendment rights.

### [3]  Right to Counsel

#### [a]  The *Edwards v. Arizona* Rule

In *Edwards v. Arizona*,[169] the police read *D* his *Miranda* warnings. Although *D* originally agreed to talk, he later told the police, "I want an attorney before making a deal." Interrogation ceased, and *D* was taken to a jail cell. The next morning, two officers came to the cell to resume questioning. When *D* said that he did not want to talk, the jail guard said "he had" to talk. The officers informed *D* of his *Miranda* rights a second time, and *D* agreed to answer questions.

The Supreme Court held that when a suspect invokes his right under *Miranda* to consult with an attorney prior to interrogation, the suspect "is not subject to further interrogation by the authorities until counsel has been made available to him, unless the accused himself initiates further communication, exchanges, or conversations with the police." The purpose of the bright-line *Edwards* rule is "to prevent police from badgering a defendant into waiving his previously asserted *Miranda* rights."[170] To the extent *Miranda* is a prophylactic rule, and the *Edwards* rule is intended to enforce *Miranda*, it constitutes a "second layer of protection"[171] *i.e.*, a double prophylaxis.[172]

The *Edwards* bright-line rule is very strict. First, it bars police-initiated interrogation, even regarding offenses unrelated to the subject of the original interrogation.[173] Second, as the Court announced in *Minnick v. Mississippi*,[174] once a suspect in custody invokes his *Miranda* right to counsel, the

---

[169] 451 U.S. 477 (1981).

[170] Michigan v. Harvey, 494 U.S. 344, 350 (1990).

[171] *Id.*

[172] Critics of *Edwards* have noted the dual prophylaxis. *See* Minnick v. Mississippi, 498 U.S. 146, 166 (1990) (Scalia, J., dissenting) ("*Edwards'* prophylactic rule [is] . . . needed to protect *Miranda*'s prophylactic right to have counsel present, which [is] needed to protect the right against *compelled self-incrimination* found (at last!) in the Constitution.").

Until Dickerson v. United States, 530 U.S. 428 (2000), it was highly plausible to argue that a violation of double-prophylaxis *Edwards* was not a violation of the Constitution. *E.g.*, Howard v. Moore, 131 F.3d 399, 414 (4th Cir. 1997). *Dickerson* provides, however, that *Miranda* is a constitutional decision even if the warnings are still characterized as "prophylactic." *See* § 24.06[C], *supra*.

[173] Arizona v. Roberson, 486 U.S. 675 (1988); *see* McNeil v. Wisconsin, 501 U.S. 171, 177 (1991) ("The *Edwards* rule . . . is *not* offense-specific: once a suspect invokes the *Miranda* right to counsel for interrogation regarding one offense, he may not be reapproached regarding *any* offense unless counsel is present.").

[174] 498 U.S. 146 (1990).

police must not only permit the suspect to consult with an attorney, but they may not re-initiate questioning *unless counsel is present.*

In short, according to *Edwards-Minnick*, once a person in custody requests counsel, it is as if a protective shield surrounds him. The police may not interrogate the suspect further about *any* crime, unless: (1) the defendant's lawyer is present, and a valid waiver is obtained; or (2) the *defendant* initiates "further communication, exchanges, or conversations with the police," after which the police obtain a valid waiver. Notice that in either eventuality the analysis returns full circle to the point immediately preceding the request for counsel: the police must obtain a voluntary, knowing, and intelligent waiver.

In the second scenario stated immediately above, what constitutes "further communication, exchanges, or conversations with the police"? Is it enough, for example, for the suspect to ask a police officer for food and water? May the police now seek to interrogate the suspect again? In *Oregon v. Bradshaw*,[175] a four-justice plurality ruled that communications, exchanges or conversations are "initiated" for purposes of the *Edwards* rule by any comment or inquiry that can "be fairly said to represent a desire . . . to open up a . . . generalized discussion relating directly or indirectly to the investigation." In contrast, comments or inquiries "relating to routine incidents of the custodial relationship," such as a request for water or to use a telephone, fall outside the scope of this definition.

The latter exclusion is a narrow one. Thus, in *Bradshaw*, the plurality determined that *D* "initiated" communications when he asked the police, "Well, what is going to happen to me now?" Although this statement apparently was intended only to find out where the police were going to take him at that time, the question was indirectly related to the general investigation. Therefore, the plurality held that the police did not act improperly by resuming their interrogation after securing a valid waiver.

### [b]   When the *Edwards* Rule Does Not Apply

### [i]   Ambiguous Request for Counsel

The Supreme Court held in *Davis v. United States*[176] that the *Edwards* rule does not apply unless a suspect unambiguously asserts his right to

---

[175] 462 U.S. 1039 (1983).

[176] 512 U.S. 452 (1994); *contra, under state constitution*, State v. Hoey, 881 P.2d 504 (Haw. 1994) (when a suspect ambiguously or equivocally requests counsel during custodial interrogation, the police must cease all questioning or seek non-substantive clarification of the suspect's request); State v. Risk, 598 N.W.2d 642 (Minn. 1999) (police must stop questioning and clarify an accused's intentions if the latter makes an ambiguous or equivocal statement during custodial interrogation that could reasonably be construed as an expression of a desire to act with the police only through counsel).

counsel. In *Davis*, *D* initially waived his *Miranda* rights and was interrogated. Ninety minutes into the questioning, *D* said, "Maybe I should talk to a lawyer." The interrogators attempted to clarify *D*'s wishes; *D* responded by saying, "No, I'm not asking for a lawyer. . . . I don't want a lawyer," after which the interrogation resumed.

The Supreme Court, 5-4, per Justice O'Connor, held that if a suspect ambiguously or equivocally asserts his *Miranda* right to counsel, as *D* did, the police may ignore the remark and continue the interrogation. The inquiry is an objective one: if the suspect's reference to a lawyer "is ambiguous or equivocal in that a reasonable officer in light of the circumstances would have understood only that the suspect *might* be invoking the right to counsel," the interrogator may ignore the reference and proceed with the questioning. The Court declined to adopt a rule requiring officers to ask clarifying questions (as occurred in the actual case), although Justice O'Connor conceded that this "will often be good police practice."

O'Connor conceded that the rule announced in *Davis* "might disadvantage some suspects who—because of fear, intimidation, lack of linguistic skills, or a variety of other reasons—will not clearly articulate their right to counsel although they actually want to have a lawyer present." Nonetheless, the Justices adopted the rule in the interest of "clarity and ease of application." She did not explain why a rule requiring the police to cease interrogation altogether, or to obtain clarification of the suspect's wishes, would be less clear or difficult to apply than the announced rule.

The *Davis* rule will have a disproportionate impact on disadvantaged groups of persons. As Professor Yale Kamisar has written, "[s]ociolinguistic research indicates that certain discrete segments of the population, such as women and a number of minority racial and ethnic groups, are far more likely than other groups to avoid strong, assertive means of expression and to use indirect and hedged speech."[177] Moreover, even among persons who do not usually use indirect modes of expression, the *Davis* rule will greatly undercut *Edwards*, because suspects undergoing custodial interrogation are "situationally powerless" and, therefore, apt often to "adopt a hedging speech register."[178]

---

[177] Kamisar, Note 11, *supra*, at 18.

[178] *Id.* Regarding the tendency of powerless persons to talk indirectly when dealing with those in power, Kamisar has also said this: "In *Fiddler on the Roof*, you will recall, Tevye the dairyman didn't come right out and say: 'Lord, make me a rich man today' or 'Lord, I want to be a wealthy man right now, before the sun sets.' No, he was rather tentative. He sort of beat around the bush. At the outset he asks: '[s]o what would have been so terrible if I had a small fortune?' At the end he asks: '[w]ould it spoil some vast, eternal plan if I were a rich man?'" Yale Kamisar, Police Interrogation and Confessions 5 (Prepared Remarks at the U.S. Law Week's Sixteenth Annual Constitutional Law Conference, Sept., 9, 1994).

Speaking for four members of the Court, Justice David Souter would have required the police to clarify a suspect's wishes in the case of an ambiguous request for counsel. In view of the fact "[a] substantial percentage of [suspects] lack anything like a confident command of the English language," Souter expressed the hope that trial courts would "sensibly" apply the rule, "without requiring criminal suspects to speak with the discrimination of an Oxford don."

### [ii]  Request for Counsel for Non-Interrogation Purposes

Not all unambiguous requests for counsel trigger the *Edwards* rule. In *McNeil v. Wisconsin*,[179] the Court stated that *Edwards* only applies if a suspect in custody expresses "his wish for the particular sort of lawyerly assistance that is the subject of *Miranda*. . . . It requires, at a minimum, some statement that can reasonably be construed to be an expression of a desire for the assistance of an attorney *in dealing with custodial interrogation by the police*."

It is essential here to distinguish between a request for counsel *under the Sixth Amendment*, a right which only comes into play after formal adversary proceedings have commenced regarding a specific offense,[180] and a request for a lawyer under *Miranda*. As *McNeil* explained, the right to counsel under the Sixth Amendment

> is to "protec[t] the unaided layman at critical confrontations" with his "expert adversary," the government, *after* "the adverse positions of government and defendant have solidified" with respect to a particular alleged crime. . . . The purpose of the *Miranda-Edwards* guarantee, on the other hand—and hence the purpose of invoking it—is to protect a quite different interest: the suspect's "desire to deal with the police only through counsel" . . . . To invoke the Sixth Amendment interest is, as a matter of *fact, not* to invoke the *Miranda-Edwards* interest.

In *McNeil, D* was arrested pursuant to a warrant charging him with armed robbery. *D* asserted his request for counsel during a bail hearing—a judicial proceeding—on the robbery charge. Thereafter, the police visited *D* at his jail cell, where he was re-advised of his *Miranda* rights. *D* signed a waiver form and answered questions regarding offenses for which he was a suspect, but for which he had not yet been formally charged.

The Court held that the *Miranda-Edwards* cease-interrogation rule did not apply in these circumstances. By requesting a lawyer at the bail hearing, the Court concluded that *D* invoked his Sixth Amendment right to counsel regarding the robbery charge. His statement could not "reasonably be

---

[179] 501 U.S. 171 (1991).

[180] *See* §§ 25.03[B] and 25.04, *infra*.

construed to be an expression of a desire for the assistance of an attorney *in dealing with custodial interrogation by the police*" on the other offenses, for which he had not yet been charged.

### [iii]   Anticipatory Request for Counsel

In *McNeil v. Wisconsin*,[181] the Supreme Court expressed doubt that the *Miranda* right to counsel can be invoked anticipatorily. The Court stated that "[m]ost rights must be asserted when the government seeks to take the actions they protect against." Therefore, without deciding the issue, the Court hinted that an assertion of the *Miranda-Edwards* right to consult with counsel might not be effective if it is "asserted initially outside the context of custodial interrogation," such as at a judicial proceeding, or in a communication sent to the police before an impending arrest.

## § 24.11   Custodial Interrogation: When *Miranda* Warnings Are Not Required

### [A]   Public-Safety Exception[182]

In *New York v. Quarles*,[183] the Supreme Court recognized a "public safety" exception to *Miranda*. In *Quarles*, a woman informed two officers shortly after midnight that she had been raped, that her assailant was armed, and that he had fled into a nearby all-night grocery store with a weapon. One of the officers entered the store and spotted a man, *D*, fitting the description of the assailant.

*D* fled to the rear of the store, with the officer in pursuit. The officer, now accompanied by three other officers, took *D* into custody and handcuffed him. When the officer discovered that *D* had an empty shoulder holster, he asked *D* (without issuing *Miranda* warnings) where the gun was. *D* nodded in the direction of some empty cartons and said "the gun is over there." The officers retrieved the weapon.

The lower courts suppressed *D*'s statement about the gun. However, the Supreme Court reversed on the ground that the custodial interrogation occurred in a situation posing a threat to the public safety and, therefore, fit within this newly recognized exception to *Miranda*. Speaking for the majority, Justice Rehnquist stated that the police "were confronted with the

---

[181] 501 U.S. 171 (1991).

[182] *See generally* Susan R. Klein, *Miranda's Exceptions in a Post-Dickerson World,* 92 J. Crim. L. & Criminology — (Fall 2001); William T. Pizzi, *The Privilege Against Self-Incrimination in a Rescue Situation,* 76 J. Crim. L. & Criminology 567 (1985); George C. Thomas III, *Separated at Birth But Siblings Nonetheless: Miranda and the Due Process Notice Cases,* 99 Mich. L. Rev. 1081 (2001).

[183] 467 U.S. 649 (1984).

immediate necessity" of finding the weapon. As long as the gun's where-abouts was unknown, it posed a "danger to the public safety: an accomplice might make use of it, a customer or employee might later come upon it."

The precise boundaries of the public-safety exception are difficult to ascertain—the Court has not ruled in any other public-safety cases—except that there must be an "objectively reasonable need to protect the police or the public from [an] immediate danger"; there must exist an "exigency requiring immediate action by the officers beyond the normal need expedi-tiously to solve a serious crime." Moreover, the questions asked by the police in such circumstances must be "reasonably prompted by a concern for the public safety."

In *Quarles*, the Court considered it irrelevant that there was no evidence that the interrogating officer was motivated by a concern for public safety when he asked about the gun. Justice Rehnquist stated that the exception "should not be made to depend on *post hoc* findings at a suppression hearing concerning the subjective motivation of the . . . officer." Indeed, the Court admitted that in emergency circumstances most officers act for a "host of different, instinctive, and largely unverifiable motives . . . [including] the desire to obtain incriminating evidence from the suspect."

The Court conceded that recognition of the public-safety exception reduces the "desirable clarity" of *Miranda*. But, "[t]he exception will not be difficult for police officers to apply because in each case it will be circumscribed by the exigency which justifies it." The Court expressed confidence that the police "can and will distinguish almost instinctively between questions necessary to secure their own safety or the safety of the public and questions designed solely to elicit testimonial evidence from a suspect." According to the majority, the newly recognized exception, "far from complicating the thought processes and the on-the-scene judgments of police officers, will simply free them to follow their legitimate instincts when confronting situations presenting a danger to the public safety."[184]

The holding in *Quarles* is dubious on its facts. Where was the exigency? The events occurred in the middle of the night in a nearly deserted market. There were no customers in the store, and the clerks were at the checkout station. At the time of the interrogation, *D* was handcuffed and surrounded by four officers. Despite the Court's concern that the gun might get into the hands of an accomplice, the police had no reason to believe that any

---

[184] More than once, the Court described the police questioning in such circumstances as "instinctual" or "instinctive." This suggests the possibility that the public-safety exception should be limited to brief questioning (in the present case, the Court expressly observed that the officer asked only one question, directly related to the gun) at the scene of the arrest.

existed. By cordoning off the area, the gun could easily have been found without questioning *D*.

Whether or not the public-safety exception is desirable, *Quarles* is a hard to justify in light of *Miranda*. *Quarles* characterized the *Miranda* warnings as prophylactic and non-constitutional in nature. In light of this, it balanced the costs and benefits of *Miranda* warnings and concluded that the benefits to the suspect of *Miranda* warnings were outweighed by the goal of protecting the public from the missing gun.

In contrast, the *Miranda* Court believed it was rendering a constitutional decision, and there is little in the *Miranda* opinion to suggest that the holding in that case was founded on any cost-benefit calculation. Indeed, the Court spoke in ringing terms about the "respect a government . . . must accord to the dignity and integrity of its citizens," and of the requirement that the government "shoulder the entire load" and "respect the inviolability of the human personality."

In light of the Court's announcement in *Dickerson v. United States* [185] that *Miranda* is, indeed, a constitutionally based decision, is *Quarles* undermined? It should be, because the bar on compelled self-incrimination is absolute—cost-benefit calculations are inappropriate. [186] As *Quarles* itself conceded, " 'the Fifth Amendment's strictures, unlike the [Fourth Amendment's], are not removed by showing reasonableness.' " [187] Nonetheless, the *Dickerson* Court stated that *Quarles* and other cases limiting the scope of *Miranda* simply

> illustrate the principle . . . that no constitutional rule is immutable. No court laying down a general rule can possibly foresee the various circumstances in which counsel will seek to apply it, and the sort of modifications represented by these cases are as much a normal part of constitutional law as the original decision." [188]

### [B]  Covert Custodial Interrogation

*Illinois v. Perkins* [189] provides that "*Miranda* warnings are not required when the suspect is unaware that he is speaking to a law enforcement officer and gives a voluntary statement."

In *Perkins*, the police obtained information that *D*, a jail inmate, had made statements to another prisoner that implicated *D* in a murder then under

---

[185] 530 U.S. 428 (2000); *see* § 24.06[C], *supra*.

[186] *See* § 23.01[B][3], *supra*.

[187] *Quarles*, 467 U.S. at 653 n.3 (quoting Fisher v. United States, 425 U.S. 391, 400 (1976)).

[188] *Dickerson*, 530 U.S. at 441.

[189] 496 U.S. 292 (1990).

investigation. The police placed X, an undercover police agent, in D's cellblock. X, posing as a burglar, was instructed to engage D in "casual conversation and report anything he said about the . . . murder." As part of the ruse, X directed a conversation to the subject of murder, and asked D whether he had ever killed anybody. In response, D admitted that he had, and then proceeded to provide details of the crime.

The Court held that D's statements to X, although the result of interrogation while in custody, and in the absence of *Miranda* warnings, were admissible at D's trial. It reasoned that "[c]onversations between suspects and undercover agents do not implicate the concerns underlying *Miranda*." In essence, for purposes of *Miranda* warnings, "custodial interrogation" involves only express questioning or its functional equivalent[190] by a known law enforcement agent.

As *Perkins* explains, the *Miranda* rule was founded on the premise that the interplay between police custody and police interrogation triggers the need to provide protections against coercion. Coercion, however, is determined from the suspect's perspective; therefore, the requisite coercion is lacking when a custodial suspect encounters a person he believes is a cellmate rather than a law enforcement officer. The Court observed that " 'when the agent carries neither badge nor gun and wears not "police blue" but the same prison gray' as the suspect, there is no '*interplay* between police interrogation and police custody.' "[191]

### [C]   Routine-Booking-Questions Exception

In *Pennsylvania v. Muniz*,[192] a four-justice plurality[193] announced a " 'routine booking question' exception which exempts from *Miranda*'s coverage questions to secure the 'biographical data necessary to complete booking or pretrial services.' "

In *Muniz*, D was arrested for driving his car under the influence of alcohol. At the police station, an officer asked D questions regarding his name, address, weight, eye color, date of birth, and age, as part of a "routine practice for receiving persons suspected of driving while intoxicated." These questions and his answers were videotaped with his knowledge, but before D was informed of his *Miranda* rights. The plurality held that these

---

[190] *See* § 24.08[A][1], *supra*.

[191] *Perkins*, 496 U.S. at 297 (quoting Yale Kamisar, *Brewer v. Williams, Massiah, and Miranda: What Is Interrogation? When Does It Matter?*, 67 Geo. L.J. 1, 67, 63 (1978).

[192] 496 U.S. 582 (1990).

[193] Justice Marshall dissented from the creation of a new *Miranda* exception. Four members of the Court (Chief Justice Rehnquist, and Justices Blackmun, Stevens, and White) did not reach the issue.

questions did not need to be preceded by *Miranda* warnings: the questions were routine, requested for record-keeping purposes only, and "reasonably related to the police's administrative concerns."

The plurality warned, however, that the mere fact that a question is asked during the booking process does not necessarily immunize it. It stated that "[w]ithout obtaining a waiver of the suspect's *Miranda* rights, the police may not ask questions, even during booking, that are designed to elicit incriminating admissions."

## § 24.12  Scope of the *Miranda* Exclusionary Rule[194]

### [A]  Impeachment Exception

The Supreme Court ruled in *Harris v. New York*[195] that a prosecutor may use a statement obtained in violation of *Miranda* to impeach a defendant who testifies at trial inconsistently with the custodial statement.

Speaking for the Court, Chief Justice Warren Burger conceded that "[s]ome comments in the *Miranda* opinion can indeed be read as indicating a bar to use of an uncounseled statement for any purpose . . . ." However, the Chief Justice characterized such language as dictum and, therefore, not controlling. Instead, Burger stated, the "shield provided by *Miranda* cannot be perverted into a license to use perjury by way of a defense, free from the risk of confrontation with prior inconsistent utterances." Once any witness, including the defendant, agrees to take the stand he must testify truthfully. If he does not, the prosecutor is entitled to use "the traditional truth-testing devices of the adversary process," including the use of prior statements to impeach the speaker's credibility. According to the Chief Justice, "[a]ssuming that the exclusionary rule has a deterrent effect on proscribed police conduct, sufficient deterrence flows when the evidence in question is made unavailable to the prosecution in its case in chief."

In other contexts, the Supreme Court has held that an incriminating statement made under compulsion in violation of the Fifth Amendment cannot be used for *any* purpose, including impeachment.[196] Therefore, although the *Harris* Court did not characterize *Miranda* as a prophylactic rule—that description did not come for three more years—the seeds of *Miranda*'s de-constitutionalization may have been planted in *Harris*.[197]

---

[194] *See generally* Klein, Note 177, *supra*; Thomas, Note 177, *supra*.

[195] 401 U.S. 222 (1971).

[196] *See* § 23.02[E][2], *infra*.

[197] As to the effect of Dickerson v. United States, 530 U.S. 428 (2000) (describing *Miranda* as a constitutional rule) on the impeachment rule, *see* the text preceding Note 183, *supra*.

## [B]   Fruit-of-the-Poisonous-Tree Doctrine[198]

### [1]   In General

The *Miranda* rule apparently supports no, or only a limited, "fruit-of-the-poisonous-tree" doctrine.[199]

This much is unambiguous. If a *Miranda* violation occurs, resulting in the exclusion of the statement secured in violation of *Miranda*, the government may nonetheless call a witness to testify at trial, even if that witness's identity was a tainted fruit of the inadmissible statement.[200] And the government may introduce a defendant's own voluntary, post-*Miranda*, admissions, even if they were obtained as a result of an earlier *Miranda* violation.[201] Although the Court has yet to say so clearly, the same rule almost certainly applies to physical evidence that is a tainted fruit of an earlier illegality.[202]

As the discussion that follows indicates, the Supreme Court's refusal to recognize a fruit-of-the-poisonous-tree doctrine in *Miranda* cases is linked to its characterization of *Miranda* as a non-constitutional rule, a description that no longer applies in light of *Dickerson v. United States*.[203] Although *Dickerson* arguably undermines the no-fruit rule, the Court has so far shrugged off any suggestion that is needs to reconsider its post-*Miranda* jurisprudence.[204]

### [2]   *Michigan v. Tucker*

In *Tucker*,[205] the police provided incomplete warnings to *D* prior to custodial interrogation. Although the questioning occurred before *Miranda* was announced, *D*'s trial took place after *Miranda* was decided; therefore, its safeguards applied retroactively to the interrogation.[206] As a

---

[198] Yale Kamisar, Response, *On the "Fruits" of Miranda Violations, Coerced Confessions, and Compelled Testimony*, 93 Mich. L. Rev. 929 (1995).

[199] *See generally* § 21.08, *supra*, for discussion of the fruit-of-the-poisonous doctrine.

[200] Michigan v. Tucker, 417 U.S. 433 (1974).

[201] Oregon v. Elstad, 470 U.S. 298 (1985).

[202] Kamisar, Note 11 *supra*, at 27 ("[t]he Court has not quite said this yet, but it came close"); and Kamisar, Note 193, *supra*, at 972 n.199 (setting out the "narrow" and "broad" reading of "*Miranda* fruit" case law, but assuming that there is no *Miranda* fruit-of-the-poisonous-tree doctrine); *accord*, State v. Yang, 608 N.W.2d. 703, 712 (Wis. App. 2000) (no fruit-of-the-poisonous-doctrine for physical evidence).

[203] 530 U.S. 428 (2000); *see* § 24.06[C], *supra*.

[204] *See* the text preceding Note 183, *supra*.

[205] 417 U.S. 433 (1974).

[206] Johnson v. New Jersey, 384 U.S. 719 (1966).

consequence, *D*'s statement obtained in violation of *Miranda* was inadmissible at his trial. In *D*'s inadmissible statement, the police obtained the name of a witness, *X*, who was later called as a prosecution witness at *D*'s trial. *Tucker* raised the question of whether *X*'s testimony was inadmissible on the basis of the *Wong Sun*[207] fruit-of-the-poisonous-tree doctrine.

*Tucker*'s analysis is noteworthy because Justice Rehnquist, writing for the Court, stated for the first time that the *Miranda* warnings were "not themselves rights protected by the Constitution but [are] instead measures to insure that the right against compulsory self-incrimination [is] protected." Therefore, the Court concluded, the only harm that occurred in the case was that the police conduct departed "from the prophylactic standards . . . laid down" in *Miranda*.

Having seemingly de-constitutionalized *Miranda*, the *Tucker* Court distinguished *Wong Sun* on the ground that the latter case involved the admissibility of a fruit of a constitutional (Fourth Amendment) violation, whereas *X*'s testimony in the present case was only a fruit of a violation of a non-constitutional prophylactic rule (*i.e.*, *Miranda*). Consequently, the Court concluded that it was not compelled by precedent to apply *Wong Sun* in the *Miranda* context.

As a matter of principle rather than precedent, the Court concluded that *X*'s testimony was admissible. First, the fruit, *X*'s testimony, was not untrustworthy, because *X* was subject to cross-examination by *D*. Second, the deterrence rationale of the exclusionary rule lost "much of its force" in light of the pre-*Miranda* context of the case because the police had acted in good faith when they provided the incomplete warnings. Third, the Court rejected "judicial integrity" as an independent basis for excluding the challenged evidence.

### [3] *Oregon v. Elstad*

In *Elstad*,[208] the police obtained an incriminating statement from *D* in violation of *Miranda*. Later, *D* was arrested and given his *Miranda* warnings. *D* waived his rights and made a second, more damaging, statement. The first statement was clearly inadmissible under *Miranda*. The issue on appeal was whether the *second* confession was also inadmissible, in part on the ground that it was a fruit of the earlier *Miranda* violation.

---

[207] Wong Sun v. United States, 371 U.S. 471 (1963).

[208] 470 U.S. 298 (1985); *contra, under the state constitution,* Commonwealth v. Smith, 593 N.E.2d 1288 (Mass. 1992) (*D*'s second custodial statement, although obtained noncoercively, is inadmissible as a fruit of an earlier confession obtained in violation of *Miranda*); State v. Smith, 834 S.W.2d 915 (Tenn. 1992) (*id.*).

The *Elstad* Court concluded that the reasoning of *Tucker* "applies with equal force when the alleged 'fruit' of a noncoercive *Miranda* violation is neither a witness *nor an article of evidence* but [as in this case] the accused's own voluntary testimony."[209] It stated that in the absence of compulsion "or improper tactics," the "twin rationales" of the *Miranda* exclusionary rule—trustworthiness and deterrence—did not call for the exclusion of *D*'s testimony, although it was a fruit of the original violation.

*Tucker* and *Elstad* involved the admissibility of volitional statements by human beings. Even in the Fourth Amendment context, the Court has treated such fruits more leniently than physical evidence.[210] A plausible case might be made, therefore, for the proposition that physical evidence, such as a gun, should still constitute an inadmissible fruit of a *Miranda* violation, subject to ordinary attenuation and inevitable discovery principles. Nonetheless, as may be observed from the italicized language in the *Elstad* quotation in the immediately preceding paragraph ("nor an article of evidence"), although the Court has never directly so held, there is probably no *Miranda* fruit doctrine, even in relation to physical evidence.

As a result of *Elstad* and *Harris v. New York*,[211] which permits the use of statements obtained in violation of *Miranda* for impeachment purposes, some police departments have openly begun training officers to "question outside *Miranda*," *i.e.*, purposely interrogate custodial suspects without providing *Miranda* warnings.[212] The justification for violating *Miranda* is this: even though any statement secured in such circumstances will be inadmissible, the *Miranda*-less statement is likely to result in far more beneficial admissible fruit—perhaps a later statement by the suspect given after *Miranda*, a clue to where a murder victim might be found, or other physical evidence linking the suspect to the crime; and the government has the ability also to use the suspect's statement for impeachment purposes. What remains to be seen is whether the Court's decision in *Dickerson*, re-constitutionalizing *Miranda* but providing no hint that it intends to turn back from these narrowing cases, will have any impact on police strategies in the interrogation room.[213]

---

[209] *Id.* at 308 (emphasis added).

[210] *See* § 21.08[D][2][e], *supra.*

[211] 401 U.S. 222 (1971); *see* § 24.12[A], *supra.*

[212] Weisselberg, Note 16, *supra*, at 132–140.

[213] *See* Charles D. Weisselberg, *In the Stationhouse After Dickerson*, 99 Mich. L. Rev. 1121 (2001).

## CHAPTER 25

# INTERROGATION LAW: SIXTH AMENDMENT RIGHT TO COUNSEL

## § 25.01 Sixth Amendment, Right to Counsel, and Interrogations: Overview [1]

The Sixth Amendment guarantees that "[i]n all criminal prosecutions, the accused shall enjoy the right . . . to have the Assistance of Counsel for his defence." This right is fundamental and applies to the states through the Fourteenth Amendment due process clause. [2]

The Sixth Amendment right to counsel is a personal right. [3] Therefore, although the Supreme Court has never so ruled, there is no serious doubt that a Sixth Amendment right-to-counsel claim may only be raised in a criminal trial by the person whose counsel right was infringed. This assumption is supported by language of the Supreme Court. In *Massiah v. United States*, [4] the seminal case in the field, the Court held that the Sixth Amendment is violated when the accused's own incriminating statement is "used by the prosecution as evidence against *him* at his trial."

As explained below, [5] the Sixth Amendment right to counsel only applies if adversary judicial criminal proceedings have commenced against the accused. [6] According to the Court, "the possibility that [an] encounter [between the government and an individual] may have important

---

[1] This chapter considers the Sixth Amendment right to counsel in the context of police interrogations. For discussion of the right to counsel in other procedural contexts, *see* § 27.02–.03 (eyewitness identification procedures) and chapter 29 (trial and on appeal), *infra*.

[2] Gideon v. Wainwright, 372 U.S. 335 (1963).

[3] Texas v. Cobb, 532 U.S. 162, 171 n. 2 (2001).

[4] 377 U.S. 201 (1964).

[5] *See* § 25.04, *infra*.

[6] There is one marginal exception to this statement. In Escobedo v. Illinois, 378 U.S. 478 (1964), the Court applied the Sixth Amendment to a post-arrest custodial interrogation that occurred prior to the initiation of adversary judicial criminal proceedings. However, the Court later re-interpreted *Escobedo* as a Fifth Amendment self-incrimination case. The holding of *Escobedo* is now limited to its facts. *See* § 24.03, *supra*.

consequences at trial, standing alone, is insufficient to trigger the Sixth Amendment right to counsel."[7]

As will be evident in the discussion that follows, in some regards Sixth Amendment jurisprudence provides a person accused of a crime with different protections in the police interrogation context than are obtained through *Miranda v. Arizona*.[8] The differences between the Sixth Amendment and *Miranda* rights to counsel are summarized in Section 25.08.

## § 25.02 *Massiah v. United States*[9]

### [A] Historical Overview

When the Supreme Court announced its holding in *Massiah v. United States*,[10] it took "a giant step in a wholly new direction"[11] in police interrogation law. *Massiah* brought the Sixth Amendment guarantee of the assistance of counsel "out of the courtroom, . . . [and] into new precincts."[12] The Court held for the first time that the Constitution is violated when government agents, in the absence of defense counsel, deliberately elicit incriminating information from a person against whom adversary judicial criminal proceedings have commenced.

*Miranda v. Arizona*,[13] decided two years after *Massiah*, temporarily eclipsed the latter case. *Massiah* moved out from behind *Miranda*'s shadows in 1977, however, when the Court applied the Sixth Amendment in exceptionally controversial circumstances in *Brewer v. Williams*.[14] Indeed,

---

[7] Moran v. Burbine, 475 U.S. 412, 432 (1986).

[8] 384 U.S. 436 (1966). *See* chapter 24, *supra*.

[9] *See generally* Office of Legal Policy, U.S. Dept. of Justice, Truth in Criminal Justice Series, Report No. 3, Report to the Attorney General on the Sixth Amendment Right to Counsel Under the *Massiah* Line of Cases, *reprinted in* 22 U. Mich. J. L. Ref. 661 (1989); Martin Bahl, Comment, *The Sixth Amendment as Constitutional Theory: Does Originalism Require that Massiah Be Abandoned?*, 82 J. Crim. L. & Criminology 423 (1991); Arnold N. Enker & Sheldon H. Elsen, *Counsel for the Suspect: Massiah v. United States and Escobedo v. Illinois*, 49 Minn. L. Rev. 47 (1964); Yale Kamisar, *Brewer v. Williams, Massiah, and Miranda: What is "Interrogation"? When Does it Matter?*, 67 Geo. L.J. 1 (1978); James J. Tomkovicz, *The Truth About Massiah*, 23 U. Mich. J. L. Ref. 641 (1990); James J. Tomkovicz, *An Adversary System Defense of the Right to Counsel Against Informants: Truth, Fair Play, and the Massiah Doctrine*, 22 U.C. Davis L. Rev. 1 (1988); H. Richard Uviller, *Evidence From the Mind of the Criminal Suspect: A Reconsideration of the Current Rules of Access and Restraint*, 87 Colum. L. Rev. 1137 (1987).

[10] 377 U.S. 201 (1964).

[11] Uviller, Note 9, *supra*, at 1155.

[12] *Id.* at 1159.

[13] 384 U.S. 436 (1966).

[14] 430 U.S. 387 (1977). *See generally* § 25.06[B], *infra*.

after *Williams*, *Massiah* "had the audacity to expand"[15] in an era of rare criminal defense successes in the Supreme Court. Although expansion of *Massiah* seems to have ended—indeed, the Court has recently begun to cut back on its potential reach[16] —it remains the leading case in the field.

## [B]　*Massiah*: The Opinion

The federal government indicted *D* for violating federal narcotics laws. *D* retained a lawyer, pleaded not guilty, and was released from custody on bail. In the meantime, *I*, who was charged in the same indictment, agreed to cooperate with the government in its continuing investigation of *D*. *I* permitted federal agents to install a listening device in his car so that they could listen while *D* (unaware of *I*'s informant status) had lengthy conversations with him. During the intercepted conversations, which occurred in the absence of *D*'s counsel, *D* made incriminating statements that were introduced at his trial over his objection.

*D* argued that admission at trial of the statements he made in *I*'s car violated various constitutional rights, including his Sixth Amendment right to counsel. The Supreme Court, per Justice Stewart, agreed with *D*'s right-to-counsel claim.

The majority opinion in *Massiah* was short and the holding was narrow. It specified at the outset that "[h]ere we deal not with a state court conviction, but with a federal case, where the specific guarantee of the Sixth Amendment directly applies." The rule announced in the federal case was that the Sixth Amendment was violated "when there was used against [*D*] at his trial evidence of his own incriminating words, which federal agents had deliberately elicited from him after he had been indicted and in the absence of his counsel."

Justice Stewart reasoned that the Sixth Amendment applied in *D*'s circumstances because the period after a suspect is formally charged with an offense and before trial is "the most critical period of the proceedings." It is during this time that "consultation, thoroughgoing investigation and preparation [are] vitally important."[17] Therefore, to deny an accused counsel during this period would deny her "effective representation by counsel at the only stage when legal aid and advice would help." Most especially, for the right of counsel to be effective, it had to apply to the surreptitious

---

[15] Tomkovicz, *An Adversary System Defense. . .*, Note 9, *supra*, at 5.

[16] *See especially* §§ 25.02[C] (the text following Note 35), 25.03[B], and 25.06[C].

[17] Notice that this description of the role of counsel in the Sixth Amendment context is broader than the *Miranda* right to counsel, the primary purpose of which is simply to assure that the suspect's Fifth Amendment right to be free from compelled self-incrimination is not violated. *See* § 24.04[B][1][b], *supra*.

conduct that occurred here. According to Justice Stewart, *D* was "more seriously imposed upon" than in a traditional encounter, because he was unaware that he was "under interrogation by a government agent."

The Court observed that the Solicitor General argued "strenuously . . . that the federal law enforcement agents had the right, if not indeed the duty, to continue their investigation of [*D*] and his alleged criminal associates even though [*D*] had been indicted." In fact, the government had reason to believe that *D* was part of a large, well-organized drug ring.

The Court accepted "and, at least for present purposes, completely approve[d] all that this argument implies." It agreed that it was "entirely proper" for the agents to continue their post-indictment investigation of *D*. It stressed that "[a]ll that we hold is that the defendant's own incriminating statements, obtained by federal agents under the circumstances here disclosed, could not constitutionally be used by the prosecution as evidence against *him* at his trial."[18] In other words, the criminal investigation could continue, but the fruits of that investigation, to the extent that they involved deliberate elicitation of the accused's own words, in the absence of counsel, regarding the indicted offense, could not be used against him at his own trial on that offense.

### [C]   Making Sense of *Massiah*: The Sixth Amendment Role of Counsel[19]

The practical effect of the *Massiah* rule is that, in the instance of surreptitious deliberate elicitation of incriminating statements made after adversary criminal proceedings have commenced against an accused, "the government either [must] reveal its presence [to the accused] and afford the opportunity to consult with counsel, or to suffer [at his trial] the exclusion of the product of its adversarial encounter with the accused."[20]

Can such a rule be defended? In his dissent, Justice Byron White criticized the majority because it barred the use by the government of "relevant, reliable, and highly probative evidence" obtained in a non-coercive environment. As a result of this case, he said, "the Constitution furnishes an important measure of protection against faithless compatriots and guarantees sporting treatment for sporting peddlers of narcotics." Justice White predicted that the effect of the *Massiah* rule would be that fewer

---

[18] Massiah v. United States, 377 U.S. 201, 207 (1964).

[19] *See generally* Martin R. Gardner, *The Sixth Amendment Right to Counsel and Its Underlying Values: Defining the Scope of Privacy Protection*, 90 J. Crim. L. & Criminology 397 (2000); William J. Stuntz, *Lawyers, Deception, and Evidence Gathering*, 79 Va. L. Rev. 1903 (1993); Uviller, Note 9, *supra*.

[20] Tomkovicz, *An Adversary System Defense. . .*, Note 9, *supra*, at 91.

confessed criminals would come forward to assist the government in their criminal investigations.

More recently, Justice Rehnquist has stated that *Massiah*'s "doctrinal underpinnings . . . have been largely left unexplained, and the result . . . is difficult to reconcile with the traditional notions of the role of an attorney."[21] Even a supporter of *Massiah* has conceded that "[t]he original . . . opinion provides a good example of . . . analytical shallowness."[22]

Indeed, how was *D*'s Sixth Amendment right to counsel violated in *Massiah*? His lawyer was not barred from the informant's automobile during the conversations. Furthermore, in light of the surreptitious nature of the police activity, it would not have served any meaningful purpose if *D*'s lawyer coincidentally *had* been present; there was little way that he could have used his expertise to protect *D*.[23] In fact, the lawyer's presence in the car could have represented a more serious risk to *D*'s Sixth Amendment rights than his absence, because the government would have been able to overhear lawyer-client confidences.[24]

According to two scholars, "[t]he real problem facing the Court in *Massiah* was not one of the right to counsel but rather the permissible extent of governmental deceit inherent in undercover work and the use of informers."[25] If this observation is accurate, *Massiah* should have rested its holding on the Fourth Amendment, or on general due process grounds. Such an approach, however, would have been inconsistent with then existing or subsequent constitutional doctrine in those fields.[26]

Is there a way to find a *Sixth Amendment* interest implicated in *Massiah*? The answer depends on what the Constitution means by the words

---

[21] United States v. Henry, 447 U.S. 264, 290 (1980) (Rehnquist, J., dissenting).

[22] Tomkovicz, *An Adversary System Defense. . .*, Note 9, *supra*, at 22.

[23] The lawyer could have told *D* not to talk to *I* on the general principle that their legal interests might eventually conflict, but she could have given this advice before the meeting in the automobile.

[24] In Weatherford v. Bursey, 429 U.S. 545 (1977), *D* and *X*, an undercover agent, participated in the vandalization of private property. In order to protect *X*'s undercover status, *X* also was charged with the offense. Prior to trial, *D* invited *X* to sit in while he discussed trial strategy with his attorney. At no time, however, did *X* pass on any of the lawyer-client conversations to the government. The Court held that under these circumstances (*i.e.*, there was "no tainted evidence in this case, no communication of defense strategy to the prosecution, and no purposeful intrusion by [*X*]"), no Sixth Amendment violation resulted.

[25] Enker & Elsen, Note 9, *supra*, at 57.

[26] Only two years after *Massiah*, Hoffa v. United States, 385 U.S. 293 (1966) reaffirmed the Fourth Amendment principle that one who talks to another person assumes the risk that the listener will betray her. *See* § 7.05[B], *supra*. *Hoffa* also rejected the claim that the use of secret government informers is a *per se* violation of the due process clause.

"assistance of counsel." In other words, what is the pretrial role of a defense attorney, and how could that role have been filled by *D*'s attorney in this case?

One scholar has helpfully identified three roles a lawyer might play in the pretrial phase of a criminal prosecution.[27] First, she can provide assistance in those encounters with the government in which her innocent client's "weakness, ignorance, or inertia"[28] threatens to result in an unjust conviction. The importance of the protect-the-innocent role of defense counsel cannot be denied, but the Court could not have had this purpose in mind in *Massiah* because there was no serious reason to fear that an innocent person would make incriminating statements in the non-coercive environment of *I*'s automobile.

Second, a lawyer can provide "preventive assistance." The concern is that an accused—whether factually innocent or not—"alone and friendless, faces the immense forces of the state arrayed against [her]."[29] The purpose of counsel here is not primarily to reduce the risk that the State's "immense forces" will crush an innocent person (that concern is satisfied by the first role of counsel), but to devise a criminal justice system for *all* accused persons, *even those who might be guilty,* that is more balanced.

The preventive-assistance concept is controversial. Critics characterize it as the "fox hunt" or "sporting" view of justice,[30] which was what Justice White had in mind in his *Massiah* dissent when he criticized the majority for "guarantee[ing] sporting treatment for sporting peddlers of narcotics." However, even if this defense role is justifiable, there was no practical way for counsel in *Massiah* to assist *D* in the "fox hunt" that was occurring in *I*'s car, because neither *D* nor counsel realized that the "game" was underway.

The third role of counsel is to provide "adversarial assistance." The premise is that once the government commits itself to a prosecution—once the investigation turns "into a hardened adversarial alignment"[31] —a form of "closure," or limitation on access to the accused, should result. The reasoning is that once the adversarial system begins, the lawyer serves as the "guardian of the fortress."[32] Therefore, she should be "the essential medium through which the demands and commitments of the sovereign are

---

[27] Uviller, Note 9, *supra,* at 1168–83.

[28] *Id.* at 1169.

[29] *Id.* at 1173.

[30] *See especially* § 24.05[B][3], *supra.*

[31] Uviller, Note 9, *supra,* at 1176.

[32] *Id.* at 1161.

communicated to the citizen."[33] According to this view, once adversarial proceedings have commenced, the prosecutor and the police "have an affirmative obligation not to act in a manner that circumvents and thereby dilutes the protection afforded by the right to counsel."[34] In particular, it is no longer appropriate for agents of the government knowingly to enter the fortress in order to obtain verbal evidence from the accused, at least in the absence of counsel or a valid waiver of the right.

*Massiah* can be justified on the latter basis. The government violated the closure concept: it deliberately elicited incriminating information from *D* after he was indicted and in his counsel's absence; and, in view of the surreptitious approach used to obtain the evidence, *D* had no meaningful way to waive his right to counsel. It must be observed, however, that the *Massiah* Court never offered this justification for the rule it announced, nor did the Court expressly recognize any broad principle of closure, as might be suggested by the "adversarial assistance" model.

The *post-Massiah* Supreme Court came very close to affirming the adversarial assistance role in *Maine v. Moulton*, when it stated that the Sixth Amendment "guarantees the accused . . . the right to rely on counsel as a 'medium' between him and the State."[35] But, in what may be the start of back-tracking on this point, the Court recently observed in *Texas v. Cobb*[36] that, in view of the fact the right to counsel is personal, "there is no 'background principle' of our Sixth Amendment jurisprudence establishing that there may be no contact between a defendant and police without [defense] counsel present."

## § 25.03    The Sixth Amendment (*Massiah*) Right to Counsel: Summary

### [A]  In General

The Sixth Amendment right to counsel has evolved since the Court announced its cautious holding in *Massiah v. United States*.[37] First, the right to counsel now applies not only to deliberate elicitation by federal agents, but also in state prosecutions, through the Fourteenth Amendment due process clause.[38] Second, although the Court in *Massiah* treated the

---

[33] Maine v. Moulton, 474 U.S. 159, 170 n.7 (1985) (quoting Brewer v. Williams, 430 U.S. 387, 415 (1977) (Stevens, J., concurring)).

[34] *Id.* at 171.

[35] *Id.* at 176.

[36] 532 U.S. 162 (2001).

[37] 377 U.S. 201 (1964).

[38] *See* Brewer v. Williams, 430 U.S. 387 (1977).

surreptitious nature of the police conduct in that case as an aggravating circumstance, it is now clear (if there was any doubt before) that the Sixth Amendment applies as well to traditional interrogations.

Subject to clarification in subsection [B] and in the chapter sections that follow, the *Massiah* rule can be summarized as follows. First, in the context of traditional interrogations—where the accused is aware that she is dealing with law enforcement agents—the Sixth Amendment renders inadmissible in the prosecution's case-in-chief any statement deliberately elicited from the defendant after commencement of adversary judicial criminal proceedings, unless the accused's lawyer is present or she knowingly and voluntarily waives her right to counsel.

In the case of covert police activity as occurred in *Massiah*, the rule is the same except that, because of the surreptitious nature of the police conduct, the "concept of a knowing and voluntary waiver of Sixth Amendment rights does not apply."[39] That is, there can never be a valid waiver of the Sixth Amendment if the accused does not know that the person with whom she is speaking is an agent of the state.

## [B] "Offense-Specific" Nature of the Right

A matter of exceeding importance is that the Sixth Amendment right to counsel specified in the preceding subsection is offense-specific. That is, in determining whether the Sixth Amendment applies in a particular circumstance, the issue is not simply whether formal judicial proceedings have commenced against the accused, but whether such proceedings have commenced in regard *to the offense that is the basis of the interrogation or surreptitious elicitation.*

The Supreme Court did not speak of the offense-specific nature of the Sixth Amendment in its early post-*Massiah* cases. For, example, in 1977, in *Brewer v. Williams*[40]—a case more fully considered below[41]—*D*, a suspect in the abduction and murder of a young girl, was arraigned on the abduction charge and thereafter subjected to conduct tantamount to an interrogation that resulted in incriminating statements relating to the child's death. Although at this point formal proceedings had not yet commenced in regard to the murder, the Supreme Court reversed *D*'s murder conviction on Sixth Amendment grounds, apparently because he had been indicted on the related abduction charge.

In 1991, in *McNeil v. Wisconsin*,[42] however, the Supreme Court explicitly characterized the Sixth Amendment as offense-specific. In *McNeil*, the

---

[39] United States v. Henry, 447 U.S. 264, 273 (1980).

[40] 430 U.S. 387 (1977).

[41] *See especially* §§ 25.05[A] and 25.06[B], *infra.*

[42] 501 U.S. 171, 175 (1991).

police questioned *D*, formally charged with armed robbery, in regard to a series of crimes for which *D* had not yet been arrested, much less formally charged. The Court held that, in view of the offense-specific nature of the right, the Sixth Amendment had not attached to the latter crimes at the time of interrogation, although it applied to the armed robbery.

The *McNeil* "offense-specific" concept was clarified in *Texas v. Cobb*.[43] The *Cobb* Court held that the Sixth Amendment does not necessarily extend to offenses that are "factually related" to those that have been actually charged. Thus, in *Williams*, the Sixth Amendment did *not* attach to the uncharged crime of murder, although the offense was inextricably intertwined with the abduction charge for which *D had* been arraigned.[44] However, the *Cobb* Court also stated that the term "offense" is "not necessarily limited to the four corners of a charging instrument." Instead, the Court announced that the meaning of the term "offense" in the Sixth Amendment counsel context is the same as in the Fifth Amendment double jeopardy ("nor shall any person be subject to the same *offence* to be twice put in jeopardy of life or limb") field.[45]

*Cobb* therefore imported the so-called *Blockburger*[46] double jeopardy rule to the Sixth Amendment. According to *Blockburger*, "where the same act or transaction constitutes a violation of two distinct statutory provisions, the test to be applied to determine whether there are two offenses or only one, is whether each provision requires proof of a fact which the other does not." Thus, if Crime 1 requires proof of elements A, B, and C, and Crime 2 contains elements A, B, and D, these are distinct offenses because each crime, as defined, requires proof of an element that the other does not (Crime 1 requires proof of element C, which Crime 2 does not; Crime 2 requires proof of element D, which Crime 1 does not). But, suppose that Crime 1 requires proof of elements A, B, and C, and Crime 2 requires proof of elements A and B. These two statutory provisions would constitute the same "offense" for purposes of double jeopardy law and—now, after *Cobb*—Sixth Amendment right-to-counsel law.

For example, suppose that *D* is indicted for assault of *V*, who died from the attack. Assume further that this offense is defined as "intentional

---

[43] 532 U.S. 162 (2001).

[44] The *Cobb* Court explained that "[t]he [*Brewer v. Williams*] Court's opinion . . . simply did not address the significance of the fact that the suspect had been arraigned only on the abduction charge, nor did the parties in any way argue this question." In view of the offense-specific nature of the right announced in *McNeil* as more fully developed in *Cobb*, *D*'s conviction for murder seemingly should not have been overturned.

[45] *See generally* § 32.07, *infra*.

[46] Blockburger v. United States, 284 U.S. 299 (1932).

application of unlawful force upon another." Under such circumstances, the police may not deliberately elicit incriminating statements from *D* in the absence of counsel or suitable waiver regarding the assault and then avoid Sixth Amendment strictures by obtaining a superseding indictment charging *D* with intent-to-kill murder of *V*. This is because, under *Blockburger*, assault (as defined above) and intent-to-kill murder are the same offense. [47] Therefore, indictment for one statutory violation serves to trigger the Sixth Amendment in regard to both statutes.

However, as the dissenters in *Cobb* warned, the Court's refusal to extend the Sixth Amendment's reach to crimes inextricably intertwined with the particular offense specified in the charging instrument permits police officials freedom to "ask the individual charged with robbery about, say, the assault of the cashier not yet charged, or about any other uncharged offense (unless under *Blockburger*'s definition it counts as the 'same crime') [committed as part of the robbery], *all without notifying counsel*" or requiring the police to seek waiver of the Sixth Amendment right. [48]

## § 25.04  "Adversary Judicial Proceedings"

In *Brewer v. Williams*, [49] the Court stated:

Whatever else it may mean, the right to counsel granted by the Sixth and Fourteenth Amendments means at least that a person is entitled to the help of a lawyer at or after the time that judicial proceedings have been initiated against him— "whether by way of formal charge, preliminary hearing, indictment, information, or arraignment." [50]

---

[47] "Assault" as defined in the text consists of the elements: (a) intent; and (b) unlawful force; intent-to-kill murder essentially involves: (a) intent; (b) unlawful force; and (c) death. Of course, the words "unlawful force" are not found in the ordinary definition of murder, but it is an implicit aspect of the concept of killing. Even this fairly straight-forward example demonstrates, as Justice Breyer observed in his dissent in *Cobb*, that "the simple-sounding *Blockburger* test has proved extraordinarily difficult to administer in practice. Judges, lawyers, and law professors often disagree about how to apply it."

[48] The *Cobb* majority accused the dissenters of giving "short shrift to the Fifth Amendment's role (as expressed in *Miranda* [*v. Arizona*] . . . .) in protecting a defendant's right to consult with counsel before talking to police." That is, even though the Sixth Amendment would not apply to the uncharged assault of the cashier in the hypothetical set out in the text, it is fair to assume that an individual charged with robbery will be informed of her *Miranda* rights and, therefore, retain the ability to refuse any and all police questioning (since *Miranda* is *not* offense-specific, *see* § 24.10[B][3][a], Note 168, *supra*). Moreover, a person in such circumstances is likely to have met with her counsel on the charged offense, and thus she has the opportunity to receive her lawyer's advice whether to invoke her right to silence in regard to uncharged offenses.

[49] 430 U.S. 387 (1977).

[50] *Id.* at 398 (quoting Kirby v. Illinois, 406 U.S. 682, 689 (1972)). For an explanation of these pretrial stages, *see* § 1.03[C], *supra*.

Despite the cautious language in this quotation—"whatever else it may mean" and "the right . . . means at least"—the Court, with one very narrow exception,[51] has shut the door on the possibility that the right-to-counsel provision might apply before judicial proceedings begin.[52]

This threshold requirement is justified on the basis of the language of the Sixth Amendment itself, which provides that "in all criminal *prosecutions* . . . the *accused* [is entitled] to have the assistance of Counsel for his *defence*." Only when the formalities occur—when the "suspect" becomes the "accused"—does the "prosecution" commence, and only then does the accused need to prepare a "defense."

Although this reading of the Sixth Amendment is disputable,[53] the Court has asserted that its interpretation of the Sixth Amendment "is far from a mere formalism. It is the starting point of our whole system of adversary criminal justice." It is at this time that the accused is "faced with the prosecutorial forces of organized society, and immersed in the intricacies of substantive and procedural criminal law."[54]

## § 25.05    "Deliberate Elicitation"[55]

### [A]    "Deliberate Elicitation" versus "Interrogation"

Although *Massiah v. United States*[56] prohibits "deliberate elicitation" —those were the words in its holding—Justice Stewart stated in the opinion that the accused in that case was "under interrogation" by *I*, the covert agent. The use of the word "interrogation" in the opinion was misleading as there was no evidence presented that *I* ever questioned *D*; instead, they had "lengthy conversations."

The Court confused matters further in *Brewer v. Williams*.[57] In *Williams*, *D* was arrested and arraigned for the abduction of a child believed to have been killed. While being transported in a police car from one part of the

---

[51] *See* Note 6, *supra.*

[52] *See* United States v. Gouveia, 467 U.S. 180 (1984).

[53] Professor Richard Uviller has pointed out that "[n]either semantics nor reason obstructs the designation of an arrest as the point of accusation in the constitutional sense." Uviller, Note 9, *supra*, at 1167. Indeed, under the Sixth Amendment, the "accused" in all "criminal prosecutions" is entitled to a speedy trial, yet *this* right has been interpreted to attach at the time of arrest or the filing of an indictment or information, whichever comes first. United States v. Marion, 404 U.S. 307 (1971).

[54] Kirby v. Illinois, 406 U.S. 682, 689 (1972).

[55] *See generally* Kamisar, Note 9, *supra*; Welsh S. White, *Interrogation Without Questions: Rhode Island v. Innis and United States v. Henry*, 78 Mich. L. Rev. 1209 (1980).

[56] 377 U.S. 201 (1964).

[57] 430 U.S. 387 (1977).

state to another, *D* was subjected to what has been characterized as "the Christian burial speech" by a police officer. In the speech, the officer prefaced his comments to *D* by saying, "I want to give you something to think about. . . ." He concluded his remarks by indicating, "I do not want you to answer me. I don't want to discuss it any further. Just think about it. . . ." In between, the officer, playing on *D*'s religious beliefs and psychological vulnerability as an escaped mental patient, expressed concern regarding the possibility that the little girl's body, which had not been discovered, would soon be buried under the Iowa winter's snow, thus depriving her parents of a chance to give the victim "a Christian burial."

At no time during the "speech" did the officer question *D*. Nonetheless, the Court described "the clear rule of *Massiah*" to be that, once judicial criminal proceedings commence, the accused "has a right to legal representation when the government interrogates him." It also stated that "no such constitutional protection would have come into play if there had been no interrogation." And, it described the burial speech as "tantamount to interrogation." Yet, in language reminiscent of *Massiah*, the Court remarked that the officer "deliberately and designedly set out to elicit information . . . just as surely as—and perhaps more effectively than—if he had formally interrogated him."

This language in *Williams* suggested the possibility that the terms "deliberate elicitation" and "interrogation" were constitutional synonyms. If they were, the Court's *Miranda* jurisprudence relating to "custodial interrogation" might have applied in the Sixth Amendment context, and vice-versa. However, in *Rhode Island v. Innis*,[58] the first Supreme Court case to define "interrogation" under *Miranda*, the Court indicated that it was erroneous to suggest "that the definition of 'interrogation' under *Miranda* is informed by this Court's [Sixth Amendment] decision[s]. . . . The definitions of 'interrogation' under the Fifth and Sixth Amendments, *if indeed the term 'interrogation' is even apt in the Sixth Amendment context*, are not necessarily interchangeable. . . ."[59]

The meaning of "deliberate elicitation" in the Sixth Amendment context is described more fully below. However, in view of the Court's warning in *Innis*, it is important to treat the Sixth Amendment and Fifth Amendment versions of the right to counsel separately.

---

[58] 446 U.S. 291 (1980).

[59] *Id.* at 300 n. 4 (emphasis added)

## [B] What Does "Deliberate" Mean?

### [1] "Deliberate" as "Purposeful"

In the most obvious situation, "deliberate elicitation" occurs when a government agent purposely elicits an incriminating statement from the accused, *i.e.*, when it is her conscious object to obtain a statement from the defendant. For example, purposeful (and, therefore, deliberate) elicitation occurs when an officer formally interrogates the accused person. Or, as in *Massiah*, it occurs when an undercover agent engages the accused in a conversation in order to obtain incriminating comments. Or, as in *Williams*, the Sixth Amendment is triggered when an officer makes statements that are designed to play on the conscience of the accused in order to induce incriminating remarks.

*Massiah*'s "deliberate elicitation" differs from the *Miranda-Innis* concept of "interrogation"[60] in that the former test centers on the subjective motivation of the officer, whereas the latter standard focuses on the suspect and is based on an objective finding that the process will likely result in incriminating information. Thus, there can be a *Miranda* "interrogation" based on negligent action by an officer, whereas the *Massiah* "deliberate elicitation" standard requires a higher standard of "culpability" by the officer.

### [2] "Deliberate" As Meaning Something Less Than "Purposeful"

#### [a] *United States v. Henry*

In *United States v. Henry*,[61] the Supreme Court examined further the concept of "deliberate elicitation." In *Henry*, the Federal Bureau of Investigation placed *I*, a paid informant, in a jail cell with *D* after the latter had been indicted. An FBI agent told *I* "to be alert to any statement" made by *D*, "but not to initiate any conversation with or question" him. However, *I* "engaged in conversation" with *D* various times, during which *D* made statements that the government sought to introduce at his trial.

In an opinion written by Chief Justice Warren Burger, the Court held that the government "deliberately elicited" the statements "within the meaning of *Massiah*." In reaching this conclusion, it focused on three facts: (1) *I* was paid on a contingent-fee basis, and thus had an incentive to obtain information from *D*; (2) *I* pretended to be a fellow inmate, which made it possible for him to engage in conversations with *D* without arousing suspicion; and (3) *D* was in custody, which "bring[s] into play subtle

---

[60] *See* § 24.08, *supra*.

[61] 447 U.S. 264 (1980).

influences that . . . make [an inmate] particularly susceptible to the ploys of undercover Government agents."

Based on these facts, the Court concluded that the government "must have known" that *I*'s proximity to *D* "likely would lead" to the incriminating statements. And, in the critical language of the opinion, the Court stated that "[b]y intentionally creating a situation likely to induce [*D*] to make incriminating statements without the assistance of counsel, the Government violated [*D*'s] Sixth Amendment right to counsel." This conclusion followed, it said, regardless of whether *I* or *D* raised the subject of the accused's criminal activities, and whether or not *I* questioned *D* about the crime or merely "engaged in general conversation about it."

A careful reading of the language of *Henry* raises questions about the meaning of the triggering term, "deliberate elicitation." If *Massiah* and *Williams* involved "purposeful" elicitation, *Henry* involved proof of no more than "knowledge" by the FBI agent that *I* would attempt to secure incriminating information. In fact, in view of the Court's statement that the government "must have known" that *I*'s conduct "likely" would result in information, the agent's state of mind might even more accurately be described as "reckless."[62] This conclusion is also consistent with the Court's statement that the government "intentionally" created a situation "likely to induce" the statements. That is, the "intent" here relates not to the elicitation but to the creation of the circumstances in which the elicitation was likely to occur.

### [b]  *Maine v. Moulton*

*Henry* was reinforced in *Maine v. Moulton*,[63] a case remarkably similar factually to *Massiah*. In *Moulton*, *D* and *I*[64] were indicted for theft and were released from custody pending trial. Unbeknownst to *D*, *I* agreed to cooperate with the prosecution and to testify against *D*.

*I* informed the police that *D* had suggested to him that a witness in the case ought to be killed. In order to obtain information regarding this proposed crime, the police received permission from *I* to install a recording device on his telephone. Thereafter, *D* telephoned *I* three times, during which conversations he commented on the pending theft charges.

---

[62] *E.g.*, Model Penal Code § 2.02(2)(c) ("A person acts recklessly . . . when he consciously disregards a substantial and unjustifiable risk [that incriminating statements] will result from his conduct").

[63] 474 U.S. 159 (1985).

[64] The last name of the surreptitious agent in *Moulton*—Colson—was the same as in *Massiah*, although they presumably were different persons.

In the last conversation, *D* asked *I* to meet with him to plan their defense in the theft case. *I* agreed and went to the meeting with a transmitter hidden on his body. During the conference, some of the discussion centered on *D*'s thoughts, by now discarded, about "eliminating" the witness, but most of the conversation "encouraged" by *I* involved the pending charges. Specifically, *I* professed a bad memory and repeatedly asked *D* to "remind him" about the details of the theft. As a consequence, *D* made various incriminating statements about the crime.

The government sought to introduce statements made by *D* on the telephone as well as during his meeting with *I*. It argued that *Massiah* and *Henry* were distinguishable on the ground that, in those cases, the police set up the encounters with the defendants, whereas here it was *D* who initiated the telephone calls and meeting.[65]

The Supreme Court, per Justice William Brennan, disagreed. It stated that the Sixth Amendment right to counsel did not depend on the identity of the instigating party. Rather, the Sixth Amendment "guarantees the accused . . . the right to rely on counsel as a 'medium' between him and the State. . . . [T]his guarantee includes the State's affirmative obligation not to act in a manner that circumvents the protections accorded the accused by invoking this right."[66]

The Court agreed that the Sixth Amendment is not violated if the government obtains incriminating information from the accused "by luck or happenstance." But, it warned, "knowing exploitation by the State of an opportunity to confront the accused without counsel being present is as much a breach of the State's obligation . . . as is the intentional creation of such an opportunity."

### [3] Summary

Based on the language of existing case law, "deliberate elicitation" for purposes of Sixth Amendment law occurs when the government through its overt or covert agent: (1) acts with the purpose of eliciting incriminating information from the accused regarding the pending charges, without regard to the likelihood that the elicitation will be successful (*Massiah*, *Williams*); (2) purposely sets up an encounter in which incriminating information is likely to be elicited (*Henry*); or (3) exploits an encounter set up by the accused with the agent that it knows is likely to result in incriminating information (*Moulton*).

---

[65] The government also argued that the statements were admissible because they were obtained during a legitimate investigation of the proposed murder. This issue is considered at § 25.07[B], *infra*.

[66] Maine v. Moulton, 474 U.S. at 176.

This being said, the most critical Sixth Amendment language—the triggering activity—remains "deliberate elicitation." Although the Court has not expressly recanted on the language in *Henry* and *Moulton*, to the extent that the current Justices are (or become) less enamored of the *Massiah* line of cases than their predecessors,[67] it is likely that the more expansive reading of the case will not sbe applied.

### [C]  What Is "Elicitation"?

### [1]  The Issue

*Massiah* did not state that the government is barred from putting one of its agents in close proximity to an accused person, outside the presence of defense counsel. It only prohibited "deliberate elicitation" of incriminating statements. What, however, constitutes "elicitation"?

*Massiah*, *Henry*, and *Moulton* involved conversations by an informant with the accused. *Williams* involved a speech given to the accused by a police officer. In each of these cases, the Court ruled that the government conduct constituted "deliberate elicitation" of the ensuing incriminating remarks. Are there even more subtle ways for the government to elicit incriminating statements from an accused?

For example, is it permissible for the police to put *I*, an informant, in the accused's jail cell and instruct her as follows: "[p]retend you are deaf and unable to communicate verbally. *D* is a blabbermouth, so just report anything that *D* says to you or others in your presence." If the agent follows these instruction—if she is a mere passive listener or "listening post"—is the Sixth Amendment violated, on the theory that the government "must have known" that "blabbermouth *D*" would talk? Alternatively, Fourth Amendment issues aside, would it be permissible for the police to install a listening device in a jail cell, in order to hear *D*'s conversations with her *non*-informant cellmate?

*Henry* observed that a listening post, as "an inanimate electronic device[,] . . . has no capability of leading the conversation into any particular subject or prompting any particular replies." Nonetheless, the Court surprisingly skirted the matter, stating that "there is no occasion to treat [the issue]; nor are we called upon to pass on the situation where an informant is placed in close proximity but makes no effort to stimulate conversations about the crime charged."[68] The Court again expressly left these questions unanswered in *Maine v. Moulton*.[69]

---

[67] *See* the text to Note 16, *supra*.

[68] United States v. Henry, 447 U.S. 264, 271 n.9 (1980).

[69] 474 U.S. at 177 n.13.

### [2]　The Court's Answer: *Kuhlmann v. Wilson*

In *Kuhlmann v. Wilson*,[70] *I*, an informant, was placed in a jail cell with instructions to "keep his ears open," to avoid asking *D* any questions, and to report to the police any statements made by *D*. The trial court found that *I* followed these instructions. Subsequently, the prosecutor sought to introduce statements made by *D* to *I* in the jail.

The Supreme Court held that the Sixth Amendment is not violated by the placement of a police agent in a jail cell with a person against whom formal charges have been brought, as long as the government does not conduct "investigatory techniques that are the equivalent of direct police interrogation." According to *Wilson*, in order to prove a violation of the Sixth Amendment, "the defendant must demonstrate that the police and their informant took some action, beyond mere listening, that was designed deliberately to elicit incriminating remarks." As there was no evidence in *Wilson* of such affirmative conduct, the Sixth Amendment was not breached. *Wilson* is distinguishable from *Henry*, because the informant in the latter case "stimulated" conversations with the accused, and from *Moulton*, where the informant asked the defendant questions to "refresh his memory."[71]

## § 25.06　Waiver of the Right to Counsel

### [A]　General Principles

There is no way for a person to waive her right to be free from police-initiated "interrogation" that she does not know is occurring.[72] Therefore, the issue of waiver does not come into play in the context of "secret interrogations," *i.e.*, when an undercover agent deliberately elicits incriminating statements from an accused, as occurred in *Massiah v. United States*,[73] *United States v. Henry*,[74] and *Maine v. Moulton*.[75]

---

[70] 477 U.S. 436 (1986).

[71] The facts in *Brewer v. Williams* suggest some lurking issues undeveloped by the Court in the case: *D* did not immediately respond to the "Christian burial speech" given in the police vehicle (see the text following Note 57, *supra*). Although the exact timing is unstated, seemingly some considerable time passed before Williams decided to speak about the whereabouts of the victim. Thus, the first question: did the officer's deliberate conduct in fact *elicit* Williams's statements or were they a free will act of a conscience-stricken man that coincidentially followed the speech? Or perhaps the burial speech triggered the suspect's conscience, which in turn caused him to speak, but then the issue lurking in the "elicitation" area is the extent to which the concept of proximate causation—here, the accused's own reasons for "coming clean"—should inform the analysis.

[72] United States v. Henry, 447 U.S. at 273.

[73] 377 U.S. 201 (1964). *See* § 25.02, *supra*.

[74] 447 U.S. 264 (1980). *See* § 25.05[B][2][a], *supra*.

[75] 474 U.S. 159 (1985). *See* § 25.05[B][2][b], *supra*.

In all other circumstances, the *Zerbst*[76] test of waiver applies to the Sixth Amendment right to counsel. That is, "[f]or the fruits of postindictment interrogations to be admissible in a prosecution's case in chief, the State must prove a voluntary, knowing, and intelligent relinquishment of the Sixth Amendment right to counsel."[77]

The difficulties arise in determining what the police must do to obtain a valid waiver and, more particularly, whether or when they may communicate—either to "deliberately elicit" incriminating statements or to seek a waiver—with a suspect who has now become, formally, "the accused." As the materials that follow demonstrate, the Court has struggled mightily with these questions; moreover, some questions remain unresolved or the law potentially in transition.

### [B] The Court's First Waiver Case: *Brewer v. Williams*

In *Brewer v. Williams*,[78] *D* was arrested and arraigned in Davenport, Iowa, for the abduction of a young girl, believed to be dead, that occurred in Des Moines. *D* received *Miranda* warnings shortly after he was arrested, and twice more later. At the arraignment in Davenport, *D* spoke briefly to an attorney, who advised him to remain silent until he saw his Des Moines lawyer. *D* also spoke by telephone to his Des Moines counsel, who gave him the same advice. The police agreed not to question *D* while they transported him to Des Moines.

On the trip, *D* told the officers in the car that he would talk to them about the crime after he arrived at his destination and spoke to his attorney. Nonetheless, an officer deliberately sought to elicit incriminating information from *D* by giving the so-called "Christian burial speech."[79] Later during the ride, apparently as the result of the officer's remarks,[80] *D* made incriminating statements and led the police to the body of the victim.[81]

The Supreme Court, per Justice Stewart, held that *D*'s incriminating statements to the police during the trip were obtained in violation of the Sixth Amendment. Adversary judicial proceedings had commenced against

---

[76] Johnson v. Zerbst, 304 U.S. 458 (1938). *See* § 4.02[A] *supra.*

[77] Michigan v. Harvey, 494 U.S. 344, 348–49 (1990).

[78] 430 U.S. 387 (1977).

[79] *See* § 25.05[A], *supra.*

[80] *But see* Note 71, *supra.*

[81] For a fascinating account of the facts regarding the crime, the Christian burial speech, and defense counsel's trial strategy, much of which is not evident in the Supreme Court opinion, *see* Phillip E. Johnson, *The Return of the "Christian Burial Speech" Case*, 32 Emory L.J. 349 (1983); Yale Kamisar, *Brewer v. Williams—A Hard Look at a Discomfiting Record*, 66 Geo. L.J. 209 (1977); *see also* Thomas N. McInnis, The Christian Burial Case (2001).

*D*, so his Sixth Amendment right to counsel had attached. The statements made were the result of deliberate elicitation (the Christian burial speech). And, although *D* could have waived his right to counsel, a valid waiver was not secured in this case.

But, why was there no valid waiver here? Under *Zerbst*, the waiver had to be "knowing and intelligent" and voluntary. *D* had been read his *Miranda* rights three times, so he knew that he had a right to assistance of counsel, and the Court agreed that he appeared to understand the warnings. Furthermore, the Court assumed that *D*'s disclosures were voluntarily made, so there was no basis to contend that he was coerced to waive his right to counsel and talk.

The Court's simple answer to the question—"Why was there no valid waiver?"—was that there *had been no waiver at all*, valid or otherwise. The Court said that "waiver requires not merely comprehension but relinquishment, and [*D*'s] consistent reliance upon the advice of counsel in dealing with the authorities refutes any suggestion that he waived that right." That is, *D* not only talked to his lawyers in both cities before he entered the police vehicle, but he told the officers in the car that he would tell them the whole story *after* he consulted with his Des Moines counsel.

But, *D* might have changed his mind after he heard the Christian burial speech. Does the Court's holding in *Williams* suggest, as Chief Justice Burger feared in dissent, that the Court "conclusively presumes a suspect is legally incompetent to change his mind and tell the truth until an attorney is present"?

Justice Stewart's opinion did not go that far. The majority criticized the officers because, despite *D*'s "express and implicit assertions of his right to counsel," the police sought to elicit incriminating statements without "prefac[ing] this effort by telling [*D*] that he had a right to the presence of a lawyer, and made no effort at all to ascertain whether [*D*] wished to relinquish that right." It would seem from this language that Stewart meant that once an accused asserts her right to counsel, a valid waiver is possible, but only if the officer reinforms the suspect of her right to counsel and secures an express waiver.

Concurring Justice Lewis Powell offered another solution: a waiver could be found if the prosecutor had proved that "police officers refrained from coercion and interrogation . . . and that [*D*] freely on his own initiative . . . confessed the crime." In short, once an accused indicates a desire to talk to counsel, as occurred here, police-initiated conversation about the crime should cease. As discussed immediately below, Justice Powell's "solution" appears to have prevailed.

## [C] When May a Waiver Be Secured?

### [1] When the Accused Requests Counsel

#### [a] The *Michigan v. Jackson* Rule

In *Brewer v. Williams*,[82] the Court held that *D* did not relinquish his Sixth Amendment right to counsel. The Court majority implied that a valid waiver could have been secured if, after *D* had expressed a wish to talk to his attorney, the police had not deliberately elicited statements from him until they had reinformed him of his rights and obtained an express waiver.

This solution apparently will not do. In *Michigan v. Jackson*,[83] the Court held that once the Sixth Amendment right to counsel attaches and the accused requests assistance of counsel, the government may no longer deliberately elicit information from her until she has consulted with her counsel, unless *she* initiates further communications, exchanges, or conversations with the government. In effect, the Court extended the protections announced in *Edwards v. Arizona*,[84] a *Miranda* waiver case, to the Sixth Amendment.

In *Jackson*, *D* was arraigned for murder. At the arraignment, as is routinely done at such a proceeding, the judge informed *D* of his right, as an indigent, to the appointment of counsel. *D* invoked the right. A notice of appointment of counsel was promptly mailed to a law firm. Before the firm received the notice, however, the police contacted *D*, read him his *Miranda* rights, and (after waiver) questioned him. Although *D* asked several times about his lawyer, he answered their questions. The Supreme Court, per Justice John Stevens, held that the waiver was invalid because the police initiated the conversation—or "private interview," as Stevens has since described it[85] —after *D* had requested counsel.

Justice Stevens justified application of the Fifth Amendment *Edwards* rule in the Sixth Amendment context by stating that the "reasons for prohibiting the interrogation of an uncounseled prisoner who has asked for the help of a lawyer are even stronger after he has been formally charged with an offense than before." Once formal charges are brought—"and a person who had previously been just a 'suspect' has become an 'accused' "—a defendant is entitled "to rely on counsel as a 'medium' between him and the State."[86] In these circumstances, the Court concluded in

---

[82] 430 U.S. 387 (1977).

[83] 475 U.S. 625 (1986).

[84] 451 U.S. 477 (1981). *See* § 24.10[B][3][a], *supra.*

[85] Patterson v. Illinois, 487 U.S. 285, 302 (1988) (dissenting opinion); Michigan v. Harvey, 494 U.S. 344, 355 (1990) (dissenting opinion).

[86] Michigan v. Jackson, 475 U.S. at 632 (quoting Maine v. Moulton, 474 U.S. 159, 176 (1985)).

*Jackson*, "the reasoning of . . . [*Edwards*] applies with even greater force
. . . ."

Notwithstanding the *Jackson* Court's emphasis on the Sixth Amendment
aspects of the case—and, indeed, the stated greater justification for the rule
in the latter context—the Supreme Court has subsequently stated that the
holding in *Jackson*, although "based on the Sixth Amendment, . . . [has]
its roots . . . in [the] Court's decisions in *Miranda* . . ., and succeeding
cases."[87] And, just as *Edwards* is a prophylactic rule designed to enforce
the *Miranda* doctrine,[88] *Jackson* is now characterized as a prophylactic rule,
albeit one attached to the Sixth Amendment.[89]

### [b]   *Jackson* (Sixth Amendment) versus *Edwards* (*Miranda*)

Although *Jackson* is based on *Edwards*, which in turn is based on
*Miranda* principles, the fact that *Jackson* is a Sixth Amendment case should
not be ignored. First, because the Sixth Amendment right to counsel is
offense-specific.[90] The *Jackson* rule only comes into play in regard to
crimes for which formal judicial proceedings have commenced. For example, in *McNeil v. Wisconsin*,[91] *D* invoked his Sixth Amendment right to
counsel regarding an armed robbery, for which the right had attached. The
Court held, however, that the police were *not* required by *Jackson* to cease
interrogation regarding other, uncharged offenses, since the Sixth Amendment did not apply as to those crimes. Under *Miranda-Edwards*, however,
once a person in custody asserts her Fifth Amendment (*Miranda*) right to
counsel, she may not be questioned regarding *any* offense, unless counsel
is present or the suspect initiates the conversation.[92]

Second, it should be observed that in *Jackson*, *D* requested counsel at
a judicial proceeding, and not at the point at which he was about to be
interviewed by the police. Presumably, *D* requested appointment of counsel
for *all* purposes relating to the criminal prosecution, and not simply (or
primarily?) to assist in any subsequent interrogation. Nonetheless, this
request was sufficient under *Jackson* to bar the police from questioning him.
In contrast, in the *Miranda* context, the *Edwards* rule only applies if the
request for a lawyer "can reasonably be construed to be an expression of
a desire for the assistance of an attorney *in dealing with custodial interrogation by the police*."[93] Presumably, the request in *Jackson*, coming as it did

---

[87] Michigan v. Harvey, 494 U.S. at 349–50.

[88] *See* § 24.10[B][3][a], *supra*.

[89] This characterization of *Jackson* has practical significance. *See* § 25.07[C], *infra*.

[90] *See* § 25.03[B], *supra*.

[91] 501 U.S. 171 (1991).

[92] *See* § 24.10[B][3][a], *supra*.

[93] McNeil v. Wisconsin, 501 U.S. at 178. *See* § 24.10[B][3][b][ii], *supra*.

at a judicial hearing, would not have sufficed under *Edwards*. Moreover, it is questionable whether a suspect may invoke her *Miranda* right to counsel at any time other than immediately prior to custodial interrogation;[94] as *Jackson* demonstrates, however, no such time limitation applies to the Sixth Amendment.

### [c] *Jackson's* Continued Vitality

The current vitality of the *Jackson* rule has been called into question by three concurring Justices in *Texas v. Cobb*.[95] Justice Kennedy (writing also for Justices Scalia and Thomas) characterized the "underlying theory" of *Jackson* as "questionable": "The *Miranda* rule, and the related preventative rule of *Edwards v. Arizona* . . . serve to protect a suspect's voluntary choice not to speak outside his lawyer's presence. The parallel rule announced in *Jackson*, however, supersedes the suspect's voluntary choice to speak with investigators."

In support of this proposition, Kennedy quoted from a post-*Jackson* case, *Patterson v. Illinois*,[96] which explained *Edwards* on the ground that it sought to "[p]reserv[e] the integrity of an accused's choice to communicate with police only through counsel," and which stated that the *Edwards* rule was not intended to "bar[] an accused from making an *initial* election as to whether he will face the State's officers during questioning with the aid of counsel, or go it alone." According to Kennedy, in *Cobb*, "[t]here is little justification for not applying the same course of reasoning with equal force to the court-made preventative rule announced in *Jackson*; for *Jackson*, after all, was a wholesale importation of the *Edwards* rule into the Sixth Amendment."

Justice Kennedy provided a second reason "to doubt the wisdom of the *Jackson* holding." He pointed to the fact that the *Jackson* rule, unlike *Edwards*, can be triggered outside the context of the interrogation process and, therefore "without reference to the suspect's choice to speak with investigators after *Miranda* warnings. . . . We ought to question the wisdom of a judge-made preventative rule to protect a suspect's desire not to speak when it cannot be shown that he had that intent." At a minimum, Kennedy suggested, "[e]ven if *Jackson* is to remain good law, its protections should apply only where a suspect has made a clear and unambiguous assertion of the right not to speak outside the presence of counsel, the same clear election required under *Edwards*."

---

[94] *See* § 24.10[B][3][b][iii], *supra*.

[95] 532 U.S. 162 (2001).

[96] 487 U.S. 285 (1988).

The *Cobb* five-Justice majority opinion did not need to reach the *Jackson* issue and, therefore, was silent on the matter. This means Chief Justice Rehnquist and Justice O'Connor—the two remaining members of the majority—fall in the "unknown vote" column.[97] The four dissenters— Justice Breyer, writing also for Justices Stevens, Souter, and Ginsburg— sharply criticized the concurring opinion's rejection of *Jackson*. It empha- sized the difference between *Jackson* and *Edwards*, namely, that the former case implicates the Sixth Amendment, a right independent of the Fifth Amendment (and even one thought to state a more compelling claim), a distinction "repeatedly recognized in our cases."

### [2] When the Accused Does Not Request Counsel

### [a] Before Counsel is Appointed or Hired

*Michigan v. Jackson*,[98] discussed in subsection [1], involved the issue of what the police must do when they wish to question a person regarding an offense for which judicial proceedings have commenced, *if the accused person has requested assistance by counsel.* But, what if the police want to interrogate the accused, and she does *not* assert her desire to consult with a lawyer? Under such circumstances, it may be necessary to distinguish between two situations: first, the case in which the accused has a lawyer (either appointed or privately hired), but has not asserted a desire to consult with her counsel prior to the interrogation; and, second, the case in which the accused does not yet have an attorney, nor has she requested one. The former case is discussed in the subsection immediately following this one.

The issue of how to deal with the second situation was raised in *Patterson v. Illinois*.[99] In *Patterson*, *D* was arrested and jailed. He was read his *Miranda* rights, after which he volunteered to answer questions. Two days later, he was indicted, triggering his Sixth Amendment right to counsel.

Shortly after indictment, a police officer informed *D* of the indictment. *D* asked the officer various questions about the charges and then began to talk about the crime. The officer interrupted *D*, repeated the *Miranda* warnings, and secured a waiver of his rights. At the time of the post- indictment questioning, *D* had not yet retained, or accepted by appointment, a lawyer to represent him.

---

[97] Justice Rehnquist, however, previously criticized *Massiah* itself, stating that it "consti- tutes such a substantial departure from the traditional concerns that underlie the Sixth Amendment guarantee that its language, if not its actual holding, should be ex-examined." United States v. Henry, 447 U.S. 264, 290 (1980) (dissenting opinion). Thus, it is very likely that the Chief Justice is prepared to overrule or narrow *Jackson* along Kennedy's lines. That leaves Justice O'Connor's as the only unknown vote in the equation.

[98] 475 U.S. 625 (1986).

[99] 487 U.S. 285 (1988).

The Court, per Justice Byron White, upheld the admissibility of the post-indictment statements. It held that *Jackson* did not bar all counsel-less interrogation after the Sixth Amendment attaches, but only questioning that occurs after the accused seeks the help of a lawyer. In effect, in the absence of such a request, the police are not prohibited from attempting to secure a waiver of an accused's Sixth Amendment rights.

Justice White contended that there is no practical difference between a person who is formally accused of a crime, and thus whose Sixth Amendment right to counsel has come into play, and a pre-indicted custodial suspect about to undergo questioning. In both cases, the individual has the right to the assistance of counsel; in both cases, that right must be honored if it is asserted; but, in the absence of the exercise of the right, the government is not barred from questioning her after obtaining a valid waiver.

Justice Stevens, the author of *Jackson*, dissented. He rejected the majority's assertion that the Fifth Amendment and Sixth Amendment rights to counsel are fundamentally the same. Quoting from *Jackson* and other Sixth Amendment cases, Justice Stevens concluded that "our prior decisions have . . . made clear that the return of a formal charge fundamentally alters the relationship between the State and the accused, conferring increased protections upon defendants in their interactions with state authorities."

Stevens and the three other dissenting Justices in *Patterson* would have held that the police may not conduct a "private interview" once formal adversary proceedings have commenced, with or without an express assertion of the right to counsel by the defendant. The dissent's position, it may be noted, is consistent with the "adversarial assistance" model of defense counsel representation that arguably best explains the rationale of *Massiah v. United States.*[100]

### [b] After Counsel is Appointed or Hired

In *Patterson*, a lawyer had not yet been retained or appointed for *D*, nor had *D* affirmatively requested counsel; therefore, the police were permitted to seek a waiver of his right to counsel and interrogate him. In a footnote in *Patterson*, however, the Court stated that it was "a matter of some significance" that *D* had not yet retained or accepted by appointment a lawyer to represent him. When an accused person is represented by counsel at the time that the police seek to question her, *Patterson* noted, "a distinct set of constitutional safeguards aimed at preserving the sanctity of the attorney-client relationship takes effect."

---

[100] *See* the text to Notes 31–35, *supra.*

Although *Patterson* did not amplify on this statement, the Court cited *Maine v. Moulton*,[101] a case that held that once adversary proceedings commence, and the accused is represented by counsel, the government is required (in *Moulton*'s words) "to rely on [defense] counsel as a 'medium' between him and the State." Thus, one can infer from *Patterson* and *Moulton* that, once the Sixth Amendment attaches and the accused has a lawyer, the government may not directly initiate communications with the accused in order to interrogate her, but must deal with her through counsel, whether or not the defendant expresses a desire for counsel's presence.

But, this reading of *Patterson-Moulton* is now in doubt. In *Texas v. Cobb*,[102] dissenting Justice Breyer summarized various "background principles" relating to the Sixth Amendment that he believed prior case law enunciated, one of which is that "once the [Sixth Amendment] right [to counsel] attaches, law enforcement officials are required, in most circumstances, to deal with the defendant through counsel rather than directly, even if the defendant has waived his Fifth Amendment rights." Breyer cited and quoted from *Jackson* and *Moulton*, which support this principle.

Chief Justice Rehnquist, writing for the majority in *Cobb*, however, responded in footnote:

> [C]ontrary to the dissent's suggestion . . . there is no 'background principle' of our Sixth Amendment jurisprudence establishing that there may be no contact between a defendant and police without counsel present. . . . Every profession is competent to define the standards of conduct for its members, but such standards are obviously not controlling in interpretation of constitutional provisions.

This language directly undermines *Moulton* and may suggest the collapse of the distinction between the "counsel hired but not requested" situation (*Moulton*) and the "no counsel hired or requested" case (*Patterson*). After *Cobb*, *Patterson* may apply in both cases. If so, the only remaining line— and one which is itself in some doubt[103] —is the one that treats "lawyer requested" (*Jackson*) cases specially.

### [D]   Elements of a Valid Waiver

### [1]   "Voluntary"

The Supreme Court has not specifically ruled on what constitutes a voluntary waiver of the Sixth Amendment right to counsel, but it will almost

---

[101] 474 U.S. 159 (1985). *See* § 25.05[B][2][b], *supra.*

[102] 532 U.S. 162 (2001).

[103] *See* § 25.06[C][1][c], *supra.*

certainly look to its *Miranda* jurisprudence, which in turn is based on general due process concepts of voluntariness.[104]

### [2] "Knowing and Intelligent"

The Sixth Amendment elements of a "knowing and intelligent" waiver are largely the same as for a waiver of a suspect's *Miranda* rights. According to *Patterson v. Illinois*,[105] at least when the accused is aware (as she was in *Patterson*) that formal proceedings have commenced against her,[106]

> [a]s a general matter, . . . an accused who is admonished with the warnings prescribed by . . . *Miranda*, . . . has been sufficiently apprised of the nature of his Sixth Amendment rights, and of the consequences of abandoning those rights, so that his waiver on this basis will be considered a knowing and intelligent one.[107]

According to *Patterson*, *Miranda* warnings convey "the sum and substance" of the Sixth Amendment right to counsel. The warnings inform the accused that she has the right to have a lawyer appointed prior to questioning and to have counsel present during questioning. The warnings also inform her of the "ultimate adverse consequence" of foregoing the right to counsel, namely that any statement she makes can be used against her. And, the warnings tell her what a lawyer can do for her, "namely, advise [the accused] to refrain from making any such statements."

Justice Stevens, with whom Justices Brennan and Marshall joined, dissented. They argued that the defense lawyer's role after adversary proceedings have begun is more multi-dimensional than the majority suggested. To the dissenters, therefore, *Miranda* warnings inadequately inform an accused of the implication of giving up the Sixth Amendment right to counsel, as distinguished from the *Miranda* right to counsel. For example, the dissent argued, *Miranda* warnings do not convey the fact "that a lawyer might examine the indictment for legal sufficiency before submitting . . . her client to interrogation or that a lawyer is likely to be more skillful in negotiating a plea bargain and that such negotiations may be most fruitful if initiated prior to any interrogation."

---

[104] *See* §§ 24.10[A][3][b] (*Miranda*), 23.03 (due process), *supra*.

[105] 487 U.S. 285 (1988).

[106] The Court stated that "we do not address the question whether or not an accused must be told that he has been indicted before a postindictment Sixth Amendment waiver will be valid." *Id.* at 296 n.8. *See* Hayes v. Commonwealth, 25 S.W.3d 463 (Ky. 2000) (an officer's failure to inform *D* that he was under indictment does not render *D*'s waiver of his Sixth Amendment right to counsel void).

[107] *Contra under the state constitution*, State v. Sanchez, 609 A.2d 400 (N.J. 1992) (the "perfunctory recitation" of *Miranda* warnings does not provide sufficient information to the accused to make a knowing and intelligent waiver of the right to counsel).

## § 25.07    Scope of the Sixth Amendment Exclusionary Rule[108]

### [A]    Right or Remedy?

With the Fourth Amendment, the *right* the Constitution provides is that "the people" shall be secure in their "persons, houses, papers, and effects" from "unreasonable searches and seizures." At one time, the Supreme Court suggested that the constitutional *remedy* for the violation of this right was exclusion of the evidence secured by the police. More recently, the Supreme Court has indicated that the exclusionary rule related to the Fourth Amendment is a judicially, not constitutionally, created remedy. An effect of separating the *remedy*—exclusion of evidence—from the Fourth Amendment *right* is that the Court could (and has) narrowed the scope of the rule of exclusion and could arguably abolish it entirely or affirm legislative efforts to do so, assuming that an adequate alternative remedy replaces it.[109] Could the same fate be in store for the Sixth Amendment?

Professor James Tomkovicz has observed that "[m]ost of the United States Supreme Court's exclusionary rule work has been in the fourth amendment area. Some decisions have involved *Miranda*'s fifth amendment-based safeguards. . . . [But], the Court has said relatively little about the premises and limits of sixth amendment exclusion."[110] And, what the Court has said on the subject is inconsistent.

In *Maine v. Moulton*,[111] the Justices stated that "[t]he Sixth Amendment protects the right of the accused not to be confronted by an agent of the State. . . . This right [is] violated as soon as the State's agent engage[s] [*D*] in conversation about the charges pending against him." According to this reading, therefore, the Sixth Amendment is violated at the moment of deliberate elicitation—accused persons have a constitutional right to be free from such efforts (absent counsel or valid waiver).

One possible implication of *Moulton* is that exclusion at trial of an uncounseled statement is "merely" a remedy for the violation of the Sixth Amendment right, which occurred prior to trial. So understood, the Sixth Amendment exclusionary rule might meet the same fate as its Fourth Amendment cousin: the Supreme Court might determine that the exclusion remedy should only be applied in those circumstances in which exclusion

---

[108] *See generally* Arnold H. Loewy, *Police-Obtained Evidence and the Constitution: Distinguishing Unconstitutionally Obtained Evidence from Unconstitutionally Used Evidence,* 87 Mich. L. Rev. 907 (1989); James J. Tomkovicz, *The Massiah Right to Exclusion: Constitutional Premises and Doctrinal Implications,* 67 N.C. L. Rev. 751 (1989).

[109] *See* §§ 21.03, 21.05–.06, *supra.*

[110] Tomkovicz, Note 108, *supra,* at 752.

[111] 474 U.S. 159 (1985).

of evidence constitutes a meaningful deterrent to government misconduct.[112]

But, *Moulton* is neither the first nor necessarily the most relevant word on the subject. Consider the language *Massiah v. United States*[113] itself. Justice Stewart stated in *Massiah* that *D*, the accused, "was denied the basic protections of that [Sixth Amendment] guarantee when there was used against him at his trial evidence of his own incriminating words." The Court, it will be remembered, "did not question" the government's assertion that "it was entirely proper to continue an investigation of the suspected criminal activities of the defendant," even after indictment.

The implication of this reading is "that the *Massiah* Court believed that a sixth amendment violation occurred at the time of, and only at the time of, admission at trial of the fruits of an uncounseled pretrial encounter."[114] Put another way, the Sixth Amendment right and the remedy are one in the same: the *Constitution itself* compels the exclusion of any statement obtained as the result of uncounseled, unwaived, deliberate elicitation after formal adversary proceedings have commenced.

Under this view, the Sixth Amendment exclusionary rule has a constitutional pedigree that the Fourth Amendment version does not. On the other hand, this reading suggests that as long as the government does not seek to introduce the fruits of such deliberate elicitation, it is free (as far as the Sixth Amendment is concerned) to deliberately elicit statements from uncounseled persons, even after the prosecution has commenced. In potential support of this interpretation, the Supreme Court recently stated that there "is no 'background principle' of our Sixth Amendment jurisprudence establishing that there may be no contact between a[n accused] defendant and police without counsel present."[115]

It appears from the crosswinds of the Court's conflicting language that more work on this topic is necessary.

---

[112] In Nix v. Williams, 467 U.S. 431 (1984), a case dealing with the scope of the Sixth Amendment exclusionary rule, the Court did, indeed, analyze the rule as it does the Fourth Amendment version, in terms of cost-benefit deterrence principles. Professor Tomkovicz concludes from his reading of this case, however, that the Court "neither endorsed nor rejected a sixth amendment *right* to exclusion, but simply reasoned that an . . . exception [to the exclusionary rule] was wholly consistent with right-based exclusion." Tomkovicz, Note 108, *supra*, at 764 (emphasis added).

[113] 377 U.S. 201 (1964).

[114] Tomkovicz, Note 108, *supra*, at 763.

[115] Texas v. Cobb, 532 U.S. 162, 171 n.2 (2001).

## [B]   When the Police Investigate "Sixth Amendment" and "Non-Sixth Amendment" Offenses

As noted before, the Sixth Amendment is offense-specific.[116] Therefore, for example, from a Sixth Amendment perspective the police may interrogate $D$, who is under indictment for Offense 1, regarding any or all uncharged offenses[117] of which they suspect $D$. And, statements made by $D$ regarding an *uncharged* offense—call it Offense 2—is admissible against her in any subsequent prosecution for that offense.

Suppose, however, in an interrogation $D$ provides the police with incriminating statements regarding both Offense 1 *and* Offense 2. May the government say that they were only seeking information about Offense 2, which they had a right to do, and therefore should be permitted to use the "inadvertent" statement they obtained regarding Offense 1? Or, suppose the government concedes (or the court finds) that their interrogation had dual purposes, improperly to obtain information on Offense 1 *and* properly to secure statements about Offense 2?

The Court observed in *Maine v. Moulton*[118] that

> [t]o allow the admission of evidence obtained from the accused in violation of his Sixth Amendment rights whenever the police assert an alternative, legitimate reason for their surveillance invites abuse by law enforcement personnel in the form of fabricated investigations and risks the evisceration of the Sixth Amendment right recognized in *Massiah*. On the other hand, to exclude evidence pertaining to charges as to which the Sixth Amendment right to counsel had not attached at the time the evidence was obtained, simply because other charges were pending at that time, would unnecessarily frustrate the public's interest in the investigation of criminal activities.

The *Moulton* Court took the "more realistic view of police investigations" that "dual purposes may exist whenever police have more than one reason to investigate someone." Therefore, in such circumstances, *Moulton* states that "incriminating statements pertaining to pending charges are inadmissible at the trial of those charges, notwithstanding the fact that the police were also investigating other crimes if, in obtaining this evidence, the State violated the Sixth Amendment by knowingly circumventing the accused's right to the assistance of counsel."[119] At the same time, incriminating

---

116 *See* § 25.03[B], *supra.*

117 *See id.* for the definition of "offense" in this context.

118 474 U.S. at 180.

119 What constitutes a *knowing* circumvention of the accused's right to counsel? The Court has not answered this question in this context. For example, what if the police only question $D$ about Offense 2 and are genuinely surprised when $D$'s answer includes statements relevant

statements regarding a crime for which the Sixth Amendment has *not* attached are *admissible*, even though the latter evidence might be considered a fruit of a constitutional violation.

### [C]  Use of Evidence for Impeachment Purposes

The Court has not yet determined whether a statement obtained in violation of the Sixth Amendment right to counsel, although inadmissible in the prosecutor's case-in-chief, may be used to impeach the defendant's false or inconsistent trial testimony. Evidence obtained in violation of the Fourth Amendment[120] or *Miranda*[121] is admissible for such purposes, but coerced confessions may not be introduced for any purpose.[122]

However the Supreme Court may resolve the impeachment rule in regard to a core violation of the Sixth Amendment, it *has* announced that the rule of *Michigan v. Jackson*[123] has an impeachment exception. In *Michigan v. Harvey*,[124] the Supreme Court held that statements secured in violation of the *Jackson* rule, which prohibits the police from interrogating an accused person after she asserts her right to counsel (unless counsel is present or the accused initiates the communication), may be introduced at trial for impeachment purposes, if the subsequent waiver was valid.

In *Harvey*, D was arraigned on rape charges, and counsel was appointed to represent him. D told an officer that he wanted to make a statement, but that he did not know whether he should first talk to his lawyer. After the officer convinced him that he did not need to talk to his lawyer because the "lawyer was going to get a copy of the statement anyway," D signed a waiver form and subsequently made incriminating statements about the crime. The prosecution conceded that these statements were taken in violation of the *Jackson* rule and, therefore, were inadmissible in the prosecutor's case-in-chief. The prosecutor used the statements, however, in cross-examination, after D testified in his own defense and provided an account of the events that conflicted with his statements to the police.

The Supreme Court characterized the Sixth Amendment *Jackson* rule as prophylactic in nature, because it was founded on a Fifth Amendment case,

---

to Offense 1? Seemingly, this is not a *knowing* circumvention of D's right to counsel and, therefore, it would seem that the police might be able to use that statement against D! On the other hand, the Supreme Court may prefer to avoid the near-impossible effort of divining an interrogator's knowledge or purpose and conclude that there is a knowing circumvention if an interrogator is aware that her questioning might lead to statements about Offense 1.

[120] *See* § 21.05[B][2][b], *supra*.

[121] *See* § 24.12[A], *supra*.

[122] *See* § 23.02[E][2], *supra*.

[123] 475 U.S. 625 (1986). *See* § 25.06[C][1][a], *supra*.

[124] 494 U.S. 344 (1990).

*Edwards v. Arizona*,[125] which was adopted as a "second layer of protection" to the *Miranda* rules. Therefore, just as a statement obtained in violation of *Miranda* is admissible for impeachment purposes, a statement secured in violation of the *Jackson* rule may be used to impeach a defendant. The *Harvey* Court concluded "that the 'search for truth in a criminal case' outweighs the 'speculative possibility' that exclusion of evidence might deter future violations of rules not compelled directly by the Constitution in the first place."

### [D]　Fruit-of-the-Poisonous-Tree Doctrine

The fruit-of-the-poisonous-tree doctrine[126] applies to violations of the Sixth Amendment right to counsel, which means that the limitations on the rule—the independent source doctrine, the inevitable discovery rule, and the attenuated connection principle—also apply, although the Supreme Court has had little occasion to discuss the basic doctrine or its limitations in the Sixth Amendment context.

The inevitable discovery rule was expressly recognized in the Sixth Amendment context in *Nix v. Williams*,[127] a follow-up case to *Brewer v. Williams*.[128] In *Williams II*, the issue was whether the body of the victim found by the police as the result of their use of the Christian burial speech was inadmissible as a fruit of the initial Sixth Amendment violation. The Court held that the victim's body could be used in *D*'s trial because the prosecutor proved by a preponderance of the evidence "that the information [including forensic tests on the body] ultimately or inevitably would have been discovered by lawful means." The Court found no reason in this case to treat the inevitable discovery doctrine differently in the Sixth Amendment context than it would have done had there been a Fourth Amendment violation instead.

### § 25.08　Right-to-Counsel Summary: Sixth Amendment versus *Miranda*

How does the Sixth Amendment right to counsel differ from the Fifth Amendment (*Miranda*) right to counsel? The Supreme Court winds have blown hot and cold in regard to this question. It has observed that "the policies underlying the two constitutional protections are quite distinct,"[129] and it has had occasion to warn that *Miranda* jurisprudence is not always

---

[125] 451 U.S. 477 (1981).

[126] *See generally* § 21.08, *supra*.

[127] 467 U.S. 431 (1984).

[128] 430 U.S. 387 (1977). *See* § 25.06[B], *supra*.

[129] Rhode Island v. Innis, 446 U.S. 291, 300 n.4 (1980).

informed by the Court's Sixth Amendment case law.[130] Indeed, the Supreme Court has conceded[131] that the impression of many courts and commentators has been that the Sixth Amendment version of the right to counsel is stronger, *i.e.*, that it is a more difficult right to relinquish, than its *Miranda* cousin.

Particularly in recent years, however, the Court has denied the latter assertion. It has stated that it "never suggested that one right is 'superior' or 'greater' than the other,"[132] and it has sometimes merged its discussion of the two rights, as if the role of defense counsel were precisely the same, before and after the prosecution commences. In some circumstances, *Miranda* law is applied in the Sixth Amendment context.[133]

Nonetheless, some differences exist between the two rights. In some circumstances, the *Miranda* right to counsel may apply when the Sixth Amendment does not, and vice-versa. Also, even now, differences exist in waiver law, as well as regarding the exclusionary rule. The following is a checklist of those key areas in which the Court has recognized differences between the Sixth Amendment and *Miranda* rights to counsel.

1. Regarding when the right attaches:

First, the Sixth Amendment right applies only after adversary judicial criminal proceedings have been initiated against the accused; the Fifth Amendment right is not so limited, so the *Miranda* right to counsel may attach earlier.

Second, the Fifth Amendment right does not attach unless the suspect is in custody; the Sixth Amendment is not so limited. Therefore, the Sixth Amendment right can attach under circumstances in which *Miranda* does not apply.

Third, the Sixth Amendment right is offense-specific (it only applies as to the offense(s) for which criminal proceedings have commenced), whereas the *Miranda* right to counsel applies to all offenses, once custodial interrogation commences. Therefore, *Miranda* potentially applies to more offenses than does the Sixth Amendment.

---

[130] *Id.*

[131] Patterson v. Illinois, 487 U.S. 285, 297 (1988).

[132] *Id.*

[133] *E.g.*, Michigan v. Jackson, 475 U.S. 625 (1986) (*Edwards v. Arizona* rule relating to waiver of *Miranda* applies to the Sixth Amendment); Patterson v. Illinois, 487 U.S. 285 (1988) (knowing and intelligent waiver of *Miranda* rights ordinarily serves as a waiver of the Sixth Amendment); Michigan v. Harvey, 494 U.S. 344 (1990) (impeachment rule, applicable to *Miranda*, applies to violations of the *Michigan v. Jackson* "prophylactic" rule).

Fourth, *Miranda* applies when the custodial suspect is "interrogated," whereas the Sixth Amendment prohibits "deliberate elicitation." The terms are not equivalent. The *Miranda* version of interrogation focuses on the suspect, and the test is an objective one based on a finding of negligence by the officer; the Sixth Amendment right focuses on the intentions of the officer, and requires proof of deliberate misconduct, although the requisite "deliberate elicitation" has been found under circumstances approaching recklessness.

Fifth, the Sixth Amendment applies to deliberate elicitation by undercover agents, which is not the case under *Miranda*.

2. Regarding waiver of the right:

First, under *Miranda*, the police do not have to cease interrogation of a suspect who requests a lawyer, unless the request occurs under circumstances in which it can reasonably be construed to be an expression for the assistance of an attorney in dealing specifically with custodial interrogation by the police. A request for Sixth Amendment counsel is not currently limited in this manner, although some Justices seem prepared to set such a limit in the future.

Second, a defendant may currently assert her Sixth Amendment right to counsel, so as to bar police questioning, during a judicial proceeding and not simply while in police custody preceding or during the interrogation. However, it is doubtful whether a suspect may initially invoke her Fifth Amendment right to counsel at any time other than immediately prior to or during police custodial interrogation.

Third, once a person successfully asserts her Fifth Amendment right to counsel regarding an offense, she may not be approached regarding any other offense, unless counsel is present; however, because the Sixth Amendment right is offense-specific, invocation of the latter right to counsel does not bar questioning regarding uncharged offenses.

3. Regarding the exclusionary rule:

Fruit-of-the poisonous-tree principles apply to Sixth Amendment violations. The doctrine does not exist or is far more limited in the *Miranda* context.

## CHAPTER 26

# PRIVILEGE AGAINST SELF-INCRIMINATION: GENERAL PRINCIPLES

## § 26.01  Fifth Amendment Self-Incrimination Clause: Overview

The Fifth Amendment to the United States Constitution provides that "[n]o person . . . shall be compelled in any criminal case to be a witness against himself . . . ." The privilege applies to the states through the Fourteenth Amendment due process clause.[1]

Generally speaking, the privilege may be raised in any proceeding, civil or criminal, formal or informal, if the testimonial evidence that would be produced there might incriminate the speaker in a criminal proceeding.[2] Consequently, legal issues regarding the Fifth Amendment privilege arise throughout the legal system.

There is an enormous body of law and scholarly literature in the field. Unfortunately, as one writer observed, "[t]he privilege against self-incrimination is much discussed but little understood."[3] It is "unlikely that anyone could argue persuasively that . . . the elements of fifth amendment law . . . fit neatly into an internally consistent, sensible whole."[4] The Fifth Amendment privilege has been described as "an unsolved riddle of vast proportions, a Gordian knot in the middle of our Bill of Rights."[5] It is "a mandate in search of a meaning."[6]

This chapter touches on the history of, the policies underlying, and the general contours of, the privilege against compulsory self-incrimination.

---

[1] Malloy v. Hogan, 378 U.S. 1 (1964).

[2] Lefkowitz v. Turley, 414 U.S. 70 (1973).

[3] Robert B. McKay, *Self-Incrimination and the New Privacy*, 1967 Sup. Ct. Rev. 193, 193.

[4] William J. Stuntz, *Self-Incrimination and Excuse*, 88 Colum. L. Rev. 1227, 1228 (1988).

[5] Akhil Reed Amar & Reneé B. Lettow, *Fifth Amendment First Principles: The Self-Incrimination Clause*, 93 Mich. L. Rev. 857, 857 (1995).

[6] *Id.* at 922.

The role of the Fifth Amendment privilege in police interrogation law is considered elsewhere in the text.[7]

## § 26.02 The Origins of the Privilege Against Self-Incrimination[8]

The origins of the Fifth Amendment self-incrimination clause "lie in a tangled web of obscure historical events."[9] Indeed, until recently, most of what lawyers thought they knew about its origins came from the writings of John Wigmore and Leonard Levy. In the past fifteen years, however, new historical research has cast doubt on aspects of the earlier received accounts.

According to Wigmore, the roots of the Fifth Amendment privilege against self-incrimination lie in a twelfth century power struggle between the Crown and the Church.[10] Levy believed that this reading of history was too narrow, and that the privilege is also the result of religious, political, constitutional, and human-rights debates that racked England during the sixteenth and seventeenth centuries.[11]

A critical factor in the development of the privilege was opposition in England to the sixteenth and seventeenth century process by which the ecclesiastical courts and the Court of Star Chamber investigated claims of heresy. Under the then-existing law, persons "could be plucked from the street"[12] and administered an "oath *ex officio*," which required them to answer truthfully all questions put to them by the court, even before they were informed of the nature of the charges against them. And, "[t]o make matters worse, the purpose of these indiscriminate procedures was often to identify and punish those whose only possible offense was theological disagreement with the crown."[13]

---

[7] *See* chapters 23–24, *supra.*

[8] *See generally* Leonard W. Levy, The Origins of the Fifth Amendment (1968); Albert W. Alschuler, *A Peculiar Privilege in Historical Perspective: The Right to Remain Silent,* 94 Mich. L. Rev. 2625 (1996); John H. Langbein, *The Historical Origins of the Privilege Against Self-Incrimination at Common Law,* 92 Mich. L. Rev. 1047 (1994); M.R.T. Macnair, *The Early Development of the Privilege Against Self-Incrimination,* 10 Oxford J. Legal Stud. 66 (1990); Eben Moglen, *Taking the Fifth: Reconsidering the Origins of the Constitutional Privilege Against Self-Incrimination,* 92 Mich. L. Rev. 1086 (1994); E.M. Morgan, *The Privilege Against Self-Incrimination,* 34 Minn. L. Rev. 1 (1949).

[9] Laurence A. Benner, *Requiem for Miranda: The Rehnquist Court's Voluntariness Doctrine in Historical Perspective,* 67 Wash. U. L.Q. 59, 68 (1989).

[10] 8 John H. Wigmore, Evidence § 2251, at 317 (McNaughton rev. 1961).

[11] Levy, Note 8, *supra,* at 42; *see* Charles T. McCormick, McCormick on Evidence § 114 (Cleary rev. 1984) (stating that the privilege was, in part, the result of "important policies of individual freedom and dignity.").

[12] Amar & Lettow, Note 5, *supra,* at 896.

[13] *Id.* at 896–97.

The oath was abolished in 1641. However, courts were still permitted to pressure witnesses to testify and to use their silence against them. Gradually, according to traditional historical accounts, opposition to the oath turned into a general rejection of the perceived "unjust, unnatural, and immoral"[14] inquisitorial requirement that persons furnish evidence to convict themselves of crimes. This English opposition to compulsory self-incrimination was imported to this country by colonists who were ardent critics of the ecclesiastical oaths. Over time, the colonies enacted laws that prohibited the oath *ex officio* as well as the use of torture to obtain confessions. By the time of the Revolution, according to Levy, the privilege was viewed by the Constitution's framers as "a self-evident truth."[15]

More modern historical accounts suggest that the Fifth Amendment privilege, at least as we know it, is a relatively new phenomenon, and may have little to do with the heroic battles for religious and human freedom of those earlier centuries. According to one revisionist view, "the true origins of the common law privilege are to be found not in the high politics of the English revolutions, but in the rise of adversary criminal procedure at the end of the eighteenth century. The privilege against self-incrimination at common law was the work of defense counsel."[16]

According to this reading of history, the criminal procedure of the sixteenth and seventeenth centuries consisted of "a set of rules and practices whose purpose and effect were to oblige the accused to respond to the charges against him."[17] In this period, the "bedrock" principle was that a person accused of crime not only was not furnished a lawyer, but was *forbidden* to have one. Indeed, during this period, "[t]he essential purpose of the criminal trial was to afford the accused an opportunity to reply in person to the charges against him."[18] The view of the time was that a defendant did not need counsel because, if he was innocent, "he will be as effective as any lawyer"[19] in explaining his case; and if he was guilty, "the very Speech, Gesture, and Countenance . . . may often help disclose the Truth . . . ."[20]

The bar on defense counsel was relaxed in 1696 in treason prosecutions. By the 1730s, defense counsel was permitted in ordinary criminal trials.[21]

---

[14] Levy, Note 8, *supra*, at 330.

[15] *Id.* at 404, 430.

[16] Langbein, Note 8, *supra*, at 1047. The description that follows draws heavily from *id.* at 1048–71.

[17] *Id.* at 1049.

[18] *Id.* at 1047.

[19] *Id.* at 1053.

[20] 2 William Hawkins, A Treatise of the Pleas of the Crown ch. 39, § 2 (1721).

[21] Langbein, Note 8, *supra*, at 1067–68.

And with the advent of defense counsel, as Professor John Langbein has put it, the criminal process shifted from an "accused speaks" trial to a "testing the prosecution" form of trial. According to this reading of history,

> [c]ounsel . . . turned a system directed at getting the defendant to attempt rebuttal of the adverse evidence into one in which the prosecutor was expected to prove his case, beyond a reasonable doubt, in the face of a learnedly uncooperative defense. This reversal of the nature of the criminal trial had as one of its consequences the creation of a right against coercive self-incrimination; it replaced a system in which . . . self-incrimination was the whole point.[22]

This historical interpretation doubtlessly adds to our understanding of the Fifth Amendment privilege. Nonetheless, one should not minimize the significance of the earlier battles for religious and human freedom because, as a result of them, "compulsory examination of the accused . . . acquired a bad name."[23] As a result of English history, American courts, especially the United States Supreme Court during certain eras, came to view the self-incrimination privilege as a highly valued right, if not also a self-evident truth.

---

[22] Moglen, Note 8, *supra*, at 1088 (explaining Langbein's thesis).

[23] Stephen J. Schulhofer, *Some Kind Words for the Privilege Against Self-Incrimination*, 26 Val. U. L. Rev. 311, 312 (1991).

## § 26.03　Is the Privilege a Good Idea?: The Controversy[24]

### [A]　In General

The Fifth Amendment self-incrimination clause is exceptionally controversial. It is, says Professor Stephen Schulhofer, "probably our most schizophrenic amendment."[25] On the one hand, the Supreme Court, particularly during the Warren Court era, "waxed eloquent"[26] about the privilege, stating that it "reflects many of our fundamental values and most noble aspirations,"[27] and that it "registers an important advance in the development of our liberty—'one of the great landmarks in man's struggle to make himself civilized.' "[28] Yet, the Supreme Court, per Justice Benjamin Cardozo once observed that "[j]ustice . . . would not perish if the accused were subject to a duty to respond to orderly inquiry."[29]

Among scholars, too, the privilege has had its eloquent advocates,[30] but it has also been the object of withering criticism. Early on, Wigmore described it as a "mark of traditional sentimentality."[31] Bentham sought

---

[24] *See generally* Erwin N. Griswold, The Fifth Amendment Today (1955); David Dolinko, *Is There a Rationale for the Privilege Against Self-Incrimination?*, 33 UCLA L. Rev. 1063 (1986); Donald A. Dripps, *Self-Incrimination and Self-Preservation: A Skeptical View*, 1991 U. Ill. L. Rev. 329; Donald A. Dripps, *Against Police Interrogation—And the Privilege Against Self-Incrimination*, 78 J. Crim. L. & Criminology 699 (1988); Henry J. Friendly, *The Fifth Amendment Tomorrow: The Case for Constitutional Change*, 37 U. Cin. L. Rev. 671 (1968); Robert S. Gerstein, *The Demise of Boyd: Self-Incrimination and Private Papers in the Burger Court*, 27 UCLA L. Rev. 343 (1979); R. Kent Greenawalt, *Silence as a Moral and Constitutional Right*, 23 Wm. & Mary L. Rev. 15 (1981); Yale Kamisar, *On the Fruits of Miranda Violations, Coerced Confessions, and Compelled Testimony*, 93 Mich. L. Rev. 929 (1995); Susan R. Klein, *Enduring Principles and Current Crises in Constitutional Criminal Procedure*, 24 Law & Social Inquiry 533 (1999); John T. McNaughton, *The Privilege Against Self-Incrimination: Its Constitutional Affectation, Raison d'Etre and Miscellaneous Implications*, 51 J. Crim. L., Criminology & Police Sci. 138 (1960); Irene Merker Rosenberg & Yale Rosenberg, *In the Beginning: The Talmudic Rule Against Self-Incrimination*, 63 N.Y.U. L. Rev. 955 (1988); Schulhofer, Note 23, *supra*; Stuntz, Note 4, *supra*; Peter W. Tague, *The Fifth Amendment: If An Aid to the Guilty Defendant, An Impediment to the Innocent One*, 78 Geo. L.J. 1 (1989); George C. Thomas III & Marshall D. Bilder, *Aristotle's Paradox and the Self-Incrimination Puzzle*, 82 J. Crim. L. & Criminology 243 (1991).

[25] Schulhofer, Note 23, *supra*, at 311.

[26] Stephen A. Saltzburg, *The Required Records Doctrine: Its Lessons for the Privilege Against Self-Incrimination*, 53 U. Chi. L. Rev. 6, 6 (1986).

[27] Murphy v. Waterfront Comm'n, 378 U.S. 52, 55 (1964).

[28] Ullmann v. United States, 350 U.S. 422, 426 (1956) (quoting Griswold, Note 24, *supra*, at 7).

[29] Palko v. Connecticut, 302 U.S. 319, 326 (1937).

[30] *E.g.*, Levy, Note 8, *supra*; Gerstein, Note 24, *supra*; Greenawalt, Note 24, *supra*.

[31] 8 John Wigmore, Note 10, *supra*, § 2251, at 317.

to trivialize the privilege by claiming that it was based on "the old woman's reason" that "tis hard upon a man to be obliged to criminate himself."[32] Modern scholars, if anything, have been even more critical. One of them has concluded that "the leading . . . efforts to justify the privilege as more than a historical relic are uniformly unsatisfactory."[33] Professor Schulhofer, only exaggerating a bit, has stated that "[i]t is hard to find anyone these days who is willing to justify and defend the privilege against self-incrimination."[34]

In view of these disparate observations, the question must be asked: *is the privilege against compelled self-incrimination defensible?* What follows is a taste of the arguments against the privilege and in its defense. However, even if the privilege is abstractly indefensible, as some critics maintain, few people suggest that it should now be abolished by constitutional amendment. As one writer has pointed out, "one does not, when he performs the surgery on one part of the body, do it without regard for the impact on other parts of the body."[35] Professor David Dolinko, a critic of the rule, has observed that "[a] rule whose existence lacks any principled justification may nevertheless come to serve important functions in the legal system as a whole, so that its repeal would do violence to the entire system."[36]

### [B] The Modern Debate

### [1] The "Cruel Trilemma" Thesis

*What the defenders of the privilege say:* The Fifth Amendment privilege "[a]t its core, . . . reflects our fierce unwillingness to subject those suspected of crime to the cruel trilemma of self-accusation, perjury or contempt."[37] That is, if there were no privilege against self-incrimination, a person could be forced (as he was in the ecclesiastical courts and the Star Chamber) to testify under oath and either admit the truth, which could result in his punishment, lie under oath (and thus be subjected to punishment for perjury), or be held in contempt of court for failing to answer the questions (and thus be jailed on the latter charge).

*Response:* It is hardly self-evident that it is cruel to require a guilty person to admit his guilt or else accept the consequences of his refusal to testify truthfully. In any case, this "cruelty"—if it is such—is far less so than many

---

[32] 7 Jeremy Bentham, Rationale of Judicial Evidence 452 (Bowring ed. 1843).

[33] Dolinko, Note 24, *supra*, at 1064.

[34] Schulhofer, Note 23, *supra*, at 311.

[35] McNaughton, Note 24, *supra*, at 153.

[36] Dolinko, Note 24, *supra*, at 1064.

[37] Pennsylvania v. Muniz, 496 U.S. 582, 596 (1990) (internal quotations marks omitted).

other "cruelties" the law uncontroversially allows. A person in a civil proceeding, for example, may be compelled to provide damaging answers to questions in discovery and on a witness stand, yet nobody considers this too cruel to permit. Perhaps more to the point, a parent may be compelled to testify at a criminal trial against his child, under penalty of contempt, even though his testimony will send a loved one to prison or Death Row. To require "a mother . . . to testify against her son and send him to the gallows"[38] is surely an example of greater psychological cruelty than requiring a criminal defendant to testify regarding his own alleged violation of a relatively minor offense.

Beyond this, to the extent that the Fifth Amendment privilege is justified on the grounds of the "cruel trilemma," it benefits only the guilty. The "innocent defendant faces no trilemma, no dilemma, in fact no problem at all."[39] He simply tells the truth.[40] Why should the Constitution provide a special privilege to the guilty?

### [2]  Compelled Self-Accusation As a Moral Wrong

*What the defenders of the privilege say:* The Fifth Amendment privilege is founded on deep moral principles supporting the right of persons to a "special zone of mental privacy,"[41] human dignity, and person autonomy. "Self-incrimination is both self-harming and self-accusing. . . .. [T]he sovereign intrudes on a narrow autonomous sphere when it encourages self-harming self-accusation."[42] Society rightly "hesitate[s] to say that someone has a moral duty to bring conviction and imprisonment upon himself."[43] Most especially, the "government impermissibly disrespects a person when it uses him as the means of his own destruction,"[44] when it "subordinates a person to the state [by using] . . . her private thoughts as the active means of her own destruction."[45]

Even if an admission of guilt is in the wrongdoer's best interests, the decision to admit culpability should be his own: "an individual ought to be autonomous in his efforts to come to terms in his own conscience with

---

[38] Amar & Lettow, Note 5, *supra*, at 890.

[39] Schulhofer, Note 23, *supra*, at 318.

[40] *But see* subsection [4], *infra*.

[41] Klein, Note 24, *supra*, at 552.

[42] George C. Thomas, III, *An Assault on the Temple of Miranda*, 85 J. Crim. L. & Criminology 807, 815 (1995).

[43] Greenawalt, Note 24, *supra*, at 36.

[44] Amar & Lettow, Note 5, *supra*, at 892.

[45] Klein, Note 24, *supra*, at 552 n.65 (summarizing an argument advanced in David Luban, Lawyers and Justice: An Ethical Study (1988)).

accusations of wrongdoing against him."[46] Our society properly has "respect for the inviolability of the human personality and of the right of each individual 'to a private enclave where he may lead a private life.' "[47]

*Response:* The preceding moral arguments are facially plausible. But, look further. First, the privilege is morally counter-intuitive: "[n]o parent would teach such a doctrine to his children; the lesson parents preach is that while a misdeed . . . will generally be forgiven, a failure to make a clean breast of it will not be."[48]

Second, civil litigants and witnesses, for example in divorce proceedings, may be required to testify to highly embarrassing—and damaging—facts and intensely personal aspects of their lives, yet the privilege does not apply in such circumstances. Third, as discussed later,[49] the government can avoid the obstacles of the Fifth Amendment by giving immunity to a witness, in which case he *can* be compelled to testify about matters that he considers to be part of his private enclave.

Finally, abolition of the privilege would not really threaten privacy. By the time of trial, the prosecutor is not interested in obtaining an "admission of wrongdoing, self-condemnation or personal feelings about the crime. What interests her are just the basic facts—where the defendant was, who he saw, what he did."[50] These are external facts, not deeply private matters.

### [3] The Privilege as a Critical Component of the Adversary System

*What the defenders of the privilege say:* The Fifth Amendment privilege is defensible on systemic grounds. It functions as a core feature of our accusatorial system of justice, specifically, by preserving a fair balance between the state and the accused in the prosecution of crime, and by reducing the risk that inhumane methods to extract testimony from persons suspected of crime will be used by the government.[51]

The privilege became an important part of the legal system once we moved from an inquisitorial system, in which criminal defendants were barred from using lawyers and judges could compel the testimony of defendants, to an adversarial one that prefers that the truth be determined

---

[46] Gerstein, Note 24, *supra*, at 347.

[47] Murphy v. Waterfront Comm'n 378 U.S. 52, 55 (1964) (quoting United States v. Grunewald, 233 F.2d 556, 581–82 (2d Cir. 1956)).

[48] Friendly, Note 24, *supra*, at 680.

[49] *See* § 26.04, *infra.*

[50] Schulhofer, Note 23, *supra*, at 320.

[51] *Id.* at 317.

by allowing the parties in dispute, through their attorneys, to present their conflicting versions of the events to the decisionmaker. In such a system, the decision should be left to the defense to determine whether it is in the defendant's best interests to testify.

The privilege against self-incrimination is also founded on the view that, if it were not for the privilege, the government, through its agents, could too easily abuse the rights of individuals caught up in criminal investigations. Without the Fifth Amendment protections, we could regress to a time when governmental overreaching was commonplace. By application of the privilege, therefore, we promote a "sense of fair play which dictates 'a fair state-individual balance by requiring the government . . . in its contest with the individual to shoulder the entire load.' "[52]

*Response:* The anti-inquisitorial arguments for the privilege do not apply in the American constitutional system. We do not have Star Chambers or heresy trials. Nor would abolition of the privilege result in inhumane treatment of suspects: if torture were used to obtain incriminating statements, the due process clause would safeguard the victim. Once one ensures against such abuses, there is no basis—other than "slogans"[53] about the adversary system—to deny the government the right to compel testimony from the defendant.

Let's look beyond the slogans. To call for a "fair balance" is simply to state the conclusion. What *is* a *fair* balance? How much advantage is an *undue* advantage for the government? Why should the government shoulder the *entire* load? Is it that we want to "boost the odds for criminals just to keep the game interesting"?[54] If so, that makes no sense.

Finally, if we are going to take the proponents' arguments seriously, we need to go further. If the government must shoulder the *entire* load, we should never compel a suspect to participate in a lineup, to give handwriting exemplars, or furnish blood, because each of these acts may serve to convict him. Yet, as discussed elsewhere,[55] the Fifth Amendment privilege against compulsory self-incrimination does *not* prevent the government from compelling any of these acts. And, few in society would want the government stripped of authority to obtain physical evidence from an accused.

---

[52] Murphy v. Waterfront Comm'n, 378 U.S. 52, 55 (1964) (quoting 8 Wigmore, Note 10, *supra*, § 2251, at 317).

[53] Amar & Lettow, Note 5, *supra*, at 893.

[54] *Id.*

[55] *See* § 26.05[D], *infra*.

### [4]  Protection of the Innocent

*What the defenders of the privilege say:* The privilege against compulsory self-incrimination, although "sometimes a 'shelter to the guilty,' is often 'a protection to the innocent.' "[56] It protects the innocent in at least two ways, one that relates to interrogation procedures by the police, and the other that focuses on a defendant's right not to testify at trial.

First, compelled testimony is inherently unreliable. Even innocent persons can be forced to utter incriminating words in order to avoid extreme pain to themselves or loved ones. It is true, as the critics point out, that the due process clause can serve to bar brutal police conduct. But, history tells us that the due process clause, standing alone, only moderated police interrogation procedures. It was only with *Miranda v. Arizona,*[57] and the forceful application of the Fifth Amendment privilege, that there was significant improvement. Professor Schulhofer suggests the following thought experiment:

> What would happen if there was no right to silence, and if officers were told that it was permissible (and perhaps therefore their duty) to use all pressures short of actually breaking the suspect's will [and, thus, violating due process]? Realistically, there can be little doubt that more abuses would occur, even though the worst abuses would still be theoretically prohibited by other rules.[58]

Second, there is a significant risk that an innocent person, forced to testify at trial, might convict himself by a bad performance on the witness stand. In the real world, it is not the case (although we might wish it to be) that innocent persons will always come across truthfully to a jury. Also, a person innocent of the crime charged—and, therefore, entitled to acquittal—might not be an entirely upstanding person. Again, a thought experiment:

> Suppose that you are representing a criminal defendant who persuades you that he is innocent. Can you think of any reason why you might prefer that your innocent client not be called to the stand? . . . Of course you can. Every lawyer can. Your client might have a highly prejudicial prior record that will become admissible once he takes the stand. There are likely to be suspicious transactions or associations that your client will have to explain. But he may look sleazy. He may be inarticulate, nervous or easily intimidated. His vague memory on some of the details may leave him vulnerable to a clever cross-examination. Most ordinary

---

[56] Murphy v. Waterfront Comm'n 378 U.S. 52, 55 (1964) (quoting Quinn v. United States, 349 U.S. 155, 162 (1955)).

[57] 384 U.S. 436 (1966).

[58] Schulhofer, Note 23, *supra,* at 326.

citizens find that being a witness in any formal proceeding is stressful and confusing. The problems are bound to be heightened when the witness happens to be on trial for his life or his liberty.[59]

*Response:* Neither of these protect-the-innocent arguments is persuasive. First, regarding coerced confessions, in most cases they serve only to corroborate other reliable evidence of the defendant's guilt. And, even without the Constitution, a state could choose to enforce a rule that coerced confessions are inadmissible at trial, but that the physical (and reliable) fruits of the coerced confession would be admissible.[60]

Second, innocent persons rarely hurt themselves on the witness stand. The "truth is consistent with itself, and everyone who is speaking the truth can tell in the main a straight story."[61] One critic has challenged advocates of the privilege to point to "a single case in all the annals of American jurisprudence where an innocent man has been, or could have been, convicted because [he was] compelled to answer . . . ."[62] Third, those concerned for the plight of the innocent should not lose sight of the fact that an innocent person accused of a crime cannot successfully compel a guilty person to testify and admit the truth, "while the guilty [can] wrap themselves in the self-incrimination clause and walk free."[63]

Finally, if the concern is for the innocent defendant who may come across poorly in front of a jury, the "problem could be solved simply by allowing the defendant to refuse to testify at trial for the jury to hear but eliciting information pretrial that could generate admissible fruit."[64]

## § 26.04  Procedures Relating to the Invocation of the Privilege[65]

"The Fifth Amendment privilege against compelled self-incrimination is not self-executing."[66] That is, the Fifth Amendment does not forbid the

---

[59] *Id.* at 330.

[60] Amar & Lettow, Note 5, *supra*, at 895.

[61] Henry T. Terry, *Constitutional Provisions Against Forcing Self-Incrimination*, 15 Yale L.J. 127, 127 (1906).

[62] Ernest C. Carman, *A Plea for Withdrawal of Constitutional Privilege from the Criminal*, 22 Minn. L. Rev. 200, 204 (1938).

[63] Akhil Reed Amar, The Constitution and Criminal Procedure: First Principles 48 (1997).

[64] Amar & Lettow, Note 5, *supra*, at 895.

[65] *See generally* Kate E. Bloch, *Fifth Amendment Compelled Statements: Modeling the Contours of Their Protected Scope*, 72 Wash. U. L.Q. 1603 (1994); Kate E. Bloch, *Police Officers Accused of Crime: Prosecutorial and Fifth Amendment Risks Posed by Police-Elicited "Use Immunized" Statements*, 1992 U. Ill. L. Rev. 625 (1992); Peter Lushing, *Testimonial Immunity and the Privilege Against Self-Incrimination: A Study in Isomorphism*, 73 J. Crim. L. & Criminology 1690 (1982).

[66] Roberts v. United States, 445 U.S. 552, 559 (1980).

*asking* of incriminating questions or the *demanding* of the production of incriminating documents.[67] Nor does it prohibit a person from voluntarily answering the questions propounded or producing the documents subpoenaed. Instead, "[a]t least where the Government has no substantial reason to believe that the requested disclosures are likely to be incriminating, the privilege may not be relied upon unless it is invoked in a timely fashion."[68]

If a person subpoenaed or otherwise compelled to testify in any formal proceeding asserts his privilege against self-incrimination, the interrogator must honor the privilege or "seek a judicial determination as to the bona fides of the witness' Fifth Amendment claim,"[69] *i.e.*, that the threat of incrimination is real.[70] If the judge determines that the privilege has been legitimately asserted, the government must permit the witness to stand on the privilege or it must apply for an immunity order.[71] An immunity order requires the witness to testify, but it also protects him at least as fully as the constitutional privilege itself.

Generally speaking, there are two forms of immunity that may be granted to a witness. The broadest form is "transactional" immunity, in which a witness is guaranteed that he will not be prosecuted for any offense that is the subject of the questioning. A narrower form of immunity is "use" immunity (or, more accurately, "use and derivative use" immunity). For example, the federal immunity statute provides that "no testimony or other information compelled under the order (or any information directly or indirectly derived from such testimony or other information) may be used against the witness in any criminal case . . . ."[72]

Under a use and derivative use immunity statute, the witness may be prosecuted for the offense for which he was questioned, but the compelled testimony is inadmissible at his criminal trial and, as well, "the statute imposes an affirmative duty on the prosecution, not merely to show that its evidence is not tainted by the prior [immunized] testimony, but 'to prove that the evidence it proposes to use is derived from a legitimate source wholly independent of the compelled testimony.' "[73]

---

[67] *See* United States v. Mandujano, 425 U.S. 564, 574 (1976).

[68] Roberts v. United States, 445 U.S. at 559.

[69] United States v. Mandujano, 425 U.S. at 575.

[70] *See* § 26.05[D][2], *infra.*

[71] Immunity is most often granted during grand jury proceedings, at which a witness— perhaps, a target of the investigation—is subpoenaed to testify, but stands on his Fifth Amendment rights.

[72] 18 U.S.C. § 6002 (1996).

[73] United States v. Hubbell, 530 U.S. 27, 40 (2000) (quoting Kastigar v. United States, 406 U.S. 441, 460 (1972).

If either form of immunity is granted, the witness must testify truthfully. If he testifies falsely, his statements may be used against him in a perjury prosecution.[74] If he refuses to testify, he may be held in contempt of court and jailed as a consequence.

The Supreme Court declared in *Kastigar v. United States* that "[t]ransactional immunity . . . affords the witness considerably broader protection than does the Fifth Amendment privilege." Instead, "immunity from use and derivative use is coextensive with the scope of the privilege against self-incrimination, and therefore is sufficient to compel testimony over a claim of the privilege."[75] As a consequence, transactional immunity is rarely granted today in the federal system and in most states.

## § 26.05    Elements of the Fifth Amendment Privilege

The Fifth Amendment to the United States Constitution provides that "[n]o person . . . shall be compelled in any criminal case to be a witness against himself . . . ."

### [A]    "No Person"

Because the Fifth Amendment begins with the words "no person," the Supreme Court has declared under the "collective entity" doctrine that artificial entities, such as corporations,[76] labor unions,[77] and partnerships,[78] may not assert the privilege against self-incrimination, although a sole proprietor may.[79] Furthermore, a custodian of an entity's records may not oppose a subpoena *duces tecum* by invoking his personal privilege against self-incrimination in order to protect the entity.[80] Nor is he entitled to assert the privilege if his claim is that production of the entity's documents will incriminate him personally.[81] In short, the collective-entity doctrine "trumps" the personal privilege.

---

[74] United States v. Mandujano, 425 U.S. 564 (1976).

[75] 406 U.S. 441, 453 (1972); *contra, requiring transactional immunity under the state constitution,* State v. Gonzalez, 853 P.2d 526 (Alaska 1993); State v. Miyasaki, 614 P.2d 915 (Haw. 1980); State v. Soriano, 684 P.2d 1220 (Or. Ct. App.), *aff'd en banc,* 693 P.2d 26 (Or. 1984); Attorney Gen. v. Colleton, 444 N.E.2d 915 (Mass. 1982); Wright v. McAdory, 536 So. 2d 897 (Miss. 1988); State v. Thrift, 440 S.E.2d 341 (S.C. 1994).

[76] Hale v. Henkel, 201 U.S. 43 (1906).

[77] United States v. White, 322 U.S. 694 (1944).

[78] Bellis v. United States, 417 U.S. 85 (1974).

[79] United States v. Doe, 465 U.S. 605 (1984).

[80] Wilson v. United States, 221 U.S. 361 (1911).

[81] Braswell v. United States, 487 U.S. 99 (1988); *contra, under the state constitution,* Commonwealth v. Doe, 544 N.E.2d 860 (Mass. 1989).

The preceding exception aside, the Fifth Amendment generally applies to any person. Therefore, any witness in a criminal trial—not only the criminal defendant—may invoke the personal privilege. Thus, as critics of the Fifth Amendment privilege like to point out,[82] an innocent defendant cannot compel a person with guilty knowledge to testify and, apparently, cannot even require the recalcitrant witness to assert the privilege in front of the jury.[83]

### [B]   "Shall Be *Compelled*"

### [1]   Nature of "Compulsion": In General

The Fifth Amendment is violated only by compulsion, more specifically, by "the use of 'physical or moral compulsion' exerted on the person asserting the privilege."[84] The required compulsion occurs if the holder of the privilege[85] is forced by subpoena to testify at trial[86] or to produce incriminating documents. In the police interrogation field, the use of physical force, psychological pressures, or deception may render a confession involuntary.[87]

A witness's free choice is also foreclosed by a threat of discharge from state employment for refusal to testify. Thus, statements given by police officers in an internal police affairs investigation of alleged traffic ticket fixing, in response to a threat of removal from office if they asserted their Fifth Amendment privilege, may not be used against them at a subsequent criminal trial. According to the Court, "[t]he option to lose their means of livelihood or to pay the penalty of self-incrimination is the antithesis of free choice to speak out or to remain silent."[88]

---

[82] *See* the text to Note 63, *supra*.

[83] Tague, Note 24, *supra*, at 5.

[84] Fisher v. United States, 425 U.S. 391, 397 (1976).

[85] Notice that the compulsion must be directed at the person who is asserting the privilege. *See* § 26.05[D][3], *infra*.

[86] Obviously, the defendant in a criminal trial is not required to take the stand. Moreover, in order that there is no penalty for the exercise of the right, neither the prosecutor nor the judge may comment adversely on the defendant's silence. Griffin v. California, 380 U.S. 609 (1965). In support of this proposition, a non-testifying defendant is entitled to a jury instruction informing jurors that they may draw no adverse inferences from the defendant's failure to testify. Carter v. Kentucky, 450 U.S. 288 (1981). Such an instruction is permitted, even over the defendant's objections. Lakeside v. Oregon, 435 U.S. 333 (1978). The *Griffin* rule also applies at sentencing. A sentencing tribunal may not draw an adverse inference from a defendant's silence with regard to determinations respecting the circumstances and details of the crime. Mitchell v. United States, 526 U.S. 314 (1999).

[87] *See* § 23.03, *supra*.

[88] Garrity v. New Jersey, 385 U.S. 493, 497 (1967).

The Fifth Amendment is probably violated as well if a person provides testimonial evidence against himself as an alternative to submitting "to a test so painful, dangerous, or severe, or so violative of religious beliefs, that almost inevitably a person would prefer 'confession.' "[89]

On the other hand, not all difficult choices are "compelled." For example, Fifth Amendment values are not violated if the government requires a driver stopped on suspicion of driving under the influence of alcohol to choose between submitting to a comparatively painless blood test, or have the refusal used against him in a criminal trial and his driving privileges revoked for up to one year.[90]

## [2]  Required-Records Doctrine[91]

Under certain circumstances, a person may not assert the privilege against self-incrimination in regard to records that he is compelled by law to keep. In a series of cases decided over the past half decade, the Supreme Court has developed the "required records" doctrine. A leading case in the development of the law was *Shapiro v. United States.*[92] In *Shapiro*, the Court upheld the constitutionality of federal regulations issued under the Emergency Price Control Act, which required certain licensed businesses to maintain records of their business activities and to make them available for inspection by the government upon request.

*Shapiro* held that the Fifth Amendment privilege does not attach to the production of records which the defendant is "required to keep, not for his private uses, but for the benefit of the public, and for public inspection." Although the Court warned that "there are limits which the Government cannot constitutionally exceed in requiring the keeping of records which may be inspected by an administrative agency," it did not indicate what those limits were.

Subsequent opinions suggest that the required-records doctrine applies if: (1) the regulatory scheme is imposed in an "essentially noncriminal and regulatory area of inquiry," rather than "in an area permeated with criminal

---

[89] South Dakota v. Neville, 459 U.S. 553, 563 (1983) (dictum).

[90] *Id.; contra,* Opinion of Justices to Senate, 591 N.E.2d 1073 (Mass. 1992) (observing that state courts are divided on the wisdom of *Neville,* and holding that evidence of a driver's refusal to submit to a chemical test or analysis of his breath is inadmissible under the state constitution). For observations on the coercion question in *Neville, see* George C. Thomas III, *A Philosophical Account of Coerced Self-Incrimination,* 5 Yale J.L. & Human. 79, 108–110 (1993); *see generally* H. Richard Uviller, *Self-Incrimination by Inference: Constitutional Restrictions on the Evidentiary Use of a Suspect's Refusal to Submit to a Search,* 81 J. Crim. L. & Criminology 37 (1990).

[91] *See generally* Saltzburg, Note 26, *supra.*

[92] 335 U.S. 1 (1948).

statutes";[93] (2) the requirements are "directed at the public at large" and not at a "selective group inherently suspect of criminal activities";[94] and (3) the records requirement is rationally related to the regulatory purpose.[95]

The required-records doctrine applies even when the information that must be disclosed could be a link in the chain of evidence leading to a criminal prosecution. For example, in *California v. Byers*,[96] the Court upheld a state hit-and-run statute, which required the driver of any motor vehicle involved in an accident to stop at the scene and report his name and address. In part, the holding was based on the four-justice plurality's determination that: (1) the statute was regulatory in character, in that it "was not intended to facilitate criminal convictions but to promote the satisfaction of civil liability"; (2) the statute was directed at the public at large; and (3) "self-reporting [was] indispensable to . . . fulfillment" of the legislative purpose.

In an expansion of the doctrine, in *Baltimore City Department of Social Services v. Bouknight*,[97] the Supreme Court ruled that a mother who had previously lost custody of her child because of suspected child abuse, but who had been permitted temporary custody of the youth subject to various court conditions, could not assert the privilege against self-incrimination to resist compliance with a subsequent juvenile court order that she produce the child or otherwise reveal its whereabouts. Primarily citing required-records cases, but also invoking language from cases applying the collective-entity doctrine,[98] the Court stated that "[w]hen a person assumes control over items that are the legitimate object of the government's non-criminal regulatory powers, the ability to invoke the privilege is reduced."

The Court concluded that once the child was adjudicated in need of assistance, "his care and safety became the particular object of the State's regulatory interests." By accepting temporary custody of the child, the mother thereby "submitted to the routine operation of the regulatory system and agreed to hold [the child] in a manner consonant with the State's regulatory interests and subject to inspection [by the juvenile court]."

---

[93] Albertson v. Subversive Activities Control Board, 382 U.S. 70, 79 (1965).

[94] *Id.*

[95] *See* Saltzburg, Note 26, *supra*, at 24–25.

[96] 402 U.S. 424 (1971).

[97] 493 U.S. 549 (1990); *see generally* Irene Merker Rosenberg, *Bouknight: Of Abused Children and the Parental Privilege Against Self-Incrimination*, 76 Iowa L. Rev. 535 (1991).

[98] *See* § 26.05[A], *supra*.

## [C] "In Any Criminal Case"

The privilege against self-incrimination does not apply if the only concern of the person asserting the claim is that the statements he is compelled to make will result in personal disgrace,[99] loss of employment,[100] or civil confinement.[101] His claim must be that the evidence he is required to produce will incriminate him in a criminal proceeding in the United States.[102]

Although the language of the Fifth Amendment might suggest that the privilege against compulsory self-incrimination may only be asserted *during* a criminal case, the Court has interpreted the Amendment to mean that the right may be asserted in any "proceeding, civil or criminal, formal or informal, where the answers might incriminate him in future criminal proceedings."[103] As a consequence, a person may invoke the Fifth Amendment privilege, among other places, in grand jury proceedings, civil trials, legislative and administrative hearings, and police stations, if the testimony he would give might be used against him in a domestic criminal trial.

## [D] "To Be a Witness Against Himself"

### [1] What Makes a Person a "Witness"

#### [a] "Testimonial or Communicative" Evidence: The Rule

"The word 'witness' in the constitutional text limits the relevant category of compelled incriminating communications to those that are 'testimonial' in character."[104] The Court explained this limitation in *Schmerber v. California*,[105] when it held that a person is not an involuntary "witness" against himself unless he is "compelled to testify . . . or otherwise provide the State with evidence of a testimonial or communicative nature." As the *Schmerber* Court explained, "[t]he distinction which has emerged, often expressed in different ways, is that the privilege is a bar against compelling

---

[99] *See* Brown v. Walker, 161 U.S. 591 (1896)

[100] Ullmann v. United States, 350 U.S. 422 (1956).

[101] Allen v. Illinois, 478 U.S. 364 (1986).

[102] A person may *not* invoke the Fifth Amendment privilege to answer legitimate questions propounded by federal or state law enforcement officers if the sole ground for refusal is that his testimony might be used against him in a criminal prosecution in a foreign country. United States v. Balsys, 524 U.S. 666 (1998); *see* Diane Marie Amann, *A Whipsaw Cuts Both Ways: The Privilege Against Self-Incrimination in an International Context*, 45 UCLA L. Rev. 1201 (1998).

[103] Lefkowitz v. Turley, 414 U.S. 70, 77 (1973).

[104] United States v. Hubbell, 530 U.S. 27, 34 (2000).

[105] 384 U.S. 757 (1966); *see generally* Peter Arenella, *Schmerber and the Privilege Against Self-Incrimination: A Reappraisal*, 20 Am. Crim. L. Rev. 31 (1982).

'communications' or 'testimony,' but that compulsion which makes a suspect or accused the source of 'real or physical evidence' does not violate it."

In *Doe v. United States*,[106] the Supreme Court explored the "testimony or communications" requirement further. It stated that "in order to be testimonial, an accused's communication must itself, explicitly or implicitly, relate a factual assertion or disclose information." *Doe* explained that "the privilege is [intended] to spare the accused from having to reveal, directly or indirectly, his knowledge of facts relating him to the offense or from having to share his thoughts and beliefs with the Government."

According to *Doe*, this definition of "testimony"—and, thus, the meaning of the "witness" requirement in the Fifth Amendment—stems from the historical point that "the privilege was intended to prevent the use of legal compulsion to extract from the accused a sworn communication of facts which would incriminate him," as occurred in the ecclesiastical courts and the Star Chamber.

The outer boundaries of the "testimony or communications" requirement remain unexplored. However, the Court stated in *Pennsylvania v. Muniz*[107] that, at its core, a person is compelled to be a "witness" against himself "at least whenever he must face the modern-day analog" of the "cruel trilemma" of self-accusation, perjury or contempt that confronted sixteenth century Star Chamber witnesses.

### [b] Application of the Rule

The line between "testimony or communications," on the one hand, and "real or physical evidence," on the other hand, is not always easy to draw. According to *Schmerber v. California*,[108] "the protection of the privilege reaches an accused's communications, whatever form they might take . . . ." The privilege "applies to both verbal and nonverbal conduct."[109]

According to the Supreme Court, "[t]here are very few instances in which a verbal statement, either oral or written, will not convey information or assert facts."[110] Most obviously, trial testimony, oral confessions to the police, and statements expressed in personal documents,[111] constitute

---

[106] 487 U.S. 201 (1988).

[107] 496 U.S. 582 (1990).

[108] 384 U.S. 757 (1966).

[109] Pennsylvania v. Muniz, 496 U.S. at 595 n.9.

[110] Doe v. United States, 487 U.S. at 213.

[111] In Boyd v. United States, 116 U.S. 616 (1886), the Supreme Court held that compelling a person to hand over private papers for use against him in a criminal trial is equivalent to compelling the person to be a "witness" against himself under the Fifth Amendment.

protectible "testimony or communications." Indeed, in view of the history of the self-incrimination clause, "[w]hatever else it may include, . . . the definition of 'testimonial' evidence . . . must encompass all responses to questions that, if asked of a sworn suspect during a criminal trial, could place the suspect in the 'cruel trilemma'."[112]

Nonetheless, not all uses of the human voice or written words are protected. For example, a person may lawfully be compelled at a lineup to utter the words expressed by the malefactor, if the purpose is to require the suspect "to use his voice as an identifying *physical* characteristic, not to speak his guilt."[113] Likewise, a person may be required to put words down on paper if the purpose of the demand is to exhibit the suspect's handwriting, another physical characteristic, for identification purposes.[114] In neither of these cases is the person compelled by the government to reveal his knowledge of facts relating to the offense or to share his thoughts or beliefs.

Non-verbal conduct, too, falls within the scope of the Fifth Amendment privilege if it "reflects the actor's communication of his thoughts to another,"[115] such as when he nods or shakes his head. On the other hand, the actor does *not* communicate his thoughts to another, and therefore the privilege does *not* apply, when the government compels him to put on clothing to see if it fits,[116] to stand in a lineup,[117] to move his eyes or walk on a straight line as part of a sobriety test,[118] or to give blood after being arrested for driving under the influence of alcohol,[119] although in each of these cases the product of the compulsion might be incriminating.

### [c]   A Closer Look at the Rule: *Pennsylvania v. Muniz*

The difficulty in drawing the line between testimonial communications and real or physical evidence is apparent in the Court's treatment of the facts in *Pennsylvania v. Muniz*.[120] In *Muniz, D*, arrested for driving under

---

[112] Pennsylvania v. Muniz, 496 U.S. at 596–97.

[113] United States v. Wade, 388 U.S. 218, 222–23 (1967) (emphasis added).

[114] United States v. Dionisio, 410 U.S. 1 (1973); Gilbert v. California, 388 U.S. 263 (1967).

[115] Pennsylvania v. Muniz, 496 U.S. at 595 n.9.

[116] Holt v. United States, 218 U.S. 245, 252–53 (1910) ("the prohibition of compelling a man in a criminal court to be witness against himself is a prohibition of the use of . . . compulsion to extort communications from him, not an exclusion of his body as evidence when it may be material").

[117] United States v. Wade, 388 U.S. 218 (1967).

[118] Pennsylvania v. Muniz, 496 U.S. 582 (1990).

[119] Schmerber v. California, 384 U.S. 757 (1966).

[120] 496 U.S. 582 (1990).

the influence of alcohol, was compelled to give his name, address, height, weight, date of birth, current age, and the date of his sixth birthday, as part of a sobriety test. *D*'s slurred answers to these questions were videotaped and introduced at his subsequent trial.

The Court, 8-1, held that *D*'s compelled answers to the questions were not inadmissible merely because the slurred nature of his speech incriminated him. *D*'s physical inability to articulate words clearly due to his lack of muscular coordination in his tongue and mouth was not a testimonial component of his responses to the questions asked. Instead, *D*'s slurred words were physical evidence of his intoxication; he was not compelled "to share his thoughts and beliefs with the Government," or to relate a factual assertion.

On the other hand, the Court also held, but only 5-4, that *D*'s answer "No, I don't," to the question, "Do you know what the date was of your sixth birthday?" *was* testimonial in nature and, therefore, implicated the Fifth Amendment. The majority was unpersuaded by the government's claim that the Fifth Amendment privilege did not apply because the police did not have an investigative interest in the actual date of *D*'s sixth birthday, nor even in *D*'s "assertion of belief that was communicated by his answer to the question." According to the government, the incriminating aspect of *D*'s answer—that his mental state was confused—concerned the physiological function of *D*'s brain, a matter "every bit as 'real or physical' as the physiological makeup up of his blood and the timbre of his voice."

The majority reasoned, however, that even if the fact to be inferred from *D*'s words related to the physical status of his brain, "[t]he correct question . . . [was] whether the incriminating inference of mental confusion [was] drawn from a testimonial act or from physical evidence." The majority concluded that *D*'s answer to the sixth-birthday question was a testimonial act, *i.e.*, his words—and not just his slurred response—supported the factual inference that his mental faculties were impaired, just as much as if he had said directly, "I cannot answer your question because I am intoxicated."

### [2] Seriousness of the Threat of Incrimination

The privilege against compulsory self-incrimination extends not only "to answers that would in themselves support a conviction . . . but likewise embraces those which would furnish a link in the chain of evidence needed to prosecute the claimant."[121] The privilege, however, "is confined to real danger and does not extend to remote possibilities out of the ordinary course of law"[122] or to imaginary concerns.[123] Although the person asserting the

---

[121] Hoffman v. United States, 341 U.S. 479, 486 (1951).

[122] Heike v. United States, 227 U.S. 131, 144 (1913).

Fifth Amendment privilege must have "reasonable cause to apprehend danger"[124] of incrimination from answering a question or producing the testimonial evidence, the privilege is to "be accorded liberal construction in favor of the right it was intended to secure."[125]

### [3]  Personal Nature of the Privilege

The Fifth Amendment privilege is "intimate and personal."[126] It "adheres basically to the person, not to information that may incriminate him."[127] As Justice Holmes once put it, "[a] party is privileged from producing the evidence [that incriminates him] but not from its production."[128]

Most of the difficult problems in this area relate to the compelled production of documents intended for use in a criminal investigation. In determining whether there is a Fifth Amendment violation one must consider the following three interrelated questions: (1) who was compelled?; (2) who is incriminated; and (3) what is the claim of incrimination—is the incriminating feature found in the documents disclosed, or is the incrimination found simply in the act of producing the documents?

For example, *D* may not successfully assert the Fifth Amendment privilege if a judge issues a subpoena directing *X*, *D*'s accountant, to produce tax records that will incriminate *D*.[129] In such a case, *X* is the victim of the compulsion (the subpoena); but the person incriminated is *D*, based on the information found in the documents that *X* was compelled to hand over to the government. Put slightly differently, in these circumstance there is no compelled *self*-incrimination: in the words of the Fifth Amendment, *X* is not being compelled to be a "witness against himself." He is being compelled to be a witness against *D*.

---

[123] Mason v. United States, 244 U.S. 362, 366 (1917) (privilege does not apply to a danger of an "imaginary and unsubstantial character"). For example, if the witness cannot be prosecuted because of the statute of limitations or the Fifth Amendment double jeopardy clause, the privilege does not apply. *See* Brown v. Walker, 161 U.S. 591 (1896). On the other hand, the mere fact that a witness intends to deny all culpability for an offense does *not* by that fact alone mean that she cannot assert the privilege; depending on the factual setting, the witness may still have "reasonable cause to apprehend danger from her answers if questioned . . . ." Ohio v. Reiner, 532 U.S. 17, 21 (2001) (*per curiam*) (internal quotations omitted).

[124] Hoffman v. United States, 341 U.S. at 486.

[125] *Id.*

[126] Couch v. United States, 409 U.S. 322, 327 (1973).

[127] *Id.* at 328.

[128] Johnson v. United States, 228 U.S. 457, 458 (1913).

[129] Couch v. United States, 409 U.S. 322 (1973).

Or, consider the case in which the Internal Revenue Service subpoenas working papers in a tax preparer's possession, some of which were prepared by the taxpayer himself, that were used in the preparation of the taxpayer's fraudulent tax returns. It is the tax preparer being compelled to produce the documents, but it is the taxpayer who is incriminated by the information found in the records themselves. It is true, of course, that some of those incriminating papers were prepared by the taxpayer—the person who *is* now a witness against himself—but they were written before the summons was issued and, therefore, constituted non-compelled self-incrimination.[130]

On the other hand, even if a business record or personal paper is voluntarily prepared by *D*, the act of producing it in response to a subpoena or warrant "has communicative aspects of its own, wholly aside from the contents of the papers produced."[131] By handing over the document, *D* concedes that the article produced exists, that he was in possession of it, and that he believes that the item he is handing over is that described in the subpoena or warrant. If such an implicit concession is incriminating, *D* may successfully assert the privilege as to the production of the documents.[132]

## § 26.06 Privilege Against Self-Incrimination: Exclusionary Rule

The Fifth Amendment privilege against compelled self-incrimination contains its own exclusionary rule. That is, the constitutional right and the remedy for its violation commingle: by its own terms, the privilege "excludes" a witness' compelled testimony against himself. And, as the result of judicial interpretation, the privilege also prohibits the use at trial of incriminating testimonial or communicative evidence compelled from the witness prior to his criminal trial.

The exclusionary rule is a stringent one. In *New Jersey v. Portash,*[133] the Supreme Court held that testimony given by a witness before a grand

---

[130] *See* Fisher v. United States, 425 U.S. 391 (1976); *see also* Andresen v. Maryland, 427 U.S. 463 (1976) (the police seized *D*'s business records from his home and office pursuant to a search warrant; there was no potential Fifth Amendment violation because *D* was not required to participate in the seizure, *i.e.*, he was not required to aid in the discovery, production, or authentication of the seized evidence; and, as for the incriminating information found in the records, they were prepared voluntarily).

[131] Fisher v. United States, 425 U.S. at 410.

[132] United States v. Doe, 465 U.S. 605 (1984); United States v. Hubbell, 120 S. Ct. 2037 (2000); *see also* Baltimore City Department of Social Services v. Bouknight, 493 U.S. 549 (1990) (the Court assumed that a court order requiring a mother suspected of child abuse to produce her child might incriminate her; the mere act of production could constitute "implicit communication of control" over the child at the moment of production, which might aid the state in criminal prosecution of *D* for child abuse).

[133] 440 U.S. 450 (1979).

jury, who was compelled to testify under an immunity statute, could not be used against him at trial, even for impeachment purposes. The no-impeachment rule undermines the state's valid interest in deterring perjury at trial. Nonetheless, the Court reasoned that because immunized testimony is "the essence of coerced testimony," the privilege against self-incrimination is implicated "in its most pristine form. Balancing [of interests], therefore, is not simply unnecessary. It is impermissible."[134]

---

[134] Notice the difference between the exclusionary rule consequences of this pristine constitutional violation and the deterrence-based exclusionary rule of the Fourth Amendment, *see* § 21.05[B][2][b] (permitting impeachment), and the exclusionary rule for *Miranda*, *see* § 24.12[A], *supra*.

CHAPTER 27

# EYEWITNESS IDENTIFICATION PROCEDURES

## § 27.01 Eyewitness Identification: The Problem and Potential Safeguards[1]

### [A] Severity of the Problem

The Supreme Court has warned that "[t]he vagaries of eyewitness identification are well known . . . ."[2] Erroneous eyewitness identification of suspects has long been recognized as one of the most serious problems in the administration of justice. A 1932 survey suggested that among 65 cases in which innocent persons were convicted, 29 of the improper verdicts were attributed to improper eyewitness identification.[3] A more recent study of wrongful convictions estimates that eyewitness misidentifications account for 52 percent of the cases surveyed.[4]

---

[1] See generally Elizabeth Loftus, Eyewitness Testimony (1979); Adult Eyewitness Testimony: Current Trends and Development (David F. Ross, et al., eds. 1994); Eyewitness Testimony: Psychological Perspectives (Gary L. Wells & Elizabeth F. Loftus eds. 1984); Jennifer L. Devenport & Steven D. Penrod, Eyewitness Identification Evidence: Evaluating Commonsense Evaluations, 3 Psychol., Pub. Pol'y & Law 338 (1997); Samuel R. Gross, Loss of Innocence: Eyewitness Identification and Proof of Guilt, 16 J. Legal Stud. 395 (1987); Ralph Norman Haber & Lyn Haber, Experiencing, Remembering and Reporting Events, 6 Psychol., Pub. Pol'y & Law 1057 (2000); Sherri Lynn Johnson, Cross-Racial Identification Errors in Criminal Cases, 69 Cornell L. Rev. 934 (1984); Felice J. Levine & June Louin Tapp, The Psychology of Criminal Identification: The Gap from Wade to Kirby, 121 U. Pa. L. Rev. 1079 (1973); Steve Penrod & Brian Cutler, Witness Confidence and Witness Accuracy: Assessing Their Forensic Relation, 1 Psychol., Pub. Pol'y, and Law 817 (1995); Gary L. Wells and Amy Bradfield, "Good, You Identified the Suspect", 83 J. Applied Psych. 360 (1998); Gary L. Wells & Eric P. Seelau, Eyewitness Identification: Psychological Research and Legal Policy on Lineups, 1 Psychol., Pub. Pol'y, & Law 765 (1995); Fredric D. Woocher, Note, Did Your Eyes Deceive You? Expert Psychological Testimony on the Unreliability of Eyewitness Identification, 29 Stan. L. Rev. 969 (1977).

[2] United States v. Wade, 388 U.S. 218, 228 (1967).

[3] Edwin M. Borchard, Convicting the Innocent 3–5 (1932).

[4] Arye Rattner, Conviction but Innocent: Wrongful Conviction and the Criminal Justice System, 12 Law & Hum. Behav. 283, 289 (1988). A dramatic example of the unreliability of eyewitness-identification testimony—only discovered by means of subsequent DNA technology— involved the 1984 rape of Jennifer Thompson, a 22-year-old college student.

In short, there is probably no police practice that results in a greater risk of wrongful conviction than the use at trial of eyewitness testimony. Yet, as will be seen in this chapter, the Supreme Court has spent relatively little time devising legal safeguards against convictions based on misidentifications. Ironically, as a constitutional matter, the Court has adopted far more rigorous rules, resulting in the exclusion of far more reliable evidence, in the areas of search-and-seizure and police interrogation than it has in the identification field, where attention is needed.

### [B] Nature of the Problem

Some eyewitness misidentifications result from the intentional use of suggestive techniques by police officers, such as by displaying a suspect in a lineup with persons who do not look like her or fit the description of the criminal given by the witness.[5]

Most misidentifications, however, are attributable to conditions beyond the control of the police, namely, the "inherent unreliability of human perception and memory and . . . human susceptibility to unintentional, and often quite subtle, suggestive influences."[6] As two observers have summarized the research data, "people quite often do not see or hear things which are presented clearly to their senses, see or hear things which are not there, do not remember things which have happened to them, and remember things which did not happen."[7]

Studies indicate that a person can simultaneously perceive only a limited number of stimuli from her environment, even if her attention level is high.[8]

---

Thompson identified Ronald Cotton as her assailant in a photographic display of a lineup, later in a physical lineup, and again at trial. Despite Cotton's claim of innocence, he was convicted and sentenced to life imprisonment. Two years later, Cotton won a new trial based on testimony that another man, a fellow inmate, had bragged about committing the rape. Cotton was convicted a second time, again based on Thompson's identification. Nine years later—eleven years after his initial incarceration—new DNA technology proved Cotton's innocence and the guilt of the fellow inmate. Thompson stated later, "I was absolutely, positively, without-a-doubt certain [Cotton] was the man who raped me. . . . And nobody was going to tell me any different. . . . I felt like my whole world had been turned upside down, like I had betrayed everybody, including myself." *Scoping Out Eyewitness Ids*, American Bar Association Journal, April, 2001, at p. 39.

[5] *E.g.,* Ludovic Kennedy, The Airman and the Carpenter 176–77 (1985) (describing the lineup in which *D*, the suspect in the kidnapping and murder of the Lindbergh baby, was identified; the police told *X*, an eyewitness to certain critical events, prior to the lineup that "we've got the right man," "[t]here isn't a man in this room who isn't convinced he is the man," and "don't say anything until I ask you if he is the man"; then, *D*, a short man, was placed "between two beefy, 6-foot [uniformed] New York policemen" for identification).

[6] Woocher, Note 1, *supra*, at 970.

[7] Levine & Tapp, Note 1, *supra*, at 1087–88.

[8] *See id.* at 1096–97.

As a consequence, it is difficult for a witness to observe concurrently the height, weight, age, and other features of a suspect at the time of a crime. Reliability is reduced further by the fact that the encounter between the witness or victim and the criminal is often brief, frequently in poorly lit conditions, and often in highly stressful circumstances. There is also substantial evidence of grave unreliability in cross-racial identification cases, *i.e.*, in which a person of one racial group seeks to identify the perpetrator of a crime of a different racial category.[9]

Another serious problem is that people tend to see what they expect to see. A hunter looking for deer may identify the silhouette of a human being as a deer, even though a non-hunter nearby, observing the same moving figure, will realize it is a human being.[10] This phenomenon is aggravated by stereotyping and prejudice: "in particularly complex or ambiguous situations, individuals will necessarily structure events to make them understandable, and in cases of ambiguity may be guided more by past experiences, needs, and expectations than by the stimuli themselves."[11] In such circumstances, a person may unconsciously "see" a person who fits the viewer's expectation of a criminal.[12]

Beyond the difficulties that arise from the original observation, human memory decays over time. Worse still, "memory . . . is an active, constructive process,"[13] in which a person tends to fill in memory gaps with new "information." People have a psychological need to reduce uncertainty and to make consistent that which is not; therefore, witnesses often unconsciously fill in memory holes with details that are inaccurate.

The police identification process itself can aggravate the situation. By its nature, a lineup "is a multiple-choice recognition test"[14] in which the eyewitness-participant often believes (or is led to believe) that there is no "none of the above" option. The effect of this is that the witness picks the "most correct answer," *i.e.*, the person who most resembles the culprit.[15] For example, in one study,[16] after a staged crime, eyewitnesses were asked

---

**9** *See generally* Johnson, Note 1, *supra*; *Special Theme: The Other-Race Effect and Contemporary Criminal Justice: Eyewitness Identification and Jury Decision Making*, 7 Psych., Pub. Pol'y, and Law 3-200 (2001); Joy L. Lindo, Note, *New Jersey Jurors are No Longer Color-Blind Regarding Eyewitness Identification*, 30 Seton Hall L. Rev. 1224 (2000).

**10** Loftus, Note 1, *supra*, at 36–37.

**11** Levine & Tapp, Note 1, *supra*, at 1108.

**12** *Id.*

**13** Woocher, Note 1, *supra*, at 983.

**14** *Id.* at 986.

**15** Loftus, Note 1, *supra* at 144.

**16** R.S. Malpass & P.G. Devine, *Eyewitness Identification: Lineup Instructions and the Absence of the Offender*, 66 J. Applied Psych. 482 (1981).

to select the offender from a lineup in which the wrongdoer was absent. When the witnesses were warned that the culprit might not be in the lineup, misidentifications occurred in 33 percent of the cases; without the warning, the error rate was 78 percent.[17]

Witnesses are also subject to socio-psychological pressures that can render identifications untrustworthy. For example, a subtle comment or action by a police officer (the authority figure), such as a change in voice intonation or even the hint of a smile, may inadvertently suggest the "right" choice in a lineup.[18]

Small-group pressures also influence the process. If witnesses are in each other's presence during the identification process,[19] there is a significant risk that once a person is identified as the perpetrator by some witnesses, others will feel an unconscious pressure to select the same individual. In turn, the uniformity in the identification strengthens the resolve of each witness to stand by her identification.[20] Then, to aggravate matters, once the identification is made, a witness ordinarily substitutes in her mind the accused's image as it appeared at the lineup for the prior image of the criminal at the time of the offense.

Finally, all of these concerns are aggravated by the fact that juries place a high value on eyewitness testimony. The results of some studies suggest, for example, that witnesses who make eyewitness identifications are believed by jurors approximately 80 percent of the time, regardless of the accuracy of the identifications.[21] According to social scientists, "[j]urors appear to overestimate the accuracy of identifications . . ., do not distinguish accurate from inaccurate eyewitnesses, and are generally insensitive to factors that influence eyewitness identification accuracy."[22]

In one study,[23] for example, three sets of jurors in a mock robbery trial

---

[17] *See also* Siegfried L. Sporer, *Eyewitness Identification Accuracy, Confidence, and Decision Times in Simultaneous and Sequential Lineups*, 78 J. Applied Psych. 22 (1993) (misidentifications occurred 39 percent of the time when eyewitnesses looked at photographs of suspects one at a time; the error rate rose to 72 percent when they were shown the same pictures together and, therefore, believed that they should pick the person who most looked like the culprit).

[18] Woocher, Note 1, *supra*, at 988.

[19] *E.g.*, Gilbert v. California, 388 U.S. 263 (1967) (*D* was identified in an auditorium containing about 100 witnesses).

[20] Woocher, Note 1, *supra*, at 988–89.

[21] Gary L. Wells, *Effects of Expert Psychological Advice on Human Performance in Judging the Validity of Eyewitness Testimony*, 4 Law & Hum. Behav. 275, 278 (1980).

[22] Penrod & Cutler, Note 1, *supra*, at 822, 819–22 (summarizing studies).

[23] Elizabeth F. Loftus, The Incredible Eyewitness, Psychol. Today, Dec. 1974, at 117–18 (as reported in Cindy J. O'Hagan, Note, *When Seeing is Not Believing: The Case for Eyewitness Expert Testimony*, 81 Geo. L.J. 741, 749–50 (1993)).

were presented the same evidence, with one exception. With the first set of jurors, there were no eyewitnesses. In the second version, one eyewitness was presented who identified the defendant, although the defense lawyer argued that the witness was mistaken. In the third case, the defense was able to show that the eyewitness had only 20/400 vision and was not wearing his glasses on the day of the crime. With the first jury (no eyewitness), only 18% of the jurors convicted the defendant; in the second case, 72 percent voted to convict; in the third case, the conviction rate only dropped to 68 percent, despite the highly doubtful nature of the eyewitness identification.

## [C]　Potential Safeguards

Social scientists have suggested various ways to reduce, although not eliminate, the risk of misidentification. For example, Gary Wells and Eric Seelau[24] have urged police departments to follow four rules in conducting lineups and photographic displays: (1) that eyewitnesses be informed by the police that the offender may not be in the lineup or photographic array; (2) that the suspect should not stand out in the display; (3) in order to avoid conscious or unconscious prompting, identifications should be conducted by someone unaware of the identity of the suspect; and (4) if a witness identifies someone, she should be asked how certain she is of her choice before other information "contaminates" her judgment.[25]

Except when constitutional rights are implicated, courts have limited authority to restrict the admission of eyewitness testimony. One federal court,[26] noting the inherent unreliability of eyewitness identifications, has recommended that district courts instruct juries on the risks associated with eyewitness testimony. The model jury instruction it attached to its decision, however, has largely been ignored by other courts. One state court has held that in a case in which a defendant's guilt is based almost exclusively on cross-racial identification by an eyewitness, the accused is entitled as a matter of law to a jury instruction on the pitfalls of such identifications.[27]

---

[24] Wells and Seelau, Note 1, *supra.*

[25] Some reform efforts are underway. In October, 2001, the State of New Jersey became the first in the country to stop using traditional lineups. Instead, individuals are presented to witnesses one at a time through one-way mirrors. The State also will no longer permit eyewitnesses to browse through photographs of suspects in "mug shot" books, but will be shown photographs one after the other. If a witness wants a second look, she will be required to view all of the photographs a second time, and ordinarily the officer showing the photographs will be one who does not know whom the suspect may be. Gina Kolata & Iver Peterson, *New Way to Insure Eyewitnesses Can ID The Right Bad Guy*, New York Times, July 21, 2001, at A1.

[26] United States v. Telfaire, 469 F.2d 552 (D.C. Cir. 1972).

[27] State v. Cromedy, 727 A.2d 457 (N.J. 1999).

Alternatively, some appellate courts have ruled that trial courts have discretion to admit expert testimony on the general unreliability of eyewitness identifications, or on the risks inherent in the identification techniques used in the particular case.[28] Some courts, however, bar such testimony as a matter of law, sometimes reasoning that the unreliability issue is clear to jurors without expert testimony.[29]

Constitutional safeguards exist. As discussed in the remainder of this chapter, the Supreme Court has found some protections against unreliable eyewitness identifications in the Sixth Amendment right-to-counsel provision, and the due process clauses of the Fifth and Fourteenth Amendment.[30]

## § 27.02 Corporeal Identification Procedures: Right to Counsel[31]

### [A] Rule

Pursuant to the so-called *Wade-Kirby*[32] doctrine discussed below, a person has a Sixth Amendment constitutional right to counsel at any corporeal identification procedure[33] conducted after, but not before, she has been indicted or equivalent adversary judicial criminal proceedings have commenced against her.[34] For shorthand, this rule may be described as providing an accused a constitutional right to counsel at all "post-indictment" lineups.

Unless counsel is present at the post-indictment lineup, or her presence is waived by the accused,[35] the prosecutor may not present evidence at trial

---

[28] *E.g.*, Johnson v. State, 526 S.E.2d 549 (Ga. 2000); *see generally* O'Hagan, Note 23, *supra.*

[29] *E.g.*, State v. Coley, 32 S.W.3d 831 (Tenn. 2000); *see also*United States v. Benitez, 741 F.2d 1312 (11th Cir. 1984).

[30] Seizure of a person from her home so that she may be placed in a lineup raises Fourth Amendment issues. See §§ 18.04–.05, *supra.* Compulsory display of a suspect's physical characteristics in a lineup does not result in "testimonial" or "communicative" evidence and, therefore, does not impinge on the person's privilege against compulsory self-incrimination. See § 26.05[D][1], *supra.*

[31] Joseph D. Grano, *Kirby, Biggers and Ash: Do Any Constitutional Safeguards Remain Against the Danger of Convicting the Innocent?*, 72 Mich. L. Rev. 719 (1974); Frank T. Read, *Lawyers at Lineups: Constitutional Necessity or Avoidable Extravagance?*, 17 UCLA L. Rev. 339 (1969); Note, *Lawyers and Lineups*, 77 Yale L.J. 390 (1967).

[32] United States v. Wade, 388 U.S. 218 (1967); Kirby v. Illinois, 406 U.S. 682 (1972).

[33] A "corporeal" identification procedure in one in which a suspect is physically presented to an eyewitness for identification. Typically, this is done by displaying the suspect in a lineup or by bringing her to the victim or eyewitness for a one-on-one confrontation.

[34] For a definition of "adversary judicial criminal proceedings," *see* § 25.04, *supra.*

[35] The waiver is valid if she voluntarily, knowingly, and intelligent relinquishes her right to counsel. *See* Johnson v. Zerbst, 304 U.S. 458 (1938).

of the results of the pretrial post-indictment identification procedure. That is, if *W* identifies *D* at a post-indictment lineup at which *D* was denied assistance of counsel, neither *W* nor anyone else may testify at trial regarding the results of the lineup.

Furthermore, if the accused is denied her right to counsel at the lineup, the prosecutor is prohibited from obtaining an *in*-court identification of the accused by the witness, unless the prosecutor proves by clear and convincing evidence that the in-court identification is not a fruit of the tainted out-of-court procedure. [36] Among the factors that a trial court may consider in determining whether the prosecutor has met her burden of proof in this regard are those listed as examples by the Supreme Court:

> [The trial court may consider] the prior opportunity [of the witness] to observe the alleged criminal act, the existence of any discrepancy between any pre-lineup description and the defendant's actual description, any identification prior to lineup of another person, the identification by picture of the defendant prior to the lineup, failure to identify the defendant on a prior occasion, and the lapse of time between the alleged act and the lineup identification. [37]

## [B]　How the Rule Developed

### [1]　The Start: *United States v. Wade*

The Supreme Court first considered the applicability of the Sixth Amendment to eyewitness identifications in *United States v. Wade*, [38] a case involving a post-indictment lineup. Quoting from *Powell v. Alabama*, [39] a case relating to the right to counsel *at trial*, the Court in *Wade*, per Justice William Brennan, stated that a person is entitled to the "guiding hand of counsel" at all critical stages of a criminal proceeding. Justice Brennan defined a "critical stage" as "any stage of the prosecution, formal or informal, in court or out, where counsel's absence might derogate from the accused's right to a fair trial."

The Court determined that absent legislative or police reform of eyewitness identification procedures, the pretrial exhibition of a suspect to a witness for identification purposes is a critical stage of the prosecution because the process is "peculiarly riddled with innumerable dangers and variable factors which might seriously, even crucially, derogate from a fair trial."

---

[36] *Wade*, 388 U.S. at 241.

[37] *Id.*

[38] 388 U.S. 218 (1967).

[39] 287 U.S. 45 (1932).

The Court expressed concern regarding the inherent unreliability of eyewitness identifications and the fact that it is seldom possible for defense counsel, if she is absent when the identification occurs, to reconstruct the procedure in order to demonstrate at trial why the witness' identification should be discounted. Justice Brennan pointed out that the identity of the other persons in a lineup may not be known or divulged to defense counsel, and it is unlikely that either the eyewitness or the defendant will have been sufficiently alert to the potential deficiencies of the process to be able to testify to any suggestive features of the lineup. As a result, counsel cannot conduct effective cross-examination of the eyewitness at trial. In passing, the Court also noted that "presence of counsel [at the lineup] itself can often avert prejudice and assure a meaningful confrontation at trial."

Justice White dissented from the Court's right-to-counsel holding. He criticized the majority for its "pervasive distrust of all official investigations," and its "treacherous and unsupported assumptions" that lineups are unreliable and that police misconduct is undiscoverable if counsel is not present. He accused the majority of basing its rule on the premise that "improper police procedures are so widespread that a broad prophylactic rule must be laid down."

Justice White also worried that the introduction of lawyers into the lineup process would hamper law enforcement. His remarks in this regard are considered in subsection [C] below.

### [2]   Turning Away from *Wade*: *Kirby v. Illinois*

In *Kirby v. Illinois*,[40] the police brought a robbery eyewitness to the police station where he identified *D*, who was sitting at a table with a police officer. This identification procedure occurred six weeks before *D* was indicted for the robbery. Speaking for the Court, Justice Potter Stewart refused to apply—or, as he put it, to "extend"—the *Wade*[41] right-to-counsel rule to this one-on-one pre-indictment confrontation. He stated that the Sixth Amendment right to counsel does not apply to police conduct that occurs prior to the initiation of formal judicial proceedings. As most lineups occur before formal charges are brought, the practical effect of *Kirby* is to render the *Wade* right-to-counsel rule largely ineffectual.

Today, in view of a long line of Sixth Amendment cases in other contexts,[42] *Kirby*'s formalistic line-drawing is not surprising, but it was at the time. Although *Wade* involved a post-indictment lineup, Justice Brennan stated in *Wade* that courts must "scrutinize *any* pretrial confrontation of

---

[40] 406 U.S. 682 (1972).

[41] United States v. Wade, 388 U.S. 218 (1967).

[42] *See especially* § 25.04, *supra.*

the accused to determine whether the presence of his counsel is necessary to preserve the defendant's basic right to a fair trial . . . ."[43] The implication of this statement is that the right to counsel could apply in pre-indictment circumstances, and this was the reading of *Wade* by many pre-*Kirby* commentators and lower courts.[44] Indeed, Justice White, dissenting in *Wade*, believed that the rule applied to pre-indictment lineups.[45] Because he believed that *Kirby* was controlled by *Wade*, Justice White dissented as well in *Kirby*.

From a policy perspective, *Kirby* is unjustifiable. The risks inherent in lineups and other identification procedures are as substantial before formal charges are brought as they are after. If defense counsel is needed at a post-indictment lineup, she is also needed at a pre-indictment identification procedure.

### [C]    The Role of Counsel In the Identification Process

In his dissent in *Wade*, Justice White expressed concern that the introduction of defense lawyers into the identification process would undermine the state's legitimate interest in conducting prompt and efficient investigations and would even make the process less trustworthy.

Justice White's prediction was based on the assumption that defense lawyers would play an active role at lineups. Because of *Wade*, he expected the process to become adversarial: attorneys would "hover over witnesses and begin their cross-examination then, menacing truthful factfinding as thoroughly as the Court fears the police now do." Furthermore, because the role of defense counsel in the adversary system is to represent her client faithfully, Justice White expected that lawyers would now advise their clients how to behave at lineups, *e.g.*, not to move or talk when requested, or even to recommend that they not appear in them. He predicted that defense lawyers would "suggest rules for the lineup[s] and . . . manage and produce [them] as best [they] can."

Justice White's reading of the majority opinion in *Wade* is overblown. The role of the defense attorney at the lineup, at least as it is described in the majority opinion, is more passive than White assumes: primarily, counsel is present so that she can later reconstruct the events and cross-examine the eyewitness at trial. She is an observer of the events, not a catalyst for change.

---

[43] *Wade*, 388 U.S. at 227.

[44] Joseph D. Grano, *A Legal Response to the Inherent Dangers of Eyewitness Identification Testimony* in Wells & Loftus, Note 1, *supra*, at 321.

[45] In *Wade*, Justice White warned that the counsel rule announced in that case "applies . . . regardless of when the identification occurs, . . . and whether before or after indictment or information."

It is true that the majority in *Wade did* state, without explaining, that the "presence of counsel [at the corporeal identification procedure] itself can often avert prejudice." That probably means only that if a lawyer is present, the police have an additional incentive to make sure that the procedure is fair to the defendant. Although there is nothing in *Wade* that suggests that a lawyer cannot make suggestions to the police to improve the procedure, there is also nothing in it that suggests that counsel has a right to be heard on such matters, much less that her suggestions must be taken.

Intriguing questions remain. First, if the role of counsel is primarily one of observation, could a police department eliminate the constitutional need for counsel by videotaping in full the lineup process?[46] Second, if Justice White's reading of *Wade* is correct—if defense counsel *may* actively participate in the lineup process—*should* she try to improve the quality of a lineup in which her client is being presented to witnesses? If the lawyer succeeds in making the lineup more reliable, this may backfire, as she would have less basis for criticizing the identification at trial, should her client be identified at the lineup. Yet, if she says nothing, does the defense effectively waive its right to object later to the process?

## § 27.03 Non-Corporeal Identification Procedures: Right to Counsel[47]

In *United States v. Ash*,[48] the Supreme Court held that, notwithstanding *United States v. Wade*,[49] a person against whom adversary judicial proceedings have been initiated is *not* entitled to the presence of counsel when the police display one or more photographs, including one of the accused, to an eyewitness to see if she can identify the culprit. According to *Ash*, such a display, although it occurs after indictment, is not a critical stage of the prosecution.

The Court explained in *Ash* that the primary purpose of the Sixth Amendment right to counsel is to provide counsel at trial, when the defendant is "confronted with both the intricacies of the law and advocacy of the public prosecutor." The right was extended to certain pretrial stages, *Ash* reasoned, once the criminal justice system became more intricate. In the case of post-indictment lineups, counsel was required because "the lineup offered opportunities for prosecuting authorities to take advantage

---

[46] It should be remembered that *Wade* stated that *absent legislative or police reform* the identification process was a critical stage of the prosecution.

[47] See generally Grano, Note 31, *supra*.

[48] 413 U.S. 300 (1973).

[49] 388 U.S. 218 (1967). See § 27.02[B][1], *supra*.

of the accused. . . . Counsel present at [the] lineup would be able to remove disabilities of the accused in precisely the same fashion that counsel compensated for the disabilities of the layman at trial."[50]

Based on this reasoning, the *Ash* Court concluded that a photographic display is not a critical stage of the prosecution. According to the majority, "[s]ince the accused himself is not present at the time of the . . . display, and asserts no right to be present, . . . no possibility arises that the accused might be misled by his lack of familiarity with the law or overpowered by his professional adversary."

The Court also rejected the assertion that the lawyer's presence at a photographic display is necessary to protect the accused's trial rights. It concluded that the risks inherent in this type of procedure are not "so pernicious" that special safeguards are required. Furthermore, because of the tangible nature of photographs, an absent defense attorney can adequately reconstruct the display in order to determine if it was suggestive.[51]

*Ash* is a questionable decision. Photographic displays, like corporeal identification procedures, are inherently unreliable.[52] And, as the dissenters in *Ash* pointed out, unless counsel or her representative is present, there is no way to know if "inflection, facial expressions, physical motions, and myriad other almost imperceptible means of communication . . . intentionally or unintentionally . . . compromise[d] the witness' objectivity."

## § 27.04   Identification Procedures: Due Process of Law[53]

The due process clause requires the exclusion at trial of evidence of a pretrial identification of the defendant if, based on the totality of the circumstances, the procedure used to obtain the identification was: (1) unnecessarily suggestive; and (2) conducive to mistaken identification.[54] This rule applies regardless of whether the identification was corporeal or non-corporeal, occurred before or after formal charges were initiated, and whether or not counsel was present.

---

[50] *Ash*, 413 U.S. at 312.

[51] If this fact justifies the holding in *Ash*, it would seem that videotaping of a post-indictment lineup should also satisfy the requirements of the Sixth Amendment. See Note 46 and the accompanying text, *supra*.

[52] See § 27.01[B], *supra*.

[53] See generally Grano, Note 31, *supra*; Charles A. Pulaski, *Neil v. Biggers: The Supreme Court Dismantles the Wade Trilogy's Due Process Protection*, 26 Stan. L. Rev. 1097 (1974); Benjamin E. Rosenberg, *Rethinking the Right to Due Process in Connection With Pretrial Identification Procedures: An Analysis and a Proposal*, 79 Ky. L.J. 259 (1991).

[54] Stovall v. Denno, 388 U.S. 293 (1967); Neil v. Biggers, 409 U.S. 188 (1972).

Under this test, as a threshold matter, a defendant must show that the police procedure was unnecessarily suggestive. For example, in *Stovall v. Denno*,[55] *D*, an African-American male, was taken to the hospital the day after *V*, an eyewitness to the stabbing murder of her husband and also a victim of a stabbing, had undergone life-saving surgery. *D* was handcuffed to one of five white police officers. *V* identified *D* as the assailant.

The Court agreed that the procedure used was highly suggestive. It noted that the "practice of showing suspects singly to persons for the purpose of identification, and not as part of a lineup has been widely condemned." Nonetheless, due process was not offended, the Court explained, because the procedure used here was "imperative"—it was *necessarily*, not *unnecessarily*, suggestive—in that the police were unsure that *V* would survive the surgery to allow a later lineup. The Court did not explain why the police could not have conducted an in-hospital lineup or, at least, have included black non-suspects in the identification procedure.

However, even if an identification procedure *is* unnecessarily suggestive, due process is not necessarily violated. As the Court explained in *Manson v. Brathwaite*,[56] "reliability is the linchpin in determining the admissibility of identification testimony." Therefore, the ultimate issue to be determined is the likelihood that a misidentification has occurred as the result of the unnecessarily suggestive process. The relevant factors in determining reliability include the opportunity of the witness to view the criminal at the time of the crime, the witness' degree of attention, the accuracy of the witness' prior description of the criminal, the level of certainty demonstrated by the witness at the confrontation, and the length of time between the crime and confrontation.[57]

If the *out*-of-court identification offends due process under the preceding analysis, it must be excluded at trial. In such circumstances, no *in*-court identification by the witness is permitted unless the government proves that the out-of-court procedure did not create "a very substantial likelihood of *irreparable* misidentification."[58] In practice, however, trial courts rarely

---

[55] 388 U.S. 293 (1967).

[56] 432 U.S. 98, 114 (1977); *contra, under the state constitution*, Commonwealth v. Johnson, 650 N.E.2d 1257 (Mass. 1995); People v. Adams, 423 N.E.2d 379 (N.Y. 1981) (both cases holding that the state constitution requires per se exclusion of unnecessarily suggestive identifications, regardless of the reliability of the identification process).

[57] Neil v. Biggers, 409 U.S. 188, 199–200 (1972); *see generally* Amy L. Bradfield & Gary L. Wells, *The Perceived Validity of Eyewitness Identification Testimony: A Test of the Five Biggers Criteria*, 24 Law & Hum. Behav. 581 (2000) (the *Biggers* factors combine with each other independently; they do not interact with each other).

[58] Simmons v. United States, 390 U.S. 377, 384 (1968) (emphasis added).

find that a police identification procedure offends due process, so *both* the pretrial and in-court identifications are allowed.

CHAPTER **28**

# ENTRAPMENT

## § 28.01 Entrapment: In General[1]

Entrapment is a criminal law defense. That is, like such defenses as insanity, duress, and self-defense, entrapment is pleaded by the defendant, and if the claim is adequately proved, he is acquitted. In short, a finding of entrapment does more than result in the exclusion of evidence at trial: it bars the successful prosecution of the defendant.

Entrapment is not a constitutional doctrine. A police officer who entraps a citizen does not, by that fact alone, violate the Constitution. As a consequence, no jurisdiction is required to recognize the defense, although all of the states and the federal courts currently allow the claim;[2] and the definition of the defense and the procedural rules relating to it can and do vary by jurisdiction.

In general, there are two divergent approaches to the defense, frequently termed the "subjective" and "objective" tests of entrapment. Although the definition of entrapment depends on which test is used, both versions usually require proof that: (1) the defendant was induced to commit the crime by a government agent (typically, an undercover police officer); (2) the defendant or, at least, a hypothetically average person, would not have

---

[1] *See generally* Ronald J. Allen, Melissa Luttrell, & Anne Kreeger, *Clarifying Entrapment*, 89 J. Crim. L. & Criminology 407 (1999); Jonathan C. Carlson, *The Act Requirement and the Foundations of the Entrapment Defense*, 73 Va. L. Rev. 1011 (1987); Gerald Dworkin, *The Serpent Beguiled Me and I Did Eat: Entrapment and the Creation of Crime*, 4 Law & Phil. 17 (1985); Paul Marcus, *The Development of Entrapment Law*, 33 Wayne L. Rev. 5 (1986); Roger Park, *The Entrapment Controversy*, 60 Minn. L. Rev. 163 (1976); C. Robton Perelli-Minetti, Comment, *Causation and Intention in the Entrapment Defense*, 28 UCLA L. Rev. 859 (1981); Mary Massaron Ross, Note, *Entrapment Reconsidered: A Nonexculpatory Defense Based on the Need for Reciprocity Between the Government and the Governed*, 35 Wayne L. Rev. 99 (1988); Louis Michael Seidman, *The Supreme Court, Entrapment, and Our Criminal Justice Dilemma*, 1981 Sup. Ct. Rev. 111; Maura F.J. Whelan, *Lead Us Not Into (Unwarranted) Temptation: A Proposal to Replace the Entrapment Defense with a Reasonable-Suspicion Requirement*, 133 U. Pa. L. Rev. 1193 (1985).

[2] Carlson, Note 1, *supra*, at 1013.

committed the offense but for the inducement; and (3) the government agent acted as he did in order to obtain evidence to prosecute the defendant.

## § 28.02 Entrapment: The Subjective Test

### [A] Rule

#### [1] In General

The Supreme Court recognized a federal defense of entrapment for the first time in 1932 in *Sorrells v. United States*,[3] when Chief Justice Charles Evans Hughes, speaking for five members of the Court, allowed an entrapment defense based on what has come to be called the "subjective" test of entrapment. The Court reaffirmed its support for the subjective version of the defense in *Sherman v. United States*[4] and *United States v. Russell.*[5]

As the Court has explained the subjective test, "[a]rtifice and stratagem may be employed to catch" criminals,[6] but a "different question is presented when the criminal design originates with the officials of the Government, and they implant in the mind of an innocent person the disposition to commit the alleged offense and induce its commission in order that they may prosecute."[7] In short, the Supreme Court distinguishes between the trap set for the "unwary criminal" (which is permitted) and for the "unwary innocent" (which is not).[8] Under the subjective test, entrapment is proved if a government agent induces an "innocent" person—a person not predisposed to commit the type of offense charged—to violate the law, so that he can be prosecuted.

#### [2] Proving Predisposition[9]

In the typical subjective entrapment prosecution, the critical issue is whether the defendant was predisposed to commit the offense charged. If he was not predisposed and yet committed the offense after some contact with government agents, this is a matter of concern to the courts. As the

---

[3] 287 U.S. 435 (1932).

[4] 356 U.S. 369 (1958).

[5] 411 U.S. 423 (1973).

[6] *Sorrells,*, 287 U.S. at 441.

[7] *Sherman*, 356 U.S. at 372 (quoting *Sorrells*, 287 U.S. at 442).

[8] *Id.* at 372–73.

[9] *See generally* Damon D. Camp, *Out of the Quagmire After Jacobson v. United States: Towards a More Balanced Entrapment Standard*, 83 J. Crim. L. & Criminology 1055 (1993); Paul Marcus, *Presenting, Back From the [Almost] Dead, the Entrapment Defense*, 47 Fla. L. Rev. 205 (1996); Paul Marcus, *Proving Entrapment Under the Predisposition Test*, 14 Am. J. Crim. L. 53 (1987).

Supreme Court explained in *Jacobson v. United States*,[10] "[w]hen the Government's quest for convictions leads to the apprehension of an otherwise law-abiding citizen who, if left to his own devices, likely would have never run afoul of the law, the courts should intervene."

Notwithstanding the preceding language in *Jacobson* and similar statements in other Court opinions, it is not the case that only an *entirely* law-abiding person can prevail with a claim of entrapment, although such a person provides a more attractive case.[11] It is enough that the defendant was not predisposed to commit the type of offense for which he was prosecuted at the time the government first approached him. A life-long pickpocket, for example, is predisposed to commit minor larcenous acts, but is not by that fact alone disposed to commit, for example, drug offenses or murder. As to these latter offenses, he is a "non-predisposed" individual.

Predisposition may be proved at trial in various ways. First, the facts of the incident itself may demonstrate the defendant's "ready complaisance"[12] to commit the crime. For example, the prosecutor may point to the defendant's non-hesitancy to commit the offense, his ready knowledge of how to commit it, or his comments leading up to the offense that demonstrate his propensity to commit the crime.

Second, predisposition may be proved by reference to the defendant's character in the community prior to the time the government approached him. This is done by the prosecutor introducing evidence, in most other circumstances inadmissible at trial, of the defendant's bad reputation in the community and/or his prior criminal record, including arrests and convictions for related offenses.[13]

An example of predisposition is seen in *United States v. Russell*.[14] In *Russell*, an undercover federal agent met *D*, who was illegally manufacturing amphetamines, and stated that he represented an organization interested in controlling the manufacture and distribution of the drugs in the Pacific

---

[10] 503 U.S. 540 (1992).

[11] In *Jacobson, id.*, the Court gratuitously described the defendant as "a 56-year-old veteran-turned-farmer, who supported his elderly father in Nebraska." Presumably, this description was included to make the reader more sympathetic to the defendant, in order to make the Court's decision to reverse the conviction of a purchaser of child pornography seem more palatable.

[12] Sherman v. United States, 356 U.S. 369, 375 (1958) (internal quotation marks omitted).

[13] On the other hand, there is some support for the proposition that a defendant is entitled to introduce evidence of prior *good* acts or conduct, including evidence of his *lack* of a criminal or arrest record, to *support* an entrapment claim. United States v. Thomas, 134 F.3d 975 (9th Cir. 1998); Sykes v. State, 739 So.2d 641 (Fla. App. 1999).

[14] 411 U.S. 423 (1973).

Northwest. The agent offered to supply *D* with a difficult-to-obtain chemical that was necessary in the production of the drug. *D* readily agreed to the arrangement. The Court held that entrapment was not proved, in view of *D*'s predisposition to commit drug offenses of the sort for which he was prosecuted.

Examples of non-predisposed persons are the defendants in *Sorrells v. United States*,[15] *Sherman v. United States*,[16] and *Jacobson*. In *Sorrells*, *D* was prosecuted for violation of the National Prohibition Act after he sold a one-half gallon jug of whiskey to a government agent who posed as a tourist. *D* sold him the liquor only after three entreaties by the agent, who had befriended him by claiming to be a former member of the World War I military division in which *D* had served. The Court stated that *D* "had no previous disposition to commit [the criminal act] but was an industrious, law-abiding citizen . . . lured [by the agent] . . . to its commission by repeated and persistent solicitation . . . ."

In *Sherman*, a government informer met *D* at a doctor's office where both men were being treated for narcotics addiction. After befriending *D*, the informer asked him if he knew of a good source of narcotics, and pleaded with *D* to supply him with the drugs. *D* turned him down various times before ultimately obtaining narcotics for the informer, based on the informer's "presumed suffering." The Court concluded that *D* was entrapped as a matter of law. It rejected the government's argument that *D* "evinced a 'ready complaisance' to accede" to the informant's request. Although *D* had previously been convicted of drug-related offenses—thus, at one time he *was* disposed to commit drug crimes—the Court considered him to be non-predisposed at the time the government agent approached him for the first time: no evidence was presented that he was still in the drug trade; no narcotics were found in a search of his apartment; he did not seek profit from the sales; and his initial hesitancy to sell the drugs did not appear to be "the natural wariness of the criminal."

In *Jacobson*, the pertinent facts were these: in February, 1984, *D* ordered by mail and received two magazines (*Bare Boys I* and *Bare Boys II*) that contained photographs of nude pre-teen and teenage boys. Receipt of these magazines, which did not depict the youths in sexual activity, was lawful under then-existing federal and state law. A few months later, Congress passed the Child Protection Act of 1984, which prohibited the receipt by mail of sexually explicit depictions of children, such as those found in the *Bare Boys* magazines. Thereafter, various federal agencies began sophisticated operations intended to arrest violators of the new law.

---

[15] 287 U.S. 435 (1932).

[16] 356 U.S. 369 (1958).

*D*'s name came to the government's attention after it obtained the mailing list from the bookstore that sold him the *Bare Boys* magazines. Beginning in January, 1985, government agents sent mail to *D* through five fictitious organizations, such as the "American Hedonist Society." Some of the mailings promoted sexual freedom, expressed opposition to censorship, and called for statutory reform of the laws relating to sexually explicit materials. Two pieces of correspondence included "sexual attitude" surveys purporting to measure the recipient's enjoyment of various sexual materials. *D* responded to the surveys, indicating that he had a moderate level of interest in "pre-teen sex" and "preteen sex-homosexual" materials, but that he was opposed to pedophilia.

The government also sent *D*, again through a fictitious organization, a bogus list of "pen pals" with similar interests in sexual materials. When *D* failed to initiate correspondence with persons from the list, a government pen-pal wrote him instead. *D* answered twice before discontinuing the correspondence. In one letter he stated that he enjoyed "male-male items," although at no time did he mention child pornography.

In March 1987—twenty-six months after the government first targeted *D*—a fictitious organization mailed *D* a brochure advertising photographs of young boys engaged in sex. *D* placed an order that was not filled, but shortly thereafter, he ordered another magazine from a second government-sponsored catalogue. *D* was arrested upon receipt of the magazine. In a subsequent search of *D*'s home, the government found the *Bare Boys* magazines purchased in 1984 and the materials sent to him from the government, but they discovered nothing else that suggested that *D* purchased or collected child pornography.

At trial, *D* pleaded entrapment. When asked why he purchased the illegal materials, he explained that "[w]ell, the statement was made [in the government correspondence] of all the trouble and the hysteria over pornography and I wanted to see what the material was." The jury rejected *D*'s entrapment claim.

The Supreme Court, 5-4, reversed *D*'s conviction. It ruled that as a matter of law the government failed to prove beyond a reasonable doubt (the burden of proof in federal trials) that *D* was predisposed to purchase child pornography prior to being contacted by government agents. Consequently, although *D* "had become predisposed to break the law by May, 1987 [the date of purchase], . . . the Government did not prove that this predisposition was independent and not the product of the attention that the Government had directed at [*D*] since . . . 1985." That is, as the Court viewed the facts, *D* *was* predisposed to commit the offense when the government offered to sell him the magazines, but he was *not* so predisposed until after the government had "softened him up" for more than two years. As one writer has put it, the government did not prove "pre-predisposition."[17]

The Court considered the *lawful* purchase of the *Bare Boys* magazines as "scant if any proof of [D]'s predisposition to commit an illegal act . . . ." These purchases indicated "a predisposition to view sexually oriented photographs that are responsive to [D's] sexual tastes; but evidence that merely indicates a generic inclination to act within a broad range, not all of which is criminal, is of little probative value in establishing predisposition." As Justice White explained, "[e]vidence of predisposition to do what once was lawful is not, by itself, sufficient to show predisposition to do what is now illegal, for there is a common understanding that most people obey the law even when they disapprove of it."

*Jacobson* is a close case. Apparently, if the government had sold D child pornography as soon as it contacted him, a jury could properly have convicted him of the crime; entrapment would not have been proven as a matter of law. Indeed, if the post-arrest search of D's house had turned up a stash of child pornography purchased from non-government sources over the years, D's conviction—even despite the government's entreaties— would probably not have been overturned.

What should the government have done differently? The Court hinted at an answer: it quoted favorably from the Attorney General Guidelines on FBI Undercover Operations, first announced in 1980, that provide that inducements should not be offered by federal officers unless "there is a reasonable indication . . . that the subject is engaging, has engaged, or is likely to engage in illegal activity of a similar type"—something like a "reasonable suspicion" standard relating to the individual being induced—or that "the opportunity for illegal activity has been structured so that there is reason for believing that persons drawn to the opportunity . . . are predisposed to engage in the contemplated illegal activity."The latter investigatory approach is one in which law enforcement agents devise a ruse that should only attract predisposed individuals, much like placing honey out so that the bees will come swarming.[18]

### [B] Rationale of the Rule

The Supreme Court has justified the acquittal of persons induced to commit crimes by the government on the ground of legislative intent: "Congress could not have intended criminal punishment for a defendant

---

[17] Camp, Note 9, *supra*, at 1083.

[18] *E.g.*, People v. Watson, 990 P.2d 1031 (Cal. 2000) (in a sting operation to catch car thieves, the police left a vehicle in a parking lot, unlocked and with the keys in the ignition; held: no entrapment).

who has committed all the elements of a proscribed offense, but was induced to commit them by the government."[19]

According to the Supreme Court, convictions in circumstances such as those set out in *Sorrells*, *Sherman*, and *Jacobson* can stand only if a court rests its interpretation of the applicable criminal statute "entirely upon the letter of the statute."[20] However, such a "[l]iteral interpretation of statutes at the expense of the reason of the law" results in "absurd consequences or flagrant injustice."[21] By passing specific criminal statutes, the Supreme Court has reasoned, Congress did not intend for the government to "use its resources to increase the criminal population by inducing people to commit crimes who otherwise would not do so."[22]

### [C]  Procedural Features of the Rule

In "subjective entrapment" jurisdictions, the issue of whether the defendant was entrapped is a question of fact, which is raised by the defendant at trial and resolved by the trier of fact, ordinarily the jury. The defendant is entitled to a jury instruction on the defense if he presents some evidence that government agents induced him to commit the offense. As this is a fairly easy standard to satisfy, the defense of entrapment typically goes to the jury. Assuming that it does, the government must disprove entrapment beyond a reasonable doubt in the federal courts and in some states.

As with any other defense, a trial judge may refuse to submit the issue of entrapment to the jury, and may acquit the defendant, if there are no factual issues in dispute and entrapment exists as a matter of law, *i.e.*, no reasonable juror could conclude that the defendant was *not* entrapped. However, if the defense goes to the jury, and the jury rejects it, the defendant can appeal, though reviews of federal appellate decisions support the conclusion that the defense is "easy to raise and supremely difficult to establish as a matter of law."[23]

If the jury accepts the defense and acquits, double jeopardy forbids appellate review. And, because an acquittal is non-appealable, jury nullification is possible when jurors finds the police techniques used to obtain evidence against the defendant especially outrageous. In such circumstances

---

[19] United States v. Russell, 411 U.S. 423, 435 (1973).

[20] Sorrells v. United States, 287 U.S. 435, 446 (1932).

[21] *Id.*

[22] United States v. Hollingsworth, 9 F.3d 593, 598 (7th Cir. 1993) (opinion of Posner, J.).

[23] Park, Note 1, *supra*, at 178 (footnote omitted). Although Professor Park's survey of the case law is quite dated, review of more recent appellate decisions does not suggest a different conclusion.

it is possible that a jury will acquit even if the defendant was predisposed to commit the offense.

## § 28.03 Entrapment: The Objective Test

### [A] Rule

For more than a half-century, the so-called "objective" version of the entrapment defense has been defended by a minority of the members of the Supreme Court. In *Sorrells v. United States*,[24] Justice Owens Roberts, speaking also for Justices Louis Brandeis and Harlan Stone, favored an objective test. In *Sherman v. United States*,[25] Justice Felix Frankfurter wrote a four-Justice concurrence in favor of the test. In *United States v. Russell*,[26] the subjective test was favored again by four Justices.

Whereas the subjective test primarily centers on the defendant—was he predisposed to commit the crime?—the objective standard focuses more on police conduct. According to Justice Frankfurter in *Sherman*, entrapment occurs when the "the police conduct . . . falls below standards, to which common feelings respond, for the proper use of governmental power." As he explained the objective approach:

> [The police] should act in such a manner as is likely to induce to the commission of crime only these persons [ready and willing to commit further crime should the occasion arise] and not others who would normally avoid crime and through self-struggle resist ordinary temptations. This test . . . [focuses on] the likelihood, objectively considered, that [the police conduct] would entrap only those ready and willing to commit crime.[27]

In evaluating police conduct according to the objective test, a court must consider how the police inducements would affect an individual. However, unlike the subjective test that focuses on the impact of police conduct on a specific person—the defendant—the question here is "whether, under the circumstances, the governmental activity would induce a hypothetical person not ready and willing to commit the crime to engage in criminal activity."[28]

The "hypothetical person" against whom the police conduct is measured apparently includes some of the characteristics of the actual defendant. For

---

[24] 287 U.S. 435 (1932).

[25] 356 U.S. 369 (1958).

[26] 411 U.S. 423 (1973).

[27] *Sherman*, 356 U.S. at 384.

[28] People v. Jamieson, 461 N.W.2d 884, 891 (Mich. 1990); *see also* United States v. Russell, 411 U.S. 423, 434 (1973) (the question is whether the police conduct "might have seduced a hypothetical individual who was not . . .predisposed" to commit the crime).

example, in *Sherman*, *D* was a drug addict in rehabilitation who distributed drugs as a favor to a government agent only after multiple pleas. The concurring Justices believed that *D* was objectively entrapped as a matter of law. This view is hard to justify if the test is understood to be whether the police conduct would have caused an average law-abiding non-addict to supply illegal drugs. The Justices' position is plausible, however, if the "hypothetical person" is described with *D*'s characteristics, as an addict seeking cure.[29]

### [B]  Rationale of the Rule

The objective standard is justified on grounds of judicial integrity and deterrence. The theme of judicial integrity was first expressed in the entrapment context by Justice Roberts in *Sorrells v. United States*,[30] when he stated that courts were obligated to enforce the defense in order to protect "the purity of its own temple."

Advocates of the objective standard argue, as well, that the acquittal of criminal defendants will deter egregious forms of police misconduct. For example, Justice Potter Stewart condemned the police conduct in *United States v. Russell*[31] on the ground that it was "precisely the type of governmental conduct that the entrapment defense is meant to prevent." Similarly, the drafters of the Model Penal Code justified their adoption of an objective standard of entrapment on the ground that "the attempt to deter wrongful conduct on the part of the government . . . provides the justification for the defense . . . ."[32]

### [C]  Procedural Features of the Rule

Many advocates of the objective test contend that the "objective" entrapment defense should be submitted to a judge rather than to the jury. They reason that courts, not jurors, should protect "the temple's purity," and that only through judicial opinions can appropriate police standards be developed. This is the approach followed by the Model Penal Code[33] and various states.[34] At least one state court has adopted a hybrid approach: a defendant must be acquitted on the ground of entrapment "if a jury finds as a matter of fact that police conduct created a substantial risk that an ordinary person not predisposed to commit a particular crime would have

---

[29] Park, Note 1, *supra*, at 174.

[30] 287 U.S. 435 (1932).

[31] 411 U.S. 423 (1973).

[32] American Law Institute, Model Penal Code and Commentaries, Comment to § 2.13, at 406–07 (1985).

[33] Model Penal Code § 2.13(2).

[34] 2 Paul H. Robinson, Criminal Law Defenses § 209(c)(2) (1984).

been caused to commit that crime, or if the trial court rules as a matter of law that police conduct exceeded the standards of proper investigation."[35]

Most states that apply the objective standard follow the lead of the Model Penal Code, which allocates the burden of proof to the defendant in entrapment cases. The Model Penal Code requires that the defendant prove entrapment by a preponderance of the evidence.

## § 28.04 Entrapment: The Debate

### [A] Overview

Controversy swirls around the defense of entrapment. Most of it relates to the question of whether the subjective or the objective standard is preferable. Although most courts follow the Supreme Court's lead and apply the subjective test, scholars overwhelmingly favor the objective version.[36] The underlying issue in the debate is whether, on the one hand, the entrapped defendant should be excused because he is "innocent" (as subjectivists maintain) or should be exculpated, despite his guilt for the offense, because of the wrongdoing of the police (as objectivists argue).

Most of the entrapment debate is of a negative nature. That is, advocates of each standard generally point to the weaknesses in the opposing position rather than to provide support for their own version of the defense. Many of the criticisms on both sides are powerful, so much so that one scholar has observed that "no member of the [Supreme] Court—and none of the numerous commentators on its work—has advanced a defense of the doctrine that is satisfactory."[37]

### [B] Criticisms of the Subjective Test

#### [1] "The Legislative Intent Rationale is Fictional"

"[I]t is painfully obvious," according to one observer, that the rationale of the subjective test, namely that Congress did not intend for its statutes to be enforced by tempting innocent persons into violations, is "wholly fictional."[38] There is nothing in legislative history to suggest that Congress intended, on the one hand, for nondisposed persons who violate its laws as the result of police inducements to be acquitted while, on the other hand, predisposed persons, subjected to the same blandishments, to be convicted.

---

[35] State v. Vallejos, 945 P.2d 957, 961 (N.M. 1997).

[36] Seidman, Note 1, *supra*, at 115 n.13.

[37] *Id.* at 112.

[38] *Id.* at 129–30; *see also* Sherman v. United States, 356 U.S. 369, 379 (1958) (Frankfurter J., dissenting) (the legislative intent theory is "sheer fiction").

The Supreme Court in *United States v. Russell*[39] virtually conceded the fictional nature of the legislative intent argument when it stated that criticism of the rationale was "not devoid of appeal." Nonetheless, it reaffirmed the subjective standard on the basis of *stare decisis*, the fact that the arguments raised against the objective test were "at least equally cogent," and because Congress, if the legislative intent rationale is unacceptable to it, can "address itself to the question and adopt any substantive definition of the defense that it may find desirable." This is hardly a spirited defense of the theoretical underpinnings of the subjective test.

### [2] "The Subjective Test Acquits Culpable Persons"

The subjective test conflicts with existing substantive criminal law concepts. An entrapped person knowingly violates the law, and he does so under circumstances that would *not* constitute compulsion if the inducing party were another private person rather than a police officer.

In the non-entrapment context, the criminal law does not excuse persons who commit crimes because of tempting offers—no matter how tempting—or who accede to minor threats.[40] The reason for this rule is that people who are tempted by others to commit crimes, or who are victims of minor threats, have sufficient free choice to be held accountable for their actions.[41] One who responds to similar temptations or threats at the hands of the government is no less culpable—he has no less free will—than a victim of private temptation.[42]

Critics of the subjective test suggest that the reason why we acquit the entrapped defendant, even as we convict another person who gives in to similar non-government inducements, is that non-coercive pressures are unacceptable if, but only if, it is the government that plays an ignoble part in producing them. That is, the heart of the entrapment claim really is that, in certain circumstances, we want to punish the government more for its conduct than we want to punish the entrapped party for his. But, this is the essence of the *objective* standard, not the *subjective* test.

### [3] "The Subjective Test Is Unfair"

Because the subjective test focuses on the criminal disposition of the defendant, the standard is unfair. It permits the prosecution to introduce

---

[39] 411 U.S. 423 (1973).

[40] Joshua Dressler, Understanding Criminal Law § 23.01 (3d ed. 2001).

[41] *See generally* Joshua Dressler, *Exegesis of the Law of Duress: Justifying the Excuse and Searching for Its Proper Limits*, 62 So. Cal. L. Rev. 1331 (1989).

[42] American Law Institute, Model Penal Code and Commentaries, Comment to § 2.13, at 406 (1985).

evidence of the defendant's bad character in the form of rumors, reputation evidence, and criminal history. Yet, evidence of this sort ordinarily is inadmissible at trial because it is only of slight probative value and is apt to be prejudicial to the rights of the defendant.[43] Even an advocate of the subjective test has conceded that courts have, "[d]espite the lack of any pressing need, . . . permitted otherwise inadmissible evidence to be introduced . . . . Some of it has been shockingly unreliable."[44]

### [C]  Criticisms of the Objective Test

#### [1]  "The Test Leads to Inappropriate Results"

Because the objective standard focuses on the conduct of the police, critics of the test argue that it can lead to inappropriate results. A hardened criminal can avoid conviction if the police behave improperly. This result is not only dangerous to society but anomalous: when the police violate the Fourth Amendment or another constitutional provision, evidence obtained as the result of the illegal police conduct is excluded, but the prosecution of the defendant may proceed. In the case of entrapment, however, police conduct of which we do not approve, *but which is not unconstitutional,*[45] prevents society from bringing the defendant to justice.

#### [2]  "The Test's Stated Rationales are Indefensible"

Critics maintain that the "purity of the temple" argument based on judicial integrity is unpersuasive. Society does not want judges to protect their temples' purity by releasing criminals to the streets. Opponents of the objective standard agree with Justice William Rehnquist who, in responding to similar "judicial integrity" claims in the Fourth Amendment context, observed that "while it is quite true that courts are not to be participants in 'dirty business,' neither are they to be ethereal vestal virgins of another world."[46] As with the Fourth Amendment, critics claims, "judicial integrity" is little more than a rephrased argument based on deterrence.[47]

The deterrence argument also fails, critics contend.[48] First, advocates of the objective standard fail to explain why courts should deter police conduct

---

[43] Evidence of prior convictions apparently has a powerful impact on jurors in "subjective entrapment" trials. *See* Eugene Borgida & Roger C. Park, *The Entrapment Defense*, 12 Law & Hum. Behav. 19 (1988) (simulated-jury study).

[44] Park, Note 1, *supra*, at 248.

[45] *See* § 28.01, *supra*.

[46] California v. Minjares, 443 U.S. 916, 924 (1979) (dissenting).

[47] United States v. Leon, 468 U.S. 897, 921 n.22 (1984) (quoting United States v. Janis, 428 U.S. 433, 459 n.35 (1976) ("[T]he question whether the use of illegally obtained evidence in judicial proceedings . . .offends the integrity of the court 'is essentially the same as the inquiry into whether exclusion would serve a deterrent purpose.' ").

[48] *See* Seidman, Note 1, *supra*, at 136–46; Park, Note 1, *supra*, at 225–39.

that is not unconstitutional or otherwise illegal. Second, the hypothetical-person test is too ambiguous to provide useful guidance to the police. Moreover, a general verdict of acquittal does not inform law enforcement agencies at what point the entrapment line is crossed.

Third, by its own standards, the objective test does not focus entirely on police conduct. Only conduct that *would cause the average person* to violate the law constitutes entrapment, a principle that seriously undercuts the deterrence goal. For example, suppose that undercover officers nab prostitutes by standing in alleys exposing their penises, or catch thieves by urinating in streets with $20 bills visibly hanging from their coat pockets. [49] Under the objective test, the police have not entrapped their "victims"—and, thus, will not be deterred—because ordinary people do not commit prostitution or theft when induced by such obnoxious conduct.

## § 28.05    Entrapment: Due Process [50]

In federal courts and states that apply the subjective standard of entrapment, no government inducements or threats—not matter how egregious—can constitute entrapment if the "victim" of the police conduct was predisposed to commit the type of offense charged. But, could it be that, at some point, entrapment-like conduct, if outrageous enough, violates the Constitution and, therefore, serves as an alternative basis to bar a prosecution, even of a predisposed individual? As far as Supreme Court case law is concerned, the answer to the question is, "perhaps." A survey of lower court opinions suggests that the answer is "theoretically yes, but virtually never."

In *United States v. Russell*,[51] D was convicted of the illegal manufacture of amphetamines after federal undercover agents furnished him with a difficult-to-obtain legal chemical necessary in the production of the narcotics. Because D was predisposed to commit the crime, an entrapment defense did not successfully lie. D argued, however, that the police violated the due process clause by supplying him with the chemical and by becoming "enmeshed in the criminal activity."

---

[49] These police actions are not fanciful. See R.T. Rybak, *Officer Nabs Prostitute Suspect with 'Unbecoming' Technique*, Minneapolis Tribune, August 30, 1980, at 3A.

[50] *See generally* Leslie W. Abramson & Lisa L. Lindeman, *Entrapment and Due Process in the Federal Courts*, 8 Am. J. Crim. L. 139 (1980); Tim A. Thomas, Annotation, *What Conduct of Federal Law Enforcement Authorities in Inducing or Co-Operating in Criminal Offense Raises Due Process Defense Distinct from Entrapment*, 97 A.L.R. Fed. 273 (1990); Dana M. Todd, Note, *In Defense of the Outrageous Government Conduct Defense in the Federal Courts*, 84 Ky. L.J. 415 (1995).

[51] 411 U.S. 423 (1973).

In an opinion for five Justices, Justice Rehnquist stated that "[w]hile we may some day be presented with a situation in which the conduct of law enforcement agents is so outrageous that due process principles would absolutely bar the government from invoking judicial processes to obtain a conviction . . . the instant case is distinctly not of that breed." Due process was not violated here, the majority concluded, because the chemical that the government furnished was lawful, harmless in itself, and not unobtainable elsewhere. As such, the government was not unduly enmeshed in the criminal activity.

Three years later, some members of the Court rethought their position in *Hampton v. United States*.[52] In *Hampton*, an undercover agent arranged for *D* to sell heroin to another undercover agent. In short, the government was involved in "[t]he beginning and the end of [the] crime." Justice Rehnquist, this time speaking only for himself, Chief Justice Burger, and Justice White, backed off from his earlier due process remarks in *Russell*. He conceded that the government played a much more significant role in the crime in the present case. Nonetheless, Rehnquist stated that the due process clause "comes into play only when the Government activity in question violates some protected right of the *defendant*," which does not occur, he reasoned, if the police act in concert with a defendant to commit a crime. If the police acted illegally here, "the remedy lies, not in freeing the equally culpable defendant, but in prosecuting the police under the applicable provisions of state or federal law."

Despite the plurality's comments, a majority of the *Hampton* Court expressed the belief that due process violations are possible, assuming the right facts. Justices Powell and Blackmun, while concurring in the judgment in the present case (in their view, this narcotics transaction did not state a due process violation), noted that they were "unwilling to join the plurality in concluding that, no matter what the circumstances, . . . due process principles . . . could [not] support a bar to conviction." The three dissenters—Justices Brennan, Stewart, and Marshall—agreed with these remarks. Justice Stevens, who joined the Court after oral arguments were heard in the case, did not participate.

Thus, after *Hampton*, at least five members of the Court were prepared to find that the government could become sufficiently enmeshed in a crime or otherwise act so outrageously that the due process clause would bar a prosecution. However, the only members of the *Hampton* Court still sitting on the bench are Justices Rehnquist and Stevens, so it is difficult to determine how the new Court would resolve the due process issue.

---

[52] 425 U.S. 484 (1976).

Defendants have raised the due process "outrageousness" claim in many federal cases involving prosecutions of crimes, such as manufacture of narcotics, prison escape, mail fraud, and illegal sale or possession of firearms. [53] Although one federal circuit has held that in the absence of binding precedent it will not recognize a due process defense, [54] nearly ever other federal circuit, and many state courts, have assumed that such a defense may lie. [55] However, only in a few cases has a due process violation been found to exist. [56]

---

[53] *See especially* Thomas, Note 50, *supra.*

[54] United States v. Tucker, 28 F.3d 1420 (6th Cir. 1994).

[55] State v. Lively, 921 P.2d 1035, 1044–1045 (Wn. 1996).

[56] *E.g.,* United States v. Twigg, 588 F.2d 373 (3rd Cir. 1978) (due process violation: government informant suggested to *D* that he set up a "speed" laboratory, and the government supplied equipment, raw materials, and expertise at no cost, and even rented a farm for the production of illegal amphetamines); State v. Lively, 921 P.2d 1035 (Wn. 1996) (a government agent took advantage of *D*, a 21-year-old vulnerable single mother who attended Alcoholics Anonymous and Narcotics Anonymous meetings, by befriending her and beginning a sexual relationship in order to involve her in police-sponsored drug activities); *see* United States v. Cuervelo, 949 F.2d 559 (2nd Cir. 1991) (in an international drug importation case, *D* was entitled to a hearing on her allegations of "outrageous governmental conduct," based on her claim that an undercover agent "sexually entrapped" her; dismissal of prosecution would be appropriate if she showed that the "government consciously set out to use sex as a weapon in its investigatory arsenal, or acquiesced in such conduct for its purposes upon learning that such a relationship existed," that the agent initiated the sexual relationship or allowed it to continue in order to further the investigation, and that the relationship was "entwined" with the criminal events).

## CHAPTER 29

# THE RIGHT TO COUNSEL: AT TRIAL AND ON APPEAL

## § 29.01  Overview: The Importance of Defense Lawyers in the Adversary System

A defense lawyer may seem to some to be "a nettlesome obstacle to the pursuit of wrongdoers."[1] Indeed, some people do not believe that she has a proper role to play during various police-citizen encounters, such as during interrogations and at lineups.[2] But the role of defense counsel at trial and in post-trial proceedings is much less in dispute: she serves to reduce the risk of wrongful convictions of innocent persons, as well as to ensure that the guilty receive due process.

In our adversarial system of justice, defense lawyers "in criminal courts are necessities, not luxuries."[3] They serve as potential equalizers in the confrontation between the government, which hires a lawyer to prosecute, and the person charged with an offense. Defense counsel serves as "an antidote to the fear, ignorance, and bewilderment"[4] felt by the ordinary defendant. Without a lawyer, the Supreme Court has observed, an innocent defendant "faces the danger of conviction because he does not know how to establish his innocence."[5] It is not an exaggeration to state, therefore, that the very legitimacy of the American criminal justice system depends in considerable part on the participation of competent, ethical defense lawyers who diligently represent their clients' best interests.

---

[1] Moran v. Burbine, 475 U.S. 412, 468 (1986) (Stevens, J., dissenting).

[2] *See* §§ 25.02[C] (police interrogations), § 27.02[C] (lineups), *supra*.

[3] Gideon v. Wainwright, 372 U.S. 335, 344 (1963).

[4] Albert W. Alschuler, *The Defense Attorney's Role in Plea Bargaining*, 84 Yale L.J. 1179, 1179 (1975).

[5] Powell v. Alabama, 287 U.S. 45, 69 (1932).

## § 29.02   The Right to Counsel: At Trial[6]

### [A]   The Right to Employ Counsel

It has always been clear that, at a minimum, the Sixth Amendment entitles an accused in a federal prosecution to employ a lawyer to assist in her defense at trial.[7] Moreover, since 1963, the right to counsel has been deemed a fundamental right of criminal justice;[8] therefore, an accused in a state prosecution has a similar Fourteenth Amendment right to retain an attorney to represent her during trial.

### [B]   Indigents: The Right to Appointed Counsel[9]

#### [1]   Overview

##### [a]   The Goal

Justice Hugo Black, speaking for the Supreme Court, wrote in 1956 that "[t]here can be no equal justice where the kind of trial a man gets depends on the amount of money he has."[10] And, given the historic correlation between race and poverty, "failure to provide adequate assistance of counsel to accused indigents draws a line not only between rich and poor, but also between white and black."[11] As a consequence, the Supreme Court has

---

[6] *See generally* William M. Beaney, The Right to Counsel in American Courts (1955); Gerald F. Uelman, *2001: A Train Ride: A Guided Tour of the Sixth Amendment Right to Counsel,* 58 Law & Contemp. Probs. 13 (1995). For a thoughtful dialogue on the role of defense counsel in representing "not just the damned but the damnable," *see* Michael E. Tigar, *Defending,* 74 Tex. L. Rev. 101 (1995), and a response by Monroe H. Freedman, *The Lawyer's Moral Obligation of Justification,* 74 Tex. L. Rev. 111 (1995).

[7] Scott v. Illinois, 440 U.S. 367, 370 (1979).

[8] Gideon v. Wainwright, 372 U.S. 335 (1963).

[9] *See generally* Committee to Review the Criminal Justice Act, Report of the Committee to Review the Criminal Justice Act, *reprinted in* 52 Crim. L. Rep. (BNA) 2265 (1993); John J. Cleary, *Federal Defender Services: Serving the System or the Client?,* 58 Law & Contemp. Probs. 65 (1995); Chester L. Mirsky, *The Political Economy and Indigent Defense: New York City, 1917-1998,* 1997 Annual Survey of American Law 891; John B. Mitchell, *Redefining the Sixth Amendment,* 67 S. Cal. L. Rev. 1215 (1994); Charles J. Ogletree, Jr., *An Essay on the New Public Defender for the 21st Century,* 58 Law & Contemp. Probs. 81 (1995); Edward C. Prado, *Process and Progress: Reviewing the Criminal Justice Act,* 58 Law & Contemp. Probs. 51 (1995); Stephen J. Schulhofer & David D. Friedman, *Rethinking Indigent Defense: Promoting Effective Representation Through Consumer Sovereignty and Freedom of Choice for All Criminal Defendants,* 31 Am. Crim. L. Rev. 73 (1993); Robert L. Spangenberg & Marea L. Beeman, *Indigent Defense Systems in the United States,* 58 Law & Contemp. Probs. 31 (1995); Kim Taylor-Thompson, Individual Actor v. Institutional Player: Alternating Visions of the Public Defender, 84 Geo. L.J. 2419 (1996).

[10] Griffin v. Illinois, 351 U.S. 12, 19 (1956).

[11] Ogletree, Note 9, *supra,* at 83.

sought over time to mandate legal assistance to indigent criminal defendants through the aegis of the Sixth Amendment.

In 1938, the Supreme Court announced in *Johnson v. Zerbst*[12] that the "Sixth Amendment withholds from federal courts, in all criminal proceedings, the power and authority to deprive an accused of his life or liberty unless he has or waives the assistance of counsel." However, the Court did not construe the Constitution to require the states (as distinguished from the federal government) to appoint counsel for indigents until its 1963 landmark decision in *Gideon v. Wainwright*,[13] described below. Until *Gideon*, legal representation of indigents in state courts was sporadic and often ineffective.[14]

### [b]    The Reality: Data Regarding Representation of Indigents

In 1986, lawyers were appointed to represent indigents in 4.4 million state cases.[15] In 1994, the national figure apparently skyrocketed to approximately 8 million.[16] In 1999, in the 100 most populous counties alone, 4.2 million state prosecutions were handled by indigent criminal defense programs.[17]

In 1989, approximately 80 percent of the nation's jail inmates reported that they had court-appointed lawyers representing them for the offenses for which they were charged.[18] In 1996, court-appointed attorneys represented 82 percent of state defendants in the 75 largest counties; in 1998, two-thirds of federal defendants were represented by court-appointed counsel.[19] Yet, based on 1988 and 1990 data, less than one penny of every

---

[12] 304 U.S. 458 (1938).

[13] 372 U.S. 335 (1963).

[14] *See generally* Beaney, Note 6, *supra*; Bertram F. Willcox & Edward J. Bloustein, *Account of a Field Study in a Rural Area of the Representation of Indigents Accused of Crime*, 59 Colum. L. Rev. 551 (1959).

[15] U.S. Department of Justice, Bureau of Justice Statistics, Criminal Defense for the Poor, 1986 1 (1988).

[16] Andrew Blum, *Defense of Indigents: Crisis Spurs Lawsuits*, National Law Journal, May 15, 1995, at A1, A26 (quoting Robert Spangenberg).

[17] U.S. Department of Justice, Bureau of Justice Statistics, Indigent Defense Services in Large Counties, 1999 1 (2000). An estimated $1.2 billion was expended on these programs. *Id.*

[18] U.S. Department of Justice, Bureau of Justice Statistics, Indigent Defense 1 (1996).

[19] U.S. Department of Justice, Bureau of Justice Statistics, Defense Counsel in Criminal Cases 1 (2000).

government dollar was spent on judicial and legal services, which includes appropriations for courts, prosecutors, and public defense counsel.[20]

Although the Supreme Court cases discussed below mandate publicly financed representation of indigents, the Court has never stated what institutional form that representation must take. As a consequence, states or counties[21] have devised three forms of public representation: public-defender programs; contract-attorney representation; and assigned-lawyer programs.[22]

A public-defender system is an organization of lawyers designated by a jurisdiction to provide representation to indigents in criminal cases.[23] In 1986, about 37 percent of the nation's counties—large or small—had such defender programs.[24]

A contract-attorney program is one in which a jurisdiction enters into an agreement with private attorneys, law firms, or bar associations to represent indigents in the community.[25] Attorneys in this system maintain a substantial private practice. They are paid either on a fixed-price basis (they agree to accept an undetermined number of cases for a determined flat fee) or on a fixed-fee-per-case basis.[26] Frequently, the fees are so low

---

[20] U.S. Department of Justice, Bureau of Justice Statistics, Justice Expenditures and Employment, 1990 1 (1992); U.S. Department of Justice, Bureau of Justice Statistics, Justice Expenditures and Employment, 1988 1 (1990). Typically, indigent criminal defense programs have received less funding than prosecutorial offices. In 1999, for example, in 89 surveyed counties, $1.1 billion was budgeted for indigent criminal defense services, whereas prosecutorial offices had budgets approximating $1.9 billion. The disparity is greater than these figures suggest, as the budgets of prosecutorial offices often do not include prosecutorial resources provided by law enforcement agencies, forensic laboratories, and the like. Indigent Defense Services in Large Counties, Note 17, *supra*, at 3. *See also* Note 21, *infra*.

[21] In some states, each county is left to develop *and fund* its own legal representation system. Overall, budgets for indigent defense systems in such states "are flat or have been cut." David E. Rovella, *Unclogging Gideon's Trumpet*, National Law Journal, Jan. 14, 2000, at A1. In one such state, Mississippi, three counties have sued the state to compel the state legislature to spend some of its surplus monies to assist counties in funding indigent defense systems. *Id.*

[22] *See generally* Robert L. Spangenberg & Patricia A. Smith, An Introduction to Indigent Defense Systems (American Bar Association 1986); Criminal Defense for the Poor, Note 15, *supra*; Schulhofer & Friedman, Note 9, *supra*, at 83–96; Spangenberg & Beeman, Note 9, *supra*, at 32–44.

[23] Spangenberg & Beeman, Note 9, *supra*, at 36.

[24] Criminal Defense for the Poor, Note 15, *supra*, at 1.

[25] Schulhofer & Friedman, Note 9, *supra*, at 89.

[26] Spangenberg & Beeman, Note 9, *supra*, at 34.

that quality representation, particularly in capital cases,[27] is difficult to obtain.[28]

Many counties have an assigned-counsel program. Here, many lawyers, often inexperienced private practitioners, are placed on a list to provide representation to poor defendants on a case-by-case basis. They are paid by the hour (usually well below ordinary rates for attorneys in the community) or receive a flat fee per case.[29]

Today, most large counties provide some combination of these programs. In 1999, 314 criminal defense programs were identified in the 100 most populated counties. About 40 percent of the programs were of the assigned-counsel variety; 39 percent were public-defender programs; and 21 percent were contract-attorney indigent criminal defense programs.[30]

### [2]    The Road to *Gideon*

### [a]    *Powell v. Alabama*

In *Powell v. Alabama*,[31] nine teenage black youths (ages 12 to 19) were prosecuted for the alleged rape of two white girls in an Alabama community that, due to the race of the parties, was "explosive with rage and vengeance."[32] The youths, described by the Court as "ignorant and illiterate," and residents of another state, were indicted, arraigned, and brought to trial in less than two weeks after the capital offenses supposedly occurred.

---

[27] *See generally* Douglas W. Vick, *Poorhouse Justice: Underfunded Indigent Defense Services and Arbitrary Death Sentences*, 43 Buff. L. Rev. 329, 377–97 (1995); *see also* § 29.07[A], *infra*.

[28] According to 1994 figures prepared by the Spangenberg Group for the ABA Bar Information Program, most states only pay court-appointed attorneys $20 to $50 per hour for their work. Worse, most states have an overall compensation cap regardless of the length or complexity of the prosecution, *e.g.*, $325 per case (Connecticut), $1000 (Alabama), and $1,250 (Illinois). In one Texas capital case, the state paid defense counsel $11.84 per hour. *See* Stephen B. Bright, *Counsel for the Poor: The Death Sentence Not for the Worst Crime but for the Worst Lawyer*, 103 Yale L.J. 1835, 1838–39 (1994). In New York, a defendant facing a life sentence may get a lawyer who spends as few as 20 hours on the case; the lawyer may get as little as $693 for the work, a figure less than the average cost for a real estate closing. Jane Fritsch & David Rhode, *Lawyers Often Fail New York's Poor*, New York Times, April 8, 2001, at A1.

[29] *See* Spangenberg & Beeman, Note 9, *supra*, at 32–34.

[30] Indigent Defense Services in Large Counties, Note 17, *supra*, at 4.

[31] 287 U.S. 45 (1932).

[32] Willcox & Bloustein, Note 14, *supra*, at 551. The case, which has come to be known as the "Scottsboro Case" (the site of the trial), has been the subject of voluminous scholarly research. *E.g.*, Dan T. Carter, Scottsboro: A Tragedy of the American South (1969); James Goodman, Stories of Scottsboro (1994); Claudia Johnson, *The Secret Courts of Men's Hearts: Code and Law in Harper Lee's To Kill a Mockingbird*, 19 Stud. Am. Fiction 129 (1991) (suggesting a relationship between the Scottsboro Case and the fictional Mockingbird trial).

As Supreme Court Justice George Sutherland explained, until the day of trial, "no lawyer had been named or definitely designated to represent the defendants." Instead, as the trial judge explained, he had "appointed all the members of the bar for the purpose of arraigning the defendants and then of course anticipated . . . [them to] continue to help the defendants if no counsel appeared." On the day of trial, two lawyers, one of whom was from out of state and unfamiliar with local law, offered to represent the youths. Once appointed, however, the lawyers were denied a continuance so that they could adequately prepare their defense. Eight of the defendants were convicted in the three one-day trials that followed and were sentenced to death.

The Court overturned the convictions. Treating the youths as constructively unrepresented by counsel at trial because the lawyers had not been given time to prepare, Justice Sutherland wrote:

> The right to be heard would be, in many cases, of little avail if it did not comprehend the right to be heard by counsel. Even the intelligent and educated layman has small and sometimes no skill in the science of law. . . . He is unfamiliar with the rules of evidence. Left without the aid of counsel he may be put on trial without a proper charge, and convicted upon incompetent evidence, or evidence irrelevant to the issue or otherwise inadmissible. He lacks both the skill and knowledge adequately to prepare his defense, even though he has a perfect one. He requires the guiding hand of counsel at every step in the proceedings against him. Without it, though he be not guilty, he faces the danger of conviction because he does not know how to establish his innocence.[33]

Despite this broad language, the Court's holding was narrow, and focused on special circumstances of the case:

> All that it is necessary now to decide, as we do decide, is that in a capital case, where the defendant is unable to employ counsel, and is incapable adequately of making his own defense because of ignorance, feeble mindedness, illiteracy, or the like, it is the duty of the court, whether requested or not, to assign counsel for him as a necessary requisite of due process of law; and that duty is not discharged by an assignment at such a time or under such circumstances as to preclude the giving of effective aid in the preparation and trial of the case.[34]

### [b]  *Betts v. Brady*

In *Betts v. Brady*,[35] the Court was invited to announce that there is a *per se* constitutional right to appointed counsel. It did not take the step.

---

[33] *Powell*, 287 U.S. at 68–69.

[34] *Id.* at 71.

[35] 316 U.S. 455 (1942).

(Matthew Bender & Co., Inc.)                                                                    (Pub.791)

In *Betts*, *D*, an indigent, was indicted for robbery. He requested, but was denied, the assistance of counsel at trial. He was convicted of robbery and sentenced to prison. *D* appealed his conviction on the ground that he was entitled to free assistance of counsel at trial.

The Supreme Court rejected the principle that "due process of law demands that in every criminal case, whatever the circumstances, a State must furnish counsel to an indigent defendant." Based on its reading of constitutional history and contemporary state practices, the Court concluded that the right to counsel was not essential to a fair trial in light of the "common understanding of those who have lived under the Anglo-American system of law."

Instead, the Court applied the special circumstances standard used in *Powell v. Alabama*.[36] It concluded that no circumstances existed in the present case to justify the appointment of counsel. Unlike the facts in *Powell*, *D* was prosecuted for a non-capital crime, and the case presented only the "simple issue" of whether *D*'s alibi claim should be believed. The Court concluded that *D*, "not helpless, . . . a man forty-three years old, [and] of ordinary intelligence," could handle his defense satisfactorily by himself.

### [3]  *Gideon v. Wainwright*

*Gideon v. Wainwright*[37] overruled *Betts v. Brady*.[38] *Gideon* brought the protections of the Sixth Amendment right to counsel to the states, through the Fourteenth Amendment due process clause. In *Gideon*, *D* was prosecuted for the felony of breaking and entering a poolroom. *D* requested, but was denied, the assistance of counsel. According to the Court, he conducted his own defense "about as well as could be expected from a layman." Nonetheless, the jury convicted him and he was sentenced to five years' imprisonment.

The Court, per Justice Hugo Black, overturned the conviction.[39] It stated that the Court in *Betts* had "made an abrupt break with its own

---

[36] 287 U.S. 45 (1932).

[37] 372 U.S. 335 (1963). *See generally* Anthony Lewis, Gideon's Trumpet (1964); Jerold H. Israel, *Gideon v. Wainwright: The "Art" of Overruling*, 1963 Sup. Ct. Rev. 211; Yale Kamisar, *Betts v. Brady Twenty Years Later: The Right to Counsel and Due Process Values*, 61 Mich. L. Rev. 219 (1962); Yale Kamisar, *The Right to Counsel and the Fourteenth Amendment: A Dialogue on "The Most Pervasive Right" of an Accused*, 30 U. Chi. L. Rev. 1 (1962).

[38] 316 U.S. 455 (1942).

[39] If a defendant is actually (as in *Gideon*) or constructively (as in *Powell v. Alabama*) denied her constitutional right to the assistance of counsel at trial, any resulting conviction must be reversed, *i.e.*, the error is *never* harmless. *See* Strickland v. Washington, 466 U.S. 668, 692 (1984). Harmless-error doctrine is discussed at § 4.03, *supra*.

well-considered precedents," especially that of *Powell v. Alabama*.[40] It described as an "obvious truth" the fact that "in our adversary system of criminal justice, any person haled into court, who is too poor to hire a lawyer, cannot be assured a fair trial unless counsel is provided for him." Justice Black observed:

> Governments . . . quite properly spend vast sums of money to establish machinery to try defendants accused of crime. Lawyers to prosecute are everywhere deemed essential to protect the public's interest in an orderly society. Similarly, there are few defendants charged with crime, few indeed, who fail to hire the best lawyers they can get to prepare and present their defenses. [The implication of this is] . . . that lawyers in criminal courts are necessities, not luxuries. The right of one charged with crime to counsel may not be deemed fundamental . . . in some countries, but it is in ours.

*D* was retried, but now with the assistance of counsel. The jury returned a not guilty verdict in one hour.[41]

### [4]   Post-*Gideon* Law: The Misdemeanor Cases

#### [a]   *Argersinger v. Hamlin*

*Gideon v. Wainwright*[42] held that an indigent has a constitutional right to assistance of counsel at trial. *Gideon*, however, involved a felony trial. In *Argersinger v. Hamlin*,[43] the Supreme Court considered the applicability of *Gideon* to misdemeanor trials. In *Argersinger*, *D*, an indigent, was charged with carrying a concealed weapon, a misdemeanor for which the maximum penalty was imprisonment for six months, a $1000 fine, or both. *D* requested, but was denied, the appointment of counsel. Consequently, *D* represented himself, was convicted, and was sentenced to 90 days in jail.

The state supreme court upheld the trial court's decision not to appoint counsel. It followed the line drawn by the United States Supreme Court in its Sixth Amendment trial-by-jury jurisprudence. In the latter field, the Supreme Court has held that the right to trial by jury applies only to "nonpetty" offenses, *i.e.*, offenses punishable by imprisonment in excess of six months.[44] The state court reasoned that the same rule should apply to the right to counsel, since it derives from the Sixth Amendment as well. Because

---

[40] 287 U.S. 45 (1932). *See* § 29.02[B][2][a], *supra*.

[41] *See* Lewis, Note 37, *supra*, at 226–37.

[42] 372 U.S. 335 (1963).

[43] 407 U.S. 25 (1972); *see generally* Lawrence Herman, The Right to Counsel in Misdemeanor Court (1974); Steven Duke, *The Right to Appointed Counsel: Argersinger and Beyond*, 12 Am. Crim. L. Rev. 601 (1975).

[44] *See* Duncan v. Louisiana, 391 U.S. 145 (1968).

*D*'s trial involved a "petty" offense (the maximum potential incarceration for the offense was imprisonment for six months), it concluded that *D* was not entitled to appointed counsel.

The Supreme Court overturned the conviction. It stated that the right to counsel "has a different genealogy" than the trial-by-jury right: "[w]hile there is historical support for limiting the . . . trial by jury [right] to 'serious criminal cases,' there is no such support for a similar limitation on the right to assistance of counsel . . . ."

The Court reasoned that although both *Gideon* and *Powell v. Alabama*[45] involved felony trials, "their rationale has relevance to any criminal trial, where an accused is deprived of his liberty." It warned that misdemeanor and petty offenses may implicate legal and constitutional issues as complex as arise when a person is prosecuted for a serious offense. The Court also expressed concern that, in view of the high volume of misdemeanor cases, defendants were becoming victims of "assembly-line justice." Therefore, the Court concluded that "even in prosecutions for offenses less serious than felonies, a fair trial may require the presence of a lawyer."

Although the reasoning of *Argersinger* could apply to all misdemeanor cases, the Court's holding was limited: "absent a knowing and intelligent waiver, no person may be imprisoned for any offense, whether classified as petty, misdemeanor, or felony, unless he was represented by counsel at his trial." In other words, an indigent is entitled to the appointment of counsel if she actually, not merely potentially, will be jailed (even for one day) if she is convicted.

Justice Lewis Powell, with whom Justice William Rehnquist joined, concurred in the result. He described the imprisonment/no-imprisonment line drawn by the majority as "illogical" and "without discernible support" in the Constitution. Justice Powell argued that not all misdemeanor cases are complex, and the line between the difficult and simple ones is not drawn on the basis of whether a defendant is sentenced to imprisonment. Although he agreed that the right to a lawyer "does not mysteriously evaporate" when an indigent is charged with a misdemeanor, he would have applied the *Powell* special circumstances rule to all petty offenses.

The concurring Justices also criticized the majority for being "disquietingly barren of details" as to how the new rule would be implemented. Under *Argersinger*, the trial judge is faced with an "awkward dilemma." She must decide before trial—before evidence is introduced—whether to appoint counsel. If she does not appoint counsel, she cannot jail a convicted defendant, no matter how justifiable such punishment might turn out to be.

---

[45] 287 U.S. 45 (1932). *See* § 29.02[B][2][a], *supra.*

If the judge wishes to retain her option to incarcerate the defendant, she must provide counsel. The concurrence predicted that the effect of the Court's decision would be to overburden local courts, exacerbate delays, and increase court congestion.

### [b]   *Scott v. Illinois*

In *Scott v. Illinois,*[46] D, an indigent, was charged with theft, a misdemeanor that carried a potential penalty of one-year imprisonment, a $500 fine, or both. Denied the assistance of counsel, D was convicted and fined $50. On appeal, D argued that although he was not imprisoned he should have been provided counsel at his trial.

D's contention was plausible. First, the Court's reasoning in *Argersinger v. Hamlin*[47] —counsel is required because of the potential complexity of misdemeanor cases and the risk of assembly-line justice—applies with equal force in non-jail cases. Second, a bright-line rule—either that a lawyer is required in all petty-offense prosecutions or, at least, whenever imprisonment is authorized—would have resolved the "awkward dilemma" noted by the concurring Justices in *Argersinger*.

Third, and perhaps most significantly, the crime for which D was prosecuted, although denominated as a misdemeanor, was not a petty offense. Because the potential penalty was one-year imprisonment, D was entitled to a jury trial. *Argersinger* had apparently concluded that the right to counsel is more encompassing than the jury-trial right; therefore, D's request for appointment of counsel should have been granted.

Nonetheless, the Supreme Court left the counsel/no-counsel line where it had been drawn in *Argersinger*. Justice Rehnquist, writing for a five-Justice majority, spoke of the Sixth Amendment in far less expansive terms than the Court did in *Gideon*. He stated that "[t]here is considerable doubt that the Sixth Amendment itself, as originally drafted by the Framers of the Bill of Rights, contemplated any guarantee other than the right of an accused in a criminal prosecution in a federal court to employ a lawyer to assist in his defense." After review of the relevant case law, the majority stated that "constitutional line drawing becomes more difficult as the reach of the Constitution is extended further, and as efforts are made to transpose lines from one area of Sixth Amendment jurisprudence to another."

The *Scott* Court described the "intentions of the *Argersinger* Court as not unmistakably clear." It concluded, however, that the case "did indeed

---

[46] 440 U.S. 367 (1979); *see generally* Lawrence Herman & Charles A. Thompson, Scott v. Illinois and the Right to Counsel: A Decision in Search of a Doctrine?, 17 Am. Crim. L. Rev. 71 (1979).

[47] 407 U.S. 25 (1972).

delimit the constitutional right to appointed counsel" to those cases resulting in actual imprisonment. And, even considering the matter anew, the Court concluded that the actual imprisonment line drawn in *Argersinger* "is eminently sound and warrants adoption . . . as the line defining the constitutional right to appointment of counsel." In short, the Constitution requires "only that no indigent criminal defendant be sentenced to a term of imprisonment unless the State has afforded him the right to assistance of appointed counsel in his defense."[48]

## § 29.03   The Right to Counsel: On Appeal

### [A]   Inapplicability of the Sixth Amendment

By its language, the Sixth Amendment does not apply to criminal appeals. The amendment entitles a person to the assistance of counsel "for his *defence*" in "criminal *prosecutions*." When the trial is completed, the "prosecution" ends; on appeal, it is the defendant/appellant who seeks to upset the status quo, and it is the prosecutor who seeks to "defend" the conviction.

Despite the inapplicability of the Sixth Amendment to criminal appeals, appellate procedures are subject to the standards of the Fourteenth Amendment equal protection and due process clauses. In *Griffin v. Illinois*,[49] the Supreme Court held that a state that requires a defendant to furnish a trial transcript to the appellate court as a condition of hearing her appeal must provide the transcript at state expense for indigents. Justice Black, writing for a four-Justice plurality, applied both due process and equal protection standards to reach this conclusion. He wrote:

> [A] State can no more discriminate on account of poverty than on account of religion, race, or color. Plainly the ability to pay costs in advance bears no rational relationship to a defendant's guilt or innocence . . . . [¶ ] There can be no equal justice where the kind of trial a man gets depends on the amount of money he has. Destitute defendants must be afforded

---

[48] A valid uncounseled misdemeanor conviction (a conviction valid despite the absence of counsel, because the defendant did not receive a jail sentence) may be used as the basis for enhancing punishment of the defendant after a subsequent, *counseled* conviction. For example, in Nichols v. United States, 511 U.S. 738 (1994), *D* pleaded guilty to a federal drug offense. Pursuant to sentencing guidelines, *D* received enhanced punishment of approximately two years because of his criminal record, which included a prior uncounseled misdemeanor conviction for which he had previously been fined, but not incarcerated. The Court upheld the additional punishment as a "logical consequence" of *Scott*, because the enhancement contained in the sentencing guidelines did "not change the penalty imposed for the earlier conviction."

[49] 351 U.S. 12 (1956).

as adequate appellate review as defendants who have money enough to buy transcripts.[50]

The *Griffin* equality principle has been applied in various contexts to ensure that indigent defendants at trial and on appeal obtain meaningful access to procedures available to nonindigents.[51] It serves as the point of departure for consideration of an indigent's right to assistance of counsel on appeal.

## [B] First Appeal

### [1] In General

A convicted defendant has no constitutional right to appeal her conviction.[52] Nonetheless, every state permits a convicted person at least one appeal of right after conviction. Thereafter, courts have discretion not to hear appeals of criminal convictions.

In *Douglas v. California*[53] the Supreme Court, per Justice Douglas, held that the Fourteenth Amendment requires a state to provide counsel for an indigent on her first statutory appeal of right. In doing so, the Court invalidated a California rule that permitted appellate courts, on the request of an indigent for the assistance of appellate counsel, to look at the trial record to determine whether the defendant would be benefitted by appointment of counsel.

The Court stated that although states do not have to provide absolute equality to the rich and the poor in their procedures, "where the merits of *the one and only appeal* an indigent has as of right are decided without benefit of counsel, we think an unconstitutional line has been drawn between rich and poor." Without distinguishing between due process and equal protection principles, the Justices concluded that it is impermissible to require an indigent appellant to "run this gantlet of a preliminary showing

---

[50] *Id.* at 17–18, 19.

[51] *E.g.*, Ake v. Oklahoma, 470 U.S. 68 (1985) (due process requires that the state provide access to a psychiatrist to an indigent defendant who makes a preliminary showing that her sanity will be an issue at trial); Mayer v. Chicago, 404 U.S. 189 (1971) (*Griffin* rule applies to payment of transcripts in appeals of misdemeanor convictions); Draper v. Washington, 372 U.S. 487 (1963) (a state rule providing for a free transcript only if the defendant can convince the trial judge that the appeal is non-frivolous violates the Fourteenth Amendment); Burns v. Ohio, 360 U.S. 252 (1959) (a state rule that requires indigent defendants to pay a fee before filing a notice of appeal violates *Griffin*); *see also* M.L.B. v. S.L.J., 519 U.S. 102 (1996) (*Griffin* rule is extended to an appeal of a ruling terminating a mother's parental rights, a "quasi-criminal" case).

[52] McKane v. Durston, 153 U.S. 684 (1894) (dictum); Jones v. Barnes, 463 U.S. 745 (1983) (dictum).

[53] 372 U.S. 353 (1963).

of merit," if persons wealthy enough to hire a lawyer do not have to face the same obstacle.

As Justice Douglas explained, the discrimination in the case was not between "possibly good and obviously bad cases," but between people rich enough to hire lawyers and those who were not. In this, the Court said, "[t]here is lacking that equality demanded by the Fourteenth Amendment . . . . The indigent . . . has only the right to a meaningless ritual, while the rich man has a meaningful appeal."

### [2]  Special Problem: Frivolous Appeals

A defendant does not have a constitutional right to demand that her attorney act unethically by prosecuting a frivolous appeal, i.e., an appeal that includes no arguable claims for reversal of the conviction.[54] In other words, she does not have a constitutional right to require her attorney to file a brief making spurious arguments. Instead, an attorney appointed to represent an indigent on direct appeal may request that the appellate court allow her to withdraw from the case. On the other hand, the Supreme Court determined in *Anders v. California*[55] that "in order to protect indigent defendants' constitutional right to appellate counsel, courts must safeguard against the risk of granting such requests in cases where the appeal is not actually frivolous."[56]

Until recently, the general understanding of *Anders* was that a state appellate procedure was constitutionally infirm unless the appointed appellate counsel, in seeking to withdraw, filed a brief referring to anything in the record that arguably supported the appeal, and including citations to case or statutory authority supporting the attorney's conclusion that the appeal was frivolous. The appellate court was also required, it seemed from *Anders*, to permit the appellant to file her own brief, raising any additional points she chose. The appellate court would then determine either that the case was "wholly frivolous" (and rule against the appellant on the merits) or determine that the appeal was not wholly frivolous, in which case new counsel would be appointed to represent the appellant and file a full brief.

In *Smith v. Robbins*,[57] however, the Court concluded that the appellate procedures described in *Anders* (as noted above) are not obligatory. States "are free to adopt different procedures, so long as those procedures adequately safeguard a defendant's right to appellate counsel." More specifically, *Smith* provides that a "State's procedure provides [adequate]

---

[54] McCoy v. Court of Appeals of Wisconsin, Dist. 1, 486 U.S. 429, 436 (1988).

[55] 386 U.S. 738 (1967).

[56] Smith v. Robbins, 528 U.S. 259, 262–263 (2000) (explaining *Anders*).

[57] 528 U.S. 259 (2000).

review so long as it reasonably ensures that an indigent's appeal will be resolved in a way that is related to the merit of that appeal."

In *Smith*, the Court upheld a new California appellate procedure that provided fewer protections than those enunciated in *Anders*. In California, if appellate counsel determines that an appeal would be frivolous, she must file a brief with the court summarizing the procedural factual history of the case, and attest that she has reviewed the record, explained the case to her client, provided the client with a copy of her brief, and informed the client of the latter's right to file a supplemental brief. The appellate court must then conduct its own review of the record. If it determines that there are no arguable issues, it affirms the conviction; if it finds arguable claims, it orders briefing on those issues.

The procedure approved in *Smith* is far less rigorous than that demanded in *Anders*. Among other matters, it does not require appellate counsel to set out any possible arguable claims. As the dissenters in *Smith* complained, the appellate counsel who seeks to withdraw is not required "to show affirmatively . . . that he has made the committed search for [arguable] issues . . . that go[es] to the heart of appellate representation in our adversary system."[58] Instead, the approved system leaves it to the appellate court to search the record for arguable issues. This process does not assure that the adversarial system will be at play on appeal, since the appellate court will not be looking at the record with an adversary's eye for finding plausible claims, as is expected of a partisan defense lawyer.

### [C] Subsequent (Discretionary) Appeals

In *Ross v. Moffitt*,[59] the Supreme Court held that the Fourteenth Amendment does not require the appointment of counsel to assist indigent appellants in discretionary state appeals and for applications for review in the United States Supreme Court. Since *Ross* was decided, the Court has extended the no-right-to-counsel principle to state *habeas corpus* proceedings.[60]

In *Ross*, the Court discussed separately the issues of due process (which "emphasizes fairness between the State and the individual dealing with the State") and equal protection (which "emphasizes disparity in treatment by a State between classes of individuals whose situations are arguably indistinguishable"), although there was little difference in the ultimate analysis.

---

[58] *Id.* at 297 (Souter, J., dissenting).

[59] 417 U.S. 600 (1974).

[60] Pennsylvania v. Finley, 481 U.S. 551 (1987); Murray v. Giarratano, 492 U.S. 1 (1989) (plurality opinion) (death penalty appeal).

In its due process discussion, the Court focused on the difference between trials and appeals: whereas states cannot dispense with trials, they do not have to permit appeals. Therefore, when appeals are permitted, it "does not automatically mean that a State then acts unfairly by refusing to provide counsel to indigent defendants at every stage of the way." According to *Ross*, the due process clause requires only that indigents not be singled out "and denied meaningful access [to appellate courts] . . . because of their poverty."

In the Court's equal protection discussion, it gave lip service to the *Griffin* equality principle,[61] but it quoted language in both *Griffin* and *Douglas v. California*[62] that indicated that absolute equality between the rich and poor is not constitutionally required. According to *Ross*, the equal protection clause does not require a state "to duplicate the legal arsenal that may be privately retained by a criminal defendant." All that the constitutional provision demands, the Court said, is that the indigent have "an adequate opportunity to present his claims fairly in the context of the . . . appellate process."

The Court conceded that "a skilled lawyer, particularly one trained in the somewhat arcane art of preparing petitions for discretionary review, would . . . prove helpful to any litigant able to employ" the lawyer. Nonetheless, it concluded that indigents on discretionary appeals have an "adequate opportunity" to present their claims (or, in due process terms, they have "meaningful access" to appellate review) without the assistance of counsel.

The Court pointed out that with discretionary appeals, the appellate court will have various documents to consider: a transcript or other record of the trial proceedings; a brief on the appellant's behalf filed by her attorney during the first (*Douglas*) appeal of right; often an opinion of the lower court disposing of the case; and any submission by the indigent herself. The Supreme Court concluded that with these materials the appellate court has "an adequate basis on which to base its decision to grant or deny review."

---

[61] *See* § 29.03[A], *supra.*

[62] 372 U.S. 353 (1963).

## § 29.04  The Right of Self-Representation[63]

### [A]  *Faretta v. California*

#### [1]  **Recognition of the Right**

In *Faretta v. California*,[64] the Supreme Court, per Justice Potter Stewart, held that a defendant has a constitutional right voluntarily and knowingly to waive her right to the assistance of counsel and to represent herself at trial. In essence, the Sixth Amendment right-to-counsel provision includes two rights: expressly, the right of a criminal defendant to the assistance of counsel; and, by implication, an independent right of self-representation that follows from waiver of the first right.

In *Faretta*, *D*, charged with theft, requested permission to represent himself at trial. The judge originally agreed to the request, but later changed his mind when *D* failed adequately to answer various questions intended to determine his knowledge of applicable procedural and evidentiary law. Represented at his trial by a public defender, *D* was convicted.

The Supreme Court reversed the conviction. It concluded that *D* had a constitutional right to represent himself. According to Justice Stewart, the Sixth Amendment "does not provide merely that a defense shall be made for the accused; it grants to the accused personally the right to make the defense." According to *Faretta*, the personal nature of the right is evident from the fact that it is the defendant—not counsel—who must be informed of the nature of the charges, who has the right to confront accusers, and who must be accorded compulsory process for obtaining witnesses. According to the Court, "[t]he right to defend is given directly to the accused; for it is he who suffers the consequences if the defense fails."

The Court also found support for the right of self-representation in the language and historical roots of the Sixth Amendment. Textually, the amendment provides that a defendant is entitled to the "assistance" of counsel. The lawyer is the assistant; the defendant is the master. Historically, the English common rule provided that no criminal defendant "can have counsel forced upon him against his will."[65] And, according to the majority, "[i]n the American colonies the insistence upon a right of self-representation was, if anything, more fervent than in England."

Justice Blackmun, joined by Chief Justice Burger and Justice Rehnquist, dissented. They argued that the fact that Sixth Amendment rights are

---

[63] *See generally* John F. Decker, *The Sixth Amendment Right to Shoot Oneself in the Foot: An Assessment of the Guarantee of Self-Representation Twenty Years After Faretta*, 6 Seton Hall Const. L.J. 483 (1996).

[64] 422 U.S. 806 (1975).

[65] *Id.* at 826 (quoting R. v. Woodward [1944] K.B. 118, 119).

personal does not "guarantee[] any particular procedural method of asserting those rights." The dissent also questioned the Court's historical analysis. In view of the fact that the framers "expressly constitutionalized the right to assistance of counsel but remained conspicuously silent on any right of self-representation," the dissenters believed that "it is at least equally plausible to conclude that the Amendment's silence . . . indicates that the Framers simply did not have the subject in mind when they drafted the language."

As a policy matter, the dissenters were troubled with the majority's holding. It stated that the Sixth Amendment does not require "the States to subordinate the solemn business of conducting a criminal prosecution to the whimsical—albeit voluntary—caprice of every accused who wishes to use his trial as a vehicle for personal or political self-gratification."

### [2]  Reflections on *Faretta*

Justice Stewart conceded in *Faretta* that "[t]here can be no blinking the fact that the right of an accused to conduct his own defense seems to cut against the grain of this Court's [prior right-to-counsel] decisions." Indeed, ironically, the Justices forming the majority in *Faretta*—an opinion that says, in essence, that defendants have the right to forego the "necessities, not luxuries"[66] of the assistance of counsel—are those who have argued most strenuously for the expansion of the right to counsel. Meanwhile, it was the dissenters—members of the Court not generally sympathetic to such extensions—who were called on to point out that "representation by counsel is essential to ensure a fair trial."

The essence of *Faretta* is that a defendant has a protectible right of autonomy. As it is the defendant, not the lawyer, who will suffer the consequences of a conviction, it is the accused's personal right to decide whether counsel is a benefit or a detriment. As Justice Stewart explained, "whatever else may be said of those who wrote the Bill of Rights, surely there can be no doubt that they understood the inestimable worth of free choice." Even if the defendant's freely-willed decision is "ultimately to his own detriment, [the] choice must be honored out of 'that respect for the individual which is the lifeblood of the law.' "[67]

In dissent, Justice Blackmun quoted the proverb that "one who is his own lawyer has a fool for a client." He needled the majority by stating that the Court "now bestows a *constitutional* right on one to make a fool of himself." Justice Stewart's answer to the dissenters was that "[p]ersonal liberties are not rooted in the law of averages." As he pointed out, "it is

---

[66] Gideon v. Wainwright, 372 U.S. 335, 344 (1963).

[67] *Faretta*, 422 U.S. at 834 (quoting Illinois v. Allen, 397 U.S. 337, 350–51 (1970)).

not inconceivable that in some rare instances, the defendant might in fact present his case more effectively by conducting his own defense."

Justice Stewart last observation is correct, of course. However, it is also true, as he conceded, that "in most criminal prosecutions defendants could better defend with counsel's guidance than by their own unskilled efforts." And, as important as the right of autonomy is, it is not the *only* value at stake in criminal trials. The majority opinion runs counter to "the established principle that the interest of the State in a criminal prosecution 'is not that it shall win a case, but that justice shall be done.' "[68] Moreover, "courts have an independent interest in ensuring that . . . legal proceedings appear fair to all who observe them."[69] *Faretta* quite arguably threatens these interests.

The current Supreme Court seems at least as divided about the wisdom of *Faretta* as the original Court. For example, in *Martinez v. Court of Appeal of California*,[70] in which the Court held that there is no comparable constitutional right of self-representation on appeal,[71] Justice Stevens, who delivered the opinion of the Court, evinced only lukewarm support for some of *Faretta*'s reasoning, particularly the historical evidence set out in the latter case. Concurring Justice Breyer, too, noted "that judges closer to the firing line have sometimes expressed dismay about the practical consequences of [*Faretta*]."[72]

Indeed, the majority's tepid support for *Faretta* motivated Justice Kennedy, in concurrence, to write that "[t]o resolve this case [of self-representation on appeal] it is unnecessary to cast doubt upon the rationale of *Faretta v. California*." And, concurring Justice Scalia stated more directly that he does "not share the apparent skepticism of [the majority] opinion concerning the judgment of the Court . . . in *Faretta v. California*."

---

[68] *Id.* at 849 (Blackmun, J., dissenting) (quoting Berger v. United States, 295 U.S. 78, 88 (1935)).

[69] Wheat v. United States, 486 U.S. 153, 160 (1988).

[70] 528 U.S. 152 (2000).

[71] The Sixth Amendment does not apply to criminal appeals, *see* § 29.03[A], *supra,* so if a right of self-representation on appeal exists it must be found in general principles of due process. The Court stated that neither the holding of *Faretta* nor its reasoning compels a state to recognize a constitutional right of self-representation on direct appeal from a criminal conviction. Although the Court conceded that *Faretta*'s concern for an individual's right of autonomy would seem to support a right of appellate self-representation, it determined that such a right is not a necessary component of a fair appellate procedure, nor are their meaningful historical roots of such a right.

[72] Martinez v. Court of Appeal of California, 528 U.S. at 164 (concurring opinion) (also *quoting* United States v. Farhad, 190 F.3d 1097, 1107 (CA9 1999): the right of self-representation "frequently . . . conflicts squarely and inherently with the right to a fair trial").

## [B]  Procedural Issues

### [1]  Informing the Accused of the Right

The right of self-representation is independent of the right to the assistance of counsel. Therefore, courts are confronted with a dilemma: must the accused be informed of both rights and then waive one of them? Although a defendant must be informed of her right to trial counsel,[73] lower courts have held that she does not need to be informed of her right of self-representation unless she clearly indicates that she is considering the option.[74]

Because self-representation is an independent right, and not simply a waiver of the right to counsel, a defendant who expresses the desire to represent herself must be permitted to do so as long as she is mentally competent to give up the right to counsel.[75] Specifically, the Court stated in *Faretta* that a defendant "should be made aware of the dangers and disadvantages of self-representation, so that the record will establish that 'he knows what he is doing and his choice is made with eyes open.' "[76]

### [2]  Timeliness of the Request

A defendant must assert her right of self-representation in timely fashion. In *Faretta*, the Court noted that *D*'s request was made "well before" the trial began. The implication is that a defendant must not only make the request before commencement of the trial, but she must make it sufficiently early that her request does not unduly delay orderly processes.

### [3]  Hybrid Representation

Courts have uniformly held that a defendant is not entitled to so-called "hybrid" representation.[77] That is, a person does not have an automatic right to assert both of her Sixth Amendment rights, *i.e.*, the right to the assistance of counsel *and* to represent herself at trial. Trial courts permit hybrid representation only as a "matter of grace."[78]

---

[73] *E.g.*, Fed. R. Crim. P. 5(c).

[74] 3 Wayne R. LaFave, Jerold H. Israel & Nancy J. King, Criminal Procedure § 11.5(b) (2d ed. 1999).

[75] The competency standard is "whether the defendant has 'sufficient present ability to consult with his lawyer with a reasonable degree of rational understanding' and has 'a rational as well as factual understanding of the proceedings against him.' " Godinzez v. Moran, 509 U.S. 389, 396 (1993) (quoting Dusky v. United States, 362 U.S. 402, 402 (1960)). *See also* § 31.02[A], *infra*.

[76] *Faretta*, 422 U.S. at 835 (quoting Adams v. United States ex. rel. McCann, 317 U.S. 269, 279 (1942)); for one example of a jury instruction that explains the pitfalls of self-representation, *see* United States v. Hayes, 231 F3d 1132, 1138–39 (9th Cir. 2000).

[77] 3 LaFave, Israel & King, Note 74, *supra*, at § 11.5(g).

[78] State v. Melson, 638 S.W.2d 342, 359 (Tenn. 1982).

### [4] Standby Counsel[79]

The Supreme Court stated in *Faretta* that a trial court may, even over the objection of the defendant, appoint standby counsel in self-representation cases. According to *Faretta*, the purpose of standby counsel is limited: to assist the defendant if and when she seeks help, and to take over the case if self-representation must be terminated during trial.

In an arguable cutback on *Faretta*, the Supreme Court in *McKaskle v. Wiggins*[80] upheld a conviction in which standby counsel provided unsolicited, and at times even unwanted, assistance. In *Wiggins*, the Court stated that the right of self-representation "exists to affirm the dignity and autonomy of the accused and to allow the presentation of what may, at least occasionally, be the accused's best possible defense." Therefore, in evaluating whether a defendant's self-representation rights have been vindicated, "the primary focus must be on whether the defendant had a fair chance to present his case in his own way."

According to *Wiggins*, the right of self-representation is not violated unless standby counsel substantially interferes with "significant tactical decisions" of the defendant, "control[s] the questioning of witnesses," speaks in defendant's place against her wishes "on . . . matter[s] of importance," or in some other way "destroy[s] the jury's perception that the defendant is representing" herself.

In *Wiggins*, the Court concluded that standby counsel did not violate *D*'s right of self-representation, although the lawyer intervened without *D*'s permission, and sometimes over his vocal objection, more than 50 times during the three-day trial. In part, the Court refused to disapprove of counsel's actions because some of the intrusions occurred outside the presence of the jury, and therefore did not destroy its perception that *D* was representing himself, and because *D* wavered during the trial, sometimes vehemently objecting to standby counsel's participation but other times inviting it.

### [5] Legal Significance of Poor Self-Representation

As explained in Section 29.07, a defendant has a constitutional right to effective assistance of counsel. However, one who chooses self-representation "cannot thereafter complain that the quality of his own defense amounted to a denial of 'effective assistance of counsel.' "[81] In

---

[79] *See generally* Anne Bowen Poulin, *The Role of Standby Counsel in Criminal Cases: In the Twilight Zone of the Criminal Justice System*, 75 N.Y.U. L. Rev. 676 (2000).

[80] 465 U.S. 168 (1984).

[81] *Faretta*, 422 U.S. at 835 n.46; McKaskle v. Wiggins, 465 U.S. at 177 n.8.

essence, a person who validly waives her right to counsel assumes the risk that, indeed, she had a "fool for a client."

### [6] Legal Effect of an Erroneous Denial of the Right

If a court wrongfully refuses to permit a defendant to represent herself at trial, or if the right is violated by standby counsel, any subsequent conviction must be reversed. The Supreme Court has reasoned that because the right of self-representation serves to affirm a defendant's personal autonomy and, indeed, is "a right that when exercised usually increases the likelihood of a trial outcome unfavorable to the defendant, its denial is not amenable to 'harmless error' analysis. The right is either respected or denied; its deprivation cannot [ever] be harmless."[82]

## § 29.05 The Right to Representation by One's Preferred Attorney[83]

### [A] In General

The Sixth Amendment comprehends the right of a nonindigent defendant "to select and be represented by one's preferred attorney."[84] With few exceptions,[85] and despite the criticism of some scholars,[86] courts have not granted indigents a similar right to choose their appointed counsel.[87]

The right of a defendant to hire and be represented by the attorney of her choice is not unqualified. First, although defense counsel "should seek to establish a relationship of trust and confidence with the accused,"[88] the Supreme Court has declared that a defendant has no Sixth Amendment right to a "meaningful" attorney-client relationship.[89]

Second, a defendant is not permitted to be represented by a non-attorney, except herself.[90] Third, a defendant may not be represented by an attorney

---

[82] McKaskle v. Wiggins, 465 U.S. at 177 n.8. For discussion of "harmless error" law generally, *see* § 4.03, *supra.*

[83] *See generally* Floyd Feeney and Patrick G. Jackson, *Public Defenders, Assigned Counsel, Retained Counsel: Does the Type of Criminal Defense Counsel Matter?*, 22 Rutgers L.J. 361 (1991); Bruce A. Green, *"Through a Glass, Darkly": How the Court Sees Motions to Disqualify Criminal Defense Lawyers,* 89 Colum. L. Rev. 1201 (1989); Schulhofer & Friedman, Note 9, *supra;* Peter W. Tague, *An Indigent's Right to the Attorney of His Choice,* 27 Stan. L. Rev. 73 (1974).

[84] Wheat v. United States, 486 U.S. 153, 159 (1988).

[85] *E.g.,* Harris v. Superior Court, 567 P.2d 750 (Cal. 1977).

[86] *E.g.,* Teague, Note 83, *supra.*

[87] 3 LaFave, Israel & King, Note 74, *supra,* at § 11.4.

[88] American Bar Association, Standards for Criminal Justice, Prosecution Function and Defense Function 4-3.1 (3d ed 1993).

[89] Morris v. Slappy, 461 U.S. 1 (1983).

[90] *See* Wheat v. United States, 486 U.S. 153, 159 (1988).

who has a conflict of interest, even if the defendant is willing to accept the risks inherent in such representation.[91]

Fourth, a defendant "may not insist on representation by an attorney he cannot afford."[92] This limitation is of particular significance in view of the enactment of statutes that permit the government to seize assets, including money that would pay for an attorney, that allegedly were obtained illegally. This issue is discussed immediately below.

### [B]  Special Problem: Seizing Lawyers' Fees

In two cases, *Caplin & Drysdale, Chartered v. United States*[93] and *United States v. Monsanto*,[94] the Supreme Court held that the right to counsel is not violated if a court, pursuant to statute,[95] grants an *ex parte* motion by the government to freeze the defendant's assets, including assets that would be used to pay for legal representation, on the ground that they were obtained as a result of illegal drug activities. Nor is the Sixth Amendment violated by an order that any monies paid to defense counsel be recaptured if the client is convicted of such drug activities.

The Court reasoned that forfeiture statutes of the sort involved in these two cases do not impinge on a defendant's constitutional right to counsel of choice, because they do not prevent the defendant from hiring any attorney whom she can afford or who is willing to represent her without assurances that she will have adequate funds. Furthermore, even if such statutes prevent her from hiring an attorney, the right to the counsel of one's choice encompasses only the right to spend one's own money, and not to spend another person's money, to hire a lawyer.

Justice Blackmun, joined by Justices Brennan, Marshall, and Stevens, dissented in the cases. They argued "that it is unseemly and unjust for the Government to beggar those it prosecutes in order to disable their defense at trial."[96] Perhaps the most intriguing feature of the dissent is its examination of the reasons why the dissenters believed that a defendant wealthy enough to hire an attorney is ordinarily better served than one who must accept appointed counsel. The implication of their comments (if accepted as true) is that, despite the Supreme Court's efforts in the middle of the twentieth century to assure that the kind of trial a person gets does not depend on the amount of money she has,[97] this is exactly what happens.

---

[91] *See* § 29.08, *infra.*

[92] *Wheat,* 486 U.S. at 159.

[93] 491 U.S. 617 (1989).

[94] 491 U.S. 600 (1989).

[95] 21 U.S.C.A. § 853 (1999).

[96] Caplin & Drysdale, Chartered v. United States, 491 U.S. at 635.

[97] Griffin v. Illinois, 351 U.S. 12, 19 (1956).

The dissenters focused on four factors. First, to be an effective advocate, an attorney needs her client's trust. Trust is fostered when a defendant can choose her own attorney. It is undermined, the dissenters stated, "[w]hen the Government insists upon the right to choose the defendant's counsel" for her. As two scholars have put it:

> Most citizens would consider it shockingly unethical for an attorney representing one side in a lawsuit to be selected or paid, even directly, by the opposing party. Yet such principles are violated routinely in this country on a massive scale. In criminal cases, the great majority of defense attorneys are paid directly or indirectly by the prosecuting party, the state.[98]

Second, the right to hire private counsel "serves to assure some modicum of equality between the government and those it chooses to prosecute." The government expends considerable resources to prosecute persons accused of crime, "[b]ut when the Government provides for appointed counsel, there is no guarantee that levels of compensation and staffing will be even average."[99]

Third, according to the dissent, the "socialization" of criminal-defense representation too easily excludes "the maverick and risk taker, [whose approach] might not fit into the structured environment of a public defender's office, or that might displease a judge whose preference for nonconfrontational styles of advocacy might influence the judge's appointment decisions."[100]

Finally, private attorneys can more easily specialize in complex areas of the criminal law than can public defenders, who need a broader—but necessarily thinner—range of skills.[101]

## § 29.06    Interference With The Right to Counsel

The right to counsel includes the right "that there . . . be no restrictions upon the function of counsel in defending a criminal prosecution in accord with the traditions of the adversary [system] . . . that has been constitutionalized in the Sixth and Fourteenth Amendments."[102] This means, among

---

[98] Schulhofer & Friedman, Note 9, *supra*, at 74 (footnote omitted).

[99] For example, in 1985, public expenditures on the defense of indigents was only 26% of that spent on their prosecution. *See* Sourcebook of Criminal Justice Statistics—1986, Table 1.1 (U.S. Dept. of Justice 1987).

[100] *Caplin & Drysdale, Chartered*, 491 U.S. at 647.

[101] Perhaps worse, indigents in most counties are not represented by Public Defenders, but receive representation from private, often relatively inexperienced, attorneys who are paid on a low hourly or flat-fee basis. *See* § 29.02[B][1][b], *supra*.

[102] Herring v. New York, 422 U.S. 853, 857 (1975).

other things, that the government may not ordinarily (1) restrict defense counsel's decision on whether, and when in the course of the presentation of the defendant's case, the accused will testify;[103] (2) prevent counsel from eliciting testimony from her client through direct examination;[104] or (3) deny counsel the opportunity to make a summation to the jury.[105]

The Constitution is also violated if a trial judge prohibits a defendant from consulting with her attorney during an overnight recess, even if the recess is called while the defendant is on the witness stand and is about to be cross-examined by the prosecutor.[106] However, the Supreme Court explained in *Perry v. Leeke*[107] that because "cross-examination often depends for its effectiveness on the ability of counsel to punch holes in a witness' testimony at just the right time, in just the right way," a judge may prohibit consultation between the defendant and her counsel during a brief same-day recess, while the accused is testifying, in order to further the truth-seeking function of the trial.

Direct interference by the government with the defendant's right to the assistance of counsel ordinarily requires automatic reversal of any resulting conviction.[108]

---

[103] Brooks v. Tennessee, 406 U.S. 605 (1972) (applying the Fifth Amendment self-incrimination and due process clauses).

[104] Ferguson v. Georgia, 365 U.S. 570 (1961).

[105] Herring v. New York, 422 U.S. 853 (1975).

[106] Geders v. United States, 425 U.S. 80 (1976).

[107] 488 U.S. 272 (1989).

[108] *E.g.*, Geders v. United States, 425 U.S. at 91–92 (reversing conviction without expressly determining whether prejudice occurred).

## § 29.07   Effective Assistance of Counsel: General Principles[109]

### [A]   Nature of the Issue

The fact "[t]hat a person who happens to be a lawyer is present at trial alongside the accused . . . is not enough to satisfy" the Sixth Amendment.[110] If the Sixth Amendment "is to serve its purpose, defendants cannot be left to the mercies of incompetent counsel."[111] The Constitution require lawyers, whether retained or appointed, to provide effective assistance to their clients at trial and on the first appeal of right.[112]

Effective representation entails various duties, among them the following. First, "the professional judgment of a lawyer should be exercised, within the bounds of the law, solely for the benefit of his or her client and free of any compromising influences and loyalties."[113] Second, a defense lawyer should interview her client early on in their relationship, keep her client informed of important developments in the case, and consult with her client on important decisions.[114]

Third, and perhaps most basically, counsel has a duty to "conduct a prompt investigation of the circumstances of the case and explore all avenues leading to facts relevant to the merits of the case and the penalty in the event of conviction,"[115] after which she must "bring to bear such

---

[109] See generally Lisa J. McIntyre, The Public Defender: The Practice of Law in the Shadows of Repute (1987); David Wasserman, The Appellate Defender as Monitor, Watchdog, and Gadfly (Occasional Papers from The Center for Research in Crime and Justice, N.Y.U. School of Law, VII, 1989); Vivian O. Berger, The Supreme Court and Defense Counsel: Old Roads, New Paths—A Dead End?, 86 Colum. L. Rev. 9 (1986); Bright, Note 28, supra; William J. Genego, The Future of Effective Assistance of Counsel: Performance Standards and Competent Representation, 22 Am. Crim. L. Rev. 181 (1984); Bruce A. Green, Lethal Fiction: The Meaning of "Counsel" in the Sixth Amendment, 78 Iowa L. Rev. 433 (1993); Michael McConville & Chester L. Mirsky, Criminal Defense of the Poor in New York City, 15 N.Y.U. Rev. L. & Soc. Change 581 (1986-87); Mirsky, Note 9, supra; Amy R. Murphy, Note, The Constitutional Failure of the Strickland Standard in Capital Cases Under the Eighth Amendment, 63 Law & Contemp. Probs. 179 (2000); Willcox & Bloustein, Note 14, supra.

[110] Strickland v. Washington, 466 U.S. 668, 685 (1984).

[111] McMann v. Richardson, 397 U.S. 759, 771 (1970).

[112] The due process clause, rather than the Sixth Amendment, entitles a convicted defendant to effective assistance of counsel on her first appeal of right. Evitts v. Lucey, 469 U.S. 387 (1985). On discretionary appeals, for which there is no constitutional right to the assistance of counsel, see § 29.03[C], supra, there is also no constitutional right to effective assistance. Id. at 396 n.7.

[113] Standards for Criminal Justice, Note 88, supra, Commentary to Standard 4-3.5, at 162.

[114] Id. at 4-3.2, 4-3.8, and 4-5.2.

[115] Id. at 4–4.1.

skill and knowledge as will render the trial a reliable adversarial process."[116]

Issues regarding the effectiveness of counsel are especially acute in the representation of indigents, who must rely on often-harried lawyers in understaffed and underfinanced Public Defender offices, or who are represented, sometimes with less than complete vigor, by private attorneys through contract or judicial appointment.[117] For example, one study reported that private attorneys assigned to represent indigents frequently failed to perform such basic tasks as interviewing their clients, investigating the facts underlying the charges, and filing written motions to suppress evidence or to discover evidence from the prosecutor.[118] One commentator has suggested that death sentences are meted out in capital cases "not for the worst crime[s] but for the worst lawyer[s],"[119] and the "worst lawyers" are usually those representing indigents. A major reason for the poor quality of representation by private counsel is the inadequate compensation provided to such attorneys.[120]

## [B] "Ineffective Assistance": The *Strickland* Test

### [1] General Principles

The Supreme Court defined "ineffective assistance of counsel" for Sixth Amendment purposes in *Strickland v. Washington*.[121] The standard announced in the case applies to criminal trials and capital sentencing

---

[116] American Bar Association, Model Rules of Professional Conduct, Rule 1.1 (1983).

[117] *See generally* § 29.02[B][1][b], *supra*.

[118] McConville & Mirsky, Note 109, *supra*, at 746–47. According to the study of New York County during the mid-1980s, lawyers assigned to represent indigents interviewed their clients in only 26 percent of homicide cases and 18 percent of all other felonies; they conducted investigations in 27 percent of homicide cases and 12 percent of other felony cases; and they filed written motions in only a quarter of the homicide cases, and in 20 percent of other cases. A New York Times study of New York City records and court cases in the year 2000 found that "almost no part of the indigent defense system functioned as it was intended": most lawyers appointed to represent indigents failed to hire private investigators to look for witnesses or evidence, did not seek experts to rebut expert prosecutorial evidence, and did not go the scene of the crime to conduct their own investigation. Most of the appointed lawyers did not make even a single visit to the jail to discuss the case with their clients. Jane Fritsch & David Rhode, Note 28, *supra*, at A1.

[119] Bright, Note 28, *supra*.

[120] For state cases, *see* Note 28, *infra*. In the federal system, there are statutory caps on compensation set out in 18 U.S.C. 3006A(d)(2) (2000) (currently, $5,200 for representation of a felony defendant before and during trial; lesser amounts are set for appellate representation).

[121] 466 U.S. 668 (1984).

hearings.[122] It also serves as the proper framework for evaluating a claim of ineffectiveness by a convicted defendant whose attorney failed to file a notice of appeal.[123]

According to the Court, the "benchmark" for evaluating a claim of ineffective assistance of counsel is "whether counsel's conduct so undermined the proper functioning of the adversarial process that the trial [or capital sentencing hearing] cannot be relied on as having produced a just result." The purpose of the Sixth Amendment right-to-counsel provision, *Strickland* states, "is simply to ensure that criminal defendants receive a fair trial."

*Strickland* announced a difficult-to-prove two-prong test for determining whether a convicted defendant received constitutionally ineffective representation. Both elements must be proved if the defendant is to show that her conviction or resulting death sentence "resulted from a breakdown in the adversary process that renders the result unreliable."

The two-pronged test is considered in detail immediately below. Two specific issues (a lawyer with a conflict of interest; and the role of ethical canons in determining the adequacy of representation) receive separate treatment.[124]

## [2]   The First Prong: Deficiency of Representation

### [a]   The Standard

A defendant must prove that her counsel's performance was constitutionally deficient, by which is meant that the "errors [were] so serious that counsel was not functioning as the 'counsel' guaranteed . . . by the Sixth Amendment."[125]

*Strickland* eschewed explicit guidelines for effective representation. According to the Court, "[n]o particular set of detailed rules for counsel's conduct can satisfactorily take into account of the variety of circumstances faced by defense counsel or the range of legitimate decisions regarding how best to represent a criminal defendant." Therefore, the inquiry is, simply, "whether counsel's assistance was reasonable considering all the circumstances."

The *Strickland* "deficiency" test is extremely difficult to prove. A convicted defendant must identify with precision the acts or omissions that

---

[122] A slightly different version of the *Strickland* test is used to evaluate the effectiveness of counsel during plea negotiations. *See* § 31.02[C][5], *infra*.

[123] Roe v. Flores-Ortega, 528 U.S. 470 (2000).

[124] *See* §§ 29.08–.09, *infra*.

[125] Strickland v. Washington, 466 U.S. at 687.

she claims were constitutionally unreasonable. Furthermore, the court evaluating a claim must consider the issue from the lawyer's perspective at the time of the act or omission, rather than "second-guess" counsel's performance with the "distorting effects of hindsight." The court's scrutiny "must be highly deferential": it "must indulge a strong presumption that counsel's conduct falls within the wide range of reasonable professional assistance."

Strategic decisions by a defense lawyer are "virtually unchallengeable" if they were made after thorough investigation of the law and facts relevant to the case. Strategic choices made after "less than complete investigation are reasonable precisely to the extent that reasonable professional judgments support the limitations on investigation." As seen below, a claim of deficiency will often center on whether a lawyer's lack of effort to investigate or to perform other tasks was a matter of strategic choice or, instead, was the result of inexcusable lack of attentiveness.

### [b]  Deficiency: Case Law

### [i]  Failure to Perform Ordinary Tasks

It is exceedingly difficult to prove that a counsel's failure to conduct ordinary tasks in defending her client constitutes Sixth Amendment "deficient" representation. The difficulties confronting a convicted defendant are evident from *Strickland* itself. Over his lawyer's objection, *D* pleaded guilty to three counts of capital murder. *D* told the judge that he had no significant prior criminal record, that he had acted under extreme stress due to economic problems in his family, but that he accepted responsibility for the crimes. The judge stated that he had "a great deal of respect" for persons who admit their responsibility, but that he was not prejudging the sentencing issue.

*D*'s objection to his lawyer's conduct related to counsel's post-plea preparation for, and conduct at, the capital sentencing hearing. *D* alleged various omissions on his lawyer's part, including counsel's failure to request a psychiatric report, to investigate and present character witnesses at the hearing, to seek a presentence investigation report, and to present "meaningful arguments" for leniency to the sentencing judge.

The Court found each of these claims unpersuasive. It was satisfied that counsel, after talking to his client and *D*'s wife and mother, made a strategic decision to argue that *D*'s emotional stress mitigated his blameworthiness for the murders, and to rely on his client's acceptance of responsibility for the crimes. Counsel's decision not to request a psychiatric report was justified because "his conversations with his client gave no indication that [*D*] had psychological problems." And, the Court found, counsel did not request a presentence report because he learned from his investigation that *D* had a somewhat more serious criminal history than *D* had disclosed to the judge. The Court stated that "although counsel understandably felt hopeless about [*D*'s] prospects, . . . nothing in the record indicates . . . that counsel's sense of hopelessness distorted his professional judgment." It concluded that the lawyer's behavior "was well within the range of professionally reasonable judgments."

The Court demonstrated even greater deference to defense counsel's judgment in *Burger v. Kemp*.[126] In *Burger*, *D*'s counsel offered no mitigating evidence whatsoever during two capital sentencing hearings, although he could have presented evidence that his client, a minor, had no adult criminal record, that his I.Q. was only 82, and that he "had an exceptionally unhappy and unstable childhood," all factors that can justify saving the life of a person convicted of murder.

*D*'s lawyer was aware of some, but not all, of his client's background. Prior to the hearing, he had talked to *D*'s mother several times, to an out-of-state lawyer who had served as his client's "Big Brother" and who had offered to come to the hearing to testify, and to a psychiatrist who had conducted a pretrial examination of his client. Counsel had also reviewed various psychologists' reports based on meetings with *D* before the crime was committed.

The Supreme Court held, over the sharp dissent of four Justices, that the lawyer's conduct was not deficient. It conceded that he "could well have made a more thorough investigation than he did." However, the Court stated that counsel's decision not to conduct an "all-out investigation" into his client's background was supported by reasonable professional judgment, in that his interviews and studies of the reports indicated that "an explanation of [*D*'s] history would not have minimized the risk of the death penalty."[127]

---

[126] 483 U.S. 776 (1987).

[127] Of course, ineffective representation claims are very fact-specific. Recently the Supreme Court upheld a trial court finding of deficient representation. In Williams (Terry) v. Taylor, 529 U.S. 362 (2000), the deficient attorney failed to discover or failed to offer mitigating evidence at the defendant 's capital sentencing hearing. For example, counsel failed to prepare for the hearing until a week beforehand, failed to uncover extensive records graphically setting out the defendant's "nightmarish" childhood, and he failed to introduce available evidence of the client's borderline mental retardation, as well as his exemplary behavior in prison, which included the defendant's assistance in cracking a prison drug ring and returning a guard's missing wallet. These failures were not the result of tactical decisions; they demonstrated that counsel did not fulfill his ethical obligation to conduct a thorough investigation of his client's background.

Lower courts occasionally find that a lawyer's lack of vigor amounts to deficient representation, although such cases often include evidence of other forms of deficiency, such as lack of knowledge of pertinent law. For example, in one capital case,[128] *D*'s lawyers, a husband and wife who had never represented a defendant in a capital proceeding, and whose primary legal experience was civil in nature, were found to have provided deficient representation: (1) they prepared no defense (although there was significant evidence to support a claim that *D* was not the killer), interviewed no witnesses, sought no discovery, and did not visit the scene of the crime; (2) because of their poor preparation, the lawyers were surprised at trial by blood evidence introduced by the state (and for which there was a possible exculpatory explanation); (3) lead counsel was outside the courtroom parking his car when a key prosecution witness testified, and yet he conducted the cross-examination of the witness; (4) during the prosecutor's closing argument, lead counsel was absent for half of the argument; (5) neither lawyer ever read the death penalty statute applicable to the case and, therefore, were surprised to learn that there was a separate sentencing hearing; and (6) they prepared no arguments in behalf of their client on the death penalty, and made only a few-seconds-long closing argument consisting of a short bible verse.

The Eleventh Circuit concluded from the preceding record that the "haphazard nature of the . . . defense, the failure to develop strategy of any consequence, and absenting themselves from crucial portions of the trial constitute[d] no representation at all." Effectively, in the language of *Strickland*, the "errors [were] so serious that counsel was not functioning as the 'counsel' guaranteed . . . by the Sixth Amendment."

### [ii]  Sleeping on the Job

Lawyers sometimes fall asleep in the courtroom. Most of the litigation in this regard focuses on the *second* prong of *Strickland* (the prejudicial effect of the lawyer's conduct), but courts appear to agree that constitutional deficiency is shown if a defendant proves that her lawyer frequently slept during trial or during significant pretrial hearings. For example, in one Second Circuit case,[129] the court found a violation based on the undisputed evidence that the defense counsel "was unconscious for numerous extended periods of time during which the defendant's interests were at stake."[130] And in a Texas criminal case, a defense lawyer fell asleep five to ten times during the trial, the longest time of which was for approximately ten

---

[128] House v. Balkcom, 725 F.2d 608 (11th Cir. 1984).

[129] Tippins v. Walker, 77 F.3d 682 (2d Cir. 1996).

[130] *Id.* at 685.

minutes, and during which time the prosecutor was questioning witnesses or presenting evidence.[131]

### [iii]  Ignorance of Relevant Law

Deficient representation linked to a counsel's ignorance of applicable law is a somewhat less daunting claim to prove than that a lawyer acted with undue vigor in her defense. For example, in *Kimmelman v. Morrison*,[132] defense counsel failed to file a timely motion to suppress evidence obtained in violation of the Fourth Amendment. The lawyer did not make the motion because he was unaware of the search that resulted in the seizure of highly incriminating evidence; his lack of knowledge of the search was the result of his failure to request discovery, which in turn was based on his mistaken belief that the prosecutor was required on his own initiative to turn over to the defense all of the incriminating evidence in his possession.

The Court reversed the conviction, holding that, although counsel's representation of his client at trial was "creditable," his failure to conduct the pretrial discovery in this case, which would have put him on notice of the incriminating evidence that might have been suppressed, was contrary to prevailing professional norms. The deficiency prong of *Strickland* was satisfied because counsel's actions were not the result of a well (or even questionably) crafted trial strategy, but were based on his legally mistaken understanding of the law of discovery.

Similarly, in *Lockhart v. Fretwell*,[133] D was sentenced to death for a robbery-murder. One of the aggravating factors that the jury found at the sentencing phase was that the murder was committed for pecuniary gain. The evidence in this regard duplicated facts already proved at the guilt phase (that D had committed a robbery) and, therefore, was inadmissible at the capital sentence phase according to case law at the time of the trial. D's attorney failed to object to introduction of this evidence, apparently because he was unaware of the relevant law. This failure by the attorney constituted deficient representation, the first prong of *Strickland*.

---

[131] Burdine v. Johnson, 66 F. Supp.2d 854 (S.D. Texas 1999), *affirmed*, 262 F.3d 336 (5th Cir. 2001); *see also* Ross v. Kemp, 393 S.E.2d 244 (Ga. 1990), and Harrison v. Zant, No. 88-V-1460 (reported in *Snoozing, Unprepared Lawyer Cited*, 77 A.B.A. J. (Feb. 1991) at 14) (death sentences were overturned due to the inadequacy of an 83-year-old counsel's representation, upon proof that he slept a "good deal" during the proceedings).

[132] 477 U.S. 365 (1986).

[133] 506 U.S. 364 (1993).

### [3]   The Second Prong: Prejudice

### [a]   The Standard

In most circumstances, a defendant must not only prove that her counsel provided deficient representation, but must also show that such deficiencies prejudiced her, in that, as *Strickland* put it, the "errors were so serious as to deprive the defendant of a fair trial, a trial whose result is reliable."[134]

To prove prejudice, "[t]he defendant must show that there is a reasonable probability that, but for counsel's unprofessional errors, the result of the proceeding would have been different." Under this test, "reasonable probability is a probability sufficient to undermine confidence in the outcome." *Strickland* rejected any mathematical formula to measure "reasonable probability," but the Court stated that the defendant must prove more than that the error "had some conceivable effect on the outcome of the proceeding"; on the other hand, she does not need to show that it is more likely than not that counsel's deficient conduct affected the outcome.

Generally speaking, in measuring prejudice a reviewing court should, according to *Strickland* "proceed on the assumption that the decisionmaker is reasonably, conscientiously, and impartially applying the standards that govern the decision." That is, it is irrelevant to the defendant's prejudice claim that the particular judge might have had an idiosyncratic approach to the law or to sentencing decisions; what matters is whether counsel's errors would have effected the outcome of a reasonable decisionmaker.

The Court indicated in *Strickland* that "[i]n certain Sixth Amendment contexts, prejudice is presumed." These cases include: (1) actual[135] or constructive[136] denial of the assistance of counsel; (2) certain forms of state interference with counsel's assistance;[137] and (3) representation by a lawyer burdened by an actual conflict of interest.[138]

In the first two circumstances, *Strickland* said, prejudice "is so likely that case-by-case inquiry into prejudice is not worth the cost. . . . Moreover,

---

[134] As one commentator has put it: "So we have come full circle back to the jurisprudence of *Betts* [*v. Brady, see* § 29.02[B][2][b], *supra*], albeit in a slightly different form. Even though all indigents facing serious charges have the right to a licensed attorney standing beside them in court, the right to an effective attorney is encompassed in the right not to be deprived of a fair trial. The substance of the sixth amendment right to the assistance of counsel is thus submerged in the due process guarantee of a fair trial, rendering the sixth amendment substantively extraneous." George C. Thomas, III, *Laying Bare the Failure of Criminal Procedure Doctrine,* 4 Crim. L. Forum 535, 553 (1993).

[135] *E.g.,* Gideon v. Wainwright, 372 U.S. 335 (1963). *See* § 29.02[B][3], *supra*.

[136] *E.g.,* Powell v. Alabama, 287 U.S. 45 (1932). *See* § 29.02[B][2][a], *supra*.

[137] *See* § 29.06, *supra*.

[138] *See* § 29.08, *infra*.

such circumstances involve impairments of the Sixth Amendment right that are easy to identify and, for that reason and because the prosecution is directly responsible, easy for the government to prevent." In the third case, "it is difficult to measure the precise effect on the defense of representation corrupted by conflicting interests." As will be seen below, sometimes lower courts have sought to use the reasoning in the presumed-prejudice cases to expand on the list of circumstances that justify such a presumption.

### [b]   Prejudice: Special Problems

### [i]   The Sleeping Lawyer

How does a court determine whether a lawyer's lack of attention at trial prejudiced her client's interests in the manner described in *Strickland*? In one case [139] in which a lawyer was asleep (or "unconscious," as the federal court put it) for extended periods of time during the trial, a state court refused to find prejudice because the defendant did not prove and, therefore, the court could not tell, "how long he slept, or what portion of the testimony he missed, if any"; nor did the defendant show how the lawyer's sleeping habits caused trial errors by defense counsel and, therefore, resulted in an unreliable, verdict.

The state court's analysis, however, was rejected by the Second Circuit, which has held that when a lawyer is asleep for "numerous" and "extended" periods of time during which the defendant's interests are at stake, "[t]hese circumstances suggest 'a breakdown in the adversarial process that our system counts on to produce just results.' " [140] The court stated that "[o]rdinarily, episodes of inattention or slumber are perfectly amenable to analysis under the *Strickland* prejudice test." But, at some point a sleeping lawyer is equivalent to no counsel at all; in such circumstances, "the ordinary analytical tools for identifying prejudice are [then] unavailable." Therefore, it held that a defendant suffers prejudice, "by presumption or otherwise, if his counsel was repeatedly unconscious at trial for periods of time in which the defendant's interests were at stake."

In another case in which the defense lawyer fell asleep as many as ten times, once for ten minutes, [141] the Fifth Circuit originally refused to presume prejudice, in part because "it is impossible to determine whether . . . counsel slept during the presentation of crucial inculpatory evidence, or during the introduction of unobjectionable, uncontested evidence," only later to conclude that a presumption of prejudice applies when there is

---

[139] Tippins v. Walker, 77 F.3d 682 (2d Cir. 1996).

[140] *Id.* at 685 (quoting *Strickland*, 466 U.S. at 696).

[141] *See* the text to Note 131, *supra*.

credible evidence that a defense lawyer has repeatedly slept during the trial.[142]

### [ii]  The Factually Guilty Defendant

*Strickland* stated that a defendant is not prejudiced unless her counsel's deficiencies rendered the trial unreliable. Does this mean that a factually guilty defendant cannot be prejudiced by ineffective representation? Put another way, suppose that a convicted defendant's claim comes down to this: "If my lawyer had provided competent representation, she would have been able to get me off by getting the evidence of my guilt excluded at trial, but she failed in this regard." Has the defendant been "prejudiced"? The Court has not been of one mind in this regard.

First, consider *Kimmelman v. Morrison*,[143] in which *D*'s lawyer failed to raise a Fourth Amendment claim that arguably would have resulted in the exclusion of reliable, but unconstitutionally seized, evidence of *D*'s guilt. As explained above,[144] counsel's error constituted deficient representation (the first prong of *Strickland*).

The Court in *Kimmelman* did not determine whether counsel's deficient conduct prejudiced his client. Instead, it remanded the case to a lower court to conduct a hearing on the matter. However, it stated that to win his Sixth Amendment claim, *D* would have to prove that it was reasonably probable that he would have won his Fourth Amendment claim if it had been properly made and, further, that in the absence of the incriminating evidence, "there is a reasonable probability that the [the factfinder] . . . would have had a reasonable doubt as to [*D*'s] guilt." In other words, a person who may have *factually* committed an offense *can* prove prejudice, if she can demonstrate that there is a reasonable probability that, but for counsel's errors, her guilt would not have been proven on the basis of *legally* admissible evidence.

Justice Powell, joined by Chief Justice Burger and Justice Rehnquist, who concurred in the judgment, disagreed with the preceding analysis. Justice Powell argued that the alleged prejudice suffered by *D* was "the absence of a windfall." The fact that *D*'s lawyer failed to make a motion that arguably would have resulted in the exclusion of reliable incriminating evidence did not affect "the fundamental fairness of the trial. . . . [O]ur reasoning in *Strickland* strongly suggests that such harm does not amount to prejudicial ineffective assistance of counsel under the Sixth Amendment."

---

[142] Burdine v. Johnson, 231 F.3d 950, 958 (5th Cir. 2000), *reversed en banc*, 262 F.3d 336 (5th Cir. 2001).

[143] 477 U.S. 365 (1986).

[144] *See* the text following Note 132, *supra*.

In contrast to *Kimmelman*, consider *Lockhart v. Fretwell*,[145] in which *D* was sentenced to death because his attorney, apparently out of ignorance, failed to object to the introduction of evidence that, under then-applicable case law, was inadmissible at *D*'s sentencing hearing. This error satisfied the first prong of *Strickland*. The Supreme Court held, however, that this deficiency did not prejudice *D* because the lower court case law that rendered the evidence inadmissible was effectively overturned by Supreme Court case law decided *after* *D*'s sentencing hearing, but *before* his Sixth Amendment ineffective-assistance claim was raised.

According to the Court, prejudice does not result if the lawyer's error "does not deprive the defendant of any substantive or procedural right to which the law entitles him"; although case law supported *D* at the time of the sentencing proceeding, that law proved to be erroneous; therefore, to grant *D*'s *Strickland* claim would be to grant him a "windfall" (the same word used by the *concurring* Justices in *Kimmelman*).

Notice the effect of the holding in *Lockhart*: *D* would have received a more favorable verdict—he would not have been sentenced to death—had his lawyer provided reasonable representation at the time of the sentencing proceeding, because the law at that time favored *D*'s interests. Notwithstanding this, *D* has suffered no legally cognizable "prejudice."

*Lockhart* is distinguishable from *Kimmelman* in a key regard: the *law* under which the defendant in *Kimmelman* was convicted, *both at the time of trial and at the time that the Sixth Amendment claim was litigated*, entitled him to a ruling that (based on reasonable probabilities) might have resulted in a more favorable verdict. In *Lockhart*, the law favored the defendant only at the time of counsel's error; and, the subsequent change in the law was not the result of legislative rethinking, but rather of Supreme Court jurisprudence that essentially demonstrated that the prior case law on which *D*'s counsel could have relied was wrong. It is this circumstance that caused the majority in *Lockhart* to treat *D*'s claim as one of being denied a "windfall."[146]

---

[145] 506 U.S. 364 (1993). *See* § 29.07[B][2][b][iii], *supra*.

[146] *See also* Williams (Terry) v. Taylor, 529 U.S. 362, 391 (2000) (rejecting the view that *Lockhart* "modified or in some way supplanted the rule set down in *Strickland*"; and explaining that *Lockhart* was based on the unusual fact that the defendant attempted to claim prejudice on the basis of a consideration—incorrect case law, corrected prior to his Sixth Amendment appeal—that ought not to have informed the prejudice inquiry).

## § 29.08  Effective Assistance of Counsel: Conflicts of Interest[147]

### [A]  Nature of the Issue

A defendant is entitled to the undivided loyalty of her attorney. However, when one attorney or law firm[148] represents multiple clients, especially if they are co-defendants, there is the possibility that the interests of the clients will clash, and that the attorney (or firm) will be unable to represent all of the clients effectively. For this reason, joint representation is generally considered unethical if representation of one client will materially limit a counsel's ability to represent another client.[149]

A breach of ethical standards, however, does not constitute a *per se* violation of the Sixth Amendment. The subsections that follow relate to the constitutional right to conflict-free legal representation.

### [B]  Pretrial Procedures to Avoid Conflicts

The Supreme Court ruled in *Holloway v. Arkansas*[150] that when an attorney representing co-defendants makes a timely pretrial motion for appointment of separate counsel, based on her assertion of a potential conflict of interest, a trial judge is required either to grant the motion or "to take adequate steps to ascertain whether the risk [is] too remote to warrant separate counsel." Failure of the judge to grant the motion or, at least, to conduct a hearing on the matter requires automatic reversal of any subsequent conviction.

According to *Holloway*, joint representation is constitutionally suspect. Because a defense lawyer is in a better position than a court to know prior to trial whether a conflict exists or may develop—she is more familiar with the facts of the case, and may become aware of a conflict as the result of confidential communications with a client—the Supreme Court generally favors the granting of motions for separate counsel. However, to protect the authority of the trial court and to avoid the possibility of abuse by

---

[147] *See generally* John Stewart Geer, *Representation of Multiple Criminal Defendants: Conflicts of Interest and the Professional Responsibilities of the Defense Attorney*, 62 Minn. L. Rev. 119 (1978); Green, Note 83, *supra*; Nancy J. Moore, *Conflicts of Interest in the Simultaneous Representation of Multiple Clients: A Proposed Solution to the Current Confusion and Controversy*, 61 Texas L. Rev. 211 (1982); Peter W. Tague, *Multiple Representation and Conflicts of Interest in Criminal Cases*, 67 Geo. L.J. 1075 (1979).

[148] Although the Supreme Court has acknowledged that "[t]here is certainly much substance to [the] argument that the appointment of two partners to represent coindictees . . . creates a possible conflict of interest," it has only assumed, but not decided, that law partners should be treated as if they were one attorney for purposes of conflict-of-interest analysis. Burger v. Kemp, 483 U.S. 776, 783 (1987).

[149] Model Rules, Note 116, *supra*, Rule 1.7(a)–(b).

[150] 435 U.S. 475 (1978).

unscrupulous attorneys, the Court stated in *Holloway* that it does not "preclude a trial court from exploring the adequacy of the basis of defense counsel's representations," as long as it can do so without requiring counsel to disclose confidential communications.

The Sixth Amendment does not require a trial court *on its own motion* to inquire into joint-representation arrangements. Unless the trial court knows or reasonably should know that a conflict exists, it "may assume [absent a motion] either that multiple representation entails no conflict or that the lawyer and his clients knowingly accept such risk of conflict as may exist."[151]

### [C]    Post-Trial Proof of a Conflict

A conviction will not be overturned on the basis of an after-trial allegation of a conflict of interest (as distinguished from a claim that the trial court refused to conduct an adequate pretrial hearing into the conflict issue, as discussed immediately above) unless the defendant demonstrates that: (1) an actual conflict of interest existed; and (2) the conflict adversely affected her lawyer's performance.[152]

As the second element stated immediately above suggests, it is not necessary for the defendant to meet the prejudice standard applied in ordinary ineffective-assistance-of-counsel cases.[153] That is, a conviction must be overturned if the conflict "adversely affected" the lawyer's performance, even if it cannot be shown that there is a reasonable probability that the trial was unreliable.

### [D]    Waiver of the Right to Conflict-Free Representation

Although representation of co-defendants by a single attorney or law firm often leads to a conflict of interest, co-defendants may nonetheless wish to be represented by the same attorney or law firm. For example, by pooling their resources, co-defendants may be able to afford an attorney whose services would otherwise be unavailable to them; or the defendants may commit themselves in advance to a united sink-or-swim strategy that reduces or eliminates the risk of conflict.

---

[151] Cuyler v. Sullivan, 446 U.S. 335, 347 (1980). This constitutional rule is less demanding than the Federal Rules of Criminal Procedure, which provide that when persons jointly charged with an offense are represented by the same attorney or by different attorneys from the same law firm, "the court shall promptly inquire with respect to such joint representation and shall personally advise each defendant of the right to the effective assistance of counsel, including separate representation." Fed. R. Crim. P. 44(c). Unless there is good cause to believe that no conflict is likely to arise, the trial court must "take such measures as may be appropriate to protect each defendant's right to counsel." *Id.*

[152] Cuyler v. Sullivan, 446 U.S. 335 (1980).

[153] *See* § 29.07[B][3], *supra.*

Nonetheless, the Supreme Court ruled in *Wheat v. United States*[154] that a trial court has the authority to disqualify defense counsel over her client's objection if it concludes that there is a serious possibility that a conflict of interest exists. Put somewhat differently, a defendant does not have unlimited authority to waive her right to conflict-free representation in order to be represented by the attorney of her choice.

In *Wheat*, *D* was indicted for participation in an alleged drug conspiracy. *C*, an attorney, represented *X* and *Y*, co-conspirators of *D*. Prior to *D*'s trial, *C* secured *X*'s acquittal on some of the conspiracy charges and helped him to negotiate a guilty plea on lesser charges. *C* also assisted *Y* to negotiate a guilty plea. A few days prior to his own trial, *D* made a timely request to substitute or add *C* as his own attorney.

The prosecutor objected to the substitution. He raised two possible conflicts of interest. First, the trial court had not yet accepted *X*'s guilty plea; if the plea were rejected, and if *X* ultimately had to go to trial, the prosecutor warned that he might need to call *D* as a witness at *X*'s trial. In such circumstances, *C* would be faced with a conflict, because he could not effectively cross-examine *D* without disclosing confidences. Second, the prosecutor indicated that he was likely to call *Y* as a witness at *D*'s trial, which would again result in a conflict. Based on these representations, the trial court refused to grant *D*'s request to substitute or add *C* as his counsel. In doing so, the trial judge conceded that "[w]ere I in [*D*'s] position, I'm sure I would want [*C*] representing me, too. He did a fantastic job in . . . [*X*'s] trial."

The Supreme Court, 5-4, upheld the trial court's decision. It stated that although the right to "be represented by one's preferred attorney is comprehended by the Sixth Amendment, the essential aim of the Amendment is to guarantee an effective advocate for each criminal defendant . . . ." Furthermore, it said, courts "have an independent interest in ensuring that criminal trials are conducted within the ethical standards of the profession and that legal proceedings appear fair to all who observe them." Yet, the latter argument was minimized by the Court in *Faretta v. California*,[155] when it held that defendants have a constitutional right of self-representation, even though (as the dissenters there argued) assertion of this right will often result in a "lawyer" having a fool for a client. In *Faretta*, the defendant's right of autonomy trumped society's interest in ensuring a fair and reliable trial; in *Wheat*, the latter interest won out.

The majority stated that when a court finds an actual conflict of interest, "there can be no doubt that it may decline a proffer of waiver, and insist

---

[154] 486 U.S. 153 (1988).

[155] 422 U.S. 806 (1975). *See* § 29.04, *supra*.

that defendants be separately represented." Furthermore, it held that, as in the present case, trial courts "must be allowed substantial latitude" to refuse waivers of conflict of interest "where a [serious] potential for conflict exists which may or may not burgeon into an actual conflict as the trial progresses."

The Court conceded that prosecutors might manufacture conflicts in order to prevent a defendant from being represented by a particularly able attorney. However, it stated that "trial courts are undoubtedly aware of this possibility, and must take it into consideration with all of the other factors which inform this sort of a decision."

### § 29.09   Effective Assistance: The Role of Ethical Canons[156]

Violation of an ethical canon by a defense lawyer does not constitute *per se* violation of the Sixth Amendment. The lesson of *Strickland v. Washington*[157] is that "[p]revailing norms of practice as reflected in American Bar Association standards and the like . . . are guides to determining what is reasonable [representation], but they are only guides."

But, what if a defendant argues that her lawyer provided ineffective assistance, and the basis of her claim is that counsel *obeyed* ethical canons? Put another way, is a lawyer immunized from a Sixth Amendment "verdict" of inadequate representation if she acts in conformity with recognized ethical rules? The issue arose in *Nix v. Whiteside*.[158]

In *Whiteside*, D was prosecuted for stabbing V to death. In conversations with C (his lawyer), D claimed that he killed V in self-defense because he believed that V was pulling a gun out from under a bed. No weapon was found on or around V, and witnesses observed no gun. Furthermore, D admitted to C that he had not actually seen the weapon. C explained that this was not fatal to D's self-defense claim, as long as he reasonably believed that the victim was armed. A week before trial, however, D told C for the first time that he saw something metallic at the time of the incident. He explained: "There was a gun. If I don't say I saw a gun, I'm dead."

C explained to D that such testimony would constitute perjury. He warned his client that if he persisted in his wish to testify in this manner, it was C's duty to advise the court of D's plan, that he "would probably be allowed

---

[156] *See generally* Brent R. Appel, The Limited Impact of Nix v. Whiteside on Attorney-Client Relations, 136 U. Pa. L. Rev. 1913 (1988); Monroe H. Freedman, *Client Confidences and Client Perjury: Some Unanswered Questions*, 136 U. Pa. L. Rev. 1939 (1988); A. Kenneth Pye, *The Role of Counsel in the Suppression of Truth*, 1978 Duke L.J. 921.

[157] 466 U.S. 668, 688 (1984). *See generally* § 29.07, *supra*.

[158] 475 U.S. 157 (1986).

to attempt to impeach that particular testimony," and that he would seek to withdraw from the case. *C*'s warnings apparently worked: although *D* testified at trial, he did not make the false claim.

*Whiteside* involves a comparatively easy perjury scenario. First, *C* had good reason to believe, based on *D*'s prior admissions, that *D*'s testimony would be perjurious. The case does not raise the question of whether *C*'s forceful actions would have been constitutionally justified if he had merely suspected perjury. Second, *C* knew of the planned perjury before trial; the case does not raise the issue of "what a lawyer must, should, or may do after his client has given [surprise] testimony that the lawyer does not believe."[159] Third, *D* testified truthfully. The case does not dispose of the problem of whether a lawyer acts properly if she convinces her client not to testify at all.

The Court unanimously agreed that *D* failed to make out a case of ineffective representation by *C*. Chief Justice Warren Burger, for five Justices, held that neither prong of the *Strickland* ineffective-representation test was proved in the case. The four concurring Justices relied solely on the prejudice prong of *Strickland*.

Regarding the first ("deficiency of representation") prong, the Chief Justice ruled that the lawyer's conduct "fell within the wide range of professional responses to threatened client perjury acceptable under the Sixth Amendment." He stated that the ethical and constitutional duty of a lawyer to be loyal to her client "is limited to legitimate, lawful conduct compatible with the very nature of a trial as a search for truth." The majority emphasized that *C*'s conduct in the case was ethically appropriate. Although a breach of an ethical canon does not by itself make out a violation of the Sixth Amendment, Chief Justice Burger stated that where "there has been no breach of any recognized professional duty, it follows that there can be no deprivation of the right to assistance of counsel under the *Strickland* standard."

Second, the Court unanimously held that *as a matter of law*, *C*'s conduct here—preventing a client from committing perjury—could not establish the prejudice required for relief under *Strickland*. As the benchmark of the inquiry under *Strickland* is the fairness of the adversary proceeding, *D* "had no valid claim that confidence in the result of his trial has been diminished by his desisting from the contemplated perjury."

---

[159] *Id.* at 191 (Stevens J., concurring).

CHAPTER **30**

# PRETRIAL RELEASE OF THE DEFENDANT

## § 30.01 Pretrial Release: Procedural Context

After a suspect is arrested and booked at the police station, he is ordinarily taken to jail. Except for minor offenses, his first opportunity to be released pending trial arises at his first appearance before a judicial officer (or "magistrate").[1] This appearance should occur "without unnecessary delay,"[2] usually within 24 hours after arrest, except on weekends.

At the hearing, the magistrate determines whether to release the arrestee "on recognizance" (on the promise that he will appear as required at criminal proceedings) or to attach conditions to his release. A common condition is that the accused deposit cash or property with the court, or post a bond provided by a commercial surety (a "bondsman") in an amount determined by the magistrate. This bond is subject to forfeiture if he fails to appear as required. The money deposited or the bond posted is called "bail."

In some states, and in the federal courts, the magistrate also has the authority to order the continued confinement of the accused pending trial ("preventive detention"), if the magistrate determines that no conditions will reasonably assure the accused's appearance as required or that his release will jeopardize the safety of another person (*e.g.*, a witness to the crime) or the community as a whole.

In the federal courts, a defendant is entitled to representation by counsel, appointed by the court if he is indigent, at the bail hearing.[3] However, it is commonplace in the state court systems to fail to provide counsel to indigents for bail proceedings.[4]

---

[1] In some jurisdictions, a person arrested for a minor offense is released if he posts bail at the police station or jail in an amount set on a fixed bail schedule.

[2] Fed. R. Crim. P. 5(a). See § 1.03[C][3], *supra*.

[3] Fed. R. Crim. P. 44(a) (right to representation at the initial appearance, at which bail is set).

[4] Douglas L. Colbert, *Thirty-five Years After Gideon: The Illusory Right to Counsel at Bail Proceedings*, 1998 U. Ill. L. Rev. 1, 9–10 (1998). This is not a new phenomenon. P. Wice, Freedom for Sale 48 (1974) (lawyers were present in only 25% of the state cases surveyed at that time).

## § 30.02   Pretrial Release: Interests at Stake

### [A]   The Community's Interest

Although the Supreme Court has stated that an accused person has a "traditional right to freedom before conviction,"[5] society has a long recognized interest in protecting the integrity of the judicial process. Therefore, it is entitled to adequate assurance that if the defendant is released he will attend trial and sentencing if convicted,[6] and that he will not intimidate witnesses and others involved in his prosecution.[7]

The community also has an interest in making sure that persons charged with crimes who are released pending trial do not commit other offenses while they are free.[8] Although the issue was once in doubt,[9] the Court now recognizes pretrial crime prevention as a constitutionally justifiable interest in regulating pretrial release.[10]

### [B]   The Arrestee's Interest

An arrestee's interest in liberty—and, therefore, in release pending trial—is a weighty one. The Supreme Court has characterized the interest as strong and fundamental.[11] One court has suggested that a detainee's fundamental interest in liberty is "second only to life itself in terms of constitutional importance."[12] Given the often poor conditions of the jails in which detainees are held,[13] persons accused of crime have a significant interest in their freedom.

---

[5] Stack v. Boyle, 342 U.S. 1, 4 (1951).

[6] Bell v. Wolfish, 441 U.S. 520, 534 (1979); see U.S. Dept. of Justice, Bureau of Justice Statistics, Felony Defendants in Large Urban Counties, 1992 (1995) (among the nation's 75 largest counties, one-fourth of defendants released prior to case disposition failed to appear in court as scheduled, and a third of these persons—or 8% of all released defendants—were still fugitives at the end of the one-year study period).

[7] United States v. Salerno, 481 U.S. 739, 753 (1987).

[8] See U.S. Dept. of Justice, Bureau of Justice Statistics, Pretrial Release of Felony Defendants, 1988 (1991) (in the 75 largest counties in the nation, 18% of the released defendants were known to have been re-arrested for a felony while free); U.S. Dept. of Justice, Bureau of Justice Statistics, Pretrial Release of Felony Defendants, 1992 (1994) (approximately one-third of all defendants released prior to trial were rearrested for a new offense, failed to appear as scheduled for at least one judicial proceeding, or violated some condition of release requiring revocation of pretrial release).

[9] See Bell v. Wolfish, 441 U.S. at 534 n.15 (expressly leaving open the issue of whether government objectives other than ensuring the defendant's presence at trial could justify pretrial detention).

[10] United States v. Salerno, 481 U.S. 739 (1987). See § 30.05, *infra*.

[11] *Id.* at 750.

[12] Van Atta v. Scott, 613 P.2d 210, 214 (Cal. 1980).

[13] For description of particularly poor jail conditions, *see id.* at 214–15; Miller v. Carson, 401 F.Supp. 835 (S.D. Fla. 1975).

An arrestee's interest in pretrial release is linked to the presumption of innocence implied by the Constitution's due process clause.[14] Although the presumption does not formally come into play until trial, the Supreme Court has observed that "[u]nless this right to bail before trial is preserved, the presumption of innocence, secured only after centuries of struggle, would lose its meaning."[15]

Moreover, confinement can hamper the defendant's or his counsel's preparation of the trial defense.[16] For example, it may be necessary for a defendant to assist his lawyer to identify and convince alibi witnesses to testify, or to search the accused's home for relevant evidence. Somewhat dated studies suggest that "some defendants unable to make bail are, for that reason alone, more likely to be convicted and, if convicted, more likely to be sentenced to jail."[17]

Finally, confinement can be emotionally and financially disruptive to the accused and his family. A defendant may lose his job if he is incarcerated pending trial; in turn, he may be unable to support his family or earn the money necessary to pay for the attorney he wishes to retain.

## § 30.03    Pretrial Release: Eighth Amendment[18]

Traditionally, persons charged with non-capital offenses have had an absolute statutory or state constitutional right to be admitted to bail.[19] As one commentator put it, "a person arrested for a [non-capital] criminal offense [has] the right to purchase his release pending trial."[20]

How expensive can the key to the jail be? The Eighth Amendment to the United States Constitution provides in part that "[e]xcessive bail shall not be required." The Supreme Court has noted in dictum that this provision "has been assumed to have application to the States through the Fourteenth

---

[14] In re Winship, 397 U.S. 358 (1970); see Joshua Dressler, Understanding Criminal Law § 7.03 (3d ed. 2001).

[15] Stack v. Boyle, 342 U.S. 1, 4 (1951).

[16] Id.

[17] Hans Zeisel, *Bail Revisited*, 1979 Am. B. Found. Res. J. 769, 779.

[18] *See generally* Caleb Foote, *The Coming Constitutional Crisis in Bail: I*, 113 U. Pa. L. Rev. 959 (1965); Hermine Herta Meyer, *Constitutionality of Pretrial Detention*, 60 Geo. L.J. 1139 (1972); Donald B. Verrilli, Jr., Note, *The Eighth Amendment and the Right to Bail: Historical Perspectives*, 82 Colum. L. Rev. 328 (1982).

[19] In most states, bail may be denied in capital offenses "where the proof is evident, or the presumption great" that the defendant is guilty of the crime. The high risk that such a person will flee if released is thought to justify this exception.

[20] Wayne H. Thomas, Jr., Bail Reform in America 11 (1976).

Amendment."[21] The matter may be moot, however, because all states, by constitution or statute, prohibit excessive bail.

In *Stack v. Boyle*,[22] the Supreme Court stated that although pretrial release is a traditional right, it is permissible for a judge to condition freedom on "adequate assurance that [the accused] will stand trial and submit to sentence if found guilty." In that context, it held that "[b]ail set at a figure higher than an amount reasonably calculated to fulfill this purpose is 'excessive' under the Eighth Amendment."

The fixing of bail must be based upon standards relevant to the purpose of assuring the presence of the defendant. In *Stack*, the Justices listed the "traditional standards" as: the nature and circumstances of the offense charged; the weight of the evidence against the accused; the accused's character; and the financial ability of the defendant to meet the bail requirements. Even during the Supreme Court's most constitutionally expansive period, however, it never ruled that the Constitution entitles an indigent to be released *without* bail if he cannot afford to meet any financial conditions.

## § 30.04 Pretrial Release: Statutory Law

### [A] Pre-Reform[23]

Until statutory reform occurred in the 1960s, magistrates typically conditioned pretrial release of defendants on the deposit of cash with the court. Usually, a defendant lacking sufficient resources to make the payment contacted a bail bondsman who, if he was satisfied that the accused was a good risk, furnished security to the court for the defendant's appearance. In exchange for this service, the bondsman usually received a nonrefundable fee in the amount of ten percent of the bond.

For example, if a magistrate set bail at $10,000, the defendant would pay the bondsman $1,000, who would then guarantee the full sum to the court. If the defendant failed to appear as required at criminal proceedings, the bond was subject to remission; unless the bondsman had obtained collateral from the arrestee, which he usually did, he lost the money. If the defendant appeared at all proceedings, the bondsman was released from his obligations. The accused, however, would not receive back his ten percent share, as this was the bondsman's fee for taking the risk. If the defendant lacked sufficient resources to pay the bondsman's fee or if the bondsman refused for any other reason to serve as his surety (*e.g.*, the

---

[21] Schilb v. Kuebel, 404 U.S. 357, 365 (1971).

[22] 342 U.S. 1 (1951).

[23] *See generally* Thomas, Note 20, *supra*.

defendant had insufficient collateral), the defendant remained in jail through the trial.

### [B]   Federal Bail Reform Act of 1966

Growing disenchantment with the pretrial release system resulted in state and federal reform during the 1960s. The first significant reform occurred in Illinois,[24] where the legislature effectively put many bondsmen out of business by permitting release of defendants who deposited ten percent of the required bond directly with the court. A defendant remained liable for the remainder of the bond if he fled. Unlike the private bondsman, however, the court returned the deposited money (less a nominal administrative fee) to the defendant upon disposition of the case, if he did not flee.

At the federal level, Congress enacted the Federal Bail Reform Act of 1966.[25] The Act announced a presumption in favor of the release of arrestees on their own recognizance. Further, it provided that conditions for release could be imposed only if the magistrate determined that they were necessary to reasonably assure the appearance of the defendant at criminal proceedings. Moreover, when conditions were deemed necessary, the law required the magistrate to attach the least restrictive condition or combination of conditions possible.

Under the 1966 statute, non-financial conditions were preferred to bail. For example, the statutory preference was that the magistrate place the defendant in the custody of a designated individual, such as an employer or clergyman who agreed to supervise him, rather than that the magistrate set bail. If the magistrate determined that financial conditions were necessary, the preferred condition was that he permit the defendant to deposit up to ten percent of the bond directly with the court, rather than that he be compelled to execute a full bond, presumably with a commercial bondsman.

### [C]   Federal Bail Reform Act of 1984

Congress amended the federal bail law in 1984.[26] It remains in effect today. The new law differs in key respects from the Bail Reform Act of 1966. First, for the first time in history, federal law authorizes the magistrate in setting conditions for release of the defendant to consider the extent to which the release "will endanger the safety of any other person or the

---

[24] Ill. Rev. Stat. ch. 38, § 110.7 (1963).

[25] 18 U.S.C. §§ 3146–3152, *repealed in part* by the Bail Reform Act of 1984, discussed in the next subsection.

[26] 18 U.S.C. §§ 3141–3150 (2000).

community."[27] Second, under specified circumstances discussed below, a magistrate may now order the pretrial detention of a defendant.

Except where preventive detention is authorized, the 1984 statute, like the old one, follows a "no or least restrictive condition" approach. The judicial officer is required to release the defendant on his own recognizance "or upon execution of an unsecured appearance bond in an amount specified by the court,"[28] unless the magistrate concludes that more restrictive conditions are necessary to reasonably assure that the defendant will not flee and/or endanger others while free.

For the first time, federal law expressly provides that "[t]he judicial officer may not impose a financial condition that results in the pretrial detention of the person."[29] Although this provision does not require a magistrate to reduce bail merely because it is difficult for the defendant to pay, Congress' apparent intention is to prohibit the use of bail as a form of *sub rosa* preventive detention. If a judge believes that the accused should be detained pending trial, he is required to follow the detention provisions set out in the Act.

The United States Department of Justice periodically provides figures on pretrial release and detentions under the federal law. In 1996, 66% of federal felony defendants were released pending trial, while 34% were denied release on preventive detention grounds. Of those released, 22% were set free on their own recognizance, 38% were released on an unsecured bond, 26% were entitled to release on financial conditions (bail), and 14% were released subject to other restrictive conditions. Among those eligible for release on bail, however, 61% were not able immediately to post the required bail, although an unspecified number of these persons presumably did later.[30]

---

[27] 18 U.S.C. § 3142(b) (2000).

[28] *Id.* An "unsecured appearance bond" is one in which the defendant promises that if he does not appear as required, he will pay in full the bond set by the court. However, he is not compelled to secure the bond with any collateral.

[29] 18 U.S.C. § 3142(c)(2) (2000).

[30] U.S. Dept. of Justice, Bureau of Justice Statistics, Federal Pretrial Release and Detention, 1996 (Feb. 1999, NCJ 168635), at 1–3.

## § 30.05    Preventive Detention

### [A]    Federal Bail Reform Act of 1984[31]

Preventive detention of persons charged with non-capital offenses was rarely authorized by statute until the 1980s. However, the Federal Bail Reform Act of 1984 permits the detention of arrestees in specified circumstances if, after a hearing, the magistrate determines that "no condition or combination of conditions will reasonably assure the appearance of the person as required and the safety of any other person and the community . . . ."[32]

According to a 1987 study of the effects of the statute on pretrial release, the percentage of persons able to post bond increased in the first year after the new law was implemented from the year immediately preceding it (63 percent compared to 50 percent). On the other hand, the percentage of persons detained pending trial rose from two percent under the old statute to 19 percent the years after the new law took effect. In 1996, the detention rate had hit 34 percent.[33] According to the Justice Department, "pretrial detention has largely been substituted for bail as a means of detaining defendants."[34]

Under the Act, the magistrate must hold a detention hearing on the motion of the prosecutor if the defendant is charged with a crime of violence, any offense for which the maximum sentence is life imprisonment or death, a drug offense for which the maximum term of imprisonment is ten years or more, or any other felony committed by a person previously convicted of two or more of the above offenses.[35] A hearing is also required on a motion of the prosecutor or on the judge's own motion in cases that involve an allegation of "a serious risk" of flight, obstruction of justice, or intimidation of a prospective witness or juror.

At the detention hearing, which ordinarily must be held at the defendant's first appearance before the magistrate,[36] the accused is entitled by statute

---

[31] *See generally* Robert S. Natalini, Comment, *Preventive Detention and Presuming Dangerousness Under the Bail Reform Act of 1984*, 134 U. Pa. L. Rev. 225 (1985); Thomas E. Scott, *Pretrial Detention Under the Bail Reform Act of 1984: An Empirical Analysis*, 27 Am. Crim. L. Rev. 1 (1989).

[32] 18 U.S.C. § 3142(e) (2000).

[33] *See* Note 30 and accompanying text, *supra*.

[34] U.S. Dept. of Justice, Bureau of Justice Statistics, Pretrial Release and Detention: The Bail Reform Act of 1984 (1988), at 1.

[35] 18 U.S.C. § 3142(f)(1) (2000).

[36] Under 18 U.S.C. § 3142(f) (1996), except for good cause, a continuance on the defendant's motion may not exceed five days, and a continuance on the motion of the prosecutor

to be represented by counsel, to testify in his own behalf, to present witnesses, and to cross-examine witnesses called by the prosecutor. Rules concerning the admissibility of evidence at criminal trials do not apply at the hearing. For example, hearsay and evidence obtained in violation of the Constitution, although ordinarily inadmissible at trial, may be introduced at the hearing.

In order to determine whether any condition or combination of conditions will reasonably assure the appearance of the defendant and the safety of others, the magistrate must take into account various factors, including the nature of the offense charged, the weight of the evidence against the defendant, and the history and characteristics of the person, including his physical and mental condition, his ties to family and the community, and whether, at the time of the current arrest, he was already on probation or parole or on pretrial release from another offense.[37]

The Act provides that the facts the judicial officer uses to support a determination that no condition or combination of conditions will reasonably assure the safety of any person and the community must be supported by clear and convincing evidence.[38] However, the Act creates two rebuttable presumptions.[39]

First, the accused is presumed to be too dangerous to be released if the prosecutor proves that the defendant has previously been convicted of one of the enumerated offenses that justifies a detention hearing, that the offense for which he was convicted was committed while he was on release pending trial for another crime, and that five years have not elapsed since the date of conviction or of release from imprisonment (whichever is later) of the prior conviction.

Second, there is a presumption that no conditions of release will reasonably assure that the defendant will not flee or commit a crime, if the magistrate determines that there is probable cause to believe that, on the present occasion, he committed one of a specified set of serious drug offenses or an offense involving the use or possession of firearms.

---

may not exceed three days. However, the failure to comply with these provisions does not require the release of a person who should otherwise be detained. The error is considered harmless, unless a court concludes from the record as a whole that it had a substantial influence on the outcome of the detention proceeding. United States v. Montalvo-Murillo, 495 U.S. 711 (1990).

[37] 18 U.S.C. § 3142(g) (2000).

[38] 18 U.S.C. § 3142(f) (2000).

[39] 18 U.S.C. § 3142(e) (2000).

If the judge orders preventive detention, he must include written findings of fact, stating the reasons for his decision.[40] The losing side in the detention hearing may immediately appeal the magistrate's order.[41]

### [B]    The Policy Debate[42]

Critics of preventive detention claim that anticipatory confinement runs contrary to the presumption of innocence, and the principle of limited government authority. Detention of a person simply on the ground that he may do something wrong in the future violates the tenet that "leaving people free to pursue their own projects, free to act in accord with their choices and to take the consequences, enhances liberty, dignity, and respect for the individual as a moral agent—albeit at the cost of increasing risk to others."[43]

Put another way, critics maintain that it is wrong to jail persons on the basis of what society fears they will do in the future, rather than for what they have done in the past. Preventive detention statutes violate society's historical belief in human free will, *i.e.*, in the belief that a person has a right to his liberty until it is proven (beyond a reasonable doubt) that he has chosen to abuse it.[44]

Even if detention were theoretically justifiable, critics maintain that it is unwise to implement detention laws today because experts lack the capacity accurately to predict future dangerousness. Professor Albert Alschuler has put it that "even funnel clouds sometimes turn around, and human beings sometimes defy predictions."[45]

---

[40] 18 U.S.C. § 3142(i) (2000).

[41] 18 U.S.C. § 3145 (2000).

[42] *See generally* Albert W. Alschuler, *Preventive Pretrial Detention and the Failure of Interest-Balancing Approaches to Due Process*, 85 Mich. L. Rev. 510 (1986); Arthur R. Angel, et al., Note, *Preventive Detention: An Empirical Analysis*, 6 Harv. C.R.-C.L. L. Rev. 300 (1971); Michael Corrado, *Punishment and the Wild Beast of Prey: The Problem of Preventive Detention*, 86 J. Crim. L. & Criminology 778 (1996); Charles Patrick Ewing, *Preventive Detention and Execution: The Constitutionality of Punishing Future Crimes*, 15 Law & Hum. Behav. 139 (1991); Jeffrey Fagan & Martin Guggenheim, *Preventive Detention and the Judicial Prediction of Dangerousness for Juveniles: A Natural Experiment*, 86 J. Crim. L. & Criminology 415 (1996); Marc Miller & Martin Guggenheim, *Pretrial Detention and Punishment*, 75 Minn. L. Rev. 335 (1990); Stephen J. Morse, *Neither Desert Nor Disease*, 5 Legal Theory 265 (1999); Stephen J. Morse, *Blame and Danger: An Essay on Preventive Detention*, 76 B.U. L. Rev. 113 (1996); Edward R. Richards, *The Jurisprudence of Prevention: The Right of Societal Self-Defense Against Dangerous Individuals*, 16 Hastings Const. L.Q. 329 (1989); Jack F. Williams, *Process and Prediction: A Return to a Fuzzy Model of Pretrial Detention*, 79 Minn. L. Rev. 325 (1994).

[43] Morse, *Blame and Danger*, Note 42, *supra*, at 117.

[44] *See* Alschuler, Note 42, *supra*, at 557.

[45] *Id.*

Specifically, according to one study, the ability of mental health professionals to predict future violence among mentally disordered females is no better than chance, and is not much better than chance with males.[46] Other studies confirm that "false positives" (the erroneous prediction that an event will occur) in regard to the prediction of future criminal behavior is quite high. According to one scholar, "[e]ven the most optimistic behavioral scientists and legal commentators now seem to believe that the accuracy of predictions of dangerousness, whether made clinically or statistically, is 'probably no better than one valid assessment out of two.' "[47]

If experts are so unsuccessful in predicting dangerousness, there is no reason to be optimistic that judges can do a better job. From a utilitarian perspective, therefore, critics contend that it is exceedingly difficult to justify anticipatory confinement (especially in light of the moral principles favoring non-confinement) on the basis of such data. Too many persons innocent of future dangerousness must be incarcerated in order to ensure the detention of dangerous individuals.

Defenders of preventive detention reason that it is hard to sustain the argument that the government should *never* have the power to detain a person prior to trial, regardless of the circumstances. For example, suppose that an extremely wealthy defendant, one who could pay any bail imposed and who is charged with being a serial rapist-murderer, tells the magistrate, "If you release me, I will be on my private jet within the day to a country that will not extradite me." Or, worse, suppose that he says, "If you release me, I will walk out the door and resume raping and killing until the day I am jailed." Are we to say that the defendant in these extreme circumstances *must* be given the opportunity to be released, even if the magistrate has good reason to believe that the threats are genuine?

Cases involving a high degree of certainty of future flight or criminal conduct, such as that posed in the hypothetical, are admittedly rare. But, if one concedes that preventive detention is justifiable in *this* example, the question no longer is whether the government has the right to preventively detain, but instead is: under what circumstances should society use its legitimate power? In short, the argument concludes, societal self-defense allows for detention. As Professor Alschuler writes, "sensible people usually do not allow murderers and highwayman to roam among them." Therefore, detention may be justifiable if—but only if—there is "substantial

---

[46] Charles W. Lodz, et al., *The Accuracy of Predictions of Violence to Others*, 269 JAMA 1007, 1009–10 (1993).

[47] Ewing, Note 42, *supra*, at 141 (quoting Christopher Slobogin, *Dangerousness and Expertise*, 133 U. Pa. L. Rev. 97, 117 (1984)).

preliminary proof" that those whom society intends to detain are, indeed, "murderers and highwaymen."[48]

## [C] The Constitutional Debate

### [1] *U.S. v. Salerno*: The Holding[49]

In *United States v. Salerno,*[50] Chief Justice William Rehnquist stated that "[i]n our society liberty is the norm, and detention prior to trial or without trial is the carefully limited exception." In *Salerno*, the Supreme Court determined that the preventive detention provisions of the Federal Bail Reform Act of 1984 constituted a carefully limited exception to the liberty norm. By a vote of 6-3, the Court rejected a facial challenge[51] that the Act violated the Fifth Amendment due process clause and the Eighth Amendment no-excessive bail provision.

### [2] Due Process

#### [a] Substantive

As Chief Justice Rehnquist explained, "substantive due process" prevents the government from engaging in conduct that 'shocks the conscience,' . . . or interferes with rights 'implicit in the concept of ordered liberty' . . . ."[52] The claim of those attacking the Bail Reform Act was that pretrial detention violates substantive due process because it authorizes impermissible punishment before trial.

The Court rejected this claim. It stated that although pretrial punishment *is* unconstitutional, "the mere fact that a person is detained does not inexorably lead to the conclusion that the government has imposed punishment." In short, not all incarceration constitutes "punishment." The Court stated that the due process clause erects no "impenetrable 'wall' in this area"; it does not lay down any "categorical imperative." Instead, the issue of whether preventive detention—incarceration in the absence of a criminal

---

[48] Alschuler, Note 42, *supra*, at 556, 557.

[49] *See generally* Michael J. Eason, Note, *Pretrial Detention: What Will Become of the Innocent?*, 78 J. Crim. L. & Criminology 1048 (1988); John B. Howard, Jr., Note, The Trial of Pretrial Dangerousness: Preventive Detention After United States v. Salerno, 75 Va. L. Rev. 639 (1989); Miller & Guggenheim, Note 42, *supra*.

[50] 481 U.S. 739 (1987).

[51] A "facial" challenge is one that asserts that the law is void on its face. As the Court observed, this is "the most difficult challenge to mount successfully, since the challenger must establish that no set of circumstances exists under which the Act would be valid." Most constitutional challenges to statutes are more limited and seek only to show that the statute is unconstitutional based on the facts of the individual case.

[52] *Salerno*, 481 U.S. at 746 (quoting Rochin v. California, 343 U.S. 165, 172 (1952), and Palko v. Connecticut, 302 U.S. 319, 325–26 (1937)).

conviction—violates substantive due process is a matter primarily of interest-balancing.

The *Salerno* Court explained that there is a three-step process for determining whether a restriction on liberty constitutes "impermissible punishment or permissible regulation." First, a court must look at legislative history to determine if Congress "expressly intended to impose punitive restrictions." Second, if no such intent is divined, a court must decide if "an alternative purpose to which [the restriction] may rationally be connected is assignable for it." Third, it must decide if the restriction is excessive "in relation to the alternative purpose assigned [to it]."[53] In this case, the majority concluded that the detention imposed by the Bail Reform Act "falls on the regulatory side of the dichotomy."

The Court quickly disposed of the issue of legislative intent. The Chief Justice, citing Senate Reports, stated simply that the "legislative history of the Bail Reform Act clearly indicates that Congress did not formulate the . . . provisions as punishment for dangerous individuals." He just as quickly found a regulatory justification for preventive detention: "Congress . . . perceived pretrial detention as a potential solution to a pressing societal problem. . . . There is no doubt that preventing danger to the community is a legitimate regulatory goal."[54]

That left the third step, namely, to resolve whether the restriction on liberty "appears excessive in relation to the alternative purpose assigned to it." The Court balanced the government's "legitimate and compelling" regulatory interest in protecting the community from harm against the individual's liberty interest. On the basis of such interest-balancing, the Court pointed out, other pretrial and nontrial restrictions on liberty have been justified: detention of persons believed to be dangerous during times of war or insurrection; incarceration of mentally disordered individuals who are dangerous to themselves or others; and detention of dangerous criminal defendants incompetent to stand trial.

The Chief Justice noted here that the provisions of the Act operate only against persons arrested for a "specific category of extremely serious offenses," and only against those who Congress has found "are far more likely [than others] to be responsible for dangerous acts in the community after arrest." Consequently, the Court concluded, the law "narrowly focuses on a particularly acute problem in which the Government interests are overwhelming."

---

[53] *Id.* at 747 (alteration in original) (quoting Kennedy v. Mendoza-Martinez, 372 U.S. 144, 168–69 (1963)).

[54] Query: Isn't crime prevention—utilitarianism—also a *penal* goal?

Weighed against this "overwhelming" and "narrowly focused" interest "is the individual's strong interest in liberty," which the Court also described as "important" and "fundamental." The majority said no more about this interest, however, except that it "may, in circumstances where the government's interest is sufficiently weighty, be subordinated to the greater needs of society." The Court concluded that when the government must prove by clear and convincing evidence, as required by the Act, "that an arrestee presents an identified and articulable threat to an individual or the community, . . . consistent with the Due Process Clause, a court may disable the arrestee from executing that threat."

### [b] Procedural

The Court dealt only briefly with the respondents' facial challenge to the procedures of the Bail Reform Act. It found the procedures "adequate to authorize the pretrial detention of at least some [persons] charged with crimes."[55]

Despite evidence that experts have great difficulty predicting dangerousness,[56] the Chief Justice indicated that "there is nothing inherently unattainable about a prediction of future criminal conduct." The majority found the procedural safeguards in the statute—*e.g.*, the defendant has a right to counsel, the right to testify and put on other evidence, and the right of cross-examination; and the magistrate is guided by statutorily enumerated factors and cannot order detention in the absence of clear and convincing evidence— to be "specifically designed to further the accuracy of that determination."

### [3] Eighth Amendment

The majority concluded that the detention provisions of the Act do not violate the Eighth Amendment prohibition of excessive bail.[57] As Chief Justice Rehnquist explained, the Amendment prohibits excessive bail, but it "says nothing about whether bail shall be available at all."

The Court accepted the premise that the primary purpose of bail is to ensure that the defendant does not flee or intimidate witnesses. But, the

---

[55] *Salerno*, 481 U.S. at 751 (alteration in original) (quoting Schall v. Martin, 467 U.S. 253, 264 (1984), in which the Court approved pretrial detention of juveniles).

[56] See § 30.05[B], *supra*.

[57] The Court raised, but did not answer, the question of "whether the Excessive Bail Clause speaks at all to Congress' power to define the classes of criminal arrestees who shall be admitted to bail." An implication of this remark is that the bail clause might apply only to *judicial* action. In dissent, Justice Marshall responded that "[t]he majority is correct that this question need not be decided today; it was decided long ago." He reasoned that because the other clauses of the Eighth Amendment—*e.g.,* the prohibition on cruel and unusual punishment—limit legislative action, the bail clause also pertains to legislation.

Eighth Amendment does not prohibit "the government from pursuing other admittedly compelling interests through regulation of pretrial release." The bail clause requires only that the magistrate's "conditions of release or detention not be 'excessive' in light of the perceived evil." In view of its earlier analysis, the Court saw no reason to invalidate the detention provisions.

### [4] Dissenting Opinions

Justice Marshall, with whom Justice Brennan joined, dissented. The two dissenters criticized the majority for what Justice Marshall described as the "sterile formalism" of "divid[ing] a unitary argument into two independent parts [the due process and excessive bail arguments] and then profess[ing] to demonstrate that the parts are individually inadequate."

Justice Marshall criticized the majority's "cramped" substantive due process analysis. He said that "[t]he majority's technique . . . is simple: merely redefine any measure which is claimed to be punishment as 'regulation,' and, magically, the Constitution no longer prohibits its imposition." According to the dissenters, "[t]he ease with which the conclusion is reached suggests the worthlessness of the achievement."

The dissenters sought to demonstrate the weakness of the majority's approach by way of hypothetical: suppose Congress were to determine that most serious crimes are committed by unemployed persons at night and, therefore, "from amongst the panoply of 'potential solutions,' " Congress were to create a dusk-to-dawn curfew applying to all unemployed people. Based on the majority opinion, as long as Congress stated that its reasons were regulatory in nature, the statute would be "entirely compatible" with the due process clause.

Justice Marshall also criticized the majority's Eighth Amendment analysis, which he described as "sophistry." According to majority, the dissent pointed out, a judge may not impose excessive bail of $1 billion, but it may deny bail altogether; yet, "the consequences are indistinguishable."

According to the dissenters, the preventive detention provisions of the Federal Bail Reform Act are unconstitutional because they undermine the presumption of innocence. Again, a hypothetical is provided: suppose that a person indicted for a crime is detained because a magistrate determines by clear and convincing evidence that he is dangerous, yet the defendant is later acquitted. In such circumstances, the dissent contended, the individual must be released, even if the evidence of his future dangerousness remains unchallenged. If he were not released, "that would allow the Government to imprison someone for uncommitted crimes based upon 'proof' not beyond a reasonable doubt."

Justice Marshall reasoned that "our fundamental principles of justice declare that the defendant is as innocent on the day before his trial as he is on the morning after his acquittal." An indictment merely indicates that there is probable cause to believe that a person has committed a crime and that the government intends to bring him to trial for that offense. It does not demonstrate beyond a reasonable doubt that the individual is guilty of the offense or that he represents a danger to the community.

Justice Stevens filed a separate dissent. He agreed with Justice Marshall that an indictment is not entitled to any weight in determining whether an individual poses a risk to the community. However, he left open the possibility that the government may have the authority to detain a person it considers dangerous if, for example, "it is a virtual certainty that he or she would otherwise kill a group of innocent people in the immediate future."

## CHAPTER 31

# PLEA BARGAINING AND GUILTY PLEAS

## § 31.01 Guilty Pleas: Overview

### [A] Procedural Context

After an accused has been indicted by a grand jury or an information is filed against her by the prosecutor, she must be arraigned on the indictment or information.[1] Although procedures vary by jurisdiction, the defendant at a federal arraignment is read the charges, a copy of the indictment or information is provided to her or her counsel, and she is asked to enter a plea to each of the charges.[2]

The defendant may plead not guilty,[3] *nolo contendere*,[4] or guilty.[5] In some jurisdictions, she may also plead not guilty by reason of insanity, a prerequisite in those states to presenting evidence of insanity at the trial. In some states and in the federal courts,[6] a defendant may enter a conditional plea of guilty or *nolo contendere*, upon approval of the court and the consent

---

[1] *See generally* § 1.03[C], *supra*.

[2] Fed. R. Crim. P. 10.

[3] The "not guilty" verdict essentially means that the prosecution has failed to meet its constitutional obligation to prove the defendant's guilt beyond a reasonable doubt. It does not necessarily mean that the factfinder has determined that the accused is factually innocent of the offense charged. For a thoughtful discussion and proposal that an acquitted defendant have the right to ask for an additional determination of her factual innocence, *see* Andrew D. Leipold, *The Problem of the Innocent, Acquitted Defendant*, 94 Nw. U. L. Rev. 1297 (2000).

[4] "*Nolo contendere*" literally means "I will not contest it [the charges]." Although it is not an admission of guilt, it has the same effect in a criminal proceeding as a guilty plea. 1A Charles Alan Wright, Federal Practice and Procedure § 177 (3d ed. 1999). The primary benefit to the defendant of a *nolo* plea is that—unlike a guilty plea—it may not be used as an admission of guilt in a civil action based on the same conduct. Under the federal rules, a defendant may plead *nolo contendere* only with the consent of the court, which is to be granted "only after due consideration of the views of the parties and the interest of the public in the effective administration of justice." Fed. R. Crim. P. 11(b).

[5] *E.g.*, Fed. R. Crim. P. 11(a)(1).

[6] Fed. R. Crim. P. 11(a)(2).

of the prosecutor. As explained later,[7] a defendant who pleads guilty waives various defects in the proceeding. The purpose of a conditional plea is to permit the defendant to appeal a specific issue that otherwise would not survive the plea. If her appeal is successful, she may withdraw her plea of guilty.

## [B] Constitutional and Policy Context

Although results vary by locality, by crime, and by year, guilty pleas are secured in an extremely high number of criminal prosecutions. In 1998, of 59,885 federal convictions, 56,256 of them—or almost 94 percent—were the result of guilty pleas or pleas of *nolo contendere*.[8] In state courts, 91 percent of all convictions were the result of guilty pleas.[9] The guilty plea process, therefore, is a matter of enormous practical significance and the subject of a number of constitutional and policy controversies.

From a constitutional perspective, a person who pleads guilty relinquishes various rights, including her Fifth Amendment privilege against self-incrimination, her due process right to be acquitted unless proven guilty beyond a reasonable doubt, and her Sixth Amendment rights to a speedy and public trial by an impartial jury, to be confronted with the witnesses against her, and to call witnesses in her own behalf. It is essential, therefore, to determine whether the procedures used to obtain guilty pleas adequately ensure that defendants waive their constitutional rights voluntarily and knowingly, rather than as the result of coercion or ignorance. Furthermore, a defendant must usually rely on her lawyer to represent her in any plea negotiations and to advise her regarding whether to plead guilty. It is essential, therefore, to make sure that she receives her constitutional right to effective assistance of counsel in the plea process.

Constitutional issues aside, the overriding policy question is whether the law should encourage, tolerate, or actively discourage guilty pleas. A risk of unknown magnitude exists that in a system that encourages or condones self-conviction, innocent persons or, at least, persons against whom there is insufficient evidence to convict, will plead guilty. Because most guilty pleas are the product of plea bargaining, most of the policy debate pertaining to guilty pleas centers on that process.[10]

---

[7] *See* § 31.04, *infra.*

[8] United States Dept. of Justice, Bureau of Justice Statistics, Sourcebook of Criminal Justice Statistics—1998 407 (1999).

[9] *Id.* at 432.

[10] *See* § 31.06, *infra.*

## § 31.02  Validity of a Guilty Plea: Constitutional Principles[11]

### [A]  In General

A defendant who pleads guilty waives various constitutional rights.[12] But, there is always a risk that a guilty plea is the result of "[i]gnorance, incomprehension, coercion, terror, inducements, [or] subtle or blatant threats."[13] Therefore, a guilty plea is not valid unless it meets constitutional safeguards. First, a defendant who intends to plead guilty must be represented by counsel or validly waive that right.[14]

Second, a criminal defendant may not plead guilty, or waive counsel in order to do so, unless she is mentally competent. The Supreme Court controversially ruled in *Godinez v. Moran*,[15] however, that the competency standard for pleading guilty or waiving the right to counsel is the same as the standard for competence to stand trial, namely, "whether the defendant has 'sufficient present ability to consult with his lawyer with a reasonable degree of rational understanding' and has 'a rational as well as factual understanding of the proceedings against him.' "[16] According to *Godinez*, there is no reason to apply a higher standard than this:

> [W]hile the decision to plead guilty is undeniably a profound one, it is no more complicated than the sum total of decisions that a defendant may be called upon to make during the course of a trial. . . . This being so, we can conceive of no basis for demanding a higher level of competence for those defendants who choose to plead guilty. If the [competency to stand trial] standard is adequate for defendants who plead not guilty, it is necessarily adequate for those who plead guilty.[17]

Third, the due process clause provides that a guilty plea is invalid unless the trial court satisfies itself that the defendant's waiver of her constitutional rights is voluntary and knowing.[18] And, fourth, at least in some cases, a

---

[11] *See generally* Albert W. Alschuler, *The Supreme Court, the Defense Attorney, and the Guilty Plea*, 47 U. Colo. L. Rev. 1 (1975); Loftus E. Becker, Jr., *Plea Bargaining and the Supreme Court*, 21 Loy. L.A. L. Rev. 757 (1988).

[12] *See* § 31.01[B], *supra*.

[13] Boykin v. Alabama, 395 U.S. 238, 242–43 (1969).

[14] *See* Moore v. Michigan, 355 U.S. 155 (1957).

[15] 509 U.S. 389 (1993). For a thoughtful analysis of *Godinez* and the ethical responsibilities of defense lawyers representing clients with mental disabilities, *see* Christopher Slobogin & Amy Mashburn, *The Criminal Defense Lawyer's Fiduciary Duty to Clients with Mental Disability*, 68 Fordham L. Rev. 1581 (2000).

[16] *Id.* at 396 (quoting Dusky v. United States, 362 U.S. 402, 402 (1960)).

[17] *Id.* at 398–99.

[18] Parke v. Raley, 506 U.S. 20, 28–29 (1992); McCarthy v. United States, 394 U.S. 459, 466 (1969).

guilty plea will not be upheld unless a factual basis for it exists.[19] The latter two conditions are considered in the subsections that follow.

Even if all of the preceding constitutional standards are satisfied, a defendant apparently does not have a federal constitutional right to forego a criminal trial by pleading guilty. In *North Carolina v. Alford*,[20] the Supreme Court stated in dictum that a "criminal defendant does not have an absolute right under the Constitution to have his [constitutionally valid] guilty plea accepted by the court, . . . although the States may by statute or otherwise confer such a right." The *Alford* Court did not indicate whether a trial judge's discretion to reject a plea is subject to constitutional restrictions.

### [B] Voluntariness of the Plea

Due process is violated if a trial judge accepts a coerced guilty plea.[21] The Supreme Court has not fully defined "voluntariness" in the guilty plea context. However, it has stated that a guilty plea is not coerced unless it was "induced by threats (or promises to discontinue improper harassment), misrepresentation . . ., or perhaps by promises that are by their nature improper as having no proper relationship to the prosecutor's business (e.g. bribes)."[22]

The Supreme Court is hesitant to invalidate guilty pleas on the basis of involuntariness because a strict standard might discourage guilty pleas and the plea bargaining process that usually precedes them. As an example of the Court's general desire to uphold guilty pleas against claims of coercion, consider *Brady v. United States*:[23] in 1959, *D* was prosecuted for kidnapping. At that time the kidnapping statute provided that a defendant could receive the death penalty if, but only if, a jury recommended the sentence.

---

[19] North Carolina v. Alford, 400 U.S. 25 (1970).

[20] *Id.* at 38 n.11.

[21] There is some dispute as to whether a coerced plea is invalid if it is the result of a threat or promise emanating from a codefendant, relative, or friend. *Compare* 1A Wright, Note 4, *supra*, at 147 ("Pressure from codefendants, rather than the prosecutor, does not invalidate a plea.") (citing cases) *with* Iaea v. Sunn, 800 F.2d 861 (9th Cir. 1986) (holding that a guilty plea coerced by a private party is invalid, but also stating that acts that might constitute coercion, if committed by a government agent, may not always be coercive if done by others) *and* United States v. Martinez-Molina, 64 F.3d 719 (1st Cir. 1995) (trial judge did not conduct an adequate inquiry into the voluntariness of the plea because of threats or pressures from co-defendants to accept a plea arrangement).

[22] Brady v. United States 397 U.S. 742, 755 (1970) (quoting Shelton v. United States, 242 F.2d 101 115 (dissenting opinion) (5th Cir. 1957), *reversed on other grounds*, 356 U.S. 26 (1958)).

[23] 397 U.S. 742 (1970).

In other words, a person could free herself from the risk of a death sentence if she waived her right to a jury trial or pleaded guilty. As a consequence, *D* pleaded guilty after learning that a co-defendant would testify against him at trial.

Nearly a decade later, the Supreme Court held in *United States v. Jackson*[24] that the death penalty portion of the kidnapping statute was unconstitutional because it placed an impermissible burden on a defendant's right to a jury trial. As a result of *Jackson*, *D* sought to vacate his plea. He claimed that he would not have pled guilty but for the statutory threat of death; and, since that threat was constitutionally impermissible (per *Jackson*), his guilty plea was similarly tainted.

The *Brady* Court rejected the argument. It stated that there was no evidence that *D* was so "gripped by fear" that, with the assistance of competent counsel, he could not "rationally weigh" the advantages of trial against the benefits of pleading guilty. The Court saw little difference between *D*'s situation and that of a defendant who is informed by her lawyer that a judge will very likely be more lenient than a jury, or of a defendant who pleads guilty on the basis of her understanding that more serious charges will be dismissed.

A lurking voluntariness issue is whether an offer by a prosecutor to dismiss serious charges in exchange for a guilty plea to a comparatively minor offense, or a promise to the defendant that she will receive a light sentence for a very serious crime, can amount to unconstitutional coercion. For example, suppose that *D* is charged with forcible rape, for which the punishment upon conviction is 20 years to life. Further suppose that the prosecutor is unsure she can prove *D*'s guilt, because the victim's poor eyesight renders her identification of the assailant questionable. Therefore, the prosecutor offers to dismiss the rape charge in exchange for a guilty plea to battery, a petty misdemeanor.

Is the guilty plea coerced? On the one hand, if we assume that *D did* commit the rape, his guilty plea looks like a rational act of free choice, in response to a similarly rational decision by the prosecutor to offer *D* a windfall in view of the victim's poor eyesight. Therefore, some commentators assert, in the absence of wrongdoing by the prosecutor (not present in this case), the potentially "coercive elements of the plea bargaining environment do not corrupt the voluntariness of the plea agreement."[25] On the other hand, the differential punishment—20-years-to-life for rape versus

---

[24] 390 U.S. 570 (1968).

[25] Robert E. Scott & William J. Stuntz, *Plea Bargaining as Contract*, 101 Yale L.J. 1909, 1920–21 (1992).

a short or no jail sentence for battery—is so substantial that it might induce even an innocent person, fearful of wrongful conviction, to plead guilty. Therefore, it is submitted, the prosecutor's "inducements start to look very much like what the ordinary person calls 'coercion.' "[26]

### [C] Knowing (Intelligent) Nature of the Plea

### [1] In General

Subject to clarification below, a guilty plea is invalid and, therefore, subject to attack on appeal, if the defendant is unaware of: (1) the nature of the charges to which she is pleading; (2) the penal consequences of the plea; or (3) the nature of the rights she is waiving by pleading guilty. However, a plea may not successfully be attacked merely on the basis that the defendant or her counsel incorrectly assessed the legal or factual circumstances surrounding the case.

### [2] Nature of the Charges

In *Henderson v. Morgan*,[27] *D*, a 19-year-old male of substantially below average intelligence, pleaded guilty to second-degree intent-to-kill murder, even as he told the court that he "meant no harm" to the victim. The Supreme Court held that, despite what it assumed to be "overwhelming evidence of guilt," *D*'s plea was constitutionally invalid because the trial judge determined that neither *D*'s defense attorney nor the prosecutor explained to him that intent was a "critical element" of the crime, nor did the record disclose that the trial judge remedied the omission. Under these circumstances, the Supreme Court stated, "the plea could not be voluntary in the sense that it constituted an intelligent admission that he committed the offense." *D* did not "receive[] 'real notice of the true nature of the charge against him, the first and most universally recognized requirement of due process.' "[28]

The holding in *Henderson* is narrow. First, the rule apparently only applies to undefined "critical" elements of the crime. The Court stated that it would not decide whether fair notice "requires a description of every element of the offense; *we assume it does not.*"[29] Second, the Court stated that its holding would have limited effect:

---

[26] Stephen J. Schulhofer, *Criminal Justice Discretion as a Regulatory System*, 17 J. Legal Stud. 43, 73 (1988).

[27] 426 U.S. 637 (1976).

[28] *Id.* at 645 (quoting Smith v. O'Grady, 312 U.S. 329, 334 (1941)). The same rule applies if the claim is that the trial judge *misinformed* a defendant regarding a critical element of a crime. Bousley v. United States, 523 U.S. 614 (1998).

[29] *Henderson*, 426 U.S. at 647 n.18 (emphasis added).

Normally the record contains either an explanation of the charge by the trial judge, or at least a representation by defense counsel that the nature of the offense has been explained to the accused. *Moreover, even without such an express representation, it may be appropriate to presume that in most cases defense counsel routinely explain the nature of the offense in sufficient detail to give the accused notice of what he is being asked to admit.* This case is unique because the trial judge found as a fact that the element of intent was not explained to respondent. [30]

In *Marshall v. Lonberger*, [31] the Court applied the *Morgan* presumption to a case in which *D*, a person of ordinary intelligence, pleaded guilty to attempted murder. Although *D* was not told expressly that the offense contained the element of "intent to kill," the trial judge did tell *D* that he was pleading to "attempt on [*V*] with a knife." The Court held that *D* was adequately informed of the nature of the charge based on the judge's comment, the fact that *D* was competently represented by counsel, and that *D* was presumed under *Morgan* to have been informed by his lawyers of the precise nature of the charge.

### [3]  Penal Consequences of the Plea

The "conventional wisdom" [32] is that a defendant must be informed of the direct, as distinguished from collateral, consequences of her guilty plea. Unfortunately, the line between "direct" and "collateral" consequences is far from settled. At a minimum, a defendant should be informed of the maximum possible sentence for the crime to which she is pleading guilty.

The specific notice requirements in the federal courts are discussed elsewhere, [33] but the majority view is that the failure of a court to inform a defendant of the direct penal consequences of the plea, even if such failure violates a statute or procedural rule, does not by itself constitute a due process violation. [34] A due process violation may occur, however, if the pleader's lack of correct information prejudiced him—primarily if he would not have pleaded guilty if he had been provided accurate sentencing information. [35]

---

[30] *Id.* at 647 (emphasis added).

[31] 459 U.S. 422 (1983).

[32] 5 Wayne R. LaFave, Jerold H. Israel & Nancy J. King, Criminal Procedure 167 (2d ed. 1999).

[33] *See* § 31.03, *infra.*

[34] *See* United States v. Timmreck, 441 U.S. 780 (1979) (formal violation of a provision of Fed. R. Crim. P. 11, relating to guilty pleas, does not in itself constitute a constitutional violation).

[35] *See id.* at 784 (noting that the error in the case did not result in a "complete miscarriage of justice"; *D* did not claim that "if he had been properly advised by the trial judge, he would not have pleaded guilty").

### [4] Nature of the Rights Being Waived

The Supreme Court pointed out in *Boykin v. Alabama*[36] that a guilty plea involves the waiver of the Fifth Amendment privilege against self-incrimination, the right to trial by jury, and the right to confront one's accusers. It further stated that "[w]e cannot presume a waiver of these three important federal rights from a silent record." Therefore, the Court reversed a conviction obtained by guilty plea of a defendant whose plea was accepted although "so far as the record shows, the judge asked no questions of [the defendant] concerning his plea, and [the defendant] did not address the court." As a result of *Boykin,* states and the federal courts have devised procedures for taking pleas that ensure that defendants who plead guilty are informed of the rights they are waiving.

Lower courts have not generally interpreted *Boykin* to require the reversal of a guilty plea merely because the trial record fails to show that the judge expressly informed the pleader of the rights being waived.[37] For example, it is apparently constitutionally sufficient if, from the record of the guilty plea proceeding supplemented by any post-plea hearings, it is evident that the defendant was aware of the consequences of the plea, regardless of how she came to this knowledge.[38]

Moreover, it should be noted that *Boykin* involved a direct appeal of the defendant's guilty plea. A different set of rules apply if a state defendant collaterally attacks her conviction in a federal habeas corpus proceeding. In *Parke v. Raley,*[39] D collaterally attacked his plea on the ground that state law required him to prove the invalidity of his guilty plea, but that no transcript of the plea proceeding was maintained by the state. Therefore, D argued, state procedures violated the *Boykin* "presumption of invalidity" of a guilty plea based on a silent record.

The Court stated that there was "no tension" between the state system and *Boykin.* It indicated that to "import *Boykin*'s presumption of invalidity into this very different context [of a federal habeas corpus proceeding] would . . . improperly ignore another presumption deeply rooted in our jurisprudence: the 'presumption of regularity' that attaches to final judgments, even when the question is waiver of constitutional rights."[40] In essence, the "presumption of regularity" in habeas proceedings overrides the *Boykin* "presumption of invalidity" in cases in which, as here, the

---

[36] 395 U.S. 238 (1969).

[37] 5 LaFave, Israel & King, Note 32, *supra,* at 177.

[38] *See* Wilkins v. Erickson, 505 F.2d 761 (9th Cir. 1974).

[39] 506 U.S. 20 (1992).

[40] *Id.* at 29.

absence of a transcript is not "suspicious." As the Court explained, *"Boykin* colloquies have been required for nearly a quarter-century." Therefore, "it defies logic to presume from the mere unavailability of a transcript . . . that the defendant was not advised of his rights."

### [5] Incorrect Legal Advice: How It Affects the Intelligence of the Plea

In *Brady v. United States*,[41] *D*, who was represented by counsel, pleaded guilty to kidnapping in order to escape a death sentence that could only be imposed by recommendation of a jury. Subsequently, a different defendant, represented by a different lawyer, refused to plead guilty to kidnapping and challenged the death penalty provision in the kidnapping statute. The Supreme Court's answer to that defendant's challenge came in *United States v. Jackson*,[42] when it ruled that, indeed, the death penalty provision of the statute was unconstitutional. *D* thereafter sought to vacate his plea. *D* argued that, in light of *Jackson*, he entered his plea unintelligently, in that his lawyer advised him incorrectly that the jury could impose the death penalty.

The Court rejected *D*'s claim. It observed that the decision to plead guilty "is heavily influenced by the defendant's appraisal of the prosecution's case against him and by the apparent likelihood of securing leniency should a guilty plea be offered and accepted. Considerations like these frequently present imponderable questions for which there are no certain answers."

The Court stated that a "defendant is not entitled to withdraw his plea merely because he discovers long after the plea has been accepted that his calculus misapprehended the quality of the State's case or the likely penalties attached to alternative courses of action." More specifically, an otherwise voluntary plea is not vulnerable to attack simply because "later judicial decisions indicate that the plea rested on a faulty premise." It is enough that the plea was based on a *competent* lawyer's advice, based on "then existing law as to possible penalties." As the Court later put it, when the intelligence of a guilty plea is at issue, the question is merely "whether that advice was within the range of competence demanded of attorneys in criminal cases."[43]

Of course, a plea *is* vulnerable to attack if the defendant can show that she *was* the victim of incompetent legal representation. The general principles in this regard are considered elsewhere in the text.[44] A guilty

---

[41] 397 U.S. 742 (1970).

[42] 390 U.S. 570 (1968).

[43] McMann v. Richardson, 397 U.S. 759, 771 (1970).

[44] *See* § 29.07, *supra*.

plea will not be vacated on the ground of ineffective representation, however, unless the defendant proves both that her counsel's representation was constitutionally deficient, and that she was prejudiced by the deficiency, *i.e.*, that "there is a reasonable probability that, but for counsel's errors, [s]he would not have pleaded guilty and would have insisted on going to trial."[45]

This prejudice test is an especially difficult standard for a pleader to overcome. How does one measure a pleader's psychological state as to whether or not she would have chosen to go to trial? Perhaps the only way to measure this is to determine whether, with proper representation, she would have been successful at trial, but this question cannot realistically be answered without seeing the full panoply of prosecutorial and defense evidence that would have been presented at the trial.[46] A far more realistic "prejudice" analysis would ask whether, but for the incompetent representation, the defendant would likely have received a better plea deal.

### [D] Factual Basis of the Plea

In general, a judge is not constitutionally required to determine whether there is a factual basis for a defendant's guilty plea, although such a requirement may be imposed by statute or judicial rule. In one circumstance, however, the Constitution *does* require a judicial determination of the factual basis for the plea, and that is when a defendant affirmatively tells the judge during the plea proceeding that she is innocent of the offense for which she is pleading guilty.

In *North Carolina v. Alford*,[47] *D* pleaded guilty to second-degree murder, although he told the judge that he did not commit the crime and that he was only pleading guilty in order to avoid the death penalty. The Supreme Court ruled that a personal admission of guilt is not constitutionally required to validate a guilty plea. Moreover, a judge may accept a guilty plea from a defendant asserting innocence, as long as the record before the judge "contains strong evidence of actual guilt." The Court did not define "strong evidence," although it did state that in the present case there was "overwhelming evidence" of *D*'s guilt. It is unlikely that the judge is required to be convinced of a defendant's guilt beyond a reasonable doubt.[48]

---

[45] Hill v. Lockhart, 474 U.S. 52, 59 (1985).

[46] Even if such information were available to an appellate court, which it is not, the *Hill* test would need to take into consideration the extent to which the pleader is a risk-taker, *i.e.*, to what extent would she have risked conviction based on the evidence?

[47] 400 U.S. 25 (1970).

[48] H. Richard Uviller, *Pleading Guilty: A Critique of Four Models*, 41 Law & Contemp. Prob. 102, 126 (1977).

## § 31.03    Obtaining a Valid Guilty Plea: Federal Procedures[49]

### [A]   Ensuring Voluntariness

Rule 11(d) of the Federal Rules of Criminal Procedure requires the trial court to withhold acceptance of a guilty plea until it determines that the plea is voluntary. The rule does not define "voluntary," except to state that it must not be the "result of force or threats or of promises apart from a plea agreement."

Rule 11 requires the judge to determine the voluntariness of the plea "by addressing the defendant personally in open court." Although the Supreme Court unanimously held in *McCarthy v. United States*[50] that a guilty plea must be set aside if the district court failed to follow this procedure, Rule 11 has since been amended to include a "harmless error" provision that provides that "[a]ny variance from the procedures required by this rule which does not affect substantial rights shall be disregarded."[51]

The Supreme Court has ruled that in federal habeas corpus proceedings, a technical violation of Rule 11 does not entitle a petitioner to relief;[52] instead, harmless error analysis applies. Although the Supreme Court has not ruled on the continued vitality of *McCarthy* in direct appeals, lower courts unanimously have ruled that *McCarthy* is superseded by the "harmless error" provision in Rule 11.[53]

### [B]   Ensuring An Intelligent Plea

Federal Rule 11(c) requires the trial court to "address the defendant personally in open court and inform the defendant of, and determine that the defendant understands," a variety of matters pertaining to the nature of the charges to which she is pleading, the penal consequences of her plea, and the constitutional rights she is waiving.

Among the requirements of Rule 11(c), the judge must inform the defendant of the nature of the charge to which she is pleading, any mandatory minimum sentence provided by law, and the maximum penalty for the offense, including any pertinent special parole provisions. The judge must also inform the defendant that she is "required to consider any applicable sentencing guidelines but may depart from those guidelines under some circumstances."

---

[49] For federal procedures relating specifically to plea bargains, *see* § 31.05[C], *infra*; *see generally* 1A Wright, Note 4, *supra*, at §§ 172–174.

[50] 394 U.S. 459 (1969).

[51] Fed. R. Crim. P. 11(h).

[52] United States v. Timmreck, 441 U.S. 780 (1979).

[53] 1A Wright, Note 4, *supra*, at 306–07.

The judge must also inform the defendant of her right to be tried by jury, which includes the right to assistance of counsel, the right to confront her accusers, and the right against compelled self-incrimination, all of which (she must be told) are waived if she pleads guilty.

Finally, if the court intends to question the defendant under oath during the plea proceeding, it must inform the defendant that her answers can later be used against her in a prosecution for perjury or false statement. However, the Supreme Court has held that the defendant's waiver of her privilege against compelled self-incrimination by pleading guilty is a narrow one: her truthful statements to the judge during the plea colloquy may not be used against her at any subsequent sentencing hearing in that case.[54]

### [C] Determining the Factual Basis of the Plea

Rule 11(f) provides that "the court should not enter a judgment upon such [guilty] plea without making such inquiry as shall satisfy it that there is a factual basis for the plea." Unlike the other Rule 11 provisions, which apply as well to pleas of *nolo contendere*, the factual-basis requirement applies exclusively to guilty pleas.

It should be observed that the rule does not require a trial judge to believe that the defendant is guilty. It is sufficient that there is a factual basis for the plea. Moreover, although a judge must not accept a guilty plea in the absence of a factual basis, she may reject a factually based guilty plea.[55]

## § 31.04 Effect of a Guilty Plea on Prior Constitutional Claims[56]

### [A] General Rule

A state defendant who pleads guilty to a criminal charge ordinarily is barred from raising a claim in federal court of a constitutional violation that occurred prior to the guilty plea, even if the claim might have served as a bar to conviction had she chosen to go to trial in the state court. The defendant is not barred, however, from proving that there was a procedural defect in the guilty plea procedure itself, or that the plea was not voluntarily or intelligently made.

For example, in *McMann v. Richardson*,[57] three defendants in New York state court pleaded guilty to their crimes because, under then applicable state law, there was no way to keep the jury from hearing their arguably

---

[54] Mitchell v. United States, 526 U.S. 314 (1999).

[55] 1A Wright, Note 4, *supra*, at 200–202; *see also* § 31.02[A], *supra*.

[56] *See generally* Peter Westen, *Away from Waiver: A Rationale for the Forfeiture of Constitutional Rights in Criminal Procedure*, 75 Mich. L. Rev. 1214 (1977).

[57] 397 U.S. 759 (1970).

coerced confessions. When this New York procedure was later declared unconstitutional,[58] and the new rule was applied retroactively, the defendants sought relief in federal court on the ground that their guilty pleas were motivated by the coerced confessions.

The Court in *McMann* was unimpressed. It treated the defendants' guilty pleas as a break in the chain of events that preceded them in the criminal process.[59] As the *McMann* Court explained, a defendant who pleads guilty "is convicted on his counseled admission in open court that he committed the crime charged against him. The prior confession [or other constitutional claim] is not the basis for the judgment . . . ."[60] The Court further stated: "It is no denigration of the right to trial to hold that when the defendant waives his state court remedies and admits his guilt, he does so under the law then existing; further, he assumes the risk of ordinary error in either his or his attorney's assessment of the law and facts."[61]

Although *McMann* used the word "waiver" in its explanation of the rule, this term is a misnomer, as the Supreme Court later recognized.[62] A waiver involves an intelligent relinquishment of a known right, which may not be involved if a defendant acts on the basis of faulty legal advice. Therefore, it is more accurate to say that the defendant who pleads guilty *forfeits* the right to assert constitutional claims pertaining to events that occurred prior to the plea.[63]

### [B] Exceptions to the General Rule

A defendant who pleads guilty is not barred in all circumstances from raising antecedent constitutional claims in federal court. First, although a defendant assumes the risk of "ordinary error" by her attorney, she does not assume the risk that her lawyer is incompetent. If her attorney's conduct does not fall within the range of competence demanded of attorneys in criminal cases and she was prejudiced as a result, she may attack her guilty plea.[64]

Second, the Supreme Court has admitted a few exceptions to its forfeiture rule, although it has struggled to explain the basis for the exceptions. In *Blackledge v. Perry*,[65] it permitted a defendant who pleaded guilty to raise

---

[58] Jackson v. Denno, 378 U.S. 368 (1964).

[59] Tollett v. Henderson, 411 U.S. 258, 267 (1973) (explaining *McMann*).

[60] *McMann*, 397 U.S. at 773.

[61] *Id.* at 774.

[62] Tollett v. Henderson, 411 U.S. at 266.

[63] Westen, Note 56, *supra*, at 1215.

[64] *See* § 31.02[C][5], *supra*.

[65] 417 U.S. 21 (1974).

a due process claim that he was the victim of prosecutorial vindictiveness in the charging process. And, in *Menna v. New York*,[66] the Court allowed a defendant to raise an antecedent double jeopardy claim, even as it warned that "[w]e do not hold that a double jeopardy claim may never be waived." On the other hand, the Court ruled in *Tollett v. Henderson*[67] that a person who pleads guilty is barred from raising a claim of racial discrimination in the selection of the grand jurors who indicted him. And, in *United States v. Broce*,[68] the Court confirmed its warning in *Menna* by holding that the defendant in *Broce* was barred from raising a double jeopardy claim in that circumstance.

How are these exceptions and non-exceptions justified? *Menna* sought to explain the distinction on the basis of "factual" versus "legal" guilt: a plea of guilty is an admission of factual guilt and therefore removes that issue from the case; it does not remove claims that the defendant, although factually guilty, may not legally be subjected to conviction and punishment.

The factual/legal distinction does not adequately explain the Court's decisions.[69] First, one reason for the prohibition on double jeopardy is to prevent factually innocent persons from being wrongfully convicted as the result of successive prosecutions.[70] Thus, a double jeopardy claim may fall on the "factual guilt" side of the line, which would mean that the defendant's claim in *Menna* should have been barred. On the other hand, the racial discrimination claim in *Tollett* can be treated as a "legal guilt" defense, since discrimination in the selection of a grand jury is constitutionally wrong, even if those whom it indicts are guilty. Beyond this, as a matter of policy, it is hard to defend a proposition that legal rights relating to factual innocence may be lost through inadvertence, whereas claims that have nothing to do with factual innocence are not barred.[71]

The Supreme Court in *Blackledge* provided a different explanation for the rules: a defendant is not barred from raising antecedent constitutional claims that go "to the very power of the State to bring the defendant into court to answer the charge brought against him." Thus, the prosecutorial vindictiveness alleged in *Blackledge*, if proved, would have barred the government from hailing the defendant into court at all on the felony charge for which he pleaded guilty. Similarly, a double jeopardy claim, if upheld,

---

[66] 423 U.S. 61 (1975).

[67] 411 U.S. 258 (1973).

[68] 488 U.S. 563 (1989).

[69] *See* Westen, Note 56, *supra*, at 1223.

[70] *See* § 32.01[D], *infra*.

[71] Louis Michael Seidman, *Factual Guilt and the Burger Court: An Examination of Continuity and Change in Criminal Procedure*, 80 Colum. L. Rev. 436, 475 (1980).

bars re-prosecution of that offense. On the other hand, in *Tollett*, the government could have cured the problem of the tainted indictment by securing a new indictment from a properly selected tribunal.

This explanation comes closer to explaining the Court's treatment of antecedent constitutional claims. However, the Justices added a wrinkle to the rule in *Broce*. In that case, *D* pleaded guilty to two separate charges of conspiracy. Thereafter, his co-defendants, who did not plead guilty, convinced the trial court that the two conspiracies were only one. In effect, this meant that *D* had been convicted and punished twice for a single offense, in violation of the double jeopardy clause. *D* argued that this double jeopardy claim was not barred in light of *Menna*.

The Supreme Court disagreed. It noted that in *Menna* and *Blackledge*—cases in which the Court held that the antecedent claims were not barred—the defendants did not "seek further proceedings at which to expand the record with new evidence." In those cases, the defendants' claims were capable of determination on the basis of the indictment and the original record before the court that accepted the guilty plea. In contract, in *Broce*, the legitimacy of *D*'s double jeopardy claim could not be proved without adding to the original record, since there was nothing in the indictments to suggest that the two conspiracies were actually one. Therefore, the Court was unwilling to permit the antecedent claim to be raised.

### [C]  Conditional Pleas

The rule that a guilty plea bars most antecedent constitutional claims creates practical difficulties for the defense and can result in wasteful allocation of judicial resources at the trial level. Ordinarily, a defendant whose pretrial motion to suppress evidence is denied cannot seek interlocutory relief, *i.e.*, she cannot appeal the denial of her motion before trial. Therefore, if the defendant wishes to preserve her constitutional claim, she must plead not guilty and go to trial, so that she can later appeal the trial court's denial of her constitutional motion, if she is convicted.

In order to avoid a trial that neither side wants, some jurisdictions, now including the federal courts,[72] permit conditional pleas of guilty. Under the Federal Rules, if the court and the prosecutor consent, the defendant may enter a conditional plea of guilty or *nolo contendere*, reserving the right, "on appeal from the judgment, to review of the adverse determination of any specified pretrial motion." If the defendant prevails on appeal, she may withdraw the plea. If she does not prevail, the plea stands.

---

[72] Fed. R. Crim. P. 11(a)(2).

## § 31.05   Plea Bargaining: General Principles[73]

### [A]   Overview

Plea bargaining is the process by which a defendant in a criminal prosecution agrees, in exchange for some official concession, to an act of self-conviction, *i.e.*, to plead guilty to one or more criminal charges.

At least since the beginning of the twentieth century, the vast majority of guilty pleas have been the result of plea negotiations between prosecutors and defendants and/or their counsel. However, because of the controversial nature of plea bargaining and related doubts about its constitutionality, the process was usually conducted *sub rosa*: the judge at arraignment would ask the defendant whether her proposed guilty plea was the result of any promises by the prosecutor; the defendant, on the advice of her counsel or the prosecutor, would state that it was not. In most cases, the judge knew that this statement was false. The result was that plea bargaining was legally unreviewable, and the defendant was required to participate in a cynical charade.

In 1970, the Supreme Court made clear that plea bargaining is not unconstitutional *per se*.[74] Now, plea negotiations usually occur above the table. However, there is considerable dispute as to whether plea bargaining is a benefit or detriment to the goals of criminal justice.

### [B]   Types of Plea Agreements

Plea negotiations generally involve "charge bargaining," "sentencing bargaining," or both. In charge bargaining, in exchange for a guilty plea to one or more charges, the prosecutor agrees to the dismissal of other charges in the indictment or information (a "dismissal agreement"), or to accept the guilty plea to a lesser degree of the charge (a "charge-reduction agreement").

Sentencing bargaining is also of two kinds. In some cases, the prosecutor agrees that, in exchange for a guilty plea, she will recommend to the judge that the latter impose the sentence agreed upon by the defendant or, less favorably to the defendant, not oppose the defendant's request for a particular sentence (a "sentencing recommendation agreement"). Alternatively, the prosecutor may agree to a specified sentence (a "sentencing agreement").

---

[73] *See generally* Albert W. Alschuler, *Plea Bargaining And Its History*. 79 Colum. L. Rev. 1 (1979); George Fisher, *Plea Bargaining's Triumph*, 109 Yale L.J. 857 (2000).

[74] Brady v. United States, 397 U.S. 742 (1970); McMann v. Richardson, 397 U.S. 759 (1970); Parker v. North Carolina, 397 U.S. 790 (1970).

## [C]   Federal Plea Agreement Procedures[75]

Federal Rule 11 permits the prosecutor and the defendant's attorney, or the defendant herself if she has waived her right to counsel, to engage in plea negotiations. The existence and nature of the plea agreement must be disclosed by the parties at the arraignment.

A judge is not required to accept a dismissal, charge-reduction, or sentencing plea agreement, although the rules are silent regarding the factors she should consider in determining whether to accept the agreement.[76] The judge may accept the agreement at the arraignment, reject it at that time, or defer a decision until she receives a presentence report.[77] If the judge rejects the plea agreement, the defendant must be given the opportunity to withdraw her plea, and she must be informed that if she does not withdraw it "the disposition of the case may be less favorable to the defendant than that contemplated by the plea agreement."[78]

A guilty plea based on a sentencing-recommendation agreement is treated differently. Such an agreement does not require the judge to commit herself to anything; therefore, in order to assure that the defendant realizes this critical fact, the judge must inform the defendant that if she does not accept the recommendation, the defendant has no right to withdraw the plea.[79]

Rule 11 also provides that evidence that the defendant entered a plea of guilty that was later withdrawn may not be introduced against her in any civil or criminal proceeding, nor may statements made by her to the prosecutor in plea negotiations, or to the judge in plea proceedings, be used against her.[80]

---

[75] *See generally* 1A Wright, Note 4, *supra*, at § 175.1.

[76] The United States Sentencing Commission recommends that no agreement be accepted unless, in the case of a sentencing agreement, the recommended sentence falls within applicable sentencing guidelines or there are "justifiable reasons" to depart from them; a dismissal agreement should not be accepted unless "the remaining charges adequately reflect the seriousness of the actual offense behavior and . . . accepting the agreement will not undermine the statutory purposes of sentencing." 18 U.S.C. App. § 6B1.2 (1995).

[77] The United States Sentencing Commission recommends deferral. 18 U.S.C. App. § 6B1.1(c) (1995). The trial court may accept the guilty plea itself while deferring a decision on the agreement itself. If it does this, the defendant has no automatic right to withdraw her guilty plea while the plea agreement is being considered. Federal Rule 32(e) provides that she must offer a "fair and just reason" for withdrawing the plea once it has been accepted. United States v. Hyde, 520 U.S. 670 (1997). *See also* Note 79, *infra*.

[78] Fed. R. Crim. P. 11(e)(4).

[79] Although the defendant has no *right* to withdraw her plea after a guilty plea is accepted, the judge may *permit* her to withdraw her plea before the sentence is imposed, if she "shows any fair and just reason" to do so. Fed. R. Crim. P. 32(e).

[80] Fed. R. Crim. P. 11(e)(6).

This exclusionary protection may be waived by a defendant. For example, in *United States v. Mezzanatto*,[81] the prosecutor would not proceed with negotiations unless *D* agreed (which he did) that any statements he made could be used to impeach any contradictory testimony he might give at trial should negotiations fail. The Supreme Court held that the agreement was valid absent some indication that *D*'s waiver was involuntary or unknowing.

### [D]  Judicial Participation In Plea Negotiations[82]

Judicial participation in the plea bargaining process is possible in various ways, in varying degrees, and at various times. For example, a judge might initiate bargaining between the prosecution and the defense, much as a judge in a civil suit seeks to bring the parties together to negotiate. She might ask the defense attorney what the prosecutor would need to do to convince her client to plead guilty, and then she might try to convince the prosecutor to accept the "offer" or to make a counter-offer. Alternatively, the judge might participate as an information provider, by answering questions about her sentencing philosophy if the defendant stands trial.

Historically, participation by judges in plea bargaining has not been uncommon. A late 1970s study found that approximately one-third of criminal trial judges attended plea discussions, usually in an active role.[83] One 1970s observer of ten cities reported that judicial participation was common in nine of them.[84] More recent surveys suggest that judicial involvement remains extensive in some jurisdictions.[85] On the other hand, the Federal Rules of Criminal Procedure prohibit judicial participation in plea agreement discussions.[86]

Judicial participation in plea bargaining is controversial. Advocates contend that it is unwise to ban judges from the process. In the final analysis they will have to approve or reject a plea agreement; therefore, it is sensible to include them in the process so that negotiations proceed fruitfully. Furthermore, when negotiations focus on a sentencing-recommendation agreement, the defense cannot easily measure the value of the prosecutor's

---

[81] 513 U.S. 196 (1995).

[82] *See generally* Albert W. Alschuler, *The Trial Judge's Role in Plea Bargaining (pt. 1)*, 76 Colum. L. Rev. 1059 (1976); Kathleen Gallagher, *Judicial Participation in Plea Bargaining: A Search for New Standards*, 9 Harv. C.R.-C.L. L. Rev. 29 (1974).

[83] John P. Ryan & James J. Alfini, *Trial Judges' Participation in Plea Bargaining: An Empirical Perspective*, 13 Law & Soc'y Rev. 479, 487 (1979).

[84] Alschuler, Note 82, *supra*, at 1061–62.

[85] *E.g.*, Allen F. Anderson, *Judicial Participation in the Plea Negotiation Process: Some Frequencies and Disposing Factors*, 10 Hamline J. Pub. L. & Pol'y 39 (1990).

[86] Fed. R. Crim. P. 11(e)(1).

offer unless it knows whether the judge is likely to accept the recommendation. Judicial participation, therefore, informs the process. It also may reduce the anxiety of the defendant by allowing her, prior to trial, to get an "authoritative statement" of her likely sentence; she does not have to wait for the trial, which one public defender has described as "a plunge from an unknown height."[87] Indeed, advocates of judicial participation ask, if the judge knows what sentence she would give if the defendant elects to go to trial, "what interests of the defendant are protected by prohibiting the judge from communicating this information to him?"[88]

Critics of judicial participation believe that they have an answer to the latter question: a bar on participation would serve the defendant's interest in not being coerced to plead guilty. They maintain that a judge is like a stick of dynamite placed in the negotiation room: she is apt to blast out a guilty plea that might not otherwise have been obtained. Judicial participation is efficient precisely because it compels defendants, already fearful, to plead guilty rather than to stand trial. What is the defendant expected to do, critics ask, if the judge is present and "suggests" that a particular offer is a good one?

Anecdotes of "judicial blasting" are plentiful. For example, in one case[89] a judge told an inexperienced attorney who was hesitant to recommend that his client accept a particular offer that "I'm not going to tell you what to do, young man, but I can tell you what *I'll* do." He then explained his sentencing philosophy, which was to double the prison sentence of anyone who stood trial. As the judge explained, "He takes some of my time—I take some of his." The defendant immediately accepted the plea offer. One moral of this story is that the judge's participation rendered the defendant's decision more informed. The opposing interpretation of it is that, although knowledge sometimes empowers, it may also coerce.

Critics of judicial participation also fear that a judge whose suggestions are rejected by the defendant will find it more difficult to conduct a fair trial. Even if she can, they find it unseemly for a judge, the neutral trial arbiter, to participate in the "horse trading," the aim of which is to avoid a trial and convict a defendant.

Advocates of judicial participation do not discount these concerns. Some proponents of judicial involvement would set limits on, but not ban, participation by judges. For example, judges might be permitted to moderate

---

[87] Alschuler, Note 82, *supra*, at 1081.

[88] Uviller, Note 48, *supra*, at 116–17.

[89] Alschuler, Note 82, *supra*, at 1089 (anecdote of Professor Dallin Oaks, University of Chicago, when he represented an indigent defendant in a drug case).

negotiations but do no more. Or, participation might be limited to stating what charges the judge would be willing to dismiss or what sentencing concessions she might be prepared to accept. Or, a "cooling off period" after a deal is reached in the judge's presence might be required. Finally, in order to maintain the appearance and reality of a fair trial, the judge participating in plea negotiations might be barred from conducting the trial, if negotiations break down.

## § 31.06 Plea Bargaining: Policy Debate

### [A] Is Plea Bargaining Inevitable?[90]

One scholar of plea bargaining recently wrote, "plea bargaining has triumphed. Bloodlessly and clandestinely, it has swept across the penal landscape and driven our vanquished jury into small pockets of resistance. Plea bargaining may be, as some chroniclers claim, the invading barbarian. But it has won all the same."[91]

If this is so, was this outcome inevitable? Or, perhaps as importantly, must critics of plea bargaining consider the battle over for good? The conventional wisdom is that plea bargaining is inevitable. The thesis is that if bargaining were not permitted, the guilty-plea rate (now more than 90 percent of all convictions[92]) would drop substantially, the resulting number of trials would increase dramatically (even a one-third reduction in plea bargains could result in a 400 percent increase in the number of trials),[93] and this would overwhelm an already beleaguered criminal justice system, causing socially unacceptable and, perhaps, even unconstitutional,[94] delays in the distribution of justice. Consequently, plea bargaining would either be reinstituted or participants in the system would return to the days when bargaining was an under-the-table, and, therefore, unregulated, phenomenon.[95]

Some studies support the inevitability thesis, particularly the claim that plea bargaining will be forced underground where it is not expressly permitted.[96] A study of a ban on prosecutorial bargaining in Alaska, which

---

[90] *See generally* Stephen J. Schulhofer, *Is Plea Bargaining Inevitable?*, 97 Harv. L. Rev. 1037 (1984).

[91] Fisher, Note 73, *supra*, at 859.

[92] *See the text to* Notes 8–9, *supra*.

[93] Scott & Stuntz, Note 25, *supra*, at 1932.

[94] "In all criminal prosecutions, the accused shall enjoy the right to a speedy . . . trial . . . ." U.S. Const. amend VI.

[95] *See* § 31.05[A], *supra*.

[96] *E.g.*, Milton Heumann & Colin Loftin, *Mandatory Sentencing and the Abolition of Plea*

purports to reach the opposite conclusion,[97] is inconclusive because the study focused on a period when judges were permitted to initiate plea bargaining. Furthermore, it is unclear whether Alaska's experiences apply in urban settings, with their congested courtrooms and crowded dockets.

On the other hand, two studies of the Philadelphia criminal justice system, one in which guilty pleas were obtained in considerably fewer cases than is the national norm, suggest that an urban criminal justice system can make trials available in most cases without insurmountable difficulties.[98] According to the author of these studies, the results throw into serious question the assumption of plea bargaining inevitability.[99]

Obviously, if plea bargaining is not inevitable, advocates of the process ought to be able to offer principled reasons why the justice system should not abolish or limit plea bargaining. Even if plea bargaining *is* inevitable, this does not render policy analysis irrelevant. If bargaining is undesirable, albeit inevitable, plea negotiations should be reduced to the extent possible, and the process that remains should be more carefully regulated. If bargaining is desirable, the law should recognize this fact and allow the process to proceed in a comparatively unfettered manner. Therefore, it is still appropriate to ask whether bargaining is good in principle.

---

*Bargaining: The Michigan Felony Firearm Statute*, 13 Law & Soc'y Rev. 393 (1979); Thomas Church, Jr., *Plea Bargains, Concessions and the Courts: Analysis of a Quasi-Experiment*, 10 Law & Soc'y Rev. 377 (1976).

[97] Michael L. Rubinstein & Teresa J. White, *Alaska's Ban on Plea Bargaining*, 13 Law & Soc'y Rev. 367 (1979).

[98] Stephen J. Schulhofer, *No Job Too Small: Justice Without Bargaining in the Lower Criminal Courts*, 1985 Am. B. Found. Res. J. 519; Schulhofer, Note 90, *supra*; *but see* Michael deCourcy Hinds, *Philadelphia Justice System Overwhelmed*, New York Times, Aug. 15, 1990, at A1 (quoting a district attorney as describing the Philadelphia criminal justice system as being "on the verge of collapse"; and reporting on a Pennsylvania Supreme Court report that, at the end of 1989, a backlog of 12,199 criminal cases existed, that the average case took 245 days from arrest to final disposition, and that one of the reasons given for the crisis was the plea-bargaining policy in that city).

[99] Schulhofer, Note 90, *supra*, at 1106.

## [B] Is Plea Bargaining Good in Principle?[100]

### [1] In Support of Plea Bargaining

The Supreme Court has described plea bargaining as "not only an essential part of the [criminal justice] process but a highly desirable part."[101] Indeed, although many (perhaps most) legal scholars are critical of plea bargaining, most of the major participants in the system—prosecutors, defense attorneys, and judges—are either "remarkably untroubled" by the process or advocates of it.[102]

First, from the defense perspective, advocates of plea bargaining contend that the negotiation process permits the accused, presumably with the assistance of counsel, to determine rationally whether "the contemplated punishment [arising from a guilty plea] is lower than the anticipated posttrial sentence, discounted by the possibility of acquittal."[103] Particularly if the risk of conviction is great, plea bargaining provides the defendant with an opportunity for minimizing her punishment, legal expenses, and anxiety.[104]

Second, plea bargaining is beneficial to the prosecutor. A prosecutor seeks to obtain the optimum level of punishment—punishment that is retributively just, provides the best deterrent bite, and/or is tailored to the rehabilitative needs of the offender—at the least cost in terms of allocation of resources.[105] In a system in which plea negotiations are permitted, she can determine the foreseeable costs of a trial, the likelihood of conviction,

---

[100] *See generally* Milton Heumann, Plea Bargaining (1978); Albert W. Alschuler, *Personal Failure, Institutional Failure, and the Sixth Amendment*, 14 N.Y.U. Rev. L. & Soc. Change 149 (1986); Albert W. Alschuler, *The Changing Plea Bargaining Debate*, 69 Cal. L. Rev. 652 (1981); Albert W. Alschuler, *The Defense Attorney's Role in Plea Bargaining*, 84 Yale L.J. 1179 (1975); Albert W. Alschuler, *The Prosecutor's Role in Plea Bargaining*, 36 U. Chi. L. Rev. 50 (1968); Gerard V. Bradley, *Plea Bargaining and the Criminal Defendant's Obligation to Plead Guilty*, 40 So. Tex. L. Rev. 65 (1999); Frank H. Easterbrook, *Plea Bargaining as Compromise*, 101 Yale L.J. 1969 (1992); Fisher, Note 73, *supra*; Stephen J. Schulhofer, *Plea Bargaining as Disaster*, 101 Yale L.J. 1979 (1992); Scott & Stuntz, Note 25, *supra*; H. Richard Uviller, *Pleading Guilty: A Critique of Four Models*, 41 Law & Contemp. Probs. 102 (1977); Welsh S. White, *A Proposal for Reform of the Plea Bargaining Process*, 119 U. Pa. L. Rev. 439 (1971); Fred C. Zacharias, *Justice in Plea Bargaining*, 39 Wm. & Mary L. Rev. 1121 (1998).

[101] Santobello v. New York, 404 U.S. 257, 261 (1971).

[102] Scott & Stuntz, Note 25, *supra*, at 1909–10.

[103] Schulhofer, Note 100, *supra*, at 1980 (but ultimately rejecting this argument).

[104] Brady v. United States, 397 U.S. 742, 752 (1970) ("For a defendant who sees slight possibility of acquittal, the advantages of pleading guilty and limiting the probable penalty are obvious—his exposure is reduced, the correctional processes can begin immediately, and the practical burdens of a trial are eliminated.").

[105] Schulhofer, Note 100, *supra*, at 1980.

and the probable sentence disposition, and then use the negotiation process to "fit the crime to the punishment."

Third, as a result of plea negotiations, society more efficiently attains the objectives of criminal punishment, by ensuring that it is more promptly imposed. And, the Supreme Court has suggested, by "the avoidance of trial, scarce judicial and prosecutorial resources are conserved for those cases in which there is a substantial issue of the defendant's guilt or in which there is substantial doubt that the State can sustain its burden of proof."[106] In short, those whose guilt is clearest are bargained out of the trial process, allowing time and energy to go to the more troubling cases. The consequence, advocates of plea bargaining assert, is that the justice system is more reliable.

Defenders of plea bargaining would have us imagine a justice system without it. There would be a huge increase in trials. Very likely, the quality of those trials would decrease dramatically, as over-burdened lawyers and judges seek to keep up with the flood of cases. As a consequence, the trial process would be less reliable than it is today. One can readily expect that, in view of the pressures such a system would place on harried defense lawyers, the higher error rate would result in the conviction of more innocent persons, especially defendants who are compelled by poverty to rely on appointed counsel,[107] even as the overall conviction rate dropped![108]

### [2] In Opposition to Plea Bargaining

### [a] Overview: Serving the Interests of the Powerful?

According to Professor George Fisher, "[l]ike most of history's victors, plea bargaining won in great part because it served the interests of the powerful."[109] Another observer of plea bargaining has put it differently, although it may add up to much the same point: principled support for plea bargaining consists of little more than the "jurisprudence of joy,"[110] in that bargaining is deemed good simply because the process pleases the participants. But, as anti-bargaining scholars point out, the real parties in interest are the defendant and the public (including the crime victim[111]); but their

---

[106] Brady v. United States, 397 U.S. at 752.

[107] Scott and Stuntz, Note 25, *supra*, at 1932–34.

[108] Because more than 90 percent of all convictions today are the result of guilty pleas, the trial conviction rate would have to be exceptionally high to maintain the overall conviction level.

[109] Fisher, Note 73, *supra*, at 859.

[110] Alschuler, *The Changing Plea Bargaining Debate*, Note 100, *supra*, at 683 n.83.

[111] Many victims are distressed when they learn that a bargain has been arranged. Recent

agents—defense lawyers and prosecutors—have goals that are often "far from congruent with those of their principals."[112]

What makes the criticisms of plea bargaining especially interesting is that they come from divergent political and philosophical camps. The "hawks" oppose the process because they believe that it prejudices the crime control interests of the community. The "doves" are concerned with the effects of plea bargaining on the accused's ability to retain her constitutional trial rights.[113]

### [b]  Sentencing Differential

The hawks oppose plea bargaining because, in their view, it results in undue leniency to criminals. The evidence of leniency is overwhelming in this regard: according to the United States Sentencing Commission, in the absence of sentencing guidelines that severely reduce judicial discretion, those who plead guilty are likely to receive a sentence from 30 to 40 percent below that which they would have received had they pleaded not guilty and been convicted at trial of the same offense.[114] Other studies support this conclusion.[115] Therefore, the hawks suggest, many wrongdoers receive a penalty far below that which is retributively justified. Reduced penalties also weaken the deterrent value of punishment.

Dovish critics of plea bargaining also attack the leniency shown defendants, but their sympathies lie with those who do *not* plead guilty. As they view it, plea bargaining unfairly burdens a defendant who chooses to assert her constitutional right to a trial. In essence, the rare defendant who forces the state to prove its case against her is penalized for her actions.

### [c]  Prosecutorial Overcharging

Many critics maintain that prosecutors overcharge defendants. As a result, the deal that a defendant receives during plea negotiations is largely illusory.

---

concern about "victims' rights" has resulted in statutory and state constitutional reforms that sometimes require the parties to consider the wishes of the victim in the resolution of criminal cases. *See generally* George P. Fletcher, With Justice for Some: Victims' Rights in Criminal Trials (1995); LeRoy L. Lamborn, *Victim Participation in the Criminal Justice Process: The Proposals for a Constitutional Amendment*, 34 Wayne L. Rev. 125 (1987); Jeffrie G. Murphy, *Getting Even: The Role of the Victim*, 7 Soc. Phil. & Pol'y 209 (1990); Stephen J. Schulhofer, *The Trouble with Trials; the Trouble with Us*, 105 Yale L.J. 825 (1995); Sarah N. Welling, *Victim Participation in Plea Bargains*, 65 Wash. U.L.Q. 301 (1987).

[112] Schulhofer, Note 100, *supra*, at 1987.

[113] *See* Thomas Church, Jr., *In Defense of "Bargain Justice"*, 13 Law & Soc'y Rev. 509, 510 (1979).

[114] United States Sentencing Commission, Supplemental Report on the Initial Sentencing Guidelines and Policy Statements 48 (1987).

[115] *See* Alschuler, *The Changing Plea Bargaining Debate*, Note 100, *supra*, at 652–56.

According to some observers, prosecutors treat the charging process "like horse trading," in which "both sides start out asking for more than they expect to get."[116] They claim that prosecutors typically divide a criminal transaction into as many offenses as they can and charge them all ("horizontal overcharging"), charge the highest degree of an offense that the evidence could even remotely permit ("vertical overcharging"), or both.

If the evidence does not support the charges filed, it is genuine overcharging. But even if there is sufficient evidence to support the charges, critics of plea bargaining reason that the purpose of the extra or heightened charges is to compel the defendant to participate in the horse trading. Ultimately, if the prosecutor succeeds, the defendant will plead guilty to an offense (or offenses) at least as serious as a jury would have convicted her at trial in a no-bargaining system. Thus, the bargain is illusory: the prosecutor ends up where she should have started or, perhaps, even better off; meanwhile, the defendant has waived her trial rights.

Plea bargaining advocates suggest that if the plea process results in the same outcome as a trial, this is good: we get the same result, just more efficiently. For critics, the point of the argument is that it is wrong in principle to tolerate a system in which defendants are falsely led to believe that society has provided them with a benefit in consideration for which they have waived their constitutional rights.

### [d]　Inadequate Representation

Defense lawyers are supposed to be equalizers. They zealously and loyally defend their clients against the State, supposedly serving as "an antidote to the fear, ignorance, and bewilderment of the impoverished and uneducated defendant."[117] Therefore, whatever chicanery the prosecutor might seek to commit in the plea bargaining process, the defense lawyer is there to prevent it.

Some critics of plea bargaining question whether the quality of representation of defendants in the bargaining process merits this optimistic, even romantic, view.[118] They suggest that defense attorneys, like other people, desire money. For a private defense attorney, there are two ways to become financially successful: develop a reputation as a high-quality trial attorney; or do a high-volume business. The latter approach is the path of least resistance. But, to handle large quantities of cases, a defense lawyer must

---

[116] Alschuler, *The Prosecutor's Role. . .*, Note 100, *supra*, at 85. Prosecutors nearly universally deny that their initial charges are inflated. *Id.*

[117] Alschuler, *The Defense Attorney's Role. . .*, Note 100, *supra*, at 1179.

[118] *See especially id.* at 1181–1270; Alschuler, *Personal Failure. . .*, Note 100, *supra*. The ideas expressed in this subsection come largely from these two articles.

try very few of them. In short, private defense attorneys too often become "pleaders." The result is that defendants receive misleading advice, or they are unduly influenced to plead guilty by their own attorneys.

Second, even the most ethical but fatigued and overwhelmed public defender, forced to deal with huge caseloads, is apt to rely too heavily on plea bargaining. Third, public defenders have an incentive to cooperate with the prosecutors with whom they deal on a daily basis; the result is that bargaining is not always in the best interests of an individual client.

Finally, lawyers, like others, do not like to be wrong, and the decision to plead guilty is never wrong, in the sense that there is no way to determine whether the client would have been acquitted or received a more lenient penalty had she proceeded to trial. In contrast, a lawyer's recommendation *not* to plead guilty can prove to be wrong, if the defendant is convicted and receives a more severe sentence than was offered by the prosecutor. Therefore, a bias exists to accept a guilty plea.[119]

### [e]  Conviction of the Innocent

Incompetent representation, noted above, enhances the risk that an innocent person will be convicted. But, critics believe that lawful plea bargaining, *i.e.*, bargaining that courts do not consider coercive, often places too much pressure on defendants—even those competently represented—especially those who are risk-averse. As a result, there is an enhanced possibility that innocent persons will plead guilty.

Consider this anecdote:[120] *D* was charged with kidnapping and forcible rape, punishable by life imprisonment. *D* continually asserted his innocence to his lawyer, and the case against him was so weak that his counsel was confident of acquittal at trial. However, the prosecutor (aware of the weakness of the case) offered *D* a deal: he would drop the rape and kidnapping charges in exchange for a guilty plea to simple battery, a thirty-day misdemeanor. Over the lawyer's objections, the defendant pleaded guilty, saying "I can't take the chance." Whether or not this story, reported as accurate, is true, the critics' point is made: a defendant who is innocent can be lawfully pressured to plead guilty as a result of hard bargaining by a prosecutor.

Advocates of plea bargaining might defend the outcome in the latter case on the ground that innocent persons are not necessarily exonerated at trial and, therefore, it is appropriate to give a defendant the opportunity to choose

---

[119] Advocates of plea bargaining do not necessarily deny the validity of the critics' concerns about the quality of defense representation. However, they believe that a no-bargaining system would aggravate the problem. *See* the text to Notes 107–108 *supra*.

[120] Alschuler, *The Prosecutor's Role. . .*, Note 100, *supra*, at 61.

whether to take the risk. Moreover, they might maintain, there is a greater risk to innocent defendants in a system in which every case goes to trial, but in a haphazard manner.[121]

## § 31.07    Plea Bargaining: Broken Deals and Withdrawn Offers

### [A]    Broken Deals

Once plea negotiations result in an agreement, the parties are expected to abide by their promises. In *Santobello v. New York*,[122] the Supreme Court announced that when a guilty plea rests in significant part "on a promise or agreement of the prosecutor, so that it can be said to be part of the inducement or consideration, such promise must be fulfilled." Indeed, *Santobello* teaches, a governmental breach of a plea agreement has constitutional overtones.

In *Santobello*, a prosecutor, in exchange for a guilty plea by *D*, agreed to make no sentencing recommendation before the judge. *D* pleaded guilty. Months later at the sentencing hearing, in violation of the agreement, a different prosecutor sought the maximum sentence, which the judge imposed. In view of the breach of the agreement, *D* sought, unsuccessfully, to vacate his plea.

The Supreme Court unanimously agreed that the prosecutor wronged *D*. However, Chief Justice Warren Burger, who delivered the opinion of the Court, failed to state what constitutional right was violated by the prosecutor's actions. Nor did he indicate what remedy ought to be granted in cases of breach. The Chief Justice stated only that in "the interests of justice" the case should be remanded to the state court to determine what relief should be granted. He suggested two possibilities: the trial court could require specific performance of the agreement, or it could grant the relief sought by *D*, namely, to vacate the plea and permit him to plead anew to the original charge.[123]

The Supreme Court attached a constitutional justification to the *Santobello* rule in *Mabry v. Johnson*.[124] In *Mabry*, the Court explained that the holding in *Santobello* was based on the proposition that a plea may be challenged under the due process clause "when it develops that the

---

[121] *See* the text to Notes 107–108, *supra*.

[122] 404 U.S. 257 (1971).

[123] Justices Marshall, Brennan and Stewart concurred in part and dissented in part. They would have required the trial court to permit *D* to withdraw his guilty plea, since that was his motion. Justice Douglas, who concurred, stated that "a court ought to accord a defendant's preference considerable, if not controlling weight" when the prosecutor breaches a deal.

[124] 467 U.S. 504 (1984).

defendant was not fairly apprised of its consequences." In other words, when a defendant pleads guilty on the basis of a promise that the prosecutor subsequently breaks, the effect of the unfulfilled promise is to render the plea invalid because it was based on "a false premise," and thus was not intelligently made.

Of course, a defendant is not entitled to relief unless there has been a breach of the agreement, and it is not always clear whether an agreement has been violated. Courts often look at plea agreements the way they would analyze any contract.[125] And, as is evident from *United States v. Benchimol*,[126] defense counsel should seek to have all aspects of a deal expressly and clearly set out if she wishes to have a remedy under *Santobello*. In *Benchimol*, the prosecutor agreed to recommend probation. At the sentencing hearing, defense counsel told the judge that the prosecutor agreed to recommend probation. In support of probation, the prosecutor said only, "That is an accurate representation [of the arrangement.]" The Court concluded that the government did not commit itself "enthusiastically" to make a particular recommendation. In short, the defendant got what he bargained for.

In especially complicated or unusual cases, a defendant may even want counsel to include an express provision mandating judicial construction of a plea agreement, in the event that the parties dispute the meaning of a provision. This is the lesson of *Ricketts v. Adamson*.[127] In *Ricketts*, *D* was charged with first-degree murder, but agreed to plead guilty to second-degree murder, in exchange for his promise to testify against his co-defendants. The agreement further provided that if *D* did not testify, the agreement was "null and void and the original charge will be *automatically* reinstated."

*D* testified, as promised, and his confederates were convicted. However, their convictions were overturned, and *D* refused to testify at their second trial. As a consequence, the government sought to vacate *D*'s second-degree murder conviction and reinstate the first-degree charge. The state supreme court granted the government's motion after it determined that the plea agreement contemplated that *D* would testify at any retrial (although this was not expressly stated in the arrangement). Once the state court so ruled, *D* agreed to testify against his colleagues, but the prosecutor (claiming a breach) chose to proceed with the first-degree murder prosecution. The United States Supreme Court let the conviction and death penalty stand.

---

[125] *See* United States v. Harvey, 791 F.2d 294 (4th Cir. 1986) (stating that contract law is applicable when a court must interpret ambiguities in a plea agreement).

[126] 471 U.S. 453 (1985).

[127] 483 U.S. 1 (1987).

## [B]  Withdrawn Offers

Although the government may not constitutionally violate a provision of a plea agreement after a defendant pleads guilty, it may permissibly revoke an offer, even after a defense acceptance, at least if there has been no detrimental reliance on the offer.

For example, in *Mabry v. Johnson*,[128] a prosecutor offered, in exchange for a guilty plea, to recommend a sentence of 21 years, to be served concurrently with other sentences already being served by *D*. After *D* accepted the offer, the prosecutor told *D*'s counsel that he had misspoken, and that he had intended to recommend a sentence of 21 years to be served *consecutively* with the other sentences. *D* rejected this new offer and elected to stand trial, but later changed his mind and pleaded guilty on the basis of the prosecutor's second offer.

*D* appealed. He argued that he was entitled to specific performance of the original deal. The Supreme Court disagreed. Unlike a case in which a prosecutor fails to live up to a promise *after* a guilty plea is entered, the guilty plea here was intelligently made, because *D* knew the conditions of the bargain (*i.e.*, that the prosecutor would recommend consecutive, not concurrent, sentences) when he pleaded guilty. Therefore, no constitutional violation occurred. Even if the prosecutor was negligent in making and withdrawing the original offer, the Court said that the due process clause "is not a code of ethics for prosecutors."

## § 31.08  Prosecutorial and Judicial Vindictiveness[129]

### [A]  Explanation of the Issue

Consider the facts in *State v. Halling*:[130] The prosecutor made a plea offer to *D* through his counsel. *D*'s lawyer informed the prosecutor that his client wished to go to trial rather than to plead guilty, and he informed her to expect "three or four days of [pre-trial] motions." The prosecutor then informed counsel, "I have a brilliant idea. I have just thought of a way to cause further evil to [your] poor [client]." She explained that, unless *D* accepted her original plea offer, she intended to charge *D* with additional crimes. Assuming that she did so, did the prosecutor act improperly?

The facts demonstrate a tension in the law. On the one hand, the law affords prosecutors substantial discretion in determining whether to

---

[128] 467 U.S. 504 (1984).

[129] *See generally* Note, *Breathing New Life Into Prosecutorial Vindictiveness Doctrine*, 114 Harv. L. Rev. 2074 (2001).

[130] 672 P.2d 1386 (Or. Ct. App. 1983).

prosecute and what charges to bring.[131] The law also tolerates, and even encourages, plea bargaining. Arguably, the prosecutor's actions in this case constituted tough, but lawful, bargaining.

On the other hand, with substantial discretion comes the power to abuse. A prosecutor might be severe for inappropriate reasons. In the *Halling* case, for example, the prosecutor's decision to "up the ante" might have been a vindictive response on her part to *D*'s unwillingness to accept her plea offer. She may have punished *D* for his insistence on his constitutional right to go to trial.

This chapter section considers the extent to which a due process clause "vindictiveness defense" is recognized in circumstances such as those in *Halling*. However, to understand the law on this subject, one must also consider prosecutorial vindictiveness more generally, *i.e.*, outside the plea-bargaining context. Furthermore, the law regarding prosecutorial vindictiveness is an off-shoot of a separate, but not entirely independent, line of Supreme Court cases pertaining to judicial vindictiveness. The issue of judicial vindictiveness is also considered here.

The early holdings of the Supreme Court in the vindictiveness area were broad and, apparently, sweeping in nature. The Court has narrowed the scope of the rules in both lines of cases. Therefore, the reader must consider the narrower version of the rules (subsection [C]), in light of the original ones (subsection [B]).

### [B] The Original Vindictiveness Rules

#### [1] Judicial Vindictiveness: The *Pearce* Principle

In *North Carolina v. Pearce*,[132] *D* successfully appealed his conviction for assault with intent to rape on the ground that his confession was improperly admitted against him at trial. On retrial, *D* was convicted again, but the judge at the second trial imposed a more severe prison sentence than was handed out after the first trial.

The Supreme Court held that a judge may not punish a defendant for successfully appealing a conviction by imposing a more severe sentence after a second trial and conviction. According to *Pearce*, due process "requires that vindictiveness against a defendant for having successfully attacked his first conviction must play no part in the sentence he receives

---

[131] *See generally* Richard S. Frase, *The Decision to File Federal Criminal Charges: A Quantitative Study of Prosecutorial Discretion*, 47 U. Chi. L. Rev. 246 (1980); John Kaplan, *The Prosecutorial Discretion—A Comment*, 60 Nw. U. L. Rev. 174 (1965); Wayne R. LaFave, *The Prosecutor's Discretion in The United States*, 18 Am. J. Comp. L. 532 (1970).

[132] 395 U.S. 711 (1969).

after a new trial." Moreover, since fear of vindictiveness may deter a defendant from exercising his right to appeal, "due process also requires that a defendant be freed of apprehension of such a retaliatory motivation on the part of the sentencing judge."

In order to deter judicial vindictiveness, the Court held in *Pearce* that a judge may not impose a more severe sentence upon a defendant after a new trial unless the reasons for doing so appear on the record and are "based upon objective information concerning identifiable conduct on the part of the defendant occurring after the time of the original sentencing proceeding." For example, applying *Pearce*, a court *may* impose a more severe penalty after a second trial if, after the first sentencing hearing, the defendant committed another crime and thereby demonstrated her heightened dangerousness. But the trial court may *not* impose a more severe penalty on the basis of new evidence introduced at the second trial regarding the defendant's involvement in the original crime.

## [2]   Prosecutorial Vindictiveness: The *Blackledge* Principle

In *Blackledge v. Perry*,[133] the Supreme Court applied the principles of *North Carolina v. Pearce*[134] to a case involving alleged prosecutorial vindictiveness. In *Blackledge*, D was convicted of assault with a deadly weapon, a misdemeanor, in a court with jurisdiction over misdemeanor prosecutions only. D exercised his right under state law to a trial *de novo* in a superior court. Prior to the second trial, the prosecutor sought and obtained a new indictment charging D with assault with a deadly weapon with the intent to kill, a felony.

D did not produce evidence that the prosecutor's motivation for seeking the higher charge was to punish him for exercising his statutory right to a new trial. Nonetheless, the Supreme Court concluded that the *Pearce* rationale—that a defendant should be free from the apprehension of retaliation for exercising a constitutional or statutory right—applied to these facts. Under *Blackledge*, a prosecutor may not bring a more serious charge after a defendant has been once tried and convicted.

This rule is not absolute, but *Blackledge* seemed to permit only a narrow exception. In a footnote, the *Blackledge* Court observed that "[t]his would clearly be a different case if the State had shown that it was impossible to proceed on the more serious charge at the outset." It gave an example: if the defendant were originally charged with battery, but prior to the second trial the victim died from his wounds, the prosecutor could charge the defendant with criminal homicide.

---

[133] 417 U.S. 21 (1974).

[134] 395 U.S. 711 (1969).

### [C] The Supreme Court Narrows the Vindictiveness Rules

### [1] *Pearce-Blackledge* Becomes a Rebuttable Presumption

The Supreme Court no longer treats the *Pearce-Blackledge*[135] rules as constitutional doctrine applicable in all cases of enhanced sentences or charges. Instead, the rules of these cases are now treated as prophylactic rules,[136] intended to prevent due process violations. That is, as the Court now explains the *Pearce-Blackledge* doctrine,[137] the Constitution is not violated unless an enhanced sentence or charge is motivated by *actual* vindictiveness toward the defendant for having exercised a constitutional or statutory right.

*Pearce* and *Blackledge* only create a rebuttable presumption of vindictiveness. This presumption is applied in those circumstances in which its objectives are "most efficaciously served,"[138] namely in those circumstances in which "there is a 'reasonable likelihood' . . . that the increase in sentence [or charge] is the product of actual vindictiveness . . . . Where there is no such reasonable likelihood, the burden remains upon the defendant to prove actual vindictiveness."[139] In other words, the due process clause *does* prohibit actual vindictiveness in judicial sentencing and prosecutorial charging; if a defendant can prove that she was the victim of such vindictiveness, due process requires that the enhanced penalty or charge be voided. However, only in *some* circumstances will the Supreme Court now *presume* such vindictiveness and require the government to rebut the presumption.

Therefore, it is now necessary to determine two matters in any alleged vindictiveness case. First, does the *Pearce-Blackledge* presumption apply? Second, if it does, did the government overcome the presumption? (If the presumption doesn't apply, the defendant is still free to prove actual vindictiveness, but the burden is on her.) These questions are discussed immediately below.

---

[135] North Carolina v. Pearce, 395 U.S. 711 (1969); Blackledge v. Perry, 417 U.S. 21 (1974).

[136] For discussion of the significance of identifying a rule as "prophylactic," *see* § 4.05, *supra.*

[137] *See especially* United States v. Goodwin, 457 U.S. 368 (1982); Texas v. McCullough, 475 U.S. 134 (1986); Alabama v. Smith, 490 U.S. 794 (1989).

[138] Texas v. McCullough, 475 U.S. at 138.

[139] Alabama v. Smith, 490 U.S. at 799–800.

## [2]    When Does the Presumption Apply?

### [a]    Judicial Vindictiveness

The presumption of judicial vindictiveness applies in those circumstances in which there is a reasonable likelihood that an increase in sentence was the result of vindictiveness. The Court has suggested various circumstances in which a "reasonable likelihood" is *not* present.

First, the presumption of judicial vindictiveness does not apply if the second sentence is imposed by a different sentencer than was involved at the first trial. This is the case if: the second sentence was imposed by a different-level court than at the original trial;[140] the first sentencer was a jury and the second one was a judge;[141] two different juries imposed the sentences;[142] or, probably, if the sentencers were different trial judges.[143]

Second, the presumption of vindictiveness does not apply, even if the same sentencer is involved, if the original (and lesser) sentence was imposed after a guilty plea. In *Alabama v. Smith*,[144] *D* pleaded guilty to charges of burglary and rape, was sentenced, but later succeeded in vacating his plea. Thereafter he pleaded not guilty, was convicted, and received a more severe sentence from the same judge. The Court held that a presumption of vindictiveness does not apply in these circumstances: the likely reason for any increase in sentence is that "the relevant sentencing information available to a judge after the plea will usually be considerably less than that available after a trial."

Third, and more generally, the presumption does not apply if special circumstances in the case suggest that there is no reasonable likelihood that the increase in sentence was the result of vindictiveness. For example, in *Texas v. McCullough*,[145] after a conviction, the trial judge granted *D*'s motion for a new trial based on prosecutorial misconduct. In view of the judge's favorable ruling on *D*'s motion, which indicated that he was not

---

[140] Colten v. Kentucky, 407 U.S. 104 (1972) (first trial was held in a misdemeanor county court; *D* was retried in a superior court of general criminal jurisdiction).

[141] Texas v. McCullough, 475 U.S. 134 (1986).

[142] Chaffin v. Stynchcombe, 412 U.S. 17 (1973).

[143] *See* Texas v. McCullough, 475 U.S. at 140 n.3. *Pearce* involved two different judges, but the *McCullough* Court suggested that this fact "may not have been drawn to the [*Pearce*] Court's attention . . . ." Therefore, it stated, "[w]e . . . decline to read *Pearce* as governing this issue." At least one state court has held that, notwithstanding *McCullough*, a presumption of vindictiveness is required under the state due process clause when the second, and more severe, sentence is imposed by a different trial judge. People v. Van Pelt, 556 N.E.2d 423 (N.Y. 1990).

[144] 490 U.S. 794 (1989).

[145] 475 U.S. 134 (1986).

hostile to $D$'s wishes for a second trial, the Supreme Court concluded that the possibility of vindictiveness in the sentencing after the second trial was too speculative to require the operation of the presumption. This conclusion was reinforced by the fact that $D$ chose to be sentenced by the judge in the second trial; $D$ did not invoke his statutory right to be sentenced by the jury.

### [b] Prosecutorial Vindictiveness

The Supreme Court has narrowed the scope of the *Blackledge v. Perry*[146] prosecutorial vindictiveness rule. In *Bordenkircher v. Hayes*,[147] the Court refused to apply the presumption in the context of pretrial plea bargaining.

In *Bordenkircher*, a prosecutor obtained an indictment of $D$ for uttering a forged instrument, a felony carrying a two-to-ten year prison sentence. In plea negotiations, the prosecutor offered to recommend a five-year prison sentence if $D$ would plead guilty, but he also told $D$'s counsel that if his client did not plead guilty, he would return to the grand jury and seek a new indictment of $D$, a prior two-time felon, under the state's habitual offender law. Under that law, $D$ was subject to a maximum sentence of life imprisonment for the present offense.

$D$ refused to plead guilty. The prosecutor went through with his threat and secured a new indictment charging $D$ with violation of the state's recidivist law. After a jury found $D$ guilty, he was sentenced to life imprisonment on the basis of his two prior felonies.

The Supreme Court distinguished *Blackledge*, which involved a "unilateral imposition of a penalty upon a defendant who had chosen to exercise a legal right to attack his original conviction," from the present situation, which the *Bordenkircher* Court described as the "give-and-take negotiation common in plea bargaining." In short, whereas the defendant in *Blackledge* was arguably punished for seeking a trial *de novo*, the defendant in *Bordenkircher* was merely the "victim" of hard pretrial plea bargaining.

The Supreme Court took the *Bordenkircher* exception to *Blackledge* a step further in *United States v. Goodwin*,[148] when it apparently placed the entire pretrial setting outside the scope of the *Blackledge* presumption. *Goodwin* did not involve the give-and-take of plea bargaining. Instead, $D$ was charged with misdemeanor assault, after which he advised the prosecutor that he desired a trial by jury, which necessitated transferring the case to a higher court and to a different prosecutor.[149] The new prosecutor

---

[146] 417 U.S. 21 (1974).

[147] 434 U.S. 357 (1978).

[148] 457 U.S. 368 (1982).

[149] Does the fact that a second prosecutor was involved take the case outside the *Black-*

obtained a new indictment based on the same incident, and charged *D* with the more serious offense of assault on a federal officer, a felony.

The Court distinguished *Blackledge* from the pre-trial setting of the present case on the ground that *Blackledge* involved a defendant's exercise of a right that "caused a complete retrial after he had been once tried and convicted." The Court reasoned that the "deep-seated bias" against retrial of issues creates "institutional pressures" that support a presumption of prosecutorial vindictiveness; such pressures are absent, the Court concluded, in the pretrial context.

### [3]   How May the Presumption Be Rebutted?

### [a]   Judicial Vindictiveness

The Supreme Court stated in dictum in *Texas v. McCullough*[150] that, notwithstanding language in *North Carolina v. Pearce*,[151] the presumption of judicial vindictiveness may be overcome on the basis of *any* objective information that justifies an increased sentence, including information relating to a defendant's conduct that occurred *before* the original sentencing proceeding. For example, it is now permissible for a judge to consider new evidence introduced at a second trial that demonstrates a defendant's greater involvement in the criminal enterprise; or she may consider evidence, not previously disclosed, of a defendant's dangerousness, although the evidence relates to conduct of the defendant that preceded the first trial.

As the Court conceded, the effect of *McCullough* is to eviscerate the *Pearce* rule because "a defendant may be more reluctant to appeal if there is a risk that new, probative evidence supporting a longer sentence may be revealed on retrial." The Court stated, however, that this "chilling effect" is not "sufficient reason to create a constitutional prohibition against considering relevant information in assessing sentences."

### [b]   Prosecutorial Vindictiveness

In *Blackledge v. Perry*,[152] the Court indicated that a prosecutor could rebut the presumption of vindictiveness in limited circumstances, namely, when the government could show that "it was impossible to proceed on the more serious charge at the outset."

---

*ledge* presumption, just as the *Pearce* presumption is now inapplicable in the case of different sentencers? *See* § 31.08[C][2][a], *supra. Goodwin* did not answer that question. However, in Thigpen v. Roberts, 468 U.S. 27 (1984), the Court held that the presumption is not inapplicable merely because of an addition in the prosecutorial team. The Court left open "the correct rule when two independent prosecutors are involved."

[150] 475 U.S. 134 (1986).

[151] 395 U.S. 711 (1969).

[152] 417 U.S. 21 (1974).

In *United States v. Goodwin*,[153] the Court described somewhat more broadly the method by which the presumption may be rebutted. The Court stated that it "could be overcome by objective evidence [in the record] justifying the prosecutor's action." Ambiguously, though, it then quoted the original, narrower language from *Blackledge*, which may imply that the Court in *Goodwin* did not intend to change the rule.

The Supreme Court has not decided a due process case in which a prosecutor has sought to overcome a presumption of vindictiveness. However, if a presumption of *judicial* vindictiveness may now be overcome on the basis of any objective information of non-vindictiveness, it is reasonable to assume that the Court will permit prosecutorial rebuttal on a similar basis.

---

[153] 457 U.S. 368, 376 n.8 (1982).

CHAPTER **32**

# DOUBLE JEOPARDY

## § 32.01  General Principles[1]

### [A]  Constitutional Text

#### [1]  In General

The Fifth Amendment provides that no person shall "be subject for the same offence to be twice put in jeopardy of life or limb." This provision, the so-called "double jeopardy clause," has roots in Greek and Roman law, as well as in English canon and common law.[2] The concept of double jeopardy "although not universal, is part of Western legal heritage, explicitly enshrined in the law of many countries."[3] The double jeopardy prohibition is a fundamental right applicable to the states through the Fourteenth Amendment due process clause.[4]

#### [2]  "In Jeopardy"

For double jeopardy purposes, a person is not "in jeopardy" of life or limb until the jury is empaneled and sworn[5] or, in a bench trial, until the first witness is sworn.[6] Consequently, the prosecutor is not constitutionally barred from appealing a pretrial dismissal of criminal charges against a defendant or from refiling charges against him, even if a court's ruling was based on the evidence that would have been introduced at trial.[7]

---

[1] *See generally* George C. Thomas III, Double Jeopardy: The History, the Law (1998); Martin L. Friedland, Double Jeopardy (1969); Akhil Reed Amar, *Double Jeopardy Law Made Simple*, 106 Yale L.J. 1807 (1997); Susan R. Klein, *Double Jeopardy's Demise*, 88 Calif. L. Rev. 1001 (2000); George C. Thomas III, *An Elegant Theory of Double Jeopardy*, 1988 U. Ill. L. Rev. 827; Peter Westen, *The Three Faces of Double Jeopardy: Reflections on Government Appeals of Criminal Sentences*, 78 Mich. L. Rev. 1001 (1980); Peter Westen & Richard Drubel, *Toward a General Theory of Double Jeopardy*, 1978 Sup. Ct. Rev. 81.

[2] Friedland, Note 1, *supra*, at 5–15.

[3] Thomas, *Elegant Theory*, Note 1, *supra*, at 837.

[4] Benton v. Maryland, 395 U.S. 784 (1969).

[5] Crist v. Bretz, 437 U.S. 28 (1978).

[6] Serfass v. United States, 420 U.S. 377 (1975).

[7] *Id.*

### [3] "Of Life or Limb"

### [a] Generally

The Fifth Amendment provides that a defendant may not be twice placed in jeopardy "of life or limb" for the "same offence."[8] Notwithstanding this life-or-limb language, the Court long ago held that the double jeopardy clause applies to *all* crimes, including those offenses for which the only potential punishment is a monetary fine.[9]

### [b] Civil versus Criminal Proceedings and Penalties[10]

A legislature "may impose both a criminal and a civil sanction in respect to the same act or omission; for the double jeopardy clause prohibits merely punishing twice, or attempting a second time to punish criminally, for the same offense."[11] Therefore, *D* may be subjected to a civil suit, and a civil sanction imposed on him, even if he was previously criminally prosecuted and punished for the same conduct.

This does mean, however, that the government may escape the dictates of the Fifth Amendment merely by denominating a proceeding as "civil." For example, the Supreme Court ruled in *Breed v. Jones*[12] that a youth may not be prosecuted in a criminal court for conduct that was the basis of a previous juvenile court proceeding because—notwithstanding "the 'civil' label-of-convenience which has been attached to juvenile proceedings"—a finding of delinquency can result in the youth's loss of liberty and stigmatization, consequences similar to a criminal conviction.

As might be expected, the Supreme Court and lower courts have struggled drawing a line between civil and criminal proceedings and, most especially,

---

[8] For the definition of "same offence," *see* § 32.07, *infra.*

[9] *See* Ex parte Lange, 85 U.S. (18 Wall.) 163 (1873); Amar, Note 1, *supra,* at 1810–11 (concluding that as long as one rejects constitutional "hyperliteralism" in favor of "faithful textualism," which "also attend[s] to the apparent purpose and logic of a given [constitutional] clause," the "life or limb" "imagery should obviously apply to imprisonment and all serious criminal punishments and should probably apply to petty criminal punishments (including criminal fines which, by their inherently stigmatic nature as 'criminal' sanctions, rob a man of his good name as well as his purse by branding him a 'criminal' "). For an argument, relying on the history of "life or limb," that the double jeopardy clause should apply only to offenses that authorize incarceration, *see* George C. Thomas III, *A Modest Proposal to Save the Double Jeopardy Clause,* 69 Wash. U. L.Q. 195, 208–20 (1991).

[10] *See generally* Carol S. Steiker, *Punishment and Procedure: Punishment Theory and the Criminal-Civil Procedural Divide,* 85 Geo. L.J. 775 (1997); Kenneth Mann, *Punitive Civil Sanctions: The Middleground Between Criminal and Civil Law,* 101 Yale L.J. 1795 (1992).

[11] Helvering v. Mitchell, 303 U.S. 391, 399 (1938).

[12] 421 U.S. 519 (1975).

between civil and criminal penalties for purposes of the double jeopardy clause. In *Hudson v. United States*,[13] the Supreme Court announced a two-step approach to the question. According to *Hudson*, "[w]hether a particular punishment is criminal or civil is, at least initially, a matter of statutory construction." The first question, therefore, is "whether the legislature 'in establishing the penalizing mechanism, indicated either expressly or impliedly a preference for one label or the other.' "[14]

Even if a legislature labels a penalty as civil, *Hudson* provides that a court must inquire "'whether the statutory scheme was so punitive either in purpose or effect' as to 'transform what was clearly intended as a civil remedy into a criminal penalty.'" In making this latter (second step) determination, the *Hudson* Court stated that factors listed in *Kennedy v. Mendoza-Martinez*[15] provided "useful guideposts":

[1] Whether the sanction involves an affirmative disability or restraint; [2] whether it has historically been regarded as a punishment; [3] whether it comes into play only on a finding of *scienter*; [4] whether its operation will promote the traditional aims of punishment—retribution and deterrence; [5] whether the behavior to which it applies is already a crime; [6] whether an alternative purpose to which it may rationally be connected is assignable for it; and [7] whether it appears excessive in relation to the alternative purpose assigned.

*Hudson* warned that "these factors must be considered in relation to the statute on its face" and that " 'only the clearest proof' will suffice to override legislative intent and transform what has been denominated a civil remedy into a criminal penalty." In light of this language in *Hudson*, there will rarely be a case in which imposition of a monetary penalty will bar a later criminal prosecution on the basis of double jeopardy.[16] For example, in *Hudson*, the Court held that the double jeopardy clause did not bar the government from, first, imposing monetary penalties on defendants for violating federal banking statutes and, later, prosecuting them for essentially the same conduct. The penalties were expressly denominated as civil (the first step

---

[13] 522 U.S. 93 (1997).

[14] *Id.* at 99 (quoting United States v. Ward, 448 U.S. 242, 248 (1980)).

[15] 372 U.S. 144, 168–169 (1963) (a non-double jeopardy case involving a statute that stripped a citizen of citizenship as a penalty for draft evasion; held: the statute was penal in nature, consequently requiring that the defendant be provided assistance to counsel and other criminal trial rights).

[16] This is not to say that a civil scheme could not be attacked on other constitutional grounds. *Hudson* noted that sanctions that are "downright irrational" could be challenged on equal protection or due process grounds, or the ground that they violate the Eighth Amendment bar on excessive fines.

of the analysis); and, taking the second step and considering the "guide-posts" listed above, the Court found "little evidence, much less the clearest proof" that the penalties were "punitive in form and effect."

The Supreme Court has also made it nearly impossible to contest civil forfeitures on the basis of double jeopardy. In *United States v. Ursery*[17] the Court ruled that the federal government could punish *D* in a criminal proceeding for violating a drug offense and then require him in a civil proceeding to forfeit assets linked to the drug crime. The *Ursery* Court observed that "[s]ince the earliest years of this Nation, Congress has authorized the Government to seek parallel *in rem* civil forfeiture actions and criminal prosecutions based upon the same underlying events." Indeed, numerous federal and state laws permit an individual to be prosecuted for a criminal offense and, simultaneously or after the criminal trial, have real or personal property linked to the criminal conduct subjected to civil forfeiture. The *Ursery* Court stated that "in a long line of cases, this Court has considered the application of the Double Jeopardy Clause to civil forfeitures, consistently concluding that the Clause does not apply to such actions because they do not impose punishment."

*Ursery* did not categorically rule out the possibility that a civil forefiture could be deemed penal. The Court stated in a footnote:

> That a forfeiture is designated as civil by Congress [or a state] and proceeds *in rem* establishes a presumption that it is not subject to double jeopardy. . . . Nevertheless, where the 'clearest proof' indicates that an *in rem* civil forfeiture is 'so punitive either in purpose or effect' as to be equivalent to a criminal proceeding, that forfeiture may be subject to the Double Jeopardy Clause.[18]

Such clear proof was not present in *Ursery*.[19] The Court pointed to various nonpunitive purposes of the drug forfeiture law: to encourage "property owners to take care in managing their property," to guarantee that property will not be used for illegal purposes, and to ensure that law violators do not profit from their misdeeds. These criteria, of course, would justify nearly any civil forfeiture scheme.

---

[17] 518 U.S. 267 (1996).

[18] *Id.* at 289–90 n.3 (quoting United States v. One Assortment of 89 Firearms, 465 U.S. 354, 365 (1984)).

[19] *But see* State v. Nunez, 2 P.3d 264 (N.M. 1999) (applying the state constitution, the court rejected the "clearest proof" requirement of *Ursery*; stated that the court should not accord any special deference to the legislature's intent for this purpose; and held that civil forfeiture of property associated with criminal drug offenses constitutes "punishment" for purposes of double jeopardy analysis).

## [B] "Dual Sovereignty" Doctrine[20]

Conduct may simultaneously constitute a violation of federal and state law. For example, the unprovoked act of *D* striking *V*, a federal officer, constitutes the federal offense of assault upon a federal officer,[21] and a state offense, such as simple assault or battery. Or, as was seen in the police beating of Rodney King in Los Angeles,[22] the actions of the officers there were chargeable with the state offenses of assault with a deadly weapon and excessive use of force by a police officer, and the federal crime[23] of violating the constitutional rights of King. As well, robbery of a federally insured bank—which is virtually any bank today—constitutes a violation of state and federal law.

Likewise, a single act may constitute a violation of criminal statutes in more than one state. For example, if *D*, while standing in state X, shoots and kills *V*, who is standing across the border in state Y, both states may claim jurisdiction to prosecute the homicide. Or, a multijurisdictional conspiracy could easily violate conspiracy laws in multiple states.

The same conduct may also simultaneously violate a state law and a local ordinance. For example, if *D* steals a painting attached to a wall in a city building, this act may constitute theft under state law and larceny of city property under a local ordinance.

In *United States v. Lanza*,[24] the Supreme Court announced the dual sovereignty doctrine, which provides that "an act denounced as a crime by both national and state sovereignties is an offense against the peace and dignity of both and may be [prosecuted and] punished by each." In effect, prosecutions under laws of separate sovereigns are prosecutions of different offenses, not reprosecutions of the "same offense." Therefore, it is permissible for the federal government to prosecute a defendant after a state prosecution of the same conduct,[25] or vice-versa,[26] regardless of the outcome of the first prosecution.

---

[20] *See generally* Akhil Reed Amar & Jonathan L. Marcus, *Double Jeopardy Law After Rodney King*, 95 Colum. L. Rev. 1, 4–27 (1995); Sandra Guerra, *The Myth of Dual Sovereignty: Multijurisdictional Drug Law Enforcement and Double Jeopardy*, 73 N.C. L. Rev. 1159 (1995).

[21] 18 U.S.C. § 111 (1996).

[22] For a brief summary of the facts in the case, with emphasis on the federal prosecution, *see* Koon v. United States, 518 U.S. 81 (1996).

[23] 18 U.S.C. § 242 (1996).

[24] 260 U.S. 377 (1922).

[25] Abbate v. United States, 359 U.S. 187 (1959).

[26] Bartkus v. Illinois, 359 U.S. 121 (1959).

The doctrine applies as well to dual state prosecutions. For example, *D* may be prosecuted for a single homicide in states X and Y, assuming that both states have adequate ties to the event to claim jurisdiction. The Fifth Amendment is not violated in such circumstances, even in the extreme case that the second prosecution is brought to secure the death penalty after the defendant received a lesser penalty for the same homicide in another state.[27]

However, a city is considered a subordinate instrumentality of the state in which it is located. Therefore, it is not an independent sovereign for purposes of the double jeopardy clause. Consequently, successive municipality and state prosecutions for the same offense ordinarily are barred.

The dual sovereignty doctrine is controversial. From a policy perspective, the doctrine may be justified on the ground that it is needed to vindicate federal interests. Thus, during the 1950s and 1960s civil rights era, when a state jury acquitted a defendant of murder or assault upon a civil rights worker, the federal government was still free to prosecute based on the same incident; likewise, the federal courts were not barred from prosecuting the police officers in the Rodney King beating after their state acquittal by a Los Angeles area jury.

Even if this feature of dual sovereignty is justifiable, it can hardly justify a federal prosecution after a state *conviction,* and the doctrine of federal supremacy arguably is threatened if a state can prosecute for an offense, based on the same conduct, after a federal acquittal.[28] Moreover as one scholar has pointed out,[29] federal and state prosecutors today often participate in multijurisdictional law enforcement efforts (*e.g.*, in drug cases); thus the argument that there are separate interests to vindicate is often a fiction.

Finally, from a defendant's personal perspective—for example, if States X and Y prosecute *D* for the same homicide—the dual sovereignty rule *seems* to authorize multiple prosecutions for the same offense. The doctrine is little more than "definitional formalism."[30] To the extent that the purpose of the double jeopardy clause is, in considerable part, to protect persons accused of crime from the anxiety, expense, and ordeal of dual prosecutions for the same offense,[31] the doctrine seems to exalt form over substance.

---

[27] Heath v. Alabama, 474 U.S. 82 (1985).

[28] Amar & Marcus, Note 20, *supra*, at 8.

[29] Guerra, Note 20, *supra*, at 1209.

[30] Amar & Marcus, Note 20, *supra*, at 6.

[31] *See* § 32.01[D], *infra*.

## [C]  Guarantees of the Double Jeopardy Clause

The Supreme Court's "favorite saying"[32] about the double jeopardy clause, adopted from a law review article,[33] and repeated frequently in its opinions, is the following:

> [T]he Fifth Amendment guarantee against double jeopardy . . . consists[s] of three separate constitutional protections. [1] It protects against a second prosecution for the same offense after acquittal. [2] It protects against a second prosecution for the same offense after conviction. [3] And it protects against multiple punishments for the same offense.[34]

It is a shame the Court often repeats this language. Professor George Thomas has explained why:

> Although [the statement] correctly indicates that double jeopardy protection extends to different procedural contexts, it implies a deceptively simple, absolute protection that does not exist under the Court's case law. It implies, for example, that "same offense" has a self-defining quality, and it does not.[35] It implies that acquittal and conviction trigger precisely the same kind of double jeopardy bar, and they do not.[36] It implies that the protection against multiple punishment is coextensive with the protection against multiple trials, and it is not.[37] The "favorite saying" is also incomplete because it omits mistrials,[38] perhaps the most often litigated and most puzzling aspect of double jeopardy.[39]

The "saying" is incomplete in two other regards: the double jeopardy clause protects against reprosecution after certain dismissals;[40] and embodied in the prohibition of double jeopardy is the doctrine of collateral estoppel.[41]

The Court has conceded that "the decisional law in the area is a veritable Sargasso Sea which could not fail to challenge the most intrepid judicial navigator,"[42] and that its holdings "can hardly be characterized as models

---

[32] Westen, Note 1, *supra*, at 1062.

[33] Comment, *Twice in Jeopardy*, 75 Yale L.J. 262, 265–66 (1965).

[34] North Carolina v. Pearce, 395 U.S. 711, 717 (1969) (footnotes omitted) (bracketed numbers supplied).

[35] The meaning of "same offense" under the double jeopardy clause is a matter of considerable complexity. *See* § 32.07, *infra*.

[36] Compare § 32.03 [acquittal] with § 32.05 [conviction], *infra*.

[37] *Compare* § 32.07 [multiple trials] *with* § 32.08 [multiple punishment], *infra*.

[38] *See* § 32.02, *infra*.

[39] Thomas, *Elegant Theory*, Note 1, *supra*, at 830–31 (footnotes omitted).

[40] *See* § 32.04, *infra*.

[41] *See* § 32.09, *infra*.

[42] Albernaz v. United States, 450 U.S. 333, 343 (1981).

of consistency and clarity."[43] The result is that the double jeopardy clause is "the embodiment of technical . . . rules that require the Government to turn square corners."[44]

## [D] Values Underlying the Double Jeopardy Clause

The Supreme Court has advanced various justifications for the double jeopardy clause, depending (in part) on the procedural context. First, reprosecution for the same offense subjects the individual "to embarrassment, expense and ordeal and compel[s] him to live in a continuing state of anxiety and insecurity."[45]

Second, reprosecution for the same offense creates an unacceptably high risk that the government will convict an innocent person by wearing him down with its superior resources.[46] Moreover, if reprosecution is allowed, the government may use "the first trial as . . . a dry run for the second prosecution,"[47] i.e., it could use the first trial to discover the strengths of the defendant's case and the weaknesses of its own, and then present its case in a better light the second time around.

Third, in the context of mistrials, the Fifth Amendment protects the defendant's "valued right to have his trial completed by a particular tribunal."[48] Once a trial begins the defendant has a "weighty"[49] interest in "being able, once and for all, to conclude his confrontation with society through the verdict of a tribunal he might believe to be favorably disposed to his fate."[50]

Fourth, the Supreme Court has stated that "a" or "the" primary purpose of the double jeopardy clause is "to preserve the finality of judgments."[51] One scholar believes that verdict finality is the "core" interest of the double jeopardy clause;[52] others believe that it "is a relatively soft [interest that] . . . can be overridden by a strong and justifiable societal interest to the contrary."[53]

---

[43] Burks v. United States, 437 U.S. 1, 9 (1978).

[44] Jones v. Thomas, 491 U.S. 376, 396 (1989) (Scalia, J., dissenting).

[45] Green v. United States, 355 U.S. 184, 187 (1957).

[46] United States v. Scott, 437 U.S. 82, 91 (1978).

[47] Ashe v. Swenson, 397 U.S. 436, 447 (1970).

[48] Wade v. Hunter, 336 U.S. 684, 689 (1949).

[49] Illinois v. Somerville, 410 U.S. 458, 471 (1973).

[50] United States v. Jorn, 400 U.S. 470, 486 (1971) (plurality).

[51] Crist v. Bretz, 437 U.S. 28, 33 (1978).

[52] Thomas, *Elegant Theory* Note 1, *supra*, at 828–29.

[53] Westen & Drubel, Note 1, *supra*, at 161.

In recent years, the Supreme Court has expressed the view that, ultimately, it is "government oppression" that triggers the double jeopardy clause.[54] Unfortunately, the "oppression" label is little more than a conclusion reached by balancing various factors: society's interest in successful prosecution of guilty persons;[55] the extent to which the government acted in good or bad faith in the initial prosecution; and the defendant's double jeopardy interests (as discussed above).[56] According to this view, reprosecution for the same offense should be permitted in the absence of serious government overreaching or harassment.[57]

## § 32.02  Reprosecution After a Mistrial[58]

### [A]  General Principles

A "mistrial" is a judicial termination of a trial before a verdict is reached, granted on the motion of either party or on the judge's own motion. The intention of a judge in granting a mistrial is "that the prosecutor will be permitted to proceed anew notwithstanding the defendant's plea of double jeopardy."[59]

The declaration of a mistrial brings into play the defendant's valued interest in having his fate decided at the first proceeding. The Supreme Court has explained the double jeopardy concerns this way:

> Even if the first trial is not completed, a second prosecution may be grossly unfair. It increases the financial and emotional burden on the accused, prolongs the period in which he is stigmatized by an unresolved accusation of wrongdoing, and may even enhance the risk that an innocent defendant may be convicted. The danger of such unfairness to the defendant exists whenever a trial is aborted before it is completed. *Consequently, as a general rule, the prosecutor is entitled to one, and only one, opportunity to require an accused to stand trial.*[60]

---

[54] *E.g.* Lockhart v. Nelson, 488 U.S. 33, 42 (1988); United States v. Scott, 437 U.S. 82, 91 (1978).

[55] Garrett v. United States, 471 U.S. 773, 796 (1985) (O'Connor, J., concurring) (the defendant's interest in finality "must accommodate the societal interest in prosecuting and convicting those who violate the law").

[56] Thomas, Note 1, *supra*, at 832–33.

[57] Garrett v. United States, 471 U.S. at 798 (O'Connor, J., concurring) (reprosecution is allowed, unless a defendant is "unduly exposed to oppressive tactics by the Government").

[58] Stephen J. Schulhofer, *Jeopardy and Mistrials*, 125 U. Pa. L. Rev. 449 (1977); Westen & Drubel, Note 1, *supra*, at 85–106.

[59] United States v. Scott, 437 U.S. 82, 92 (1978).

[60] Arizona v. Washington, 434 U.S. 497, 503–05 (1978) (footnotes deleted) (emphasis added).

The "general rule" stated in the italicized language is only partially accurate. First, as discussed in the next subsection, an exception to this rule exists, one that is so broadly interpreted that it is invoked far more often than the general rule itself. Second, the general bar on reprosecution following a mistrial—as limited as that prohibition is—only applies if the mistrial was granted over the defendant's objection. As discussed in subsection [C], when a defendant requests a mistrial or consents to one, the general rule (subject to one exception) is that double jeopardy does *not* bar retrial.

## [B] Mistrials Over the Defendant's Objection

### [1] The "Manifest Necessity" Standard

In *United States v. Perez*,[61] the seminal Supreme Court case in the field, a mistrial was declared over *D*'s objection because the jury could not reach a verdict. The Court upheld the right of the government to reprosecute *D*, holding for the first time that the double jeopardy clause is not an absolute bar to reprosecution after a mistrial declared over the defendant's objection.

According to *Perez*, reprosecution following a defendant-opposed mistrial is permitted if a "manifest necessity" existed for terminating the trial or, in other words, if "the ends of public justice would otherwise be defeated." *Perez* stated that the trial judge may exercise "sound discretion on the subject." However, the Court warned that in view of a defendant's weighty interest in not being subjected to a second prosecution, the power to declare a mistrial "ought to be used [only] with the greatest caution, under urgent circumstances, and for very plain and obvious causes."

### [2] "Manifest Necessity": The Case Law

#### [a] The Early Cases

Although *Perez*[62] appeared to state only a limited exception to the general rule, post-*Perez* case law belies that appearance. Indeed, until 1963, the Court upheld every retrial that followed the grant of a defense-opposed mistrial that it considered.[63]

In the early years, the Court justified mistrials for a variety of reasons, including the following circumstances that occurred or were discovered after jeopardy attached: the jury was unable to reach a verdict;[64] the defendant failed to plead to the indictment;[65] a juror served on the grand jury that

---

[61] 22 U.S. (9 Wheat) 579 (1824).

[62] *Id.*

[63] Schulhofer, Note 58, *supra*, at 459.

[64] Besides *Perez*, *see* Dreyer v. Illinois, 187 U.S. 71 (1902).

[65] Lovato v. New Mexico, 242 U.S. 199 (1916).

had indicted the defendant; [66] a *petit* juror knew the defendant personally; [67] and two co-defendants, previously tried and convicted but not yet sentenced, and who were called as witnesses by the prosecutor in a trial of another defendant, asserted their constitutional privilege not to testify until their sentences were imposed. [68]

The most questionable decision during this period may have been *Gori v. United States*. [69] In *Gori*, the trial judge abruptly declared a mistrial over *D*'s objection during the prosecutor's examination of a witness, because the judge feared that the questioning would ultimately lead to testimony prejudicial to *D*'s rights. As no improper question had yet been asked, much less answered, an appellate court found that the judge acted "overassiduous-[ly]," "premature[ly]," "too hastily," and "overzealous[ly]." Despite this characterization, the Supreme Court upheld the trial judge's actions on the basis of manifest necessity.

The *Gori* Court observed that the mistrial "order was the product of the trial judge's extreme solicitude—an overeager solicitude, it may be—in favor of the accused." Describing the judge's actions as "neither apparently justified nor clearly erroneous," the majority stated that it was "unwilling, where it clearly appears that a mistrial has been granted in the sole interest of the defendant, to hold that its necessary consequence is to bar all retrial." Thus, the Court minimized or ignored the warning in *Perez* that mistrials ought to be declared only "with the greatest caution, under urgent circumstances, and for very plain and obvious causes."

### [b] The Temporary "Radical Transformation"

Two years after *Gori*[70] was decided, the Supreme Court "radically transformed the jurisprudence of mistrials"[71] —or, so it appeared—in *Downum v. United States*. [72] In *Downum*, immediately after the jury was impaneled and sworn, the prosecutor requested a mistrial because his key witness had not yet been subpoenaed. The motion was granted over *D*'s objection.

The Supreme Court held that the Fifth Amendment barred *D*'s reprosecution. In language reminiscent of *United States v. Perez*,[73] the Court declared

---

[66] Thompson v. United States, 155 U.S. 271 (1894).

[67] Simmons v. United States, 142 U.S. 148 (1891).

[68] Brock v. North Carolina, 344 U.S. 424 (1953), *overruled in part on other grounds*, Benton v. Maryland, 395 U.S. 784 (1969)..

[69] 367 U.S. 364 (1961).

[70] *Id.*

[71] Schulhofer, Note 58, *supra*, at 463.

[72] 372 U.S. 734 (1963).

[73] 22 U.S. (9 Wheat) 579 (1824). *See* § 32.02[B][1], *supra*.

that mistrials should be granted "only in very extraordinary and striking circumstances,"[74] which it concluded were absent in the present case because the prosecutor had been aware of the subpoena problem prior to attachment of jeopardy. Furthermore, the *Downum* Court announced that it would "resolve any doubt 'in favor of the liberty of the citizen, rather than exercise what would be an unlimited, uncertain, and arbitrary judicial discretion.' "[75]

The Supreme Court followed this stricter approach in *United States v. Jorn*.[76] In *Jorn*, the judge expressed concern during the trial that various government witnesses had not been adequately informed of their privilege against self-incrimination. Therefore, he declared a mistrial so that they could consult with attorneys. According to the plurality, the trial judge abused his discretion because he did not conduct a "scrupulous" search for alternative remedies to the perceived problem.

### [c]  The Supreme Court Turns Direction Again

Two years after *Jorn*,[77] the Supreme Court reversed directions again in *Illinois v. Somerville*.[78] In *Somerville*, the day after the jury was sworn in *D*'s theft trial, the prosecutor discovered that the indictment was defective, because it failed to allege that *D* acted with the specific intent to steal. Under Illinois law, this defect in the indictment could not be cured by amendment. Consequently, over *D*'s objection, the judge granted the prosecutor's motion for a mistrial, so that a new indictment could be secured. A few weeks later, *D* was retried and convicted.

The Supreme Court conceded that there was no "mechanical formula" for determining when manifest necessity exists for a mistrial. However, it stated that it was "possible to distill from [the prior cases] . . . a general approach" to the problem: "[a] trial judge properly exercises his discretion to declare a mistrial if an impartial verdict cannot be reached, or if a verdict of conviction could be reached but would have to be reversed on appeal due to an obvious procedural error in the trial."[79] For example, under this standard, manifest necessity for a mistrial exists when an impartial verdict is impossible because the jury is hopelessly deadlocked or because of juror bias. Likewise, a mistrial is proper if a subsequent conviction "would

---

[74] *Downum*, 372 U.S. at 736 (quoting United States v. Coolidge, 25 Fed. Cas. 622, 623 (1815)).

[75] *Id.* at 738 (quoting United States v. Watson, 28 Fed. Cas. 499, 501 (1868)).

[76] 400 U.S. 470 (1971).

[77] *Id.*

[78] 410 U.S. 458 (1973).

[79] *Id.* at 464.

automatically" be overturned by an appellate court, such as when it is discovered during trial that the defendant failed to plead to the indictment or, as in *Somerville*, because he was tried on the basis of a fatally deficient indictment.

*Somerville* is "exceedingly difficult to reconcile"[80] with *Downum*[81] and *Jorn*, the two cases decided during the Court's "radical" period, when it placed a very high value on the defendant's interest in having his fate settled at the first trial. *Somerville* distinguished *Downum* on the ground that the latter case involved a situation that "len[t] itself to prosecutorial manipulation," in that the mistrial—declared so that the prosecutor could subpoena his key witness—"operated . . . to allow the prosecution an opportunity to strengthen its case." In *Somerville*, there was no suggestion that the state rule barring the amendment of indictments "could be manipulated so as to prejudice the defendant."

The Court in *Somerville* distinguished *Jorn* on the basis that the judge in that case failed to consider alternatives to a mistrial—granted so that government witnesses could consult with attorneys before they testified— such as a brief continuance. In contrast, in *Somerville*, the Court concluded that the trial judge had no option but to declare the mistrial.[82]

Although *D*'s retrial was upheld in *Somerville*, the opinion does contain some language that can prove helpful to a defendant asserting a double jeopardy claim in a sympathetic court. The Supreme Court stated that a defendant's interest in having his fate determined at the first trial is a "weighty one." It warned that the determination to abort a proceeding "is not one be to be lightly undertaken." It also indicated that the fact that a defendant cannot prove prejudice beyond that which would ordinarily occur from any reprosecution does not "preclude . . . invocation of the double jeopardy bar in the absence of some important countervailing interest of proper judicial administration."

Five years after *Somerville*, the Supreme Court revisited the thorny mistrial thicket. In *Arizona v. Washington*,[83] *D*'s attorney made improper remarks in his opening statement to the jury. As a consequence, the trial judge declared a mistrial over *D*'s objection, although in doing so he did not expressly state that was there was a manifest necessity for his order,

---

[80] Schulhofer, Note 58, *supra*, at 468.

[81] Downum v. United States, 372 U.S. 734 (1963).

[82] But, in view of *D*'s valued right to have his fate decided on the present occasion, the trial judge could (and, according to the *Somerville* dissenters, should) have allowed the case to run its course, since *D* might have been acquitted, thus negating the need for a new trial.

[83] 434 U.S. 497 (1978).

nor did he indicate whether he had considered other remedies, such as an instruction cautioning the jury to disregard the improper comments made by defense counsel. Nonetheless, the Supreme Court held that the double jeopardy clause did not bar reprosecution.

*Washington* can be justified on the basis of *Somerville*'s "general approach": perhaps due to *D*'s attorney's improper remarks, an impartial verdict was impossible. But, in view of the "weighty" interests at stake, the Court could have held that the decision to abort the proceeding was, in *Somerville*'s words, too "lightly undertaken"—after all, the trial judge never indicated it considered less extreme remedies before declaring the mistrial—particularly in view of the *Downum* Court's warning that it would "resolve any doubt in favor of the liberty of the citizen."

*Washington* provides insights into the Supreme Court's view of the proper role of appellate courts in scrutinizing mistrials. First, the Court stated that the burden of proof is on the government to prove the existence of a manifest necessity. However, as is now obvious, the word "necessity" is not taken literally. According to the *Washington* Court, "we assume that there are degrees of necessity and we require a 'high degree' before concluding that a mistrial is appropriate."

Second, the extent to which an appellate court should scrutinize a judge's mistrial ruling depends on the justification for the mistrial. According to *Washington*, "the strictest scrutiny is appropriate when the basis for the mistrial is the unavailability of critical prosecution evidence, or when there is reason to believe that the prosecutor is using the superior resources of the State to harass or to achieve a tactical advantage over the accused." Thus, applying this standard, strict scrutiny was appropriate in *Downum* (involving an unavailable prosecutorial witness), and the Court's lesser scrutiny in *Gori* was justified on the ground that the mistrial there was declared "in the sole interest of the defendant."

*Washington* provides help in understanding other mistrial circumstances. A mistrial granted because of a hung jury—"long considered the classic basis for a proper mistrial"[84] —requires virtually no appellate scrutiny because of "society's [compelling] interest in giving the prosecution one complete opportunity to convict those who have violated its laws."

Where do the facts in *Washington* fit in? The judge here had to determine whether *D*'s remarks biased the jury. Because a trial judge is more conversant with the subjective factors relating to juror bias, his "determination is entitled to special respect." The Court concluded that the judge here

---

[84] *Id.* at 509.

acted "responsibly and deliberately," rather than "irrationally," "irresponsibly," or "precipitately." Although he did not expressly state that the mistrial was necessary, nor that he had considered alternatives to his order, the Court determined that the record as a whole demonstrated that the trial judge "accorded careful consideration to [*D*'s] interest in having the trial concluded in a single proceeding." One additional factor in support of the Court's conclusion was that *D* did "not attempt to demonstrate specific prejudice from the mistrial ruling, other than the harm which always accompanies retrial."

### [3]  Making Sense of the Case Law

The manifest necessity standard cannot be applied mechanistically or without regard to the particular facts of the case. Nonetheless, four factors are of particular importance in the resolution of mistrial cases:[85] (1) whether the government was responsible for the difficulty that gave rise to the motion for the mistrial; (2) whether the motivation of the party associated with the "difficulty" was wrongful, *e.g.*, the prosecutor intended to provoke the mistrial or, at least, the case is one in which there was a potential for manipulation; (3) whether the defendant suffered special prejudice from the mistrial; and (4) whether there were meaningful alternatives to the mistrial. A mistrial is probably improper (and, thus, double jeopardy will bar reprosecution) if there is a finding against the government on factors (1) and (2) (as in *Downum*[86] ) or on (1) and (4) (as in *Jorn*[87] ), but not on the basis of factor (1) alone (as in *Somerville*[88] ).

In view of *Washington*,[89] a mistrial might be improper in some circumstances even if there is no finding against the government on factor (1), i.e., even if the defense, rather than the government, is responsible for the difficulty resulting in the mistrial. Reprosecution might be barred if the defendant suffered extraordinary prejudice as the result of the mistrial (factor 3) and suitable alternative remedies existed (factor 4), unless the defendant acted in bad faith (factor 2).

### [C]  Mistrials With the Defendant's Consent

### [1]  General Rule

As explained in *United States v. Dinitz*,[90] subject to one exception discussed in the next subsection, a defendant who requests a mistrial or

---

[85] Schulhofer, Note 58, *supra*, at 468–69.

[86] Downum v. United States, 372 U.S. 734 (1963). *See* § 32.02[B][2][b], *supra*.

[87] United States v. Jorn, 400 U.S. 470 (1971). *See* § 32.02[B][2][b], *supra*.

[88] Illinois v. Somerville, 410 U.S. 458 (1973). *See* § 32.02[B][2][c], *supra*.

[89] Arizona v. Washington, 434 U.S. 497 (1978). *See* § 32.02[B][2][c], *supra*.

[90] 424 U.S. 600 (1976)

who consents to one may not object on double jeopardy grounds to the institution of a second trial. A defendant's decision to request or consent to a termination of the proceedings serves as a deliberate relinquishment of his constitutional interest in obtaining a verdict at the first trial. In short, in such circumstances, "the 'manifest necessity' standard has no place in the application of the Double Jeopardy Clause."[91]

Arguably, this rule is unfair if a defendant's request for, or condonation of, a mistrial is the result of prosecutorial or judicial error that seriously prejudiced the defendant's capacity to obtain a fair trial and possible acquittal. Under these circumstances, a defendant's waiver of his double jeopardy right seemingly is involuntary. The Court's response in *Dinitz* was that "traditional waiver concepts have little relevance where the defendant must determine whether or not to request or consent to a mistrial in response to judicial or prosecutorial error." According to the Court, "[t]he important consideration [for double jeopardy purposes] . . . is that the defendant retain primary control over the course to be followed in the event of such error."

In other words, if the defendant decides that, because of prejudicial error, an acquittal is no longer realistic, he may prefer to have the proceedings terminated immediately, rather than to complete the trial, almost certainly be convicted, and then face the anxiety, expense, and delay of an appeal, which if successful would result in a retrial.[92] As long as the decision whether to continue the trial primarily rests with the defendant, his rights are adequately protected.

### [2] Exception: Intent to Provoke a Mistrial Motion[93]

In *Dinitz*, the Supreme Court noted an exception to the general rule that there is no bar to reprosecution when a defendant moves for a mistrial or consents to one being granted:

> The Double Jeopardy Clause . . . protect[s] a defendant against govern-
> mental actions intended to provoke mistrial requests . . . . It bars retrials
> where "bad-faith conduct by judge or prosecutor" . . . threatens the

---

[91] Oregon v. Kennedy, 456 U.S. 667, 672 (1982).

[92] The ordinary rule is that reprosecution is permitted after a defendant successfully appeals his conviction. *See* § 32.05[A], *infra*.

[93] *See generally* James F. Ponsoldt, *When Guilt Should Be Irrelevant: Government Overreaching as a Bar to Reprosecution Under the Double Jeopardy Clause After Oregon v. Kennedy*, 69 Cornell L. Rev. 76 (1983); Kenneth Rosenthal, *Prosecutor Misconduct, Convictions, and Double Jeopardy: Case Studies in an Emerging Jurisprudence*, 71 Temple L. Rev. 887 (1998).

"[h]arrassment of an accused by successive prosecutions or declaration of a mistrial . . . ."[94]

However, in *Oregon v. Kennedy*,[95] the Supreme Court controversially[96] narrowed the exception. In *Kennedy*, the trial judge granted *D*'s motion for a mistrial immediately after the prosecutor improperly asked a witness whether the reason he did not do business with *D* was "because [*D*] is a crook?" Prior to retrial, *D* moved to bar reprosecution on double jeopardy grounds. The trial judge denied the motion because the prosecutor had not intended to provoke the mistrial by his question. However, an appellate court, relying on the full *Dinitz* statement quoted above, ruled in *D*'s favor because it found that the prosecutor's question was motivated by bad faith or was undertaken to harass or prejudice *D*.

The Supreme Court held that *D* could be reprosecuted. Justice Rehnquist, for the Court, held that reprosecution is barred, even when a mistrial is declared at the defendant's request, if the prosecutor or the judge intended to provoke or goad the mistrial motion. However, it rejected the implication in *Dinitz* that reprosecution is also barred upon the "more generalized standard of 'bad faith conduct' or 'harassment' on the part of the judge or prosecutor."

The Court rejected the "bad faith" and "harassment" tests because they "offer virtually no standards for their application." The majority reasoned that "[e]very act on the part of a rational prosecutor during a trial is designed

---

[94] United States v. Dinitz, 424 U.S. at 611 (alteration in original) (quoting United States v. Jorn, 400 U.S. 470, 485 (1971)).

[95] 456 U.S. 667 (1982).

[96] Various states, including Oregon when the *Kennedy* case was remanded, have rejected the rule announced in *Kennedy* in favor of broader double jeopardy protection based on state constitutional grounds: Pool v. Superior Court, 677 P.2d 261, 271 (Ariz. 1984) (reprosecution is barred if the prosecutor's improper prejudicial conduct was knowing and pursued "for any improper purpose with indifference to a significant resulting danger of mistrial or reversal"); State v. Rogan, 984 P.2d 1231 (Hawaii 1999) (reprosecution after a mistrial or reversal on appeal, based on prosecutorial misconduct, is barred if the misconduct was so egregious that the defendant was denied a fair trial); State v. Breit, 930 P.2d 792, 795 (N.M. 1996) (reprosecution is barred in *Kennedy* circumstances, as well as when a prosecutor knows that his conduct is improper and acts "in willful disregard of the resulting mistrial, retrial, or reversal"); State v. Kennedy, 666 P.2d 1316 (Or. 1983) (reprosecution is barred if the prosecutor either intended or was indifferent to the danger of a resulting mistrial); Commonwealth v. Martorano, 741 A.2d 1221 (Pa. 1999) (reprosecution is barred when the conduct of the prosecutor is intentionally undertaken to prejudice the defendant to the point of denial of a fair trial); Bauder v. State, 921 S.W.2d 696 (Tex. Crim. App. 1996) (retrial is prohibited if the prosecutor intended to induce the motion for mistrial or "when the prosecutor was aware but consciously disregarded the risk that an objectionable event for which he was responsible would require a mistrial at defendant's request").

to 'prejudice' the defendant by placing before the judge or jury evidence leading to a finding of his guilt."[97] Also, if the more general standards were used, a trial court might hesitate to grant a mistrial motion because it would know that by doing so it would "all but inevitably bring with it an attempt to bar a second trial." As a result, fewer mistrial motions would be granted, and more defendants would be compelled to complete their tainted trials.

Four Justices, although concurring in the judgment that the misconduct in the present case did not justify application of the double jeopardy clause, sharply criticized the majority's narrow rule. They argued that the Court's test was inadequate because it would not bar reprosecution if a prosecutor purposely injected prejudice into a trial in order to obtain a conviction, rather than to cause a mistrial. Likewise, the Fifth Amendment would not bar retrial if the prosecutor intended to harass the defendant, but was indifferent regarding whether a mistrial was declared. According to these Justices, a defendant's double jeopardy interests should outweigh the society's interest in obtaining a judgment on the merits in a case of prosecutorial misconduct.

Realistically, does *Kennedy* foreclose a finding that reprosecution is barred after a defense motion for a mistrial? The concurring Justices believed so, because "[i]t is almost inconceivable that a defendant could prove that the prosecutor's deliberate misconduct was motivated by an intent to provoke a mistrial instead of an intent simply to prejudice the defendant." In this regard, Justice Lewis Powell, although joining the majority opinion, wrote a separate concurrence in which he stated that "[b]ecause 'subjective' intent often may be unknowable, I emphasize that a court . . . should rely primarily upon the objective facts and circumstances of the particular case." In view of the 5-4 split on the double jeopardy standard, Powell's recommendation to trial judges—one that could reduce somewhat the defendant's burden—should not be ignored.

---

[97] But surely this is not what is commonly meant by "prejudice." There is considerable difference between, on the one hand, a prosecutor seeking to introduce admissible evidence incriminating the defendant and, on the other hand, seeking to impair the defendant's ability to obtain a fair trial by the use of improper prosecutorial tactics.

## § 32.03  Reprosecution After an Acquittal[98]

### [A]  Rule

### [1]  In General

Acquittals are accorded "special weight" in double jeopardy jurisprudence.[99] It has been the unequivocal rule since *United States v. Ball*[100] that a defendant who is acquitted of an offense may not be prosecuted again for the same offense.[101]

At the present time, the bar on reprosecution after an acquittal is absolute.[102] The prohibition applies whether the acquittal is the result of: (1) a "not guilty" verdict by the jury, or by a judge in a bench trial; (2) an "implied" acquittal by the judge or jury;[103] or (3) a ruling by the judge, whatever label he attaches to it, that "represents a resolution [in the defendant's favor], . . . of some or all of the factual elements of the offense charged."[104] An example of the latter variety of acquittal is a ruling (however denominated) by a judge in a jury trial that there is insufficient evidence to establish the defendant's guilt.[105]

The bar on reprosecution after an acquittal applies even if the verdict or ruling is "based upon an egregiously erroneous foundation,"[106] such as when a judge, who lacks the authority to do so, directs a verdict of acquittal before the prosecution has rested its case.[107]

Similarly, an acquitted defendant may not be retried, "even if the legal rulings underlying the acquittal were erroneous."[108] For example,

---

[98] *See generally* Office of Legal Policy, U.S. Dep't of Justice, Truth in Criminal Justice Series, Report No. 6, Report to the Attorney General on Double Jeopardy and Government Appeals of Acquittals, *reprinted in* 22 U. Mich. J.L. Ref. 831 (1989); Anne Bowen Poulin, *Double Jeopardy and Judicial Accountability: When Is an Acquittal Not an Acquittal?*, 27 Ariz. St. L.J. 953 (1995); David S. Rudstein, *Double Jeopardy and the Fraudulently-Obtained Acquittal*, 60 Mo. L. Rev. 607 (1995); Westen, Note 1, *supra*, at 1004–23; Westen & Drubel, Note 1, *supra*, at 122–55.

[99] United States v. DiFrancesco, 449 U.S. 117, 129 (1980).

[100] 163 U.S. 662 (1896).

[101] Of course, an acquitted defendant *may* be prosecuted for a *different* offense. Sometimes, however, two different statutory offenses are considered the "same offense" for purposes of double jeopardy. *See* § 32.07, *infra*.

[102] *But see* § 32.03[B], *infra*.

[103] *See* § 32.05[C], *infra*.

[104] United States v. Martin Linen Supply Co., 430 U.S. 564, 571 (1977).

[105] Smalis v. Pennsylvania, 476 U.S. 140, 144 (1986).

[106] Fong Foo v. United States, 369 U.S. 141, 143 (1962).

[107] *Id.*

[108] Sanabria v. United States, 437 U.S. 54, 64 (1978)

reprosecution is barred if a judge acquits a defendant of criminal reckless-ness, even if the verdict was based on the judge's legally erroneous understanding of the definition of "recklessness."

Reprosecution is also prohibited if the verdict was the result of the judge's erroneous exclusion of evidence favorable to the prosecution at trial.[109] As the Supreme Court has stated, "the fact that 'the acquittal may result from erroneous evidentiary rulings or erroneous interpretations of governing legal principles,'. . . affects the accuracy of that determination, but it does not alter its essential character."[110]

### [2] Appealing an Acquittal

Although *retrial* after an acquittal is always barred, the double jeopardy clause does not prohibit the government from *appealing* an acquittal if the defendant would *not* be exposed to a second trial if the appeal were successful. For example, if a jury returns a guilty verdict, after which the judge grants *D*'s motion for a judgment of acquittal notwithstanding the verdict, the government may appeal the judicial acquittal.[111] If the appeal is successful, no new trial is required, as the original conviction may be reinstated.

In contrast, the government may *not* appeal a judgment of acquittal granted by the trial court following the declaration of a mistrial due to a deadlocked jury, because a new trial would be required if the appeal of the acquittal were successful.[112] However, the line that separates the mistrial cases from the acquittal rule can prove thin, indeed. Thus, the failure of the defense to file a timely motion for judgment of acquittal following a mistrial can prove fatal to a double jeopardy claim. For example, in *United States v. Sanford,*[113] *D* failed to move for judgment of acquittal within the requisite seven days after the jury was discharged for failing to reach a verdict.[114] Instead, *D* waited until immediately prior to the second trial, at which time he successfully sought dismissal of the indictment on the basis of the evidence developed at the original trial. Although the trial judge's ruling might have been treated as an acquittal, the Court did not characterize it that way. Instead, because of the delayed timing of the

---

[109] *Id.*

[110] United States v. Scott, 437 U.S. 82, 98 (1978).

[111] United States v. Wilson, 420 U.S. 332, 336 (1975) (the rule applies to any post-conviction motion favorable to the defendant, including an acquittal); *see* United States v. Scott, 437 U.S. at 91 n.7.

[112] United States v. Martin Linen Supply Co., 430 U.S. 564 (1977).

[113] 429 U.S. 14 (1976).

[114] Fed. R. Crim. P. 29(c).

motion, the Court characterized the case as one involving a mistrial in which a manifest necessity (hung jury) justified the second trial. It then treated the judge's ruling as a *pre*trial dismissal of the new prosecution, which, like any other pretrial action, is not subject to the double jeopardy clause.[115]

### [B]  Should the Rule Be Modified?

In *United States v. Scott*,[116] the Supreme Court explained the prohibition on reprosecution following an acquittal this way:

> To permit a second trial after an acquittal, however mistaken the acquittal may have been, would present an unacceptably high risk that the Government, with its vastly superior resources, might wear down the defendant so that "even though innocent he may be found guilty."

As has been forcefully argued,[117] this rationale is questionable in light of the contrasting rule that a defendant who successfully appeals a wrongful *conviction* ordinarily may be reprosecuted.[118] There is no reason to believe that a defendant who has been wrongfully convicted as the result of prejudicial trial error is more likely to be guilty than one who is wrongfully acquitted as the result of a ruling prejudicial to the government.

Nor can the rule adequately be justified, as the dissenters in *Scott* sought to do, by claiming "that the second trial would present all the untoward consequences the Clause was designed to prevent," such as allowing the prosecutor to strengthen his case, and "to subject the defendant to the expense and anxiety of a second trial." This argument fails because in other double jeopardy contexts, such as after a mistrial,[119] these concerns are not ordinarily considered weighty enough to override society's interest in bringing potentially guilty persons to justice.

Two commentators have argued that the most persuasive rationale for the rule against reprosecution following a jury acquittal, a rationale that the Court now acknowledges,[120] is that it "may be a product of the jury's legitimate authority to acquit against the evidence,"[121] that is, to nullify the law.

The "jury nullification" doctrine provides that a jury—the moral conscience of the community—may properly exercise its prerogative to

---

[115] *See* § 32.01[A][2], *supra*.

[116] 437 U.S. 82, 91 (1978) (quoting Green v. United States, 355 U.S. 184, 188 (1957)).

[117] Westen & Drubel, Note 1, *supra*, at 124–29.

[118] *See* § 32.05[A], *infra*.

[119] *See* § 32.02, *supra*.

[120] *See* United States v. DiFrancesco, 449 U.S. 117, 130 n.11 (favorably quoting Westen, Note 1, *supra*, at 1012, 1063).

[121] Westen & Drubel, Note 1, *supra*, at 129.

disregard uncontradicted evidence and the legal instructions of the judge in order to acquit a defendant. Historically, juries have used their nullification power to acquit defendants charged with unpopular crimes, or out of sympathy for a defendant and his circumstances, or due to dislike for the victim, or even as a means of punishing the government for some perceived impropriety in the prosecution. If jury nullification is legitimate, then it follows that no verdict of acquittal by a jury that nullifies the law can truly be wrong, and thus there *is* no legitimate basis for reprosecution in such cases. And, since jury deliberations are secret, there is no way to know for sure whether an acquittal was based on nullification; thus, the double jeopardy rule ensures that nullification can occur unhampered.

The difficulty with this justification for the double jeopardy acquittal rule is that is presupposes that jury nullification *is* legitimate. Jurors have the *power* to nullify the law precisely because of the existence of the no-reprosecution-after-acquittal rule. But, is this power *legitimate*? Jury nullification is highly controversial.[122] Most courts today consider nullification an undesirable byproduct of the double jeopardy rule. Moreover, even if nullification *is* proper, the doctrine cannot justify the bar on reprosecution after an erroneous acquittal by a *judge*, who has never been thought to have the right to acquit against the evidence. Thus, even allowing for jury nullification, the acquittal rule might more properly be limited to "not guilty" verdicts by juries.

Moreover, at least in extreme cases, the absolute nature of the acquittal rule is difficult to defend. Consider *People v. Aleman*:[123] *D*, a reputed crime syndicate assassin, was acquitted of murder in a bench trial. Several years later, federal investigators uncovered evidence that the trial judge in the case has accepted a $10,000 bribe to acquit *D*. The judge committed suicide, whereupon the prosecutor obtained a second indictment of *D for the same offense*. *D* sought to dismiss the prosecution on double jeopardy grounds, but the state court allowed the second prosecution to proceed. (*D* was convicted at the second trial and sentenced to a term of 100 to 300 years' imprisonment.) The appellate court avoided the double jeopardy rule by reasoning that the first trial was a sham; as the result of the fraud or collusion, *D* was never in genuine jeopardy for the offense. Therefore, reprosecution did not subject *D* to *double* jeopardy.

The no-reprosecution rule is one to which the Court has "clung tenaciously,"[124] even in cases involving bench trials where the acquittal followed

---

[122] *See* Joshua Dressler, Understanding Criminal Law 5–9 (3rd ed. 2001).

[123] 667 N.E.2d 615 (Ill. App. Ct. 1996); 729 N.E.2d 20 (Ill. App. Ct. 2000), *cert. denied*, 531 U.S. 1152 (2001).

[124] Thomas, Note 1, *supra*, at 852.

erroneous legal rulings. It remains to be seen whether the United States Supreme Court will devise a limited exception to the acquittal doctrine.

## § 32.04 Reprosecution After a Dismissal

### [A] Nature of a "Dismissal"

A dismissal often takes on the appearances of a mistrial or an acquittal. Like a mistrial, a dismissal involves a judicial termination of the trial before a verdict is reached. However, unlike a mistrial, the granting of a dismissal "contemplates that the proceedings will terminate then and there in favor of the defendant,"[125] such as when a prosecution is dismissed due to government misconduct.

Like an acquittal, a dismissal involves a termination of a trial in favor of the defendant under circumstances in which it is assumed by the trial court that no further prosecution of the defendant for the offense will occur. The difference lies in the fact that a dismissal, but not an acquittal, involves a termination of the trial in the defendant's favor "on a basis unrelated to factual guilt or innocence."[126] For example, a ruling during the trial that the proceedings must be terminated because of preindictment delay[127] constitutes a dismissal[128] and not an acquittal, regardless of the trial court's characterization of the motion.[129]

### [B] General Rules

### [1] Dismissal on the Defendant's Motion

In *United States v. Jenkins*,[130] the Supreme Court held that the government is barred from appealing a dismissal. The Court concluded that an appeal would violate the double jeopardy clause because if it were successful the defendant would be required to undergo the expense, ordeal, and anxiety of a second prosecution.

---

[125] United States v. Scott, 437 U.S. 82, 94 (1978).

[126] *Id.* at 99.

[127] *See* United States v. Wilson, 420 U.S. 332 (1975).

[128] Usually, dismissal motions must be made prior to trial, *e.g.*, Fed. R. Crim. P. 12(b), and thus before jeopardy attaches. However, some motions to dismiss may be raised for the first time during trial, *e.g.*, *id.* 12(b)(2) (the indictment fails to show jurisdiction in the court). Furthermore, a judge may reconsider a pretrial motion for dismissal after jeopardy attaches, *e.g.*, Lee v. United States, 432 U.S. 23 (1977), or the defendant may raise a pretrial motion again after the trial begins. *E.g.*, United States v. Scott, 437 U.S. 82 (1978).

[129] *See also* State v. Kruelski, 737 A.2d 377 (Conn. 1999) ("acquittal" by judge on statute of limitations grounds after the trial began constitutes a dismissal and, therefore, is subject to the dismissal rules discussed *infra* in the text).

[130] 420 U.S. 358 (1975).

Three years later, the Court overruled *Jenkins* in *United States v. Scott*.[131] The *Scott* Court concluded that the concerns expressed in *Jenkins*, while appropriate in other procedural circumstances, do not apply to the situation "in which the defendant is responsible for the second prosecution" by seeking a dismissal of the charges against him. The latter circumstance, the Court reasoned, "is scarcely a picture of an all-powerful state relentlessly pursuing a defendant who had either been found not guilty or who had at least insisted on having the issue of guilt submitted to the first trier of fact." As with mistrials,[132] "the Double Jeopardy Clause, which guards against Government oppression, does not relieve a defendant from the consequences of his voluntary choice."

### [2] Dismissal Without the Defendant's Consent

A judge will rarely dismiss criminal charges against a defendant during a trial, except on the latter's motion or with his consent. However, suppose that a judge, on his own motion, dismisses a prosecution during trial due to government misconduct without obtaining the defendant's approval. May the prosecutor appeal the dismissal and, if successful on appeal, reprosecute the defendant for the same offense?

The Supreme Court has not answered this question. However, when charges are dismissed without the defendant's consent, the defendant is denied primary control over his fate. Therefore, the reasoning of *United States v. Scott*[133] does not apply in such circumstances. At least one court[134] has held that a dismissal without "a significant level of participation by the defendant in bringing about a termination of his trial prior to a determination on the merits," bars further proceedings. It is submitted here that the Supreme Court might apply some version of the "manifest necessity" standard used in mistrial cases in such circumstances.[135]

### § 32.05 Reprosecution After a Conviction

#### [A] General Rule

The government may not reprosecute a convicted defendant for the same offense if he does not appeal his conviction or if his appeal is

---

[131] 437 U.S. 82 (1978).

[132] *See* § 32.02[C][1], *supra*.

[133] 437 U.S. 82 (1978).

[134] United States v. Dahlstrum, 655 F.2d 971 (9th Cir. 1981).

[135] *See* Thomas, Note 1, *supra*, at 859 (classifying dismissals and mistrials as "no-verdict terminations" and arguing that typical dismissals and mistrials "have identical double jeopardy implications").

unsuccessful.[136] However, it is a "well-established part of our constitutional jurisprudence"[137] that, subject to one or possibly two exceptions discussed in subsection [B], the double jeopardy clause does not bar reprosecution of a defendant who successfully appeals his conviction on the basis of prejudicial error in the prior proceeding.[138] Although the Supreme Court has offered various explanations for the rule,[139] the modern explanation is as follows:

> Corresponding to the right of an accused to be given a fair trial is the societal interest in punishing one whose guilt is clear after he has obtained such a trial. It would be a high price indeed for society to pay were every accused granted immunity from punishment because of any defect sufficient to constitute reversible error in the proceedings leading to conviction.[140]

### [B] When Reprosecution Is Barred

### [1] Insufficiency of the Evidence

### [a] The *Burks* Principle

The Supreme Court ruled in *Burks v. United States*[141] that the government is barred from reprosecuting a previously convicted defendant if an appellate court reverses the conviction on the sole ground that the evidence presented at the trial was insufficient to sustain the guilty verdict. The *Burks* rule also applies if a trial judge, rather than an appellate court, grants a new trial on the basis of evidentiary insufficiency.[142]

The *Burks* rule applies because, in the circumstances in which it obtains, the reversal of the conviction (or the granting of the motion for a new trial) "is in effect a determination that the government's case against the

---

[136] Of course, a defendant *may* be prosecuted for a *different* offense. Sometimes, however, two different statutory offenses are considered the "same offense" for purposes of double jeopardy. *See* § 32.07, *infra*.

[137] United States v. Tateo, 377 U.S. 463, 465 (1964).

[138] United States v. Ball, 163 U.S. 662 (1896).

[139] The Court has explained the rule on waiver principles. Trono v. United States, 199 U.S. 521, 533–34 (1905). Because it is unfair to treat a defendant's appeal as a voluntary waiver of his double jeopardy rights when the appeal is taken in response to government-caused prejudicial error, this argument is rarely advanced any longer. It has also been argued that the jeopardy of the first trial continues through the appeal and second trial (and any subsequent convictions, reversals, and retrials). Kepner v. United States, 195 U.S. 100, 134–37 (1904) (Holmes, J., dissenting).

[140] United States v. Tateo, 377 U.S. at 466.

[141] 437 U.S. 1 (1978).

[142] Hudson v. Louisiana, 450 U.S. 40 (1981).

defendant was so lacking that the trial court should have entered a judgment of acquittal, rather than submitting the case to the jury."[143] Therefore, although convicted, the defendant's case is subsumed within the acquittal principles of the double jeopardy clause.

### [b] When *Burks* Does Not Apply

The *Burks* rule does not apply "beyond the procedural setting in which it arose."[144] Therefore, reprosecution is *not* barred if the appellate court or trial judge reverses the conviction on the basis of the weight, rather than the sufficiency, of the evidence.[145] That is, if a court concludes that sufficient evidence was introduced at trial to justify a conviction, reprosecution is allowed even though the court, serving as a "thirteenth juror" (as is permitted in some states) would have acquitted the defendant.

Nor does *Burks* apply after a mistrial is granted. For example, in *Richardson v. United States*[146] a mistrial was granted due to a hung jury. The trial court subsequently denied *D*'s motion for a judgment of acquittal based on insufficiency of the evidence. The Supreme Court held that *D* was not entitled to appeal the denial of the latter motion, stating that *Burks* was not intended to overturn the Court's long history of mistrial jurisprudence, which has "its own sources and logic."

The Court also considered *Burks* inapplicable in *Lockhart v. Nelson*.[147] In *Lockhart*, an appellate court overturned *D*'s conviction on the ground that evidence was erroneously and prejudicially introduced against him at trial. It further held that in the absence of that evidence there were insufficient grounds to convict *D*; therefore, applying *Burks*, it barred reprosecution.

The Supreme Court reversed the lower court's double jeopardy ruling. Distinguishing *Burks*, which involved a conviction overturned *solely* on the basis of evidentiary insufficiency, the Court ruled that reprosecution *is* permitted after a successful appeal by a defendant as long as "the evidence offered by the State and admitted by the trial court—whether erroneously or not—would have been sufficient to sustain a guilty verdict."[148]

The *Lockhart* Court concluded that its holding constituted a proper accommodation of the competing interests, in that it "recreates the situation

---

[143] Lockhart v. Nelson, 488 U.S. 33, 39 (1988).

[144] Richardson v. United States, 468 U.S. 317, 323 (1984).

[145] Tibbs v. Florida, 457 U.S. 31 (1982).

[146] 468 U.S. 317 (1984).

[147] 488 U.S. 33 (1988).

[148] *Id.* at 34.

that would have been obtained if the trial court had [properly] excluded the evidence." Under such circumstances, the defendant is provided an opportunity to obtain a new trial, and the government is given the chance to present other evidence that might have justified the guilty verdict, but which was held back because it did not appear necessary in light of the trial court's erroneous evidentiary rulings.

The Court hinted in *Lockhart* at another area for litigation regarding the scope of the *Burks* rule: "whether the rule that retrial is prohibited after a conviction is set aside by an *appellate* court for evidentiary insufficiency . . . is applicable when the determination . . . is made instead by a federal habeas court in a collateral attack on a state conviction . . . ."[149] The Court assumed, without deciding, an affirmative answer to this question.

### [2] Prosecutorial Misconduct

A highly plausible argument can be made that reprosecution after a successful appeal should be barred in the case of certain forms of prosecutorial trial misconduct. For example, assume that a prosecutor is aware that the trial is going poorly for the government, so he purposely infects the trial with prejudicial information, in order to goad *D* into requesting a mistrial. If *D* makes such a motion and it is granted, reprosecution is barred under the principles of *Oregon v. Kennedy*.[150]

Suppose, however, that the judge denies the mistrial motion, and allows the trial to proceed to a judgment of conviction, with an ineffectual cautionary instruction to the jury to disregard the prejudicial information. If *D* appeals, and the appellate court rules that the mistrial motion should have been granted because of the prosecutorial misconduct, logic would suggest that the *Kennedy* mistrial doctrine should apply to bar reprosecution, even in the context of a conviction. In this hypothetical scenario, *D* has experienced more, not less, double jeopardy harm than in the *Kennedy* case, as he has been forced to undergo the ordeal of a completed trial, conviction, and appeal, due to the judge's error compounding the prosecutorial misconduct. To date, the Supreme Court has not resolved a case involving analogous facts.

### [C] Special Problem: Convictions With Implied Acquittals

### [1] Verdict Acquittal

A criminal conviction can simultaneously result in an implied acquittal of a greater offense. For example, if *D* is charged with first-degree murder and the jury convicts him of second-degree murder, the conviction of the

---

[149] *Id.* at 38 n.6.

[150] 456 U.S. 667 (1982). *See* § 32.02[C][2], *supra*.

latter offense serves as an implied acquittal of the greater charge.[151] In such circumstances, if *D* successfully appeals from his second-degree murder conviction, the reprosecution-after-*conviction* rules apply to the *second*-degree murder charge—*D* may be reprosecuted for that offense—but the reprosecution-after-*acquittal* ban applies to the *first*-degree charge, of which he was implicitly acquitted.

Notwithstanding the implied acquittal rule, if *D* is wrongfully retried for the greater offense (first-degree murder) and again convicted, the Supreme Court has determined that, rather than impose a third trial on the defendant, the appropriate remedy is to reduce the conviction to "a lesser included offense which is not jeopardy barred [*e.g.*, second-degree murder], [unless] . . . the defendant [is able] to demonstrate a reasonable probability that he would not have been convicted of the nonjeopardy-barred offense absent the presence of the jeopardy-barred offense."[152]

### [2] Sentence "Acquittal"

Ordinarily, the "implied acquittal" concept has no application to resentencing after a defendant is reprosecuted following a successful appeal of a conviction. For example, if a judge imposes a five-year prison sentence at *D*'s first trial, although the maximum penalty for the crime is 20 years' imprisonment, this sentence is not treated as if *D* was acquitted of 15 years of imprisonment. Double jeopardy is not violated, therefore, if the judge imposes a more severe punishment, up to the maximum allowed under the law, after any subsequent reprosecution and conviction.[153]

A different rule applies in the capital-sentencing context. A typical capital-sentencing proceeding is conducted like a trial: after a defendant is convicted of a capital offense, a separate hearing is held at which the prosecutor must prove to the trier of fact beyond a reasonable doubt that aggravating factual circumstances exist, and that they outweigh whatever mitigating facts the defendant may prove at the hearing. The trier of fact, usually a jury, then deliberates on whether to impose (or recommend) the penalty of death or life imprisonment.

The Supreme Court held in *Bullington v. Missouri*[154] that a determination at such a trial-like proceeding that the convicted defendant should be sentenced to life imprisonment is comparable to an acquittal of the "verdict" of death: it has "the hallmarks of the trial on guilt or innocence." Therefore,

---

[151] Green v. United States, 355 U.S. 184 (1957).

[152] Morris v. Mathews, 475 U.S. 237, 246–47 (1986).

[153] North Carolina v. Pearce, 395 U.S. 711 (1969). The more severe sentence may raise due process concerns, however. *See* § 31.08, *supra*.

[154] 451 U.S. 430 (1981).

if the defendant succeeds in overturning his murder conviction for any reason, the state may not seek the death penalty on reprosecution of the capital offense.

The Supreme Court emphasized the limited scope of the *Bullington* holding in *Monge v. California*.[155] *Monge* involved California's "three-strikes law," which provides that a convicted felon with one prior conviction for a serious felony (the first "strike") shall have his prison term for the "second strike" doubled. Under state law, a number of procedural safeguards surround the assessment of prior conviction allegations, including the right to a jury trial, the right to confront witnesses, the privilege against self-incrimination, and the requirement that the prosecutor prove the prior conviction allegation beyond a reasonable doubt.

The *Monge* Court stated that the rationale of *Bullington* does not apply to noncapital sentencing proceedings, even if such proceedings have the "hallmarks" of a trial identified in that case. The Court stated that "a critical component of our reasoning in [*Bullington*] was the capital sentencing context": the penalty phase of a capital trial "is in many respects a continuation of the trial on guilt or innocence of capital murder"; and "because the death penalty is unique 'in both its severity and finality,' we have recognized an acute need for reliability in capital sentencing proceedings."

## § 32.06  Government Appeals of Criminal Sentences[156]

The federal government has no right of appeal in criminal proceedings, absent explicit statutory authority.[157] Congress (as many states now do) has provided authority for government appeals in criminal cases, except "where the double jeopardy clause of the United States Constitution prohibits further prosecution."[158]

The federal government may appeal a final sentence, following a conviction, if it believes that the sentence imposed was in violation of law or sentencing guidelines, was "imposed as a result of an incorrect application of the sentencing guidelines," or was otherwise "plainly unreasonable."[159] If an appellate court agrees, it remands the case to the district court for further sentencing proceedings.

---

[155] 524 U.S. 721 (1998).

[156] *See generally* James A. Strazzella, *The Relationship of Double Jeopardy to Prosecution Appeals*, 73 Notre Dame L. Rev. 1 (1997); Westen, Note 1, *supra*.

[157] United States v. Scott, 437 U.S. 82, 84–85 (1978).

[158] 18 U.S.C. § 3731 (1996).

[159] 18 U.S.C. § 3742 (1996).

The Supreme Court upheld a similar sentencing statute in *United States v. DiFrancesco*.[160] The Court stated that "a sentence does not have the qualities of constitutional finality that attend an acquittal." It also reasoned that the government's right to appeal the sentence does not involve the sort of government oppression that the double jeopardy clause bars.

## § 32.07 Multiple Prosecutions of the "Same Offense"[161]

### [A] An Overview to the Problems Ahead

The "same offense" language of the Fifth Amendment—"nor shall any person be subject *for the same offense* to be twice put in jeopardy of life or limb"—has led lawyers into a quagmire. First, there is what is sometimes described as the "unit of prosecution" problem. Consider a simple case first. Assume *D* robs *V1* on Day 1, *V2* on Day 2, and so on for five days. *D*, of course, has committed the same offense—robbery—on five different occasions. Obviously, the double jeopardy clause does not mean by the words "the same offense" to bar the government from prosecuting *D* for five counts of robbery. These are separate offenses for purposes of double jeopardy.

But, change the facts slightly: suppose that *D* enters a grocery store and walks up to five different cashiers and points a gun at each in order to obtain money. Do we still treat this as five robberies, or is it now just one offense? The answer is that nothing has changed: there were five victims, so there have been five robberies. Therefore, *D* may be punished for all five robberies without offending the double jeopardy clause. Indeed, in most circumstances, the government may constitutionally subject *D* to successive prosecutions of these separate robberies,[162] even though the crimes were committed in a single criminal transaction.[163]

---

[160] 449 U.S. 117 (1980).

[161] *See generally* Amar & Marcus, Note 20, *supra*, at 28–49; Susan R. Klein & Katherine P. Chiarello, *Successive Prosecutions and Compound Criminal Statutes: A Functional Test*, 77 Texas L. Rev.333 (1998); Lawrence A. Locke, *On Leo Katz, Double Jeopardy, and the Blockburger Test*, 9 Law & Phil. 295 (1990); George C. Thomas III, *A Blameworthy Act Approach to the Double Jeopardy Same Offense Problem*, 83 Cal. L. Rev. 1027 (1995); Thomas, Note 9, supra; Westen & Drubel, Note 1, *supra*, at 111–22. For purposes of clarity, the text uses the American spelling of "offense," although the English spelling ("offence") is used in the original version of the Fifth Amendment.

[162] In one circumstance, the double jeopardy clause *will* bar multiple prosecutions in this example. *See* § 32.09, *infra*.

[163] United States v. Dixon, 509 U.S. 688, 704–05 (1993). Some members of the Court have argued that the government should not be permitted to bring successive prosecutions in such circumstances. *E.g., see*, Ashe v. Swenson, 397 U.S. 436, 448–460 (1970) (Brennan, Douglas, and Marshall, JJ., concurring). However, the Court has "steadfastly refused to adopt the 'single transaction' view of the Double Jeopardy Clause." Garrett v. United States, 471 U.S. 773, 790 (1985).

But, sometimes a prosecutor may "split the atom" a little too finely. When D steals V's six-pack of beer, is this one theft or six? *This* is the unit-of-prosecution issue. The constitutional answer here comes down to nothing more than a judicial effort to devise a sensible reading of a criminal statute in light of the court's best efforts to divine legislative intent. Almost certainly we would conclude that the legislature intended to treat this as one theft. But, what should a court do with an ordinance that makes it an offense "to sell beer without a license"—is each sale by the unlicensed bartender a separate offense, no matter how many sales are amassed?[164] Or, what if it is an offense to "tear, cut, or otherwise injure any mail bag with the intent to rob or steal any such mail." What if D cuts once into each of five different mail bags sitting next to each other—is this five different offenses?[165] What if D cuts five times into a single bag? Unit-of-prosecutions issues can be very difficult to resolve sensibly.

There is a second double jeopardy "same offense" issue that has perplexed and confounded the courts even more deeply. A single act may constitute a violation of two or more distinct statutory provisions. For example, if *D1* assaults *V1* with a gun, he simultaneously commits the crimes of "assault" and "assault with a deadly weapon." If V happens to be a police officer, *D1*'s act may also violate a statute prohibiting assaults upon a law enforcement officer. Similarly, when *D2* burglarizes *V2*'s home, he also commits the crime of trespass.

Although it is possible that the Supreme Court might have concluded that these are different offenses—they are, after all, distinct provisions in the penal code—the Supreme Court observed in *Brown v. Ohio*[166] that "[i]t has long been understood that separate statutory crimes need not be identical . . . in order to be the same within the meaning of the constitutional prohibition." In other words, the fact that an act or series of acts is prohibited under two or more distinct provisions of a criminal code does not *in itself* mean that the conduct constitutes separate offenses for Fifth Amendment purposes.

This chapter section considers the Fifth Amendment meaning of the term "same offense" in this context. But, even here we must divide the issue into two: even when we know what is meant by the term "same offense," one must ask whether the double jeopardy bar applies only to multiple *prosecutions* for the "same offense" (the topic of this chapter section) or

---

[164] State v. Broeder, 90 Mo. App. 169 (1901) (multiple charges permitted).

[165] Ebeling v. Morgan, 237 U.S. 625 (1915) (multiple charges, convictions and sentences permitted).

[166] 432 U.S. 161, 164 (1977).

whether it also applies if the government seeks to impose multiple *punishment* of a defendant at a *single* trial for the "same offense." The latter issue is left for consideration in Section 32.08.

### [B] "Same Offense": The *Blockburger* Rule

*Blockburger v. United States*[167] provides that two distinct statutory provisions constitute separate offenses if "each provision requires proof of a fact which the other does not." That is, if Crime 1 requires proof of facts A, B, and C, and Crime 2 requires proof of facts A, B, and D, the two crimes are separate offenses, because each statute includes an element that the other does not (elements C and D, respectively). For example, "assault with the intent to kill" and "assault with a deadly weapon" are separate offenses because each crime requires proof of a fact that the other does not (intent to kill, and use of a deadly weapon, respectively.)

On the other hand, "[i]f application of th[e *Blockburger*] test reveals that [two] offenses have identical statutory elements or that one is a lesser included offense of the other, then the inquiry must cease, and the subsequent prosecution is barred."[168] That is, if Crime 1 requires proof of elements A, B, and C, and Crime 2 requires proof of the same elements[169] or, simply, of elements A and B, these crimes constitute the "same offense" for double jeopardy purposes. An example of the latter situation is *Brown v. Ohio*:[170] *D* stole an automobile. Nine days later he was apprehended. *D* pleaded guilty to the offense of joyriding. Subsequently, he was prosecuted for auto theft, based on the same incident.[171] Under Ohio law, joyriding consisted of taking or operating a vehicle without the owner's consent; auto theft consisted of taking or operating a vehicle without the owner's consent *with the intent to steal the car.* Under *Blockburger*, therefore, the two crimes were the same offense: joyriding was a lesser-included crime of the other.[172] Therefore, the government was forbidden

---

[167] 284 U.S. 299 (1932).

[168] Grady v. Corbin, 495 U.S. 508, 516 (1990), *overruled on other grounds*, United States v. Dixon, 509 U.S. 688 (1993).

[169] Of course, duplicative statutes should not exist in a well-drafted criminal code.

[170] 432 U.S. 161 (1977).

[171] Notice that this case involves a potential unit-of-prosecution (see § 32.07[A], *supra*) issue. Presumably, during the nine days *D* had the car, he turned off the ignition and exited the vehicle many times. *D* was only charged with one count of joyriding, presumably because Ohio law treated joyriding as a continuing offense.

[172] Notice that this would not be the case if joyriding were defined as "taking or operating a vehicle without the owner's consent, *with the intent to temporarily deprive the owner of its use.*" In this hypothetical situation, the offenses of joyriding and auto theft each include an element that the other does not: for joyriding, the government would have to prove that

to bring the second prosecution. Furthermore, the sequence of the successive prosecutions is constitutionally immaterial: conviction of either crime bars subsequent prosecution of the other, absent a relevant exception to the rule.

### [C]   "Same Offense": Beyond *Blockburger*

#### [1]   *Harris v. Oklahoma*: A Minor Variation on the *Blockburger* Theme

Under *Blockburger*,[173] two offenses are the same for double jeopardy purposes if they have identical statutory elements or if one crime is a lesser-included offense of the other.

Consider, however, *Harris v. Oklahoma*.[174] *D* killed *V* during the commission of a robbery, for which he was convicted of felony murder. Later, he was prosecuted for the predicate robbery. In a "terse,"[175] three paragraph *per curiam* opinion, the Court unanimously held that the robbery prosecution was barred by the double jeopardy clause.

Under a strict application of the *Blockburger* test, the two crimes—felony murder and robbery—were not the "same offense." The felony-murder statute prohibited the killing of a human being during the attempted commission of an enumerated felony, including (but not limited to) robbery. Put slightly differently, the crime of "felony murder" consisted of elements A (a killing of a human being by the defendant), B1, B2, or B3 (the attempted commission of an enumerated felony), and C (a causal connection between A and B1 or B2 or B3). If one looks exclusively at the statutory definition of the offenses, as *Blockburger* requires, the crimes of "felony murder" and "robbery" each require proof of an element that the other does not: felony murder requires proof of a killing (which robbery does not); robbery requires proof of a forcible taking of another's personal property (a fact not necessary to prove felony murder, since proof of the commission of a different enumerated felony will suffice).

How is *Harris* explained? Evidently, the Court looked beyond the statutory elements of the two crimes. Instead of defining "felony murder" in a factual vacuum, it considered the elements of this offense in light of

---

the defendant intended to temporarily (not permanently) deprive the owner of the use of the car; for theft, the government would have to prove that the defendant intended to permanently (not temporarily) deprive the owner of the use of the vehicle. Thus, we would have separate offenses—one requiring proof of A (taking or operating the vehicle), B (without the owner's consent), and C (intent to temporarily deprive), and the other requiring evidence of A, B, and D (intent to permanently deprive).

[173] Blockburger v. United States, 284 U.S. 299 (1932). See § 32.07[B], *supra*.

[174] 433 U.S. 682 (1977).

[175] United States v. Dixon, 509 U.S. 688, 698 (1993).

the theory of the prosecution in *this* case: because the alleged felony murder involved a robbery, robbery *in this prosecution* was a lesser-included offense of felony murder. Therefore, the subsequent robbery prosecution was barred.

### [2] *Grady v. Corbin*: A Broad (but Temporary) Addition to *Blockburger*

*Harris v. Oklahoma* narrowly extended the scope of the *Blockburger* test. In 1990, however, in *Grady v. Corbin*,[176] the Court announced an additional test for determining when distinct criminal statutes constitute the "same offense" for purposes of barring dual prosecutions. In *Corbin*, *D* drove his automobile across a double yellow line, striking two oncoming vehicles. As a result, *D* received two traffic tickets, one of which charged him with the misdemeanor offense of driving while intoxicated, and the second of which charged him with failing to keep right of the median.

Hours after the accident, a driver of one of the cars struck by *D*'s vehicle died from injuries stemming from the incident. However, the prosecutor involved in the homicide investigation failed to inform the judge hearing the traffic offenses or the prosecutor covering that court of the fatality. Three weeks after the accident, *D* pleaded guilty to the traffic offenses.

Subsequently, *D* was indicted for the offense of reckless manslaughter. In a bill of particulars,[177] the prosecutor specified three acts on which he would rely to prove that the homicide was reckless: (1) that *D* drove his vehicle in an intoxicated condition; (2) that *D* did not keep his vehicle to the right of the median; and (3) that *D* drove too fast during a heavy rain.

Under *Blockburger*, the homicide prosecution was not barred: "reckless manslaughter," on the one hand, and "driving while intoxicated" and "failing to keep to the right," on the other hand, are separate offenses. By definition, manslaughter requires proof of a fact—a killing—that is not a statutory element of either driving offense. In turn, the driving offenses involve conduct—intoxication and failure to stay to the right, respectively—that are not statutory elements of manslaughter.

Even under *Harris*, the second prosecution was permissible. In *Harris*, the offense involved in the second prosecution—robbery—was an express, albeit disjunctive, element of felony murder, the offense involved in the initial prosecution. That is, the felony murder statute expressly required

---

[176] 495 U.S. 508 (1990), *overruled by* United States v. Dixon, 509 U.S. 688 (1993).

[177] In the context of a criminal prosecution, a "bill of particulars" is a written specification of the facts that the prosecutor intends to prove to support the charges set out in the indictment. Under federal rules and in various states, a trial court may order the government to file a bill of particulars after an indictment is issued. Fed. R. Crim. P. 7(f).

proof of the attempted commission of robbery *or* rape *or* arson *or* some other specifically enumerated felony. In *Corbin*, however, neither "driving while intoxicated" nor "failing to keep to the right of the median" was an element (disjunctive or otherwise) of the offense of reckless manslaughter.

Nonetheless, the Supreme Court held, 5-4, that the second prosecution was barred by the double jeopardy clause because, based on the bill of particulars filed by the prosecutor, it was evident that the state would seek to prove reckless manslaughter on the basis of the conduct—driving while intoxicated and crossing the center line—for which the defendant had already been prosecuted. The majority stated that even if two criminal statutes do not constitute the "same offense" under *Blockburger*, "the Double Jeopardy Clause bars a subsequent prosecution if, to establish an essential element of an offense charged in that prosecution, the government will prove conduct that constitutes an offense for which the defendant has already been prosecuted."

### [3]  *United States v. Dixon*: Back to *Harris*?

*Grady v. Corbin* had a short shelf life. In *United States v. Dixon*,[178] a severely divided Supreme Court overruled *Corbin*. Justice Scalia delivered the *coup de grace* for the Court, stating that "[t]he 'same-conduct' rule [*Corbin*] announced is wholly inconsistent with earlier Supreme Court precedent and with the clear common-law understanding of double jeopardy."

*Dixon* involved two consolidated appeals, in which defendants were prosecuted for criminal offenses after they had been convicted of criminal contempt based on the same conduct. In one case, *D1* was arrested for murder, but released on bond. One condition of his release was that he not commit any criminal offense while free. While awaiting his murder trial, *D1* was arrested again, this time for felony cocaine possession with the intent to distribute. Thereafter, the court that had released *D1* pending his murder trial took evidence on the cocaine charge, determined that *D1* had been in possession of cocaine in violation of the law, and, therefore, found him guilty of criminal contempt, an element of which was that a "person who has been conditionally released . . . and who has *violated a condition of release* [here, the condition that *D1* not commit any criminal offense] shall be subject to . . . prosecution for contempt of court." Thereafter, the government sought to prosecute *D1* on the cocaine charge. *D1* moved to dismiss the indictment on double jeopardy grounds.

In the second appeal, *D2*'s estranged wife obtained a civil protection order (CPO), which required him not to "assault . . . or in any manner threaten"

_____

[178] 509 U.S. 688 (1993).

her. Later, based on allegations that *D2* assaulted and threatened additional injury to his wife on various occasions, *D2* was convicted of criminal contempt for violating the CPO. At the contempt proceeding, the trial judge stated that the elements of contempt for purposes of the present case were: (1) knowledge of the protective order; and (2) "willful violation of one of its conditions, here simple assault as defined by the criminal code." *D2* was subsequently indicted for simple assault, assault with intent to kill, and on multiple counts of threatening to injure another.

The five-Justice majority split amongst themselves regarding some of the offenses. What they agreed on, however, is that *Corbin* should be overruled; and, as a result, they agreed that prosecution of certain charges against *D2*, barred under *Corbin*, could proceed.

The majority agreed that if *Corbin* were good law the government could not prosecute *D2* for the offense of "assault with intent to kill" or for threatening his wife, because *Corbin* prohibited "'a subsequent prosecution if, to establish an essential element of an offense charged in that prosecution [here, assault as an element of assault with intent to kill, or threatening as an element of threatening bodily injury], the government will prove conduct that constitutes an offense for which the defendant has already been prosecuted [here, the assault and threatening, which conduct constituted the offense of violating the CPO].'"[179] With *Corbin* dead, however, the prosecution of these offenses could proceed.

What about the prosecution of *D1* on the cocaine charge, and of *D2* for simple assault? Justice Scalia, in an opinion that was joined only by Justice Kennedy, stated that these prosecutions were barred by *Harris v. Oklahoma*. In *D1*'s case, an element of criminal contempt was the violation of a condition of release; one condition of release was that *D1* not violate any criminal statute; therefore, effectively, the cocaine offense (indeed, any offense specified in the criminal code) was a lesser-included offense of criminal contempt. Similarly, in *D2*'s case, assault was a lesser-included offense of criminal contempt for violation of the CPO, which required *D2* not to assault or threaten his wife.

The three remaining *Dixon* Justices who voted to overrule *Corbin* (Chief Justice Rehnquist, and Justices Sandra O'Connor and Clarence Thomas), interpreted *Harris* more narrowly. According to them, *Harris* did not apply to the present circumstances. They stated that they would "limit *Harris* to the context in which it arose: where the crimes in question are analogous to greater and lesser included offenses. The crimes at issue here bear no such resemblance."[180] As these Justices explained:

---

[179] *Id.* at 703–04 (brackets in original) (quoting Grady v. Corbin, 495 U.S. 508, 510 (1990)).
[180] *Id.* at 714.

[In *Harris*,] [w]e construed this generic reference to some felony [in the felony-murder statute] as incorporating the statutory elements of the various felonies upon which a felony-murder conviction could rest. . . . The criminal contempt provision involved here, by contrast, contains no such generic reference which by definition incorporates the statutory elements of assault or drug distribution.

Unless we are to accept the extraordinary view that the three-paragraph *per curiam* in *Harris* was intended to overrule *sub silentio* our previous decisions that looked to the statutory elements of the offenses charged in applying *Blockburger*, we are bound to conclude . . . that the *ratio decidendi* of our *Harris* decision was that the two crimes there were akin to greater and lesser included offenses. The crimes at issue here [contempt, and the "lesser" offenses of cocaine possession for distribution and assault], however, cannot be viewed as greater and lesser included offenses, either intuitively or logically.[181]

With *Corbin* dead and *Blockburger* the ruling standard, where does *Dixon* leave *Harris*? In terms of the *Dixon* opinion itself, Justices Scalia and Kennedy seemingly are joined by the four dissenters in interpreting *Harris* more broadly it was construed by Justices Rehnquist, O'Connor, and Thomas.[182] Therefore, at this time, *Harris*—indeed, the slightly broader version of it applied in *Dixon*—is good law. However, in view of post-*Dixon* departures from the Court, the role of *Harris* in double jeopardy law remains unstable.

## [D]  Exceptions to the General Rule

Even if two statutory provisions constitute the "same offense" under the applicable law, multiple prosecutions are not barred in all circumstances. First, in *Brown v. Ohio*,[183] the Court suggested that "[a]n exception may exist where the State is unable to proceed on the more serious charge at the outset because the additional facts necessary to sustain that charge have not occurred or have not been discovered despite the exercise of due diligence." For example, if *D* is prosecuted and convicted of attempted murder of *V*, after which *V* dies as the result of wounds inflicted upon him by *D*, a murder prosecution is not barred.[184]

---

[181] *Id.* at 717–18.

[182] *See id.* at 734 n.8 (White and Stevens, JJ.); *Id.* at 741 (Blackmun, J.); *Id.* at 757 (Souter and Stevens, JJ.).

[183] 432 U.S. 161, 169 n.7 (1977).

[184] *E.g.*, People v. Harding, 506 N.W.2d 482 (Mich. 1993) (*D* was convicted of attempted murder of *V*, during the commission of a felony; four years later, *V* died when he was the victim of another assault, this time by *X*; based on evidence that *V*'s death was the result of injury to his heart caused in the original attempted murder, *D* was prosecuted for felony-murder of *V*; the court held that the *Brown* exception applied to these facts).

Consider also *Garrett v. United States*: [185] *D* pleaded guilty to a drug charge. He was later prosecuted for the offense of "continuing criminal enterprise" (CCE), which requires proof of the commission of three or more violations of specified offenses within a set period of time. The Court assumed that the drug charge was a lesser-included offense of CCE; therefore, reprosecution would ordinarily have been barred. A plurality held, however, that the *Brown* exception applied because, at the time of the first prosecution, the CCE crime set out in the indictment had not yet been completed. The plurality considered it irrelevant that "the Government could [at the time of the first prosecution] have successfully indicted and prosecuted [*D*] for a different continuing criminal enterprise," namely, one ending at a somewhat earlier date.

Second, it is important to remember that the rule discussed in this chapter section arises when a defendant is prosecuted for the "same offense" (as defined in this chapter section) after a conviction *that is not the subject of a successful appeal.* The no-successive-prosecution rule does not apply if "a defendant is retried on the same charge after a mistrial, . . . dismissal . . ., or after a conviction is reversed on appeal." [186] For example, in *Montana v. Hall,* [187] *D* was convicted of incest. *D* appealed the conviction successfully on the ground that the sexual acts charged against him did not constitute incest within the meaning of the statute. Consequently, the state prosecuted *D* for sexual assault, an offense that the state court determined was the same as incest under the *Blockburger* test. The Supreme Court allowed the second prosecution to proceed, however, on the ground that *D* had appealed his conviction of incest; therefore, it was appropriate to apply the ordinary rule that reprosecution is permitted after a conviction is overturned. [188]

Third, the double jeopardy clause is not violated when the defendant requests separate trials on the greater and lesser offenses, or "in connection with his opposition to trial together, fails to raise the issue that one offense might be a lesser included offense of the other." [189]

---

[185] 471 U.S. 773 (1985).

[186] Brown v. Ohio, 432 U.S. at 161 n.5.

[187] 481 U.S. 400 (1987).

[188] *See* § 32.05, *supra.*

[189] Jeffers v. United States, 432 U.S. 137, 152 (1977) (plurality).

## § 32.08   Excessive or Multiple Punishments for the "Same Offense"[190]

### [A]   Excessive Punishment

### [1]   In General

In *Ex parte Lange,*[191] *D* was convicted of an offense punishable by a fine of $200 *or* a one-year prison term. However, the judge imposed a fine of $200 *and* sentenced *D* to one year in prison. *D* paid the fine and was incarcerated for five days before the trial court vacated the earlier judgment and re-sentenced *D* to one year in prison, commencing from the date of the second judgment. The fine, however, could not be returned because it had passed into the Treasury. Effectively, therefore, *D* suffered punishment of $200, and one year and five days in prison.

The Supreme Court held that *D*'s punishment violated the Fifth Amendment double jeopardy clause prohibition on multiple punishment. Although the case could be interpreted in various ways, *Lange* now "stands for the uncontested proposition that the Double Jeopardy Clause prohibits punishment in excess of that authorized by the legislature."[192] *D*'s punishment was excessive on two accounts: he was fined and imprisoned, which the statute did not permit; and he was subjected to imprisonment greater than that permitted under the law.

### [2]   Credit For Time Served

The holding in *Ex parte Lange,*[193] in particular the judge's failure to credit *D*'s five days already served on the first judgment, operated as the basis for the Supreme Court's holding in *North Carolina v. Pearce,*[194] which expressly provides that the double jeopardy clause is violated "when punishment already exacted for an offense is not fully 'credited' in imposing sentence upon a new conviction for the same offense."

In *Pearce*, *D* was convicted of an offense and sentenced to a prison term of 12 to 15 years. While serving his sentence, *D* successfully appealed the conviction. *D* was retried and again convicted. This time, the trial judge

---

[190] *See generally* George C. Thomas III, *A Unified Theory of Multiple Punishment*, 47 U. Pitt. L. Rev. 1 (1985); George C. Thomas III, *Multiple Punishments for the Same Offense: The Analysis After Missouri v. Hunter*, 62 Wash. U. L.Q. 79 (1984). For purposes of clarity, the text uses the American spelling of "offense," although the English spelling ("offence") is used in the original version of the Fifth Amendment.

[191] 85 U.S. (18 Wall.) 163 (1873).

[192] Jones v. Thomas, 491 U.S. 376, 383 (1989).

[193] 85 U.S. (18 Wall.) 163 (1873). *See* § 32.08[A][1], *supra.*

[194] 395 U.S. 711 (1969).

sentenced *D* to imprisonment of eight years, "which, when added to the time [*D*] had already spent in prison, . . . amounted to a longer total sentence than that originally imposed."[195] In effect, the trial judge did not credit *D* for the entire time he served while appealing the first conviction. This failure, *Pearce* stated, constituted a violation of the double jeopardy clause.

*Pearce* arguably goes further than should be required under the Fifth Amendment. Credit for time served clearly should have been granted if *D* had received the maximum punishment for his offense upon the second conviction: in such circumstances, without credit, *D* would have served a sentence in excess of that authorized by the legislature, in clear violation of *Lange*.

But, *Pearce* went further by requiring credit in *all* cases. For example, suppose that *D* is sentenced after a second conviction to five years in prison for an offense punishable by imprisonment up to ten years. Suppose further that *D* receives no credit for one year served before the first conviction was overturned. The effect of this no-credit sentence is that *D* will serve six years in prison, *which is still within the maximum punishment allowed by the legislature.* As a matter of double jeopardy principles, there ought to be no difference between sentencing *D* the second time to six years' imprisonment with one year of credit for time already served, or to sentence him (as hypothesized) to five years with no credit. Nonetheless, under *Pearce*, if the judge wants *D* to serve a total of six years, he must follow the former approach.

## [B]  Multiple Punishments

### [1]  In General

As explained in Section 32.07, a single act may constitute a violation of two or more statutory provisions. Furthermore, under the rule announced in *Blockburger v. United States*,[196] separate crimes constitute the "same offense" for double jeopardy purposes if they contain identical statutory elements, or if one offense is a lesser-included offense of the other.

The Supreme Court ruled in *Missouri v. Hunter*[197] that imposition of cumulative punishment (as distinguished from multiple prosecutions) for two crimes that constitute the "same offense" under the *Blockburger* test is not in itself a violation of the double jeopardy clause. For example, in *Hunter*, *D* was prosecuted in a single trial for armed robbery and "armed

---

[195] *Id.* at 713.

[196] 284 U.S. 299 (1932). *See* § 32.07[B], *supra.*

[197] 459 U.S. 359 (1983).

criminal action." The latter crime, which was treated as a lesser-included offense of robbery under the *Blockburger* test, expressly provided that punishment imposed for it "shall be in addition to any punishment provided by law for the crime committed . . . with . . . a dangerous or deadly weapon."

The Supreme Court in *Hunter* held that punishment for multiple crimes, although a "single offense" under *Blockburger*, is not barred "[w]here . . . a legislature specifically authorizes cumulative punishment under two statutes." According to the Court, in such circumstances, "a court's task of statutory construction is at an end and the prosecutor may seek and the trial court or jury may impose cumulative punishment . . . ."

Thus, although the government is generally required to *prosecute* a defendant for two "same offense" crimes in a single prosecution, *punishment* for both crimes after a *single* trial is not barred if the legislature intended to permit it. Essentially, the *Blockburger* "same offense" test is a constitutional principle as it relates to multiple *prosecutions*; on the matter of cumulative punishments as part of a single prosecution, however, *Blockburger* is a rule of statutory construction.

### [2]    Sentence Enhancement for Uncharged Criminal Conduct

In *Witte v. United States*,[198] D pleaded guilty to a federal marijuana charge. The trial judge, consistent with the federal sentencing guidelines, sentenced D to a higher-than-ordinary prison term on the basis of his finding that D was involved in a continuing drug conspiracy involving importation of cocaine. Subsequently, D was indicted for conspiring and attempting to import cocaine. D sought to dismiss the indictment on the ground that, if convicted, punishment for the cocaine charges would result in multiple punishment, as he had already received a heightened sentence at the first trial on the basis of this criminal conduct.

The Supreme Court stated that, as long as a defendant's sentence falls within the legislatively authorized punishment range, "consideration of offender-specific information at sentencing . . . does not result in 'punishment' for such conduct." Therefore, it did not violate the double jeopardy clause to punish D (for the first time) for cocaine importation at the second trial.

### § 32.09    Collateral Estoppel

#### [A]    Nature of the Doctrine

According to *Ashe v. Swenson*,[199] the doctrine of collateral estoppel is embodied in the guarantee against double jeopardy. As the Court explained

---

[198] 515 U.S. 389 (1995).

[199] 397 U.S. 436 (1970).

the concept, collateral estoppel "means simply that when an issue of ultimate fact has once been determined by a valid and final judgment, that issue cannot again be litigated between the same parties in any future lawsuit."

The facts in *Ashe* demonstrate how the doctrine is applied. In that case, six poker players were robbed at the home of one of the victims by three or four armed men. *D* and three other men were charged with six counts of armed robbery, one count for each victim at the poker game.

The prosecutor could have joined all six robbery counts in a single prosecution.[200] Instead he chose to prosecute *D* for each robbery seriatim. At the first trial for robbery of one victim, *D*'s sole defense was that he was not at the scene of the crime, *i.e.*, that he was misidentified as one of the robbers. The jury acquitted *D*.

When the prosecutor sought to bring *D* to trial again for the robbery of another poker player, *D* moved to bar the second prosecution. Because each robbery constituted a separate offense, the prosecutor's multiple prosecution strategy did not offend ordinary double jeopardy principles.[201] Nonetheless, the Court held that the doctrine of collateral estoppel barred further criminal proceedings against *D*.

As the Court explained in *Ashe*, in order to apply the doctrine of collateral estoppel, a court must examine all of the relevant matters in the case in order to determine "whether a rational jury could have grounded its verdict upon an issue other than that which the defendant seeks to foreclose from consideration." In this case, a realistic interpretation of the facts could "lead to but one conclusion," namely that the jury did not accept the prosecutor's claim that *D* was one of the persons in the house. Therefore, as that issue could no longer be relitigated, there was no basis to prosecute *D* for the remaining robberies.

The collateral estoppel doctrine is *not* a double-edged sword in criminal proceedings. That is, the *government* is *not* permitted to take advantage of the collateral estoppel doctrine in criminal cases.[202] For example, in *Ashe*, if *D* had been convicted rather than acquitted at the first trial—if the jury

---

[200] Under federal rules and in most states, two or more offenses "based on the same act or transaction" may be charged in the same indictment and, therefore, prosecuted in a single trial. Fed. R. Crim. P. 8(a). If such joinder would be prejudicial to the interests of either party, the court may sever the charges, subject to double jeopardy principles. Fed. R. Crim. P. 14.

[201] The double jeopardy clause does not require that multiple offenses stemming from the same incident be prosecuted in a single trial. *See* Note 163, *supra* and accompanying text.

[202] Simpson v. Florida, 403 U.S. 384 (1971).

had been convinced beyond a reasonable doubt that *D* had been one of the robbers—*D* could still have raised his alibi claim at subsequent trials.

### [B] Limits on Application of the Doctrine

The collateral estoppel doctrine is less expansive than traditional double jeopardy protection involving the same offense. First, it can only be invoked if a rational jury could not have grounded its verdict on any basis other than the claim that the defendant seeks to foreclose from further consideration. If a defendant provides multiple exculpatory claims, the jury's general verdict of acquittal is too ambiguous to justify use of the collateral estoppel doctrine. [203]

Second, the doctrine applies only if the issue in question has been adjudicated to a valid and final judgment. It does not apply if the first prosecution is concluded by a guilty plea, because in such circumstances there is no "adjudication on the merits after full trial," [204] and a guilty plea would rarely resolve an issue of ultimate fact in the defendant's favor. [205]

Third, the doctrine does not apply in a proceeding in which a lower standard of proof is permitted than at a criminal trial. For example, even if *D* is acquitted of an offense, he may not invoke collateral estoppel to bar a forfeiture proceeding in which the government must prove by only a preponderance of the evidence that *D* committed the crime for which he was acquitted earlier. [206]

Similarly, consider the facts in *Dowling v. United States*. [207] In *Dowling*, a man wearing a ski mask burglarized *V*'s home. During the crime, *V*

---

[203] In this regard, consider Schiro v. Farley, 510 U.S. 222 (1994): *D* admitted he raped and killed *V*. He was charged in separate counts with intentional murder and felony murder (which does not require proof of intent). The jury was given verdict forms for both counts. It convicted *D* of felony murder; it left the "intentional murder" form blank. In the death penalty phase of the trial, the prosecutor sought to prove that *D* killed *V* intentionally (an aggravating factor that could be used to invoke the death penalty). The trial judge sentenced *D* to death on that basis. *D* argued on appeal that the government was collaterally estopped from arguing that the killing was intentional, in view of the jury's verdict at the guilt phase.

The Court held that *D* had "not met his burden of establishing the factual predicate for the application of the doctrine [of collateral estoppel], . . . namely, that an 'issue of ultimate fact has once been determined' in his favor." Among the Court's reasons for its holding was that the fact that the jury found *D* guilty of felony murder did not necessarily amount to a finding by the jury that the killing was not intentional; the jury might have considered the felony murder count first, without considering the issue of intent.

[204] Ohio v. Johnson, 467 U.S. 493, 500 n.9 (1984).

[205] A defendant who pleads guilty to a lesser-included offense would not be able to demonstrate an implied acquittal of the greater offense because jeopardy never attached regarding the greater offense. Implied acquittals are considered at § 32.05[C], *supra*.

[206] United States v. One Assortment of 89 Firearms, 465 U.S. 354 (1984).

[207] 493 U.S. 342 (1990).

unmasked the intruder, whom she identified at trial as *D*. Despite this testimony, *D* was acquitted. Later, *D* was prosecuted for an unrelated bank robbery during which the perpetrator also wore a ski mask. An eyewitness to that crime observed the culprit pull off the mask after he departed the bank. The witness identified *D* as the robber. At the second trial, in order to buttress this identification claim, the government introduced *V*'s testimony regarding the earlier burglary of which *D* had been acquitted. This evidence was admitted pursuant to a state rule permitting proof of uncharged misconduct in order to show identity or for any other purpose other than to demonstrate the defendant's bad character.

The Supreme Court held that the doctrine of collateral estoppel, even if otherwise applicable to the case, did not bar introduction of evidence that tended to prove that *D* committed the prior crime. The acquittal at the first trial proved only that the jury had a reasonable doubt regarding *D*'s guilt for that offense; under the applicable evidentiary code, however, the prior misconduct evidence was admissible at the second trial if a jury "could reasonably conclude" that *D* committed the previous offense, a lesser burden of proof.

# TABLE OF CASES

[References are to Sections.]

# D

# FEDERAL RULES OF CRIMINAL PROCEDURE

[Text references are to Sections]

# FEDERAL STATUTES

[Text references are to Sections]

# UNDERSTANDING CRIMINAL PROCEDURE

## INDEX

(Matthew Bender & Co., Inc.)

(Rel.3—4/02 Pub.791)

# INDEX

[References are to sections.]

## A

**ADMINISTRATIVE SEARCHES**
Generally . . . 19.02

**AERIAL SURVEILLANCE**
Generally . . . 7.08
Helicopters . . . 7.08[C]

**ALCOHOL TESTING** (See RANDOM SUSPI-
CIONLESS SEARCHES AND SEIZURES)

**APPEALS**
Generally . . . 1.03[C][9]
Right to counsel during . . . 29.03

**ARRAIGNMENT**
Generally . . . 1.03[C][3], 1.03[C][6]

**ARRESTS** (See also SEIZURE)
Common law and statutory rules . . . 10.02
Defined . . . 10.01
Effectuating
    Force against arrestee in making . . . . .
      10.07[B]
    General constitutional rules . . . 10.07[A]
    Knock-and-announce principle . . . . . .
      10.07[A]
*Terry* stops distinguished . . . 18.04
Warrant requirement
    Exigent circumstances . . . 10.05[B][2]
    Hot pursuit . . . 10.05[B][2][a]
    In home . . . 10.05
    Overview . . . 10.03
    Public places . . . 10.04
    Third-party residence . . . 10.06

**AUTOMOBILE CHECKPOINTS**
Border searches . . . 19.03
Drug interdiction . . . 19.04[C]
License and vehicle registration . . . 19.03[A]
Sobriety . . . 19.03[B]

**AUTOMOBILE SEARCHES**
"Automobile exception" to warrant requirement
    Generally . . . 14.01[B]-[C]
    Lesser-expectation-of-privacy rationale
      . . . 14.05, 14.06
    Mobility rationale . . . 14.02, 14.03, 14.04
    Overview . . . 14.01[A]
    Probable cause requirement . . . 14.01[D]

**AUTOMOBILE SEARCHES**—Cont.
Border . . . 19.03
Containers found during . . . 14.07
Incident to an arrest . . . 13.02[C][2][b], 13.05
Inventories . . . 16.01, 16.02
Weapons searches in . . . 18.07

## B

**BAIL** (See PRETRIAL RELEASE)

**BEEPERS** (See ELECTRONIC SURVEIL-
LANCE)

**BILL OF RIGHTS**
Incorporation of (See INCORPORATION OF
BILL OF RIGHTS)

**BODY SEARCHES**
Fingernail scrapings . . . 12.03
Intrusions into . . . 12.02
Pat-downs . . . 18.06[B]

**BORDER SEARCHES**
At border . . . 19.03[A]
Fixed interior checkpoints . . . 19.03[B][3]
Near border . . . 19.03[B]
Roving border patrols . . . 19.03[B][2]

**BRIGHT-LINE RULES** (See CRIMINAL PRO-
CEDURE, GENERALLY)

## C

**CAR SEARCHES** (See AUTOMOBILE
SEARCHES)

**CHECKPOINTS** (See AUTOMOBILE CHECK-
POINTS)

**COERCED CONFESSIONS** (See INTERRO-
GATIONS)

**COLLATERAL ESTOPPEL** (See DOUBLE
JEOPARDY CLAUSE)

**COMMUNITY CARETAKING FUNCTION**
Generally . . . 12.01
House entries . . . 12.04

**COMPLAINT**
Generally . . . 1.03[C][1]

(Rel.3—4/02 Pub.791)

[References are to sections.]

[References are to sections.]

[References are to sections.]

[References are to sections.]

(Rel.3—4/02 Pub.791)

[References are to sections.]

[References are to sections.]

# S

[References are to sections.]

[References are to sections.]

# W

**WAIVER** (See also specific constitutional rights)
Generally . . . 4.02
Fourth Amendment . . . 17.02[B]

**WIRETAPPING** (See ELECTRONIC SUR-
VEILLANCE)